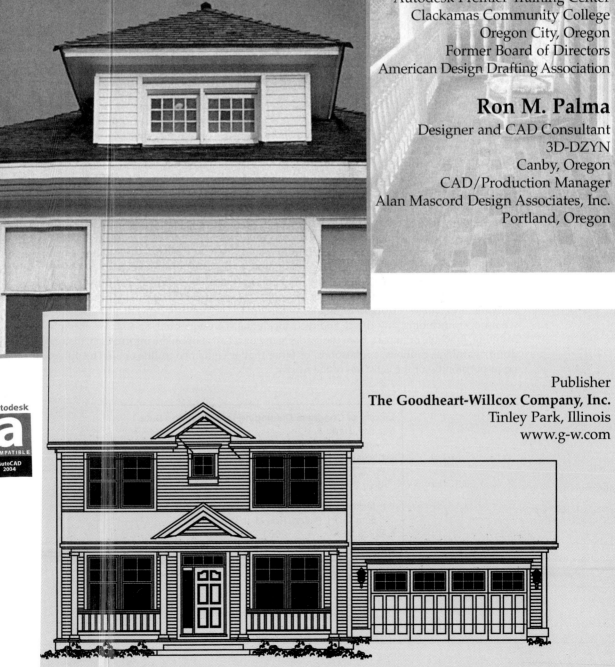

# Architectural Drafting Using AutoCAD

Drafting/Design/Presentation

AutoCAD 2004

by
**David A. Madsen**
Faculty Emeritus
Former Chairperson
Drafting Technology
Autodesk Premier Training Center
Clackamas Community College
Oregon City, Oregon
Former Board of Directors
American Design Drafting Association

**Ron M. Palma**
Designer and CAD Consultant
3D-DZYN
Canby, Oregon
CAD/Production Manager
Alan Mascord Design Associates, Inc.
Portland, Oregon

Publisher
**The Goodheart-Willcox Company, Inc.**
Tinley Park, Illinois
www.g-w.com

autodesk
**a**
COMPATIBLE
AutoCAD
2004

Library of Congress Catalog Card Number 2003060998
International Standard Book Number 1-59070-310-3

1 2 3 4 5 6 7 8 9 – 04 – 08 07 06 05 04

Cover image: James D'Addio/CORBIS

**Goodheart-Willcox Publisher Brand Disclaimer:** Brand names, company names, and illustrations for products and services included in this text are provided for educational purposes only, and do not represent or imply endorsement or recommendation by the authors or the publisher.

**The Goodheart-Willcox Company, Inc. Safety Notice:** The reader is expressly advised to carefully read, understand, and apply all safety precautions and warnings described in this book or that might also be indicated in undertaking the activities and exercises described herein to minimize risk of personal injury or injury to others. Common sense and good judgment should also be exercised and applied to help avoid all potential hazards. The reader should always refer to the appropriate manufacturer's technical information, directions, and recommendations; then proceed with care to follow specific equipment operating instructions. The reader should understand these notices and cautions are not exhaustive.

The publisher makes no warranty or representation whatsoever, either expressed or implied, including but not limited to equipment, procedures, and applications described or referred to herein, their quality, performance, merchantability, or fitness for a particular purpose. The publisher assumes no responsibility for any changes, errors, or omissions in this book. The publisher specifically disclaims any liability whatsoever, including any direct, indirect, incidental, consequential, special, or exemplary damages resulting, in whole or in part, from the reader's use or reliance upon the information, instructions, procedures, warnings, cautions, applications, or other matter contained in this book. The publisher assumes no responsibility for the activities of the reader.

**Library of Congress Cataloging-in-Publication Data**
Madsen, David A.
    Architectural drafting using AutoCAD : drafting/design/presentation / by David A. Madsen, Ron M. Palma.
    p. cm.
    ISBN 1-59070-310-3

    1. Architectural drawing—Computer-aided design.
    2. AutoCAD. I. Palma, Ron M. II. Title.
NA2728.M347          2003
720'.28'40285—dc22

                                    2003060998

# Introduction

*Architectural Drafting Using AutoCAD* will teach you how to use AutoCAD to create architectural drawings for residential and light commercial construction. You will learn how to use the basic tools provided in AutoCAD, and you will learn how to customize AutoCAD for your specific architectural applications. Topics are covered in an easy-to-understand sequence and progress in a way that allows you to become comfortable with the commands as your knowledge builds from one chapter to the next.

With *Architectural Drafting Using AutoCAD*, you learn AutoCAD commands and become familiar with information in other areas:

- The history of architectural drafting.
- Architectural design coordination.
- Architectural careers and education paths.
- The architectural design process.
- Architectural standards.
- Ergonomics.
- Office practices for architectural firms.
- Preliminary planning and sketches.
- Creating and managing symbol libraries.
- Preliminary design.
- Floor plans.
- Foundation plans.
- Elevations.
- Schedules.
- Structural and framing plans.
- Electrical, plumbing, and HVAC plans.

## Fonts Used in This Text

Different typefaces are used throughout this text to define terms and identify AutoCAD commands. Important terms always appear in *bold-italic face, serif* type. AutoCAD menus, commands, variables, dialog box names, and toolbar buttons are printed in **bold-face, sans serif** type. File names, directory folder names, paths, and keyboard-entry items appear in the body of the text in Roman, sans serif type. Keyboard keys are shown inside of square brackets [ ] and appear in Roman, sans serif type. For example, [Enter] means to press the Enter key.

Prompt sequences are set apart from the body text with space above and below, and appear in Roman, sans serif type. Keyboard entry items in prompts appear in **bold-face, sans-serif** type. In prompts, the [Enter] key is represented by the ↵ symbol.

In addition, commands, menus, and dialog boxes related to Microsoft® Windows® appear in Roman, sans serif type.

# Introducing the AutoCAD Commands

There are several ways to select AutoCAD drawing and editing commands. Selecting commands from the toolbars, pull-down menus, or the digitizer tablet template menu is slightly different from entering them from the keyboard. All AutoCAD commands and related options in this text are introduced by providing all of the commonly active command entry methods.

In many examples, command entries are shown as if they are typed at the keyboard. This allows the text to present the keyboard shortcuts, full command name, and prompts that appear on screen. Commands, options, and values you must enter are given in bold text, as shown below. The available keyboard shortcuts are given first to reinforce the quickest way for you to enter commands at the keyboard. Pressing the [Enter] (return) key is indicated with the ↵ symbol.

> Command: **l** *or* **line**↵
> From point: **2,2**↵
> To point: **4,2**↵
> To point: ↵

General input, such as picking a point or selecting an object, is presented in italic, serif font, as shown below.

> Command: **l** *or* **line**↵
> From point: *(pick a point)*
> To point: *(pick another point)*
> To point: ↵

The command line, pull-down menu, and toolbar button menu entry methods are presented throughout the text. When a command is introduced, these methods are illustrated in the margin next to the text reference. The toolbar in which the button is located is also identified. The example in the margin next to this paragraph illustrates the various methods of initiating the **LINE** command.

Some commands and functions are handled more efficiently by picking a toolbar button or a menu command. Many of these procedures are described in numbered, step-by-step instructions.

# Flexibility in Design

Flexibility is the key word when using *Architectural Drafting Using AutoCAD*. This text is an excellent training aid for individual instruction, as well as classroom instruction. *Architectural Drafting Using AutoCAD* teaches you how to apply AutoCAD to common architectural drafting tasks and projects found in residential and commercial construction. It is also an invaluable resource for any professional using AutoCAD for architectural applications.

# Features of the Text

When working through the text, you will see a variety of notices. These notices include Professional Tips and Notes that help you develop your AutoCAD skills.

These ideas and suggestions are aimed at increasing your productivity and enhancing your use of AutoCAD commands and techniques.

When entering input at the Command prompt, use the [Backspace] key to correct typing errors. To cancel an active command, press the [Esc] key. For some commands, you may need to press the [Esc] key twice to return to the Command prompt.

*Architectural Drafting Using AutoCAD* provides several ways for you to evaluate your performance. Included are the following:

- **Exercises.** Each chapter contains in-text Exercises. These Exercises instruct you to perform tasks that reinforce the material just presented. You can work through the Exercises at your own pace. The Exercises take you through the development of a complete set of working drawings for a residential project. You can do a portion of the Exercises, or you can do them in their entirety.
- **Chapter Tests.** Each chapter includes a written test at the end of the chapter. The questions require you to give the proper definition, command, option, or response. The chapter tests can be used as open-book questions for review, or to challenge your knowledge of the chapter content.
- **Drawing Problems.** There are a variety of drafting and design problems at the end of each chapter. These are presented as real-world residential and commercial architectural projects. The problems are designed to make you think, solve problems, use design techniques, research, and use proper drafting standards. The drawing problems allow you to complete one or more sets of working drawings for residential and commercial construction projects.

# About the Authors

David A. Madsen is Faculty Emeritus, the former Chairperson of Drafting Technology and the Autodesk Premier Training Center at Clackamas Community College and former member of the American Design and Drafting Association Board of Directors. David was an instructor and a department chair at Clackamas Community College for nearly 30 years. In addition to community college experience, David was a Drafting Technology instructor at Centennial High School in Gresham, Oregon. David also has extensive experience in mechanical drafting, architectural design and drafting, and construction practices. He is the author of several Goodheart-Willcox drafting and design textbooks, including *Geometric Dimensioning and Tolerancing,* and coauthor of the *AutoCAD and its Applications* series (Releases 10, 11, 12, 13, and 14; AutoCAD 2000/2000i; and AutoCAD 2002 and 2004 editions) and *AutoCAD Essentials.*

Ron M. Palma is an Autodesk Certified Instructor and the owner and operator of 3D-DZYN in Canby, Oregon. Ron specializes in the professional training of companies and individuals on the Autodesk AEC product line. Ron has been a home designer in the Pacific Northwest since 1988, and has extensive CAD management experience.

# Acknowledgment

The authors want to give special thanks to the following people for their professional support:

- Jon Epley and Alan Mascord, Alan Mascord Design Associates, Inc.
- Cynthia Bankey, Cynthia Bankey Architect, Inc.

Ron would like to thank his coauthor David Madsen for partnering on this project, and providing him with the encouragement and patience to see him through it. Ron would also like to thank his wife, Lisa, and his children, Eddie and Jessica, for their support, love, and understanding while working through this project.

# Brief Contents

Architectural drafters create many types of drawings. The type of drawing shown here, called an *elevation*, allows the client to easily visualize how the finished building will appear.

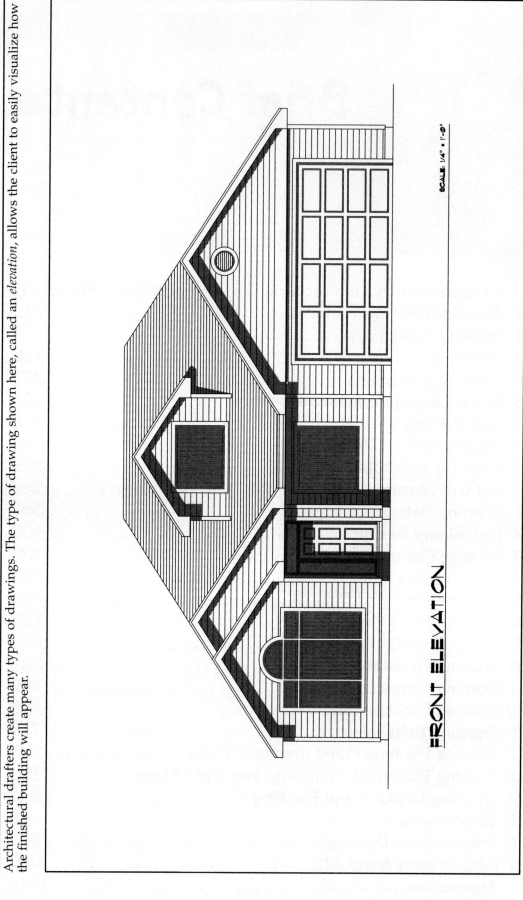

FRONT ELEVATION

SCALE: 1/4" = 1'-0"

# Expanded Contents

# 1

# Introduction to Architectural Drafting with AutoCAD

## Learning Objectives

After completing this chapter, you will be able to:

- Define *architectural drafting.*
- Describe general stages in the history of architectural drafting.
- List the advantages of CAD over manual drafting.
- Explain the concept of architectural Web-based collaboration.
- Describe careers related to architectural drafting.
- List specific technical skills and general work skills needed for a successful career.
- Explain the importance of leadership and the characteristics of a leader.
- Define *entrepreneurship* and list the skills required by an entrepreneur.
- Outline and explain the architectural design process.
- Identify the types of drawings commonly contained in a set of working drawings.
- Explain the purpose of architectural standards.
- Discuss the proper CAD workstation setup to help reduce strain in your wrists, arms, neck, back, legs, and eyes.
- Identify several professional organizations related to architecture.

## Important Terms

architect
architectural designer
architectural drafter
architectural drafting
CAD manager
computer-aided drafting (CAD)
construction documents
construction specifications
drafting
entrepreneurship
ergonomics
internal systems administrator

Internet
intranet
leadership
manual drafting
software
standards
system administrator
virtual reality
Web page
Web-based collaboration
working drawings
World Wide Web (Web)

# The Evolution of Architectural Drafting

Drawings are used to express ideas and designs. Throughout history, a variety of instruments and media have been used to create drawings. In ancient times, drawings were created on stone walls, clay tablets, animal skin, and papyrus. In recent times, drawings have been created using pens and pencils on paper, vellum, and film. Today, many drawings are created using computers.

*Drafting* is the process of creating drawings of objects, structures, or systems that an architect, engineer, or designer has visualized. *Architectural drafting* is the process of representing engineering works, buildings, plans, and details by means of construction drawings. An *architectural drafter* creates these architectural drawings.

## Early Architectural Drawings

Early architectural drawings were an art form, as well as a construction tool. Architectural drafters used tools such as T squares, triangles, pencils, and ink pens to prepare drawings. Drawings were often created on cloth or paper.

Drafters created basic floor plans, precise elevations, and elaborate construction details. Plans included room names, basic room dimensions, key construction dimensions, and a graphic scale. **Figure 1-1** shows the floor plan drawings of a simple early American cottage.

Early elevations displayed the construction materials in a rendering. The drafter often included trees and other landscape features in these drawings. See **Figure 1-2**. Early construction details provided the pictorial illustrations needed for the craftsperson creating elements of the building facade. **Figure 1-3** shows details an architectural drafter created in the mid-1800s.

---

**Figure 1-1.**
The floor plans of a simple early American cottage.

Architectural Drafting Using AutoCAD

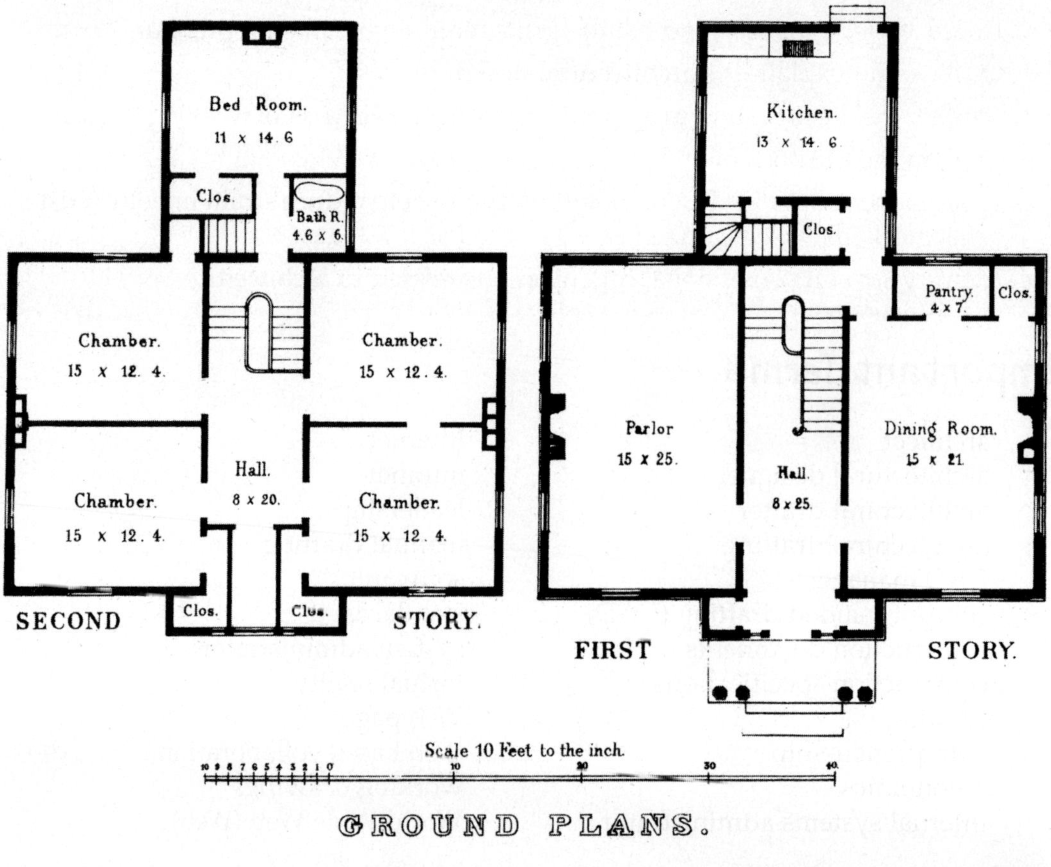

**Figure 1-2.**
Early architectural elevations displayed many details of the building. The architectural drafters often included trees, fences, and other landscaping in the elevation.

**Figure 1-3.**
Construction details created by an architectural drafter in the mid-1800s.

## Manual Drafting

More recently, architectural drafters have used pencils and pens, along with tools such as T squares and drafting machines, to prepare drawings. These drawings are often created on drafting paper called *vellum*. This type of drafting, in which a drafter uses drafting instruments to create drawings, is called **manual drafting. Figure 1-4** shows an architectural drafter working at a drafting table.

**Figure 1-4.**
An architectural drafter working at a traditional drafting table.

## Computer-Aided Drafting

Today, most architectural drafters create drawings with the aid of a computer and drafting software. **Computer-aided drafting (CAD)** is the process of creating drawings using computer software.

> *Computer-aided drafting* (CAD) and *computer-aided design and drafting* (CADD) are terms that can be used interchangeably. This text uses *CAD* to mean *computer-aided drafting, computer-aided design,* and *computer-aided design and drafting.*

In making the transition from manual drafting to CAD, companies faced several concerns. One concern was that CAD would remove the drafter's artistic impression from the drawing. Drafters soon discovered, however, that CAD drawings are both artistic and professional in appearance. **Figure 1-5** shows an architectural elevation drawn using AutoCAD. Notice the artistic quality of the drawing. CAD has revolutionized the practice of architectural drafting and will continue to do so in the future. There are many advantages to using CAD in architectural drafting:

- **Increased productivity.** The productivity with CAD is generally greater than that with manual drafting. The use of standard symbols and details, ease of revision, and automatic creation of schedules and bills of materials can greatly increase a drafter's productivity.
- **Improved coordination.** By using layers and referenced drawings, the construction documents can be connected. Thus, a change to the floor plan can be automatically made to the framing plan, electrical plan, and plumbing plan.

**Figure 1-5.**
An architectural elevation drawn using AutoCAD. Notice the artistic quality of the drawing, including the lettering that appears hand drawn. (Alan Mascord Design Associates, Inc.)

FRONT ELEVATION
SCALE : 1/4" = 1'-0"

- **Superior accuracy.** When used correctly, CAD results in an extremely precise drawing. This level of precision is far more difficult to attain with manual drafting.
- **Better consistency.** By developing some basic standards, all CAD drafters can produce drawings in a uniform style. Thus, all drawings for a project appear to have been drawn by the same drafter, even if several drafters were involved. With manual drafting, each drafter has unique drafting and lettering practices, so drawings are inconsistent.
- **Accessible data.** The data representing the objects in the drawing are stored in electronic files. This data can be accessed and used to analyze objects in the drawing. For example, the area of a roof or parking lot can be calculated automatically.

## What is AutoCAD?

*Software* is the list of instructions that determines what you can do with your computer. Most computer programs are called *software*. There are many CAD software programs available to help you visualize and communicate your ideas. AutoCAD® is drafting and design software made by Autodesk, Inc. It is the world's leading CAD software and an asset for both architects and architectural drafters if they are trained in its use.

## Architectural design with CAD

CAD software programs offer a wide variety of applications to make the architectural design and drafting process efficient. As you create a CAD drawing, the software program creates a database containing the locations and properties of objects within the drawing. This information can be used for applications in addition to its original purpose. For example, the location and properties of a wall can be specified as you create a floor plan. This data can then be used to create a wall section, 3D model, rendering, or bill of materials.

All applications access the same database, so objects need to be defined only once. If the various applications could not share the data, the model would need to be constructed from scratch for each application. As shown in **Figure 1-6,** however, advanced applications can build on the data from more basic applications. A single database may be used for the following applications:

- **2D drawings.** As plans, sections, elevations, and details are created, the properties of objects are stored in the database.
- **Schedules.** Window, door, and finish schedules can be automatically compiled if tags and other information are stored properly.
- **Component lists with quality calculations.** Bills of materials and material quantities can be automatically computed.

**Figure 1-6.**
This chart shows how CAD data from a 2D drawing (such as a floor plan) can be used as a base for more advanced applications.

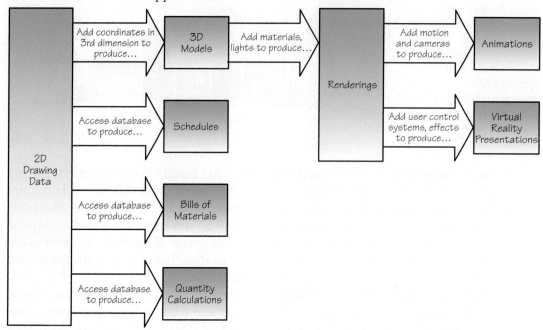

- **3D models.** A 2D plan drawing can be used as a base for a 3D model.
- **Renderings.** By assigning material properties to an existing 2D or 3D model, a realistic rendering can be created for presentation and marketing.
- **Animations.** Walk-through or fly-through animations can be based on rendered 3D models. These animations appear as if created by filming with a video camera while moving through the structure.
- **Virtual reality.** *Virtual reality* refers to an artificial environment with the appearance and feel of a real environment. By creating a realistic rendered 3D model and adding additional sound and feel components, a client wearing special virtual reality goggles, earphones, and gloves can "walk" through a virtual building. The client could listen to footsteps on a marble floor, open heavy oak doors, and feel the bumpy texture of a stucco wall.

Most projects do not require all these applications. A simple rendering of the building's exterior may be included for commercial and large residential projects. Normally, a fly-through animation would only be created for a large commercial project. A virtual reality model would only be used if requested for a very large commercial project and would most likely be created by a firm specializing in virtual reality.

## Web-based architectural collaboration

One of the most time-consuming tasks in an architectural project is managing drawings and other documents. Hundreds of drawings and documents can be issued during the design process. These documents must be shared among the architectural firm, client, contractors, and building officials. The coordination of this information can be a huge task.

*Web-based collaboration* allows information to be shared using the Internet and World Wide Web. The *Internet* is a global network of computers. The *World Wide Web (Web)* is a system of Internet servers supporting documents created in Hypertext Markup Language (HTML). This programming language allows for links between these documents, called *Web pages.* The Web provides a very effective forum for sharing and accessing information.

The architectural field is beginning to see the development of Web-based collaboration systems. These systems allow architects, designers, drafters, product suppliers, building contractors, and clients to communicate and share information. Documents and drawings can be stored as Web pages. Access to these Web pages can be limited to only the appropriate project personnel. Even if the project participants are located throughout the world, Web-based collaboration can be very successful.

Web-based collaboration also impacts the relationship of the architect and the client. Because the work product is visible on the Web, the owner can view the progress at any time. The client can also involve more people in the review of the work. This model of practice enhances the client's involvement in the process and improves the overall sense of teamwork.

# Careers in Architecture

Successfully completing an architectural drafting course provides some valuable skills. These skills are required for several careers in the architectural field and can also be useful for careers in related fields. Some of these careers are discussed in the following sections.

In addition to specific technical skills, a good employee must also have strong general work skills. Leadership skills are needed for career growth, and entrepreneurial skills are needed for anyone starting a business venture. These skills are also discussed in the following sections.

## Career Opportunities

Career opportunities in the field of architecture are wide and varied. The following information identifies typical career paths and related educational requirements in the architectural field. The following are some careers that use architectural drafting skills:

- Architect.
- Architectural designer.
- Architectural drafter.
- CAD manager.

### Architect

*Architects* plan, design, and supervise the construction of buildings and other structures. The table in **Figure 1-7** lists the types of residential, commercial, and industrial structures architects design. The responsibilities of an architect vary, depending on the architect's experience and the size of the architectural firm.

In the planning stage, an architect may meet with clients to develop a preliminary plan for the project. The architect may estimate the cost of the project to determine if the client's budget is realistic. The architect may be involved in obtaining bids, selecting a contractor, and preparing contracts.

After the planning stage, the design phase begins. The architect must be able to visualize the final structure. Construction documents are then created. The architect may prepare the drawings personally or oversee the work of architectural designers and drafters. The architect also writes *construction specifications*, which describe the requirements for materials and construction procedures.

Building contractors construct the building based on the architect's drawings and specifications. The architect may supervise the construction, **Figure 1-8.** Sometimes, the contractor may want to modify the drawings or specifications. For

**Figure 1-7.**
This table lists examples of residential, commercial, industrial, and institutional structures designed by architects. Some architects specialize in a single type of structure, such as hospitals, schools, or apartment complexes.

| Structures Designed by Architects | | | |
|---|---|---|---|
| **Residential** | **Commercial** | **Industrial** | **Institutional** |
| Houses | Office buildings | Factories | Schools |
| Townhouses | Airport terminals | | Churches |
| Apartment complexes | | | Hospitals |

**Figure 1-8.**
An architect reviews drawings with contractors at the construction site. Architects often oversee construction and work with building contractors to solve problems. (DiNisco Design Partnership)

example, the contractor may prefer to use an installation procedure different from the specified procedure or want to substitute for a specified material. In these cases, the architect must approve the change. Once construction is complete and the client has possession of the building, the architect may still be involved with the building. The client may consult with the architect on maintenance issues, remodeling, or future additions.

Architects must be licensed by the state in which they practice. Licensing requirements vary from state to state, but generally there are three requirements:

- Graduation from an accredited school of architecture (generally a five-year college program).
- Professional experience under the supervision of a registered architect (generally three years of experience are required).
- Acceptable performance on the Architect Registration Examination (ARE).

Candidates must complete the professional experience component before applying to take the examination. Those who do not have a college degree in architecture can become licensed architects by taking the exam after five to seven years of professional experience.

# Architectural designer

The responsibilities of an *architectural designer* vary among architectural firms. Some states have specific licensing requirements for architectural designers, while other states have none. In nearly all cases, however, the abilities and responsibilities of an architectural designer are greater than those of an architectural drafter, but less than those of an architect.

Generally, an architectural designer works under the direct supervision of an architect or engineer. Designers may have responsibilities similar to those of architects. A designer's responsibilities may include the following:
- Supervising drafters.
- Working with clients.
- Designing projects.
- Preparing drawings.

Architectural designers often have their own businesses designing residential and light commercial buildings. State laws vary on the types and sizes of buildings designers can create.

Architectural designers normally begin their careers as architectural drafters. After several years of experience, a drafter with strong architectural skills may be promoted to designer. Although architectural designers normally do not have degrees in architecture, completing some architectural design courses is extremely beneficial.

# Architectural drafter

Architectural drafters prepare construction drawings for structures such as homes and office buildings. Drafters create the drawings based on sketches, specifications, codes, and calculations previously made by architects or designers. Construction workers then use these drawings.

An architectural drafter can have a variety of responsibilities, depending on the amount of experience he or she has. Architectural drafters with several years of experience often work directly with the architect or designer and clients in the development of the design. Entry-level drafters usually do routine work under close supervision. An architect, designer, or experienced drafter provides directions and reviews drawings. With more experience, drafters perform more challenging work with less supervision. They may be required to exercise more judgment and perform calculations when preparing and modifying drawings. Many employers pay for continuing education. By learning in the office and completing appropriate coursework, an architectural drafter may acquire the skills needed to advance to the level of architectural designer or even acquire the skills needed to become a licensed architect.

# CAD manager

With CAD being integrated into more architectural offices, a new career path has emerged. Most companies have a person designated as the *CAD manager, system administrator,* or *internal systems administrator.* The CAD manager is normally a CAD expert with the ability to customize CAD, troubleshoot equipment, and train others. This person usually has the following responsibilities:
- Develop and monitor operating procedures.
- Troubleshoot hardware problems and perform minor repairs.
- Solve software problems.
- Supervise the CAD network.
- Implement CAD standards.
- Customize AutoCAD to suit specific company needs.

- Perform in-house training.
- Select new hardware and software.
- Remain up-to-date on trends and practices.
- Establish and monitor drawing management, symbol libraries, and numbering conventions.

The CAD manager may have the same formal education as an architectural drafter, plus additional computer skills and training. This computer training may include training in computer science and computer programming. In some cases, the CAD manager may be an architect.

## Additional occupations for drafters

In addition to the career paths and opportunities previously described, there are several fields that make use of the skills learned in architectural drafting. Many of these careers also have levels corresponding to drafter, designer, and architect. The highest career level in some of these fields is engineer. The educational and licensing requirements for engineers and architects are similar. The most common engineers in the construction industry are structural engineers, civil engineers, and mechanical engineers.

One advantage of a drafting education is the long-range opportunities. A combination of drafting and AutoCAD is an excellent stepping-stone into related fields or management positions. Many drafting graduates move into management, sales, estimating, or design within the first five years of employment. A drafter may move into customizing and programming company software and symbol libraries. This could even lead to system management, system analyst, CAD sales, or CAD training. The following list provides a brief introduction to some drafting careers. While the following descriptions relate to the drafter level, there is also a designer and architect or engineer level for each category.

- **Civil Drafter.** A civil drafter prepares detailed construction drawings used in the planning and construction of highways, river and harbor improvements, flood control drainage, and other civil engineering projects. Civil drawings include topographic profiles, maps, and specification sheets. Civil drafters also plot maps and charts showing profiles and cross sections. They also draw details of structures and installations such as roads, culverts, fresh water supply and sewage disposal systems, dikes, wharves, and breakwaters. Responsibilities also include calculating volume of excavation and fills and preparing charts and hauling diagrams used in earthmoving operations. The civil drafter may accompany a survey crew in the field. The engineering title for this career path is *civil engineer*. **Figure 1-9** shows a typical civil drawing produced with AutoCAD.
- **Electrical Drafter.** Electrical drafters prepare electrical equipment drawings and wiring diagrams or schematics used by electrical construction crews. These drawings may be used to install or repair electrical equipment and wiring in communication centers, commercial and residential buildings, and electrical distribution centers. The engineering title for this career path is *electrical engineer*. **Figure 1-10** shows a typical electrical drawing produced with AutoCAD.
- **HVAC Drafter.** HVAC drafters specialize in drawing plans for the installation of heating, ventilating, and air conditioning (HVAC) equipment. At the design level, this person may calculate heat loss and gain for buildings to determine equipment specifications. This career may also involve designing and drafting installation plans for refrigeration equipment. The engineering position is commonly referred to as a *mechanical engineer*. **Figure 1-11** shows a typical HVAC plan created with AutoCAD.

## Figure 1-9.
This civil drawing shows the intersection of two streets and several lots within a subdivision. A section illustrates sidewalk, curb, and street design.

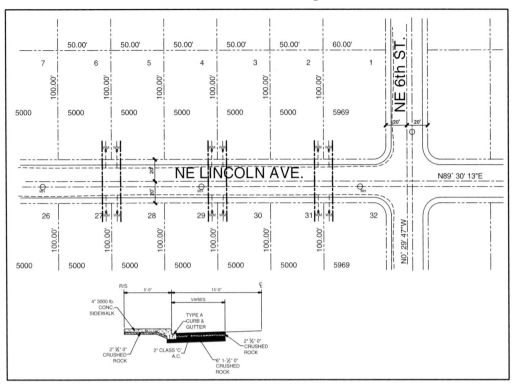

## Figure 1-10.
This portion of a residential electrical plan shows the locations of switches, lighting fixtures, receptacles, and other electrical devices. (EC Company)

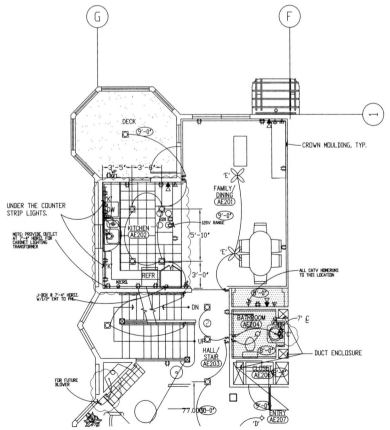

**Figure 1-11.**
This portion of an HVAC plan shows the ductwork needed for a commercial installation. (MCEI)

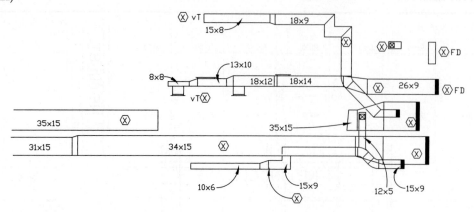

- **Interior Designer.** Interior designers plan and select interior finishes, furnishings, and lighting for residential and commercial buildings. They normally work directly with the architect on the interior design of a proposed building. **Figure 1-12** displays a drawing created by an interior designer. The educational path of the interior designer is normally different from that of the drafter and architect. Two-year associate's degree programs and four-year bachelor's degree programs in interior design normally provide training in design, furnishing, fabrics, and art.
- **Landscape Drafter.** Landscape drafters work with landscape architects to design and arrange the natural environment. They prepare drawings for site designs around buildings, grading and drainage plans, exterior lighting plans, paving plans, irrigation plans, and planting plans. They also design garden layouts, parks, and recreation areas. The professional title for this field is *landscape architect*. **Figure 1-13** shows a typical landscape plan.

**Figure 1-12.**
A drawing of the interior layout for an office building.

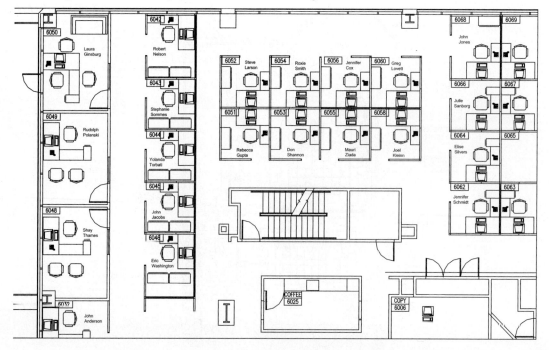

**Figure 1-13.**
This residential
landscape plan
shows the location
of trees, shrubs, and
the various types of
ground cover.

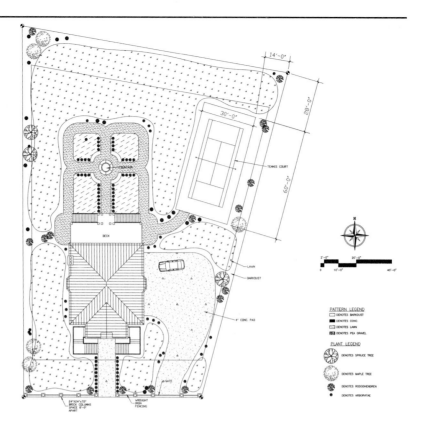

- **Piping Drafter.** Piping drafters create drawings used for plumbing and piping installations. The drawings are normally used in commercial and industrial applications, rather than in residential applications. The engineer involved in the field is a mechanical engineer who specializes in piping installations. **Figure 1-14** shows a plumbing plan drawn using AutoCAD.
- **Structural Drafter.** Structural drafters create plans and details for buildings made of structural steel, concrete, masonry, wood, and other structural materials. The drawings commonly include plans and details for foundations, floor framing, roof framing, and other structural elements. The engineering career path for this discipline is structural engineer. A typical structural detail drawing is shown in **Figure 1-15.**

**Figure 1-14.**
A portion of a piping plan for a commercial building. (MCEI)

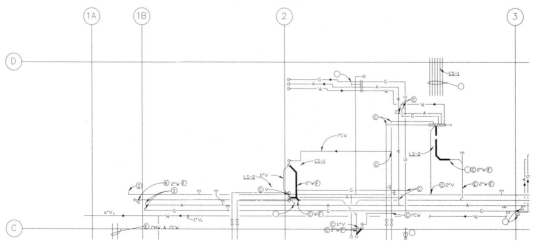

**Figure 1-15.**
Structural drafters prepare details showing connections between structural members.

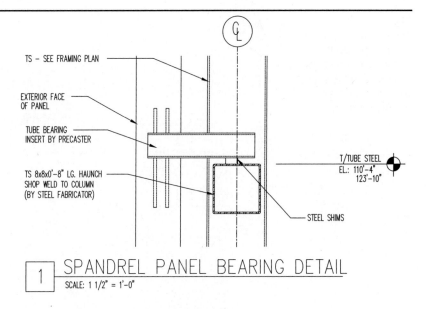

TS – SEE FRAMING PLAN

EXTERIOR FACE OF PANEL

TUBE BEARING INSERT BY PRECASTER

TS 8x8x0'–8" LG. HAUNCH SHOP WELD TO COLUMN (BY STEEL FABRICATOR)

T/TUBE STEEL
EL.: 110'–4"
123'–10"

STEEL SHIMS

1 SPANDREL PANEL BEARING DETAIL
SCALE: 1 1/2" = 1'-0"

## Skills Required for Architectural Drafting

Architectural drafting training can be found in high schools, community colleges, and some colleges and universities. Generally, employers prefer some post–high school training in drafting and other technical areas. Training in the following areas is useful for an architectural drafter:

- Mathematics.
- Science.
- Engineering technology.
- Computer technology.
- CAD drafting.
- Building codes and engineering standards.

In addition, communication and problem-solving skills are required. Artistic ability is helpful, along with knowledge of construction methods. Architectural drafters should have good interpersonal skills because they work closely with clients, architects, engineers, surveyors, and other professionals. See **Figure 1-16.**

**Figure 1-16.**
An architect and architectural drafter discuss a project with the clients. Communication and teamwork are important in the architectural field. (DiNisco Design Partnership)

## General Work Skills

In addition to the specific technical skills required to become an architectural drafter, many general qualities are needed to be successful. The following qualities reflect the professional behavior generally required for success and advancement in the workplace:

- **Cooperative.** An employee must cooperate with supervisors, other employees, and customers. An architectural drafter must work well with architects, designers, other drafters, and clients.
- **Dependable.** A dependable employee is timely, completes all assignments, and sets realistic goals for completing projects. A dependable employee is trusted by others. A drafter who is late for work, ignores assignments, or fails to meet deadlines is not dependable.
- **Dedicated.** Good employees put an honest effort into their work. They do not spend their work time having extended casual conversations with their coworkers or visiting inappropriate Web sites.
- **Respectful.** In order to be respected, employees must show respect for others, the company, and themselves.

These general skills are as important as specific job skills. Developing these skills is essential to being successful in any career.

## Leadership

Teamwork is an important aspect of nearly all businesses. Within an architectural firm, architects, designers, drafters, and office administrators must work together if the firm is to be successful. Every employee has a specific role, and all employees must work together.

*Leadership* is the ability to guide or direct. Employees who manage or supervise others must have strong leadership skills. Even employees who do not manage others benefit from developing their leadership skills. Possessing leadership skills is a requirement for career growth. The following are some practices that reflect leadership skills:

- **Exercising motivation.** A leader must be able to motivate others. Treating others fairly, praising others when appropriate, maintaining a positive attitude, and involving others in decisions all help to motivate people.
- **Accomplishing goals.** A leader must be able to define goals and then see that they are accomplished. Assigning tasks according to each team member's abilities and limitations helps to complete projects more efficiently.
- **Solving problems.** A leader must be able to address problems as they occur. A leader may involve others to help solve the problems, but must see that a solution is found.
- **Recognizing limitations.** Leaders must recognize their own weaknesses and be willing to rely on others to help in those areas.
- **Acting as a role model.** A leader must serve as a role model for other employees through both words and actions. Leaders must always behave in a manner deserving of respect.

## Entrepreneurship

*Entrepreneurship* is the act of organizing, managing, and accepting risks of a business. There are many opportunities for entrepreneurship in the architectural field. After gaining sufficient experience with an architectural firm, some architects and designers choose to begin their own businesses. At first, the architect may simply create a home office and begin attracting clients. As the number of clients grows, the architect may begin renting a small office and employing a drafter and receptionist. If the business continues to grow, more architects, designers, and drafters may be needed.

Architectural drafters also have entrepreneurial opportunities. Some architects with their own businesses may need drafting help on a part-time basis. Larger architectural firms may use outside drafting sources when there are too many projects for the full-time drafters to handle. It is fairly easy for an experienced architectural drafter to begin establishing contacts with firms that can use a reliable drafting service.

There are several advantages to starting your own business:

- It is often more satisfying to manage your own business, rather than working for someone else.
- Since you are the boss, you are not at the mercy of others' judgment for important decisions.
- If you manage your business well, there is good opportunity for greater financial rewards.

Many new businesses, however, fail. There are many reasons why businesses fail. There may be little demand for the products or services the new venture offers. There may be too much existing competition in the market. The entrepreneur may have underestimated business costs and obtained insufficient financing. Often, the entrepreneur does not have sufficient management skills or lacks the specific technical skills required for the business.

There are other disadvantages to starting your own business. You may need to work longer hours, particularly when the business is first started. There are many responsibilities, especially if you hire employees. Finally, the income the business generates may fluctuate greatly. To be a successful entrepreneur, you must possess the following characteristics:

- **Organized.** Normally, an entrepreneur must manage the business and also be involved in producing products or providing service. Remaining organized is essential.
- **Responsible.** An entrepreneur must be willing to accept responsibility for all aspects of the business. When you run your own business, there is no one to whom you can "pass the buck."
- **Knowledgeable.** An entrepreneur must be knowledgeable in the product or service being provided. If competitors are more knowledgeable, the business will likely fail.
- **Goal oriented.** An entrepreneur must set both personal goals and business goals and be able to meet these goals.
- **Able to lead.** In order to have any chance of success, an entrepreneur must possess strong leadership skills. These skills were discussed in the previous section.
- **Able to work hard.** An entrepreneur must be able to put in long hours when necessary.

# Architectural Design Process

The design of an architectural project commonly goes through several stages. For small, simple projects, each stage may take anywhere from an hour to a week. On large projects, each stage could take weeks or even months. The design process can be separated into the following phases:

- Consultation.
- Preliminary design.
- Drawing production.

## Consultation

A project begins with an initial consultation between the architect and the client. The client provides the basic background information needed to begin the design. This information includes fundamental design ideas of the client, the type of architectural design, the number of square feet, the desired room arrangement, and a proposed budget. The architect may make suggestions based on experience with similar projects.

## Preliminary Design

When the architect has a solid understanding of the client's needs and a contract has been signed, the preliminary design work begins. The preliminary design includes an evaluation of the site and research of local building codes and zoning ordinances. All general design considerations must be determined at this stage.

The preliminary design then continues with sketches, informal hand drawings, or simple CAD drawings of floor plans and perhaps some elevations. The preliminary drawings are normally done as quickly as possible. The architect meets with the clients to determine if the preliminary design meets their expectations. Once the preliminary design has been approved, the architect continues with the initial working drawings.

## Drawing Production

The terms **construction documents** and **working drawings** refer to the set of drawings needed to construct the building. The initial documents are known as *preliminary drawings.* They contain the basic elements of the design. This includes the beginning of the floor plans and elevations with key features and dimensions. Often, these drawings are used to obtain a construction loan and building permits. An architect, a designer, or an experienced drafter can draw the initial working drawings. An initial floor plan is shown in **Figure 1-17.**

The entry-level architectural drafter can often take over once the initial working drawings are approved and work is ready to begin on the final working drawings. The final working drawings are the drawings from which the building is constructed. They are drawn after the client approves the initial working drawings.

**Professional Tip**

The arrangement of drawings within the set of working drawings varies among architectural firms. It is common, however, to have the drawings in the following order:
1. Site plan.
2. Exterior elevations.
3. Floor plans.
4. Foundation plan.
5. Sections.
6. Details.
7. Interior elevations.

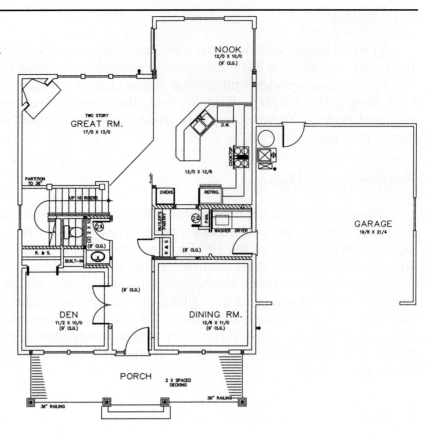

**Figure 1-17.**
The initial floor plan for a residence. (Alan Mascord Design Associates, Inc.)

# Architectural Drawings

The set of working drawings contains several types of drawings, along with the necessary notes and schedules. Notes are written items on a drawing providing additional explanation or clarification. Schedules are tabular lists that may provide specifications for materials and installations. They are commonly placed with the floor plan if space is available. The notes, details, and interior elevations are often placed on sheets where space is available or together on one sheet. The following sections identify the elements of a set of working drawings for a residential structure.

## Site Plans

The site plan (also called *plot plan)* shows the location of the building on the property. A surveyor provides much of the information for the site plan. Generally, the site plan includes some or all of the following features:
- Property lines.
- Setback requirements and easements.
- Contour lines showing ground elevation.
- Basic building dimensions and distances from property lines.
- Utilities.
- Streets, driveways, sidewalks, and fences.
- North arrow.
- Trees and shrubs.

**Figure 1-18** shows a typical site plan.

**Figure 1-18.**
This residential site plan shows property lines, utilities, and setback distances.

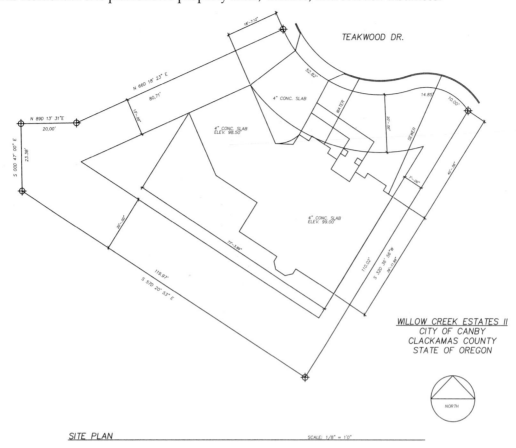

SITE PLAN                                                        SCALE: 1/8" = 1'0"

## Floor Plans

Floor plans show the layout and size of rooms within the building. They also show the locations of doors and windows. Some floor plans show the door and window sizes directly on the plan. Others include door and window schedules keyed to the floor plan with symbols. Additional information on the size, manufacturer, and model numbers for doors and windows is included in the door and window schedules.

For simple residential designs, the floor plan may also show the framing, electrical, and plumbing systems and interior design elements, such as cabinets, appliances, and finishes. See **Figure 1-19.** These items may also include schedules.

For complex residences or commercial designs, the floor plan may include wall, window, and door locations. In this case, the floor plan is referred to as a *background* or *base drawing* and is complemented by the following drawings:

- **Electrical plan.** This drawing specifies the location of electrical panels, receptacles, lighting fixtures, and switches. It also identifies the type and size of conduit runs and the number and size of wires within each run of conduit. Schedules for the electrical panel and lighting fixtures may also be included.
- **Plumbing plan.** This drawing shows the size and type of piping used in the supply and drain plumbing systems. In addition to the piping, the locations of the water meter, main shutoff valve, and water heater are included. For large projects, a plumbing fixture schedule may be needed.
- **HVAC plan.** This drawing includes the location and size of supply and return ductwork and registers. Heating and air conditioning units are also identified on the HVAC plan.

**Figure 1-19.**
This residential floor plan includes electrical, plumbing, and HVAC design. (Alan Mascord Design Associates, Inc.)

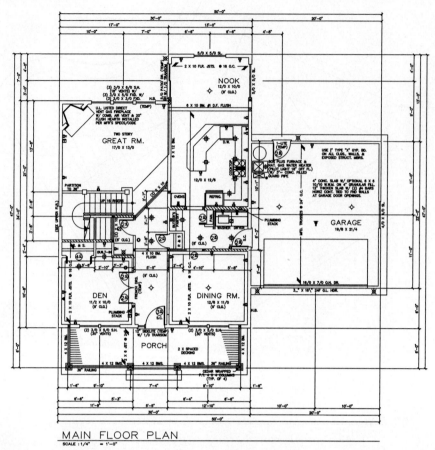

MAIN FLOOR PLAN
SCALE : 1/4" = 1'-0"

- **Reflected ceiling plan.** This type of plan is normally reserved for commercial designs with drop ceilings. This drawing shows the location of lighting fixtures and ceiling panels.

The plumbing and HVAC plans may be combined into a single plan called a *mechanical plan*. The number of plans required normally depends on the size and complexity of the design.

## Exterior Elevations

The exterior elevations show the building as it appears from the outside. Elevations show floor to ceiling dimensions, roof slopes, and exterior construction materials. The front elevation is normally quite detailed, but the other elevations may be drawn with less detail to help save time. A front elevation is illustrated in **Figure 1-5.**

## Foundation Plans

Foundation plans show the construction below the first floor. The construction materials and related dimensions are provided on the foundation plan, as shown in **Figure 1-20.** Foundation plans may include a foundation section, which illustrates the foundation wall and footing dimensions and the size, location, and spacing of steel reinforcing bars.

**Figure 1-20.**
The foundation plan for the floor plan shown in **Figure 1-19**. (Alan Mascord Design Associates, Inc.)

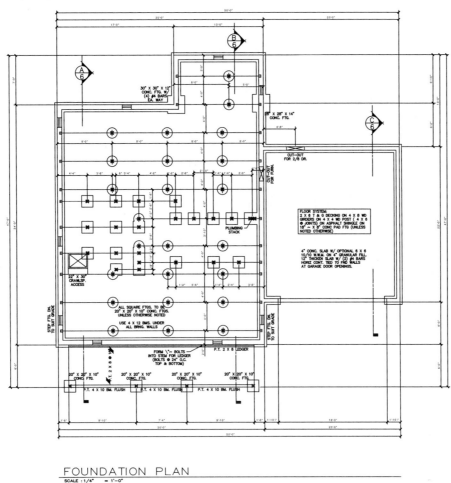

FOUNDATION PLAN

SCALE : 1/4" = 1'-0"

## Framing Plans

For small residential designs, the floor plan normally shows the location and size of framing members. More complex designs, however, require detailed floor framing plans and roof framing plans. These framing plans show the sizes and locations of the structural members composing the floor or roof. **Figure 1-21** shows a typical floor framing plan.

## Sections

A section illustrates construction elements as if a slice were made through the building and part of the structure were removed. It may show the entire width of the building or illustrate the construction of a specific feature, such as a wall. Sections clarify how building components are assembled. **Figure 1-22** shows a section of the house displayed in **Figure 1-19**.

**Figure 1-21.**
A main floor framing plan. (Alan Mascord Design Associates, Inc.)

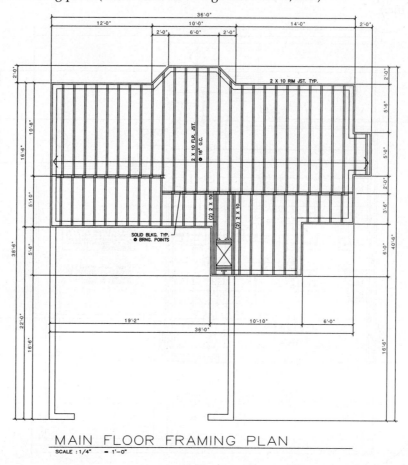

MAIN FLOOR FRAMING PLAN
SCALE : 1/4" = 1'-0"

**Figure 1-22.**
This section is taken near the left side of the floor plan shown in **Figure 1-19**. (Alan Mascord Design Associates, Inc.)

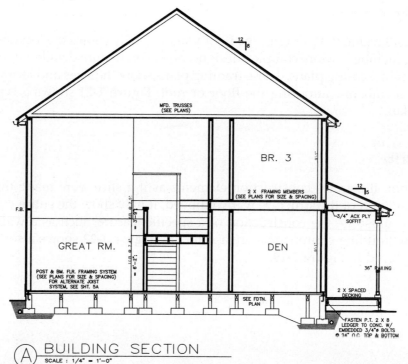

Ⓐ BUILDING SECTION
SCALE : 1/4" = 1'-0"

**Figure 1-23.**
This stair construction detail is drawn on a larger scale than a section. This allows relatively small or complex details to be shown clearly. (Alan Mascord Design Associates, Inc.)

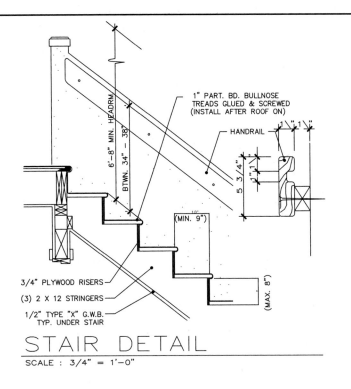

1" PART. BD. BULLNOSE
TREADS GLUED & SCREWED
(INSTALL AFTER ROOF ON)

HANDRAIL

6'-8" MIN. HEADRM.

BTWN. 34" - 38"

5 3/4"

(MIN. 9")

(MAX. 8")

3/4" PLYWOOD RISERS

(3) 2 X 12 STRINGERS

1/2" TYPE "X" G.W.B.
TYP. UNDER STAIR

STAIR DETAIL
SCALE : 3/4" = 1'-0"

## Details

Details are large-scale drawings illustrating a specific construction assembly or area of the structure. They are drawn on a larger scale than plans, so relatively small dimensions and materials are more apparent. Details are normally provided for stairs, fireplaces, retaining walls, and unusual eaves. **Figure 1-23** shows a detail for residential construction.

## Interior Elevations

Interior elevations show interior design elements such as cabinets and wood-work. These drawings show dimensions, construction materials and practices, appliances, fixtures, and related details. **Figure 1-24** shows cabinet elevations and related construction details.

**Figure 1-24.**
Interior cabinet elevations. (Alan Mascord Design Associates, Inc.)

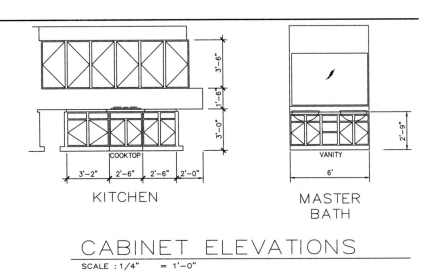

3'-6"

1'-6"

3'-0"

COOKTOP

3'-2"   2'-6"   2'-6"   2'-0"

KITCHEN

2'-9"

VANITY

6'

MASTER
BATH

CABINET ELEVATIONS
SCALE : 1/4"    = 1'-0"

**Figure 1-25.**
This table shows
some common
topics addressed by
CAD standards.

| Typical Areas Covered by Standards | |
|---|---|
| **Drafting** | **File Management** |
| Standard symbols | File naming system |
| Title blocks | Folder and file organization |
| Linetypes | Adding new symbols and details |
| Blocks/Symbols | Backup procedures |
| Lettering heights and styles | Plotting procedures |
| Layer settings | Template files |
| Sheet sizes and scales | |
| Typical details | |
| Dimensioning practices and styles | |

# Architectural and CAD Standards

All architectural firms use some type of standards. **Standards** are rules or guidelines for design and drafting. They may be developed for drafting procedures, drawing appearance, and file management. Some typical procedures defined by standards are listed in the table in **Figure 1-25.** Using standards improves consistency and efficiency. Often, architectural firms develop their own standards to ensure consistent practices and drawings within the office.

 **Note**     Each chapter of this textbook covers related office standards that should be considered when drawing with AutoCAD.

In most cases, office standards are based on standards developed by organizations such as the American Institute of Architects (AIA), the National CAD Standard (NCS), American National Standards Institute (ANSI), Construction Specifications Institute (CSI), or General Service Administration (GSA). Architectural drafting standards are needed for manual drafting and CAD drafting. These standards may be printed and bound into a book or stored on an intranet so all drafters can access them from their computers. An **intranet** is a relatively small network of computers, usually within a company, enabling each drafter access to standards on an internal office Web page. Each drafter has access to the standards for use as a reference.

One of the main advantages of CAD is the ability to reuse standard symbols and details. Once a symbol or detail is created for a drawing, it can be saved and then used for future drawings. As new symbols are created, they are added to the collection of standard symbols. **Figure 1-26** shows an example of a page from a typical office standards library.

**Figure 1-26.**
This drawing contains standard symbols, which can be copied into other drawings.

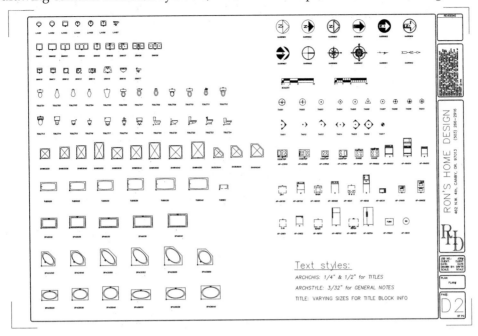

# Safety and Health in the Architectural Office

Architectural drafters usually work in comfortable offices furnished to accommodate their tasks. In order to avoid computer malfunctions, the office should be air-conditioned, well ventilated, and as dust-free as practical. Antistatic carpets may also be used to avoid a static charge between the operator and computer. These conditions make for a fairly comfortable office.

CAD drafters spend most of their time working at computer workstations. A good CAD workstation has reference manuals, computer hardware, and a layout table arranged in an organized manner. A drafting table with a drafting machine or parallel straightedge is also helpful in the layout area. This offers you a place to sketch designs and reference prints.

Normally, the CAD workstations are networked. A computer network is a group of connected computers that can share electronic data (such as drawing files, memos, and e-mail messages) and hardware resources (such as printers, plotters, scanners, and external storage devices). Small offices often have only one or two plotters, which all drafters share. The noise of plotters can be disturbing, so plotters are normally located in a separate room, near the workstations. Some companies have a plotter room that plots drawings from the user's disks upon request. Other companies place the plotter in a central location with small office workstations around the plotter. Still others prefer to have the plotters near individual workstations surrounded by acoustical partition walls or partial walls.

## The Ergonomic Environment

Like other workers who spend long periods of time doing detailed work with computers, drafters may be susceptible to eyestrain, back discomfort, and hand and wrist problems. *Ergonomics* is the science of adapting the workstation to fit the needs of the drafter. Applying ergonomic principles results in a comfortable and efficient environment.

**Figure 1-27.**
A recommended
workstation setup.

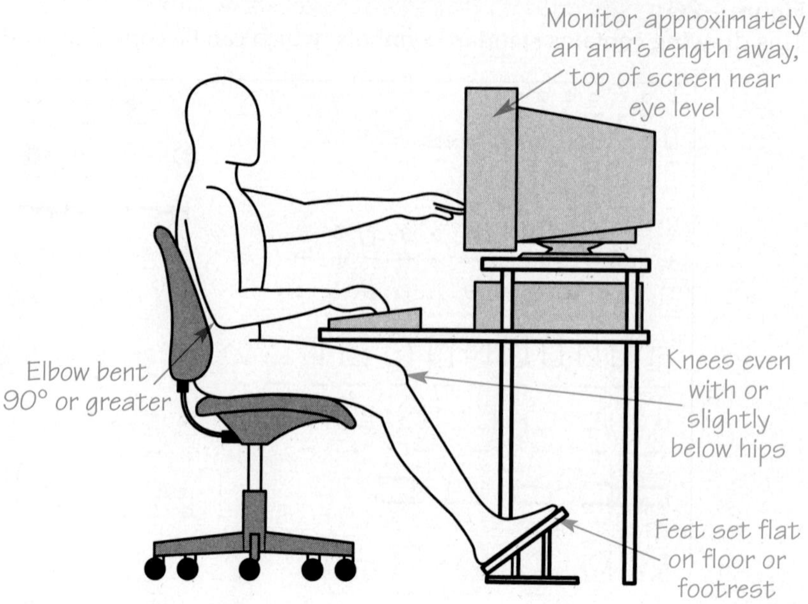

Monitor approximately
an arm's length away,
top of screen near
eye level

Elbow bent
90° or greater

Knees even
with or
slightly
below hips

Feet set flat
on floor or
footrest

There are many types of ergonomic accessories that may improve a computer workstation. In addition, a few things can be done to create a comfortable environment and help prevent injury or strain to the operator's body. **Figure 1-27** shows the recommended setup of an ergonomic workstation. The following sections list specific guidelines to help prevent injuries for various body parts.

## Eyes

- Position the monitor to minimize glare from overhead lights, windows, and other light sources. Reduce light intensity by turning off some lights or closing blinds and shades. You should be able to see images clearly without glare.
- Position the monitor so it is 18" to 30" from your eyes. This is about an arm's length. To help reduce eyestrain, look away from the monitor every 15 to 20 minutes and focus on an object at least 20' away for one to two minutes.

## Wrists and arms

- Forearms should be parallel to the floor.
- Periodically stretch your arms, wrists, and shoulders.
- Try using an ergonomic keyboard and mouse. This kind of keyboard keeps the wrists in a normal body position, and such a mouse will fit the hands more comfortably.

## Neck

- Adjust the monitor so your head is level, not leaning forward or back. The top of the screen should be near your line of sight.

## Back

- Use a comfortable chair providing good back support. The chair should be adjustable and provide armrests.

Architectural Drafting Using AutoCAD

- Sit up straight. This maintains good posture and reduces strain. Think about good posture until it becomes common practice.
- Try standing up, stretching, and walking every hour. This will also reduce strain.

## Legs

- Keep your thighs parallel to the ground.
- Rest your feet flat on the floor or use a footrest.
- When taking a break, walk around. This will stretch the muscles and promote circulation through your body.

Make the workstation comfortable and practice these tips. Try to keep your stress level low. Increased stress can contribute to tension, which may aggravate physical problems. Take a break periodically to help reduce muscle fatigue and tension. Some stretching exercises can help if you feel pain and discomfort. Relaxing activities such as yoga, biofeedback, and massage may also help reduce muscle strain. You should consult with your doctor for further advice and recommendations.

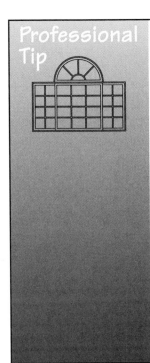

**Professional Tip**

The United States Copyright Office protects computer software. You do not actually own the software you buy. You are buying a license to use the software. Unless otherwise indicated in the agreement, this means you can use the software on only one computer in one location at a time. It is illegal to make or distribute copies of copyrighted material without authorization. For example, when you buy a single copy of AutoCAD, the copy is to be used on only one computer and cannot be copied throughout the office, given or sold to a friend, or distributed in any other way. You are allowed to make a backup copy for safekeeping in case something happens to the original, but you cannot copy the software in any other way.

Stealing software is the same as shoplifting. Software companies rely on the sale of their products to help keep their businesses running and to continue research and development for product improvement. Be sure you read the licensing agreement of any software you buy and use the product in a lawful manner.

## Student and Professional Organizations

There are several professional and educational organizations related to architectural drafting. Many of the professional organizations have student membership and student chapters. The following is a partial list of organizations that can provide valuable information about careers and educational opportunities in architecture and architectural drafting.

## ADDA

The American Design Drafting Association (ADDA) is pledged to meeting and serving the professional growth and advancement of the individual working in the design drafting community. The ADDA is the only membership organization exclusively for all disciplines of professional drafters. This organization also maintains a drafter certification program. Individuals who wish to become certified must pass the Drafter Certification Test, which is administered periodically at ADDA-authorized test sites. Applicants are tested on their knowledge and understanding of basic drafting concepts, such as geometric construction, working drawings, and architectural terms and standards. Although employers normally do not require drafters to be certified, certification demonstrates that nationally recognized standards have been achieved. For more information about the ADDA, including student chapters, curriculum certification, national conference, and membership, use the following contact information:

American Design Drafting Association
P.O. Box 11937
Columbia, SC 29211
www.adda.org

## AIA

The American Institute of Architects (AIA) has been advancing the value of architects and architecture for more than 135 years through AIA member resources and as the collective voice of the profession. Contact the following for more information about the AIA:

American Institute of Architects
1735 New York Avenue NW
Washington, DC 20006
www.e-architect.com

## SARA

The Society of American Registered Architects (SARA) was founded in 1956 as a professional society that includes the participation of all architects, regardless of their roles in the architectural community. Contact the following for more information about SARA:

Society of American Registered Architects
305 E. 46th Street
New York, NY
www.sara-national.org

## AIBD

Since 1950, the American Institute of Building Design (AIBD) has provided building designers with educational resources, design standards, and a code of ethics. Today, the AIBD is a nationally recognized association with professional and associate members in 47 states and throughout Canada, as well as Europe, Asia, and Australia. The AIBD promotes public awareness of the building design profession and educates members about new and improved materials and methods of construction.

The AIBD also enforces a certification program for professional building designers. For those who have chosen the building design profession, there is no greater evidence of competency than achieving the status of Certified Professional Building Designer (CPBD). Contact the following for more information about the AIBD:

American Institute of Building Design
991 Post Road East
Westport, Connecticut 06880
www.aibd.org

## NCS

The National CAD Standard (NCS) is a relatively young organization focused on the management of electronic or CAD drawings. The standards, first printed in 1999, provide a means of drawing organization and standards to manage a project through a building's entire life cycle. The standard is a merger of three separate standards: the American Institute of Architect's CAD layering guidelines, the Construction Specifications Institute's Uniform Drawing System, and the U.S. Department of Defense's Tri-Services CADD/GIS Technology Centers plotting guidelines. For more information regarding this resource, go to the following Web site:
www.nationalcadstandard.org

## Other Organizations

The following are additional organizations that can be contacted for professional and educational opportunities:

American Institute of Landscape Architects
501 E. San Juan Avenue
Phoenix, AZ 85012

American Society of Landscape Architects
636 Eye Street, NW
Washington, DC 20001-3736
www.asla.org

Association of Collegiate Schools of Architecture
1735 New York Avenue NW
Washington, DC 20006
www.acsa-arch.org

# Chapter Test

*Answer the following questions on a separate sheet of paper.*

1. Define *architectural drafting*.
2. Briefly describe the evolution of architectural drafting.
3. Define *software*.
4. What is AutoCAD?
5. List five advantages of using CAD in architecture.
6. How does Web-based collaboration affect the relationship between the architect and client?
7. Generally speaking, what three requirements must be met before a person can become a licensed architect?
8. Describe the type of work entry-level drafters generally perform.
9. List five responsibilities of a CAD manager.
10. In addition to CAD skills, what other types of training are desirable for a CAD manager?
11. List the types of drawings the following types of drafters create:
    A. Civil drafter
    B. Electrical drafter
    C. HVAC drafter
    D. Interior designer
    E. Landscape drafter
    F. Piping drafter
    G. Structural drafter
12. List five academic areas of study and training employers prefer for architectural drafters.
13. List four general work skills needed for success in the workplace.
14. Define *leadership*.
15. List five characteristics of a leader.
16. Define *entrepreneurship*.
17. List three advantages of entrepreneurship.
18. List three reasons why a business may fail.
19. List six skills needed to be a successful entrepreneur.
20. Describe the basic steps in the architectural design process.
21. What is the purpose of the consultation between the architect and the client?
22. Why is it important to research the site, building codes, and zoning restrictions during the preliminary design phase?
23. Define *working drawings*.
24. What is normally included in the initial working drawings?
25. Identify the drawing that typically shows the location of the building on the property, along with roads, walks, driveways, and utilities.

26. Identify at least six types of drawings contained in a set of working drawings.
27. When are separate electrical plans, plumbing plans, and HVAC plans used?
28. Name the plan that shows the construction below the floor plan.
29. Name the type of drawing that illustrates construction methods and materials by showing a cut through the entire building.
30. What is the difference between a section and a detail?
31. Define *standards.*
32. Why are standards used?
33. List five topics office standards normally address.
34. Why is it a good idea to locate a plotter in a room separate from the CAD workstations?
35. Define *ergonomics.*
36. List two ways to minimize eyestrain caused by the CAD workstation monitor.
37. Identify two ways to help reduce wrist and arm tension when working at a CAD workstation.
38. What does ADDA stand for?
39. What does AIA stand for?
40. What does SARA stand for?

# Chapter Problems

1. Sketch or draw an example of a recommended ergonomic CAD workstation.
2. Research and write a 250-word essay on one of the following topics, using graphic examples as appropriate:
   - History of architectural drafting.
   - Transition from manual drafting to CAD.
   - Architectural Web-based collaboration.
   - Architect profession.
   - Architectural drafter profession.
   - Civil drafting.
   - Electrical drafting.
   - HVAC drafting.
   - Interior design.
   - Landscape drafting.
   - Plumbing drafting.
   - Structural drafting.
   - Architectural design process.
   - Set of working drawings.
   - Architectural standards.
   - Ergonomics for computer users.
   - Computer workstation exercises.
   - American Design Drafting Association.
   - American Institute of Architects.
   - Society of American Registered Architects.
   - American Institute of Building Design.
   - The National CAD Standard.

Floor plan drawings for commercial projects such as this office building originate from preliminary designs or sketches. They show the locations of walls, doors, and windows and are used in the later development of elevations and other types of drawings. (Autodesk, Inc.)

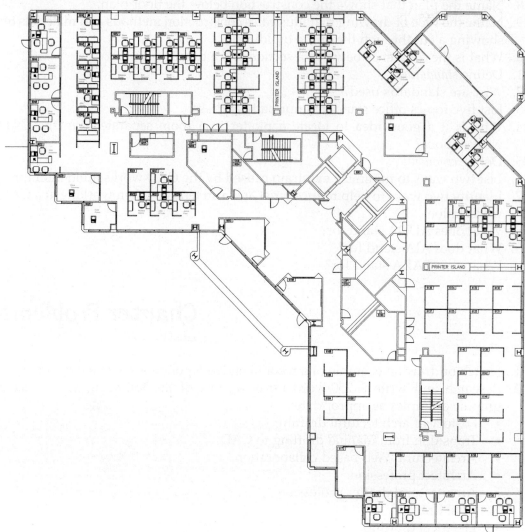

Architectural Drafting Using AutoCAD

# CHAPTER 2

# The AutoCAD Environment

## Learning Objectives

After completing this chapter, you will be able to:

- Launch AutoCAD.
- Create a new drawing.
- Open an existing drawing.
- Identify the various features in the AutoCAD window.
- Access commands using pull-down menus.
- Identify dialog box features.
- Save drawing files.
- Use the AutoCAD help system.

## Important Terms

cascading menu
command window
desktop
desktop icon
dialog box
docked
double-click
floating

flyout
grab bar
menu accelerator key
pull-down menu
shortcut menu
toolbar
tooltip

The AutoCAD installation program creates a *desktop icon* that is displayed on the Windows desktop. The term *desktop* refers to the background on your screen when you are using Windows. The screen is like your real desktop, and everything you need is there for your use. To launch AutoCAD, simply double-click on the desktop icon. See **Figure 2-1.**

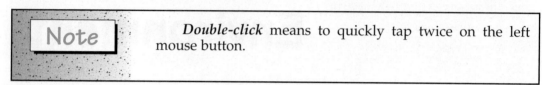

| Note | *Double-click* means to quickly tap twice on the left mouse button. |

**Figure 2-1.**
Double-click on the desktop icon to launch AutoCAD.

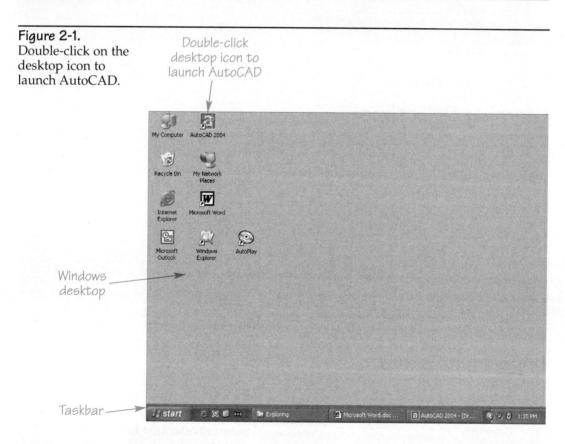

Another method for starting AutoCAD is to pick the Start button in the lower-left corner of the Windows desktop. This displays the Start menu. Select Programs from the Start menu to display the Programs menu. Move the pointer to Autodesk and click to show the Autodesk menu. Pick AutoCAD 2004 from the list, and then select AutoCAD 2004 to load the software. See **Figure 2-2.** Either of these methods launches the AutoCAD software. Once AutoCAD has loaded, you're ready to start working.

Figure 2-2.
Launching AutoCAD from the Start menu.

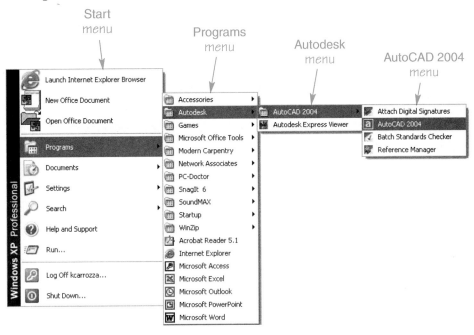

# The AutoCAD Window

The AutoCAD window is similar to other windows within the Windows operating system. Picking the small control icon in the upper-left corner displays a standard window control menu, and the icons in the upper-right corner are used for minimizing, maximizing, and closing the program window or individual drawing window. Window sizing operations are done as with any other Windows application.

AutoCAD uses the familiar Windows interface, with buttons, pull-down menus, and dialog boxes. These items are discussed in detail in this section. Learning the layout, appearance, and proper use of these features allows you to master AutoCAD quickly. **Figure 2-3** shows important features of the AutoCAD window.

## Window Layout

The AutoCAD window layout provides a large drawing area. The drawing area is bordered by *toolbars* at the left and top of the screen and the *command window* at the bottom. See **Figure 2-3**.

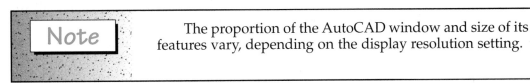

Note    The proportion of the AutoCAD window and size of its features vary, depending on the display resolution setting.

Many features of the AutoCAD window can be resized and moved within the window. These features are called *floating* features. Floating features are outlined by a standard Windows border and display a title bar at the top.

When you launch AutoCAD for the first time, the AutoCAD window is displayed in a floating position on the desktop. A smaller window within the AutoCAD window displays the drawing area for the currently open drawing file.

**Figure 2-3.**
The AutoCAD window contains many features and tools.

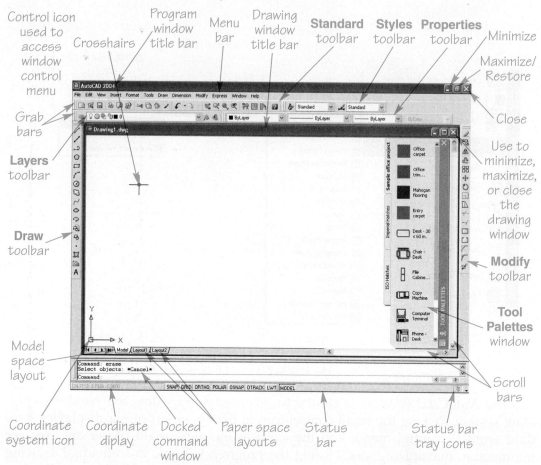

Floating windows are moved and adjusted for size in the same manner as any other Windows program. Drawing windows, however, can be adjusted and positioned only within the AutoCAD window.

Some floating features, such as toolbars, can also be *docked* around the edges of the AutoCAD window. Docked toolbars do not display a title bar. Instead, they display a *grab bar,* the two thin bars at the top or left edge of the docked toolbar. To place a docked toolbar in a floating position, you can double-click on the grab bar. You also can press and hold the pick button while pointing at the grab bar, and then move your mouse to drag the toolbar away from the edge of the window. To dock a floating toolbar, double-click on the title bar, or press and hold the pick button while pointing at the title bar and drag it to an edge of the drawing area. Wait until the toolbar outline changes to a thin outline, and then release the pick button. Toolbars may be moved or docked at any time as needed. The following list describes several components of the AutoCAD window. Look at **Figure 2-3** and your own AutoCAD window as you review these features:

- **Command window.** In its default position, this window is docked at the bottom of the AutoCAD window. It displays command entries and prompts for input. Your primary communications with AutoCAD are displayed in the command window.
- **Menu bar.** The menu bar is located below the title bar and displays a number of menu names. As with standard Windows menus, use the cursor to point at a menu name and press the pick button. This causes a *pull-down menu* to be displayed. Each pull-down menu contains AutoCAD commands.

- **Scroll bars.** The scroll bars allow you to adjust your view of the drawing area.
- **Crosshairs.** This is your primary means of pointing to objects and selecting locations within a drawing.
- **Coordinate system icon.** This indicates the current coordinate system drawing plane and helps to determine point locations.
- **Toolbars.** Toolbars contain various buttons that activate AutoCAD commands. These toolbars can be moved, resized, modified, hidden, or docked as needed.
- **Status bar.** This contains several buttons that display the current state of specific settings and allows access for changing them. When a pull-down menu item is highlighted or you are pointing at a toolbar button, a brief explanation (help tip) for the item is shown at the left end of the status bar.
- **Coordinate display.** This display field, found on the status bar, shows the XYZ crosshairs location.
- **Standard toolbar.** In the default AutoCAD window configuration, the **Standard** toolbar appears above the **Layers** toolbars. When you move your pointing device to the toolbar, the crosshairs change to the familiar Windows pointer. As you move the pointer across a toolbar button, a 3D button is displayed around the previously flat button. Holding the pointer motionless over a toolbar button for a moment displays a *tooltip,* which shows the name of the button in a small box at the pointer location.

   Some buttons show a small black triangle in the lower-right corner. These buttons are called *flyouts.* Press and hold the pick button while pointing at a flyout to display a set of related buttons.
- **Styles toolbar.** In the default AutoCAD screen configuration, the **Styles** toolbar appears to the right of the **Standard** toolbar. This toolbar contains buttons and display fields relative to text and dimension styles.
- **Layers and Properties toolbars.** In the default AutoCAD window configuration, the **Layers** and **Properties** toolbars appear just above the drawing area, below the **Standard** and **Styles** toolbars. These toolbars contain buttons and display fields for setting and adjusting the properties of objects in a drawing.

## Exercise 2-1

◆ Start AutoCAD.
◆ Look at all the features of the AutoCAD window.
◆ Keep AutoCAD open for the next exercise. If you must quit, pick **Exit** in the **File** pull-down menu, and then pick **No** in the **AutoCAD** alert box.

## Pull-Down Menus

The AutoCAD pull-down menus are located on the menu bar at the top of the AutoCAD window. As with a toolbar, when you move the cursor to the menu bar, the crosshairs change to the pointer. The menu bar, **Figure 2-4,** contains 11 pull-down menu items: **File, Edit, View, Insert, Format, Tools, Draw, Dimension, Modify, Window,** and **Help.**

Most of the available menu selections can be found in both the toolbars and pull-down menus. Some menu selections, however, are found in only one of these two menu areas, so it is important to be familiar with the layout and use of both toolbars and pull-down menus. To see how a pull-down menu works, move the pointer to the **Draw** menu and press the left mouse (pick) button. A pull-down menu appears below **Draw,** as shown in **Figure 2-5A.** Commands are easily selected by picking a menu item with the pointer.

**Figure 2-4.**
The AutoCAD menu bar. To access the pull-down menus, place the pointer on the menu title and press the pick button.

File Edit View Insert Format Tools Draw Dimension Modify Window Help

Notice that several of the commands in the **Draw** pull-down menu have a small arrow to the right. When one of these items is selected, a *cascading menu* appears. A cascading menu has additional options for the previous selection, as shown in **Figure 2-5B.**

An ellipsis (...) follows some menu selections. If you pick one of these items, a dialog box is displayed. If you pick the wrong pull-down menu, simply move the pointer to the one you want. The first menu is removed, and the new menu is displayed. The pull-down menu disappears after you pick an item in the menu, pick a point in the drawing area, or type on the keyboard.

**Figure 2-5.**
Using a pull-down menu. A—Items in a pull-down menu. B—When selecting an item with an arrow, a cascading menu with more items appears.

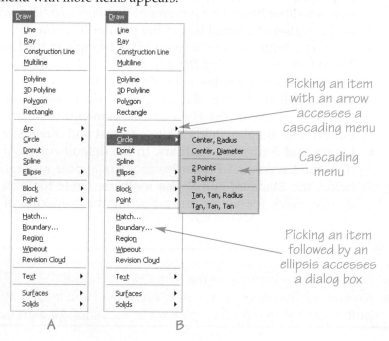

Picking an item with an arrow accesses a cascading menu

Cascading menu

Picking an item followed by an ellipsis accesses a dialog box

A                    B

**Professional Tip**

You can also select a pull-down menu item by holding the pick button down while moving the pointer to the desired selection and releasing the pick button.

## Accessing pull-down menus from the keyboard

It is also possible to use the keyboard to access pull-down menu items by typing shortcuts. These shortcut keystrokes are called *menu accelerator keys*. They allow access to any pull-down menu selection using an [Alt]+[*key*] combination on the keyboard. For example, pressing [Alt]+[F] accesses the **File** pull-down menu, and pressing [Alt]+[V] accesses the **View** pull-down menu. For AutoCAD releases prior to 2004, the menu accelerator keys were automatically displayed. One character of each pull-down menu title or command was underlined on screen. To display the accelerator keys with an underline in AutoCAD 2004, you need to press the [Alt] key.

Once a pull-down menu is displayed, a menu item can be selected using a single character key. For example, suppose you want to draw a circle by selecting the center point and the radius. Referring once again to **Figure 2-5B**, first press [Alt]+[D] to access the **Draw** pull-down menu. Press [C] to access the **Circle** cascading menu. Finally, press [R] to select the **Center, Radius** option.

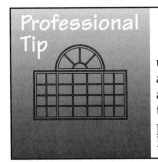
**Professional Tip**

Once a pull-down menu is displayed, you can use the up, down, right, and left arrow keys to move between items and display cascading menus. When an item followed by an arrow is highlighted, press the right arrow key to display the cascading menu. Remove the cascading menu by pressing the left arrow key. Press [Enter] to select a highlighted item.

## Exercise 2-2

◆ Continue from Exercise 2-1 or start AutoCAD as instructed in Exercise 2-1.
◆ Using the mouse and pointer, open each pull-down menu and read the commands found in each menu without picking any options.
◆ Open each pull-down menu using the menu accelerator keys.
◆ If you access a command, dialog box, or other feature, press the [Esc] key on your keyboard to clear the activity and resume this exercise.
◆ Keep AutoCAD open for the next exercise. If you must quit, pick **Exit** in the **File** pull-down menu, and then pick **No** in the **AutoCAD** alert box.

## Dialog Boxes

*Dialog boxes* are features containing a variety of devices used to provide information to AutoCAD. You can change settings, specify properties, and select items using dialog boxes. This eliminates typing, saving time and increasing productivity.

Buttons in a dialog box followed by an ellipsis (...) display another dialog box when picked. The second dialog box is displayed on top of the original dialog box, much like laying one sheet of paper on top of another. You must make a selection from the second dialog box before returning to the original dialog box. You can close a dialog box at any time by picking the **Cancel** button or the close "X" button in the upper-right corner.

**Note** Pressing the "X" button closes a dialog box without saving the modified settings. Always pick the **OK** button to accept changes. If there is not an **OK** button, the "X" button applies the settings and closes the dialog box.

Dialog boxes contain several standard items for input and selections. If you take a few minutes to review the following brief descriptions, you will find it much easier to work with the dialog boxes:

- **Tabs.** A dialog box tab is much like an index tab used to separate sections of a notebook. Many dialog boxes contain two or more "pages" or "panels," each with a tab at the top. Each tab displays a new set of related options. See **Figure 2-6.** While the dialog box is displayed, you can switch between tabs in order to select options. Pick the **OK** button to apply the settings and dismiss the dialog box.

- **Command buttons.** Command buttons are normally located at the bottom of the dialog box. When you pick a command button, something happens immediately. The most common command buttons are **OK** and **Cancel**. Another common button is **Help**. See **Figure 2-6.** A button with a dark border is the default. Pressing the [Enter] key accepts the default. If a button is "grayed-out," it cannot be selected.

  Buttons can also lead to other features. A button with an ellipsis (**...**) accesses another dialog box. A button with an arrow symbol (**<**) requires you to pick a point or select an object in the drawing area.

- **Radio buttons.** When you press a selector button on your car radio, the station changes. Only one station can play at a time. Likewise, only one item in a group of radio buttons can be highlighted or active at one time. See **Figure 2-6.**

**Figure 2-6.**
This dialog box includes tabs, command buttons, radio buttons, check boxes, and text boxes.

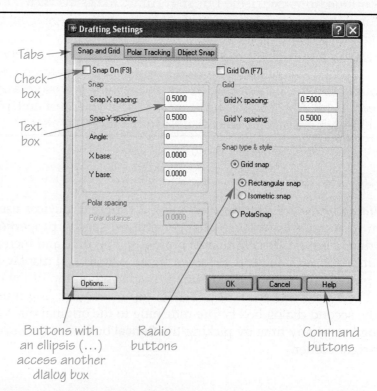

- **Check boxes.** A check box, or toggle, displays a "✔" when it is on (active). The option is off if the box is empty. See **Figure 2-6.**
- **Text boxes.** You can enter a name or single line of information in a text box. See **Figure 2-6.** To enter text in a text box, place the pointer in the text box and press the pick button. When the currently selected text box is empty, the cursor appears as a flashing vertical bar positioned at the far left side of the box. If there is existing text in the box, the text is highlighted. Any characters you type replace the highlighted text.
- **List boxes.** A list box contains a list of items or options. You can scan through the list using the scroll bar (if present) or the keyboard arrow keys. Highlight the desired item with the arrow keys and press [Enter]. You also can simply select the item with the pointer. See **Figure 2-7A.**
- **Drop-down lists.** A drop-down list contains a list of options, but only one item is initially shown. The remaining items are hidden until you pick the drop-down arrow. When you pick the drop-down arrow, the drop-down list is displayed below the initial item. See **Figure 2-7B.** You can then pick from the expanded list or use the scroll bar to find the item you need.
- **Preview box or image tile.** A preview box is an area of a dialog box displaying a "picture" of the item you select, such as a hatching style, linetype, or text font. For many image tiles, picking anywhere on the image changes the associated setting and updates the image accordingly. Some image tiles are more interactive and respond based on the specific location you pick on the image. See **Figure 2-8.**

**Figure 2-7.**
This dialog box includes a list box and a drop-down list. A—The drop-down list displays only the selected option. B—To change the selection, pick the drop-down arrow to display the drop-down list. Use the scroll bar to view additional options.

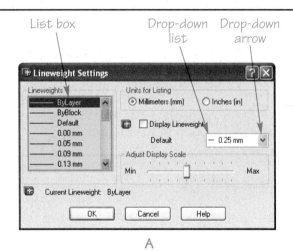

A

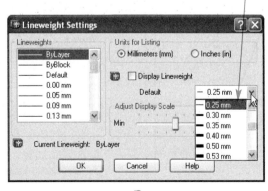

B

**Figure 2-8.**
The image tile shows a "preview" of the selected setting. Some image tiles allow selections right on the preview.

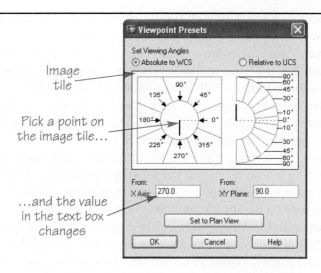

Image tile

Pick a point on the image tile...

...and the value in the text box changes

- **Alerts.** Alerts can be displayed in two forms. A note may appear in the lower-left corner of the original dialog box, or a separate alert dialog box may appear.
- **... (Ellipsis) buttons.** Some dialog box features have an ellipsis button displayed adjacently. The ellipsis button provides access to a related dialog box. See **Figure 2-9.**
- **Help.** If you are unsure of any features of a dialog box, pick the ? button in the upper-right corner of the dialog box. When the question mark appears next to the pointer, you can pick any feature in the dialog box to see a description of what it does. **Figure 2-10** shows how this feature is used.

Note — Another method for displaying information about features in a dialog box is to point at the feature and right-click. If help information is available, the shortcut menu displays the **What's This?** option, which displays a description of the feature.

**Figure 2-9.**
Picking the ... (ellipsis) button in a dialog box opens another dialog box.

The ... (ellipsis) button opens another related dialog box

**Figure 2-10.**
Using the **?** button.
A—Pick the question mark button, and a question mark appears next to the pointer. B— Pick an item in the dialog box to display a brief description.

Question mark cursor

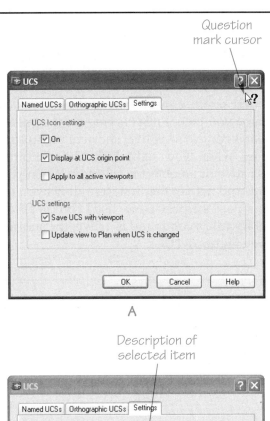

A

Description of selected item

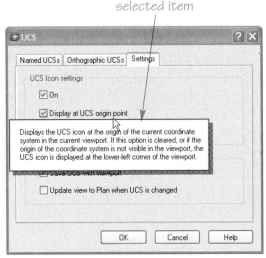

B

## Exercise 2-3

- ◆ Continue from Exercise 2-2 or start AutoCAD as instructed in Exercise 2-1.
- ◆ Open a variety of dialog boxes and observe the features identified in the previous discussion.
- ◆ You may make selections or change options in the dialog boxes if you wish, but this is not required. This is just an opportunity for you to see what different dialog boxes contain.
- ◆ You can close a dialog box at any time by picking the **Cancel** button or the "X" button in the upper-right corner. If you activate something and you wish to exit, press the [Esc] key on your keyboard to exit the command or activity.
- ◆ Keep AutoCAD open for the next exercise. If you must quit, pick **Exit** in the **File** pull-down menu, and then pick **No** in the **AutoCAD** alert box.

## Shortcut Menus

AutoCAD makes extensive use of *shortcut menus* to simplify and accelerate command entries. Sometimes referred to as "cursor menus" because they are displayed at the cursor location, these context sensitive menus are accessed by right-clicking. *Context sensitive* means the menu reflects commands or options relating to the item or area you pick. *Right-clicking* means pressing the right mouse button.

Because it is context sensitive, shortcut menu content varies based on the location of the pointer when you right-click and conditions such as whether or not a command is active or an object is selected. When you right-click in the drawing area with no command active, the first item displayed on the shortcut menu is typically an option to repeat the previously used command or operation. See **Figure 2-11A.** If you right-click while a command is active, the shortcut menu contains options for the command. See **Figure 2-11B.**

**Figure 2-11.**
Context sensitive shortcut menus appear by right-clicking the mouse. A—If a command is not active when right-clicking, the top menu item allows you to repeat the last command. B—When right-clicking during an active command, the shortcut menu displays options for that command. This shortcut menu appears when the **PLINE** command is active.

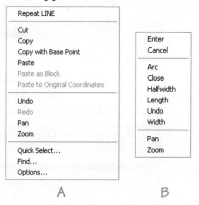

Shortcut menus are discussed where they apply throughout this text. To help familiarize yourself with this powerful AutoCAD feature, try right-clicking at different times while you are learning to use new AutoCAD commands or when practicing dialog box operations. You can significantly increase your productivity in AutoCAD by learning to use these features effectively.

## Exercise 2-4

◆ Continue from Exercise 2-3 or start AutoCAD as instructed in Exercise 2-1.
◆ Access and view the contents of shortcut menus by right-clicking in the following locations:
◆ Command window
◆ Drawing area
◆ Toolbar buttons
◆ You can close a shortcut menu by pressing [Esc] or picking in an area away from the menu.
◆ Keep AutoCAD open for the next exercise. If you must quit, pick **Exit** in the **File** pull-down menu, and then pick **No** in the **AutoCAD** alert box.

## Creating New Drawings

To create a new drawing, pick the **QNew** button from the **Standard** toolbar, select **New...** from the **File** pull-down menu, enter new at the Command prompt, or use the [Ctrl]+[N] key combination. Using the **NEW** command opens the **Select template** dialog box, **Figure 2-12.** New drawings are started from AutoCAD files referred to as *templates.* To start a new drawing file, pick a template in the **Select template** dialog box, and then pick the **Open** button. If you are not sure which template to use, use the acad.dwt template for imperial drawings and the acadiso.dwt template file for metric drawings.

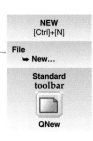

**NEW**
[Ctrl]+[N]

**File**
↳ New...

**Standard toolbar**

QNew

Figure 2-12.
When starting a new drawing, the **Select template** dialog box allows you to start a drawing file from a predefined template.

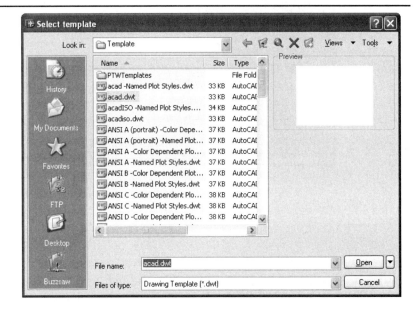

## Template Files

Template files store standard drawing settings, like units of measurement, text settings, and dimension settings. They can also contain predefined drawing layouts, title blocks, print or plot settings, and other common drawing components. When you begin a drawing using a template, all the settings and contents of the template file are added to the new drawing. Using a template means the drawing setup process is already complete and you are ready to begin drafting immediately. In addition to reducing drawing setup time, templates also help to maintain consistent standards in each of your drawings.

OPEN
[Ctrl]+[O]

File
➡ Open...

Standard toolbar

Open

When the AutoCAD program opens, the default template file is displayed (acad.dwt). Most of the time, you will need to open an existing drawing file to continue working on it or modify it. The **Select File** dialog box provides a simple means of locating and selecting files. To access this dialog box, pick the **Open** button in the **Standard** toolbar, select **Open...** from the **File** pull-down menu, type open at the Command prompt, or use the [Ctrl]+[O] key combination. The **Select File** dialog box is shown in **Figure 2-13**.

**Figure 2-13.**
The **Select File** dialog box provides many options for accessing files.

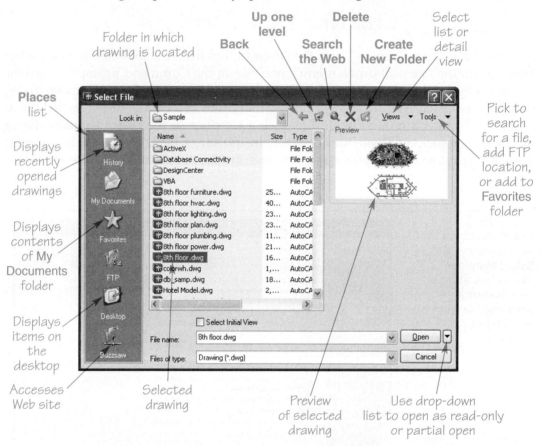

By double-clicking a folder name in the list, you can "open" it. Its contents are then displayed in the list box where items can be selected. The **Look in:** drop-down list displays the directory tree and allows you to browse for a storage device or folder. Once a file name is selected in the list box, it appears in the **File name:** text box, and its image appears in the **Preview** box. When selecting more than one file name, each file name appears in the **File name:** text box in quotation marks.

The five buttons next to the **Look in:** drop-down list allow you to go back to the previously displayed folder, move up one folder level, search the Web, delete the selected item, and create a new folder. Use the **Views** drop-down menu to select a list or detail format for the list box. The **Tools** drop-down menu includes options for searching for files, adding FTP locations, and adding items to your Favorites folder.

The **Places** list, located along the left side of the **Select File** dialog box, provides instant access to certain folders. The following buttons are available:

- **History.** Pick this button to list drawing files opened recently from the **Select File** dialog box.
- **My Documents.** Displays the files and folders contained in the My Documents folder.
- **Favorites.** Displays files and folders located in the Windows\Favorites folder.
- **FTP.** Displays available FTP (file transfer protocol) sites. To add or modify the listed FTP sites, select **Add/Modify FTP Locations** from the **Tools** drop-down menu in the **Select File** dialog box.
- **Desktop.** Pick this button to list the files, folders, and drives located on your desktop.
- **Buzzsaw.** Pick this button to display projects on the Buzzsaw Web site. Buzzsaw.com is designed for the building industry. After setting up a project hosting account, users can access project drawings from the Web site. This allows the various companies involved in the construction process to have instant access to the drawing files.

The **OPEN** command is not the only command that accesses the **Select File** dialog box. Many commands requiring file selection access this dialog box. Be sure to explore and become comfortable with the dialog box features and options.

# Saving Drawings

Periodically saving your drawing protects your work by writing the existing status of your drawing to the hard disk while remaining in the AutoCAD window. It is a good idea to save your drawing every 10 minutes. *This is very important!* If there is a power failure, a severe editing error, or other problems, all the work done after your last save will be lost. If you save only once an hour, a power failure could result in an hour of lost work. Saving your drawing every 10 minutes results in less lost work if a problem occurs. *Please take this seriously.* Do not be one of the people who loses a lot of work because you do not save frequently. Also, back up your work at least once a day. It is best to have two backup copies.

There are two commands that allow you to save your work: **QSAVE** and **SAVEAS**. In addition, when ending your drawing session, AutoCAD provides a warning asking if you want to save changes to the drawing. This gives you a final option to either save or not save changes to the drawing.

## Using the QSAVE Command

**QSAVE** stands for *quick save.* The **QSAVE** command is accessed by picking the **Save** button from the **Standard** toolbar, picking **Save** from the **File** pull-down menu, typing qsave at the Command prompt, or pressing the [Ctrl]+[S] key combination. The **QSAVE** command response varies, depending on whether or not the drawing has been previously saved. If the current drawing has been saved, the **QSAVE** command updates the file based on the current state of the drawing. In this situation, **QSAVE** issues no prompts and displays no messages. If the current drawing has not yet been saved, the **QSAVE** command displays the **Save Drawing As** dialog box, **Figure 2-14.** You must complete three steps in order to save your file:
1. Select the folder in which the file is to be saved.
2. Select the type of file to save, such as drawing (DWG) or template (DWT).
3. Enter a name for the file.

QSAVE
[Ctrl]+[S]

File
→ Save

Standard
toolbar

Save

**Figure 2-14.**
The **Save Drawing As** dialog box is used to assign a name to a drawing.

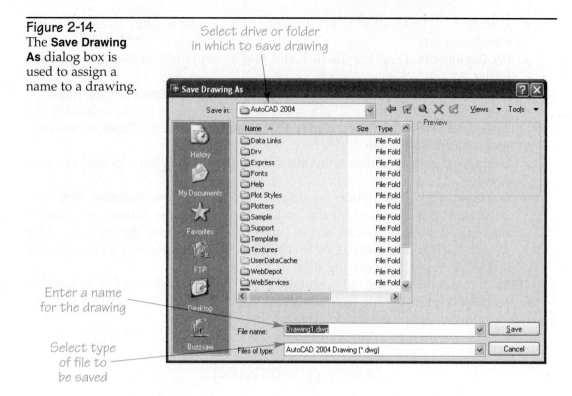

Select drive or folder in which to save drawing

Enter a name for the drawing

Select type of file to be saved

## Using the **SAVEAS** Command

The **SAVEAS** command is accessed by picking **Save As...** from the **File** pull-down menu or typing saveas or save at the Command prompt. This command always displays the **Save Drawing As** dialog box, **Figure 2-14.** If the current drawing has already been saved, the current name and location are displayed. Confirm that the **Save in:** box displays the desired drive and folder and the **Files of type:** box displays the desired file type. Type the new drawing name in the **File name:** text box and pick the **Save** button. The **SAVEAS** command is used in the following situations:

- The current drawing already has a name, and you need to save it with a different name.
- You need to save the current drawing in an alternate format, such as a drawing file for AutoCAD 2000, a DXF file, or a drawing template file.
- You want to save the drawing to a different drive.
- You open one of the drawing template files to create a new drawing.

If you try to save the current drawing using the same name and location as another drawing file, AutoCAD issues a warning message in an alert box. You can either cancel the operation or replace the current drawing with the one on which you are working. If you actually need to replace the existing file, pick the **Yes** button to overwrite the file with the information in the current drawing. If you do not wish to overwrite the file, pick the **No** button to return to the **Save Drawing As** dialog box. Pick the **Cancel** button to cancel the operation. *Be very careful*—if you pick the **Yes** button, the current drawing replaces the other drawing.

**Note**

If you need to send the file to someone who has an earlier release of AutoCAD, the **SAVEAS** command must be used, and the appropriate option must be selected from the **Files of type:** drop-down list.

## Exercise 2-5

◆ Continue from Exercise 2-4 or start AutoCAD as instructed in Exercise 2-1.
◆ Carefully review the previous discussion as you use each of the following commands.
◆ Use the **SAVEAS** command.
◆ Type test in the **File name:** text box.
◆ Pick the **Save** button. The current drawing is saved with the name test.
◆ Use the **QSAVE** command and observe the results. The test drawing is automatically saved without displaying the **Save Drawing As** dialog box.
◆ Use the **SAVEAS** command again. The **Save Drawing As** dialog box appears, and test.dwg should be displayed in the **File name:** text box.
◆ Pick the **Save** button.
◆ This displays the **Save Drawing As** alert box. Think carefully about what will happen if you pick either the **Yes** or **No** button.
◆ Pick the **No** button.
◆ Keep AutoCAD open for the next exercise. If you must quit, pick **Exit** in the **File** pull-down menu, and then pick **No** in the **AutoCAD** alert box.

# Getting Help

HELP
?
[F1]

Help
↳ Help

Standard
toolbar

Help

If you need help with a specific command, option, or program feature, AutoCAD provides a powerful and convenient online help system. To access help, pick the **Help** button in the **Standard** toolbar, select **Help** from the **Help** pull-down menu, enter ? or help at the Command prompt, or press the [F1] key. The **AutoCAD 2004 Help** window consists of two frames, **Figure 2-15.** The left frame, which has five tabs, is used to locate help topics. The right frame displays the selected help topics. In addition to the two frames, the following buttons are located in the **AutoCAD 2004 Help** window:

- **Hide/Show.** This button controls the visibility of the left frame. When you pick **Hide**, the left frame disappears, the **Show** button replaces the **Hide** button, and the buttons appear above the right frame. Pick the **Show** button to view the left frame.
- **Back.** Pick this button to view the previously displayed help topic.
- **Forward.** Pick this button to access pages that were active when the **Back** button was picked. This button becomes active once the **Back** button is used.
- **Home.** Displays the home help page in the right frame.
- **Print.** If you want to print a help topic, pick this button. You must then specify if you want to print the selected help topic or the selected heading and all subtopics.
- **Options.** This button contains a menu with a variety of items. Pick **Hide Tabs** to remove the left frame. Use **Forward** and **Back** to navigate help topics. Select **Home** to return to the AutoCAD 2004 Help page. Pick **Stop** to interrupt a help topic being loaded. **Refresh** regenerates the help topic. **Internet Options...** accesses the Windows **Internet Options** dialog box. Select **Print...** to bring up the dialog box to print a help topic. Choose **Search Highlight Off** if you do not wish to see the words you searched for highlighted in the help topic.

**Figure 2-15.**
The **AutoCAD 2004 Help** window.

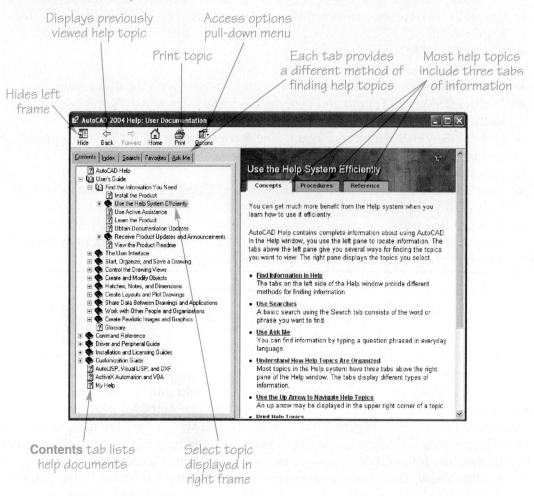

Hides left frame

Displays previously viewed help topic

Print topic

Access options pull-down menu

Each tab provides a different method of finding help topics

Most help topics include three tabs of information

**Contents** tab lists help documents

Select topic displayed in right frame

## Locating Help Topics

The left frame is used to navigate through the help documentation to find the desired help topic. This frame has five tabs. Each tab provides a different method of finding help topics.

The **Contents** tab lists each of the help documents within the AutoCAD help system. The following documents are available:

- **AutoCAD Help.** This document provides a general introduction to the help section.
- **User's Guide.** This is the most useful help area for most AutoCAD users. The User's Guide contains many subtopics explaining how various tasks are accomplished using AutoCAD. New AutoCAD users should explore the User's Guide to become comfortable using the program.
- **Command Reference.** This guide contains an alphabetical listing of commands, system variables, and command aliases, along with information on utilities and standard libraries.
- **Driver and Peripheral Guide.** This reference describes techniques of installing and configuring pointing devices, printers, plotters, and external databases.
- **Installation and Licensing Guides.** This area contains information on doing stand-alone and network installations.

- **Customization Guide.** This document provides direction in customizing the AutoCAD environment, aliases, and menus, along with an introduction to programming languages.
- **AutoLISP, Visual LISP, and DXF.** This help area provides access to four documents used for advanced customization and programming:
  - AutoLISP Reference.
  - AutoLISP Developer's Guide.
  - AutoLISP Tutorial.
  - DXF Reference.
- **ActiveX Automation and VBA.** This area provides access to three documents used for advanced customization and programming:
  - ActiveX and VBA Developer's Guide.
  - ActiveX and VBA Reference.
  - Connectivity Automation Reference.
- **My Help.** This option allows you to create your own group of help topics.

When you first view the **Contents** tab, the nine help documents are listed. A small plus symbol and a closed book symbol precede five of the document names. These symbols indicate that these documents are condensed. To expand these documents, pick the plus sign or double-click on the document name. This expands the documents, and subtopics are listed. If a subtopic has a plus symbol, it can also be expanded to reveal subtopics within the subtopic. When a topic is picked, the right frame shows the help topic.

The **Index** tab provides an alphabetical listing of the general topics addressed in the AutoCAD help system. Type in the topic, and the index list automatically finds the corresponding index entry. Double-click on the item in the index list to access the **Topics Found** dialog box. This dialog box lists the help topics related to the selected index entry, along with the help document in which the topic is located. Double-click on a help topic to display it in the right frame.

The **Search** tab can be used to search for specific words or phrases. Type the search entry into the **Type in the word(s) to search for:** text box. Pick the arrow button next to the text box to select the AND, OR, NEAR, and NOT search operators. After typing the search entry, pick the **List Topics** button to list all topics containing the search entry. Double-click on a listed help topic (or select the topic and pick the **Display** button) to have the topic displayed in the right frame.

The **Favorites** tab can be used to list help topics for future reference. To save a help topic, display the topic in the right frame, access the **Favorites** tab, and then pick the **Add** button. The topic is listed in the **Topics:** window. When you want to access this topic in the future, simply access the **Favorites** tab and select the topic from the list. This is much easier than navigating through the **Contents** tab to find a help topic. Use the **Remove** button to delete help topics from the **Favorites** tab.

You can sort help topics by posing a question or typing a phrase in the **Ask Me** tab. First, use the **List of components to search:** drop-down list to select the help documents most likely to contain the desired help information. Normally, the User's Guide or Command Reference contains help topics on basic issues. Type the question you want answered in the **Type in a question and press Enter** text box. You can also enter phrases. Press [Enter], and hyperlinks to help topics are listed in the window. Pick a hyperlink to display the help topic in the right frame.

## Help Topic Features

Help topics generally display three tabs in the right frame. See **Figure 2-15.** The **Concepts** tab contains the explanation of the concept. The **Procedures** tab provides step-by-step instruction for completing tasks related to the topic. The **Reference** tab has links to related commands and system variables. Each tab contains links allowing you to quickly find the precise information you need.

Some help topics display an arrow graphic in the upper-right corner. Left and right arrows display the topic before or after (respectively) the current topic in the help content organization. An up arrow displays the help topic one level above the current topic in the topic organization.

Finally, each help topic contains a **Comments?** link. If you wish to send a comment regarding the help topic to Autodesk Technical Publications, pick this link. Type the comment in the dialog box that appears and pick the **Send Comment** button. Note that these comments are not intended to serve as technical support.

Another form of help is **Active Assistance**, which can be accessed by selecting **Active Assistance** from the **Help** pull-down menu. When you enter a command, the **Active Assistance** window opens and displays content related to the command.

## Using the Communication Center

Product updates and announcements can be sent to you over the Web using the **Communication Center**. To access the **Communication Center**, pick the icon in the lower-right corner of the AutoCAD window, **Figure 2-16.** This displays the **Communication Center** window.

Figure 2-16.
The **Communication Center** allows you to get product information from the Web.

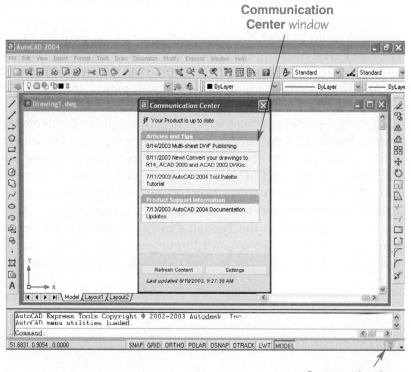

Communication Center *window*

Communication Center *icon*

Architectural Drafting Using AutoCAD

To configure the **Communication Center**, pick **Specify your country and preferred update frequency.** This opens the **Configuration Settings** dialog box. Select your country and how often you would like the **Communication Center** to check for new information. Pick the **OK** button, and then select **Connect to the Internet and download available information.** AutoCAD then searches for the latest information. When this is finished, pick **Specify which information channels you wish to view.** This opens the **Channels** tab of the **Configuration Settings** dialog box. Check the options on which you wish to receive information, and then pick the **OK** button. The **Communication Center** should then tell you your product is up to date, and it may contain links to available information. After the **Communication Center** has been configured, you can check for updates by opening the **Communication Center** and picking the **Refresh Content** button in the lower left-hand corner.

# Chapter Test

*Answer the following questions on a separate sheet of paper.*

1. List two methods of launching AutoCAD.
2. Identify two ways to place a docked toolbar in a floating position.
3. Explain two ways to dock a floating toolbar.
4. How does a floating toolbar change in appearance when it is docked?
5. What is the function of the command window?
6. What happens when you pick a pull-down menu item that is followed by an ellipsis?
7. In the AutoCAD window, where is the coordinate display located?
8. What is a *tooltip?*
9. What is a *flyout?*
10. List the six toolbars displayed in the AutoCAD window by default.
11. How do you know if a pull-down menu item has a cascading menu with it?
12. Identify three ways to make a pull-down menu disappear.
13. What combination of keys would you press to select the **Erase** command from the **Modify** pull-down menu?
14. What does an arrow (<) on a dialog box button represent?
15. How do you access an item in a drop-down list?
16. What happens if you type new text in a text box while existing text is highlighted?
17. What is the function of the **?** button in the upper-right corner of a dialog box?
18. How are shortcut menus displayed?
19. Define *context sensitive.*
20. What is a *template file?*
21. How do you open a folder in the **Select File** dialog box?
22. How often should you save your work?
23. Why is it important to save your work periodically?
24. Name the command you would use if you were working on a named drawing and you wanted to update the file based on the current state of the drawing.
25. Name the command you would use if the current drawing already had a name and you needed to save it under a different name.
26. Give the name of the command you would use if you needed to save the current drawing in an alternate format, such as AutoCAD 2000.
27. What command would you use if you wanted to save the current drawing to a different drive?

28. What happens if you try to save the current drawing using the same name and location as an existing drawing file?
29. Identify four ways to access the **AutoCAD 2004 Help** window.

# Chapter Problems

*For questions 1–8, identify the following items in the AutoCAD window.*

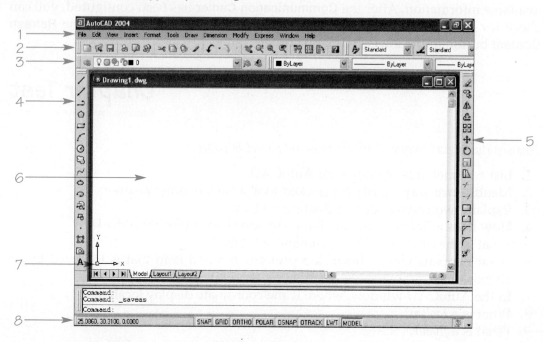

*For questions 9–12, identify the dialog box features.*

9.

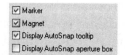

10.

11.

12.

*For questions 13–20, use the online help system and write the descriptions of the following commands exactly as given in the* **Command Reference** *help document.*

13. **ARC**
14. **AREA**
15. **ERASE**
16. **LINE**
17. **PLOT**
18. **QUIT**
19. **QSAVE**
20. **SAVEAS**

Drawing templates provide a quick way to start a new drawing with predefined settings. The standard templates available in AutoCAD include two architectural templates based on named and color-dependent plot styles. Each template is set up for a 36" × 24" drawing sheet, as shown below, with units set to feet and inches. A predrawn title block is provided.

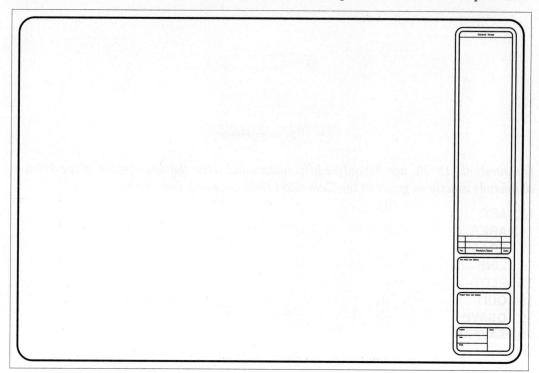

# Drawing Basics

## Learning Objectives

After completing this chapter, you will be able to:

- Use the **LINE** command to draw several different geometric shapes.
- Use absolute, relative, and polar coordinate point entry systems to draw geometry in AutoCAD.
- Specify point locations using direct distance entry and polar tracking.
- Set different types of linear and angular units.
- Use the **ERASE** command to remove geometry.
- Undo operations with the **U** command.
- Draw circles using the **CIRCLE** command.
- Draw arcs using the **ARC** command.
- Use the **PLINE** command to draw polylines and polyarcs.
- Draw polygons using the **POLYGON** command.
- Draw rectangles using the **RECTANG** command.
- Draw ellipses using the **ELLIPSE** command.
- Use zooming and panning techniques.
- Plot a drawing.

## Important Terms

absolute coordinates
alignment path
arc
bearing
Cartesian coordinate system
chamfer
circumference
circumscribed
command aliases
diameter
direct distance entry

fillet
included angle
inscribed
layout
model space
origin
pan displacement
paper space
pick box
point entry
point of tangency
polar coordinates

polar tracking
polygon
polyline
radius
realtime pan
realtime zoom
regular polygon
relative coordinates
selection set
tangent
transparent command

CAD drafters have electronic tools that allow them to draw geometry such as aight lines, circles, and ellipses. These electronic tools are known as *drawing mands* in AutoCAD. In addition to drawing commands, AutoCAD also provides ls, or commands, that allow you to change how drawn geometry appears.

Drawing commands are used to create objects, and editing commands are used modify objects. For example, erasing, moving, and copying are all editing cesses. This chapter introduces you to the basic drawing and editing commands round in AutoCAD. You will also learn how to adjust the display in the AutoCAD window. Future chapters use these tools to create architectural drawings.

# Drawing Lines

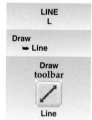

LINE
L

Draw
➡ Line

Draw
toolbar

Line

The **LINE** command allows you to draw a straight line between two selected points. The process of selecting points is called *point entry*. After selecting the **LINE** command, simply enter the endpoints of the line using any of the point entry methods discussed in the next section. The **LINE** command can be accessed by picking the **Line** button in the **Draw** toolbar, picking **Line** in the **Draw** pull-down menu, or entering l or line at the Command prompt.

When you use the **LINE** command, AutoCAD prompts you to specify a first point. The prompt is displayed in the command window. Using the pick button on your pointing device (usually the left mouse button), select a point in the drawing area. This establishes the first point of your line. The Command prompt now asks for the next point (Specify next point or [Undo]:). As you move the pointing device, a temporary line is attached from the first point picked to the crosshairs. This "rubberband line" shows where the line would be located if the second endpoint was selected at the crosshairs position. Pick a second point with your pick button. This establishes a line between the two points you selected. Notice the command window displays another Specify next point or [Undo]: prompt. Continue selecting additional points if you want to connect a series of lines. To complete the **LINE** command, right-click and select **Enter** from the shortcut menu. You can also press the [Enter] key, the [Esc] key, or the space bar. The following command sequence is used for the **LINE** command:

Command: **l** *or* **line↵**
Specify first point: *(select the first point)*
Specify next point or [Undo]: *(select the second point)*
Specify next point or [Undo]: *(select a third point, or press* [Enter], [Esc], *or the space bar to finish)*
Command: *(this appears if you pressed* [Enter], [Esc], *or the space bar at the previous prompt)*

**Professional Tip**

AutoCAD provides a set of abbreviated commands called *command aliases.* A command alias is a one-, two-, or three-letter abbreviation for a command. Using command aliases allows you to enter commands more quickly. For example, instead of typing line at the Command prompt, it is faster to type l. Becoming familiar with the available command aliases can help you become more productive with AutoCAD. Appendix J lists the command aliases in AutoCAD 2004.

As just explained, there are several ways to end the **LINE** command. Most commands allow you to end the command by pressing the [Enter] key or the space bar. The space bar acts as the [Enter] key in AutoCAD, except when creating text. All commands in AutoCAD also allow you to end the command by pressing the [Esc] key.

> **Note**
>
> When entering input at the Command prompt, use the [Backspace] key to correct typing errors. To cancel an active command, press the [Esc] key. For some commands, you may need to press the [Esc] key twice to return to the Command prompt.

# Point Entry Methods

There are several point entry techniques. Being familiar and skillful with these methods is very important. A combination of point entry techniques should be used to help reduce drawing time.

Each of the point entry methods uses the Cartesian, or rectangular, coordinate system. The *Cartesian coordinate system* is based on three intersecting axes. A point location is defined by its distance from the intersection point, called the *origin,* in respect to each of these axes. **Figure 3-1** illustrates the three intersecting axes. In standard two-dimensional (2D) drafting applications, objects are drawn in the XY plane, and the Z axis is not referenced. Using the Z axis in three-dimensional drawing is discussed in Chapter 25.

In 2D drafting, the origin divides the coordinate system into four quadrants within the XY plane. Points are located in relation to the origin (0,0), where X = 0 and Y = 0. **Figure 3-2** shows the X,Y values of points located in the Cartesian coordinate system.

When starting a drawing in AutoCAD, the origin is usually at the lower-left corner of the drawing. This setup places all points in the upper-right quadrant, where both X and Y coordinate values are positive. See **Figure 3-3.** Methods of establishing points in the Cartesian coordinate system include using absolute coordinates, relative coordinates, and polar coordinates.

**Figure 3-1.**
The Cartesian coordinate system uses three axes (X, Y, and Z) to define point locations in 3D space. The three axes meet at the origin (0,0,0). Normally, 2D drawings are created in the XY plane.

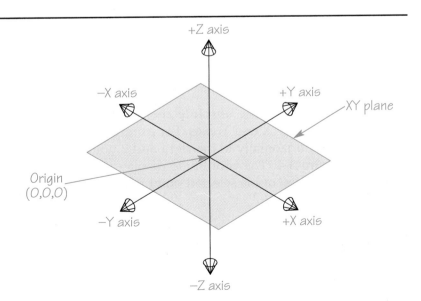

Figure 3-2.
The four quadrants
within the XY
plane.

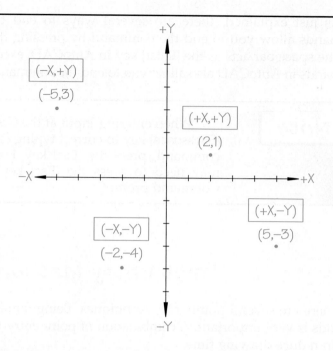

Figure 3-3.
By default, the
origin of the XY
plane is located in
the lower-left corner
of the drawing area.

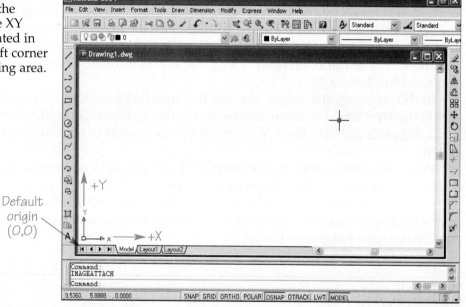

## Using Absolute Coordinates

To locate points using *absolute coordinates,* measure their distance from the origin (0,0) along the X and Y axes. For example, a point at X = 4 and Y = 2 (4,2) is located 4 units horizontally to the right and 2 units vertically up from the origin, as shown in **Figure 3-4.** The coordinate display on the status bar (lower-left corner) registers the location of the selected point in X, Y, and Z coordinates.

## Figure 3-4.

Locating points with absolute coordinates. Absolute coordinates identify location relative to the origin.

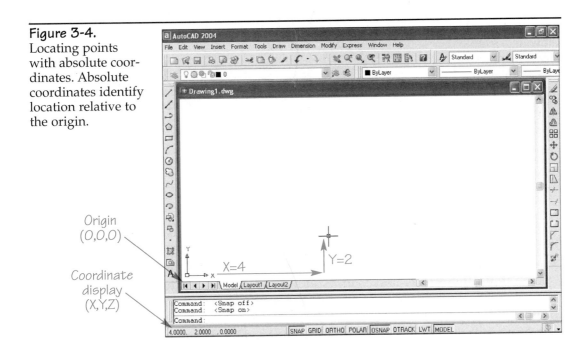

The discussion and examples in this chapter reference only the X and Y coordinates for 2D drafting. Also note that the coordinate display reflects the current system of working units (decimal units, in this case). Remember, when the absolute coordinate system is used, each point is located from 0,0. Follow through these commands and point placements at your computer as you refer to **Figure 3-5A.**

Command: **l** *or* **line**↵
Specify first point: **2,2**↵
Specify next point or [Undo]: **4,4**↵
Specify next point or [Undo]: **6,2**↵
Specify next point or [Close/Undo]: **2,2**↵
Specify next point or [Close/Undo]: ↵
Command:

## Exercise 3-1

◆ Start a new drawing using a template or startup option of your own choice.
◆ Given the absolute coordinates in the chart below, use the **LINE** command to draw the object.
◆ Save the drawing as ex3-1.
◆ Use the **CLOSE** command to close the drawing.

| Point | Coordinates | Point | Coordinates |
|-------|-------------|-------|-------------|
| 1 | 0,0 | 5 | 0,2 |
| 2 | 9,0 | 6 | 0,1.5 |
| 3 | 9.5,.5 | 7 | .25,.5 |
| 4 | 9.5,2 | 8 | 0,0 |

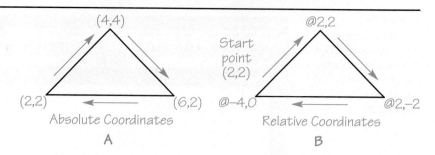

**Figure 3-5.**
Drawing a simple shape using the **LINE** command.
A—Using absolute coordinates.
B—Using relative coordinates.

## Using Relative Coordinates

*Relative coordinates* are points located from the previous position, rather than from the origin. For example, in **Figure 3-4**, you located absolute point 4,2. To draw a line from this point 2 units to the right, you need to tell AutoCAD to draw a line 2 units along the X axis and 0 units along the Y axis, starting where the line is currently (4,2). For relative coordinates, the @ symbol must precede your entry. To specify the next point from absolute coordinate 4,2, you would type @2,0. This draws a line 2 units horizontally to the right from 4,2. The @ symbol can be selected by holding the [Shift] key and pressing the [2] key at the top of the keyboard.

The relationship of points in the Cartesian coordinate system shown in **Figure 3-2** must be clearly understood before using this method. For example, if you wanted to draw a line from a previous point horizontally to the left, you would need to type in the @ symbol, followed by a –X,0 value. To draw a line down vertically, you would need to type the @ symbol, followed by a 0,–Y value. The following command sequence would be used to draw the triangle in **Figure 3-5B** using relative coordinate entry:

```
Command: l or line↵
Specify first point: 2,2↵
Specify next point or [Undo]: @2,2↵
Specify next point or [Undo]: @2,–2↵
Specify next point or [Close/Undo]: @–4,0↵
Specify next point or [Close/Undo]: ↵
Command:
```

## Exercise 3-2

◆ Start a new drawing using a template or startup option of your own choice.
◆ Use the **LINE** command to draw an object using the relative coordinates given in the chart below.
◆ Save the drawing as ex3-2.
◆ Use the **CLOSE** command to close the drawing.

| Point | Coordinates | Point | Coordinates |
|-------|-------------|-------|-------------|
| 1 | 1,1 | 5 | @–9.5,0 |
| 2 | @9,0 | 6 | @0,–.5 |
| 3 | @.5,.5 | 7 | @.25,–1 |
| 4 | @0,1.5 | 8 | @–.25,–.5 |

## Using Polar Tracking

*Polar tracking* is similar to Ortho mode, except you are not limited to horizontal or vertical directions. With polar tracking on, you can cause the drawing crosshairs to "snap" to any predefined angle increment. To turn on polar tracking, pick the **POLAR** button on the status bar or use the [F10] function key at the top of your keyboard. Polar tracking provides visual aids as you draw. After a command has been entered and the first point has been picked, AutoCAD displays an *alignment path* (dotted line) and tooltip when the cursor crosses the default polar angle increments of 0°, 90°, 180°, and 270°.

To set other angles for polar tracking, right-click on the **POLAR** button on the status bar and select **Settings...** from the shortcut menu. This displays the **Drafting Settings** dialog box. You can also access the **Drafting Settings** dialog box by picking **Drafting Settings...** in the **Tools** pull-down menu or entering dsettings. Pick the **Polar Tracking** tab.

Change the increment angle in the **Increment angle:** drop-down list. See **Figure 3-10.** Now when the cursor crosses any specified angle, an alignment path and tooltip are displayed. If you pick a point while the alignment path is displayed, you draw a straight line along the path.

**Figure 3-10.**
The polar tracking settings. Select an increment angle for the cursor to "snap" to.

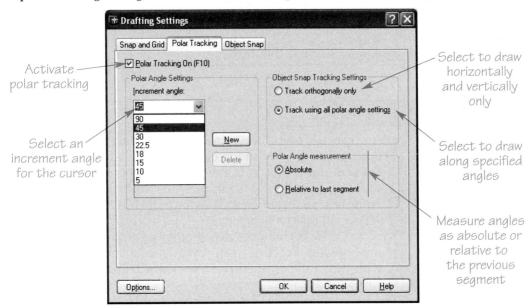

After you start the **LINE** command and move the cursor in alignment with a polar tracking angle, all you have to do is type the desired distance value and press [Enter] to have the line drawn. With a 45° angle increment setting, polar tracking is used as follows to draw the lines shown in **Figure 3-11**:

Command: **l** *or* **line.**↵
Specify first point: *(pick a point)*
Specify next point or [Undo]: **1** *(drag the crosshairs while watching the dotted line and tooltip; at 0°, press [Enter])*
Specify next point or [Undo]: **1** *(drag the crosshairs and press [Enter] at 45°)*
Specify next point or [Close/Undo]: **1** *(drag the crosshairs and press [Enter] at 135°)*
Specify next point or [Close/Undo]: **1** *(drag the crosshairs and press [Enter] at 180°)*
Specify next point or [Close/Undo]: **1** *(drag the crosshairs and press [Enter] at 225°)*
Specify next point or [Close/Undo]: **1** *(drag the crosshairs and press [Enter] at 315°)*
Specify next point or [Close/Undo]: ↵

**Figure 3-11.**
Using polar tracking to draw lines at predefined angle increments. A—After picking the starting point for the line, the second point "snaps" to the displayed alignment path. B—Drawing the second line segment. C—The completed object.

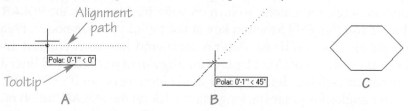

## Exercise 3-6

- ◆ Start a new drawing using a template or startup option of your own choice.
- ◆ Draw an equilateral triangle (three equal sides and angles). Ortho mode must be off to do this.
- ◆ Draw a 3″ × 2″ (76 mm × 50 mm) rectangle, using the screen cursor for point entry, with Ortho mode off. Draw a second rectangle with Ortho mode on. Compare the difference.
- ◆ Use direct distance entry to draw a rectangle similar to **Figure 3-9.**
- ◆ Turn Ortho mode off and turn polar tracking on.
- ◆ Draw a 3″ × 2″ (76 mm × 50 mm) rectangle using polar tracking.
- ◆ Save the drawing as ex3-6.
- ◆ Use the **CLOSE** command to close the drawing.

**Professional Tip**

Practice using the different point entry techniques and decide which method works best for certain situations. Keep in mind that you may mix methods to enhance your drawing speed. For example, absolute coordinates may work best to locate an initial point or draw a simple shape. These calculations are easy. Polar coordinates may work better to locate features in a circular pattern or at an angular relationship. Practice using Ortho mode and polar tracking with direct distance entry to see the advantages and disadvantages of each.

## Using the Close Line Option

A *polygon* is a closed figure with at least three sides. Triangles and rectangles are examples of polygons. Once you have drawn two or more line segments, the endpoint of the last line segment can be connected automatically to the first line segment using the **Close** option. To use this option, type c or close on the command line. In **Figure 3-12,** the last line is drawn using the **Close** option as follows:

Command: **l** *or* **line.**↵
Specify first point: (*pick Point 1*)
Specify next point or [Undo]: (*pick Point 2*)
Specify next point or [Undo]: (*pick Point 3*)
Specify next point or [Close/Undo]: (*pick Point 4*)
Specify next point or [Close/Undo]: **c.**↵
Command:

**Figure 3-12.**
Using the **Close**
option to complete
the box.

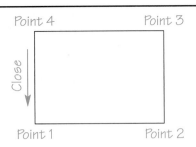

## Undoing the Previously Drawn Line

When drawing a series of lines, you may find that you made an error. To delete the mistake while still in the **LINE** command, type u at the Specify next point or [Undo]: prompt and press [Enter]. Doing this removes the previously drawn line and allows you to continue from the previous point. You can use the **Undo** option repeatedly to continue deleting line segments until you are back to the first point.

```
Command: l or line↵
Specify first point: (Pick Point 1)
Specify next point or [Undo]: (Pick Point 2)
Specify next point or [Undo]: (Pick Point 3)
Specify next point or [Close/Undo]: (Pick Point 4)
Specify next point or [Close/Undo]: u↵ (deletes Point 4)
Specify next point or [Close/Undo]: u↵ (deletes Point 3)
Specify next point or [Undo]: (Pick new Point 3)
Specify next point or [Close/Undo]: (Pick new Point 4)
Specify next point or [Close/Undo]: ↵
```

## Exercise 3-7

◆ Start a new drawing using a template or startup option of your own choice.
◆ Experiment drawing lines using the following guidelines and options:
   ◆ Draw one triangle and one rectangle using the **Close** option.
   ◆ Draw eight connected lines. Use the **Undo** option to remove the last four lines while remaining in the **LINE** command. Finally, draw four new connected lines.
◆ Save the drawing as ex3-7.
◆ Use the **CLOSE** command to close the drawing.

# Drawing Units

So far in this chapter, you have seen how to draw lines and use the Cartesian coordinate system when drawing lines. By default, the coordinate display is shown in decimal units, such as 1,2 or 1.5,2.75. AutoCAD can also recognize whole number input in feet and inches.

Units are set in the **Drawing Units** dialog box, **Figure 3-13A.** This dialog box is accessed by picking **Units...** in the **Format** pull-down menu or entering un or units at the Command prompt. Notice the default linear units are set to **Decimal**, and the angular units are set to **Decimal Degrees**. Using these units, AutoCAD recognizes the input of 1 to be 1 unit. In AutoCAD, 1 unit could be 1″, 1 mm, 1 m, or 1 mile. Most AutoCAD users generally think of 1 unit to be either 1″ or 1 mm.

units
un

Format
➥ Units...

**Figure 3-13.**
The **Drawing Units** dialog box. A—By default, AutoCAD is set for decimal units. B—For architectural drafting, use architectural (feet and inches) units. Set the precision appropriate for the drawing.

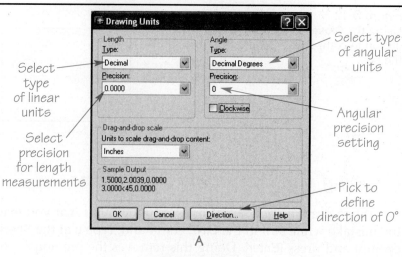

Select type of linear units

Select type of angular units

Select precision for length measurements

Angular precision setting

Pick to define direction of 0°

A

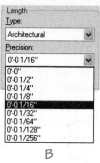

B

## Length Units

In architecture, lengths are commonly measured in feet and inches. To set AutoCAD to display and accept input in inches and feet, select **Architectural** from the **Type:** drop-down list in the **Length** area. Use the **Precision:** drop-down list to specify the linear units precision. See **Figure 3-13B.** To change the type of angle, select the **Type:** and **Precision:** drop-down lists in the **Angle** area.

When working with architectural units, there are several formats for entering distances. For example, if the length of a line is one foot six and one-half inches long, you can enter any of the following values:

- 1'6–1/2
- 1'6.5
- 1'6–1/2"
- 1'–6–1/2
- 1'–6–1/2"

A "foot" unit must be followed by the foot mark ('), and the whole number and fractional portions of the "inch" value must be separated by a dash. Lengths less than one inch can be entered as either fractions or decimals. The inch mark (") *may* follow an inch value, and a dash *may* separate the foot and inch units. These marks, however, are unnecessary.

**Professional Tip**

When using architectural units, placing the inch mark (") after an inch value is acceptable, but unnecessary. AutoCAD recognizes any number without a foot or inch mark as being a decimal inch. Often, it takes more time and reduces productivity if the inch mark is used.

The following list describes the different types of units available in AutoCAD and the format of typed distances when using these units:

- **Architectural.** Architectural, structural, and other drawings use these units when measurements are in feet, inches, and fractional inches. The initial default precision is 1/16". Values are typed as feet and inches. They are entered as 16'8,22'6 or 24'6–1/2,18'8–3/4. Notice a dash separates the inches from the fractional parts of an inch, as in 8–3/4.
- **Decimal.** These units are used to create drawings in decimal inches or millimeters. Decimal units are normally used on mechanical drawings for manufacturing. Values do not include unit marks. They are simply entered as 3,8 or 3.005,2.
- **Engineering.** These units are often used in civil drafting projects, such as maps, plot plans, dam and bridge construction, and topography. Values are in feet and decimal inches. They are entered as 80'6.5,42'.
- **Fractional.** This option is used for drawings that have fractional parts of any common unit of measure. The initial default precision is 1/16. Values to be typed are in fractions. They are entered as 6–1/2,8–1/4.
- **Scientific.** These units are used when very large or small values are applied to the drawing. These applications take place in industries such as chemical engineering and astronomy. Values to be typed are base numbers, followed by an E+$xx$, where $xx$ is the power of ten by which the base number is multiplied. An example of an entry using scientific units is 1.55E+04.

## Angular Units

The following list describes the different types of angular input available in AutoCAD. In architectural drafting, angles are normally expressed in decimal degrees. Surveyor's units may be used for some architectural applications.

- **Decimal Degrees.** This is the default setting. It is normally used in architectural or mechanical drafting. Values to be typed are in whole numbers. A valid entry in AutoCAD is 3'0"<45.
- **Deg/Min/Sec.** This style is sometimes used in mechanical, architectural, structural, and civil drafting. There are 60 minutes in 1 degree and 60 seconds in 1 minute. Values to be typed are in number of degrees/number of minutes/number of seconds. A valid entry in AutoCAD is @50'<24d33'13".
- **Grads.** *Grad* is the abbreviation for *gradient*. Like degrees, gradients are another unit of angular measure. A full circle has 400 gradients, so a gradient is slightly smaller than a degree. When entering gradient values, the angular value is followed by a *g*. These values are entered as @12<30g.
- **Radians.** A radian is an angular unit of measure in which $2\pi$ radians = 360°, and $\pi$ radians = 180°. For example, a 90° angle has $\pi/2$ radians. Values are followed by an *r*. They are entered as @6'1–1/2"<23r.
- **Surveyor's Units.** Surveyor angles are measured using bearings. A *bearing* is the direction of a line with respect to one of the quadrants of a compass. Bearings are measured from either north or south, in units of degrees, minutes, and seconds. An angle measured 55°45'22" from north toward west is expressed as N55d45'22"W. An angle measured 25°30'10" from south toward east is expressed as S25d30'10"E.

In AutoCAD, angles are measured counterclockwise, with 0° pointing to the right (east) by default. If you want to change the 0° direction, pick the **Direction...** button in the **Drawing Units** dialog box. This accesses the **Direction Control** dialog box, **Figure 3-14.** Select the compass direction for 0°, or select **Other** to select two points on screen or to enter an angle in the text box.

**Figure 3-14.**
Picking the
**Direction...** button
in the **Drawing Units**
dialog box displays
the **Direction Control**
dialog box.

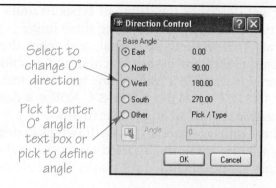

*Select to change 0° direction*

*Pick to enter 0° angle in text box or pick to define angle*

## Exercise 3-8

◆ Start a new drawing using a template or startup option of your own choice.
◆ Experiment drawing lines using the following guidelines and options:
  ◆ Set the length units to **Architectural** and the angular units to **Decimal Degrees**. Draw one triangle and one rectangle.
  ◆ Set the length units to **Architectural** and the angular units to **Surveyor's Units**. Draw one triangle and one rectangle.
  ◆ Set the length units to **Fractional** and the angular units to **Deg/Min/Sec**. Draw one triangle and one rectangle.
◆ Save the drawing as ex3-8.
◆ Use the **CLOSE** command to close the drawing.

# Introduction to Editing

*Editing* is the procedure used to correct mistakes or revise an existing drawing. There are many editing functions that help increase productivity. The basic editing commands **ERASE**, **OOPS**, and **U** are introduced in the next sections.

To edit a drawing, you must select items to modify. The Select objects: prompt appears whenever you need to select items for modification in an editing command sequence. Whether you select one object or hundreds of objects, you are creating a selection set. A *selection set* is a group of objects that have been selected for modification.

## Using the ERASE Command

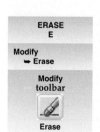

ERASE
E

Modify
➥ Erase

Modify
toolbar

Erase

Using the **ERASE** command is similar to using an eraser to remove unwanted information in manual drafting. With the **ERASE** command, however, you have a second chance. If you erase the wrong item, it can be brought back with the **OOPS** command. Access the **ERASE** command by picking the **Erase** button in the **Modify** toolbar, selecting **Erase** in the **Modify** pull-down menu, or entering e or erase at the Command prompt. When you enter the **ERASE** command, you are prompted to select an object to be erased, as follows:

Command: **e** *or* **erase**↵
Select objects: *(select the object(s) to be erased)*
Select objects: ↵
Command:

When the Select objects: prompt appears, a small box replaces the screen crosshairs. This box is referred to as the *pick box.* Move the pick box over the item to be erased and pick it. The object is "highlighted." Press the [Enter] key or right-click, and the object is erased.

Architectural Drafting Using AutoCAD

**Figure 3-15.**
Using the **ERASE** command to erase an object. A—Object and crosshairs before starting the **ERASE** command. B—Crosshairs change to pick box. C—Selected object becomes highlighted. D—Object erased.

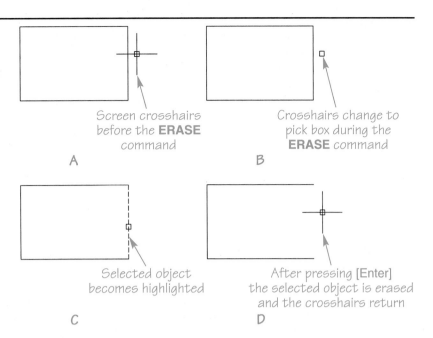

Screen crosshairs before the **ERASE** command

A

Crosshairs change to pick box during the **ERASE** command

B

Selected object becomes highlighted

C

After pressing [Enter] the selected object is erased and the crosshairs return

D

After you pick the first object, the Select objects: prompt is redisplayed. You can then select another object to erase, as shown in **Figure 3-15.** If you are finished selecting objects, press the [Enter] key to finish creating the selection set. The **ERASE** operation is completed, and you are returned to the Command prompt.

> The terms *object* and *entity* are used interchangeably in relation to AutoCAD. An object, or entity, is a predefined element you place in a drawing by means of a single command. For example, a line, circle, arc, or single line of text is an object, or entity.

## Using the OOPS Command

The **OOPS** command brings back the last object you erased. It is issued by entering oops at the Command prompt. If you erased several objects in the same command sequence, all are brought back to the screen. Only the objects erased in the last erase procedure can be returned using the **OOPS** command.

OOPS

## Using the U Command

While the **OOPS** command brings back the last object(s) you erased, the **U** command undoes the last command. The **U** command is issued by picking the **Undo** button in the **Standard** toolbar, selecting **Undo** from the **Edit** pull-down menu, entering u at the Command prompt, or using the [Ctrl]+[Z] key combination. **OOPS** can only be used one time in sequence, while **U** can be issued until every command used since the editing session began has been undone. Even **OOPS** can be undone with the **U** command.

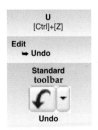

U
[Ctrl]+[Z]

Edit
↳ Undo

Standard toolbar

Undo

## Exercise 3-9

◆ Open drawing ex3-8.
◆ Erase a few of the lines.
◆ Draw some new lines.
◆ Use the **OOPS** command to bring back the last objects erased.
◆ Draw some more lines.
◆ Use the **U** command as many times as needed to undo all operations.
◆ Use the **CLOSE** command to close the drawing.

# Drawing Circles

Before you can draw circles, you must be familiar with the terms used to identify the characteristics of circles. A circle is an object in which all points along the circle are located the same distance from a center point. The *radius* is the distance from the center point to any point on the circle. The *diameter* is the length of a line drawn across the circle through the center point. It is always twice as large as the radius. The *circumference* is the perimeter, or the distance around the circle.

The **CIRCLE** command is used by picking the **Circle** button in the **Draw** toolbar, selecting **Circle** from the **Draw** pull-down menu, or entering c or circle at the Command prompt. There are six different methods for creating a circle. The method used normally depends on the known information and the drafter's familiarity with each method. The six methods are available in the **Circle** cascading menu, **Figure 3-16.**

Options for commands can also be found in brackets following a prompt. The options for the **CIRCLE** command include [3P/2P/Ttr (tan tan radius)]. To access an option at the Command prompt, type the number or uppercase letter shown for the desired option, and then press the [Enter] key.

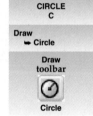

CIRCLE
C

Draw
➥ Circle

Draw
toolbar

Circle

**Figure 3-16.**
The **Circle** cascading
menu in the **Draw**
pull-down menu.

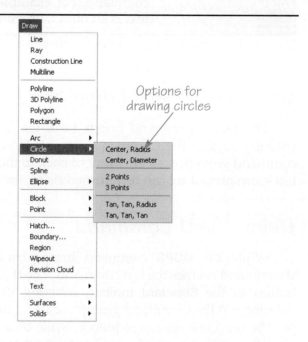

Architectural Drafting Using AutoCAD

**Figure 3-17.**
Drawing a circle by
specifying the
center point and
either the radius or
diameter.

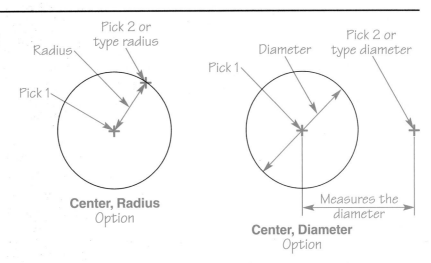

## Specifying a Center Point and a Second Point

The first two methods of creating a circle are **Center, Radius** and **Center, Diameter**. These methods are illustrated in **Figure 3-17.** After accessing the **CIRCLE** command, pick the center point for the circle, or enter the coordinates and press [Enter]. Once the center is established, the Specify radius of circle or [Diameter]: prompt appears. Specify a radius by entering the radius at the command line and pressing [Enter]. You can also specify a radius by picking a point with the crosshairs.

Command: **c** *or* **circle**↵
Specify center point for circle or [3P/2P/Ttr (tan tan radius)]: *(select a center point)*
Specify radius of circle or [Diameter] *<current>*: *(drag the circle to the desired radius and pick, or type the radius size and press* [Enter]*)*

If you prefer to specify the diameter, type d at the prompt, and then enter the diameter at the prompt line. You can also pick the diameter with the crosshairs. The following is the prompt sequence:

Command: **c** *or* **circle**↵
Specify center point for circle or [3P/2P/Ttr (tan tan radius)]: *(select a center point)*
Specify radius of circle or [Diameter] *<current>*: **d**↵
Specify diameter of circle *<current>*: *(drag the circle to the desired diameter and pick, or type the diameter size and press* [Enter]*)*

Watch the screen carefully when using the **Center, Diameter** option. The crosshairs cursor measures the diameter, but the circle passes midway between the center and the cursor. The **Center, Diameter** option is convenient because most circle dimensions are given as diameters.

Note

The radius value you enter is stored as the **CIRCLERAD** system variable. This system variable is the default radius setting the next time you use the **CIRCLE** command. If you use the **Diameter** option, the previous default setting is converted to a diameter. If **CIRCLERAD** is set to zero, no default radius is provided in the **CIRCLE** command prompts.

## Specifying Points on the Circle

The third and fourth options for drawing circles are the **2 Points** and **3 Points** options. A two-point circle is drawn by picking two points on opposite sides of the circle. The distance between the two points is the diameter, and the center point of the circle is located between the two points. A three-point circle is drawn through three selected points. Both options are shown in **Figure 3-18.**

The **2 Points** option is useful if the diameter of the circle is known and the center is difficult to find. One example of this is locating a circle between two lines. To use this option, select **2 Points** from the **Circle** cascading menu, or enter the following at the Command prompt:

Command: **c** *or* **circle**⏎
Specify center point for circle or [3P/2P/Ttr (tan tan radius)]: **2p**⏎
Specify first end point of circle's diameter: *(select a point)*
Specify second end point of circle's diameter: *(select a point)*

If three points on the circumference of a circle are known, the **3 Points** option is the best method to use. The three points can be selected in any order. See **Figure 3-18.** The first two points selected establish the limits in which AutoCAD must keep the circle when specifying the third point. The command sequence is as follows:

Command: **c** *or* **circle**⏎
Specify center point for circle or [3P/2P/Ttr (tan tan radius)]: **3p**⏎
Specify first point on circle: *(select a point)*
Specify second point on circle: *(select a point)*
Specify third point on circle: *(select a point)*

**Figure 3-18.**
Drawing a circle by specifying points on the circle.

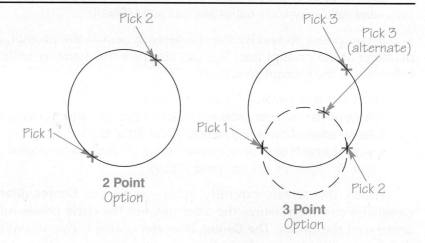

Pick 2

Pick 3

Pick 3
(alternate)

Pick 1

Pick 1

**2 Point**
Option

Pick 2

**3 Point**
Option

| Note | Remember that whenever AutoCAD prompts for a point location, Cartesian coordinates, direct distance entry, and picking a point are all valid types of input. |
|---|---|

# Drawing a Circle Tangent to Objects

The term *tangent* refers to a line, circle, or arc that comes into contact with an arc or a circle at only one point. That point is called the *point of tangency.* A line drawn from the circle's center to the point of tangency is perpendicular to the tangent line. A line drawn between the centers of two tangent circles passes through the point of tangency. You can draw a circle tangent to lines, circles, or arcs. There are two options for drawing circles tangent to existing objects: the **Tan, Tan, Radius** option and the **Tan, Tan, Tan** option.

The **Tan, Tan, Radius** option (**Ttr** option) draws a circle tangent to two objects with a specific radius. Once the **Tan, Tan, Radius** option is selected, select the lines, or line and arc, to which the new circle will be tangent. The radius of the circle is also required. To assist you in picking the three objects, AutoCAD uses the Deferred Tangent object snap mode by default. Object snap modes are covered in Chapter 4. When you see the Deferred Tangent symbol, move it to the objects you want to pick. Refer to **Figure 3-19** as you follow the command sequence:

> Command: **c** *or* **circle**↵
> Specify center point for circle or [3P/2P/Ttr (tan tan radius)]: **t**↵
> Specify point on object for first tangent of circle: *(pick the first line, circle, or arc)*
> Specify point on object for second tangent of circle: *(pick the second line, circle, or arc)*
> Specify radius of circle <current>: *(type a radius value and press [Enter])*

If the radius entered is too small, AutoCAD gives you the message: Circle does not exist. AutoCAD automatically calculates the radius of the circle.

---

**Figure 3-19.**
Two examples of drawing circles tangent to two objects using the **Tan, Tan, Radius** option.

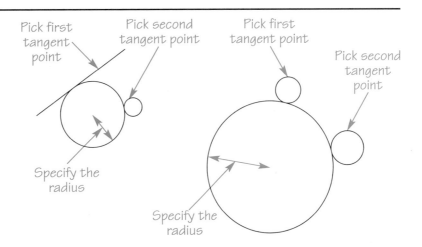

Pick first tangent point

Pick second tangent point

Specify the radius

Pick first tangent point

Pick second tangent point

Specify the radius

---

The **Tan, Tan, Tan** option allows you to draw a circle tangent to three existing objects. See **Figure 3-20**. This option is only available in the **Circle** cascading menu. You can, however, duplicate this option at the Command prompt by selecting the **3 Points** option and then using the Tangent object snap mode for the three picks. Object snap modes are covered in Chapter 4.

> Command: **c** *or* **circle**↵
> Specify center point for circle or [3P/2P/Ttr (tan tan radius)]: **3p**↵
> Specify first point on circle: **tan**↵
> to *(pick an object)*
> Specify second point on circle: **tan**↵
> to *(pick an object)*
> Specify third point on circle: **tan**↵
> to *(pick an object)*
> Command:

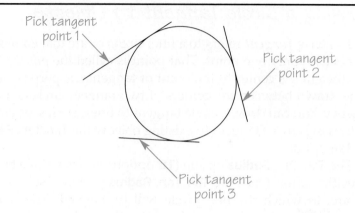

**Figure 3-20.**
An example of drawing a circle tangent to three given objects.

Pick tangent point 1

Pick tangent point 2

Pick tangent point 3

## Using the @ Symbol to Specify the Last Coordinates

The @ symbol can be used to input the last coordinates entered. For example, suppose you want to draw a circle with a center at the end of the line just drawn. Enter the @ symbol when asked for a center point. The command sequence is as follows:

Command: **l** *or* **line**↵
Specify first point: **4,4**↵
Specify next point or [Undo]: **8,4**↵
Specify next point or [Undo]: ↵
Command: **c** *or* **circle**↵
Specify center point for circle or [3P/2P/Ttr (tan tan radius)]: **@**↵

The @ symbol automatically issues the coordinate 8,4 (the endpoint of the line) as the center of the circle. The 8,4 value is saved in the **LASTPOINT** system variable. The @ symbol retrieves the **LASTPOINT** value.

Another application of the @ symbol is drawing concentric circles (circles that have the same center). To do this, draw a circle using the **Center, Radius** or **Center, Diameter** option. Enter the **CIRCLE** command again and type @ when asked for the center point. This automatically places the center of the new circle at the center of the previous circle.

## Exercise 3-10

◆ Start a new drawing using a template or startup option of your own choice.
◆ Set the units to **Architectural**.
◆ Use the **Center, Radius** option of the **CIRCLE** command to draw a circle with a 6″ radius.
◆ Use the **Center, Diameter** option of the **CIRCLE** command to draw a circle with a 1′-4″ diameter.
◆ Draw two vertical parallel lines 2″ apart. Use the **2 Points** option of the **CIRCLE** command to draw a circle tangent to the two lines.
◆ Use the **3 Points** option of the **CIRCLE** command to draw a circle touching the lower endpoints of the two lines and the center point of the two-point circle.
◆ Use the **Tangent, Tangent, Radius** option of the **CIRCLE** command to draw a circle with a 2″ radius tangent to the three-point circle and one of the vertical lines.
◆ Draw a third vertical line 2″ from one of the existing lines. Use the **Tan, Tan, Tan** option to draw a circle tangent to the two outer lines and the three-point circle.
◆ Draw a line. Use the **Center, Radius** option of the **CIRCLE** command and the @ symbol to place the circle's center at the endpoint of the line.
◆ Draw three concentric circles using @ and the **CIRCLE** command.
◆ Save the drawing as ex3-10.
◆ Use the **CLOSE** command to close the drawing.

# Drawing Arcs

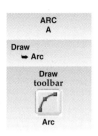

An *arc* is defined as any portion of a circle. The **ARC** command can be accessed by selecting **Arc** from the **Draw** pull-down menu. There are 11 arc construction options accessible in the **Arc** cascading menu, **Figure 3-21.** The **ARC** command can also be accessed by picking the **Arc** button in the **Draw** toolbar or entering a or arc at the Command prompt. The **3 Points** option is the default when using the toolbar button or the Command prompt.

**Figure 3-21.**
The **Arc** cascading menu in the **Draw** pull-down menu.

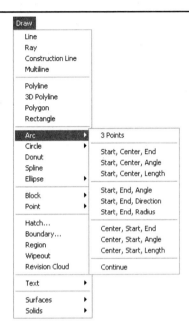

## Drawing a Three-Point Arc

The **3 Points** option asks for the start point, a second point along the arc, and then the endpoint. See **Figure 3-22.** The arc can be drawn clockwise or counterclockwise, and it is dragged into position as the endpoint is located. The command sequence is as follows:

Command: **a** *or* **arc**↵
Specify start point of arc or [Center]: *(select the first point on the arc)*
Specify second point of arc or [Center/End]: *(select a second point on the arc)*
Select end point of arc: *(select the arc's endpoint)*
Command:

**Figure 3-22.**
Drawing an arc by picking three points.

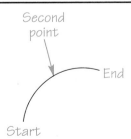

# Drawing Arcs Using Arc Properties

To draw an arc, you must define the three properties of the arc: the start point, the endpoint, and the amount of curvature. AutoCAD provides many different methods of specifying these properties.

- **Start point.** In all methods of drawing arcs, the start point is defined explicitly.
- **Endpoint.** The endpoint of the arc can be defined in three ways: by picking the endpoint (**End**), defining the arc's angle (**Angle**), or defining the chord length of the arc (**Length**). See **Figure 3-23.**

---

**Figure 3-23.**
The endpoint of an arc can be specified in any one of three ways: by specifying the coordinate of the endpoint, entering the included angle, or typing the length of the arc.

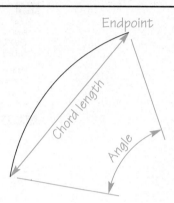

---

- **Amount of curvature.** The amount of curvature determines how much the arc "bows" between the start point and the endpoint. This can be expressed as the arc's radius (**Radius**) or center point (**Center**), or it can be expressed by defining the tangent direction at the arc's start point (**Direction**). See **Figure 3-24.**

The **Arc** cascading menu lists nine command options in which these arc properties are identified. These options correspond to the "option paths" available when using the **ARC** command at the Command prompt. Notice, however, that six of these options define identical properties. The only difference between the options is the order of selection. See **Figure 3-25.**

Regardless of the option used to draw an arc, you must specify the start point. In addition, the center point or endpoint must also be specified. The following describes each arc entry option:

- **Start.** Use this option to specify the location of the start point of the arc. Unless you are using the **3 Points** option or the **Direction** option, the arc will be drawn in a counterclockwise direction by default. Therefore, you must select the correct end of the arc as the start point.

---

**Figure 3-24.**
The curvature of an arc can be specified in any one of three ways: by picking the center point, entering the radius, or setting the direction tangent to the start point.

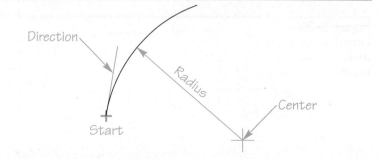

---

**Figure 3-25.**
Of the nine three-item options in the **Arc** cascading menu, six define the same properties. The only difference is the order in which the start point and center point are selected.

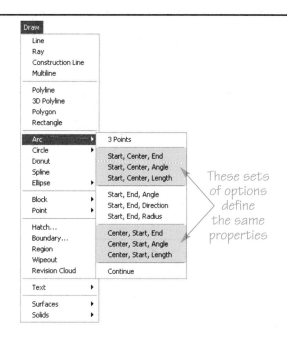

These sets of options define the same properties

- **Center.** Use this option to specify the center point of the arc. Picking the start and center points establishes the arc's radius.
- **End.** Use this option to specify the endpoint of the arc. The point selected for the endpoint determines the arc length. If the center point of the arc has already been established, the selected point does not need to be on the radius of the arc, **Figure 3-26.**
- **Angle.** The *included angle* is an angle formed between the center, start point, and endpoint of the arc. Positive angles are drawn counterclockwise; negative angles are drawn clockwise. See **Figure 3-27.**
- **Length.** This option is useful if you know the center point or radius of the arc, but do not know the angle. A *chord* is a straight line joining two points on an arc. A positive chord length gives the smallest possible arc with that length. A negative chord length results in the largest possible arc. See **Figure 3-28.**
- **Direction.** An arc can be drawn by picking the start point, picking the endpoint, and entering the direction of rotation in degrees. The arc is started tangent to the direction specified, as shown in **Figure 3-29.** This tangent direction defines the radius and center point.
- **Radius.** Use this option to specify the radius of the arc. This option is useful if you know the start point and endpoint of the arc, but do not know the center point, angle, or direction of rotation. The radius can be specified by entering a length. It can also be specified by moving the pointing device clockwise or counterclockwise and clicking to specify a distance.

**Figure 3-26.**
When selecting the arc endpoint after selecting the start point and center point, the point selected does not need to be on the arc.

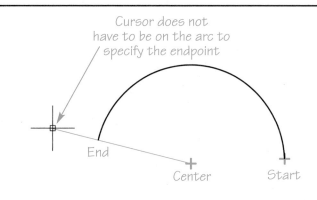

Cursor does not have to be on the arc to specify the endpoint

End

Center          Start

**Figure 3-27.**
Positive angles result in a counterclockwise arc; negative angles produce a clockwise arc.

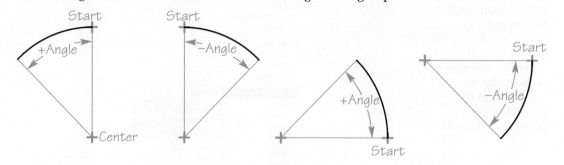

**Figure 3-28.**
A positive chord length results in the smallest possible arc. A negative chord length produces the largest possible arc.

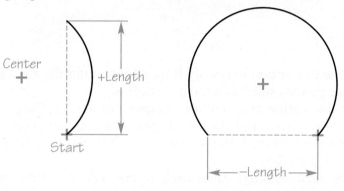

**Figure 3-29.**
After picking the start point and endpoint, the curvature of the arc can be specified by defining the tangent direction of the arc at the start point.

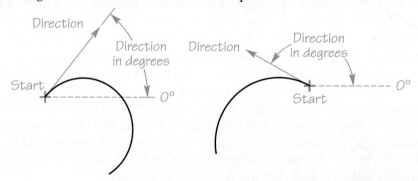

If you use the **Arc** button or the command line to access the **ARC** command, the following prompt is displayed:

Command: **a** *or* **arc.↵**
Specify start point of arc or [Center]:

Select the start point, or type c and press [Enter] to select a center point. If you enter the start point initially, you are given the option of entering a second point (**3 Points** option), center point, or endpoint. In the following command sequence, the **End** option is selected:

Command: **a** *or* **arc.**⏎
Specify start point of arc or [Center]: *(pick start point)*
Specify second point of arc or [Center/End]: **e.**⏎
Specify end point of arc: *(pick endpoint)*
Specify center point of arc or [Angle/Direction/Radius]:

After selecting the start point and endpoint, you have four options for completing the arc: center point, angle, direction, or radius. Note that this command line sequence corresponds to the following pull-down menu options:

- **Start, Center, End**
- **Start, End, Angle**
- **Start, End, Direction**
- **Start, End, Radius**
- **Center, Start, End**

If you select the **Center** option at the first prompt, you must pick the start point after picking the center point:

Command: **a** *or* **arc.**⏎
Specify start point of arc or [Center]: **c.**⏎
Specify center point of arc: *(pick center point using cursor or by entering coordinates at the command line)*
Specify start point of arc: *(pick start point using cursor or by entering coordinates at the command line)*
Specify end point of arc or [Angle/chord Length]:

Regardless of the order in which you select the start point and center point, you have three options to complete the arc: endpoint, angle, or chord length. Note that this command line sequence corresponds to the following pull-down menu options:

- **Start, Center, End**
- **Start, Center, Angle**
- **Start, Center, Length**
- **Center, Start, End**
- **Center, Start, Angle**
- **Center, Start, Length**

## Continuing Arcs from a Previously Drawn Arc or Line

An arc can be continued from the previous arc or line. To do this, pick **Continue** from the **Arc** cascading menu in the **Draw** pull-down menu. The **Continue** option can also be accessed by beginning the **ARC** command and then pressing the [Enter] key, pressing the space bar, or selecting **Enter** from the shortcut menu.

When a series of arcs are drawn in this manner, consecutive arcs are tangent. The start point and direction are taken from the endpoint and direction of the previous arc. See **Figure 3-30**.

The **Continue** option can also be used to quickly draw an arc tangent to the endpoint of a previously drawn line. See **Figure 3-31**. The command sequence is as follows:

Command: **l** *or* **line.**⏎
Specify first point: *(select a point)*
Specify next point or [Undo]: *(select a second point)*
Specify next point or [Undo]: ⏎
Command: **a** *or* **arc.**⏎
Specify start point of arc or [Center]: *(press the space bar or [Enter] to place the start point of the arc at the end of the previous line)*
Specify end point of arc: *(select the endpoint of the arc)*
Command:

---

**Figure 3-30.**
Using the **Continue** option to draw three connected arcs.

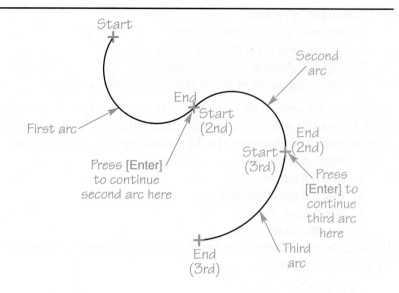

**Figure 3-31.**
An arc continuing from the previous line. Point 2 is the start of the arc, and Point 3 is the end of the arc.

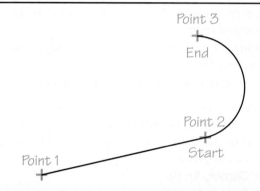

## Exercise 3-11

◆ Start a new drawing using a template or startup option of your own choice.
◆ Set the units to **Architectural**.
◆ Use the **3 Points** option of the **ARC** command to draw several arcs.
◆ Use the **Start, Center, End** option of the **ARC** command to draw several arcs.
◆ Draw an arc with a chord length of 5".
◆ Draw an arc with a tangent direction of 50°.
◆ Draw an arc with an included angle of 120°.
◆ Draw an arc with a radius of 4".
◆ Use the **ARC** command and the **Continue** option to draw the arcs shown in **Figure 3-30**.
◆ Use the **ARC** command and the **Continue** option as described in the text to draw an arc connected to a previously drawn line, as shown in **Figure 3-31**.
◆ Save the drawing as ex3-11.
◆ Use the **CLOSE** command to close the drawing.

Architectural Drafting Using AutoCAD

# Drawing Polylines

The term *polyline* is composed of the prefix *poly-* and the word *line*. *Poly-* means *many*. A **polyline** is a single object that can be made up of one or more varied-width line or arc segments, all "glued" together. The **PLINE** command is used to draw polylines and any related objects made up of line segments. Polylines have advantages over normal lines for the following reasons:

- Polylines can be drawn as thick or tapered lines.
- They can be edited using advanced editing features.
- Closed polygons can be drawn.
- The area or perimeter of a polyline object can be determined easily.
- Arcs and straight lines of varying thicknesses can be joined as single objects.
- Polylines can be used to create special custom symbols and graphics.

The **PLINE** command is similar to the **LINE** command. There are additional options, however, and all segments of a polyline are treated as a single object. To draw a polyline, you can pick the **Polyline** button from the **Draw** toolbar, pick **Polyline** from the **Draw** pull-down menu, or type pl or pline at the Command prompt:

PLINE
PL

Draw
➥ Polyline

Draw
toolbar

Polyline

```
Command: pl or pline↵
Specify start point: (select a point)
Current line-width is 0.0000
Specify next point or [Arc/Halfwidth/Length/Undo/Width]: (select the next point)
```

A line width of 0.0000 or 0'-0" produces a line of minimum width. If this is acceptable, you may select the endpoint of the line. If additional line segments are added to the first line, the endpoint of the first line automatically becomes the starting point of the next line. Press [Enter] to end the **PLINE** command and return to the Command prompt.

## Setting the Polyline Width

When the **Width** option of the **PLINE** command is selected, you are asked to specify the starting and ending widths of the polyline. The specified starting width becomes the default setting for the ending width. Therefore, to keep the polyline the same width, press [Enter] at the second prompt. If a tapered polyline is desired, enter different values for the starting and ending widths. The following command sequence draws the polyline shown in **Figure 3-32A.** Notice that the starting and ending points are located at the center of the polyline.

```
Command: pl or pline↵
Specify start point: 4,4↵
Current line-width is 0.0000
Specify next point or [Arc/Halfwidth/Length/Undo/Width]: w↵
Specify starting width <0.0000>: .25↵
Specify ending width <0.2500>: ↵
Specify next point or [Arc/Halfwidth/Length/Undo/Width]: 4,8↵
Specify next point or [Arc/Close/Halfwidth/Length/Undo/Width]: ↵
Command:
```

Enter different starting and ending widths if you want to draw a tapered polyline. The polyline in **Figure 3-32B** has a starting width of 0.25 and an ending width of 0.5. The **Width** option of the **PLINE** command can be used to draw an arrow by specifying 0 as the starting width and then using any desired ending width.

Figure 3-32.
A—A polyline with constant width. B—A tapered polyline. C—Using the **Halfwidth** option.

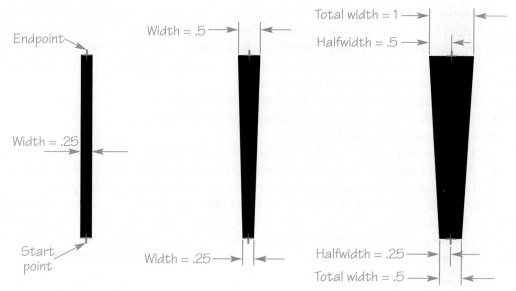

The **Halfwidth** option of the **PLINE** command allows you to specify the width of the polyline from the center to one side. After picking the first point of the polyline, enter the **Halfwidth** option and specify values for the starting and ending halfwidths. Notice the polyline in **Figure 3-32C** is twice as wide as the polyline in **Figure 3-32B**.

Specify next point or [Arc/Close/Halfwidth/Length/Undo/Width]: **h**⏎
Specify starting half-width <*current*>: **.25**⏎
Specify ending half-width <0.2500>: **.5**⏎

**Note**

Once a polyline width has been specified, the value becomes the default width value for all future polylines. To change the width back to the AutoCAD default, enter the **Width** option and specify a 0 starting width and a 0 ending width.

## Using the Length Option

The **Length** option of the **PLINE** command allows you to draw a polyline having the same angle as the previous polyline. After drawing a polyline, reissue the **PLINE** command and pick a starting point. Enter the **Length** option and give the desired length:

Command: **pl** *or* **pline**⏎
Specify start point: *(pick a starting point)*
Current line-width is *current*
Specify next point or [Arc/Halfwidth/Length/Undo/Width]: **l**⏎
Specify length of line: *(type any desired length and press* [Enter]*)*
Specify next point or [Arc/Close/Halfwidth/Length/Undo/Width]: ⏎
Command:

The polyline is drawn at the same angle as the previous polyline and at the length you specify. If there are no previously drawn polylines in the drawing session, the polyline is drawn at 0°.

## Using the Arc Option

The **Arc** option of the **PLINE** command allows you to add arcs to the polyline being drawn. Upon entering the **Arc** option, additional options become available that are specific to how the arc is to be drawn. The following command sequence draws the line-arc-line object shown in **Figure 3-33**.

Command: **pl** *or* **pline**↵
Specify start point: **2,2**↵
Current line-width is *current*
Specify next point or [Arc/Halfwidth/Length/Undo/Width]: **4,2**↵
Specify next point or [Arc/Close/Halfwidth/Length/Undo/Width]: **a**↵
Specify endpoint of arc or
[Angle/CEnter/CLose/Direction/Halfwidth/Line/Radius/Second pt/Undo/Width]: **@2,2**↵
Specify endpoint of arc or
[Angle/CEnter/CLose/Direction/Halfwidth/Line/Radius/Second pt/Undo/Width]: **l**↵
Specify next point or [Arc/Close/Halfwidth/Length/Undo/Width]: **@0,2**↵
Specify next point or [Arc/Close/Halfwidth/Length/Undo/Width]: ↵
Command:

**Figure 3-33.**
The **Arc** option of the **PLINE** command allows you to draw polyline arcs.

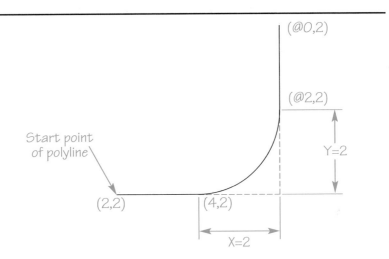

Once the arc option has been entered, the standard polyline options change to options relating to arcs. The following is a description of the arc options:

- **Angle.** Allows you to specify the included angle for the arc.
- **Center.** Allows you to specify the center point of the polyline arc.
- **Close.** Closes the polyline with an arc segment.
- **Direction.** Allows you to specify a starting direction for the arc.
- **Halfwidth.** Allows you to specify a halfwidth for the arc.
- **Line.** Allows you to resume drawing polyline line segments and use the default **PLINE** command options.
- **Radius.** Allows you to specify the radius of the arc.
- **Second pt.** Allows you to select a second and then a third point for the arc.
- **Undo.** Undoes the last arc segment drawn.
- **Width.** Allows you to specify the width of the arc segment.

## Undoing Previously Drawn Polylines

While inside the **PLINE** command, you can use the **Undo** option to erase the last polyline segment drawn. To do so, enter u at the prompt line, and then press [Enter]. Each time you use the **Undo** option, another polyline segment is erased. You can use the **Undo** option to remove all polyline segments up to the first point of the polyline. The segments are removed in reverse order (from the order in which they were drawn).

## Closing Polylines

The **Close** option of the **PLINE** command draws a line segment from the last point selected to the starting point of the polyline. In order for the **Close** option to work, a minimum of two polyline segments must be drawn. The following command sequence closes the polyline shown in **Figure 3-34.**

```
Command: pl or pline↵
Specify start point: 2,2↵
Current line-width is current
Specify next point or [Arc/ Halfwidth/Length/Undo/Width]: @3<0↵
Specify next point or [Arc/Close/Halfwidth/Length/Undo/Width]: a↵
Specify endpoint of arc or
[Angle/CEnter/CLose/Direction/Halfwidth/Line/Radius/Second pt/Undo/Width]: @0,2↵
Specify endpoint of arc or
[Angle/CEnter/CLose/Direction/Halfwidth/Line/Radius/Second pt/Undo/Width]: l↵
Specify next point or [Arc/Close/Halfwidth/Length/Undo/Width]: c↵
Command:
```

**Figure 3-34.**
Using the **Close** option in the **PLINE** command.

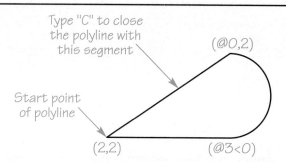

Type "C" to close the polyline with this segment

(@0,2)

Start point of polyline

(2,2)          (@3<0)

## Exercise 3-12

- Start a new drawing using a template or startup option of your own choice.
- Set the units to **Architectural.**
- Use the **PLINE** command to draw several objects of your own design. Vary the width for each object.
- Draw three different types of arrowheads by specifying different starting and ending widths.
- Set the polyline width to 1/8". Draw a single polyline. Using the **Length** option, draw two more polylines with the same width and a length of 4".
- Draw a polyline with a width of 0, a straight line segment, an arc segment, and then a straight line segment again.
- Save the drawing as ex3-12.
- Use the **CLOSE** command to close the drawing.

Architectural Drafting Using AutoCAD

# Drawing Regular Polygons

A *regular polygon* is any closed-plane geometric figure with three or more equal sides and equal angles. For example, a hexagon is a six-sided regular polygon. The **POLYGON** command is used to draw any regular polygon with up to 1,024 sides.

The **POLYGON** command can be accessed by selecting **Polygon** from the **Draw** pull-down menu, picking the **Polygon** button in the **Draw** toolbar, or entering pol or polygon at the Command prompt. Regardless of the method used to select the command, you are first prompted for the number of sides. If you want an octagon, which is a polygon with eight sides, enter 8, as follows:

```
Command: pol or polygon↵
Enter number of sides <current>: 8↵
```

The number of sides you enter becomes the default for the next time you use the **POLYGON** command. Next, AutoCAD prompts for the edge or center of the polygon. If you reply by picking a point on the screen, this point becomes the center of the polygon. You are then asked if you want to have the polygon inscribed within or circumscribed outside of an imaginary circle. See **Figure 3-35**. A polygon is *inscribed* when it is drawn inside a circle, with its corners touching the circle. *Circumscribed* polygons are drawn outside of a circle, with the sides of the polygon tangent to the circle. You must then specify the radius of the circle. The command continues as follows:

```
Specify center of polygon or [Edge]: (pick center of polygon)
Enter an option [Inscribed in circle/Circumscribed about circle] <current>: (respond with
    i or c and press [Enter])
Specify radius of circle: (type the radius, such as 2, and press [Enter]; or pick a point on
    the screen at the desired distance from the center)
```

POLYGON
POL

Draw
→ Polygon

Draw
toolbar

Polygon

**Figure 3-35.**
Drawing an inscribed and a circumscribed polygon.

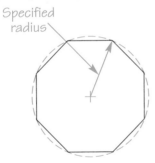

Specified radius

Inscribed Polygon

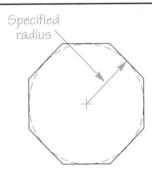

Specified radius

Circumscribed Polygon

**Note**    It is important to remember that although you are specifying a polygon with a center and a radius, a circle is not being drawn. Polygons do not have centers like circles and arcs.

The **I** or **C** option you select becomes the default for the next polygon. The Specify center of polygon or [Edge]: prompt allows you to pick the center or specify the edge. Notice that picking the center is the default. If you want to draw the polygon along one of the edges of the object, specify the **Edge** option and pick the edge endpoints, as follows:

```
Specify center of polygon or [Edge]: e↵
Specify first endpoint of edge: (pick a point)
Specify second endpoint of edge: (pick a second point)
```

After you pick the endpoints of one side, the rest of the polygon sides are drawn counterclockwise. Polygons are polylines and can be easily edited using the **PEDIT** (polyline edit) command, which is discussed in Chapter 6. For example, a polygon can be given a width using the **Width** option of the **PEDIT** command.

Polygons can be used for a number of objects in architecture, such as a turret in a Victorian house, a fountain, or a deck. To draw a polygon to be dimensioned across the flats, use the **Circumscribed about circle** option. The radius you enter is equal to one-half the distance across the flats. The distance across the corners (in the **Inscribed in circle** option) is specified when the polygon must be confined within a circular area. One example is the boundary of a swimming pool deck. Notice the distance across the flats and the distance across the corners in **Figure 3-36.**

**Figure 3-36.**
Specifying the distance across the flats and between the corners of a polygon.

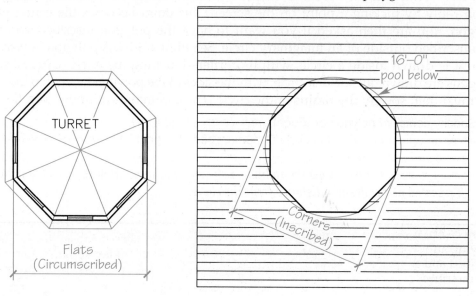

## Exercise 3-13

◆ Start a new drawing using a template or startup option of your own choice.
◆ Set the units to **Architectural** and **Decimal Degrees**.
◆ Draw a hexagon with a distance of 3'-0" across the flats. Draw another hexagon measuring 3'-0" across the corners.
◆ Draw an octagon with a horizontal edge that is 1'-6" long.
◆ Draw a pentagon circumscribed about a circle having a 2-1/4" diameter.
◆ Save the drawing as ex3-13.
◆ Use the **CLOSE** command to close the drawing.

# Drawing Rectangles

REC
RECTANG
RECTANGLE

Draw
➥ Rectangle

Draw
toolbar

Rectangle

The **RECTANG** command allows you to easily draw rectangles. When using this command, pick one corner and then the opposite corner. See **Figure 3-37.** The **RECTANG** command can be accessed by picking **Rectangle** in the **Draw** pull-down menu, picking the **Rectangle** button in the **Draw** toolbar, or entering rec, rectang, or rectangle at the Command prompt:

**Figure 3-37.**
Using the **RECTANG**
command. Simply
pick opposite
corners of the
rectangle.

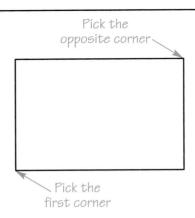

Pick the
opposite corner

Pick the
first corner

Command: **rec**, **rectang**, *or* **rectangle**.↵
Specify first corner point or [Chamfer/Elevation/Fillet/Thickness/Width]: *(pick a point for*
*the first corner of the rectangle)*
Specify other corner point or [Dimensions]: *(Pick a point for the opposite corner)*
Command:

Keep in mind that Cartesian coordinates can be used to specify points for rectangles. For example, if a specific size rectangle is needed, such as a 4″ × 3″ rectangle, the following sequence would apply:

Command: **rec**, **rectang**, *or* **rectangle**.↵
Specify first corner point or [Chamfer/Elevation/Fillet/Thickness/Width]: *(pick a point for*
*the first corner of the rectangle)*
Specify other corner point or [Dimensions]: **@4,3**.↵
Command:

Rectangles are polylines and can be edited using the **PEDIT** command. Since a rectangle is a polyline, it is treated as one object until exploded. After it is exploded, the individual sides can then be edited separately. The **EXPLODE** command is discussed in Chapter 6.

## Specifying Rectangle Dimensions

AutoCAD provides a **Dimensions** option for the **RECTANG** command. The option is available after the first corner of the rectangle is picked:

Command: **rec**, **rectang**, *or* **rectangle**.↵
Specify first corner point or [Chamfer/Elevation/Fillet/Thickness/Width]: *(pick first corner*
*point)*
Specify other corner point or [Dimensions]:

Enter d to access the **Dimensions** option. You are then prompted to enter the length and width of the rectangle. In the following example, a 5 × 3 rectangle is specified:

Specify other corner point or [Dimensions]: **d**.↵
Specify length for rectangles <*current*>: **5**.↵
Specify width for rectangles <*current*>: **3**.↵
Specify other corner point or [Dimensions]: *(move crosshairs to the desired quadrant*
*and pick a point)*

After specifying the length and width, the Specify other corner point or [Dimensions]: prompt is displayed. If you wish to change the dimensions, select the **Dimensions** option. If the dimensions are correct, you can specify the other corner point to complete the rectangle. When using the **Dimensions** option, the second corner point determines which of four possible rectangles is drawn.

## Drawing Rectangles with Line Width

The **Width** option of the **RECTANG** command is used to specify the width of the rectangle lines. Setting line width for rectangles is similar to using the **Width** option in the **PLINE** command. The following sequence is used to create a rectangle with .25 wide lines:

Command: **rec**, **rectang**, *or* **rectangle**.↵
Specify first corner point or [Chamfer/Elevation/Fillet/Thickness/Width]: **w**.↵
Specify line width for rectangles <*current*>: **.25**.↵

You can press [Enter] at the Specify line width for rectangles <*current*>: prompt to have the rectangle polylines drawn with the default polyline width. The default polyline width for rectangles is zero, similar to polylines. If you enter a value at this prompt, the rectangle will be drawn with the specified width. After setting the rectangle width, you can either select another option or draw the rectangle. Continue selecting options until you have set the characteristics correctly, and then draw the rectangle.

## Drawing Chamfered Rectangles

A *chamfer* is an angled corner on an object. Drawing chamfers is covered in detail in Chapter 6. This is a brief introduction to drawing chamfers on rectangles. To draw chamfers on rectangles, use the **Chamfer** option of the **RECTANG** command. The rectangle created will have chamfers drawn automatically.

After you select the **Chamfer** option, you must provide the chamfer distances, **Figure 3-38.** The command sequence is as follows:

Command: **rec**, **rectang**, *or* **rectangle**.↵
Specify first corner point or [Chamfer/Elevation/Fillet/Thickness/Width]: **c**.↵
Specify first chamfer distance for rectangles <*current*>: *(enter the first chamfer distance from the corner of the rectangle)*
Specify second chamfer distance for rectangles <*current*>: *(enter the second chamfer distance from the corner of the rectangle)*
Specify first corner point or [Chamfer/Elevation/Fillet/Thickness/Width]:

After setting the chamfer distances, you can either draw the rectangle or select another option. If you select the **Fillet** option, the chamfers will not be drawn.

The AutoCAD default chamfer distance is zero. If the default for the first chamfer distance is zero and you enter a different value, the new distance becomes the default for the second chamfer distance. A chamfer can have two different distance values for each side. If the two distance values are the same, a 45° chamfer is added to each corner of the rectangle.

**Figure 3-38.**
A chamfer is an angled corner. The chamfer distance is measured from the corner of the rectangle to the beginning or end of the chamfer.

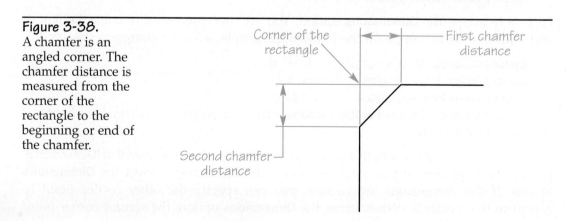

Architectural Drafting Using AutoCAD

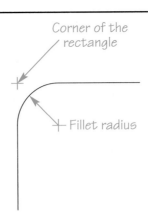

**Figure 3-39.**
A fillet is a rounded corner.

Corner of the rectangle

Fillet radius

## Drawing Filleted Rectangles

A *fillet* is a rounded corner on an object, **Figure 3-39.** Drawing fillets is covered in detail in Chapter 6. This is a brief introduction to drawing fillets on rectangles.

Fillets are automatically drawn on rectangles using the **Fillet** option of the **RECTANG** command. After selecting the option, you must enter the fillet radius:

Command: **rec**, **rectang**, *or* **rectangle.**⏎
Specify first corner point or [Chamfer/Elevation/Fillet/Thickness/Width]: **f.**⏎
Specify fillet radius for rectangles <*current*>: *(enter a fillet radius or press* [Enter] *to accept the default)*
Specify first corner point or [Chamfer/Elevation/Fillet/Thickness/Width]:

The default fillet radius is the radius of the previously drawn rectangle. Once a fillet radius is specified, the **RECTANG** command automatically draws fillets on rectangles. In order to draw rectangles without fillets, the fillet radius must be set to zero.

## Additional **RECTANG** Options

There are two other options available when using the **RECTANG** command. These options remain effective for future uses of the command:

- **Elevation.** This option sets the elevation of the rectangle along the Z axis (up off of the XY drawing plane). The default value is zero.
- **Thickness.** This option gives the rectangle depth along the Z axis (the thickness). The default value is zero.

Any combination of these five options can be used to draw a single rectangle. For example, a rectangle can have 3" fillets and a 1/4" line width.

Note — Once you have set an option for the **RECTANG** command, this becomes the default for the next rectangle you draw. Set the **Chamfer**, **Elevation**, **Fillet**, **Thickness**, and **Width** options back to zero, and new rectangles will be drawn with the AutoCAD defaults.

## Exercise 3-14

◆ Start a new drawing using a template or startup option of your own choice.
◆ Set the units to **Architectural.**
◆ Use the **RECTANG** command to draw a rectangle.
◆ Use the **RECTANG** command to draw a rectangle with a 1/8" line width.
◆ Use the **RECTANG** command to draw rectangles with fillets and chamfers.
◆ Save the drawing as ex3-14.
◆ Use the **CLOSE** command to close the drawing.

# Drawing Ellipses

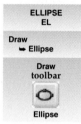

ELLIPSE
EL

Draw
➡ Ellipse

Draw
toolbar

Ellipse

When a circle is viewed at an angle, an elliptical shape is seen. For example, a 30° ellipse is created if a circle is rotated 30° from the line of sight. The parts of an ellipse are shown in **Figure 3-40.** The **ELLIPSE** command can be accessed by selecting **Ellipse** from the **Draw** pull-down menu, picking the **Ellipse** button in the **Draw** toolbar, or entering el or ellipse at the Command prompt. An ellipse can be drawn using three different **ELLIPSE** command options. These options are available at the Command prompt or in the **Ellipse** cascading menu, **Figure 3-41.**

**Figure 3-40.**
Parts of an ellipse.

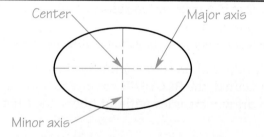

**Figure 3-41.**
The options for drawing an ellipse are available in the **Ellipse** cascading menu in the **Draw** pull-down menu.

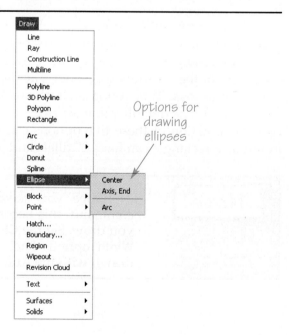

# Drawing an Ellipse Using the **Axis, End** Option

The **Axis, End** option establishes the first axis and one endpoint of the second axis. The first axis may be either the major or minor axis, depending on what is entered for the second axis. The longer of the two axes is always the major axis. After you pick the first axis, the ellipse is dragged by the cursor until the third point is picked. The command sequence for the ellipses in **Figure 3-42** is as follows:

Command: **el** or **ellipse.**↵
Specify axis endpoint of ellipse or [Arc/Center]: *(select an axis endpoint)*
Specify other endpoint of axis: *(select the other endpoint of the axis)*
Specify distance to other axis or [Rotation]: *(select a distance from the midpoint of the first axis to the end of the second axis and press* [Enter]*)*

If you respond to the Specify distance to other axis or [Rotation]: prompt with r for rotation, AutoCAD assumes you have selected the major axis with the first two points. The next prompt requests the angle that the corresponding circle is rotated from the line of sight. The command sequence is as follows:

Command: **el** or **ellipse.**↵
Specify axis endpoint of ellipse or [Arc/Center]: *(select a major axis endpoint)*
Specify other endpoint of axis: *(select the other endpoint of the major axis)*
Specify distance to other axis or [Rotation]: **r**↵
Specify rotation around major axis: *(type a rotation angle, such as* 30*, and press* [Enter]*)*

The 30 response draws an ellipse representing a circle rotated 30° from the line of sight. A 0 response draws an ellipse with the minor axis equal to the major axis. This is a circle. AutoCAD rejects any rotation angle between 89.42° and 90.57° or 269.42° and 270.57°. **Figure 3-43** shows the relationship between several ellipses having the same major axis length, but different rotation angles.

---

**Figure 3-42.**
Constructing identical ellipses by choosing different axis endpoints.

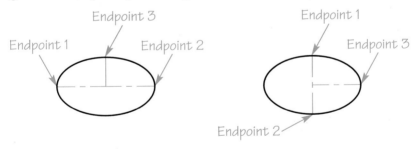

---

**Figure 3-43.**
Ellipse rotation angles.

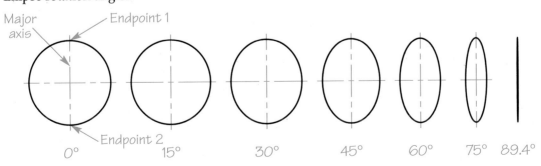

---

## Drawing an Ellipse Using the **Center** Option

An ellipse can also be constructed by specifying the center point and one endpoint for each of the two axes. See **Figure 3-44.** To use this option, select **Center** from the **Ellipse** cascading menu in the **Draw** pull-down menu. The command sequence for this option is as follows:

Specify axis endpoint of ellipse or [Arc/Center]: **c↵**
Specify center of ellipse: *(select the ellipse center point)*
Specify endpoint of axis: *(select the endpoint of one axis)*
Specify distance to other axis or [Rotation]: *(select the endpoint of the other axis)*

The **Rotation** option can be used instead of selecting the second axis endpoint.

**Figure 3-44.**
Drawing an ellipse
by picking the
center and endpoint
of two axes.

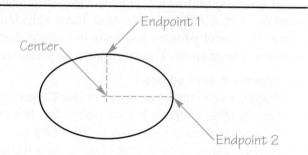

## Drawing Elliptical Arcs

The **Arc** option of the **ELLIPSE** command is used to draw elliptical arcs. The command sequence for the **Arc** option is as follows:

Command: **el** *or* **ellipse.↵**
Specify axis endpoint of ellipse or [Arc/Center]: **a↵**
Specify axis endpoint of elliptical arc or [Center]: *(pick the first axis endpoint)*
Specify other endpoint of axis: *(pick the second axis endpoint)*
Specify distance to other axis or [Rotation]: *(pick the distance for the second axis)*
Specify start angle or [Parameter]: **0↵**
Specify end angle or [Parameter/Included angle]: **90↵**
Command:

Once the second endpoint of the first axis is picked, you can drag the shape of a full ellipse. This can be used to help you visualize the other axis. The distance for the second axis is from the ellipse center to the point picked. Enter a start angle. The start and end angles are the angular relation between the ellipse center and where the arc begins. The angle of the elliptical arc is established from the angle of the first axis. A 0° start angle is the same as the first endpoint of the first axis. A 45° start angle is 45° counterclockwise from the first endpoint of the first axis. End angles are also established counterclockwise from the start point. **Figure 3-45** shows the elliptical arc drawn with the previous command sequence and displays samples of different start and end angle arcs.

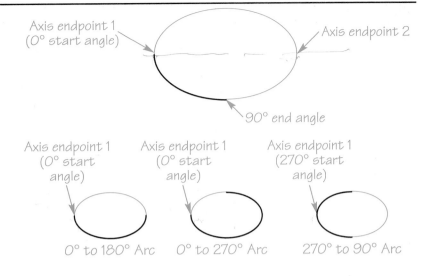

**Figure 3-45.**
Drawing elliptical arcs with the **Arc** option of the **ELLIPSE** command. Note the three examples at the bottom using different start and end angles.

Axis endpoint 1
(0° start angle)

Axis endpoint 2

90° end angle

Axis endpoint 1
(0° start
angle)

Axis endpoint 1
(0° start
angle)

Axis endpoint 1
(270° start
angle)

0° to 180° Arc

0° to 270° Arc

270° to 90° Arc

## Exercise 3-15

◆ Start a new drawing using a template or startup option of your own choice.
◆ Set the units to **Architectural**.
◆ Use the **Axis, End** option of the **ELLIPSE** command to draw the ellipses shown in **Figure 3-42**.
◆ Use the **Center** and **Rotation** options of the **ELLIPSE** command to draw some ellipses similar to **Figure 3-43**.
◆ Use the **Center** option of the **ELLIPSE** command to draw the ellipse shown in **Figure 3-44**.
◆ Use the **Arc** option of the **ELLIPSE** command to draw the following elliptical arcs:
  ◆ Use axis endpoints, axis distance, start angle = 0, and end angle = 90, similar to **Figure 3-45**.
  ◆ Use the same options as in the previous instructions to draw a 0° to 180° arc, a 0° to 270° arc, and a 270° to 90° arc, similar to the samples in **Figure 3-45**.
  ◆ Save the drawing as ex3-15.
  ◆ Use the **CLOSE** command to close the drawing.

# Viewing Your Drawing

The ability to "zoom in" (magnify) or "zoom out" of a drawing allows architectural designers to move around and display various sections of a drawing. The **ZOOM** command is a helpful tool you will use often. The different options of the **ZOOM** command are discussed in the next sections.

## The ZOOM Options

Each of the **ZOOM** options can be accessed by its corresponding button in the **Standard** toolbar or by selecting the option in the **Zoom** cascading menu from the **View** pull-down menu. All the buttons in the **Zoom** flyout are also found in the **Zoom** toolbar. See **Figure 3-46**. All **ZOOM** options except **In** and **Out** are available at the Command prompt:

ZOOM
Z

View
➥ Zoom

Command: **z** *or* **zoom**↵
Specify corner of window, enter a scale factor (nX or nXP), or
    [All/Center/Dynamic/Extents/Previous/Scale/Window] <real time>:

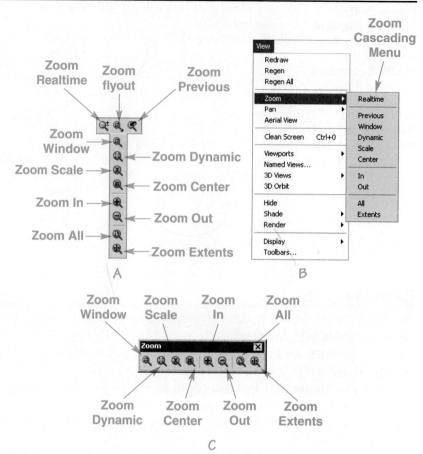

**Figure 3-46.**
**ZOOM** command options. A—The **Zoom** flyout button on the **Standard** toolbar. B—The **Zoom** cascading menu in the **Draw** pull-down menu. C—The **Zoom** toolbar contains the same buttons as the **Zoom** flyout.

The following provides an explanation of each **ZOOM** option:
- **real time.** The default option allows you to perform realtime zooming. This interactive zooming is discussed later in this chapter.
- **All.** Zooms to the edge of the drawing limits. If objects are drawn beyond the limits, the **All** option zooms to the edges of your geometry. Always use this option after you change the drawing limits. Drawing limits are discussed in Chapter 11.
- **Center.** Zooms the center of the display screen to a picked point. If you want to zoom to the center of an area of the drawing and magnify the view as well, pick the center and height of the area in the drawing. Rather than a height, a magnification factor can be entered, by typing a number followed by an *x*, such as 4x. The current value represents the height of the screen in drawing units. Entering a smaller number enlarges the image size, while a larger number reduces it. The command sequence is as follows:

> [All/Center/Dynamic/Extents/Previous/Scale/Window] <real time>: **c.**↵
> Specify center point: (*pick a center point*)
> Enter magnification or height <*current*>: **4x.**↵
> Command:

- **Dynamic.** Allows for a graphic pan and zoom with the use of a view box representing the screen.
- **Extents.** Zooms to the extents (or edges) of the geometry in a drawing. This is the portion of the drawing area containing drawing objects.
- **Previous.** Returns to the previous display. You can go back to up to 10 displays, one at a time.
- **Scale.** The following prompt appears when you select the **Scale** option:

> Enter a scale factor (nX or nXP):

There are two options: **nX** and **nXP**. The **nX** option scales the display relative to the current display. To use this option, type a positive number, type x, and then press [Enter]. For example, enter 2x to magnify the current display two times. To reduce the display, enter a number less than one. For example, if you enter .5x, objects appear half as large as they did in the previous display.

The **nXP** option is used in conjunction with model space and paper space. It scales a drawing in model space, relative to paper space, and is used primarily in the layout of scaled multiview drawings. A detailed discussion of this option is given in Chapter 24. Both of the **Scale** options can be entered at the initial **ZOOM** command prompt. For example, enter the following to enlarge the current display by a factor of three:

Command: **z** *or* **zoom**↵
Specify corner of window, enter a scale factor (nX or nXP), or
[All/Center/Dynamic/Extents/Previous/Scale/Window] <real time>: **3x**↵
Command:

- **Window.** Pick opposite corners of a box. Objects in the box enlarge to fill the display. The **Window** option is the default if you pick a point on the screen upon entering the **ZOOM** command.
- **In.** This option is available only on the toolbar and the pull-down menu. It automatically executes a 2X zoom scale factor.
- **Out.** This option is available only on the toolbar and the pull-down menu. It automatically executes a .5X zoom scale factor.

## Performing realtime zoom

When using the command line, the default option of the **ZOOM** command is **real time**. A *realtime zoom* can be viewed as it is performed. It is activated by pressing [Enter] after entering the **ZOOM** command, picking the **Zoom Realtime** button in the **Standard** toolbar, picking **Realtime** in the **Zoom** cascading menu in the **View** pull-down menu, or right-clicking in the drawing area and selecting **Zoom** in the shortcut menu. Realtime zooming allows you to see the model move on the screen as you zoom. It is the quickest and easiest method for adjusting the magnification of drawings on the screen.

The Zoom cursor is a magnifying glass icon with a plus and minus sign, and it is displayed when realtime zoom is executed. Press and hold the left mouse button (pick button) and move the pointer up to zoom in (enlarge) and down to zoom out (reduce). When you have achieved the display you want, release the button. If the display needs further adjustment after the initial zoom, press and hold the left mouse button again and move the pointer to get the desired display. To exit once you are done, press the [Esc] key, press the [Enter] key, or right-click and pick **Exit** from the shortcut menu.

If you right-click while the Zoom cursor is active, a shortcut menu is displayed. See **Figure 3-47**. This menu appears at the cursor location and contains six viewing options.

- **Pan.** Activates the **Realtime** option of the **PAN** command. This allows you to adjust the placement of the drawing on the screen. If additional zooming is required, right-click again to display the shortcut menu and pick **Zoom**. In this manner, you can toggle back and forth between **Pan** and **Zoom Realtime** to accurately adjust the view. A detailed explanation of the **PAN** command is given later in this chapter.
- **Zoom.** Activates the **Realtime** option of the **ZOOM** command. A check appears to the left of this option if it is active.

Figure 3-47.
This shortcut menu
containing six
viewing options is
displayed if you
right-click while the
Zoom cursor is
active.

| |
|---|
| Exit |
| Pan |
| ✓ Zoom |
| 3D Orbit |
| Zoom Window |
| Zoom Original |
| Zoom Extents |

- **3D Orbit.** When this is selected, AutoCAD allows you to change your point of view around your drawing. Similar to **Zoom**, this option is used to move around a 3D object. Orbiting the view is discussed in Chapter 25.
- **Zoom Window.** Activates the **Zoom Window** option and changes the cursor display to a pointer next to a rectangle. You can pick opposite corners of a window, but you must press and hold the pick button and drag the window box to the opposite corner. You then can release the pick button.
- **Zoom Original.** Restores the previous display before any realtime zooming or panning had occurred. This is a handy function if the current display is not to your liking and it would be easier to start over than to make further adjustments.
- **Zoom Extents.** Zooms to the extents of the drawing geometry.

## Enlarging with a window

The **Zoom Window** option requires you to pick opposite corners of a rectangular window enclosing the area to be zoomed. The first point you pick is automatically accepted as the first corner of the zoom window. After this corner is picked, move the mouse, and a box appears, showing the area to be displayed once the second corner is picked. The box grows and shrinks as you move the pointing device. When the second corner is picked, the center of the window becomes the center of the new screen display. **Figure 3-48** shows **Zoom Window** used on a drawing.

Figure 3-48.
Using the **Window** option of the **ZOOM** command. A—Select the corners of a window. B—The selected window fills the drawing screen. To return to the original view, use the **Previous** option of the **ZOOM** command.

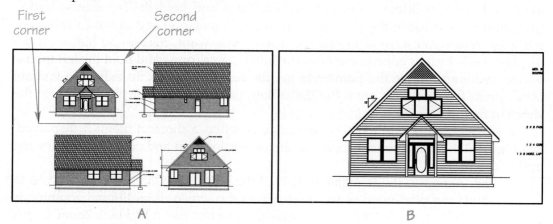

First corner

Second corner

A

B

## Exercise 3-16

◆ Start AutoCAD and load a drawing from a previous exercise or drawing problem.
  ◆ Enlarge and reduce the drawing using **Zoom Realtime**.
  ◆ Move around the drawing using **Pan Realtime**.
  ◆ Select **Zoom Window** and enlarge a portion of the drawing.
  ◆ Select **Zoom Window** again, to move in closer to a detail.
  ◆ Use the **Previous** option of the **ZOOM** command to return to the last display.
  ◆ Select **Zoom Extents** to show only the drawing entities.
  ◆ Select the **All** option of the **ZOOM** command to display the entire drawing limits.
◆ Save the drawing as ex3-16.
  ◆ Use the **CLOSE** command to close the drawing.

## Moving around the Display Screen

The **PAN** command allows you to move your viewpoint around the drawing without changing the magnification factor. You can then view objects lying outside the edges of the display screen.

## Performing realtime pan

A *realtime pan* allows you to see the drawing move on the screen as you pan. It is the quickest and easiest method for adjusting the view on the screen. To activate realtime panning, pick **Realtime** from the **Pan** cascading menu in the **View** pull-down menu, pick the **Pan Realtime** button on the **Standard** toolbar, or enter p or pan at the Command prompt.

After starting the command, press and hold the pick button. Move the pointing device in the direction you wish to pan. The pan icon of the hand is displayed when a realtime pan is used. A right-click displays the shortcut menu shown in **Figure 3-47,** with the check mark next to **Pan** instead of **Zoom**.

If you pan to the edge of your drawing, a bar is displayed on one side of the hand cursor. The bar correlates to the side of the drawing. For example, if you reach the left side of the drawing, a bar and arrow appear on the left side of the hand.

PAN
P

View
➡ Pan
➡ Realtime

Standard
toolbar

Pan Realtime

## Picking the pan displacement

The *pan displacement* is the distance the drawing is moved on the screen. You can pick the displacement by selecting **Point** from the **Pan** cascading menu in the **View** pull-down menu or by entering –p or –pan at the Command prompt. The following prompt appears:

Command: **–p** *or* **–pan**↵
Specify base point or displacement:

You can specify a base point by picking a point or entering absolute coordinates. You are then prompted to select a second point. The display window is moved the distance between the points. You can also enter the displacement, or the distance the display window is to be moved, by giving coordinates. The coordinates can be relative, polar, or absolute.

–PAN
–P

View
➡ Pan
➡ Point

**Figure 3-49.**
The **PAN** options can be found in the **Pan** cascading menu of the **View** pull-down menu.

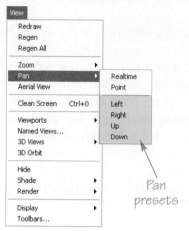

Pan presets

## Using pan presets

The **Pan** cascading menu in the **View** pull-down menu includes four preset directional options: **Left**, **Right**, **Up**, and **Down**. See **Figure 3-49.** Select one of the options to move the display in the indicated direction.

## Using scroll bars to pan

The scroll bars found at the bottom and to the right of the drawing area can also be used to pan the display. See **Figure 3-50.** Pick the arrows at the end of the scroll bar to pan in small increments. Select the scroll bar itself to pan in larger increments. Position the cursor over the box in the scroll bar, pick the left button and hold it, and then move the mouse to see realtime panning in the horizontal or vertical direction.

**Figure 3-50.**
Use the scroll bars to pan the drawing display.

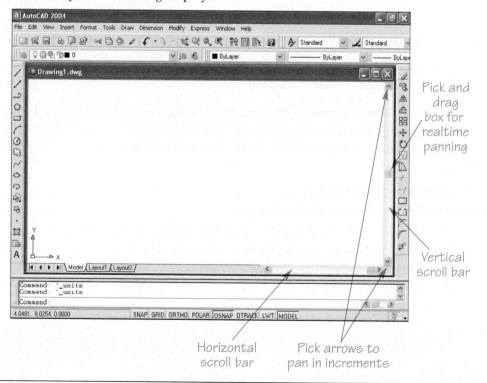

Pick and drag box for realtime panning

Vertical scroll bar

Horizontal scroll bar

Pick arrows to pan in increments

Architectural Drafting Using AutoCAD

AutoCAD supports the IntelliMouse. This mouse has a wheel between the two mouse buttons. The IntelliMouse provides you with zoom and pan capabilities. The IntelliMouse has these basic functions in addition to the standard operation of the two buttons:

- Roll the wheel forward (away from you) to zoom in.
- Roll the wheel backward (toward you) to zoom out.
- Press and hold the wheel button down and move the mouse to pan.
- Double-click on the wheel to zoom to the drawing extents.

## Using Transparent Display Commands

To begin a new command, you usually need to complete or cancel the current command. Most menu picks automatically cancel the command in progress before initiating the new one. Some commands, however, function without canceling an active command.

A *transparent command* temporarily interrupts the active command. After the transparent command is completed, the interrupted command is resumed. Therefore, it is not necessary to cancel the initial command. Many display commands can be used transparently, including **PAN** and several **ZOOM** options.

Suppose that, while drawing a line, you need to place a point somewhere off the screen. One option is to cancel the **LINE** command. You can then zoom out to see more of the drawing and select **LINE** again. A more efficient method is to use **PAN** or **ZOOM** while still in the **LINE** command. An example of drawing a line to a point off the screen is as follows:

Command: **l** *or* **line.**↵
Specify first point: *(pick a point)*
Specify next point or [Undo]: *(pick the **Pan Realtime** button or enter* 'pan*)*
>>Press ESC or ENTER to exit, or right-click to display shortcut menu. *(pan to the location desired, and then press* [Enter]*)*
Resuming LINE command.
Specify next point or [Undo]: *(pick a point)*
Specify next point or [Undo]: ↵
Command:

The double prompt (>>) indicates a command has been put on hold while you are using a transparent command. The transparent command must be completed before the original command resumes. At that time, the double prompt disappears.

The above procedure is similar when using the **ZOOM** command. When typed at the keyboard, an apostrophe (') is entered before the transparent command. To use the **ZOOM** command transparently, enter 'z or 'zoom.

## Regenerating the Display

Often, when zooming into your drawing, circles and arcs appear segmented. AutoCAD "segments" curved objects in the drawing because it can redisplay straight line segments faster than it can calculate curved objects for display. It is important to note that your circles and arcs are truly not straight line segments. AutoCAD is simply displaying them this way to help increase your productivity. When you regenerate the drawing, you are telling AutoCAD to display your curved objects as circles and arcs. The **REGEN** command also is used when you can no longer pan to a side or you have zoomed out far enough that AutoCAD is requesting you to regenerate.

To regenerate the screen, the **REGEN** command is used. This command recalculates all drawing object coordinates and regenerates the display based on the current zoom magnification. To access the **REGEN** command, pick **Regen** from the **View** pull-down menu or enter re or regen at the Command prompt. The screen is immediately regenerated.

# Introduction to Printing and Plotting

A drawing created with CAD can exist in two distinct forms: hard copy and soft copy. The term *hard copy* refers to a physical drawing a printer or plotter produces on paper. The term *soft copy* refers to the computer software version of the drawing, or the actual data file. The soft copy can only be displayed on the computer monitor, making it inconvenient to use for many manufacturing and construction purposes. If the power to the computer is turned off, the soft copy drawing is no longer displayed.

A hard copy drawing is extremely versatile. It can be rolled up or folded and taken down to the shop floor or out to a construction site. A hard copy drawing can be checked without a computer or CAD software. Although CAD is the standard throughout the world for generating drawings, the hard copy drawing is still a vital tool in industry.

The information found in this section is provided to give you only the basics so you can make your first plot. Chapter 24 explores the detailed aspects of printing and plotting architectural drawings. Prints and plots are made using the **Plot** dialog box. Access this dialog box by selecting **Plot...** in the **File** pull-down menu, picking the **Plot** button in the **Standard** toolbar, pressing the [Ctrl]+[P] key combination, or entering plot at the Command prompt. You can also right-click on the **Model** tab or a layout tab and select **Plot...** from the shortcut menu.

The first step in making an AutoCAD drawing is to create a model. The model is composed of various objects, such as lines, circles, and text. The model (or drawing) is created in an environment called *model space.* See **Figure 3-51.**

Once the model is completed, a layout can be created. A *layout* can contain various views of the model at different scales, a title block, and other annotations. In addition, the layout includes page setup information, such as paper size and margins. The layout also has plotter configuration data, which is information related to the specific model of printer or plotter being used. Layouts are produced using the layout tabs at the bottom of the drawing area. They are created in an environment called *paper space,* and a single drawing can have many layouts.

Drawings can be plotted from the **Model** tab of the drawing area or from one of the layout tabs. The following discussion addresses plotting from the **Model** tab only. Creating and plotting layouts is explained in detail in Chapter 24.

Architectural Drafting Using AutoCAD

**Figure 3-51.**
When the **Model** tab is active, you are working in model space.

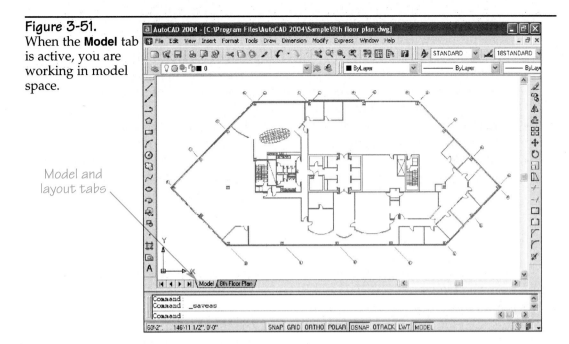

Model and layout tabs

## Plot Device *Tab*

The **Plot** dialog box is shown in **Figure 3-52** with the **Plot Device** tab displayed. All the features of this tab are discussed in detail in Chapter 24. The following is a brief introduction to some of the features:

- **Plotter configuration.** This area displays the name of the currently selected printing device and allows you to select a different plotter or printer. For now, it is assumed that your instructor or CAD system manager has assigned the plotter configuration.

**Figure 3-52.**
The **Plot** dialog box with the **Plot Device** tab selected.

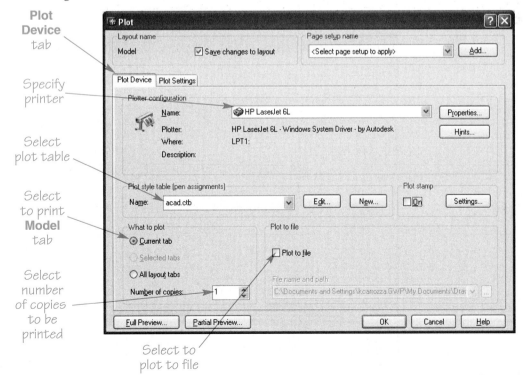

Plot Device tab

Specify printer

Select plot table

Select to print **Model** tab

Select number of copies to be printed

Select to plot to file

- **Plot style table (pen assignments).** All objects created in AutoCAD have a plot style property, just as all objects have layer and color properties. The plot style property determines how the object is plotted. The plot style table contains definitions for a collection of plot styles. This area displays the name of the currently selected plot style table and allows you to select a different table. This topic is described in detail in Chapter 24.
- **What to plot.** The **Current tab** option is used to plot from the **Model** tab. You can adjust the **Number of copies:** setting to make multiple plots.
- **Plot to file.** If you select the **Plot to file** check box, you can write your plot to a file, rather than to a printing device. This is useful because many print companies can take the resulting plot file and make hard copy prints for you.

## Making a Plot

There are many plotting options available. In this section, one method of creating a plot from the **Model** tab is discussed. Refer to **Figure 3-53** as you read through the following plotting procedure:

1. Access the **Plot** dialog box and select the **Plot Settings** tab.
2. Check the plot device and paper size specifications in the **Paper size and paper units** area.
3. Select what is to be plotted in the **Plot area** section. The following options are available:
   - **Limits.** This option plots everything inside the defined drawing limits.
   - **Extents.** This option plots only the area of the drawing where objects are drawn.
   - **Display.** This option plots the current screen display.
   - **View.** This option plots a saved view.

**Figure 3-53.**
The **Plot** dialog box with the **Plot Settings** tab selected.

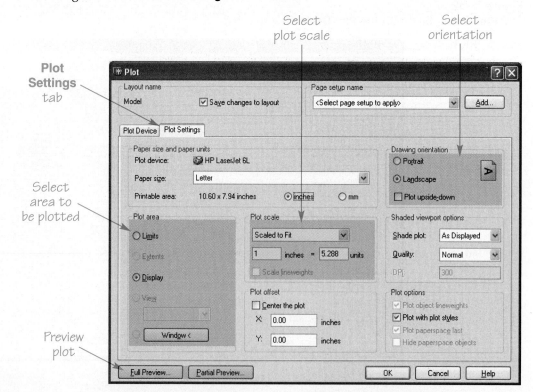

Architectural Drafting Using AutoCAD

- **Window.** Pick the **Window** button to manually select a rectangular area of the drawing to plot. When you pick this button, the drawing window returns, and you can select the windowed area to plot. After you select the second corner of the window, the **Plot** dialog box returns.
4. Select an option in the **Drawing orientation** area. Choose **Portrait** or **Landscape** to orient your drawing vertically (portrait) or horizontally (landscape). The **Plot upside-down** option rotates the paper 180°.
5. Set the scale in the **Plot scale** area. Because you draw at full scale in AutoCAD, you typically need to scale drawings either up or down to fit the paper. Scale is measured as a ratio of either inches or millimeters to drawing units. Select a predefined scale from the **Plot scale** drop-down list, or enter your own values into the **Plot scale** custom fields. Choose **Scaled to Fit** from the **Plot scale** drop-down list to let AutoCAD automatically shrink or stretch the plot area to fill the paper.
6. If desired, use the **Plot offset** area to center the plot or to set additional left and bottom margins.
7. Preview the plot. Pick the **Full Preview…** button to display the sheet as it will look when it is plotted, **Figure 3-54.** The cursor appears as a magnifying glass with a plus and minus sign. The plot preview image zooms if you hold the left mouse button and move the cursor. You can send the drawing directly to the plotter from here. To do this, right-click and pick **Plot** from the shortcut menu. Press the [Esc] or [Enter] key, or right-click and pick **Exit** from the shortcut menu to exit the preview. The **Partial Preview…** button displays the **Partial Plot Preview** dialog box, **Figure 3-55.** This shows the area of the paper and the area of the plotted drawing. To exit a partial plot preview, press the [Esc] or [Enter] key, or pick the **OK** button.
8. Pick the **OK** button in the **Plot** dialog box to send the data to the plotting device.

Before you pick the **OK** button to send your drawing to the plotter, there are several items you should check:
- Printer or plotter is plugged in.
- Cable from your computer to printer or plotter is secure.
- Printer has paper.
- Paper is properly loaded in the plotter, and grips or clamps are in place.
- Ink cartridges or plotter pens are inserted correctly.
- Plotter area is clear for paper movement.

**Figure 3-54.**
A full preview of the plot shows exactly how the drawing will appear on the plotted paper.

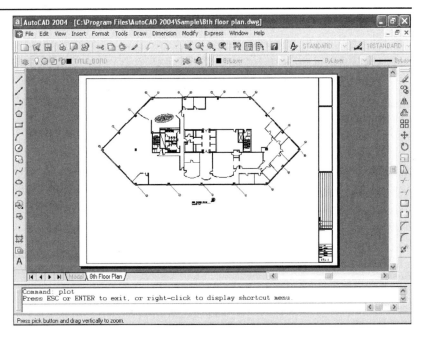

**Figure 3-55.**
The **Partial Plot Preview** dialog box shows the locations of the paper margins and the area covered by the drawing.

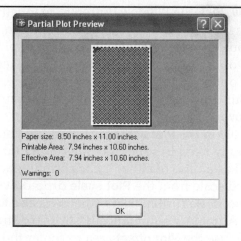

Paper size: 8.50 inches x 11.00 inches.
Printable Area: 7.94 inches x 10.60 inches.
Effective Area: 7.94 inches x 10.60 inches.

Warnings: 0

OK

**Professional Tip**

You can stop a plot in progress at any time by using the [Esc] key. Keep in mind that it may take a while for some plotters or printers to terminate the plot, depending on how much of the drawing file has already been sent. Turning the plotter off purges all plot data from the plotter's internal buffer.

## Exercise 3-17

◆ Open any of your previous drawings.
◆ Access the **Plot** dialog box.
◆ Set the plot scale to **Scaled to Fit**, and set the plot area to **Display**.
◆ Pick the **Partial Preview...** button and observe the display. Press the [Esc] key.
◆ Pick the **Full Preview...** button and observe the results. A full representation of your drawing should be displayed as it will appear when printed on the paper. Press the [Esc] key.
◆ Experiment by changing the drawing orientation and viewing a full preview after each change.
◆ Select the **Window** button and window a small portion of your drawing.
◆ Do another full preview to see the results. End the preview.
◆ Set the plot area to **Display** and preview the drawing. Make a print if a printer is available for your use.
    ◆ Close the drawing.

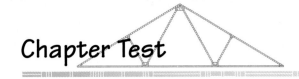
*Answer the following questions on a separate sheet of paper.*

1. Identify three ways to access the **LINE** command.
2. When using the **LINE** command, what is the term that identifies the stretchable, temporary line connecting the first point you pick to the cursor?
3. Give at least three ways to exit the **LINE** command and return to the Command prompt.
4. Give the command alias for the **LINE** command.
5. If you type the **LINE** command as linr, how do you change it to line before pressing [Enter]?
6. How do you cancel a command?
7. Name the Cartesian coordinate system that measures all distances from the origin.
8. Name the Cartesian coordinate system that locates points using X,Y coordinates from the previous point.
9. Name the Cartesian coordinate system that locates points using a distance and an angle.
10. Give the point entry you would type at the keyboard if you wanted the point to be 4 units to the right of the previous point.
11. Give the point entry you would type at the keyboard if you wanted the point to be 4 units at 30° from the previous point.
12. Identify two ways to turn the coordinate display on and off.
13. When the **LINE** command is started and you pick the first point, the coordinate display shows the location of that point. How do you get the coordinate display to provide the distance and angle from the first point to the cursor location?
14. What does the Ortho mode do?
15. Identify three ways to turn Ortho mode on and off.
16. Explain the advantage of drawing a rectangle with the Ortho mode on.
17. What is the process called that allows you to enter point locations by dragging the cursor in the direction of the new point and typing the distance to the new point?
18. Name the process that allows the crosshairs to snap to any predefined angle increment.
19. Name the option used to automatically connect the endpoint of the last line segment to the start of the first segment.
20. How do you remove a previously drawn line while still in the **LINE** command?
21. List two ways to access the **Drawing Units** dialog box.
22. Identify the type of linear units generally used in architecture.
23. What do you type at the command line to specify a distance of two feet eight inches?
24. What do you type at the command line to specify a distance of two feet eight and one-half inches?
25. Define *editing*.
26. Identify at least three ways to access the **ERASE** command.
27. What is the small box at the cursor location called when using the **ERASE** command?
28. How do you know when an object has been selected for erasing?
29. Name the command that brings back the last object you erased.
30. How many commands can you undo with the **U** command?
31. What is the command alias for the **CIRCLE** command?
32. Identify the default option for drawing a circle.
33. What symbol is used to input the coordinates last entered?
34. Give the command alias for the **ARC** command.
35. What is the default option when accessing the **ARC** command from the toolbar or at the Command prompt?

36. Identify the term related to the angle formed between the center, start point, and endpoint of an arc.
37. What is the term that means a straight line between two points on an arc?
38. If you use the **Start, End, Angle** option to draw an arc, a positive angle produces an arc in which direction?
39. How do you draw an arc that is automatically continued from a previously drawn arc or line?
40. Name the command used to draw polylines.
41. Explain how you would draw a polyline that looks like an arrow.
42. Identify the **PLINE** command option used to draw another polyline with the same angle as the previous polyline.
43. Name the **PLINE** command option that allows you to draw arc polylines.
44. Identify a quick way to go back and correct the polyline while remaining in the command.
45. Give the **PLINE** command option that allows you to automatically draw a segment from the last point selected to the starting point of the polyline.
46. Name the command used to draw regular polygons.
47. What does the first prompt request when using the command identified in question number 46?
48. What option would you use when drawing a regular polygon and you know the distance across the flats?
49. Name the command that allows you to draw a rectangle by picking one corner and then the other.
50. Name the option that allows you to draw angled corners on a rectangle.
51. Name the option that allows you to draw rounded corners on a rectangle.
52. Identify two ways to access the **ELLIPSE** command.
53. Name the option you would use if you wanted to draw an ellipse representing a circle rotated 30° from the line of sight.
54. Identify the command and option used for drawing an elliptical arc.
55. Name the **ZOOM** command option that zooms to the edge of the drawing limits.
56. What is the **ZOOM** command option that allows you to pick the opposite corners of a box surrounding the portion of the drawing you want to view?
57. What does realtime zoom allow you to do?
58. Identify two ways to exit realtime zoom.
59. Name the command that allows you to move the drawing around without changing the magnification.
60. What does the cursor look like when using realtime pan?
61. Define *pan displacement*.
62. What happens when you use pan presets?
63. How do you use the scroll bar to move the display in small increments?
64. How do you use the scroll bar to move the display in large increments?
65. What is a *transparent command*?
66. How do you enter a transparent command at the keyboard?
67. What command do you use to smooth out circles and arcs if your curved objects begin to look like circles and arcs with straight segments?
68. Give the terminology that refers to a physical drawing a printer or plotter produces on paper.
69. What is the terminology referring to the computer software version of the drawing, or the actual data file?
70. Identify at least three ways to access the **Plot** dialog box.
71. What is *model space?*
72. Describe a layout.
73. Identify the tab you would pick to access the place for producing a layout.
74. Give the name of the environment where layouts are created.

75. Identify the tab of the **Plot** dialog box where you can select the desired plotter or printer to use.
76. Name the tab of the **Plot** dialog box where you can select the area of the drawing you want printed.
77. Identify the tab of the **Plot** dialog box where you can select the orientation of the plot.
78. Name the option in the **Plot area** section of the **Plot** dialog box that allows you to plot everything inside the defined drawing limits.
79. Give the name of the option in the **Plot area** section of the **Plot** dialog box that allows you to plot what you see on the screen.
80. Name the option in the **Plot area** section of the **Plot** dialog box that allows you to put a box around the area you want to print or plot.
81. Identify the drawing orientation you would use if you wanted the drawing printed vertically.
82. What button would you pick in the **Plot** dialog box if you wanted to see the sheet as it would look when plotted?
83. How do you send the drawing directly to the plotter from the full plot preview?
84. How do you stop a plot in process?

# Chapter Problems

1. Use the **LINE** command to draw the object using the absolute coordinates given in the following chart. Save the drawing as p3-1.

| Point | Coordinates | Point | Coordinates |
|-------|-------------|-------|-------------|
| 1 | 1–1/2,3–1/2 | 5 | 4,9–1/2 |
| 2 | 6–1/2,3–1/2 | 6 | 1,7 |
| 3 | 6–1/2,7 | 7 | 1–1/2,7 |
| 4 | 7,7 | 8 | 1–1/2,3–1/2 |

2. Use the **LINE** command to draw the object using the relative coordinates given in the following chart. Save the drawing as p3-2.

| Point | Coordinates | Point | Coordinates |
|-------|-------------|-------|-------------|
| 1 | 1–1/2,3–1/2 | 5 | @–3,2–1/2 |
| 2 | @5,0 | 6 | @–3,–2–1/2 |
| 3 | @0,3–1/2 | 7 | @1/2,0 |
| 4 | @1/2,0 | 8 | @0,–3–1/2 |

3. Use the **LINE** command to draw the object using the polar coordinates given in the following chart. Save the drawing as p3-3.

| Point | Coordinates | Point | Coordinates |
|-------|-------------|-------|-------------|
| 1 | 1–1/2,3–1/2 | 5 | @3–7/8<140 |
| 2 | @5<0 | 6 | @3–7/8<220 |
| 3 | @3–1/2<90 | 7 | @1/2<0 |
| 4 | @1/2<0 | 8 | @3–1/2<270 |

4. Use the **LINE** command to draw the object using the coordinates given in the following chart. Save the drawing as p3-4.

| Point | Coordinates | Point | Coordinates |
|-------|-------------|-------|-------------|
| 1 | 1–1/2,3–1/2 | 5 | @–3,2–1/2 |
| 2 | @5<0 | 6 | @–3,–2–1/2 |
| 3 | @0,3–1/2 | 7 | @1/2<0 |
| 4 | @1/2<0 | 8 | Use the Close option. |

*The following drawings can be used on projects later in this text. Draw the objects without dimensions or notes. Determine the location and size of features when this information is not provided. Make these features proportional to the given sketches. Save the drawings as p3-5, p3-6, etc.*

5.

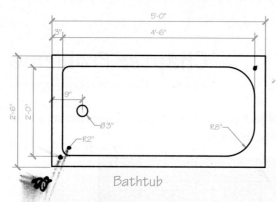

Bathtub

6.

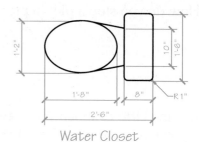

Water Closet

7.

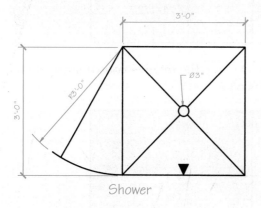

Shower

8.

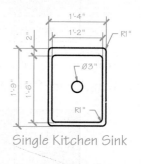

Single Kitchen Sink

9.

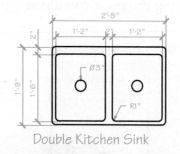

Double Kitchen Sink

10.

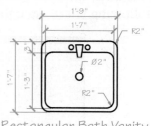

Rectangular Bath Vanity

**11.**

Round Bath Vanity

**12.**

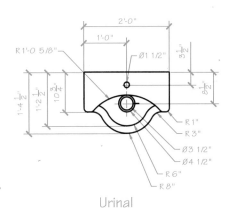

Oval Bath Vanity

**13.**

Hexagonal Bath Vanity

**14.**

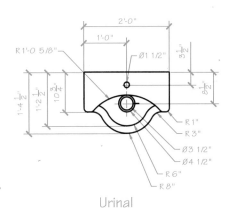

Urinal

**15.**

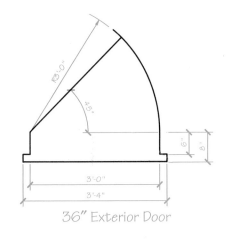

36″ Exterior Door

**16.**

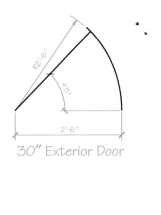

30″ Exterior Door

**17.**

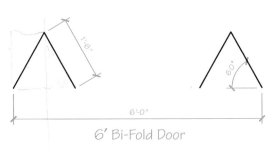

6′ Bi-Fold Door

**18.**

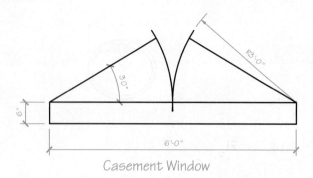

Casement Window

**19.**

Double-Hung Window

**20.**

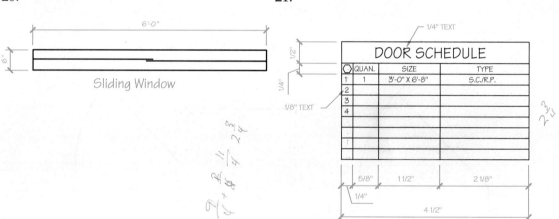

Sliding Window

**21.**

| QUAN. | SIZE | TYPE |
|-------|------|------|
| DOOR SCHEDULE | | |
| 1    1 | 3'-0" X 6'-8" | S.C./R.P. |
| 2 | | |
| 3 | | |
| 4 | | |
| | | |
| | | |
| | | |
| | | |

1/4" TEXT
1/2"
1/4"
1/8" TEXT
5/8"   1 1/2"   2 1/8"
1/4"
4 1/2"

**22.**

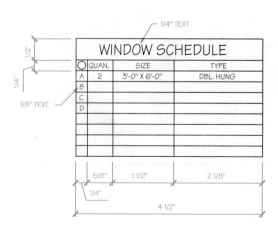

| QUAN. | SIZE | TYPE |
|-------|------|------|
| WINDOW SCHEDULE | | |
| A    2 | 3'-0" X 6'-0" | DBL. HUNG |
| B | | |
| C | | |
| D | | |
| | | |
| | | |
| | | |
| | | |

1/4" TEXT
1/2"
1/4"
1/8" TEXT
5/8"   1 1/2"   2 1/8"
1/4"
4 1/2"

23.

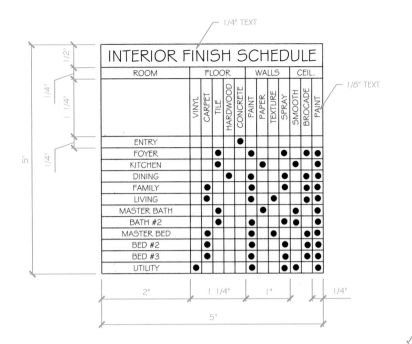

## INTERIOR FINISH SCHEDULE

| ROOM | FLOOR | | | | | WALLS | | | | CEIL. | | |
|---|---|---|---|---|---|---|---|---|---|---|---|---|
| | VINYL | CARPET | TILE | HARDWOOD | CONCRETE | PAINT | PAPER | TEXTURE | SPRAY | SMOOTH | BROCADE | PAINT |
| ENTRY | | | | | ● | | | | | | | |
| FOYER | | ● | | | | ● | | | ● | | ● | ● |
| KITCHEN | | | ● | | | | ● | | | ● | | |
| DINING | | | | ● | | ● | | | ● | | ● | ● |
| FAMILY | ● | | | | | ● | | | ● | | ● | ● |
| LIVING | ● | | | | | ● | | ● | | ● | | ● |
| MASTER BATH | | | ● | | | | | ● | | | ● | ● |
| BATH #2 | | | ● | | | ● | | | | ● | | ● |
| MASTER BED | | ● | | | | ● | | ● | | | ● | ● |
| BED #2 | | ● | | | | ● | | | ● | ● | | ● |
| BED #3 | | ● | | | | ● | | | ● | | ● | ● |
| UTILITY | ● | | | | | ● | | | | ● | ● | ● |

24.

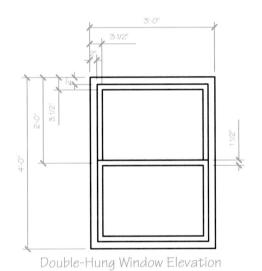

Double-Hung Window Elevation

**25.**

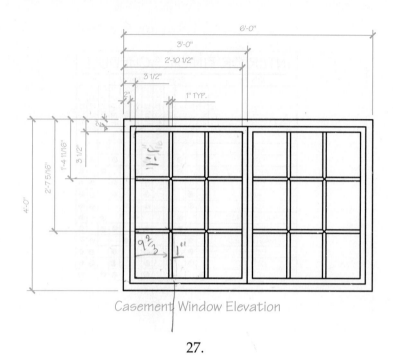

Casement Window Elevation

**26.**

Exterior Door Elevation

**27.**

Duplex Convenience Outlet

**28.**

Special Outlet

**29.**

Ceiling Outlet

30.

Surface-Mounted Fixture

31.

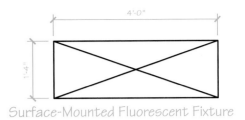

Surface-Mounted Fluorescent Fixture

32.

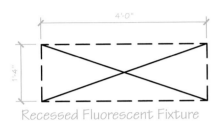

Recessed Fluorescent Fixture

33.

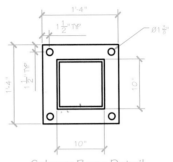

Column Base Detail

34.

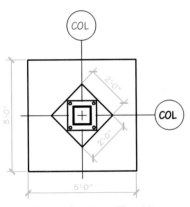

Column Footing Plan View

35.

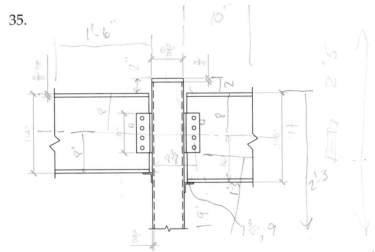

Steel Beam Connection Detail

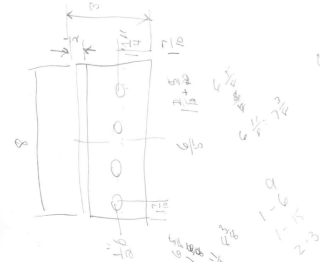

36.

Polyline Arrows

# CHAPTER 4

# Creating Accurate Drawings

## Learning Objectives

After completing this chapter, you will be able to:

- Set up a grid system.
- Snap to points on the screen.
- Use the object snap tools to create accurate drawings.
- Recognize and use AutoSnap markers.
- Access object snaps from toolbar buttons, from shortcut menus, and by typing.
- Use object snap overrides.
- Work with extended and apparent intersections.
- Use the Extension object snap to acquire points and create extensions.
- Set and use running object snaps.
- Use multiple object snap modes.
- Use AutoTrack to locate points.
- Snap to specific angles with a polar snap.

## Important Terms

acquired point
aperture
apparent intersection
AutoSnap
AutoTrack
deferred tangency
extension path
markers

object snap
object snap override
object snap tracking
quadrant
running object snap modes
snap grid
tracking

# Establishing a Grid on the Screen

AutoCAD provides a grid, or pattern of dots, on the screen to help you lay out geometry in the drawing. When the grid is activated, a pattern of dots appears in the drawing area, as shown in **Figure 4-1.** The grid pattern shows only within the drawing limits to help clearly define the working area. Grid spacing between dots can be adjusted.

**Figure 4-1.**
Dots represent the grid spacing.

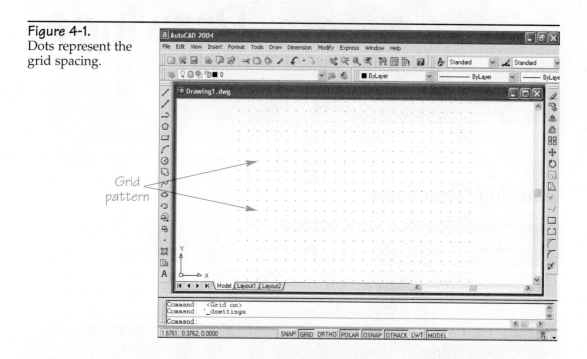

Grid pattern

**Figure 4-2** shows the **Snap and Grid** tab of the **Drafting Settings** dialog box. This dialog box can be used to turn the grid on and off and set the grid spacing. To access the **Drafting Settings** dialog box, select **Drafting Settings...** from the **Tools** pull-down menu, right-click on the **GRID** or **SNAP** button in the status bar and select **Settings...** from the shortcut menu, or enter dsettings, ds, or se at the Command prompt. The grid can be turned on (displayed) or off (not displayed) by selecting or deselecting the **Grid On (F7)** check box. Other methods for turning the grid on and off include picking the **GRID** button on the status bar, using the [Ctrl]+[G] key combination, pressing the [F7] function key, right-clicking on the **GRID** button in the status bar and selecting **On** or **Off** from the shortcut menu, and using the **ON** and **OFF** options of the **GRID** command.

The grid spacing can be set in the **Grid** area of the **Drafting Settings** dialog box. You can also set the grid spacing using the **GRID** command. Entering grid at the Command prompt provides the following prompt:

Command: **grid**↵
Specify grid spacing(X) or [ON/OFF/Snap/Aspect] <*current*>: **.25**↵

You can press [Enter] to accept the default spacing value shown in brackets or enter a new value, as shown. If the grid spacing you enter is too close to display on the screen, you get the Grid too dense to display message. In this case, a larger grid spacing is required.

Architectural Drafting Using AutoCAD

**Figure 4-2.**
Grid settings can be made in the **Snap and Grid** tab of the **Drafting Settings** dialog box.

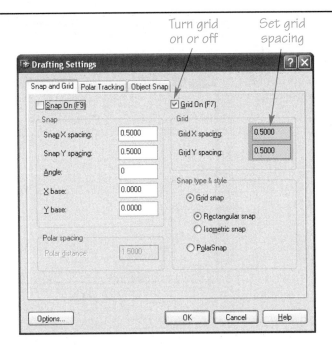

Turn grid on or off

Set grid spacing

## Setting Different Values for Horizontal and Vertical Grid Spacing

To set different values for horizontal and vertical grid spacing, enter the appropriate values in the **Grid X spacing:** and **Grid Y spacing:** text boxes in the **Drafting Settings** dialog box. This can also be done using the **GRID** command. Enter a (for the **Aspect** option) to set different values for the horizontal and vertical grid spacing. For example, suppose you want a horizontal spacing of 1 and a vertical spacing of 0.5. Enter the following:

Command: **grid**↵
Specify grid spacing(X) or [ON/OFF/Snap/Aspect] *<current>*: **a**↵
Specify the horizontal spacing(X) *<current>*: **1**↵
Specify the vertical spacing(Y) *<current>*: **.5**↵

This **Aspect** option provides the grid spacing shown in **Figure 4-3.**

## Setting Increments for Cursor Movement

When you move your pointing device, the crosshairs move freely on the screen. It is hard to place a point accurately with this free cursor movement. You can set up an invisible grid that allows the cursor to move, or "snap," only in exact increments. This is called the *snap grid.* The snap grid is different from the grid established with the **GRID** command. It controls the movement of the crosshairs. The grid discussed in the previous section is only a visual guide. The snap grid and grid settings can, however, be used together. The AutoCAD defaults provide the same settings for both.

Properly setting the snap grid can greatly increase your drawing speed and accuracy. The snap grid spacing can be set in the **Snap and Grid** tab of the **Drafting Settings** dialog box. See **Figure 4-4.** Enter the snap spacing values in the **Snap X spacing:** and **Snap Y spacing:** text boxes.

**Figure 4-3.**
The X and Y grid spacing can be set to different values. Notice the horizontal spacing is greater than the vertical spacing.

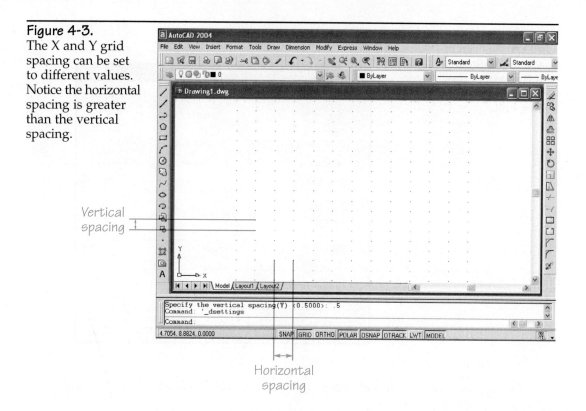

Vertical spacing

Horizontal spacing

**Figure 4-4.**
Snap grid settings can be made in the **Snap and Grid** tab of the **Drafting Settings** dialog box.

Turn snap on and off

Set snap spacing

Set snap angle (rotation of crosshairs)

Set base point for snap grid

Select type of snap grid

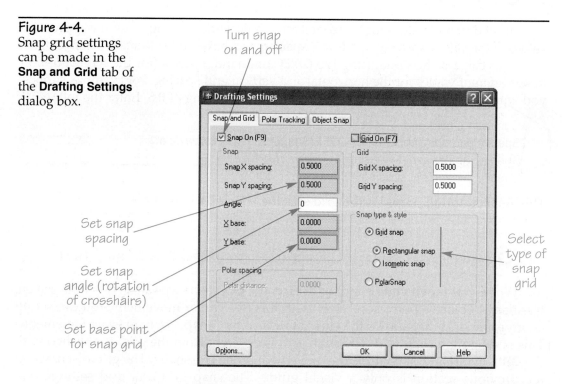

The **SNAP** command can also be used to set the invisible snap grid. Entering snap gives you the following prompt:

Command: **snap↵**
Specify snap spacing or [ON/OFF/Aspect/Rotate/Style/Type] *<current>*:

Pressing [Enter] accepts the value shown in brackets. The value you set remains the same until changed. The **OFF** option turns snap off, but the same snap spacing is again in effect when you turn snap back on. The snap spacing can be turned on or off at any time by clicking the **SNAP** button on the status bar, pressing [Ctrl]+[B], pressing function key [F9], or deselecting the **Snap On (F9)** check box in the **Drafting Settings** dialog box.

## Setting Different Values for Horizontal and Vertical Snap Spacing

The snap grid is usually set up with equal horizontal and vertical snap spacing. It is possible, however, to set different values for horizontal and vertical snap spacing. To do this, enter different values in the **Snap X spacing:** and **Snap Y spacing:** text boxes in the **Drafting Settings** dialog box. This can also be done using the **Aspect** option of the **SNAP** command:

Command: **snap**↵
Specify snap spacing or [ON/OFF/Aspect/Rotate/Style/Type] <*current*>: **a**↵
Specify horizontal spacing <*current*>: **.5**↵
Specify vertical spacing <*current*>: **.25**↵

**Professional Tip**

The most effective use of the snap grid quite often comes from setting X and Y spacing equal to the lowest increment of the majority of the feature dimensions, such as 1″ in an architectural application or 1′-0″ in a civil engineering application. If many horizontal features conform to one increment, and many vertical features conform to another, a corresponding snap grid can be set up using different X and Y values.

## Rotating the Snap Grid

The normal snap grid pattern consists of horizontal rows and vertical columns. Another option, however, is to rotate the snap grid. This technique is helpful when drawing an auxiliary view at an angle to other views of the drawing. When the snap grid is rotated, you are given the option of setting a new base point. The base point is the pivot around which the snap grid is rotated. It may be more convenient to set the base point at the location where you will begin the view.

Using the **Drafting Settings** dialog box, enter the snap angle in the **Angle:** text box and the new base point in the **X base:** and **Y base:** text boxes. These values can also be set using the **Rotate** option of the **SNAP** command, as follows:

Command: **snap**↵
Specify snap spacing or [ON/OFF/Aspect/Rotate/Style/Type] <A>: **r**↵
Specify base point <0.0000,0.0000>: (*press* [Enter], *enter a new coordinate value, or pick a new base point*)
Specify rotation angle <0>: **45**↵

The grid automatically rotates counterclockwise about the base point when a positive rotation angle is given and clockwise when a negative rotation angle is given. **Figure 4-5** shows the relationship between the regular and rotated snap grids. Remember, the snap grid is invisible.

## Setting the Snap Type and Style

The **Snap type & style** area of the **Drafting Settings** dialog box allows you to select one of two types of snap grids: **Grid snap** or **PolarSnap**. Polar snap allows you to snap to precise distances along alignment paths when using polar tracking. Polar tracking is discussed later in this chapter. Grid snap has two styles: **Rectangular snap** and **Isometric snap**. Rectangular snap is the standard style. The isometric pattern is useful when creating isometric drawings. Isometric snap rotates the crosshairs into a left, right, and top plane to aid in the creation of isometric drawings. Select the radio button(s) for the snap type and style you desire and pick the **OK** button. You can also use the **Type** and **Style** options of the **SNAP** command to change these settings at the Command prompt. Use the **Type** option to select **Polar** or **Grid** snap and the **Style** option to select **Standard** (rectangular) or **Isometric**.

---

**Figure 4-5.**
The snap grid is usually horizontal rows and vertical columns. It can be rotated, however, to help you draw. Notice the angle of the crosshairs. (The snap grid is invisible, but the dots are displayed when the grid is on.)

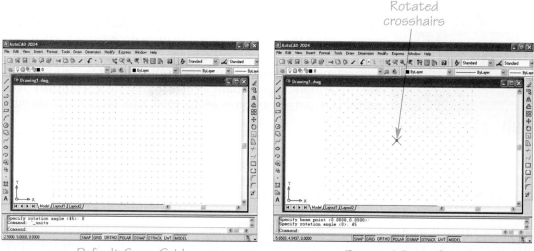

Default Snap Grid          Rotated Snap Grid

## Setting the Grid Spacing Relative to the Snap Spacing

The visible grid can be set to coincide with the snap grid by choosing the **Snap** option after entering the **GRID** command. You can also set the grid spacing as a multiple of the snap units by entering the number of snap units between grid points. For example, 2x places grid points at every other snap unit. If the snap spacing is 0.25, and you specify 2x at the Specify grid spacing(X) or [ON/OFF/Snap/Aspect] <current>: prompt, the grid spacing will be 0.5 units.

Command: **grid**↵
Specify grid spacing(X) or [ON/OFF/Snap/Aspect] <current>: **2x**↵

## Exercise 4-1

◆ Start a new drawing using a template or startup option of your own choice.
◆ Set the units to **Architectural**.
◆ Set the grid spacing to 0.5.
◆ Set the snap spacing to 0.25.
◆ Use the **LINE** command to draw two sets of four connected line segments.
◆ Turn snap off and draw two sets of three connected line segments. Notice that when snap is activated, the cursor "jumps" exactly at 0.25 intervals.
◆ Save the drawing as ex4-1.
◆ Use the **CLOSE** command to close the drawing.

**Professional Tip**

The snap and grid spacing may be set at different values to complement each other. For example, the grid may be set at 6", and the snap may be set at 1". With this type of format, each plays a separate role in assisting drawing layout. This may also keep the grid from being too dense. You can quickly change these values at any time to have them best assist you. Remember, if the message Grid too dense to display is shown on the command line, increase the grid spacing.

## Factors to Consider when Setting Drawing Aids

The following factors influence drawing aid settings:
- **Drawing units.** If the units are decimal inches, set the grid and snap values to standard decimal increments, such as 0.0625, 0.125, 0.25, 0.5, and 1 or 0.05, 0.1, 0.2, 0.5, and 1. For architectural units, use settings such as 1", 6", and 12" or 1', 2', 4', 5', and 10' increments.
- **Drawing size.** A very large drawing might have a 4'-0" grid spacing, while a small drawing may use a 1" or less spacing.
- **Value of the smallest dimension.** If the smallest dimension is 1", an appropriate snap value would be 1", with a grid spacing of 6" or 12".
- **Ability to change settings.** You can change the snap and grid values at any time without changing the location of points or lines already drawn. This should be done when larger or smaller values would assist you with a certain part of the drawing. For example, suppose a few of the dimensions are in 6" multiples, but the rest of the dimensions are 48" multiples. Change the snap spacing from 48" to 6" when laying out the smaller dimensions.
- **Preparation.** Always preparing a rough sketch of the drawing before working with AutoCAD will save you time on the entire project. A sketch can help you plan the drawing layout. When you start working in AutoCAD, use the visible grid to help you place views and lay out the drawing.
- **Efficiency.** Use whatever method works best and fastest when setting or changing the drawing aids.

# Snapping to Specific Features

Object snap is one of the most useful tools found in AutoCAD. It increases your drafting ability, performance, accuracy, and productivity. The term *object snap* refers to the cursor's ability to "snap" exactly to a specific point or place on an object. The advantage of object snap is that you do not have to pick an exact point.

The *AutoSnap*™ feature is enabled by default. With AutoSnap active, *markers* are displayed while using an object snap mode. These visual cues identify the current object snap mode.

**Figure 4-6** shows two examples of markers AutoSnap provides. The endpoint of a line object is being picked in **Figure 4-6A.** The marker for an Endpoint object snap is shown as a square when the cursor is placed close to the line object. After a brief pause, a tooltip is displayed, indicating the name of the object snap mode. In **Figure 4-6B,** a point tangent to an existing circle is being selected. The AutoSnap marker for a tangency point is shown as a circle with a tangent horizontal line.

Another visual cue displayed with some object snaps is an alignment path. An *alignment path* is a dashed line showing the path upon which an object would be drawn if aligned as desired with another object. For example, you see a parallel alignment path when using the Parallel object snap. An *extension path* is a type of alignment path displayed when using the Extension object snap mode to find the imaginary extension of an existing object.

---

**Figure 4-6.**
AutoSnap markers and tooltips provide visual cues to identify the active object snap mode. A—When using the Endpoint object snap mode, moving the cursor close to a line object displays a marker and tooltip. B—When drawing a line to be tangent to a circle, the Tangent object snap marker and tooltip appear when the cursor is close to the circle.

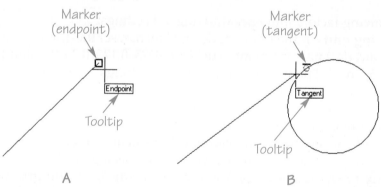

## Object Snap Modes

Object snap modes determine the point the cursor snaps to when selecting a point. These modes can be activated using the following methods:

- **Command line.** Object snap modes can be specified at the Command prompt when AutoCAD is requesting a point selection. Enter the first three letters of the object snap mode to activate it.
- **Shortcut menu.** Object snap modes can be selected from the **Object Snap** shortcut menu, which is shown in **Figure 4-7.** This menu is activated by holding down the [Shift] key and right-clicking.
- **Toolbar.** Object snap overrides are also available as buttons in the **Object Snap** toolbar, **Figure 4-8.**

## Figure 4-7.
The **Object Snap** shortcut menu provides quick access to object snap modes.

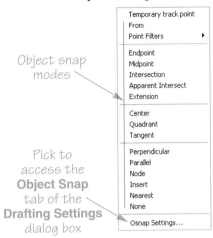

Object snap modes

Pick to access the **Object Snap** tab of the **Drafting Settings** dialog box

## Figure 4-8.
The **Object Snap** toolbar.

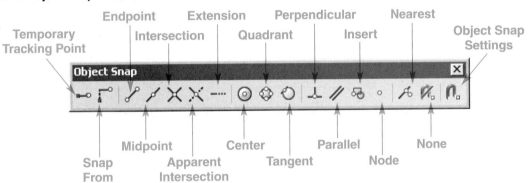

Temporary Tracking Point
Endpoint
Intersection
Extension
Quadrant
Perpendicular
Insert
Nearest
Object Snap Settings

Snap From
Midpoint
Apparent Intersection
Center
Tangent
Parallel
Node
None

**Professional Tip**

If you have a three-button mouse, the middle mouse button performs a zoom or pan by default. If desired, the middle mouse button can "pop up" the **Object Snap** shortcut menu shown in **Figure 4-7**. To change the button setting, enter the following at the Command prompt:

Command: **mbuttonpan**↵
Enter new value for MBUTTONPAN <1>: **0**↵
Command:

This changes the setting of the **MBUTTONPAN** system variable. To return to the default button setting, reset the system variable to 1.

To activate the **Object Snap** toolbar, right-click on an existing toolbar button, and then select **Object Snap** from the shortcut menu. You can keep the **Object Snap** toolbar floating, or you can dock it at the edge of the drawing area for convenience. *Object snap override* refers to the entry of an object snap mode when AutoCAD is prompting for a point location. Object snap overrides are active for a single point selection, and they override any previously set running object snap modes for that one entry.

*Running object snap modes* are object snap modes that are active for all point selections. Running object snap modes are discussed later in this section.

The table in **Figure 4-9** summarizes the object snap modes. Included with each mode is the marker that appears on screen and its button from the **Object Snap** toolbar. Each object snap mode selects a different portion of an object. Only the first three letters are required to activate an object snap when typing in the object snap at the prompt line.

**Figure 4-9.**
The object snap modes.

| Object Snap Modes | | | |
|---|---|---|---|
| **Mode** | **Marker** | **Button** | **Description** |
| **Endpoint** | □ | | Finds the nearest endpoint of a line, arc, elliptical arc, spline, ellipse, ray, solid, or multiline. |
| **Midpoint** | △ | | Finds the middle point of any object having two endpoints, such as a line, arc, elliptical arc, spline, ray, solid, xline, or multiline. |
| **Center** | ○ | | Locates the center point of curved objects, such as circles, arcs, ellipses, elliptical arcs, and radial solids. |
| **Quadrant** | ◇ | | Picks the closest of the four quadrant points that can be found on circles, arcs, elliptical arcs, ellipses, and radial solids. (Not all of these objects may have all four quadrants.) |
| **Intersection** | ✕ | | Picks the closest intersection of two objects. |
| **Apparent Intersection** | ⊠ | | Selects a visual intersection between two objects that appear to intersect on screen in the current view, but may not actually intersect each other in 3D space. |
| **Extension** | ＋ | | Finds a point along the imaginary extension of an existing line or arc. (This is used in conjunction with another object snap such as endpoint or midpoint.) |
| **Insertion** | ⌐⌐ | | Finds the insertion point of text objects and blocks. |
| **Perpendicular** | ⌐ | | Finds a point that is perpendicular to an object from the previously picked point. |
| **Parallel** | ∥ | | Used to find any point along an imaginary line parallel to an existing line or polyline. |
| **Tangent** | ○̄ | | Finds points of tangency between radial and linear objects. |
| **Nearest** | ⋈ | | Locates the point on an object closest to the crosshairs. |
| **Node** | ⊗ | | Picks a point object drawn with the **POINT** command. |
| **None** | | | Turns running object snap off for the current point to be picked. |

Architectural Drafting Using AutoCAD

Remember that object snap overrides are not commands, but are used in conjunction with commands. If you enter mid or per at the Command prompt, AutoCAD displays an Unknown command error message. If AutoCAD is expecting a point entry, however, an Endpoint object snap allows you to snap to one of the ends of an existing line.

Practice with the different object snap modes to find which works best in various situations. Object snap can be used during many commands, such as **LINE**, **CIRCLE**, **ARC**, **MOVE**, **COPY**, and **INSERT**. The most common object snap uses are discussed in the following sections.

## Endpoint object snap

In many cases, you need to connect a line, an arc, or the center point of a circle to the endpoint of an existing line or arc. Select the Endpoint object snap mode and move the cursor past the midpoint of the line or arc, toward the end to be picked. A small square marks the endpoint that will be picked.

In **Figure 4-10,** the following command sequence is used to connect a line to the endpoint of an existing line:

Command: **l** *or* **line.**⌐
Specify first point: *(pick a point)*
Specify next point or [Undo]: *(pick the* **Snap to Endpoint** *button from the* **Object Snap** *toolbar, enter* end, *or pick* **Endpoint** *from the* **Object Snap** *shortcut menu)*
of *(move the cursor near the end of the existing line until the marker shows, and pick)*
Specify next point or [Undo]: ⌐
Command:

The Endpoint object snap can be used to quickly select the endpoints of all types of lines and arcs. It is often selected as a running object snap.

## Midpoint object snap

The Midpoint object snap mode finds and picks the midpoint of a line, polyline, or arc. Enter mid at the prompt line, pick the **Snap to Midpoint** button from the **Object Snap** toolbar, or select **Midpoint** from the **Object Snap** shortcut menu to activate this object snap. Position the cursor near the midpoint of the object you want to snap to, and a small triangle marks the midpoint to which the line will snap. See **Figure 4-11.**

**Figure 4-10.**
Using the Endpoint object snap.

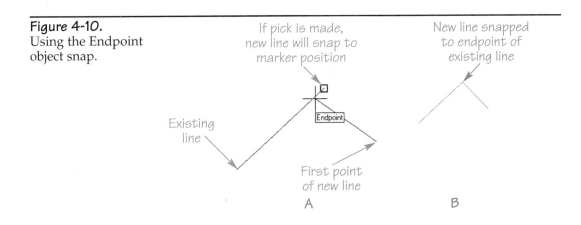

**Figure 4-11.**
Using the Midpoint object snap.

Triangle marks midpoint snap location

First point of new line

New line snaps to midpoint

Existing line

Midpoint

A

B

## Exercise 4-2

◆ Start a new drawing using a template or startup option of your own choice.
◆ Set the units to **Architectural**.
◆ Use the Endpoint and Midpoint object snap modes to draw the object shown below. Draw Line 1, and then draw Line 2 connecting to the endpoint of Line 1. Draw Line 3 from the endpoint of Line 2 to the midpoint of Line 1. Draw Arc A with one end connected to the endpoint of Line 1.
◆ Save the drawing as ex4-2.
◆ Use the **CLOSE** command to close the drawing.

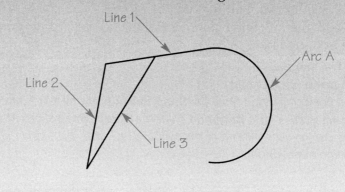

Line 1

Arc A

Line 2

Line 3

## Center object snap

The Center object snap mode allows you to snap to the center point of a circle, ellipse, elliptical arc, or arc. The mode is activated by entering cen at the selection prompt, picking the **Snap to Center** button from the **Object Snap** toolbar, or picking **Center** from the **Object Snap** shortcut menu. Move the cursor onto the object whose center point is to be located. A small circle marks the center point.

Be sure to move the cursor near the object, *not* the center point of the object. For example, when locating the center of a large circle, the Center object snap mode *may not* locate the center if the cursor is not near the perimeter of the circle. In **Figure 4-12,** the Center object snap is used to draw a line to the center of a circle.

## Quadrant object snap

A *quadrant* is a quarter section of a circle, ellipse, elliptical arc, polyline arc, or arc. The Quadrant object snap mode finds the 0°, 90°, 180°, and 270° positions on a circle or arc, **Figure 4-13.** When picking quadrants, locate the cursor on the circle or arc near the intended quadrant. For example, **Figure 4-14** illustrates the use of the Quadrant object snap mode to locate the center point of a new circle at the quadrant of an existing circle. The command sequence is given.

**Figure 4-12.**
Using the Center object snap.

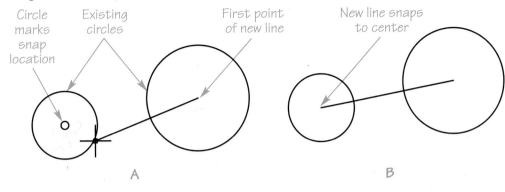

**Figure 4-13.**
The quadrants of a circle.

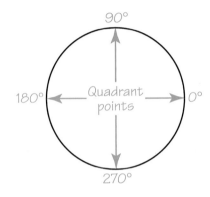

**Figure 4-14.**
Using the Quadrant object snap.

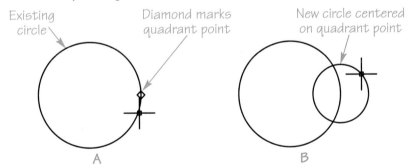

Command: **c** *or* **circle**↵
Specify center point for circle or [3P/2P/Ttr (tan tan radius)]: *(pick the* **Snap to Quadrant** *button from the* **Object Snap** *toolbar, enter* qua, *or pick* **Quadrant** *from the* **Object Snap** *shortcut menu)*
of *(move the cursor near the desired quadrant, and pick)*
Specify radius of circle or [Diameter] *<current>*: *(pick a radius)*

**Note**

Quadrant positions are unaffected by the current angle zero direction, but always coincide with the current world coordinate system (WCS). The quadrant points of a circle or arc are at the top, bottom, left, and right, regardless of the rotation of the object. The quadrant points of ellipses and elliptical arcs, however, rotate with the object.

## Exercise 4-3

◆ Start a new drawing using a template or startup option of your own choice.
◆ Set the units to **Architectural**.
◆ Use the Center and Quadrant object snap modes for the following:
  ◆ Draw two separate circles side by side, and refer to the one on the left as Circle A and the one on the right as Circle B.
  ◆ Draw a line from the center of Circle A to the 180° quadrant of Circle B.
  ◆ Draw a line from the center of Circle B to the 270° quadrant of Circle B, to the 270° quadrant of Circle A, and finally to the center of Circle A.
◆ Save the drawing as ex4-3.
◆ Use the **CLOSE** command to close the drawing.

## Intersection object snap

The Intersection object snap is used to snap to the intersection of two or more objects. This mode is activated by typing int at the selection prompt, picking the **Snap to Intersection** button from the **Object Snap** toolbar, or picking **Intersection** from the **Object Snap** shortcut menu. Move the cursor near the intersection of two objects. A small X marks the intersection. See **Figure 4-15.**

When picking a point for an Intersection object snap, the X appears only when the cursor is close to the intersection point of two objects. If the cursor is near an object, but not close to an actual intersection, the tooltip reads Extended Intersection, and the AutoSnap marker is followed by an ellipsis (...). When using the Extended Intersection object snap, you can select the objects one at a time, and then the intersection point is found. This is especially useful when two objects do not actually intersect, and you need to access the point where these objects would intersect if they were extended. **Figure 4-16** shows the use of the Extended Intersection object snap to find an intersection point between a line and an arc.

If the intersection point is not in the currently visible screen area, the AutoSnap marker is not displayed when pointing to the second object. AutoSnap, however, still allows you to confirm the point before picking. Keeping the cursor motionless for a moment displays the Intersection tooltip, and this supports the fact that the two objects do actually intersect somewhere beyond the currently visible area. When selecting two objects that could not intersect, no AutoSnap marker or tooltip is displayed, and no intersection point is found if the pick is made.

**Figure 4-15.**
Using the Intersection object snap.

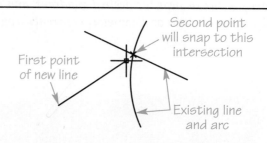

First point of new line

Second point will snap to this intersection

Existing line and arc

**Figure 4-16.**
Finding the extended intersection of two objects. A—Select the first object. B—When the second object is selected, the extended intersection becomes the snap point. C—The completed line.

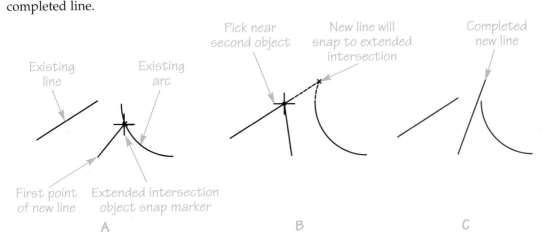

## Apparent Intersection object snap

The *apparent intersection* is the point where two objects created in 3D space appear to intersect based on the currently displayed view. Three-dimensional objects that are far apart may appear to intersect when viewed from certain angles. Whether they intersect or not, this option returns the coordinate point where the objects appear to intersect. This is a valuable option when working with 3D drawings. Creating and editing 3D objects is discussed in Chapter 25.

## Extension object snap

The Extension object snap is used to find any point along the imaginary extension of an existing line, polyline, or polyline arc. This mode is activated by entering ext at the selection prompt, picking the **Snap to Extension** button from the **Object Snap** toolbar, or picking **Extension** from the **Object Snap** shortcut menu. The Extension object snap differs from most other snaps because it requires more than one selection point. The initial point, called the *acquired point,* is not selected in the typical manner. Rather, it is found by simply moving the crosshairs over the surface of the line or arc from which the new object is to be extended. When the object is found, a (+) symbol marks the location. The last point, which is the actual snap point, is located somewhere along the extension path. The *extension path,* represented by a dashed line or arc, extends from the acquired point to the current location of the mouse.

**Figure 4-17** shows an example of the Extension object snap being used on both a polyline arc and a rectangle. The first acquired point is found by moving the cursor directly over the endpoint of the arc and entering ext. When the Extension: tooltip is displayed, the (+) marker becomes visible at the end of the arc. The second acquired point is found in the same manner at the corner of the rectangle. Move the cursor to the corner, and the Extension: tooltip appears. Dragging the cursor slowly from left to right allows the intersection of both extension paths to be displayed as dashed lines, as shown in **Figure 4-17.**

**Figure 4-17.**
The Extension object snap being used on an arc and a rectangle. Line A begins at the point on the arc where the top line of the rectangle would intersect it. Line B is started 1" away from the corner of the rectangle using the Extension object snap and direct distance entry.

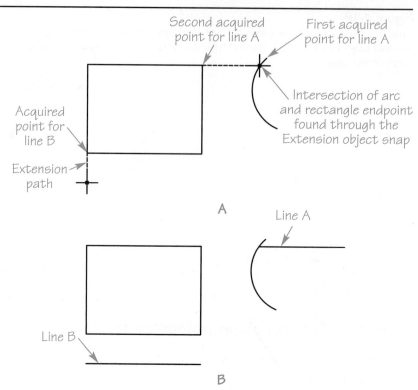

## Exercise 4-4

◆ Start a new drawing using a template or startup option of your own choice.
◆ Set the units to **Architectural**.
◆ Draw a rectangle with a polyline arc to the right of the rectangle, similar to **Figure 4-17A**.
◆ Use the Extension object snap mode to draw Line A and Line B, similar to **Figure 4-17B**.
◆ Save the drawing as ex4-4.
◆ Use the **CLOSE** command to close the drawing.

## Perpendicular object snap

A common geometric construction technique is to draw one object perpendicular to another. This is done using the Perpendicular object snap mode. This mode is activated by entering per at the selection prompt, picking the **Snap to Perpendicular** button from the **Object Snap** toolbar, or picking **Perpendicular** from the **Object Snap** shortcut menu. A small right-angle symbol appears at the snap point. This mode can be used with arcs, elliptical arcs, ellipses, lines, polylines, rectangles, or circles.

**Figure 4-18** shows an example of the Perpendicular object snap being used for the endpoint of a line. The endpoint is located so the new line is perpendicular to the existing line. It is important to understand that perpendicularity is measured at the point of intersection, so it is possible to draw a line perpendicular to a circle or an arc.

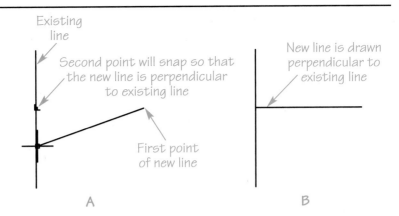

**Figure 4-18.**
Drawing a line from a point perpendicular to an existing line. The Perpendicular object snap mode is used to select the second endpoint.

Existing line

Second point will snap so that the new line is perpendicular to existing line

New line is drawn perpendicular to existing line

First point of new line

A

B

## Exercise 4-5

◆ Start a new drawing using a template or startup option of your own choice.
◆ Set the units to **Architectural**.
◆ Draw a horizontal line, and then draw a circle above the line. Add a new line from the circle's center, perpendicular to the first line.
◆ Draw two intersecting lines and a separate circle. Add a line from the circle's center to the intersection of the lines.
◆ Save the drawing as **ex4-5**.
◆ Use the **CLOSE** command to close the drawing.

## Tangent object snap

The term *tangent* refers to a line that touches an arc or a circle at only one point, or an arc or a circle that touches another arc or circle at only one point. The Tangent object snap aligns objects tangentially. This mode is activated by entering tan at the selection prompt, picking the **Snap to Tangent** button from the **Object Snap** toolbar, or picking **Tangent** from the **Object Snap** shortcut menu. A small circle with a horizontal line appears at the snap point.

In **Figure 4-19,** the endpoint of a line is located using the Tangent object snap mode. The first point is selected normally. The Tangent object snap is then activated, and the cursor is placed near the tangent point on the circle. AutoCAD determines the tangency point and places the snap point (and the endpoint) there.

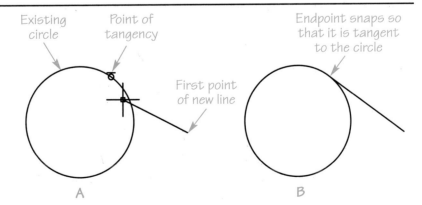

**Figure 4-19.**
Using the Tangent object snap.

Existing circle

Point of tangency

Endpoint snaps so that it is tangent to the circle

First point of new line

A

B

When creating an object tangent to another object, multiple points may be needed to fix the tangency point. For example, the point where a line is tangent to a circle cannot be found without knowing the locations of both ends of the line. Until both points have been specified, the object snap specification is for *deferred tangency*. Once both endpoints are known, the tangency is calculated, and the object is drawn in the correct location. In **Figure 4-20,** a line is drawn tangent to two circles. The command sequence is as follows:

Command: **l** *or* **line.**⏎
Specify first point: *(pick the* **Snap to Tangent** *button from the* **Object Snap** *toolbar, enter* tan, *or pick* **Tangent** *from the* **Object Snap** *shortcut menu)*
to *(pick the first circle)*
Specify next point or [Undo]: *(pick the* **Snap to Tangent** *button from the* **Object Snap** *toolbar, enter* tan, *or pick* **Tangent** *from the* **Object Snap** *shortcut menu)*
to *(pick the second circle)*
Specify next point or [Undo]: ⏎
Command:

Figure 4-20.
Drawing a line tangent to two circles.

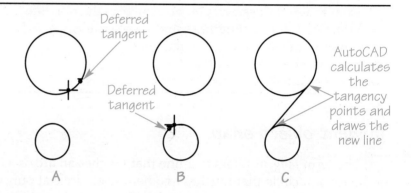

Deferred tangent

Deferred tangent

AutoCAD calculates the tangency points and draws the new line

A      B      C

## Exercise 4-6

◆ Start a new drawing using a template or startup option of your own choice.
◆ Set the units to **Architectural**.
◆ Draw a line tangent to an existing circle.
◆ Draw two circles, and then draw a line tangent to both of the circles.
◆ Use the Tangent object snap to draw two lines that are tangent to the circles, but do not cross.
◆ Save the drawing as ex4-6.
◆ Use the **CLOSE** command to close the drawing.

## Parallel object snap

The process of drawing, moving, or copying objects that are not horizontal or vertical is improved with the Parallel object snap mode. This option is used to find any point along an imaginary line that is parallel to an existing line or polyline. The Parallel object snap is activated by entering par at the selection prompt, picking the **Parallel** button, or picking **Parallel** from the **Object Snap** shortcut menu.

The Parallel object snap is similar to the Extension object snap because it requires more than one selection point. The first point, called the *acquired point,* is found by pausing the crosshairs above the line to which the new object is to be parallel. When the object is found, and you move the crosshairs in a direction parallel to the existing line, a (//) symbol marks the existing line. The last point, which is the actual snap point, is located anywhere along the alignment path, which is represented by a dashed line. When the alignment path is displayed, the Parallel object snap marker appears on the initial line. Now you pick the second point of the parallel line. **Figure 4-21** shows an example of the Parallel object snap being used to draw a line parallel to an existing line. The following command sequence is used:

Command: **l** *or* **line.**↵
Specify first point: *(pick the first point of the new line)*
Specify next point or [Undo]: **par**↵
to *(move the cursor over the existing line until you see the acquired point symbol and move the cursor near the first endpoint of the new line; at this time, the alignment path and snap marker are displayed; pick the endpoint of the new line)*
Specify next point or [Undo]: ↵
Command:

**Figure 4-21.**
Using the Parallel object snap to draw a line parallel to an existing line.
A—Select the first endpoint for the new line, and then move the crosshairs near the existing line to acquire a point.
B—After the parallel point is acquired, move the crosshairs near the location of the parallel line, and an alignment path appears.

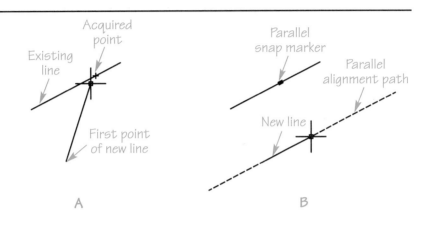

## Exercise 4-7

◆ Start a new drawing using a template or startup option of your own choice.
◆ Set the units to **Architectural**.
◆ Draw a line at any angle, similar to the existing line in **Figure 4-21A**.
◆ Use the Parallel object snap option to draw a line parallel to the existing line, similar to **Figure 4-21B**.
◆ Save the drawing as ex4-7.
◆ Use the **CLOSE** command to close the drawing.

## Node object snap

Point objects and dimension points can be snapped to, using the Node object snap mode. When you want to snap to a point or dimension point, simply use the Node object snap and move the crosshairs over the point or end of the dimension.

## Nearest object snap

When you need to specify a point that is on an object, but cannot be located with any of the other object snap modes, the Nearest object snap mode can be used. This object snap locates the point on the object closest to the crosshairs location. It should be used when you want an object to touch an existing object, but the location of the intersection is not critical.

Consider drawing a line object that is to end on another line. Trying to pick the point with the crosshairs is inaccurate because you are relying only on your screen and cursor resolution. The line you draw may fall short or extend past the line. Using the Nearest object snap mode ensures the point is precisely on the object.

## Setting Running Object Snaps

The previous discussion explained how to use object snaps by activating the individual mode at the selection prompt. If you plan to use object snaps continuously, however, you can set running object snaps. When you preset the running object snap modes, AutoCAD automatically activates them at all point selection prompts.

Running object snaps are set in the **Object Snap** tab of the **Drafting Settings** dialog box. To access this dialog box, pick **Drafting Settings...** from the **Tools** pull-down menu; pick the **Object Snap Settings** button from the **Object Snap** toolbar; right-click on the **OSNAP** or **OTRACK** button on the status bar and select **Settings...** from the shortcut menu; pick **Osnap Settings...** from the **Object Snap** shortcut menu; or enter os, osnap, or ddosnap at the Command prompt. You can also enter dsettings, ds, or se at the Command prompt to access the **Drafting Settings** dialog box.

The **Object Snap** tab of the **Drafting Settings** dialog box is shown in **Figure 4-22.** Notice the Endpoint, Intersection, Extension, and Parallel modes are active. You can use this dialog box at any time to discontinue a running object snap or to set additional modes.

**Figure 4-22.**
Running object snap modes are set in the **Drafting Settings** dialog box.

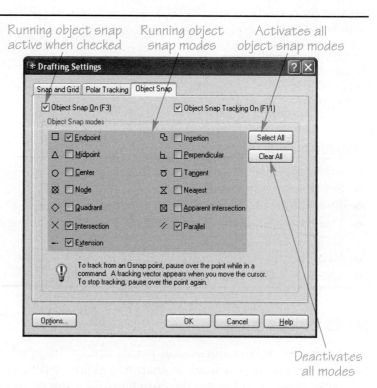

Running object snap active when checked

Running object snap modes

Activates all object snap modes

Deactivates all modes

## Toggling, disabling, and overriding running object snap modes

A running object snap is active at all point selection prompts, but is temporarily suspended when an object snap override is entered. The override is temporary and active for a single point selection only. All current running object snap modes are reactivated for the next pick.

To make a single point selection without the effects of any running object snap modes, use the None object snap mode. When you need to make several point specifications without the aid of the running object snaps, you can toggle them off. The advantages of this method are that you can make several picks, and you can restore the same running object snap modes by toggling them back on. Toggle the running object snaps on and off by picking the **OSNAP** button on the status bar, right-clicking on the **OSNAP** button and picking **On** or **Off** from the shortcut menu, picking the **Object Snap On (F3)** check box in the **Drafting Settings** dialog box, or pressing the [F3] key on your keyboard.

You can remove the active checks in the **Drafting Settings** dialog box as needed to disable running object snaps. You can also pick the **Clear All** button to disable all running modes. Select desired running object snaps by picking the associated box or pick the **Select All** button to activate all object snaps.

## Using multiple object snap modes

As shown with the examples of running object snap modes, more than one object snap mode can be made active at once. When multiple modes are running at the same time, each mode is checked for possible points, and the closest point is selected. For example, assume the Endpoint and Midpoint object snap modes are active. The AutoSnap marker locates either an endpoint or the midpoint of a line, depending on which is closest to the crosshairs location. This can cause conflicts between some object snap modes. For example, no matter where you pick a circle, the closest quadrant point is always closer than the center of the circle. This means that when the Quadrant and Center object snaps are both active, a quadrant point is always selected.

The Nearest object snap mode causes conflicts with almost every other mode. The Nearest mode does not move the selection point to a nearby feature of an object, but picks the point on the object closest to the current cursor location. This means the Nearest object snap mode always locates the closest point.

The [Tab] key on your keyboard can be used to cycle through available snap points. This works well when multiple object snap modes are active. For example, use this feature if you are trying to select the intersection between two objects where several other objects intersect nearby. When an AutoSnap marker appears, press the [Tab] key until the desired point is marked.

## Exercise 4-8

- ◆ Start a new drawing using a template or startup option of your own choice.
- ◆ Set the units to **Architectural**.
- ◆ Set the Endpoint, Midpoint, and Perpendicular running object snaps and practice using them in at least two situations. Drawings similar to **Figure 4-10, Figure 4-11,** and **Figure 4-18** can be used.
- ◆ Change the running object snaps to Center and Tangent, and use each twice in creating a simple drawing. Drawings similar to **Figure 4-12** and **Figure 4-20** can be used.
- ◆ Discontinue the running object snaps.
- ◆ Save the drawing as ex4-8.
- ◆ Use the **CLOSE** command to close the drawing.

**Professional Tip**

Use object snap modes when drawing and editing. With practice, using object snaps becomes second nature and greatly increases your productivity and accuracy.

## AutoSnap Settings

The AutoSnap features make object snaps much easier to use. If you do not wish to have the additional visual cues while using object snaps, however, you can turn the AutoSnap features off. AutoCAD also allows you to customize the appearance and functionality of the AutoSnap features. To do so, pick the **Options...** button in the **Object Snap** tab of the **Drafting Settings** dialog box to access the **Drafting** tab of the **Options** dialog box. This tab is shown in **Figure 4-23**. The **AutoSnap Settings** area contains several options. The settings are described as follows:

- **Marker.** Toggles the display of AutoSnap markers when snapping to an object.
- **Magnet.** Toggles the AutoSnap magnet. When active, the magnet snaps the cursor to the closest object snap point.
- **Display AutoSnap tooltip.** Toggles the tooltip display.
- **Display AutoSnap aperture box.** Toggles the display of the aperture. By default, the aperture is turned off so the object snap points can be seen more clearly.

The marker size and color can also be adjusted to suit your needs. For example, the default marker color is yellow, but this is difficult to see if you have the graphics screen background set to white. Pick the drop-down arrow and select the desired color. At higher screen resolutions, a larger marker size improves visibility. Move the slider at the **AutoSnap Marker Size** area to change the size.

**Figure 4-23.**
Setting AutoSnap features.

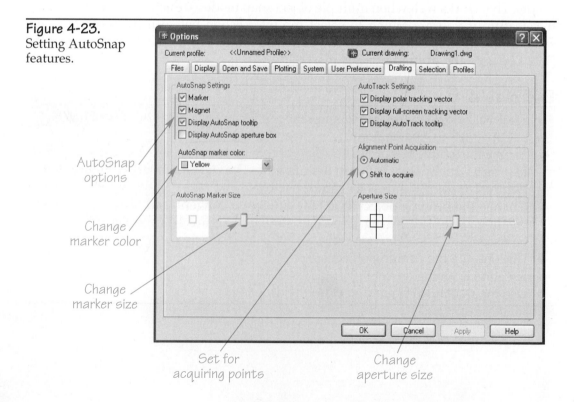

AutoSnap options

Change marker color

Change marker size

Set for acquiring points

Change aperture size

The **Alignment Point Acquisition** area contains two options. These options control how a point will be acquired when using the Extension and Parallel object snap modes. These options are described below:

- **Automatic.** When this option is selected, points are automatically acquired by leaving the crosshairs over the area you are trying to acquire and pausing.
- **Shift to acquire.** This option requires you to press the [Shift] key in order to acquire a point.

## Exercise 4-9

◆ Start a new drawing using a template or startup option of your own choice.
◆ Open the **Drafting Settings** dialog box, and then open the **Options** dialog box.
◆ Move the **AutoSnap Marker Size** slider and watch the image change to represent the marker size.
◆ Change the marker color to red.
◆ Use the newly revised marker size and color to draw objects of your choice with the object snaps.
◆ Save the drawing as ex4-9.

## Changing the aperture size

When selecting a point using object snaps, the cursor must be within a specific range of the desired point before it is located. The object snap detection system finds everything within a square area centered at the crosshairs location. This square area is called the *aperture* and is invisible by default.

To display the aperture, activate the **Display AutoSnap aperture box** check box in the **Drafting** tab of the **Options** dialog box. Having the aperture visible may be helpful when you are first learning to work with object snaps. To change the size of the aperture, move the slider in the **Aperture Size** area. Increasing or decreasing the size of the aperture controls how close or far away the crosshairs need to be from an object in order for AutoCAD to find the object snap point.

Keep in mind that the *aperture* and the *pick box* are different. The aperture is displayed on the screen when object snap modes are active. The pick box appears on the screen for any command activating the Select objects: prompt (such as the **ERASE** command).

## Exercise 4-10

◆ Open ex4-7.
◆ Display the aperture.
◆ Reduce the aperture size. Draw lines to existing objects using the object snap modes of your choice.
◆ Increase the aperture size to the maximum value. Again, draw lines to the existing objects using the object snap modes of your choice.
◆ Observe the difference in aperture size. Determine your personal preference of the default, small, and large settings.
◆ Save the drawing as ex4-10.

# Using Temporary Tracking to Locate Points

*Tracking* is a system allowing you to visually locate points in a drawing, relative to other points. It creates a new point using the X coordinate of one tracking point and the Y coordinate of another. The tracking feature can be used at any point specification prompt, just like object snaps. Tracking can also be used in combination with object snaps. To activate temporary tracking, pick the **Temporary Tracking Point** button from the **Object Snap** toolbar, enter tt, or pick **Temporary track point** from the **Object Snap** shortcut menu.

As an example, tracking can be used to place a circle at the center of a rectangle. See **Figure 4-24.** The center of the rectangle corresponds to the X coordinate of the midpoint of the horizontal lines. The Y coordinate corresponds to the Y coordinate of the midpoint of the vertical lines. Temporary tracking can be used to combine these two points to find the center of the rectangle, using this sequence:

Command: **c** *or* **circle**↵
Specify center point for circle or [3P/2P/Ttr (tan tan radius)]: **tt**↵
Specify temporary OTRACK point: **mid**↵
of *(pick one of the vertical lines and move the cursor horizontally)*
Specify center point for circle or [3P/2P/Ttr (tan tan radius)]: **tt**↵
Specify temporary OTRACK point: **mid**↵
of *(pick one of the horizontal lines and move the cursor vertically)*
Specify center point for circle or [3P/2P/Ttr (tan tan radius)]: *(select the point where the two alignment paths cross or intersect)*
Specify radius of circle or [Diameter] <current>: ↵
Command:

The direction of the orthogonal line determines whether the X or Y component is used. In the previous example, after picking the first tracking point, the cursor is moved horizontally. This means the Y axis value of the point is being used, and tracking is now ready for an X coordinate specification.

After moving the cursor horizontally, you may notice movement is locked in a horizontal mode. If you need to move the cursor vertically, move the cursor back to the previously picked point, and then drag vertically. Use this method any time you need to switch between horizontal and vertical movement.

---

**Figure 4-24.**
Using temporary tracking to locate the center of a rectangle. A—The midpoint of the left line is acquired. B—The midpoint of the bottom line is acquired. C—The center point of the circle is located at the intersection of the alignment paths.

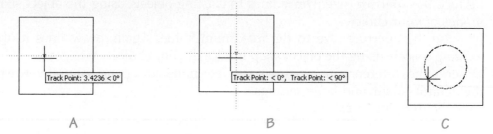

A          B          C

## Using the From Selection Option

The From selection mode is another tracking tool that can be used to locate points based on existing geometry. The From selection mode allows you to establish a relative coordinate, polar coordinate, or direct distance entry from a specified reference base point. Access the From selection mode by selecting the **Snap From** button in the **Object Snap** toolbar, selecting **From** in the **Object Snap** shortcut menu, or entering fro at a point selection prompt. The example in **Figure 4-25** shows the center point for a circle being established as a polar distance from the midpoint of an existing line. The command sequence is shown here:

Command: **c** *or* **circle**↵
Specify center point for circle or [3P/2P/Ttr (tan tan radius)]: **fro**↵
Base point: **mid**↵
of *(pick line)*
<Offset>: **@2<45**↵
Specify radius of circle or [Diameter] <*current*>: **.75**↵
Command:

Figure 4-25.
Using the From selection mode to locate a point 2" away from the midpoint of a line at 45°.

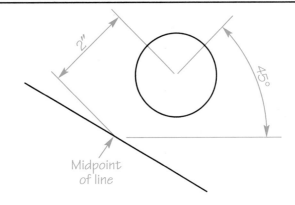

Midpoint
of line

## Exercise 4-11

◆ Start a new drawing using a template or startup option of your own choice.
◆ Draw a rectangle similar to the one in **Figure 4-24.**
◆ Use temporary tracking to locate the center of the rectangle and draw a circle with its center at that location.
◆ Draw a line with a length and angle similar to **Figure 4-25.**
◆ Use the From selection mode to draw a 1" diameter circle with its center 2 units and 45° from the midpoint of the line, similar to **Figure 4-25.**
◆ Save the drawing as ex4-11.

# Using AutoTrack to Locate Points

The temporary tracking mode, discussed earlier, allows the relative placement of a point for a single task. The *AutoTrack*™ mode enables this feature to be activated at all times, similar to running object snaps. The purpose of tracking is to reduce the need for construction lines and keyboard entry when drawing geometry.

There are two AutoTrack modes: object snap tracking and polar tracking. Both modes provide alignment paths to aid in exact point location, relative to existing points. Any command requiring a point selection, such as the **LINE, CIRCLE, COPY,** or **MOVE** command, can make use of these modes.

## Object Snap Tracking

*Object snap tracking* is always used in conjunction with object snaps. When this mode is active, placing the crosshairs near an AutoSnap marker and pausing acquires a point. Once a point is acquired, horizontal and vertical alignment paths are available for locating points.

This mode is toggled on and off with the [F11] keyboard key or the **OTRACK** button on the status bar. It is only available for points selected by the currently active object snap modes. When running object snaps are active, all selected object snap modes are available for use with object snap tracking. These modes are not available for object snap tracking, however, if running object snaps are deactivated. In **Figure 4-26,** object snap tracking is used with the Endpoint and Midpoint running object snaps to start a line at the imaginary intersection of the middle of the vertical line and the end of the horizontal line. The running object snap modes are set before the following command sequence is initiated, and the **OSNAP** and **OTRACK** buttons on the status bar are active.

Command: **l** *or* **line.⏎**
Specify first point: *(acquire endpoint, acquire midpoint, move crosshairs to where the endpoint and midpoint would cross, and pick the start point)*
Specify next point or [Undo]: *(pick a second point)*
Specify next point or [Undo]: ⏎
Command:

**Figure 4-26.**
Using object snap tracking to locate the start point of a line. A—The endpoint and midpoints of two lines are acquired to locate the imaginary intersection. B—The line is started at the imaginary intersection of the two points.

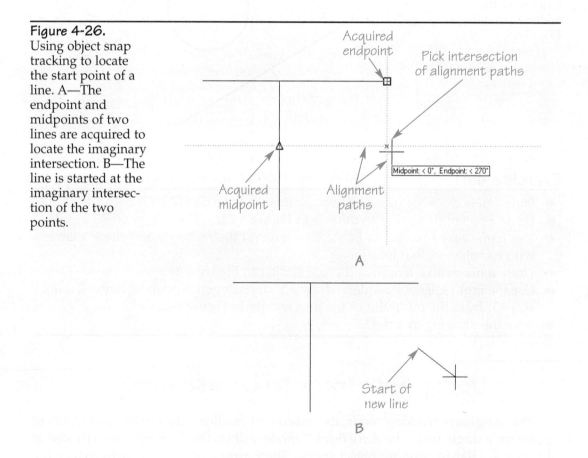

**Professional Tip**

AutoTrack is similar in performance to the Extension object snap. Experiment with a combination of just the Endpoint object snap mode and AutoTrack. Try a combination of Endpoint and Extension object snap modes without AutoTrack to see the difference. Notice that without object snap tracking, you cannot drag in a direction perpendicular to an endpoint.

## Exercise 4-12

◆ Start a drawing using a template or startup option of your own choice.
◆ Set the Endpoint and Midpoint running object snaps.
◆ Draw two lines as shown in **Figure 4-26A**. Start a line similar to the line in **Figure 4-26B**.
◆ Use object snap tracking to draw the end of the line to the imaginary intersection of the Midpoint and Endpoint of the two existing lines on the other side of the vertical line.
◆ Save the drawing as ex4-12.

## Polar Tracking

Ortho mode (discussed in Chapter 3) forces the cursor movement to orthogonal (horizontal and vertical) orientations. When Ortho mode is turned on, and the **LINE** command is in use, all new line segments are drawn at either 0°, 90°, 180°, or 270°. Polar tracking works in much the same way, but allows for a greater range of angles.

Polar tracking can be turned on and off by selecting the **POLAR** button from the status bar or using the [F10] keyboard key. AutoCAD automatically turns Ortho mode off when polar tracking is on and turns polar tracking off when Ortho mode is on. You cannot use polar tracking and Ortho mode at the same time.

When polar tracking is turned on, the cursor snaps to preset incremental angles when a point is being located relative to another point. For example, when using the **LINE** command, polar tracking is not active for the start point selection, but is available for the second and following point selections. Polar alignment paths are displayed as dashed lines whenever the cursor comes into alignment with any of these preset angles.

To set incremental angles, use the **Polar Tracking** tab in the **Drafting Settings** dialog box. See **Figure 4-27**. The following features are found in the **Polar Tracking** tab:

• **Polar Tracking On (F10).** Check this box, press the [F10] key, or pick the **POLAR** button on the status bar to turn polar tracking on.
• **Polar Angle Settings area.** This area of the dialog box allows you to set the desired polar angle increments. It contains the following items:
  • **Increment angle.** This drop-down list is set at 90, by default. This setting provides angle increments every 90°. Open the drop-down list to use a variety of preset angles. The angle set in **Figure 4-27** is 30, which sets polar tracking in 30° increments.

**Figure 4-27.**
The **Polar Tracking** tab of the **Drafting Settings** dialog box.

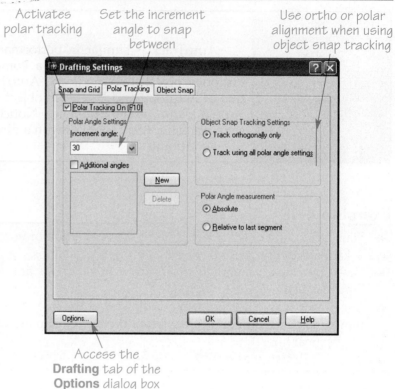

Activates polar tracking

Set the increment angle to snap between

Use ortho or polar alignment when using object snap tracking

Access the **Drafting** tab of the **Options** dialog box

- **Additional angles.** This check box activates your own angle increments. To do this, pick the **New** button to open a text box in the window. Type the desired angle. Pick the **New** button each time you want to add another angle. The additional angles are used together with the incremental angle setting when you use polar tracking. Use the **Delete** button to remove angles from the list. You can make the additional angles inactive by turning off the **Additional angles** check box.
- **Object Snap Tracking Settings area.** This area is used to set the angles available with object snap tracking. If **Track orthogonally only** is selected, only horizontal and vertical alignment paths are active when using object snap tracking. If **Track using all polar angle settings** is selected, alignment paths for all polar snap angles are active when using object snap tracking.
- **Polar Angle measurement area.** This setting determines if the polar snap increments are constant or relative to the previous segment. If **Absolute** is selected, the polar snap angles are measured from the base angle of 0° set for the drawing. If **Relative to last segment** is checked, each increment angle is measured from a base angle established by the previously drawn segment.

**Figure 4-28** shows an example using polar tracking with 30° angle increments to draw a parallelogram by using the following command sequence:

Command: **l** or **line.**↵
Specify first point: (select the first point)
Specify next point or [Undo]: (drag the cursor to the right while the polar alignment path indicates <0°) **3.**↵
Specify next point or [Undo]: (drag the cursor to the 60° polar alignment path) **1.5.**↵
Specify next point or [Close/Undo]: (drag the cursor to the left while the polar alignment path indicates <180°) **3.**↵
Specify next point or [Close/Undo]: **c.**↵
Command:

**Figure 4-28.**
Using polar tracking with 30° angle increments to draw a parallelogram. A—After the side is drawn, the alignment path and direct distance entry are used to create the second side. B—A horizontal alignment path is used for the third point. C—The parallelogram is completed with the **Close** option.

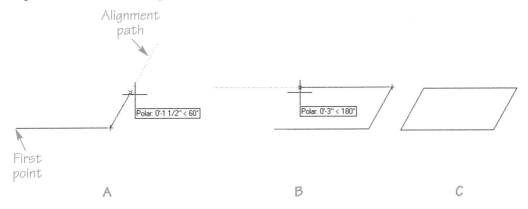

## Exercise 4-13

◆ Start a drawing using a template or startup option of your own choice.
◆ Open the **Polar Tracking** tab of the **Drafting Settings** dialog box and set the increment angle to 30.
◆ Use polar tracking to draw a parallelogram similar to **Figure 4-28.**
◆ Save the drawing as ex4-13.

## Polar tracking with polar snaps

Polar tracking can also be used in conjunction with polar snaps. If polar snaps are used when drawing the parallelogram in **Figure 4-28,** there is no need to type the length of the line, because you set both the angle and length increments. The desired angle and length increments are established in the **Snap and Grid** tab of the **Drafting Settings** dialog box. See **Figure 4-29.**

**Figure 4-29.**
The **Snap and Grid** tab of the **Drafting Settings** dialog box is used to set the polar snap spacing.

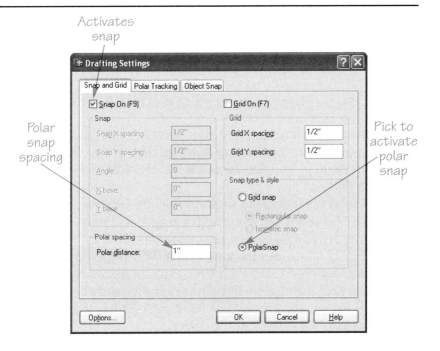

Polar snap is activated by picking the **PolarSnap** radio button in the **Snap type & style** area of the dialog box. Picking this button activates the **Polar spacing** area and deactivates the **Snap** area. The length of the polar snap increment is set in the **Polar distance:** box.

## Using polar tracking overrides

It takes some time to set up the polar tracking and polar snap options, but it is worth the effort if you have several objects to draw that can take advantage of this feature. If you want to perform polar tracking for only one point, you can use the polar tracking override to do this easily. This works for the specified angle if polar tracking is on or off. A polar tracking override is done by entering a left angle bracket (<), followed by the desired angle, when AutoCAD asks you to specify a point. The following command sequence uses a 30° override to draw a line 2″ long:

Command: **l** *or* **line.**↵
Specify first point: *(pick a start point for the line)*
Specify next point or [Undo]: **<30**↵
Angle override: 30
Specify next point or [Undo]: *(move the cursor in the desired direction)* **2.**↵
Specify next point or [Undo]: ↵
Command:

## Exercise 4-14

◆ Start a drawing using a template or startup option of your own choice.
◆ Open the **Polar Tracking** tab of the **Drafting Settings** dialog box and set the increment angle to 60.
◆ Open the **Snap and Grid** tab of the **Drafting Settings** dialog box to set the polar distance at 1.5″.
◆ Use polar snap to draw a parallelogram similar to **Figure 4-28.**
◆ Use the polar tracking overrides to draw the following connected lines:
  ◆ Start from a point of your choice and draw a line 1.125″ long at a 67° angle.
  ◆ Continue with a line 1.125″ long at 293°.
  ◆ Continue with a line 1.125″ long at 67°.
  ◆ Continue with a line 1.125″ long at 293°.
  ◆ Exit the **LINE** command.
◆ Save the drawing as ex4-14.

## AutoTrack Settings

The settings controlling the function of AutoTrack can be accessed through the **Options...** button in the **Drafting Settings** dialog box. This opens the **Options** dialog box to the **Drafting** tab. See **Figure 4-30.** The following options are available in the **AutoTrack Settings** area:

• **Display polar tracking vector.** When this feature is selected, the alignment path is displayed when using object snap tracking. When this option is off, no polar tracking path is displayed.
• **Display full-screen tracking vector.** When this option is selected, the alignment path for object snap tracking extends across the length of the screen. If not checked, the alignment paths are shown only between the acquired point and the cursor location. Polar tracking vectors always extend from the original point to the extents of the screen.

**Figure 4-30.**
The **Drafting** tab in the **Options** dialog box contains the AutoTrack settings.

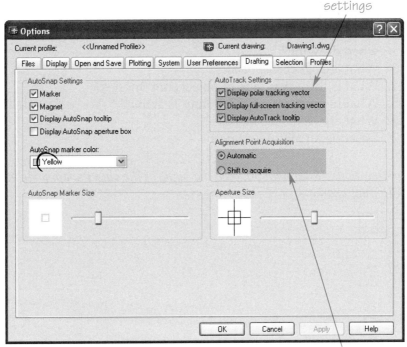

AutoTrack settings

Alignment point settings

- **Display AutoTrack tooltip.** When this box is checked, a temporary tooltip is displayed with the AutoTrack alignment paths.

The options in the **Alignment Point Acquisition** area determine how the object snap tracking alignment paths are selected:

- **Automatic.** When this option is selected, points are acquired whenever the cursor is paused over an object snap point.
- **Shift to acquire.** When this option is selected, the [Shift] key must be pressed to acquire an object snap point and use object snap tracking. AutoSnap markers are still displayed, and normal object snap can be used without pressing the [Shift] key. If many running object snaps are set, it may be useful to use this option to reduce the number of paths displayed across the screen.

# Chapter Test

*Answer the following questions on a separate sheet of paper.*

1. AutoCAD provides a pattern of dots on the screen to help you lay out geometry in the drawing. What is this feature called?
2. Name the dialog box where the spacing can be established for the pattern of dots.
3. Identify three ways to turn on and off the pattern of dots.
4. Name the invisible grid that allows the cursor to move, or "snap," only in exact increments.
5. Name the dialog box where the snap spacing can be set.
6. Why is it possible to pick a point more accurately if snap is on than if it is off?
7. Identify three ways to turn snap on and off.
8. What is the result of selecting the **Snap** option of the **GRID** command?
9. When using the **GRID** command, what do you enter if you want the grid spacing to be twice the snap spacing?

10. List three commonly used grid and snap settings for architectural drawings.
11. Give an appropriate snap and grid spacing if the smallest dimension on the drawing is 1″.
12. Why is it a good idea to change the snap and grid spacing as needed to assist you when drawing?
13. What are *object snap modes?*
14. What is the advantage of object snap modes?
15. What happens when AutoSnap is active?
16. What are *AutoSnap markers?*
17. Describe an alignment path.

*In Questions 18 through 30, give the name of the object snap mode identified by the AutoSnap markers.*

18. □

19. △

20. ○

21. ◇

22. ✕

23. ⊠

24. ✚

25. ⌐┘

26. ┗

27. ∥

28. ⌒

29. ⧖

30. ⊗

31. How do you display the **Object Snap** shortcut menu?
32. How do you display the **Object Snap** toolbar if it is not already displayed?
33. How do you activate a specific object snap by typing, when AutoCAD prompts for a location or selection?
34. What is an *object snap override?*
35. What are *running object snaps?*
36. Define *quadrant.*
37. Identify the positions on a circle or arc the Quadrant object snap finds.
38. When using the Center object snap to find the center of a circle, do you move the cursor near the center of the circle or the perimeter of the circle?
39. When using the Extension object snap, what is the initial point called that is found by moving the cursor over the line or arc from which the new object is to be extended?
40. When using the Extension object snap, what marks the location when the object is found?
41. Name the object snap option that allows you to draw one object at 90° to another.
42. Give the term meaning a line that touches an arc or a circle at only one point, or an arc or a circle that touches another arc or circle at only one point.
43. How long is an object snap override active?
44. Name the object snap mode that allows you to make a single point selection without the effects of any running object snap modes.
45. What is the effect of picking the **OSNAP** button on the status bar?
46. How does AutoCAD decide which running object snap mode to use when multiple object snap modes are active?
47. How do you cycle through the available snap points when multiple object snap modes are active?
48. What is the AutoSnap magnet?
49. How do you access the **Options** dialog box for customizing the AutoSnap settings?
50. How do you turn off the AutoSnap marker, magnet, and tooltip?
51. How do you change the AutoSnap marker color?
52. What is the difference between the aperture and the pick box?
53. Define *tracking.*
54. Identify two ways to activate temporary tracking.
55. What is the purpose of the From selection mode?
56. What is the difference between temporary tracking and AutoTrack?
57. List the two AutoTrack modes.
58. Is object snap tracking available if running object snaps are deactivated?
59. How does object snap tracking work?
60. How do you turn object snap tracking on and off?
61. How does polar tracking work?
62. How do you turn polar tracking on and off?
63. What happens to Ortho mode if polar tracking is turned on?
64. What do polar alignment paths look like?
65. What is the default incremental angle for polar tracking?
66. How do you set an incremental angle of 30° for polar tracking?
67. If object snap tracking is set for only horizontal and vertical alignment paths, how do you change it to match the polar snap angles?
68. What is the difference between regular polar tracking and polar tracking with snaps?
69. How do you activate polar snaps?
70. Where is the length of the polar snap increment set?
71. What is a *polar tracking override?*
72. How is a polar tracking override performed?
73. What does *shift to acquire* mean?

*For questions 74 through 80, provide the AutoCAD object snap mode(s) you would use to accomplish the given task.*

74. Draw a circle with its center at the end of an existing line.
75. Draw a line from the center of an existing circle to the center of an existing line.
76. Draw a line from the 90° position on an existing circle to the point of tangency on an existing arc.
77. Draw a hexagon with its center placed where two lines cross.
78. Draw a line beginning 1″ beyond the endpoint of an existing line.
79. Draw a line from the 270° position on an existing circle and at a right angle to an existing line.
80. Draw a line parallel to an existing line.

# Chapter Problems

1. Draw the following figure. Use a snap setting of 1″ and a grid spacing of 2″. Use the Endpoint and Perpendicular running object snap modes. Save the drawing as p4-1.

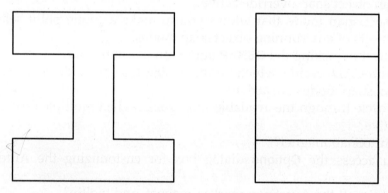

2. Draw the column. Use a snap setting of 1/8″ and a grid spacing of 1″. Use the Endpoint, Intersection, and Perpendicular running object snap modes. Save the drawing as p4-2.

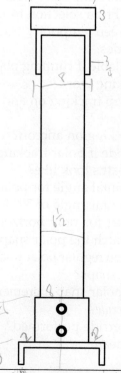

3. Draw the landscape plan. Use a snap setting of 1/8" and a grid spacing of 1". Use the Endpoint, Intersection, Extension, and Perpendicular running object snap modes. Do not draw dimensions. Scale is not important. Save the drawing as p4-3.

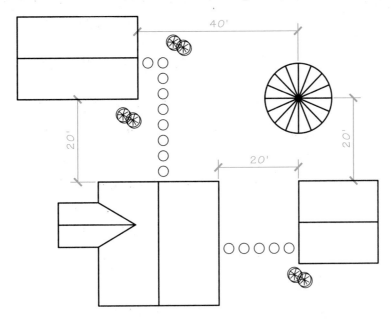

*Draw the following problems based on the given information. Use the given dimensions and dimensional information, and determine the rest of the dimensions as desired and proportional to the given examples. Use your own practical experience and items around the home to determine the size of features such as sinks, water heaters, and stair treads. Establish grid and snap settings to help you create each drawing. Use the object snaps and other accuracy tools discussed in this chapter as needed to create each drawing. Do not draw notes or dimensions. Save each drawing using the problem number, such as p4-4 for Problem 4-4.*

4.

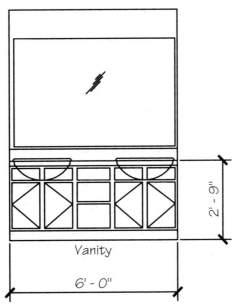

Vanity

Master Bath Cabinet Elevation

5.

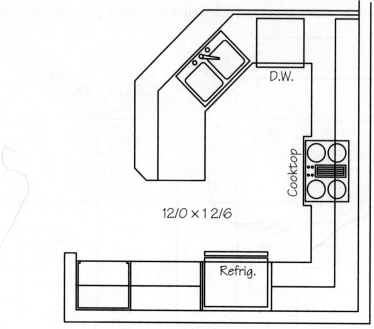

D.W.

Cooktop

12/0 × 12/6

Refrig.

Kitchen Floor Plan

6.

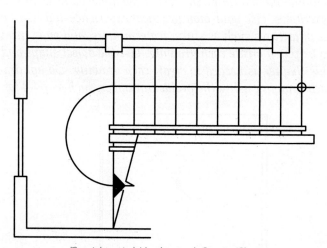

Residential U-shaped Stair Plan

7.

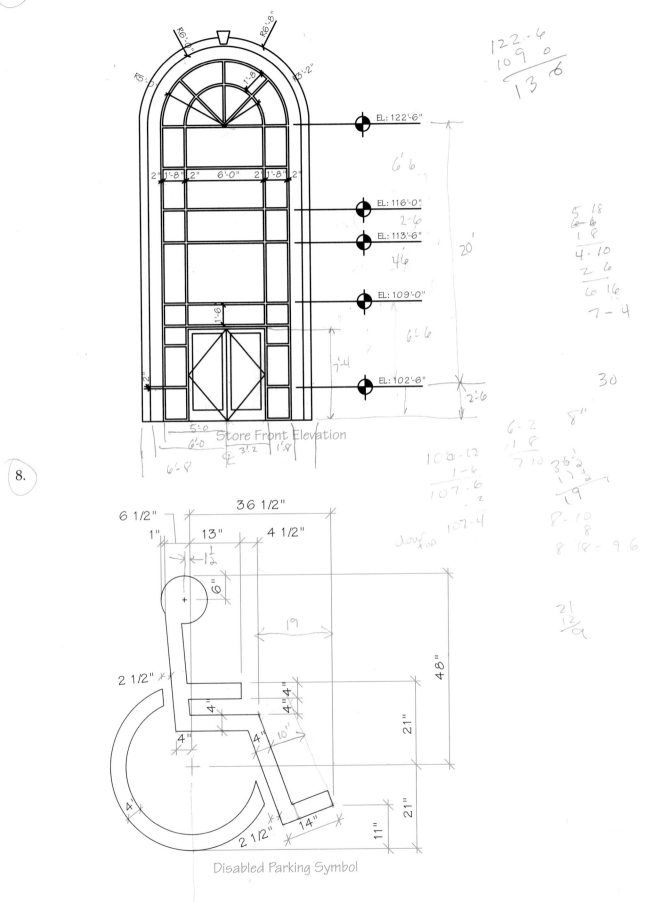

Store Front Elevation

8.

Disabled Parking Symbol

9.

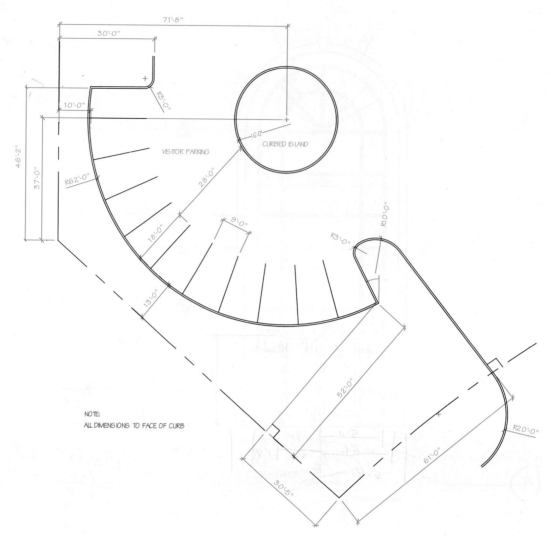

71'-8"

30'-0"

10'-0"

R3'-0"

46'-2"

37'-0"

R62'-0"

VISITOR PARKING

CURBED ISLAND

16'-0"

28'-0"

9'-0"

18'-0"

13'-0"

R3'-0"

R10'-0"

52'-0"

NOTE:
ALL DIMENSIONS TO FACE OF CURB

30'-5"

61'-0"

R20'-0"

Parking Plan

# Layer Management

## Learning Objectives

After completing this chapter, you will be able to:

- Explain how layers are used in a drawing.
- Create layer-naming conventions.
- Create and manage layers.
- Assign layer properties and settings.
- Load linetypes into your drawing.
- Assign lineweights to objects and layers.
- Apply layer filters.
- Modify object properties.

## Important Terms

absolute
as-built drawing
ByBlock
ByLayer
current layer
explicit color

global
layer
layer filter
linetype
lineweight
logical color

## An Introduction to Layers

In manual drafting, different elements or components of drawings can be separated by placing them on different sheets. This is called an *overlay system,* where each sheet is perfectly aligned with the others. The overlay system in AutoCAD uses what are called *layers.* A *layer* is defined as a logical grouping of data. Layers contain various object property settings that allow every object created in a drawing to be assigned to a specific layer group. Objects placed on a layer will adopt the properties of the layer to which they have been assigned. Each layer containing objects can be displayed and plotted individually or in any desired combination of layers.

Layers are used for managing visual information in a drawing. All the layers can be reproduced together to reflect the entire design drawing. Individual layers might also be reproduced to show specific details or components of the design, based on who needs to see what information. Using layers increases productivity in several ways:

- Specific information can be grouped on separate layers. For example, the floor plan walls can be drawn on one layer, the electrical plan symbols on a second layer, and the plumbing fixtures on a third layer.
- Several plot sheets can be displayed from the same drawing file by modifying layer visibility.
- The layers in a drawing can be reproduced individually or combined in any desired format. For example, the floor plan and electrical plan can be reproduced together and sent to an electrical contractor for a bid. The floor plan and plumbing plan can be reproduced together and sent to the plumbing contractor.
- Each layer can be assigned a different color, linetype, and lineweight to help improve clarity.
- Each layer can be plotted in a different color, while some layers may not be plotted at all.
- Selected layers can be turned off or frozen to decrease the amount of information displayed on the screen or to speed up screen regeneration.
- Changes can be made to a layer quickly, often while the client watches.

## Layers Used in Architecture

In architectural drafting, there can be over 100 layers in a single drawing. Each of the following items might be created on its own unique layer:

- Floor plans
- Foundation plans
- Partition layouts
- Plumbing systems
- Electrical systems
- Structural systems
- Roof drainage systems
- Reflected ceilings
- HVAC systems

These systems can be broken down further into layers for walls, windows, doors, dimensions, and notes. Interior designers may use layers for floor plans, interior partitions, and furniture. A structural engineer might use wall, beam, framing, and detail layers. **Figure 5-1** shows an example of the use of layers.

## Current Layer

When you draw an object, it is automatically drawn on the *current layer*. The current layer is listed in the **Layer Control** drop-down list on the **Layers** toolbar. See **Figure 5-2.** In drawings containing multiple layers, you can select which layer is the current layer.

As you have worked through the exercises in this book, you may have noticed that 0 appears in the **Layer Control** drop-down list. The 0 layer is the AutoCAD default layer. Until another layer is defined and set current, all objects in the drawing are created on the 0 layer.

**Figure 5-1.**
AutoCAD objects on different layers can be used in conjunction with each other to create any number of drawings. For example, the dimension layer may be turned off for the client, but turned on for the contractor. (Alan Mascord Design Associates, Inc.)

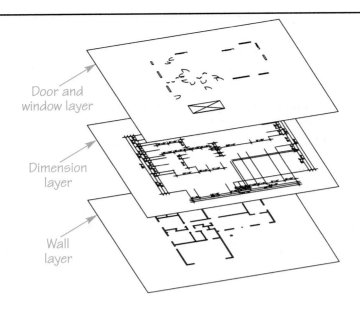

Door and window layer

Dimension layer

Wall layer

**Figure 5-2.**
The **Layers** toolbar. Layer 0 is the AutoCAD default layer.

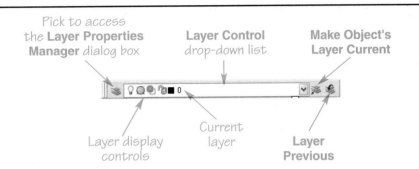

Pick to access the **Layer Properties Manager** dialog box

**Layer Control** drop-down list

**Make Object's Layer Current**

Layer display controls

Current layer

**Layer Previous**

## Naming Layers

When creating layers, you can use a layer name identifying the type of object placed on the layer. Layer names can have up to 255 characters and include letters, numbers, spaces, and other special characters. Some typical architectural, structural, and civil drafting layer names are as follows:

| Architectural | Structural | Civil |
|---------------|------------|-------|
| Walls | Beams | Property Line |
| Windows | Columns | Structures |
| Doors | Steel | Roads |
| Electrical | Hangers | Water |
| Plumbing | Footings | Contours |
| Furniture | Hold-downs | Gas |
| Lighting | Straps | Elevations |

For very simple drawings, layers can be named by linetype and color. For example, the layer name Object-White might have an object line (Continuous linetype) drawn in white. The linetype and color number, such as Object-7, can also be used. Another option is to assign the layer a numerical value. For example, object lines can be 0, hidden lines can be 1, and centerlines can be 2. If you use this method, keep a written record of the numbering system for reference. Most of your drawings will be too complex for this application.

Layers can also be given more complex names. The name might include the drawing number, color code, and layer content. The name Dwg100-2-Dimen could refer to drawing DWG100, color 2, and the Dimension layer. Some companies create layers for each floor or level of a building. In these types of layering systems, certain groups of layers have a code prefix associated with the layer name. Using this method, door, window, note, title, and wall layers may be identified with the prefix 1-, which identifies first floor layers, or M-, which relates to main floor layers. For example, the layers 1-Wall, 1-Door, and 1-Window could refer to the wall, door, and window layers for the first floor plan. M-Elec, M-Furn, and M-Note could refer to the main floor electrical, furniture, and note layers. The following are some examples of layer names using this method:

| Layer Name | Description |
|---|---|
| 1-Wall | First floor walls |
| 1-Door | First floor doors |
| 2-Wind | Second floor windows |
| 2-Dims | Second floor dimensions |
| M-Note | Main floor notes |
| U-Anno | Upper floor annotations |
| F-Wall | Foundation walls |

The American Institute of Architects (AIA) has developed a layer-naming system for the architecture industry. This system is outlined in the AIA's *CAD Layer Guidelines* publication. This document provides guidance in the naming and usage conventions for layers.

In the AIA layer-naming system, each layer name includes up to four fields:
- Discipline code
- Major group
- Minor group (optional)
- Status group (optional)

**Figure 5-3** shows an example of a layer name based on the AIA guidelines. Appendix A of this book provides an introduction to this standard.

**Figure 5-3.**
The AIA layer-naming system includes discipline codes and major groups, along with optional minor groups and status codes.

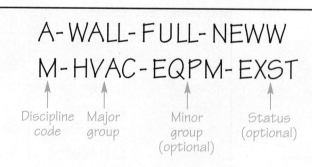

**Professional Tip**

In releases of AutoCAD prior to AutoCAD 2000, layer names could be no longer than 31 characters and could not contain spaces. If you save an AutoCAD 2004 drawing in the AutoCAD R12/LT2 DXF format, AutoCAD replaces any disallowed characters with underscores (_) and shortens the layer names to 31 characters.

# Layer Management

LAYER
LA

Format
→ Layer...

Layers
toolbar

Layer Properties
Manager

You can create and modify layers in the **Layer Properties Manager** dialog box. See **Figure 5-4.** To display this dialog box, pick the **Layer Properties Manager** button in the **Layers** toolbar, select **Layer...** from the **Format** pull-down menu, or enter la or layer at the Command prompt.

Only one layer, the 0 layer, is required in an AutoCAD drawing. This layer cannot be renamed or purged from the drawing. As discussed earlier, however, it is normal to have more than one layer in a drawing. When drawing, the most important layer is the *current layer* because whatever you draw is placed on this layer. It is useful to think of the current layer as the top layer.

**Figure 5-4.**
Use the **Layer Properties Manager** dialog box to create new layers, set layer status, and define layer properties.

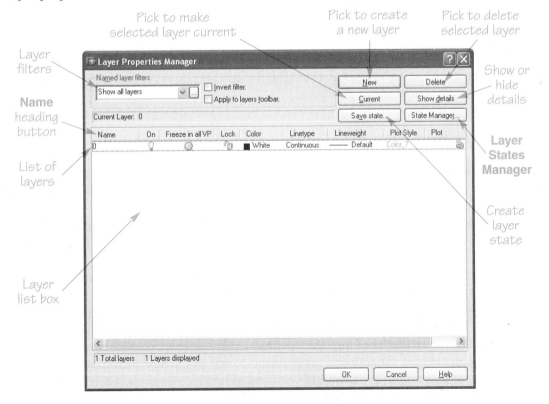

## Creating Layers

Layers should be added to a drawing to meet the needs of the current drawing project. To add a new layer, pick the **New** button in the **Layer Properties Manager** dialog box. A new layer listing appears, using a default name of Layer1. See **Figure 5-5.** Type a new name, and press the [Enter] key or pick the **OK** button.

You can also type several new layer names at the same time. To do so, type a layer name, and then press the comma key. This adds a new layer to the list and starts a new layer name entry. Entering several layer names in this manner is much faster because it keeps you from having to pick the **New** button each time. Press the [Enter] key when you are finished typing the new layer names. By pressing the heading button **Name**, the layers are sorted alphabetically.

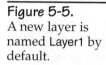

**Figure 5-5.**
A new layer is named Layer1 by default.

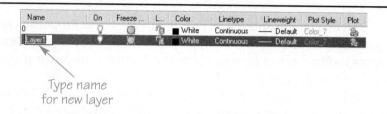

Type name
for new layer

**Note**

Selecting any of the headings in the layer list controls sorting. Each time the **Layer Properties Manager** dialog box is reopened, however, the layers are sorted alphabetically.

## Deleting Layers

Deleting a layer not in use is a simple process. First, select the layer. Pick the **Delete** button. The layer is erased from the list box. If the layer is not removed, it is being used somewhere in the drawing.

## Setting the Current Layer

You can set a layer current using the **Layer Properties Manager** dialog box, the **Layer Control** drop-down list in the **Layers** toolbar, or the **Make Object's Layer Current** button on the **Layers** toolbar. Use whichever method is most convenient. In the **Layer Properties Manager** dialog box, you set a layer as current by double-clicking the layer name or by selecting the layer name in the layer list and then picking the **Current** button.

You can also make a layer current using the **Layer Control** drop-down list located in the **Layers** toolbar. The **Layer Control** drop-down list displays the name of the current layer. Pick the drop-down arrow, and a layer list appears, as shown in **Figure 5-6.** Pick a layer name from the list, and that layer is set current. When many layers are defined in the drawing, the vertical scroll bar can be used to move up and down through the list. Selecting a layer name to set as current automatically closes the list and returns you to the drawing window. When a command is active, the drop-down button is grayed out, and the list is not available. The **Layer Control** drop-down list has the same status icons as the **Layer Properties Manager** dialog box. By picking an icon, you can change the state of the layer.

**Figure 5-6.**
The **Layer Control** drop-down list is located to the left side of the **Layers** toolbar. All layers are listed with icons representing their state and color. Pick a layer name to make it the current layer.

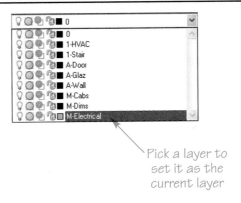

*Pick a layer to set it as the current layer*

Another quick way to set the current layer is to use the **Make Object's Layer Current** button in the **Layers** toolbar. When you pick this button, AutoCAD asks you to select an object on the layer you want to make current. Pick an object on the desired layer, and its layer becomes the current layer.

Layers toolbar

Make Object's Layer Current

Note

You can view context-specific help by picking the **Help** button in the upper-right corner of the **Layer Properties Manager** dialog box and then picking the area of the dialog box where you want help.

## Exercise 5-1

- ◆ Start a new drawing using a template or startup option of your own choice.
- ◆ Open the **Layer Properties Manager** dialog box.
- ◆ Create the layers listed below. Enter most layer names by typing them consecutively, with a comma between each layer name. Enter a couple of the names by picking the **New** button after each entry.
  - ◆ A-Wall
  - ◆ A-Door
  - ◆ A-Glazing
  - ◆ 1-Electrical
  - ◆ 1-HVAC
  - ◆ F-Footing
  - ◆ F-Beam
  - ◆ S-Prop
  - ◆ S-Contour
- ◆ Press the **Name** heading button to list the layer names in alphabetical/numerical order.
- ◆ Close the **Layer Properties Manager** dialog box.
- ◆ Save as ex5-1.
- ◆ Close the drawing.

# Viewing the Status of Layers

The status of each layer is displayed with icons in both the **Layer Properties Manager** dialog box and the **Layer Control** drop-down list in the **Layers** toolbar. See **Figure 5-7.** If you position the pointer over a column header for a moment, a tooltip appears and tells what the icon column represents. Picking an icon can change the related layer settings.

- **Changing the layer name.** The layer name list box contains all the layers in the drawing. To change an existing name, pick the name once to highlight it, pause for a moment, and then pick it again. When you pick the second time, the layer name is highlighted with a text box and cursor. Enter a new name. The 0 layer cannot be renamed.

**Figure 5-7.**
Icons in the **Layer Properties Manager** dialog box and the **Layer Control** drop-down list identify layer settings. Pick an icon to toggle or change the setting.

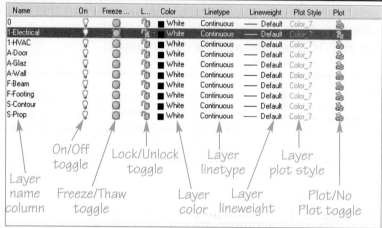

**Layer Properties Manager** dialog box

A

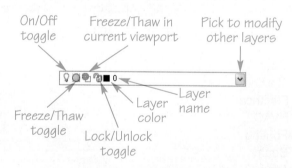

**Layer Control** drop-down list

B

- **Turn a layer On or Off.** The lightbulb icon shows whether a layer is on or off. The yellow lightbulb means the layer is on; objects drawn on that layer are displayed on screen and can be plotted. If you pick on a yellow lightbulb, it turns gray, turning the layer off. If a layer is off, objects on the layer are not displayed on screen or plotted. Objects on a layer that has been turned off can still be edited when using advanced selection techniques and are regenerated when a drawing regeneration occurs.

Architectural Drafting Using AutoCAD

- **Freeze or thaw in ALL viewports.** Layers are further classified as thawed or frozen. Similar to the off setting, frozen layers are not displayed or plotted. Objects on a frozen layer, however, cannot be edited and are not regenerated when the drawing regenerates. Freezing layers can greatly speed up your system performance. The snowflake icon is displayed when a layer is frozen. A thawed layer's objects are displayed on screen. The sun icon is displayed for thawed layers. Picking the sun or snowflake icon toggles the setting.

Objects on frozen layers cannot be modified, but objects on layers turned off can be modified. For example, if you access the **ERASE** command and enter all at the Select objects: prompt, objects on layers that are turned off are also erased. Objects on frozen layers are not erased.

- **Lock or Unlock a layer.** Layers are unlocked by default, but you can pick on the unlocked padlock to lock it. A locked layer remains visible, but objects on that layer cannot be edited. New objects can be added to a locked layer, but they become locked after being drawn. Layers are commonly locked for the purpose of tracing or referencing existing drawings.

  Often, there are differences between a completed construction project and the project design drawings. Items changed during the construction phase might not be reflected in the design drawings. In addition, there may be slight variations in dimensions, details, and locations. After construction is completed, *as-built drawings* are created to detail the actual construction. When creating as-built drawings, the layers from the original design drawings can be locked and used as reference.
- **Color of layer.** The color swatch shows the default color for objects on the layer. When you need to change the layer color, pick the swatch to display the **Select Color** dialog box. Working with colors is discussed later in this chapter.
- **Linetype.** The linetype setting for the layer is shown in the **Linetype** list. Picking the linetype name opens the **Select Linetype** dialog box, where you can specify a new linetype. Working with linetypes is discussed later in this chapter.
- **Lineweight.** The current lineweight setting for the layer is shown in the **Lineweight** list. Picking the lineweight name opens the **Lineweight** dialog box, where you can specify a new lineweight. Working with lineweights is discussed later in this chapter.
- **Plot Style.** This setting determines the plot style for the layer. The plot style setting is disabled when you are working with color-dependent plot styles (the **PSTYLEPOLICY** system variable is set to 1). Otherwise, picking the plot style displays the **Select Plot Style** dialog box. Plot styles are discussed in Chapter 24.
- **Plot.** Select this toggle to turn off plotting for a particular layer. The "no plot" symbol is displayed when the layer is not available to be plotted. The layer is still displayed on screen.

- **Freeze or thaw in current viewport.** These settings for floating model space views on layouts are detailed in Chapter 24. The options are visible only when a layout tab is active.

## Exercise 5-2

◆ Open ex5-1.
◆ Open the **Layer Properties Manager** dialog box.
◆ Select the **?** button and pick each item in the dialog box. Read the help tip that appears.
◆ Pick each icon to see it change settings or give you an AutoCAD message. Change each back to the original setting.
◆ Pick the color swatch to open the **Select Color** dialog box. Look at the dialog box, and then pick **Cancel** to exit the dialog box.
◆ Pick a linetype name to open the **Select Linetype** dialog box. Pick the **Cancel** button to exit the dialog box.
◆ Pick a lineweight name to open the **Lineweight** dialog box. Pick the **Cancel** button to exit the dialog box.
◆ Exit AutoCAD, or keep this drawing open for the next exercise.

## Working with Layers

When you change a layer setting, the change affects all selected layers. Select layer names using the same techniques used in file dialog boxes. You can highlight a single name by picking it. Picking another name deselects the first layer and selects the new layer. You can use the [Shift] key to select two layers and all layers between them. Holding the [Ctrl] key while picking layer names selects or deselects a name without affecting any other selections.

A shortcut menu is also available while your cursor is in the layer list area of the **Layer Properties Manager** dialog box. Right-click to display the shortcut menu shown in **Figure 5-8.** The following options are available:

- **New Layer.** Creates a new layer.
- **Select All.** Selects all layers.
- **Clear All.** Deselects all layers.
- **Select all but current.** Selects all layers, except the current layer.
- **Invert selection.** Deselects all highlighted layers and highlights all deselected layers.
- **Invert layer filter.** Inverts the current filter setting. Filters are discussed later in this chapter.
- **Layer filters.** Displays a submenu with the following predefined filters:
  - **Show all layers**
  - **Show all used layers**
  - **Show all Xref dependent layers**
- **Save layer states.** Accesses the **Save Layer States** dialog box. Layer states are discussed later in this chapter.

**Figure 5-8.**
Right-click in the list box of the **Layer Properties Manager** dialog box to access this shortcut menu.

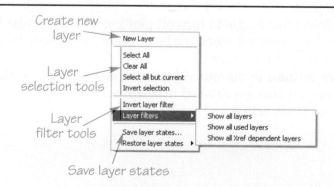

## Exercise 5-3

◆ Open ex5-1 if it is not already open.
◆ Open the **Layer Properties Manager** dialog box.
◆ Pick layer names to highlight each individually.
◆ Pick the first layer. Press and hold the [Shift] key, and pick a group of consecutive layer names.
◆ Right-click in the **Layer Properties Manager** dialog box and select **Clear All** from the shortcut menu.
◆ Press and hold the [Ctrl] key to pick a group of nonsequential layer names.
◆ Position the cursor in the layer list area and right-click. Try out the options in the shortcut menu.
◆ Exit AutoCAD, or keep this drawing open for the next exercise.

## Setting the Layer Color

The number of layer colors available depends on your graphics card and monitor. Color systems usually support at least 256 colors, while many graphics cards support up to 16.7 million colors. Colors should highlight the important features on the drawing and not cause eyestrain. Standard colors that can cause eyestrain include bright colors like yellow and cyan.

To change a layer color, select the layer name(s), and then pick the color swatch for one of the highlighted layer names. This displays the **Select Color** dialog box, as shown in **Figure 5-9**. This dialog box includes three different color tabs from which a color can be selected for use in your highlighted layer. These tabs are the **Index Color** tab, **True Color** tab, and **Color Books** tab. Each of these tabs includes different methods of obtaining colors for assignment to a layer. Each of the tabs is described in the following sections.

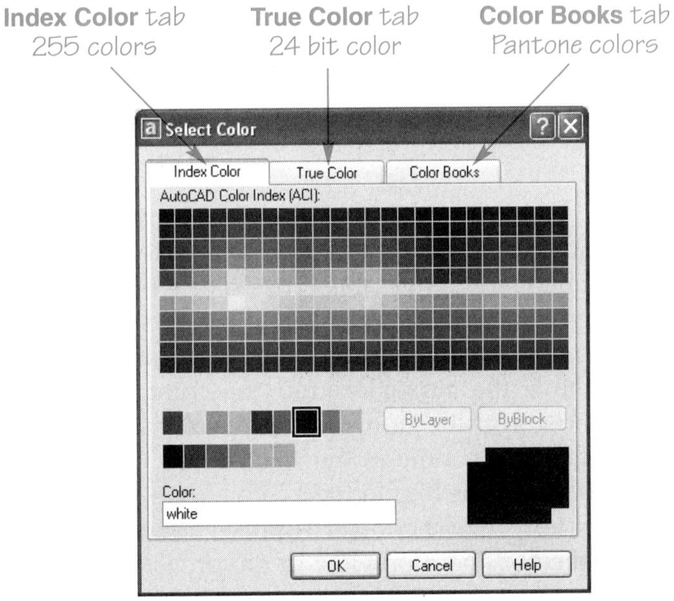

**Figure 5-9.**
Layer color is assigned using the **Select Color** dialog box.

Index Color tab
255 colors

True Color tab
24 bit color

Color Books tab
Pantone colors

**Figure 5-10.**
The **Index Color** tab in the **Select Color** dialog box includes 255 color swatches.

Selected color

Red, green, and blue colors used to mix selected color

Color index number

Standard colors #1–9

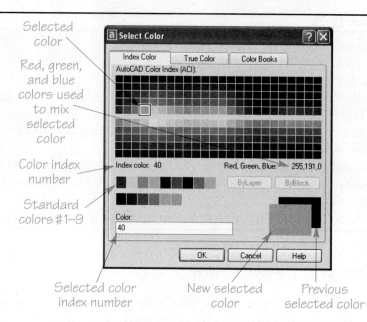

Selected color index number

New selected color

Previous selected color

## Index Color tab

This tab includes 255 color swatches from which you can choose a color. See **Figure 5-10.** This tab is commonly referred to as the *AutoCAD Color Index (ACI),* as layer colors are coded by name and number. The first seven colors in the ACI include both a numerical index number and a name:

| Number | Color |
|--------|---------|
| 1 | Red |
| 2 | Yellow |
| 3 | Green |
| 4 | Cyan |
| 5 | Blue |
| 6 | Magenta |
| 7 | White |

To select a color, you can pick the color swatch displaying the desired color or enter the color name or number in the **Color:** text box. The first seven basic colors were listed previously in the table. The color white (number 7) refers to white if the graphics screen background is black, and it refers to black if the background is white. All other colors can be accessed by their ACI numbers.

As you move the cursor around the color swatches, the **Index color:** note is updated to show you the number of the color over which the cursor is hovering. Beside the **Index color:** note is the **Red, Green, Blue:** note. This indicates the RGB numbers used to mix the highlighted color. Once you pick a color, the color is entered into the **Color:** text box. The lower-right section of the tab includes a preview of the newly selected color and a preview of the previously assigned color. Two additional buttons are also included: **ByLayer** and **ByBlock**. These are special object settings that are assigned to geometry in the drawing, but cannot be assigned to a layer name.

**Note**

**ByLayer** and **ByBlock** are logical settings representing the color, linetype, or lineweight assigned to an AutoCAD layer or block insertion. *ByLayer* means "use the color, linetype, or lineweight of the object's layer." *ByBlock* means "use the color, linetype, or lineweight assigned to the block insertion." **ByLayer** and **ByBlock** are assigned to objects in the drawing through the **Properties** toolbar and cannot be assigned to layers because they already represent the settings assigned to individual layers.

Practice using the ACI numbering system by picking a color swatch and seeing what number appears in the **Color:** text box. After selecting a color, pick the **OK** button when ready. The color you picked is now displayed as the color swatch for the highlighted layer name in the **Layer Properties Manager** dialog box.

### True Color tab

The **True Color** tab allows you to specify a true color (24 bit color) using either the **HSL** (Hue, Saturation, and Luminance) or **RGB** (Red, Green, Blue) color model. **Figure 5-11** displays the **True Color** tab with the **HSL** and **RGB** color models selected. The **HSL** color model includes three text boxes that allow you to control the properties for the color. The *hue* represents a specific wavelength of light within the visible spectrum. Valid **Hue:** values range from 0–360 degrees. The *saturation* refers to the purity of the color. Valid **Saturation:** values range from 0–100%. Finally, the *luminance* specifies the brightness of the color. Valid **Luminance:** values range from 0–100%, where 0% represents black, 100% represents white, and 50% represents the optimal brightness of the color.

Instead of adjusting the HSL colors through the text boxes, you can also move the cursor in the spectrum preview screen and along the luminance slider bar to pick the approximate color you are after. The true color specified is then translated to RGB values, which are displayed in the **Color:** text box. The **RGB** color model includes three text boxes and three slider bars. Adjusting the value in the **Red:**, **Green:**, and **Blue:** text boxes causes the slider bars to be adjusted with the mixed color displayed in the new color preview. The cursor can also be used to slide the marker along each bar to mix the colors.

### Color Books tab

The **Color Books** tab allows you to use third-party color books to specify a color. See **Figure 5-12.** The **Color book:** drop-down list includes several different color books, such as **PANTONE** and **RAL** books. Once a book has been selected, the available colors within the book are displayed. You can pick an area on the color slider or use the up and down keys to browse through the book. To select the color, use your pick button to pick on top of one of the color book swatches. As a color is selected, the equivalent RGB values are displayed on the right side of the tab, and the color is updated in the new color preview.

**Figure 5-11.**
The **True Color** tab in the **Select Color** dialog box allows you to specify a 24 bit color. A—The **Color model:** drop-down list is set to **HSL**. B—The **Color model:** drop-down list is set to **RGB**.

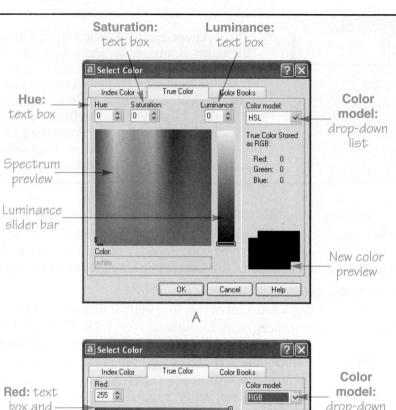

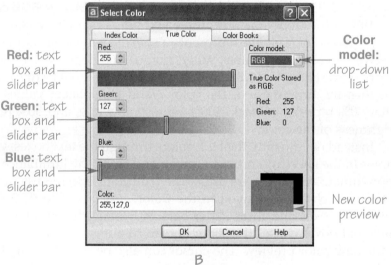

**Figure 5-12.**
The **Color Books** tab of the **Select Color** dialog box allows you to use third-party color books to choose a color.

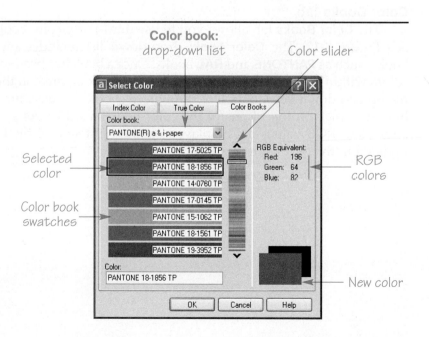

## Exercise 5-4

◆ Open ex5-1 if it is not already open.
◆ Open the **Layer Properties Manager** dialog box.
◆ Highlight one or more layer names.
◆ Pick the color swatch of one of the highlighted layers to open the **Select Color** dialog box.
◆ Select a new color for the layer from the **Index Color** tab.
◆ Pick the **OK** button. Notice the layer color swatch is changed to match your color selection.
◆ Assign other layers colors using colors from the **True Color** and **Color Books** tabs.
◆ Save your work and exit AutoCAD, or keep this drawing open for the next exercise.

## Setting the Layer Linetype and Lineweight

AutoCAD provides standard linetypes that can be used at any time to match the standards for your drawing. You can also create your own custom linetypes. Chapter 27 discusses how to create your own custom linetypes. In order to achieve different line widths, it is necessary to assign lineweights. Assigning lineweights is discussed later in this section.

### Linetype and lineweight standards

*Linetypes* in AutoCAD are line styles used to represent various features and objects. They come in many different configurations, such as solid lines and dashed lines. There are also specialty linetypes representing hot water lines, fence lines, and railroad track lines. These lines are broken periodically with a letter or symbol identifying the type of line.

*Lineweight* is line thickness or width. For common architectural applications, there are three lineweights: thin, medium, and thick. Each one of these types can be further divided by varying the weights in each category.

- **Thin lines.** Thin lines are typically used for dimension and extension lines, leaders, and break lines. The weight for thin lines is usually set from 0.3 mm to 0.5 mm. Dimension, extension, and leader lines are occasionally set to the heavier side of the thin category.
- **Medium lines.** Medium lines are typically used for lettering, arrowheads, object lines, centerlines, dashed lines, and hidden lines. The weight for medium lines is usually set from 0.5 mm to 0.7 mm. Object lines are generally at the higher end of the medium line category.
- **Thick lines.** Thick lines are typically used for cutting-plane lines, border lines, site lines, and detail callouts. The weight for thick lines is usually set from 0.7 mm to 1.0 mm.

These lineweights are general guidelines only. Determination of lineweights should be decided by what looks best on the finished print and coordinated with company standards. **Figure 5-13** provides examples of various objects and lineweights.

**Figure 5-13.**
Examples of
different
lineweights.

| Thin Lines | Medium Lines | Thick Lines |
|---|---|---|
| 2" ⟵———⟶ | ─── ─ ─── | ─────── |
| Dimensions | Centerlines | Border lines |
| ~~~~~⌒~~~~~ | ─ ─ ─ ─ ─ ─ ─ | ───◯─── |
| Break Lines | Hidden Lines | Detail Lines |
| ──────── | **NOTES** | ── ─ ── ─ ── |
| Construction Lines | Text | Site Lines |

## AutoCAD linetypes

AutoCAD maintains its standard linetypes in an external file named acad.lin. Before any of these linetypes can be used, they must be loaded. One of AutoCAD's linetypes is required and cannot be deleted from the drawing. The Continuous linetype represents solid lines with no breaks.

The AutoCAD linetypes are shown in **Figure 5-14.** Standard linetypes use only dashes, dots, and gaps. Complex linetypes can also contain special shapes and text.

**Professional Tip**

Two linetype definition files are available: acad.lin and acadiso.lin. The ACAD_ISO linetypes found in both files are identical, but the non-ISO linetype definitions are scaled up 25.4 times in the acadiso.lin file. The scale factor of 25.4 is used to convert from inches to millimeters. The ACAD_ISO linetypes are for metric drawings; if they are used in a US Customary (English) scaled drawing, the linetype scale will need to be modified. The **LTSCALE** system variable controls linetype scaling. This is discussed later in this chapter.

## Changing linetype assignments

To change linetype assignments, select the layer name you want to change and pick its linetype name. This displays the **Select Linetype** dialog box, **Figure 5-15.** The first time you use this dialog box, you may find only the Continuous linetype listed in the **Loaded linetypes** list box. You may need to load additional linetypes before they can be used in the drawing. If you need to add linetypes not included in the list, pick the **Load...** button to display the **Load or Reload Linetypes** dialog box, **Figure 5-16.** The standard, complex, and ACAD_ISO linetypes are listed in the **Available Linetypes** list.

**Note**

The acad.lin file is used by default in the **Load or Reload Linetypes** dialog box. You can switch to the ISO library by picking the **File...** button. This displays the **Select Linetype File** dialog box, where you can select the acadiso.lin file. You can also select custom .lin files.

**Figure 5-14.**
The AutoCAD linetype library contains standard, complex, and ISO linetypes.

| Standard Linetypes | | |
|---|---|---|
| Continuous ————————— | | |
| Border —— —— —— —— —— | Divide — ·· — ·· — ·· — ·· — |
| Border2 —— — — — — — — | Divide2 —·—·—·—·—·—·—·— |
| Borderx2 —— —— —— —— | Dividex2 — ·· — ·· — ·· — |
| Center —— — —— — —— — | Dot ···················· |
| Center2 —— — —— — —— — | Dot2 ···························· |
| Centerx2 —— —— — —— | Dotx2 · · · · · · · · · |
| Dashdot —· —· —· —· —· | Hidden — — — — — — — — |
| Dashdot2 —·—·—·—·—·—· | Hidden2 ——————————— |
| Dashdotx2 —— · —— · —— · | Hiddenx2 — — — — — — — |
| Dashed —— — — — — — | Phantom ———— — — ———— |
| Dashed2 — — — — — — — — | Phantom2 —— - - —— - - —— |
| Dashedx2 —— —— —— —— | Phantomx2 ———— — — ———— |

| Complex Linetypes | ISO Linetypes | |
|---|---|---|
| Fenceline1 —o——o——o— | Acad_iso02w100 — — — — — — — |
| Fenceline2 —□——□——□— | Acad_iso03w100 — — — — — |
| Gas_line —— GAS —— GAS —— | Acad_iso04w100 —— — —— — —— |
| Hot_water_supply —— HW —— HW —— | Acad_iso05w100 —— — —— — —— |
| | Acad_iso06w100 — — — — — |
| | Acad_iso07w100 ···················· |
| Tracks ++++++++++++++++ | Acad_iso08w100 —— — —— — —— |
| | Acad_iso09w100 —— — —— — —— |
| | Acad_iso10w100 — · — · — · — · |
| Zigzag /\/\/\/\/\/\ | Acad_iso11w100 — · — · — · — · |
| | Acad_iso12w100 — · · — · · — · · |
| | Acad_iso13w100 — · · — · · — · · |
| | Acad_iso14w100 — · — · — · — · |
| Batting 〰〰〰〰〰〰 | Acad_iso15w100 — · · — · · — · · |

**Figure 5-15.**
The **Select Linetype** dialog box lists all linetypes currently loaded in the drawing.

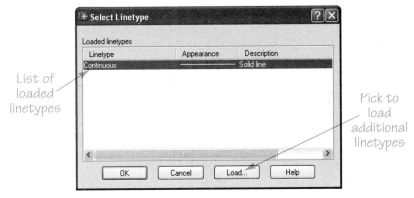

List of loaded linetypes

Pick to load additional linetypes

**Figure 5-16.**
Linetypes must be
loaded into the
drawing using the
**Load or Reload**
**Linetypes** dialog
box.

*Select
to list
linetypes
stored in
acad.lin,
acadiso.lin,
or a
custom
LIN file*

*Select
linetype(s)
to load
into
drawing*

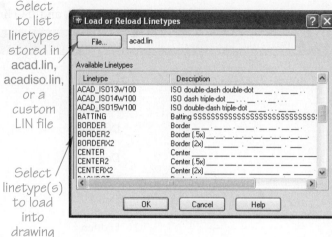

Use the down arrow to look at all the linetypes. Select the linetypes you want to load. Use the [Ctrl] and [Shift] keys to select multiple linetypes as needed. Pick the **OK** button to return to the **Select Linetype** dialog box, where the linetypes you selected are listed. See **Figure 5-17.**

In the **Select Linetype** dialog box, pick the desired linetype, and then pick **OK.** The new linetype is assigned to your selected layer(s) in the **Layer Properties Manager** dialog box. See **Figure 5-18.**

## Managing linetypes

LINETYPE
LT

Format
↳ Linetype...

The **Linetype Manager** dialog box is a convenient place to load and access linetypes. This dialog box can be accessed by selecting **Linetype...** from the **Format** pulldown menu, selecting **Other...** in the **Linetype Control** drop-down list in the **Properties** toolbar, or entering lt or linetype at the Command prompt. See **Figure 5-19.**

This dialog box is similar to the **Layer Properties Manager** dialog box. Picking the **Load...** button opens the **Load or Reload Linetypes** dialog box. Picking the **Delete** button deletes any selected linetypes not being used in the drawing.

**Figure 5-17.**
Linetypes loaded
from the **Load or**
**Reload Linetypes**
dialog box are
added to the **Select**
**Linetype** dialog box.

*Loaded
linetypes
are listed*

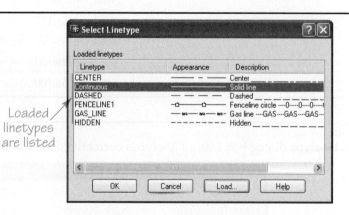

## Figure 5-18.
Objects drawn on the M-Electrical layer will now be drawn with the color Cyan and a CENTER linetype.

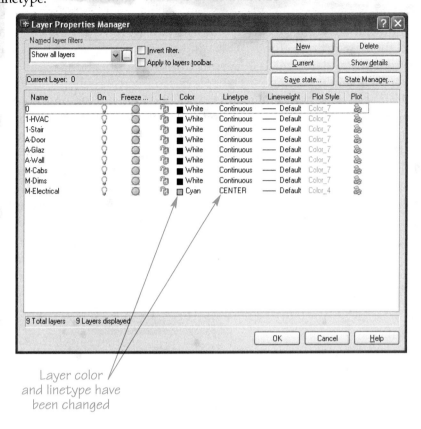

Layer color and linetype have been changed

## Figure 5-19.
Use the **Linetype Manager** dialog box to load linetypes, delete linetypes, and set linetypes as current.

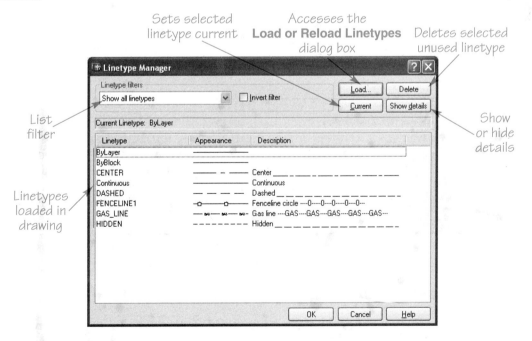

Sets selected linetype current

Accesses the **Load or Reload Linetypes** dialog box

Deletes selected unused linetype

List filter

Show or hide details

Linetypes loaded in drawing

## Changing lineweight assignments

As with a linetype, objects can also have a lineweight. *Lineweight* adds width to objects for display and plotting. Lineweights can be set for objects or assigned to layers. Assigning lineweights to layers allows you to have the objects on specific layers set to their own lineweights. This allows you to control the display of line thickness to match standards related to your drafting application.

The layer lineweight settings are displayed on screen when the lineweight is turned on. To toggle on-screen lineweights, pick the **LWT** button on the status bar, or right-click on the **LWT** button and pick the **On** or **Off** option from the shortcut menu. To change lineweight assignments for a layer, select the layer in the **Layer Properties Manager** and pick its lineweight setting. This displays the **Lineweight** dialog box, **Figure 5-20.** Scroll through the **Lineweight** list to select the desired lineweight.

The **Lineweight** dialog box displays fixed lineweights available in AutoCAD for you to apply to the selected layer. The Default lineweight is the lineweight initially assigned to a layer when it is created. The area near the bottom of the **Lineweight** dialog box displays the original and new lineweight settings for the layer. In **Figure 5-20,** this area shows the lineweight setting will be changed from Default to 0.13 mm.

Figure 5-20.
Use the **Lineweight** dialog box to select the lineweight setting for a layer.

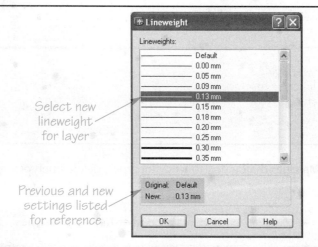

Select new lineweight for layer

Previous and new settings listed for reference

Professional Tip

Layers are meant to simplify the drafting process. They separate different details of the drawing and can reduce the complexity of what is displayed. If you set colors and linetypes for each layer, do not override and mix object linetypes and colors on the same layer. Doing so can mislead you and your colleagues when trying to find certain details.

## Setting the current lineweight

The current lineweight is set in the **Lineweight Settings** dialog box, **Figure 5-21.** The **Lineweight Settings** dialog box can be accessed by picking **Lineweight...** from the **Format** pull-down menu, entering lw or lweight at the Command prompt, or right-clicking on the **LWT** button on the status bar and then selecting **Settings...** in the shortcut menu.

LWEIGHT
LW

Format
↳ Lineweight...

Architectural Drafting Using AutoCAD

**Figure 5-21.**
Set the current lineweight using the **Lineweight Settings** dialog box.

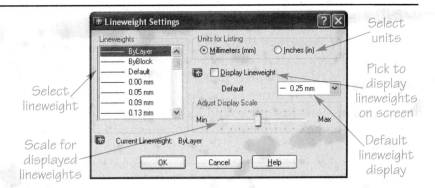

The following describes the features of the **Lineweight Settings** dialog box:

- **Lineweights** drop-down list. Set the current lineweight by selecting the desired setting from the list. If the lineweight is set to ByLayer, the object lineweight corresponds to the lineweight of its layer. Settings other than ByLayer, ByBlock, or Default are used as overrides.
- **Units for Listing** area. This area allows you to display lineweight thickness in **Millimeters (mm)** or **Inches (in)**.
- **Display Lineweight** check box. This is another way to turn the visibility of lineweights on or off. Check this box to turn lineweights on in the drawing.
- **Default** drop-down list. Select a lineweight default value from the drop-down list. This becomes the default lineweight for layers. The initial default setting is **0.25 mm** (or **0.010"**).
- **Adjust Display Scale** area. The scale allows you to adjust the lineweight display scale to improve the appearance of different lineweight widths. Adjustment of the lineweight display scale toward the maximum value can reduce AutoCAD performance. A minimum setting or a setting near the middle of the scale may be preferred.
- **Current Lineweight:** area. This indicates the current lineweight setting.

Note

The **Properties** toolbar displays the current color, linetype, lineweight, and plot style. If the color, linetype, and lineweight are set to ByLayer, newly drawn objects will assume the layer settings for color, linetype, and lineweight. This is the preferred way to assign object properties because the layer settings can determine the properties of multiple objects. An object can have any of these properties overridden by changing the ByLayer value to the desired value.

## Exercise 5-5

- ◆ Open ex5-1 if it is not already open.
- ◆ Open the **Select Linetype** dialog box and notice the default linetype.
- ◆ Pick the **Load...** button and load FENCELINE1, CENTER, DASHED, HIDDEN, and PHANTOM.
- ◆ Pick the **OK** button.
- ◆ Apply the HIDDEN, CENTER, and PHANTOM linetypes to the layers of your choice.
- ◆ Apply the lineweight of 0.80 mm to the M-Wall layer.
- ◆ Open the **Lineweight Settings** dialog box and experiment with lineweight settings. Draw a few lines after each setting to see the results.
- ◆ Save your work and exit AutoCAD, or keep this drawing open for the next exercise.

## Using Layer Details

The **Layer Properties Manager** dialog box contains a **Show details** button. When this button is selected, a new area is displayed at the bottom of the existing dialog box, as shown in **Figure 5-22**. In addition, the **Show details** button changes to a **Hide details** button. The features of the **Details** area are disabled unless one or more of the layers in the layer list are highlighted. The **Details** area provides an alternate way of entering the same information that can be entered in the upper area.

**Figure 5-22.**
You can set layer properties and status in the **Details** area of the **Layer Properties Manager** dialog box.

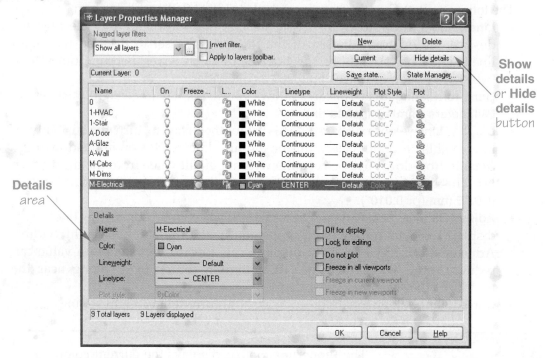

## Layer Filters

In some applications, large numbers of layer names may be used to assist in drawing information management. Having all layer names showing at the same time in the layer list can make it difficult to work with your drawing layers. *Layer filters* are used to screen, or filter out, any layers you do not want displayed in the **Layer Properties Manager** dialog box. The **Named layer filters** area of the **Layer Properties Manager** provides options for filtering out unwanted layer names. See **Figure 5-23**. The default options are explained below:

- **Show all layers.** This is the default option, and it shows all defined layer names.
- **Show all used layers.** The current layer and any layers containing drawing objects are displayed.
- **Show all Xref dependent layers.** Xrefs are discussed in Chapter 17. This option displays all layers brought in with externally referenced drawings.
- **Invert filter.** In addition to the default layer filter options, you can also invert, or reverse, the layer filter setting. For example, there is a choice to show all used layers, but what if you want to show all unused layers? In this case, you would choose the **Show all used layers** option, and then you would check the **Invert filter** check box to invert, or reverse, your choice.
- **Apply to layers toolbar.** Check this toggle if you want only the layers that match the current filter displayed in the **Layer Control** drop-down list in the **Layers** toolbar.

Architectural Drafting Using AutoCAD

**Figure 5-23.**
The **Named layer filters** area provides options for filtering layers.

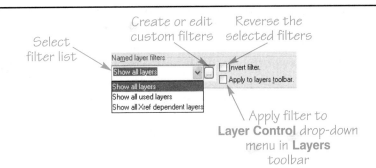

Select filter list

Create or edit custom filters

Reverse the selected filters

Apply filter to **Layer Control** drop-down menu in **Layers** toolbar

Perhaps the most powerful aspect of the **Named layer filters** area is the feature allowing you to create and save custom filters. To create or edit a custom layer filter, select the ellipsis (...) button to the right of the drop-down arrow. Picking this button displays the **Named Layer Filters** dialog box, **Figure 5-24.**

For example, you could define a filter that displays only layers with names beginning with the number *1*. To create a layer filter with these properties, press the ellipsis (...) button to display the **Named Layer Filters** dialog box, and enter the values displayed in **Figure 5-24.** Pick the **Add** button when finished, and then pick the **Close** button to exit the **Named Layer Filters** dialog box. You can select the layer filter named 1st floor layers from the filter list in the **Layer Properties Manager** dialog box whenever you want to hide layers that do not meet these requirements. The following is an explanation of the various features of the **Named Layer Filters** dialog box:

- **Filter name.** Filter names are saved in this list. To create a new filter, type a name in the text box and pick the **Add** button. To delete an existing filter, select the name in the list and pick the **Delete** button. Use the **Reset** button to clear all user-defined filter settings. Picking the **Delete All** button deletes all user-defined filters.

- **Layer name.** Use this filter to display layers by name. For example, a single layer name can be entered in this text box if that is the only layer to be listed. Wild card characters can be used to filter a specific group of layers. For example, the layer name M* would filter all layers beginning with *M*, such as M-Wall01, M-Wall02, and M-Wall03. Multiple layers can be filtered by placing a comma to separate the layer values. For example, an entry of Door,Window,M* would display the Door and Window layers, plus all layers beginning with *M*.

**Figure 5-24.**
You can create custom filters using the **Named Layer Filters** dialog box.

Select existing filter or enter name for new filter

Enter text string for layer names to pass filter

Define layer status to pass filter

Define layer properties to pass filter

Add or update a filter

Delete a filter

Reset default values for filter

Named Layer Filters

Filter name: 1st floor layers    Add

Layer name: 1*    Delete / Reset / Delete All

On/Off: Both
Freeze/Thaw: Both
Current viewport: Both
New viewport: Both
Lock/Unlock: Both
Plot: Both
Color: *
Lineweight: *
Linetype: *
Plot style: *

Close    Help

- **On/Off.** Use this filter to display names of layers that are either on or off. The default for this setting is to display both cases.
- **Freeze/Thaw.** Use this filter to display names of either frozen or thawed layers.
- **Current viewport.** Use this filter to display names of layers frozen or thawed in the current viewport. (Viewports are discussed later in this text.)
- **New viewport.** Use this filter to display names of layers frozen or thawed in new viewports.
- **Lock/Unlock.** Use this filter to display names of either locked or unlocked layers.
- **Plot.** Use this filter to display names of layers set to plot or not to plot.
- **Color.** Use this filter to display layer names by color designation. Use color numbers or names. For example, you can use red or 1.
- **Lineweight.** Use this filter to display layer names by lineweight designation.
- **Linetype.** Use this filter to display layer names by linetype.
- **Plot style.** Use this filter to display layer names by plot style.

## Exercise 5-6

◆ Open ex5-1 if it is not already open.
◆ Create a named layer filter called Architectural layers. In the **Named Layer Filters** dialog box, enter A* in the **Layer name** text box, and leave the other settings at the default values.
◆ Select the **Apply to layers toolbar** check box in the **Layer Properties Manager** and see the results in the **Layers** toolbar layer list. Deselect the **Apply to layers toolbar** check box and look at the results in the **Layers** toolbar layer list.
◆ Save the exercise as ex5-6.

## Layer States

Layer settings, such as on/off, frozen/thawed, and locked/unlocked, determine whether or not a layer is displayed, plotted, and editable. The status of layer settings for all layers in the drawing can be saved as a named *layer state*. Once a layer state is saved, the settings can be reset by selecting the layer state.

For example, a basic architectural drawing uses the layers shown in **Figure 5-25.** From this drawing file, three different drawings are plotted: a floor plan, a plumbing plan, and an electrical plan. The following chart shows the layer settings for each of the three drawings:

| Layer Name | Floor Plan | Plumbing Plan | Electrical Plan |
|---|---|---|---|
| 0 | Off | Off | Off |
| Dimension-Electrical | Frozen | Frozen | On |
| Dimension-Floor Plan | On | Frozen | Frozen |
| Dimension-Plumbing | Frozen | On | Frozen |
| Electrical | Frozen | Frozen | On |
| Floor Plan Notes | On | Frozen | Frozen |
| Plumbing | Frozen | On | Frozen |
| Title Block | On | Locked | Locked |
| Walls | On | Locked | Locked |
| Windows and Doors | On | Frozen | Frozen |

Architectural Drafting Using AutoCAD

**Figure 5-25.**
Layers for a basic architectural drawing.

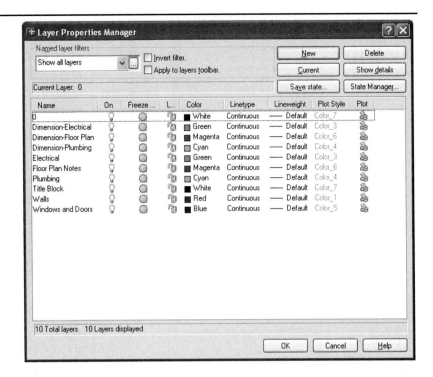

Each of the three groups of settings can be saved as an individual layer state. Once the layer state is created, the settings can be restored by simply restoring the layer state. This is easier than changing the settings for each layer individually.

To save a layer state, first set the layer settings you wish to save. Pick the **Save state...** button to access the **Save Layer States** dialog box. See **Figure 5-26.** Enter a name for the layer state and pick the settings and properties to be saved. Only saved settings and properties are reset when the layer state is restored. For this example, the three layer states (with settings) shown in **Figure 5-27** are created.

Once a layer state is saved, it can be restored at any time. By restoring a layer state, the layer settings are automatically changed to match the settings saved in the layer state. To restore a layer state, pick the **State Manager...** button in the **Layer Properties Manager** dialog box. This accesses the **Layer States Manager** dialog box, **Figure 5-28.** Select a layer state from the **Layer states** list and pick one of the following buttons:

- **Restore.** Restores the settings saved in the selected layer state.
- **Edit.** Accesses the **Edit layer state** dialog box, where you can select which settings and properties are saved in the layer state. You cannot change the value of layer settings in this dialog box.

**Figure 5-26.**
Only selected settings and properties are saved in the layer state. The settings not saved are not reset when the layer state is restored.

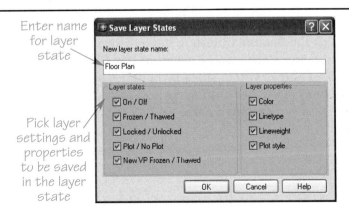

**Figure 5-27.**
The layer states and saved layer settings.

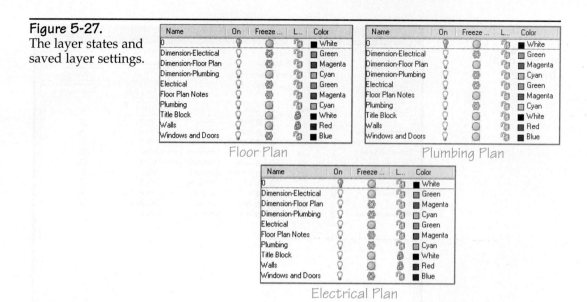

Floor Plan

Plumbing Plan

Electrical Plan

**Figure 5-28.**
Use the **Layer States Manager** dialog box to restore, modify, import, or export existing layer states.

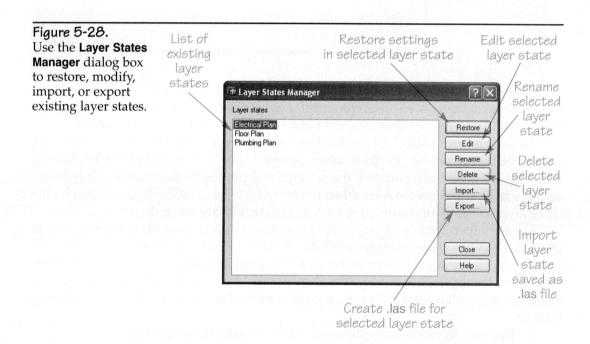

List of existing layer states

Restore settings in selected layer state

Edit selected layer state

Rename selected layer state

Delete selected layer state

Import layer state saved as .las file

Create .las file for selected layer state

- **Rename.** Allows you to rename the layer state.
- **Delete.** Deletes the selected layer state.
- **Import.** Accesses a standard file selection dialog box where you can select an .las file containing an existing layer state. Imported layer states are listed in the **Layer states** list in the **Layer State Manager**. Select the imported layer state and pick the **Restore** button to have the settings restored.
- **Export.** Layer states can be saved as .las files and imported into other drawings. This allows you to share layer states between drawings containing identical layers. Pick this button to access a standard file selection dialog box, where you can specify a name and location for the .las file.

# Changing Object Properties

You should always draw objects on an appropriate layer, but layer settings are not permanent. If needed, you can change an object's layer. You can also change other properties of the object, such as color, linetype, and lineweight. These properties can be modified using the **Properties** toolbar or the **Properties** window.

To modify properties using the **Properties** toolbar, select the object first, and then use the drop-down lists to change the property. After you have changed the properties, press [Esc] to deselect the object.

Before modifying an object's properties in the **Properties** window, you must first display the window. To display the **Properties** window, pick the **Properties** button in the **Standard** toolbar; select **Properties** from the **Tools** or **Modify** pull-down menu; enter props, pr, ch, mo, or properties at the Command prompt; or use the [Ctrl]+[1] key combination. Double-clicking on most objects selects the object and opens the **Properties** window. If an object has been selected, you can also right-click and pick **Properties** from the shortcut menu. When you do this, AutoCAD displays the **Properties** window, **Figure 5-29A**.

The properties of the selected object are listed in the **Properties** window. The specific properties listed vary, depending on the type of object selected. Properties such as **Color**, **Layer**, and **Linetype** are listed in the **General** category.

To modify a particular object property, first find the property in the **Properties** window, and then select its value. Depending on the type of value, a specific editing method is activated. Use this tool to change the value. For example, if you want to change an object's layer, pick the **Layer** property to highlight it, as in **Figure 5-29B**. A drop-down arrow is displayed to the right of the layer name. Pick the arrow to access the drop-down list, and pick the layer name you want to use for the selected object's layer. You can use this same process to change the color, linetype, or lineweight of a selected object or objects.

PROPERTIES
PROPS
PR
CH
MO
[Ctrl]+[1]

Tools
➥ Properties
Modify
➥ Properties

Standard
toolbar

Properties

---

**Figure 5-29.**
The **Properties** window is used to modify the properties of the selected object. A—Properties are arranged in categories. B—Changing the layer of the object.

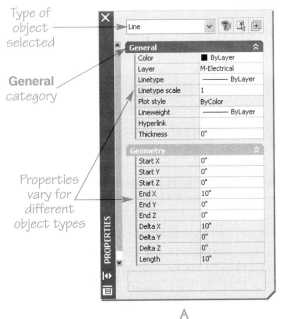

---

You can work in AutoCAD with the **Properties** window open and available for use. By picking and holding on the title bar while you move the mouse, you can move the **Properties** window. This window can also be hidden by right-clicking on the title bar and selecting **Auto-hide** from the shortcut menu. If you want to close the **Properties** window, select the X in the title bar.

Note

Modifying object properties using the **Properties** window is covered in greater depth in Chapter 7.

## Exercise 5-7

◆ Open ex5-1 if it is not already open.
◆ Use the **Layer Control** drop-down list in the **Layers** toolbar to experiment with making different layers current. Draw an object each time you change to a new current layer. Draw objects based on what you have already learned, such as line segments, circles, and polylines.
◆ Select an object and change its layer using the **Layer Control** drop-down list. Do this again, but this time, select more than one object and change the layer in the **Properties** window.
◆ Use the **Properties** window to make other changes to objects, such as color and linetype.
◆ Save your work and exit AutoCAD, or keep this drawing open for the next exercise.

# Overriding Layer Settings

Colors, linetypes, and lineweights reference layer settings by default. This means when you create a layer, you also establish a color, linetype, and lineweight to go with the layer. This is what it means when the color, linetype, and lineweight are specified as ByLayer. This is the most common method for managing these settings.

Sometimes, however, you may need objects with color, linetype, or lineweight properties different from the layer settings. In such a situation, the color, linetype, and lineweight can be set to an absolute value, and current layer settings are ignored. The term *absolute*, as used here and in future content, refers to an object being assigned specific properties that are not reliant on a layer or block for their definition.

## Setting Color

The current object color can be easily set by selecting the **Color Control** drop-down list from the **Properties** toolbar. See **Figure 5-30.** The default setting is ByLayer. This is the recommended setting for most applications. To change this setting, pick another color from the list. If the color you want is not in the list, pick **Select Color...** to display the **Select Color** dialog box. You can also access the **Select Color** dialog box by entering col or color at the Command prompt or by picking **Color...** from the **Format** pull-down menu. Once a color other than ByLayer is specified, all new objects are drawn in the specified color, regardless of the current layer settings.

**Figure 5-30.**
The current object color is easily set using the **Color Control** drop-down list in the **Properties** toolbar. This control box is also used to change the color of any selected objects.

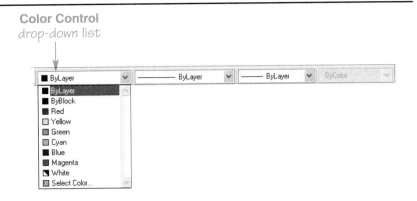

Color Control drop-down list

## Exercise 5-8

◆ Start a new drawing using a template or startup option of your own choice.
◆ Set up the following four layers using the **Layer Properties Manager** dialog box. Use the following settings:

| Layer name | Linetype | Color |
|------------|----------|-------|
| Object | Continuous | White |
| Hidden | HIDDEN | Red |
| Center | CENTER | Yellow |
| Phantom | PHANTOM | Cyan |

◆ Draw the objects shown below using approximate dimensions. Place the objects on the layers that have their linetypes.

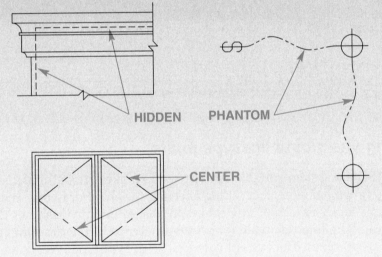

HIDDEN    PHANTOM

CENTER

◆ Save the drawing as **ex5-8**.

## Setting Linetype

Similar to the way you can set the current object color, you can set the current object linetype to be separate from the layer settings. To set the current object linetype, pick the **Linetype Control** drop-down list from the **Properties** toolbar and select the desired linetype. See **Figure 5-31.** If the linetype you want has not been loaded into the current drawing yet, it will not appear in the listing.

**Figure 5-31.**
The current object linetype is easily set by opening the **Linetype Control** drop-down list in the **Properties** toolbar. Only linetypes loaded into the current drawing are listed here.

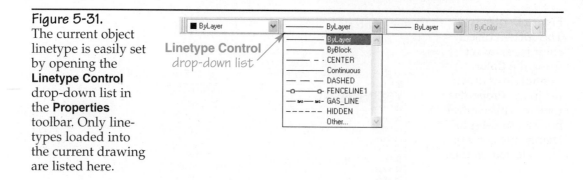

Linetype Control drop-down list

## Setting the linetype scale

The linetype scale sets the lengths of dashes and spaces in linetypes. The default object linetype scale factor is 1.0. As with color, the linetype scale can be changed at the object level. One reason for changing the default linetype scale is to make your drawing more closely match standard drafting practices.

Earlier, you were introduced to the **Properties** window. When a line object is selected to modify, a **Linetype scale** property is listed. You can change the linetype scale of the object by entering a new value in this field. A value less than 1.0 makes the dashes and spaces smaller than those of the default linetype scale setting, while a value greater than 1.0 makes the dashes and spaces larger. Using this, you can experiment with different linetype scales until you achieve the desired results. Be careful when changing linetype scales to avoid making your drawing look odd, with a variety of line formats. **Figure 5-32** shows different linetype scale factors.

**Figure 5-32.**
This table shows the effect of linetype scale.

| Scale Factor | Line |
|:---:|:---:|
| 0.5 | —— – – – —— – – – —— – – – —— |
| 1.0 | —— – – —— – – —— – – —— |
| 2.0 | —————  ——  ————— |

## Changing the global linetype scale

The **LTSCALE** system variable can be used to make a global change to the linetype scale. The term *global* refers to a setting affecting the entire drawing. The default global linetype scale factor is 1.0000. Any line with dashes initially assumes this factor.

To change the linetype scale for all the linetypes in the drawing, enter ltscale at the Command prompt. The current value is listed. Type a new value and press [Enter]. A Regenerating model. message appears on the command line, as the global linetype scale is changed for all lines on the drawing.

The global linetype scale (**LTSCALE**) setting does not override the linetype scale property for a single line object—it provides additional scaling. An object's linetype is the product of the linetype object property and the global linetype scale. When the **Properties** window is displayed, and no object is selected (No selection), the linetype scale setting sets the current linetype scale, not the global linetype scale. That is, this sets the object-level linetype scale for the next line drawn.

Architectural Drafting Using AutoCAD

## Setting Lineweight

Similar to the way you can set the current object linetype, you can set the current object lineweight to differ from the layer settings. To set the current object lineweight, pick the **Lineweight Control** drop-down list from the **Properties** toolbar and select the desired lineweight. See **Figure 5-33.** Any new objects created now assume the current lineweight, regardless of the current layer settings.

**Figure 5-33.**
The current object lineweight is easily set using the **Lineweight Control** drop-down list in the **Layers** toolbar.

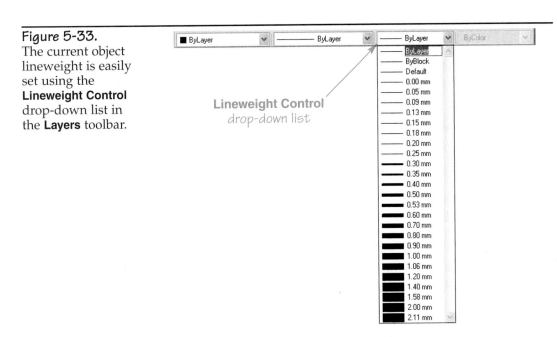

Lineweight Control drop-down list

**Note** Colors, linetypes, and lineweights are often set as ByLayer. A ByLayer color is known as a *logical color,* while colors such as red are known as *explicit colors.* If an object uses ByLayer as its color, the object assumes the color of its layer. Explicit properties override logical properties. Therefore, if an object's color is set *explicitly* to red, it appears red, regardless of the object's layer. Change its color to ByLayer, and it uses the layer color. *It is a common AutoCAD mistake for users to set the color, linetype, or lineweight to some value other than ByLayer and then wonder why new objects do not use the settings of the current layer!*

## Undoing Changes to Layer Settings

You can undo changes to layer settings using the **LAYERP** command. To access the **LAYERP** command, pick the **Layer Previous** button in the **Layers** toolbar or enter layerp at the Command prompt. The **LAYERP** command undoes the previous change or set of changes made in the **Layer Properties Manager** dialog box or the **Layer Control** drop-down list in the **Layers** toolbar. For example, if you change the current layer from Walls to Dimensions using the **Layer Control** drop-down list, picking the **Layer Previous** button resets Walls as the current layer. If you need to freeze a group of layers prior to plotting, you can freeze the layers using the **Layer Properties Manager** dialog box, plot the drawing, and then "thaw" the layers with the **LAYERP**

LAYERP

Layers toolbar

Layer Previous

command. The **LAYERP** command can be used multiple times to undo several layer setting changes. The **LAYERPMODE** command must be set to the **ON** option in order for the **LAYERP** command to function.

## Exercise 5-9

◆ Open ex5-8.
◆ Change the **LTSCALE** system variable to 0.5, to 1.5, and then back to 1. Observe the effect to the lines each time it is changed.
◆ Using the **Properties** window, change the linetype scale of only the hidden line to 0.5, to 1.5, and then back to 1.
◆ Using the **Properties** window, change the linetype scale of only the centerline to 0.5, to 1.5, and then back to 1.
◆ Experiment with other linetype scales if you wish, and then change them back to 1.
◆ Save the drawing as ex5-9.

## Additional Layering Tools

In addition to the standard layering tools discussed throughout this chapter, there are several AutoCAD Express Tools useful for working with layers. If the Express Tools are installed with AutoCAD 2004, the **Express** pull-down menu includes a **Layers** cascading menu. The tools in this menu are described as follows:

• **Layer Manager.** The **Layer Manager...** option allows you to create layer states within the drawing. Choosing it opens the **Layer Manager: Save and Restore Layer Settings** dialog box. This is very similar to using the **Save state...** and **State Manager...** buttons in the **Layer Properties Manager**. This utility was available in releases prior to AutoCAD 2000 as a means of creating and managing layer states before the command was added to standard AutoCAD.

• **Layer Walk.** Selecting this command opens the **LayerWalk - Layers:** dialog box. See **Figure 5-34A.** This tool lists all the layers in the drawing in a list box. Selecting a layer name in the list causes all the layers in the drawing to be

**Figure 5-34.**
A—The **LayerWalk - Layers:** dialog box lists all the layers in the drawing in a list box. B—The **LayerWalk - Layers:** dialog box allows you to enter filter criteria to screen for layer names with specific characters. The list box then displays the layers meeting your criteria.

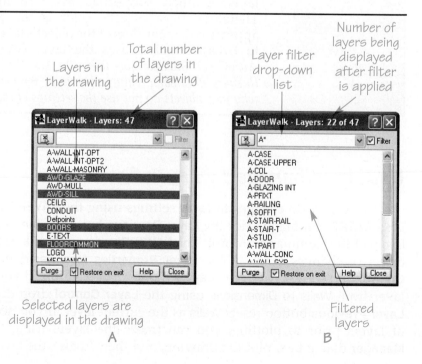

Layers in the drawing

Total number of layers in the drawing

Layer filter drop-down list

Number of layers being displayed after filter is applied

Selected layers are displayed in the drawing

A

Filtered layers

B

turned off, except for the selected layer. This provides a means for you to "walk" through a drawing full of layers to see which objects are drawn on which layers. Using the [Shift] or [Ctrl] keys to select layer names causes the objects on those layers to display. You can also enter a character in the filter list to have the **LayerWalk** routine filter for layers with specific characters. Layers meeting your filter criteria are then displayed in the list box, as shown in **Figure 5-34B**.

- **Layer Match.** Using this command allows you to select objects that need their layer to match another object's layer. First, select the objects whose layers will be changed, and then select an object whose layer will be matched.
- **Change to Current Layer.** This command allows you to pick objects on a layer and have them moved to the current layer instead.
- **Copy Objects to New Layer.** Use this command to copy objects in the drawing to a new layer and move the copies to a new location. After selecting the objects you want to copy, this command will display the **COPYTOLAYER** dialog box, where you can select the layer to which the objects will be moved. After selecting the layer, you have the opportunity to choose a base point from which to move the objects, and you can specify a displacement point or new location for the copied objects.
- **Layer Isolate.** This command turns off all the layers in the drawing, except for the layer of an object you pick.
- **Isolate Layer to Current Viewport.** This command is similar to the **Layer Isolate** command, but it freezes the selected layer in all paper space viewports, except the current viewport. Layer control for paper space viewports is discussed later in this text.
- **Layer Off.** You can use this command when you desire to turn off a layer. Select an object whose layer you wish to turn off, and the layer will be turned off.
- **Turn All Layers On.** This command turns on all layers that have been turned off.
- **Layer Freeze.** Similar to the **Layer Off** command, this command freezes the layer of an object you select.
- **Thaw All Layers.** This command thaws all frozen layers in the drawing.
- **Layer Lock.** Use this command to lock the layer of an object you select.
- **Layer Unlock.** Use this command to unlock any locked layers in the drawing.
- **Layer Merge.** This command allows you to merge objects on two layers to a single layer. First, select the objects needing to be moved to a different layer. Next, select an object on the layer where you want the first selected objects to be merged. Once you have done this, the layer the first selected objects were on is deleted from the drawing.
- **Layer Delete.** This command deletes all objects on a layer you choose and then deletes the selected layer.

This is a brief description of these commands. Getting to know these will help you become more productive when manipulating layer displays. For additional information on these commands and other Express Tools, access the **Help** command at the bottom of the **Express** pull-down menu.

# Chapter Test

*Answer the following questions on a separate piece of paper.*

1. Define *layers*.
2. List five ways layers can be used to increase productivity.
3. What is the name of the AutoCAD default layer?
4. Layer names can have up to how many characters?
5. Identify the AIA publication that provides layer conventions.
6. Identify two ways to open the **Layer Properties Manager** dialog box.
7. Define *current layer*.
8. Describe the process for adding a layer named Wall to a drawing.
9. How do you delete a layer?
10. Identify two ways to set a layer as current.
11. What is the difference between turning a layer off and freezing the layer?
12. How do you change a layer's color?
13. Define *linetype*.
14. What does *ByLayer* mean?
15. How do you load linetypes?
16. How do you change a layer's linetype?
17. Define *lineweight*.
18. How can you control the display of lineweights on screen?
19. What is the purpose of layer filters?
20. Identify a case when it might be a good idea to filter out some layer names.
21. How do you modify the properties of an object using the **Properties** toolbar?
22. Identify five ways to access the **Properties** window.
23. How do you change an object's layer if the object has been selected, and the **Properties** window is open?
24. How can you change the linetype scale of an individual line in the drawing?
25. Name the system variable used to change the linetype scale of all lines in a drawing.

# Chapter Problems

1. Create the following layers: Book, Chair, Computer, Desk, and Lamp. Assign any color desired to each layer. Create the following drawing, placing the objects on the appropriate layers. Scale is not important. Do not draw notes. Save the drawing as p5-2.

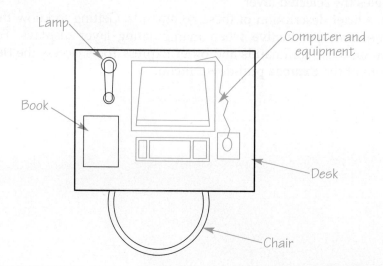

Architectural Drafting Using AutoCAD

2. Create the following layers: Bolts, Foundation, Framing, Hidden, Nailing, Plywood, and Straps. Assign any color desired to each layer. Assign the HIDDEN linetype to the Hidden layer, the HIDDEN2 linetype to the Bolts layer, and the DOT2 linetype to the Nailing layer. Create the following drawing, placing the objects on the appropriate layers. Scale is not important. Do not draw notes. Save the drawing as p5-3.

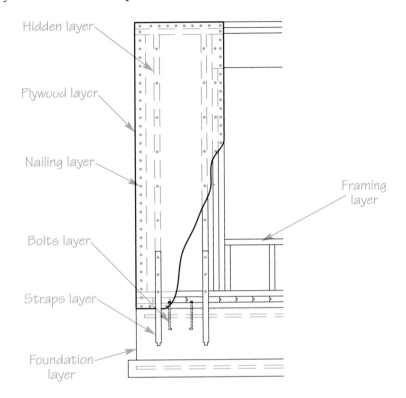

3. Open the drawings of your choice, or those assigned by your instructor, from Chapters 3 and 4, and assign the objects to layers of your choice using the **Properties** window and the **Properties** toolbar. Establish layer names and colors, as discussed in this chapter.

4. Establish a template that has layers set up to match the preferred standards of your company or school. If there are no specific standards available, use one of the layer name formats described in this chapter or the AIA layer guidelines provided in Appendix A of this book. Save the template as architectural layers for use when starting future drawings.

Different drawings making up a single project are easily distinguished through the use of layers. Standard naming conventions and color assignments are used to clarify the content.

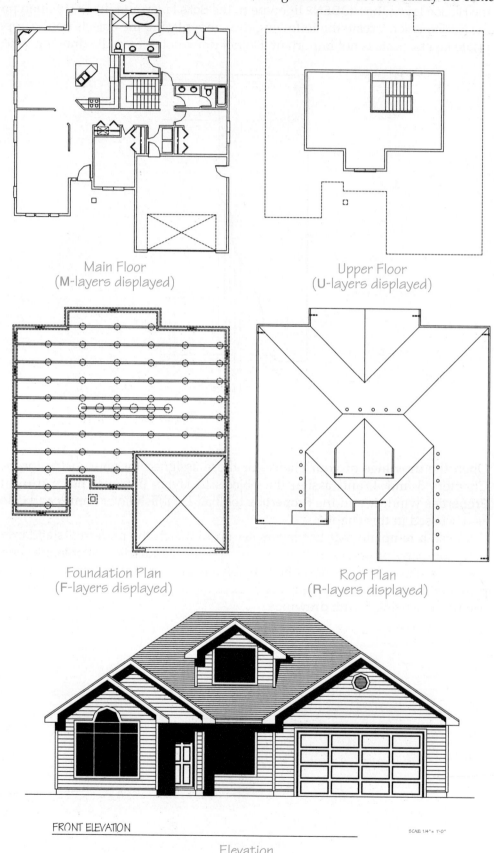

Main Floor
(M-layers displayed)

Upper Floor
(U-layers displayed)

Foundation Plan
(F-layers displayed)

Roof Plan
(R-layers displayed)

FRONT ELEVATION                          SCALE 1/4" = 1'-0"

Elevation
(E-layers displayed)

# Basic Editing Commands

## Learning Objectives

After completing this chapter, you will be able to:

- Relocate objects using the **MOVE** command.
- Make single and multiple copies of existing objects using the **COPY** command.
- Use different methods to select objects for editing.
- Use object cycling to select overlapping geometry.
- Understand the use of the Quick Select feature.
- Change the angular position of an object using the **ROTATE** command.
- Change the size of an object using the **SCALE** command.
- Modify the length of an object using the **STRETCH** command.
- Create a mirror image of objects.
- Use the **EXPLODE** command to break up objects.
- Remove a portion of a line, circle, or arc using the **BREAK** command.
- Use the **TRIM** and **EXTEND** commands to edit an object.
- Modify the length of an object using the **LENGTHEN** command.
- Use the **PEDIT** command to modify polylines.

## Important Terms

base point
boundary edge
curve fitting
cutting edge
cycling
displacement
filter

implied intersection
mirror line
point of tangency
polygon
qualifying object
stacked objects
polyline vertex

This chapter explains commands and methods for changing a drawing. With manual drafting techniques, editing and modifying a drawing can take hours or even days. AutoCAD makes the same editing tasks simpler and quicker. In Chapter 3 you learned how to draw and erase lines. The **ERASE** command is one of the most commonly used editing commands.

This chapter will show you the methods used to select objects in order to modify them. You will also learn how to move, copy, rotate, scale, and create a mirror image of an existing object, plus a few other commands used to modify geometry. These features are found in the **Modify** toolbar and the **Modify** pull-down menu.

> **Note**
>
> This chapter describes most AutoCAD editing commands. However, some editing commands are discussed in other chapters. The **FILLET** and **CHAMFER** commands are covered in Chapter 16. The **ARRAY** command is discussed in Chapter 18.

# Moving an Object

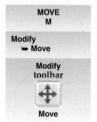

In many situations, you may find that the location of a view or feature is not where you want it. This problem is easy to fix using the **MOVE** command. You can access the **MOVE** command by picking the **Move** button in the **Modify** toolbar, picking **Move** from the **Modify** pull-down menu, or entering m or move at the Command prompt.

After the **MOVE** command is accessed, AutoCAD asks you to select the objects to be moved. Pick the objects you would like moved. Once the items are selected, press [Enter] to end the selection process. The next prompt requests the base point. The *base point* provides a reference point. Most drafters select a point on an object, the corner of a view, or the center of a circle using object snap modes. The next prompt asks for the second point of displacement. This is the new position for the objects. All selected objects are moved the distance from the base point to the displacement point. The *displacement* is the direction and distance that you move the object.

The following **MOVE** operation relates to the object shown in **Figure 6-1.** As the base point is picked, the object is automatically dragged into position. This is the command sequence:

**Figure 6-1.**
Using the **MOVE** command. When you select the object to be moved, it becomes highlighted. You pick the base point and move the object to the second point.

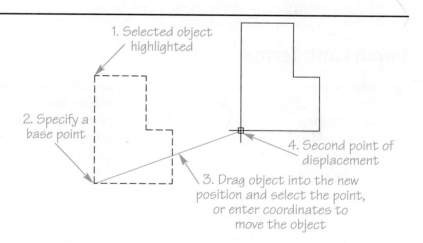

1. Selected object highlighted
2. Specify a base point
3. Drag object into the new position and select the point, or enter coordinates to move the object
4. Second point of displacement

Command: **m** *or* **move**↵
Select objects: *(select the object or objects to be moved)*
Select objects: ↵
Specify base point or displacement: *(enter coordinates or pick a point on screen)*
Specify second point of displacement or <use first point as displacement>: *(establish the new position by entering coordinates or picking a second point on screen)*
Command:

## Using the First Point as Displacement

In the previous **MOVE** command, you selected a base point and then selected a second point of displacement. The object moved the distance and direction that you specified. You can also move the object relative to the first point. The coordinates you use to select the base point are automatically used as the coordinates for the direction and distance when moving the object. The following command sequence moves an object 2″ along the X axis and 4″ along the Y axis:

Command: **m** *or* **move**↵
Select objects: *(select the objects to move)*
Select objects: ↵
Specify base point or displacement: **2,4**↵
Specify second point of displacement or <use first point as displacement>: ↵
Command:

**Professional Tip**
Always use object snap modes to your best advantage with editing commands. For example, suppose you want to move an object from the corner of an object to the center point of a circle. Use the Endpoint object snap to select the corner as the base point and the Center object snap to select the center of the circle as the second point of displacement.

## Copying Objects

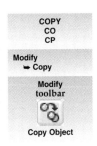
COPY
CO
CP

Modify
↳ Copy

Modify toolbar

Copy Object

The **COPY** command is used to make a copy of an existing object or objects. To access the **COPY** command, pick the **Copy** button in the **Modify** toolbar, select **Copy** from the **Modify** pull-down menu, or enter co, cp, or copy at the Command prompt. The command prompts are the same as those for the **MOVE** command. However, when a second point of displacement is picked, the original object remains and a copy is drawn. The following command sequence is illustrated in **Figure 6-2**:

Command: **co**, **cp**, *or* **copy**↵
Select objects: *(select the objects to be copied)*
Select objects: ↵
Specify base point or displacement, or [Multiple]: *(select base point or enter displacement)*
Specify second point of displacement or <use first point as displacement>: *(pick second point or press* [Enter] *if displacement was specified)*
Command:

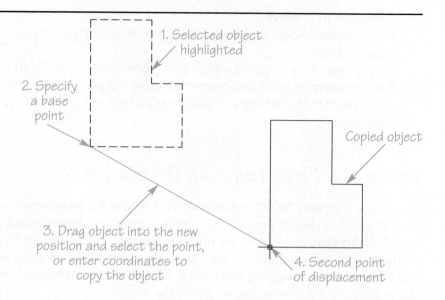

**Figure 6-2.**
Using the **COPY** command.

1. Selected object highlighted

2. Specify a base point

3. Drag object into the new position and select the point, or enter coordinates to copy the object

Copied object

4. Second point of displacement

The **COPY** command is similar to the **MOVE** command. However, instead of moving the selected objects, you are copying them to a new location. The placement of the copied object is determined by specifying either two points or a displacement.

## Making Multiple Copies

To make several copies of the same object, select the **Multiple** option of the **COPY** command by entering m at the Specify base point or displacement, or [Multiple]: prompt. The prompt for a second point repeats. When you have made all the copies needed, press [Enter]. The results are shown in **Figure 6-3.**

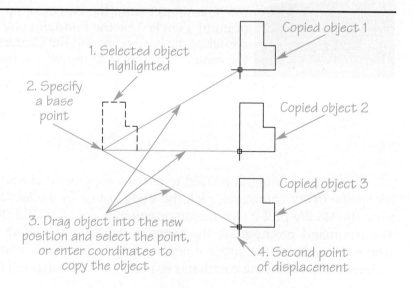

**Figure 6-3.**
Using the **Multiple** option in the **COPY** command.

1. Selected object highlighted

2. Specify a base point

3. Drag object into the new position and select the point, or enter coordinates to copy the object

Copied object 1

Copied object 2

Copied object 3

4. Second point of displacement

Architectural Drafting Using AutoCAD

## Exercise 6-1

◆ Start a new drawing using a template or startup option of your own choice.
◆ Set architectural units.
◆ Set the Endpoint and Intersection running object snap modes.
◆ Draw a square and an equilateral triangle (equal sides and angles) using the **POLYGON** command.
◆ Move the square to a new location that is 3″ to the right and 2″ up (use the relative coordinates @3,2).
◆ Move the triangle by specifying a displacement of 2,4 at the Specify base point or displacement prompt.
◆ Copy the triangle from one of its corners to a corner of the new square position.
◆ Move all features to a new position in the upper-left corner of the screen.
◆ Copy the original triangle by specifying the coordinates 2,4 at the Specify base point or displacement prompt.
◆ Make four copies of the square anywhere on the screen. The new copies should not touch other objects.
◆ Save the drawing as ex6-1.

# Selection Methods

So far, we have looked at three different modifying commands: **ERASE**, **MOVE**, and **COPY**. As you worked with these commands, did you notice a pattern? Before the commands would execute, they required you to select objects to be modified. The same is true of all modifying commands. In Chapter 3, you were introduced to the **ERASE** command. In order to select items to be erased, you needed to "pick" them. Often, picking objects can get a bit tedious, especially if there are a number of items that need to be moved, copied, or erased.

There are a number of options available for selecting objects. You have already looked at the first option. This is the ability to move the pick box directly over the object and pick it. The next section describes the other options available.

## Making a Single Selection Automatically

Normally, AutoCAD lets you pick as many items as you want for a selection set, and the selected items are highlighted to let you know what has been picked. You also have the option of selecting a single item and having it automatically edited without first being highlighted. To do this, enter si (for Single) at the Select objects: prompt. To select several items with this method, use the **Window** or **Crossing** selection options (discussed later in this chapter). The command sequence is as follows:

Command: **e** *or* **erase.**↵
Select objects: **si**↵
Select objects: *(pick an individual item, or use the* **Window** *or* **Crossing** *option to pick several items)*
Command:

Notice that the Select objects: prompt did not return after the items were picked. The entire group is automatically edited (erased in this example) when you press [Enter] or pick the second corner of a window or crossing box.

**Professional Tip**

The **Single** selection option is not commonly used because picking an object and pressing [Enter] requires fewer keystrokes than entering si and pressing [Enter]. The **Single** selection option is most commonly used when developing menu macros that require selection of a single object. Menu macros are discussed in Chapter 27.

## Using the Last Selection Option

The **Last** selection option saves time if you need to erase, move, or copy the last object drawn. For example, suppose you draw a line and then want to move it. The **Last** selection option automatically selects the object. The **Last** selection option can be selected by entering l at the Select objects: prompt:

```
Command: m or move↵
Select objects: l↵
1 found
Select objects: ↵
Specify base point or displacement: (select a base point)
Specify second point of displacement or <use first point as displacement>: (select a dis-
    placement point)
Command:
```

Keep in mind that using the **Last** selection option only highlights the last visible object drawn. You must press [Enter] for the object to be moved.

## Exercise 6-2

◆ Start a new drawing using a template or startup option of your own choice.
◆ Set architectural units.
◆ Set the Endpoint and Intersection running object snaps.
◆ Use the **LINE** command to draw the objects in part A of the illustration at the end of the exercise. Do not dimension.
◆ Use the **MOVE** and **COPY** commands to create the object in part B of the illustration.
◆ Use the **Single** selection option to copy one of the lines to a new location.
◆ Use the **ERASE** command with the **Last** selection option to erase the last object created.
◆ Save the drawing as ex6-2.

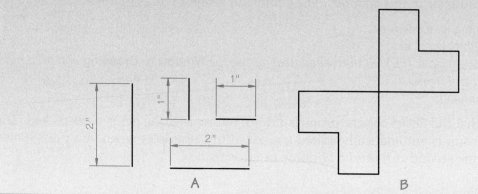

## Using the **Window** Selection Option

The **Window** selection option can be used at any Select objects: prompt. This option allows you to select single objects or groups of objects by drawing a box, or window, around them. All objects entirely *within* the window are selected. If a portion of an object projects outside the window, the object is not selected. The command sequence looks like this:

Command: **m** *or* **move.**↵
Select objects: *(select a point below and to the left of the object(s) to be moved)*

When the Select objects: prompt is shown, select a point clearly below and to the left of the object to be edited. The cursor is replaced with a window. One corner of the window is fixed at the point you selected. The opposite corner of the window follows the movement of the pointing device. Move the pointing device forward and to the right. This causes the selection window to expand. Note that the window is composed of solid lines. The following prompt appears:

Specify opposite corner: *(pick the other corner to the right of the object(s) to be moved)*
Select objects: ↵
Specify base point or displacement: *(pick a base point)*
Specify second point of displacement or <use first point as displacement>: *(pick a displacement point)*
Command:

When the Specify opposite corner: prompt is shown, move the pointing device forward and to the right so the window totally encloses the object(s) to be erased. Then, pick to locate the second corner. All objects within the window become highlighted. When finished, press [Enter] to complete the **MOVE** command. **Figure 6-4** shows an example of using the **Window** selection option with the **ERASE** command.

You can also manually specify the **Window** selection option from the command line. You need to do this if the **PICKAUTO** system variable (discussed later in this chapter) is set to 0. The command sequence is as follows:

Command: **e** *or* **erase.**↵
Select objects: **w.**↵
Specify first corner: *(select a point outside of the object)*
Specify opposite corner: *(move the cursor to the left or right, and pick the other corner)*
Select objects: ↵
Command:

---

**Figure 6-4.**
Using the **Window** selection option with the **ERASE** command.

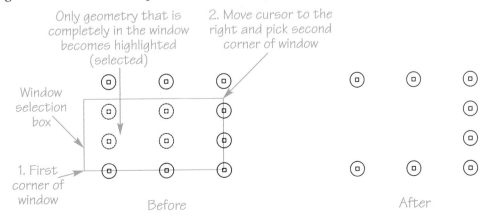

When you enter the **Window** selection option manually, the first point you pick does not need to be to the left of the objects being selected. The "box" remains the selection window whether you move the cursor to the left or right.

## Using the **Crossing** Selection Option

The **Crossing** selection option is similar to the **Window** selection option. However, objects within the box and those *crossing* the box are selected. The crossing box outline is dotted to distinguish it from the solid outline of the selection window. The command sequence for the **Crossing** selection option is as follows:

Command: **co, cp,** *or* **copy.**↵
Select objects: *(pick a point to the right of the object(s) to be copied)*

When the Select objects: prompt is shown, select a point below and to the right of the object to be erased. After you select the first point, move the pointing device forward and to the left. The crossing box expands as you move the pointing device. The next prompt appears:

Specify opposite corner: *(move the cursor to the left so that the box encloses or crosses the objects to be copied and pick)*
Select objects: ↵
Specify base point or displacement, or [Multiple]: *(select base point or enter displacement)*
Specify second point of displacement or <use first point as displacement>: *(pick second point or press [Enter] if displacement was specified)*
Command:

Unlike the selection window, the crossing box does not need to enclose the entire object to select it. The crossing box need only "cross" part of the object. **Figure 6-5** shows how to use the **Crossing** selection option.

You can also manually specify the **Crossing** selection option from the command line. You need to do this if the **PICKAUTO** variable (discussed later in this chapter) is set to 0. The command sequence is as follows:

Command: **m** *or* **move.**↵
Select objects: **c.**↵
Specify first corner: *(pick a point outside of the object)*
Specify opposite corner: *(move cursor to the right or left and pick the other corner)*
Select objects: ↵
Specify base point or displacement: *(pick a base point)*

---

**Figure 6-5.**
Using the **Crossing** selection option to erase objects.

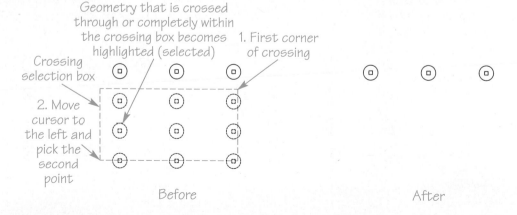

Specify second point of displacement or <use first point as displacement>: *(pick a displacement point)*
  Command:

When you manually enter the **Crossing** selection option, the first point you pick does not need to be to the right of the object(s) being edited. The "box" remains the crossing box whether you move the cursor to the left or right.

## Using the PICKAUTO System Variable

The **PICKAUTO** system variable controls automatic windowing when the Select objects: prompt appears. The **PICKAUTO** settings are on (1) and off (0). Change the **PICKAUTO** value by entering pickauto at the Command prompt and then entering the new value. By default, **PICKAUTO** is set to 1. At this setting, you automatically use a selection window if the cursor is pulled to the right of the first corner picked, or a crossing box if the cursor is pulled to the left of the first corner picked.

You can still use the **Window** or **Crossing** selection options when **PICKAUTO** is off (0). To do this, enter w for **Window** or c for **Crossing** at the Select objects: prompt, and proceed as previously discussed.

## Using the Box Selection Option

Another way to begin the **Window** or **Crossing** selection option is to enter box at the Select objects: prompt. You are then prompted to pick the first corner, which can be a left corner of a selection window or a right corner of a crossing box. Using the **Box** option accomplishes the same function as the automatic **Window** or **Crossing** selection option. The command sequence is as follows:

Command: **e** *or* **erase**↵
Select objects: **box**↵
Specify first corner: *(pick the left corner of a selection window or the right corner of a crossing box)*
Specify opposite corner: *(pick the opposite corner)*
Select objects: ↵
Command:

## Exercise 6-3

- ◆ Start a new drawing using a template or startup option of your own choice.
- ◆ Set architectural units.
- ◆ Set the Endpoint and Intersection running object snaps.
- ◆ Set the **PICKAUTO** system variable to 0 (off).
- ◆ Draw a 2″ × 2″ square using the **LINE** command with relative coordinates and the **Close** option.
- ◆ Enter erase at the Command prompt and use the **Window** selection option. Place the window around the entire square to erase it.
- ◆ Draw a 4″ × 3″ rectangle using the **LINE** command, Ortho mode, and direct distance entry.
- ◆ Using the **Crossing** selection option, move three of the four lines 4″ up.
- ◆ Set the **PICKAUTO** system variable to 1 (on).
- ◆ Using an automatic window selection, copy the single remaining line 4″ up.
- ◆ Draw a 3″ × 2″ rectangle using the **LINE** command and Snap mode.
- ◆ Erase three sides of the 3″ × 2″ rectangle using the automatic crossing selection option.
- ◆ Save the drawing as ex6-3.

## Using the Window Polygon *Selection Option*

The **Window** selection option requires that you place a rectangle completely around the objects to be modified. Sometimes, it is awkward to place a rectangle around the items to modify. When this situation occurs, you can place a polygon of your own design around the objects with the **Window Polygon** selection option. A *polygon* is a closed figure with three or more sides.

To use the **Window Polygon** selection option, enter wp at the Select objects: prompt. Then draw a polygon that encloses the objects. As you pick corners, the polygon drags into place. The command sequence for erasing the squares shown in **Figure 6-6** is as follows:

> Command: **e** *or* **erase.**⏎
> Select objects: **wp.**⏎
> First polygon point: *(pick Point 1)*
> Specify endpoint of line or [Undo]: *(pick Point 2)*
> Specify endpoint of line or [Undo]: *(pick Point 3)*
> Specify endpoint of line or [Undo]: *(pick Point 4)*
> Specify endpoint of line or [Undo]: *(pick Point 5)*
> Specify endpoint of line or [Undo]: *(pick Point 6)*
> Specify endpoint of line or [Undo]: *(pick Point 7)*
> Specify endpoint of line or [Undo]: *(pick Point 8)*
> Specify endpoint of line or [Undo]: ⏎
> Select objects: ⏎

If you do not like the last polygon point you picked, use the **Undo** option by entering u at the Specify endpoint of line or [Undo]: prompt.

## Using the Crossing Polygon *Selection Option*

The **Crossing** selection option lets you place a rectangle around or through the objects to be modified. Sometimes it is difficult to place a rectangle around or through the items to be modified without coming into contact with other objects. When you want to use the features of the **Crossing** selection option, but prefer to use a polygon instead of a rectangle, enter cp at the Select objects: prompt. Then, draw a polygon that encloses or crosses the objects to be modified. As you pick the points, the polygon drags into place. The crossing polygon is a dashed rubberband cursor.

---

**Figure 6-6.**
Using the **Window Polygon** selection option to erase objects.

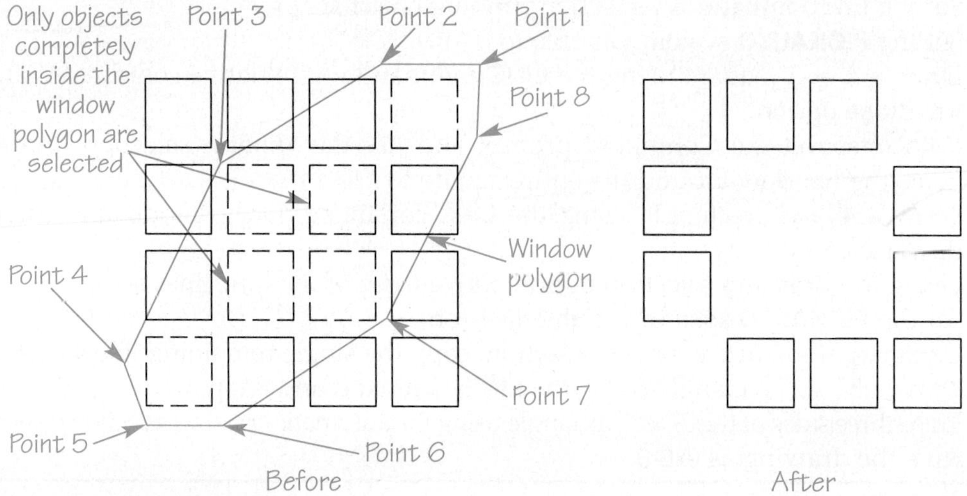

Architectural Drafting Using AutoCAD

Suppose you want to copy all but the corner boxes in **Figure 6-7**. The command sequence to copy these boxes is as follows:

Command: **co**, **cp**, *or* **copy**↵
Select objects: **cp**↵
First polygon point: *(pick Point 1)*
Specify endpoint of line or [Undo]: *(pick Point 2)*
Specify endpoint of line or [Undo]: *(pick Point 3)*
Specify endpoint of line or [Undo]: *(pick Point 4)*
Specify endpoint of line or [Undo]: *(pick Point 5)*
Specify endpoint of line or [Undo]: *(pick Point 6)*
Specify endpoint of line or [Undo]: *(pick Point 7)*
Specify endpoint of line or [Undo]: *(pick Point 8)*
Specify endpoint of line or [Undo]: ↵
Select objects: ↵

To change the last point you picked, enter u at the Specify endpoint of line or [Undo]: prompt.

**Figure 6-7.**
Using the **Crossing Polygon** selection option. All objects within or crossed by the polygon are selected.

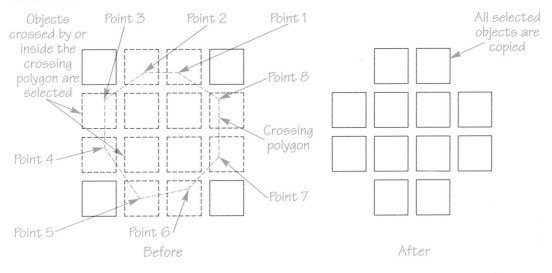

**Professional Tip**

When using the **Window Polygon** or **Crossing Polygon** selection option, AutoCAD does not allow you to select a point that causes the lines of the selection polygon to intersect each other. Pick locations that do not result in an intersection. Use the **Undo** option if you need to go back and relocate a preceding pick point.

## Using the Fence Selection Option

The **Fence** selection option provides another way of selecting objects. When using the **Fence** selection option, you simply need to place a fence through the objects you want to select. Anything that the fence passes through is included in the selection set. The fence can be straight or staggered, as shown in **Figure 6-8.** To activate this selection option, enter f at the Select objects: prompt:

> Command: **e** *or* **erase.**↵
> Select objects: **f.**↵
> First fence point: *(pick Point 1)*
> Specify endpoint of line or [Undo]: *(pick Point 2)*
> Specify endpoint of line or [Undo]: *(pick Point 3)*
> Specify endpoint of line or [Undo]: *(pick Point 4)*
> Specify endpoint of line or [Undo]: *(pick Point 5)*
> Specify endpoint of line or [Undo]: *(pick Point 6)*
> Specify endpoint of line or [Undo]: *(pick Point 7)*
> Specify endpoint of line or [Undo]: *(pick Point 8)*
> Specify endpoint of line or [Undo]: *(pick Point 9)*
> Specify endpoint of line or [Undo]: *(pick Point 10)*
> Specify endpoint of line or [Undo]: ↵
> Select objects: ↵
> Command:

**Figure 6-8.**
Using the **Fence** selection option to erase objects. The fence can be a straight or staggered line.

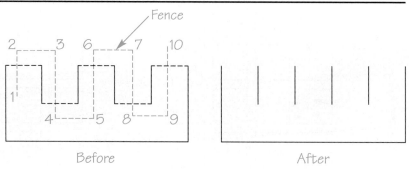

Before

After

## Exercise 6-4

◆ Start a new drawing using a template or startup option of your own choice.
◆ Set architectural units.
◆ Set the Endpoint and Intersection running object snaps.
◆ Draw a group of boxes similar to the one shown in **Figure 6-6.**
◆ Use the **Window Polygon** selection option to erase the items indicated in the figure.
◆ Undo the previous step to restore the group of boxes.
◆ Use the **Crossing Polygon** selection option to copy the items indicated in **Figure 6-7.**
◆ Draw an object similar to the one shown in **Figure 6-8.**
◆ Use the **Fence** selection option to erase the items indicated in the figure.
◆ Save the drawing as ex6-4.

Architectural Drafting Using AutoCAD

## Removing from and Adding to the Selection Set

When editing a drawing, a common mistake is to accidentally select an object that you do not want to select. The simplest way to remove one or more objects from the current selection set is to hold down the [Shift] key and reselect the objects. This is possible only for individual picks and automatic windows and crossings. For an automatic window or crossing, the [Shift] key must be held down while picking the first corner, and can then be released for picking the second corner. If you accidentally remove the wrong object from the selection set, release the [Shift] key and pick it again.

To use other methods for removing objects from a selection set, or for specialized selection needs, you can switch to the Remove mode by entering r at the Select objects: prompt. This changes the Select objects: prompt to Remove objects: as follows:

Command: **m** *or* **move**↵
Select objects: *(pick several objects using any technique)*
Select objects: **r**↵
Remove objects: *(pick the objects you want removed from the selection set)*
Remove objects: ↵

Switch back to the selection mode by entering a, for Add mode, at the Remove objects: prompt. This restores the Select objects: prompt and allows you to select additional objects. This is how the Add mode works:

Remove objects: **a**↵
Select objects: *(continue selecting objects as needed)*
Select objects: ↵
Command:

## Using the Previous Selection

Often, sequential editing operations need to be carried out on a specific group of objects. In this case, the **Previous** selection option allows you to select the same object(s) you just edited. You can select the **Previous** selection option by entering p at the Select objects: prompt. In the following example, a group of objects is moved and then copied:

Command: **m** *or* **move**↵
Select objects: *(pick several objects using any selection technique)*
Select objects: ↵
Specify base point or displacement: *(select a base point)*
Specify second point of displacement or <use first point as displacement>: *(pick second point)*
Command: **co**, **cp**, *or* **copy**↵
Select objects: **p**↵
Select objects: ↵
Specify base point or displacement, or [Multiple]: *(select base point)*
Specify second point of displacement or <use first point as displacement>: *(pick second point)*
Command:

## Selecting All Objects in a Drawing

Sometimes you may want to select every object in the drawing. This can be accomplished using the **All** selection option. To use this option, enter all at the Select objects: prompt as follows:

Command: **m** *or* **move.**↵
Select objects: **all**↵
Select objects: ↵

This procedure moves everything on the drawing. You can use the Remove mode at the second Select objects: prompt to remove certain objects from the set. You can also enter all after entering r to remove all objects from the set.

## Exercise 6-5

◆ Start a new drawing using a template or startup option of your own choice.
◆ Set architectural units.
◆ Draw an object similar to the one shown in **Figure 6-8.**
◆ Use the **Single** selection option to erase one line.
◆ Use the **Single** selection option with a fence to erase any two lines.
◆ Experiment using the Remove and Add selection modes by selecting six items to copy, removing two of the items from the selection set, and then adding three new entities. Copy the items 4" to the left and 3" down.
◆ Use the **Previous** option to move the previous selection 4" to the right and 3" up.
◆ Use the **All** selection option to erase everything from the drawing.
◆ Use the **U** or **OOPS** command to get everything back that you erased.
◆ Save the drawing as ex6-5.

## Cycling through Stacked Objects

*Stacked objects* occur when one feature, such as a line, overlays another in a 2D drawing. These lines have the same Z values, so one is no higher or lower than the other. However, the last object drawn appears to be on top of all others.

When a point on an object is picked in select mode, the database is scanned, and the first object found is the object selected. Additional picks only duplicate the original results. Unless the **Window**, **Crossing**, **Window Polygon**, **Crossing Polygon**, **Fence**, or **Multiple** selection option is used, the underlying objects are inaccessible.

Note | When selecting objects to be modified, AutoCAD only accepts qualifying objects. A *qualifying object* is an object on an unlocked layer that passes through the pick box area at the point selected.

One way of dealing with stacked objects is to let AutoCAD cycle through the overlapping objects. *Cycling* is repeatedly selecting one item from a series of stacked objects until the desired object is highlighted. This works best when several objects cross at the same place or are very close together. This method also works very well for objects that are overlapping one another or are stacked.

To cycle through objects, hold down the [Ctrl] key while you make your first pick. If there are two or more objects found crossing through the pick box area, the top object is highlighted. Now, you can release the [Ctrl] key. When you pick again, the next object is highlighted. Every time you pick, another object becomes highlighted.

Architectural Drafting Using AutoCAD

In this way, you cycle through all the objects. When you have the desired object highlighted, press [Enter] to end the cycling process and return to the Select objects: prompt. Press [Enter] again to return to the Command prompt.

The following command sequence is used to move one of the circles in **Figure 6-9.** The same technique can be used for any editing function:

Command: **m** *or* **move.**↵
Select objects: *(hold down the* [Ctrl] *key and pick)* <Cycle on> *(pick until the desired object is highlighted, and then press* [Enter]*)*
<Cycle off>1 found
Select objects: *(select additional objects or press* [Enter]*)* ↵
Specify base point or displacement: *(select a base point)*
Specify second point of displacement or <use first point as displacement>:
    *(pick second point)*
Command:

---

**Figure 6-9.**
Cycling through a series of stacked objects until the desired object is highlighted.

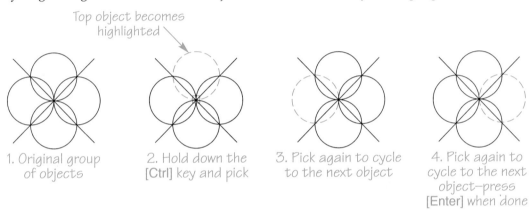

*Top object becomes highlighted*

1. Original group of objects
2. Hold down the [Ctrl] key and pick
3. Pick again to cycle to the next object
4. Pick again to cycle to the next object—press [Enter] when done

## Using Quick Select to Create Selection Sets

The term *filter* means to remove or combine certain values or objects to create a new value or object. One way to filter for objects with specific properties in a drawing is by using the **Quick Select** dialog box. With the Quick Select feature, you can quickly create a selection set based on the filtering criteria you specify. To access the **Quick Select** dialog box, select **Quick Select...** from the **Tools** pull-down menu, enter qselect at the Command prompt, or right-click in the drawing area and choose **Quick Select...** from the shortcut menu. This displays the **Quick Select** dialog box, **Figure 6-10.** You can also access the **Quick Select** dialog box by picking the **Quick Select** button in the **Properties** window.

QSELECT

Tools
↳ Quick Select...

A selection set can be defined in several ways using the **Quick Select** dialog box. You can pick the **Select objects** button and select the objects on screen. You can select a specific object type (such as text, line, or circle) to be selected throughout the drawing. You can also specify a particular property value (such as a color or layer) that objects must possess in order to be selected. Once the selection criteria is defined, you can use the radio buttons in the **How to apply** area to include or exclude the defined objects.

**Figure 6-10.**
You can define selection sets in the **Quick Select** dialog box.

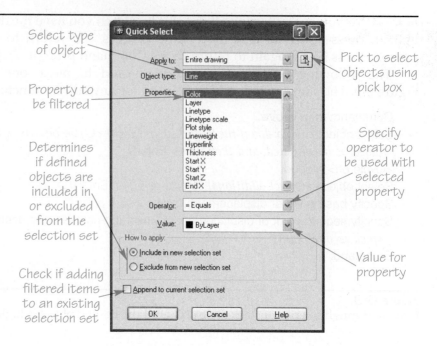

Select type of object

Property to be filtered

Determines if defined objects are included in or excluded from the selection set

Check if adding filtered items to an existing selection set

Pick to select objects using pick box

Specify operator to be used with selected property

Value for property

Look at **Figure 6-11** as you refer to the following step-by-step example, which uses the **Quick Select** dialog box to select objects that are green:

1. Select **Quick Select...** from the **Tools** pull-down menu to open the **Quick Select** dialog box.
2. In the **Apply to:** drop-down list, select **Entire drawing**. If you access the **Quick Select** dialog box after a selection set is defined, there is also a **Current selection** option that allows you to create a subset of the existing selection set.
3. Under the **Object type:** drop-down list, select **Multiple**. This allows you to select any object type. The drop-down list contains all the object types contained in the drawing.
4. In the **Properties:** list, select **Color**. The items in the **Properties:** list vary depending on which object type is specified.
5. In the **Operator:** drop-down list, select **= Equals**.
6. In the **Value:** drop-down list, select **Green**. This drop-down list contains values of the selected property.
7. In the **How to apply:** area, select the **Include in new selection set** radio button.
8. Pick the **OK** button.

AutoCAD selects all objects with the color green, as shown in **Figure 6-11B.**

**Figure 6-11.**
Creating selection sets with the **Quick Select** dialog box. A—Objects in drawing. B—Selection set containing objects that have a green color property. C—Line objects added to initial selection set. The unselected objects are polylines.

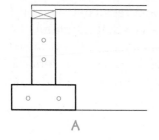
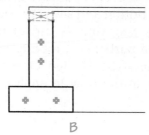
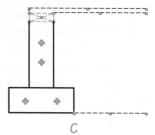

A                                    B                                    C

Once a set of objects has been selected, the **Quick Select** dialog box can be used to refine the selection set. Use the **Exclude from new selection set** option to exclude objects, or use the **Append to current selection set** option to add objects. The following procedure refines the selection set to also include black lines:

1. While the initial set of objects is selected, right-click in the drawing area and select **Quick Select...** from the shortcut menu to open the **Quick Select** dialog box.
2. Activate the **Append to current selection set** check box. AutoCAD automatically selects the **Entire drawing** option in the **Apply to:** drop-down list.
3. Select **Line** in the **Object type:** drop-down list, **Color** in the **Properties:** drop-down list, **= Equals** in the **Operator:** drop-down list, and **Black** in the **Value:** drop-down list.
4. In the **How to apply:** area, select the **Include in new selection set** radio button.
5. Pick the **OK** button. The selection now appears as shown in **Figure 6-11C.**

## Exercise 6-6

◆ Start a new drawing using a template or startup option of your own choice.
◆ Set architectural units.
◆ Set the Endpoint and Intersection running object snaps.
◆ Create two layers named Red and Yellow. Assign the following colors and linetypes:
   ◆ Red layer = Red color and Continuous linetype.
   ◆ Yellow layer = Yellow color and Hidden linetype.
◆ Draw two circles on the Red layer. Draw two lines and two circles on the Yellow layer.
◆ Use the **Quick Select** dialog box to create a new selection set of circles on the Red layer.
◆ Use the **Quick Select** dialog box to filter for multiple objects on the Yellow layer and append this filter to the current selection set.
◆ Use the **Copy** command to copy these objects to a new location.
◆ Use the **Quick Select** dialog box to create a new selection of circles with a color property equal to ByLayer.
◆ Save the drawing as ex6-6.

# Rotating Objects

Design changes often require an object, feature, or view to be rotated. For example, an office furniture layout may have to be moved, copied, or rotated for an interior design. AutoCAD allows you to easily revise the layout to get the final design.

To rotate selected objects, pick the **Rotate** button on the **Modify** toolbar, select **Rotate** from the **Modify** pull-down menu, or enter ro or rotate at the Command prompt. Objects can be selected using any of the selection options previously mentioned. Once the objects are selected, pick a base point to rotate around and enter a rotation angle. A positive rotation angle revolves the object counterclockwise. A negative rotation angle revolves the object clockwise. See **Figure 6-12.** The **ROTATE** command sequence appears as follows:

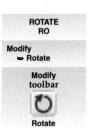

ROTATE
RO

Modify
➥ Rotate

Modify
toolbar

Rotate

Command: **ro** *or* **rotate.**↵
Current positive angle in UCS: ANGDIR = counterclockwise, ANGBASE = 0
Select objects: *(select the objects)*
Select objects: ↵
Specify base point: *(pick the base point or enter coordinates and press* [Enter]*)*
Specify rotation angle or [Reference]: *(enter a positive or negative rotation angle and press* [Enter]*, or pick a point on screen)*
Command:

**Figure 6-12.**
When using the **ROTATE** command, a positive rotation angle produces counterclockwise rotation. A negative rotation angle produces clockwise rotation.

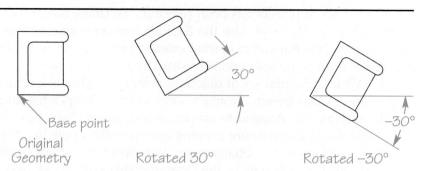

Base point

Original Geometry

Rotated 30°

Rotated –30°

If an object is already rotated and you want a different angle, you can do this in two ways. Both ways involve using the **Reference** option when prompted for a rotation angle. The first way is to specify the existing angle of the object and then the new angle, **Figure 6-13A**:

    Specify rotation angle or [Reference]: **r**⏎
    Specify the reference angle <0>: **45**⏎
    Specify the new angle: **90**⏎

The other method is used if the objects are rotated at an unknown angle and need to be rotated at a new angle. Select the objects to be rotated, select a base point, access the **Reference** option, and then pick two points along the unknown angle to use as a reference, **Figure 6-13B**:

    Specify rotation angle or [Reference]: **r**⏎
    Specify the reference angle <0>: *(pick reference point)*
    Specify second point: *(pick the other reference point)*
    Specify the new angle: **90**⏎

## Exercise 6-7

◆ Start a new drawing using a template or startup option of your own choice.
◆ Set architectural units.
◆ Set the Endpoint and Intersection running object snaps.
◆ Draw a 2 1/4″ unit square.
◆ Rotate the square to 75°. Then, using the **Reference** option, rotate the square to 90°. Finally rotate the square back to 0°.
◆ Save the drawing as ex6-7.

**Figure 6-13.**
Using the **Reference** option of the **ROTATE** command.
A—Entering the reference angle.
B—Selecting points along an unknown angle to determine a reference angle.

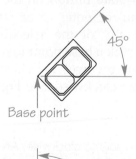
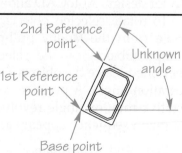

45°

Base point

2nd Reference point

1st Reference point

Unknown angle

Base point

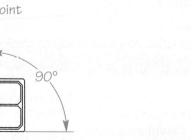
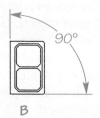

90°

90°

A

B

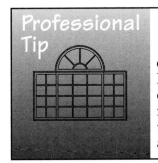
# Changing the Size of Objects

A convenient editing command that saves hours of drafting time is the **SCALE** command. This command lets you change the size of an object or the complete drawing. The **SCALE** command proportionately enlarges or reduces the entire object. If associative dimensioning is used, the dimensions also change to reflect the new size. Dimensions are discussed in Chapter 15.

To scale objects, pick the **Scale** button in the **Modify** toolbar, select **Scale** from the **Modify** pull-down menu, or enter sc or scale at the Command prompt. The command sequence is as follows:

SCALE
SC

Modify
↪ Scale

Modify
toolbar

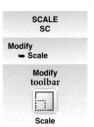

Scale

> Command: **sc** *or* **scale**↵
> Select objects: *(select objects to be scaled)*
> Select objects: ↵
> Specify base point: *(select the base point)*
> Specify scale factor or [Reference]:

Specifying the scale factor is the default option. Enter a number to indicate the amount of enlargement or reduction. For example, to double the scale, enter 2 at the Specify scale factor or [Reference]: prompt, as shown in **Figure 6-14.** The following chart shows sample scale factors:

| Scale Factor | Resulting Size |
|---|---|
| 10 | 10 times bigger |
| 5 | 5 times bigger |
| 2 | 2 times bigger |
| 1 | Equal to existing size |
| .75 | 3/4 of original size |
| .5 | 1/2 of original size |
| .25 | 1/4 of original size |

When executing the **SCALE** command, the selection of the base point is critical. When an object is scaled, it is scaled in relation to the base point. In most cases, the base point should be placed on a feature of an object, such as a corner, using object snaps.

**Figure 6-14.**
Using the **SCALE** command. The base point does not move but all objects are scaled in relationship to this point.

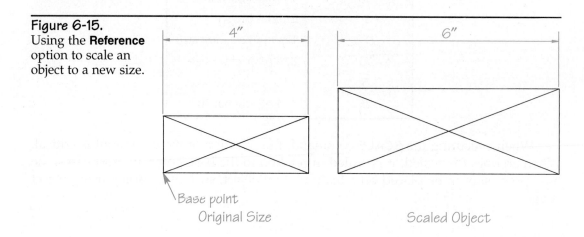

Base point

Original Size

Scaled Twice Original Size

## Using the **Reference** *Option*

An object can also be scaled by specifying a new size in relation to an existing dimension. For example, suppose you have a piece of lumber that is 4" in length and you need to make it 6" in length. To do so, use the **Reference** option in the following manner, as shown in **Figure 6-15:**

> Specify scale factor or [Reference]: **r**↵
> Specify reference length <1>: **4**↵
> Specify new length: **6**↵
> Command:

Chapter 12 explains how to scale an object of an unknown size using the **Reference** option.

**Note**    The **SCALE** command changes all dimensions of an object proportionately. To change only the width or length of an object, use the **STRETCH** command or the **LENGTHEN** command. These commands are explained later in this chapter.

**Figure 6-15.**
Using the **Reference** option to scale an object to a new size.

4"

6"

Base point

Original Size

Scaled Object

## Exercise 6-8

◆ Start a new drawing using a template or startup option of your own choice.
◆ Set architectural units.
◆ Set the Endpoint and Intersection running object snap modes.
◆ Draw two ∅2″ circles and two 2 1/4″ long squares.
◆ Triple the size of one of the circles using the center of the circle as the base point.
◆ Decrease the size of the other circle by one-half, using one of its own quadrants as the base point.
◆ Double the size of one square.
◆ Use the **Reference** option to make the other square 3 1/4″ long.
◆ Save the drawing as ex6-8.

# Stretching Objects

The **SCALE** command changes the length and width of an object proportionately. The **STRETCH** command changes only one dimension of an object. In architectural design, room sizes may be stretched to increase the square footage. In interior design, a table may need to be stretched to a new length.

When using the **STRETCH** command, you can select objects with a crossing window or crossing polygon. To use a crossing window, enter c at the Select objects: prompt or use the automatic selection window by picking the first corner to the right of the items to be stretched.

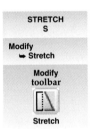

STRETCH
S

Modify
➡ Stretch

Modify
toolbar

Stretch

To access the **STRETCH** command, pick the **Stretch** button in the **Modify** toolbar, select **Stretch** from the **Modify** pull-down menu, or enter s or stretch at the Command prompt. The command sequence is as follows:

Command: **s** *or* **stretch.**↵
Select objects to stretch by crossing-window or crossing-polygon...
Select objects: *(select the first corner of a crossing window)*
Specify opposite corner: *(pick the second corner)*
Select objects: ↵

Select only the portion of the object to be stretched, as shown in **Figure 6-16**. If you select the entire object, the **STRETCH** command works like the **MOVE** command and moves all objects within the crossing box.

After selecting the objects, you are asked to pick the base point. This is the point from which the object is stretched. Then, pick a new position for the base point. As you move the cursor, the object is stretched or compressed. Pick the new point, use coordinates to stretch the objects to a new location, or use direct distance entry (drag cursor in the direction of travel and enter the distance to stretch) to establish the stretching distance. The command sequence after selecting objects is as follows:

Specify base point or displacement: *(pick the base point for the stretch to begin)*
Specify second point of displacement or <use first point as displacement>: *(pick a*
    *point, enter in coordinates, or use direct distance entry)*
Command:

The example in **Figure 6-16** shows the object being stretched. This is a common use of the **STRETCH** command. You can also use the **STRETCH** command to reduce the size of an object by stretching in the opposite direction.

**Figure 6-16.**
Using the **STRETCH** command. A—Picking a new point for the stretch. B—Using coordinates to stretch the object 2″. C—Using direct distance entry to stretch the object 1-1/4″.

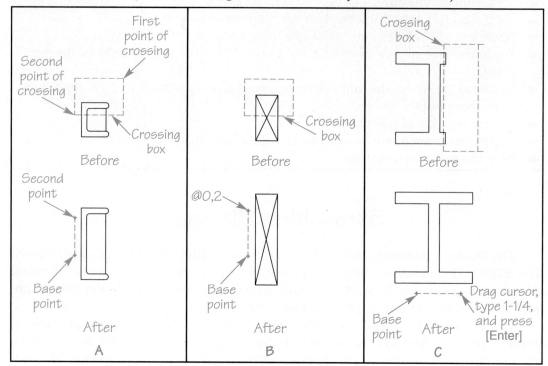

| Note | When using the **STRETCH** command, AutoCAD allows you to select as many crossings as desired. However, only the objects that were selected in the last crossing are stretched. All other selections are ignored. Therefore, it might take several uses of the **STRETCH** command to stretch several different areas in your drawing. |
|---|---|

# Drawing a Mirror Image of an Object

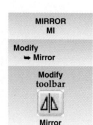

MIRROR
MI

Modify
➥ Mirror

Modify
toolbar

Mirror

It is often necessary to draw an object in a reflected, or mirrored, position. The **MIRROR** command performs this task. Mirroring an entire drawing is common in architectural drafting when a client wants a plan drawn in reverse.

The **MIRROR** command is accessed by picking the **Mirror** button in the **Modify** toolbar, by selecting **Mirror** in the **Modify** pull-down menu, or by entering mi or mirror at the Command prompt.

## Selecting the Mirror Line

When you enter the **MIRROR** command, you select the objects to be mirrored and then select a mirror line. The *mirror line* is the hinge about which objects are reflected. The objects and any space between the objects and the mirror line are reflected, **Figure 6-17.**

**Figure 6-17.**
When mirroring an object, specify two points to be used as the "hinge" line.

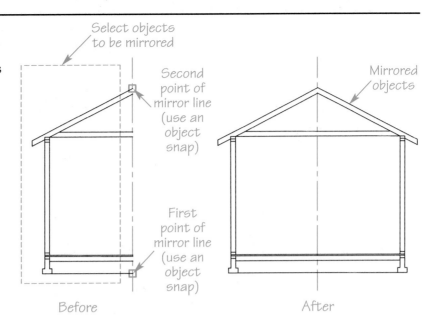

Select objects to be mirrored

Second point of mirror line (use an object snap)

First point of mirror line (use an object snap)

Mirrored objects

Before

After

The mirror line can be placed at any angle. Once you pick the first endpoint, a mirrored image appears and moves with the cursor. After you select the second mirror line endpoint, you have the option to delete the original objects. Refer to **Figure 6-18** and the following command sequence:

Command: **mi** *or* **mirror**↵
Select objects: *(select objects to be mirrored)*
Select objects: ↵
Specify first point of mirror line: *(pick the first point on the mirror line)*
Specify second point of mirror line: *(pick the second point on the mirror line)*
Delete source objects? [Yes/No] <N>: *(type Y and press [Enter] to delete the original objects, or press [Enter] to accept the default and keep the original objects)*
Command:

**Figure 6-18.**
Using the **MIRROR** command. You have the option of keeping the original items or deleting them.

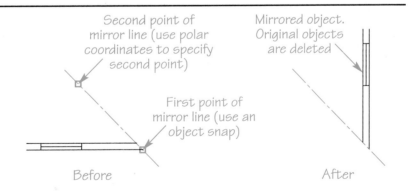

Second point of mirror line (use polar coordinates to specify second point)

First point of mirror line (use an object snap)

Mirrored object. Original objects are deleted

Before

After

## Exercise 6-9

◆ Start a new drawing using a template or startup option of your own choice.
◆ Set architectural units.
◆ Set the Endpoint and Intersection running object snaps.
◆ Draw the objects shown at the bottom of the exercise. Do not draw dimensions.
◆ Mirror the objects using the mirror line.
◆ Save the drawing as ex6-9.

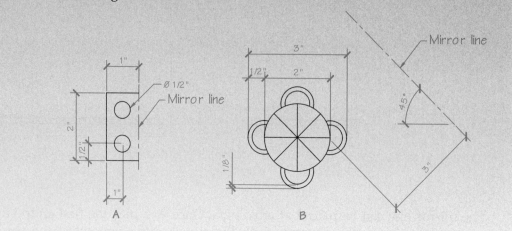

## Mirroring Text

Normally, the **MIRROR** command reverses any text associated with the selected object. Backward text is generally not acceptable, although it is used for reverse imaging. To keep the text readable, the **MIRRTEXT** system variable must be set to zero. There are two values for **MIRRTEXT**, as shown in **Figure 6-19:**

- **1.** Text is mirrored in relation to the original object.
- **0.** Mirrors the location of the text but prevents text from being reversed. This is the default value.

To draw a mirror image of an existing object and leave the text readable, set the **MIRRTEXT** variable to 0 by entering mirrtext at the Command prompt and entering 0. Then, proceed to use the **MIRROR** command.

**Figure 6-19.**
The **MIRRTEXT** system variable controls how text is mirrored.

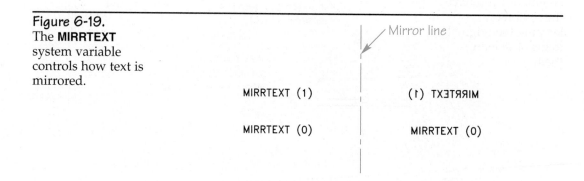

Architectural Drafting Using AutoCAD

## Exercise 6-10

◆ Start a new drawing.
◆ Set architectural units.
◆ Set the Endpoint and Intersection running object snaps.
◆ Make a drawing similar to the "original" object shown at the bottom of the exercise.
◆ Set the **MIRRTEXT** system variable to 0.
◆ Mirror the objects as shown.
◆ Save the drawing as ex6-10.

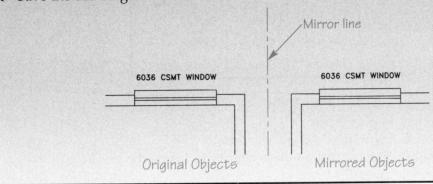

# Using the EXPLODE Command

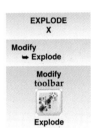
The **EXPLODE** command is used to break apart any existing polyline, block, or dimension. Blocks and dimensions are covered later in this text. To access the **EXPLODE** command, pick the **Explode** button in the **Modify** toolbar, select **Explode** from the **Modify** pull-down menu, or enter x or explode at the Command prompt as follows:

Command: **x** *or* **explode**↵
Select objects: *(pick a polyline, rectangle, or polygon)*
Select objects: ↵

When the object is exploded, the component objects are quickly redrawn. The individual entities can now be changed. To see if the **EXPLODE** command worked properly, select any single segment of the exploded object. If the item you select highlights, the **EXPLODE** command "exploded" the object to its most basic form. Lines, arcs, circles, ellipses, and text cannot be exploded. These are already in their most basic forms.

**Professional Tip**

Another command that explodes objects is the **XPLODE** command. The difference between the **XPLODE** command and the **EXPLODE** command is that the **XPLODE** command allows you to explode an object and specify the properties of the exploded objects. The command can only be accessed by entering xp or xplode at the Command prompt. After selecting the object to be exploded, you can set the color, layer, or linetype properties of the resulting objects.

---

## Exercise 6-11

◆ Start a new drawing using a template or startup option of your own choice.
◆ Set architectural units.
◆ Set the Endpoint and Intersection running object snaps.
◆ Create the following layers:

| Layer | Color | Linetype |
|---|---|---|
| Lines | Red | Continuous |
| Circles | Yellow | Continuous |
| Rectangles | Green | Hidden |
| Polygons | Cyan | Center |
| Polylines | Blue | Continuous |

◆ Create a line on the Lines layer, a circle on the Circles layer, etc.
◆ Create a rectangle with fillets.
◆ Create a polyline with line and arc segments.
◆ Use the **EXPLODE** command on these objects and view the results.
◆ Save the drawing as ex6-11.

# Removing a Section from an Object

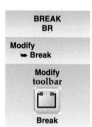

BREAK
BR

Modify
➡ Break

Modify
toolbar

Break

The **BREAK** command is used to remove a portion of a line, circle, arc, or polyline. This command can also be used to break a single object into two separate objects. The **BREAK** command can be accessed by picking the **Break** button in the **Modify** toolbar, by selecting **Break** in the **Modify** pull-down menu, or by entering br or break at the Command prompt.

When using the **BREAK** command, the following prompts appear:

Command: **br** *or* **break.**↵
Select object: *(pick the object)*
Specify second break point or [First point]: *(pick the second break point or enter f to select the first break point)*

The **BREAK** command requires you to select the object to be broken, the first break point, and the second break point. When you select the object, the point you pick is the first break point by default. If you wish to select a different first break point, enter f at the Specify second break point or [First point]: prompt to select the **First point** option. After both break points are specified, the part of the object between the two points is deleted. See **Figure 6-20.**

The **BREAK** command can also be used to split an object in two without removing a portion. This is done by selecting the same point as both the first and second break points. This can be accomplished by entering @ at the Specify second break point: prompt or by picking the **Break at Point** button in the **Modify** toolbar. The @ symbol repeats the coordinates of the previously selected point. The results of the following command sequence are shown in **Figure 6-21:**

Modify
toolbar

Break at Point

Command: **br** *or* **break.**↵
Select object: *(pick the object)*
Specify second break point or [First point]: **@**↵
Command:

---

**Figure 6-20.**
Using the **BREAK** command to break an object.
A—Selecting the object and the first point with the same pick. B—Using the **First point** option.

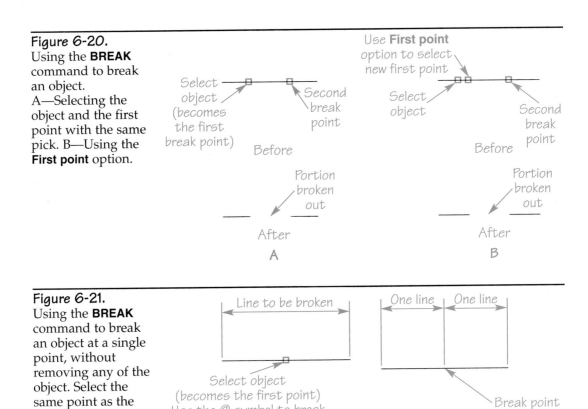

**Figure 6-21.**
Using the **BREAK** command to break an object at a single point, without removing any of the object. Select the same point as the first break point by using the @ symbol.

When breaking arcs or circles, always work in a counterclockwise direction. Otherwise, you may break the portion of the arc or circle that you want to keep. To break off the end of a line or arc, pick the first point on the object. Then, pick the second point slightly beyond the end to be cut off, **Figure 6-22.** When you pick a second point that is not on the object, AutoCAD selects the point on the object nearest to the point you picked.

To break a line from the point of intersection with another line, use the Intersection object snap mode as follows:

Command: **br** *or* **break.↵**
Select object: *(pick the line)*
Specify second break point or [First point]: **int.↵**
of *(move the aperture to the intersection and pick)*
Command:

**Figure 6-22.**
Using the **BREAK** command on circles and arcs.

The line is now broken between the first point and the point of intersection.

## Exercise 6-12

◆ Start a new drawing.
◆ Set architectural units.
◆ Draw two horizontal lines and use the **BREAK** command to break each line at two points, similar to **Figure 6-20**.
◆ Draw two horizontal lines and use the **BREAK** command to break each line at one point, similar to **Figure 6-21**.
◆ Draw two circles and an arc and break each similar to **Figure 6-22**.
◆ Save the drawing as ex6-12.

# Trimming Sections of Lines, Circles, and Arcs

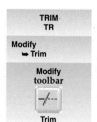

TRIM
TR

Modify
➡ Trim

Modify
toolbar

Trim

The **TRIM** command cuts lines, polylines, circles, arcs, and ellipses from a cutting edge or plane. To access the **TRIM** command, pick the **Trim** button in the **Modify** toolbar, pick **Trim** from the **Modify** pull-down menu, or enter tr or trim at the Command prompt.

The command requires that you pick a "cutting edge" and the object(s) to trim. The *cutting edge* is an object that defines the edge to which objects are trimmed. A cutting edge can be an object such as a line, arc, or text. The **TRIM** command can be thought of as a paper cutter. When using a paper cutter, the blade edge becomes the cutting edge that is used to "trim" paper. If two corners of an object overrun, select two cutting edges and two objects. Refer to **Figure 6-23** as you go through the following sequence:

Command: **tr** *or* **trim**↵
Current settings: Projection = UCS, Edge = None
Select cutting edges...
Select objects: (*pick first cutting edge*)
Select objects: (*pick second cutting edge*)
Select objects: ↵
Select object to trim or shift-select to extend or [Project/Edge/Undo]: (*pick the first object to trim*)
Select object to trim or shift-select to extend or [Project/Edge/Undo]: (*pick the second object to trim*)
Select object to trim or shift-select to extend or [Project/Edge/Undo]: ↵
Command:

**Figure 6-23.**
Using the **TRIM** command. Note the cutting edges.

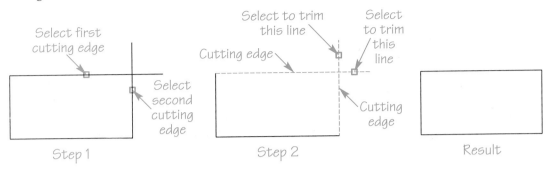

You can access the **EXTEND** command while using the **TRIM** command. After selecting the cutting edge, hold the [Shift] key while selecting an object to extend the object to the cutting edge. The **EXTEND** command is discussed later in this chapter.

## Trimming to an Implied Intersection

An *implied intersection* is the point where two or more objects would cross if extended. Trimming to an implied intersection is possible using the **Edge** option of the **TRIM** command. When you enter the **Edge** option, the choices are **Extend** and **No extend**. When **Extend** is active, AutoCAD checks to see if the cutting edge object will extend to intersect the object being trimmed. If so, the implied intersection point can be used to trim the object. This does not change the cutting edge object at all. The command sequence for the **TRIM** operation shown in **Figure 6-24** is as follows:

```
Command: tr or trim.↵
Current settings: Projection = UCS, Edge = None
Select cutting edges...
Select objects: (pick the cutting edge)
Select objects: ↵
Select object to trim or shift-select to extend or [Project/Edge/Undo]: e↵
Enter an implied edge extension mode [Extend/No extend]: e↵
Select object to trim or shift-select to extend or [Project/Edge/Undo]: (pick the object to trim)
Select object to trim or shift-select to extend or [Project/Edge/Undo]: ↵
Command:
```

**Figure 6-24.**
Trimming to an implied intersection.

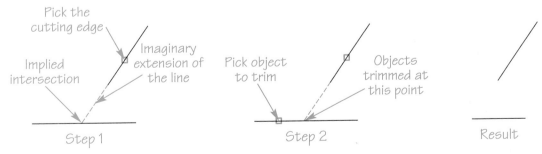

The **No extend** option only takes into consideration cutting edges that cross the object being trimmed. When this option is active, objects that do not cross a cutting edge are not trimmed.

## Using the Undo Option

The **TRIM** command has an **Undo** option that allows you to cancel the previous trimming without leaving the command. This is useful when the result of a trim is not what you expected. To undo the previous trim, simply enter u immediately after performing an unwanted trim. The trimmed portion returns and you can continue trimming other objects:

Command: **tr** *or* **trim.**↵
Current settings: Projection = UCS, Edge = Extend
Select cutting edges...
Select objects: *(pick the first cutting edge)*
Select objects: ↵
Select object to trim or shift-select to extend or [Project/Edge/Undo]: *(pick the object to trim)*
Select object to trim or shift-select to extend or [Project/Edge/Undo]: **u**↵
Command has been completely undone.
Select object to trim or shift-select to extend or [Project/Edge/Undo]: *(pick the object to trim)*
Select object to trim or shift-select to extend or [Project/Edge/Undo]: ↵
Command:

## Using the Project Mode

In a 3D drawing environment, some lines may appear to intersect, but may not actually intersect as they are drawn "up" on the Z axis. In such a case, using the **Project** option of the **TRIM** command allows trimming operations. This option allows cutting edges to project to an imaginary plane in a specified direction so that objects not drawn in the same plane can be trimmed. Using AutoCAD for 3D drawing is discussed in Chapter 25.

# Extending Lines

The **EXTEND** command is the opposite of the **TRIM** command. The **EXTEND** command is used to lengthen lines, elliptical arcs, rays, open polylines, and arcs to meet other objects. **EXTEND** does not work on closed polylines because an unconnected endpoint does not exist.

EXTEND
EX

Modify
➡ Extend

Modify
toolbar

Extend

To use the **EXTEND** command, pick the **Extend** button in the **Modify** toolbar, select **Extend** from the **Modify** pull-down menu, or enter ex or extend at the Command prompt. The command format is similar to the **TRIM** command. The difference is you are asked to select boundary edges, as opposed to cutting edges. *Boundary edges* are objects such as lines, arcs, or text to which the selected objects are extended. The command sequence is shown below and illustrated in **Figure 6-25**:

Command: **ex** *or* **extend.**↵
Current settings: Projection = UCS, Edge = Extend
Select boundary edges...
Select objects: *(pick the boundary edge)*
Select objects: ↵
Select object to extend or shift-select to trim or [Project/Edge/Undo]: *(pick the object to extend)*
Select object to extend or shift-select to trim or [Project/Edge/Undo]: ↵
Command:

**Figure 6-25.**
Using the **EXTEND** command. Note the boundary edges.

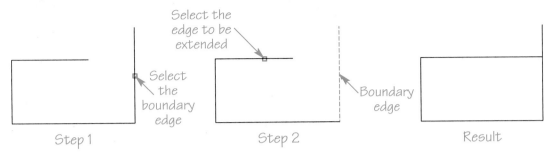

If there is nothing for the selected line to meet, AutoCAD gives the message No edge in that direction or Object does not intersect an edge.

You can access the **TRIM** command while using the **EXTEND** command. After selecting the boundary edge, hold the [Shift] key while selecting an object to trim the object to the boundary edge.

## Extending to an Implied Intersection

You can extend an object to an implied intersection using the **Edge** option in the **EXTEND** command. When you enter the **Edge** option, the choices are **Extend** and **No extend**, just as with the **TRIM** command. When **Extend** is active, the boundary edge object is checked to see if it intersects when extended. If so, the implied intersection point can be used as the boundary for the object to be extended, as shown in **Figure 6-26.** This will not change the boundary edge object, but simply uses it as an imaginary edge.

```
Command: ex or extend↵
Current settings: Projection = UCS, Edge = None
Select boundary edges...
Select objects: (pick the boundary edge)
Select objects: ↵
Select object to extend or shift-select to trim or [Project/Edge/Undo]: e↵
Enter implied edge extension mode [Extend/No extend] <No extend>: e↵
Select object to extend or shift-select to trim or [Project/Edge/Undo]: (pick the object to
    extend)
Select object to extend or shift-select to trim or [Project/Edge/Undo]: ↵
Command:
```

**Figure 6-26.**
Extending to an implied intersection.

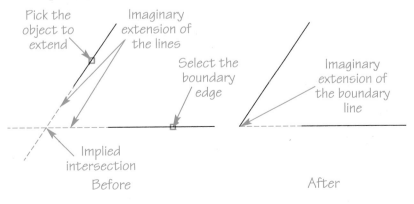

## Using the Undo Option

The **Undo** option in the **EXTEND** command can be used to reverse the previous operation without leaving the **EXTEND** command. The command sequence is the same as discussed for the **TRIM** command.

## Using the Project Mode of the EXTEND Command

In a 3D drawing, some lines may appear to intersect in a given view, but may not actually intersect in the Z axis (up off of the XY plane). In such a case, you can use the **Project** option as explained for the **TRIM** command.

**Professional Tip**

The **TRIM** and **EXTEND** commands have a convenient "smart mode." To use the smart mode, press [Enter] rather than selecting a cutting or boundary edge. This selects all the objects in the drawing as cutting edges for the **TRIM** command and as boundary edges for the **EXTEND** command. Then, when an object to trim or extend is picked, AutoCAD searches for the nearest intersecting object or implied intersection in the direction of your pick. AutoCAD then uses this object as the cutting or boundary edge. Trimming can be done between two actual or implied intersections, but not between a combination of one actual and one implied intersection.

## Exercise 6-13

- ◆ Start a new drawing using a template or startup option of your own choice.
- ◆ Set architectural units.
- ◆ Draw the objects shown at the bottom of the exercise.
- ◆ Use the **TRIM** command on the first set of objects.
- ◆ Use the **EXTEND** command on the second set of objects.
- ◆ Save the drawing as ex6-13.

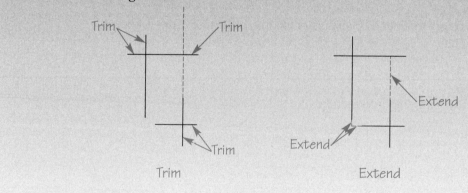

# Changing the Length of an Object

The **LENGTHEN** command can be used to change the length of objects and the included angle of an arc. Only one object can be lengthened at a time. The **LENGTHEN** command does not affect closed objects. For example, you can lengthen a line, polyline, arc, elliptical arc, or spline, but you cannot lengthen a closed polygon or circle.

To access the **LENGTHEN** command, pick **Lengthen** from the **Modify** pull-down menu or enter len or lengthen at the Command prompt. When you select an object, AutoCAD gives you the current length if the object is linear or the included angle if the object is an arc:

LENGTHEN
LEN

Modify
➥ Lengthen

Command: **len** *or* **lengthen**↵
Select an object or [DElta/Percent/Total/DYnamic]: *(pick an object)*
Current length: *current*
Select an object or [DElta/Percent/Total/DYnamic]:

Each option is described below:

- **Delta.** The **Delta** option allows you to specify a positive or negative change in length measured from the endpoint of the selected object. The lengthening or shortening happens closest to the selection point and changes the length by the amount entered. See **Figure 6-27.**

Command: **len** *or* **lengthen**↵
Select an object or [DElta/Percent/Total/DYnamic]: **de**↵
Enter delta length or [Angle] <*current*> *(enter the desired length, 3/4 for example)*
Select an object to change or [Undo]: *(pick the object)*
Select an object to change or [Undo]: *(select another object to lengthen or press [Enter] to exit command)*
Command:

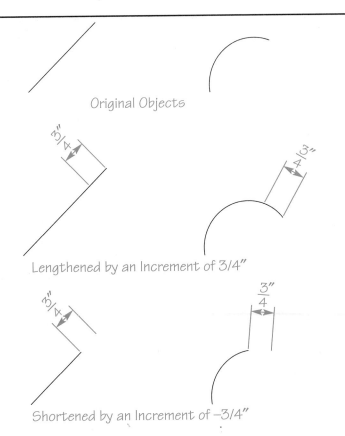

Figure 6-27.
Using the **Delta** option of the **LENGTHEN** command.

Original Objects

Lengthened by an Increment of 3/4″

Shortened by an Increment of −3/4″

---

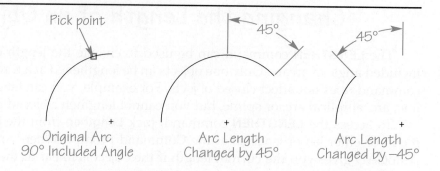

**Figure 6-28.**
Using the **Angle** suboption of the **LENGTHEN** command's **Delta** option.

Pick point

Original Arc
90° Included Angle

45°
Arc Length
Changed by 45°

45°
Arc Length
Changed by −45°

The **Delta** option has an **Angle** suboption that lets you change the included angle of an arc by a specified angle. The results of the following command sequence are shown in **Figure 6-28:**

Command: **len** *or* **lengthen.**⏎
Select an object or [DElta/Percent/Total/DYnamic]: **de.**⏎
Enter delta length or [Angle] *<current>*: **a.**⏎
Enter delta angle *<current>*: *(enter an angle, such as 45)*
Select an object to change or [Undo]: *(pick the arc)*
Select an object to change or [Undo]: ⏎
Command:

- **Percent.** The **Percent** option allows you to change the length of an object or the angle of an arc by a specified percentage. The original length is 100%. You can make the object shorter by specifying less than 100% or longer by specifying more than 100%. Look at **Figure 6-29** and follow this command sequence:

Command: **len** *or* **lengthen.**⏎
Select an object or [DElta/Percent/Total/DYnamic]: **p.**⏎
Enter percent length *<current>*: **125.**⏎
Select an object to change or [Undo]: *(pick the object)*
Select an object to change or [Undo]: ⏎
Command:

**Figure 6-29.**
Using the **Percent** option of the **LENGTHEN** command.

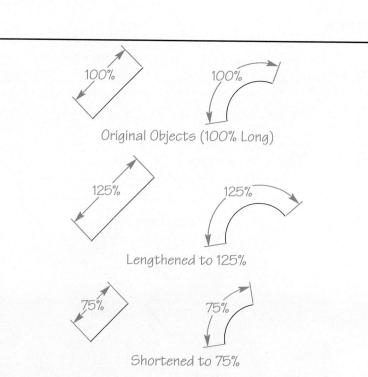

100%     100%

Original Objects (100% Long)

125%     125%

Lengthened to 125%

75%     75%

Shortened to 75%

Architectural Drafting Using AutoCAD

**Figure 6-30.**
Using the **Total**
option of the
**LENGTHEN**
command.

Original Object (3″ long)

Lengthened to 3 3/4″

Shortened to 2 1/4″

- **Total.** The **Total** option allows you to set the total length or angle. You do not have to select the object before entering one of the options, but doing so lets you know the current length of the line or angle of the arc. See **Figure 6-30.**

  Command: **len** *or* **lengthen.**↵
  Select an object or [DElta/Percent/Total/DYnamic]: **t.**↵
  Specify total length or [Angle] <current>: *(enter a new length, such as 3.75. If the*
     *object is an angle, enter* a *and then an angle at the next prompt)*
  Select an object to change or [Undo]: *(pick the object)*
  Select an object to change or [Undo]: ↵
  Command:

- **Dynamic.** This option lets you drag the endpoint of the object to the desired length or angle with the cursor. See **Figure 6-31.** It is helpful to have the grid and snap set to usable increments and Ortho mode turned off when using this option. This is the command sequence:

**Figure 6-31.**
Using the **Dynamic**
option of the
**LENGTHEN**
command.

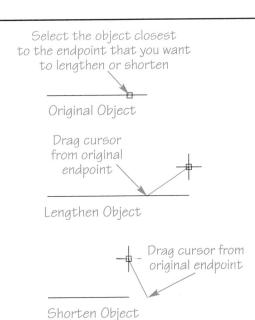

Select the object closest
to the endpoint that you want
to lengthen or shorten

Original Object

Drag cursor
from original
endpoint

Lengthen Object

Drag cursor from
original endpoint

Shorten Object

---

Command: **len** *or* **lengthen**.⏎
Select an object or [DElta/Percent/Total/DYnamic]: **dy**.⏎
Select an object to change or [Undo]: *(pick the object)*
Specify new end point *(move the cursor to the desired length and pick)*
Select an object to change or [Undo]: .⏎
Command:

## Exercise 6-14

- ◆ Start a new drawing using a template or startup option of your own choice.
- ◆ Set architectural units.
- ◆ Use the **LENGTHEN** command and the following options to draw objects similar to the ones specified in the given figure numbers. (Note: Use the **COPY** command to make two copies of each original object, one for lengthening and one for shortening.)
  - ◆ **Delta.** Figure 6-27 (change length) and **Figure 6-28** (change included angle).
  - ◆ **Percent.** Figure 6-29.
  - ◆ **Total.** Figure 6-30.
  - ◆ **Dynamic.** Figure 6-31.
- ◆ Save the drawing as ex6-14.

# Revising Polylines

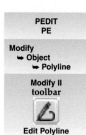

PEDIT
PE

Modify
➥ Object
➥ Polyline

Modify II
toolbar

Edit Polyline

Polylines are drawn as single segments. A polyline joined to another polyline might then be joined to a polyline arc. Even though you draw connecting segments, AutoCAD puts them all together. The result is one polyline treated as a single object. When editing a polyline, you must edit it as one object or divide it into its individual segments. These changes are made with the **PEDIT** and **EXPLODE** commands. The **PEDIT** command is accessed by picking the **Edit Polyline** button from the **Modify II** toolbar, by selecting **Polyline** from the **Object** cascading menu of the **Modify** pull-down menu, or by entering pe or pedit at the Command prompt. You can also select a polyline and then right-click in the drawing area to display a shortcut menu. Then, choose **Polyline Edit**. The **PEDIT** command sequence is as follows:

Command: **pe** *or* **pedit**.⏎
Select polyline or [Multiple]: *(select the polyline)*

If you use the pick box on a wide polyline, you must place it on the edge of a polyline segment, rather than in the center. If the object you select is an individual line or arc object, the following message is displayed:

Object selected is not a polyline
Do you want to turn it into one? <Y>

Entering y or pressing [Enter] turns the selected object into a polyline. Type n and press [Enter] to leave the object as is.

**Professional Tip**

A group of connected lines and arcs can be turned into a continuous polyline by using the **PEDIT Join** option. This option is discussed later in this chapter.

A polyline can be edited as a single object, or it can be divided into individual segments for editing. This section discusses the options for changing the entire polyline. The command sequence is as follows:

Command: **pe** *or* **pedit.**↵
Select polyline or [Multiple]: *(pick a polyline)*
Enter an option [Close/Join/Width/Edit vertex/Fit/Spline/Decurve/Ltype gen/Undo]:

There is no default option for the **PEDIT** command—you must enter one of the options. Pressing [Enter] returns you to the Command prompt.

The **Multiple** option of the **PEDIT** command allows you to edit more than one polyline at a time. The command sequence appears as follows:

Command: **pe** *or* **pedit.**↵
Select polyline or [Multiple]: **m**↵
Select objects: *(select polylines)*
Select objects: ↵
Enter an option [Close/Join/Width/Edit vertex/Fit/Spline/Decurve/Ltype gen/Undo]:

All selected polylines are modified based on the options you select.

## Opening and Closing Polylines

You may decide that you need to close an open polyline, or that you need to reopen a closed polyline. These functions are performed with the **Open** and **Close** options of the **PEDIT** command.

If you select a polyline that is already closed, AutoCAD displays the **Open** option along with the other **PEDIT** command options. Enter this option to open the polyline. If you select an open polyline, the **Close** option is displayed instead of the **Open** option. Enter c to close the polyline. Open and closed polylines are shown in **Figure 6-32.**

The **Open** option is not displayed if you select a polyline that was closed by manually snapping to the endpoint of the first segment. It is only available if the polygon was closed using the **Close** option of the **PLINE** command.

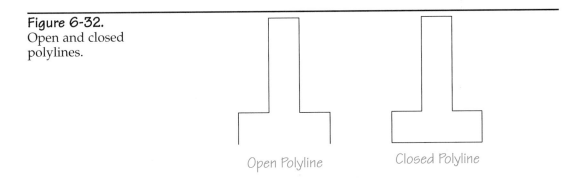

**Figure 6-32.**
Open and closed polylines.

Open Polyline        Closed Polyline

## Joining Polylines to Other Polylines, Lines, and Arcs

Polylines, lines, and arcs that are connected can be joined to create a single polyline using the **Join** option of the **PEDIT** command. This option works only if the polyline and other existing objects touch each other at their endpoints. They cannot cross, nor can there be any spaces or breaks between the segments. See **Figure 6-33.** The command sequence to join objects to a polyline and turn them into a single object is as follows:

**Figure 6-33.**
Using the **Join** option of the **PEDIT** command. A—Joining segments with matching endpoints. B—These segments cannot be joined.

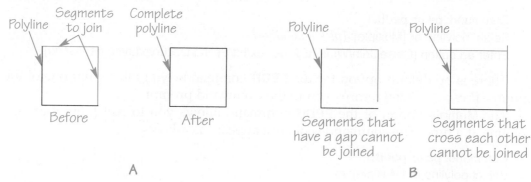

Command: **pe** *or* **pedit.**⏎
Select polyline or [Multiple]: *(select the original polyline)*
Enter an option [Close/Join/Width/Edit vertex/Fit/Spline/Decurve/Ltype gen/Undo]: **j.**⏎
Select objects: *(select all of the objects to be joined)*
Select objects: ⏎
*n* segments added to polyline
Enter an option [Close/Join/Width/Edit vertex/Fit/Spline/Decurve/Ltype gen/Undo]: ⏎
Command:

Select each object to be joined or group the objects with one of the selection set options. The original polyline can be included in the selection set, but it does not need to be. See **Figure 6-34.**

**Professional Tip**

Once items have been joined into a continuous polyline, the polyline can be closed using the **PEDIT Close** option.

**Figure 6-34.**
Joining a polyline to individual line segments.

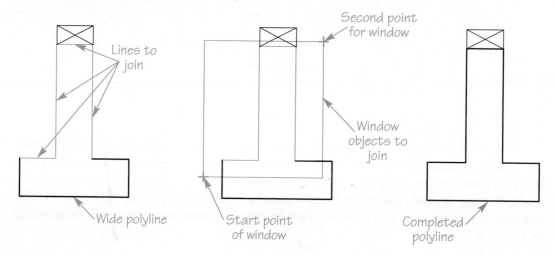

## Changing the Width of a Polyline

The **Width** option of the **PEDIT** command allows you to change the polyline width. The width of the original polyline can be constant or it can vary. To change a polyline from a 1/16″ width to a 1/8″ width, follow these steps:

Command: **pe** *or* **pedit**⏎
Select polyline or [Multiple]: *(pick the polyline)*
Enter an option [Close/Join/Width/Edit vertex/Fit/Spline/Decurve/Ltype gen/Undo]: **w**⏎
Specify new width for all segments: **1/8**⏎
Enter an option [Close/Join/Width/Edit vertex/Fit/Spline/Decurve/Ltype gen/Undo]: ⏎
Command:

An unedited polyline and a new polyline after using the **PEDIT Width** option are shown in **Figure 6-35**.

Circles drawn with the **CIRCLE** command cannot be changed to polylines for editing purposes. Polyline circles can be created by using the **PLINE Arc** option and drawing two 180° arcs, or by using the **DONUT** command. The **DONUT** command is discussed in Chapter 18. You can change the width of donuts by picking each donut individually and using the **PEDIT Width** option as previously discussed.

**Figure 6-35.**
Changing the width of a polyline from 1/16″ to 1/8″.

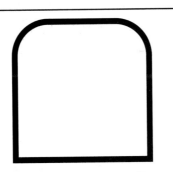 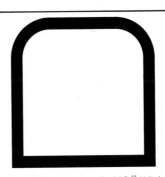

Existing Polyline with 1/16″ Width          Edited Polyline with 1/8″ Width

## Exercise 6-15

◆ Start a new drawing using a template or startup option of your own choice.
◆ Set architectural units.
◆ Draw a series of connected lines and arcs. Then, use the **Join** option of the **PEDIT** command to change these items to a single polyline. Finally, change the width of the polyline.
◆ Draw a closed polyline. Use the **Close** option to draw the final segment.
◆ Use the **Open** option of the **PEDIT** command to open the polyline, and use the **Close** option to close it again.
◆ Save the drawing as ex6-15.

## Editing a Polyline Vertex or Point of Tangency

The **Edit vertex** option of the **PEDIT** command is used to edit polyline vertices and points of tangency. A *polyline vertex* is where straight polyline segments meet and a *point of tangency* is where straight polyline segments or polyline arcs join other polyline arcs. When you enter the **Edit vertex** option, an "X" marker appears at the first polyline vertex or point of tangency. The **Edit vertex** option has 10 additional options, as shown in the following command sequence:

Command: **pe** *or* **pedit.**⏎
Select polyline or [Multiple]: *(pick the polyline)*
Enter an option [Close/Join/Width/Edit vertex/Fit/Spline/Decurve/Ltype gen/Undo]: **e.**⏎
Enter a vertex editing option
  [Next/Previous/Break/Insert/Move/Regen/Straighten/Tangent/Width/eXit] <N>:

The functions of the **Edit vertex** options are as follows:
- **Next.** Moves the "X" marker on screen to the next vertex or point of tangency on the polyline.
- **Previous.** Moves the marker to the previous vertex or point of tangency on the polyline.
- **Break.** Breaks a portion out of the polyline.
- **Insert.** Adds a new polyline vertex.
- **Move.** Moves a polyline vertex to a new location.
- **Regen.** Generates the revised version of the polyline.
- **Straighten.** Straightens polyline segments.
- **Tangent.** Specifies a tangent direction for curve fitting when using the **PEDIT Fit** option.
- **Width.** Changes a polyline segment width.
- **eXit.** Returns the **PEDIT** command prompt.

Only the current point identified by the "X" marker is affected by these editing functions. In **Figure 6-36,** the marker is moved in the same direction the polyline was created (in this case clockwise) using the **Next** option. If you edit the vertices of a polyline and nothing appears to happen, use the **Regen** option to regenerate the polyline.

**Figure 6-36.** Using the **Next** and **Previous** vertex editing options to specify polyline vertices. Note the different positions of the "X" marker.

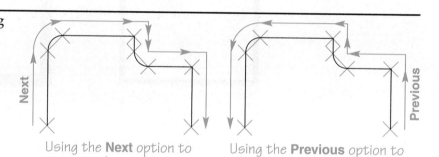

Using the **Next** option to move to the next vertex

Using the **Previous** option to move to the previous vertex

## Making Breaks in a Polyline

You can break out a portion of a polyline by using the **Break** option after entering the **Edit vertex** option. First, use the **Next** or **Previous** option to move the "X" marker to the correct vertex, as shown in the following sequence:

Enter an option [Close/Join/Width/Edit vertex/Fit/Spline/Decurve/Ltype gen/Undo]: **e.**⏎
Enter a vertex editing option
  [Next/Previous/Break/Insert/Move/Regen/Straighten/Tangent/Width/eXit] <N>: *(press* [Enter] *to move the "X" marker to the position where you want the break to begin)*
Enter a vertex editing option
  [Next/Previous/Break/Insert/Move/Regen/Straighten/Tangent/Width/eXit] <N>: **b.**⏎

AutoCAD accepts the highlighted vertex as the first break point. The sequence continues as follows:

Enter an option [Next/Previous/Go/eXit] <N>: *(move the "X" marker to the next or previous vertex)*

**Figure 6-37.**
Using the **Break** vertex option to break out a portion of a polyline.

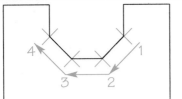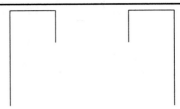

Using the **Previous** option to move to vertex "1". Enter the **Break** option to begin the break. Use the **Next** option to move to vertex "4". Enter the **Go** option to perform the break.

Original polyline broken into two separate segments

Move the marker to the vertex you want to designate as the second break point. Then, enter g for **Go**. This instructs AutoCAD to remove the portion of the polyline between the two selected vertices. The results of the following command sequence are illustrated in **Figure 6-37:**

Enter a vertex editing option
    [Next/Previous/Break/Insert/Move/Regen/Straighten/Tangent/Width/eXit] <N>: **b**↵
    *(specifies Point 1)*
Enter an option [Next/Previous/Go/eXit] <N>:↵ *(specifies Point 2)*
Enter an option [Next/Previous/Go/eXit] <N>: ↵ *(specifies Point 3)*
Enter an option [Next/Previous/Go/eXit] <N>: ↵ *(specifies Point 4)*
Enter an option [Next/Previous/Go/eXit] <N>: **g**↵ *(breaks the polyline between Points 1 and 4)*

## Inserting a New Vertex in a Polyline

The **Insert** vertex editing option is used to add a new vertex to a polyline. First, use the **Next** and **Previous** options to locate the vertex that will precede the vertex you wish to add. Refer to **Figure 6-38** as you go through the following command sequence:

Enter an option [Close/Join/Width/Edit vertex/Fit/Spline/Decurve/Ltype gen/Undo]: **e**↵
Enter a vertex editing option
    [Next/Previous/Break/Insert/Move/Regen/Straighten/Tangent/Width/eXit] <N>: *(move the "X" marker to the desired location)*
Enter a vertex editing option
    [Next/Previous/Break/Insert/Move/Regen/Straighten/Tangent/Width/eXit] <N>: **i**↵
Specify location for new vertex: *(pick the new vertex location using your pointing device or enter the coordinates)*
Enter a vertex editing option
    [Next/Previous/Break/Insert/Move/Regen/Straighten/Tangent/Width/eXit] <N>: **x**↵

**Figure 6-38.**
Using the **Insert** vertex option to add a new vertex to a polyline.

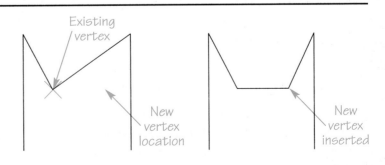

Existing vertex

New vertex location

New vertex inserted

## Moving a Polyline Vertex

The **Move** vertex editing option enables you to move a polyline vertex to a desired location. This option is similar to the **Insert** option. The "X" marker must first be placed on the vertex you want to move. Then, you can enter the **Move** option and specify the new location. The results of the following sequence are shown in **Figure 6-39**:

Enter an option [Close/Join/Width/Edit vertex/Fit/Spline/Decurve/Ltype gen/Undo]: **e.**↵
Enter a vertex editing option
    [Next/Previous/Break/Insert/Move/Regen/Straighten/Tangent/Width/eXit] <N>: *(move the "X" marker to the vertex to be moved)*
Enter a vertex editing option
    [Next/Previous/Break/Insert/Move/Regen/Straighten/Tangent/Width/eXit] <N>: **m.**↵
Specify new location for marked vertex: *(pick the desired location with your pointing device or enter the coordinates)*
Enter a vertex editing option
    [Next/Previous/Break/Insert/Move/Regen/Straighten/Tangent/Width/eXit] <N>: **x.**↵

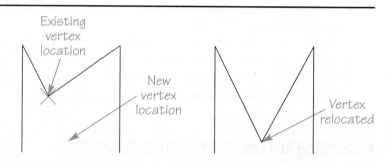

**Figure 6-39.**
Using the **Move vertex** option to move a polyline vertex to a new location.

## Straightening Polyline Segments or Arcs

The **Straighten** vertex editing option allows you to straighten polyline segments or arcs between two points. The command sequence is as follows:

Enter an option [Close/Join/Width/Edit vertex/Fit/Spline/Decurve/Ltype gen/Undo]: **e.**↵
Enter a vertex editing option
    [Next/Previous/Break/Insert/Move/Regen/Straighten/Tangent/Width/eXit] <N>: *(move the "X" marker to the first point of the segments to be straightened)*
Enter a vertex editing option
    [Next/Previous/Break/Insert/Move/Regen/Straighten/Tangent/Width/eXit] <N>: **s.**↵
Enter an option [Next/Previous/Go/eXit] <N>: *(move the "X" marker to the last point of the segments to be straightened)*
Enter an option [Next/Previous/Go/eXit] <N>: **g.**↵

If the "X" marker is not moved before g is entered, AutoCAD straightens the segment from the first marked point to the next vertex. This provides a quick way to straighten an arc. See **Figure 6-40.**

## Changing Polyline Segment Widths

The **Width** vertex editing option is the only option that changes the starting and ending widths of an individual polyline segment. To change a segment width, move the "X" marker to the beginning vertex of the segment to be altered. Then, enter the **Width** option and specify the new width. The command sequence is as follows:

**Figure 6-40.**
The **Straighten vertex** option is used to straighten polyline segments.

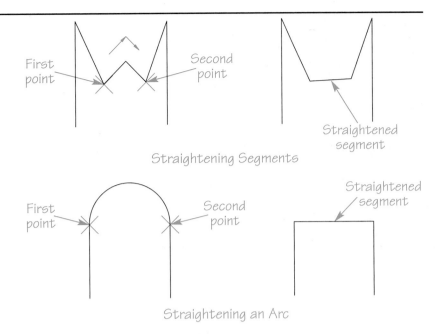

Straightening Segments

Straightening an Arc

Enter an option [Close/Join/Width/Edit vertex/Fit/Spline/Decurve/Ltype gen/Undo]: **e.↵**
Enter a vertex editing option
    [Next/Previous/Break/Insert/Move/Regen/Straighten/Tangent/Width/eXit] <N>: *(move the "X" marker to the beginning vertex of the segment to be changed)*
Enter a vertex editing option
    [Next/Previous/Break/Insert/Move/Regen/Straighten/Tangent/Width/eXit] <N>: **w.↵**
Specify starting width for next segment <*current width of segment*>: *(enter the revised starting width and press* [Enter]*)*
Specify ending width for next segment <*revised starting width*>: *(enter the revised ending width and press* [Enter]*, or press* [Enter] *to keep the width the same as the starting width)*
Enter a vertex editing option
    [Next/Previous/Break/Insert/Move/Regen/Straighten/Tangent/Width/eXit] <N>: **r.↵**

    Notice that the starting width default value is the current width of the segment to be changed. The ending width default value is the same as the revised starting width. If nothing appears to happen to the segment when you specify the ending width and press [Enter], enter the **Regen** option to have AutoCAD draw the revised polyline. See **Figure 6-41.**

**Figure 6-41.**
Changing the width of a polyline segment with the **Width** option. Use the **Regen** option to display the change.

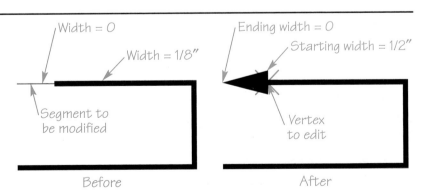

Before

After

## Exercise 6-16

◆ Start a new drawing using a template or startup option of your own choice.
◆ Set architectural units.
◆ Draw a polyline with a series of segments. Draw the polyline with at least eight vertices and three arcs.
◆ Issue the **PEDIT** command and enter the **Edit vertex** option. Move the "X" marker around using the **Next** and **Previous** options.
◆ Break the polyline between any three points. Then, undo the breaks.
◆ Insert a new vertex in the polyline.
◆ Move one vertex of the polyline.
◆ Straighten one arc segment or at least three line segments.
◆ Change the starting and ending widths of one segment.
◆ Save the drawing as ex6-16.

## Making Smooth Curves out of Polylines

In some situations, you may need to convert a polyline into a series of smooth curves. One example of this would be to make contour lines on a site plan. Contour lines are drawn by creating a smooth curve through a series of points. This process is called *curve fitting* and is accomplished using the **PEDIT Fit** option and the **Tangent** vertex editing option.

The **Fit** option allows you to construct pairs of arcs passing through control points. You can specify the control points, or you can simply use the vertices of the polyline. Closely spaced control points produce a smooth curve.

Prior to curve fitting, each vertex can be given a tangent direction. AutoCAD then fits the curve based on the tangent directions that you set. However, you do not need to enter tangent directions. Specifying tangent directions is a way to edit vertices when the **PEDIT Fit** option does not produce the best results.

The **Tangent** vertex editing option is used to edit tangent directions. After entering the **PEDIT** command and the **Edit vertex** option, move the "X" marker to each vertex to be changed. Enter the **Tangent** option for each specified vertex and enter a tangent direction in degrees, or pick a point in the expected direction. The direction you choose is then indicated by an arrow placed at the vertex.

Enter an option [Close/Join/Width/Edit vertex/Fit/Spline/Decurve/Ltype gen/Undo]: **e**↵
Enter a vertex editing option
   [Next/Previous/Break/Insert/Move/Regen/Straighten/Tangent/Width/eXit] <N>: (*move the "X" marker to the desired vertex*)
Enter a vertex editing option
   [Next/Previous/Break/Insert/Move/Regen/Straighten/Tangent/Width/eXit] <N>: **t**↵
Specify direction of vertex tangent: (*specify a direction in positive or negative degrees and press* [Enter], *or pick a point in the desired direction*)

Continue by moving the marker to each vertex that you want to change, entering the **Tangent** option for each vertex and selecting a tangent direction. Once the tangent directions are given for all vertices to be changed, exit the vertex editing options and select the **Fit** option:

Enter a vertex editing option
   [Next/Previous/Break/Insert/Move/Regen/Straighten/Tangent/Width/eXit] <N>: **x**↵
Enter an option [Close/Join/Width/Edit vertex/Fit/Spline/Decurve/Ltype gen/Undo]: **f**↵

**Figure 6-42.**
Using the **PEDIT Fit** option to turn straight-segment polylines into fit-curve polylines.

Existing Polylines    Polylines after Curve Fitting

You can also enter the **PEDIT** command, select a polyline, and then enter the **Fit** option without adjusting tangencies if desired. The polyline shown in **Figure 6-42** was made into a smooth curve using the following steps:

Command: **pe** *or* **pedit**.↵
Select polyline or [Multiple]: *(pick the polyline to be edited)*
Enter an option [Close/Join/Width/Edit vertex/Fit/Spline/Decurve/Ltype gen/Undo]: **f**↵

If the resulting curve does not look like what you had anticipated, enter the **Edit vertex** option. Then, make changes using the various vertex editing options as necessary.

## Using the **PEDIT Spline** Option

When a polyline is edited with the **PEDIT Fit** option, the resulting curve passes through polyline vertices. The **PEDIT Spline** option also smoothes the corners of a straight-segment polyline. However, this option produces different results. The resulting curve passes through the first and last control points or vertices only. However, the curve *pulls* toward the other vertices (but does not pass through them). The **Spline** option is used as follows:

Command: **pe** *or* **pedit**.↵
Select polyline or [Multiple]: *(pick the polyline to be edited)*
Enter an option [Close/Join/Width/Edit vertex/Fit/Spline/Decurve/Ltype gen/Undo]: **s**↵

The results of using the **Fit** and **Spline** options on the same polyline are illustrated in **Figure 6-43.**

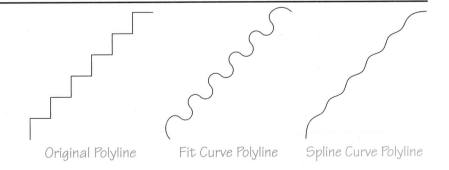

**Figure 6-43.**
A comparison of polylines edited with the **Fit** and **Spline** options.

Original Polyline    Fit Curve Polyline    Spline Curve Polyline

---

# Straightening All Segments of a Polyline

The **PEDIT Decurve** option returns a polyline edited with the **Fit** or **Spline** options to its original form. However, the information entered for tangent directions is kept for future reference. You can also use the **Decurve** option to straighten the segments of a polyarc. See **Figure 6-44**.

Command: **pe** *or* **pedit**↵
Select polyline or [Multiple]: *(pick the polyline to be edited)*
Enter an option [Close/Join/Width/Edit vertex/Fit/Spline/Decurve/Ltype gen/Undo]: **d**↵

**Figure 6-44.**
The **Decurve** option is used to straighten the curved segments of a poly-line.

 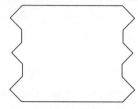

Original Polyline Arc

Polyline Arc after Using the **Decurve** Option

**Professional Tip**

If you make a mistake while editing a polyline, remember that the **Undo** option is available inside the **PEDIT** command. Using the **Undo** option more than once allows you to step backward through each option used. Press [Enter] to return to the Command prompt. The **UNDO** command can also be used at the Command prompt to undo the effects of the last **PEDIT** command.

## Exercise 6-17

◆ Start a new drawing using a template or startup option of your own choice.
◆ Set architectural units.
◆ Draw a polyline with at least five vertices. Make the polyline smooth using the **Fit** option of the **PEDIT** command.
◆ Return the polyline to its original form using the **PEDIT Decurve** option.
◆ Practice with the **Undo** option by first drawing a series of polyline segments. After using the **PEDIT** command to make several changes, use the **Undo** option to return to the original polyline.
◆ Save the drawing as ex6-17.

# Changing the Appearance of Polyline Linetypes

The **PEDIT Ltype gen** (linetype generation) option determines how linetypes other than Continuous appear in relation to the vertices of a polyline. For example, when a Center linetype is used and the **Ltype gen** option is disabled, the polyline has a long dash at each vertex. When the **Ltype gen** option is activated, the polyline is generated with the lengths of dashes producing a constant pattern in relation to the vertices. The difference between having the **Ltype gen** option off and on is illustrated in **Figure 6-45**. Also shown are the effects these settings have on spline curves. To turn the **Ltype gen** option on, use the following procedure:

Architectural Drafting Using AutoCAD

**Figure 6-45.**
A comparison of
polylines with the
**Ltype gen** option on
and off.

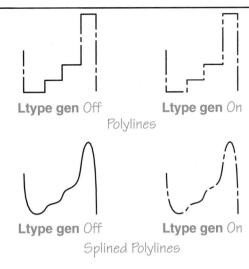

Ltype gen *Off*  Ltype gen *On*
Polylines

Ltype gen *Off*  Ltype gen *On*
Splined Polylines

Command: **pe** *or* **pedit**↵
Select polyline or [Multiple]: *(pick the polyline)*
Enter an option [Close/Join/Width/Edit vertex/Fit/Spline/Decurve/Ltype gen/Undo]: **l**↵
Enter polyline linetype generation option [ON/OFF] <Off>: **on**↵

You can also change the **Ltype gen** option setting with the **PLINEGEN** system variable. This variable must be set before the desired polyline is drawn (changing the setting only affects new polylines). The settings for the **PLINEGEN** system variable are 0 (off) and 1 (on).

## Exercise 6-18

◆ Start a new drawing using a template or startup option of your own choice.
◆ Set architectural units.
◆ Draw a polyline and a splined polyline similar to the left side of **Figure 6-45**.
◆ Turn the **Ltype gen** option off and on to observe the results.
◆ Save the drawing as ex6-18.

# Chapter Test

*Answer the following questions on a separate sheet of paper.*

1. Identify the toolbar and pull-down menu where the commands are found that allow you to edit geometry.
2. Give the command alias for the **MOVE** command.
3. What is the function of the base point?
4. Define *displacement*.
5. What is the second point of displacement?
6. What happens when using the **MOVE** command if you enter 3,5 at the Specify base point or displacement: prompt and then press [Enter] at the Specify second point of displacement or <use first point as displacement>: prompt?
7. Give the command aliases for the **COPY** command.
8. How do you make several copies of the same object while using the **COPY** command?
9. What do you enter at the Select objects: prompt to select a single item and have it automatically edited without first being highlighted?
10. Name the selection option that allows you to select the previously drawn object.
11. Briefly describe the difference in function between the **Window** and **Crossing** selection options.

12. Which selection option is established automatically when you pick a point and then move the cursor to the right?
13. Describe the difference in appearance between the window box and crossing box.
14. What is the **PICKAUTO** setting that allows you to automatically use the **Window** and **Crossing** selection options?
15. Define *polygon*.
16. Name the selection option that allows you to place a line through any objects that you want to select.
17. Which key do you hold down while picking a selected item to remove it from the selection set?
18. What do you enter at the Select objects: prompt to activate the Remove objects: prompt?
19. Name the selection option that allows you to select the same objects that you had selected in the last operation.
20. Name the selection option that allows you to select everything in the drawing.
21. Define *stacked objects*.
22. Define *cycling*.
23. How do you cycle through stacked objects?
24. Define *filter*.
25. How do you access the **Quick Select** dialog box from the **Properties** window?
26. Give the command alias for the **ROTATE** command.
27. When using the **ROTATE** command, in what direction does a positive rotation angle rotate the object?
28. Identify the command alias for accessing the **SCALE** command.
29. Name the **SCALE** command's default option.
30. What do you enter for a scale factor to scale an object to twice its original size?
31. What do you enter for a scale factor to scale an object to half its original size?
32. Name the **SCALE** command option you would use to scale an object from 4″ to 6″.
33. Identify the command alias for accessing the **STRETCH** command.
34. What selection options can you use when selecting objects to stretch?
35. How does the **STRETCH** command act if you select the entire object?
36. Identify the command alias for accessing the **MIRROR** command.
37. Define *mirror line*.
38. If you want text to be truly mirrored, what variable controls this and what should the value be set to?
39. Give the command alias for the **BREAK** command.
40. When you pick an object using the **BREAK** command, where is the first break point by default?
41. How do you select a new first break point when using the **BREAK** command?
42. How do you use the **BREAK** command to split an object in two without removing a portion?
43. In what direction should you pick the first and second break points when breaking a portion out of an arc or circle?
44. Give the command alias for the **TRIM** command.
45. Define *cutting edge*.
46. Define *implied intersection*.
47. Name the **TRIM** command option that allows you to trim to an implied intersection.
48. Name the **TRIM** command option that allows you to cancel the previous trimming operation without leaving the command.
49. Give the command alias for the **EXTEND** command.
50. Define *boundary edge*.
51. Name the **EXTEND** command option that allows you to extend to an implied intersection.
52. Give the command alias for the **LENGTHEN** command.
53. Identify the **LENGTHEN** command option that allows you to specify the amount of change in length.

54. Identify the **LENGTHEN** command option that allows you to change the length of an object or the angle of an arc by a specified percentage.
55. Give the **LENGTHEN** command option that allows you to set the total length or angle.
56. Identify the **LENGTHEN** command option that allows you to drag the endpoint of the object to the desired length or angle.
57. Give the command alias for the **PEDIT** command.
58. Name the **PEDIT** option that allows you to close an open polyline.
59. Name the **PEDIT** option that allows you to bring two separate but connecting polylines together to create a single polyline.
60. Define *polyline vertex*.
61. Define *point of tangency*.
62. What appears on the screen when you enter the **PEDIT Edit vertex** option?
63. Name the **Edit vertex** option that adds a new polyline vertex.
64. Name the two **PEDIT** command options that change a straight-segment polyline into a curved polyline.
65. Name the **PEDIT** command option that determines how linetypes other than continuous appear.

# Chapter Problems

*Start a new drawing for each problem, unless indicated otherwise.*

1. Draw Object A using the **LINE** and **ARC** commands. Make sure that the corners overrun and the arc is centered over, but does not touch, the lines. Then use the **TRIM**, **EXTEND**, **COPY**, and **MOVE** commands to make the object look like Object B. Save the drawing as p6-1.

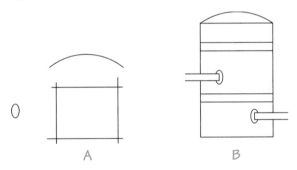

A          B

2. Open drawing p6-1 for further editing. Using the **STRETCH** command, change the shape to Object B. Make a copy of the new revision. Change the copy to represent Object C. Save the drawing as p6-2.

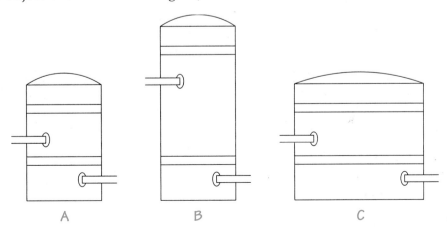

A          B          C

3. Draw the parking lot arrows shown below using lines and arcs. Use the **PEDIT** command to join the lines and arcs. Give the new polylines a width. Save the drawing as p6-3.

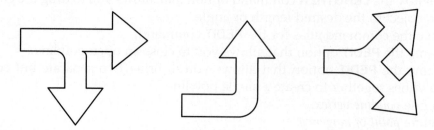

4. Draw the symbol shown below. Use the **PEDIT** command to join the line and arc segments. Then give the polylines a width. Save the drawing as p6-4.

5. Open p3-24. Use the **STRETCH** command to change the size of the window. Save the drawing as p6-5.
6. Open p6-5. Use the **MIRROR** command to mirror a copy beside the original window. Save the drawing as p6-6.
7. Open drawing p3-25. Copy the window to the side. Use the **SCALE** reference option to scale the 6'-0" width to be 4'-0". Stretch the new window to a height of 3'-0". Save the drawing as p6-7.
8. Open drawing p3-26. Use the **MIRROR** command to create a double door. Use any modifying commands to create a new design on the doors. Save the drawing as p6-8.
9. Use the **LINE** command to draw the patio shown as Object A below without dimensions. Use the **PEDIT** command to join the patio lines together. Create two copies, one for Object A and one for Object B. For Object B, use the **PEDIT Fit** option. For Object C, use the **PEDIT Spline** option. Finally, straighten out the patio lines. Save the drawing as p6-9.

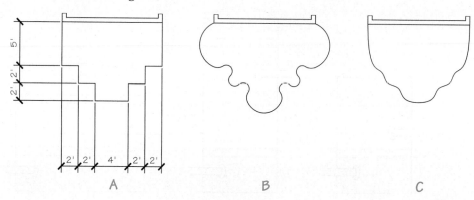

# CHAPTER 7

# Grip Editing

## Learning Objectives

After completing this chapter, you will be able to:

◆ Use the Stretch, Move, Rotate, Scale, and Mirror grip modes to perform automatic editing.
◆ Use the **Copy** option with grip modes.
◆ Perform automatic editing with the **Properties** window.
◆ Copy objects between drawings.
◆ Set selection mode options.
◆ Control object sorting methods.

## Important Terms

copy and paste
drawing database
grips
noun/verb selection

selected grips
unselected grips
verb/noun selection

In Chapter 6, you learned how to use basic editing commands to perform a variety of editing activities in AutoCAD. These commands give you maximum flexibility and increase productivity. However, this chapter takes editing a step further by explaining how to use grips to quickly edit an object.

## Automatic Editing with Grips

The use of grips can help speed the editing process in a drawing. *Grips* are small boxes that appear at key locations on a selected object. For example, the grips on a line are located at the endpoints and midpoint. The grips can be picked and used to modify the object. When grips are used for editing, the object is first selected to activate the grips. Then, any of the small boxes can be picked to perform stretch, copy, move, rotate, scale, or mirror operations.

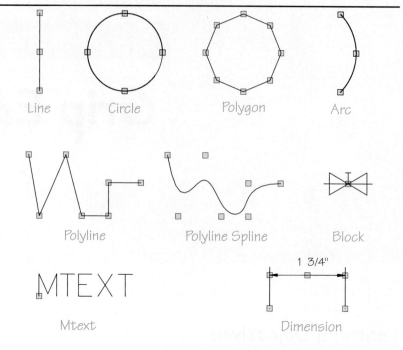

**Figure 7-1.**
Grips are placed at important locations on objects.

Line    Circle    Polygon    Arc

Polyline    Polyline Spline    Block

MTEXT

Mtext

1 3/4"

Dimension

Grips can be used as long as there is no command currently active. You can pick any object to activate its grips. **Figure 7-1** shows grip locations on several different objects. For text and blocks, the grip is located at the insertion point. Text and blocks will be discussed in future chapters.

## Warm and Hot Grips

The grips displayed when you first pick an object are called *unselected grips*. They are referred to as "warm" because they have not yet been selected for modification. Unselected grips appear as filled-in squares and are blue by default. See **Figure 7-2**.

After you pick a grip, it becomes a *selected grip*. Selected grips are referred to as "hot" because they are selected and ready for modification. A selected grip appears as a filled-in square and is red by default. Multiple grips can be selected (made hot) and then edited as a group, even if they belong to different objects.

When an object is selected and the warm grips are displayed, moving the crosshairs over one of the warm grips and pausing changes the grip color. This is referred to as the hover grip color, which is green by default. This feature is helpful when there are a lot of grips close together and you want to make sure you select the correct one.

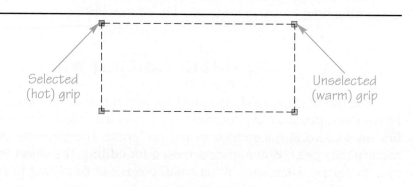

**Figure 7-2.**
Different colors are used to identify grips depending on the selection made. Selected (hot) grips are red by default. Unselected (warm) grips are blue by default. Actual colors are not shown.

Selected (hot) grip

Unselected (warm) grip

To activate an object's grips, move the pick box to the desired object and pick it. You can pick objects individually, or use a window or crossing box to select objects. The selected objects are highlighted and the unselected (warm) grips are displayed. To select a grip (make it hot), move the pick box to one of the unselected grips and pick it. When you pick a grip, the command line displays the following prompt:

```
** STRETCH **
Specify stretch point or [Base point/Copy/Undo/eXit]:
```

It is from this and similar prompts that editing actions can be carried out on grips. The following are some general rules and guidelines that can help make grips work for you:

- Be sure the **GRIPS** system variable is on.
- Pick an object or group of objects to activate grips. Objects in the selection set are highlighted with warm grips.
- Pick a warm grip to make it hot.
- Make multiple grips hot by holding the [Shift] key while picking warm grips.
- Hold the [Shift] key and pick a hot grip to make it warm. This allows you to deactivate individual hot grips.
- All selected objects (objects with warm grips) are affected by editing actions.
- To remove objects from the selection set, hold down the [Shift] key and pick the object. This turns the highlight off and deactivates the object's grips.
- Return objects to the selection set by picking them again.
- To deactivate all of the grips, press the [Esc] key. This also deselects all objects.

## Grip Modes

The Stretch mode is the first grip mode that is activated when you pick on a hot grip. If you were to move your pointing device while this prompt is displayed, the hot grip would be repositioned, stretching the object. However, other grip modes—Move, Rotate, Scale, and Mirror—are also available to automatically edit objects. To use one of the other modes, pick an object and make one of its grips hot. When you see the ** STRETCH ** prompt, press [Enter] or the space bar to cycle through the grip mode options like this:

```
** STRETCH **
Specify stretch point or [Base point/Copy/Undo/eXit]: ↵
** MOVE **
Specify move point or [Base point/Copy/Undo/eXit]: ↵
** ROTATE **
Specify rotation angle or [Base point/Copy/Undo/Reference/eXit]: ↵
** SCALE **
Specify scale factor or [Base point/Copy/Undo/Reference/eXit]: ↵
** MIRROR **
Specify second point or [Base point/Copy/Undo/eXit]: ↵
```

When the appropriate prompt is displayed, you can carry out the desired operation. The grip modes can also be accessed by right-clicking and selecting the appropriate mode from the grips shortcut menu, shown in **Figure 7-3.** This menu is only available after a grip has been turned into a selected (hot) grip.

The shortcut menu allows you to access the five grip modes without using the keyboard. After the shortcut menu is displayed, pick either **Move, Mirror, Rotate, Scale,** or **Stretch** as needed. The **Base Point, Copy,** and **Undo** options are also available in the grips shortcut menu. These options are discussed in detail later in the chapter. An added bonus in the grips shortcut menu is the **Properties...** option.

**Figure 7-3.**
The grips shortcut menu appears when a grip is selected and you right-click.

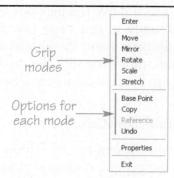

Grip modes

Options for each mode

Selecting this opens the **Properties** window, where you can change properties of the objects being edited. Selecting the **Exit** option closes the grips shortcut menu and deactivates the hot grip.

## Stretching an Object with Grips

As discussed earlier, the Stretch mode is the first grip mode activated when you pick a hot grip. When you pick a grip, the command line displays the following prompt:

** STRETCH **
Specify stretch point or [Base point/Copy/Undo/eXit]:

When this prompt is displayed, all you have to do is move the cursor to stretch the selected object, as shown in **Figure 7-4.**

 **Note** In the Stretch grip mode, if you pick the middle grip of a line or the center grip of a circle, the entire object will be moved, not stretched, as you move the cursor.

**Figure 7-4.**
Using the grips Stretch mode.

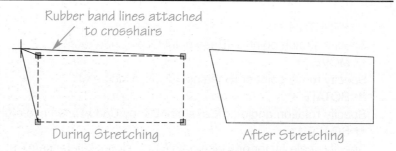

Rubber band lines attached to crosshairs

During Stretching

After Stretching

The options available with the Stretch grip mode are also available in all other grip modes (Move, Rotate, Scale, and Mirror). Later sections in this chapter will discuss the specific uses for each option. The following are brief descriptions of each option:

- **Base point.** When an unselected grip is turned into a selected grip, that grip becomes the base point for any operations performed. Type b and press [Enter] to select a new base point.
- **Copy.** Using the **Copy** option allows you to create multiple copies while stretching, moving, rotating, scaling, or mirroring objects. Type c and press [Enter] to activate this option.

Architectural Drafting Using AutoCAD

- **Undo.** Type u and press [Enter] to undo the previous operation.
- **eXit.** Type x and press [Enter] to exit the command. This deactivates the selected (hot) grip but does not affect the unselected (warm) grips. You can also use the [Esc] key to cancel the command. Canceling twice deactivates the selected and the unselected grips and returns the Command prompt.

Occasionally you will want to stretch multiple grips on an object. If the grips need to be stretched the same distance and in the same direction, such as when extending a rectangle, the grips can be stretched simultaneously. To do this, hold down the [Shift] key while selecting each grip to be stretched. After you select all the necessary grips, release the [Shift] key. Pick one of the hot grips and stretch the object as necessary.

**Figure 7-5** shows how you can move a grip to stretch the features of a selected object. Step 1 in **Figure 7-5A** stretches the first corner and Step 2 stretches the second corner. **Figure 7-5B** demonstrates how the same results can be achieved by stretching multiple grips simultaneously.

**Professional Tip**

When editing with grips, you can enter coordinates or use polar tracking with direct distance entry to help improve your accuracy. Remember that all coordinate entry methods work with grip editing.

**Figure 7-5.**
Stretching an object. A—Select individual grips to stretch the corners. B—Select several grips by holding the [Shift] key to modify all of the hot grip points.

2. Select this grip

3. Pick hot grip to activate the Stretch mode

3. Stretch to here

2. Select these grips by holding down the [Shift] key

1. Pick object to activate grips

1. Pick object to activate grips

Step 1

Step 1

1. Select this grip

2. Stretch to here

1. Stretch to here

2. Stretch to here

Step 2

Step 2

A

B

## Exercise 7-1

◆ Start a new drawing using a template or startup option of your choice.
◆ Set architectural units.
◆ Draw a line with coordinates X = 2, Y = 4 and X = 2, Y = 7. Draw a circle with the center at X = 5.5, Y = 5.5, with a radius of 1.5. Finally, draw an arc with its center at X = 8.5, Y = 5.5, a start point of X = 9.5, Y = 4, and an endpoint of X = 9.5, Y = 7.
◆ Make sure grips are enabled.
◆ Experiment with the grips Stretch mode by picking the points as follows:
　◆ Line—Pick the ends first and then the middle to see what happens.
　◆ Circle—Pick one of the quadrants, and then the center.
　◆ Arc—Pick the ends and the middle.
　◆ Line, Circle, Arc—Hold the [Shift] key down and pick an endpoint of the line and arc and a quadrant of the circle.
◆ Save the drawing as ex7-1.

## Moving an Object with Grips

If you want to move an object with grips, select the object, pick a grip to use as the base point, and then press [Enter] or the space bar to cycle through the commands until you get to this prompt:

** MOVE **
Specify move point or [Base point/Copy/Undo/eXit]:

The selected grip becomes the base point. Then, the object is moved to a new point by picking the new location. For accuracy, you may want to use an object snap mode or coordinate entry to place the object in a new location. The Move mode is illustrated in **Figure 7-6.** If you accidentally pick the wrong grip or want to have a base point other than the selected grip, type b and press [Enter] for the **Base point** option. Then, pick a new base point. You can also access the Move mode and select the **Base Point** option directly from the shortcut menu.

> **Note**
> With the exception of the Stretch grip mode, the grip mode operations modify all selected objects (objects with warm grips), whether the objects have a hot grip or not. This can be helpful if many objects need to be moved, rotated, scaled, or mirrored from a common base point. If grip points on several objects need to be stretched, the grip points to be modified must be hot.

## Exercise 7-2

◆ Start a new drawing using a template or startup option of your choice.
◆ Set architectural units.
◆ Draw a circle with a diameter of 1.5 and its center at X = 2, Y = 3.
◆ Use grips to move the circle 2 units to the right.
◆ Save the drawing as ex7-2.

      

**Figure 7-6.**
The Move mode.
The selected grip
becomes the base
point for the move.
Here, the center of
the circle is moved
to the midpoint of
the line.

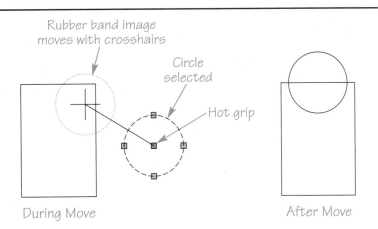

## Copying an Object with Grips

The **Copy** option is found in each of the grip modes. The **Copy** option allows you to make multiple copies of the object you are modifying. The following shows how the **Copy** option is used with the Stretch mode:

```
** STRETCH (multiple) **
Specify stretch point or [Base point/Copy/Undo/eXit]: c↵
```

The **Copy** option in the Move mode is the true form of the **COPY** command. You can activate the **Copy** option by entering c as follows:

```
** MOVE **
Specify move point or [Base point/Copy/Undo/eXit]: c↵
** MOVE (multiple) **
Specify move point or [Base point/Copy/Undo/eXit]: (make as many copies as desired
    and enter x, press [Esc], or select Exit from the grips shortcut menu to exit)
```

Holding down the [Shift] key while performing the first grip mode operation or selecting **Copy** from the grips shortcut menu also activates the **Copy** option. The **Copy** option works similarly in each of the grip modes. Try it with each mode to see what happens.

**Professional Tip**

When in the **Copy** option of the Move mode, if you make the first copy and hold down the [Shift] key while making subsequent copies, the distance of the first copy automatically becomes the snap spacing for the additional copies.

## Exercise 7-3

- ◆ Start a new drawing using a template or startup option of your choice.
- ◆ Set architectural units.
- ◆ Use the **RECTANG** command to draw the objects labeled A, B, C, and D in the figure at the end of the exercise. Do not draw dimensions.
- ◆ Use the **Copy** option of the Stretch grip mode to make Object A look similar to the example at the right.
- ◆ Use the **Copy** option of the Stretch grip mode to make Object B look similar to the example at the right. Make two grips hot for this to work.
- ◆ Use the **Copy** option of the Move mode to make multiple copies to the right of Object C by using coordinate entry or direct distance entry.
- ◆ Use the Move mode while holding down the [Shift] key to make multiple copies to the right of Object D.
- ◆ Save the drawing as ex7-3.

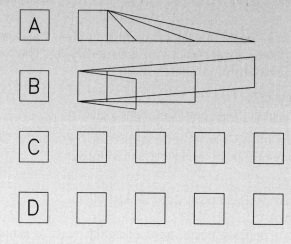

## Rotating an Object with Grips

To use grips to rotate an object, select the object, pick a grip to use as the base point, and press [Enter] or the space bar until you see this prompt:

** ROTATE **
Specify rotation angle or [Base point/Copy/Undo/Reference/eXit]:

Now, move your pointing device to rotate the object. Pick the desired rotation point, or enter a rotation angle.

Type r and press [Enter] if you want to use the **Reference** option. The **Reference** option may be used when the object is already rotated at an unknown angle and you want to rotate it to a new angle. To use the **Reference** option, enter r at the Command prompt or right-click and select **Reference** from the shortcut menu. AutoCAD prompts you to specify a reference angle. Using object snaps, snap to the endpoints of the object that define the unknown angle. Then, enter the new desired angle. **Figure 7-7** shows the Rotate mode options.

The **Reference** option of the **ROTATE** command is explained fully in Chapter 6.

## Exercise 7-4

- Start a new drawing using a template or startup option of your choice.
- Set architectural units.
- Set the polar tracking to an increment value of 45°.
- Use the **RECTANG** command to draw a rectangle similar to the one shown at the left of **Figure 7-7.** Orient the long sides so they are at 0°.
- Use grips to rotate the object 45°.
- Rotate the object again to any angle.
- Use the **Reference** option to rotate the object so that it is oriented to a 45° angle.
- Save the drawing as ex7-4.

**Figure 7-7.**
The rotation angle and **Reference** options of the Rotate grip mode.

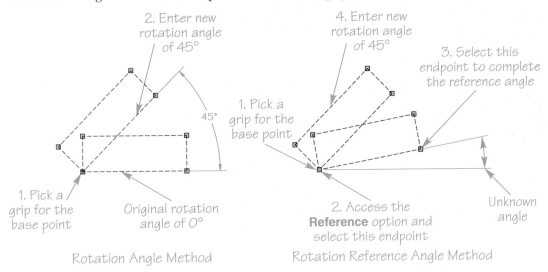

2. Enter new rotation angle of 45°

4. Enter new rotation angle of 45°

3. Select this endpoint to complete the reference angle

1. Pick a grip for the base point

45°

1. Pick a grip for the base point

Original rotation angle of 0°

2. Access the **Reference** option and select this endpoint

Unknown angle

Rotation Angle Method

Rotation Reference Angle Method

## Scaling an Object with Grips

If you want to scale an object with grips, select the object(s) to be scaled, then select a grip to make hot. Cycle through the editing options until you get this prompt:

\*\* SCALE \*\*
Specify scale factor or [Base point/Copy/Undo/Reference/eXit]:

Move the crosshairs to increase or decrease the size of the object and pick when the object is dragged to the desired size. You can also enter a scale factor at the prompt line. You can use the **Reference** option for the Scale mode if you do not know the size or scale of an object but know the desired scale or size. When using the **Reference** option, the reference length is the current length of the object, and the new length is the desired length.

The selected base point remains in the same place when the object is scaled. **Figure 7-8** shows the two Scale mode options.

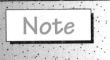

Note      The **Reference** option of the **SCALE** command is explained fully in Chapter 6.

Figure 7-8.
Options for the Scale grip mode include using a scale factor or reference length.

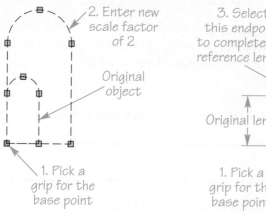

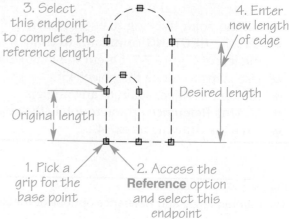

Using the Scale Factor Method

Using the Scale Factor Reference Method

## Exercise 7-5

◆ Start a new drawing using a template or startup option of your choice.
◆ Set architectural units.
◆ Using the **PLINE** command, draw an object similar to the original object on the left in **Figure 7-8.**
◆ Activate grips to make a copy of the object to the right of the original.
◆ Scale the first object using a scale factor of 1.5.
◆ Use the **Reference** option to scale the second object to any height.
◆ Save the drawing as ex7-5.

## Mirroring an Object with Grips

When using grips to mirror an object, the selected grip becomes the first point of the mirror line. To use the Mirror grip mode, select the object to be mirrored. Next, select a grip to be used as the first point of the mirror line. Then, press [Enter] or the space bar to cycle through the editing commands until you get this prompt:

\*\* MIRROR \*\*
Specify second point or [Base point/Copy/Undo/eXit]:

Select a second point that defines the second point of the mirror line. If a different first mirror line point is desired, use the **Base point** option to reset the first point of the mirror line. Pick another grip or any point on the screen as the second point of the mirror line. See **Figure 7-9.** The standard **MIRROR** command gives you the option to delete the old objects, but the Mirror grip mode does not. The old objects are deleted automatically. If you want to keep the original object while mirroring, use the **Copy** option of the Mirror mode.

## Exercise 7-6

◆ Start a new drawing using a template or startup option of your choice.
◆ Set architectural units.
◆ Draw a shape similar to the original object in **Figure 7-9.**
◆ Use grips to mirror the object along the centerline.
◆ Save the drawing as ex7-6.

**Figure 7-9.**
When using the Mirror grip mode, the selected grip becomes the first point of the mirror line and the original object is automatically deleted.

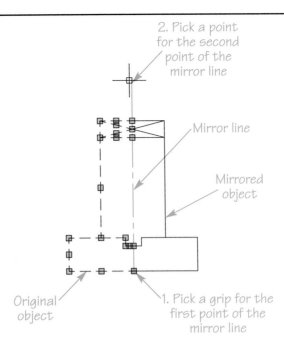

2. Pick a point for the second point of the mirror line

Mirror line

Mirrored object

Original object

1. Pick a grip for the first point of the mirror line

## The Properties Window

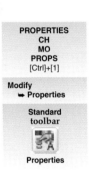

PROPERTIES
CH
MO
PROPS
[Ctrl]+[1]

Modify
↳ Properties

Standard toolbar

Properties

An object or objects can be edited automatically using the **Properties** window. To edit an object using the **Properties** window, pick the **Properties** button from the **Standard** toolbar, select **Properties** from the **Modify** pull-down menu, or enter mo, ch, props, or properties at the Command prompt. You can also toggle the **Properties** window on and off using the [Ctrl]+[1] key combination. If an object or objects have already been selected, you can also access the **Properties** window by right-clicking and selecting **Properties** from the shortcut menu. The **Properties** window opens automatically when you double-click on most objects.

The **Properties** window appears as shown in **Figure 7-10.** Like a toolbar, it can be docked in the drawing area.

While the **Properties** window is displayed, you can enter commands and continue to work in AutoCAD. You can close the **Properties** window by picking the "X" in the upper corner. The "X" may be on either side of the window, depending on which side of the screen the window is on.

**Figure 7-10.**
The **Properties** window can be used to modify object properties.

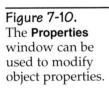

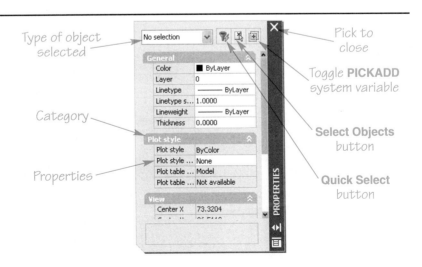

Type of object selected

Category

Properties

Pick to close

Toggle **PICKADD** system variable

Select Objects button

Quick Select button

When you access the **Properties** window without first selecting an object, No selection appears in the top drop-down list. This means that AutoCAD does not have any objects selected to modify. The four categories—**General**, **Plot style**, **View**, and **Misc**—list the current settings for the drawing. Underneath each category is a list of drawing properties. For example, in **Figure 7-10**, ByLayer is the current color in the **General** category. To change a property, pick an object or drawing property within a specific category. Once a property to be modified has been selected, a description of what that property does is shown at the bottom of the **Properties** window.

Depending on the property that is selected, one of the following methods is used to set the new value, as shown in **Figure 7-11**:

- A drop-down arrow appears. Pick the drop-down arrow and select one of the values in the list.
- A **Pick Point** button allows you to pick a new coordinate location.
- A text box is used to input a new value.

The upper-right portion of the **Properties** window displays three buttons. The **Quick Select** button accesses the **Quick Select** dialog box, where you can create object selection sets. The **Quick Select** dialog box is covered in Chapter 6. The **Select Objects** button changes the cursor to a pick box so you can select objects. The third button allows you to toggle the value of the **PICKADD** system variable. This setting determines if a picked object is added to the current selection set or if it replaces the current selection set.

## Using the **Properties** Window to Modify an Object

The previous discussion introduced you to the **Properties** window. The following explains how to change object properties in the **Properties** window. In order to modify an object, the **Properties** window must be open and an object must be selected. For example, if a circle and a line are drawn, and you need to modify the circle, first pick the circle to make its grips appear, and then open the **Properties** window.

**Figure 7-11.**
Different methods of changing properties. A—A drop-down arrow contains a list of options. B—A **Pick Point** button allows you to pick a coordinate location. C—A text box allows you to enter a new value.

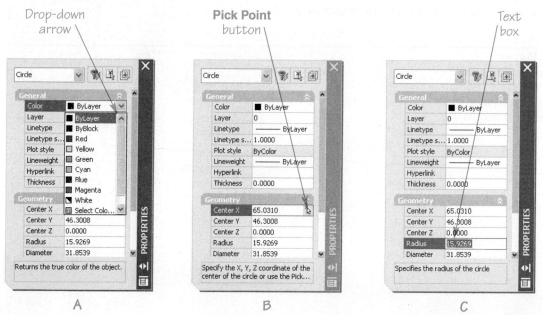

Architectural Drafting Using AutoCAD

The **Properties** window displays the categories that can be modified for the circle. All objects have a **General** category. The **General** category allows you to modify properties such as color, layer, linetype, linetype scale, plot style, lineweight, hyperlink, and thickness. For example, the following procedure changes the color of the circle:

1. Select the **Color** property in the window by picking on the word **Color**. A drop-down arrow appears to the right of the current color.
2. Select the drop-down arrow, and a list of available colors appears.
3. Select the new color. If the desired color is not in the list, pick **Select Color...** from the bottom of the list. This displays the **Select Color** dialog box, from which a color can be chosen. Once a color has been selected, the **Properties** window displays the current color for the circle.
4. Move the cursor off the **Properties** window and press the [Esc] key to deactivate the grips and have the new color setting take effect.

The following is a list of the properties available in the **General** category and brief instructions for changing them:

- **Color.** Pick this property to display a drop-down arrow and select a color from the list. At the bottom of the drop-down list is the Select Color... option, which displays the **Select Color** dialog box.
- **Layer.** Pick the drop-down arrow and select the desired layer for the object.
- **Linetype.** Pick the drop-down arrow and select the desired linetype for the object.
- **Linetype scale.** To change the object's linetype scale, highlight the value and enter a new scale value. As discussed in Chapter 5, the linetype scale for an individual object is a multiplier of the **LTSCALE** system variable.
- **Plot style.** Picking this property displays a drop-down arrow with various plot styles. Initially, only one style is available: ByColor. In order to create a list of plot styles, you must create a plot style table. Plotting and plot styles are discussed in Chapter 24.
- **Lineweight.** Pick the drop-down arrow and select the desired lineweight for the object from the drop-down list. Lineweights are discussed in Chapter 5.
- **Hyperlink.** Picking on this property displays a ... (ellipsis) button. Picking the button accesses the **Insert Hyperlink** dialog box. Use this dialog box to add a hyperlink, description, or URL address to an object.
- **Thickness.** This property allows you to change the thickness of a 3D object in a text box. Thickness is discussed in Chapter 25.

As stated earlier, all objects have a **General** category. Depending on the type of object that has been selected, other categories may also be displayed. One of the most common categories is **Geometry**. See **Figure 7-12.** The properties within the **Geometry** category vary, depending on the type of object. Typically, there are three properties that allow you to change the absolute coordinates for the object by specifying the X, Y, and Z coordinates. Picking one of these properties displays a **Pick Point** button. The button allows you to pick a point in your drawing for the new location. You can also enter the value for the coordinate in the text box instead of using the **Pick Point** button.

When multiple objects are selected, you can use the **Properties** window to modify all the objects, or you can pick only one type of the selected objects to be modified. The drop-down list at the top of the **Properties** window displays the types of objects selected. See **Figure 7-13.** Select All to change the properties of all of the selected objects. To modify only one object type, select the appropriate type from the drop-down list.

When all the changes to the object have been made, position the cursor off of the **Properties** window and press the [Esc] button to clear the grips and remove the object from the **Properties** window. This displays the object in the drawing window, with the desired changes.

**Figure 7-12.**
The **Properties** window with a line object selected. Only two categories can be modified for the line object: **General** and **Geometry**.

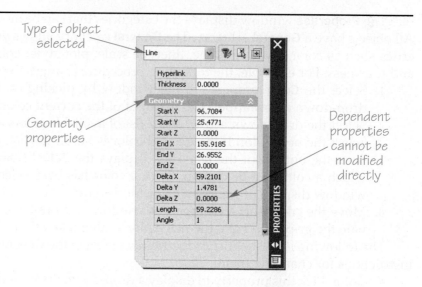

Type of object selected

Geometry properties

Dependent properties cannot be modified directly

**Figure 7-13.**
The **Properties** window with three objects selected. You can edit the objects by type by selecting **Line (1)**, **Circle (1)**, or **Arc (1)** from the drop-down list. You can also edit all the objects at the same time by selecting **All (3)**.

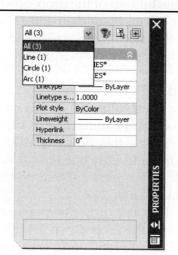

**Note**

The **Properties** window is discussed where appropriate throughout this text.

## Exercise 7-7

- Start a new drawing using a template or startup option of your choice.
- Set architectural units.
- Create a layer named Line and a layer named Circle.
- Draw a line with endpoint coordinates X = 2, Y = 3, and X = 2, Y = 6 on the Line layer.
- Draw a circle with a radius of 1.250 and a center location of X = 6, Y = 4.5 on the Circle layer.
- Use the **Properties** window to edit the line as follows:
  - Change the start point to X = 6-3/4″, Y = 3-3/4″.
  - Change the endpoint to X = 6-3/4″, Y = 6-3/4″.
  - Change the layer to the Circle layer.
- Use the **Properties** window to edit the circle as follows:
  - Change the center location to X = 7-1/8″, Y = 5-1/4″.
  - Change the radius to 3/8″.
  - Change the color to Cyan.
- Save the drawing as ex7-7.

**Professional Tip**

Using the **Properties** window is a quick way to move geometry that was drawn on the wrong layer to the correct layer.

# Editing between Multiple Drawings

One of the advantages of AutoCAD is the capability of editing more than one drawing at a time. This allows you to copy objects from one drawing to another drawing. You can also refer to one drawing to obtain information (such as a distance) while working in a different drawing.

To take a look at how this works, first open ex7-6, and then open ex7-7. Two drawings have now been opened in AutoCAD. In the **Window** pull-down menu, pick **Tile Horizontally.** This "tiles" the two open drawings as shown in **Figure 7-14.**

## Copying Objects between Drawings

The Windows *copy and paste* function is used to copy an object from one drawing to another. For example, if you want to copy the circle from drawing ex7-7 to drawing ex7-6, you first select the circle. Once the circle is selected, right-click to get the shortcut menu shown in **Figure 7-15.**

The shortcut menu has two options that allow you to copy to the Windows Clipboard:

- **Copy.** This option takes selected objects from AutoCAD and places them on the Windows Clipboard, allowing them to be used in another application or another AutoCAD drawing.

**Figure 7-14.**
Multiple drawings can be tiled to make editing easier.

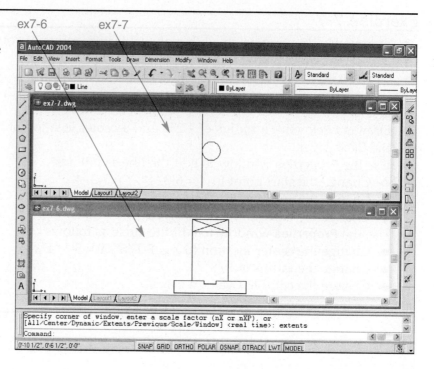

**Figure 7-15.**
Right-click to access this shortcut menu after selecting an object to be copied into another drawing.

Windows copy and paste functions

AutoCAD editing commands

Access the **Properties** window

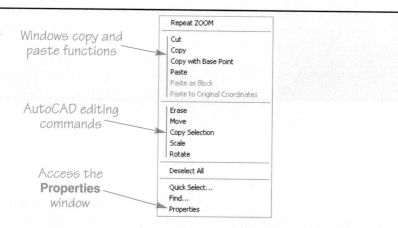

- **Copy with Base Point.** This option also copies the selected objects to the Clipboard, but allows you to specify a base point to position the copied object when it is pasted. When using this option, AutoCAD prompts you to select a base point. Select a logical base point, such as a corner or center point of the object.

Once you have selected one of the two copy options, make the second drawing active by picking in its window. Right-click to display the shortcut menu shown in **Figure 7-16.** Notice that the copy options remain available, but three paste options appear below the copy options. The paste options are only available if there is something on the Clipboard. The following are brief descriptions of the three options:

- **Paste.** This option pastes any information from the Clipboard into the current drawing. If the **Copy with Base Point** option was used to place objects on the Clipboard, then the objects being pasted are attached to the crosshairs at the specified base point.
- **Paste as Block.** This option "joins" all objects that are pasted into the drawing. The pasted objects act like a block, in that multiple objects are joined together to form one object. Blocks are covered in Chapter 9. Use the **EXPLODE** command to break the objects into their individual components.

**Figure 7-16.**
Right-click to access this shortcut menu. Select one of the paste options to paste an object from the Windows Clipboard into the current drawing.

*Paste options* →

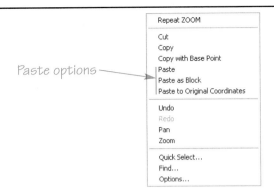

| Repeat ZOOM |
| --- |
| Cut |
| Copy |
| Copy with Base Point |
| Paste |
| Paste as Block |
| Paste to Original Coordinates |
| Undo |
| Redo |
| Pan |
| Zoom |
| Quick Select... |
| Find... |
| Options... |

- **Paste to Original Coordinates.** This option pastes the objects to the same coordinates from which they were copied in the original drawing.

You can also copy objects between drawings using the drag-and-drop method. To do this, first open both drawings and tile them. Select the object to be copied, and then press and hold the right mouse button. Move the cursor to the other drawing and release the right mouse button. A menu pops up with choices of where to place the copied object. See **Figure 7-17.** The choices are described below:

- **Copy Here.** This option places the dragged object at the cursor position where the right mouse button is released.
- **Paste as Block.** Places the dragged objects into the new drawing as a block (all objects are grouped together).
- **Paste to Orig Coords.** This option places the dragged objects into the new drawing at the same coordinates as their coordinates in the original drawing.
- **Cancel.** Cancels the drag-and-drop operation.

The drag and drop copy and paste feature only works when the **Noun/verb selection** check box is checked in the **Selection** tab of the **Options** dialog box. Selection settings are described in detail in the following section.

**Figure 7-17.**
This shortcut menu appears when copying an object between drawings using the drag-and-drop method.

| Copy Here |
| --- |
| Paste as Block |
| Paste to Orig Coords |
| Cancel |

# Exercise 7-8

- ◆ Open drawings ex7-6 and ex7-7, and tile the drawings horizontally.
- ◆ Select the circle.
- ◆ Use the **Properties** window to make the circle in ex7-7 green.
- ◆ Right-click and select **Copy with Base Point**. Select the center of the circle as the base point.
- ◆ Use the [Ctrl]+[Tab] key combination to make ex7-6 active.
- ◆ Right-click and select **Paste** from the shortcut menu. Pick a new location for the circle.
- ◆ Select the rectangle and "X" in ex7-6 and copy them to the Clipboard.
- ◆ Use the **Paste as Block** option to paste the objects into the ex7-7 drawing.
- ◆ Pick either the newly pasted rectangle or the "X" and notice that they are selected together as a group.
- ◆ Save the drawing as ex7-8.

# Selection Settings

You can control grip and general selection settings in the **Selection** tab of the **Options** dialog box. The **Options** dialog box is opened by picking **Options...** in the **Tools** pull-down menu, right-clicking and selecting **Options...** from the shortcut menu, or entering options at the Command prompt. You can access the **Selection** tab of the **Options** dialog box directly by entering gr or ddgrips at the Command prompt. The **Selection** tab in the **Options** dialog box is shown in **Figure 7-18**.

**Figure 7-18.**
The **Selection Modes** area of the **Selection** tab in the **Options** dialog box.

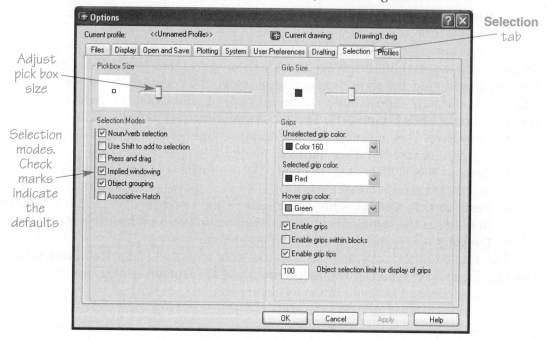

## General Selection Settings

When the **Selection** tab is selected, the left-hand side of the **Options** dialog box contains general selection controls. The **Pickbox Size** slider changes the size of the pick box, which is used to select objects. The sample in the image tile gets smaller or larger as you move the slider. Stop when you have the desired size.

The **Selection Modes** area of the **Selection** tab in the **Options** dialog box allows you to control the way that you use editing commands. See **Figure 7-18**. Select or deselect the following options based on your own preferences:

- **Noun/verb selection.** When you first select objects and then enter a command, it is referred to as *noun/verb selection*. A "✓" in this check box means that the noun/verb method is active. When using *verb/noun selection*, you enter the command before selecting the object. If you remove the "✓" from the **Noun/verb selection** check box, you must first enter a command before selecting the objects to be affected.

 Some editing commands, such as **FILLET, CHAMFER, OFFSET, EXTEND,** and **TRIM,** *require* that you enter the command before you select the object.

- **Use Shift to add to selection.** When this check box is off, every object or group of objects you select is highlighted and added to the selection set for modifying. If you check this check box, it changes the way AutoCAD accepts objects you pick. For example, the first object or group of objects you pick is highlighted and becomes the selection set. If you pick an additional object or group of objects, it is highlighted, but the first one is removed from the selection set. This means that each object or group of objects you pick replaces the current selection set. If you want to add more items to the selection set, you must hold down the [Shift] key as you pick them.
- **Press and drag.** With **Press and drag** on, you create a selection window by picking the first corner, then moving the cursor while holding down the pick button. Release the pick button when you have the desired selection window. This option is off by default, allowing you to create a window or crossing box by only picking the corners.
- **Implied windowing.** This option is on by default. This means that you can automatically create a window box by picking the first point and moving the cursor to the right to pick the second point, or make a crossing box by picking the first point and moving the cursor to the left to pick the second point.
- **Object grouping.** This option controls whether or not AutoCAD recognizes grouped objects as singular objects. When off, the individual elements of a group can be selected for separate editing without having to first explode the group. The **GROUP** command is discussed in Chapter 13. This option is active by default.
- **Associative hatch.** The default is off, which means that if an associative hatch is moved, the hatch boundary does not move with it. Select this toggle if you want all objects defining the boundary of an associative hatch to move when you move the hatch pattern. It is a good idea to have this on for most applications. Hatches and hatch boundaries are fully explained in Chapter 19.

## Grip Settings

The **Selection** tab of the **Options** dialog box contains controls for adjusting the appearance and function of grips. See **Figure 7-19**. The **Grip Size** slider in the **Selection** tab of the **Options** dialog box lets you change the size of the grips. The sample in the image tile gets smaller or larger as you move the slider. Change the grip size to whatever works best for your drawing. Very small grip boxes may be difficult to pick. However, the grips may overlap if they are too large.

The **Grips** area appears below the **Grip Size** slider. Check or uncheck the **Enable grips** check box to turn grips on or off. When grips are enabled, grip boxes appear on an object that is selected.

Pick the **Enable grips within blocks** check box to have grips displayed on every object within a block. A *block* is a special symbol designed for multiple use. Blocks are discussed in detail in Chapter 9. When this check box is off, the grip location for a block is at the insertion point.

The **Enable grip tips** check box affects only special custom objects that support grip tips. Standard AutoCAD objects are not affected by this option.

The three drop-down color lists allow you to change the colors of grips. The **Unselected grip color:** drop-down list is used to select the color of warm grips. The **Selected grip color:** drop-down list is used to select the color of hot grips. The **Hover grip color:** drop-down list is used to select the color of a grip when the cursor pauses over it.

The **Object selection limit for display of grips** setting in the **Grips** area sets the maximum number of objects in an initial selection set for which grips are displayed. This setting is 100 by default. This means that if 101 (or more) objects are selected at the same time, the grips are not displayed. However, if 100 or fewer objects are selected at the same time, additional objects can then be added to the selection set and their grips will be displayed.

Figure 7-19.
Figure 7-19.
The **Selection** tab of the **Options** dialog box contains grip control settings.

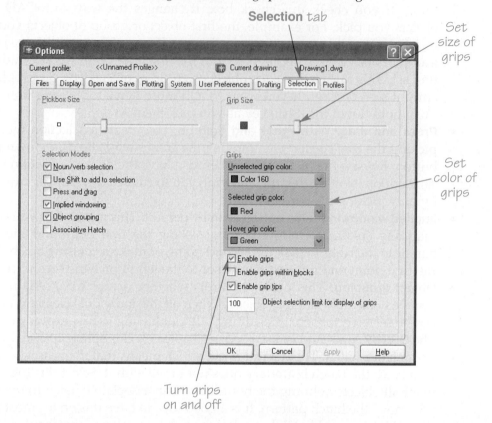

# Setting Object Sorting Methods

The **Object Sorting Methods** area shown in **Figure 7-20** appears when you pick the **User Preferences** tab in the **Options** dialog box. The check boxes in the **Object Sorting Methods** area allow you to control the order in which objects are displayed or plotted. The following are brief descriptions of the check boxes:

- **Object selection.** Objects selected using a windowing method are placed in the selection set in the order they occur in the drawing database.
- **Object snap.** Object snap modes find objects in the order they occur in the drawing database.
- **Regens.** Objects are displayed by a drawing regeneration in the order they occur in the drawing database.
- **Plotting.** Objects are plotted in the order they occur in the drawing database.

By default, all of the options are on. This should be adequate in most situations. In very large drawing files (files that contain a lot of objects), it may be desirable to uncheck some or all of the options. Since object sorting takes time, in large files you may notice a decrease in performance when selecting objects.

Objects are sorted as they appear in the drawing database. The *drawing database* contains information defining all objects and settings in a drawing. It is automatically created each time an object is drawn, objects are modified, or the drawing is regenerated. This database is not accessible by the drafter.

**Figure 7-20.**
The **User Preferences** tab of the **Options** dialog box.

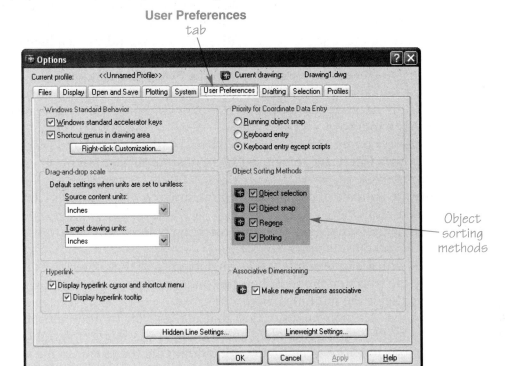

Chapter Test

*Answer the following questions on a separate sheet of paper.*

1. Define *grips*.
2. How do you toggle grips on and off?
3. What are unselected grips?
4. When does a grip become hot?
5. How do you remove a highlighted object from a selection set?
6. Name the first grip mode that is activated when you pick a grip.
7. What is the function of the **Base point** option?
8. What does the **Copy** option of the grip modes do?
9. How do you make more than one grip hot at the same time?
10. How do you remove hot grips from the selection set?
11. When the Stretch grip mode is active, explain how to access the Move mode.
12. How do you access the grips shortcut menu?
13. What does the **Undo** option of the grips shortcut menu do?
14. Briefly discuss what happens when you pick the **Properties** option in the grips shortcut menu.
15. Name the grip mode for which the **Copy** option is the true form of the **COPY** command.
16. When using the Move grips mode, how can you set a snap spacing for multiple copies?
17. Identify two ways to scale an object when using the Scale grip mode, other than with the **Reference** option.
18. When using the Mirror grip mode, what is special about the selected grip?
19. When using the Mirror grip mode, are the original objects automatically deleted or automatically kept?
20. What is the function of the **Copy** option of the Mirror grip mode?

21. Identify the toolbar button that opens the **Properties** window.
22. When can you access the **Properties** window from the shortcut menu?
23. What does it mean when No selection is specified at the top of the list in the **Properties** window?
24. Briefly outline the sequence of activities that you would use to change the color of a circle using the **Properties** window.
25. How do you change an object's layer in the **Properties** window?
26. Give the sequence of activities to use if you want to copy a circle from one drawing to another. Assume that the drawings are both displayed in the AutoCAD window.
27. Name the option that takes selected objects from AutoCAD and places them on the Windows Clipboard to be used in another application or another AutoCAD drawing.
28. Identify the option that pastes any information from the Windows Clipboard into the current drawing.
29. Explain the drag-and-drop process of copying objects between drawings.
30. How do you adjust the pick box size?
31. Give the term that refers to first selecting objects and then entering the command.
32. Identify the selection mode option that requires that you hold down the [Shift] key when selecting multiple objects.
33. Identify the selection mode option that allows you to automatically create a window by picking the first point and moving the cursor to the right, or make a crossing box by picking the first point and moving the cursor to the left.
34. How do you change the size of grips?
35. What is the purpose of the **Object Sorting Methods** area of the **User Preferences** tab in the **Options** dialog box?

# Chapter Problems

1. Draw the objects shown at A below and then use the Stretch grip mode to make them look like the objects at B. Do not include dimensions. Save the drawing as p7-1.

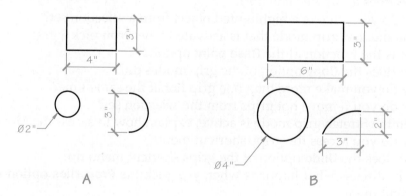

2. Draw the object shown at A below. Then, using the **Copy** option of the Move grip mode, copy the object to the position shown at B. Edit Object A so that it resembles Object C. Edit Object B so that it looks like Object D. Do not include dimensions. Save the drawing as p7-2.

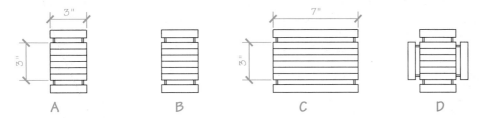

3. Draw the object shown at A below. Do not be concerned about scale. Then copy the object, without rotating it, to a position at B indicated by the dashed lines. Then, rotate the object 45°. Copy the rotated object at B to the position at C indicated by the dashed lines. Use the **Reference** option to rotate the object at C to 25° as shown. Save the drawing as p7-3.

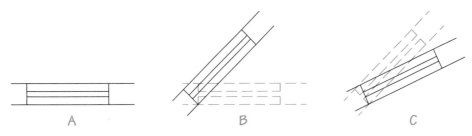

4. Draw the individual objects (vertical line, horizontal line, circle, arc, and "C" shape) at A below using the dimensions given. Then, use grip modes to create the object shown at B. Do not include dimensions. Save the drawing as p7-4.

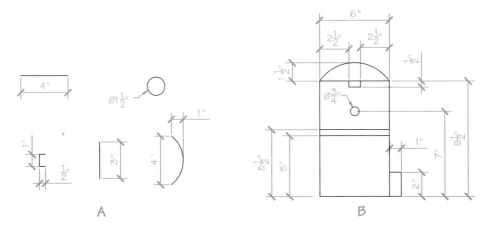

5. Use the completed drawing from Problem 7-4. Erase everything except the completed object and move it to a position similar to A below. Copy the object two times to positions B and C. Use the Scale grip mode to scale the object at B to 50% of its original size. Use the **Reference** option of the Scale grip mode to enlarge the object at C from the existing 9-1/2″ length to a 11-1/2″ length as shown in C. Do not include dimensions. Save as p7-5.

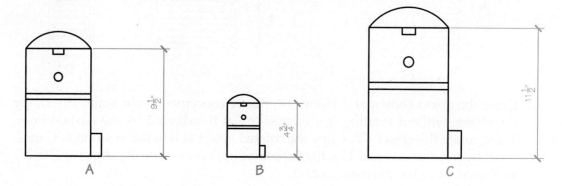

6. Draw the workspace layout shown at A. Use the Mirror grip mode to complete the four quadrants as shown at B. Place the desks and chairs on a layer named Furniture. Save the drawing as p7-6.

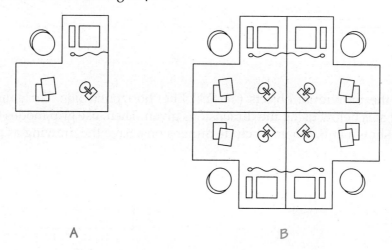

# Placing Text on Drawings

## Learning Objectives

After completing this chapter, you will be able to:

- Use and discuss proper text standards.
- Use the **TEXT** command to create single-line text.
- Make multiple lines of text with the **MTEXT** command.
- Create text styles using the **Text Style** dialog box.
- Edit existing text.
- Change text properties using the **Properties** window.
- Check your spelling.
- Search for and replace text material automatically.

## Important Terms

Big Fonts
command line editing
composition
control code
font
justify
line text
multiline text
reactive text

scaleable
selected text
text
text baseline
text boundary
text editor
text style
tolerance stack
word wrap

Words and notes on drawings have traditionally been added by hand lettering. This is a slow, time-consuming task. CAD software has reduced the tedious nature of adding notes to a drawing. In CAD, lettering is referred to as *text*.

There are advantages of computer-generated text over hand-lettering techniques. When performed by computer, lettering is faster, often easier to read, and normally more consistent. This chapter shows how text can be added to drawings.

# Text Standards

Company standards often dictate how text appears on a drawing. The heights of letters vary depending on the plotting scale of the drawing. Text heights should be large enough so the text on the finished drawing can be easily read. The following lettering heights are recommended as a general guideline for plotted text:

| Item | Plotted Text Height |
|---|---|
| Main titles | 1/4″ to 1/2″ |
| Subtitles | 3/16″ to 1/4″ |
| Notes and general lettering | 3/32″ to 5/32″ |
| | (1/8″ common) |
| Sheet number in title block | 1/2″ to 1″ |

When plotting drawings at smaller scales such as 1/8″ = 1′-0″ or 3/32″ = 1′-0″, increase the lettering heights for additional clarity. For example, increase the general lettering from 3/32″ to 1/8″ or even 3/16″.

Company standards normally specify the type of text fonts used on drawings. A *font* is a style of lettering. AutoCAD includes three architectural stylized fonts:

- CityBlueprint
- CountryBlueprint
- Stylus BT

These fonts make text in your drawing appear hand lettered. Other fonts that appear hand lettered can be purchased from computer stores or downloaded from the Internet. **Figure 8-1** shows examples of fonts. Fonts are discussed in greater detail later in this chapter.

Vertical or inclined text may be used on a drawing, depending on company preference. See **Figure 8-2.** One or the other is recommended, but do not use both. Computer-generated text offers a variety of styles for specific purposes, such as titles, general notes, and captions. Text on a drawing is normally uppercase, but lowercase letters are used in some applications.

Numbers in dimensions and notes are the same height as the general notes. Fractions can also be created in AutoCAD with either a horizontal or diagonal fraction bar. A dash or space is usually placed between the whole number and the fraction. See **Figure 8-3.**

**Figure 8-1.**
Examples of fonts, including AutoCAD's standard architectural fonts.

| Fonts Supplied with AutoCAD | | Fonts from Other Sources |
|---|---|---|
| Sample of CityBlueprint font | Sample of RomanS font | Sample of Archisel font |
| Sample of CountryBlueprint font | Sample of Arial font | Sample of Archsty font |
| Sample of Stylus BT font | Sample of Times New Roman font | |
| Sample of Italic font | | |

**Figure 8-2.**
Vertical and inclined text.

VERTICAL TEXT WITH LETTERS AND NUMBERS: 123...

*INCLINED TEXT WITH LETTERS AND NUMBERS: 123...*

**Figure 8-3.**
Examples of various methods of representing numbers and fractions.

| Architectural | Engineering | Decimal and Fractional |
|---|---|---|
| 2'-3 1/2" | 2'6.75" | 2.75 |
| 2'-3½" | 2'0.5625" | 2-3/4 |
| 2'-3$\frac{1}{2}$" | 2.5625' | 2$\frac{3}{4}$ |

# Text Composition

*Composition* refers to the spacing, layout, and appearance of the text. With manual lettering, it is necessary to space letters correctly. Spacing is performed automatically with computer-generated text.

Notes should be placed horizontally on the drawing to make reading easier. In some cases, notes may be placed vertically as long as the vertical text can be read from the right side of the sheet. AutoCAD automatically sets the horizontal line spacing. This helps maintain the identity of individual notes.

The term *justify* means to align the text in relation to the starting point. For example, left-justified text is aligned along the left edge, and right-justified text is aligned along the right edge. Most lines of text are left-justified. **Figure 8-4** shows examples of justified text.

# Using AutoCAD to Draw Text

There are two types of text objects in AutoCAD. With *line text*, each line of text is a separate object. With *multiline text*, a single text object can consist of several lines. Line text is entered at the prompt line using the **TEXT** command. Multiline text is created in the multiline text editor, which is accessed using the **MTEXT** command. These commands are used differently, but their options are similar. Both line text and multiline text objects can be assigned text styles, which define the appearance of the text.

**Figure 8-4.**
Examples of text justification.

| Left Justification | Center Justification | Right Justification |

# Creating Line Text

The **TEXT** command is used to create line text. When using the **TEXT** command, you can see the text on the screen as you type. Each line of text is a single text object. Line text is most useful for text items that require only one line of text, or multiple lines if each line is a separate text object. If the text has multiple lines or requires mixed fonts, sizes, or colors, multiline text should be used.

The **TEXT** command can be issued by picking the **Single Line Text** button from the **Text** toolbar, selecting **Single Line Text** from the **Text** cascading menu in the **Draw** pull-down menu, or entering text at the Command prompt as follows:

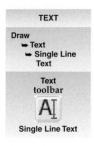

Command: **text**↵
Current text style: *current* Text height: *current*
Specify start point of text or [Justify/Style]: *(pick a starting point for text)*
Specify height <*current*>: *(enter a text height value or press [Enter])*
Specify rotation angle of text <0>: *(enter a rotation value or press [Enter])*
Enter text: *(type text)* ↵
Enter text: *(type the next line of text or press [Enter] to complete)*
Command:

When the Enter text: prompt appears, a text cursor equal in size to the specified text height appears on the screen at the text start point. The **TEXT** command can be used to enter multiple lines of text by pressing [Enter] at the end of each line. The Enter text: prompt is repeated for the next line of text. Press [Enter] twice to end the command. You can cancel the **TEXT** command at any time by pressing the [Esc] key. This action erases any incomplete lines of text.

A great advantage of line text is that multiple lines of text can be entered with each line being a separate text object at different locations. This allows you to enter multiple lines in a single prompt sequence, but then edit each line individually.

While in the **TEXT** command, the crosshairs can be moved independently of the text cursor. Selecting a new start point completes the line of text being entered and begins a new line at the selected point. Thus, multiple lines of text may be entered anywhere in the drawing without exiting the command. This can save drafting time. The following are a few aspects of the **TEXT** command to remember:

- When you end the **TEXT** command, the entered text is erased from the screen, then regenerated.
- Regardless of the type of justification selected, the cursor appears as if the text is left-justified. However, when you end the **TEXT** command, the text disappears and is then regenerated with the alignment you requested. Justification is discussed later in this chapter.
- When you use a control code sequence for a symbol, the control code, not the symbol, is displayed. When you complete the command, the text disappears and is then regenerated showing the proper symbol. Control codes are discussed later in this chapter.
- If you cancel the **TEXT** command, an incomplete line is deleted.

| Note | The **TEXT** command can also be activated by entering dt or dtext at the Command prompt. |

## The **Start Point** *option*

After entering the **TEXT** command, the Specify start point of text or [Justify/Style]: prompt appears. The default option allows you to select a point on the screen where you want the text to begin. This point becomes the lower-left corner of the text. After you pick the start point, the next prompt reads:

Specify height *<current>*:

This prompt allows you to select the text height. The default value is 3/16″ if using architectural units or 0.2000 if using decimal units. The previously selected letter height is displayed as the current value. If you want letters that are 1/8″ high, enter 1/8 or .125 at the Specify height: prompt. The next prompt follows:

Specify rotation angle of text <0>:

The default value for the rotation angle is 0, which places the text horizontally. The rotation values rotate text in a counterclockwise direction. The text pivots about the starting point as shown in **Figure 8-5.**

The last prompt is the following:

Enter text:

Type the desired text and press [Enter]. If no other justification is selected, the text is left-justified.

**Figure 8-5.**
Different rotation angles for text. The starting point is indicated with a grip box.

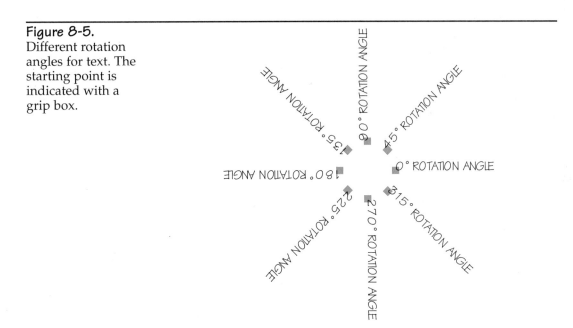

## The **Justify** *option*

Justification is how a piece of text appears in relation to the start point. The **TEXT** command offers a variety of justification options. Left justification is the default, which places the text to the right of the start point. If you want another option, enter j at the Specify start point of text [Justify/Style]: prompt. When you select the **Justify** option, you can use one of several text alignment options. These options can be seen in the command sequence below, and are explained in the next sections:

Command: **text, dt,** *or* **dtext.**↵
Current text style: *current* Text height: *current*
Specify start point of text or [Justify/Style]: **j**↵
Enter an option [Align/Fit/Center/Middle/Right/TL/TC/TR/ML/MC/MR/BL/BC/BR]:

- **Align (A).** When this option is selected, you are prompted to select two points between which the text string is confined. The two points are the ends of the *text baseline* (bottom edge of the text). The start and endpoints can be placed horizontally or at an angle. AutoCAD automatically adjusts the text width to fit between the selected points. The text height is also changed with this option. The height varies according to the distance between the points and the number of characters. See **Figure 8-6A.**

**Figure 8-6.**
Examples of aligned and fit text. A—In aligned text, letters are scaled horizontally and vertically to stretch between two points. B—In fit text, the text width is adjusted automatically between the two points.

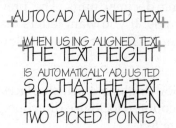

**Professional Tip**

> **TEXT** is not recommended for aligned text because the text height for each line is adjusted according to the width. One line may run into another.

- **Fit (F).** This option is similar to the **Align** option, but the text height does not change. After entering the endpoints for the text baseline, a Specify height: prompt allows you to enter the text height. AutoCAD adjusts the letter width to fit between the two given points, while keeping the text height constant. See **Figure 8-6B.**
- **Center (C).** This option allows you to select the center point for the baseline of the text. Enter the letter height and rotation angle after picking the center point. This example uses a 1/2″ height and a 0° rotation angle. The prompts appear as follows:

Enter an option [Align/Fit/Center/Middle/Right/TL/TC/TR/ML/MC/MR/BL/BC/BR]: **c**↵
Specify center point of text: *(pick a point)*
Specify height *<current>*: **.5**↵
Specify rotation angle of text *<current>*: **0**↵
Enter text:

- **Middle (M).** This option allows the text to be placed both horizontally and vertically from the selected middle point. The letter height and rotation can also be changed. The command sequence is similar to the sequence for the **Center** option.
- **Right (R).** This option justifies text at the lower-right corner of the text, allowing it to be placed to the left from the selected point. The point is entered at the Specify right endpoint of text baseline: prompt. The letter height and rotation can also be entered. The command sequence is similar to the sequence for the **Start point** option. **Figure 8-7** compares the **Center, Middle,** and **Right** options.

Architectural Drafting Using AutoCAD

**Figure 8-7.**
Three justification options with starting points shown. A—The **Center** justification option.
B—The **Middle** justification option. C—The **Right** justification option.

CENTER JUSTIFIED TEXT

A

MIDDLE JUSTIFIED TEXT

B

RIGHT JUSTIFIED TEXT

C

## Other text alignment options

There are a number of text alignment options that allow you to place text on a drawing in relation to the top, bottom, middle, left side, or right side of the text. These alignment options are shown in **Figure 8-8.** These options are shown as abbreviations that correlate to the **TEXT** command sequence. To use one of these options, type the two letters for the desired option and press [Enter].

**Figure 8-8.**
Using the **TL, TC, TR, ML, MC, MR, BL, BC,** and **BR** justification options.

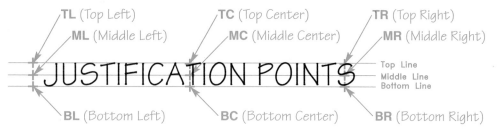

## Professional Tip

If you already know which text alignment option you want to use, you can enter it at the Specify start point of text or [Justify/Style]: prompt without accessing the **Justify** option. Just type the letter or letters of the desired option and press [Enter].

## Special symbols and formatting

Many drafting applications require special symbols for text and dimensions. When creating single-line text with the **TEXT** command, *control codes* are used to add symbols and additional formatting.

A *control code* is a sequence of characters used to identify special symbols or formatting. Control codes consist of two percent signs (%%) followed by a third character. The third character represents the symbol or formatting. The following table lists some of the available control codes:

| Control Code | Description | Symbol |
|---|---|---|
| %%d | Degrees symbol | ° |
| %%p | Plus/minus sign | ± |
| %%c | Diameter symbol | ⌀ |
| %%u | Underscore toggle | |
| %%o | Overscore toggle | |

For example, in order to add the note ⌀2.75, type %%c2.75 at the Enter text: prompt. When the text appears on screen, the control code (%%c) is replaced with the diameter symbol (⌀). See **Figure 8-9A.**

Text can be underscored (underlined) or overscored by typing a control code in front of the line of text. For example, the note <u>UNDERSCORE TEXT</u> must be entered as %%UUNDERSCORE TEXT. The resulting text is shown in **Figure 8-9B.** A line of text may require both underscoring and overscoring. For example, the text entry %%O%%ULINE OF TEXT produces the note with both underscore and overscore.

The %%u and %%o control codes are toggles that turn underscoring and overscoring on and off. Type %%u preceding a word or phrase to turn underscoring on. Type %%u after the desired word or phrase to turn underscoring off. Any text following the second %%u then appears without underscoring. For example, <u>DETAIL A</u> BEAM CONNECTION is entered as %%UDETAIL A%%U BEAM CONNECTION.

A single percent sign can be added normally. However, when a percent sign must precede another control sequence, %%% is used to force a single percent sign. For example, in order to type the note 25%±2%, you must enter 25%%%%P2%.

Symbols can also be inserted into a drawing with the multiline text editor using the **MTEXT** command. Multiline text is discussed later in this chapter.

**Figure 8-9.**
A—The control code %%C creates the ⌀ (diameter) symbol. B—The control sequence %%U underscores the text.

%%C2.75 = ⌀2.75

A

%%UUNDERSCORE TEXT = <u>UNDERSCORE TEXT</u>

B

**Professional Tip**

Many drafters prefer to underline view labels or drawing titles such as <u>SECTION A-A</u> or <u>FIRST FLOOR PLAN</u>. Rather than drawing a line under the text, use underscoring and the **Center** justification option. The view labels are automatically underlined and centered under the views or details they identify.

# Command line editing

*Command line editing* is the process of entering or modifying text at the Command prompt without typing each individual letter. The following lists the functions of editing keys when you are working in the command window:

- **[Delete].** Deletes the character to the right of the text cursor.
- **[Backspace].** Deletes the character to the left of the text cursor.
- **[←].** The left arrow key moves the cursor left through the text currently on the command line. Doing this allows you to reposition the cursor to insert text or words that were skipped when entering the text.
- **[→].** After using the left arrow key, the right arrow key moves the cursor back to the right.
- **[Home].** Moves the cursor to the home position, which is in front of the first character typed at the prompt line.
- **[End].** Moves the cursor back to the far right, at the very end of the text typed at the prompt line.
- **[Insert].** Toggles the command line between Insert mode and Overwrite mode. In Insert mode, new text is inserted at the cursor position, and any text existing to the right of the cursor is moved to the right. When in Overwrite mode, new text entered replaces the character at the cursor position.
- **[↑].** The up arrow key moves backward through previously typed commands, allowing them to become a text entry. You might think of it as moving *up* the list of previous text.
- **[↓].** After moving backward through any number of previous lines, the down arrow key moves forward again. You might think of this as moving back *down* the list of previously entered text.
- **[Page Up].** Does not directly affect the actual prompt line, but moves up in the list of history lines (the lines that show the previous prompt lines) by whatever number of lines is currently displayed. History lines are the lines that show the previous prompt lines.
- **[Page Down].** Used in the same manner as the [Page Up] key, except it moves back down the history list.

These command line editing functions can be used when entering single-line text. In addition, the space bar does not function as the [Enter] key when the **TEXT** command is active. If Insert mode is active, the space bar inserts a space in the single-line text at the cursor position. If Overwrite mode is active, the space bar replaces the character to the right of the cursor with a space.

## Exercise 8-1

◆ Start a new drawing using a template or startup option of your own choice.
◆ Set architectural units.
◆ Use the **TEXT** command to type the following lines of text exactly as shown. Use 1/4″ letter height and 0° rotation.

> LETTERING HAS TYPICALLY BEEN A SLOW, TIME-CONSUMING
> TASK. COMPUTER-AIDED DRAFTING HAS REDUCED THE
> TEDIOUS NATURE OF PREPARING LETTERING ON A
> DRAWING. IN CAD, LETTERING IS REFERRED TO AS TEXT.
> COMPUTER-GENERATED TEXT IS FAST, CONSISTENT, AND
> EASIER TO READ.

◆ Use the **TEXT** command to type the following information. Each time, change the text option to obtain the format given. Use 1/2″ letter height and 0° rotation.

> AUTOCAD TEXT LEFT-JUSTIFIED USING THE START POINT OPTION.
> AUTOCAD TEXT RIGHT-JUSTIFIED USING THE RIGHT OPTION.
> AUTOCAD TEXT ALIGNED USING THE ALIGN OPTION.
> AUTOCAD TEXT CENTERED USING THE CENTER OPTION.
> AUTOCAD FIT TEXT USING THE FIT OPTION.
> AUTOCAD TEXT USING THE MIDDLE OPTION.

◆ Use the **TEXT** command to type the following information. Each time, change the text option to obtain the format given in each statement. Use 1/2″ letter height and 0° rotation.

> AUTOCAD TOP/LEFT OPTION.
> AUTOCAD TOP/CENTER OPTION.
> AUTOCAD TOP/RIGHT OPTION.
> AUTOCAD MIDDLE/LEFT OPTION.
> AUTOCAD MIDDLE/CENTER OPTION.
> AUTOCAD MIDDLE/RIGHT OPTION.
> AUTOCAD BOTTOM/LEFT OPTION.
> AUTOCAD BOTTOM/CENTER OPTION.
> AUTOCAD BOTTOM/RIGHT OPTION.

◆ Save the drawing as ex8-1.

## Creating Multiline Text

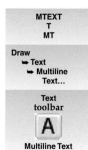

MTEXT
T
MT

Draw
➥ Text
➥ Multiline
Text...

Text
toolbar

A
Multiline Text

The **MTEXT** command is used to create multiline text objects. Instead of each line being an individual object, all the lines are one object or one paragraph of text. The **MTEXT** command is accessed by picking the **Multiline Text** button in the **Text** toolbar, picking **Multiline Text...** in the **Text** cascading menu of the **Draw** pull-down menu, or entering t, mt, or mtext at the Command prompt.

After entering the **MTEXT** command, AutoCAD asks you to specify the first and second corners of the text boundary. The *text boundary* is an imaginary box within which the multiline text is placed. When you pick the first corner of the text boundary, the cursor changes to a box with grayed-out letters representing the current text height. Move the box until you have the desired size for your paragraph and pick the opposite corner. See **Figure 8-10.**

When drawing the boundary window for multiline text, an arrow in the window shows the direction of text flow. While the width of the rectangle drawn provides a limit to the width of the text paragraphs, it does not affect the possible height. The rectangle height is automatically resized to fit the actual text entered. The *direction of text flow* indicates how the paragraph is expanded if necessary to accommodate additional text. The flow of the text is based on the justification of the multiline text. This is the command sequence:

Architectural Drafting Using AutoCAD

**Figure 8-10.**
The text boundary is a box in which the multiline text is placed. The arrow indicates the direction the text will flow as it is typed.

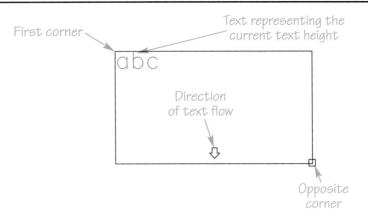

First corner

Text representing the current text height

abc

Direction of text flow

Opposite corner

Command: **t**, **mt**, *or* **mtext.**↵
Current text style: *current* Text height: *current*
Specify first corner: *(pick the first corner)*
Specify opposite corner or [Height/Justify/Line spacing/Rotation/Style/Width]: *(pick the other corner)*

After picking the text boundary, the multiline text editor appears. See **Figure 8-11.** The multiline text editor is divided into two parts: the **Text Formatting** toolbar and the *text editor*. The **Text Formatting** toolbar controls the properties of text entered into the text editor. The text editor includes a paragraph ruler containing indent and tab stops and an indent marker. A cursor is located within the text editor. This cursor identifies the height set in the **Text Formatting** toolbar. This is where text is entered to create a paragraph.

When entering text, you can move the cursor down to a new line by pressing [Enter]. A new line is also created when the text extends past the right side of the text boundary. AutoCAD automatically moves the cursor to the next line, which is called *word wrap*.

When the text editor is filled with text and a new line is added, previous lines are hidden and a scroll bar is displayed at the right. Use the scroll bar to move up and down to access lines in the text editor. Pressing [Enter] causes a new line to be entered. Pressing [Enter] twice creates a blank line between lines of text. Tabs can also be used to line up different columns of text. When finished entering text in the text editor, pick the **OK** button in the **Text Formatting** toolbar to exit.

**Figure 8-11.**
The multiline text editor consists of the **Text Formatting** toolbar and an area for entering text.

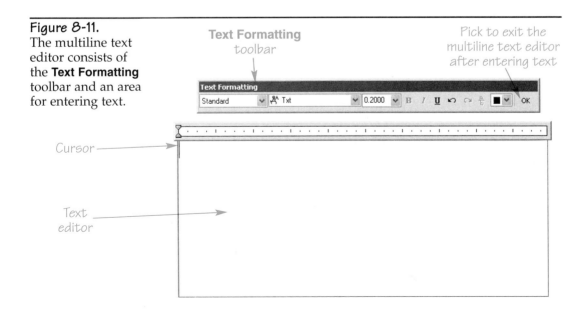

Text Formatting toolbar

Pick to exit the multiline text editor after entering text

Cursor

Text editor

## Exercise 8-2

◆ Start a new drawing using a template or startup option of your own choice.
◆ Set architectural units.
◆ Enter the **MTEXT** command and create a text boundary 4″ wide and 2″ high.
◆ In the multiline text editor, enter several lines of text of your own choosing. Place a blank line between paragraphs or notes.
◆ Enter enough text or press the [Enter] key several times so that the scroll bar is displayed on the right.
◆ Pick the **OK** button when done to see the text displayed on screen.
◆ Save the drawing as ex8-2.

## Modifying and formatting text

When entering text in the multiline text editor, the **Text Formatting** toolbar can be used to control the properties of the text. Additional text controls can also be accessed by right-clicking in the text editor window to display the text editor shortcut menu. This shortcut menu is discussed in the next section.

While in the multiline text editor, there are a number of keystroke combinations available. These combinations are as follows:

| Keystroke | Function |
| --- | --- |
| [Tab] | Moves the cursor to the next indent or tab location. |
| [↑] [←] [↓] [→] | Arrow keys move the cursor through the text one position in the direction indicated by the arrow. |
| [Ctrl]+[→]<br>[Ctrl]+[←] | Moves the cursor one word in the direction indicated. |
| [Home] | Moves the cursor to the start of the current line. |
| [End] | Moves the cursor to the end of the current line. |
| [Delete] | Deletes the character immediately to the right of the cursor. |
| [Backspace] | Deletes the character immediately to the left of the cursor. |
| [Ctrl]+[Delete] | Deletes the word immediately to the right of the cursor. |
| [Ctrl]+[Backspace] | Deletes the word immediately to the left of the cursor. |
| [Ctrl]+[C] | Copies the selection to the Clipboard. The Clipboard is an internal storage area that temporarily stores information that you copy or cut from a document. |
| [Ctrl]+[V] | Pastes the Clipboard contents to the selection or the current cursor location. |
| [Ctrl]+[X] | Cuts the selection to the Clipboard. |
| [Ctrl]+[Z] | Undoes the previous action. |
| [Enter] | Ends the current paragraph, starting a new one on the next line. |
| [Page Up]<br>[Page Down] | These keys move the cursor up or down 28 rows in the indicated direction. |
| [Ctrl]+[Page Up]<br>[Ctrl]+[Page Down] | These keys move the cursor to the top or bottom of the currently visible page of text. |
| [Ctrl]+[Home] | Moves the cursor to Line 1, Column 1. |
| [Ctrl]+[End] | Moves the cursor to the last character position. |
| [Ctrl]+[A] | Selects all text in the current multiline text object. |
| [Shift]+[→]<br>[Shift]+[←] | Selects or deselects text. Increases or decreases the selection one character at a time, depending on the direction indicated. |
| [Shift]+[↑]<br>[Shift]+[↓] | Selects or deselects text. Increases or decreases the selection one line at a time, depending on the direction indicated. |
| [Ctrl]+[Shift]+[→]<br>[Ctrl]+[Shift]+[←] | Selects or deselects text. Increases or decreases the selection one word at a time, depending on the direction indicated. |
| [Esc] | Closes the multiline text editor, negating any changes made. |

**Professional Tip**

      Text can be pasted from any text-based application into the multiline text editor. For example, you can copy text from an application such as Microsoft® Word and then paste it into the multiline text editor. The pasted text retains its properties. Likewise, text copied or cut from the multiline text editor can be pasted into another text-based application. This can be very useful if someone has already created specification notes in another program other than AutoCAD and the same notes need to be placed in your drawings.

      As you move the cursor into the editing window, it changes to a text cursor. If you have used other Windows text editors, this is a familiar cursor. Pointing to a character position within the text and pressing the pick button causes the cursor to be placed at the selected location. You can then begin typing or editing as needed. If you begin typing where the text cursor is initially placed, your text begins in the upper-left corner of the text boundary.

      Text is selected in the same way as with most standard Windows text editors. Place the cursor at one end of the desired selection, and then press and hold the pick button. Drag the cursor until the desired text is highlighted, and then release the pick button. Now, any editing operations you perform affect the highlighted text. For example, a copy or cut operation places the highlighted text on the Clipboard. One other way to highlight text is to move your mouse to the word you would like to highlight and double-click on it. To entirely replace the highlighted text with new text, either paste the new text from the Clipboard or begin typing. The selection is erased and the new text appears in its place.

      As you type in the multiline text editor, the text cursor moves to the right. When the cursor gets to the end of the text window, the line of text moves to the left, allowing you to continue typing. Notice the scroll bar below the text window. Move the scroll bar to the left or right as needed to display hidden text.

      **Figure 8-12** illustrates the features found in the **Text Formatting** toolbar. These features are described below. Keep in mind that *selected text* refers to text that you have highlighted in the text editor window.

- **Style list.** This drop-down includes a list of the different text styles in the drawing. A text style is a type of font usage definition. It controls what font is used and determines whether the text appears vertical, inclined, or backwards. Text styles are covered in greater depth later in this chapter. Selecting a style from this list sets the current **Font** list setting to the type of font the style is using.

**Figure 8-12.**
The **Text Formatting** toolbar.

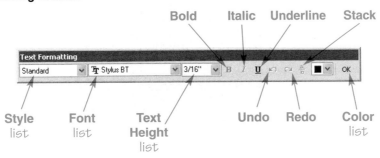

- **Font list.** Pick the drop-down arrow to access the list of available text fonts. Picking one of the fonts changes any selected text to the new font. The font can also be set current for any new text entered. This overrides the font used in the current style. Txt is the default text font.
- **Text Height list.** Use this list to specify the height of selected or new text. This overrides the current text height setting and the text height set within the text style. You can enter a new height or choose one from the drop-down list.
- **Bold.** Pick this button to have the selected text become bold. This only works with some TrueType® fonts. The AutoCAD shape fonts do not have this capability. (TrueType and shape fonts are discussed later in this chapter.)
- **Italic.** Pick this button to have the selected text become italic. This only works with some TrueType fonts. The shape fonts do not have this capability.
- **Underline.** Picking this button underlines selected text.

> **Note**
>
> If you select text that is already bold, picking the **Bold** button returns the text to its normal appearance. This is also true for italic and underline formatting.

- **Undo.** Pick this button to undo the previous activity. Press again to redo the undone activity.
- **Redo.** When picked, this button redoes a previously undone operation.
- **Stack.** This button allows selected text to be stacked vertically or diagonally. To use this feature for drawing a vertically stacked fraction, place a forward slash between the top (numerator) and bottom (denominator) items. Then select the text with your pointing device and pick the button. This button is also used for unstacking text that has been previously stacked. You can also use the caret (^) character between characters if you want to stack the items without a dividing line. This is called a *tolerance stack*. Typing a number sign (#) between selected numbers results in a diagonal fraction bar. See **Figure 8-13.**
- **Color list.** The text color is set as ByLayer as default, but you can change the text color by picking one of the colors found in the **Color** drop-down list. Selected text or any new text is now created with a color.

## Using the text editor shortcut menu

The text editor shortcut menu was introduced in the previous section. This menu is accessed by right-clicking while the cursor is in the text editor window. See **Figure 8-14.** This shortcut menu is divided into six sections and includes a **Help** option.

**Figure 8-13.**
Different types of stacked items.

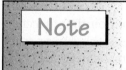

| | Typed Text | Stacked Text |
|---|---|---|
| Vertical Fraction | 1/2 | $\frac{1}{2}$ |
| Tolerance Fraction | 1^2 | $\frac{1}{2}$ |
| Diagonal Fraction | 1#2 | $^1/_2$ |

Architectural Drafting Using AutoCAD

**Figure 8-14.**
The text editor
shortcut menu.

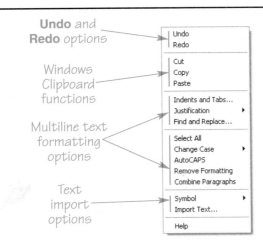

Undo and
Redo options

Windows
Clipboard
functions

Multiline text
formatting
options

Text
import
options

The top section includes the **Undo** and **Redo** options also found in the **Text Formatting** toolbar. These commands allow you to undo an operation or redo an undo operation. The second section includes the Windows Clipboard functions. These allow you to cut, copy, or paste text. The remaining options in the text editor shortcut menu are used to modify multiline text, search for and replace text, and import text and symbols.

## Modifying multiline text properties

The third and fourth sections in the text editor shortcut menu control indentation, justification, and other formatting options for multiline text. Also included is a find and replace tool that locates text and replaces it with a different string of text. The options are described as follows:

- **Indents and Tabs….** Selecting this option opens the **Indents and Tabs** dialog box. See **Figure 8-15.** This dialog box allows you to set up the indentation for the first line of a paragraph of text as well as the remaining portion of a paragraph. The setting in the **First line:** text box is used each time a new paragraph is started. As text is entered and wrapped to the next line, the setting in the **Paragraph:** text box is used. The **Tab stop position** area allows you to set tab stops for an existing paragraph or for new lines of text. To set a new tab, enter a value in the text box and pick the **Set** button. Picking the **Clear** button removes the highlighted tab.
- **Justification.** Selecting this option displays a cascading menu of justification options. These options are similar to the text justification options discussed earlier, except they apply to the entire paragraph of text. **Figure 8-16** displays the different justification options and how they relate to multiline text.

**Figure 8-15.**
The **Indents and Tabs** dialog box is used to set up paragraph indentations and tab stops.

Specify
indentation
of first line
of paragraph

Specify
indentation
of paragraph

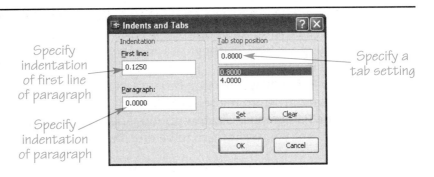

Specify a
tab setting

**Figure 8-16.**
The multiline text justification options.

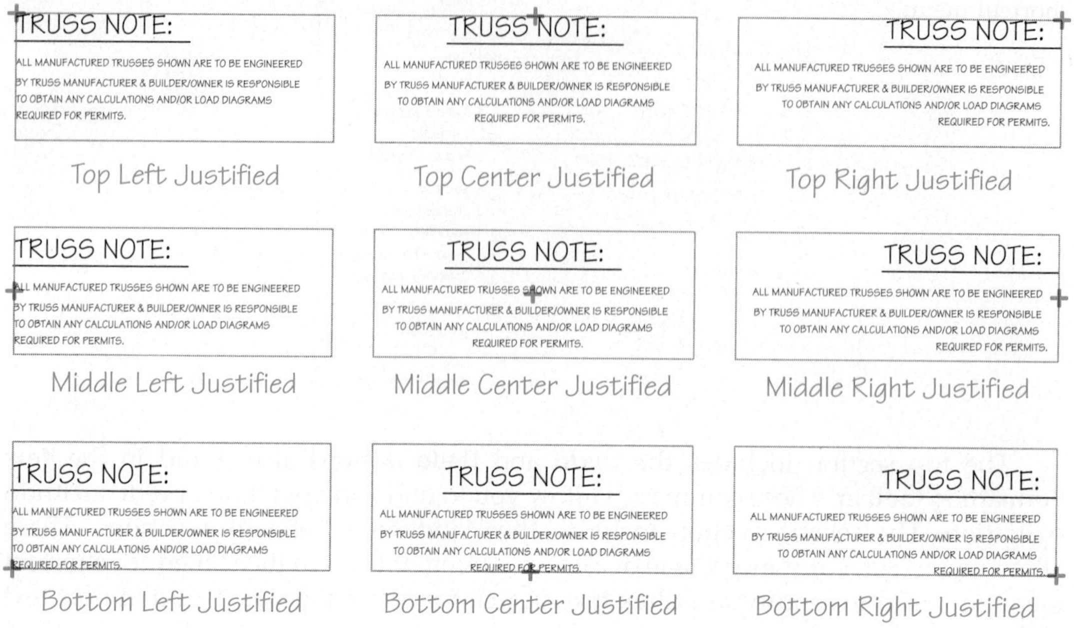

Top Left Justified

Top Center Justified

Top Right Justified

Middle Left Justified

Middle Center Justified

Middle Right Justified

Bottom Left Justified

Bottom Center Justified

Bottom Right Justified

- **Find and Replace.** When this option is selected, the **Replace** dialog box is displayed. See **Figure 8-17.** Enter the text you are searching for in the **Find what:** text box. Then pick the **Find Next** button to find and highlight the text. Next, enter the new text in the **Replace with:** text box. Pick the **Replace** button to replace the highlighted text or pick the **Replace All** button to replace all instances of text that match the search criteria.

  The **Match whole word only** check box is used to specify a search for a whole word, and not part of another word. For example, if the **Match whole word only** option is not checked, a search for the word *the* finds those letters wherever they occur—including as part of other words, such as o<u>the</u>r or we<u>ath</u>er. You can also check the **Match case** check box if you are searching for text that is case specific.

- **Select All.** Pick this option to select and highlight the entire contents of the text window.

- **Change Case.** Selecting this option displays a cascading menu with two options: **UPPERCASE** and **lowercase**. The **UPPERCASE** option changes all selected text to uppercase, and the **lowercase** option changes all selected text to lowercase.

- **AutoCAPS.** As discussed earlier in this chapter, notes in drawings are often displayed in uppercase text. When selected, this option turns on the [Caps Lock] setting on the keyboard so that multiline text is entered in uppercase. The [Caps Lock] setting remains on until you exit the multiline text editor and is reactivated after you enter the **MTEXT** command again. This prevents text from being written in uppercase in other programs after exiting the **MTEXT** command.

- **Remove Formatting.** Selecting this option removes any bold, italic, and underline formatting from the selected text.

- **Combine Paragraphs.** Use this option when you have two or more paragraphs selected and you want them to be one paragraph.

**Figure 8-17.**
Using the **Find and Replace** option for multiline text. A—Enter the text to find and the replacement text. B—Pick the **Replace** button to replace the selected text.

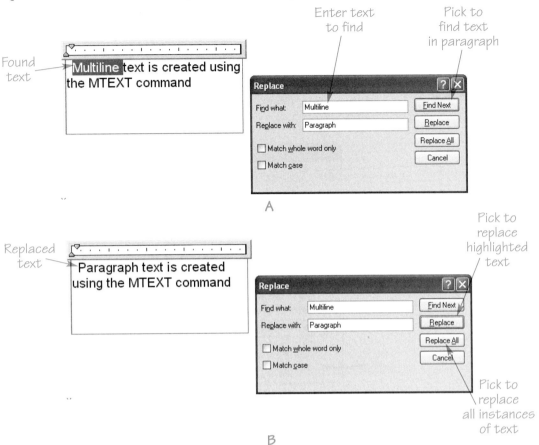

A

B

**Note**

The width of the text boundary can be changed in the multiline text editor after entering the **MTEXT** command and picking the two boundary corners. To specify a new width for a paragraph, right-click over the text editor ruler and select the **Set Mtext Width...** option. Enter a new width in the **Set Mtext Width** dialog box. As an alternative, you can move the cursor to the right side of the text editor window so that it changes to a resize cursor. When the cursor changes to a double arrow, press and hold the pick button to stretch the text editor to a wider or more narrow size.

## Importing text and symbols

The fifth section in the text editor shortcut menu includes options for adding symbols to multiline text and importing text. These two options are described as follows:

- **Symbol.** Picking this option displays a cascading menu for inserting symbols at the text cursor location. See **Figure 8-18.** This menu can be used to insert the degrees, plus/minus, or diameter symbol. The **Non-breaking Space** option keeps two separate words together. Selecting **Other...** opens the **Character Map** dialog box, **Figure 8-19.** To use this dialog box, pick the desired TrueType symbols from the **Font:** drop-down list. The following are the steps for using one or more symbols:

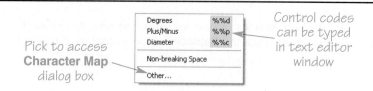

Figure 8-18.
The **Symbol**
shortcut menu
options.

Pick to access
**Character Map**
dialog box

Control codes
can be typed
in text editor
window

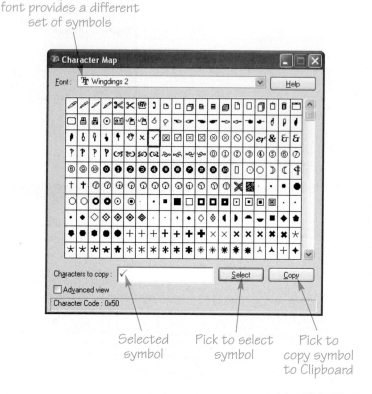

Figure 8-19.
The **Character Map**
dialog box.

Selecting a different
font provides a different
set of symbols

Selected
symbol

Pick to select
symbol

Pick to
copy symbol
to Clipboard

1. Pick the desired symbol(s) and then pick the **Select** button. Any symbols selected are displayed in the **Characters to Copy:** box.
2. Pick the **Copy** button to have the selected symbol or symbols copied to the Clipboard.
3. Close the dialog box.
4. In the multiline text editor, place the text cursor where you want the symbol(s) to be displayed.
5. Move the screen cursor to anywhere inside the text window and right-click to display the text editor shortcut menu, then pick **Paste** to paste the selection at the cursor location.

- **Import Text....** This option allows you to import text from an existing text file directly into the multiline text editor. The text file can be either a standard ASCII text file (TXT file) or a rich text format (RTF) file. The imported text becomes a part of the current multiline text object.

  When this option is selected, the **Select File** dialog box is displayed. Select the text file to be imported. If you import text while a portion of text is highlighted in the text editor, the **Inserting Text** dialog box appears. See **Figure 8-20.** This dialog box allows you to replace the highlighted text with the imported text, have the inserted text be placed after the highlighted text, or replace all of the text in the text editor with the text being inserted.

Architectural Drafting Using AutoCAD

**Figure 8-20.**
When importing text into the multi-line text editor while text is highlighted, the **Inserting Text** dialog box provides insertion options.

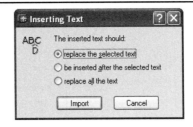

## Exercise 8-3

◆ Start a new drawing using a template or startup option of your own choice.
◆ Set architectural units.
◆ Use the **MTEXT** command to create a text boundary 8″ wide by 2″ high.
◆ Type the following text paragraph:

> Entering a paragraph of text is quick and easy with the MTEXT command. The MTEXT command opens the multiline text editor, where text is typed and edited as needed. The MTEXT command is accessed by picking Multiline Text in the Text cascading menu of the Draw pull-down menu, by picking the Multiline Text button in the Draw toolbar, or by entering MTEXT at the Command prompt.

◆ Use the text editor shortcut menu to select the entire paragraph. Then, change the height to 1/8″ and the font to CityBlueprint.
◆ Select the entire paragraph again and this time change the font to Arial. Now notice that the **Bold** and **Italic** buttons are active. This is because the Arial font is a TrueType font that has these options available.
◆ Make every occurrence of the word MTEXT bold.
◆ Add the following statement to your paragraph:

> The Multiline Text Editor also makes it easy to enter the symbols for degrees (°), plus/minus (±), diameter (∅), greater than (>), and Omega (Ω).

◆ Pick the **OK** button.
◆ Save the drawing as ex8-3.

## Modifying stacked text

As previously discussed, stacked fractions and other types of stacked text can be created in the multiline text editor by picking the **Stack** button in the **Text Formatting** toolbar. The text editor shortcut menu includes additional options for stacked text. If a selected fraction is not yet stacked, the **Stack** option is available in the menu. If the selected fraction is already stacked, the **Unstack** and **Properties** options are available. The **Properties** option accesses the **Stack Properties** dialog box. See **Figure 8-21**. The options in this dialog box allow you to modify the contents and appearance of the stacked text. You can also specify automatic stacking for fractional values and text you want to stack in the text editor.

The values in the **Text** area represent the current values for the top and bottom parts of the stacked text. The options in the **Appearance** area allow you to set the format, alignment, and size of the stacked text. The format can be set to **Fraction (Horizontal)**, **Fraction (Diagonal)**, or **Tolerance** by selecting the related option in the **Style** drop-down list. The fraction alignment is set to **Center** by default in the **Position** drop-down list. This centers the fraction vertically with the text line. The alignment can be changed to **Top** or **Bottom** to align the fraction with the top of the text line or the text baseline. The setting in the **Text size** drop-down list specifies the size of the

Figure 8-21.
The **Stack Properties** dialog box.

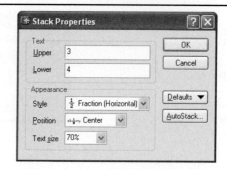

stacked text as a percentage of the text height. Picking the **Defaults** button allows you to save the settings as the default settings or restore the original defaults.

Picking the **AutoStack...** button accesses the **AutoStack Properties** dialog box. See **Figure 8-22.** This dialog box allows you to specify automatic stacking and contains the following options:

- **Enable AutoStacking.** When activated, this option stacks fractions automatically as you type.
- **Remove leading blank:.** This option removes a blank between a whole number and a fraction.
- **Convert it to a diagonal fraction.** This option converts an expression with the slash character to a diagonal fraction when AutoStack mode is on.
- **Convert it to a horizontal fraction.** This option converts an expression with the slash character to a horizontal fraction when AutoStack mode is on.
- **Don't show this dialog again; always use these settings.** This option suppresses the display of the **AutoStack Properties** dialog box when a fraction is entered in the text editor. The current property settings are maintained when this option is activated.

Figure 8-22.
The **AutoStack Properties** dialog box.

Check to activate Autostacking

Select the style for fractions

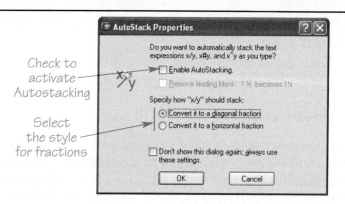

Architectural Drafting Using AutoCAD

## Exercise 8-4

◆ Start a new drawing using a template or startup option of your own choice.
◆ Set architectural units.
◆ Use the **MTEXT** command to create a text boundary 8″ wide by 2″ high.
◆ Type the following text paragraph:

> Multiline text is created using the MTEXT command. This
> provides you the opportunity to place several lines of text
> on a drawing and have all the lines act as one text object. It
> also gives you the convenience of entering and editing the
> text in the multiline text editor. Fractions can also be
> added, such as a diagonal 1/2″ fraction, a horizontal 1/2″
> fraction, or a stacked tolerance with the value .001/.002.

◆ Change the width to 4″ and observe the effect.
◆ Change the width back to 8″.
◆ Change the justification and view the results. Change the justification back to top left.
◆ Using stacked text, modify the fractions to reflect a diagonal, horizontal, and tolerance style.
◆ Pick the **OK** button.
◆ Save the drawing as ex8-4.

## Setting multiline text options at the prompt line

When creating text with the **MTEXT** command, you can preassign some of the settings so they do not have to be made within the text editor. These options are available from the command line when you begin creating the text boundary. Two of these options are not available anywhere else except from the command line.

After picking the first boundary corner, the Specify opposite corner or [Height/Justify/Line spacing/Rotation/Style/Width]: prompt is displayed. You can select any of the options by entering the appropriate letter at the prompt. A value specified with the **Width** option automatically sets the multiline text boundary width and opens the multiline text editor.

The two options available at the Command prompt that are not available in the text editor are **Line spacing** and **Rotation**. The **Rotation** option allows you to specify a rotation angle for the text in degrees. The **Line spacing** option is used to control line spacing for newly created text. The **At least** option automatically adds spaces between lines based on the height of the characters in the line. The **Exactly** option forces the line spacing to be the same for all lines of multiline text within the object. After selecting one of these options, the Enter line spacing factor or distance <1x>: prompt appears. A value followed by an "X" specifies the spacing increment. This spacing increment is the vertical distance from the bottom of one line to the bottom of the next line. For example, single-spaced lines have a value of 1x, and double-spaced lines have a value of 2x. The command sequence is as follows:

Command: **t, mt,** *or* **mtext**↵
Current text style: *current* Text height: *current*
Specify first corner: *(pick the first boundary corner)*
Specify opposite corner or [Height/Justify/Line spacing/Rotation/Style/Width]: **l**↵
Enter line spacing type [At least/Exactly] <At least>: **e**↵
Enter line spacing factor or distance <1x>: **2x**↵
Specify opposite corner or [Height/Justify/Line spacing/Rotation/Style/Width]: *(pick the second boundary corner)*

# AutoCAD Text Fonts

As discussed earlier in this chapter, AutoCAD is installed with several fonts that appear similar to lettering in a hand-lettered architectural drawing. In addition to these hand-lettered fonts, there are a number of other fonts that can be used in your drawings. AutoCAD shape (SHX) fonts are created with a series of straight line segments, making them easier to regenerate than TrueType fonts. The standard AutoCAD text fonts are shown in **Figure 8-23**. These font files have SHX file extensions.

The Txt font is the AutoCAD default. The Txt font is rough in appearance and may not be the best choice for your application, even though it requires less time to regenerate than other fonts. The Romans (roman simplex) font is smoother than Txt. It closely duplicates the single-stroke lettering that has long been the standard for most drafting. The complex and triplex fonts are multiple-stroke fonts for titles and subtitles. The gothic and italic fonts are ornamental styles. In addition, AutoCAD provides several standard symbol fonts.

TrueType fonts use lines and arcs to create the characters. These types of fonts have an outline and are *scaleable*. This means that the font can be displayed on screen or printed at any size and still maintain proportion. TrueType fonts have an outline, but they appear filled in the drawing area. When you plot or print, the fonts can be filled or shown as an outline. The **TEXTFILL** system variable controls this appearance. The **TEXTFILL** default is 1, which draws filled fonts. A setting of 0 draws the font outlines.

Samples of several TrueType fonts are shown in **Figure 8-24**. Many TrueType fonts are installed with AutoCAD. Additional TrueType fonts may be installed with other software programs. Therefore, the TrueType fonts available to you will vary from computer to computer.

**Figure 8-23.**
Standard AutoCAD text and symbol fonts.

| | | |
|---|---|---|
| | Fast Fonts | |
| Txt | ABCDabcd12345 | |
| Monotext | ABCDabcd12345 | |

| | Gothic Fonts | |
|---|---|---|
| Gothice | ABCDabcd12345 | |
| Gothicg | ABCDabcd12345 | |
| Gothici | ABCDabcd12345 | |

| | Simplex Fonts | |
|---|---|---|
| Romans | ABCDabcd12345 | |
| Scripts | ABCDabcd12345 | |
| Greeks | ABXΔαβχδ12345 | |
| Italic | ABCDabcd12345 | |
| Simplex | ABCDabcd12345 | |

| | Duplex Fonts | |
|---|---|---|
| Romand | ABCDabcd12345 | |

| | ISO Fonts | |
|---|---|---|
| Isocp | ABCDabcd12345 | |
| Isocp2 | ABCDabcd12345 | |
| Isocp3 | ABCDabcd12345 | |
| Isoct | A B C D a b c d 1 2 3 4 5 | |
| Isoct2 | A B C D a b c d 1 2 3 4 5 | |
| Isoct3 | A B C D a b c d 1 2 3 4 5 | |

| | Complex Fonts | |
|---|---|---|
| Romanc | ABCDabcd12345 | |
| Italicc | ABCDabcd12345 | |
| Scriptc | ABCDabcd12345 | |
| Greekc | ABXΔαβχδ12345 | |
| Complex | ABCDabcd12345 | |

| | Symbolic Fonts | |
|---|---|---|
| Symusic | ⊙♀♀⊕✷"ϲ12345 | |
| Symap | ⊓⊿△✲⚡⚷12345 | |
| Symath | ·‖⊢←↓∂∇12345 | |
| Symeteo | ➤╲╲—12345 | |
| Symusic | ·⸴°·⸴°12345 | |
| GDT | ABCD∠⊥◿⌓12345 | |

| | Triplex Fonts | |
|---|---|---|
| Romant | ABCDabcd12345 | |
| Italict | ABCDabcd12345 | |

**Figure 8-24.**

Some of the many TrueType fonts available.

| | | | |
|---|---|---|---|
| Algerian | **ABCDABCD12345** | Goudy Old Style | ABCDabcd12345 |
| Arial | ABCDabcd12345 | Lucida Bright | ABCDabcd12345 |
| Arial (Bold) | **ABCDabcd12345** | Monospac821 BT | ABCDabcd12345 |
| BankGothic Lt BT | ABCDABCD12345 | PanRoman | ABCDabcd12345 |
| Bernard Condensed | **ABCDabcd12345** | Perpetua | ABCDabcd12345 |
| Bookman Old Style | ABCDabcd12345 | Rockwell | **ABCDabcd12345** |
| Calisto MT | ABCDabcd12345 | Romantic | ABCDabcd12345 |
| Century Gothic | ABCDabcd12345 | Stylus BT | ABCDabcd12345 |
| City Blueprint | ABCDabcd12345 | Swis721 BdOul BT | ABCDabcd12345 |
| Comic Sans MS | ABCDabcd12345 | Swis721 BLK BT | **ABCDabcd12345** |
| Commercial MT | ±°′″©®©®●●-■▇ | Swis721 BT | ABCDabcd12345 |
| CommercialScript BT | *ABCDabcd12345* | Symbol | ABXΔαβχδ12345 |
| CountryBlueprint | ABCDabcd12345 | Tahoma | ABCDabcd12345 |
| Courier New | ABCDabcd12345 | Technic | ABCDABCD12345 |
| Dutch801 RM BT | **ABCDabcd12345** | Times New Roman | ABCDabcd12345 |
| EuroRoman | ABCDabcd12345 | UniversalMath1 BT | ABΨΔαβψδ+−×÷= |
| French Scripr MT | *ABCDabcd12345* | Verdana | ABCDabcd12345 |
| Garamond | ABCDabcd12345 | Vineta BT | **ABCDabcd12345** |

**Professional Tip**

TrueType and other complex text styles can be very taxing on system resources. This can slow down display changes and significantly increase drawing regeneration time. Use these styles only when necessary. When you must use complex text styles, set your system variables to speed-optimizing settings.

# AutoCAD Text Styles

A *text style* is a set of predefined properties assigned to a font. A text style includes settings for properties such as the text height, width, and obliquing angle (slant). You may have several text styles that use the same font, but different settings for other characteristics. By default, the Standard text style uses the Txt font with a width of 1 and a 0° obliquing angle.

## Text Style *Dialog Box*

STYLE
ST

Format
➥ Text Style...

Styles
toolbar

Text Style Manager

The **Text Style** dialog box is used to create and modify text styles. To access this dialog box, pick the **Text Style Manager** button in the **Styles** toolbar, select **Text Style...** from the **Format** pull-down menu, or enter st or style at the Command prompt.

The **Text Style** dialog box is shown in **Figure 8-25.** The following describes the features found in this dialog box:

- **Style Name area.** Set a new text style current by making a selection from the drop-down list. Use the **New...** button to create a new text style and the **Rename...** button to rename a selected style. If you need to delete a style, use the **Delete** button.

**Figure 8-25.**
The **Text Style** dialog box is used to set the characteristics of a text style.

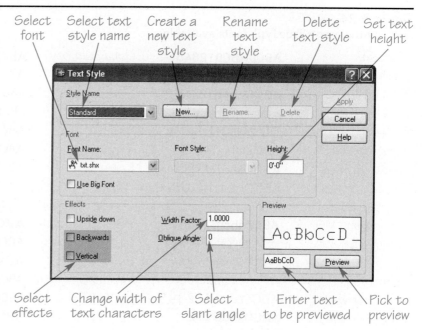

Select font · Select text style name · Create a new text style · Rename text style · Delete text style · Set text height

Select effects · Change width of text characters · Select slant angle · Enter text to be previewed · Pick to preview

- **Font area.** This area is where you select an available font, the style of the selected font, and the text height.
  - **Font Name.** This drop-down list is used to access the available fonts. The default font is txt.shx. All shape fonts are identified with an AutoCAD compass symbol, while the TrueType fonts have a double "T" TrueType symbol.
  - **Font Style.** This drop-down list is inactive unless the selected font has font style options available, such as bold or italic. None of the shape fonts have additional options, but some of the TrueType fonts do. For example, the SansSerif font has Regular, Bold, BoldOblique, and Oblique options. Each option provides the font with a different appearance.
  - **Height.** This text box is used to set the text height. The default is 0'-0". This allows you to set the text height while using the **TEXT** and **MTEXT** commands. When a height is specified, any text created with this style is always created at the specified height. Setting a text height value other than zero saves time during the command process, but also eliminates your flexibility.

**Professional Tip**

If a height other than 0'-0" is specified for the text style, any text created using this style looks to the text style for its height. It is highly recommended that a text height value of 0'-0" be used for text styles to be used in dimension styles. Dimension styles allow you to specify a text height value for the annotation text. By specifying a text height with the text style, the dimension text height is overridden. Dimensioning and dimension styles are covered in Chapter 15.

- **Use Big Font.** Asian and other large format fonts (called *Big Fonts*) are activated with this check box. Big Fonts define many symbols not available in normal font files. When this check box is selected, the **Font Style** drop-down list changes to a **Big Font** drop-down list.

Architectural Drafting Using AutoCAD

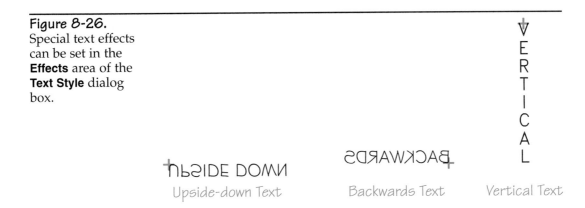

**Figure 8-26.**
Special text effects can be set in the **Effects** area of the **Text Style** dialog box.

Upside-down Text

Backwards Text

Vertical Text

- **Effects area.** This area provides more text format options. It contains the following items, which are illustrated in **Figure 8-26**:
  - **Upside down.** This check box is off by default. When it is checked, the text you draw is placed upside down.
  - **Backwards.** When the box is checked, text that you draw is placed backwards.
  - **Vertical.** This check box is only available for shape fonts—it is inactive for TrueType fonts. A check in this box makes text vertical. Text on drawings is normally placed horizontally, but vertical text can be used for special effects and graphic designs. Vertical text works best when the rotation angle is 270°.

Note | The multiline text editor displays text horizontally, right-side up, and forward. Any special effects take effect when you exit the editor.

- **Width Factor.** This text box provides a value that defines the text character width relative to the height. A width factor of 1 is the default. A width factor greater than 1 expands the characters, and a value less than 1 compresses the characters. See **Figure 8-27**.
- **Oblique Angle.** This text box allows you to set an angle at which text is slanted. The zero default draws characters vertically. A value greater than 0 slants the characters to the right, while a negative value slants characters to the left. See **Figure 8-28**. Some fonts, such as the Italic shape font, are already slanted.

**Figure 8-27.**
Examples of text width factors.

| Width Factor | Text |
|---|---|
| 1 | ABCDEFGHIJKLMN |
| .5 | ABCDEFGHIJKLMNOPQRSTUVWXYZ |
| 1.5 | ABCDEFGH |
| 2 | ABCDEF |

**Figure 8-28.**
Examples of text obliquing angles.

| Obliquing Angle | Text |
|:---:|:---:|
| 0 | ABCDEFGHIJKLMNOPQRSTUVWXYZ |
| 15° | ABCDEFGHIJKLMNOPQRSTUVWXYZ |
| −15° | ABCDEFGHIJKLMNOPQRSTUVWXYZ |

**Professional Tip**

Some companies (especially structural drafting companies) like to slant text 15° to the right. Also, water features named on maps often use text that is slanted to the right.

- **Preview area.** The preview image allows you to see how the selected font or style appears. This is a very convenient way to see what the font looks like before using it in a new style. **Figure 8-29** shows previews of various fonts. Specific characters can also be previewed. Simply type the characters in the preview text box and then pick the **Preview** button.

**Figure 8-29.**
The **Preview** area shows a sample of the selected font.
A—CityBlueprint font.
B—Stylus BT font.
C—Archstyle font.

A        B        C

## Exercise 8-5

◆ Start a new drawing using a template or startup option of your own choice.
◆ Set architectural units.
◆ Open the **Text Style** dialog box.
◆ Access the **Font Name** drop-down list and select a few different fonts to see their image in the preview tile. Pick the Arial font and then open the **Font Style** drop-down list. Pick each of the options as you watch the preview image change to represent your selection.
◆ Turn the **Upside down** and **Backwards** check boxes on and off while you watch the preview image.
◆ Change the width factor to 2, 0.5, and back to 1 while you watch the **Preview** image.
◆ Change the obliquing angle to 15, 30, −15, −30, and then back to 0 while you watch the **Preview** image.
◆ Type your own desired characters in the preview text box to the left of the **Preview** button and then pick the button.
◆ Pick the **Close** button.
◆ Exit AutoCAD or leave this drawing open for the next exercise.

## Creating a New Text Style

If you start a new drawing with the AutoCAD default template, the only text style that is available is the Standard style. The Standard text style is based on the txt.shx font, which is not very attractive. This may not suit your needs and is not commonly used in industry.

What if you want to create a text style for general notes on architectural drawings using the Stylus BT font with an obliquing angle of 15°? This style could be named General Notes. Always record the names and details of the text styles you create for future reference.

Text style names can have up to 255 characters, including letters, numbers, dashes (–), underscores (_), and dollar signs ($). You can enter uppercase or lowercase letters. The following explains the steps used to create this text style:

1. Access the **Text Style** dialog box. Standard is the current style, with the txt.shx font and a zero text height.
2. Pick the **New...** button. This opens the **New Text Style** dialog box. Notice style1 is in the **Style Name:** text box. You can keep a text style name such as style1 or style2, but this is not descriptive. Type General Notes in the box and then pick the **OK** button. General Notes is now displayed in the **Style Name** text box of the **Text Style** dialog box.
3. Select Stylus BT from the **Font Name** drop-down list.
4. Enter a 15° obliquing angle in the **Oblique Angle** text box. **Figure 8-30** shows the new text style.
5. Pick the **Apply** button and then pick the **Close** button. This creates a new text style and sets it current. The new General Notes text style is now part of your drawing.

If you want to create a similar text style for the titles of the drawings, you might consider a text style named Titles. For this style, use a font such as Times New Roman. The company where you work or your school may have specific requirements for the creation of text styles.

**Figure 8-30.**
These settings define the General Notes text style.

Pick to close dialog box

Pick to apply changes to the text style

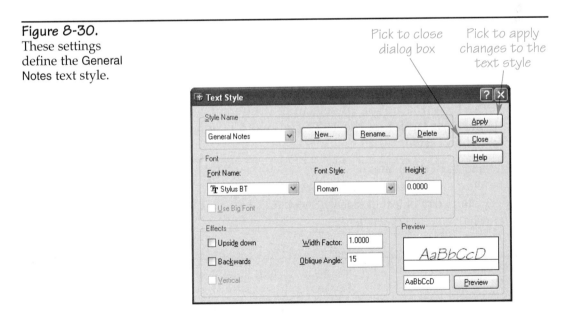

You can make the text style name the same as the font name if you wish. In some cases, this is a clear and concise way of knowing what font is being used for the style. If a font is used in more than one text style, you can include additional information in the text style name. For example, the text style name Stylus BT could correspond to a style using the standard Stylus BT font, while the Stylus BT Oblique text style adds an obliquing angle to the font.

## Exercise 8-6

◆ Start a new drawing using a template or startup option of your own choice.
◆ Set architectural units.
◆ Open the **Text Style** dialog box.
◆ Create a text style named General Notes to be used for any general notations. Create a text style named Titles to be used for the titles of drawings.
◆ For the General Notes style, set the font to Stylus BT and use an obliquing angle of 15°.
◆ For the Titles style, set the font to Times New Roman and use an obliquing angle of 15°.
◆ Save the drawing as ex8-6.

## Applying Text Styles

When you close the **Text Style** dialog box, the style listed in the **Style Name** drop-down list becomes the current text style. This text style becomes the default selection when you use the **TEXT** and **MTEXT** commands.

You can make a text style current at any time by using the **Text Style Control** drop-down list in the **Styles** toolbar, **Figure 8-31.** This toolbar is displayed by default in the drawing area. This toolbar includes the **Text Style Manager** button and options for creating and managing dimension styles. The **Text Style Control** drop-down list indicates the current text style. Any new text that is entered defaults to the style listed.

You also have the option of selecting a different text style when creating text objects. If the **Style** option of the **TEXT** command is entered, you can select a previously created text style:

```
Command: text, dt, or dtext
Current text style: "General Notes" Text height: 0'-0 3/16"
Specify start point of text or [Justify/Style]: s↵
Enter style name or [?] <current>:
```

**Figure 8-31.**
The **Styles** toolbar includes the **Text Style Control** drop-down list, which indicates the current text style.

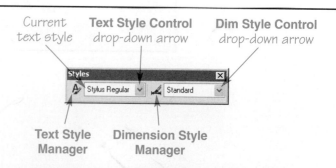

Current text style    **Text Style Control** drop-down arrow    **Dim Style Control** drop-down arrow

**Text Style Manager**    **Dimension Style Manager**

Architectural Drafting Using AutoCAD

Enter the name of an existing style, enter ? to see a list of styles, or press [Enter] to keep the existing style. After entering ?, you can type the specific text style(s) to list, or press [Enter] to display all the available text styles. The style name, font, height, width factor, obliquing angle, and generation of each of the available text styles is then shown in the **AutoCAD Text Window**.

When you are creating multiline text, the available text styles are provided in the **Style** list of the **Text Formatting** toolbar in the multiline text editor.

### Exercise 8-7

◆ Open ex8-6.dwg.
◆ Pick on the **Text Style Control** drop-down arrow to display the list of available text styles in the drawing. Make the General Notes style current.
◆ Enter the **TEXT** command and use the **Style** option to display the available text styles. Look through the list to see what is available. Press the [F2] key to return to the drawing area.
◆ Open the multiline text editor and access the **Style** list. Look through the list of available text styles.
◆ Exit AutoCAD or leave this drawing open for the next exercise.

## Changing, Renaming, and Deleting Text Styles

You can change the settings for a text style after it has been defined. To do this, access the **Text Style** dialog box and select the style you wish to change. Change the appropriate settings, and then pick the **Apply** button. The text style is redefined using the new settings.

Changing a text style will affect existing text objects. The changes are applied to new text added or any existing text in the drawing.

Existing text styles are easily renamed in the **Text Style** dialog box. Select the desired style name in the **Style Name** drop-down list and pick the **Rename...** button. This opens the **Rename Text Style** dialog box. Change the text style name in the **Style Name:** text box and pick the **OK** button.

 Styles can also be renamed using the **Text styles** option in the **Rename** dialog box. This dialog box is accessed by selecting **Rename...** from the **Format** pull-down menu or by entering rename at the Command prompt.

You can delete a text style by picking the style name in the **Text Style** dialog box and then picking the **Delete** button. If you try to delete a text style that has already been used to create text objects in the drawing, AutoCAD gives you the following message:

Style in use, can't be deleted.

This means that there are text objects in the drawing that are using this style. If you want to delete the style, change the text objects in the drawing to a different style. You cannot delete or rename the Standard style.

# Revising Text

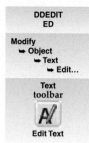

DDEDIT
ED

Modify
➥ Object
  ➥ Text
    ➥ Edit...

Text
toolbar

Edit Text

Text editing is accomplished using the **DDEDIT** command. **DDEDIT** is accessed by selecting the **Object** cascading menu in the **Modify** pull-down menu followed by **Text** and then **Edit...**, entering ed or ddedit at the Command prompt, or picking the **Edit Text** button on the **Text** toolbar. You can also edit text by selecting the text object, right-clicking, and then selecting **Mtext Edit...** or **Text Edit...** from the shortcut menu.

When editing text, AutoCAD first asks you to select an annotation object. Select any text, leader, or dimension object to be edited. Single-line text (drawn with the **TEXT** command) is edited in the **Edit Text** dialog box. See **Figure 8-32**. Modify the text displayed in the box and pick the **OK** button to display the change.

Multiline text is edited in the multiline text editor using the techniques discussed earlier in this chapter. Text created as part of a dimension or leader is multiline text.

**Figure 8-32.**
The **DDEDIT** command activates the **Edit Text** dialog box if the selected text was created with the **TEXT** command.

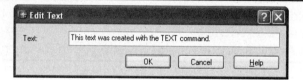

## Exercise 8-8

◆ Open ex8-6.dwg.
◆ Use the **TEXT** command to place the following text:

    *3068 SOLID CORE PANELED ENTRY DOOR SC306 ACME DOOR CO.*

◆ Use the **DDEDIT** command to change the text to read as follows:

    *3'-0" × 6'-8" STEEL FRAME PANELED ENTRY DOOR ER44 CECO ENTRY SYSTEMS*

◆ Change the font used in each of the text styles to a font of your choosing. Observe what happens to any existing text in the drawing.
◆ Save the drawing as ex8-8.

# Changing Text Properties

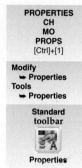

PROPERTIES
CH
MO
PROPS
[Ctrl]+[1]

Modify
➥ Properties
Tools
➥ Properties

Standard
toolbar

Properties

The **Properties** window can also be used to change text properties. To access the **Properties** window, pick the **Properties** button on the **Standard** toolbar, select **Properties** from the **Modify** pull-down menu, select **Properties** from the **Tools** pull-down menu, or enter ch, mo, props, or properties at the Command prompt. The [Ctrl]+[1] key combination can also be used to display the **Properties** window. You can also open the **Properties** window by selecting the desired text, right-clicking, and selecting **Properties** from the shortcut menu.

**Note**

For a general introduction to the **Properties** window and techniques for modifying properties within it, refer to Chapter 7.

---

**Figure 8-33.**

You can modify text properties in the **Properties** window. Notice that the available properties for single-line text are different from those for multiline text.

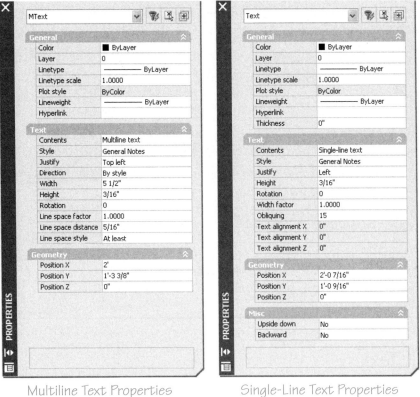

Multiline Text Properties
A

Single-Line Text Properties
B

**Figure 8-33** shows the properties listed for both single-line and multiline text objects. Notice that the type of text object (MText or Text) is listed in the drop-down list at the top of the **Properties** window. The properties are listed in the following categories:

- **General.** These general properties are found in nearly all AutoCAD object types.
- **Text.** This category lists text-specific properties. Select Contents to edit the text, or pick Style to change the text style.
- **Geometry.** The geometry properties specify the XYZ coordinates of the text insertion point.
- **Misc.** The miscellaneous properties—the **Upside down** and **Backward** effects—are available for single-line text only.

Note

Notice that there is no Font property listed. When using the **Properties** window, the only way you can change the text font is indirectly, using the Style property.

## Exercise 8-9

- ◆ Open ex8-8.dwg.
- ◆ Use the **MTEXT** command to place the following text on your drawing (incorrectly as shown) using the General Notes text style. Insert the first boundary corner at 1,4 and the opposite corner at 9.5,2.5. Use 1/8" high text.

  1.  USE MIN. OF TWO 2X4 STUDS AS BEAM SUPPORTS AT BRG WALLS.
  2.  ALL WINDOW & DOOR HDRS TO BE 4X12 (U.N.O.).
  3.  ALL EXT. WALLS TO BE 2X6 STUDS @ 16" ON CENTER (U.N.O.).
  4.  ALL INT. WALLS TO BE 2X4 STUDS AT 24" O.C. (U.N.O.).

- ◆ Use the **Properties** window to modify the above text as follows:
  - ◆ Change the text to read (note changes shown in color):

    1.  USE MIN. OF (2) 2X4 STUDS AS BEAM SUPPORTS AT BRG WALLS.
    2.  ALL WINDOW AND DOOR HEADERS TO BE 4X12 (U.N.O.).
    3.  ALL EXTERIOR WALLS TO BE 2X6 STUDS @ 16" O.C. (U.N.O.).
    4.  ALL INTERIOR WALLS TO BE 2X4 STUDS @ 24" O.C. (U.N.O.).

  - ◆ Change the color to Red.
  - ◆ Change the justification to Bottom right.
  - ◆ Change the insertion point to 8,2.
- ◆ Save the drawing as ex8-9.

## Scaling Text

**SCALETEXT**

Modify
➥ Object
  ➥ Text
    ➥ Scale

Text
toolbar

Scale Text

Changing the height of text objects can be accomplished using the **SCALETEXT** command. This command allows you to scale text objects in relation to their individual insertion points or in relation to a single base point. **SCALETEXT** is accessed by picking **Scale** from the **Text** cascading menu under the **Object** cascading menu in the **Modify** pull-down menu, entering scaletext at the Command prompt, or selecting the **Scale Text** button on the **Text** toolbar.

**SCALETEXT** works with single-line and multiline text objects. You can select both types of text objects simultaneously when using the **SCALETEXT** command. The prompts for the **SCALETEXT** command are as follows:

Command: **scaletext**↵
Select objects: *(select the text object(s) to be scaled)*
Select objects: ↵
Enter a base point option for scaling [Existing/Left/Center/Middle/Right/TL/TC/
TR/ML/MC/MR/BL/BC/BR] <Existing>: *(specify justification for base point)*
Specify new height or [Match object/Scale factor] <*default*>: *(specify scaling option)*
Command:

Using the **Existing** option scales the text objects based on their existing justification setting as the base point. Thus, the text is scaled in relation to its own justification setting.

After specifying the justification to be used as the base point, AutoCAD prompts for the scaling type. The **Specify new height** (default) option allows you to type a new value for the text height. All the selected text objects change to the new text height. The **Match object** option allows you to pick an existing text object. The selected text object's height adopts the text height from the picked text object. Use the **Scale factor** option to scale text objects to a different height in relation to their current heights. Using a scale factor of 2 scales all the selected text objects to twice their current size.

## Changing Text Justification

If you use the **Properties** window to change the justification setting of a text object, the text object moves to adjust to the new justification point. The justification point does not move. To change the justification point without moving the text, use the **JUSTIFYTEXT** command. **JUSTIFYTEXT** is accessed by picking **Justify** from the **Text** cascading menu under the **Object** cascading menu in the **Modify** pull-down menu, entering justifytext at the Command prompt, or selecting the **Justify Text** button on the **Text** toolbar. After entering the command and selecting a text object, you are prompted for a new justification option.

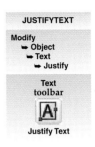

JUSTIFYTEXT

Modify
&rarr; Object
&rarr; Text
&rarr; Justify

Text
toolbar

Justify Text

# Checking Your Spelling

You have been introduced to editing text on the drawing using the **DDEDIT** command and the **Properties** window. You can use these methods to change lines of text and even correct spelling errors. However, AutoCAD has a powerful and convenient tool for checking the spelling on your drawing.

You can check spelling using the **SPELL** command. To access this command, select **Spelling** from the **Tools** pull-down menu or enter sp or spell at the Command prompt. After entering the command, you are asked to select the text to be checked. You need to pick each line of single-line text or make one pick on multiline text to select the entire paragraph. You can use the **All** selection option to select all text objects.

SPELL
SP

Tools
&rarr; Spelling

After selecting the text objects to be checked, the **Check Spelling** dialog box appears. See **Figure 8-34.** The **Current word** area lists a word that may be spelled incorrectly. Suggestions are listed in the text window.

To change the spelling of a word, you can either select a choice from the suggestions or you can edit the word in the text box. Then, pick one of the following buttons to move on to the next word:

- **Ignore.** Pick this button to leave the current word unchanged.
- **Ignore All.** Pick this button to leave the current word unchanged and to ignore any other occurrences of the word.
- **Change.** Pick this button to replace the current word with the word in the **Suggestions:** text box.
- **Change All.** Pick this button if you want to replace the current word with the word in the **Suggestions:** text box throughout the entire selection set.

**Figure 8-34.**
The **Check Spelling** dialog box provides options for addressing potential misspellings.

Word being questioned

Enter correct spelling

Suggested replacements

Add current word to custom dictionary

Sentence containing word

Pick to ignore current word

Replace current word with corrected text

List similar words in **Suggestions:** text box

Change dictionary or modify custom dictionary

**Check Spelling**

Current dictionary: American English

Current word
mispelled.

Cancel

Help

Suggestions:
misspelled.

misspelled.

Ignore       Ignore All

Change       Change All

Add       Lookup

Change Dictionaries...

Context
This word is mispelled.

- **Add.** Pick this button to add the current word to the custom dictionary. You can add words with up to 63 characters to the custom dictionary.
- **Lookup.** Select this button to list words that are similar to a word selected in the **Suggestions:** text box.

AutoCAD provides you with several dictionaries: one American English, two British English, and two French. The current dictionary is listed at the top of the **Check Spelling** dialog box. To select a different dictionary, modify entries in the custom dictionary, or create an additional custom dictionary, pick the **Change Dictionaries...** button. This accesses the **Change Dictionaries** dialog box.

In addition to the main dictionary, AutoCAD also uses a custom dictionary. The custom dictionary contains words that are specific to AutoCAD and drafting applications. The default custom dictionary is named sample.cus. The terms in the custom dictionary file can be modified using the **Custom dictionary words** area.

You can create your own custom dictionary by creating a text file with a .cus file extension using a standard text editor, such as Windows Notepad or WordPad. If you use a word processor such as Microsoft Word, be sure to save the file as *text only*, with no special text formatting or printer codes.

Professional Tip

You can create custom dictionaries for various disciplines. For example, when working on a plumbing drawing, common abbreviations and brand names might be added to a plumb.cus file. A separate file named arch.cus might contain common architectural abbreviations and frequently used brand names.

## Exercise 8-10

◆ Start a new drawing using a template or startup option of your own choice.
◆ Set architectural units.
◆ Use the **MTEXT** command to type the following short paragraph with spelling errors.

> FLOR SISTEMS TO BE 1 1/8" PLIWOOD TONGUUE AND GROOV ON 4X8 GURDERS ON 4X4 POSTS ON ASFALT SHINGLES ON 18" X 9" DIAMEETER CONCREET FOOTINGS UNLESS NOTED OTHERWISE.

◆ Check the spelling and correct the misspelled words.
◆ Save the drawing as ex8-10.

## Finding and Replacing Text

You can use the **SPELL** command to check and correct the spelling of text in a drawing. But if you want to find a piece of text in your drawing and replace it with an alternate piece of text, you should use the **FIND** command.

To find a string of text in the drawing, select **Find...** from the **Edit** pull-down menu, enter find at the Command prompt, or select the **Find and Replace** button from the **Text** toolbar. After you enter the command, AutoCAD displays the **Find and Replace** dialog box. See **Figure 8-35.**

FIND

Edit
↳ Find...

Text toolbar

Find and Replace

Architectural Drafting Using AutoCAD

Figure 8-35.
The **Find and Replace** dialog box. Notice that find and replace strings are not case sensitive.

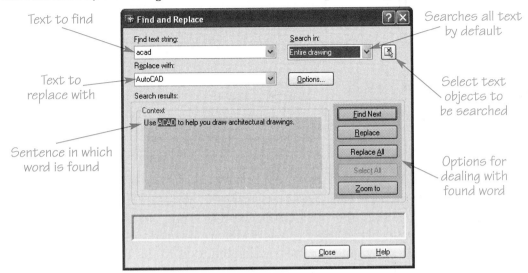

Text to find

Text to replace with

Sentence in which word is found

Searches all text by default

Select text objects to be searched

Options for dealing with found word

Enter the text to be found and the text to replace it. By default, AutoCAD searches the entire drawing, but you can also limit the search to specific text objects. The following features are available in the **Find and Replace** dialog box:

- **Find/Find Next.** This button allows you to find the text that you enter in the **Find text string:** text box. Once you find the first instance of the text, the **Find** button becomes the **Find Next** button, which you can use to find the next instance.
- **Replace.** This button allows you to replace found text with the text entered in the **Replace with:** text box.
- **Replace All.** Pick this button to find and replace all instances of the text.
- **Select All.** This button allows you to find and select all objects containing instances of the text in the **Find text string:** text box. This option is available only when searching the current selection. When you pick this button, the dialog box closes and AutoCAD displays a message indicating the number of objects found and selected.
- **Zoom to.** Picking this button displays the area in the drawing that contains the found text.

Picking the **Options...** button accesses the **Find and Replace Options** dialog box. In this dialog box, you can select the types of objects to be searched. You can also specify additional search criteria. See **Figure 8-36** for additional details.

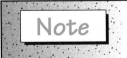

Note

The find and replace strings are saved with the drawing file and may be reused.

**Figure 8-36.**
The **Find and Replace Options** dialog box.

*Types of objects to be searched*

*Additional search options*

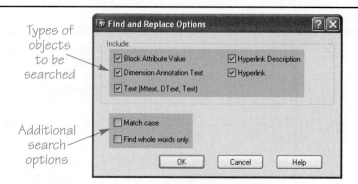

# Using Text Express Tools

Throughout this text, the AutoCAD Express Tools in AutoCAD 2004 are discussed where applicable. If the Express Tools are installed, they can be accessed from the **Express** pull-down menu. The text-related tools in the **Text** cascading menu under the **Express** pull-down menu are shown in **Figure 8-37.** These tools are discussed in the following sections.

## Using Reactive Text

*Reactive text* is text that is created from an ASCII text file or a DIESEL expression. *ASCII* (American Standard Code for Information Interchange) is a form of code that allows you to type values for text similar to text created with a word processing program. ASCII text editors such as Windows Notepad can be used to write text and save the file as a TXT file. A *DIESEL expression* is a type of programming code that looks at AutoCAD variables to determine a function.

Reactive text can be created with the **RTEXT** command. To use this command, select **Remote Text** from the **Text** cascading menu in the **Express** pull-down menu or enter rtext at the Command prompt. The following sequence is used to bring an ASCII text file into an AutoCAD drawing as a piece of reactive text.

**RTEXT**

Express
➥ Text
  ➥ Remote Text

Command: **rtext↵**
Current settings: Style=Romand Height=3/16" Rotation=0
Enter an option [Style/Height/Rotation/File/Diesel] <File>: **f↵**

You can then select a file in the **Select text file** dialog box. Browse for a file with a .txt extension, highlight it, and pick the **Open** button. The following prompts are displayed:

**Figure 8-37.**
The **Text** cascading menu in the **Express** pull-down menu.

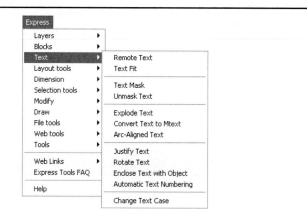

Architectural Drafting Using AutoCAD

Specify start point of RText: *(pick a start point for the text)*
Current values: Style=Romand Height=3/16" Rotation=0
Enter an option [Style/Height/Rotation/Edit]: ↵
Command:

This adds a piece of reactive text into the drawing. The reactive text maintains a link back to the file that was used for the text object.

In order to modify reactive text, the **RTEDIT** command is used. This command can be accessed by entering rtedit at the Command prompt. The **RTEDIT** command options are described as follows:

- **Style.** Used to specify a new style for the reactive text.
- **Height.** Allows you to change the height of the reactive text object.
- **Rotation.** Allows you to rotate the text.
- **Edit.** When this option is entered, the ASCII file is opened for editing.

Using a DIESEL expression for reactive text is more powerful than a TXT file because it is an interactive code that is updated each time the drawing file is opened. *DIESEL* stands for Direct Interpretively Evaluated String Expression Language. An example of a DIESEL expression is a string that displays the drawing name of the drawing file or the current date. To specify a DIESEL expression with reactive text, the following command sequence is used:

Command: **rtext**↵
Current settings: Style=Romand Height=3/16" Rotation=0
Enter an option [Style/Height/Rotation/File/Diesel] <File>: **d**↵

This opens the **Edit Rtext** dialog box. See **Figure 8-38**. The following expression is entered to display the name of the drawing in the drawing file:

Drawing file: $(getvar, "dwgname")

After entering an expression, pick **OK**. You are then prompted for a start point for the text. The resulting text appears in the drawing as follows:

Drawing file: Drawing1.dwg

As with text from a TXT file, you can change the style, height, or rotation of the resulting reactive text, or you can edit the original DIESEL expression. Other examples of reactive text DIESEL expressions are shown below. To include the folder path with the drawing file name, use the following DIESEL expression:

Drawing file: $(getvar, "dwgprefix")$(getvar, "dwgname")

**Figure 8-38.**
The **Edit RText** dialog box allows you to enter a DIESEL expression.

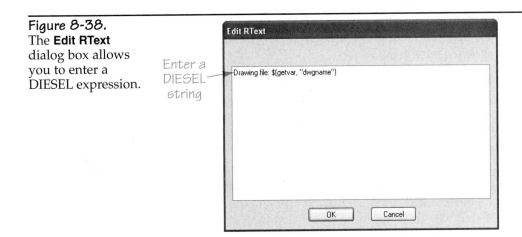

Enter a DIESEL string

Edit RText

Drawing file: $(getvar, "dwgname")

OK    Cancel

The resulting text appears in the drawing as follows:

Drawing file: D:\Drawings\A-FP1.dwg

To show the date and the time that the drawing was opened, use the following DIESEL expression:

$(edtime, 0, MON DD"," YYYY - H:MMam/pm)

The resulting text appears in the drawing as follows:

Jul 09, 2003 - 11:12pm

Additional reactive text DIESEL expressions can be found in the **AutoCAD Express Tools Help** window.

## Using the TEXTFIT Command

TEXTFIT

Express
➡ Text
    ➡ Text Fit

The **TEXTFIT** command allows you to stretch or shrink single-line text objects by specifying new start and end points for the text. To access this command, select **Text Fit** from the **Text** cascading menu in the **Express** pull-down menu or enter textfit at the Command prompt. The command sequence is as follows:

Command: **textfit**↵
Select Text to stretch or shrink: *(select a string of single-line text)*
Specify end point or [Start point]: **s**↵
Specify new starting point: *(select a new start point)*
ending point: *(select a new endpoint)*
Command:

## Creating a Text Mask

TEXTMASK

Express
➡ Text
    ➡ Text Mask

You may find it necessary to mask objects behind text when the text overlaps other objects. When using a text mask, any objects behind the text do not display through the text. A text mask can be created with the **TEXTMASK** command. This command can be used with single-line or multiline text. To access the **TEXTMASK** command, select **Text Mask** from the **Text** cascading menu in the **Express** pull-down menu or enter textmask at the Command prompt. The following sequence is used to create a mask behind text:

Command: **textmask**↵
Current settings: Offset factor = 0.0625, Mask type = Wipeout
Select text objects to mask or [Masktype/Offset]: *(select one or more text objects or enter m to specify a mask type)*

There are three different types of objects that can be used as a mask. To access the options, enter the **Masktype** option. The following options are available:
- **Wipeout.** This is the default option. When used, it applies a mask with a rectangular frame displaying the background color of the drawing area.
- **3dface.** This option places a 3D face behind the text. Three-dimensional faces are discussed in Chapter 25.
- **Solid.** This option creates a mask with a 2D solid in a specified color.

When creating a text mask, AutoCAD offsets the mask a specified distance from the edges of the text. To change the offset distance, enter o at the Select text objects to mask or [Masktype/Offset]: prompt. Then, enter a new value when the Enter offset factor relative to text height *<current>*: prompt appears. After specifying a mask type and offset distance, you are prompted to select the objects to mask:

Select text objects to mask or [Masktype/Offset]: *(select one or more text objects)*
1 found
Current settings: Offset factor = 0.0625, Mask type = Wipeout
Select text objects to mask or [Masktype/Offset]: ↵
1 text items have been masked with a Wipeout.

You can remove a mask from text that has been masked with the **TEXTMASK** command. To do so, use the **TEXTUNMASK** command. To access this command, select **Unmask Text** from the **Text** cascading menu in the **Express** pull-down menu or enter textunmask at the Command prompt.

## Exploding Text

You can explode single-line or multiline text into individual lines, plines, and arcs. To explode a text object, select **Explode Text** from the **Text** cascading menu in the **Express** pull-down menu or enter txtexp at the Command prompt.

## Converting Single-Line Text to Multiline Text

Single lines of text created with the **TEXT** command can be combined into a single multiline text object. Single-line text is converted to multiline text with the **TXT2MTXT** command. This command can be accessed by selecting **Convert Text to Mtext** from the **Text** cascading menu in the **Express** pull-down menu or by entering txt2mtxt at the Command prompt.

## Aligning Text with an Arc

You can draw curved text with the **ARCTEXT** command. To access this command, select **Arc-Aligned Text** from the **Text** cascading menu in the **Express** pull-down menu or enter arctext at the Command prompt. You are prompted to select an arc after entering the command. You can then enter the text and alter its appearance using the **ArcAlignedText Workshop-Create** dialog box. See **Figure 8-39.** This dialog box includes alignment and formatting options for the text.

The pick buttons across the top of the dialog box control the text location relative to the arc and its length. You can specify backwards text, align the text with the left or right side of the arc, fit the text, or center the text. You can also orient the text with the convex or concave side of the arc, set the direction of the text, and apply text formatting options. The drop-down lists allow you to specify the style, font, and color of the text.

Figure 8-39.
The **ArcAlignedText Workshop-Create** dialog box.

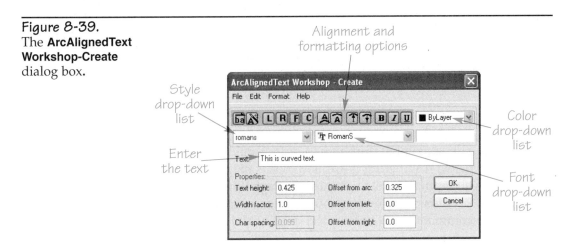

The text to be aligned with the arc is entered in the **Text:** text box. The options in the **Properties:** area control the text height, width, spacing, and offset distances.

When you are finished making settings for the curved text, pick the **OK** button. If the text needs to be modified, reenter the **ARCTEXT** command and select the curved text. After you are finished aligning the text, the arc used to curve the text can be erased if desired.

## Justifying Text

You can specify a new justification option for existing single-line text, multiline text, or attributes by using the **TJUST** command. Attributes are discussed in Chapter 21. The **TJUST** command changes the text justification without relocating the text. It is very similar to the **JUSTIFYTEXT** command discussed earlier in this chapter. To access the **TJUST** command, select **Justify Text** from the **Text** cascading menu in the **Express** pull-down menu or enter tjust at the Command prompt.

## Rotating Text

Single-line text objects, multiline text objects, and attributes can be rotated about their insertion points at a specified angle using the **TORIENT** command. To access this command, select **Rotate Text** from the **Text** cascading menu in the **Express** pull-down menu or enter torient at the Command prompt. The following command sequence rotates five pieces of text 308:

Command: **torient**↵
Select TEXT, MTEXT, ATTDEF, or BLOCK inserts w/ attributes…
Select objects: *(pick the text objects to be rotated)*
Select objects: ↵
New absolute rotation <Most Readable>: **30**↵
5 objects modified.
Command:

The **Most Readable** option orients the text to the most readable right-side up, right-reading orientation.

## Placing an Object around Text

You can enclose one or more pieces of text with a surrounding object using the **TCIRCLE** command. This command allows you to enclose each selected text object with a circle, slot, or rectangle. You can enclose single-line text, multiline text, or attributes. If you are enclosing several text objects, you can make the size of the surrounding objects constant or variable in relation to the size of the text objects. To access the **TCIRCLE** command, select **Enclose Text with Object** from the **Text** cascading menu in the **Express** pull-down menu or enter tcircle at the Command prompt.

## Automatically Numbering Text Strings

You can add sequential numbers to individual lines of text or to each line within multiline text. Text numbering is applied in this manner with the **TCOUNT** command. To access this command, select **Automatic Text Numbering** from the **Text** cascading menu in the **Express** pull-down menu or enter tcount at the Command prompt. After entering the command, you must select objects and then specify a sorting method:

Architectural Drafting Using AutoCAD

Command: **tcount**⏎
Select objects: *(pick the text objects to be numbered)*
5 found
Select objects: ⏎
Sort selected objects by [X/Y/Select-order] *<current>*:

The sorting options available are described as follows:
- **X**. Numbers are placed according to the order of increasing X coordinate values of the selected text.
- **Y**. Numbers are placed according to the order of decreasing Y coordinate values of the selected text.
- **Select-order.** Numbers are placed according to the order in which the text was selected.

After specifying the sorting method, the following prompt is displayed:

Specify starting number and increment (Start, increment) <1,1>: *(Enter the starting number followed by a comma, then the incremental number)*

The next prompt allows you to specify the placement of the numbers:

Placement of numbers in text [Overwrite/Prefix/Suffix/Find&replace..] *<current>*: *(Enter an option or press* [Enter] *for the default)*

The placement options are described as follows:
- **Overwrite.** The selected text is replaced with a number.
- **Prefix.** A number is added to the beginning of the line.
- **Suffix.** A number is added to the end of the line.
- **Find&replace.** A specified text string is replaced with a number.

After completing the command, numbers are added to the selected strings of text.

## Changing Case

The **TCASE** command is similar to the **Change Case** option in the multiline text editor. However, this command can be used to change the case of single-line text or multiline text, attributes, and dimension text. To access the **TCASE** command, select **Change Text Case** from the **Text** cascading menu in the **Express** pull-down menu or enter tcase at the Command prompt. After selecting the text to change, the **TCASE – change text case** dialog box is displayed. See **Figure 8-40**. This dialog box provides you with five case options to apply to the text. Select an option and pick **OK** to apply the changes.

TCASE

Express
➥ Text
➥ Change Text
Case

**Figure 8-40.**
The **TCASE –
change text case**
dialog box allows
you to change the
case of selected text.

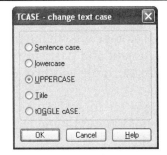

# Additional Text Tips

Text presentation is important on any drawing. It is a good idea to plan your drawing using rough sketches to allow room for text and notes. Some things to consider when designing the drawing layout include the following:

- Arrange views accurately.
- Arrange text to avoid crowding.
- Place related notes in groups to make the drawing easy to read.
- Place all general notes in a common location.
- Always use the spell checker.

# Chapter Test

*Answer the following questions on a separate sheet of paper.*

1. Identify three advantages of computer-generated text over freehand lettering.
2. Give the recommended lettering heights for notes and general text.
3. Define *font*.
4. Name the three types of architectural fonts included with AutoCAD.
5. Define *justify* as related to text.
6. Give two ways to access the **TEXT** command.
7. Identify two ways to start a new line of text when using the **TEXT** command.
8. Explain the difference between the **Fit** and **Align** justification options of the **TEXT** command.
9. Explain the difference between the **Center** and **BC** justification options of the **TEXT** command.

*For Questions 10–14, give the entry you would type at the* Enter text: *prompt when using the* **TEXT** *command to produce the given text string:*

10. 30°
11. 1.375±.005
12. Ø24
13. <u>NOT FOR CONSTRUCTION</u>
14. <u>DETAIL A</u> FRAME CONNECTION
15. Name the command used to create multiline text objects.
16. How does the width of the text boundary affect what you type for multiline text?
17. What happens if the multiline text that you are entering exceeds the text boundary length?
18. What does the arrow in the multiline text boundary window indicate?
19. Name the internal storage area that temporarily stores information that you copy or cut from a document and paste into another.
20. When you are in the multiline text editor, how do you open the text editor shortcut menu?
21. How do you change the font of a word in the multiline text editor?
22. If text is already bold, how do you change it back to standard formatting in the multiline text editor?
23. How do you create a vertically stacked fraction in the multiline text editor?
24. How do you insert a diameter symbol when using the multiline text editor?
25. Explain how to insert a document file from a word processor program such as Microsoft Word into the multiline text editor.
26. How do you enable automatic stacking of fractions?
27. What is the default AutoCAD font?

28. Name the font that closely duplicates single-stroke lettering.
29. Compare and contrast shape fonts and TrueType fonts.
30. Define *text style*.
31. What is the AutoCAD default text style?
32. What is the purpose of the **Preview** area in the **Text Style** dialog box?
33. How would you specify a text style with a double width factor?
34. How would you specify a text style with a 15° slant to the right?
35. How would you specify a text style with vertical text?
36. Describe how you would create a text style that has the name STYLUSBT-125_15, uses the Stylus BT font, and has a fixed height of .125, a text width of 1.25, and an obliquing angle of 15.
37. How do you rename a text style in the **Text Style** dialog box?
38. How do you delete a text style in the **Text Style** dialog box?
39. Identify the command that lets you edit existing single-line text in the **Edit Text** dialog box or multiline text in the multiline text editor.
40. How do you change the coordinates of a text object's insertion point by using the **Properties** window?
41. How do you make a single-line text object appear backwards by using the **Properties** window?
42. When using the **SCALETEXT** command, which base point option would you select to scale the text object(s) in relation to the current justification setting?
43. What is the difference between using the **JUSTIFYTEXT** command and using the **Properties** window to change the justification point of a text object?
44. Identify two ways to access the AutoCAD spell checker.
45. What do you do if you are checking the spelling of words in your drawing and the spell checker identifies a correct abbreviation in the **Current word** area?
46. What is the purpose of the **Add** button in the **Check Spelling** dialog box?
47. How do you change the main dictionary for use in the **Check Spelling** dialog box?
48. Name the command that allows you to find a piece of text and replace it with an alternate piece of text.
49. What Express Tools command allows you to convert single lines of text into a multiline text object?
50. List three items to consider when placing text on a drawing.

# Chapter Problems

1. Use the **TEXT** command to type the following text. Change the text style to represent each of the four fonts as shown. Use a 3/16″ text height. Save the drawing as p8-1.

   TXT–AUTOCAD'S DEFAULT TEXT FONT WHICH IS AVAILABLE FOR USE WHEN YOU BEGIN A DRAWING.

   ROMANS–SMOOTHER THAN TXT FONT AND CLOSELY DUPLICATES THE SINGLE–STROKE LETTERING THAT HAS BEEN THE STANDARD FOR DRAFTING.

   TIMES NEW ROMAN-A MULTISTROKE DECORATIVE FONT THAT IS GOOD FOR USE IN DRAWING TITLES.

   STYLUS BT-A FONT OFTEN USED IN ARCHITECTURAL DRAWINGS THAT SIMULATES HAND LETTERING.

2. Create text styles with the settings described in the following lines of text. Then use the **TEXT** command to create the text. Use a 3/16" text height. Save the drawing as p8-2.

Txt—Double width

Monotext—Slant to the left 30°

*Romans—Slant to the right 30°*

Romand—Backwards

CityBlueprint-Underscored and overscored

Stylus BT-USE 16d NAILS @ 10" O.C.

Times New Roman-12"Ø DECORATIVE COLUMN

3. Create text styles with a 3/8" height using the following fonts:
   - Arial
   - BankGothic Lt BT
   - CityBlueprint
   - Stylus BT
   - Swis721 BdOul BT
   - Vineta BT
   - Wingdings
   Use the **TEXT** command to type the complete alphabet, numerals 0 through 9, and the diameter, degree, and plus/minus symbols for the text fonts. For the Wingdings font, type the symbols corresponding to the complete alphabet and numerals 0 through 9. Save the drawing as p8-3.

4. Use the **MTEXT** command to type the following text using a text style with the Stylus BT font and a 3/16" text height. The heading text height is 1/4". After typing the text exactly as shown, edit the text as follows:
A. Change the \ in item 7 to 1/2.
B. Change the [ in item 8 to 1.
C. Change the 1/2 in item 8 to 3/4.
D. Change the ^ in item 10 to a degree symbol.
E. Check your spelling after making the changes.
F. Save the drawing as p8-4.

## COMMON FRAMING NOTES:

1. ALL FRAMING LUMBER TO BE DFL#2 OR BETTER.
2. ALL HEATED WALLS @ HEATED LIVING AREAS TO BE 2 X 6 @ 24" O.C.
3. ALL EXTERIOR HEADERS TO BE (2) 2 X 12 U.N.O., W/2" RIGID INSULATION BACKING UNLESS NOTED OTHERWISE.
4. ALL SHEAR PANELS TO BE 1/2" CDX PLYWD. W/8d @ 4" O.C. @ EDGE, HDRS, & BLK'G AND 8d @ 8" O.C. @ FIELD U.N.O.
5. ALL METAL CONNECTORS TO BE SIMPSON CO. OR EQUAL.
6. ALL TRUSSES TO BE 24" O.C. SUBMIT TRUSS CALCS TO BUILDING DEPT. PRIOR TO ERECTION.
7. PLYWOOD ROOF SHEATHING TO BE \ STD. GRADE 32/16 PLYWD. LAID PERPENDICULAR TO RAFTERS. NAIL W/8d @ 6" O.C. @ EDGES AND 12" O.C. @ FIELD.
8. PROVIDE [ 1/2" STD. GRADE T&G PLYWD. FLOOR SHEATHING LAID PERP. TO FLOOR JOISTS. NAIL W/10d @ 6" O.C. @ EDGES AND BLK'G AND 12" O.C. @ FIELD.
9. BLOCK ALL WALLS OVER 10'-0" HIGH AT MID.
10. LET-IN BRACES TO BE 1 X 4 DIAG. BRACES @45 ^ FOR ALL INTERIOR LOAD BEARING WALLS.

5. Draw the following door schedule. Create a text style with the *Stylus BT* font. Create separate layers for the text and lines. Draw the elliptical symbols in the Number column. Save the drawing as p8-5.

### DOOR SCHEDULE

| Number | Opening Size | Type | Thickness | Construction |
|--------|--------------|------|-----------|--------------|
| 01 | 3'-0" x 6'-8" | SINGLE SWING | 1 3/4 | Solid Core |
| 02 | 2'-8" x 6'-8" | SINGLE SWING | 1 3/4 | Hollow Core |
| 03 | 2'-8" x 6'-8" | SINGLE SWING | 1 3/4 | Hollow Metal |
| 04 | 2'-8" x 6'-8" | SINGLE SWING | 1 3/4 | Hollow Core |
| 05 | 2'-6" x 6'-8" | SINGLE SWING | 1 3/4 | Hollow Core |
| 06 | 2'-6" x 6'-8" | SINGLE SWING | 1 3/4 | Hollow Core |
| 07 | 2'-4" x 6'-8" | SINGLE SWING | 1 3/4 | Hollow Core |
| 08 | 2'-4" x 6'-8" | SINGLE SWING | 1 3/4 | Hollow Core |
| 09 | 4'-0" x 6'-8" | Bifold Double Louver | 1 3/4 | Hollow Core |

6. Draw the following window schedule. Create a text style with the *Stylus BT* font. Create separate layers for the text and lines. Draw the hexagonal symbols in the Number column. Save the drawing as p8-6.

### Window Schedule

| Number | Opening Size | Type | Construction | Glass |
|--------|--------------|------|--------------|-------|
| 1 | 5'-0" x 6'-0" | | Vinyl & Wood | Clear Plate |
| 2 | 3'-0" x 5'-0" | | Vinyl & Wood | Clear Plate |
| 3 | 3'-0" x 5'-0" | | Vinyl & Wood | Clear Plate |
| 4 | 3'-0" x 5'-0" | | Vinyl & Wood | Clear Plate |
| 5 | 4'-0" x 4'-6" | | Vinyl & Wood | Clear Plate |
| 6 | 4'-0" x 4'-6" | | Vinyl & Wood | Clear Plate |
| 7 | 3'-0" x 5'-0" | | Vinyl & Wood | Clear Plate |
| 8 | 3'-0" x 5'-0" | | Vinyl & Wood | Clear Plate |
| 9 | 1'-0" x 3'-0" | | Vinyl & Wood | Clear Plate |

7. Draw the following finish schedule. Create a text style with the *Stylus BT* font. Create separate layers for the text and lines. Save the drawing as p8-7.

### INTERIOR FINISH SCHEDULE

| ROOM | FLOOR | | | | | WALLS | | | CEIL. | |
|------|-------|-------|------|----------|----------|-------|-------|---------|--------|-------|
|      | VINYL | CARPET | TILE | HARDWOOD | CONCRETE | PAINT | PAPER | TEXTURE | SMOOTH | BROCADE | PAINT |
| FOYER | | O | | | | | O | | O | |
| KITCHEN | O | | | | | | O | | | O |
| DINING | | | | O | | O | | | O | |
| FAMILY | | O | | | O | | | | | O |
| LIVING | | | | O | | | O | | | O |
| MSTR BATH | O | | | | O | | | | | O |
| BATH # 2 | O | | | | O | | | | | O |
| MSTR BED | | O | | | O | | | | | O |
| BED # 2 | | O | | | O | | | | | O |
| BED # 3 | | O | | | O | | | | | O |

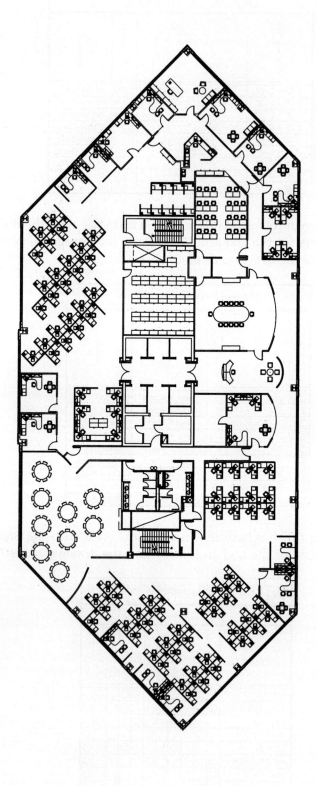

Symbols used to represent various types of objects in drawings are called blocks in AutoCAD. Many of the objects shown in this floor plan drawing, such as the office doors, computer workstations, tables, and file cabinets, were created as blocks and inserted into the drawing as needed. This greatly reduces drawing time and allows different drafters to use standard drawing content in a number of projects. (Autodesk, Inc.)

# Creating Symbols

## Learning Objectives

After completing this chapter, you will be able to:

- Create and save blocks.
- Insert blocks into a drawing.
- Edit a block and update it in a drawing.
- Create blocks that are saved independently from the drawing.
- Purge unused objects from a drawing.

## Important Terms

block
block reference
circular reference
global block
graphic symbols
in-place reference editing
nesting

real block
schematic block
symbol library
unit block
wblock
working set

One of the greatest benefits of AutoCAD is the ability to store symbols for future use. These symbols are called *blocks*. A block can be inserted into a drawing, scaled, and rotated in one operation. If a block is edited, drawings containing the block can be updated to include the new version. There are two types of blocks used in AutoCAD. A *block* created with the **BLOCK** command is stored within a drawing. A *wblock* created with the **WBLOCK** command is saved as a separate drawing file. Both types of blocks can be used to create a *symbol library,* which is a related group of symbols. This chapter discusses how symbols designed for repeated use are constructed into blocks or wblocks and inserted into drawings.

# Creating Symbols as Blocks

The ability to draw and store symbols is one of the greatest time-saving features of AutoCAD. The **BLOCK** command is used to create a symbol and keep it within the current drawing file. The block can then be inserted as many times as needed into the drawing in which it was defined using the **INSERT** command. This type of block can also be accessed for insertion into another drawing using **DesignCenter** and the **Tool Palettes** window. **DesignCenter** and tool palettes are discussed in Chapter 10.

The **WBLOCK** command is used to create a symbol as a wblock and store it as a *separate drawing file (DWG file)*. When saved, the wblock can then be inserted into any drawing using the **INSERT** command or **DesignCenter**. Upon insertion, symbols saved as wblocks or blocks can be scaled and rotated to meet the drawing requirements.

## Constructing Blocks

A block can be any shape, symbol, or group of objects that you use more than once. Before constructing a block, review the drawing you are working on. This is where a sketch of your drawing can be useful. Look for any shapes, components, notes, and assemblies that are used more than once. These objects can be drawn once and then saved as blocks.

Existing drawings can also be used as blocks in the current drawing. This is accomplished by using the **INSERT** command to select a previously saved DWG file. When inserted, the file becomes a block in the current drawing. This procedure is explained in detail later in this chapter.

## Block Creation Criteria

Before drawing a block, you need to determine the following criteria:
- What layer should the block objects be created on?
- What color setting should be assigned to the objects: ByLayer, ByBlock, or a specific color?
- What linetype setting should be assigned to the objects: ByLayer, ByBlock, or a specific linetype?
- What lineweight setting should be used: ByLayer, ByBlock, or a specific lineweight?

It is very important to make sure the correct layer, color, linetype, and lineweight settings are applied when creating and inserting blocks. Blocks can be created so that when they are inserted into a drawing, they inherit both the layer on which they are inserted and the properties of that layer. If the objects used for the block are originally created on the 0 layer, the block will assume the properties of the layer it is inserted on only. If the objects for the block are originally created on a layer *other* than the 0 layer, the objects belong to the layer the block is inserted on, but they retain the properties of the layer(s) the objects were created on. The latter method typically is a managerial nightmare, because a group of objects (a block) belongs to one layer but has the properties of a different layer. Typically, objects for a block are created on the 0 layer.

Once the layer for the block has been chosen, you need to decide how the block will obtain its color, linetype, and lineweight properties. It is undesirable for the properties of the original objects to override the properties of the layer on which the block is inserted. This can happen if the block objects are drawn using a color, linetype, or lineweight setting other than ByLayer or ByBlock.

By default, objects drawn in AutoCAD are created with the color, linetype, and lineweight settings set to ByLayer. When drawing block objects in ByLayer mode, on the 0 layer, you are telling the objects to use the current layer's color, linetype, and lineweight properties when the block is inserted. When the block is inserted on a different layer, such as the 1 layer, it inherits the color, linetype, and lineweight settings of that layer. If you try to change the color, linetype, or lineweight of the block using the **Properties** window, nothing happens because the original block objects are still looking to the layer upon which the block was inserted for the display properties. You must explode the block into its individual components to change the properties of the original objects.

To set the color to ByLayer when creating a block, pick ByLayer in the **Color Control** drop-down list of the **Properties** toolbar. You can also enter color at the Command prompt or pick **Color...** from the **Format** pull-down menu to access the **Select Color** dialog box. Then, pick the **ByLayer** button.

To set the linetype to ByLayer when creating a block, pick ByLayer in the **Linetype Control** drop-down list of the **Properties** toolbar. You can also enter linetype at the Command prompt or pick **Linetype...** from the **Format** pull-down menu to display the **Linetype Manager** dialog box. Then, select ByLayer in the **Linetype** list and pick the **Current** button.

To set the lineweight to ByLayer when creating a block, pick ByLayer in the **Lineweight Control** drop-down list of the **Properties** toolbar. You can also type lineweight at the Command prompt or pick **Lineweight...** from the **Format** pull-down menu to display the **Lineweight Settings** dialog box. Then, select ByLayer in the **Lineweights** list and pick the **OK** button.

Blocks can also be created with the color, linetype, and lineweight settings set to ByBlock. As is the case with blocks created in ByLayer mode, blocks created in ByBlock mode assume the layer on which they are inserted. However, a block created in ByBlock mode inherits the current color, linetype, and lineweight settings when it is inserted into a drawing, regardless of the current layer setting. In addition, if the inserted block needs to be displayed with a different color, linetype, or lineweight, those properties can be changed using the **Properties** window without exploding the block.

Creating a block in ByBlock mode tells the block objects to use the color, linetype, and lineweight properties assigned to the block insertion. If the current properties are set to ByLayer when the block is inserted, the block inherits the properties of the current layer. However, when the current properties are not set to ByLayer, they override the properties of the current layer and are assigned to the block when the block is inserted. For example, if a block is created with the color set to ByBlock, it will inherit the current color setting when it is inserted even if the current setting is different from the color assigned to the current layer.

To set the color, linetype, or lineweight to ByBlock when creating a block, make the setting in the appropriate drop-down list in the **Properties** toolbar. You may also use the **Select Color**, **Linetype Manager**, and **Lineweight Settings** dialog boxes.

In Chapter 5, you learned that objects are most commonly drawn using the ByLayer setting for the color, linetype, and lineweight properties, because the current layer should already have the ByLayer settings applied. When creating a block, the most desirable procedure is to draw the block on the 0 layer using the ByLayer setting for object colors, linetypes, and lineweights. This way, when the block is inserted into a drawing, the block takes on the current layer properties just as if you were drawing on the current layer.

If it is important to be able to change the color, linetype, or lineweight of a block after it is inserted, draw the block objects on the 0 layer using the ByBlock setting for object colors, linetypes, and lineweights.

## Drawing the Block Components

Draw the objects making up a block as you would any other drawing objects. If you want the block to have the color and linetype of the layer on which it is inserted, be sure to set the 0 layer current before you begin drawing the block. If you forget to do this and draw the objects on another layer, simply use the **Properties** window or the **Layers** toolbar to place all the objects on the 0 layer before creating the block. Also, make sure the object color, linetype, and lineweight properties are set to ByLayer or ByBlock.

Once the current settings are made, you can create the symbol and then turn it into a block. When you finish drawing the object, determine a logical location on or around the symbol to use as an insertion point. When you insert the block into a drawing, the symbol is attached to the screen cursor at its insertion point. This allows you to select a location for the symbol. The point should represent the logical point of insertion for the symbol. This is often a corner feature, a midpoint, or a center of a circle. Several examples of commonly used blocks with their insertion points highlighted are shown in **Figure 9-1.** Note that the insertion points shown do not appear on the screen when you insert a block.

**Figure 9-1.**
Common architectural drafting symbols and their logical insertion points for placement into the drawing. The insertion points are shown here for reference only and do not appear in the drawing.

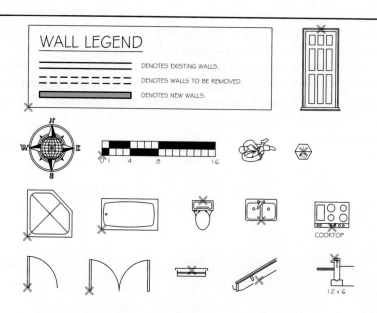

## Creating Blocks

When you draw a shape or symbol, you have not yet created a block. You have only created the object(s) that will be used in the definition of the block. To save the object as a block, pick the **Make Block** button in the **Draw** toolbar, pick **Make...** from the **Block** cascading menu in the **Draw** pull-down menu, or enter b, block, or bmake at the Command prompt. Any one of these methods displays the **Block Definition** dialog box, **Figure 9-2.**

This dialog box allows you to create a block that is stored within a drawing file. Creating wblocks is discussed later in this chapter. The process for defining a block is as follows:

1. In the **Name:** text box, enter a name for the block, such as Bathtub. The name cannot exceed 255 characters. It can include numbers, letters, and spaces, as well as the dollar sign ($), hyphen (-), and underscore (_). The block name can be a description of what the block is, or a series of number and letter combinations indicating the type of symbol the block is representing. Appendix F of this text describes a system of naming blocks that is recommended by the Construction Specifications Institute (CSI).

2. In the **Base point** area, enter absolute coordinates for the insertion base point of the block or pick the **Pick point** button to use the pointing device to select an insertion point. Remember that this is the point at which the block is attached to the cursor when inserting the block.

3. In the **Objects** area, pick the **Select objects** button to use the pointing device to select objects for the block definition. The drawing area returns and you are prompted to select objects. Select all the objects that will make up the block. Press [Enter] when you are done. The **Block Definition** dialog box reopens, and the number of objects selected is shown in the **Objects** area. If you want to create a selection set, use the **Quick Select** button to define a filter for the selection set.

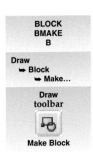

BLOCK
BMAKE
B

Draw
➥ Block
    ➥ Make...

Draw
toolbar

Make Block

---

**Figure 9-2.**
Blocks are created using the **Block Definition** dialog box.

Enter a name for the block

Pick to display a list of blocks in the drawing

Pick to select an insertion base point

**Quick Select** button

Enter absolute coordinates for the insertion point

Pick to select objects for the block

Select the type of drag-and-drop units when using **DesignCenter**

Specify whether to create a preview image of the block

Pick to attach a hyperlink to the block

Enter a description for the block

4. In the **Objects** area, specify whether to retain, convert, or delete the selected objects. If you want to keep the selected objects in the current drawing and in their original state, pick the **Retain** radio button. If you want to replace the selected objects with the block definition you are creating, pick the **Convert to block** radio button. If you want to remove the selected objects after the block is defined, pick the **Delete** radio button.

5. In the **Preview icon** area, specify whether to create an icon from the block definition. The purpose of the icon is to provide a preview image when using **DesignCenter**. **DesignCenter** is discussed in Chapter 10. You may want icons only for your most important blocks, but you can have an icon for every block if you wish. To omit an icon from the block definition, pick the **Do not include an icon** radio button. To save an icon with the block definition, pick the **Create icon from block geometry** radio button. An image of the icon is then displayed to the right.

6. Use the **Drag-and-drop units:** drop-down list to specify the type of units **DesignCenter** uses when inserting the block. This is discussed in Chapter 10.

7. In the **Description:** text box, enter a textual description to help identify the block for easy reference, such as This is a 36"X60" bathtub.

8. If you wish to attach a hyperlink to the block, pick the **Hyperlink...** button. Picking this button displays the **Insert Hyperlink** dialog box, which can be used to "link" a block or any part of the block to an associated file. As an example, a block may be hyperlinked to a detail drawing or a bill of materials listing additional information about the block. Hyperlinks are discussed in more detail in Chapter 27.

9. After you have finished defining the block, pick **OK**.

The **Convert to block** radio button in the **Block Definition** dialog box is active by default. If you select the **Delete** option and then decide that you want to keep the original block objects in the drawing after you have defined the block, you can enter the **OOPS** command. This returns the original objects to the screen, whereas entering u at the Command prompt or picking the **Undo** button from the **Standard** toolbar removes the block from the drawing.

To verify that the block is saved properly, access the **Block Definition** dialog box again. Pick the **Name:** drop-down list button to display a list of all blocks in the current drawing. See **Figure 9-3.** The block names are organized in numerical and alphabetical order. If there are more than six blocks in the drawing, a scroll bar appears to the right of the list so you can access the remaining blocks.

Try stepping through the process of creating a block again. Draw a 1″ square and name it 1-Insq. See **Figure 9-4.** After creating the block, be sure to confirm that the 1-Insq block was saved by checking the drop-down list in the **Block Definition** dialog box.

**Professional Tip**

Blocks can be used when creating other blocks. Suppose you design an individual unit apartment that is used repeatedly to create the whole building. You can insert existing blocks, such as appliances, into the unit and then save the entire apartment as a block. This is called *nesting*, where larger blocks contain smaller blocks. The larger block must be given a name that is different from that of any of the smaller blocks. Proper planning and knowledge of all existing blocks can speed up the drawing process and the creation of complex drawings.

**Figure 9-3.**
A list of blocks in
the current drawing
is accessed by
picking the **Name:**
drop-down list
button in the **Block
Definition** dialog
box.

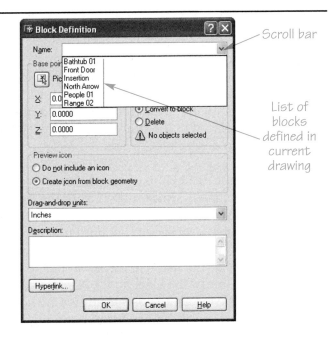

Scroll bar

List of
blocks
defined in
current
drawing

**Figure 9-4.**
Drawing a 1" square and defining it as a block. A—Draw the block on the 0 layer with the
color, linetype, and lineweight set to ByLayer. B—After entering the **BLOCK** command, give
the block a name in the **Block Definition** dialog box and pick an insertion base point. C—Pick
the **Select objects** button and select the square. Use any selection methods available. In this
case, a window is used.

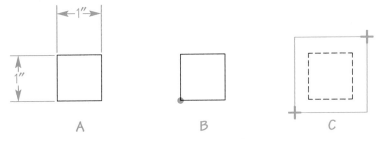

# Exercise 9-1

- Start a new drawing using a template or startup option of your own choice.
- Specify architectural units.
- Set the 0 layer current.
- Set the current color, linetype, and lineweight to ByLayer.
- Draw a 1" square with a 1" diameter circle inside.
- Create a block of the square and circle, and name it Column.
- Pick the center of the circle as the insertion base point.
- Save the drawing as ex9-1.

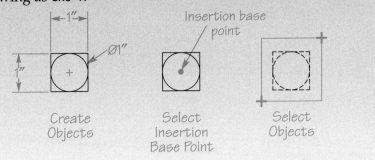

Insertion base
point

Create
Objects

Select
Insertion
Base Point

Select
Objects

# Using Blocks in a Drawing

Once a block has been created, it is easy to insert it into a drawing. First, determine a proper size and rotation angle for the block. Blocks are normally inserted on specific layers, so set the proper layer *before* inserting the block. Once a block has been inserted into a drawing, it is referred to as a ***block reference***.

Blocks are placed in the drawing with the **INSERT** command. **DesignCenter** may also be used to insert blocks and wblocks. Using **DesignCenter** is discussed in Chapter 10.

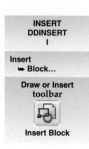
To access the **INSERT** command, enter i, insert, or ddinsert at the Command prompt, pick the **Insert Block** button from the **Draw** or **Insert** toolbar, or pick **Block...** from the **Insert** pull-down menu. This displays the **Insert** dialog box, **Figure 9-5.**

Pick the **Name:** drop-down list button to access the defined blocks in the current drawing. Highlight the name of the block you wish to insert. If there are more than six block names in the list, use the scroll bar to display additional blocks. You may also enter the name of the block in the **Name:** text box, or pick the **Browse...** button to insert a block saved as a separate drawing file. Once the desired block has been chosen, you must specify the insertion location, scale, and rotation angle. You can also specify whether to explode the block upon inserting it. The option buttons and other features in the **Insert** dialog box are described as follows:

- **Browse... button.** Pick this button to display the **Select Drawing File** dialog box. Browse through hard drives and network drives for any drawing files to be inserted into the drawing.
- **Insertion point area.** If the **Specify On-screen** check box is activated, AutoCAD prompts you to pick an insertion point on the drawing screen and insert the block dynamically. If you wish to insert the block using absolute coordinates, disable the check box and enter the appropriate coordinates in the **X:**, **Y:**, and **Z:** text boxes. Entering coordinates in this manner is referred to as using *preset values.* If preset values are used, the block is immediately inserted at the specified coordinates when you pick **OK**.

---

**Figure 9-5.**
The **Insert** dialog box allows you to select and prepare a block for insertion. Select the block you wish to insert from the drop-down list or enter the block name in the **Name:** text box.

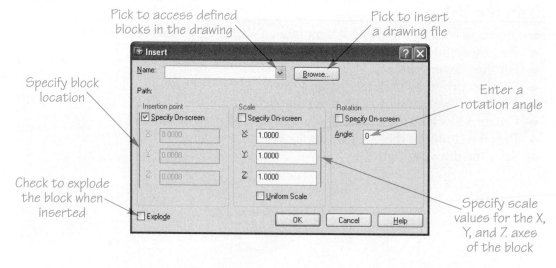

---

- **Scale area.** The **Scale** area allows you to specify scale values for the block along the X, Y, and Z axes. By default, the **Specify On-screen** check box is inactive. This causes the block to be inserted at a one-to-one scale once the insertion point has been selected. If you want to be prompted for the scale at the command line when inserting the block, activate the **Specify On-screen** check box. If the check box is inactive, you can enter scale values in the **X:**, **Y:**, and **Z:** text boxes. If you activate the **Uniform Scale** check box, you can simply specify a scale value for the X axis. The same value is then used for the Y and Z axes when the block is inserted.
- **Rotation area.** The **Rotation** area allows you to insert the block at a specified angle. By default, the **Specify On-screen** check box is inactive and the block is inserted at an angle of zero. If you want to use a different angle, enter a value in the **Angle:** text box. If you want to be prompted for the rotation angle at the command line when inserting the block, activate the **Specify On-screen** check box.
- **Explode check box.** When a block is created, it is saved as a single object. Therefore, it is defined as a single object when inserted into the drawing, no matter how many objects were used to create the block. This can help you keep the file size smaller. Activate the **Explode** check box if you wish to explode the block into its original objects for editing purposes. If you explode the block upon insertion, the individual objects assume their original properties, such as the original layer, color, and linetype settings used to create the objects.

When you pick the **OK** button, prompts appear for any values to be specified on screen as defined in the **Insert** dialog box. If you are specifying the insertion point on screen, the following prompt appears:

Specify insertion point or [Scale/X/Y/Z/Rotate/PScale/PX/PY/PZ/PRotate]: *(pick the point to insert the block)*

If you select one of the options, the new value entered overrides any setting in the **Insert** dialog box. The following options are available:

- **Scale.** This option affects the overall scale of the X, Y, and Z axes.
- **X.** Entering this option affects only the scale along the X axis.
- **Y.** Entering this option affects only the scale along the Y axis.
- **Z.** Entering this option affects only the scale along the Z axis.
- **Rotate.** This option sets the rotation angle.
- **PScale.** This option allows you to preview the scale values of the X, Y, and Z axes. You are then prompted to enter the actual scale factors.
- **PX.** This option allows you to preview the scale of the X axis. You are then prompted to enter the actual scale factor.
- **PY.** This option allows you to preview the scale of the Y axis. You are then prompted to enter the actual scale factor.
- **PZ.** This option allows you to preview the scale of the Z axis. You are then prompted to enter the actual scale factor.
- **PRotate.** This option is used to preview the rotation angle. You are then prompted to enter the actual rotation angle.

If you are specifying the scale factor on screen, the following prompt appears:

Enter X scale factor, specify opposite corner, or [Corner/XYZ] <1>: *(pick a point, or enter a value for the scale)*

Moving the cursor scales the block dynamically as it is dragged. If you want to scale the block in this manner, pick a point when the object appears correct. If you enter an X scale factor or press [Enter] to accept the default scale value, you are then prompted with the following:

Enter Y scale factor <use X scale factor>: *(enter a value or press [Enter] to accept the same scale specified for the X axis)*

---

The X and Y scale factors allow you to stretch or compress the block to suit your needs. If you want the block to be three times its size along the X axis and two times its size along the Y axis, respond with the following:

Enter X scale factor, specify opposite corner, or [Corner/XYZ] <1>: **3.**↵
Enter Y scale factor <use X scale factor>: **2.**↵

Notice that the prompt for the Y scale factor allows you to accept the X scale factor for the Y axis by simply pressing [Enter]. The object shown in **Figure 9-6** was given several different X and Y scale factors using the **INSERT** command.

If you enter the **Rotate** option or check the **Specify On-screen** check box in the **Rotation** area of the **Insert** dialog box, you are prompted to enter a rotation angle for the block. If you are specifying the rotation angle on screen, the following prompt appears:

Specify rotation angle <0>: *(pick a point, enter a value for the rotation angle and press [Enter], or press [Enter] to accept the default angle)*

**Figure 9-6.**
A comparison of different X and Y scale factors used for inserting the Column block from Exercise 9-1.

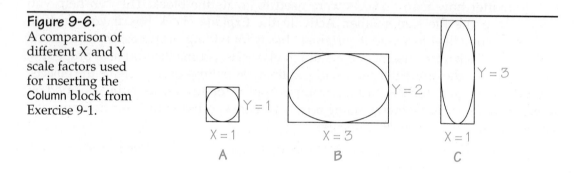

## Block Insertion Options

The scaling options available when inserting a block enable you to size or change the appearance of the block as needed. For example, it is possible to create a mirror image of a block by simply entering a negative value for the scale factor when inserting the block. For instance, entering -1 for both the X scale factor and the Y scale factor mirrors the block to the opposite quadrant of the original orientation and retains the original size. Different mirroring techniques are shown in **Figure 9-7.** The insertion point is indicated by a dot.

**Figure 9-7.**
Negative and positive scale factors have different effects when used to insert a block.

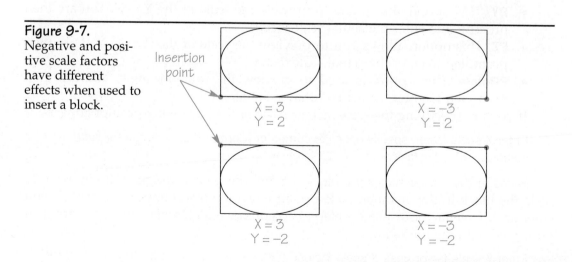

An approximate dynamic scaling technique is made possible by using the **Corner** option inside the **INSERT** command sequence. You can size the block dynamically as you move the cursor if the **DRAGMODE** system variable is set to **Auto**. Use the **Corner** option as follows:

Enter X scale factor, specify opposite corner, or [Corner/XYZ] <1>: **c**↵
Specify opposite corner: *(move the cursor to change the size of the block and pick a point or enter absolute coordinates)*

If you pick a point on screen, be sure to pick a point above and to the right of the insertion point to insert the block as drawn. Picking a corner point below or to the left of the insertion point generates a mirror image such as those shown in **Figure 9-7**.

In addition to the scaling options previously discussed, a block that is being inserted can be classified as one of three types: a *real block*, a *schematic block*, or a *unit block*. A **real block** is a block that is originally drawn at full scale. It is then inserted into the drawing using a scale factor of 1 for both the X and Y axes. Examples of real blocks could include a car design, a bathtub, or a detail drawing. See **Figure 9-8**.

A *schematic block* is a block that is originally drawn at a one-to-one paper scale. *Paper scale* refers to the size the symbol is to appear on the final plot. For example, if a detail tag is to be 1/2″ in diameter on the finished plot, it should be drawn at its full scale of 1/2″. It is then inserted into the drawing using the scale factor of the drawing for both the X and Y scale values. The scale factor is calculated by determining the scale at which the drawing will be plotted and is always the reciprocal of the drawing scale. For example, if the drawing is to be plotted at a scale of 1/4″ = 1′-0″, the scale factor is 48. This is determined by dividing 1′-0″ by 1/4″, which equals 48 (1/4″) segments. Scale factors are discussed in greater detail in Chapter 11. Appendix K also provides examples of scale factors for the most common drawing scales used in architectural and civil drafting.

Schematic blocks are commonly referred to as *graphic symbols*. **Graphic symbols** are drawing symbols that point the print reader to notes, a particular design feature, or general information. Graphic symbols are drawn in the form of annotation symbols such as section bubbles, detail bubbles, or typical notes. The development of graphic symbols should be consistent throughout a project and should observe office standards. This maintains consistency in a set of drawings and sets the standards for how drawings are created. Examples of typical graphic symbols used in a set of architectural drawings are shown in **Figure 9-9**.

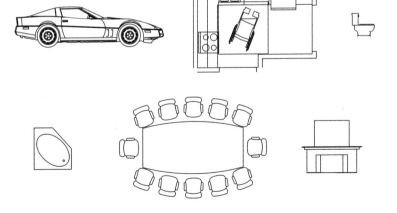

**Figure 9-8.**
Examples of real blocks. The blocks are drawn at full scale and inserted using a value of 1 for both the X and Y scale factors.

**Figure 9-9.**
Examples of graphic symbols, also known as schematic blocks. When these symbols are inserted into a drawing, the scale factor of the drawing is used for the X and Y scale values.

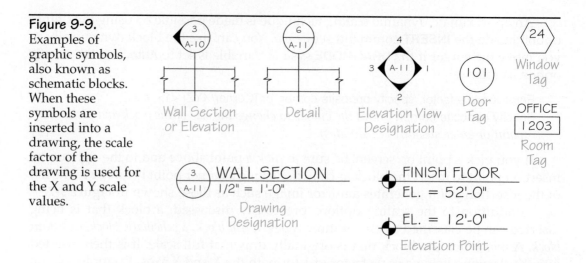

Wall Section or Elevation

Detail

Elevation View Designation

Door Tag

Window Tag

OFFICE
1203
Room Tag

WALL SECTION
1/2" = 1'-0"
Drawing Designation

FINISH FLOOR
EL. = 52'-0"

EL. = 12'-0"
Elevation Point

A *unit block* is a block that is drawn within a 1" square so that it can be inserted into a drawing using any value for the X, Y, and Z scale values. There are three different types of unit blocks: *1D unit blocks*, *2D unit blocks*, and *3D unit blocks*. A 1D unit block is a 1" horizontal or vertical line object that is turned into a block. It is then inserted into the drawing and given any scale value on the X axis if it is a horizontal line or any scale value on the Y axis if it is a vertical line. See **Figure 9-10.**

A 2D unit block is any object (or group of objects) drawn to fit inside a 1" × 1" square. When a 2D unit block is then inserted into a drawing, it can be given any scale value on both the X and Y axes. Examples of 2D unit blocks could include simple door or window blocks that are scaled to any size when inserted. For example, if a simple door is drawn to fit inside a 1" × 1" square, it can be inserted into a drawing and scaled 30 times on both the X and Y axes to make it a 2'-6" (30") door. See **Figure 9-11.**

A 3D unit block is any three-dimensional object that can fit inside a 1" cube. A 3D unit block can be inserted into a drawing using different scale values for the X, Y, and Z axes. Examples of 3D unit blocks could include framing members for a three-dimensional drawing, or columns. See **Figure 9-12.** Three-dimensional drawing is discussed in Chapter 25.

**Figure 9-10.**
Examples of 1D unit blocks.

1"
Not to scale
Horizontal line

30"
Insertion point
X = 30
Y = 0
Horizontal Line Scaled 30x on X Axis

15"
Insertion point
X = 0
Y = 15
Vertical Line Scaled 15x on Y Axis

1"
Not to scale
Vertical line

Original 1D Unit Blocks

**Figure 9-11.**
Examples of 2D unit blocks.

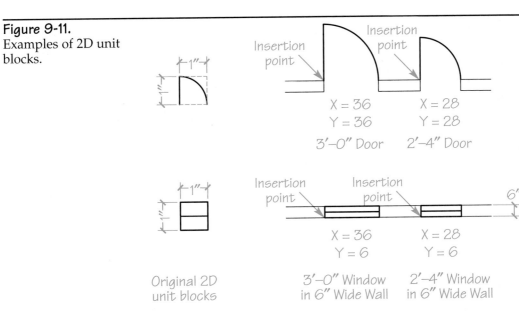

Insertion point

Insertion point

X = 36
Y = 36

X = 28
Y = 28

3'–0" Door    2'–4" Door

Insertion point

Insertion point

6"

X = 36
Y = 6

X = 28
Y = 6

Original 2D unit blocks

3'–0" Window in 6" Wide Wall

2'–4" Window in 6" Wide Wall

**Figure 9-12.**
Examples of 3D unit blocks.

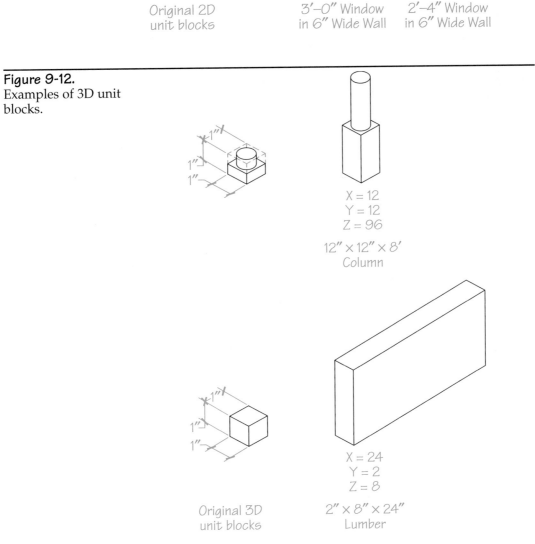

X = 12
Y = 12
Z = 96

12" × 12" × 8'
Column

X = 24
Y = 2
Z = 8

Original 3D unit blocks

2" × 8" × 24"
Lumber

## Exercise 9-2

◆ Start a new drawing using a template or startup option of your own choice.
◆ Specify architectural units.
◆ Set the 0 layer current.
◆ Set the current color, linetype, and lineweight to ByLayer.
◆ Draw the toilet block shown in Figure A. Pick an insertion base point as shown and name the block Toilet.
◆ Create a layer named Plumbing, assign it a color, and set it current.
◆ Insert the Toilet block into the drawing using a scale factor of 1 for both the X and Y axes.
◆ Set the 0 layer current.
◆ Set the current color, linetype, and lineweight to ByLayer.
◆ Draw the framing block shown in Figure B. Pick an insertion base point as shown and name the block Framing.
◆ Create a layer named Structural, assign it a color, and set it current.
◆ Insert the Framing block into the drawing using scale factors of 2 for the X axis and 6 for the Y axis.
◆ Insert the Framing block into the drawing using scale factors of 4 for the X axis and 12 for the Y axis.
◆ Save the drawing as ex9-2a. Close the drawing.
◆ Start a new drawing. Specify architectural units.
◆ Create three layers named A-bloc, A-flor-pfix, and S-jois. Assign each one a different color.
◆ Set the A-bloc layer current.
◆ Insert the ex9-2a drawing into the current drawing. Enter a scale factor of 1 for both the X and Y axes and specify a rotation angle of 45°.
◆ Set the A-flor-pfix layer current. Insert the Toilet block into the drawing using a scale factor of 1 for both the X and Y axes.
◆ Set the S-jois layer current. Insert the Framing block into the drawing using scale factors of 2 for the X axis and 4 for the Y axis.
◆ Save the drawing as ex9-2b.

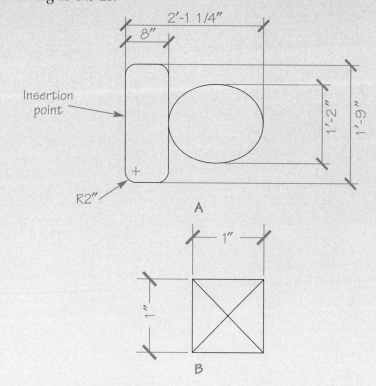

A

B

## The Effects of Layers on Blocks

As explained earlier in this chapter, unless blocks are drawn on the 0 layer, they retain the property characteristics of the layer(s) on which they are drawn. In addition, you have learned that all objects in AutoCAD are created in ByLayer mode by default. This means that the object color and linetype properties are dictated by the layer on which the object is created. For example, suppose a block named Sink is drawn on the layer Plumbing with the layer color set to red and the linetype set to dashed. When inserted, the block appears red and dashed, no matter what layer it is inserted on. If different colors, linetypes, or even layers are used in a block, they also remain the same when the block is inserted on a different layer. Therefore, a block defined in ByLayer mode on a layer other than the 0 layer retains its properties when inserted into a drawing. If the layer (or layers) included in the inserted block do not exist in the drawing, AutoCAD automatically creates them.

For a block to assume the property characteristics of the layer it is inserted on, it *must be* created on the 0 layer. Suppose you create the Sink block on the 0 layer and insert it on the 1 layer. The block becomes part of the 1 layer and thus assumes the color and linetype of that layer. Exploding the Sink block returns the objects back to the 0 layer and to the original color and linetype assigned to the 0 layer.

An exception occurs if objects within the block are drawn using an explicit color or linetype; in other words, the objects are not drawn using the default ByLayer mode. If this is the case, the objects making up the Sink block will retain their original properties upon insertion, and they will retain the same properties if the block is exploded.

## Changing the Properties of a Block

If you insert a block on the wrong layer, you can use the **Properties** window to modify it. Select the block to modify, right-click, and select **Properties** from the shortcut menu. You may also pick the **Properties** button in the **Standard** toolbar. The **Properties** window appears with the block properties listed. See **Figure 9-13.** Notice that Block Reference is specified in the drop-down list. You can now modify the selected block.

To modify the layer of the selected block, pick **Layer** in the **General** category. A drop-down arrow appears, allowing you to access the layer you want to use for the block. Once the new layer has been selected, close the **Properties** window. The block is changed to the proper layer.

You may also want to change the color, linetype, or lineweight of a block. In order to do this, the block must first have been created on the 0 layer with the color, linetype, or lineweight set to ByBlock. When the block is initially inserted, it takes the color, linetype, and lineweight of the layer it is inserted on if the current properties are set to ByLayer. If the block was created on a layer other than the 0 layer, it retains its original color and linetype.

If you want to change the color, linetype, or lineweight of an inserted block, you can access the **Properties** window and select the corresponding property in the **General** section after selecting the block. Select the desired setting from the corresponding drop-down list.

**Professional Tip**

If you want to change the properties of several blocks, you can use the **Quick Select** dialog box to create a selection set of block reference objects. Once the blocks are selected, change the properties using the **Properties** window or the **Properties** toolbar.

---

**Figure 9-13.**
The **Properties** window allows you to change the layer assigned to an inserted block.

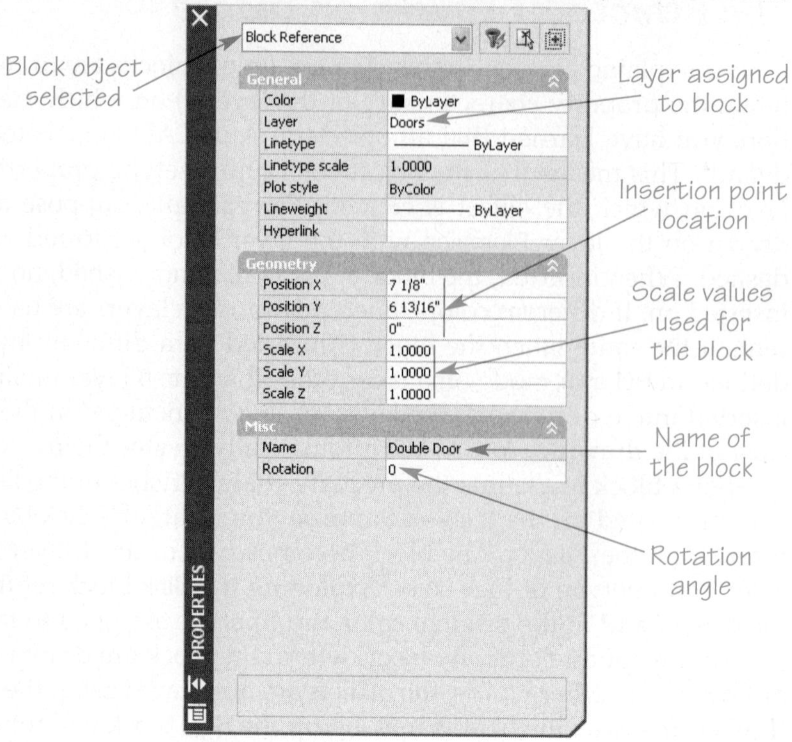

Block object selected

Layer assigned to block

Insertion point location

Scale values used for the block

Name of the block

Rotation angle

## Inserting Multiple Copies of a Block

The **INSERT** command is used to insert one block into the drawing at a time. AutoCAD also provides a means of inserting a block into the drawing and arraying multiple copies of the block at once. This can be done with the **MINSERT** (multiple insert) command. This method of inserting and arraying blocks saves time and disk space. To access the **MINSERT** command, enter minsert at the Command prompt.

An example of an application using the **MINSERT** command is the arrangement of desks on a drawing. Suppose you want to draw the layout of desks shown in **Figure 9-14.** First, specify architectural units and set the limits to 30′,22′. Draw a 4′ × 3′ rectangle on the 0 layer with the color, linetype, and lineweight set to ByBlock, and save the object as a block named Desk. The arrangement is to be three rows and four columns. Make the horizontal spacing between desks 2′, and the vertical spacing 4′. Then, enter minsert at the Command prompt. Use the following command sequence:

Command: **minsert**↵
Enter block name or [?] <current>: **desk**↵
Specify insertion point or [Scale/X/Y/Z/Rotate/PScale/PX/PY/PZ/PRotate]: *(pick a point)*
Enter X scale factor, specify opposite corner, or [Corner/XYZ] <1>: ↵
Enter Y scale factor <use X scale factor>: ↵
Specify rotation angle <0>: ↵
Enter number of rows (—-) <1>: **3**↵
Enter number of columns (|||) <1>: **4**↵
Enter distance between rows or specify unit cell (—-): **7'**↵
Specify distance between columns (|||): **6'**↵

The resulting arrangement is shown in **Figure 9-14.** The complete pattern takes on the characteristics of a block, except that an array created with the **MINSERT** command cannot be exploded. Since the array cannot be exploded, you can use the **Properties** window to modify the number of rows and columns, change the spacing

**Figure 9-14.**
To create an arrangement of desks, first create a block named Desk and then use the
**MINSERT** command.

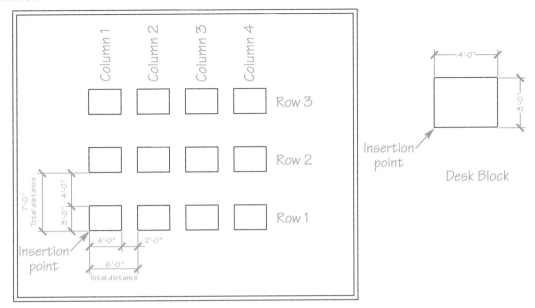

between objects, or change the layer, color, linetype, or lineweight properties. If the
initial block is rotated, all arrayed objects are also rotated about their insertion points.
If the arrayed objects are rotated about the insertion point while using the **MINSERT**
command, all objects are aligned on that point.

**Professional Tip**

    As an alternative to the previous example, if you are
working with different desk sizes, a 2D unit block may
serve your purposes better than a block drawn to exact size.
To create a 5′ × 3′-6″ (60″ × 42″) desk, for example, insert a
one-unit square block using either the **INSERT** or **MINSERT**
command, and enter a scale factor of 60 for the X axis and a
scale factor of 42 for the Y axis. A 2D unit block can be used
in this manner for a variety of objects.

## Exercise 9-3

- Start a new drawing using a template or startup option of your own choice.
- Specify architectural units.
- Set the 0 layer current. Set the current color, linetype, and lineweight to ByLayer.
- Set the limits to 0,0 for the lower-left corner and 80',60' for the upper-right corner. Then, perform a **ZOOM All**.
- Draw the chair shown as a block and name it Chair.
- Create a new layer named Seating. Assign the layer a color and set it current.
- Use the **MINSERT** command twice to create the theater arrangement. The sides of the chairs should touch. Each row on either side of the aisle should have 10 chairs. The spacing between rows is 6'. The width of the center aisle is 5'.
- Consider where you should insert the first chair to obtain the pattern.
- Save the drawing as ex9-3.

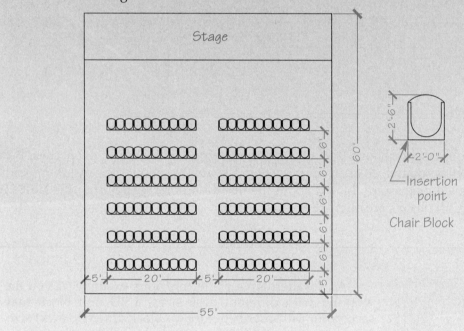

## Inserting an Entire Drawing

As explained earlier in this chapter, the **INSERT** command can be used to insert an entire drawing file into the current drawing. To do so, enter the **INSERT** command and pick the **Browse...** button in the **Insert** dialog box to access the **Select Drawing File** dialog box. You can then select a drawing file to insert.

When one drawing is inserted into another, the inserted drawing becomes a block reference in the current drawing. As a block, it may be moved to a new location with a single pick. The drawing is also inserted on the current layer, but it does not inherit the color, linetype, or lineweight properties of that layer unless items in the drawing you are inserting are drawn on the 0 layer. You can explode the inserted drawing back to its original objects if desired. Once exploded, the drawing objects revert to their original layers. A drawing that is inserted brings any existing block definitions, layers, linetypes, text styles, and dimension styles into the current drawing.

By default, every drawing has an insertion point located at 0,0,0. This is the insertion point used for a drawing file when you insert it into the current drawing. If you want to change the insertion point of the drawing that is to be inserted, use the **BASE** command to redefine the insertion base point. Open the original drawing file and access the **BASE** command by selecting **Base** from the **Block** cascading menu in the **Draw** pull-down menu, or by entering base at the Command prompt as follows:

**BASE**

Draw
➥ Block
  ➥ Base

                                   Architectural Drafting Using AutoCAD

Command: **base**↵
Enter base point <0'-0", 0'-0", 0'-0">: *(pick a point or enter new coordinates)*

The new point becomes the insertion base point for the drawing. Now insert this drawing into another drawing. Notice the insertion point is at the new location.

**Professional Tip**

When working on a drawing, it is common practice in industry to refer to other drawings to check features or dimensions. In many instances, the prints are not available and must be produced. You can avoid such delays by using the **INSERT** command. When you need to reference another drawing, simply insert it into your current drawing. When you are done checking the features or dimensions you need, simply use the **ERASE** command to erase the inserted drawing, or use the **UNDO** command to undo the **INSERT** operation.

## Exercise 9-4

◆ Open ex9-2a.
◆ Create a layer named Bathtub, assign it color number 30, and set it current.
◆ Draw a 5' × 3' rectangle. Insert the Toilet block next to the rectangle. Make a new block of the two objects and name it Bathroom.
◆ Erase all objects on screen and set the 0 layer current. Insert both the Toilet and Bathroom blocks.
◆ The Bathroom block should have color 30 because it was created on the Bathtub layer. The Toilet block should have the color white because it was created on the 0 layer and inserted on the 0 layer, taking on the color of the 0 layer.
◆ Set the Bathtub layer current and insert the Toilet block. It should have the color 30 because it was created on the 0 layer and inserted on the Bathtub layer, assuming the color of the Bathtub layer.
◆ Enter the **BASE** command. Choose an insertion base point slightly above and to the right of the objects on screen.
◆ Save the drawing as ex9-4a.
◆ Start a new drawing and save it with the file name Bathrooms.
◆ Insert drawing ex9-4a into your new drawing. The insertion point used is the one you established using the **BASE** command.
◆ Enter any editing command and select a line on one of the Toilet blocks. The entire drawing should be highlighted, since it is actually one large block.
◆ Save the drawing as ex9-4b.

## Editing Blocks

You may encounter situations where a block needs to be edited after it has been inserted into a drawing. For example, a change in design may warrant a change to the block, or perhaps the block was not originally created on the 0 layer. The most simple way to edit a block is to use the **EXPLODE** command to break the block into its individual components, or to explode the block upon insertion as described earlier in this chapter. However, there may be cases where you wish to edit a block reference so that the original block definition is changed and the changes are applied to other existing block references, as well as future insertions of the block. This process is known as *in-place reference editing* and is accomplished with the **REFEDIT** command.

In-place reference editing allows you to make minor changes to blocks, wblocks, or drawings that have been inserted in the current drawing. Wblocks and inserted drawings can be edited without the need to open the original file and redefine the block. However, if major changes are necessary, it is better to edit the original block or wblock and redefine it rather than to use reference editing with a block reference. In addition, in-place editing cannot be used on blocks that have been inserted with the **MINSERT** command. Redefining blocks is discussed later in this chapter.

If you do not use in-place editing, blocks must first be broken into their original components before they can be edited. Two methods can be used to break blocks apart. One involves the **INSERT** command and the **Explode** option in the **Insert** dialog box. This method is used at the time of insertion. The second method involves the **EXPLODE** command and can be done at any time.

## Editing Blocks In-Place

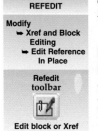

REFEDIT

Modify
➥ Xref and Block
   Editing
➥ Edit Reference
   In Place

Refedit
toolbar

Edit block or Xref

Blocks can be edited in-place using the **REFEDIT** command. This command allows you to select a block reference and extract individual components for editing without exploding the block. Changes made during the editing sequence can then be "saved back" to the original block definition. Any revisions made are applied immediately to the selected block reference and to other insertions of the block in the same drawing. In this way, you can quickly edit a block reference and update other insertions of the block at the same time.

The **REFEDIT** command is accessed by picking the **Edit block or Xref** button in the **Refedit** toolbar, selecting **Xref and Block Editing** and then **Edit Reference In-place** in the **Modify** pull-down menu, or by entering refedit at the Command prompt. To display the **Refedit** toolbar, right-click on any displayed toolbar button and pick **Refedit**. See **Figure 9-15.**

The buttons on the **Refedit** toolbar are used during the in-place reference editing sequence when revising blocks and *xrefs*, or externally referenced drawings. External references are discussed in detail in Chapter 17. The following is displayed after entering the **REFEDIT** command:

Command: **refedit.**↵
Select reference: *(select the block to edit)*

After selecting a block, the **Reference Edit** dialog box is displayed. See **Figure 9-16.** Listed in the **Reference name:** window are the names of the selected block and any references nested within the block. You can cycle through different nesting levels by picking the plus sign (+) next to the block icon. An image of the selected block is displayed in the **Preview** area.

The two radio button options in the **Path:** area are used to control which objects from the block are available for editing. The **Automatically select all nested objects** option makes all the block objects available for editing. If you only want to edit certain block objects, activate the **Prompt to select nested objects** option. When this option is selected, the Select nested objects: prompt is displayed after you pick the **OK**

---

Figure 9-15.
The **Refedit** toolbar is used for in-place reference editing.

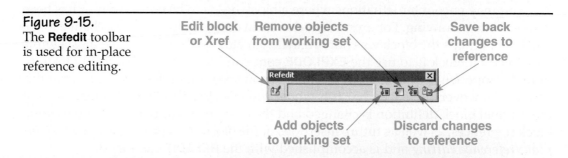

Edit block
or Xref

Remove objects
from working set

Save back
changes to
reference

Add objects
to working set

Discard changes
to reference

**Figure 9-16.**
The **Reference Edit**
dialog box.

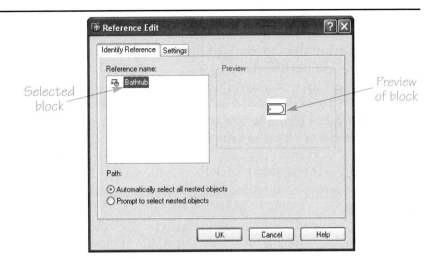

Selected block

Preview of block

button. This prompt asks you to pick objects that belong to the previously selected block. Pick any geometry of the object to be edited and press [Enter]. The nested objects that you select make up the *working set.* If multiple instances of the same block are displayed in the drawing, be sure to pick objects from the one you originally selected.

The **Settings** tab of the **Reference Edit** dialog box provides three additional options. The **Create unique layer, style, and block names** option controls the naming of selected layers and objects that are *extracted,* or temporarily removed from the drawing, for editing purposes. If this check box is selected, layer and object names are given the prefix $n$, with $n$ representing an incremented number. This is similar to the renaming method used when an external reference is bound to a drawing. External references are discussed in Chapter 17.

The **Display attribute definitions for editing** option is available when a block object with attributes has been selected in the **Identify Reference** tab of the **Reference Edit** dialog box. When this option is checked, it allows for the editing of attributes and attribute definitions. This includes the attribute tag, prompt, and default value. Attributes are covered in Chapter 21.

To prevent from accidentally editing objects that do not belong to the working set, activate the **Lock objects not in working set** option. This makes all objects outside of the working set unavailable for editing when in reference editing mode.

When you have selected a block for editing, pick **OK** to close the dialog box. For example, assume you wish to revise the Bathroom block created in Exercise 9-4 by changing the dimensions of the bathtub and adding a sink. After selecting the Bathroom block, the following prompt appears if the **Prompt to select nested objects** option is active:

Select nested objects: *(select the rectangle or objects making up the bathtub within the block and press* [Enter]*)*

If multiple insertions of the Bathroom block are displayed, be sure to pick objects from the reference you originally selected. After selecting nested objects, the **Refedit** toolbar appears, if it is not already displayed.

Select nested objects: ↵
*n* items selected
Use REFCLOSE or the Refedit toolbar to end reference editing session.
Command:

When the Command prompt returns, all objects in the drawing are grayed out, except the bathtub you selected. Any selected objects belong to the working set. You can now use any drawing or editing commands to alter the bathtub as desired. For this example, change the dimensions of the bathtub from 5′ × 3′ to 5′ × 2′-6″.

Any object that is drawn during the in-place edit is automatically added to the working set. You may add any objects that are grayed out to the working set by picking the **Add objects to working set** button from the **Refedit** toolbar. To remove objects from the working set during the edit, pick the **Remove objects from working set** button.

To add a sink to the Bathroom block, draw a 3′ × 2′ rectangle with a 1′-6″ diameter circle in the center next to the toilet. This object will be automatically added to the working set.

When you are through making changes, pick the **Save back changes to reference** button from the **Refedit** toolbar. An AutoCAD alert appears. Pick **OK** to continue with the save. If you decide to exit the reference editing session without saving changes, pick the **Discard changes to reference** button from the **Refedit** toolbar. You can also use the **REFCLOSE** command to save or discard changes to the working set and exit reference editing.

The changes to the edited Bathroom block are displayed immediately. These changes will also appear in other insertions of the same block in the drawing and in future insertions of the block.

## Exploding a Block during Insertion

If you wish to edit the individual objects of a block at the time of insertion, you can insert a block and explode it in a single operation. This is accomplished by checking the **Explode** check box in the **Insert** dialog box, as discussed earlier in this chapter. Another alternative is to use the **–INSERT** command. Using this command is very similar to using the **Insert** dialog box, but it allows you to insert a block by answering prompts at the command line. If you wish to explode a block upon insertion using the **–INSERT** command, enter an asterisk (*) before the block name as follows:

```
Command: –insert↵
Enter block name or [?] <current>: *desk↵
Specify insertion point for block: (pick a point)
Specify scale factor for XYZ axes: (specify the scale and press [Enter])
Specify rotation angle <0>: ↵
```

The inserted objects are not part of a block. They are individual objects that have their original properties and can now be edited.

## Using the EXPLODE Command

EXPLODE
X

Modify
↦ Explode

Modify
toolbar

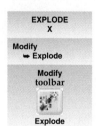

Explode

The **EXPLODE** command is used to break apart any existing block, polyline, or dimension. To access this command, pick the **Explode** button from the **Modify** toolbar, select **Explode** from the **Modify** pull-down menu, or enter x or explode at the Command prompt as follows:

```
Command: x or explode↵
Select objects: (pick the block)
Select objects: ↵
```

When the block is exploded, the component objects are quickly redrawn. The individual objects can now be changed individually. To see if the **EXPLODE** command worked properly, select any object that was formerly part of the block. Only that object should be highlighted. If so, the block was exploded properly.

## Redefining Existing Blocks

A situation can arise where you discover that the original definition of a block must be changed. As previously discussed, redefining a block by editing its original components may be more suitable than using in-place reference editing with a selected block reference. This is an easy process, even if you have placed the block on a drawing many times. To redefine a saved block, follow this procedure:

1. Insert the block to be redefined anywhere in your drawing.
2. Make sure that you know where the insertion point of the block is located. You can determine the insertion point location by drawing a line from the insertion point of the block using the Insert object snap. Then, simply cancel the **LINE** command.
3. Explode the inserted block using the **EXPLODE** command.
4. Edit the block as needed.
5. Recreate the block definition using the **BLOCK** command.
6. Give the block the same name and the same insertion point it originally had.
7. Select the objects to be included in the block.
8. Pick **OK** to close the **Insert** dialog box. When a message from AutoCAD appears and asks if you want to redefine the block, pick **Yes**.
9. When the **BLOCK** command is complete, all insertions of the block are updated.

A common mistake is to forget to explode the block before editing the block and then trying to redefine it. When you try to create the block again with the same name, an alert box indicating the block references itself is displayed. This means you are trying to create a block that already exists. Once you press the **OK** button, the alert box disappears and the **Block Definition** dialog box is redisplayed. Press the **Cancel** button, explode the block that is to be redefined, and try again.

## Understanding the Circular Reference Error

As described in the previous example, when you try to redefine a block that already exists and use the same name without exploding the block, AutoCAD informs you that the block references itself. The concept of a block *referencing itself* may be a little difficult to grasp at first without fully understanding how AutoCAD works with blocks. A block can be composed of any objects, and can be defined to include several blocks grouped together into one block. When using the **BLOCK** command to create a block that will include an existing block, AutoCAD must make a list of all the objects that make up the new block. This means that AutoCAD must refer to any existing block definitions that are selected to be part of the new block. If you select a complete block of the block being redefined as one of the component objects for the new definition, a problem occurs. You are trying to redefine a block name using a previous version of the block with the same name. In other words, the new block refers to the same block name of one of the blocks you are including in the new definition, or *references itself*.

## The Correct Way of Redefining a Block

Assume you create a block named Box that is composed of four line objects in the shape of a square, and then insert it. You then decide that the block needs to be changed so that it contains a small circle in the lower-left corner. If the original Box block is exploded, all that is left are the four line objects. After drawing the required circle, you can enter the **BLOCK** command and recreate a block named Box by selecting the four lines and the circle as the component objects. Redefining a block destroys the old definition and creates a new one. Any blocks with the same name are redefined with the updated changes. Make sure you want to redefine the block before agreeing to do so. Otherwise, give the block a new name. The correct way to redefine a block is shown in **Figure 9-17.**

Alternatively, assume you do not explode the block, but still draw the circle and try to redefine the block. By selecting the intact Box block *and* the circle, a new block named Box would now be a block reference of the Box block with a circle. The old block definition of Box has not been destroyed, but a new definition has been attempted. Thus, AutoCAD is trying to define a new block named Box by using an instance of the Box block. This is referred to as a *circular reference,* and is what is meant by a block referencing itself. Refer to **Figure 9-17.**

## Creating Permanent Global Blocks

As discussed earlier in this chapter, blocks created with the **BLOCK** command are stored in the drawing in which they are constructed. In addition, as previously discussed, you may insert any drawing file into another drawing. If a drawing file containing block definitions is inserted into a new drawing, the blocks are also brought into the new drawing. This allows you to access any symbols saved as blocks and bring them into a drawing provided you know where the parent drawing is located. However, you may want to create symbols so that they are stored as independent drawing files.

**Figure 9-17.**
A—The correct procedure for redefining a block. B—Redefining a block that has not first been exploded creates an invalid circular reference.

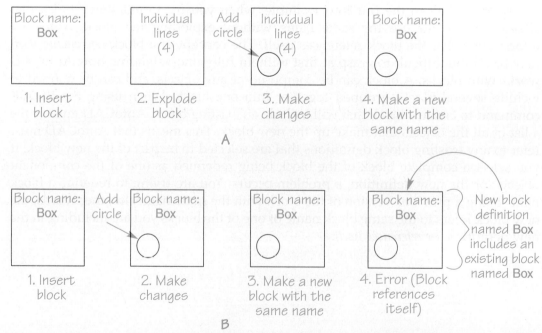

Architectural Drafting Using AutoCAD

The **WBLOCK** (write block) command allows you to create a drawing file out of a block. This type of block is known as a *global block.* You can also use the **WBLOCK** command to create a global block from any object that is not first saved as a block. The resulting drawing file can then be inserted as a block into any drawing by entering the **INSERT** command and selecting the **Browse...** button in the **Insert** dialog box.

There are several ways to use the **WBLOCK** command. To see how the first method works, open drawing ex9-1. Convert the Column block to a global block by making it a separate drawing file. Use the following procedure:

Command: **w** *or* **wblock**↵

The **Write Block** dialog box appears, **Figure 9-18.** This dialog box is similar to the **Block Definition** dialog box. Pick the **Block:** option button, and then select the Column block from the drop-down list in the **Source** area. Enter the location for the resulting drawing file and its name by using the **File name and path:** text box. Instead of typing the full file location and name, pick the ellipsis button to the right of the **File name and path:** text box. In the **Browse for Drawing File** dialog box, navigate to the folder in which you want to store the file and enter a name for the file in the **File name:** text box. Pick the **Save** button to return to the **Write Block** dialog box. If you want to insert the block at a specific unit size when using **DesignCenter**, select the type of units in the **Insert units:** drop-down list. **DesignCenter** is discussed in Chapter 10. When you are finished, pick **OK**.

The above sequence wrote a new block, with the name Col, to a drawing file on disk. You can now use the **INSERT** command to insert the new wblock (DWG file) into the current drawing or any other drawing.

**Note** When another drawing is inserted into the current drawing, the inserted drawing acts as a block. It is a single object and its individual components cannot be edited unless the block is exploded.

**Figure 9-18.**
Using the **Write Block** dialog box to create a wblock from an existing block. The column is saved as a DWG file.

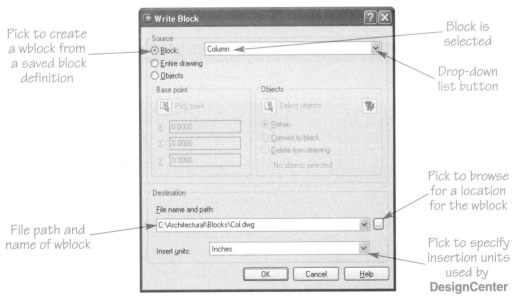

Pick to create a wblock from a saved block definition

Block is selected

Drop-down list button

Pick to browse for a location for the wblock

File path and name of wblock

Pick to specify insertion units used by **DesignCenter**

When you access the **Write Block** dialog box and select a block from the drop-down list, AutoCAD assumes the new drawing file will have the same name and lists it in the **File name and path:** text box. Decide whether to use the name of the selected block for the drawing file or enter a new name.

## Creating a New Wblock

Suppose you want to create a wblock from a set of objects you have just drawn, but you have not yet made a block of them. The following sequence is used to save the selected object(s) as a drawing file. First, enter the **WBLOCK** command and select the **Objects** option button in the **Write Block** dialog box. This option button is active by default. Pick the **Select objects** button to select the objects for the drawing file. Next, pick the **Pick point** button to select the insertion point for the wblock. You can also enter absolute coordinates in the **X:**, **Y:**, and **Z:** text boxes. Then, give the file a name and location in the **File name and path:** text box. If the path shown is not where you want to save the file, access the **Browse for Drawing File** dialog box by picking the button next to the drop-down arrow. Select the type of units that **DesignCenter** will use to insert the block in the **Insert units:** drop-down list. When you are through, pick **OK**. See **Figure 9-19.**

This sequence is the same as that used with the **BLOCK** command. However, the wblock is saved to disk as a drawing file, *not* as a block in the current drawing. Be sure to specify the correct file path in the **File name and path:** text box when using the **Write Block** dialog box. A drawing file named Desk that is saved in the Blocks folder on the c: drive, for example, is saved as c:\Blocks\Desk.

## Storing a Drawing as a Wblock

An entire drawing can also be stored as a wblock. To do this, enter the **WBLOCK** command and pick the **Entire drawing** option button in the **Write Block** dialog box. Give the wblock a name and the location it is to be saved to in the **File name and path:** text box. To specify a location for the new drawing file, access the **Browse for Drawing**

**Figure 9-19.**
Using the **Write Block** dialog box to create a wblock from selected objects without first defining them as a block.

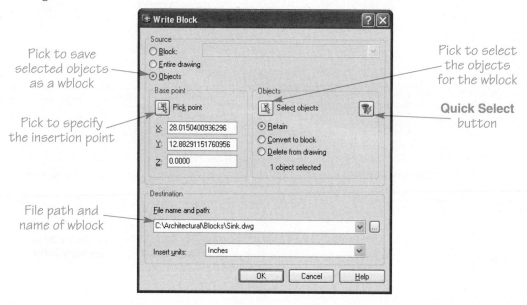

Architectural Drafting Using AutoCAD

**File** dialog box or accept the path displayed. Select the type of units **DesignCenter** will use to insert the block in the **Insert units:** drop-down list, and pick **OK** when you are through. Refer to **Figures 9-18** and **9-19**.

In this case, the entire drawing is saved to disk as if you had used the **SAVE** command. The difference is that any unused block definitions are deleted from the drawing. If the drawing contains any unused blocks, this method reduces the size of a drawing considerably.

**Professional Tip**

Using the **Entire drawing** wblock option at the end of a project is a good way to remove any named objects that are unused in your drawing to reduce the file size. Use this routine when you have completed a drawing and decide that the unused blocks, layers, and styles are no longer needed. The **PURGE** command can also be used to remove any unused layers, linetypes, text styles, dimension styles, multiline styles, plot styles, blocks, and shapes from the current drawing. The **PURGE** command is discussed later in this chapter.

## Exercise 9-5

◆ Open drawing ex9-2a.
◆ Create a wblock named Toilet using the existing block of the same name.
◆ Use Windows Explorer to list your drawing files. Be sure Toilet.dwg is listed.
◆ Start a new drawing. Create a layer named A-pfix, give it a color, and set it current.
◆ Insert the Toilet.dwg drawing file into the current drawing.
◆ Save the drawing as ex9-5.

# Renaming Blocks and Other Named Objects

As discussed in the previous section, a block is a named object. Blocks, layers, linetypes, text styles, and other named objects can be renamed using the **RENAME** command. Access this command by selecting **Rename...** from the **Format** pull-down menu or by entering ren or rename at the Command prompt. This displays the **Rename** dialog box, **Figure 9-20.**

To change the name of the Tub5026 block to Pbtub001, select Blocks in the **Named Objects** list. A list of blocks defined in the current drawing then appears in the **Items** list. Pick Tub5026 to highlight it in the list. When this name appears in the **Old Name:** text box, enter the new block name Pbtub001 in the **Rename To:** text box. Pick the **Rename To:** button and the new block name appears in the **Items** list. Pick **OK** to exit the **Rename** dialog box.

**Note**

Since AutoCAD does not permit the renaming of the 0 layer or the Continuous linetype, these two named objects do not appear in the **Items** list in the **Rename** dialog box.

**Figure 9-20.**
The **Rename** dialog box allows you to change the name of a block or any other named object.

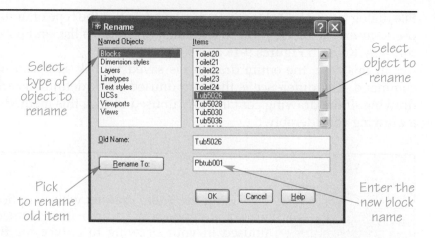

Select type of object to rename

Select object to rename

Pick to rename old item

Enter the new block name

**Professional Tip**

Use the **Rename** dialog box to rename any items that do not conform to your standard naming conventions. Layers, linetypes, text styles, and blocks can all be renamed. Often, when working with drawings from consultants or vendors, the naming conventions may not meet your standards. Change the object names with the **RENAME** command.

# Deleting Named Objects

In many drawing sessions, not all of the named objects in a drawing are used. For example, your drawing may contain several layers, text styles, and blocks that are not used. Since these objects occupy disk space, it is good practice to delete or *purge* the unused objects with the **PURGE** command at the end of the project.

Entering the **PURGE** command displays the **Purge** dialog box. See **Figure 9-21.** To access the **PURGE** command, pick **Purge...** from the **Drawing Utilities** cascading menu in the **File** pull-down menu or enter pu or purge at the Command prompt.

The radio buttons at the top of the **Purge** dialog box are used to specify how content in the drawing is listed in the main window. You may view content that can be purged or content that cannot be purged by selecting the appropriate radio button.

Specific items that can be purged may be located by picking the **View items you can purge** radio button and using the tree view listing in the main window. First, identify the type of object you wish to purge, and then pick the plus sign (+) next to the related icon to display each of the unused objects within that category. Before purging, select the **Confirm each item to be purged** check box at the bottom of the dialog box to have an opportunity to review each item before it is deleted.

As an example, if you want to purge a block named Window from your drawing, pick the plus sign next to the blocks category in the main window. The block will be listed provided it is unused in the drawing. Highlight the block name and pick the **Purge** button to delete the item.

If you wish to purge nested items, pick the **Purge nested items** check box. If you want to purge all unused items in the drawing, pick the **Purge All** button. This is a good way to clean up a finished drawing and conserve disk space.

**PURGE**
**PU**

**File**
➡ **Drawing Utilities**
  ➡ **Purge...**

**Figure 9-21.**
The **Purge** dialog box is used to purge unused named objects from a drawing.

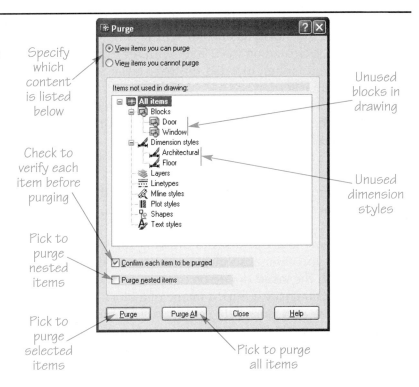

Specify which content is listed below

Unused blocks in drawing

Check to verify each item before purging

Pick to purge nested items

Unused dimension styles

Pick to purge selected items

Pick to purge all items

**Professional Tip**

When purging an item, it may take several steps to purge it from the drawing. For example, assume you created a block named Door from objects created on the A-Door layer, and deleted the original objects. If you never used the block, you can quickly purge the Door block. However, because the block was created on the A-Door layer, that layer cannot be purged until the block is purged first. After the block has been purged, the layer A-Door can then be purged.

If you find that you cannot purge a layer, one possible cause is that objects used to create a block were created on that layer and still exist in the drawing. This is another good reason to *never* create objects for a block on any layer other than the 0 layer.

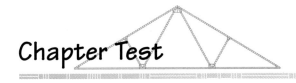

## Chapter Test

*Answer the following questions on a separate sheet of paper.*

1. What is a *block?*
2. Briefly explain the difference between a *block* and a *wblock* and identify the commands used to create the two.
3. What is a *symbol library?*
4. The objects making up a block should always be created on which layer?
5. By default, what setting is used for the object color, linetype, and lineweight properties when a block is created?

6. If you wish to assign a different object color to a block after it is inserted without exploding the block, what color setting should be used when creating the block?

7. If a block is created on the 0 layer with the default color, linetype, and lineweight settings and is then inserted on the 1 layer, which layer will be assigned to the block upon insertion?

8. List three ways to access the **Block Definition** dialog box.

9. What is the purpose of the **Convert to block** radio button in the **Block Definition** dialog box?

10. How can you verify that a block is saved properly after it is created?

11. What is *nesting?*

12. What command is used to place blocks in a drawing?

13. A block or wblock that has been inserted into a drawing is referred to as a block _____.

14. Explain how to access a saved drawing file for insertion into a drawing.

15. How can you enter absolute coordinates for the insertion point when inserting a block with the **Insert** dialog box?

16. How do you create a mirror image of a block when inserting the block?

17. What is the difference between a *real block* and a *unit block?*

18. If a block contains layers that do not already exist in the current drawing, what happens to the layers when the block is inserted?

19. What is the purpose of the **MINSERT** command?

20. When one drawing is inserted into another, what must be done before the inserted drawing can be edited?

21. What command can be used to change the insertion base point of a drawing that is to be inserted into another drawing?

22. What command is used to break apart any existing block?

23. Explain the purpose of *in-place reference editing.*

24. Which dialog box is accessed with the **REFEDIT** command?

25. What is the purpose of the **Add objects to working set** button on the **Refedit** toolbar?

26. When using the **–INSERT** command, what is the effect of entering an asterisk before the block name?

27. When creating a wblock, what type of file is saved?

28. What is a *circular reference error?* How is it avoided when redefining a block?

29. If a block named Door is to be saved as a wblock in the Office folder on the c: drive, what is the proper path to use when saving the wblock?

30. Explain how to create a wblock from objects that have not been previously saved as a block.

31. Which option button in the **Write Block** dialog box allows you to save the current drawing as a wblock?

32. What is the purpose of the **RENAME** command?

33. Which command is used to remove unused objects from a drawing?

## Chapter Problems

1. Select 10 of the architectural symbols you created as drawing problems in Chapter 3 and create a wblock for each symbol. If you did not complete any drawing problems in Chapter 3, do so now. If the objects for the symbols were not originally created on the 0 layer, place all objects on the 0 layer before using the **WBLOCK** command. Designate a logical insertion point and write a short description for each symbol. Save each file with a name that matches the name of the symbol. Place the files in a new folder named Symbols.

2. Obtain a set of residential architectural drawings that are properly drawn and scaled. Create a variety of blocks for the symbols used on the drawings. Save these blocks as wblocks in a folder named Residential Symbols.

3. Obtain a set of light commercial architectural drawings that are properly drawn and scaled. Create a variety of blocks for the symbols used on the drawings. Save these blocks as wblocks in a folder named Commercial Symbols.

4. Create a new drawing based on the illustration provided. The drawing shows an arrangement of steel columns on a concrete floor slab for a new building. The steel columns are represented as I-shaped symbols. They are arranged in "bay lines" (labeled A through G) and "column lines" (labeled 1 through 3). The width of a bay is 24'-0". Tags identify the bay and column lines. Use the following guidelines:

   A.   Draw the steel column symbol and save it as a block.

   B.   Use the **MINSERT** command to place the symbols in the drawing.

   C.   Save the drawing as p9-4.

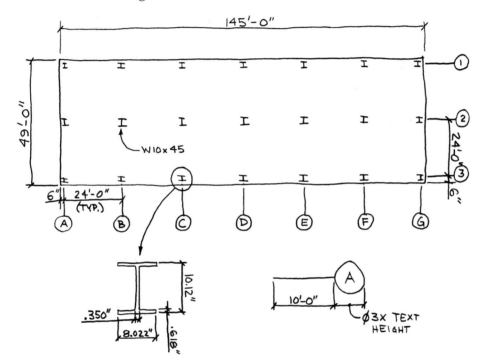

5. Create an office layout drawing from the illustration provided. Draw the desk, chair, computer, window, and door shown and save each object as a block. Create a computer workstation from the desk, chair, and computer blocks and save it as a block. Then, draw the office using the **INSERT** and **MINSERT** commands and the dimensions shown. Enter scale values for the blocks when inserted as necessary. Save the drawing as p9-5.

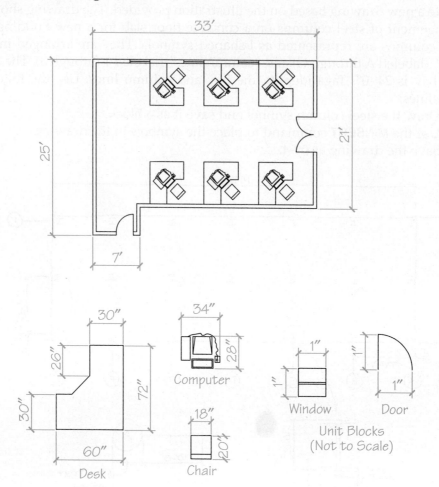

# CHAPTER 10

# Symbol Libraries, DesignCenter, and Tool Palettes

## Learning Objectives

After completing this chapter, you will be able to:

- Develop a storage system for symbols designed for repeated use.
- Construct and use a symbol library of blocks.
- Import blocks and other types of content from existing drawings using **DesignCenter**.
- Create tool palettes and use them to store and insert blocks.
- Manage and customize content used in **DesignCenter** and the **Tool Palettes** window.

## Important Terms

bitmaps
drag and drop
pixels
raster images
symbol library
tool palettes
vector image

As you build your skills with AutoCAD and begin using more architectural drafting symbols in your drawings, you will find it very useful to assemble a storage system for symbols and other content that can be used repeatedly. In Chapter 9, you learned how to create symbols as blocks and save them within drawings or as separate drawing files. It is important to remember that *blocks* are stored in the drawing in which they were created, and *wblocks* are saved as separate drawing files. As you create and use more symbols, you will want to develop a storage system that provides convenient access to them. Groups of blocks can be stored in several different ways. If you save symbols as wblocks, you can create a system of folders for the wblock files on a local or network computer drive. If you save symbols as blocks, you can store entire groups of block definitions in drawing files known as *symbol libraries*. The latter method is typically more efficient and is explained in detail in this chapter.

No matter which storage method you use, symbol libraries and individual wblock files can be managed and accessed effectively with **DesignCenter** and the **Tool Palettes** window. This chapter introduces **DesignCenter** and tool palettes and discusses how they are used to insert symbols and other content into drawings.

# Storing Symbols as Files

As you learned in Chapter 9, a symbol created as a wblock with the **WBLOCK** command is saved as a drawing file, while a block created with the **BLOCK** command is stored in the drawing in which it is defined. Wblocks are useful when you wish to maintain each symbol as a separate drawing file. For example, wblocks present an advantage over blocks when you want to insert symbols one at a time without searching for blocks that are saved with others in a symbol library.

When using the **WBLOCK** command, you must provide a name for the resulting drawing file and specify a path where it will be saved. Wblock files should be saved using standard naming conventions that make it easy to identify the file contents. In addition, each file should be saved to a folder created specifically for wblocks. Folders used for wblocks should be kept separate from folders containing other drawing files, and they should be named to reflect the types of symbols stored. A good idea is to create a folder structure with a root folder named Blocks, as shown in **Figure 10-1.** Notice that the folder shown is a subfolder of the ACAD Custom folder. Also, notice that the subfolders in the Blocks folder are named based on the type of symbols they contain.

Storing symbols in this manner makes them easy to locate and share with others. When a symbol needs to be inserted with the **INSERT** command, it can be easily accessed by navigating to the correct folder using the **Select Drawing File** dialog box.

The most efficient way to organize wblocks is to place them on a computer network drive that can be accessed by multiple users. As an alternative, if a network is not in place, the wblock files can be saved to writable compact discs (CDs) and loaded onto each user's computer. This ensures that symbols drawn to company standards are readily available to users of the network or to individual workstations. When symbols need to be updated, the original drawing files can be edited, and any drawings using the symbols can be similarly updated to reflect the changes.

**Figure 10-1.**
An efficient way to store blocks saved as drawing files is to create a Blocks folder containing folders for each type of symbol on the hard drive.

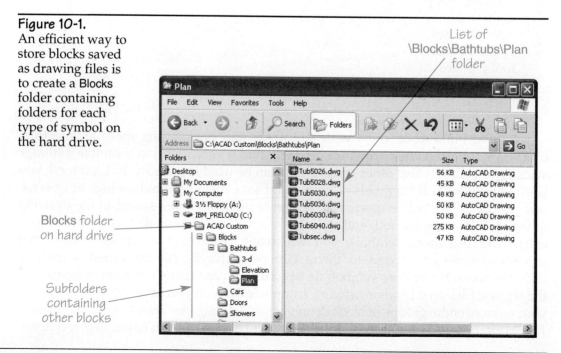

Architectural Drafting Using AutoCAD

If symbols are being accessed by multiple users, printed hard copies of the symbols should be distributed as necessary. When a symbol is revised, users should be informed of the changes and updated printouts should be provided. In addition, a backup system for the files should be applied by the network server or by individual users. The following guidelines should also be observed if a network is not in place:

- All workstations should have folders and files with the same names.
- One person should be assigned to update files and copy them to all workstation hard drives when necessary.
- Drawing files should be copied onto each workstation's hard drive from a master disk.

## Assembling a Symbol Library

A *symbol library* is a set of related block definitions stored in a single drawing file and used repeatedly in drawings. Blocks compiled in a typical symbol library may represent a collection of shapes, views, or symbols. An architectural symbol library, for instance, may contain the following types of symbols:

- Bathroom fixtures and accessories
- Doors and windows
- Electrical symbols
- Landscaping symbols
- Structural material symbols
- Tags and annotation symbols

A sample architectural symbol library is shown in **Figure 10-2**. This type of symbol library is created as a single drawing file with entire sets of blocks. Each symbol represents a bathroom fixture that is drawn separately and saved as a block. Note that the name of each symbol is provided, along with the location of the insertion

**Figure 10-2.**
An architectural symbol library composed of blocks of bathroom fixtures. The insertion base points are shown for reference only and are not part of the drawing.

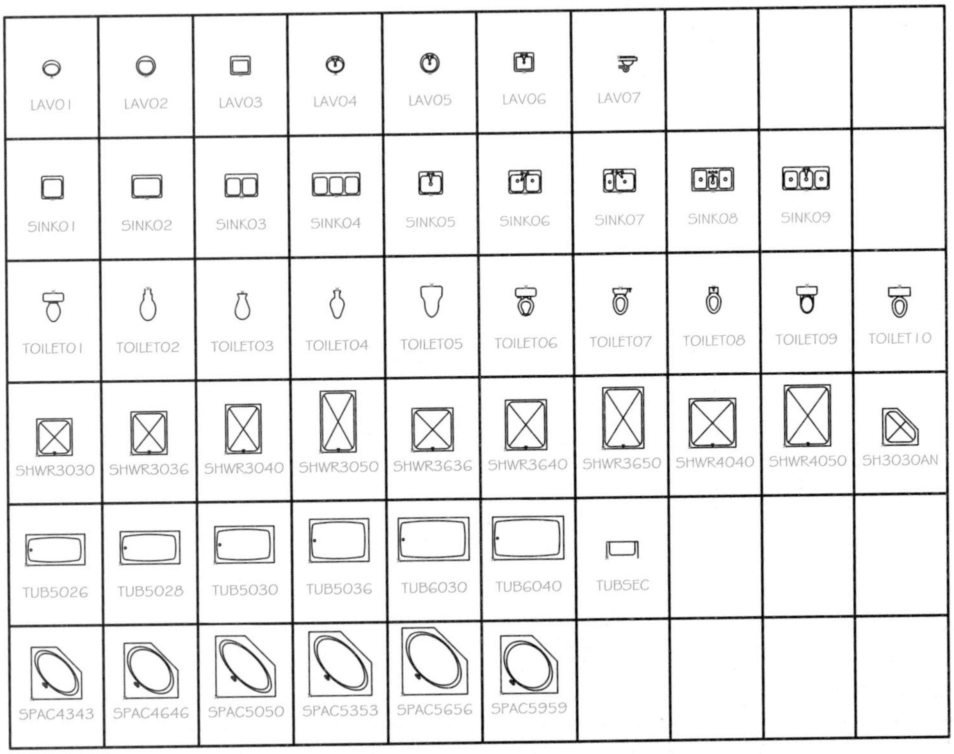

point used for inserting the block. When the entire symbol library, or drawing file, is inserted into a drawing, the blocks provided become a part of the current drawing and can be inserted, located, and scaled as necessary.

To construct a symbol library, you must first decide what symbols the file will contain. Also, you need to determine how and where the symbol library will be stored. The symbols should be drawn to company standards and should be arranged neatly in rows or columns. Each block should be identified with a name, and the insertion point locations should be highlighted. However, this information should remain separate from the actual block definitions. Finally, the symbol library should be named using standard conventions. For example, a drawing file named Sinks could be used for a symbol library containing blocks of sink fixtures.

Assembling blocks into a symbol library is an efficient way to manage drawing content and share it with others. Placing several symbol libraries on a computer network drive, for example, enables many users to access the symbols and other information within each library. As is the case with a storage system of wblock files, this also ensures that symbols drawn to company standards are readily available to users of the network. As with wblocks, printed copies of the symbol library can be distributed to everyone using the symbols. An architectural symbol library listing is shown in **Figure 10-3**. Larger copies of symbol library listings used in offices are commonly placed on a wall or bulletin board.

When symbol libraries are revised, the original blocks and drawings containing references of the blocks can be updated as needed, and new listings can be provided. The same guidelines previously discussed for managing wblock files should be observed when saving symbol libraries to network drives or individual workstations.

There are several advantages to using blocks in a symbol library rather than wblock files. Using blocks saves disk space, because a complete drawing file occupies considerably more disk space than a block, and a symbol library can contain many blocks. Another advantage is that when the file is inserted into a drawing, all blocks in the symbol library are also inserted into the drawing at once.

**Figure 10-3.**
A typical symbol library listing distributed to architectural drafters.

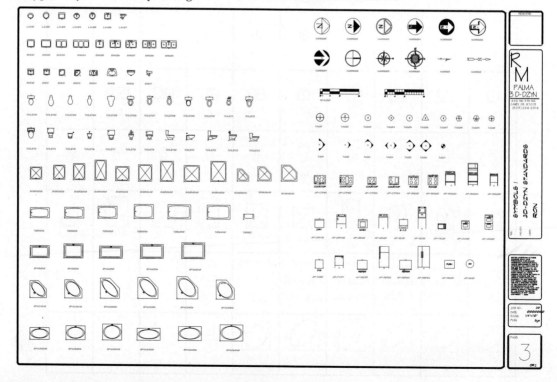

One of the biggest advantages of creating a symbol library from blocks is that individual blocks within the file can be listed separately and inserted with **DesignCenter**. Using **DesignCenter** allows you to browse the content of each file and insert any number of blocks into the current drawing without inserting the entire file. You can also create tool palettes of blocks from one or more files using **DesignCenter** and the **Tool Palettes** window. These tools are discussed later in this chapter.

A number of symbol libraries are installed with AutoCAD. They are available as DWG files in the AutoCAD 2004\Sample\DesignCenter folder. There are 15 different files containing blocks for architectural symbols and other types of content. The blocks in each symbol library can be accessed with **DesignCenter**. Other symbol libraries are available on the DesignCenter Online Web page. This feature allows you to download drafting symbols from manufacturers and catalogs online. The DesignCenter Online Web page can be accessed from the **DC Online** tab in **DesignCenter**. **DesignCenter** is discussed in the next section.

You can quickly copy a symbol library into a new drawing without subsequently displaying the block objects by using the **INSERT** command. The incoming blocks are not displayed, they are only included as *definitions* in the drawing file. After entering the **INSERT** command and locating the file, activate the **Specify On-screen** check box in the **Insert** dialog box and pick the **OK** button. When the drawing area returns, press the [Esc] key. The drawing is not inserted on screen, but the block definitions are now included in the new file. You can verify this by reentering the **INSERT** command and accessing the named objects listed in the **Name:** drop-down list in the **Insert** dialog box.

# Introduction to DesignCenter

**DesignCenter** is a powerful drawing information manager that allows you to effectively reuse and share drawing content. One of the primary benefits of AutoCAD is that once something has been created, you can use it repeatedly in any number of drawings or drawing projects. Many types of drawing elements are similar or the same in numerous drawings, such as common drawing details, sections, architectural symbols, and drawing layouts. **DesignCenter** lets you conveniently access drawing content and "drag and drop" it from one drawing to another. *Drag and drop* is a feature that allows you to perform tasks by picking and holding the pick button while you drag an item to where you want it, and then releasing the pick button to drop it in the desired location.

**DesignCenter** is used to manage several types of drawing content, including blocks, dimension styles, layers, layouts, linetypes, text styles, and externally referenced drawings. External references are discussed in Chapter 17. You can insert any item from the available content types into the current drawing by accessing the item and dragging and dropping it into the drawing. Raster images such as BMP, JPG, TGA, TIF, and GIF files can also be searched for, viewed, and added to a drawing using **DesignCenter**.

ADCENTER
ADC
[Ctrl]+[2]

Tools
➥ DesignCenter

Standard
toolbar

DesignCenter

**DesignCenter** is activated by picking the **DesignCenter** button on the **Standard** toolbar, selecting **DesignCenter** from the **Tools** pull-down menu, entering adc or adcenter at the Command prompt, or using the [Ctrl]+[2] key combination. When you first open **DesignCenter**, it is displayed in a floating state in the AutoCAD drawing area, **Figure 10-4A**. You can resize the **DesignCenter** window as desired, or you can place it in a docked position by double-clicking on the title bar. When docked, **DesignCenter** is placed on the left side of the drawing area. See **Figure 10-4B**.

**Figure 10-4.**
A—When you first open **DesignCenter** in AutoCAD, it appears in a floating state in the drawing area. The **DesignCenter** window can be resized or moved into a docked position.
B—**DesignCenter** in a docked state.

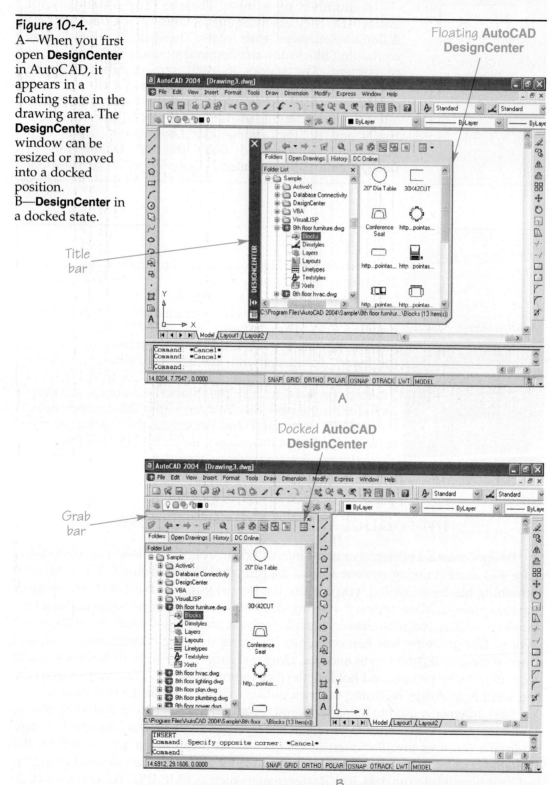

# Using DesignCenter

It is not necessary to open a drawing in AutoCAD in order to view or access its content. **DesignCenter** allows you to directly load content from any accessible drawing. You can use **DesignCenter** to browse through existing drawing files and view their content, or you can use its advanced search tools to look for specific drawing content. Once **DesignCenter** is opened, content can be dragged and dropped into any open drawing. See **Figure 10-5**.

**Figure 10-5.**
**DesignCenter** is used to list drawing file content that can be copied into a drawing.

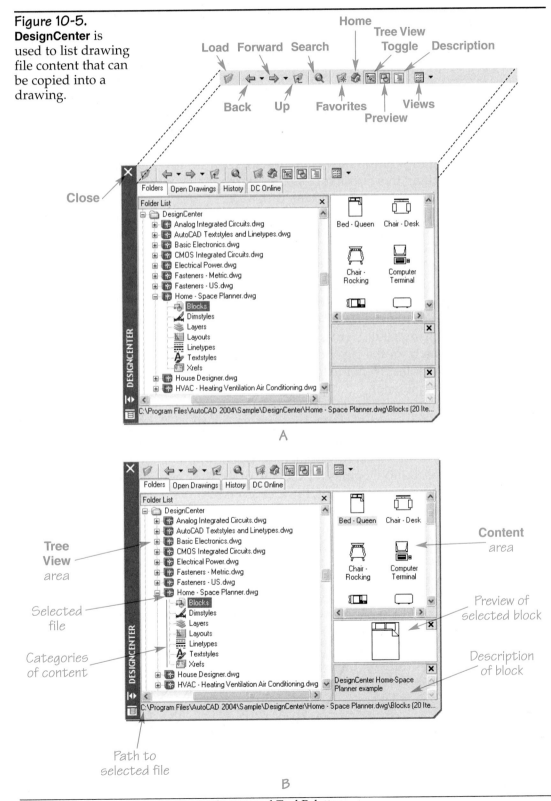

The **Tree View** area on the left side of the **DesignCenter** window is used to navigate to drawing files. The right side of **DesignCenter** is called the **Content** area. This area displays the available content from what is selected in the **Tree View** area. If a folder is selected on the **Tree View** side, the **Content** area displays all the drawing files within that folder. If a named object category is selected within a drawing file, such as Blocks, then the **Content** area displays all the blocks that are in that drawing file.

The **DesignCenter** toolbar buttons and tabs contain features for navigating to drawing file content. There are also viewing options for determining how content is displayed. **Figure 10-5** shows the button options available on the **DesignCenter** toolbar. The following features are used for navigation:

- **Load**. Picking this button displays the **Load** dialog box. Selecting a file and picking **Open** makes the drawing file active in **DesignCenter**.
- **Back.** Picking this button shows the last drawing file content that was selected. Picking the **Back** down arrow shows a list of the previous drawing file content.
- **Forward.** If the **Back** button has been used, this button is available. Picking it shows the last drawing file content that was selected. Picking the **Forward** down arrow shows a list of the previous drawing file content.
- **Up.** Picking this button moves up one folder from the current one.
- **Search.** Picking this button opens the **Search** dialog box, which allows you to search for drawings by specifying different criteria.
- **Favorites.** Picking this button displays the content of the **Favorites** folder. Content can be added to the **Favorites** folder by right-clicking over an item in the **Tree View** or **Content** area and selecting **Add to Favorites** from the right-click menu. This could be a drive letter, a folder, a drawing file, or any named objects within a drawing file, such as Blocks or Layers.
- **Home.** Picking the **Home** button moves to the *home* content in **DesignCenter**. By default, *home* is the DesignCenter folder located in the AutoCAD 2004\Sample folder. To change this, right-click over an item in the **Tree View** area and select **Set as Home** from the right-click menu. This could be a drive letter, a folder, or a drawing file. The home location should be your most commonly accessed item in **DesignCenter**.

The last four buttons on the **DesignCenter** toolbar control viewing options within the **DesignCenter** window. Refer to **Figure 10-5**. The options are described as follows:

- **Tree View Toggle.** This button controls the display of the **Tree View** area. The toggle only works when the **Folders** or **Open Drawings** tab is current.
- **Preview.** This button toggles the display of the **Preview** area. If no preview was saved for the selected content, the area is empty.
- **Description.** This button toggles the display of the **Description** area. If a description was given when the selected content was created, this is the text that is displayed. If no description was saved, it will read No description found.
- **Views.** This button is used to control how the content is displayed in the **Content** area.

When **DesignCenter** is opened, the active tab is set to **Folders**. This shows the hierarchy of files and folder on your computer, including network drives. Navigating in the **Folder List** view is very similar to using Windows Explorer. The **Open Drawings** tab displays all the open drawing files in the current AutoCAD session. The most recently accessed files through **DesignCenter** are listed by picking the **History** tab. The **DC Online** tab gives you access to the DesignCenter Online Web page, where you can download drawing content from the Internet.

To locate an item and copy it into a drawing, pick the plus sign (+) next to the drawing icon in the **Tree View** area to view the content categories for that drawing. Each category of drawing content is listed with a representative icon. The categories include Blocks, Dimstyles, Layers, Layouts, Linetypes, Textstyles, and Xrefs. Highlight the category corresponding to the type of item you want to access. You can then pick on the item in the **Content** area, hold the pick button, and drag the item to insert it into the current drawing.

## Exercise 10-1

◆ Start a new drawing using a template or startup option of your own choice.
◆ Open **DesignCenter**.
◆ Double-click on the title bar to dock **DesignCenter** if it is not already docked.
◆ Use the **Tree View** area to browse through different folders and drawings on the hard drive.
◆ Pick the **Preview** button to display a preview image of a selected item in the **Content** area.
◆ Pick the **Description** button to display a description of a selected item.
◆ Experiment with the various **Content** area viewing options using the **Views** button.
◆ Close **DesignCenter**. Do not save the drawing.

## Inserting Blocks and Drawings Using DesignCenter

As previously discussed, blocks or drawing files can be readily located and previewed before they are inserted using **DesignCenter**. You can easily insert blocks or entire drawings into the current drawing using the drag-and-drop method. You can also browse through existing drawings for blocks, display images of blocks and drawings, and access other information about saved blocks or files.

To view blocks that belong in a drawing, navigate to the drawing in the **Tree View** area and click on the Blocks icon for the drawing or double-click on the Blocks icon in the **Content** area. Refer to **Figure 10-5.** You can then use the **Preview, Description**, and **Views** buttons in the **DesignCenter** toolbar to display different types of information for each block in the drawing.

Once the desired block has been found in the **Content** area, pick on the block and use drag and drop to insert it into the current drawing. The block is inserted at the location you pick when you release the pick button. It is inserted based on the type of insertion units specified when creating the block. For example, if the original block was created as a 1″ × 1″ square, and the insertion units specified were feet, then the block will be a 12″ × 12″ square when inserted with **DesignCenter**. A block inserted from **DesignCenter** is inserted into the drawing on the current layer.

You can also specify insertion point coordinates, scale values, and a rotation angle when inserting a block from **DesignCenter**. To do so, double-click on the preview icon for the block in the **Content** area. This displays the **Insert** dialog box, which can be used to specify the insertion point, scale, and rotation angle of the block. If you want to explode the block upon insertion, pick the **Explode** check box in the **Insert** dialog box.

You can also insert a block by highlighting the preview icon and right-clicking, which displays a shortcut menu. Picking **Insert Block...** from the shortcut menu accesses the **Insert** dialog box. Picking **Copy** allows you to copy the block to the Windows Clipboard and paste it in the drawing. After selecting **Copy**, move the cursor to the location in the drawing where you want to insert the block, right-click, and select **Paste** or **Paste as Block** from the shortcut menu. You are then prompted for the insertion point on the command line. If you select **Paste to Original Coordinates** from the shortcut menu, the block is inserted at the same coordinates from which it was copied in the original drawing.

Entire drawings can also be inserted using **DesignCenter**. To insert a drawing, select the folder where it is stored. Any drawings in the selected folder will be displayed in the **Content** area with preview icons. See **Figure 10-6**. Highlight the drawing icon and use drag and drop to insert the file into the current drawing. When inserting an entire drawing, you are prompted for the insertion point, scale values, and rotation angle on the command line.

As with blocks, you can enter the insertion values in the **Insert** dialog box when inserting a drawing from **DesignCenter**. To use the **Insert** dialog box, select the drawing file in the **Content** area, right-click on its icon, and pick **Insert as Block...** from the shortcut menu. This inserts the drawing as a block reference in the current drawing. You can also attach the drawing to the current drawing as an external reference by picking **Attach as Xref...** from the shortcut menu. External references are discussed in Chapter 17.

**Figure 10-6.**
Using **DesignCenter** to access drawing files stored in a specific folder.

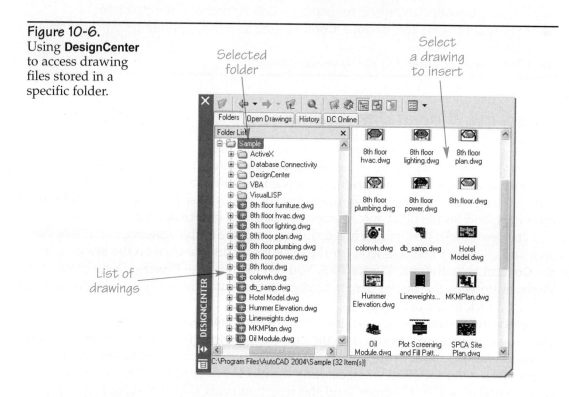

## Exercise 10-2

◆ Start a new drawing using a template or startup option of your own choice.
◆ Open **DesignCenter**.
◆ Access the DesignCenter folder located in the AutoCAD 2004 \Sample folder.
◆ Browse through the content in each drawing.
◆ Locate the file Home-Space Planner.dwg and access the Blocks content.
◆ Drag and drop several blocks from the **Content** area into the current drawing.
◆ Insert several blocks into the current drawing using the **Insert** dialog box.
◆ Select the DesignCenter folder again to list the drawings in the **Content** area.
◆ Locate the file House Designer.dwg and drag and drop the entire drawing into the current drawing.
◆ Close **DesignCenter**. Save the file as ex10-2.

Architectural Drafting Using AutoCAD

# Using the Search Dialog Box

As previously discussed, selecting the **Search** button in the **DesignCenter** toolbar displays the **Search** dialog box. See **Figure 10-7**. This dialog box can be used to locate drawings, blocks, and other content on any drive by specifying search criteria. The content can then be loaded into **DesignCenter**. This is a useful feature when you are unsure of the exact location of a drawing file, or when you know the name of a block but cannot find the file where it is stored.

The **Look for** drop-down list at the top of the **Search** dialog box is used to specify the type of content to locate. In addition to blocks and drawings, you can search for existing dimension styles, layers, layouts, linetypes, text styles, external references, hatch patterns, and hatch pattern files. Hatch patterns are discussed in Chapter 19.

When searching for a drawing, three tabs appear in the **Search** dialog box. The **Drawings** tab allows you to conduct a basic search for a particular drawing by typing the file name in the **Search for the word(s)** text box and selecting **File Name** from the **In the field(s)** drop-down list. If you want to search for a drawing by title, subject, author, or keywords, select the desired criteria using the **In the field(s)** drop-down list. This criteria relates to information stored for the drawing in the **Drawing Properties** dialog box.

Once the search information has been specified in the **Drawings** tab, you can select a drive to search in the **In** drop-down list. You can specify the search to include subfolders by checking the **Search subfolders** check box. You can also search in a specific folder by picking the **Browse...** button. To begin the search, pick the **Search Now** button. Picking the **New Search** button allows you to enter criteria for a new search. When the search is complete, any drawings matching the criteria you specified appear in the window at the bottom of the dialog box. You can then double-click on a file name to display the drawing and its contents in **DesignCenter**.

**Figure 10-7.**
The **Search** dialog box allows you to search for drawing files and content to be loaded into **DesignCenter**.

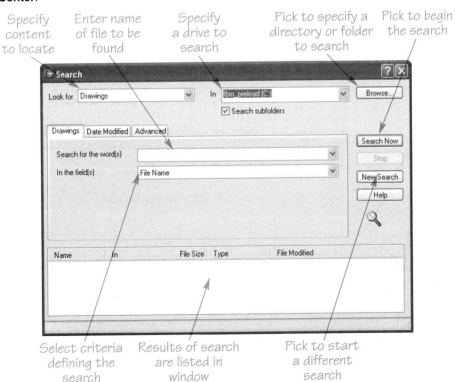

The **Date Modified** and **Advanced** tabs are also available in the **Search** dialog box when searching for drawing files. In the **Date Modified** tab, you can set up a search to look for drawings created or modified between dates you specify. This criteria is used in conjunction with the information you provide in the **Drawings** tab. The **Advanced** tab is used to further refine the search. You can specify for AutoCAD to also look for a certain block name, a block or drawing description, or any attribute information in addition to the specified file name in the **Drawings** tab. Attributes are discussed in Chapter 21. You can also specify to search for certain text within the file or limit the search to a specific file size.

When searching for items other than drawing files or hatch pattern files as specified in the **Look for** drop-down list, only one tab appears in the **Search** dialog box. For example, if you are searching for blocks only, the **Blocks** tab appears as shown in **Figure 10-8**. This tab allows you to enter a block name and search for it using a specified drive and folder(s). Note that in the figure shown, an asterisk is entered as a wild card character after the search name to access all blocks including chair in the block name.

A combined search for blocks and drawings can also be conducted by selecting **Drawings and Blocks** in the **Look for** drop-down list. This type of search can be used when similar names are used for blocks and separately saved files and you are unsure how a symbol is stored.

**Figure 10-8.**
Searching for a block with the **Search** dialog box.

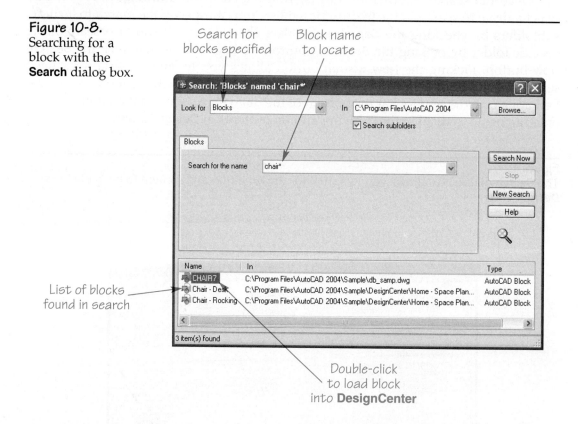

Search for blocks specified

Block name to locate

List of blocks found in search

Double-click to load block into **DesignCenter**

## Exercise 10-3

◆ Begin a new drawing and open **DesignCenter**.
◆ Access the **Search** dialog box.
◆ Perform a search for drawing files that begin with Floor by using the search string floor*. Search for any files created between the dates of Jan. 1, 2000 and the current date.
◆ Double-click on the first item listed to browse through the drawing for content.
◆ Drag and drop different types of content into your drawing.
◆ Close **DesignCenter**. Do not save the drawing.

# Importing Layers, Linetypes, and Text Styles

In Chapter 5, you learned how to create and manage layers and load and assign linetypes in drawing files. In some cases, you may find it useful to use a layer or linetype from another drawing when working on a similar drawing. You may also want to access text styles from other drawings when creating text in a new drawing. Text styles are discussed in Chapter 8. You can use **DesignCenter** to import any existing layers, linetypes, and text styles you wish to apply in the current drawing.

It is important to remember that each time you create a new drawing, frequently duplicated objects such as layers do not have to be recreated. With **DesignCenter**, you have the ability to reuse previously created content from any stored drawing. You can access specific items and import them through dragging and dropping. This saves you time and allows you to access items that are already drawn to current standards.

To reuse layers from another drawing, use the **DesignCenter** tree view to browse for the drawing file. Then, highlight the Layers category underneath the file name or double-click on the Layers icon in the **Content** area. See **Figure 10-9**. You can then drag and drop the desired layers from the **Content** area into the drawing. You can also double-click on a layer icon to insert a layer individually. To select more than one layer at a time, hold down the [Shift] key and pick the first and last icon in a group. This selects all of the layers between the first and last pick. You can also hold down the [Ctrl] key to select multiple icons individually. Right-clicking on a layer icon in the **Content** area allows you to add the layer using a shortcut menu.

Once the layers have been imported, they become available in the active drawing. If a layer name that is being inserted already exists in the destination drawing, that layer name and its settings are ignored. The existing settings for the layer are preserved and a message indicating that the duplicate settings were ignored is displayed on the command line.

Linetypes from a separate drawing file can be inserted into the current drawing with **DesignCenter** using the same procedure for inserting layers. In the tree view, select the drawing containing the linetypes to be copied. Then, select the Linetypes category to display the available linetypes in the **Content** area. Select the linetypes to be copied, and then drag and drop them into the drawing. You can also double-click on a linetype icon to add the linetype, or you can right-click to use a shortcut menu. If the linetype already exists in the destination drawing, the existing settings are preserved and the duplicate linetype is ignored.

**Figure 10-9.**
Adding layers to a drawing with **DesignCenter**.

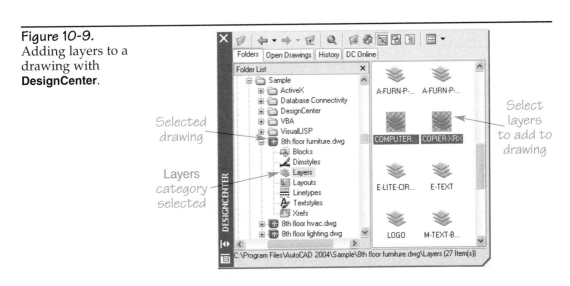

*Selected drawing*

*Layers category selected*

*Select layers to add to drawing*

Text styles can be inserted from one drawing into another with **DesignCenter** using the same process for inserting layers and linetypes. First, select the drawing file containing the text styles you want to use. Then, select the Textstyles category to display the available text styles in the **Content** area. Drag and drop the text styles, or double-click or right-click on the text style icons to add the desired styles to the current drawing. Duplicate definitions are ignored if the text style name already exists in the drawing.

When you import a text style into a drawing, it does not become the current style. You can use the **STYLE** command to set the new text style current.

### Exercise 10-4

◆ Open the drawing file 8th floor plan.dwg located in the AutoCAD 2004\Sample folder. Keep the file open while you start a new drawing.
◆ Open **DesignCenter** in the new drawing.
◆ Pick the **Open Drawings** tab in the **DesignCenter** window to list the open drawings in the tree view. Display the layers available in 8th floor plan.dwg in the **Content** area.
◆ Use the [Ctrl] key to select several layers in the **Content** area, and then drag and drop them into the new drawing.
◆ Using the **Layers** toolbar, view the layers defined in the new drawing to confirm that the layers from 8th floor plan.dwg were imported.
◆ Display the linetypes available in 8th floor plan.dwg in the **Content** area.
◆ Select the Batting, Dashed, and Hidden linetypes and drag and drop them into the new drawing.
◆ Save the drawing as ex10-4.

## Inserting Dimension Styles and Layouts

Dimension styles and layouts can be imported from existing drawing files into a new drawing using **DesignCenter**. Dimension styles are used to format the way dimensions appear in a drawing and are discussed in Chapter 15. Layouts are used to set up drawings for plotting purposes and are discussed in Chapter 24.

The procedure for importing dimension styles into a drawing with **DesignCenter** is similar to that used for blocks, layers, linetypes, and text styles. Once the drawing containing the dimension styles is located in the **DesignCenter** tree view, highlight the Dimstyles category to display available dimension styles in the **Content** area. You can then select the desired dimension styles and drag and drop them into the drawing. You can also double-click on the dimension style icons to insert the styles individually, or you can right-click to use the shortcut menu.

Layouts are added to drawings from **DesignCenter** in the same manner after locating an existing drawing in the tree view and selecting the Layouts category. A layout that is inserted becomes a part of the new drawing, and a layout tab with the corresponding name is added to the bottom of the drawing area. Any objects drawn in the layout will also be inserted, along with any layers associated with the layout.

## Adding Raster Images with DesignCenter

Drawings produced in AutoCAD are generated from vector images. A *vector image* is made up of objects defined by XYZ coordinates, where the objects are composed of points connected by straight lines. However, AutoCAD also has the ability to display raster images in a drawing. *Raster images* are generated from dots, or *pixels*, and contain no XYZ coordinate values. *Pixels,* or *picture elements,* are the single points of color displayed by a computer monitor. Raster images are created with pixels and are saved as image files commonly referred to as *bitmaps*. Raster images such as BMP, JPG, TGA, TIF, and GIF files can be incorporated into an AutoCAD drawing and used in applications requiring high-quality images or presentation graphics. You can use **DesignCenter** to browse for raster images and bring them into a drawing.

Raster images are not readily listed in **DesignCenter** as usable content. To insert a raster image into a drawing, you must browse for the folder containing the image you wish to use. See **Figure 10-10.** When the image has been found and selected in the tree view, you can drag and drop it into the drawing, or you can double-click to access the **Image** dialog box. This dialog box is similar to the **Insert** dialog box and is used to specify insertion values for the image. You can also right-click on the image icon and pick **Attach Image…** from the shortcut menu to use the **Image** dialog box, or you can pick **Copy** to copy the image to the Clipboard.

When inserted, a raster image is not actually stored in the content of a drawing. It is attached to the current drawing and *referenced* in the same way an external reference is referenced by AutoCAD. External references are discussed in Chapter 17. After a raster image is attached to a drawing, the folder path to the corresponding image file is stored, allowing AutoCAD to load the image file whenever the drawing is opened.

## Browsing the Internet for Content

You can search for files on the Internet and download content using the features of **DesignCenter**. As discussed earlier in this chapter, picking the **Load** button in the **DesignCenter** toolbar displays the **Load** dialog box. This is a standard file selection dialog box that allows you to load any drawing in **DesignCenter** and list its content. It is very similar to the **Select File** dialog box. Picking the **Search the Web** button accesses the **Select Hyperlink** Web browser, which you can use to enter a Web site address and search for other AutoCAD drawings or image files. You can then download a file from a Web site, save it, and load its contents into **DesignCenter**.

**Figure 10-10.**
Browsing for raster images using **DesignCenter**.

Drag into drawing or double-click to open **Image** dialog box

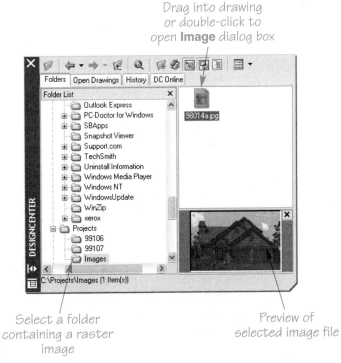

Select a folder containing a raster image

Preview of selected image file

# Customizing Content Used in DesignCenter

As you learned in Chapter 9, when creating a block using the **Block Definition** dialog box, the **Drag-and-drop units:** option allows you to specify the type of units AutoCAD uses when inserting the block with **DesignCenter**. You can use this setting to set the value at which your block is scaled when inserted from **DesignCenter**. For example, suppose you create a 1″ unit block and you always want the block to be inserted as a 1′-0″ square block when inserting it from **DesignCenter**. When creating the block, specify **Feet** for the **Drag-and-drop units:** setting so that the block is inserted at 12 times its original size. If you want to be able to insert the block without a preset scale value when using **DesignCenter**, set the **Drag-and-drop units:** option to **Unitless**.

You can also use the **User Preferences** tab in the **Options** dialog box to set insertion unit values for blocks inserted from **DesignCenter**. In the **Drag-and-drop scale** area, the **Source content units:** and **Target drawing units:** settings are used for blocks that are created with the **Drag-and-drop units:** option set to **Unitless**. For each block defined without insertion units specified, AutoCAD assumes the original block was created with the units setting in the **Source content units:** drop-down list. The setting in the **Target drawing units:** drop-down list is then used for the insertion units when the same block is inserted from **DesignCenter**. For example, assume you have drawn a 1″ square and saved it as a block with the **Drag-and-drop units:** option set to **Unitless**. If the **Source content units:** option is set to **Feet**, then **DesignCenter** assumes the original 1″ square block is 1′-0″ square. If the **Target drawing units:** option is set to **Yards**, then that block is inserted as a 3′-0″ square block from **DesignCenter**. In this case, the 1′-0″ square block is scaled up to three times its size because it is inserted using yards as the insertion units.

## Creating a Block Preview

A preview image of a block is displayed in **DesignCenter** when the block is created with the corresponding setting active in the **Block Definition** dialog box. By default, blocks are created in this manner when using the **BLOCK** command. You may find that blocks stored in drawings created with older versions of AutoCAD do not include a preview icon when viewed in **DesignCenter**. If a block does not have a preview icon, you can create one with the **BLOCKICON** command. This command is accessed by entering blockicon at the Command prompt. To create a preview icon of a block, open the drawing where it is stored and use the following sequence:

Command: **blockicon**↵
Enter block names <*>: *(enter the name of the block)*.↵
1 block updated.

## Using Sources of Predefined Content

If you are a new user of AutoCAD and unsure of where to start when creating blocks and symbol libraries, you may want to access the predefined symbols supplied in AutoCAD. In addition to the symbol library drawing files provided in the AutoCAD Sample\DesignCenter folder, there are several sample architectural drawings stored in the Sample folder. These drawings contain useful samples of blocks, layers, text styles, and dimension styles. They can be used as a starting point for creating your own architectural symbols and symbol libraries. Take some time to browse through the Sample folder and study how the files and blocks were created.

**Note**

The Internet is a very useful source for different types of drawing content. A number of sources provide free blocks and drawing files for AutoCAD users. Try searching for AutoCAD drawings or blocks if you have Internet access. Shareware Web sites such as www.cadalog.com, www.caddepot.com, and www.pointa.autodesk.com can be used to begin assembling symbol libraries. *Note:* The addresses for these Web sites are the most current available at the time of publication and are subject to change.

# Using Tool Palettes

As you have learned in this chapter, **DesignCenter** provides a useful way to copy items from a saved drawing into the current one. You can also insert frequently used drawing content from custom storage spaces called *tool palettes*. **Tool palettes** are tabbed areas in the **Tool Palettes** window used to store blocks and hatch patterns for insertion into drawings. You can create a number of tool palettes with customized settings. For example, you can store blocks with a variety of different scale settings and object properties. After creating a tool palette, you can add blocks to it from **DesignCenter**.

To display the **Tool Palettes** window, pick **Tool Palettes** from the **Standard** toolbar, select **Tool Palettes Window** from the **Tools** pull-down menu, enter tp or toolpalettes at the Command prompt, or use the [Ctrl]+[3] key combination. The **Tool Palettes** window is shown in **Figure 10-11**.

The tool palettes in the **Tool Palettes** window are arranged in tabs. By default, there are three tool palettes available. To insert a block from a tool palette, select the tab in which the block resides. Then, place the cursor over the block image and pick once. Move the cursor into the drawing area and pick again to place the block. Dragging and dropping can also be used, but is not necessary. When a block is selected in a tool palette, the block is attached to the crosshairs once the cursor is moved into the drawing area. The location where the crosshairs and the block are connected is defined by the insertion point of the block. Object snaps can also be used to precisely set a block into place.

TOOLPALETTES
TP
[Ctrl]+[3]

**Tools**
➥ Tool Palettes
Window

**Standard
toolbar**

**Tool Palettes**

**Figure 10-11.**
The **Tool Palettes** window. Tool palettes contain blocks and hatch patterns and are organized into tabs.

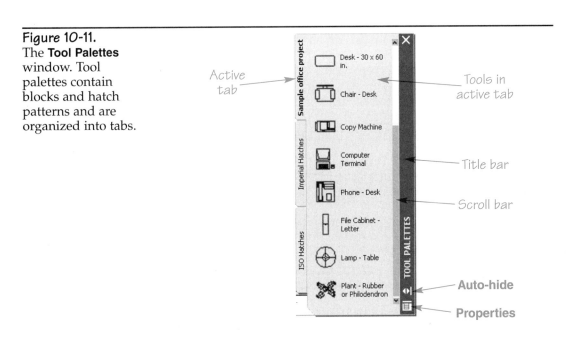

When inserting a block in this manner, you can access scaling and rotation options for the block at the command line before picking an insertion point. Enter s to scale the block along the XYZ axes or r to specify a rotation angle for the block.

## Exercise 10-5

◆ Start a new drawing using a template or startup option of your own choice.
◆ Open the **Tool Palettes** window.
◆ Pick the **Sample office project** tab.
◆ Insert the Computer Terminal block into the drawing.
◆ Insert the Phone-Desk block into the drawing.
◆ Do not save the drawing.

## Modifying the Appearance of the Tool Palettes Window

By default, only the vertical title bar of the **Tool Palettes** window is visible when it is opened. When the cursor is moved over the title bar, the tool palette tabs are displayed. Once the cursor is outside of the window, the tool palette tabs disappear again. This is controlled by a feature called **Auto-hide**. This setting can be toggled by picking the **Auto-hide** button on the title bar. You can also pick **Properties** at the bottom of the title bar and select **Auto-hide** from the shortcut menu. See **Figure 10-12**.

The **Properties** shortcut menu contains several other options that affect the appearance of the **Tool Palettes** window. The **Rename** option allows you to rename the window. The **Allow Docking** option determines whether the window can be docked. When checked, the window is dockable. The window can also be moved, resized, or closed in the same manner as any AutoCAD toolbar. You can use the cursor or the related option in the shortcut menu. The **Transparency...** option allows you to adjust the transparency of the **Tool Palettes** window. Selecting this option opens the **Transparency** dialog box, **Figure 10-13**. To set the transparency, adjust the **Transparency Level** slider. Moving the slider to the right makes the window more transparent.

**Figure 10-12.**
The **Properties**
shortcut menu.

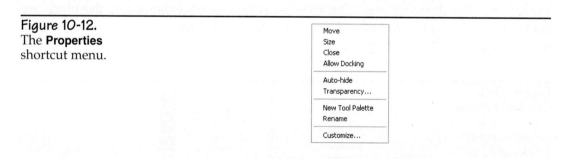

**Figure 10-13.**
The transparency
level of the **Tool
Palettes** window
can be set in the
**Transparency** dialog
box.

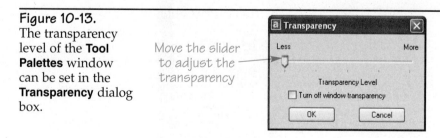

The **New Tool Palette** and **Customize...** options in the **Properties** shortcut menu allow you to create palettes, import or export palettes, and arrange the order of palettes in the **Tool Palettes** window. These options are discussed in the *Creating and Arranging Palettes* section.

## Locating and Viewing Content

As previously discussed, each tool palette has its own tab. There are a number of ways to navigate through the tools, or content, in each palette. In addition, viewing options are available to display the content in different ways.

To view the content in a palette, click on the related tab to open it. If the **Tool Palettes** window contains more palettes than what is displayed on screen, pick on the edge of the lowest tab to display a selection menu listing the palette tabs. Locate the name of the tab to access the related palette.

You can navigate through the tools in each palette by using one of two scroll methods. If all of the content of a selected palette is not visible at once, the remainder can be viewed by using the scroll bar or the scroll hand. The scroll hand appears when the cursor is placed in an empty area of a palette. Picking and dragging scrolls the palette up and down.

By default, the tools in each palette are represented by icons. The appearance of the tools can be adjusted to suit user preference. To access the viewing options in a palette, right-click in the palette to display the shortcut menu. See **Figure 10-14**. This shortcut menu contains some of the same options available in the **Properties** shortcut menu. The **View Options...** listing is used to set viewing options. The options in the lower areas of the menu are used to create, delete, rename, and rearrange tool palettes. These options and the **Paste** option are discussed in the sections that follow.

Picking **View Options...** displays the **View Options** dialog box, **Figure 10-15**. The size of the preview image for a tool can be adjusted by moving the **Image size:** slider. The **View style:** radio button options control how the content is displayed. The three options are described as follows:

- **Icon only**. This setting displays just the icon (a preview image).
- **Icon with text**. This setting displays the icon and the name of the tool.
- **List view**. This setting displays the icon and the name of each tool in the palette in a single-column format.

In the **Apply to:** drop-down list, you can specify how the view settings are assigned. The settings can be applied to the current palette only or to all palettes.

**Figure 10-14.**
This shortcut menu is displayed by right-clicking within a tool palette.

Allow Docking

Auto-hide
Transparency...
View Options...

Paste

New Tool Palette
Delete Tool Palette
Rename Tool Palette

Customize...

**Figure 10-15.**
Settings in the **View Options** dialog box control how content is displayed in the **Tool Palettes** window.

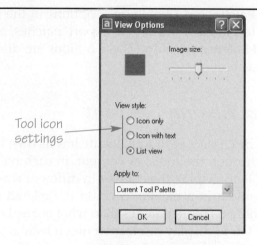

Tool icon settings

## Creating and Arranging Palettes

There are three sample tool palettes provided by AutoCAD in the **Tool Palettes** window. Using a simple procedure, you can quickly create new palettes and assign blocks and hatch patterns to them from **DesignCenter**. To create a new palette, pick **Properties** on the **Tool Palettes** title bar or right-click in a tool palette. Select **New Tool Palette** from the shortcut menu. Refer to **Figure 10-14**. You are then prompted to enter a name for the tool palette tab. Choose a name that identifies the content the palette will store. Adding blocks to a tool palette is discussed in the next section.

You can rename or delete existing palettes and change the order in which they appear. You can also import a palette saved as a file and place it in the **Tool Palettes** window. To access the palette tab options, right-click in a palette and select the **Customize...** option. This opens the AutoCAD **Customize** dialog box with the **Tool Palettes** tab current. See **Figure 10-16**. The palette tabs are listed in the **Tool Palettes:** list. To modify a tab, highlight its name in the list. The options available in the **Customize** dialog box are described as follows:

- **Up**. Picking this button moves the selected palette up in the **Tool Palettes:** list. This rearranges the order of the palette tabs.
- **Down**. Picking this button moves the selected palette down in the **Tool Palettes:** list.

**Figure 10-16.**
The **Tool Palettes** tab of the **Customize** dialog box.

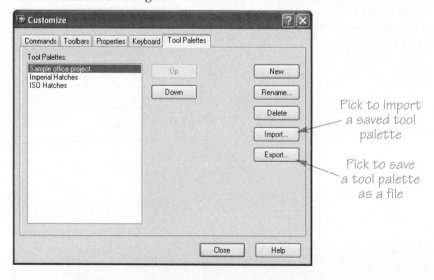

Pick to import a saved tool palette

Pick to save a tool palette as a file

- **New**. Picking this button creates a new tool palette.
- **Rename**. Picking this button allows you to rename the selected palette.
- **Delete**. Picking this button permanently deletes the selected palette.
- **Import**. Picking this button allows you to import a tool palette that has been saved (exported) using the **Import Tool Palette** dialog box.
- **Export**. Picking this button allows you to export, or save, the selected palette as a file using the **Export Tool Palette** dialog box.

When you create a new tool palette, it is good practice to export it as a file to create a backup copy. Exporting a tool palette saves it to a file with an .xtp extension. When saving, you must specify a file location.

When new content is added to or deleted from a tool palette, you can export it again to update the saved file. In a multiple AutoCAD user environment, tool palettes can be imported and exported to maximize efficiency. For example, on one workstation, tool palettes can be created and then exported to a network drive. The tool palettes can then be imported to other workstations.

## Adding Blocks to a Palette

**DesignCenter** is used to add blocks and hatch patterns to tool palettes. You can use **DesignCenter** to create individual tools as well as a new palette. For example, a palette can be created with all the blocks in a single drawing file by right-clicking on the drawing file name in **DesignCenter** and selecting **Create Tool Palette** from the shortcut menu. See **Figure 10-17**. In the example shown, a new palette is created from the House Designer file. The resulting palette consists of all the blocks in the file and has the same name as the file. A palette can also be created in this manner by expanding the contents of a drawing file in the **Tree View** area and right-clicking over the Blocks listing in either the **Tree View** area or the **Content** area. When the shortcut menu appears, select **Create Tool Palette**.

Individual blocks can be added to a palette from **DesignCenter** by using drag and drop. First, display the blocks to be added in the **Content** area of **DesignCenter**. Then, open the **Tool Palettes** window and display the palette that will store the blocks. Finally, drag each block from **DesignCenter** and drop it into the palette. If the palette is not already created, you can right-click on the block icon and select **Create Tool Palette** from the shortcut menu. This creates a new palette containing the selected block in a single operation. You are then prompted for a new name for the palette.

Figure 10-17.
Right-clicking on a drawing in **DesignCenter** and selecting **Create Tool Palette** creates a new tool palette with the name of the drawing file. All the blocks that are defined in the drawing become tools in the palette.

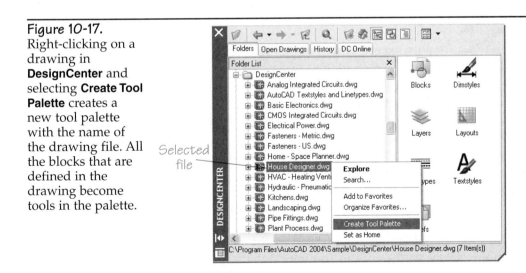

An entire drawing file can be added to a palette from **DesignCenter** by picking the folder where the file resides in the **Tree View** area and then dragging the file from the **Content** area into a palette. When the file is inserted into a drawing from the **Tool Palettes** window, it becomes a block in the drawing.

If you have multiple drawing files in a folder and want to create a palette that consists of all of the blocks combined from all of the drawing files, navigate to the folder in the **Tree View** area of **DesignCenter.** Next, right-click over the folder and select **Create Tool Palette of Blocks**. A new palette is created in the **Tool Palettes** window with the name of the folder.

 A block that has been added to a tool palette is directly linked to the drawing file in which it resides. If the block has been modified in the source file, inserting it from a tool palette inserts the updated block. The preview image in the palette does not reflect changes to the block. To update the icon, the tool must be deleted and then reinserted from **DesignCenter**, or its properties must be changed in the **Tool Properties** window. This procedure is discussed in the next section.

## Exercise 10-6

◆ Open **DesignCenter** and move it to the left side of the drawing area.
◆ Open the **Tool Palettes** window and move it to the right side of the drawing area.
◆ In **DesignCenter**, open the **Folders** tab and navigate to the AutoCAD 2004\Sample\DesignCenter folder.
◆ Right-click over the House Designer.dwg file and select **Create Tool Palette**.
◆ Create a new tool palette and name it My Blocks.
◆ In **DesignCenter**, select the Home-Space Planner.dwg file.
◆ In the **Content** area, double-click on Blocks to display the blocks in the Home-Space Planner.dwg file.
◆ Drag as many blocks as you wish from **DesignCenter** into the My Blocks palette.
◆ Save the drawing as ex10-6.

## Modifying Tools and Tool Properties

When working with several different palettes in the **Tool Palettes** window, it may be useful to copy or move the content of one palette to another. In addition, you may want to change the properties of blocks in certain palettes so that they vary from those in the source file or other palettes. Blocks residing in tool palettes can be modified to have different properties when inserted, such as different scales and rotation angles. Hatch patterns can be modified in the same manner. For example, you may want to specify a different angle for an inserted pattern. The properties override the defined object properties when the object is inserted.

A tool within a palette can be copied, moved, deleted, or renamed by right-clicking on the tool icon. This displays a tool shortcut menu, **Figure 10-18.** The **Cut** option is used to remove a tool from one palette and move it to another. After picking **Cut**, select another palette tab, right-click in the palette, and select **Paste** from the shortcut menu to move the tool to the new palette. The **Copy** option is used in the same way as the **Cut** option, except a copy is placed in the new palette and the tool remains in the original palette.

Architectural Drafting Using AutoCAD

**Figure 10-18.**
The tool icon shortcut menu displays options for modifying the selected tool.

| |
|---|
| Cut |
| Copy |
| Delete Tool |
| Rename |
| Properties... |

**Figure 10-19.**
A—The **Tool Properties** window for a block tool. B—The **Tool Properties** window for a hatch pattern tool.

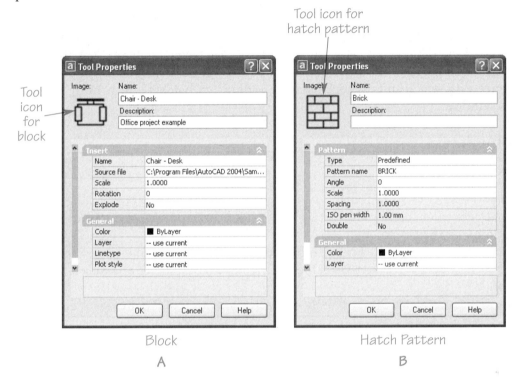

Block

A

Hatch Pattern

B

To delete a tool, right-click on its icon and select **Delete Tool** from the shortcut menu. When this option is selected, an alert dialog box appears. Selecting **OK** permanently deletes the tool.

To rename a tool, right-click on its icon and select **Rename** from the shortcut menu. Depending on the viewing option set in the **View Options** dialog box, the name of the tool may be displayed with the tool in the palette. If the name is not displayed, picking **Rename** temporarily displays the tool name so it can be renamed.

The properties of a tool can be viewed and modified by right-clicking on its icon and selecting **Properties...** from the shortcut menu. This opens the **Tool Properties** window. See **Figure 10-19**. The properties displayed depend on whether a block or hatch pattern is selected. In either case, a preview of the tool appears in the **Image:** area, and the name appears in the **Name:** text box. A description may be entered for the object in the **Description:** text box if desired.

In the **Tool Properties** window for a block, the first category is labeled **Insert**. See **Figure 10-19A**. The properties that appear are described as follows:

- **Name**. This is the name of the block in the source drawing file that will be inserted. It has to be the exact name of a block that has been defined in the source file.

- **Source file**. This is the location and name of the drawing file in which the block resides. To modify this setting, select the **Source file** setting. Then pick the ellipsis (**...**) button. This opens the **Select Linked Drawing** dialog box, which allows you to change the source drawing file.
- **Scale**. This value specifies the scale of the block in relation to the size at which the block was created.
- **Rotation**. This value specifies the rotation angle used when the block is inserted.
- **Explode**. This setting determines whether the block is exploded when inserted. The default setting is **No**.

In the **Tool Properties** window for a hatch pattern, the first category is labeled **Pattern**. See **Figure 10-19B**. The settings correspond to the options specified in the **Boundary Hatch** dialog box. Hatch patterns are discussed in Chapter 19.

The **Tool Properties** window has identical property settings in the **General** category for blocks and hatch patterns. These are the **Color**, **Layer**, **Linetype**, **Plot style**, and **Lineweight** settings. As with other object properties, these settings may be modified to produce different results when inserting a block or hatch pattern from the **Tool Palettes** window.

## Exercise 10-7

- Open ex10-6.
- Open the **Tool Palettes** window.
- Open the **Sample office project** palette.
- Right-click over the Phone-Desk tool and pick **Copy** from the shortcut menu.
- Open the My Blocks palette.
- Right-click in the palette and select **Paste** from the shortcut menu.
- Right-click over the Phone-Desk tool in the My Blocks palette and select **Delete Tool**.
- Right-click in the My Blocks palette and select **Delete Tool Palette**.

## Adding Hatch Patterns to a Palette

Hatch patterns can be added to the **Tool Palettes** window from **DesignCenter** using the same procedures involved with blocks. The pattern must first be defined in an AutoCAD hatch pattern file. Hatch pattern files have a PAT extension. The hatch patterns provided with AutoCAD are stored in the acad.pat and acadiso.pat files. These files must be first located in **DesignCenter** to access AutoCAD's predefined hatch patterns. By default, these files are AutoCAD support files stored in the Support File Search Path folder. This path location can be determined by accessing the **Files** tab in the **Options** dialog box and identifying the path listed under Support File Search Path.

Once a hatch pattern file is located, its contents can be displayed in the **Content** area of **DesignCenter**. You can then add the hatch patterns to a tool palette.

To create a palette that contains all of the hatch patterns in a single PAT file, right-click on the hatch pattern file in the **Tree View** area and select **Create Tool Palette of Hatch Patterns** from the shortcut menu. To add an individual hatch pattern to a palette, drag and drop the pattern from the **Content** area into the desired palette.

# Chapter Test

*Answer the following questions on a separate sheet of paper.*

1. What command is used to create a symbol and store it in the drawing in which it is created? What command is used to create a symbol and save it as a separate drawing file?
2. Define *symbol library*.
3. Name two advantages of storing blocks in a symbol library in comparison to storing them as individual drawing files.
4. Explain how to use the **INSERT** command to copy a symbol library into a drawing without displaying the blocks stored in the file.
5. Other than blocks, name three types of content that are listed with each drawing file in **DesignCenter**.
6. Identify two ways to open **DesignCenter**.
7. How can you display the tree view in **DesignCenter**?
8. Where is the **Content** area located in **DesignCenter**?
9. Explain how to view blocks that belong in a drawing in **DesignCenter**.
10. How can you load the content of drawings that are currently open in AutoCAD in **DesignCenter**?
11. Describe two ways to insert a block that is loaded in **DesignCenter** into the current drawing.
12. What is the purpose of the **Search** dialog box?
13. What happens when you insert a layer from one drawing into another and the layer already exists in the destination drawing?
14. Briefly explain how to bring a raster image into a drawing with **DesignCenter**.
15. How is the **Load** dialog box accessed?
16. How do you access the **Select Hyperlink** Web browser from **DesignCenter**?
17. If you create a 1″ unit block but you always want the block to be inserted as a 1′-0″ square block when inserting it from **DesignCenter**, what setting should you use for the **Drag-and-drop units:** option in the **Block Definition** dialog box?
18. What command can be used to create a block preview icon?
19. Other than a block, what type of AutoCAD object can be stored in a tool palette?
20. How do you insert a block from a tool palette into the current drawing?
21. Explain the purpose of exporting a tool palette as a file.
22. What is the best way to create a tool palette that consists of all the blocks in a drawing file?

---

# Chapter Problems

1. Create a symbol library containing architectural or structural symbols. Use architectural symbols such as doors, windows, and fixtures, or structural symbols such as steel shapes, bolts, and standard footings. Create text to identify all symbols and place them in an orderly arrangement. Save the symbol library file using an appropriate name, such as Arch-lib or Stru-lib. Then, after checking with your instructor, draw a problem using the library. Use **DesignCenter** to insert the blocks as you need them into your drawing. As an alternative, you may insert the entire symbol library file into your drawing to have access to all of the blocks and other content. Save the drawing problem you create as p10-1.

2. Open p9-5 from Chapter 9 and use the existing blocks to create a symbol library of office furniture and common architectural symbols. Identify the symbols and place them in an orderly arrangement in the new drawing. Save the symbol library file as Office-lib.

# Drawing Setup

## Learning Objectives

After completing this chapter, you will be able to:

- Plan an AutoCAD drawing.
- Use an AutoCAD template.
- Manage drawings in the Multiple Design Environment (MDE).
- Use the **UNITS** command.
- Manage and use scale factors.
- Set up the model space drawing area through the **LIMITS** command.
- Create a template.
- Open an existing drawing.

## Important Terms

American National Standards Institute
bearing
Deutsches Institut fur Normung
drawing template
gradient
grads
Guo Biao
International Standards Organization
Japanese Industrial Standard
layout space
model space
model space drawing limits
prototype drawing
Multiple Design Environment (MDE)
multiple document interface (MDI)
radian
sheet size
template

# Planning Your AutoCAD Drawing

Effective planning can greatly reduce the amount of time it takes to set up and complete a drawing. Drawing setup involves many factors that affect the quality and accuracy of your final drawing. AutoCAD helps make this planning process easy by providing a variety of setup options that help you begin a drawing. Even with these options, you still need to know the basic elements that make up your drawing. Some basic planning decisions include the following:

- The sheet size on which the drawing will be plotted.
- The planned plotting scale.
- The units of measure being used.
- The precision required for the drawing.
- The name of the drawing.

This chapter discusses all of these AutoCAD setup options. It also provides an opportunity to experiment with them.

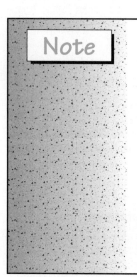

AutoCAD provides a *Multiple Design Environment* **(MDE).** This means that AutoCAD can have many different drawings open at the same time. Each open drawing occupies an individual drawing window within the AutoCAD program window. An introduction to managing the MDE is provided later in this chapter.

In this chapter, you will start several new drawings. When you start a new drawing, AutoCAD assigns a temporary name of Drawing1.dwg. The second drawing you start is given a temporary name of Drawing2.dwg, the third is named Drawing3.dwg, and so on. You can assign a different name when you save the drawing file. If you exit from AutoCAD, you may be asked if you want to save each of the drawings that you started. For the discussion in this chapter, you should answer **No** to each prompt.

# Starting a New Drawing

When AutoCAD 2004 is initially started, a new blank drawing is opened and ready for use. The drawing is based on the acad.dwt (English) template. This is a basic drawing having a 12″ × 9″ drawing area and using decimal units for linear measurement. You can then set all other drawing specifications, such as layers, units, or a new drawing area as needed.

NEW
[Ctrl]+[N]

File
➥ New...

Standard
toolbar

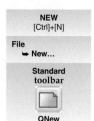

QNew

There will be times when you need to start a new drawing for a detail, floor plan, or elevation drawing. To create a new drawing, use the **NEW** command. Pick the **QNew** button from the **Standard** toolbar, select **New...** from the **File** pull-down menu, enter new at the Command prompt, or use the [Ctrl]+[N] key combination. This opens the **Select template** dialog box, which displays a list of available drawing templates. See **Figure 11-1.**

A *template* is a file that contains standard settings such as drawing area, layer names, dimension and text styles, and any linetypes that are applied to the new drawing. AutoCAD supplies a selection of templates based on accepted industry standards, but you can also create your own template or use an existing drawing file as a template.

**Figure 11-1.**
The **Select template** dialog box is used to start a new drawing from a template.

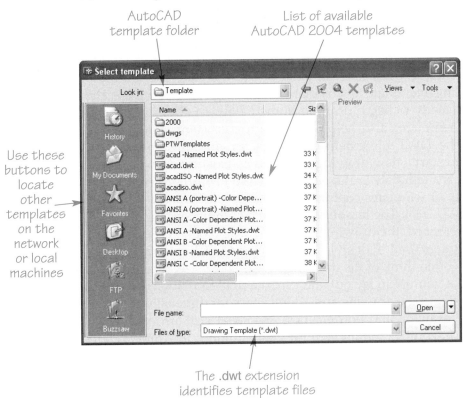

AutoCAD
template folder

List of available
AutoCAD 2004 templates

Use these
buttons to
locate
other
templates
on the
network
or local
machines

The .dwt extension
identifies template files

To start a new drawing, select a template from the list and then pick the **Open** button. This starts a new blank drawing with a new default name, such as Drawing1.dwg or Drawing2.dwg. You can change the drawing name when you save the drawing.

**Professional Tip**

AutoCAD 2004 includes two Architectural-specific templates: Architectural, English units – Color Dependent Plot Styles.dwt and Architectural, English units – Named plot Styles.dwt. These two templates start a new drawing opened to a layout tab with a title block. The initial model space drawing area is 12″× 9″ and the units are set to Architectural. This chapter explains how to further set up a drawing. Chapter 24 explains the differences between model and layout space and how to use layout space.

## Exercise 11-1

◆ Start AutoCAD if it is not already started.
◆ Pick the **QNew** button to access the **Select template** dialog box.
◆ Select the Architectural, English units – Color Dependent Plot Styles.dwt template.
◆ Select the **Model** tab.
◆ Save the drawing as ex11-1.dwg.

## Using an AutoCAD Template

In AutoCAD 2004, templates store standard drawing settings and may contain predefined drawing layouts, title blocks, layers, and other common drawing components. Anything that you normally must set up in a new drawing or during the drawing process can be saved in a template. When you begin a drawing using a template, all the settings and contents of the template file are added to the new drawing. Using a template means that the drawing setup process is already complete and you are ready to begin drafting immediately. In addition to reducing drawing setup time, templates also help to maintain consistent standards in each of your drawings. The DWT file extension stands for *drawing template.* AutoCAD also allows you to start a new drawing based on an existing drawing file. A drawing file that is used as a template is also referred to as a *prototype drawing.*

A variety of templates conforming to accepted industry standards are included with AutoCAD 2004. The template files use a naming system indicating the drafting standard referenced, the drawing size of the title block in the preset layout, and the plot style settings used. Plot styles are discussed in Chapter 24.

Drafters often think of the drawing size as sheet size. The *sheet size* is the size of the paper that you use to lay out and plot the final drawing. The sheet size takes into account the size of the drawing and added space for dimensions, notes, and clear area between the drawing and border lines. The sheet size also includes the title block, revision block, zoning, and an area for general notes. In AutoCAD, the sheet size is specified in the **Page Setup** dialog box when defining your drawing layout. The **Page Setup** dialog box is discussed in Chapter 24.

The ANSI A, DIN, Gb, ISO, and JIS templates provide a layout with the title block located in the lower-right corner of an 8-1/2″ × 11″ sheet. The architectural and generic templates provide a title block on the right side of a 36″ × 24″ sheet, which is common in the architectural industry.

The template list also contains the acad.dwt and acad – Named Plot Styles.dwt templates for starting a drawing using feet and inches, and the acadiso.dwt and acadISO – Named Plot Styles.dwt option for using metric units. These templates include two generic layouts without title blocks.

All of the templates usually have values for the following drawing elements:
- Standard layouts with a border and title block.
- Grid and snap settings.
- Units and angle values.
- Text standards and general notes.
- Dimensioning settings.

A template lets you start a drawing project with little or no drawing setup being required. Sometimes, you may use a template that starts with some or most of the required settings for the new drawing. After referencing the desired template, you can adjust your drawing settings as needed for the type of drawing being created. When going through this text, you will discover many ways to adjust AutoCAD to match individual needs and professional applications. Such adjustments can be used to build customized templates. Creating a template is discussed later in this chapter.

 You can also start a new drawing using the **Quick Setup** wizard or the **Advanced Setup** wizard. To use the wizards, you must set the **STARTUP** and **FILEDIA** system variables to 1. Then, you will be given the option of using a wizard when you start a new drawing.

Architectural Drafting Using AutoCAD

## Exercise 11-2

◆ Access the **Select template** dialog box.

◆ Go through the template list and pick each template. Notice how the preview image changes to represent the template.

◆ Pick a template that interests you and start a new drawing. For example, pick an architectural template or one of the generic templates.

◆ The AutoCAD screen now displays the layout, border, and title block as defined in the selected template. Note the title block and border have been placed on a layout tab.

◆ Pick the **Model** tab to make model space active.

◆ Close the template without saving when finished.

## Choosing a Template

Before starting an AutoCAD drawing, there should be some consideration of which template to use. Consider the differences in the following templates:

- ANSI: The *American National Standards Institute* has created a set of standards that relate to programming languages, Electronic Data Interchange (EDI), telecommunications, and the physical properties of hardware. In the AutoCAD environment, the templates include the different size drawing sheets that fall under this standard. These templates establish decimal inch units, include a standard title block, and have dimension and text styles that conform to the standard.

- DIN: The *Deutsches Institut fur Normung* (German Standards Institute) is a standard that originated in Germany and is used in engineering, construction, manufacturing, and testing applications throughout the world. The templates included with AutoCAD include the different drawing sheet sizes designated by this standard. The templates establish decimal millimeter units, include title blocks, and define dimension styles, layers, and text styles that conform to the standard.

- Gb: The *Guo Biao* (Codes of China) is a series of standards issued by the government of China to provide a common technical basis for the processing of electronic information. The templates establish decimal millimeter units, include a variety of drawing sheet sizes with title blocks, and have dimension styles, layers, and text styles that conform to the standard.

- ISO: The *International Standards Organization* is an international standard used in all industrial, engineering, and construction fields, with the exception of the electrical and electronics industry. This standard is common throughout the United States and the world. The templates establish decimal millimeter units, contain drawing sheets of the specified sizes with title blocks, and have dimension styles, layers, and text styles that conform to the standard.

- JIS: The *Japanese Industrial Standard* is used in commercial, engineering, research and development, construction, and governmental applications in Japan. The available templates establish decimal millimeter units, include different size drawing sheets with title blocks, and have text styles, dimension styles, and layers that conform to the standard.

- Metric Layout Template: This template is a standard millimeter unit template that includes layers, text styles, a dimension style, and several layout sheets that represent the DIN, ISO, and JIS drawing sheets with their appropriate title blocks. This template is a good template to use if you are creating a metric scaled drawing, as it provides a variety of metric drawing sheet sizes and title blocks.

- Generic: The two generic templates are both set up for use with decimal inches. They include a standard dimension style, text styles, layers, and a title block setup for a 24″ × 32″ drawing sheet. The significant difference between the two templates is that one uses a Color Dependent plot style and the other uses Named plot styles. Plot styles are covered in Chapter 24.
- Architectural: As with the generic templates, both of the architectural templates are set up for a 36″ × 24″ drawing sheet. They include title blocks, layers, dimension styles, and text styles. As with the generic templates, they each use a different plot style. These templates are automatically set up to use architectural feet and inches rather than decimal inches. Either of these templates can be a good starting point if you are creating a drawing that uses feet and inches rather than metric units.
- Acad: The acad templates include four different templates. The acad.dwt and the acad – Named Plot Styles.dwt templates establish decimal inch units. The acadiso.dwt and the acadISO – Named Plot Styles.dwt templates establish decimal millimeter units. None of these templates includes a title block or layers, but each one includes standard dimension and text styles. These templates are good "start from scratch" templates, because they do not include any preset information and are ready for customization using your school, work, or personal standards.

Templates are good starting points for beginning new drawings because many setup functions are already built in, so all you need to do is pick the template and start the drawing.

Later in this chapter, you will learn to create your own personal template that can be used for the exercises in the book and any future projects you create.

# Multiple Design Environment (MDE)

AutoCAD allows you to have multiple drawings open at the same time. This feature is referred to as the *Multiple Design Environment (MDE)*, which is sometimes called a *multiple document interface*, or *MDI*.

Most drafting projects are composed of a number of drawings, and each drawing presents a different aspect of the project. For example, in an architectural drafting project, required drawings might include a site plan, floor plan, elevations and sections, electrical and plumbing plans, and assorted detail drawings. The drawings in such projects are closely related to one another. By opening two or more of these drawings at the same time, you can easily reference information contained in the existing drawings while working on a new drawing. AutoCAD even allows you to directly copy all or part of the contents from one drawing directly into another using a simple drag-and-drop operation.

There are many ways to increase your drafting productivity through effective use of the MDE. The drag-and-drop features of AutoCAD, covered in Chapter 7, enable you to copy information from one drawing to another. The following section introduces the features and behaviors of the MDE.

## Controlling Drawing Windows

Each drawing you open or start in AutoCAD is placed in its own drawing window. New AutoCAD drawing windows are maximized by default. This means that the drawing area fills the inside of the main AutoCAD window. When an additional drawing is opened, it becomes the top drawing window. The name of the current drawing is displayed on the left-hand side of the AutoCAD title bar. Picking the **Restore Down** button cascades the drawing windows, with the drawing names visible on the left-hand side of the drawing window title bars.

Architectural Drafting Using AutoCAD

**Figure 11-2.**
Drawing window
control options.

| | Window Control Buttons | | |
|---|---|---|---|
| **Button** | **Function** | **Description** | |
|  | Display window control menu | Displays a pull-down menu with control options. | |
| | Minimize | Reduces the drawing window to a small title bar at the bottom of the AutoCAD window. | |
|  | Maximize | Displays the drawing window at largest possible size, and hides the title bar. | |
|  | Restore | Returns the drawing window to a floating state, at the previous size and position. | |
|  | Close | Closes the drawing, and provides an opportunity to save the drawing if it has been changed. | |

| | Window Control Buttons | | |
|---|---|---|---|
| **Button** | **Function** | **Description** | |
|  ↕ | Size window vertically | Press and hold the pick button while pointing at the top or bottom border of the drawing window, then move the mouse. | |
|  ↔ | Size window horizontally | Press and hold the pick button while pointing at the left or right border of the drawing window, then move the mouse. | |
|  ↖ | Size window diagonally | Press and hold the pick button while pointing at any of the four corners of the drawing window border, then move the mouse. | |
|  ✛ | Move window | Press and hold the pick button while pointing at the title bar, then move the mouse. | |

AutoCAD's drawing windows have the same control options as program windows on your desktop. They can be resized, moved, minimized, maximized, restored, and closed using the same methods used for program windows on your desktop. **Figure 11-2** shows a summary of the standard window control functions available for drawing windows.

The drawing windows and the AutoCAD program window have the same relationship as program windows have with the Windows desktop. When a drawing window is maximized, it fills the available area in the AutoCAD program window. Minimizing a drawing window displays it as a small title bar at the bottom of AutoCAD's drawing window and behind any maximized drawings. Drawing windows cannot be moved outside the AutoCAD program window. **Figure 11-3** illustrates drawing windows in a floating state and minimized.

To work on any currently open drawing, just pick its title bar if it is currently visible. You can also quickly cycle through open drawings by pressing either the [Ctrl]+[F6] or [Ctrl]+[Tab] key combination. To go directly to a specific drawing when the title bars are not visible, access the **Window** pull-down menu in AutoCAD. The name of each open drawing file is displayed, and the currently active drawing shows a check mark next to it. See **Figure 11-4A.** Pick the name of the desired drawing to make it current. Up to nine drawing names are displayed on this menu. If more than nine drawings are open, a **More Windows...** selection is displayed. Picking this displays the **Select Window** dialog box, shown in **Figure 11-4B.**

**Figure 11-3.**
Drawing windows can be displayed in several ways. A—By default, the drawings are displayed in floating windows. B—Minimized drawing windows are displayed as a reduced size title bar. Pick the title bar to display a window control menu.

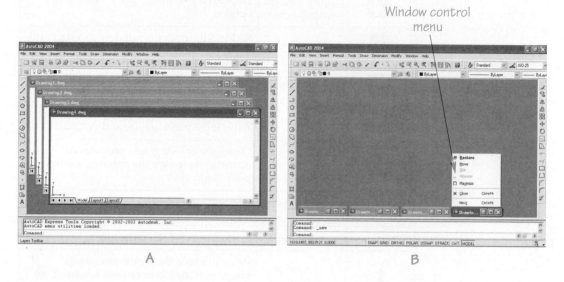

A

B

**Figure 11-4.**
Selecting the drawing to be active. A—Pick the name of the drawing from the **Window** pull-down menu to make it current. B—When more than nine drawings are open, pick **More Windows...** from the **Window** pull-down menu to display the **Select Window** dialog box.

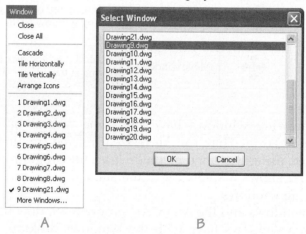

A                                    B

The additional control options available in the **Window** pull-down menu include:
- **Cascade.** Drawing windows that are not currently minimized are arranged in a cascade of floating windows, with the currently active drawing placed at the front. Refer to **Figure 11-3A.**
- **Tile Horizontally.** Drawing windows that are not currently minimized are made as wide as possible and positioned one above another, with the currently active drawing window placed in the top position.
- **Tile Vertically.** Drawing windows that are not currently minimized are made as tall as possible and positioned side-by-side, with the currently active drawing window placed in the left position.
- **Arrange Icons.** Arranges minimized drawings neatly along the bottom of the AutoCAD drawing window area.

**Figure 11-5.**
Tiled drawing windows. A—Three drawing windows tiled horizontally. B—Three drawing
windows tiled vertically. C—Four drawing windows tiled horizontally or vertically.

The effects of tiling the drawing window display varies based on the number of
windows being tiled and whether they are tiled horizontally or vertically. See
**Figure 11-5.**

 Typically, you can change the active drawing as desired. However, there are some situations when you cannot switch between drawings. For example, you cannot switch drawings during a dialog box session. You must either complete or cancel the dialog box before switching is possible.

## Exercise 11-3

- Open ex11-1.dwg.
- Pick the **Window** pull-down menu. Check to see how many drawing files are currently open.
- Access the **NEW** command and open the following templates:
  - ANSI B – Color Dependent Plot Styles.dwt
  - Architectural, English units – Color Dependent Plot Styles.dwt
  - DIN A4 – Named Plot Styles.dwt
  - Generic 24in x 32in Title Block – Color Dependent Plot Styles.dwt
  - ISO A1 – Named Plot Styles.dwt
  - Metric layout templates.dwt
- Use the **Window** pull-down menu to switch between drawings. Use the [Ctrl]+[F6] and the [Ctrl]+[Tab] key combinations to cycle between drawings.
- Pick the **Cascade** option from the **Window** pull-down menu to cascade the currently open drawing windows. Pick the **Tile Horizontally** and **Tile Vertically** options and observe the results of each action.
- Use the **Close** button to close all except four drawing windows without saving any changes. Pick the **Tile Horizontally** and **Tile Vertically** options and observe the results. Close one more drawing, repeat the tile operations, and observe the results.
- Minimize the remaining three drawings. Move the minimized drawings to different locations in the drawing window. Pick the **Arrange Icons** option and notice the new placement of the icons.
- Maximize one of the three drawing windows. Switch to another drawing using any desired method.
- Close two of the drawing windows without saving changes. Use the **Restore** button to place the drawing in a floating state. Resize the drawing window and move it to a new location. Double-click on the title bar of the drawing window.
- Close the last drawing window without saving changes.

# Changing Drawing Settings

After selecting one of the templates mentioned previously, you are ready to begin drawing. The use of the default templates is a convenient way to initially start a drawing with a few settings already in place. However, these settings may need to be changed while working on the drawing or when the drawing is finished. The drawing units may be changed at any time with the **UNITS** command, and the model space drawing limits can be changed with the **LIMITS** command.

## Changing Units

As discussed in Chapter 3, the **UNITS** command is the quickest way to set the drawing units and angles. The **UNITS** command opens the **Drawing Units** dialog box for easy control of the settings. This command can be accessed by picking **Units...** in the **Format** pull-down menu or by entering un or units at the Command prompt. The **Drawing Units** dialog box is shown in **Figure 11-6.**

Linear units are specified in the **Length** area of the **Drawing Units** dialog box. Decimal units are the default if starting a drawing using any of the acad, ANSI, DIN, Gb, Generic, ISO, JIS, or metric templates. Select the desired linear drawing units format from the **Type:** drop-down list and use the **Precision:** drop-down list to specify the linear drawing units precision. Access the **Type:** and **Precision:** drop-down lists

**Figure 11-6.**
The **UNITS** command accesses the **Drawing Units** dialog box.

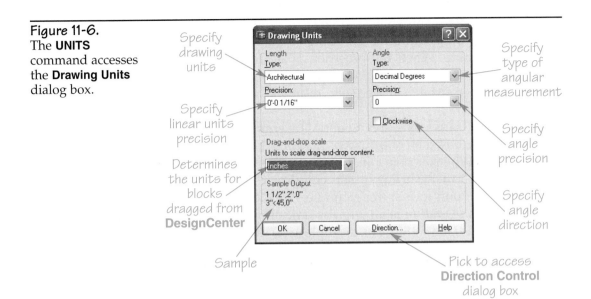

Specify drawing units

Specify linear units precision

Determines the units for blocks dragged from **DesignCenter**

Sample

Specify type of angular measurement

Specify angle precision

Specify angle direction

Pick to access **Direction Control** dialog box

located in the **Angle** area of the **Drawing Units** dialog box to set the desired angular units format and precision. Selecting the **Clockwise** check box changes the direction for angular measurements to clockwise from the default of counterclockwise. The linear unit and angle types are described as follows:

- **Decimal.** These units are used to create drawings in decimal inches or millimeters. Decimal units are normally used on mechanical drawings for manufacturing or when creating metric drawings. The default precision is four decimal places. When drawing using Cartesian coordinates, the values entered must be in decimal unit format.

- **Engineering.** These units are often used in civil drafting projects such as maps, site plans, dam and bridge construction, and topography. The default precision is four decimal places. When drawing using Cartesian coordinates, the values entered must be in feet and decimal inch format, such as 24'-6.5". The inch mark is not required.

- **Architectural.** Architectural, structural, and other drawings use these units when measurements are in feet, inches, and fractional inches. The default precision is 1/16". When drawing using Cartesian coordinates, the values entered must be in feet and inches, such as 36'9-1/2".

- **Fractional.** This option is used for drawings that have fractional parts of any common unit of measure. The initial default precision is 1/16. When drawing using Cartesian coordinates, the values entered must be in whole numbers and fractions, such as 3-1/2.

- **Scientific.** These units are used when very large or small values are applied to the drawing. These applications take place in such fields as chemical engineering and astronomy. The initial default precision is four decimal places. The value 0.0000E+01 means that the base number is multiplied by 10 to the first power. When drawing using Cartesian coordinates, the values entered must include E+ the power (e.g., 11.134E+01,12E+04).

- **Decimal Degrees.** This is the default degree setting. It is normally used in mechanical drafting where degrees and decimal parts of a degree are commonly used. When drawing using polar coordinates, the values entered must be in decimal-unit format, such as 24.0'<45.

- **Deg/Min/Sec.** This style is sometimes used in mechanical, architectural, structural, and civil drafting. There are 60 minutes in one degree and 60 seconds in one minute. When the precision is set for more accuracy, the minutes and seconds are displayed. When drawing using polar coordinates, the values entered must be in degrees, minutes, and seconds unit format, such as 75'<25d36'23".
- **Grads.** *Grads* is the abbreviation for *gradient*. Gradients are units of angular measure based on one quarter of a circle having 100 grads. A full circle has 400 grads. When working in gradients, the letter g follows the angular value. When drawing using polar coordinates, the values entered must be in gradient unit format (for example, 25'<250.5g).
- **Radians.** A *radian* is an angular unit of measure in which $2\pi$ radians $= 360°$, and $\pi$ radians $= 180°$. For example, a 90° angle has $\pi/2$ radians. Changing the precision displays the radian value rounded to the specified decimal place. When drawing using polar coordinates, the values entered must be in radian unit format, such as 6"<3.14r (180°).
- **Surveyor.** Surveyor angles are measured using bearings. A *bearing* is the direction of a line with respect to one of the quadrants of a compass. Bearings are measured clockwise or counterclockwise (depending on the quadrant), beginning from either north or south. Bearings are measured in degrees, minutes, and seconds. An angle measured 55°45'22" from north toward west is expressed as N55°45'22"W. An angle measured 25°30'10" from south toward east is expressed as S25°30'10"E. Use the **Precision:** drop-down list to set measurement to degrees, degrees/minutes, degree/minutes/seconds, or to set decimal display accuracy of the seconds part of the measurement. When drawing using polar coordinates, the values entered must be in surveyor unit format (for example, 255'<N30d23'15"W).

When you set the units, the coordinate display in the lower-left corner of the AutoCAD window will show the absolute coordinates in the selected unit of choice. The unit format that you select is used for entering coordinates on the command line when drawing geometry.

 **Note** When using relative coordinates with the polar coordinate system, place the @ symbol before distance, such as @23'<45 or @23'<.8r.

The **Drag-and-drop scale** area controls the scale at which a block will be inserted into your drawing when dragging and dropping the block from **DesignCenter**. For example, if a 1" square was drawn and turned into a block and you decided to use feet as the insertion units, then the block would be scaled to a 1'-0" square. Blocks are discussed in Chapter 9.

Pick the **Direction...** button to access the **Direction Control** dialog box. See **Figure 11-7.** The standard **East**, **North**, **West**, and **South** options are listed as radio buttons. Pick one of these buttons to set the angle 0 direction. The **Other** radio button activates the **Angle:** text box and the **Angle** button. The **Angle:** text box allows an angle for the zero direction to be entered. The **Angle** button allows two points on the screen to be picked for establishing the angle zero direction.

Architectural Drafting Using AutoCAD

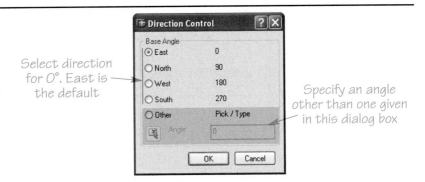

**Figure 11-7.**
Picking the
**Direction...** button in
the **Drawing Units**
dialog box displays
the **Direction Control**
dialog box.

*Select direction for 0°. East is the default*

*Specify an angle other than one given in this dialog box*

## Understanding and Finding the Scale Factor

A scale factor is a numerical value that is used in the proper scaling of text, dimension objects such as dimension text and arrowheads, and the size of the model space limits. When drawing geometry in AutoCAD, the objects are always drawn full scale. For example, a 50'-0" × 30'-0" building is drawn 50' × 30'. After the building is drawn, the notes and text are added. Assume that the text needs to be plotted so that it is 1/8" high. If 1/8" high text is placed into the drawing of the 50' × 30' building, the text would be so small in the plotted drawing that you could not read it. This is where the scale factor becomes important.

The scale factor of the drawing should already be established by the time you are ready to add text and dimensions to the drawing. To make the text readable on the plotted paper, the desired plotted text height of 1/8" is multiplied by the scale factor to determine the overall height of the text in the model space drawing. The scale factor is also used in scaling dimensions. Using the scale factor with dimensions is discussed in Chapter 15.

**Note**

It is recommended that you determine the plotting scale and scale factor of the drawing when you begin the drawing. If you find the drawing scale does not give you the desired results when plotted, you need to update the dimensions and text.

The scale factor can be determined by first deciding on the drawing scale for the plotted drawing. The scale factor is then determined by dividing the plotted units into the drawing units. The formula below demonstrates this principle:

plotted units × scale factor = drawing units
scale factor = drawing units ÷ plotted units

An architectural drawing to be plotted at a scale of 1/4" = 1'-0" has a scale factor calculated as follows:

1/4" × scale factor = 1'-0"
.25" × scale factor = 12" *(convert to inches)*
scale factor = 12 ÷ .25
scale factor = 48

An architectural drawing to be plotted at a scale of 1/8" = 1'-0" has a scale factor calculated as follows:

1/8" × scale factor = 1'-0"
.125" × scale factor = 12" *(convert to inches)*
scale factor = 12 ÷ .125
scale factor = 96

---

*Chapter 11   Drawing Setup*

The scale factor of a civil engineering drawing that has a scale of 1″ = 20′ is calculated as follows:

1" × scale factor = 20'
1" × scale factor = 240" *(convert to inches)*
scale factor = 240 ÷ 1
scale factor = 240

The scale factor for a drawing that has a scale of 1 mm = 20 mm is calculated as follows:

1 mm × scale factor = 20 mm
scale factor = 20

Once the scale factor of the drawing has been determined, multiply the height at which you want the text to appear by the scale factor. For example, if text height is to be 1/8″ on the plotted drawing, multiply the plotted text height by the scale factor.

1/8" × 48 = 6" (If the scale factor is 48, 6″ text will be 1/8″ in the plotted drawing.)
1/8" × 96 = 12" (If the scale factor is 96, 12″ text will be 1/8″ in the plotted drawing.)
1/8" × 240 = 30" (If the scale factor is 240, 30″ text will be 1/8″ in the plotted drawing.)
1/8" × 20 = 2.5" = 63.5 mm (25.4 mm / 1" × 2.5") (If the scale factor is 20, 63.5 mm text will be 1/8″ in the plotted drawing.)

If the text is not scaled by the scale factor, it most likely will not be readable in the plotted drawing. The full-size architectural drawing ends up being plotted $1/n$ its size, reducing the text by the same factor. This makes the text on the finished drawing so small that it cannot be read. Therefore, you must multiply the desired plotted text height by the scale factor in order to get text that appears in correct proportion on the drawing.

Remember, plotted scale, scale factors, and text heights should be determined before beginning a drawing. Once the scale factor has been determined, it is applied to the text heights, dimension object sizes, block scaling, and model space limits. Refer to the charts in Appendix K to find some of the most common scale factors and text heights for architectural and civil engineering drawings.

## Changing Model Space Limits

AutoCAD refers to the drawings you create as *models.* Models are drawn full size in *model space.* Model space is active when the **Model** tab is selected at the bottom of the screen. When you finish drawing the model, you then switch to *layout space,* where the drawing layout is organized so it can be printed on paper. Model space and layout space are fully explained in Chapter 24 of this text. All text material prior to Chapter 24 is based on model space being active.

An AutoCAD drawing is created actual size using the desired unit of measure. If you are drawing an object that is measured in feet and inches, you draw using feet and inches in AutoCAD. If you are creating a metric drawing, you draw using decimal units to represent millimeters. You draw the objects full-size regardless of the type of drawing, the units used, or the size of the final layout on paper. AutoCAD allows you to specify the size of the actual area required for your drawing, and refers to this as the *model space drawing limits.*

When using any of the AutoCAD templates, the model space drawing limits are initially set for a small area. The actual drawing area varies between templates, but the settings are generally too small for architectural applications. If you turn on the drawing grid in model space, it displays the current drawing limits or model space drawing limits in the drawing.

The drawing limits provide you with a general drawing area where you can begin planning a drawing. The limits represent a scaled version of the sheet size that you will print. For example, the acad.dwt limits are set up to a 12″× 9″ size and the acadiso.dwt limits are 420 mm × 297 mm. These sizes are too small to draw a real full-scale building.

The model space drawing limits can be changed using the **LIMITS** command. The **LIMITS** command is accessed by entering limits at the Command prompt or by picking **Drawing Limits** in the **Format** pull-down menu.

The **LIMITS** command asks you to specify the coordinates for the lower-left corner and the upper-right corner of the drawing area. The lower-left corner is usually set to 0,0 but you can specify a different Cartesian coordinate if desired. Press [Enter] to accept the 0,0 value for the lower-left corner default, or enter a new value. The upper-right corner usually identifies the upper-right corner of the drawing area. If you want a 17″ × 11″ drawing area, the upper-right corner setting is 17,11. The first value is the horizontal measurement (X axis) and the second value is the vertical measurement (Y axis) of the limits. Each value is separated by a comma. The command works like this:

```
Command: limits↵
Reset Model space limits:
Specify lower left corner or [ON/OFF] <0.0000,0.0000>: ↵
Specify upper right corner <12.0000,9.0000>: 17,11↵
Command:
```

Once the limits have been changed, a **Zoom All** should be performed to zoom to the edges of the limits (the edges of the "paper" in model space).

The **LIMITS** command can also be used to turn the limits on or off by entering on or off at the prompt. When the limits are turned on, AutoCAD restricts you from drawing outside of the rectangular area defined by the limits settings. Limits are typically turned off for most drafting applications.

## Calculating the Drawing Area and Limits

Just as text is scaled to actual size in the model space drawing, the plotted paper size is also multiplied by the scale factor to set the drawing limits. To calculate the available drawing area of a sheet of paper at a specific scale, use this formula:

scale factor × media size = limits

For example, the limits of a B-size (17″ × 11″) sheet of paper at 1/4″ = 1′-0″ scale (scale factor = 48) can be calculated as follows:

48 × 17″ = 816″ (X axis)
48 × 11″ = 528″ (Y axis)

Thus, the limits of a B-size sheet at the scale of 1/4″ = 1′-0″ are 816,528. The limits can also be expressed in feet if using architectural units. C-size sheets are 24″ × 18″, which can also be expressed as 2′ × 1′-6″. Multiplying the foot size of the sheet by the scale factor will determine the limits. The following example calculates the limits for a C-size sheet at a scale of 1/8″ = 1′-0″ (scale factor = 96):

2′ × 96 = 192′ (X axis)
1′-6″ × 96 = 144′ (Y axis)

Model space limits are not required before drawing a building but can be used in conjunction with the **GRID** command to help determine if your building will fit on the selected sheet of paper at a particular scale. Refer to the charts in Appendix K to find the limits for common scales on various paper sizes used in the architectural and civil engineering fields.

## Sheet Sizes

Drawing sheets vary between offices, depending on the type of work being performed, and the type of reproduction used. The most common sheet sizes are B size for check plots, and C, D, or E size for finished documents. The "D" and "E" sizes are typically used for large buildings. A title block and border is typically added to the sheet when entering the page setup/plot stage of the drawing process.

**Professional Tip**

Metric drawing sheets are numbered as A4, A3, A2, A1, and A0. The A3 sheet size is common for check plots, and the A2 and A1 sizes are common for finished plotted documents. The A0 sheet size can be used for large architectural projects.

When sheets are created so the drawings are read horizontally, they are usually bound together on the left side. A typical border is 3/8" to 1/2" from the edge of the sheet on three sides, and 1" to 1-1/2" from the binding edge of the sheet. The title block can be located at the bottom or the right edge of the paper. The title block is where pertinent information for the drawing is kept. The title block is usually 1-1/2" to 2" wide and along the right edge of the sheet. This allows for more drawing area on the sheet. Setting up a title block on a plotted sheet of paper is discussed in Chapter 24.

Along with the use of a variety of title block locations and sizes, sheet sizes also vary between offices. Some offices choose to base the sheet sizes on standard rolls of plotter paper, such as 24" or 36" wide rolls. Other offices base the sheet sizes on traditional office paper sizes such as 17" × 11". Also, offices in the United States and around the world use sheets in a variety of metric sizes. **Figure 11-8** shows the most common sheet sizes used in architectural drafting.

No matter which paper size, location of borders, or title block sizes and locations you use, remember that a standard is being created. The key to standards is that they establish a consistency in your drawings.

**Figure 11-8.**
A—Sheet sizes based on traditional office paper.
B—Sheet sizes based on standard rolls of plotter paper.

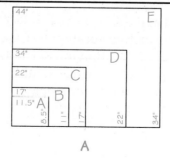

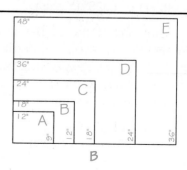

A

B

The following list provides some professional guidelines that you can use to set the drawing area width and length based on different applications:

- **Inch and Metric drawings.** Calculate the total width and length of the objects included in all views with extra space between views and room for dimensions and notes. Use these values for your drawing area settings.
- **Architectural drawings.** The actual size of architectural drawings is based on feet and inch measurements. If you are drawing a floor plan that is 48' × 24', allow 12' on each side for dimensions and notes, making the total drawing area 72' × 48'. When you select architectural units, AutoCAD automatically sets up the drawing for you to draw in feet and inches.
- **Civil drawings.** The actual sizes of civil drawings used for mapping are often measured in units of feet. The drawing limits can be calculated in the same manner as limits for architectural drawings. Civil drawings often represent very large areas, such as a site plan that requires 200' × 100' to accommodate all of the property lines, dimensions, and notes.

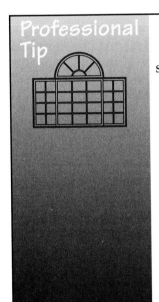

Professional Tip

Use the following steps as a guide for setting up and starting a new drawing:

- Determine the scale at which you plan to plot the drawing.
- Determine the scale factor.
- Use the **NEW** command to start a new drawing.
- Set the drawing units.
- Determine the size of paper available to print on the printer/plotter.
- Determine and set the model space drawing limits.
- Perform a **Zoom All**.
- Set the grid and snap as desired.
- Set any running object snap modes needed.
- Create any layers and linetypes needed.
- Start drawing.

## Exercise 11-4

◆ Open AutoCAD if it is not already open. Select a template of your choice.
◆ Open the **Drawing Units** dialog box and make the linear units architectural. Set the angular measure to decimal degrees and the angular precision to 3. Specify the angular direction as counterclockwise.
◆ Pick **OK** to exit the **Drawing Units** dialog box.
◆ Use the **LIMITS** command to scale a 36" × 24" sheet of paper at a scale of 1/4"=1'-0". Use 0,0 as the lower-left corner of the paper.
◆ Save the drawing as ex11-4.

# Creating a Template

Depending on the types of drawing projects you work with, there are many settings that are the same from one drawing to the next. These can include snap and grid settings, text styles, layers, and many other setup features. With most companies, standard borders and title blocks are used in all drawings. To save drawing setup time, custom templates are used.

The word *template* is defined as a model on which something is based. In AutoCAD, a *drawing template* is a model upon which other drawings are based. When you use a template, all the settings saved in the template are applied to your new drawing. The template file can supply any information that is normally specified and saved in a drawing file, such as units settings. Many of the AutoCAD templates already have standard borders and title blocks. The template drawing contains the setup options that you would normally set up in a new drawing. All of these settings should match your company or school specifications and should meet the requirements of your drawing applications.

If none of the predefined templates meets your needs, you can create and save your own custom templates. AutoCAD allows you to save *any* drawing as a template. A drawing template should be developed whenever a number of drawing applications require the same setup procedures. The template then allows the setup to be applied to any number of future drawings. Creating templates increases drafting productivity by decreasing setup requirements.

The simplest way to create a template is to begin a drawing using the acad.dwt or the acadiso.dwt template. This will start a drawing with only the default settings such as the 0 layer, no user-defined linetypes, the standard text and dimension styles, decimal drawing units, and limits that are set to 12" × 9" (or 420 mm × 297 mm for metric). Begin by setting up the drawing units and model space limits. Think about the layers that are required, and what layer should be current when the template is opened. Load any linetypes you plan on using. Create text styles and make current the style that is to be the default. Create any dimension styles that will be used. Dimension styles are covered in Chapter 15. Set the running object snaps that are to be on when you open the template. Anything that you normally have to set up should be included in a template.

**Figure 11-9** is a list of features to consider adding or setting up in a template. This is only a partial list of the most common settings to include in a template. As you become familiar with more commands and system variables, you may decide to set other variables and options current.

**Professional Tip**

Generalized templates that set the units, limits, snap, and grid to specifications are useful, but keep in mind that you can create any number of drawing templates. Templates that contain more detailed settings can dramatically increase drafting productivity.

Once you have set up your template, you need to save the drawing. Use the **SAVEAS** command to save the drawing as a template. In the **Save Drawing As** dialog box, change the type of drawing you are saving in the **Files of type:** drop-down list from the default DWG file to **AutoCAD Drawing Template File (*.dwt)**. See **Figure 11-10.**

Architectural Drafting Using AutoCAD

**Figure 11-9.**
A partial list of the
most common
settings to include
in a template.

| Command | Description |
|---|---|
| | **Considerations for Creating Templates** |
| **UNITS** | Select the default units and angular settings to use. |
| **LIMITS** | Determine the paper size available. |
| **SNAP** | Set the appropriate snap spacing. |
| **GRID** | Set the appropriate grid spacing. |
| **OSNAP** | Set any running object snaps. |
| **POLAR** (button) | Set the AutoSnap increment angle. |
| **TILEMODE** | Set to 1 if you want to start drawing in model space. Set to 0 if you want to start in the first layout tab. (You can also select the tab you want to be in when starting the template.) |
| **LAYER** | Create the layers to be used. List all the layer names, colors, linetypes, and lineweights. Set the layer that you want to be current. |
| **COLOR** | Set the current color (usually set to ByLayer). |
| **LINETYPE** | Load any linetypes you use. |
| **STYLE** | Create text styles, and set the style you want to be current. |
| **DIMSTYLE** | Create dimension styles, and set the dimension style you want to be current. |
| **BLOCK** (optional) | Insert any block definitions that will be used in the drawing. This is optional as it could make the drawing file too large if you insert all the blocks that you use. |
| **DDPTYPE** | Select the type of point style you will use when using the **DIVIDE** and **MEASURE** commands. |
| **MIRRTEXT** | Set to 0 to only mirror the text locations and not the text when using the **MIRROR** command. |
| **EDGEMODE** | Set to 1 to have AutoCAD project an imaginary line to objects when using the **TRIM** or **EXTEND** commands. |
| **FILLET** (radius) | Set the default fillet radius. |
| **CHAMFER** | Set the **Distance** and **Angle** options. |
| **TRIMMODE** | Set to 1 to trim the corners of geometry when using the **FILLET** or **CHAMFER** commands. |
| **PLINE** | Set the polyline width. |
| **RECTANG** | Set the rectangle width, chamfer distances, or fillet radius. |
| **BASE** | Set the drawing's insertion base point. (Typically 0,0 is OK.) |
| **BLIPMODE** | Turn on blips if desired. |

Once the **AutoCAD Drawing Template File (\*.dwt)** extension has been selected, AutoCAD will change the **Save in:** location to the Template folder. Enter a name for the drawing template in the **File name:** text box and pick the **Save** button. This opens the **Template Description** dialog box, **Figure 11-11.** Enter a description for the template, such as 36" × 24" paper. The **Measurement** drop-down list contains two options: **English** and **Metric.** If **English** is selected, then AutoCAD uses English-scaled hatches and linetypes. If **Metric** is chosen, AutoCAD uses metrically scaled hatches and linetypes. Press the **OK** button when finished.

**Figure 11-10.**
Selecting the template extension from the **Files of type:** drop-down list in the **Save Drawing As** dialog box.

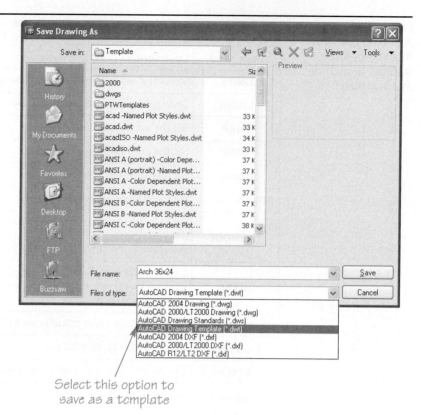

Select this option to save as a template

**Figure 11-11.**
The **Template Description** dialog box.

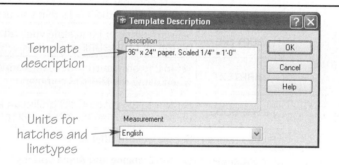

Template description

Units for hatches and linetypes

Your new template file is now available when you start a new drawing and can be found in the templates list. If after using the template you need to make changes to the file, open the DWT file and make the desired changes. Then, save the file as a template again. Remember that a template is a "living" document. It is constantly changed and updated. As new, productive ideas or standards become established in your office or class, implement them into your template.

## Exercise 11-5

◆ Open AutoCAD if it is not already open. Start a drawing with the acad.dwt or acadiso.dwt template file.
◆ Using the list in **Figure 11-9,** begin making the settings that you will need in the template.
◆ Set the limits for a 34" × 22" sheet of paper using a scale of 1/4" = 1'-0".
◆ Create layers that you will use frequently. See Appendix A for AIA layer naming conventions.
◆ Save the template as Arch_34"x22".dwt.
◆ Give the template a description.

*Answer the following questions on a separate sheet of paper.*

1. Identify at least four basic planning decisions.
2. Name the command that you can use to start a new drawing if you are already in an AutoCAD session.
3. Define *template*.
4. What does MDE stand for and what does it do?
5. What is *model space*?
6. What is *layout space*?
7. What are the model space drawing limits?
8. How do you enter 24′ at 45 degrees using polar coordinates?
9. How do you enter 24′ at 45 degrees 36 minutes and 15 seconds NW using polar coordinates?
10. Briefly explain the advantage of using a template.
11. Define *sheet size*.
12. How are multiple drawings displayed when they are opened at the same time?
13. Where is the name of each drawing displayed when multiple drawings are open?
14. How do you work on a currently open drawing that is not in the top drawing window?
15. What does the **Window** pull-down menu **Tile Horizontally** option do?
16. What does the **Window** pull-down menu **Cascade** option do?
17. Define *scale factor*.
18. Calculate the scale factor for a scale of 1/4″ = 1′-0″. Show your calculations.
19. Calculate the scale factor for a scale of 1″ = 20′. Show your calculations.
20. Calculate the scale factor for a scale of 1 mm = 20 mm. Show your calculations.
21. If you want 1/8″ high text on your plotted drawing, what height text do you specify if the final drawing scale is 1/4″ = 1′-0″? Show your calculations.
22. If you want 1/8″ high text on your plotted drawing, what height text do you specify if the final drawing scale is 1 mm = 20 mm? Show your calculations.
23. What command do you use to save a template that you have created?
24. Give the **Save as type** option that you should select when saving a template file.

# Chapter Problems

*The following problems can be saved as templates for future use. For Problems 1–5, use the* acad.dwt *or* acadiso.dwt *template as a starting point where appropriate.*

1. Create a template with an 11″ × 8.5″ area and decimal units. Name it A Size (H) Inches.dwt and include A size setup (horizontal) for decimal units for its description. You now have a template for doing inch drawings on 11″ × 8.5″ sheets.
2. Create a template with an 8.5″ × 11″ area and decimal units. Name it A Size (V) Inches.dwt and include A size setup (vertical) for decimal for its description. You now have a template for doing inch drawings on 8.5″ × 11″ (vertical) sheets.
3. Create a template with a 594 mm × 420 mm area and decimal units. Name it A2 Size Metric.dwt and include A2 size metric setup for its description. You now have a template for doing metric (millimeters) drawings on 594 mm × 420 mm (A2) sheets.
4. Create a template for a 17″ × 11″ area at a scale of 1/4″ = 1′-0″ (scale factor of 48). Use architectural units with 1/16″ precision, decimal degrees with 0 precision,

and default angular measure and orientation. Set the limits to 0,0 and 68',44'. Name it Arch_B-Size_17x11.dwt and include 17" × 11" paper. Scaled to 1/4" = 1'-0", architectural units for its description. You now have a template for doing drawings that will be plotted at a scale of 1/4" = 1'-0" on a 17" × 11" (B) sheet.

5. Create a template for a 22" × 17" area at a scale of 1/4" = 1'-0" (scale factor of 48). Use architectural units with 1/16" precision, decimal degrees with 0 precision, and default angular measure and orientation. Set the limits to 0,0 and 88',68'. Name it Arch_C-Size_22x17.dwt and include 22" × 17" paper. Scaled to 1/4" = 1'-0", architectural units for its description. You now have a template for doing drawings that will be plotted at a scale of 1/4" = 1'-0" on a 22" × 17" (C) sheet.

*For Problems 6–10, create a new template using an existing template as a model.*

6. Begin a new drawing and select the acad.dwt template. Use the **UNITS** command to set architectural units with 1/16" precision and decimal angles with 0 precision. The direction control should be set to the default values. Set the limits to 0,0 and 136',88'. Name the template Arch_D-Size_34x22.dwt and include 34" × 22" paper. Scaled to 1/4" = 1'-0", architectural units for its description. You now have a template for doing drawings that will be plotted at a scale of 1/4" = 1'-0" on a 34" × 22" (D) sheet.

7. Begin a new drawing and select the acad.dwt template. Use the **UNITS** command to set engineering units with 0'-0.00" precision and surveyor's units with N0d00'00"E precision. The direction control should be set to the default values. Set the limits to 0,0 and 360',240'. Name the template Eng_B-Size_18x12.dwt and include 18" × 12" paper. Scaled to 1" = 20'-0", engineering units, surveyor's angles for its description. You now have a template for doing drawings that will be plotted at a scale of 1" = 20'-0" on an 18" × 12" (B) sheet.

8. Begin a new drawing and select the acad.dwt template. Use the **UNITS** command to set engineering units with 0'-0.00" precision and surveyor's units with N0d00'00"E precision. The direction control should be set to the default values. Set the limits to 0,0 and 480',360'. Name the template Eng_C-Size_24x18.dwt and include 24" × 18" paper. Scaled to 1" = 20'-0", engineering units, surveyor's angles for its description. You now have a template for doing drawings that will be plotted at a scale of 1" = 20'-0" on a 24" × 18" (C) sheet.

9. Start a new drawing using the Architectural, English units – Color Dependent Plot Style.dwt template. Access the **Model space** tab. Use the **UNITS** command to set engineering units with 0'-0.00" precision and surveyor's units with N0d00'00"E precision. The direction control should be set to the default values. Set the limits to 0,0 and 720',480'. Name the template Eng_D-Size_36x24.dwt and include 36" × 24" paper. Scaled to 1" = 20'-0", engineering units, surveyor's angles for its description. You now have a template for doing drawings that will be plotted at a scale of 1" = 20'-0" on a 36" × 24" (D) sheet.

10. Start a new drawing using the Architectural, English units – Color Dependent Plot Style.dwt template. Access the **Model space** tab. Use the **UNITS** command to set architectural units with 1/16" precision and decimal angles with 0 precision. The direction control should be set to the default values. Set the limits to 0,0 and 144',96'. Name the template Arch_D-Size_36x24.dwt and include 36" × 24" paper. Scaled to 1/4" = 1'-0", architectural units, decimal angles for its description. You now have a template for doing drawings that will be plotted at a scale of 1/4" = 1'-0" on a 36" × 24" (D) sheet.

# CHAPTER 12

# Preliminary Design

## Learning Objectives

After completing this chapter, you will be able to:

- Create bubble diagrams.
- Create preliminary design sketches from bubble diagrams.
- Insert images into AutoCAD.
- Change the display order of AutoCAD objects.
- Control the display of images.
- Measure distances with the **DIST** command.
- Calculate the square footage of a building with the **AREA** command.
- Use the **BOUNDARY** command to establish areas.
- Use the **LIST** command to get information about an AutoCAD object.

## Important Terms

blips
boundary set
bubble diagram
clipping boundary
conceptual design
design criteria

islands
preliminary design
raster images
scanner
vector images

This text takes a small building project through the construction documentation process. In addition, in the chapters that follow, several building projects are presented as end-of-chapter problems. These projects can be developed using the principles discussed in successive chapters. This chapter discusses the conceptual, or preliminary, design phase. The chapters that follow address other steps in the architectural design process, from drawing floor plans, elevations, and sections all the way to plotting.

# Introduction to the Planning Process

The *conceptual design,* also called *preliminary design,* begins once the design criteria have been established for the building. *Design criteria* are guidelines or rules for the design process determined by the client and the architect. Some factors considered when establishing the design criteria are the desired style, client needs, financial considerations, and available materials.

The conceptual design process often begins with a bubble diagram. A *bubble diagram* is usually a freehand sketch showing the proposed floor plan layout. Rooms are represented as sketched circles or blocks, known as *bubbles.* See **Figure 12-1.** Bubble diagrams can also be created in a paint program or drawn with circles and rectangles in AutoCAD. Sketching programs are also available, including Architectural Studio from Autodesk and SketchUp from @Last Software. The architect may make several bubble diagrams until one of the designs provides a satisfactory arrangement.

## Creating a Design Sketch in AutoCAD

The next step of the conceptual design is to lay out a design sketch from the bubble diagram. This sketch allows the architect to see if the bubble diagram converts to a scaled sketch. During this stage of planning, the actual room sizes are taken into consideration.

AutoCAD can be used as a quick layout tool by referring to the bubble diagram and using a series of rectangles, polygons, circles, and lines to approximate the size of the rooms. These simple diagrams can later be used in the development of the construction documents. See **Figure 12-2.**

**Figure 12-1.**
Bubble diagrams are created in the preliminary design phase. A—A diagram created with circles. B—A diagram drawn by sketching.

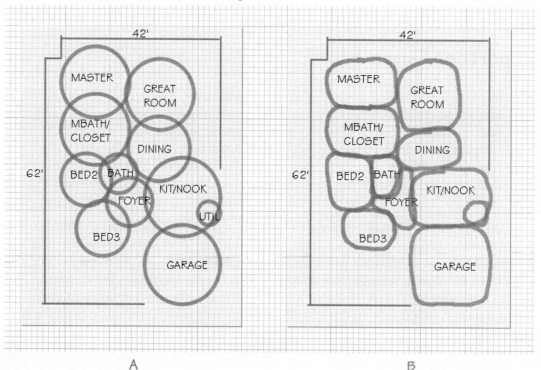

A                                        B

**Figure 12-2.**
A simple design sketch of a small house using rectangles and polylines to lay out the basic room sizes and orientation. Some detail is added to help convey the idea of the layout.

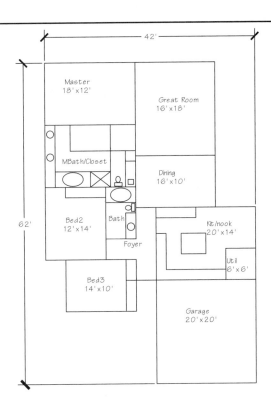

You can use the **RECTANG** command and relative coordinates to lay out rooms. For example, if a room is to be 12'-0" × 18'-0", use the following process:

Command: **rectang**↵
Specify first corner point or [Chamfer/Elevation/Fillet/Thickness/Width]: *(pick a point in the drawing)*
Specify other corner point or [Dimensions]: **@12',18'**↵
Command:

Details such as cabinetry and stair locations can be drawn with polylines or lines. Items such as toilets and sinks can be inserted into the design sketch using predrawn symbols.

**Professional Tip**

Often, the architect or designer refers to the hand-sketched bubble diagram for approximate sizes and arrangement of rooms and spaces when creating the design sketch in AutoCAD. If the bubble diagram has been created with approximate proportions, use an architect's scale to transfer proportions to the AutoCAD design sketch.

## Using Bubble Diagrams in AutoCAD

A *scanner* is a device that takes a picture or image and converts it into digital form. Once the image has been saved as an electronic file, it can be stored and viewed using a computer. The **IMAGE** command is used to bring an image into AutoCAD.

There are two basic types of images. *Raster images* are composed of many tiny dots. *Vector images* are composed of geometric shapes, such as lines and circles. AutoCAD drawings are vector images.

A bubble diagram can be scanned to create an electronic file. The file can then be inserted into AutoCAD. You can trace over the image using lines, rectangles, polylines, and other AutoCAD objects.

In this example, the bubble diagram for the house is a scanned image that is brought into AutoCAD. It is scaled and then traced with standard AutoCAD objects.

## Inserting Images

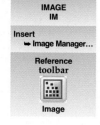

Before inserting a scanned image, it is a good idea to create a layer for the image. Set this layer current before inserting the image.

The **Image Manager** dialog box provides tools for locating, inserting, and removing image files. Use the **IMAGE** command to access this dialog box by selecting **Image Manager...** from the **Insert** pull-down menu, entering im or image at the Command prompt, or picking the **Image** button on the **Reference** toolbar. The **Image Manager** dialog box is shown in **Figure 12-3**.

To add an image to an AutoCAD drawing, select the **Attach...** button in the **Image Manager** dialog box. This opens the **Select Image File** dialog box, **Figure 12-4**.

**Figure 12-3.**
The **Image Manager** dialog box provides tools for inserting and removing image files.

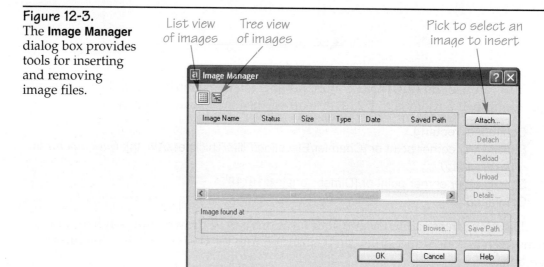

**Figure 12-4.**
The **Select Image File** dialog box allows you to browse through folders to select and open an image file.

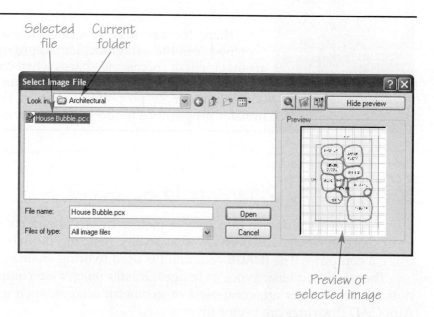

**Note**

You can also access the **Select Image File** dialog box by selecting **Raster Image...** from the **Insert** pull-down menu.

Browse through folders on the computer to locate the image file. Select the image and then pick the **Open** button. This displays the **Image** dialog box shown in **Figure 12-5**.

The **Image** dialog box indicates which image file is being inserted and the different parameters for the insertion. The features in this dialog box are described as follows:

- **Browse... button.** Picking this button opens the **Select Image File** dialog box, where you can select a different image file.
- **Retain Path check box.** When this check box is selected, AutoCAD saves the folder path for the image file in the drawing. If the **Retain Path** check box is not selected, AutoCAD searches through only the support file search path for the image file when the drawing is opened.
- **Insertion point area.** This area allows you to specify the insertion point for the selected image. If the **Specify on-screen** check box is checked, AutoCAD prompts you for a location for the image. Uncheck this box to specify the absolute coordinates for the lower-left corner of the image.
- **Scale area.** This area allows you to specify the scale factor for the selected image. If the **Specify on-screen** check box is checked, AutoCAD prompts you for a scale for the image after the insertion point has been selected. Uncheck this check box to specify a scale in the dialog box.
- **Rotation area.** This area allows you to specify the rotation angle of the image. If the **Specify on-screen** check box is checked, AutoCAD prompts you for a rotation angle for the image after the scale has been entered. Uncheck this check box to specify a rotation in the dialog box.
- **Details button.** Pick this button to display the **Image Information** area, which provides information regarding the image width, height, and resolution.

**Figure 12-5.**
The **Image** dialog box indicates the settings to be used for placing the image.

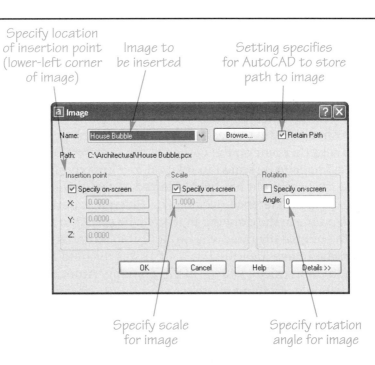

When you pick the **OK** button, the dialog box closes and AutoCAD prompts for information to be specified on screen. The following prompt sequence is shown if the insertion point and scale are specified on screen:

> Specify insertion point <0,0>: *(pick a point in the drawing)*
> Base image size: Width: *current*, Height: *current*, Inches
> Specify scale factor <1>: *(enter a scale or pick a point to scale the image)*

This places the image into your drawing. Notice that there is a border around the image in the current color. Do not be overly concerned with the scale at this point; you can use the **SCALE** command to accurately scale the image. **Figure 12-6** illustrates the bubble diagram image inserted into a drawing.

**Figure 12-6.**
The bubble diagram image inserted into the drawing.

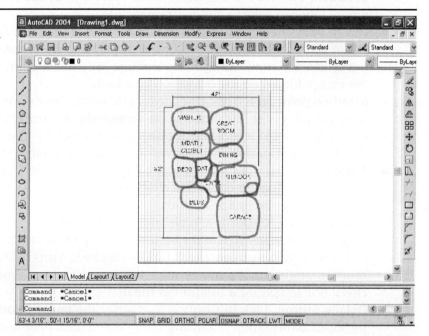

## Scaling the Image

Before the image can be traced over with rectangles and lines, the image needs to be scaled so that it is approximately full scale in AutoCAD. Use the **SCALE** command to do this. When you enter the **SCALE** command, AutoCAD prompts you to select objects. Select the image border. This selects the image. Now, press the [Enter] key when finished selecting objects to be scaled. When prompted for a base point, it is useful to select a point on the corner of the sketched building. See **Figure 12-7.** This allows the image to be scaled in relation to a known point on the image.

Once the base point has been selected, AutoCAD prompts for a scale factor. You can also use the **Reference** option. The **Reference** option allows you to pick (reference) two points in the drawing that are to be scaled to a specific length. For example, assume the bubble diagram was brought into AutoCAD and was not full scale. Two points on the image identified as a 40′ distance could be selected with the reference option, and then scaled to 40′-0″ in the drawing. AutoCAD then scales all the selected objects, scaling everything relative to the length specified.

**Figure 12-7.**
When using the **SCALE** command with the bubble diagram image, pick a base point on a corner of the sketched building. Use a dimensioned distance with the **Reference** option.

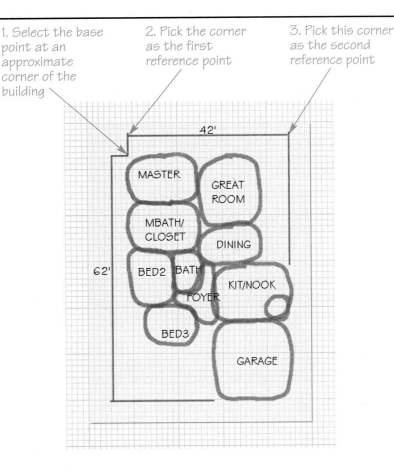

1. Select the base point at an approximate corner of the building

2. Pick the corner as the first reference point

3. Pick this corner as the second reference point

In this case, the bubble diagram has a few dimensions noting approximate sizes. These can be used to scale the image. Refer to **Figure 12-7** as you follow through the prompt sequence:

    Command: **sc** *or* **scale**↵
    Select objects: *(pick the image border)*
    1 found
    Select objects: ↵
    Specify base point: *(pick a corner of the building)*
    Specify scale factor or [Reference]: **r**↵
    Specify reference length <1>: *(pick the upper-left corner of the building)*
    Specify second point: *(pick the upper-right corner of the building)*
    Specify new length: **42'**↵
    Command:

Once the length has been entered, AutoCAD scales the image to a full scale. You may have to zoom out of the drawing to see the full-scaled image.

Note — When scaling an image with the **Reference** option, the image may not be 100% accurate. If the image is a sketch with rough sizes, it is not drawn precisely. Also, scaling the image increases the line width and length. However, the **Reference** option is a good starting place when you plan to trace over an image. When tracing over an image with AutoCAD objects, always draw the objects as the correct size.

## Creating an AutoCAD Sketch from an Image

Once the image of the bubble diagram has been inserted into the AutoCAD drawing and scaled, you can create a more accurate sketch. With this method, rather than referring to a hand-drawn sketch, the image has been scaled in AutoCAD and can be traced.

Use a series of rectangles, polygons, and lines to trace over the image. Using drawing aids such as running object snap modes, Snap mode, and polar tracking can be helpful in laying out the sketch.

Tracing over the image may not be completely accurate. Use the image as a guide, but draw objects based on the dimensions included in the sketch. Use rectangles and relative coordinates to draw correct room sizes.

After tracing the bubble diagram, you no longer need the image. You can either freeze the layer containing the image or *detach* the image. This is discussed later in this chapter. You can then add text to the design sketch. Rooms should be labeled by name and size. Most layer conventions require a separate layer for text. This layer can be given a name such as A-Anno-Sket, text, or notes. The finished sketch for the house should appear similar to **Figure 12-2**.

## Exercise 12-1

- Start the Microsoft Paint program. (From the Windows Start menu, select Programs, then Accessories, and finally Paint.)
- Use the Microsoft Paint program to sketch a bubble diagram of the house similar to the one in **Figure 12-1**. Include the dimensions to be used as a reference for scale.
- Save the file as House Bubble.bmp.
- Start a new drawing using one of your templates.
- Set architectural units.
- Set the limits to 144′ × 96′ (use a 36″ × 24″ sheet with a scale factor of 48).
- Create a layer called X-Image, assign a color, and set it current.
- Insert the House Bubble.bmp image into the drawing.
- Use the **SCALE** command with the **Reference** option to scale the image.
- Create a layer called M-Sketch, assign a color, and set it current.
- Using rectangles, lines, and polylines, draw a sketch for the house similar to **Figure 12-2**. Use the image as a reference for room locations and sizes.
- Create a layer named M-Notes. Add room names and sizes.
- Save the drawing as ex12-1.

**Professional Tip**

If the dimensions supplied in the bubble diagram are incorrect, alert the architect or designer. The sizes may reflect design criteria that cannot change due to lot size, client preference, or building codes. Do not make changes without the original designer's approval. In some offices, drafters may add minor walls, fixtures, and other items to the preliminary sketches.

# Managing Images in a Drawing

Suppose after the first bubble diagram was inserted into AutoCAD, the architects decided that they would like to also see an image of the site plan in the drawing. When the site plan is inserted, it covers the bubble diagram and sketch, as shown in **Figure 12-8.** In order to view the bubble diagram, you must change the display order of the images.

**Figure 12-8.**
The site plan brought into the drawing with the bubble diagram. The bubble diagram is "hidden" by the site plan.

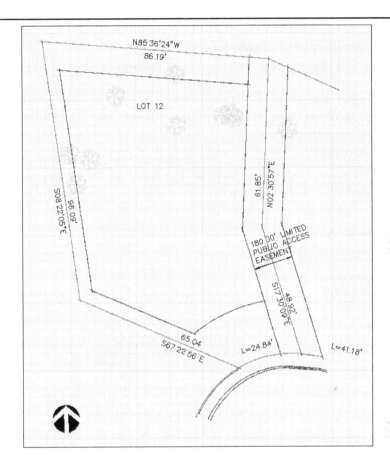

| Note | It should be noted that the site plan is being brought into the drawing to serve as a reference only. This gives the designers an understanding of whether or not their ideas are valid. Due to the scaling, images cannot be completely accurate. The site plan should be drawn separately in AutoCAD later during the construction document phase. For more information on site plans, refer to Chapter 14. |
| --- | --- |

# Changing the Display Order of Objects

When drawing in AutoCAD, the object last created or inserted is displayed above any previously drawn objects. In this case, the last object inserted is the site plan. The **DRAWORDER** command allows you to select which objects are displayed in front of other objects.

The **DRAWORDER** command can be accessed by selecting an option from the **Display Order** cascading menu in the **Tools** pull-down menu, picking the **Draworder** button in the **Modify II** toolbar, or entering dr or draworder at the Command prompt. The following command sequence moves the site plan to the back of the drawing:

Command: **dr** *or* **draworder.**⏎
Select objects: *(pick the site plan image border)*
1 found
Select objects: ⏎
Enter object ordering option [Above object/Under object/Front/Back] <Back>: ⏎
Regenerating model.
Command:

This sends the site plan to the back of the drawing, displaying the bubble diagram and design sketch on top of the site plan. See **Figure 12-9**.

**Figure 12-9.**
The site plan moved to the "back" of the drawing with the **DRAWORDER** command.

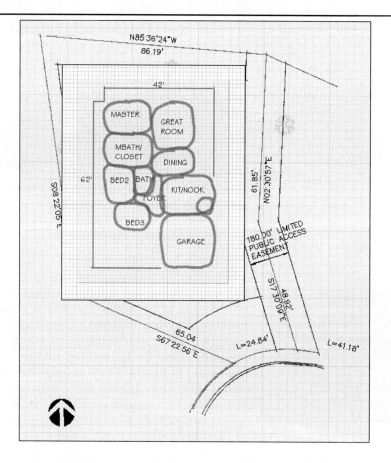

The **DRAWORDER** command options are also available in the **Display Order** cascading menu in the **Tools** pull-down menu. The following is a description of the **DRAWORDER** options:

- **Bring Above Object**. This option moves selected objects above another object.
- **Send Under Object**. This option moves selected objects below another object.
- **Bring to Front**. This option moves selected objects to the front of the drawing.
- **Send to Back**. This option moves the selected objects to the back of the drawing.

**Note** The **DRAWORDER** command may need to be used on several objects until the "order" of objects is displayed correctly. When an object is modified, it is moved to the front of the drawing.

### Exercise 12-2

◆ Open ex12-1.
◆ Use the **DRAWORDER** command to change the display order of the house sketch and bubble diagram.
◆ Experiment with the other **DRAWORDER** options by inserting another image into the drawing.
◆ Save the drawing as ex12-2.

## Managing Images

The **Image Manager** is used to manage a number of images in your drawing. Images contained in the drawing can be displayed in two ways. See **Figure 12-10**. List view displays the image name, along with specific details such as the file path, whether or not the image is loaded, and the file size, file type, and creation date. Tree view lists the drawing name and the names of the images contained in the drawing. The display method is selected using the buttons in the upper-left corner of the **Image Manager** dialog box.

## Removing an Image

Now that the sketch has been completed and the site plan has been added to the drawing, there is no more need for the bubble diagram. Use the **Image Manager** to delete an image from a drawing. In the **Image Manager** dialog box, select the image to be removed from the list. The buttons to the right of the dialog box become enabled. See **Figure 12-11**. Select the **Detach** button to detach the image from the drawing. Press the **OK** button when finished. This removes the selected image from the drawing. See **Figure 12-12**.

The remaining options and features in the **Image Manager** include the following:

- **Unload.** This option removes the image from the drawing, but the image remains listed in the **Image Manager** dialog box. The image name, folder location, insertion point, and scale remain with the drawing. If an image has been unloaded and you want to insert it into the drawing again, use the **Reload** option.
- **Reload.** This option reloads an image that has been unloaded. If the image has not been unloaded, the most recent version of the file is reloaded. Reloading an image updates the image to reflect any changes made to the original image file.
- **Details.** This option displays the **Image File Details** dialog box. This dialog box contains information regarding the image, including the file name and path, file size, and image size.
- **Image found at area.** This area displays the full folder path for the image file.
  - **Browse.** This option allows you to browse for a different path location for an image file. If the image was brought into the drawing without the **Retain Path** check box checked, the **Browse** button can be used to locate the file path location.

**Figure 12-10.**
The **Image Manager** displays the names of all images in the drawing. A—Images displayed in list view. B—Images displayed in tree view.

List View
*button*

Tree View
*button*

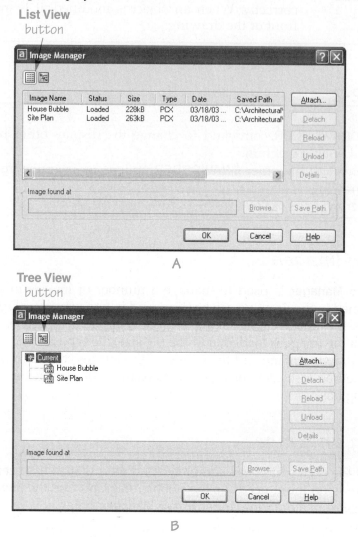

A

B

**Figure 12-11.**
Enable the buttons on the right of the **Image Manager** dialog box by selecting one of the listed images.

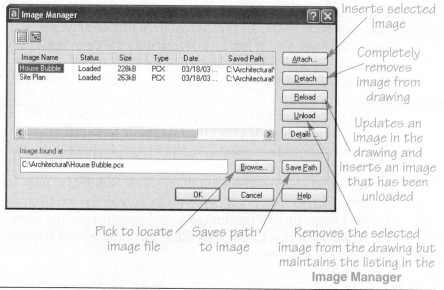

Inserts selected image

Completely removes image from drawing

Updates an image in the drawing and inserts an image that has been unloaded

Pick to locate image file

Saves path to image

Removes the selected image from the drawing but maintains the listing in the **Image Manager**

**Figure 12-12.**
The bubble diagram
image is detached
from the drawing.

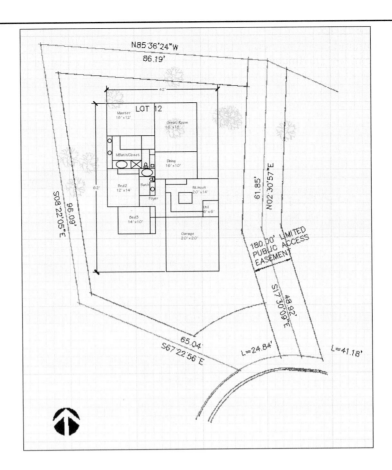

- **Save Path.** After a path has been located, you can save the path so AutoCAD can locate the file in the future.

## Controlling the Display of Images

Along with freezing and thawing layers, unloading and reloading images, and controlling their display order, there are a few other ways to control the appearance of images. You can adjust the image properties, select which portion of the image to display, and control the display of the image border.

Commands used to modify images can be accessed from the **Reference** toolbar and by selecting the **Image** cascading menu from the **Object** cascading menu in the **Modify** pull-down menu. You can also pick an image border and right-click to access a shortcut menu with an **Image** cascading menu. See **Figure 12-13**.

### Adjusting Images

The **Image Adjust** dialog box is used to adjust the brightness, contrast, and fade of an image. You can access this dialog box by picking the **Image Adjust** button in the **Reference** toolbar, by selecting **Image** and then **Adjust...** from the **Object** cascading menu in the **Modify** pull-down menu, or by entering iad or imageadjust at the Command prompt. You can also select an image in the drawing area, right-click, and select **Adjust** from the **Image** cascading menu in the shortcut menu. The **Image Adjust** dialog box is shown in **Figure 12-14.**

Adjust the brightness, contrast, and fade of the selected image by moving the slider bars. A preview of the image is displayed in the dialog box, allowing you to preview your changes before exiting the dialog box. If you need to reset the changes back to the default values, pick the **Reset** button.

IMAGEADJUST
IAD

Modify
↪ Object
↪ Image
↪ Adjust...

Reference
toolbar

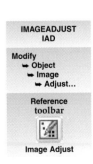

Image Adjust

**Figure 12-13.**
Commands used to modify images can be accessed in several ways. A—The **Reference** toolbar. B—The **Image** cascading menu. C—A shortcut menu is displayed by selecting an image in the drawing area and right-clicking.

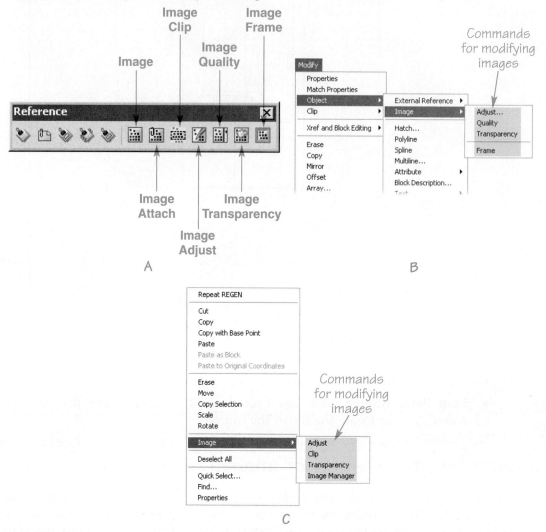

**Figure 12-14.**
The **Image Adjust** dialog box is used to control the appearance of the image.

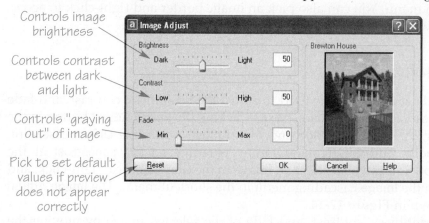

# Clipping Images

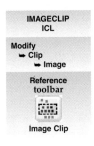

IMAGECLIP
ICL

**Modify**
➥ Clip
➥ Image

Reference
toolbar

Image Clip

Another useful tool for images is the **IMAGECLIP** command. This command allows you to trim, or clip, a portion of the image so it does not display in the drawing. To access the command, pick the **Image Clip** button in the **Reference** toolbar, select **Image** from the **Clip** cascading menu in the **Modify** pull-down menu, or enter icl or imageclip at the Command prompt. You can also highlight an image in the drawing area, right-click, and select **Image** and then **Clip** from the shortcut menu.

When clipping an image, you define a *clipping boundary.* Only the portion of the image within the clipping boundary is displayed after the clipping procedure. You have a choice of creating a rectangular or polygonal clipping boundary. If the image portion you want displayed is rectangular, use a rectangular boundary by picking two corner points. If the image portion is not rectangular, use a polygonal boundary and pick the points needed to define the boundary. When you finish selecting points for the boundary, press the [Enter] key. This clips away the portion of the image outside the clipping boundary.

For example, the following sequence clips a portion of the site plan image using the polygonal option:

> Command: **icl** *or* **imageclip**↵
> Select image to clip: *(pick the border of the image to be clipped)*
> Enter image clipping option [ON/OFF/Delete/New boundary] <New>: ↵
> Enter clipping type [Polygonal/Rectangular] <Rectangular>: **p**↵
> Specify first point: *(pick a point on the image)*
> Specify next point or [Undo]: *(pick a point on the image)*
> Specify next point or [Undo]: *(pick a point on the image)*
> Specify next point or [Close/Undo]: *(continue picking points until the boundary is defined)*
> Specify next point or [Close/Undo]: ↵

The clipped site plan image is shown in **Figure 12-15.**

**Figure 12-15.**
Clipping the site plan image using a polygonal clipping boundary.

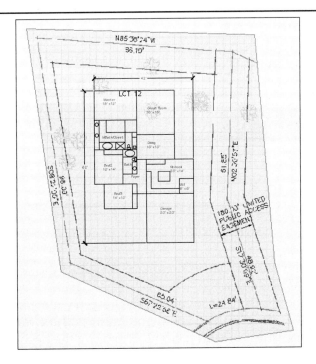

The **Delete** option removes an existing clipping boundary, displaying the entire image. To remove a clipping boundary temporarily, use the **OFF** option. You can then use the **ON** option to reactivate a boundary that has been turned off.

Only one clipping boundary can be associated with an image at any time. If the **IMAGECLIP** command has already been used on an image and a new clipping is desired, accessing the **New boundary** option causes AutoCAD to display the prompt Delete old boundary?. Press the [Enter] key to accept the default value of **Yes**, which deletes the old boundary. You can then specify a new boundary. If you select the **No** option, the command ends.

## Controlling the Image Border Display

The only way to select an image for editing is by picking the image frame. In order for an image to be selected for standard editing commands—such as **MOVE**, **COPY**, **ROTATE** and **DRAWORDER**—the image frame must be displayed. However, if the image frame is displayed when you plot a drawing, the frame is also plotted. Therefore, there are times when you want to deactivate the display of image frames.

IMAGEFRAME

Modify
→ Object
→ Image
→ Frame

Reference
toolbar

Image Frame

The **IMAGEFRAME** command controls the display of image frames. You can access this command by picking the **Image Frame** button in the **Reference** toolbar, selecting **Frame** from the **Image** cascading menu in the **Object** cascading menu of the **Modify** pull-down menu, or by entering imageframe at the Command prompt.

AutoCAD displays the prompt Enter image frame setting [ON/OFF]. Enter off to turn off all image frames in the drawing. Once image frames have been turned off, images cannot be selected.

> **Note**
>
> If image frames are turned off, selecting one of the image commands (such as **IMAGECLIP** or **IMAGEADJUST**) automatically turns on the image frames.

> **Professional Tip**
>
> If an image is displayed in front of standard AutoCAD objects, you can change the display order while image frames are not displayed by selecting the objects and moving them in front of the image. Use the Window or Crossing selection option to select objects hidden by the image.

## Exercise 12-3

◆ Open ex12-1.
◆ Use the **DRAWORDER** command to bring the bubble diagram to the front of the drawing.
◆ Use the **IMAGEADJUST** command to adjust the brightness and contrast of the bubble diagram.
◆ Use the **IMAGECLIP** command to clip away the edges of the image.
◆ Use the **IMAGEFRAME** command to turn off the frame.
◆ Use the **DRAWORDER** command to bring the design sketch objects to the front of the drawing.
◆ Save the drawing as ex12-3.

Architectural Drafting Using AutoCAD

# Obtaining Information from the Sketch

As the design process progresses toward the construction document phase, it is often important to begin finalizing details of the building, such as accurate room sizes and square footages. The following section walks you through the process of obtaining information from the sketched drawings.

## Measuring Distances

DIST
DI

Tools
➥ Inquiry
➥ Distance

Inquiry
toolbar

Distance

The **DIST** command measures the distance between two points. This command can be used to measure the length of a wall, the interior dimensions of a room, or the distance between a building and a property line. Often, the **DIST** command can be used to verify room sizes and building dimensions in the design sketch.

To access the **DIST** command, pick the **Distance** button in the **Inquiry** toolbar, select **Distance** from the **Inquiry** cascading menu in the **Tools** pull-down menu, or enter di or dist at the Command prompt.

Once the **DIST** command has been activated, AutoCAD prompts you to specify two points. AutoCAD measures the distance between these two points and returns the value in the command window. In the following command sequence, the **DIST** command is used to measure a distance in a floor plan sketch. Refer to **Figure 12-16**.

Command: **di** *or* **dist.**⏎
Specify first point: *(pick the first point)*
Specify second point: *(pick the second point)*
Distance = 18'-0", Angle in XY Plane = 0.00, Angle from XY Plane = 0.00
Delta X = 18'-0", Delta Y = 0'-0", Delta Z = 0'-0"

**Figure 12-16.**
When you use the **DIST** command, use object snap modes to ensure accurate point selection.

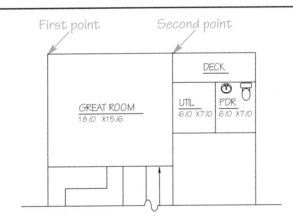

Once the second point has been picked, AutoCAD returns the distance between the two points. Other values are provided along with the distance. See **Figure 12-17** for a description of these other values.

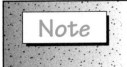

Note    When measuring distances, it is often a good idea to use object snap modes to establish accurate points for measurement.

**Figure 12-17.**
These diagrams illustrate the values reported by the **DIST** command.

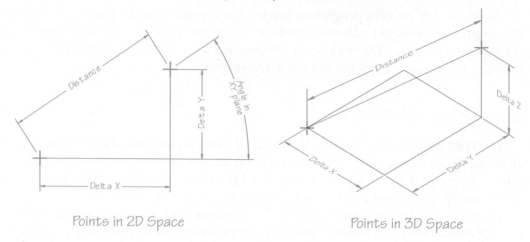

Points in 2D Space          Points in 3D Space

## Exercise 12-4

◆ Open ex12-3.
◆ Use the **DIST** command to verify the overall width and length of the house.
◆ Verify the room sizes using the **DIST** command. If the distances are wrong, use the **MOVE**, **ERASE**, and **COPY** commands to adjust the objects.
◆ Save the drawing as ex12-4.

## Obtaining the Square Footage of a Building

Once the design sketch is complete and the room sizes have been verified, it is often necessary to obtain the square footage of the building. The **AREA** command is used for this purpose.

Before using the **AREA** command, you may want to make several settings for tools that can help when finding areas. The running object snap modes Endpoint, Midpoint, and Perpendicular can be helpful when obtaining area. A second tool that can be helpful is the display of *blips*. *Blips* are temporary marks that appear on screen at each point in your drawing where you have picked a point.

Use the **BLIPMODE** command to turn blips on and off. Enter blipmode at the Command prompt, and then enter on or off to control the display of blips. When Blip mode is on, a blip is displayed every time a point is picked. Blips do not print and can be removed from the screen by entering r or redraw at the Command prompt. See **Figure 12-18**.

Now that the running object snap modes are set and Blip mode is activated, the **AREA** command can be used to measure the total area on the main floor of the house. To access the **AREA** command, select the **Area** button in the **Inquiry** toolbar, select **Area** from the **Inquiry** cascading menu in the **Tools** pull-down menu, or enter aa or area at the Command prompt. AutoCAD returns the prompt below:

Specify first corner point or [Object/Add/Subtract]:

The default prompt requests the first corner point to be used in the area calculation. Pick a corner of the building. Continue selecting points around the perimeter of the building until the last corner has been selected. AutoCAD automatically closes the area by connecting the first and last points. When the last point has been picked, press [Enter] to end the command. AutoCAD provides the area and perimeter of the selected area:

**AREA**
**AA**

**Tools**
↳ Inquiry
  ↳ Area

**Inquiry**
**toolbar**

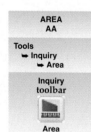

**Area**

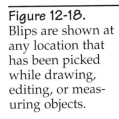

**Figure 12-18.**
Blips are shown at any location that has been picked while drawing, editing, or measuring objects.

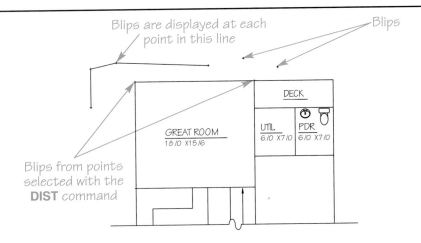

Blips are displayed at each point in this line

Blips

Blips from points selected with the **DIST** command

Area = 289152.00 square in. (2008.0000 square ft.), Perimeter = 220'-0"
Command:

**Figure 12-19** shows the points picked to find the area of the house. The blips serve as visual reminders of the points defining the area.

**Figure 12-19.**
When Blip mode is on and the **AREA** command is used, AutoCAD displays a blip at each point that is picked.

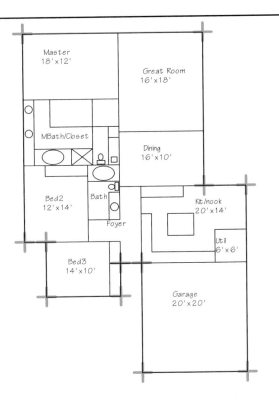

| Note | If you are using architectural units, AutoCAD displays area in square inches and square feet. If you are using decimal units, AutoCAD displays area as square units. |

## Adding and Subtracting Areas

The **AREA** command has an **Add** option and a **Subtract** option. Use the **Add** option to add a series of areas together. Use the **Subtract** option to remove a section of a selected area. In **Figure 12-20**, the area of the garage is subtracted from the total area of the house measured in **Figure 12-19**. To begin this process, access the **AREA** command, and select the **Add** option to start the Add mode. The prompt sequence is as follows:

Command: **aa** *or* **area**↵
Specify first corner point or [Object/Add/Subtract]: **a**↵
Specify first corner point or [Object/Subtract]: *(pick the first point of the area)*
Specify next corner point or press ENTER for total (ADD mode): *(pick points to define the total area)*

Notice that AutoCAD recognizes that you are in Add mode. Continue picking points to measure the total area of the house, as shown in **Figure 12-19**. When finished selecting points, press the [Enter] key. AutoCAD returns the total area and perimeter of the added area, but remains in the **AREA** command so you can add another area or go into Subtract mode.

Area = 289152.00 square in. (2008.0000 square ft.), Perimeter = 220'-0"
Total area = 289152.00 square in. (2008.0000 square ft.)
Specify first corner point or [Object/Subtract]:

Enter s to enter the Subtract mode and select the points that are to be subtracted from the total area measured in the Add mode. Refer to **Figure 12-20**.

Specify first corner point or [Object/Subtract]: **s**↵
Specify first corner point or [Object/Add]: *(pick the first point of the area to be subtracted)*
Specify next corner point or press ENTER for total (SUBTRACT mode): *(pick points to define the area to be subtracted)*

**Figure 12-20.**
The area of the garage is subtracted from the total area of the house by using the Add and Subtract modes of the **AREA** command.

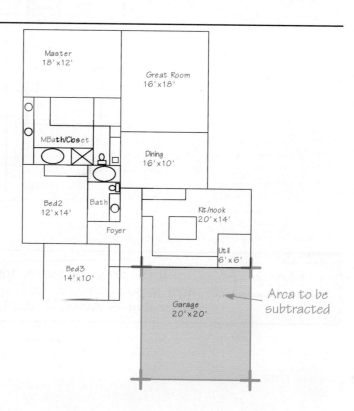

Architectural Drafting Using AutoCAD

When finished selecting the points to be subtracted, press the [Enter] key. AutoCAD returns the area and perimeter of the subtracted area, and then the total area of the house minus the subtracted area:

Area = 57600.00 square in. (400.0000 square ft.), Perimeter = 80'-0"
Total area = 231552.00 square in. (1608.0000 square ft.)

When completely finished obtaining the total area, press the [Enter] key to exit the **AREA** command.

## Exercise 12-5

◆ Open ex12-4.
◆ Use the **AREA** command to obtain the total area of the house.
◆ Use the **AREA** command with the Add mode to obtain the area of the house again, then enter the Subtract mode to subtract the garage area.
◆ Use the **MTEXT** command to place a note indicating the square footages of the house and garage areas.
◆ Save the drawing as ex12-5.

## Calculating the Area of a Closed Object

The **Object** option of the **AREA** command allows you to find an area of a closed object. For example, you can quickly calculate the area of a polyline, circle, rectangle, or polygon.

If an area is going to be measured, polylines are often used to define different spaces of the building. The polylines can then be used to quickly find the areas of individual rooms. Before obtaining specific room sizes from the house plan, create a layer for the polylines that will define the perimeters of each room or space. A layer called M-Area is created, assigned a color, and set current.

To create the polyline perimeters, the **PLINE** command can be used. You can also use the **BOUNDARY** command. To use the **BOUNDARY** command, pick **Boundary...** from the **Draw** pull-down menu or enter bo or boundary at the Command prompt. This displays the **Boundary Creation** dialog box, **Figure 12-21**. The **Object type** drop-down list contains two settings: Polyline and Region. The Polyline setting is the default. If the option is set to Polyline, AutoCAD creates a polyline around the area. If it is set to Region, AutoCAD creates a closed 2D area. Regions may be used in the creation of 3D objects.

Boundary
BO

Draw
➥ Boundary...

Figure 12-21.
Use the **Boundary Creation** dialog box to create polyline boundaries and regions.

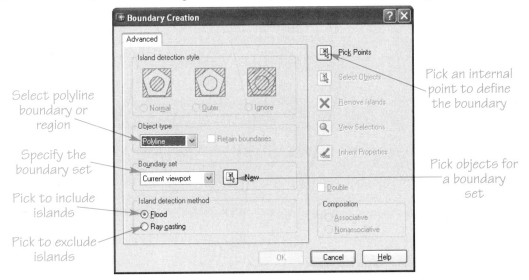

The **Boundary set** drop-down list has the Current viewport setting active. A *boundary set* is the portion of the drawing or area that AutoCAD evaluates when defining a boundary. The Current viewport option defines the boundary set from everything visible in the current viewport. The **New** button allows you to define a boundary set. When you pick this button, the **Boundary Creation** dialog box closes and you can select the objects to be included in the boundary set. After you are done selecting objects, press [Enter]. The **Boundary Creation** dialog box returns with Existing set listed in the **Boundary set** drop-down list. This means that the boundary set is defined from the objects that you selected. By creating a boundary set, AutoCAD evaluates only a portion of the objects on screen in order to create the boundary, which speeds up the process.

The **Island detection method** area is used to specify whether objects within the boundary are used as boundary objects. Objects inside a boundary are called *islands*. See **Figure 12-22**. There are two options in the **Island detection method** area. Activate the **Flood** radio button if you want islands to be included as boundary objects. Activate the **Ray casting** radio button if you do not want to include islands as boundary objects.

The only other active feature in the **Boundary Creation** dialog box is the **Pick Points** button, located in the upper-right corner. When you pick this button, the **Boundary Creation** dialog box closes and the Select internal point: prompt appears. If the point you pick is inside a closed polygon, the boundary is highlighted, as shown in **Figure 12-23**. If the point you pick is not within a closed polygon, the **Boundary Definition Error** alert box appears. Pick the **OK** button, correct the problem by closing the area in which you want to pick, and try picking the internal point again. When you are finished selecting internal points, press [Enter] and new polylines are traced over the top of the closed objects. See **Figure 12-24**. The shaded portions in this example represent the boundary areas created for the rooms and spaces of the house.

**Figure 12-22.**
Objects within a boundary (islands) can be included or excluded when defining a boundary.

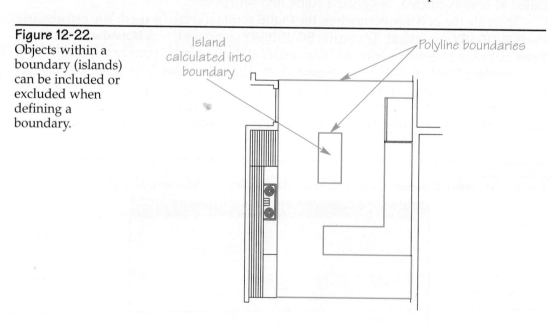

Island calculated into boundary

Polyline boundaries

Architectural Drafting Using AutoCAD

**Figure 12-23.**
When you select a point inside a closed polygon, the boundary is highlighted, indicating where the boundary will be created.

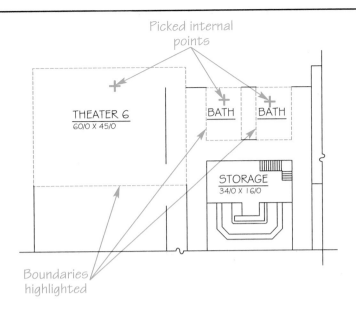

**Figure 12-24.**
Polyline boundary objects created for each room and space of the house plan.

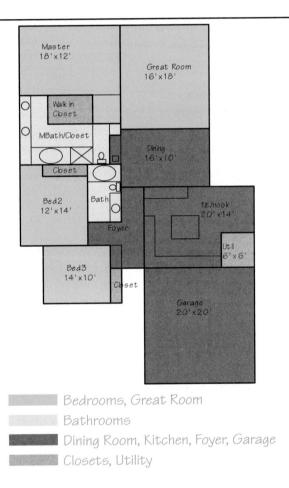

Now that the boundaries have been created, the layers containing the original objects can be frozen so only the boundaries are displayed. In **Figure 12-25**, area calculations are made for each room and space in the house. To obtain the area values, use the **AREA** command with the **Object** option. Only one object can be selected at a time when using the **Object** option.

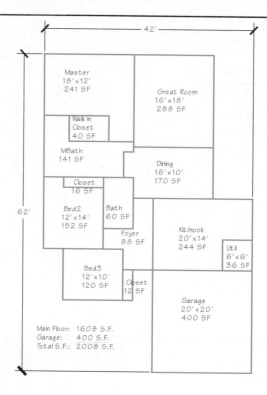

**Figure 12-25.**
Calculate the square footage of each room and space using the polyline boundary objects.

The figure shows a floor plan with the following labeled rooms:

- Master 18'×12' 241 SF
- Great Room 16'×18' 288 SF
- Walk in Closet 40 SF
- MBath 141 SF
- Dining 16'×10' 170 SF
- Closet 16 SF
- Bed2 12'×14' 152 SF
- Bath 60 SF
- Foyer 88 SF
- Kit/nook 20'×14' 244 SF
- Util 6'×6' 36 SF
- Bed3 12'×10' 120 SF
- Closet 12 SF
- Garage 20'×20' 400 SF

Overall dimensions: 42' and 62'

Main Floor: 1608 S.F.
Garage: 400 S.F.
Total S.F.: 2008 S.F.

Command: **aa** *or* **area**↵
Specify first corner point or [Object/Add/Subtract]: **o**↵
Select objects: *(pick an object to obtain an area)*
Area = *nn.nn* square in. (*nn.nn* square ft.), Perimeter = *n′-n″*

If several areas are to be added together, use the **Add** option to access the Add mode, then use the **Object** option while in Add mode to select several boundaries to be added together:

Command: **area**↵
Specify first corner point or [Object/Add/Subtract]: **a**↵
Specify first corner point or [Object/Subtract]: **o**↵
(ADD mode) Select objects: *(pick the first boundary)*
Area = *nn.nn* square in. (*nn.nn* square ft.), Perimeter = *n′- n″*
Total area = *nn.nn* square in. (*nn.nn* square ft.)
(ADD mode) Select objects: *(pick additional boundaries until all are selected)*
Area = *nn.nn* square in. (*nn.nn* square ft.), Perimeter = *n′- n″*
Total area = *nn.nn* square in. (*nn.nn* square ft.)
(ADD mode) Select objects: ↵
Specify first corner point or [Object/Subtract]: ↵

**Professional Tip**

Finding square footage is an important process in architectural drafting. Without an accurate square footage, the amounts of materials for a project could be inadequately ordered and priced. The square footage of a building is also important for contractor bids and local building jurisdiction requirements for lighting, ventilating, and landscaping.

## Exercise 12-6

- Open ex12-5.
- Freeze the X-Image layer, where the image is located.
- Use the **DIST** command to verify the overall width and depth of the house plan and the room sizes.
- Use the **MOVE**, **COPY**, and **ERASE** commands respectively to adjust the drawing as needed.
- Create a layer called M-Area, assign a color, and set the layer current.
- Use the **BOUNDARY** and **POLYLINE** commands to create polyline boundaries around the rooms of the house plan.
- Freeze the M-Sketch layer.
- Use the **AREA** command in Add mode with the **Object** option to obtain the square footage of each room and space in the house.
- Set the M-Notes layer current. Use the **MTEXT** command to create a note of the square footage for each room in the house.
- Save the drawing as ex12-6.

## Listing Geometry

The **LIST** command allows you to display information about any AutoCAD object. Lines, polylines, text, blocks, circles, and rectangles all have specific properties. For example, listing a line object displays properties such as layer, starting and ending locations, length, and angle. The **LIST** command can be accessed by picking the **List** button in the **Inquiry** toolbar, selecting **List** in the **Inquiry** cascading menu in the **Tools** pull-down menu, or entering li, ls, or list at the Command prompt. The **LIST** command sequence is as follows:

LIST
LI
LS

Tools
➥ Inquiry
➥ List

Inquiry
toolbar

List

Command: **li**, **ls**, *or* **list**↵
Select objects: (*pick the first object to be listed*)
Select objects: ↵

The following information is shown for a line and an arc:

```
LINE                          Layer: layer name
                              Space: Model space

          Handle = nn
  from  point,    X=n'-n"    Y=n'-n"    Z=n'-n"
    to  point,    X=n'-n"    Y=n'-n"    Z=n'-n"
Length = n'-n", Angle in XY Plane = nn.nn
Delta X = n'-n", Delta Y = n'-n", Delta Z = n'-n"


ARC                           Layer: layer name
                              Space: Model space

          Handle = nn
center  point,    X=n'-n"    Y=n'-n"    Z=n'-n"
radius  n'-n"
 start  angle     nn.nn
   end  angle     nn.nn
length  n'-n"
```

The **LIST** command is especially useful when the length of a line or radius of an arc is desired. The **LIST** command can be used on any type of AutoCAD object. Practice using the **LIST** command on different types of objects.

## Exercise 12-7

◆ Open a previous exercise or drawing that contains several different types of objects.

◆ Use the **LIST** command to get information about some of the objects.

◆ Close the drawing without saving.

# Chapter Test

*Answer the following questions on a separate piece of paper.*

1. List three factors used to determine the design criteria in a building project.
2. Define *bubble diagram.*
3. What is a *raster image?*
4. What is a *scanner?*
5. How do you access the **Image Manager** dialog box?
6. Name the command that you can use to make the image approximately full size in AutoCAD.
7. For the image list in the **Image Manager** dialog box, which option displays more information: list view or tree view?
8. What is the purpose of the **DRAWORDER** command?
9. Explain the difference between detaching and unloading an image.
10. Which dialog box includes controls for the brightness, contrast, and fade of an image?
11. List the two types of clipping boundaries.
12. Name the command that controls display of image borders.
13. Name the command that is used to determine the distance between two points.
14. Name the command that is used for calculating area.
15. What units are given by AutoCAD when calculating area with architectural units?
16. When determining the total area of several separate regions, which command option would you use?
17. Define *blips.*
18. Name the command used to turn blips on or off.
19. Name the command that can be used to remove blips from the screen.
20. In addition to the **PLINE** command, name a command that can be used to create a polyline perimeter around an area.
21. Define *boundary set.*
22. What are *islands?*
23. What is the purpose of the **Flood** option in the **Island detection method** area of the **Boundary Creation** dialog box?
24. What is the purpose of the **DRAWORDER** command?

*The drawing problems in this chapter involve four projects: two residential projects, one multifamily housing project, and one commercial project. In this chapter, you will create the project design sketch. This design sketch will be used as a base to build on for drawing problems in future chapters.*

1. Prepare a design sketch for the residence shown using the following procedure. Then, calculate the living area.
   A. Start a new drawing using one of your templates.
   B. Set architectural units.
   C. Set the limits to 144',96'. (The scale factor for the drawing is 48.)
   D. Create a layer named M-Sketch and set it current.
   E. Draw the following diagram as a design sketch. Do not dimension.
   F. Add the fixtures, doors, windows, and text on the M-Sketch layer. Be more concerned with locations than sizes. You will be adjusting these later in future chapters.
   G. Create a layer named M-Area and set it current.
   H. Draw a polyline around the living space of the house. Do not include the garage.
   I. Obtain the area of the house. Create text in the drawing to note the square footage.
   J. Save the drawing as 12-ResA.

Project

Residential A

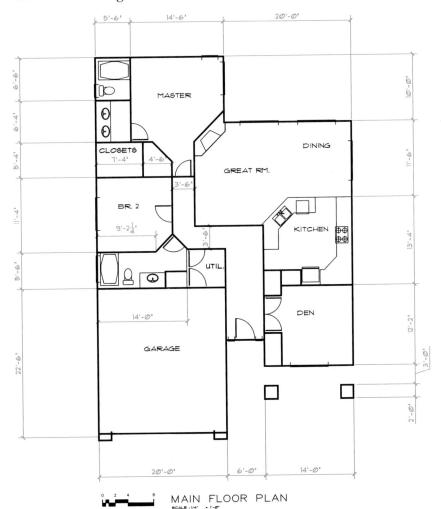

MAIN FLOOR PLAN
SCALE : 1/4" = 1'-0"

(Alan Mascord Design Associates, Inc.)

2. Residential Project B includes a second floor. You will add the upper floor plan into the same drawing as the main floor plan and use layer management to display the appropriate geometry.

A. Start a new drawing using one of your templates.
B. Set architectural units.
C. Set the limits to 144',96'. (The scale factor for the drawing is 48.)
D. Create layers named M-Sketch, U-Sketch, M-Area, and U-Area.
E. Set the M-Sketch layer current and create a design sketch for the main level. Add the fixtures, doors, windows, and text. Be more concerned with locations than sizes. You will be adjusting these later in future chapters. Do not dimension.
F. Set the M-Area layer current and draw a polyline around the living space of the main level.
G. Obtain the area of the main level. Create text in the drawing to note the square footage of the main level.
H. Lock the M-Sketch layer. Freeze the M-Area layer.
I. Set the U-Sketch layer current and create a design sketch for the upper level (shown on the following page). Be sure to line up the upper level and the main level. Change the color of the M-Sketch layer to make it easier to differentiate between the layers.
J. Freeze the M-Sketch layer when done referencing.
K. Determine the area of the upper floor house minus the staircase. The staircase has already been calculated at the main floor level. Use text in the drawing to note the square footage.
L. Save the drawing as 12-ResB.

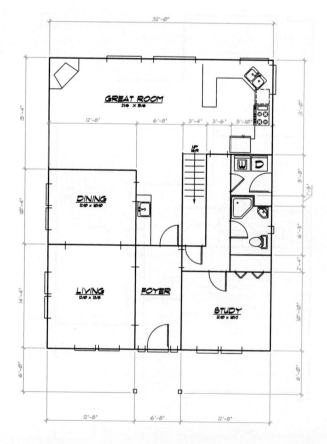

MAIN FLOOR                                                          SCALE: 1/4" = 1'-0"

(3D-DZYN)

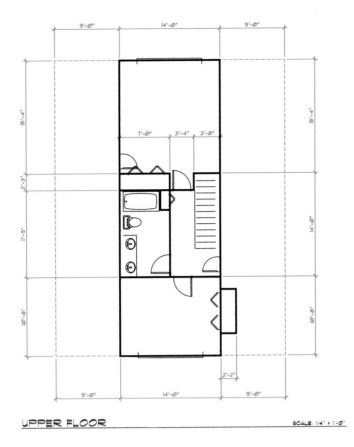

UPPER FLOOR                                    SCALE: 1/4" = 1'-0"

(3D-DZYN)

3.  The Multifamily Residence Project uses the AIA layer naming convention.
    A.  Start a new drawing using one of your templates.
    B.  Set architectural units.
    C.  Set the limits to 144',96'. (The scale factor for the drawing is 48).
    D.  Create layers named **A-Flor-Sket** and **A-Area**. Set the **A-Flor-Sket** layer current.
    E.  Draw a design sketch of the plan shown.
    F.  Determine the area of each of the three units and the total area. Record the square footage values with text.
    G.  Save the drawing as **12-Multifamily**.

Project

Multifamily

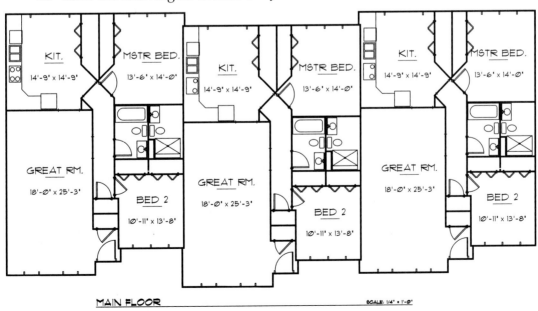

MAIN FLOOR                                     SCALE: 1/4" = 1'-0"

(3D-DZYN)

4. The Commercial Project involves the main and upper levels of a small commercial structure. The two plans will be created as separate drawings.

   A. Start a new drawing using architectural units. Set the limits to 288',192'. (The scale factor is 96).

   B. Create layers named A-Flor-Sket and A-Area. Set the A-Flor-Sket layer current.

   C. Draw a design sketch of the main level plan shown below without dimensions.

   D. Obtain the area of the main floor and use text to record the square footage.

   E. Save the drawing as 12-Commercial-Main.

   F. Create a new drawing using the same units, limits, and layers used in 12-Commercial-Main.

   G. Insert the 12-Commercial-Main drawing at a location of 0,0 and a scale of 1.

   H. Draw a design sketch of the upper level plan shown on the following page using the main floor as a reference. Do not dimension.

   I. Erase the 12-Commercial-Main drawing and purge the drawing.

   J. Obtain the area of the upper floor and use text to record the square footage.

   K. Save the drawing as 12-Commercial-Upper.

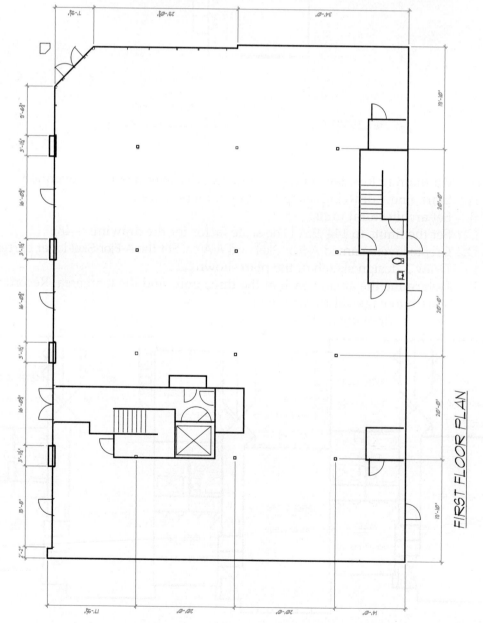

FIRST FLOOR PLAN

(Cynthia Bankey Architect, Inc.)

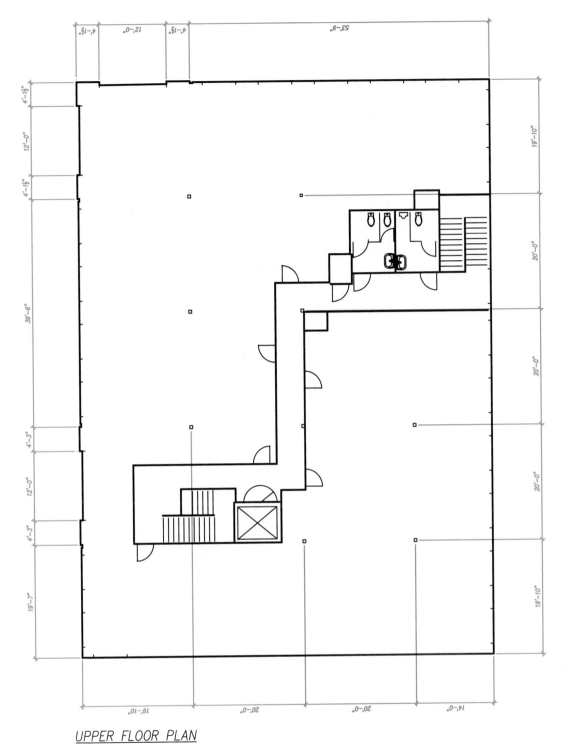

UPPER FLOOR PLAN

(Cynthia Bankey Architect, Inc.)

This chart lists the units of measure that can be converted using the **CVUNIT** function. This function, discussed in Chapter 13, is used with the AutoCAD geometry calculator. The units listed here are defined in the acad.unt file. You can customize this file to have additional units of measure available for conversion.

## Units Defined for Conversion with CVUNIT function

### Basic SI Units

meter(s), metre(s), m
kilogram(s), kg
second(s), sec
ampere(s), amp(s)
kelvin, k
candela, cd

### Derived SI Units

celsius, centigrade, c
rankine
fahrenheit
gram(s), gm, g
newton(s), n
pascal, pa
joule(s)

### Exponent Synonyms

square, sq
cubic, cu

### Units of Volume

barrel(s), bbl
board_f(oot.eet), fbm
bushel(s), bu
centiliter(s), cl
cord(s)
cc
decistere(s)
dekaliter(s), dal
dekastere(s)
dram(s)
dry_pint(s)
dry_quart(s)
firkin(s)
gallon(s), gal
gill(s)
hectoliter(s)
hogshead(s), hhd
kilderkin(s)
kiloliter(s)
liter(s)
milliliter(s), ml
minim(s)
fluid_ounce(s)
peck(s)
pint(s), fluid_pint(s)
pottle(s)
puncheon(s)
quart(s), qt, fluid_quart(s)
register_ton(s)
seam(s)
stere(s)
tun(s)

### Circular Measure

circle(s)
radian(s)
degree(s)
grad(s)
quadrant(s)

### Units of Length

Angstrom(s)
astronomical_unit(s), au
bolt(s)
cable(s)
caliber
centimeter(s), centimetre(s), cm(s)
chain(s)
cubit(s)
decimeter(s), decimetre(s), dm
dekameter(s), dekametre(s), dam
fathom(s), fath
f(oot.eet), ft, '
furlong(s), fur
gigameter(s), gigametre(s)
hand(s)
hectometer(s), hectometre(s), hm
inch(es), in(s), "
kilometer(s), kilometre(s), km
league_nautical
league_statute
light_year(s)
link(s)
microinch(es)
micron(s)
mil(s)
mile_nautical, inm
mile_statute, mile(s), mi
millimeter(s), millimetre(s), mm(s)
millimicron(s), nanometer(s),
   nanometre(s), nm(s)
pace(s)
palm(s)
parsec(s)
perch(es)
pica(s)
point(s)
rod(s), pole(s)
rope(s)
skein(s)
span(s)
survey_f(oot.eet)
yard(s), yd

### Units of Time

centur(y.ies)
day(s)
decade(s)
fortnight(s)
hour(s), hr
milleni(um.a)
minute(s), min
sidereal_year(s)
tropical_year(s)
week(s), wk
year(s), yr

### Solid Measure

sphere(s)
hemisphere(s)
steradian(s)

### Units of Area

acre(s)
are(s)
barn(s)
centare(s)
hectare(s)
rood(s)
section(s)
township(s)

### Units of Mass

dalton(s)
dyne(s)
grain(s)
hundredweight(s), cwt
long_ton(s)
ounce_weight, ounce(s), oz
ounce_troy
pennyweight(s), dwt, pwt
poundal(s)
pound(s), lb
scruple(s)
slug(s)
stone
ton(s)
tonn(e.es)

### Units of Frequency

hertz, hz

### Electromagnetic Units

coulomb(s)
farad(s)
henr(y.ies)
ohm(s)
siemens
tesla(s)
volt(s), v
watt(s), w
weber(s)

### Dimensionless Prefixes

deca
hecto
kilo
mega
giga
tera
peta
exa

### Fractions

deci
centi
milli
micro
nano
pico
femto
atto

# CHAPTER 13

# Interior Planning

## Learning Objectives

After completing this chapter, you will be able to:

- Explain the space planning process.
- Formulate a design program.
- Use the AutoCAD geometry calculator.
- Create a space diagram.
- Discuss the importance of a furniture symbol library.
- Use the **GROUP** command to group blocks.
- Create object selection filters.

## Important Terms

design program
filter
geometry calculator
group
grouping

interior layout
nesting
relative operator
space diagram
space planning

Interior planning can be broken down into two areas: space planning and interior layout. *Space planning* is the study of space and how the flow of space works in an architectural design. *Interior layout* uses the space plan and establishes the layout of furniture, equipment, and electrical and mechanical fixtures.

## Space Planning

Space planning is an architectural specialty. Some architectural firms provide a space planning service, while others do not. Space planning is a study of the internal relationships that make a space work for the client. It is not the same as interior layout. The architect/space planner studies the client's needs and prepares flow diagrams and text describing the internal relationships and functions of the space. The space planning process involves studying the following:

- **General space requirements.** Space can be divided into departments, and the departments are then divided into areas such as storage, office, and support areas. The required square footage for each area is specified.
- **Adjacency requirements.** The space planner must study the relationships between areas and within departments. *Adjacent spaces* are spaces or areas located next to each other. *Near spaces* should not be separated by more than one space.
- **Functionality requirements.** Together with the client, the space planner must analyze the operation and functions of the client's business and make sure that the space plan fulfills these requirements.
- **Flexibility.** In most instances, the space plan must include provisions for flexibility of interior space and potential future expansion.
- **Equipment/machinery.** The space plan must take into account any large equipment or machinery that will be installed.
- **Traffic patterns.** Human foot traffic, vehicular traffic, and special materials traffic all have a substantial impact on the space plan.

After evaluating the client's needs, create a design program. The *design program* lists the required spaces for the building. For each space, note an approximate square footage, adjacency requirements, and any other considerations.

Suppose your client is an engineering firm. After consultation with the client, a simplified version of the design program is developed. The following items identify a design program for this example:

- A large open DRAFTING space is required. This space should be approximately 8000 square feet (SF).
- Near the drafting space is the PRINT room. The print room should be located in a remote place away from offices and the public because it is noisy. The print room should be 250 SF.
- A SHOP space for building models is required near the print room and the drafting space. This shop space should be approximately 250 SF.
- Four private OFFICES are required. These offices are to be near the entry, adjacent to one another, and near the drafting space.
- The RECEPTION area should be large enough to hold two work desks and all the office files. The reception area should be 250 SF.
- A small ENTRY lobby with seating for four clients is required. It should be adjacent to the foyer and near the reception area.
- The FOYER lobby should be adjacent to the reception area.
- A small CONFERENCE room is also required. This conference room should have a table large enough to seat 14 people.
- The ACCOUNTING department requires a 300 SF space.
- Two RESTROOMS occupying a total of 240 SF (15′ ×16′) are needed.

You can use the above criteria as a basis for the development of the plan. One of the first things to create is a 1′-0″ unit block for spaces. In Chapter 9, you learned how to create and use 1″ unit blocks. In this case, creating a 1′-0″ unit block makes it easier to create large spaces. For example, a 1′-0″ unit block can be scaled by 12 along the X axis and by 16 along the Y axis to create a 12′ × 16′ room equaling 192 square feet. **Figure 13-1** displays the 1′-0″ unit block. Remember to create the block on layer 0 and use either ByBlock or ByLayer colors, linetypes, and lineweights.

Professional Tip

You can also use the **RECTANG** command to create spaces. Pick the first corner point and then use relative coordinates to specify the other corner of the space. For example, if a space is 12′ × 10′, enter @12',10' for the second corner point.

Architectural Drafting Using AutoCAD

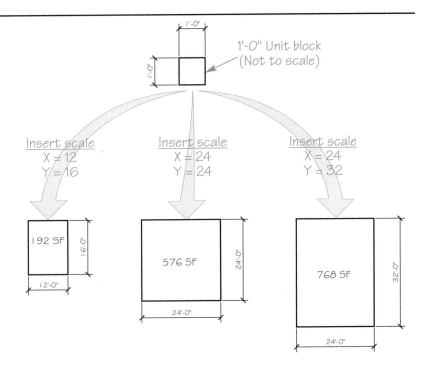

**Figure 13-1.**
A 1'-0" unit block can be inserted at different scales to produce different sized spaces.

# Using the AutoCAD Calculator

When inserting a unit block, the insertion scale can be variable and based on objects or locations in a drawing, or it can be based on a given square footage as in space planning. An AutoCAD feature known as the *geometry calculator* can be used to help determine the room size for a given square footage.

AutoCAD's geometry calculator allows you to extract and use existing information in your drawing. The geometry calculator also allows you to perform basic mathematical calculations at the command line. In addition, you can also supply an expression as input to a prompt.

Access the geometry calculator by entering cal at the Command prompt. You are then prompted for an expression. After you enter the mathematical expression and press [Enter], AutoCAD automatically simplifies the expression, as shown in the following example:

Command: **cal**⏎
>> Expression: **2+2**⏎
4
Command:

## Basics of the Geometry Calculator

To use the geometry calculator, you must understand the ordering and format of an expression. The geometry calculator evaluates expressions according to the standard mathematical rules of precedence. This means that expressions within parentheses are simplified first, starting with the innermost set and proceeding outward. Mathematical operators are evaluated in the standard order: exponents first, multiplication and division next, followed by addition and subtraction. Operators of equal precedence are evaluated from left to right.

## Making Numeric Entries

The same methods of entering numeric values at AutoCAD prompts are acceptable for calculator expressions. When entering feet and inches, either of the accepted formats can be used. This means that 5'-6" can also be entered as 5'6". The 5'-6" value can also be entered as inches by entering 66. When a number expressed in feet and inches is entered, AutoCAD automatically converts to inches:

```
Command: cal↵
>> Expression: 24'-6"↵
294.0
```

> **Note**
> You must press [Enter] to complete an entry at the Expression: prompt. Pressing the space bar adds a space to your entry; it does not act as a return at this prompt.

## Using Basic Math Functions

The basic mathematical functions used in numeric expressions include addition, subtraction, multiplication, division, and exponential notation. Parentheses are used to group symbols and values into sets. The symbols used for the basic mathematical operators are shown in the following table:

| Symbol | Function | Example |
|--------|----------|---------|
| + | Addition | 3+26 |
| − | Subtraction | 270–15.3 |
| * | Multiplication | 4*156 |
| / | Division | 256/16 |
| ^ | Exponent | 22.6^3 |
| ( ) | Grouped expressions | 2*(16+2^3) |

The following examples use each type of mathematical function shown in the previous table:

```
Command: cal↵
>> Expression: 24'+12'↵
432.0 (inches)
```

```
Command: cal↵
>> Expression: 18'6"–12'3"↵
75.0 (inches)
```

```
Command: cal↵
>> Expression: 12*18.25↵
219.0
```

```
Command: cal↵
>> Expression: 250/25↵
10.0
```

Command: **cal⏎**
\>\> Expression: **9^2⏎**
81.0

Command: **cal⏎**
\>\> Expression: **(24'+12')/12⏎**
36.0 *(inches)*

**Professional Tip**

The geometry calculator has limits when working with integer values. (An *integer* is a number with no decimal or fractional part.) Numeric values greater than 32,767 or less than –32,768 must be presented as real numbers. When working with values outside this range, enter a decimal point and a zero (.0) after the value.

## Exercise 13-1

◆ Open a drawing and use the **CAL** command to make the following calculations:
  A. 24'-6" + 18'-4"
  B. 16.875 – 7.375
  C. 1'-4" + 9"
  D. (25.75 ÷ 4) + (5.625 × 3)
  E. (4'-8" × 3) + (3'-9" ÷ 3)

## Determining Room Size from Square Footage

The space planning process assigns a square footage to each area or room. In order to create a preliminary design sketch, the square footage must be converted into room dimensions. If you know the square footage and you select one dimension for a room, you can calculate the second dimension. For example, if an office needs to have an area of 150 SF and you want the office to be 10' wide, calculate the second dimension by dividing the square footage by the width. When you enter the numbers using the geometry calculator, express all numbers in units of feet and do not include the foot mark symbol ('). For example:

Command: **cal⏎**
\>\> Expression: **150/10⏎**
15.0

The foot marks cannot be used in this application because you do not include units for the square footage value. The result returned by AutoCAD is also expressed in feet. Thus, the office in this example measures 10'-0" × 15'-0" and has a square footage of 150 SF.

## Exercise 13-2

◆ The following lists the square footage and width for a room. Use the geometry calculator to find the remaining room dimension:
   A.   250 SF ÷ 25'-0"
   B.   300 SF ÷ 15'-0"
   C.   320 SF ÷ 20'-0"
   D.   288 SF ÷ 18'-0"
   E.   400 SF ÷ 20'-0"
   F.   120 SF ÷ 12'-0"

## Making Unit Conversions

The calculator has a **CVUNIT** function that lets you convert one type of unit into another. For example, inches can be converted to millimeters, or liters can be converted to gallons. The formula for the **CVUNIT** function is:

CVUNIT(value,from_units,to_units)

The following example converts 4.7 kilometers to the equivalent number of feet:

Command: **cal**↵
>> Expression: **cvunit(4.7,kilometers,feet)** ↵
15419.9

If the units of measure you specify are either incompatible or are not defined in the acad.unt file, an error message is displayed and the prompt is reissued.

The **CVUNIT** function can work with units of distance, angles, volume, mass, time, and frequency. The units available for conversion are specified in the file acad.unt found in the AutoCAD 2004 Support folder. This file can be opened with Microsoft Notepad and can be edited to include additional units of measure if needed. Microsoft Notepad can be accessed from AutoCAD by entering notepad at the Command prompt. The command sequence is as follows:

Command: **notepad**↵
File to edit: *(enter a path and file name or press* [Enter] *to open Microsoft Notepad)*

There are more complex features of the geometry calculator available. These are discussed later in this text.

## Exercise 13-3

◆ Start a new drawing and use the geometry calculator to make the following conversions:
   ◆ 8.625" to millimeters
   ◆ 34.5 mm to inches
   ◆ 5.5 kilometers to miles
   ◆ 12 gallons to liters
   ◆ 47 hours to minutes

## Arranging Spaces

A *space diagram* is a sketch or drawing representing the spaces and adjacency requirements specified in the design program. You can create a space diagram based on a preliminary design program. Any changes made to the design program must be reflected in the space diagram.

To create a space diagram, start a new drawing and create a layer for the space diagram. Create a unit block and then insert and scale the block to create a rectangle for each space. Add text listing the name, square footage, and dimensions for each space. Use the geometry calculator as needed to determine room sizes from the required square footages. Add arrows to the space diagram to indicate the adjacency relationships between the spaces. **Figure 13-2** illustrates a space diagram for the sample design program developed earlier in this chapter.

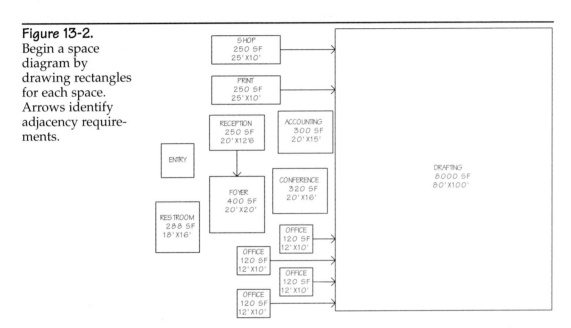

**Figure 13-2.**
Begin a space diagram by drawing rectangles for each space. Arrows identify adjacency requirements.

The square footages of the entry, foyer, and conference room are not defined in the design program. The conference room is defined only by the furniture to be used. You need to determine the size of a 14-seat conference table to develop the space diagram for the conference room. Furniture catalogs can be used to make this decision. A 20′ × 16′ area is determined to be sufficient to hold a conference table with 14 chairs. Thus, the conference space becomes 320 SF. A foyer space of 200 SF is designated as a working number only and can change during the space planning process.

The addition of space names, sizes, and square footages can aid in the preliminary stages of space planning. Be generous with your space allocations in the preliminary stages of design. The client may want to add features, such as a storage room or coffee bar. The designer is probably not prepared to make specific furniture selections at this point, but has the spaces sketched in the drawing and can now arrange the pieces to determine a space design.

Now that most of the spaces are defined, you can arrange the space diagram to develop your space plan. A designer generally selects three or four layouts for consideration. **Figure 13-3** shows one possible configuration for the engineering office.

**Figure 13-3.**
This space diagram shows one possible arrangement of spaces. Several arrangements should be considered before making a final decision.

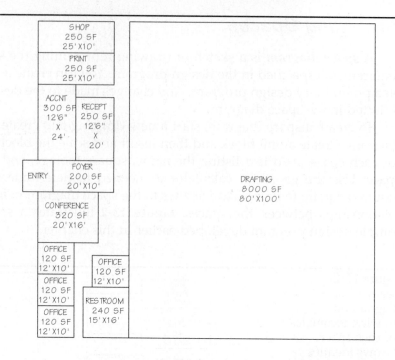

## Exercise 13-4

- ◆ Create a space diagram based on the design program discussed in the text with the following changes:
  - ◆ Change the DRAFTING room area to 5000 SF.
  - ◆ Change the CONFERENCE room area to 216 SF.
  - ◆ Change the RESTROOM area to 216 SF.
  - ◆ Adjust the FOYER room area as needed.
- ◆ Save your drawing as ex13-4.

**Professional Tip**

If space planning is a big part of your drawing process, begin creating blocks with tag names, square footages, and sizes for common rooms. Place these in a space planning folder or a space planning drawing file. This allows you to create a library of spaces that can be easily inserted into new drawings.

## Interior Layout

As the spaces and their dimensions are finalized, interior layout can begin. *Interior layout* is the selection and placement of furnishings within a space.

Interior designers have thousands of products to consider. A furniture catalog library often exceeds the size of an architectural library. The selection of furniture is generally based on product design, cost, product availability, and suitability to the project.

A great deal of the interior designer's time is spent managing this library. Furniture manufacturers are constantly updating and adding features to their product line. Many manufacturers create AutoCAD block libraries for their products. Sources on the Internet also provide thousands of furniture blocks.

Architectural Drafting Using AutoCAD

**Figure 13-4.**
The Home-Space Planner drawing found in the Sample\DesignCenter folder contains some generic furniture blocks.

AutoCAD provides some generic libraries of furniture blocks in drawings located in the Sample\DesignCenter folder. The Sample office project tool palette also includes several office furniture blocks. **Figure 13-4** displays a few blocks found in the Home-Space Planner drawing. As discussed in Chapter 10, DesignCenter's **DC Online** tab provides access to manufacturer web sites where blocks can be downloaded for insertion into drawings. Standard blocks can be modified to match a specific manufacturer's sizes.

## Developing a Furniture Library

The organization of blocks is an important consideration in the development of company standards. When organizing furniture blocks, separate the furniture into groups. For example, if you are responsible for the furniture layout of an office building, there may be several different types of desks and chairs available. Create one folder on the hard drive for desk blocks and another folder for chair blocks. This makes locating the type of block easy when using **DesignCenter**. Another alternative is to create a drawing file or tool palette for each category of block symbols. For example, a single drawing or tool palette could contain all desk blocks.

**Professional Tip**

As you compile a drawing of symbols, you may want to create a tool palette from the file so that the symbols are readily available in the **Tool Palettes** window. This reduces the time spent locating the blocks through **DesignCenter**.

## Exercise 13-5

◆ Open ex13-4.
◆ Create several office furniture blocks for a typical workstation. Include a desk, lamp, computer, and chair.
◆ Create a conference table with chairs around it.
◆ Create cubicle panels for the work areas. Typical panel lengths include 2′, 3′, 4′, 5′, and 6′.
◆ Create one 8′ × 8′ drafting workstation in the drafting area.
◆ Add the conference table and chairs to the CONFERENCE room.
◆ Add several pieces of furniture to one office.
◆ Create a couch, chair, plant, and coffee table for the FOYER.
◆ Add two desks for the RECEPTION area.
◆ Save the drawing as ex13-5.

## Grouping Blocks Together

When creating drawings for interior layouts, many furniture blocks are scattered throughout the drawing. There are instances where it is useful to combine several blocks into a single object. For example, in some offices, furniture is allocated to one person and moves with the person during an office move. The blocks for the chair, desk, telephone, and computer within an office can be linked together and selected with a single pick. The process of linking separate objects to form a single selection object is called *grouping*.

The **GROUP** command is used to group blocks together. If one piece of furniture in the group is selected, all blocks in the group are selected. This is particularly helpful when one employee is moving across the building and all of the employee's furniture must be moved.

A group is similar to a block. Individual objects included in the group are all part of the group. However, the group is not one object (as are the elements of a block). A group maintains the characteristics of all of the individual objects that make up the group. Thus, objects within a single group can maintain individual property settings, such as layer, color, and linetype.

A *group* is a named selection set. Groups are saved with a drawing, so they exist between multiple drawing sessions. Objects can be members of more than one group and groups can be nested. *Nesting* means including one group as part of another group. It is used to place smaller groups into larger groups for easier editing.

An object can exist in more than one group. This can create interesting situations. For example, a desk block and chair block are grouped together, and then the chair is also grouped with a file cabinet. Moving the first group moves the desk and chair, and moving the second group moves the chair and file cabinet.

Grouping can be helpful when you want objects to be selectable as a block but still maintain their individuality. The **GROUP** command allows you to turn the group specification on or off. This is not possible with a block. Once a block has been exploded, it must be redefined or reinserted.

GROUP
G

The **GROUP** command can be accessed by entering g or group at the Command prompt. Either of these entry methods displays the **Object Grouping** dialog box, **Figure 13-5**.

There are many elements found in the **Object Grouping** dialog box. The **Group Name** text box displays the existing groups and lists whether the group is selectable. If a group is selectable, picking any object in it selects the entire group. Making a group not selectable allows the individual objects to be edited.

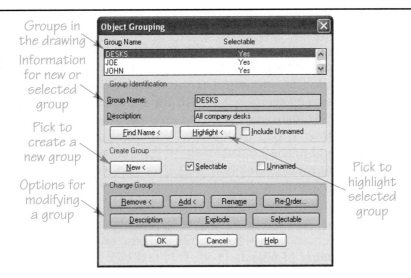

The **Group Identification** area has several components:
- **Group Name: text box.** This text box displays the name of a selected group. When creating a new group, enter the name of the new group in this box.
- **Description: text box.** This text box displays a description of the selected group. This area is also used to enter a description when creating a new group.
- **Find Name button.** When you pick this button, a Pick a member of a group: prompt appears. Pick an object and the **Group Member List** dialog box lists any groups with which the object is associated.
- **Highlight button.** Pick this button to highlight all members of the selected group. This allows you to see the drawing objects contained in the group. Then pick the **Continue** button or press [Enter] to return to the **Object Grouping** dialog box.
- **Include Unnamed check box.** When checked, this check box causes unnamed groups to be listed with named groups. Unnamed groups are created when you copy a group. (You are not only copying the objects belonging to the group, you are also copying the group association.) Unnamed groups are given a default name by AutoCAD in the format: *A$x$, where $x$ is an integer value that increases with each new group (for example, *A6). Unnamed groups can be named later using the **Rename** option.

The **Create Group** area contains the following options for creating a new group:
- **New button.** This button creates a new group. To create a new group, first enter a new name and description in the **Group Identification** area. Pick the **New** button, and AutoCAD issues a Select objects for grouping: prompt. Pick the objects to be included in the group. The new group is added into the list at the top of the **Object Grouping** dialog box.
- **Selectable check box.** A check in this check box sets the initial status of the **Selectable** value as Yes for the new group. A selectable group is selected if any object in the group is picked. Uncheck this check box to specify a group that is not selectable, where objects within the group can be selected and modified individually.
- **Unnamed check box.** This check box indicates whether the new group is named. If this box is checked, AutoCAD assigns a name.

The **Change Group** area of the **Object Grouping** dialog box contains the options for changing a group. The buttons are not highlighted until a group is selected in the **Group Name** text box. The options used to modify groups are described as follows:
- **Remove.** Pick this button to remove objects from a group definition.

- **Add.** This button allows objects to be added to a group definition.
- **Rename.** Pick this button to change the name of an existing group. Unnamed groups can be renamed if the **Include Unnamed** check box is selected.
- **Re-Order.** When defining a group, objects are numbered in the order they are selected. The first object is numbered 0, not 1. The **Re-Order** button allows objects to be reordered within the group. For example, if a group contains a set of text instructions, you can reorder the text to suit the steps that are used. The **Order Group** dialog box is displayed when you pick this button. See **Figure 13-6**. The main elements of this dialog box are briefly described as follows:
  - **Remove from position (0-$n$).** This text box allows you to enter the position number of the object to be reordered, where $n$ is the total number of objects found in the group.
  - **Enter new position number for the object (0-$n$).** This text box allows you to enter a new position number for the object.
  - **Number of objects (1-$n$).** This text box allows you to specify the object or range of objects to reorder.
  - **Re-Order.** Picking this button reorders the objects in the group.
  - **Highlight.** Picking this button allows you to sequence through the objects in the group and determine position numbers. See **Figure 13-7.**
  - **Reverse Order.** Picking this button reverses the order of all members in the group.
- **Description.** Pick this button to update the group with the new description entered in the **Description:** text box.
- **Explode.** Pick this button to delete the selected group definition, but not the group's objects. The group name is removed and the original group is exploded. By selecting the **Include Unnamed** check box, unnamed groups are displayed and can then be exploded, if needed.
- **Selectable.** Pick this button to toggle the selectable value of a group. This changes the value in the **Selectable** list.

**Figure 13-6.**
The **Order Group** dialog box allows you to reorder the objects in a group.

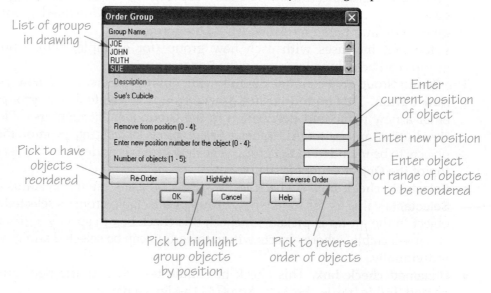

**Figure 13-7.**
Position numbers for objects in a group can be determined by cycling through the group.

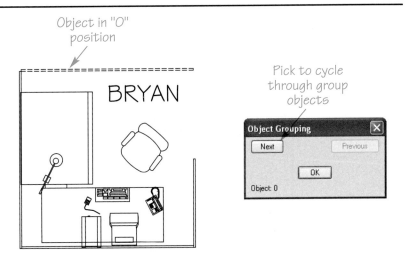

## Exercise 13-6

- ◆ Open ex13-5.
- ◆ Copy the drafting workstation four times.
- ◆ Use the **GROUP** command to create a group named DESKS. Make the group not selectable. Pick the **New** button and select all the desks.
- ◆ Use the **GROUP** command to create four groups with unique employee names. For each group, assign the objects within a workstation.
- ◆ Make all five groups selectable.
- ◆ Move the cubicles around the drafting area.
- ◆ Make the employee groups not selectable.
- ◆ Move a desk in the DESKS group.
- ◆ Make the DESKS group not selectable, and then move one desk.
- ◆ Explode the DESKS group and make the employee groups selectable.
- ◆ Save the drawing as ex13-6.

## Using a Filter to Select Objects

A *filter* is a set of properties or values that are needed for a specific object to be selected. Filters are created with the **FILTER** command. Similar to the **Quick Select** feature discussed in Chapter 6, this command allows you to find objects based on filter criteria. The advantage of the **FILTER** command is that filter lists can be created and saved in the drawing for later use. These filter lists are accessed at any Select object: prompt. The **FILTER** command can also be used transparently by entering 'filter at the Select object: prompt.

The **FILTER** command is accessed by entering fi or filter at the Command prompt. This opens the **Object Selection Filters** dialog box, **Figure 13-8.**

The three major areas of the **Object Selection Filters** dialog box are the list box, the **Select Filter** area, and the **Named Filters** area. The list box is where the current filter list data is displayed, the **Select Filter** area is used to specify filter criteria, and the **Named Filters** area is used to save filters for future use.

FILTER
FI

### Entering Filter Data

The **Select Filter** area of the **Object Selection Filters** dialog box is where filter data is entered. The drop-down list and edit boxes can be used to enter the values for the filters. Objects in a drawing can even be selected to develop a filter.

Figure 13-8.
The **Object Selection Filters** dialog box.

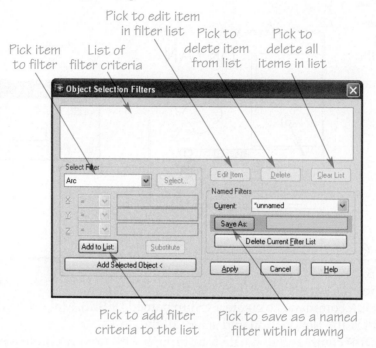

Pick to edit item in filter list

Pick to delete item from list

Pick to delete all items in list

Pick item to filter

List of filter criteria

Pick to add filter criteria to the list

Pick to save as a named filter within drawing

The three edit boxes correspond to X, Y, and Z point coordinates and other property settings. They are enabled as needed for entering different types of filter information. When the filter drop-down list reads Arc, it refers to an object type. Since no further information is required about the object type, the edit boxes are all disabled.

Setting the filter to Arc Center enables all three edit boxes, which are used to define the center point. When Arc Radius is selected, only the top edit box is enabled because only a single value is required. An example of each of these situations is shown in **Figure 13-9.**

For many filter specifications—such as layers, linetypes, and other object properties—the **Select...** button is enabled. The **Select...** button displays the appropriate dialog box for showing the available options. For example, if Color is the specified filter, picking the **Select...** button displays the standard **Select Color** dialog box. Once the desired filter and value are specified, pick the **Add to List:** button to add the new item to the existing filter list.

To use an existing object as a basis for a filter list, pick the **Add Selected Object** button. This gives you a Select object: prompt. Once an object is selected, you are returned to the **Object Selection Filters** dialog box. The information from the selected

Figure 13-9.
Examples of filter items. A point filter accesses the **X:**, **Y:**, and **Z:** edit boxes.

Object Filter
Edit Boxes Deactivated

Point Filter
All Three Edit Boxes Activated

Distance/Length Filter
One Edit Box Active

object is placed in the filter list. Since you may not need all of the filter list specifications that result from picking an object, the filter list can now be edited as needed. Editing the filter list is covered later in this chapter.

To introduce you to selection filters, the following example creates a simple filter list that selects only text objects.

Command: **fi** *or* **filter**↵

This displays the **Object Selection Filters** dialog box. In the **Select Filter** area, pick the drop-down list to see the selection filter options. From this list, select Text. To add this specification to the filter list, pick the **Add to List:** button. The list box now displays this selection criteria as Object = Text. See **Figure 13-10.** This shows that only text objects will be selected. To use the selection filter, pick the **Apply** button, and the following prompt is issued:

Applying filter to selection.
Select objects: *(window around the objects or enter* all*)*

The prompt tells you that the filter is active. In **Figure 13-11,** a selection window is created around a group of lines, blocks, and text. Because the filter is set to allow only text objects, all other object types are filtered out of the selection. AutoCAD reports the number of objects found and the number selected:

45 found 40 were filtered out.

To exit the filtered selection, press [Enter] at the Select objects: prompt. The message Exiting filtered selection appears on the command line and the selected objects are displayed with grips.

Filter lists can be expanded to select only objects with specific properties. The next example creates a filter list that selects only block objects that belong to a specific layer. Use the following steps:

1. Enter the **FILTER** command and clear the filter list by picking the **Clear List** button.
2. From the drop-down list in the **Select Filter** area, select Block, and then pick the **Add to List** button. This adds the filter Object = Block to the list.
3. Select Layer from the drop-down list, then pick the **Select...** button to display the **Select Layer(s)** dialog box.

**Figure 13-10.**
Setting a filter so that only text objects are selected.

Selection set criteria

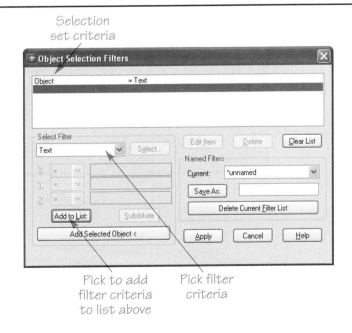

Pick to add filter criteria to list above

Pick filter criteria

**Figure 13-11.**
All objects are filtered out except the text objects. Selected objects are shown here in color.

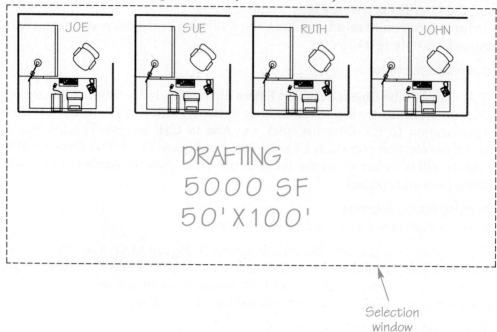

Selection
window

4. Select the A-Furn-Desk layer, pick the **OK** button, and then pick the **Add to List** button. The **Object Selection Filters** dialog box should appear as shown in **Figure 13-12.**

By adding more filters to the filter list, a filter can be extremely specific when needed. Filters for a specific location or a specific text string can be useful when selecting items in very large, complex drawings.

**Figure 13-12.**
Block objects on the A-Furn-Desk layer will be selected with this filter when applied.

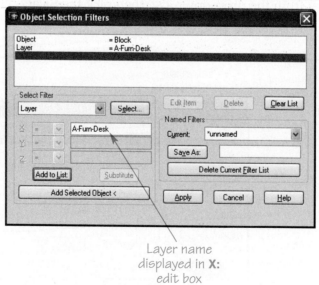

Layer name
displayed in **X:**
edit box

## Exercise 13-7

◆ Open ex13-6.
◆ Use the **FILTER** command to create a filter that selects only text.
◆ Use a selection window around all objects and observe which ones are selected.
◆ Create a layer named A-Furn-Desk.
◆ Use the **FILTER** command to create a filter for a block name. Use the **Select...** button to open the **Select Block Name(s)** dialog box and choose the desk block name. Apply the filter.
◆ With the desk blocks selected, right-click and select **Properties** from the shortcut menu. Change the layer of the desks to A-Furn-Desk.
◆ Save the drawing as ex13-7.

## Working with Relative Operators

The term *relative operator* refers to a function that determines the relationship between data items. These relationships include equality, inequality, greater than, less than, and combinations such as *greater than or equal to* and *less than or equal to*. Each of the three edit boxes in the **Select Filter** area are preceded by a relative operator drop-down list. An appropriate relative operator can be selected for each data field.

For example, a relative operator can be used to select all arcs that have a radius of 2.5 or greater. To do this, the filter specification is Arc Radius with 2.5 entered in the enabled edit box. Then, select the greater than or equal to symbol (>=) from the relative operator drop-down list. See **Figure 13-13**.

**Figure 13-13.**
Applying relative operator functions to the filter criteria in the **Object Selection Filters** dialog box.

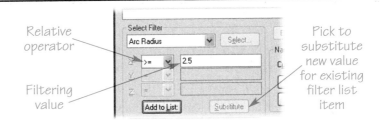

Relative operator

Filtering value

Pick to substitute new value for existing filter list item

The following chart shows the relative operator functions:

| Symbol | Meaning |
|--------|---------|
| = | Equal to |
| != | Not equal to |
| < | Less than |
| <= | Less than or equal to |
| > | Greater than |
| >= | Greater than or equal to |
| × | Equal to any value |

## Editing the Filter List

Editing capabilities allow you to modify and delete filter list items. If you accidentally enter an incorrect filter specification in the **Object Selection Filters** dialog box, you can easily correct it using these steps:

1. Pick the item in the filter list that you need to edit, then pick the **Edit Item** button. The values for the selected specification are displayed in the **Select Filter** area and can be freely edited.
2. Change the values as necessary.
3. Pick the **Substitute** button when finished. The edited filter specification is substituted for the highlighted item. Be sure to pick **Substitute**, and not **Add to List**; otherwise, you end up with two different values for the same filter specification in the filter list.

To remove an item from the filter list, highlight it and select the **Delete** button. Only one filter specification can be deleted at a time using this method. If you need to remove all of the current specifications and start over, pick the **Clear List** button.

## Creating Named Filters

In any CAD project, it is always important to benefit from work you have already done. By reusing previous work instead of repeating the work to produce duplicate results, you increase your efficiency and overall productivity levels.

Complex filter lists can be time-consuming to develop. AutoCAD allows you to name and save filter lists. The **Named Filters** area of the **Object Selection Filters** dialog box is used to create and manage these lists.

When you have created a filter list that you plan to use again, it should be named and saved. When the filter list is completed and tested, follow these steps to name and save the list:

1. Pick the edit box to the right of the **Save As:** button to make it current.
2. Enter a short, descriptive name in the edit box. The name for a filter list can be up to 18 characters in length. Named filters created in this manner are stored in a file named filter.nfl and are available to all drawings until deleted.
3. Pick the **Save As:** button to save the named filter.

To delete a filter list, make it current by picking the filter name from the **Current:** drop-down list, and then pick the button labeled **Delete Current Filter List**.

## Exercise 13-8

◆ Open ex13-7.
◆ Change the text to 12″ high text.
◆ Create a filter that filters for all text objects with a height equal to 12″.
◆ Save the filter as 12in_high_text.
◆ Save the drawing as ex13-8.

## Using Filters on a Drawing

Filters can increase productivity, but you must learn to recognize situations when they can be used. Imagine that you have just created the interior layout in **Figure 13-14.** You are then asked to change all of the text inside the cubicles to a new layer and text style. You could use the **Properties** window and individually select each piece of text in every cubicle, but you decide to use the **FILTER** command to make the job easier.

**Figure 13-14.**
An interior layout requiring modification to the cubicle names.

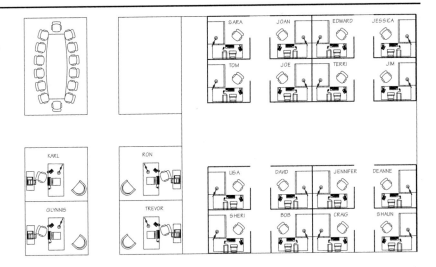

The **FILTER** command opens the **Object Selection Filters** dialog box, where you can use the following steps:

1. Pick the **Add Selected Object** button. The drawing returns with a Select object: prompt. Pick a text element in one of the cubicles.
2. The dialog box returns and displays the characteristics of the text you picked. Highlight items such as Text Position, Text Value, Normal Vector, and Text Rotation and pick the **Delete** button for each. See **Figure 13-15.** These filters are not needed because they limit the filter list to specific aspects of the selected text object.
3. Enter a filter name, such as Text, in the **Save As:** text box and then pick the **Save As:** button. Text becomes the current filter name.
4. Pick the **Apply** button. The drawing returns and this prompt is given:

Select object:
Applying filter to selection.
Select objects: *(window all of the drawing text to be included in the selection set or enter all)*

**Figure 13-15.**
Deleting selection filters that are too specific. Note that only one filter can be deleted at a time.

*Delete highlighted filters*

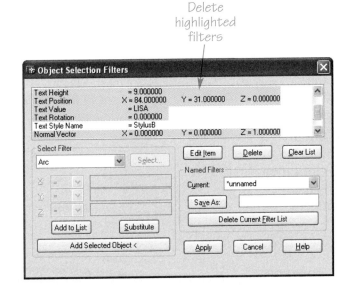

The text within the drawing is now highlighted, and the following prompt appears:

> Select objects: Specify opposite corner: 219 found
> 199 were filtered out.
> Select objects: ↵
> Command:

5. The highlighted text returns and the items that were previously highlighted become part of the selection set.
6. Use the **Properties** window to change the style and layer assigned to the text. The revised interior layout is shown in **Figure 13-16**.

**Figure 13-16.**
The revised interior layout. All text is updated to a new layer and text style.

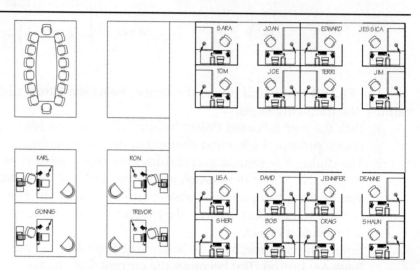

## Chapter Test

*Answer the following questions on a separate sheet of paper.*

1. Define *space planning.*
2. List five items that must be considered when space planning.
3. What is a *design program?*
4. Identify the command that is used to access the geometry calculator.
5. List three ways that the value *five feet six inches* can be entered in the geometry calculator.

*In Questions 6 through 10, give the symbol used in the geometry calculator to access the function identified.*

6. Addition.
7. Subtraction.
8. Multiplication.
9. Division.
10. Exponent.

11. Define *integer.*

*For Questions 12 through 15, use the geometry calculator to solve the given problem.*

12. A bedroom is 12′ wide and 180 SF. What is the length of the bedroom?
13. A dining room is 16′ wide and 400 SF. What is the length of the dining room?

14. Convert 12'-6" to millimeters.
15. Convert 220' to meters.

16. What items are included in a space diagram?
17. Define *interior layouts*.
18. Why is it a good idea to create folders on the hard drive for different types of furniture blocks?
19. What is another alternative to placing blocks in folders?
20. Define *group*.
21. Describe the difference between a group and a block.
22. Define *nesting*.
23. What does it mean when a group is selectable?
24. What is the purpose of the **FILTER** command?
25. In which file are named filters saved?

# Chapter Problems

1. Create a space diagram for the following design program. Save the diagram as p13-1.

| Room Name | Square Footage | Adjacent To |
| --- | --- | --- |
| WORK area | 2500 SF | ACCOUNTING office |
| (7) PRIVATE offices | 120 SF each | CONFERENCE room |
| CONFERENCE room | 200 SF | |
| ACCOUNTING office | 700 SF | |
| LOBBY | 250 SF | RECEPTION area |
| RECEPTION area | 500 SF | PRIVATE offices |

2. Create a space diagram for the following design program. Save the diagram as p13-2.

| Room Name | Square Footage | Adjacent To |
| --- | --- | --- |
| ENGINEERING area | 4000 SF | ACCOUNTING office |
| (5) PRIVATE offices | 120 SF each | CONFERENCE room |
| CONFERENCE room | 225 SF | |
| ACCOUNTING office | 300 SF | |
| LOBBY | 250 SF | RECEPTION area |
| RECEPTION area | 300 SF | PRIVATE offices |

3. Open p13-1 and design the furniture layout for one of the PRIVATE offices and the ACCOUNTING office. Include plants and 20 lineal feet of file cabinets in the ACCOUNTING office.
4. Open p13-2 and design the furniture layout for the ENGINEERING area and LOBBY area.

5. Create the following interior layout of a doctor's office. Use the **GROUP** command to group the furniture in each room together.

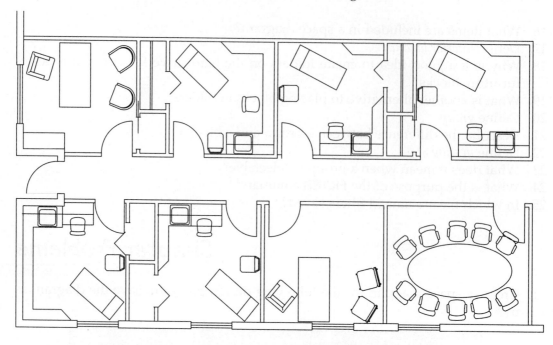

6. Draw an interior layout for an office similar to the office shown below. Use the following layers:

| Layer | Objects |
| --- | --- |
| I-Furn-Char | Chairs |
| I-Furn-Free | Freestanding desks, credenzas, etc. |
| I-Furn-File | File systems |
| I-Furn-Stor | Storage units |

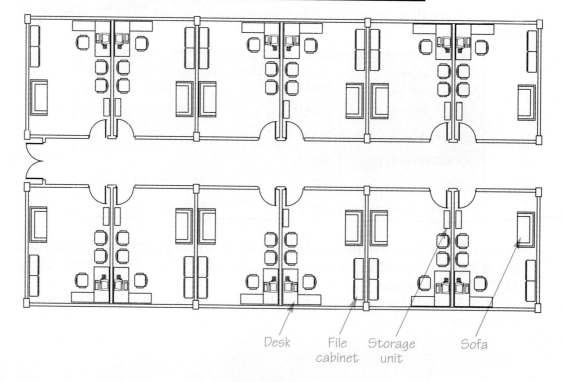

Desk    File cabinet    Storage unit    Sofa

7. Create an interior layout for a drafting workroom similar to the following workroom. Use the following layers:

| Layer | Objects |
|-------|---------|
| I-Furn-Char | Chairs |
| I-Furn-Free | Freestanding desks, credenzas, etc. |
| I-Furn-Pnls | Cubicle panels |
| I-Furn-Plnt | Interior plants |

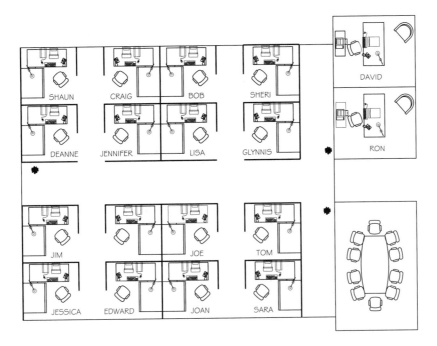

8. Develop an interior layout for a MASTER BEDROOM that measures 16′ × 18′. You can base the interior layout on the sample below or create a completely original layout.

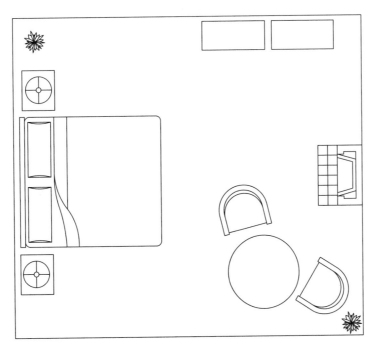

9. Develop an interior layout for a DINING ROOM measuring 12′ × 14′ and a LIVING ROOM measuring 14′ × 18′. You can base the interior layout on the sample below or create a completely original layout.

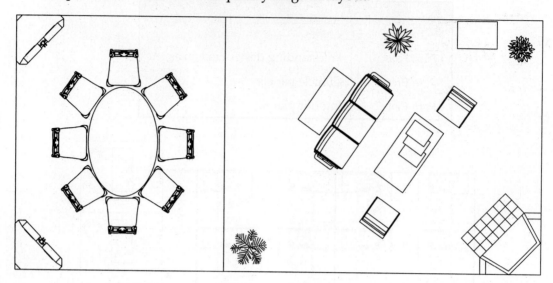

Architectural Drafting Using AutoCAD

# Drawing Site Plans

## Learning Objectives

After completing this chapter, you will be able to:

- List features of site plans.
- Draw and label property lines.
- Use the **OFFSET** command to establish setbacks.
- Identify factors affecting site location and orientation.
- Use the **SPLINE** command to draw contour lines.
- Draw curbs, gutters, sidewalks, and landscape strips.
- Design and draw parking spaces.

## Important Terms

bearing
buildable area
chord length
contour interval
contour lines
curb cuts
easement
elevation
grade
gutter
index contour lines
intermediate contour lines
lot

lot and block
metes and bounds
plot
point objects
property lines
rectangular system
setback
site
site orientation
site plan
surveyor's units
tolerance
walk

A *site* is an area of land with defined limits used for a construction project. The terms *lot* and *plot* are also used when referring to a site. The *site plan* specifies the size, location, and configuration of the site, along with the location of the structure on the site.

In this chapter, you will learn how to create commercial and residential site plans. The features included on typical site plans are discussed, along with specific AutoCAD techniques used to produce these features.

# Beginning a Site Plan Drawing

Site plans can be drawn on sheet sizes ranging from 8 1/2" × 11" up to 36" × 48" depending on the purpose of the plan, type of construction (residential or commercial), local government guidelines, and lending institution requirements. For residential construction, many local planning departments require the site plan to be printed on an 8 1/2" × 11" sheet. Commercial projects often contain size and detail requiring a larger sheet. Typical architectural sheet sizes are 18" × 24", 24" × 36", and 36" × 48".

Site plans are generally created and plotted using a civil engineering scale. The scale depends on the following characteristics:

- Sheet size.
- Site dimensions.
- Amount of information required.
- Details required.

Site plans typically have a scale ranging from 1" = 10' (1:50 metric) to 1" = 100' (1:1000 metric). Common scales for residential and commercial site plans are 1" = 10', 1" = 100', and 1" = 200'. The drawing of a subdivision of land that has many individual sites is often drawn at a 1" = 1000' scale.

The American Institute of Architects (AIA) CAD Layer Guidelines has established the heading Civil Engineering and Site Work as the major group for CAD layers for site plan applications:

| Layer Name | Description |
|---|---|
| C-Prop | Property lines and survey benchmarks |
| C-Topo | Proposed contour lines and elevations |
| C-Bldg | Proposed building footprint |
| C-Pkng | Parking lots |
| C-Road | Roads |
| C-Strm | Storm drainage, catch basins, and manholes |
| C-Comm | Site communications systems, such as telephone systems |
| C-Watr | Domestic water |
| C-Fire | Fire protection system |
| C-Ngas | Natural gas system |
| C-Sswr | Sanitary sewer system |
| C-Elev | Elevations |
| C-Sect | Sections |
| C-Detl | Details |
| C-Psit | Site plan |
| C-Putl | Site utility plan |
| C-PPav | Paving plan |

Architectural Drafting Using AutoCAD

Landscape plans also have CAD layer designations. The following tables list some common landscaping layers:

| Layer Name | Description |
|---|---|
| L-Plnt | Plant and landscape material |
| L-Irrg | Irrigation system |
| L-Walk | Walks and steps |

A typical AutoCAD site plan template has the following components:
- Site plan layers.
- Site plan linetypes.
- Text styles.
- Title block and border.

## Site Plan Features

The features included on a site plan vary, depending on the project requirements. Some features generally included on site plans are the following:
- Property lines
- Structures
- Elevations
- Contour lines
- Streets, driveways, curbs, and sidewalks
- Utility lines

All of these features are normally found on both residential and commercial site plans. A commercial site plan is drawn with the same components as the residential site plan, but generally contains more information. Commercial site plans may contain details for grading, parking lots, sidewalk curbing, landscaping, fire protection systems, and access to local roads.

### Property Lines

The site is normally described by at least one of three legal descriptions. The most common system is the *metes and bounds* system, which defines property lines by length and bearing. A *lot and block* description identifies the site by a block number and lot number within the particular subdivision. The *rectangular system* uses longitude and latitude lines to divide land into square townships (measuring 6 miles on each side) and sections (1 mile per side). *Property lines* identify the site boundaries.

### Bearings

*Bearing* is a method of expressing direction by specifying the angle and direction from due north or due south. For example, the bearing N 30° E specifies a direction 30° east of due north. This and other bearings are shown in **Figure 14-1.**

The angle component of the bearing is expressed in degree/minute/second format. These units of angular measure are very accurate. There are 360 degrees in a complete revolution, 60 minutes in each degree, and 60 seconds in each minute. Surveyors and civil engineers normally use these units when measuring a site.

## Figure 14-1.

Bearings identify direction by the angle from north or south. Compass directions are normally identified as due north, due south, etc.

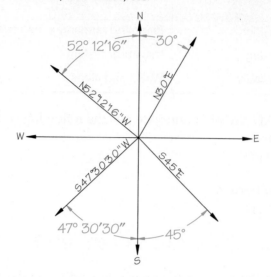

In AutoCAD, bearings are called *surveyor's units.* You can enter an angle in surveyor's units at the Command prompt. The entry format is illustrated in **Figure 14-2.** Surveyor's units normally include two compass directions and an angle expressed in degree/minute/second format. The degree component is followed by a *d,* the minute portion is followed by a foot mark ('), and the second portion is followed by an inch mark ("). The *d* can be omitted when there are no minute and second components. A compass direction can be expressed with only the first letter of the direction (such as *s* for south). When the length and bearing are known, relative polar coordinates are normally used to draw property lines.

 **Note**

The setting for angular units in the **Drawing Units** dialog box determines only the units used for AutoCAD displays such as status bar coordinates, command line prompts, and **LIST** command responses. Regardless of the angular units selected in the **Drawing Units** dialog box, you can always enter angular measurements in surveyor's units at the Command prompt.

## Figure 14-2.

Examples of surveyor's unit format for angle expressions and relative polar coordinate entry.

| | Surveyor's units with degrees, minutes, and seconds | When the angle has no minute or second component, the "d" can be omitted | When the angle corresponds to a compass direction, the single direction is sufficient |
|---|---|---|---|
| Angle Entries | n52d12'16"w | s45w | n |
| Relative Polar Coordinate Entries | @80.25'<s34d12'15"w | @41"<n12e | @15'<w |

Architectural Drafting Using AutoCAD

# Drawing Property Lines

Property boundary lengths are generally measured in feet and hundredths of a foot. For example, a measurement of 120'-6" is listed as 120.50'. The surveyor's measurements are generally provided in this decimal format. When entering these units, be sure to use the foot symbol ('). If you do not, AutoCAD interprets the measurement as inches.

Property lines can be drawn as lines, arcs, or polylines using a Phantom linetype and a heavy lineweight. You can use the **LINE, ARC,** or **PLINE** command. For rectangular sites, you can use the **RECTANG** command to draw the property lines. The following prompt sequence produces the property lines shown in **Figure 14-3**. The final boundary line is drawn as an arc. Drawing curved property lines is discussed in the next section.

```
Command: l or line↵
Specify first point: (pick the start point)
Specify next point or [Undo]: @48.92'< n17d30'9"w↵
Specify next point or [Undo]: @61.85'<n2d30'57"e↵
Specify next point or [Undo]: @86.19'<n85d36'24"w↵
Specify next point or [Undo]: @96.09'<s8d22'5"e↵
Specify next point or [Undo]: @65.04'<s67d22'56"e↵
Specify next point or [Undo]: ↵
Command: a or arc↵
Specify start point of arc or [Center]: (pick the original start point)
Specify second point of arc or [Center/End]: e↵
Specify end point of arc: (pick the last line's endpoint)
Specify center point of arc or [Angle/Direction/Radius]: r↵
Specify radius of arc: 40'↵
Command:
```

**Figure 14-3.**
Property lines are labeled with length and bearing. Bearings are based on identifying one corner of the site as a starting point and then drawing connecting lines.

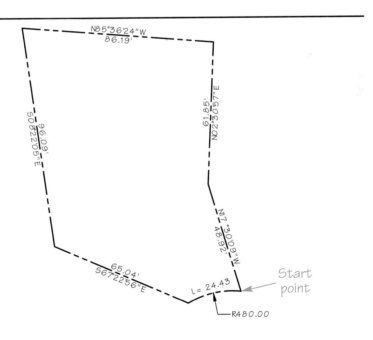

Due to the rounding of measurements by surveyors and the rounding of values entered in AutoCAD, the starting and ending points of a property boundary may not match exactly when the previously discussed procedure is used. To have the points coincide, use the **Close** option for the last property line segment.

## Curved Property Lines

As shown in **Figure 14-3,** property lines are not always straight. They can also be arcs. Surveyors normally describe arcs by radius and chord length. Radius measures the amount of curvature, and *chord length* is the straight-line distance between the endpoints of the arc. These properties are shown in **Figure 14-4.**

To draw a curved property line, use the **ARC** command. Pick the first endpoint, and then use relative polar coordinates (using the chord length and bearing) to pick the second endpoint. After picking the endpoints, use the **Radius** option to enter the radius. The following prompt sequence creates the curved property line shown in **Figure 14-5:**

Command: **a** *or* **arc**⏎
Specify start point of arc or [Center]: *(pick a starting point)* ⏎
Specify second point of arc or [Center/End]: **e**⏎
Specify end point of arc: **@88'<s43d38'15"w**⏎
Specify center point of arc or [Angle/Direction/Radius]: **r**⏎
Specify radius of arc: **100'**⏎

Figure 14-4.
When the property boundary is an arc, it is described by its radius and chord length.

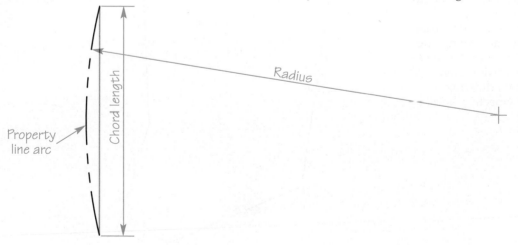

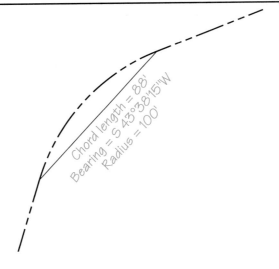

**Figure 14-5.**
Using the **ARC** command to draw curved property lines.

Chord length = 88'
Bearing = S 43°38'15"W
Radius = 100'

## Labeling Property Lines

It is standard practice to label property lines by length and bearing. The labels should be centered at the midpoint and aligned with the property line. This can be accomplished using the **MTEXT** command and the following procedure:

1. Enter t at the Command prompt to begin the **MTEXT** command.
2. Pick the midpoint of the property line as the first corner point.
3. Before picking the second corner point, enter r to access the **Rotation** option.
4. At the Specify rotation angle: prompt, pick the endpoint of the property line that will be closest to the end of the label.
5. After specifying the rotation angle, access the **Justify** option and select the middle center (MC) justification.
6. Pick the midpoint of the property line as the second corner point.
7. In the **Multiline Text Editor**, enter the text for the length of the property line, press [Enter], and then enter the text for the bearing.
8. Set the correct text font and height.
9. Pick the **OK** button.

The text is now centered and aligned with the property line. If the labels are too close to the property line, they may be difficult to read. If this is the case, change the line spacing of the text. This can be done with the **Properties** window.

## Exercise 14-1

◆ Start a new drawing using one of your templates.
◆ Use a 1″ = 10′-0″ drawing scale (the scale factor is 120).
◆ Set limits of 0,0 and 360′,240′ (use a 36″ × 24″ sheet).
◆ Create a layer named Site-Propline with a PhantomX2 linetype. Set this layer current.
◆ Set the **LTSCALE** system variable to 120.
◆ Draw the property boundaries shown in **Figure 14-3**.
◆ Create a layer named Site-Notes.
◆ Add labels similar to those shown in **Figure 14-3**. Use a text height of 30″ (1/4″ × 120).
◆ Save the drawing as ex14-1.

## Setbacks and Easements

In almost all cases, building codes do not allow you to erect a structure right next to the property line. The minimum allowable distance between a property line and a building is called the *setback*. No buildings can be placed within the setback area. Setbacks are specified in local building codes and normally depend on the property use. For example, a residential lot may have smaller setbacks than an industrial lot.

In addition, a portion of the site may include an easement. An *easement* is an area of the site to which another party has legal access. Most easements are provided for utility companies. For example, if telephone poles are located along one of the property lines, there will be an easement below the lines so the telephone company has the right to access their wires at any time. In this case, the easement would be wide enough for a repair truck. No buildings or permanent structures should be located on an easement.

Setbacks can be drawn on a Setback or Construction layer so they can be frozen or turned off when not in use. The easiest method of adding setbacks to your drawing is by using the **OFFSET** command.

### Offsetting Objects

The **OFFSET** command is used to create concentric circles, arcs, and polylines, and parallel lines. The command creates a copy at a specified distance from the original object. In this example, the **OFFSET** command is used to offset setbacks from existing property lines.

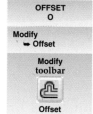

OFFSET
O

Modify
➥ Offset

Modify
toolbar

Offset

The **OFFSET** command is accessed by selecting **Offset** from the **Modify** pull-down menu, picking the **Offset** button in the **Modify** toolbar, or by entering o or offset at the Command prompt.

When the command is first accessed, you are prompted to enter an offset distance. This is the distance from the original object that you want the new object to be copied. Once a distance has been specified, select the object you want to offset. Finally, select the side of the original object where the new object should be placed. **Figure 14-6** illustrates the use of the **OFFSET** command.

**Figure 14-6.**
Examples of offsetting different types of objects.

| | Original Object | Pick Object and Side to Offset | Offset Object |
|---|---|---|---|
| Circle | ○ | Side to offset / Select object | Offset object |
| Line | / | / + | // |
| Polyline | ⊥ | + | ⊥ |

# Drawing Setbacks

Often, building codes specify different setbacks for the front, sides, and back of the site. For the site shown in **Figure 14-7,** a 25′ front setback, 10′ side setback, and 10′ rear setback are required. There is also a 7′-6″ wide easement along the right edge of the property. The following prompt sequence shows how the **OFFSET** command is used to create the front and rear setbacks:

Command: **o** *or* **offset**⏎
Specify offset distance or [Through] <*current*>: **25′**⏎
Select object to offset or <exit>: *(pick the front property line)*
Specify point on side to offset: *(pick the side of the property line for the setback)*
Select object to offset or <exit>: ⏎
Command: *(press* [Enter] *to reenter the* **OFFSET** *command)*
Specify offset distance or [Through] <10′-0″>: **15′**⏎
Select object to offset or <exit>: *(pick the rear property line)*
Specify point on side to offset: *(pick the side of the property line for the setback)*
Select object to offset or <exit>: ⏎
Command:

The left-side and right-side setbacks are created in the same manner. An offset distance of 10′ is used.

Once the setbacks have been created, use the **TRIM** and **EXTEND** commands as appropriate to trim or extend the setback lines where they cross. Use the **Layer Control** drop-down list in the **Layers** toolbar to assign the setbacks to the correct layer. The completed setbacks are shown in **Figure 14-8.**

The area within the setbacks is called the buildable area. The *buildable area* is the area in which structures can be located.

---

**Figure 14-7.**
Add setbacks (shown in color) by offsetting the property lines.

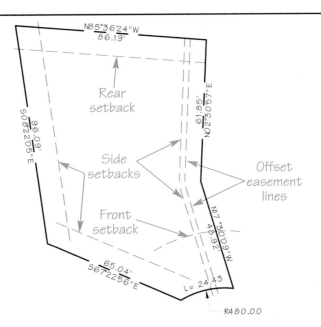

**Figure 14-8.**
Trim the offset lines to complete the setbacks. The area in which buildings can be located is shaded.

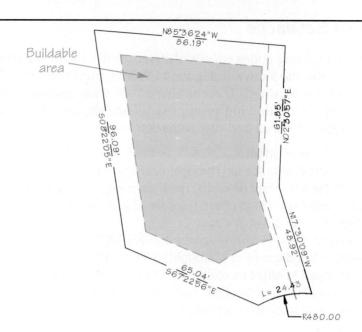

Buildable area

## Exercise 14-2

◆ Open ex14-1.
◆ Use the **OFFSET** command to offset lines for the property boundary 25′ from the front, 10′ on the sides, and 15′ from the rear.
◆ Create a 7′-6″ easement along the right edge of the property.
◆ Create a layer named Site-Setback with a Hidden linetype.
◆ Use the **Layer Control** drop-down list in the **Layers** toolbar to change the setback lines to the Site-Setback layer.
◆ Use the **TRIM** and **EXTEND** commands to clean up the setback lines.
◆ Your drawing should look like **Figure 14-8.** Save your drawing as ex14-2.

## Placing the Structure

Now that the property boundaries and setback requirements have been established, the structure can be added to the site plan. If you are creating the site plan early in the design process, insert a bubble diagram to verify that the structure fits within the buildable area. Even though preliminary calculations have been made to determine if the structure fits, this allows you to confirm the calculations.

**Professional Tip**

Normally, setbacks apply to building lines (walls). In some cases, setbacks apply to roof overhangs. Always check the local building codes.

## Site Orientation

*Site orientation* is the placement of a structure on the property. When determining the site orientation, you must take into account physical and environmental relationships. The following factors must be considered:

- **Terrain.** Existing geographical features, such as land contour, trees, water, and existing structures, may affect the site orientation. For example, structures are normally positioned at the highest elevation on the site so that rainwater drains away from the structure.
- **Sun.** The direction of the sun relative to the house may affect orientation of the structure. For example, in North America, the south side of the structure is exposed to direct sunlight.
- **View.** The environment surrounding the site can affect orientation. For example, an ocean side residence may be oriented so the dining room windows offer a breathtaking view of the water.
- **Wind.** The prevailing wind direction can affect orientation. For example, in the central part of the United States, cold winds generally come from the north and warmer winds come from south.
- **Sound.** Any existing or future sources of noise in the area near the site should be considered when orienting the structure. For example, when orienting a residence, bedrooms should be located away from the side of the house exposed to noise from a highway or set of railroad tracks.

In addition to these factors, the site orientation must also take into account all applicable legal requirements. Local building codes and zoning ordinances contain specific requirements that must be followed. An inspector reviews construction to make sure these requirements are satisfied. If the construction does not comply with building code requirements, the inspector can stop construction on the project until the requirements are satisfied.

## Drawing the Structure

Once you have a general idea of the location and orientation of the building, you can add it to the site plan. The structure's outline is commonly referred to as the building footprint. Create a layer with a descriptive name for the footprint, such as Site-Structure.

To draw a structure on a site plan, create an outline of the structure's exterior walls. The building outline should be a solid, thick line.

Structures are illustrated on site plans in several different ways, depending on the drafting standards being used. **Figure 14-9** illustrates the following items, which may be included:

- **Roof overhang.** The roof overhang is often included on the site plan. This helps ensure that the structure does not extend over the setbacks. The roof overhang is drawn as a thin hidden line. You can offset the building outline to quickly establish the roof overhang.
- **Section lines.** Sometimes, the area within the outline of the structure is highlighted with section lines. Section lines are normally not used if roof details are shown.
- **Roof details.** If the structure has a complex roof, the site plan often shows the roof intersections at ridges, hips, and valleys.

If you have already created a design sketch for the building, you can insert it into the site plan as a block to use as a guide. Then, use the **PLINE** command to trace the outline. The polyline should be on a layer for structures. After creating the outline, delete the block and purge it from the drawing. In **Figure 14-10**, the house structure created in Chapter 12 is added to the site plan.

---

*Chapter 14   Drawing Site Plans*

## Figure 14-9.
A—The roof overhang of a structure is often included on a site plan. Section lines may be used to clearly identify the structure. B—You can include roof details for structures with complex or unusual roofs. In this case, section lines are normally not used.

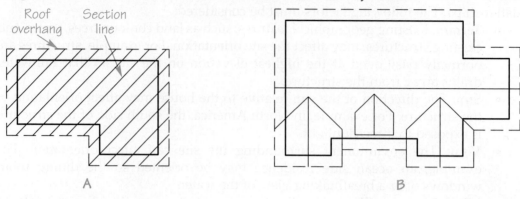

## Figure 14-10.
The site plan with the building outline (footprint).

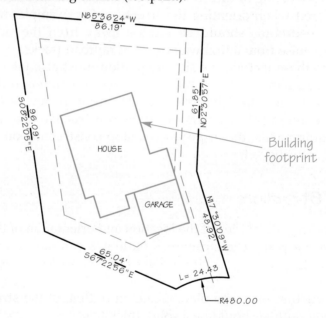

## Exercise 14-3

◆ Open ex14-2.
◆ Create a layer named Site-Structure and set it current.
◆ Use the **INSERT** command to insert ex12-6.
◆ Use the inserted house drawing as a reference and trace the outline of the design sketch with a polyline.
◆ Delete and purge ex12-6.
◆ Use the **MOVE** and **ROTATE** commands as appropriate to locate the house as shown in **Figure 14-10.**
◆ Label the structure using the Site-Notes layer.
◆ Your drawing should look like **Figure 14-10.** Save your drawing as ex14-3.

Architectural Drafting Using AutoCAD

# Elevations and Contour Lines

In addition to property lines, setbacks, and structures, some other graphical information must be added to the site plan. In most situations, a site plan should include elevations. An *elevation* is the height of land at a particular location or the height of a permanent horizontal surface, such as a concrete slab. Elevations provide the relative differences in height between points on the building site. The elevations are measured relative to either a known benchmark elevation or an arbitrary permanent elevation.

Elevations are normally expressed in units of feet with two decimal places. The exact location of the elevation measurement is identified by a symbol on the site plan. The symbol may be a small dot, cross, or X.

Site plans normally include elevations for the corners of the property. The elevation of the structure may also be included. **Figure 14-11** shows a site plan with elevations.

In some cases, contour lines are required to show the slope of the land and lot drainage. *Contour lines* are lines on a map or drawing representing points of equal ground elevation. On small site plans, contour lines are normally drawn for each foot of elevation. See **Figure 14-12.**

The surveyor or civil engineer usually provides the contour information in either electronic format or hard copy format. The architect seldom has to go to the site and measure the elevations for contour reference.

*Contour interval* is the vertical distance between adjacent contour lines. There are normally two types of contour intervals: major contour intervals and minor contour intervals. Major contour lines are also called *index contour lines*, because the line is broken along its length and the elevation value is inserted for reference. Major contour lines are displayed at every 5th or 10th contour line and are generally a heavier lineweight. Minor contour lines are shown at each of the contour intervals. Minor contour lines are also referred to as *intermediate contour lines.* For example, if a site is laid out in 2' elevation increments, the minor contour lines are shown every 2' in elevation. This is referred to as a 2' contour interval.

Contour lines can be drawn solid, as centerlines, or dashed. The index contour lines are generally thicker than the intermediate contour lines. The index contour line is also broken along its length and the contour elevation value is inserted. Contours representing new grade are normally displayed using a dashed linetype. The term *grade* when used for this purpose means the ground elevation on the site. A new grade occurs when an existing contour is changed.

**Figure 14-11.**
Elevations added at the corners of the property lines.

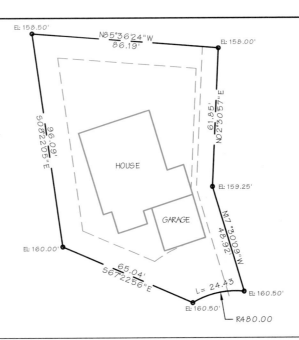

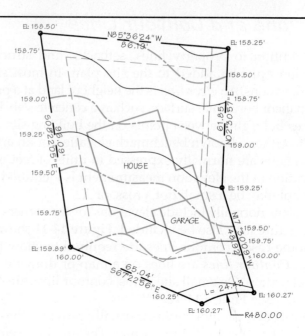

**Figure 14-12.**
Contour lines identify points of equal elevation on the site. Major contour lines (shown in color) have a heavier lineweight than minor contour lines.

## Drawing Contour Lines

Contour lines can be drawn with the **SPLINE** command. To access the **SPLINE** command, pick the **Spline** button in the **Draw** toolbar, pick **Spline** from the **Draw** pull-down menu, or enter spl or spline at the Command prompt. A spline is created by specifying the control points along the curve using any standard coordinate entry method:

> Command: **spl** *or* **spline**↵
> Specify first point or [Object]: **2,2**↵
> Specify next point: **4,4**↵
> Specify next point or [Close/Fit tolerance] <start tangent>: **6,2**↵
> Specify next point or [Close/Fit tolerance] <start tangent>: ↵
> Specify start tangent: ↵
> Specify end tangent: ↵
> Command:

When you have given all of the necessary points along the spline, press [Enter] to end the point specification process. Next, you are prompted to enter the start tangency and end tangency. Specifying the tangents changes the direction in which the spline curve begins and ends. Pressing [Enter] at these prompts accepts the default direction, as calculated by AutoCAD, for the specified curve. The results of the previous command sequence are shown in **Figure 14-13.**

**Figure 14-13.**
A spline drawn with the **SPLINE** command, using the AutoCAD defaults for the start and end tangents.

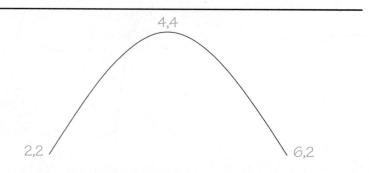

Architectural Drafting Using AutoCAD

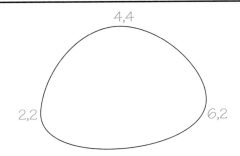

**Figure 14-14.**
Using the **Close** option of the **SPLINE** command with AutoCAD default tangents to draw a closed spline.

4,4

2,2

6,2

## Drawing Closed Splines

The **Close** option of the **SPLINE** command allows you to draw closed splines, **Figure 14-14.** The command sequence is as follows:

Command: **spl** *or* **spline**↵
Specify first point or [Object]: **2,2**↵
Specify next point: **4,4**↵
Specify next point or [Close/Fit tolerance] <start tangent>: **6,2**↵
Specify next point or [Close/Fit tolerance] <start tangent>: **c**↵
Specify tangent: ↵
Command:

After closing a spline, you are prompted to specify a tangent direction for the start/end point of the spline. Pressing [Enter] accepts the AutoCAD default.

## Altering the **Fit Tolerance** Specifications

Different results can be achieved when drawing splines by altering the specifications used with the **Fit Tolerance** option. The outcomes of different settings vary, depending on the configuration of the individual spline object. The setting specifies a *tolerance* within which the spline curves as it passes through the control points. The spline control points also act as grips. Select a spline to display the grips so you can see the control points. Control points can be used to change the appearance of a spline.

## Specifying the Start and End Tangents

The previous examples using the **SPLINE** command used AutoCAD's default start and end tangents. You can set start and end tangent directions by entering values at the prompts that appear after you pick the points of the spline. The tangency is based on the tangent direction of the selected point. The results of using the horizontal and vertical tangent directions with Ortho mode are shown in **Figure 14-15.** The following command sequence is used:

Command: **spl** *or* **spline**↵
Specify first point or [Object]: **2,2**↵
Specify next point: **4,4**↵
Specify next point or [Close/Fit tolerance] <start tangent>: **6,2**↵
Specify next point or [Close/Fit tolerance] <start tangent>: ↵
Specify start tangent: *(move cursor in tangent direction and press* [Enter]*)*
Specify end tangent: *(move cursor in tangent direction and press* [Enter]*)*
Command:

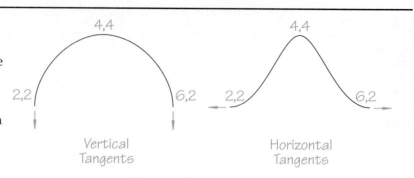

**Figure 14-15.**
These splines were drawn through the same points but have different start and end tangent directions. The tangent directions, which can be specified using Ortho mode, are shown as arrows.

4,4

4,4

2,2

6,2

2,2

6,2

Vertical
Tangents

Horizontal
Tangents

The above examples use coordinate entry to place spline points. Picking points along a site plan also creates splines that can be used to represent contour lines.

Note

You can also draw contour lines by drawing a series of polyline segments between selected points along the proposed contour lines. The contour line is then smoothed out using the **PEDIT** command **Fit** option or **Spline** option. Refer to Chapter 6 for a review on using the **PLINE** and **PEDIT** commands.

## Exercise 14-4

◆ Open ex14-3.
◆ Create two layers named Site-Major and Site-Minor.
◆ Using the new layers, add major and minor contour lines to the site plan as shown in **Figure 14-12.**
◆ Add the elevation marks in the corners and at each contour line interval as shown in **Figure 14-12.**
◆ Use the Site-Notes layer for the elevation marks.
◆ Save the drawing as ex14-4.

## Drawing Streets, Curbs, and Sidewalks

Once the property lines and building location have been established, streets, sidewalks, curbs, and gutters are added to the site plan. In addition to the location of these features, site plans may also include a description (such as 4" CONC WALK) and finish elevation.

Normally, streets and roads are located by their centerlines. Use the Center linetype and draw a line at the location of the center of the street. Include the centerline symbol and label the street using large letters (1/4" minimum). The street is dimensioned on each side of the centerline to the curb or edge of the pavement.

Curbs are generally 6" wide. *Curb cuts* are areas where curbs are lowered to accommodate a driveway or other access, such as a wheelchair ramp. These are usually represented by a diagonal line drawn from the street to the innermost line of a sidewalk. This represents the slope down to the street. The *gutter* is a sloped piece of paving or concrete along the road next to the curb. Rainwater drains from the street to the gutter and then along the gutter to a storm drain.

Sidewalks on residential property are generally 3′–5′ wide. Those on commercial property are normally 5′–10′ wide. You can use the **OFFSET** command to offset building lines and property lines to create one side of the sidewalk. Create a new layer for the concrete sidewalk with a descriptive name, such as C-Walk. Use the drop-down lists in the **Object Properties** toolbar to change the layer of the new line. Then, set the offset distance to the sidewalk width and offset the sidewalk edge to create the second edge.

**Figure 14-16** displays a site plan with sidewalks and curbing applied.

**Figure 14-16.**
The site plan with a sidewalk, curbing, and gutter drawn. A driveway and walkway are also added.

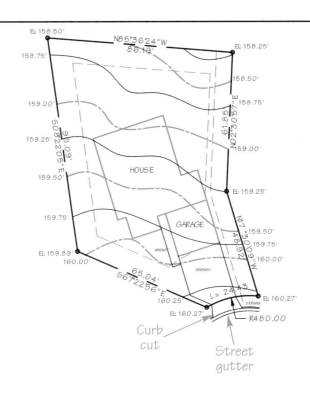

## Exercise 14-5

◆ Open ex14-4.
◆ Create the following layers:
  ◆ Site-Road Curb
  ◆ Site-Concrete Slab
  ◆ Site-Road Drain
◆ Offset the front property line to the outside of the site 5′ for the street sidewalk. Draw a driveway slab and walkway to the house.
◆ Offset the street sidewalk 6″ toward the street for the curb. Add a curb cut from the curb to the driveway.
◆ Offset the curb lines 16″ to the outside for the rain gutter.
◆ Use the **TRIM** and **EXTEND** commands to clean up the offset lines.
◆ Use the **Properties** window to place the sidewalk lines on the Site-Concrete Slab layer.
◆ Use the **Properties** window to place the curb lines on the Site-Road Curb layer.
◆ Use the **Properties** window to place the gutter lines on the Site-Road Drain layer.
◆ Do not dimension.
◆ Save as ex14-5.

# Parking Lot Development

Parking lots are normally included in commercial site plans. While the major consideration in the development of the parking lot is the number of parking spaces that can be created on the site, other considerations such as accessibility, pedestrian aisles, and landscaping must be considered. The following items should be considered in the development of a parking lot:

- **Parking spaces.** Parking spaces (or stalls) are necessary on a commercial site plan. Parking spaces vary in size and patterns. A typical parking space ranges in width between 8′ and 10′, with a length between 14′ and 18′. The angle of a parking space can vary between 45° and 90°. See **Figure 14-17.**
- **ADA parking spaces.** The Americans with Disabilities Act (ADA) parking requirements need to be considered in the development of a parking lot. ADA parking spaces are wider than standard parking spaces to allow for accessibility. These spaces need to be at least 11′ wide with a 5′ wide accessible area beside the parking space. The number of ADA spaces required is usually a percentage of the total number of spaces in the parking lot. See local building codes and regulations for more information.
- **Traffic considerations.** When developing a parking lot, the method of vehicular travel also needs to be considered. This can be broken down into two categories: one-way parking layout and two-way parking layout. Vehicle turning radius also needs to be considered in the parking layout. The following describes considerations for vehicular traffic:
  - **One-way layout.** A one-way parking layout is typically used in small parking lots and limits the vehicular travel to one direction between parking spaces. The lane width generally ranges from 14′ to 18′. See **Figure 14-18.**
  - **Two-way layout.** Two-way parking layouts are used in parking lots where there is more room for additional traffic between parking spaces. The width for two-way travel is generally 28′ to 36′. See **Figure 14-18.**
  - **Turning radii.** As vehicles turn from one lane to the next, enough room needs to be allocated for easy maneuvering of the vehicle. Turning radius varies depending on the sizes of lanes the vehicle is turning from and into. A turning radius for a vehicle turning from a single lane to a single lane can vary in size from 15′ to 19′ for the inside radius and 30′ to 35′ for the outside radius. See **Figure 14-19.**

**Figure 14-17.**
Typical parking space details.

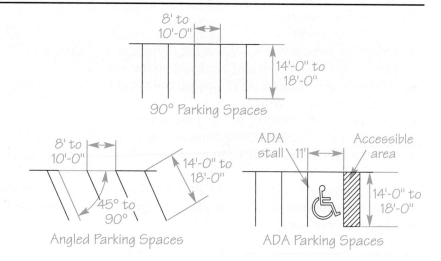

Architectural Drafting Using AutoCAD

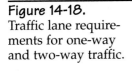

**Figure 14-18.**
Traffic lane require-
ments for one-way
and two-way traffic.

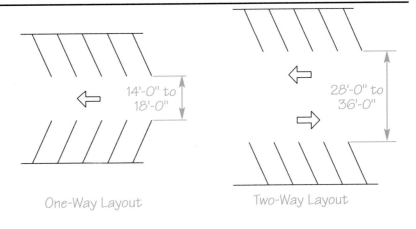

14'-0" to 18'-0"

28'-0" to 36'-0"

One-Way Layout

Two-Way Layout

**Figure 14-19.**
Turning radius is an
important consider-
ation in parking lot
design.

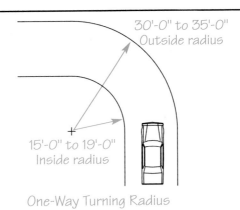

30'-0" to 35'-0"
Outside radius

15'-0" to 19'-0"
Inside radius

One-Way Turning Radius

After parking spaces and traffic flow have been determined, a few additional factors should be considered. The following provides a description of some of the additional considerations. See **Figure 14-20.**

- **Curbing.** Curbing is usually a concrete division between the head of a parking space and another parking space, walkway, or landscaping. Curbs can vary in shape and size. When drawn in a site plan, they are generally drawn 6″ wide. Curbing can also be a wheel stop at the head of a parking stall to keep the vehicle from advancing too far into or past the stall.

**Figure 14-20.**
Typical parking lot
details.

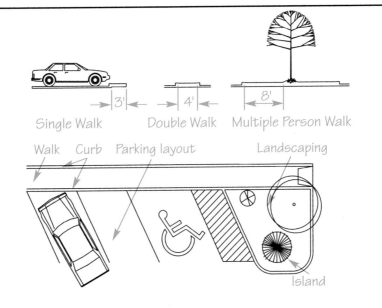

Single Walk 3'

Double Walk 4'

Multiple Person Walk 8'

Walk    Curb    Parking layout    Landscaping

Island

- **Walks.** After a person has parked the vehicle, an area should be designated for access to the building. This area is called a *walk*. Although not required in a parking lot, a walk can add a safe and aesthetically pleasing component to the parking lot. Walks vary in width from 3′ to 8′. Walks that are placed between two opposing parking stalls may include a curb on each side.
- **Islands.** An island is an area in the parking lot that can aid in breaking up the parking lot into manageable parking stall layouts for efficient traffic flow. Islands are also used for landscaping to break up the monotonous look of a large parking lot. Islands vary in size and shape and are often placed at the end of a string of parking stalls, separating the stall layout from the traffic access ways.
- **Landscaping.** Landscaping is often placed in islands. Landscaping consideration in a parking lot should include a diversified mixture of overhead trees, flowering trees, evergreen trees, shrubs, and ground cover. Avoid using plants that drop fruit or sap.

In AutoCAD, the **DIVIDE** and **MEASURE** commands can aid in the layout of parking spaces. These commands place point objects along a line, polyline, arc, or circle at a specified interval. The following sections explain these commands.

## Drawing Points

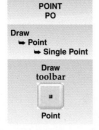

*Point objects* are objects located at a single coordinate. Point objects normally serve as reference points used to draw lines or other objects. Use the Node object snap mode to snap to point objects. You can use the **POINT** command to draw points.

To draw a single point, pick the **Point** button on the **Draw** toolbar, select **Single Point** from the **Point** cascading menu in the **Draw** pull-down menu, or enter po or point at the Command prompt. A Specify a point: prompt appears. Pick a location with the cursor or enter a coordinate value.

You can also draw multiple points by selecting **Multiple Point** from the **Point** cascading menu in the **Draw** pull-down menu. With this option, the Specify a point: prompt is repeated, and you can draw multiple points. To end the command, press the [Esc] key.

By default, points appear as dots in the drawing area. The point style determines how points are displayed and plotted. You can change the point style using the **Point Style** dialog box. Select **Point Style...** from the **Format** pull-down menu to access the **Point Style** dialog box. This dialog box is shown in **Figure 14-21**.

Figure 14-21.
Use the **Point Style** dialog box to select the point style and size.

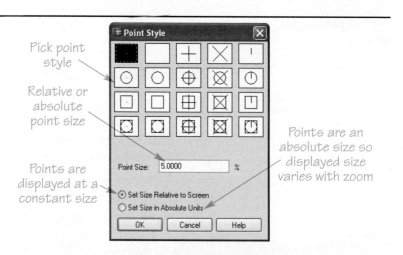

Pick point style

Relative or absolute point size

Points are displayed at a constant size

Points are an absolute size so displayed size varies with zoom

Architectural Drafting Using AutoCAD

The **Point Style** dialog box contains 20 different point styles. The current point style is highlighted. To change the style, pick the graphic image in the dialog box.

Set the point size by entering a value in the **Point Size:** text box. Pick the **Set Size Relative to Screen** option button if you want the point size to change in relation to different zoom scale factors. When this option is selected, the on-screen point marker size remains constant. Picking the **Set Size in Absolute Units** option button makes the point appear in an actual size. When this option is selected, the on-screen size of the point marker changes as you zoom.

## Dividing Objects

A line, circle, arc, or polyline can be divided into an equal number of segments using the **DIVIDE** command. To access the **DIVIDE** command, select **Divide** from the **Point** cascading menu of the **Draw** pull-down menu or enter div or divide at the Command prompt.

DIVIDE
DIV

Draw
➥ Point
➥ Divide

The **DIVIDE** command does not physically break an object into multiple parts. It places point objects or blocks at the locations where the breaks would occur if the object were actually divided into multiple segments.

Suppose you have drawn a line and want to divide it into seven equal parts. Enter the **DIVIDE** command and select the object to divide. Then, enter the number of segments. Refer to **Figure 14-22.** The procedure is as follows:

Command: **div** *or* **divide**↵
Select object to divide: *(pick the object)*
Enter the number of segments or [Block]: **7**↵
Command:

Once you have added the points using the **DIVIDE** command, use the Node object snap mode to snap new geometry to the points.

The **Block** option of the **DIVIDE** command allows you to place a block at each division point. After entering this option, you are asked if the block is to be aligned with the object. After the number of segments is given, the object is divided with the blocks. See **Figure 14-23.**

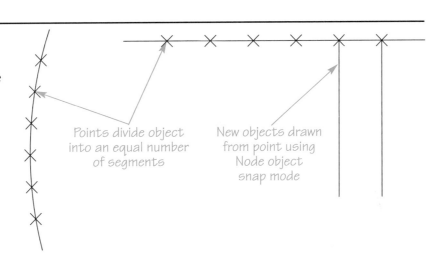

Figure 14-22.
Using the **DIVIDE** command. Note that the point style has been changed from dots to Xs. Dots are not commonly used because they are difficult to see.

Points divide object into an equal number of segments

New objects drawn from point using Node object snap mode

**Figure 14-23.**
Dividing an object using a block.

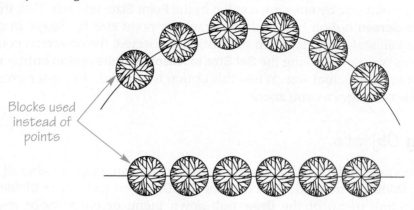

Blocks used
instead of
points

## Dividing Objects at Specified Distances

MEASURE
ME

Draw
➡ Point
➡ Measure

The **MEASURE** command is similar to the **DIVIDE** command. As discussed in the previous section, the **DIVIDE** command divides an object into a specified number of parts. The **MEASURE** command also places points along an object, but the points are spaced at a specified distance. This is the best option for laying out parking spaces because you can specify the width of the space.

The **MEASURE** command is accessed by picking **Measure** from the **Point** cascading menu of the **Draw** pull-down menu, or by typing me or measure at the Command prompt. The line shown in **Figure 14-24** is measured with 8'-0" segments as follows:

Command: **me** *or* **measure**↵
Select object to measure: *(pick an object)*
Specify length of segment or [Block]: **8'**↵

Measuring begins at the end closest to where the object is picked. All increments are equal to the entered segment length except the last segment, which may be shorter.

Blocks can be inserted at the given distances using the **Block** option of the **MEASURE** command. You can use this option when drawing parking spaces if you first create a block for the space dividers. This is shown in **Figure 14-25.**

**Figure 14-24.**
Using the **MEASURE** command. Notice that the last segment may be shorter than the others, depending upon the total length of the object.

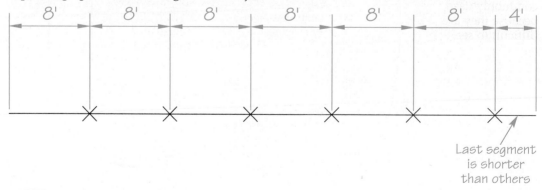

8'   8'   8'   8'   8'   8'   4'

Last segment
is shorter
than others

**Figure 14-25.**
Inserting a block representing a parking space divider with the **MEASURE** command.

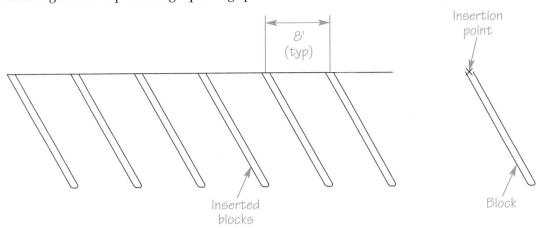

## Exercise 14-6

◆ Open ex14-5.
◆ Create a layer named Site-Landscape and set it current.
◆ Use **DesignCenter** to locate the Landscaping.dwg drawing in the AutoCAD 2004\Sample\DesignCenter folder.
◆ Drag and drop some of the landscaping blocks into your drawing. (Note: You may want to explode the tree block, scale it down, and redefine the tree block to make it smaller.)
◆ Use the **LIST** command to determine the block names. Make a note of the names.
◆ Use the **DIVIDE** command to make a few rows of plants along the easement of the site plan as shown.
◆ Use the **MEASURE** command to create a stepping-stone path along the right side of the garage using a measured distance of 2'-0".
◆ Ensure the block insertions are on the Site-Landscape layer.
◆ Adjust any notes as required.
◆ Save the drawing as ex14-6.

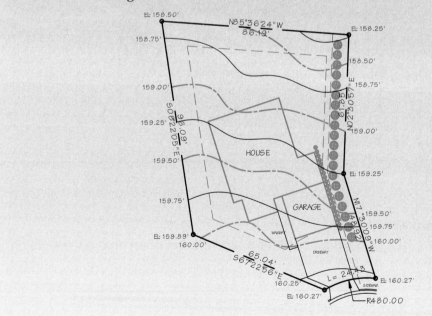

## Other Site Plan Features

In addition to the items discussed earlier in this chapter, a site plan can include many other features. The following items are normally included on both residential and commercial site plans. See **Figure 14-26.**

- North arrow
- Legal description and address of property
- Utility lines (electric, gas, water, and sewer)
- Well location
- Septic tank and drain field locations
- Proposed methods of drainage and rain drains
- Dimensions

If the site is wooded, existing tree locations may be included. Trees to be removed may be identified. Check with your local code official to determine the site plan requirements for your area.

You will need to add dimensions to the site in order for the construction crews to know where to place the building on the lot, and for plan review by your local building official. Dimensioning is covered in Chapter 15.

**Figure 14-26.**
The site plan with utility lines and a legal description added.

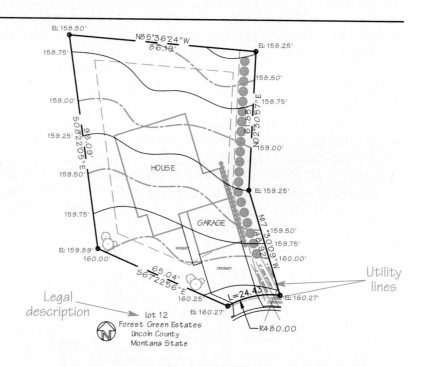

## Exercise 14-7

- ◆ Open ex14-6.
- ◆ Referring to **Figure 14-26**, add a north arrow, additional trees, and a legal description.
- ◆ Create a Site-Utilities layer.
- ◆ Add a water line, gas line, septic line, and storm drain line as shown in **Figure 14-26.**
- ◆ Save the drawing as ex14-7.

Architectural Drafting Using AutoCAD

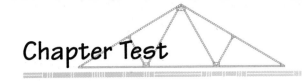
*Answer the following questions on a separate sheet of paper.*

1. Define *site*.
2. Name two terms that are the same as *site*.
3. Identify at least five items that are commonly found on a site plan.
4. Identify the coordinate entry system that is commonly used to lay out property lines.
5. Give the polar coordinate entry used to draw a property line that is 80′-0″ long at an angle of 45°13′33″ in the northwest quadrant.
6. Name the term that refers to a straight line between the end points of an arc.
7. Identify two pieces of information that are normally given for drawing arc property lines.
8. Define *setback*.
9. Define *easement*.
10. Describe the general purpose of setbacks.
11. Name the command that is easiest to use when drawing setbacks.
12. Define *site orientation*.
13. Identify at least four characteristics related to site orientation.
14. How are the property corner elevations identified?
15. Define *contour lines*.
16. Name the command that can be used to draw contour lines.
17. Major contour lines are also called what?
18. Describe the difference between the display of major and minor contour lines.
19. Identify the term that refers to the vertical distance between adjacent contour lines.
20. Name the term that is used to identify areas where curbs are lowered to accommodate a driveway or other access, such as a wheelchair ramp.
21. Give the range of width and length for a typical parking space.
22. In which dialog box can you set the appearance of point objects?
23. Why is the default dot point style a poor choice?
24. Name the command that divides an object into a specified number of parts.
25. Name the command that places points at a specified distance along an object.

# Chapter Problems

1. Start a new drawing using one of your templates. Use the following procedure to create the site plan.
   A. Set engineering and surveyor's units.
   B. Set the limits to 144′,96′. (The scale factor for the drawing is 48.)
   C. Draw the following site plan with appropriate layers. Use a 20′ front, 5′ side, and 15′ rear setback.
   D. Insert the 12-ResA drawing to trace the building outline. Erase and purge the block when done.
   E. Do not dimension.
   F. Save the drawing as 14-ResA.

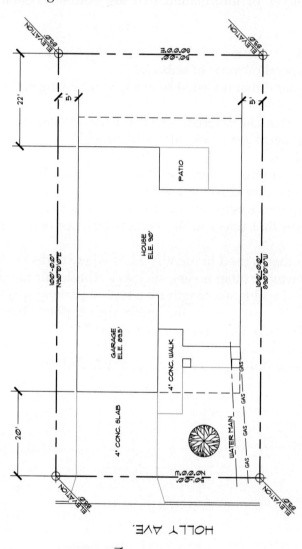

(Alan Mascord Design Associates, Inc.)

2. Start a new drawing using one of your templates. Use the following procedure to create the site plan.

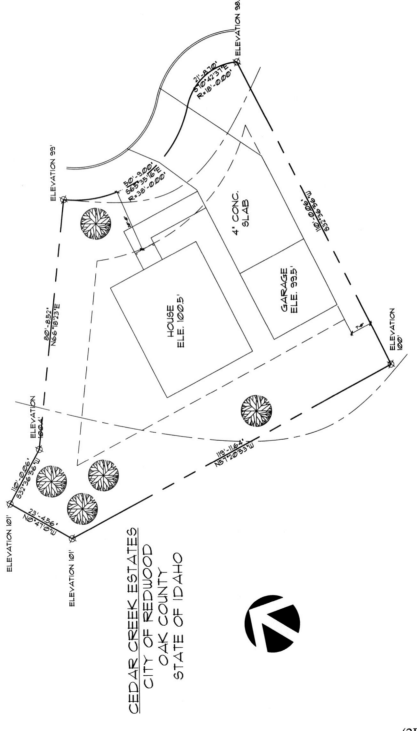

   A. Set engineering and surveyor's units.

   B. Set the limits to 288′,192′. (The scale factor for the drawing is 96.)

   C. Draw the following site plan with appropriate layers. Use a 20′ front, 13′ right side, 7′ left side, and 20′ rear setback.

   D. Insert the 12-ResB drawing to trace the building outline. Erase and purge the block when done.

   E. Do not dimension.

   F. Save the drawing as 14-ResB.

(3D-DZYN)

3. Start a new drawing using one of your templates. Use the following procedure to create the site plan.
   A. Set engineering and surveyor's units.
   B. Set the limits to 288',192'. (The scale factor for the drawing is 96.)
   C. Draw the following site plan with appropriate layers. Use a 30' front, 10' right side, 10' left side, and 15' rear setback.
   D. Insert the 12-Multifamily drawing to trace the building outline. Erase and purge the block when done.
   E. Do not dimension.
   F. Save the drawing as 14-Multifamily.

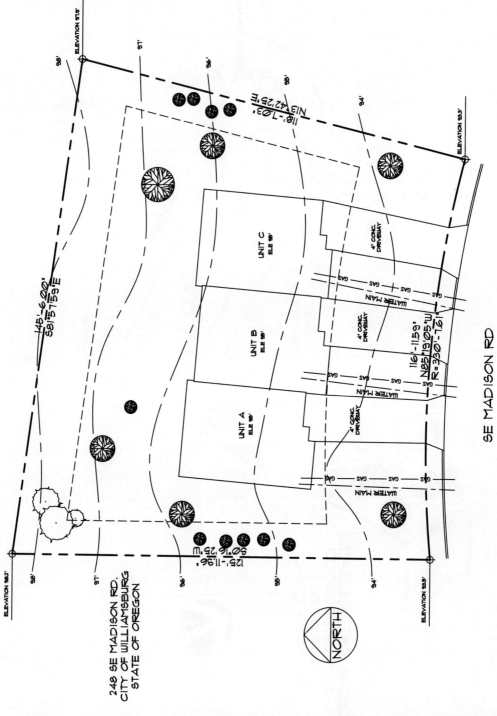

(3D-DZYN)

4. Start a new drawing using one of your templates. Use the following procedure to create the site plan.

   A. Set engineering and surveyor's units.
   B. Set the limits to 288′,192′. (The scale factor for the drawing is 96.)
   C. Draw the following site plan with appropriate layers.
   D. Insert the 12-Commercial-Main drawing to trace the building outline. Erase and purge the block when done.
   E. Do not dimension.
   F. Save the drawing as 14-Commercial.

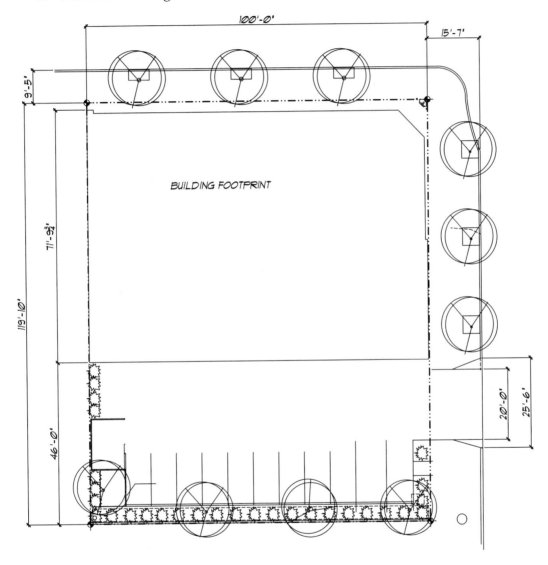

BUILDING FOOTPRINT

(Cynthia Bankey Architect, Inc.)

Dimensions and notes on detail drawings provide construction information for a specific portion of the building. This drawing details the construction of a staircase.

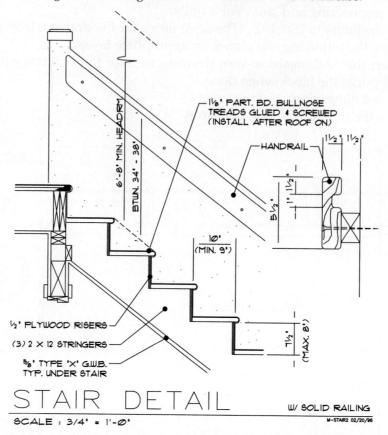

6'-8" MIN. HEADRM

BTWN. 34" - 38"

1⅛" PART. BD. BULLNOSE TREADS GLUED & SCREWED (INSTALL AFTER ROOF ON)

HANDRAIL

1½" 1½"

1½"

5½"

1"

1½"

10" (MIN. 9")

½" PLYWOOD RISERS

(3) 2 X 12 STRINGERS

⅝" TYPE 'X' G.W.B. TYP. UNDER STAIR

7½" (MAX. 8")

# STAIR DETAIL

W/ SOLID RAILING

SCALE : 3/4" = 1'-0"

M-STAIR2 02/20/96

# CHAPTER 15

# Dimensioning and Dimension Styles

## Learning Objectives

After completing this chapter, you will be able to:

- Control the appearance of dimensions.
- Create and use dimension styles.
- Set the appropriate units and fractional values for dimensions.
- Use **DesignCenter** to transfer dimension styles between drawings.
- Add linear, angular, diameter, and radius dimensions to a drawing.
- Add dimensions for multiple items using the **QDIM** command.
- Dimension arcs and circles.
- Use the **QLEADER** command to draw specific notes with linked leader lines.
- Create dimension style overrides.
- Edit dimensions.

## Important Terms

aligned dimensioning
alternate units
angular dimensioning
arrowless dimensions
associative dimension
baseline dimensions
block
chain dimensioning
child
child dimension style
datum dimensioning

dimension styles
dual dimensioning
equal bilateral
location dimensions
override
parent
parent dimension style
prefixes
suffixes
unidirectional dimensioning

Dimensions are provided to describe the size, shape, and location of features on a building or structure. The dimensions in a drawing may consist of numerical values, lines, symbols, and notes. Typical AutoCAD dimensioning features and characteristics are shown in **Figure 15-1.**

When referring to architectural practices, the term *AEC* (architecture, engineering, and construction) is often used. Each AEC field, such as architectural, civil, and structural, uses a different type of dimensioning technique. It is important for a drafter to adhere to company and industry standards when placing dimensions.

AutoCAD's dimensioning functions provide you with unlimited flexibility to dimension linear distances, circles, and arcs. You can also place notes with arrows and leader lines pointing to features. Dimension styles allow you to control the height, width, style, and spacing of individual components of a dimension.

When you dimension objects with AutoCAD, the objects are automatically measured exactly as you have them drawn. This makes it important for you to create accurate original designs and drawings. Use the object snaps to your best advantage when dimensioning.

**Figure 15-1.**
Dimensions describe size and location of different building components.

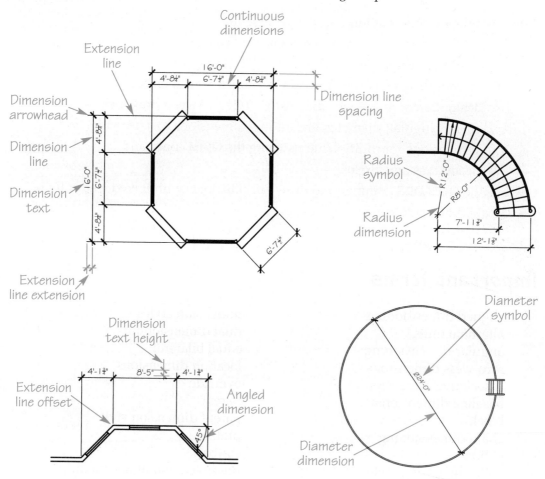

Architectural Drafting Using AutoCAD

**Note** Throughout this chapter, you will be presented with a number of dialog boxes and their options. The corresponding command or option that can be entered at the Command prompt will be shown in brackets as well. For example, in the **Lines and Arrows** tab of the **New Dimension Style** dialog box, you will be given the option to change the color of the dimension lines. In the dialog box, this is done in the **Dimension Lines** area using the **Color** drop-down list. From the Command prompt, you enter dimcldr. The **Color (DIMCLRD)** setting is presented in this chapter.

# Dimension Arrangement

Dimensions are used to communicate information about the drawing. Different industries and companies apply similar techniques for presenting dimensions. The two most accepted arrangements of dimension text are unidirectional and aligned.

## Unidirectional Dimensioning

*Unidirectional dimensioning* is where dimensions are read from one direction. This system typically is used in the mechanical drafting field. All dimension numbers and notes are placed horizontally on the drawing. They are read from the bottom of the sheet.

Unidirectional dimensions normally have arrowheads on the ends of dimension lines. The dimension number is usually centered in a break near the center of the dimension line. See **Figure 15-2.**

**Figure 15-2.**
When applying unidirectional dimensions, all dimension numbers and notes are placed horizontally on the drawing.

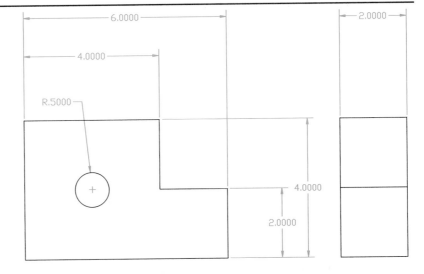

## Aligned Dimensioning

*__Aligned dimensioning__* is where the dimension numbers are lined up with the dimension lines. This system is typically used for architectural and structural drawings. The dimension numbers for horizontal dimensions read horizontally. Dimension numbers for vertical dimensions are placed so they are read from the right side of the sheet. See **Figure 15-3.** Numbers for dimensions placed at an angle read at the same angle as the dimension line. Notes usually read horizontally.

When using the aligned system, terminate dimension lines with tick marks, dots, or arrowheads. In architectural drafting, the dimension number is generally placed above the dimension line and tick marks are used. This is explained more in the following discussion.

**Figure 15-3.**
In the aligned dimensioning system, dimension numbers for horizontal dimensions are read horizontally. Dimension numbers for vertical dimensions are read from the right side of the print.

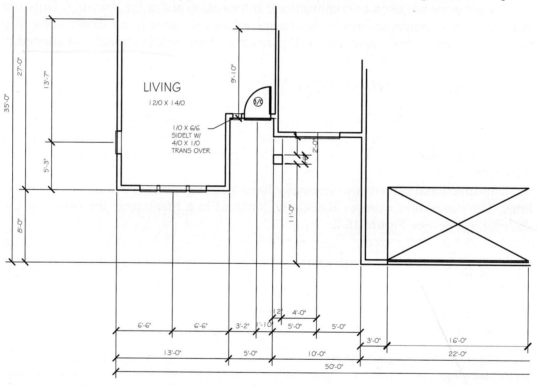

## Placement of Dimensions

The placement of dimensions in architecture is very important. Dimensions should be placed so there is no confusion when reading the plans. Generally, there are four or five levels of dimensioning strings when dimensioning the exterior of a building. These include overall dimensions, major building corner dimensions, minor building corner and interior wall dimensions, and wall opening dimensions. See **Figure 15-4.** Additional dimension strings may be added to aid in reading of the print.

Interior building dimensions are not as strict as the exterior dimensions. Generally, interior walls that cannot be dimensioned from the exterior of the building are placed along a single string of dimensions within the building.

Architectural Drafting Using AutoCAD

**Figure 15-4.**
When dimensioning architectural drawings, there are different strings of dimensions that are used to dimension various portions of the drawing.

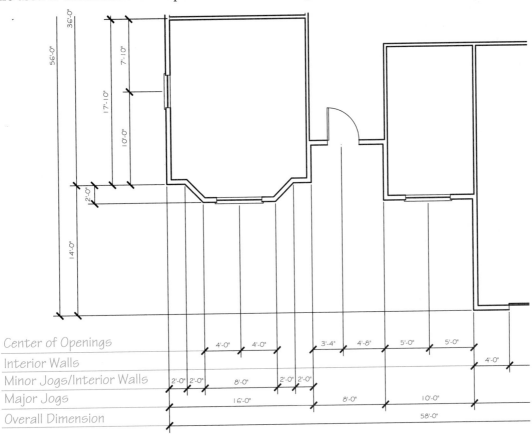

# Dimension Styles

The appearance of dimensions, from the size and the style of the text to the color of the dimension line, is controlled by over 70 different settings. Dimension settings are changed to achieve the desired dimension appearance for your drafting application. *Dimension styles* are saved configurations of these settings. For example, the dimension style for civil or structural drafting may have the Romans text font and dimension lines capped with arrowheads. The dimension text in this case is placed between the dimension line. The dimension style for architectural drafting may use the CityBlueprint, CountryBlueprint, or Stylus BT text font and dimension lines terminated with tick marks. The dimension text in this case is placed above the dimension line.

The dimension style can have dimensions based on national or international standards, or it may adhere to company or school standards and applications. The dimensioning practice that AutoCAD defaults to is based on American National Standards Institute (ANSI) standards and is called the Standard dimension style. This dimension style uses the AutoCAD default settings and variables.

# Creating Dimension Styles

You might think of dimension styles as the dimensioning standards that you use. Dimension styles are usually established for a specific type of drafting field or application. You can customize dimension styles to correspond to architectural, structural, or civil drafting standards, or to your own company or school standards.

D
DST
DDIM
DIMSTY
DIMSTYLE

Format
➥ Dimension
Style...
Dimension
➥ Style...

Styles
toolbar

Dimension Style
Manager

Dimension styles are created using the **Dimension Style Manager** dialog box. See **Figure 15-5.** This dialog box is accessed by picking the **Dimension Style Manager** button in the **Styles** toolbar, by picking **Dimension Style...** in the **Format** pull-down menu, by picking **Style...** in the **Dimension** pull-down menu, or by entering d, dst, ddim, dimsty, or dimstyle at the Command prompt.

The current dimension style, Standard, is noted at the top of the **Dimension Style Manager** dialog box. The **Styles:** list box displays the dimension styles found within the current drawing. The **List:** drop-down list controls whether all styles or only the styles in use are displayed in the **Styles:** list box.

If there are external reference drawings (xrefs) within the current drawing, the **Don't list styles in Xrefs** box can be checked to eliminate xref-dependent dimension styles from the **Styles:** list box. This is often valuable because xref dimension styles cannot be used to create new dimension objects. External references are discussed in Chapter 17.

**Figure 15-5.**
The **Dimension Style Manager** dialog box. The Standard dimension style is the AutoCAD default.

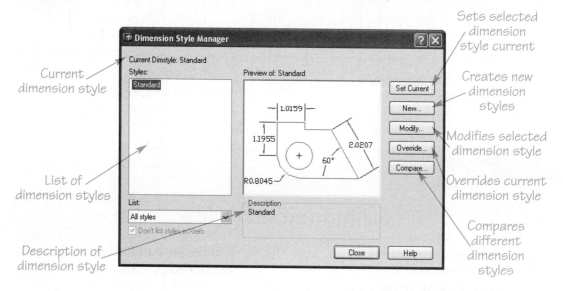

The **Description** box and **Preview of:** image provide information about the selected dimension style. The Standard dimension style is the AutoCAD default. If you change any of the AutoCAD default dimension settings without first creating a new dimension style, the changes are automatically stored in a dimension style override. A dimension style override occurs when you make temporary changes to an existing dimension style. The following describes additional options found in the **Dimension Style Manager:**

- **Set Current** button. This button makes the selected dimension style current in the **Styles:** list box. When a dimension style is current, any new dimensions are created with that style. Existing dimensions created with a different style are not affected by a change to the current style. Xref-dependent dimension styles cannot be set current.
- **New...** button. This button is used to create a new dimension style. When you pick this button, the **Create New Dimension Style** dialog box is displayed. See **Figure 15-6.** The following features are available in this dialog box:
  - **New Style Name** text box. Use this to name the new dimension style. Use a descriptive name, such as Architectural or Civil.

**Figure 15-6.**
The **Create New Dimension Style** dialog box. Type in a new name and base the settings on the Standard dimension style. Set the overall dimension style for all dimensions before making a "substyle" for individual dimension types.

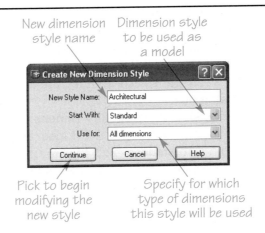

New dimension style name

Dimension style to be used as a model

Pick to begin modifying the new style

Specify for which type of dimensions this style will be used

- **Start With:** drop-down list. This option helps you save time by basing the settings for a new style upon an existing dimension style. Xref dimension styles can be selected from this dialog box only if they were displayed in the **Dimension Style Manager**.
- **Use for:** drop-down list. The choices in this drop-down list are **All dimensions**, **Linear dimensions**, **Angular dimensions**, **Radius dimensions**, **Diameter dimensions**, **Ordinate dimensions**, and **Leaders and Tolerances**. Use the **All dimensions** option to create a new dimension style that governs how all dimensions are to appear. If you select one of the other options, you create a "substyle" of the overall dimension style specified in the **Start With:** drop-down list. The settings in the new style are applied to the dimension type selected in this drop-down list.
- **Continue** button. Pick this button to access the **New Dimension Style** dialog box and begin setting up your new dimension style. This is discussed later in this section.

**Professional Tip**

It is a good idea to create a dimension style for architectural drafting, because architectural dimensions can have their own "character." First create a style with settings that affect all the different types of dimensions, and then make "substyles" based upon any special needs for the different dimension types.

- **Modify...** button. Selecting this button opens the **Modify Dimension Style** dialog box, which allows you to make changes to the style currently selected. Xref styles cannot be modified.
- **Override** button. An *override* is a temporary change to the current style settings. Picking this button opens the **Override Current Style** dialog box. This button is only available for the style listed as current. Including a text suffix, such as NOT TO SCALE, for just a few of the dimensions on a drawing is an example of an override. Once an override is created, it is made current and is displayed as a branch, called the *child,* of the style from which it is created. The overall dimension style from which the child is created is called the *parent.* The override settings are lost when any other style, including the parent, is selected to become current again.

- **Compare...** button. Sometimes it is useful to view the details of two styles to determine why one is not behaving as the other. When the **Compare...** button is selected, you can compare two styles by entering the name of one style in the **Compare:** box and the name of the other in the **With:** box. Only the differences between the selected styles are displayed in the **Compare Dimension Styles** dialog box.

The **New Dimension Style**, **Modify Dimension Style**, and **Override Current Style** dialog boxes have the same six tabs: **Lines and Arrows**, **Text**, **Fit**, **Primary Units**, **Alternate Units**, and **Tolerances**. See **Figure 15-7**. The **Lines and Arrows**, **Text**, **Fit**, **Primary Units**, **Alternate Units**, and **Tolerances** tabs access the settings used for changing the way dimensions are displayed.

An alternative method of defining the dimension settings is to access the corresponding dimension system variables directly at the Command prompt. For example, **DIMSCALE** is a system variable that can be used to change the **Use overall scale of:** setting in the **Fit** tab. In this book, the system variables are noted in parenthesis where applicable. Using the dialog boxes provides you with visual descriptions of the dimension variables, and is the preferred method of establishing and changing dimension styles. The following shows an example of setting the dimension variable for overall scale at the command line:

Command: **dimscale**⏎
Enter new value for DIMSCALE <current>: (enter a new value)

**Figure 15-7.**
The **Lines and Arrows** tab of the **New Dimension Style** dialog box.

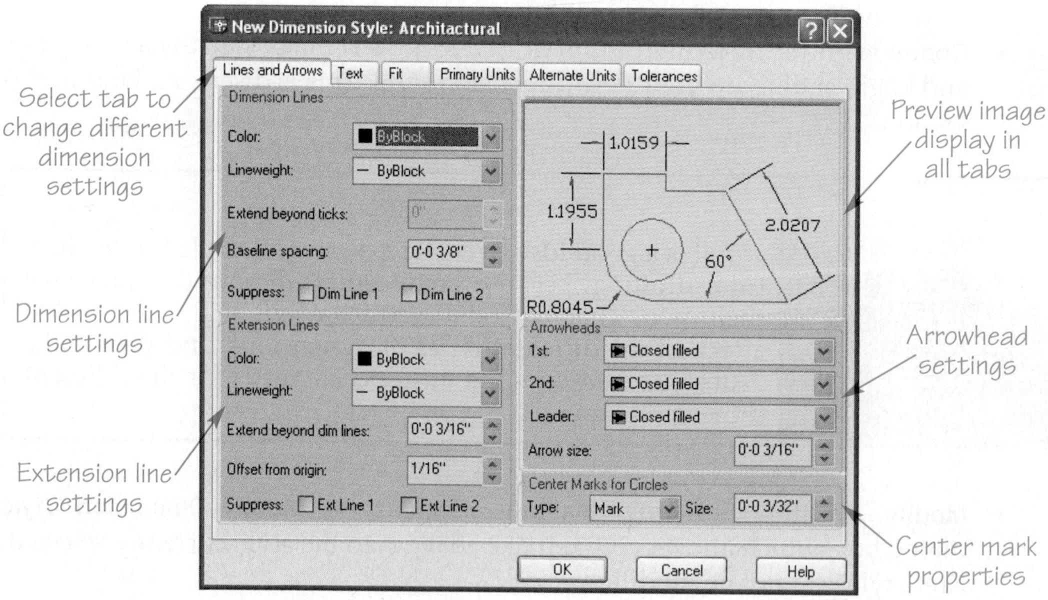

Architectural Drafting Using AutoCAD

## Exercise 15-1

- Start a new drawing using one of your templates.
- Open the **Dimension Style Manager** dialog box and notice Standard as the current dimension style.
- Create a new style named Architectural. The new style should be based on the Standard style and used for all dimensions.
- Pick the **Continue** button to access the **New Dimension Style: Architectural** dialog box.
- Press the **OK** button to return to the **Dimension Style Manager** dialog box.
- Highlight the Architectural style in the **Styles:** box and then pick the **Set Current** button.
- Pick the **Close** button to return to the drawing and save the drawing as ex15-1.

## Using the Lines and Arrows Tab

When the **New** (or **Modify**) button is selected from the **Dimension Style Manager** dialog box, the **New** (or **Modify**) **Dimension Style** dialog box and its six tabs are displayed. As adjustments are made to the current dimension style, an image on each tab updates to graphically reflect those changes. The **Lines and Arrows** tab controls all settings for the display of the dimension and extension lines, arrowheads, leaders, and center marks of dimension strings. Refer to **Figure 15-7.**

The **Dimension Lines** area is used to change the format of the dimension line with the following settings:

- **Color (DIMCLRD).** By default, the dimension line color is assigned to ByBlock. The ByBlock color setting means that the color assigned to the drawn dimension is used for the component objects of the dimension, in this case the dimension line. All associative dimensions are created as block objects. Blocks are symbols designed for multiple use and are discussed in Chapter 9. Associative dimensions are discussed later in this chapter. If the current entity color is set to ByLayer when the dimension block is created, it comes in with a ByLayer setting. The component objects of the dimension then take on the color of the layer the dimension is created on. If the current object color is an absolute color, the component objects of the block take on that specific color regardless of the layer where the dimension is created.

- **Lineweight (DIMLWD).** By default, the dimension line lineweight is assigned to ByBlock. If the current object lineweight is set to ByLayer when the dimension block is created, it comes in with a ByLayer setting. The component objects of the dimension then take on the lineweight of the layer where the dimensions are created. If the current object lineweight is an absolute lineweight, the component objects of the dimension take on that specific lineweight regardless of the layer where the dimension is created.

- **Extend beyond ticks (DIMDLE).** This text box is active when you are using tick marks or oblique arrowheads instead of standard arrowheads. Architectural tick marks or oblique arrowheads are often used when dimensioning architectural drawings. The different settings for arrowhead styles are explained later in this section. In this style of dimensioning, the dimension lines often cross through the extension lines. The extension represents how far the dimension line extends beyond the extension line. Some architectural offices use this practice. See **Figure 15-8.** The 0.00 default is used to draw dimensions that do not extend past the extension lines.

---

**Figure 15-8.**
Using the **Extend beyond ticks** setting to allow the dimension line to extend past the extension line. With the default value of 0, the dimension line does not extend past the extension line.

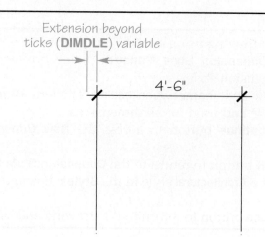

Extension beyond ticks (**DIMDLE**) variable

4'-6"

- **Baseline spacing (DIMDLI).** This text box allows you to change the spacing between the dimension lines of baseline dimensions. *Baseline dimensions* are dimensions that all begin at the same location (the baseline). The default spacing is .38. AutoCAD automatically spaces the dimension lines this distance when you use the **DIMBASELINE** command. This command is discussed later in this chapter. The default value is generally too close for most drawings. Try other values such as .5 (1/2″) to help make the drawing easy to read. **Figure 15-9** shows the dimension line spacing for baseline dimensions.

**Figure 15-9.**
The **Baseline spacing** setting controls the spacing between dimension lines.

Baseline spacing (**DIMDLI**) variable

52'-0"

36'-0"

12'-0"

Baseline

Note

It is important to note that any size setting that you make to dimension components should be made using the same size they will appear on the final plot. In the previous baseline spacing example, if you want to have a 1/2″ spacing between dimension lines, then specify that the spacing is 1/2″. Later in this chapter, you will learn how to apply the scale factor of the drawing to a dimension style.

- **Suppress.** This option has two toggles that keep either the first, second, or both dimension lines and their arrowheads from being displayed. The **Dim Line 1** (**DIMSD1**) and **Dim Line 2** (**DIMSD2**) check boxes refer to the first and second points picked when the dimension is created. Both dimension lines are displayed by default. The results of using these options are shown in **Figure 15-10**.

**Figure 15-10.**
Using the **Dim Line 1** and **Dim Line 2** dimensioning settings.

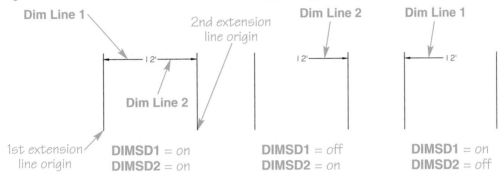

The **Extension Lines** area of the **Lines and Arrows** tab is used to change the format of the extension lines with the following dimension settings:
- **Color** (**DIMCLRE**). The color setting made here controls the extension line color. The default value is ByBlock.
- **Lineweight** (**DIMLWE**). The lineweight setting controls the lineweight of the extension lines.
- **Extend beyond dim lines** (**DIMEXE**). This text box is used to set the extension line extension, which is the distance the extension line runs past the dimension line. See **Figure 15-11**. The default value is 0.18, and an extension line extension of .125 (1/8″) is common on most drawings.
- **Offset from origin** (**DIMEXO**). This text box is used to change the distance between the object and the beginning of the extension line. See **Figure 15-11**. Most applications require this small offset. The default is .0625 (1/16″).

**Figure 15-11.**
The extension line extension (**Extend beyond dim lines**) and the extension line offset (**Offset from origin**).

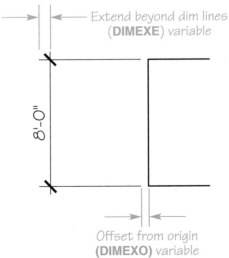

- **Suppress.** This option is used to suppress either the first, second, or both extension lines using the **Ext Line 1** (**DIMSE1**) and **Ext Line 2** (**DIMSE2**) check boxes. Extension lines are displayed by default. An extension line might be suppressed, for example, if it coincides with an object line. See **Figure 15-12.**

The **Arrowheads** area provides several different arrowhead options and controls the arrowhead size. Use the appropriate drop-down list to select the arrowhead used for the **1st** arrowhead (**DIMBLK1**), **2nd** arrowhead (**DIMBLK2**), and **Leader** arrowhead (**DIMDRBLK**). The default arrowhead is Closed Filled, and other options are shown in **Figure 15-13.** If you pick a new arrowhead in the **1st:** drop-down list, AutoCAD automatically makes the same selection for the **2nd:** drop-down list. Check your drafting standards before selecting the appropriate arrowhead. Architectural drawings commonly use architectural ticks, oblique arrowheads, closed filled arrowheads, or dots on dimension lines. The closed filled arrowhead or dot is typically used on leaders. Leaders are discussed later in this chapter.

Notice in **Figure 15-13** there is no example of the **User Arrow...** option. This option is used to access an arrowhead of your own design. For this to work, you must first design an arrowhead that fits inside a 1″ square (unit block) with a dimension line "tail" of 1″ in length, and save it as a block. Blocks are discussed in Chapter 9 of this text. When you pick the **User Arrow...** option in the **Arrowheads** list, the **Select Custom Arrow Block** dialog box is displayed. Enter the name of your custom arrow block in the **Select from Drawing Blocks:** text box and then pick **OK** to have the arrow used on the drawing.

When you access the Oblique or Architectural tick arrowhead options, the **Extend beyond ticks:** text box in the **Dimension Lines** area is activated. This allows you to enter a value so the dimension line projects beyond the extension line. The default value is zero, but some architectural companies like to project the dimension line past the extension line by setting this to a desired value.

The **Arrow size:** text box (**DIMASZ**) allows you to change the size of arrowheads. The default value is .18. An arrowhead size of .125 or .1875 (1/8″ or 3/16″) is common. **Figure 15-14** shows the arrowhead size value.

The **Center Marks for Circles** area (**DIMCEN**) of the **Lines and Arrows** tab allows you to select the way center marks are placed in circles and arcs. The **Type:** setting has the following options:
- **None.** No center marks are to be placed in circles and arcs.
- **Mark.** This option is used to place only center marks without lines.
- **Line.** This option places center marks and centerlines.

**Figure 15-12.**
Suppressing extension lines.

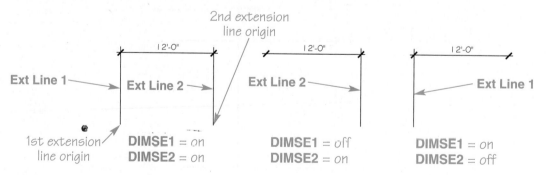

Architectural Drafting Using AutoCAD

**Figure 15-13.**
Examples of dimensions drawn using the options found in the **Arrowhead** drop-down list.

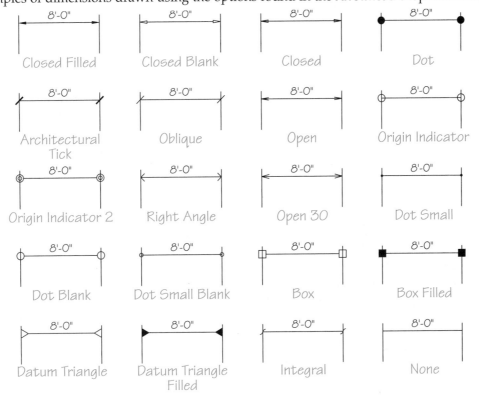

**Figure 15-14.**
Specifying an arrowhead size.

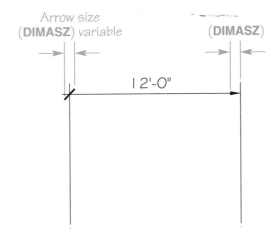

After selecting either the Mark or Line center mark option, you can place center marks on circles and arcs by using the **DIMCENTER** command. The results of drawing center marks and centerlines are shown in **Figure 15-15**. The **Size:** text box is used to change the size of the center mark and centerline. The default size is .09. The size specification controls the Mark and Line options in different ways. Refer to **Figure 15-15**.

cs and circles displayed with center marks and centerlines.

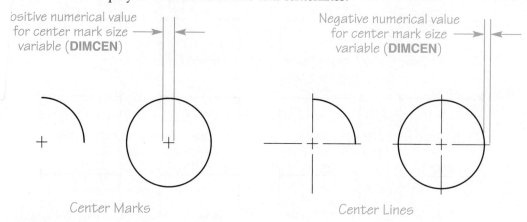

Positive numerical value for center mark size → variable (**DIMCEN**)

Negative numerical value for center mark size → variable (**DIMCEN**)

Center Marks                    Center Lines

## Exercise 15-2

◆ Open ex15-1.
◆ Access the **Dimension Style Manager** dialog box. The Architectural style should be current. Select the **Modify...** button.
◆ This will open the **Modify Dimension Style: Architectural** dialog box.
◆ Use the **Lines and Arrows** tab to make the following settings:

| Setting | Architectural |
|---|---|
| Dimension Arrowheads | Architectural Tick, Oblique, Dot, or Closed Filled |
| Leader Arrowheads | Closed Filled or Dot |
| Dimension line extension | 1/8″ |
| Dimension line spacing | 1/2″ |
| Extension line extension | 1/8″ |
| Extension line offset | 1/16″ |
| Arrowhead size | 3/16″ |
| Center marks | Mark |
| Center mark size | 1/4″ |

◆ Pick the **OK** button, and close the **Dimension Style Manager** dialog box.
◆ Save the drawing as ex15-2.

## Using the Text Tab

Changes can be made to dimension text by picking the **Text** tab in the **Modify Dimension Style** dialog box. See **Figure 15-16.** Remember, these settings can also be made from the **Text** tab in the **New Dimension Style** dialog box when the style is initially created. The **Text Appearance** area is used to set the dimension text style, color, height, and frame. The following explains each of the options:

● **Text style (DIMTXSTY).** This drop-down list is used to select the dimension text style. The Standard text style is the default. Text styles must be loaded in the current drawing before they are available for use in dimension text. If there is not a text style available, pick the ellipsis button (...) to the right of the drop-down

Figure 15-16.
The **Text** tab of the **Modify Dimension Style: Architectural** dialog box. This tab is also found in the **New Dimension Style:** dialog box.

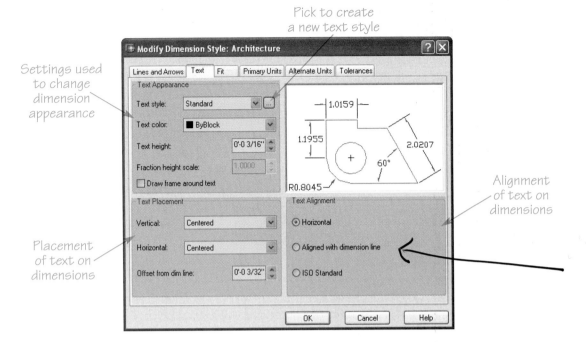

*Pick to create a new text style*

*Settings used to change dimension appearance*

*Alignment of text on dimensions*

*Placement of text on dimensions*

list. This opens the **Text Style** dialog box, where text styles can be created. Text styles are discussed in Chapter 8.

- **Text color** (**DIMCLRT**). This drop-down list contains nine basic colors for changing the color of the dimension text. The dimension color default is ByBlock. If another color is desired, pick the **Select Color...** option to access the **Select Color** dialog box.

- **Text height** (**DIMTXT**). This text box is used to set the height of the dimension text. Dimension text height is commonly the same as the text height found on the rest of the drawing, except for titles, which are larger. The default dimension text height is .18, which is an acceptable standard. Many companies use a text height of .125 or .09375 (1/8″ or 3/32″) for general notes and dimensions, while some companies use a text height of .15625 (5/32″) for additional clarity.

- **Fraction height scale** (**DIMTFAC**). This setting controls the height of fractions when using Architectural or Fractional unit dimensions. The value in this box is multiplied by the dimension text height value to determine the height of the fraction. A value of 1.0 creates overall fractions that are two times the text height as regular (nonfractional) dimension text. This is the normally accepted standard. A value less than 1.0 makes the overall fraction smaller than the regular dimension text height.

- **Draw frame around text** (**DIMGAP**). Check this box to have a rectangle around the text. The distance between the text and the frame is determined by the setting for the **Offset from dim line** value. This is discussed later in this section.

The **Text Placement** area of the **Text** tab is used to place the text relative to the dimension line. See **Figure 15-17.** The preview image changes to represent the selections you make. The **Vertical:** (**DIMTAD**) drop-down list has the following options for the vertical justification:

- **Centered.** This option is the default and places dimension text centered in a gap provided in the dimension line. This is the dimensioning practice commonly used in mechanical drafting and many other fields.

**Figure 15-17.**
Dimension text justification options. A—Vertical justification options, with horizontal centered justifications. B—Horizontal justification options, with the vertical centered justifications.

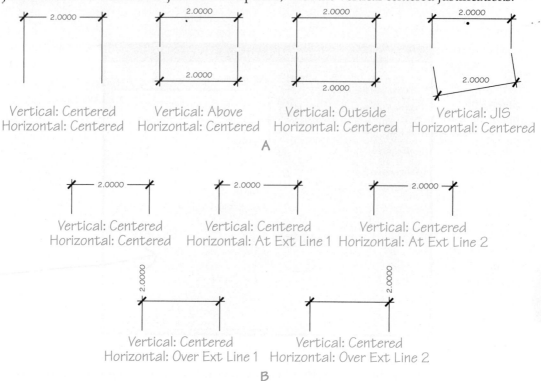

- **Above.** This option is generally used for architectural drafting and building construction, in which the dimension text is placed above the dimension line. This places the dimension text horizontally and above horizontal dimension lines and in a gap provided in vertical and angled dimension lines. *Aligned dimensioning* is commonly used in architectural drafting. This is where the dimension text is aligned (parallel) with the dimension lines and all text reads from either the bottom or right side of the sheet. An additional setting for this type of dimensioning is discussed later in this chapter.
- **Outside.** This option places the dimension text outside the dimension line and either above or below a horizontal dimension line or to the right or left of a vertical dimension line, depending on which way you move the cursor.
- **JIS.** This option is used when dimensioning for the Japanese Industrial Standards.

The **Horizontal:** (**DIMJUST**) drop-down list has the following options for the horizontal justification:

- **Centered.** This option is the AutoCAD default. It places dimension text centered along the dimension line.
- **At Ext Line 1.** This option locates the text next to the extension line placed first.
- **At Ext Line 2.** This option locates the text next to the extension line placed second.
- **Over Ext Line 1.** This option places the text aligned with and over the first extension line. This practice is not commonly used.
- **Over Ext Line 2.** This option places the text aligned with and over the second extension line. This practice is not commonly used.

Architectural Drafting Using AutoCAD

The **Offset from dim line: (DIMGAP)** text box is used to set the gap between the dimension line and the dimension text, the distance between the leader shoulder and the text, and the space between the dimension frame and the text. The default gap is .09 (3/32"). The gap should be set to half the text height. **Figure 15-18** shows the gap in a linear and leader dimension.

The **Text Alignment** area (**DIMTOH** and **DIMTIH**) of the **Text** tab allows you to control the alignment of dimension text. This area is used when you want to draw unidirectional dimensions or aligned dimensions. These types of dimensions were discussed earlier in this chapter. The **Horizontal** option draws unidirectional dimensions commonly used for mechanical manufacturing drafting applications. The **Aligned with dimension line** option creates aligned dimensions, which are typically used for architectural dimensioning. The **ISO Standard** option creates aligned dimensions when the text falls between the extension lines and horizontal dimensions when the text falls outside the extension lines.

**Figure 15-18.**
The offset from dimension line variable (**DIMGAP**) is the gap displayed in a linear dimension and a leader line.

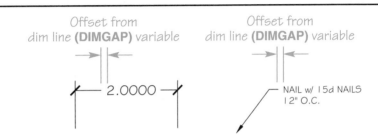

## Exercise 15-3

- ◆ Open ex15-2.
- ◆ Create a text style named Arch. Use the Stylus BT font.
- ◆ Access the **Dimension Style Manager** dialog box. The Architectural style should be current. Select the **Modify...** button. This will open the **Modify Dimension Style: Architectural** dialog box.
- ◆ Use the **Text** tab to make the following settings:

| Setting | Architectural |
|---|---|
| **Text style:** | Arch |
| **Text color:** | ByBlock |
| **Text height:** | 1/8" |
| **Vertical:** | Above |
| **Horizontal:** | Centered |
| **Offset from dim line:** | 3/32" |
| **Text Alignment** | Aligned with dimension line |

- ◆ Pick the **OK** button, and close the **Dimension Style Manager** dialog box.
- ◆ Save the drawing as ex15-3.

The **Fit** tab in the **Modify** (or **New**) **Dimension Style** dialog box is used to establish the way dimension text appears on the drawing and how arrowheads are placed. The **Fit** tab is shown in **Figure 15-19** with default settings.

The **Fit Options** area (**DIMATFIT**) of the **Fit** tab controls how text and arrows should behave if they cannot fit between two extension lines. The effects of the fit option you choose are most obvious on dimensions where space is limited.

Read the message that AutoCAD gives you in the **Fit Options** area. This should help you understand how each option acts. Watch the preview image change as you try each of the following options:

- **Either the text or the arrows, whichever fits best (DIMATFIT = 3).** This default setting allows AutoCAD to place text and dimension lines with arrowheads inside extension lines if space is available. If space is limited, dimension lines with arrowheads are placed outside the extension lines before the text. Both the text and arrowheads are placed outside the extension lines if there is not enough space between extension lines.
- **Arrows (DIMATFIT = 1).** The text, dimension line, and arrowheads are placed inside the extension lines if there is enough space. The text is placed outside of the extension lines if there is enough space for only the arrowheads and dimension line inside the extension lines. Both the text and arrowheads are placed outside the extension lines if there is not enough room for anything inside.
- **Text (DIMATFIT = 2).** The text, dimension line, and arrowheads are placed inside the extension lines if there is enough space for everything. If there is enough space for only the text inside the extension lines, then the dimension lines and arrowheads are placed outside. Both the text and arrowheads are placed outside if there is not enough room for the text inside.
- **Both text and arrows (DIMATFIT = 0).** When this option is used, AutoCAD places the text, dimension line, and arrowheads inside the extension lines if there is enough space. If the text and the arrowheads cannot fit between the extension lines, then they are placed outside the extension lines.

**Figure 15-19.**
The **Fit** tab of the **New Dimension Style: Architectural** dialog box.

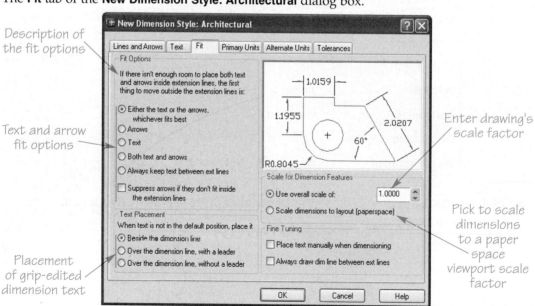

512     

- **Always keep text between ext lines (DIMTIX).** This option always places the dimension text between the extension lines whether there is room or not. This may cause problems when there is limited space between extension lines, because the text may be placed over the extension line.
- **Suppress arrows if they don't fit inside the extension lines (DIMSOXD).** This option removes the arrowheads if they do not fit inside the extension lines. Use this with caution, because it can create dimensions that violate standards.

Sometimes it becomes necessary to move the dimension text from its default position. The text can be moved by grip editing the text portion of the dimension. The options in the **Text Placement** area (**DIMTMOVE**) of the **Fit** tab instruct AutoCAD how to handle these grip-editing situations. The following options are available:

- **Beside the dimension line (DIMTMOVE = 0).** When the dimension text is grip edited and moved, the text is constrained to move with the dimension line and can only be placed within the same plane as the dimension line. As the text is moved, the dimension line will move to stay in line with the text.
- **Over the dimension line, with a leader (DIMTMOVE = 1).** When the dimension text is grip edited and moved, the text can be moved in any direction away from the dimension line. A leader line is then created that connects the text back to the dimension line.
- **Over the dimension line, without a leader (DIMTMOVE = 2).** When the dimension text is grip edited and moved, the text can be moved in any direction away from the dimension line without a connecting leader.

Professional Tip

To return the dimension text to its default position, select the text, right-click to choose the **Dim Text position** shortcut menu option, and then select **Home text**.

The **Scale for Dimension Features** area of the **Fit** tab is used to set the scale factor for all dimension features in the entire drawing. The **Use overall scale of:** (**DIMSCALE** > 0) option sets a *multiplier* for dimension settings, such as text height, arrowhead size, and the offset from origin. The value placed here is the *scale factor* of the drawing. For example, if the height of the dimensioning text is set to .125 (1/8″) and the value for the overall scale is set to 100, then the dimension text can be measured within the drawing to be 12 1/2″ (100 × .125). If the drawing is then plotted and the plot scale is set to 1=100, the size of the dimension text on the plotted paper measures 1/100 its size, which would be 1/8″.

Note

As discussed earlier in this chapter, any sizes in the **Dimension Styles Manager** dialog box should be the actual plotted paper sizes. The **Use overall scale of:** area uses the *scale factor* of the drawing as a multiplier of the dimension settings. Scale factors are discussed in Chapter 11. See Appendix K for a list of common scales and their scale factors.

If you are dimensioning in a floating viewport in a layout tab, select the **Scale dimensions to layout (paperspace)** (**DIMSCALE** = 0) option. It allows the overall scale of dimensions to adjust based on the active floating viewport by setting the overall scale equal to the viewport scale factor. Layout space and viewports are discussed in Chapter 24.

The **Fine Tuning** area of the **Fit** tab provides you with maximum flexibility in controlling where you want to place dimension text. The **Place text manually when dimensioning** (**DIMUPT**) option gives you control over text placement and dimension line length outside extension lines. After the dimension line has been placed, the text can be placed where you want it, such as beside the extension lines, or outside of the extension lines.

The **Always draw dim line between ext lines** (**DIMTOFL**) option forces AutoCAD to place the dimension line inside the extension lines, even when the text and arrowheads are outside. The default application is with the dimension line and arrowheads outside the extension lines. **Figure 15-20** shows the difference between checked and unchecked. Architectural firms usually prefer forcing the dimension line inside the extension lines.

**Figure 15-20.**
The effects of the **Always draw dim line between ext lines** option in the **Fit** tab.

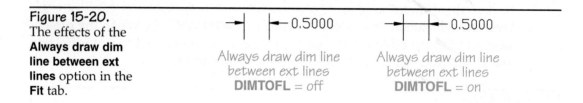

Always draw dim line between ext lines
**DIMTOFL** = off

Always draw dim line between ext lines
**DIMTOFL** = on

## Exercise 15-4

◆ Open ex15-3.
◆ Access the **Dimension Style Manager** dialog box. The Architectural style should be current. Select the **Modify...** button.
◆ This will open the **Modify Dimension Style: Architectural** dialog box.
◆ Use the **Fit** tab to make the following settings:

| Setting | Architectural |
|---|---|
| **Fit Options** | Either the text or the arrows, whichever fits best |
| **Text Placement** | Over the dimension line, without a leader |
| **Scale for Dimension Features** | Use overall scale of: 48 (1/4″ = 1′-0″ = scale factor of 48) |
| **Fine Tuning** | Always draw dim line between ext lines |

◆ Pick the **OK** button, and close the **Dimension Style Manager** dialog box.
◆ Save the drawing as ex15-4.

## Using the Primary Units Tab

The **Primary Units** tab is where the settings for the type of AutoCAD dimensioning units can be set up. The **UNITS** command allows you to draw new geometry using Architectural, Fractional, or Decimal units. The **Primary Units** tab is where the unit setting for your main (primary) dimension text is specified. The following section explains the function of each of the options in the **Primary Units** tab of the **New** (or **Modify**) **Dimension Style** dialog box. See **Figure 15-21**.

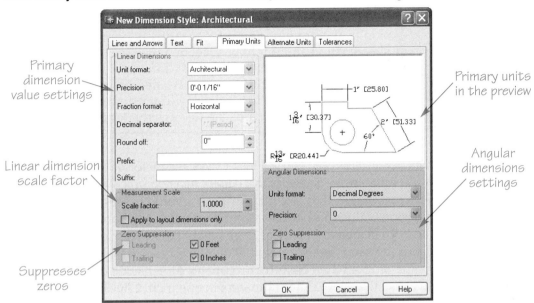

*Primary dimension value settings*

*Linear dimension scale factor*

*Suppresses zeros*

*Primary units in the preview*

*Angular dimensions settings*

The **Linear Dimensions** area of the **Primary Units** tab is used to set units for linear dimensions. The following discusses each of the setting options:

- **Unit format (DIMLUNIT/DIMALTU).** Use this drop-down list to select the type of units for dimension text. The default is Decimal units. The options include Scientific, Decimal, Engineering, Architectural, Fractional, and Windows Desktop units. Architectural units are most commonly used in architectural drawings and engineering units are most commonly used in civil and GIS drawings.
- **Precision (DIMDEC/DIMALTD).** Use this drop-down list to determine how many zeros follow the decimal place when decimal units are selected. If using Decimal units, the default is 0.0000. When Architectural or Fractional units are selected, the precision values are related to the smallest desired fractional denominator. The default is 1/16″, but you can choose other options ranging from 1/256″ to 1/2″, or 0″ if you want no fractional values displayed. A variety of dimension precisions can be found on the same drawing.
- **Fraction format (DIMFRAC).** The options for controlling the display of fractions are Diagonal, Horizontal, and Not Stacked. This choice is only available if the Architectural or Fractional style is selected for the unit format.
- **Decimal separator (DIMDSEP).** Decimal numbers may use commas, periods, or spaces as separators. The '.' (Period) option is the default. This option is only available if using Decimal units.
- **Round off (DIMRND/DIMALTRND).** Use this text box to have all numbers rounded to a specified value. The default is zero, which means that no rounding takes place and all dimensions are placed exactly as measured. If you enter a value of .1, all dimensions are rounded to the closest .1 unit. For example, an actual measurement of 1.188 is rounded to 1.2.
- **Prefix (DIMPOST/DIMAPOST).** *Prefixes* are special notes or designations placed in front of the dimension text. A typical prefix might be 3X, meaning three times. When a prefix is used on a diameter or radius dimension, the prefix replaces the ∅ (diameter) or R (radius) symbol.
- **Suffix (DIMPOST/DIMAPOST).** *Suffixes* are special notes or designations placed after the dimension text. A typical suffix might be NTS, the abbreviation for *Not to Scale*. The abbreviation mm can also be used when metric dimensions are placed on an inch drawing.

- **Measurement Scale.** This area is used to set the scale factor of linear dimension values. Set the value in the **Scale factor: (DIMLFAC)** text box. Dimension values display the actual length they are measuring if a value is set to 1. If it is set to 2, the dimension values are twice as much as the measured amount. For example, an actual measurement of 2 inches is displayed as 2 with a scale factor of 1, but the same measurement is displayed as 4 when the scale factor is 2. Set a value of 25.4 when creating millimeter dimensions of an inch-based drawing, because there are 25.4 millimeters in one inch. Checking the **Apply to layout dimensions only (DIMLFAC < 0)** check box makes the linear scale factor active only when dimensioning in a layout tab. This causes dimensions placed on a layout tab to display the actual size of the object being measured, even though the object may be scaled on the layout sheet.

- **Zero Suppression (DIMZIN/DIMALTZ).** There are four check boxes in this area used to suppress leading and trailing zeros in dimensions based on the primary units.

  - **Leading.** This check box is off by default, which leaves a leading zero on decimal unit numerals less than one, such as 0.5. Check this box to remove the 0 on decimal units less than one. The result is a decimal dimension, such as .5.

  - **Trailing.** This check box is off by default, which leaves zeros after the decimal point based upon the precision setting.

  - **0 Feet.** This check box is on by default, and removes the leading zero in architectural or engineering unit dimensions when there are zero feet. For example, when **0 Feet** is on, a measurement reads 11″. If **0 Feet** is off, the same dimension reads 0′-11″. This option is not available when using the Decimal unit format.

  - **0 Inches.** This check box is on by default, and removes the zero when the inch part of feet and inch dimensions is zero, such as 12′. If this check box is off, the same dimension reads 12′-0″. This option is not available when the unit format is Decimal.

The **Angular Dimensions** area of the **Primary Units** tab is used to set the desired type of angular units for dimensioning. The **UNITS** command does not control the type of angular units used for dimensioning. The following settings are found in this area:

- **Units format (DIMAUNIT).** The default setting is Decimal Degrees and the other options are Deg/Min/Sec, Gradians, and Radians.
- **Precision (DIMADEC).** Sets the desired precision for the angular dimension value display. Select an option from the drop-down list. This is similar to the precision for linear dimensions.
- **Zero Suppression (DIMAZIN).** This area is used to keep or remove leading or trailing zeros for angular dimension values.

## Exercise 15-5

◆ Open ex15-4.
◆ Access the **Dimension Style Manager** dialog box. The Architectural style should be current. Select the **Modify...** button. This will open the **Modify Dimension Style: Architectural** dialog box.
◆ Use the **Primary Units** tab to make the following settings:

| Setting | Architectural |
|---|---|
| Unit Format: | Architectural |
| Precision | 1/16″ |
| Fraction Format: | Diagonal |
| Round off | 0 |
| Measurement Scale | 1 |
| Zero Suppression | Uncheck 0 inches |
| Units format: | Decimal Degrees |
| Precision | 0.00 |
| Zero Suppression | Activate Leading |

◆ In the **Text** tab, set the **Fraction height scale** to 0.5.
◆ Pick the **OK** button, and close the **Dimension Style Manager** dialog box.
◆ Save the drawing as ex15-5.

## Using the **Alternate Units** Tab

The **Alternate Units** tab is used to set up and display alternate units on a dimension. See **Figure 15-22.** *Alternate units* have inch measurements followed by millimeters in brackets. This is referred to as *dual dimensioning*. By default, when alternate dimensions are used, a metric equivalent of the inch dimension is shown in brackets beside the primary unit number.

To activate the settings for alternate units, check the **Display Alternate Units (DIMALT)** check box. The **Alternate Units** area has many of the same settings found in the **Primary Units** tab. The **Multiplier for alt units (DIMALTF)** setting is the value used to multiply with the primary unit to establish the value for the alternate unit. The default is 25.4, because multiplying inch values by 25.4 converts them to millimeters (25.4 millimeters in each inch). The **Placement** area controls the location of the alternate unit. The two options are **After primary value** and **Below primary value.** See **Figure 15-23.**

**Figure 15-22.**
The **Alternate Units** tab of the **New Dimension Style: Architectural** dialog box.

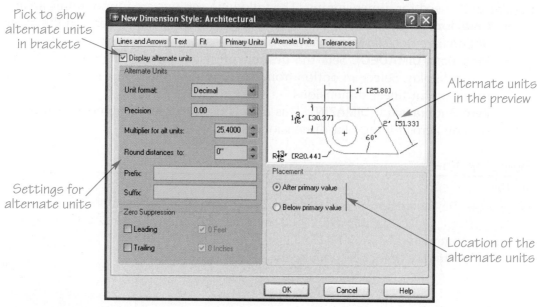

Pick to show alternate units in brackets

Settings for alternate units

Alternate units in the preview

Location of the alternate units

**Figure 15-23.**
Alternate dimension locations.

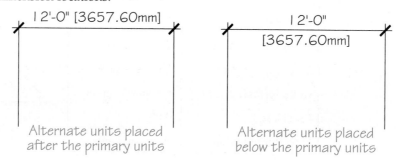

Alternate units placed after the primary units

Alternate units placed below the primary units

## Using the Tolerances Tab

The **Tolerances** tab can be used to apply a tolerance method to your drawing. Tolerances are typically used in mechanical drafting practices but can also apply to some architectural applications. See **Figure 15-24.** The following describes the options in the **Tolerances** tab:

- **Method. None** is the default option. This means that no tolerance method is used for dimensions. As a result, most of the options in this area are disabled. Other dimensioning methods can be selected by picking the drop-down arrow. If **Symmetrical, Deviation, Limits,** or **Basic** is selected from the **Method:** drop-down list, the resulting preview image shows the method selected. **Figure 15-25** provides an example of each type of tolerance.
  - **None.** No tolerances are applied to the dimensions.
  - **Symmetrical (DIMTOL).** This method is used to draw a plus/minus tolerance that is an equal bilateral tolerance for a dimension. *Equal bilateral* means the plus tolerance is the same as the minus tolerance.
  - **Deviation (DIMTOL).** This method is used to create a bilateral plus/minus tolerance, which means the plus value is different than the minus value.
  - **Limits (DIMLIM).** This method is used when a dimension must fit between an upper value and a lower value.

Figure 15-24.
The **Tolerances** tab
in the **New
Dimension Style:
Architectural** dialog
box.

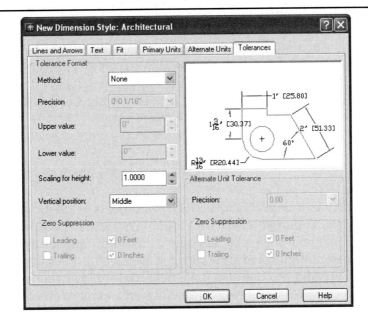

Figure 15-25.
Different types of
tolerance dimen-
sioning.

Symmetrical
Tolerance

Deviation
Tolerance

Limits Tolerance

Basic
Dimension

- **Basic.** This method is used for a theoretically perfect dimension and is used in geometric dimensioning and tolerancing (GD&T). This type of dimension places a box around a dimension.
- **Precision.** This setting determines how accurately the tolerance will be dimensioned.
- **Upper value (DIMTP).** This setting becomes available when choosing the deviation or limits tolerance method. It is used for specifying the tolerance value for **Symmetrical** dimensions or the plus value for **Deviation** and **Limit** tolerances.
- **Lower value (DIMTM).** This value becomes available when choosing the deviation or limits tolerance method and specifies the minus value in the tolerance.
- **Scaling for height.** This sets the size of the tolerance in relationship to the overall dimension text size. A value of .5 will create the tolerance half the height of the overall dimension text. Changing this value also affects the **Fraction height scale** setting in the **Text** tab.
- **Vertical Position.** This setting changes the justification of the tolerance. Options include **Bottom**, **Middle**, and **Top**.

- **Zero Suppression.** These settings control the placement of leading or trailing zeros in the tolerance.

The **Alternate Unit Tolerance** area controls tolerances in alternate units. Change the precision and the zero suppression values as appropriate.

After completing the information on all tabs, select the **OK** button to return to the **Dimension Style Manager** dialog box. Select **Set Current** to have all new dimensions take on the qualities of the newly created style.

# Creating Substyles

The previous section described the process of creating a parent, or global, dimension style. A *parent dimension style* lays down the rules for each type of dimensioning command to establish how dimensions appear in the drawing. For example, if the parent dimension style uses the architectural tick arrowhead, linear dimensions and radius dimensions also have tick marks. However, a substyle allows you to use the closed filled arrow for a radius dimension by overriding the global setting in the parent dimension style. The substyle is sometimes referred to as the *child dimension style,* because it is subordinate to the parent.

The child dimension style (substyle) can modify the rules set by the parent dimension style. In the previous case, if closed filled arrows for radius dimensions are desired instead of the tick marks, you will create a child dimension style. A parent dimension style must exist before a child dimension style can be created. To create a child dimension style, access the **Dimension Style Manager** dialog box. Access the **Create New Dimension Style** dialog box by selecting the **New...** button. In the **Start With:** drop-down list, select the parent style to be modified. Then in the **Use for:** list box, select the type of dimension you would like to override. With the closed filled arrow example, select Radius dimensions. Notice that the **New Style Name:** area is grayed out. AutoCAD makes this a dimension override, because the rules for the parent radius dimensions are being broken. See **Figure 15-26.**

Pick the **Continue** button when finished to access the **New Dimension Style** dialog box. This is the same dialog box that you used when creating new dimension styles. The only difference is that some areas are grayed out. The areas that are grayed out mean that these settings do not affect the type of dimension you are overriding. See **Figure 15-27.** Go through the tabs making the appropriate changes desired for the child style (substyle).

Figure 15-26.
The **Create New Dimension Style** dialog box for creating a child dimension style.

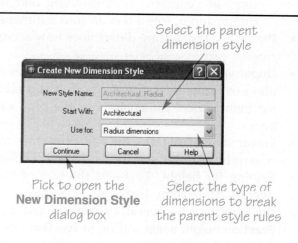

Select the parent
dimension style

Pick to open the
**New Dimension Style**
dialog box

Select the type of
dimensions to break
the parent style rules

Architectural Drafting Using AutoCAD

**Figure 15-27.**
The **Lines and Arrows** tab with some options grayed out.

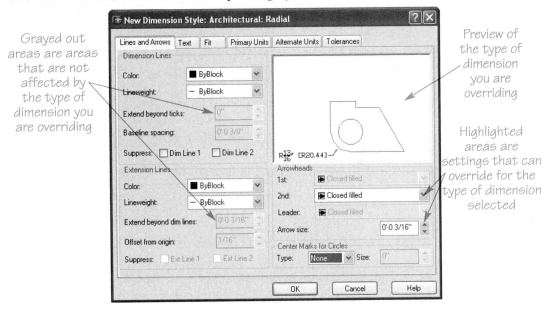

Grayed out areas are areas that are not affected by the type of dimension you are overriding

Preview of the type of dimension you are overriding

Highlighted areas are settings that can override for the type of dimension selected

When finished, press the **OK** button to return to the **Dimension Style Manager** dialog box. Notice that Architectural (parent dimension style) now has Radial (child dimension style) listed beneath it. See **Figure 15-28.**

**Figure 15-28.**
The parent dimension style controls all aspects of a dimension. The child dimension style affects how radius dimensions will appear.

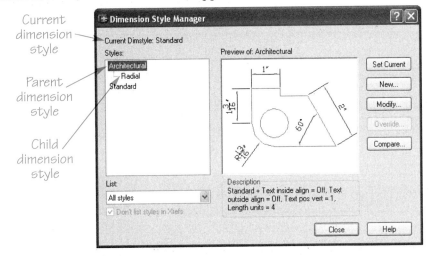

Current dimension style

Parent dimension style

Child dimension style

## Exercise 15-6

◆ Open ex15-5.
◆ Access the **Dimension Style Manager** dialog box. The Architectural style should be current. Select the **New...** button to open the **New Dimension Style** dialog box.
◆ Start with the Architectural style and override the radius dimensions. Change the 2nd arrowheads to a closed filled arrow, and change the vertical text placement to centered.
◆ Pick the **OK** button to return to the **Dimension Style Manager** dialog box.
◆ Create a child style for angular and diameter dimensions. Change the 1st arrowheads and 2nd arrowheads to closed filled arrows, and change the vertical text placement to centered.
◆ Pick the **Close** button and save the drawing as ex15-6.

## Making Your Own Dimension Styles

Creating and recording dimension styles is part of your AutoCAD management responsibility. You should carefully evaluate the items contained in the dimensions for the type of drawings you do. During this process, be sure to carefully check company, school, or national standards to verify the accuracy of your plan. Based on what you have learned in this chapter, make a list of features and values for the dimensioning settings you use. When you are ready, use the **Dimension Style Manager** dialog box to establish dimension styles that are named to suit your drafting practices. **Figure 15-29** provides possible dimension style settings for architectural, civil engineering, and metric drafting applications.

**Figure 15-29.**
Common dimension settings for civil and architectural dimension styles.

| Setting | Architectural | Civil | Metric |
|---|---|---|---|
| Dimension line spacing | 1/2″ | .75 | 12.7 mm |
| Extension line extension | 1/8″ | .125 | 3.175 mm |
| Extension line offset | 3/32″ | .125 | 2.38 mm |
| Arrowheads | Oblique, Architectural Tick, or Right Angle | Closed, Closed Filled, or Dot | Oblique, Architectural Tick, Closed, Closed Filled or Right Angle |
| Arrowhead size | 1/8″ | .125 | 3.175 mm |
| Center | Mark | Line | Line |
| Center size | 1/4″ | .25 | 6.35 mm |
| Vertical justification | Above | Above | Above |
| Text alignment | Aligned with dimension line | Aligned with dimension line | ISO Standard |
| Primary units | Architectural | Engineering | Decimal |
| Dimension precision | 1/16″ | 0.00 | 1.58 mm |
| Zero suppression | Feet check on Inches check off | Leading check off Trailing check off | Leading check on Trailing check off |
| Angles | Decimal Degrees | Deg/Min/Sec | Decimal Degrees |
| Text style | Stylus BT | Romans | Romans |
| Text height | 1/8″ or 3/32″ | .125 | 3.175 mm or 2.38 mm |
| Text gap | 1/16″ | .1 | 1.58 mm |

When a variety of dimension styles have been created, you can easily switch between dimension styles by using the **Dim Style Control** drop-down list in the **Styles** toolbar. Pick the down arrow and select the desired dimension style. You can also change the dimension style of a dimension in your drawing. Pick the dimension you wish to change to access the grip control, and then pick the desired style from the **Dim Style Control** drop-down list.

Another way to change the dimension style of an existing dimension is to use the **UPDATE** command. This command changes the dimension style of the selected dimension to the current style. The **UPDATE** command can be accessed by picking **Dimension Update** from the **Dimension** toolbar, by selecting **Update** from the **Dimension** pull-down menu, or by entering dim at the Command prompt followed by entering update at the Dim: prompt.

Dimension styles should be created in your template drawings. They are then available for use whenever a drawing is started from the template.

**DesignCenter** can be used as a way to copy existing dimension styles from one drawing to another. To do this, find the drawing that contains the desired dimension style, then drag and drop the style into your drawing. Refer to Chapter 10 for more information on **DesignCenter**.

## Exercise 15-7

- Create your own dimension style settings list for the type of drafting you perform. Confirm optional settings with your instructor or supervisor.
- Open the **Dimension Style Manager** dialog box and change the settings as needed to match the list you created.
- Save the dimension style with a name that describes the list you made.
- Save the drawing as ex15-7.

# Drawing Dimensions with AutoCAD

AutoCAD has a variety of dimensioning applications that fall into five fundamental categories: linear, angular, diameter, radius, and ordinate dimensioning. These applications allow you to perform nearly every type of dimensioning practice needed for architecture.

# Drawing Linear Dimensions

Linear means straight. In most cases, dimensions measure straight distances, such as horizontal, vertical, or angled surfaces. The **DIMLINEAR** command allows you to measure the length of an object and place extension lines, dimension lines, dimension text, and arrowheads automatically. To do this, pick the **Linear Dimension** button in the **Dimension** toolbar, select **Linear** from the **Dimension** pull-down menu, or enter dli or dimlinear at the Command prompt as follows:

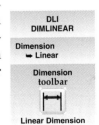

Command: **dli** or **dimlinear**↵
Specify first extension line origin or <select object>: *(pick the origin of the first extension line)*
Specify second extension line origin: *(pick the origin of the second extension line)*

The points you pick are the extension line origins. See **Figure 15-30.** Place the crosshairs directly on the corners of the object where the extension lines begin. Use object snap modes for accuracy.

The **DIMLINEAR** command allows you to generate horizontal, vertical, or rotated dimensions. After selecting the object or points of origin for dimensioning, the following prompt appears:

Specify dimension line location or [Mtext/Text/Angle/Horizontal/Vertical/Rotated]:

These options are outlined as follows:

- **Specify dimension line location.** This is the default. Simply drag the dimension line to a desired location and pick. See **Figure 15-31.** This is where preliminary plan sheets and sketches help you determine proper distances around the object or building to avoid crowding of dimensions. The extension lines, dimension line, dimension text, and arrowheads are automatically drawn.
- **Mtext.** This option accesses the multiline text editor. See **Figure 15-32.** Here you can provide specific measurement, content, or text format for the dimension. See Chapter 8 for a complete description of the multiline text editor. The chevrons (< >) represent the current dimension value. If you want the current dimension value changed, delete the chevrons and type the new value. If you want the chevrons to be part of the dimension text, type the new value inside, before, or after the chevrons.
- **Text.** This option uses the command line to change dimension text. This is convenient if you prefer to type in the desired text rather than use the multiline text editor. The **Text** and **Mtext** options both create multiline text objects. The **Text** option displays the current dimension value in brackets and allows you to accept this value or type a new value. The command sequence works like this:

Specify dimension line location or [Mtext/Text/Angle/Horizontal/Vertical/_Rotated]: t↵
Enter dimension text <4'-0">:

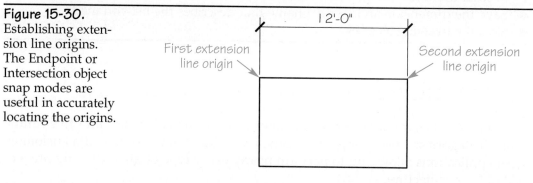

**Figure 15-30.**
Establishing extension line origins. The Endpoint or Intersection object snap modes are useful in accurately locating the origins.

First extension line origin

Second extension line origin

12'-0"

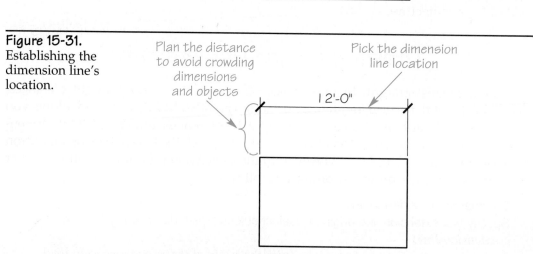

**Figure 15-31.**
Establishing the dimension line's location.

Plan the distance to avoid crowding dimensions and objects

Pick the dimension line location

12'-0"

**Figure 15-32.**
When using the **Mtext** option, the multiline text editor dialog box appears. The chevrons (< >) represent the dimension value AutoCAD has calculated.

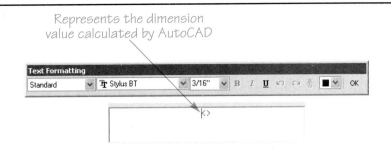

Represents the dimension value calculated by AutoCAD

Pressing [Enter] accepts the current value. Add a suffix, such as (OC), as follows:

Enter dimension text <4'-0">: **<>(OC)** ↵

- **Angle.** This option allows you to change the dimension text angle. This option can be used when creating rotated dimensions or for adjusting the dimension text to a desired angle. The sequence is as follows:

Specify dimension line location or [Mtext/Text/Angle/Horizontal/Vertical/_Rotated]: **a**↵
Specify angle of dimension text: *(enter desired angle)*

- **Horizontal.** This option sets the dimension to a horizontal distance only. This may be helpful when dimensioning the horizontal distance of an angled surface. The **Mtext**, **Text**, and **Angle** options are available again in case you want to change the dimension text value or angle.
- **Vertical.** This option sets the dimension being created to a vertical distance only. This option may be helpful when dimensioning the vertical distance of an angled surface. Like the **Horizontal** option, the **Mtext**, **Text**, and **Angle** options are available.
- **Rotated.** This option allows an angle to be specified for the dimension line. A practical application is dimensioning to angled surfaces and auxiliary views. This technique is different from other dimensioning commands because you are asked to provide a dimension line angle. See **Figure 15-33**. The command sequence looks like this:

**Figure 15-33.**
Rotating a dimension for an angled view.

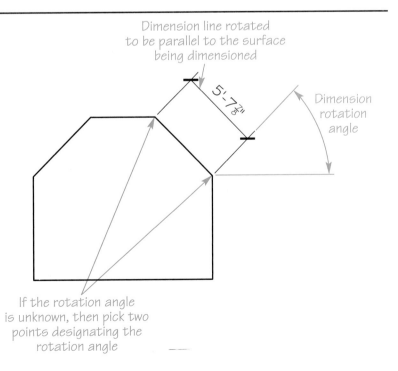

Dimension line rotated to be parallel to the surface being dimensioned

Dimension rotation angle

If the rotation angle is unknown, then pick two points designating the rotation angle

Specify dimension line location or [Mtext/Text/Angle/Horizontal/Vertical/_Rotated]: r↵
Specify angle of dimension line <0>: *(enter a value, such as 45, or pick two points*
*on the line to be dimensioned)*

## Exercise 15-8

◆ Start a new drawing using one of your templates.
◆ Use **DesignCenter** to drag and drop the Architectural dimension style from ex15-6 into your drawing.
◆ Draw and dimension the two objects below.

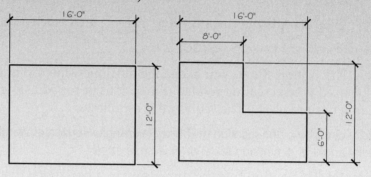

◆ Draw and dimension an object similar to **Figure 15-30** using the **Text** option to change the dimension text to read 12'-0" (NTS).
◆ Save the drawing as ex15-8.

## Selecting an Object to Dimension

In the previous discussion, the extension line origins were picked in order to establish the extents of the dimension. One of the more powerful options of AutoCAD allows you to pick a single line, circle, or arc to dimension. This works when you are using the **DIMLINEAR** command as well as the **DIMALIGNED** and **QDIM** commands, which are discussed later in this chapter. You can use this AutoCAD feature any time you see the Specify first extension line origin or <select object>: prompt. Press [Enter] and select the object being dimensioned. When you select a line or arc, AutoCAD automatically begins the extension lines from the endpoints. If you pick a circle, the extension lines are drawn from the closest quadrant and its opposite quadrant. See **Figure 15-34**.

**Figure 15-34.**
AutoCAD can automatically determine the extension line origins if you select a line, arc, or circle.

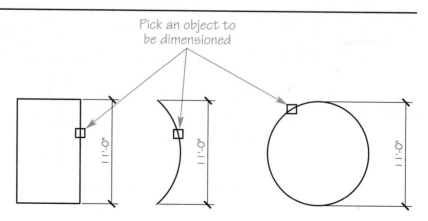

# Exercise 15-9

◆ Open ex15-8.
◆ Draw and dimension the three objects shown using the **select object** option. Dimension the objects exactly as shown.
◆ Save the drawing as ex15-9.

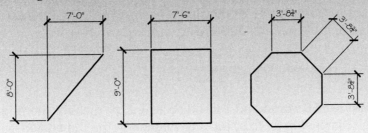

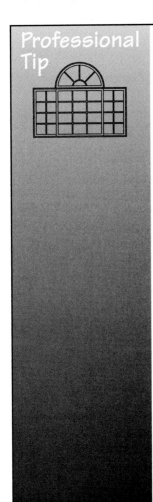

Dimensioning in AutoCAD should be performed as accurately and neatly as possible. You can achieve consistently professional results by using the following guidelines:

- Always construct drawing geometry accurately. Never round decimal values when entering locations, distances, or angles. For example, enter .4375 for 7/16, rather than .44.
- Set the desired precision level before beginning dimensioning. Most drawings have varying levels of precision for specific drawing features, so select the most common precision level to start with, and adjust the precision as needed for each dimension.
- Always use the precision drawing aids to ensure the accuracy of dimensions. If the point being dimensioned does not coincide with a snap point or a known coordinate, use an appropriate object snap override.
- *Never* type a different dimension value than what appears in the brackets. If a dimension needs to change, revise the drawing or dimensioning variables accordingly. The ability to change the dimension in the brackets is provided by AutoCAD so that a different text format can be specified for the dimension. Prefixes and suffixes can also be added to the dimension in the brackets. A typical example of a prefix might be to specify the number of times a dimension occurs, such as 4X 2'-0". Other examples of this capability appear later in this chapter.

# Dimensioning Angled Surfaces and Auxiliary Views

When dimensioning an object drawn at an angle, it may be necessary to align the dimension line with the surface. For example, auxiliary views are normally placed at an angle. In order to properly dimension these features, the **DIMALIGNED** command or the **Rotated** option of the **DIMLINEAR** command can be used.

## Using the DIMALIGNED Command

The **DIMALIGNED** command can be accessed by picking the **Aligned Dimension** button on the **Dimension** toolbar, picking **Aligned** in the **Dimension** pull-down menu, or entering dal or dimaligned at the Command prompt. The results of the **DIMALIGNED** command are displayed in **Figure 15-35.** The following shows the command sequence:

Command: **dal** *or* **dimaligned.**↵
Specify first extension line origin or <select object>: *(pick the first extension line origin)*
Specify second extension line origin: *(pick the second extension line origin)*
Specify dimension line location or [Mtext/Text/Angle]: *(pick the dimension line location)*
Dimension text = 5' 7-7/8"
Command:

Figure 15-35.
The **DIMALIGNED** dimension command allows you to place dimension lines parallel to angled features.

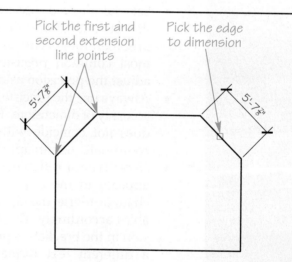

Pick the first and second extension line points

Pick the edge to dimension

# Exercise 15-10

◆ Open ex15-9.
◆ Draw the objects shown below. Object A is a hexagon using the **Edge** option of the **POLYGON** command. The absolute coordinates for Object B are provided.

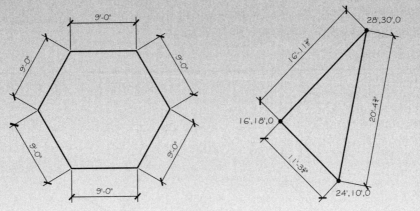

◆ Use the **DIMALIGNED** command to dimension Object A. Use the **Rotate** option of the **DIMLINEAR** command to dimension Object B.
◆ Save the drawing as ex15-10.

# Dimensioning Angles

*Angular dimensioning* locates one corner with a dimension and provides the value of the angle in degrees. See **Figure 15-36.** You can dimension the angle between any two nonparallel lines. The intersection of the lines is the angle's vertex. AutoCAD automatically draws extension lines if they are needed.

The type of angular unit depends on the criteria set within the dimension style. To access the **DIMANGULAR** command, pick the **Angular Dimension** button in the **Dimension** toolbar, pick **Angular** in the **Dimension** pull-down menu, or enter dan or dimangular at the Command prompt. Refer to **Figure 15-36A** as you read the following sequence:

DAN
DIMANGULAR

Dimension
➡ Angular

Dimension
toolbar

Angular Dimension

Command: **dan** *or* **dimangular**↵
Select arc, circle, line, or <specify vertex>: *(pick the first leg of the angle to be dimensioned)*
Select second line: *(pick the second leg of the angle to be dimensioned)*
Specify dimension arc line location or [Mtext/Text/Angle]: *(pick the desired location of the dimension line arc)*
Dimension text = 45
Command:

**Figure 15-36.**
Two examples of drawing angular dimensions.

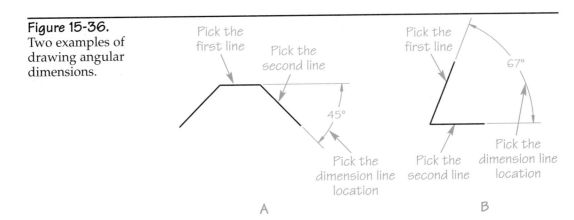

When you are prompted to pick the dimension line arc location, AutoCAD places the dimension text, dimension line arc, and arrowheads inside the extension lines if there is enough space. If there is not enough space between extension lines for the arrowheads and text, AutoCAD automatically places the arrowheads outside and the text inside the extension lines. If space is very tight, AutoCAD may place the dimension line arc and arrowheads inside and the text outside, or may place everything outside of the extension lines. See **Figure 15-37.**

**Figure 15-37.**
The dimension line location determines where the dimension line arc, text, and arrow are displayed.

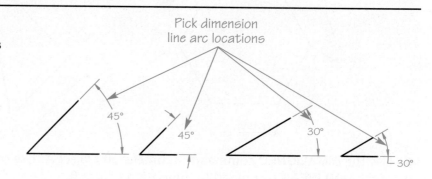

## Placing Angular Dimensions on Arcs

The **DIMANGULAR** command can be used to dimension the included angle of an arc. The arc's center point becomes the angle vertex and the two arc endpoints are the origin points for the extension lines. See **Figure 15-38.** The command sequence is as follows:

Command: **dan** *or* **dimangular**↵
Select arc, circle, line, or <specify vertex>: *(pick the arc)*
Specify dimension arc line location or [Mtext/Text/Angle]: *(pick the desired dimension line location)*
Dimension text = 44
Command:

**Figure 15-38.**
Placing angular dimensions on arcs.

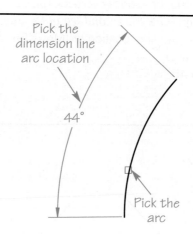

Architectural Drafting Using AutoCAD

## Placing Angular Dimensions on Circles

The **DIMANGULAR** command can also be used to dimension a portion of a circle. The circle's center point becomes the angle vertex and two picked points are the origin points for the extension lines. See **Figure 15-39.** The command sequence is as follows:

Command: **dan** *or* **dimangular**↵
Select arc, circle, line, or <specify vertex>: *(pick the circle)*

The point you pick on the circle becomes the endpoint of the first extension line. You are then asked for the second angle endpoint. This becomes the endpoint of the second extension line:

Specify second angle endpoint: *(pick the second point)*
Specify dimension arc line location or [Mtext/Text/Angle]: *(pick the desired dimension line location)*
Dimension text = 122
Command:

Figure 15-39.
Placing angular dimensions on circles.

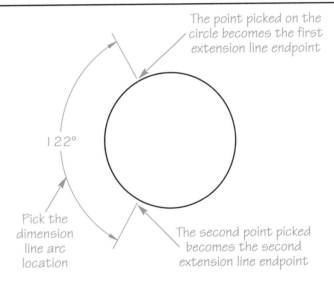

The point picked on the circle becomes the first extension line endpoint

122°

Pick the dimension line arc location

The second point picked becomes the second extension line endpoint

**Professional Tip**

Using angular dimensioning for circles increases the number of possible solutions for a given dimensioning requirement, but the actual uses are limited. One professional application is dimensioning an angle from a quadrant point to a particular feature without having to first draw a line to dimension. Another benefit of this option is the ability to specify angles that exceed 180°.

## Angular Dimensioning through Three Points

You can also establish an angular dimension through three points. The points are the angle vertex and the two angle line endpoints. See **Figure 15-40.** To do this, press [Enter] after the Select arc, circle, line, or <specify vertex>: prompt:

Command: **dan** *or* **dimangular**↵
Select arc, circle, line, or <specify vertex>: ↵
Specify angle vertex: *(pick a vertex point and a "rubber band" connects between the vertex and the cursor to help locate the first point)*
Specify first angle endpoint: *(pick the first endpoint)*
Specify second angle endpoint: *(pick the second endpoint)*
Specify dimension arc line location or [Mtext/Text/Angle]: *(pick the desired dimension line location)*
Dimension text = 65

This method also dimensions angles over 180°.

**Figure 15-40.**
Angular dimensions using three points.

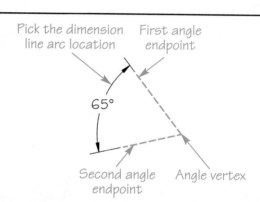

Pick the dimension line arc location    First angle endpoint

65°

Second angle endpoint    Angle vertex

## Exercise 15-11

◆ Start a new drawing using one of your templates.
◆ Use **DesignCenter** to import the Architectural dimension style from ex15-6.
◆ Draw the object below and use the **DIMLINEAR** and **DIMANGULAR** dimensioning commands to dimension the object exactly as shown.
◆ Save the drawing as ex15-11.

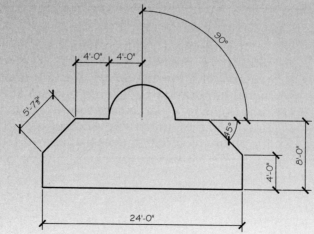

# Location Dimensions

*Location dimensions* are used to locate features on an object or plan from a common measuring point. Location dimensioning can be broken down into two types: datum and chain.

In *datum dimensioning,* locations are measured from a known point. See **Figure 15-41.** Datum dimensioning can be seen most often in mechanical drafting and occasionally in civil engineering drawings when dimensioning the contour intervals of a site. AutoCAD refers to datum dimensions as baseline or ordinate dimensions. Datum dimensions use the **DIMBASELINE** or **DIMORDINATE** command.

*Chain dimensioning* uses a series of dimensions where each successive dimension continues from the previous dimension. Chain dimensioning is also often called *point-to-point dimensioning.* Chain dimensions use two different dimension commands, **DIMBASELINE** and **DIMCONTINUE.** With continuous dimensions, interior walls, windows, and doors can be dimensioned to their centers from an exterior wall. See **Figure 15-42.**

**Figure 15-41.**
Using datum dimensions for a cross section of a site plan.

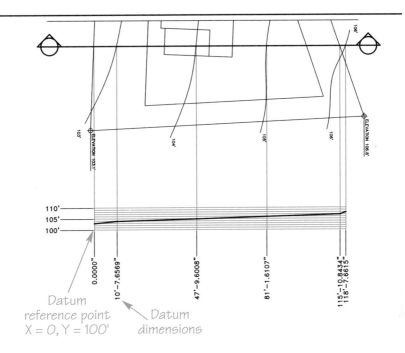

## Using Arrowless Dimensions

AutoCAD refers to arrowless dimensions as ordinate dimensions. *Arrowless dimensions* are dimensions that do not have the traditional extension lines, dimension lines, and arrowheads. These dimensions use only an extension line and dimension value. The dimension for each feature originates from a common starting place, called a datum. This type of dimensioning is commonly done in the precision sheet metal industry and occasionally in the civil engineering field. To use ordinate dimensions, select the **Ordinate Dimension** button on the **Dimension** toolbar, pick **Ordinate** from the **Dimension** pull-down menu, or enter dimord or dimordinate at the Command prompt. The following sequence is used to dimension the items in **Figure 15-43A:**

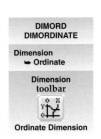

DIMORD
DIMORDINATE

Dimension
➥ Ordinate

Dimension
toolbar

Ordinate Dimension

Command: **dimord** *or* **dimordinate.**↵
Specify feature location: *(pick the desired feature to dimension)*
Specify leader endpoint or [Xdatum/Ydatum/Mtext/Text/Angle]: *(pick the desired dimension leader line endpoint)*
Dimension text = 16'-0 7/8"

---

**Figure 15-42.**
Using chain dimensions to dimension a floor plan.

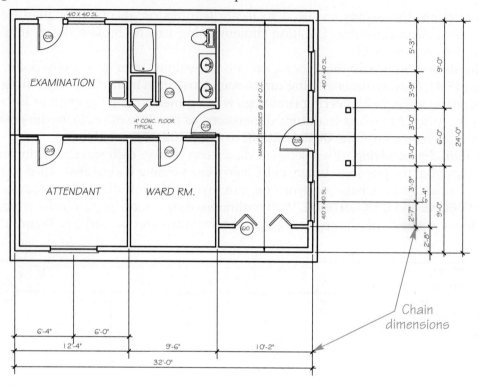

**Figure 15-43.**
A—Placing an ordinate dimension. B—Move the UCS to the new 0,0 measuring point before using ordinate dimensions.

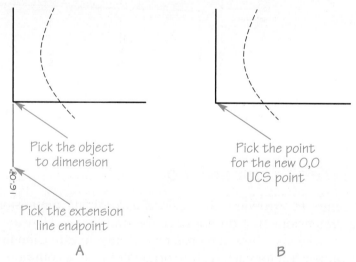

Pick the object
to dimension

Pick the extension
line endpoint

Pick the point
for the new 0,0
UCS point

A

B

Notice that the value for the dimension does not start at 0′-0″. Ordinate dimensions begin measuring from the current user coordinate system (UCS). In order for the first ordinate dimension to be measured as 0, the UCS origin (0,0 point) needs to be moved to the corner of the object you are trying to dimension.

To move the UCS, pick the **Origin UCS** button on the **UCS** toolbar, select **Origin** from the **New UCS** cascading menu in the **Tools** pull-down menu, or enter ucs at the Command prompt. The following sequence moves the UCS origin to the corner of the site plan in **Figure 15-43B.**

Tools
→ New UCS
→ Origin

UCS
toolbar

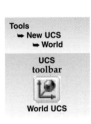

Origin UCS

```
Command: ucs↵
Current ucs name: *WORLD*
Enter an option [New/Move/orthoGraphic/Prev/Restore/Save/Del/Apply/?/World]
<World>: n↵
Specify origin of new UCS or [ZAxis/3point/OBject/Face/View/X/Y/Z] <0,0,0>: (pick the
    desired 0,0 point)
```

After the UCS has been moved to its new 0,0 point, use ordinate dimensions to finish dimensioning the drawing. Any new ordinate dimensions are now measured relative to the new 0,0 point. If you want to place the UCS back to the AutoCAD world origin, enter ucs at the Command prompt and enter w, pick the **World UCS** button in the **UCS** toolbar, or pick **World** from the **New UCS** cascading menu in the **Tools** pull-down menu. This will place the UCS at the world origin 0,0 point and not change the ordinate dimensions. See **Figure 15-44.**

Tools
→ New UCS
→ World

UCS
toolbar

World UCS

**Figure 15-44.**
The site plan finished with ordinate dimensions.

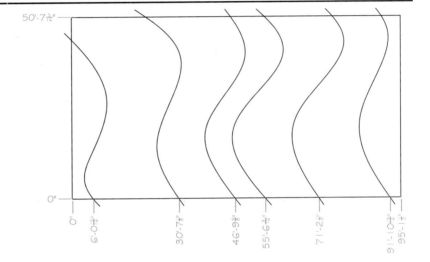

## Using Baseline Dimensions

The **DIMBASELINE** command is used for drawing datum dimensions as introduced earlier. This dimensioning system places all dimensions from a common measuring point. To create baseline dimensions, pick the **Baseline Dimension** button in the **Dimension** toolbar, pick **Baseline** in the **Dimension** pull-down menu, or enter dba or dimbaseline at the Command prompt. Baseline dimensions can be created with linear, ordinate, and angular dimensions.

DBA
DIMBASELINE

Dimension
→ Baseline

Dimension
toolbar

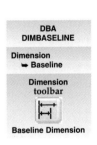

Baseline Dimension

When you enter the **DIMBASELINE** command, you are prompted with Specify a second extension line origin. This command assumes that the first extension line of the last drawn dimension is the baseline for new dimensions. Picking a second extension line creates a second dimension spaced away from the previous dimension using the same first extension line as the baseline. Therefore, a dimension must exist before using **DIMBASELINE**. You need to draw the first dimension using the **DIMLINEAR** command. AutoCAD uses the last drawn dimension as the base dimension, unless you specify a different one. You can add additional datum dimensions to the previous dimension. AutoCAD automatically spaces and places the extension lines, dimension lines, arrowheads, and numbers. For example, to dimension the series of horizontal baseline dimensions shown in **Figure 15-45**, use the following procedure:

Command: **dli** *or* **dimlinear**↵
Specify first extension line origin or <select object>: *(pick the first extension line origin)*
Specify second extension line origin: *(pick the second extension line origin)*
Specify dimension line location or [Mtext/Text/Angle/Horizontal/Vertical/Rotated]: *(pick the dimension line location)*
Dimension text = 4'-0"
Command: **dba** *or* **dimbaseline**↵
Specify a second extension line origin or [Undo/Select] <Select>: *(pick the next second extension line origin)*
Dimension text = 20'-6"
Specify a second extension line origin or [Undo/Select] <Select>: *(pick the next second extension line origin)*
Dimension text = 27'-6"
Specify a second extension line origin or [Undo/Select] <Select>: *(pick the next second extension line origin)*
Dimension text = 32'-0"
Specify a second extension line origin or [Undo/Select] <Select>: *(pick the next second extension line origin)*
Dimension text = 40'-0"
Specify a second extension line origin or [Undo/Select] <Select>: ↵
Select base dimension: ↵
Command:

**Figure 15-45.**
Using the **DIMBASELINE** command. AutoCAD automatically spaces and places the extension lines, arrowheads, and dimension values.

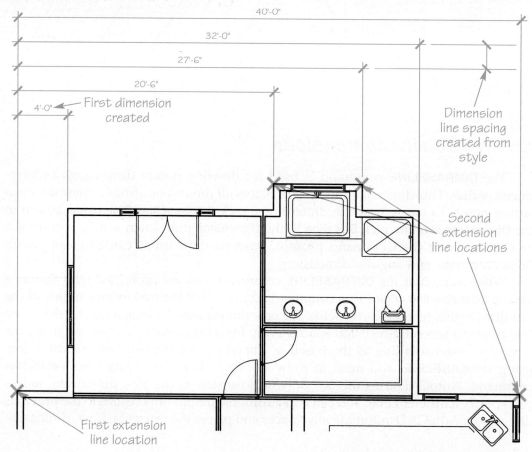

Architectural Drafting Using AutoCAD

You can continue to add baseline dimensions until you press [Enter] twice to return to the Command prompt. If you want to come back later and add baseline dimensions to an existing dimension other than the most recently drawn dimension, you can use the **Select** option by pressing [Enter] at the first prompt. At the Select base dimension: prompt, pick the extension line to serve as the baseline. Then select the new second extension line origins as described in this section. Baseline dimensioning is commonly used in mechanical drafting, but can be used to lay out architectural dimension strings. Refer to **Figure 15-4.**

## Using Continuous Dimensions

In AutoCAD, chain dimensions are called continuous dimensions. Chain dimensions string together dimensions from the last extension line drawn. When creating chain dimensions, you will receive the same prompts and options received while creating baseline dimensions. You need to draw the first dimension using the **DIMLINEAR** command. Chain dimensioning is shown in **Figure 15-46.** To create chain dimensions, pick the **Continue Dimension** button in the **Dimension** toolbar, pick **Continue** in the **Dimension** pull-down menu, or enter dco or dimcontinue at the Command prompt. Continue dimensions can be created with linear, ordinate, and angular dimensions. Use the **Undo** option in the **DIMBASELINE** or **DIMCONTINUE** commands to undo previously drawn dimensions.

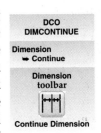

**Figure 15-46.**
Using the **DIMCONTINUE** command to finish dimensioning the floor plan.

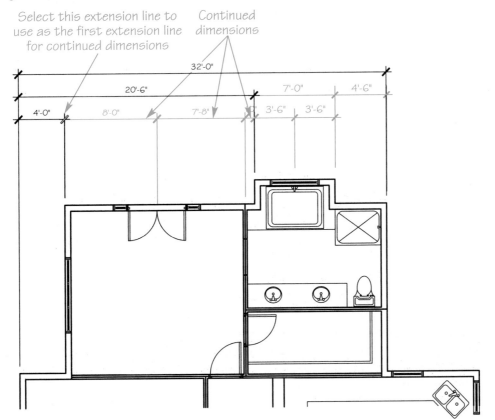

## Using QDIM to Dimension

QDIM

Dimension
➥ Quick Dimension

Dimension
toolbar

Quick Dimension

The **QDIM** command makes continuous and baseline dimensioning even easier by eliminating the need to define the exact points being dimensioned. This command also simplifies radius and diameter dimensioning. Often, the points that need to be selected for dimensioning are the endpoint of a line or the center of an arc. AutoCAD automates the process of point selection in the **QDIM** command by finding those points for you. To access the **QDIM** command, select **Quick Dimension** from the **Dimension** pull-down menu, pick the **Quick Dimension** button from the **Dimension** toolbar, or enter qdim at the Command prompt.

The type of geometry selected affects the **QDIM** output. If a single polyline is selected, **QDIM** attempts to draw linear dimensions to each vertex of the polyline. If a single arc or circle is selected, **QDIM** draws a radius or diameter dimension. If multiple objects are selected, linear dimensions are drawn to the vertex of every line or polyline and to the center of every arc or circle. In each case, AutoCAD finds the points automatically. The command line sequence is as follows:

Command: **qdim**↵
Select geometry to dimension: *(pick several lines, polylines, arcs, and/or circles)*
Specify dimension line position, or
 [Continuous/Staggered/Baseline/Ordinate/Radius/Diameter/datumPoint/Edit]
 <Continuous>: *(pick a position for the dimension lines)*

**Figure 15-47** shows examples of different types of objects being dimensioned with the **QDIM** command. The upper dimensions are created by selecting each object separately. The lower dimensions are created by selecting all objects at once. The **Continuous, Staggered, Baseline, Ordinate, Radius,** and **Diameter** options relate to the different modes of dimensioning discussed earlier in this chapter. The top dimensions on Object A were dimensioned with the **Baseline** option of the **QDIM** command. The command sequence is as follows:

Command: **qdim**↵
Select geometry to dimension: *(pick Object A (polyline))*
Specify dimension line position, or [Continuous/Staggered/Baseline/Ordinate/Radius/
 Diameter/datumPoint/Edit] <Continuous>: **b**↵
Specify dimension line position, or [Continuous/Staggered/Baseline/Ordinate/Radius/
 Diameter/datumPoint/Edit] <Staggered>: *(pick a vertical or horizontal position for the
 dimension line)*
Command:

The **QDIM** command also can be used as a way to edit any existing associative dimension. Access the **QDIM** command and select any existing dimensions. Choose one of the options, such as **Continuous, Staggered,** or **Baseline,** and then the location of the first dimension line. The existing associative dimensions are updated to reflect your changes. The term *associative dimension* means that all components of the

**Figure 15-47.**
The **QDIM** command can dimension multiple features or objects at the same time.

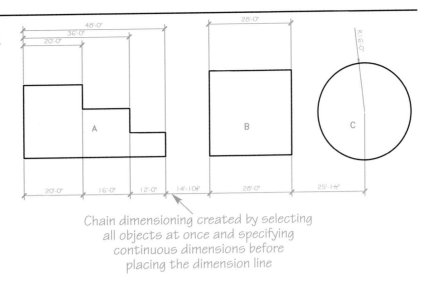

Chain dimensioning created by selecting all objects at once and specifying continuous dimensions before placing the dimension line

dimension act as a single object. This includes the dimension line, extension lines, arrowheads, and text. In addition, an associative dimension is updated when the dimension object is edited. The dimension value is automatically changed to reflect the edit. Associative dimensions are discussed in more detail later in this chapter.

## Drawing Center Dashes or Centerlines in a Circle or Arc

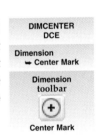

When small circles or arcs are dimensioned, the **DIMDIAMETER** and **DIMRADIUS** commands leave center dashes. These commands are discussed in the sections that follow. If the dimension of a large circle crosses through the center, the dashes are left out. To draw center dashes and centerlines, pick the **Center Mark** button in the **Dimension** toolbar, pick **Center Mark** in the **Dimension** pull-down menu, or enter dce or dimcenter at the Command prompt. The command sequence is as follows:

    Command: **dce** or **dimcenter**↵
    Select arc or circle: (pick the arc or circle)
    Command:

When the circle or arc is picked, center marks are automatically drawn. The size of the center marks, or the amount that the centerlines extend outside the circle or arc, is controlled by the **Center Marks for Circles** area in the **Lines and Arrows** tab of the **Modify Dimension Style** dialog box. **Figure 15-48** shows the difference between drawing center marks and centerlines in arcs and circles.

## Dimensioning Circles

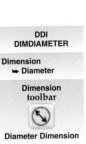

Circles are normally dimensioned with a diameter. Diameter dimensions are produced by picking the **Diameter Dimension** button on the **Dimension** toolbar, picking **Diameter** in the **Dimension** pull-down menu, or entering ddi or dimdiameter at the Command prompt. You are then prompted to select the arc or circle.

When using the **DIMDIAMETER** command, a leader line and diameter dimension value are attached to the cursor when you pick the desired circle or arc. You can drag the leader to any desired location and length before picking where you want it. The resulting leader points to the center of the circle or arc. See **Figure 15-49**. The command sequence is as follows:

**Figure 15-48.**
Arcs and circles displayed with center marks and centerlines.

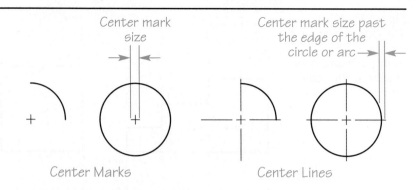

Center Marks          Center Lines

**Figure 15-49.**
Using the **DIMDIAMETER** command.

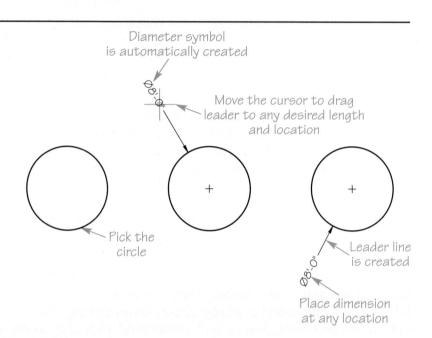

Command: **ddi** *or* **dimdiameter**⏎
Select arc or circle: *(pick the circle)*
Dimension text = 8'-0"
Specify dimension line location or [Mtext/Text/Angle]: *(pick the dimension line location)*
Command:

You are also given the **Mtext**, **Text**, and **Angle** options that were introduced earlier in this chapter. Use the **Mtext** or **Text** option if you want to change the text value. Use the **Angle** option if you want to change the angle of the text.

## Exercise 15-12

◆ Start a new drawing using one of your templates.
◆ Use **DesignCenter** to import the Architectural dimension style from ex15-6.
◆ Draw and dimension an object similar to **Figure 15-49**.
◆ Save the drawing as ex15-12.

# Dimensioning Arcs

DRA
DIMRADIUS

Dimension
➥ Radius

Dimension
toolbar

Radius Dimension

The standard for dimensioning arcs is a radius dimension. A radius dimension is placed with the **DIMRADIUS** command. Access this command by picking the **Radius Dimension** button on the **Dimension** toolbar, by picking **Radius** in the **Dimension** pull-down menu, or by entering dra or dimradius at the Command prompt.

When using the **DIMRADIUS** command, you are prompted to Select arc or circle. A leader line and radius dimension value are attached to the cursor when you pick the desired arc or circle. You can drag the leader to any desired location and length before picking where you want it. The resulting leader points to the center of the arc or circle. See **Figure 15-50.** The command sequence is as follows:

Command: **dra** *or* **dimradius**↵
Select arc or circle: *(pick an arc)*
Specify dimension line location or [Mtext/Text/Angle]: *(drag the leader to a desired location and pick)*
Dimension text = 0.750
Command:

**Figure 15-50.**
Using the
**DIMRADIUS**
command to
dimension arcs.

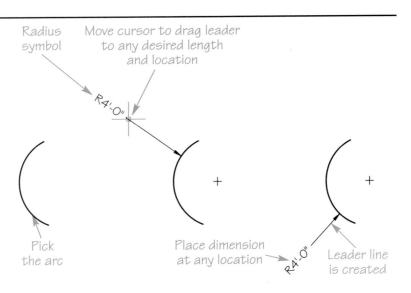

You are also given the **Mtext**, **Text**, and **Angle** options that were introduced earlier in this chapter. Use the **Mtext** or **Text** option if you want to change the text value. Use the **Angle** option if you want to change the angle of the text.

## Exercise 15-13

◆ Open ex15-12.
◆ Draw and dimension objects similar to **Figure 15-50.**
◆ Save the drawing as ex15-13.

# Drawing Leader Lines

The **DIMDIAMETER** and **DIMRADIUS** commands automatically place dimensions with leaders on objects in the drawing. The **QLEADER** command allows you to place a leader line anywhere you desire in the drawing. You can also place single or multiple lines of text with the leader. This command is ideal for the following situations:

- When adding specific notes to the drawing.
- When a leader line must be staggered to go around other drawing features.
- Where several leader lines are required from one note to several similar objects.
- When making custom leader lines.
- When drawing curved leaders.

The **QLEADER** command creates leader lines and related notes that are considered complex objects. This command provides the flexibility to place a detail bubble block or multiple lines of text with the leader. Some of the leader line characteristics, such as arrowhead size, are controlled by the dimension style settings. Other features, such as the leader format and annotation style, are controlled by the **Settings** option within the **QLEADER** command.

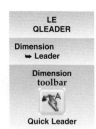

LE
QLEADER

Dimension
➥ Leader

Dimension
toolbar

Quick Leader

To access the **QLEADER** command, pick the **Quick Leader** button in the **Dimension** toolbar, select **Leader** in the **Dimension** pull-down menu, or enter le or qleader at the Command prompt. The initial prompts look like those used with the **LINE** command. This allows you to pick where the leader starts and ends.

By default, AutoCAD draws a straight-line leader, but you also have the option of drawing curved leaders. Curved leaders are commonly used in architectural drafting. The command sequence begins like this:

Command: **le** *or* **qleader**↵
Specify first leader point, or [Settings]<Settings>: *(pick the leader start point)*
Specify next point: *(pick the second leader point, which is the start of the leader shoulder)*
Specify next point: *(press [Enter] and the shoulder is drawn automatically)*
Specify text width <0.0000>: ↵
Enter first line of annotation text <Mtext>: *(enter text)*
Enter next line of annotation text: ↵

In this example, AutoCAD automatically draws a leader shoulder in front of the text.

## QLEADER *Settings*

The **Settings** option can be used to give you greater control over the leader and the text associated with the leader. For example, the leader can be set to have the first segment always drawn at a 45° angle and the second segment (or shoulder) always drawn at 0°.

When you select the **Settings** option of the **QLEADER** command, the **Leader Settings** dialog box is displayed. This dialog box has three tabs: **Annotation**, **Leader Line & Arrow**, and **Attachment**. The appearance of the arrow and leader line is determined by the settings in the **Leader Line & Arrow** tab. The settings found in the **Annotation** and **Attachment** tabs determine the appearance of the text portion of the leader.

### Leader Line and Arrow Settings

The **Leader Line & Arrow** tab of the **Leader Settings** dialog box is shown in **Figure 15-51.** The settings in this tab determine the type of arrowhead, type of leader line, angles for the leader line and shoulder, and number of requested points.

Architectural Drafting Using AutoCAD

Figure 15-51.
The **Leader Line & Arrow** tab of the **Leader Settings** dialog box.

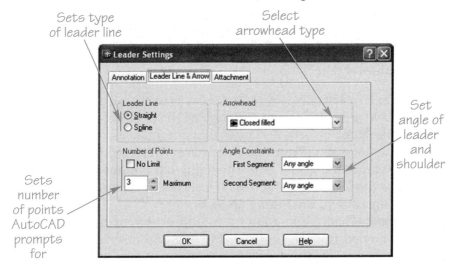

The **Leader Line** area is used to specify either a line leader or spline leader. Spline leaders are curved, and are commonly used in architectural drafting. **Figure 15-52** shows examples of the spline and straight leader lines.

You can also set the maximum number of vertices on the leader line. This is set in the **Number of Points** area. Set the maximum number of vertices in the **Maximum** text box, or select the **No Limit** check box to have no maximum number. After the maximum number is reached, the **QLEADER** command automatically stops drawing the leader and asks for text information. To use less than the maximum number of points, press the [Enter] key at the Specify next point prompt. If the leader is a line object, a value of three for the maximum number of points defines a maximum total of two line segments.

The **Arrowhead** area uses the default value assigned to leaders within the current dimension style. To change the appearance of the arrowhead, open the drop-down list to display the full range of choices. Changing the **Arrowhead** setting creates a dimension style override, which is discussed later in this chapter.

Figure 15-52.
The type of leader line (straight or splined) is set in the **Leader Line & Arrow** tab of the **Leader Settings** dialog box.

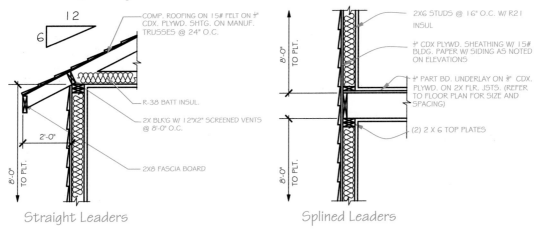

The first two segments of the leader line can be held to certain angles. These angles are set in the **Angle Constraints** area. The options for each segment are Any angle, Horizontal, 90, 45, 30, or 15. The Ortho mode setting overrides the angle constraints, so it is advisable to turn Ortho mode off while using the **QLEADER** command.

## Leader text settings

The **Annotation** and **Attachment** tabs control the way text is used with the leader line. The **Annotation** tab contains settings that specify the type of object used for annotation, additional options for **Mtext** objects, and tools that automatically repeat annotations. See **Figure 15-53**. The **Annotation Type** area determines which type of object is inserted and attached to the end of the leader line. The following options are available:

- **MText.** This is the default setting, which inserts a multiline text object after the leader lines are drawn. See **Figure 15-54A**.
- **Copy an Object.** This option allows a multiline text, text, block, or tolerance object to be copied from the current drawing and inserted at the end of the current leader line. This is useful when the same note or symbol is required in many places throughout a drawing. After drawing the leader line, the Select an object to copy: prompt appears. The selected object is placed at the end of the shoulder. See **Figure 15-54B**.
- **Tolerance.** This displays the **Geometric Tolerance** dialog box for creation of a feature control frame. See **Figure 15-54C**. When this option is chosen, the **Geometric Tolerance** dialog box appears, allowing you to select tolerancing information. This is used in the mechanical drafting field.

Figure 15-53.
The **Annotation** tab of the **Leader Settings** dialog box.

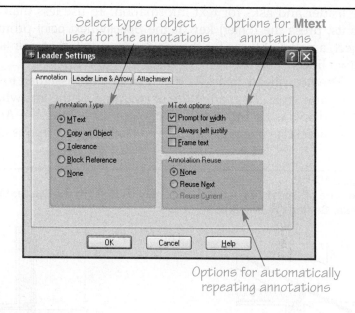

Select type of object used for the annotations

Options for **Mtext** annotations

Options for automatically repeating annotations

Figure 15-54.
The annotation object is selected in the **Annotation** tab of the **Leader Settings** dialog box.

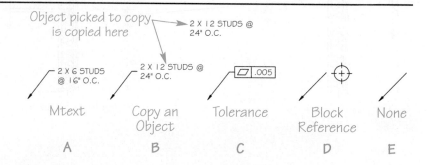

Object picked to copy is copied here

2 X 12 STUDS @ 24" O.C.

2 X 6 STUDS @ 16" O.C.

2 X 12 STUDS @ 24" O.C.

.005

Mtext

Copy an Object

Tolerance

Block Reference

None

A          B          C          D          E

- **Block Reference.** This option inserts a specified block at the end of the leader. A *block* is a symbol that was previously created and saved. Blocks can be inserted into other drawings. They are discussed in detail in Chapter 9 of this text. Blocks can be scaled during the insertion process. A special symbol block called Target is inserted in **Figure 15-54D.**
- **None.** This option ends the leader with no annotation of any kind. See **Figure 15-54E.** This option can be used as a way to create multiple leaders for a single leader annotation, as shown in **Figure 15-55.**

You can automatically repeat the previous leader annotation using the options in the **Annotation Reuse** area. The default option is **None.** This allows you to specify the annotation when creating a leader. If you wish to use an annotation repeatedly, select the **Reuse Next** option and then create the first leader and annotation. When you create another leader, the setting automatically changes to **Reuse Current**, and the annotation is inserted automatically. The annotation is repeated for all new leaders until the **Annotation Reuse** setting is changed back to **None.**

The **MText options** area of the **Annotation** tab is only available if **MText** is selected as the annotation type. These settings can be overridden by selecting the **Mtext** option during the **QLEADER** command. The following options are available:

- **Prompt for width.** If checked, you are prompted to define the size of the mtext box. If this option is not checked, a value of 0 (no text wrapping) is assigned to the mtext box.
- **Always left justify.** Forces the mtext to be left justified, regardless of the direction of the leader line.
- **Frame text.** Creates a box around the mtext text box. The default properties of the frame are controlled by the settings of the current dimension style.

The **Attachment** tab has options for specifying the point where the leader line shoulder meets an mtext annotation object. See **Figure 15-56.** The **Attachment** tab is only available when the **MText** option is selected in the **Annotation Type** area. This tab contains options that determine how the mtext object is positioned relative to the endpoint of the leader line shoulder.

**Figure 15-55.**
Use the **None** anno-
tation option when
drawing multiple
leaders.

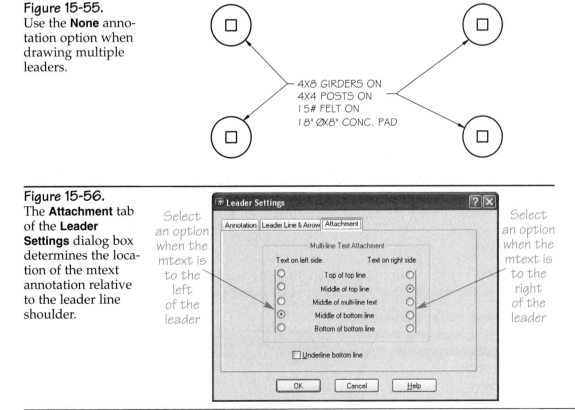

**Figure 15-56.**
The **Attachment** tab
of the **Leader**
**Settings** dialog box
determines the loca-
tion of the mtext
annotation relative
to the leader line
shoulder.

Different options can be specified for mtext to the right of the leader line and mtext to the left of the leader line. The **Underline bottom line** option causes a line to be drawn along the bottom of the mtext box. When this check box is selected, the choices for text on the left and right side become grayed out.

Professional Tip

Common drafting practice is to use the **Middle of bottom line** option for left-sided text and the **Middle of top line** option for right-sided text. These are the default settings.

## Exercise 15-14

◆ Start a new drawing using one of your templates.
◆ Use **DesignCenter** to import the Architectural dimension style from ex15-6.
◆ Use the **QLEADER** command to do the following:
 ◆ Draw multiple straight-line and splined leaders similar to those shown in **Figure 15-52**.
 ◆ Draw multiple leaders with a note similar to those shown in **Figure 15-55**.
 ◆ Experiment by drawing a leader with each of the settings in the **Attachment** tab of the **Leader Settings** dialog box.
◆ Save the drawing as ex15-14.

# Overriding Existing Dimensioning Variables

Generally, it is appropriate to have one or more dimensioning variables set to perform specific tasks that relate to your dimensioning practices. However, situations may arise where it is necessary to alter dimensioning variables to modify one or more specific dimensions on the final drawing. For example, assume you have the value for **Offset from origin (DIMEXO)** set at 1/16". However, you have three specific dimensions in your final drawing that require a 0 **Offset from the origin** setting. You can pick these three dimensions and alter the **DIMEXO** variable exclusively using the **DIMOVERRIDE** command. The command works as follows:

Command: **dov** *or* **dimoverride.**↵
Enter dimension variable name to override or [Clear overrides]: **dimexo.**↵
Enter new value for dimension variable <1/16">: **0.**↵
Enter dimension variable name to override: *(type another variable name to override or press* [Enter]*)*
Select objects: *(select the dimension or dimensions to override)*
Select objects: ↵
Command:

The **DIMEXO** variable automatically changes from 1/16" to 0 on the three selected dimensions. You can also clear any previous overrides by using the **Clear overrides** option:

Command: **dov** *or* **dimoverride.**↵
Enter dimension variable name to override or [Clear overrides]: **c.**↵
Select objects: *(select the dimension or dimensions to clear an override)*
Select objects: ↵
Command:

Depending on the nature of the change, it may be better to use the **Dimension Style Manager** dialog box rather than the **DIMOVERRIDE** command. In the dialog box, you can pick an existing style, change the variable, and then make a new style.

Sometimes it is also better to generate a new style, because certain situations require specific dimension styles in order to prevent conflicts with drawing geometry or dimension crowding. For example, if a number of the dimensions in the current drawing all require the same overrides, generating a new dimension style is a good idea. If only one or two dimensions need the same overrides, using the **DIMOVERRIDE** command may be more productive.

## Using the **Properties** Window to Alter Dimensions

A much simpler way of overriding dimensions is through the use of the **Properties** window. If you see a dimension that needs to be altered, select the dimension, and right-click to access **Properties** from the shortcut menu. This displays the **Properties** window with the dimension properties that are available for modification. See **Figure 15-57**.

**Figure 15-57.**
Using the **Properties** window to override dimension variables.

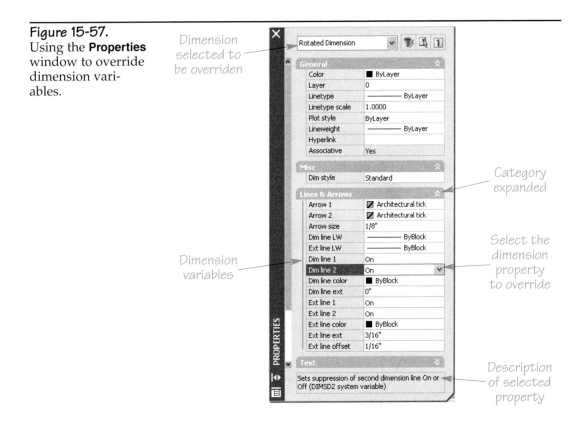

For example, if you are dimensioning the width of a hallway, you do not need the extension lines, because the dimension tick marks have been placed on the wall lines. To remove the extension line, right-click on the dimension, and select **Properties** from the shortcut menu. In the **Properties** window, select the **Lines & Arrows** category, and then turn the extension lines off using the Ext line 1 and Ext line 2 properties. This turns off the extension lines for just the one dimension that was selected. New dimensions are still drawn with extension lines.

**Professional Tip**

Right-clicking on a property in the **Properties** window accesses a shortcut menu. This menu allows you to close the **Properties** window, undo changes to that property, or open a property description area at the bottom of the window.

## Exercise 15-15

◆ Start a new drawing using one of your templates.
◆ Create and save a dimension style with dimensioning values set as follows:
  ◆ Arrowhead size = .1
  ◆ Text offset from dimension line = .05
  ◆ Dimension line extend beyond ticks = .12
  ◆ Dimension line baseline spacing = .5
  ◆ Extension line offset from origin = .06
◆ Make a drawing similar to **Figure 15-47.**
◆ Use the **QDIM** command with the baseline option to dimension the objects.
◆ After completing the entire drawing with the dimensioning values set as required, use the **DIMOVERRIDE** command to change only the **Extension Line offset from origin:** value to 0 on all dimensions except the overall dimensions.
◆ Use the **Properties** window to change a few of the dimension arrowheads to dots.
◆ Use the **Properties** window to turn off a few extension lines on different dimensions.
◆ Save the drawing as ex15-15.

# Editing Dimensioned Objects and Dimensions

As discussed earlier in this chapter, an associative dimension is made up of a group of individual elements and treated as a single object. When an associative dimension is selected for editing, the entire group of elements is highlighted. If you use the **ERASE** command, for example, you can pick the dimension as a single object and erase all the elements at once.

One benefit of associative dimensioning is that it permits existing dimensions to be updated as an object is edited. This means that when a dimensioned object is edited the dimension value automatically changes to match the edit. The automatic update is only applied if you accepted the default text value during the original dimension placement, or if you kept the value represented by chevrons (< >) in the multiline text editor. This provides you with an important advantage when editing an associative-dimensioned drawing. Any changes to objects are automatically transferred to the dimensions.

Architectural Drafting Using AutoCAD

Associative dimensioning is controlled by the **DIMASSOC** dimension variable or by selecting the **Make new dimensions associative** option in the **Associative Dimensioning** area of the **User Preferences** tab in the **Options** dialog box.

There are three settings for the **DIMASSOC** dimension variable: 0, 1, and 2. A setting of 0 turns off associative dimensioning. In this case, elements of the dimension are created separately, as if the dimension is exploded. The dimension is not updated when the object is edited. With a setting of 1, the components that make up a dimension are grouped together, but the dimension is not associated with an object. If you edit the object, you also have to edit the dimension. If **DIMASSOC** is set to 2, the components that make up a dimension are grouped together, and the dimension is associated with the object. If the object is stretched, trimmed, or extended, the dimension updates automatically. An associative dimension also updates when using grips or the **MOVE**, **MIRROR**, **ROTATE**, or **SCALE** commands.

 Associative dimensions in paper space attached to model space objects also automatically update when the object is edited.

Nonassociative dimensions can be converted to associative dimensions using the **DIMREASSOCIATE** command. To access this command, select **Reassociate Dimensions** from the **Dimension** pull-down menu or enter dre or dimreassociate at the Command prompt. You are prompted to select the dimensions to be associated. After selecting the dimensions, an X marker appears at the first extension line endpoint. Select the point on an object with which to associate this extension line. Then, select the associated point for the second extension line. Use the **next** option to advance to the next definition point. When a definition point has been associated, the X marker appears in a box.

**DIMREASSOCIATE**
**DRE**

**Dimension**
➥ **Reassociate Dimensions**

You can also use the **Select object** option to select an object with which to associate the dimension. The extension line endpoints are then automatically associated with the object endpoints.

To disassociate a dimension from an object, enter dda or disassociate at the Command prompt and then select the dimension. The dimension objects will still be grouped together, but the dimension will not be associated with an object.

## Editing Dimension Text

The **DIMTEDIT** command allows you to change the placement and orientation of an existing dimension text value. To access the **DIMTEDIT** command, pick the **Dimension Text Edit** button from the **Dimension** toolbar, pick one of the options from the **Align Text** cascading menu in the **Dimension** pull-down menu, or enter dimtedit at the Command prompt. Enter the command and then select the dimension to be edited.

**DIMTEDIT**

**Dimension**
➥ **Align Text**

**Dimension toolbar**

**Dimension Text Edit**

If you are editing an associative dimension, the text of the selected dimension automatically drags with the screen cursor. This allows you to relocate the text with your pointing device. You can also select the following command line options:

- **Left.** Moves horizontal text to the left and vertical text down.
- **Right.** Moves horizontal text to the right and vertical text up.
- **Center.** Centers text on the dimension line.
- **Home.** Text that has been changed from its original position can be moved back to the original place with this option.
- **Angle.** Allows you to place dimension text at an angle. This option asks for a rotation angle for the text.

The **DIMEDIT** command can also be used to edit the dimension text value or placement, or the extension lines of an existing dimension. To access the **DIMEDIT** command, pick the **Dimension Edit** button in the **Dimension** toolbar, or enter ded, dimed, or dimedit at the Command prompt:

Command: ↵
Enter type of dimension editing [Home/New/Rotate/Oblique]<Home>:

This command has the following options for editing individual or multiple dimensions:

- **Home.** This is the default option that moves dimension text back to where it originated.
- **New.** Allows you to specify new dimension text. When you enter this option, the **Multiline Text Editor** is displayed for you to use.
- **Rotate.** Allows you to rotate the dimension text.
- **Oblique.** Allows you to change the angle of extension lines. This option can also be accessed by picking **Oblique** from the **Dimension** pull-down menu.

## Exploding a Dimension

If you find it necessary to edit the parts of an associative dimension, you can use the **EXPLODE** command to break the dimension into individual parts. To access the **EXPLODE** command, enter x or explode at the Command prompt.

**Professional Tip**

Use extreme caution when exploding an associative dimension. An exploded dimension loses all of its associativity with associated features. A better way to edit the individual parts of an associative dimension is to use the **Properties** window.

## Dimension Express Tools

Throughout this text, the AutoCAD Express Tools in AutoCAD 2004 have been introduced for different productivity gains. The **Express** pull-down menu includes a few commands specific to dimensions. These tools can be found in the **Dimension** cascading menu, **Figure 15-58.** They are discussed in the following sections.

**Figure 15-58.**
The **Dimension** options in the **Express** pull-down menu.

## Leader Tools

The leader tools found in the **Express** pull-down menu include three commands to aid you in working with leaders. These commands allow you to attach a leader line to an annotation, detach a leader from an annotation, and globally attach leaders to annotations. The commands are described as follows:

- **Attach Leader to Annotation.** This command is used to connect a leader line to an existing mtext, tolerance, or block object. This command also can be accessed at the Command prompt by entering **QLATTACH**. Once the command is accessed, you are prompted to Select a leader. Select a leader line that is not connected to an annotation object. After selecting the leader line, you are prompted to Select Annotation. Pick the mtext, tolerance, or block object to which the leader is to be attached. The result is a leader line attached to an annotation object.

  When attaching a leader to an mtext or tolerance object, the leader line will jump to the default attachment point. If attaching to a block the result will not be as apparent. The leader stays in its original position but is attached to the block. Use grip editing to stretch the tail to the desired location in relation to the block object as needed.

- **Detach Leaders from Annotation.** This command allows you to detach any number of leader lines from their associated annotation objects. This command also can be accessed at the Command prompt by entering **QLDETACHSET**.

- **Global Attach Leader to Annotation.** This command is similar to the **Attach Leader to Annotation** command, except multiple leader lines can be selected and attached to annotations. When using this command, AutoCAD locates the nearest mtext, tolerance, or block object to each of the selected leader lines and attaches them. This command also can be accessed at the Command prompt by entering **QLATTACHSET**.

## Dimension Style Tools

The **Dimstyle Export** and **Dimstyle Import** commands work with existing dimension styles in the drawing. The **Dimstyle Export...** command allows you to export the values of a dimension style as textual values in an ASCII text file. The exported dimension style is assigned a .dim file extension for importation into another drawing file. The **Dimstyle Import...** command allows you to import a previously saved .dim file.

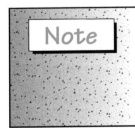

Note

The **Dimstyle Export** and **Dimstyle Import** commands create an ASCII text file that contains the dimension style information that can be used in other drawings. With the advent of **DesignCenter**, these commands are rarely used now as **DesignCenter** allows you to drag and drop a dimension style from one drawing to another.

## Resetting Dimension Text Values

The last command in the **Dimension** cascading menu is **Reset Dim Text Value**. This command also can be accessed at the Command prompt by entering **DIMREASSOC**. This command allows you to change any edited dimension text to its original default value. For example, suppose someone created a dimension and edited the text by removing the chevrons (<>) and placing a different value in their place. The **Reset Dim Text Value** command can be used to change the edited text back to the chevrons, allowing you to see the actual value of the dimension.

# Chapter Test

*Answer the following questions on a separate sheet of paper.*

1. What is the name of the AutoCAD default dimension style?
2. Name the dialog box where dimension styles are created.
3. What does it mean when a dimension style is set current?
4. Which dialog box allows you to make changes to the dimension style that is currently selected?
5. Describe the function of the **Extend beyond ticks** option.
6. What does the **Extend beyond dim line** option control?
7. What must happen before a text style can be used in a dimension style?
8. Identify at least two possible AutoCAD fonts that can be used to look like architectural hand lettering.
9. What is the dimension text placement commonly used for architectural drafting?
10. To what is the measurement scale factor set so that dimension values are equal to the actual length measured?
11. Explain how you can create a substyle of your architectural dimension style. Rather than global architectural ticks, the desired substyle should have closed filled arrowheads for radius dimensions.
12. Describe how to switch between dimension styles using the **Styles** toolbar.
13. When providing specific measurement, content, or text format for a dimension, what do the chevrons (< >) in the multiline text editor represent?
14. What command allows you to create arrowless dimensions?
15. In AutoCAD, what are datum dimensions called and what command allows you to draw them?
16. In AutoCAD, what are continuous dimensions called and what command allows you to draw them?
17. What must exist before a continuous dimension can be placed on a drawing?
18. What command allows you to draw center dashes and centerlines?
19. What command is used to dimension circles?
20. What command is used to dimension arcs?
21. Name the command that allows you to draw a leader line where you desire and place single or multiple lines of text with the leader.
22. What is the default leader line option?
23. Name the command that allows you to override existing dimensioning variables.
24. In addition to the command identified in Question 23, describe another method to alter existing dimensions using the **Properties** window.
25. Name the system variable that determines whether associative dimensions are created.
26. Identify two commands that allow you to edit dimension text.

1. Open 14-ResA.
    A. Create a dimension style similar to the architectural dimension style created in this chapter. In the **Fit** tab, use the scale factor of 48 in the **Use overall scale of:** text box.
    B. Dimension the site plan as shown below. Place all dimensions on a layer named Site-Dims.
    C. Save the drawing as 15-ResA.

Residential A

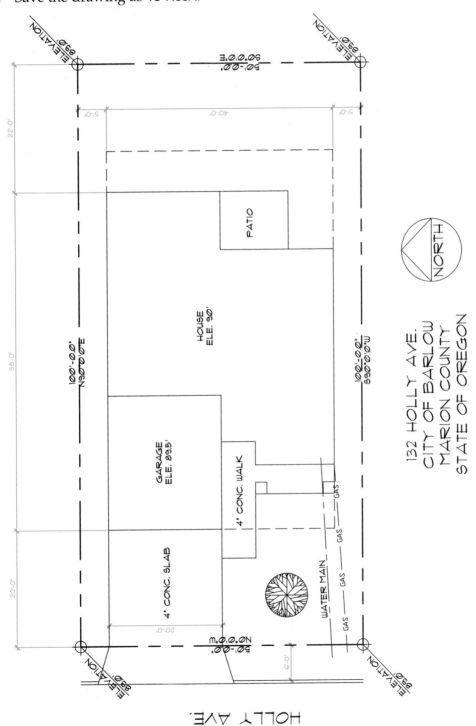

(Alan Mascord Design Associates, Inc.)

Project

Residential B

2. Open 14-ResB.
   A. Create a dimension style similar to the architectural dimension style created in this chapter. In the **Fit** tab, use the scale factor of 96 in the **Use overall scale of:** text box.
   B. Dimension the site plan as shown below. Place all dimensions on a layer named Dims.
   C. Save the drawing as 15-ResB.

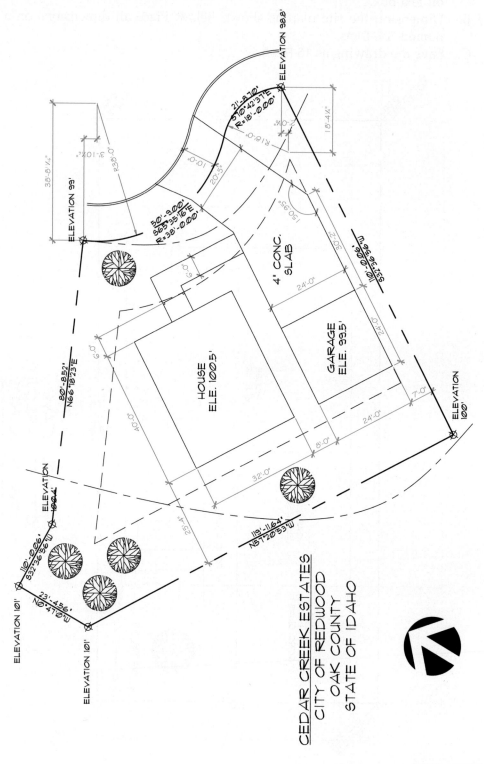

(3D-DZYN)

3. Open 14-Multifamily.
   A. Create a dimension style similar to the architectural dimension style created in this chapter. In the **Fit** tab, use the scale factor of 96 in the **Use overall scale of:** text box.
   B. Dimension the site plan as shown below. Place all dimensions on a layer named C-Anno-Dims.
   C. Save the drawing as 15-Multifamily.

Multifamily

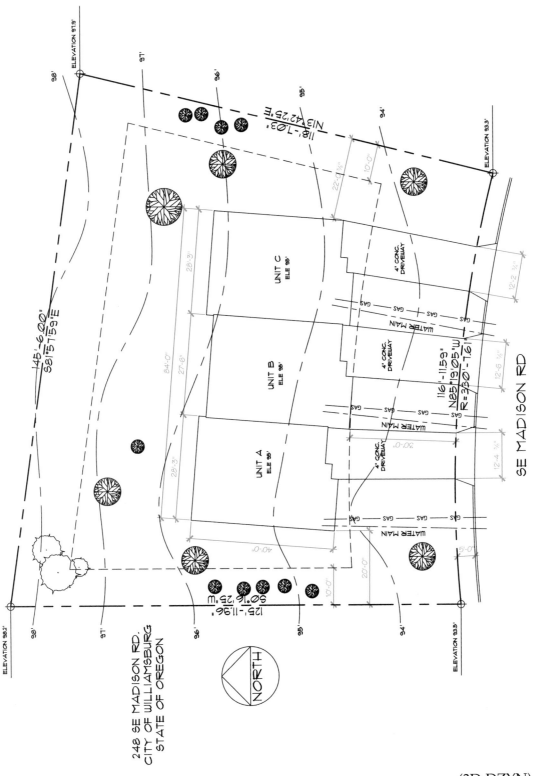

(3D-DZYN)

4. Open 14-Commercial.
A. Create a dimension style similar to the architectural dimension style created in this chapter. In the **Fit** tab, use the scale factor of 96 in the **Use overall scale of:** text box.
B. Dimension the site plan as shown below. Place all dimensions on a layer named C-Anno-Dims.
C. Save the drawing as 15-Commercial.

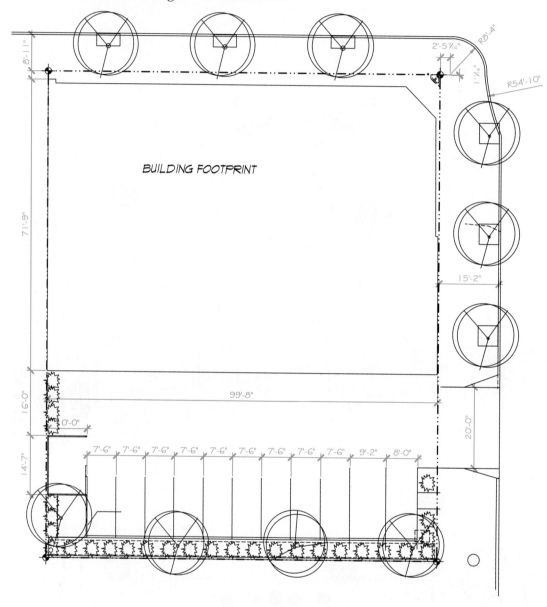

(Cynthia Bankey Architect, Inc.)

# CHAPTER 16

# Drawing Floor Plans

## Learning Objectives

After completing this chapter, you will be able to:

◆ Completely describe a floor plan.
◆ Draw walls using lines and polylines.
◆ Use the **OFFSET** command to construct walls.
◆ Create rounded corners using the **FILLET** command.
◆ Use the **CHAMFER** command to create angled features.
◆ Search for information with the **FILTER** command.
◆ Use the **MATCHPROP** command to "paint" properties to other objects.

## Important Terms

base cabinets
continuous dimensioning
cutting plane
destination object
dimension strings
fillets
floor plan
general notes
islands

local notes
plumbing plan
riser
source object
specific notes
total rise
tread
upper cabinets
wall-hung cabinets

A *floor plan* is a two-dimensional representation of a building layout, as viewed from above. It consists of wall placement, door and window location, cabinets, plumbing fixtures, detail symbols, and dimensions. To create the floor plan, the building is "cut" horizontally at approximately eye level. See **Figure 16-1.** This allows the viewer to see where doors, windows, and cabinets are placed within the building. In a multistory building, each floor is "cut" horizontally and its top removed. This allows the viewer to see wall placement on each floor.

**Figure 16-1.**
Floor plans are developed by "cutting off" the top portion of a building and looking straight down at the floor. (3D-DZYN)

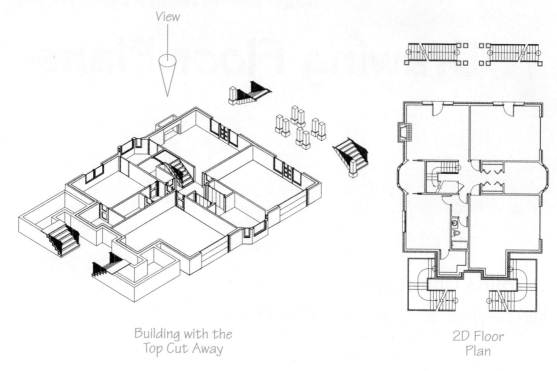

Building with the
Top Cut Away

2D Floor
Plan

The horizontal cut is called the *cutting plane.* You can think of the cutting plane as a saw cutting horizontally through the building. The top portion of the building is then removed. The bottom portion of the building represents the floor plan. The elevation of the cutting plane can vary, especially if there is a design feature you want to show in the floor plan. For example, if a single room is two stories high, the cutting plane can be adjusted to show this feature.

# Drawing Walls

Walls are generally drawn as two parallel lines. The type of wall construction material determines the distance between the two lines. For example, if the walls are to be made of wood, the distance between the lines is determined by the thickness of the framing members. Common framing members are 4" thick for a 2 × 4, or 6" thick for a 2 × 6. In other words, the parallel lines for a 2 × 4 wall are drawn 4" apart. See **Figure 16-2.** In wood frame construction, studs are not shown in a wall to reduce clutter in the drawing. In steel construction, the wall thickness is drawn similar to that for wood construction. However, structural columns ("studs") are shown inside the walls so the builder knows where to place these items.

With AutoCAD, you can draw the space between wall lines equal to the exact wall construction materials, if desired. For example, a 2 × 6 exterior stud wall with 1/2" interior gypsum, 1/2" sheathing, and 1/2" exterior siding measures:

5-1/2" (actual dimension of a 2 × 6 wood stud is 1-1/2" × 5-1/2")
   1/2" gypsum
   1/2" sheathing
 + 1/2" siding
   7"

**Figure 16-2.**
Types of wall construction and their typical thickness.

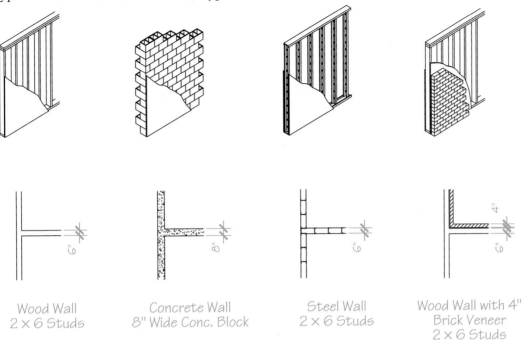

Wood Wall
2 × 6 Studs

Concrete Wall
8" Wide Conc. Block

Steel Wall
2 × 6 Studs

Wood Wall with 4"
Brick Veneer
2 × 6 Studs
4" Brick

A 2 × 4 interior stud wall with 1/2" gypsum on each side measures:

3-1/2"  (actual dimension of a 2 × 4 wood stud is 1-1/2" × 3-1/2")
  1/2"  gypsum
+ 1/2"  gypsum
4-1/2"

In concrete or masonry construction, the distance between the lines is the thickness of the concrete block or slab. If the construction material is concrete, a fill or hatch pattern representing concrete can be applied to the walls.

If brick veneer is used in construction, two additional lines are drawn on the outside of the wall. These lines represent the brick and an airspace between the exterior wall and the brick. Brick can also be drawn with a hatch pattern to represent the material.

## Laying out the Exterior Wall Lines

To start laying out walls, draw the outer perimeter of the building with lines or a polyline. This provides the overall area of the building exterior that can be arranged within the model space limits. Leave room around the building perimeter for notes and dimensions. If you initially created a design sketch, the drawing can be opened and traced using lines or polylines on the appropriate Wall layer. In **Figure 16-3A**, an exterior wall layout is created. In **Figure 16-3B,** a polyline is traced over the top of a design sketch.

After the exterior wall lines are laid out, double-check distances using the **DIST** or **LIST** command. The **DIST** and **LIST** commands are covered in Chapter 12. Once all the distances have been verified, the parallel line representing the interior walls can be created.

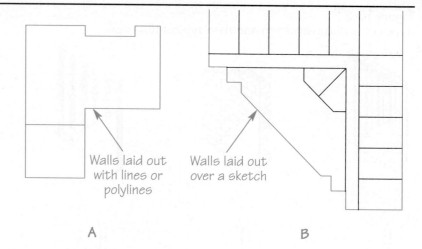

**Figure 16-3.**
A—A layout of exterior wall lines.
B—Tracing a design sketch for the exterior wall lines.

Walls laid out with lines or polylines

Walls laid out over a sketch

A                    B

## Drawing Parallel Lines and Curves

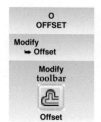

O
OFFSET

Modify
→ Offset

Modify
toolbar

Offset

One of the most often used modifying commands in architectural drafting is the **OFFSET** command. This command can be used to offset the exterior walls to the inside of the building, thus creating the interior walls. The **OFFSET** command can also be used to draw concentric circles, arcs, curves, polylines, and other parallel lines. Access the command by picking **Offset** in the **Modify** pull-down menu, picking the **Offset** button in the **Modify** toolbar, or entering o or offset at the Command prompt. The following prompt appears.

Command: **o** *or* **offset.**↵
Specify offset distance or [Through] *<current>*:

Enter a distance desired between the original object and the new object, or pick a point for the parallel object to be drawn through. In the case of residential wood construction, use a width of 6″ for the wall offset. If the building is constructed of masonry, determine the width of the masonry and use it for the offset. Typically, masonry construction uses 8″ wide walls for smaller buildings and 12″ wide walls for larger construction. The following example shows drawing two parallel lines a distance of 1″ apart. Refer to **Figure 16-4.**

Command: **o** *or* **offset.**↵
Specify offset distance or [Through] *<current>*: **1**↵
Select object to offset or *<exit>*: *(pick the object)*
Specify point on side to offset: *(pick on the side of the object where the offset is to be drawn)*
Select object to offset or *<exit>*: *(select another object to offset or press* [Enter] *to end the command)*

When the Select object to offset or *<exit>*: prompt appears, the screen cursor turns into a pick box. After the object is picked, the screen cursor turns back into crosshairs. No other selection option, such as window or crossing, works with the **OFFSET** command.

Another **OFFSET** command option is to pick a point through which the offset is drawn. Use the **Through** option as follows to produce the results shown in **Figure 16-5.**

Command: **o** *or* **offset.**↵
Specify offset distance or [Through] *<current>*: **t.**↵
Select object to offset or *<exit>*: *(pick the object)*
Specify through point: *(pick the point or distance through which the offset will be drawn)*
Select object to offset or *<exit>*: ↵

**Figure 16-4.**
A—Offsetting an exterior perimeter drawn as a line. B—Offsetting an exterior perimeter drawn as a polyline.

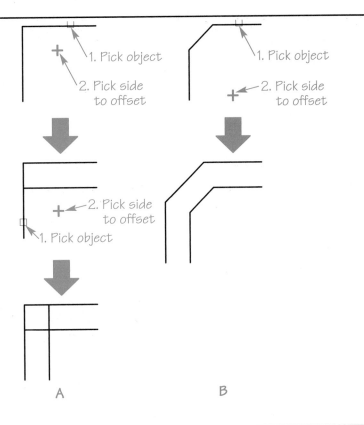

**Figure 16-5.**
Offsetting an object by specifying the "through" point. A—Original circle and line. B—End result.

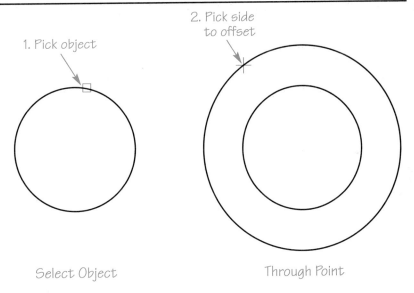

Object snap modes can also assist in drawing an offset. For example, suppose you have a circle and a line, and want to draw a concentric circle tangent to the line. Refer to **Figure 16-6** as you go through the following command sequence.

Command: **o** *or* **offset.**↲
Specify offset distance or [Through] <*current*>: **quadrant.**↲
of (*pick the existing circle*)
Specify second point: **perpendicular.**↲
to (*pick the existing line*)
Select object to offset or <exit>: (*pick the existing circle*)
Specify point on side to offset: (*pick between the circle and line*)
Select object to offset or <exit>: ↲
Command:

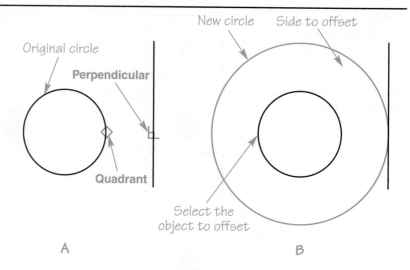

**Figure 16-6.**
Using the **OFFSET** command to draw a concentric circle tangent to a line. A—Picking the "through" point. B—End result.

Original circle

Perpendicular

Quadrant

New circle     Side to offset

Select the object to offset

A                                    B

When possible, draw the outer perimeter of the building as a polyline. This will make it easier to "clean up" the corners of the walls. If the perimeter is drawn with lines, the **TRIM** command must be used to clean up the corners of the walls. See **Figure 16-7.**

## Exercise 16-1

◆ Open ex12-6 you created in Chapter 12.
◆ Create a new layer named M-Walls and set it current.
◆ Use the **PLINE** command to trace the outer perimeter of the house. Trace a line over the inside garage wall.
◆ Lock the M-Area layer.
◆ The house will be created with 2 × 6 wood construction. Use the **OFFSET** command to offset the outside perimeter into the building 6".
◆ Clean up the wall intersections at the garage area. Double-check the outside lengths.
◆ Save the drawing as ex16-1.

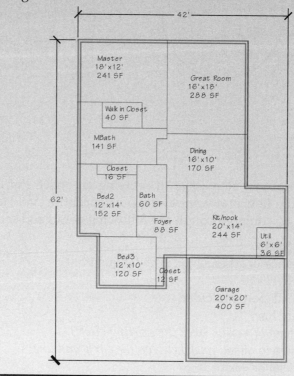

Architectural Drafting Using AutoCAD

**Figure 16-7.**
A—An offset poly-
line produces a
clean corner.
B—Offset lines
produce corners
that need to be
cleaned up with the
**TRIM** command.

Use the **TRIM**
command to clean
up the corners of
the building

Corner cleaned up
after using the
**TRIM** command

Polylines

Lines

A

B

In Exercise 16-1, you are instructed to create new wall lines by tracing directly on top of an existing design sketch. The new wall lines are placed on a new layer. This allows you to keep the original sketch and the final drawings in one file for easier drawing management. Keeping everything in one file works well in smaller architectural offices where only a few drafters work on a project.

In larger architectural firms, many drafters can be working on different parts of the project. These large firms often keep different plans separate. In this way, each group of drafters can work on the drawings that have been assigned. In Chapter 17, the referencing of drawings will be discussed.

## Laying out the Interior Wall Lines

Once the exterior walls are laid out and checked, the interior walls can be drawn. You can offset the exterior walls (parallel lines) the width of each room. The exterior wall lines can also be copied the correct distance.

Interior walls in wood construction are typically 4″ wide. If another construction method is used, determine the width of the interior walls from the material being used. Do not forget to confirm the sizes of the rooms with the **DIST** command.

The design sketch provides rough room sizes for planning. If the rooms are not quite the size that was noted in the sketch, try adjusting the interior walls accordingly. Once you start offsetting wall widths and room sizes, one of the most significant changes to the design sketch is that the room sizes may change and the areas get shifted. You may need to consult with the architect, designer, or your teacher if the wall widths drastically affect the design of the plan. Generally, if a sketch has been given dimensions, the interior dimensions change before the exterior dimensions.

**Figure 16-8** displays the new walls for the plan. Notice that the room sizes have been updated to reflect the new interior room sizes from their original sketched-in areas.

**Professional Tip**

If the design sketch is a little rough, try drawing new lines using tracking or object snap tracking. Tracking and object snap tracking are discussed in Chapter 4.

**Figure 16-8.**
The main floor of
the house with the
exterior and interior
walls laid out.

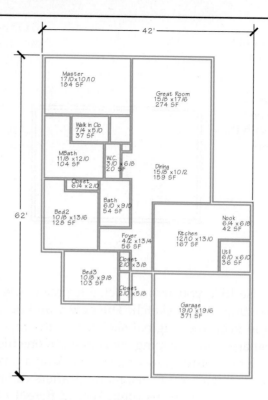

## Exercise 16-2

- ◆ Open ex16-1.
- ◆ Draw the interior walls for the house using a 4" wide wall.
- ◆ If you are offsetting any of the exterior wall lines, you may wish to explode the polyline into separate lines to make it easier to offset the individual lines.
- ◆ Use the **TRIM** and **EXTEND** commands as required to complete the design.
- ◆ Refer to your design sketch lines and **Figure 16-8** for the layout.
- ◆ Freeze the M-Area layer when finished.
- ◆ Do not dimension the drawing.
- ◆ Save the drawing as ex16-2.

## Drawing Rounded Corners

AutoCAD refers to rounded corners as *fillets.* In architectural drafting, fillets can be used to make rounded walls or corners. By changing the fillet radius to 0, the **FILLET** command can also aid in the cleanup of wall intersections by squaring the corners.

To access the **FILLET** command, pick the **Fillet** button on the **Modify** toolbar, select **Fillet** from the **Modify** pull-down menu, or enter f or fillet at the Command prompt. Fillets are sized by radius. The default radius is 0'-0". A new radius is specified first by entering the **Radius** option as follows.

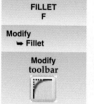

FILLET
F

Modify
➥ Fillet

Modify
toolbar

Fillet

> Command: **f** *or* **fillet.**⏎
> Current settings: Mode = TRIM, Radius = *current*
> Select first object or [Polyline/Radius/Trim/mUltiple]: **r.**⏎
> Specify fillet radius <*current*>: *(type the fillet radius and press* [Enter], *or press* [Enter]
>     *to accept the current value)*

Once the fillet radius has been established, fillet the objects as follows. Refer to **Figure 16-9.**

**Figure 16-9.**
Several examples of using the **FILLET** command.

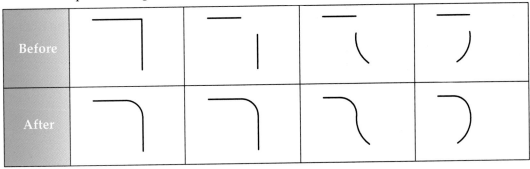

Select first object or [Polyline/Radius/Trim/mUltiple]: *(pick the first object to be filleted)*
Select second object: *(pick the other object to be filleted)*
Command:

## Rounding the Corners of a Polyline

Fillets can be drawn at all corners of a closed polyline by entering the **Polyline** option of the **FILLET** command. The current fillet radius is used for this option. The command sequence is as follows. See **Figure 16-10**.

Command: **f** *or* **fillet.**⏎
Current settings: Mode = TRIM, Radius = *current*
Select first object or [Polyline/Radius/Trim/mUltiple]: **p**⏎
Select 2D polyline: *(pick the polyline)*
*n* lines were filleted
Command:

AutoCAD tells you how many lines were filleted. Then, the Command prompt returns. If the polyline was drawn without using the **Close** option, the first corner is not filleted.

**Figure 16-10.**
Using the **Polyline** option of the **FILLET** command.

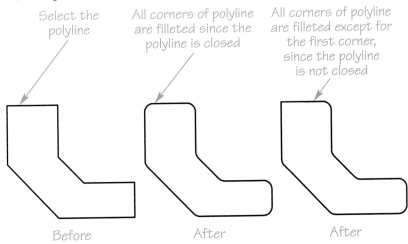

Select the polyline

All corners of polyline are filleted since the polyline is closed

All corners of polyline are filleted except for the first corner, since the polyline is not closed

Before    After    After

## Making Multiple Fillets

By default, only one fillet is created at a time unless you use the **Polyline** option to fillet multiple corners of a polyline. If you have several lines that need to be filleted, the **mUltiple** option can be used to add fillets to several corners. The following command sequence is used to create multiple fillets:

Command: **f** *or* **fillet.⏎**
Current settings: Mode = TRIM, Radius = *current*
Select first object or [Polyline/Radius/Trim/mUltiple]: **u⏎**
Select first object or [Polyline/Radius/Trim/mUltiple]: *(pick the first object)*
Select second object: *(pick the second object)*
Select first object or [Polyline/Radius/Trim/mUltiple]: *(pick another first object)*
Select second object: *(pick the second object)*
Select first object or [Polyline/Radius/Trim/mUltiple]: ⏎
Command:

## Setting the Fillet Trim Mode

The **TRIMMODE** system variable controls how the **FILLET** command trims object segments extending beyond the fillet. When **TRIMMODE** is set to 1, the portions of the objects extending beyond the fillet are trimmed. When **TRIMMODE** is set to 0, the objects are not changed after the fillet is created, as shown in **Figure 16-11**. The **TRIMMODE** system variable can be set with the **Trim** option of the **FILLET** command.

Command: **f** *or* **fillet.⏎**
Current settings: Mode = TRIM, Radius = *current*
Select first object or [Polyline/Radius/Trim/mUltiple]: **t.⏎**
Enter Trim mode option [Trim/No trim] <Trim>: **n.⏎** *(this sets TRIMMODE to 0)*
Select first object or [Polyline/Radius/Trim/mUltiple]: *(pick the first object)*
Select second object: *(pick the second object)*
Command:

If the lines to be filleted do not connect at the corner, they are automatically extended when **TRIMMODE** is set to 1 (**Trim**). However, they are not extended when **TRIMMODE** is set to 0 (**No trim**). If you do not want a separation between the line and the filleted corner, extend the lines to the corner before filleting.

## Filleting Parallel Lines

A fillet can be drawn between parallel lines. If **TRIMMODE** is set to 1 (**Trim**), the longer line is trimmed to match the length of the shorter line. If **TRIMMODE** is set to 0 (**No trim**), the original lines are unchanged.

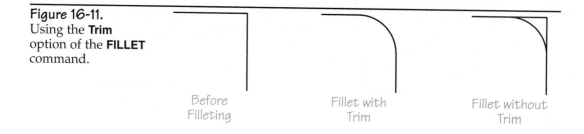

**Figure 16-11.**
Using the **Trim** option of the **FILLET** command.

Before Filleting

Fillet with Trim

Fillet without Trim

The radius of a fillet between parallel lines is always one-half the distance between the two lines, regardless of the radius setting for the **FILLET** command. Also, the fillet between two parallel lines is always an arc. Therefore, if the fillet radius is set to 0, an arc is drawn between the lines, not a square corner.

## Exercise 16-3

◆ Start a new drawing using one of your architectural templates.
◆ Create a layer named A-Wall, and set it current.
◆ Draw the plan shown using the dimensions provided.
◆ The interior walls will be created with 2 × 4 wood construction. The exterior walls will be created with 2 × 6 wood construction.
◆ Use the **TRIM**, **EXTEND**, and **FILLET** commands to clean up the wall intersections.
◆ Do not dimension the drawing.
◆ Save the drawing as ex16-3.

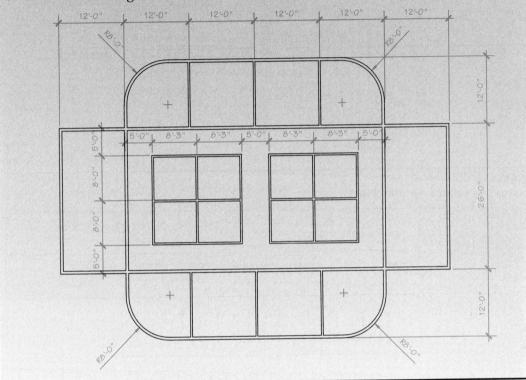

# Adding Doors and Windows

The next step in the development of a floor plan is the addition of doors, windows, and any openings in the walls. **Figure 16-12** shows some typical doors and windows in a three-dimensional view and how they look in the floor plan.

It is best to first draw doors and windows as blocks. Then, insert the block into your drawing. See **Figure 16-13.** The blocks can either be unit blocks scaled to the desired size, or they can be real blocks inserted at full scale.

The advantage of using unit blocks is that there are less blocks to be managed. However, the display of the doors or windows varies as the scale changes. For example, window glass should always be the same thickness. However, when windows are drawn as unit blocks, the glass thickness will vary when the blocks are scaled. **Figure 16-14** shows the difference in glass width when a window drawn as a unit block is inserted into a 4″ and an 8″ wall.

---

### Figure 16-12.
Doors and windows in plan view and the typical cutting plane.

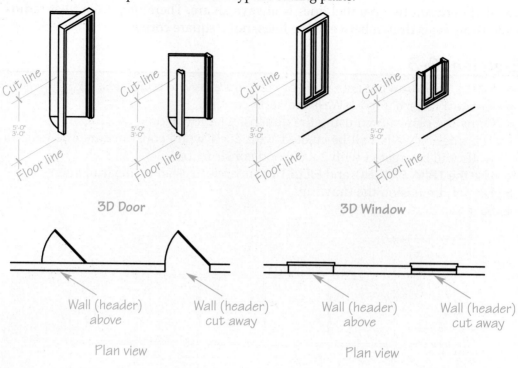

**Figure 16-13.**
Sample door and window blocks.

| | | | | | | | | | | | |
|---|---|---|---|---|---|---|---|---|---|---|---|
| **Bi-Fold Doors** | 1'-8" | 2'-0" | 2'-2" | 2'-4" | 2'-6" | 2'-8" | 3'-0" | 3'-0" | 4'-0" | 5'-0" | 6'-0" |
| **Sliding Doors** | 4'-0" | 5'-0" | 6'-0" | 8'-0" | 5'-0" | 6'-0" | 8'-0" | | | | |
| **Single Swing Doors** | 1'-6" | 2'-0" | 2'-2" | 2'-4" | 2'-6" | 2'-8" | 2'-10" | 3'-0" | 3'-6" | | |
| **Double Swing Doors** | 3'-0" | 4'-0" | 4'-4" | 4'-8" | 5'-0" | 5'-4" | 5'-8" | 6'-0" | 7'-0" | | |
| **Pocket Doors** | 2'-0" | 2'-2" | 2'-4" | 2'-6" | 2'-8" | 2'-10" | 3'-0" | | | | |
| **4″ Wide Windows** | 10" | 1'-6" | 2'-0" | 2'-6" | 3'-0" | 3'-6" | 4'-0" | 5'-0" | 6'-0" | 8'-0" | |
| **6″ Wide Windows** | 10" | 1'-6" | 2'-0" | 2'-6" | 3'-0" | 3'-6" | 4'-0" | 5'-0" | 6'-0" | 8'-0" | |

The advantage of using real blocks for doors and windows is the scale of the display does not change with wall thickness. A disadvantage is any change made to the door or window must be made to *all* door and window blocks.

The block insertion point for a door or window can be at the midpoint or endpoint of the block. To a large degree, this depends on personal preference. However, for some blocks, one of the two points may make it easier to place the block into a wall.

Architectural Drafting Using AutoCAD

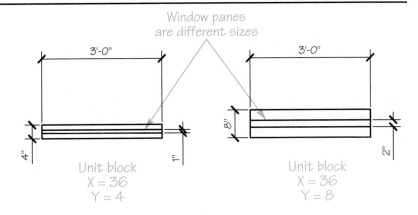

**Figure 16-14.**
If a window is drawn as a unit block, when the block is scaled, the glass is incorrectly scaled as well.

Window panes are different sizes

3'-0"

4"

1"

Unit block
X = 36
Y = 4

3'-0"

8"

2"

Unit block
X = 36
Y = 8

## Inserting Door and Window Blocks

Before the door and window blocks are inserted, the wall openings must be created. The opening widths can be established by offsetting wall lines to the correct dimensions. This procedure is demonstrated in **Figure 16-15A.** Excess lines can then be trimmed, leaving only the door jambs and window frames. The opening is trimmed because the wall (header) above the door or window is not displayed on the floor plan. The door and window locations for the house floor plan are shown in **Figure 16-15B.**

Once the openings have been placed in the drawing, create a layer for the doors and windows. Then, use the **INSERT** command to place the door and window blocks into the openings. If the door and window blocks are created in a block library, use **DesignCenter** to drag and drop the blocks into the drawing. If they are stored in tool palettes, use the **Tool Palettes** window. The drawing from **Figure 16-15B** is shown with the doors and windows added in **Figure 16-16.**

**Professional Tip**

Instead of creating the openings first, the doors and windows can be inserted and placed in the drawing using tracking or the AutoTrack feature described in Chapter 4. Use tracking when prompted for the insertion point of the block, and track a distance from a corner of the walls to where the opening is to be placed. Then draw the jamb lines and trim out the header.

## Exercise 16-4

- ◆ Open ex16-2.
- ◆ Create the following layers:
    - ◆ M-Doors
    - ◆ M-Windows
- ◆ Create door and window blocks to your liking, remembering to create them on the 0 layer. Use **Figure 16-13** as a guide.
- ◆ Create the door and window openings.
- ◆ Insert the doors and windows into your drawing. Ensure the blocks are on the appropriate layers.
- ◆ Your drawing should look like **Figure 16-16.**
- ◆ Save the drawing as ex16-4.

## Figure 16-15.

A—Using the **OFFSET** command to locate door and window openings and the **TRIM** command to clean up the openings. B—The door and window openings are placed in the floor plan with the headers trimmed out.

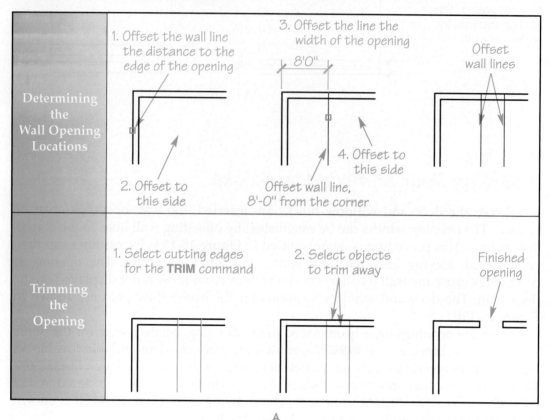

A

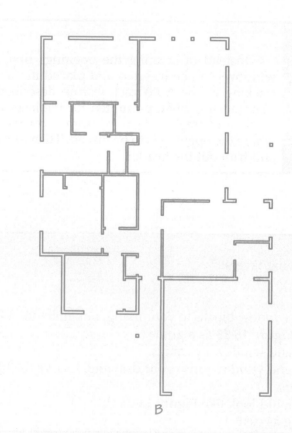

B

**Figure 16-16.**
Doors and windows
are inserted into the
floor plan.

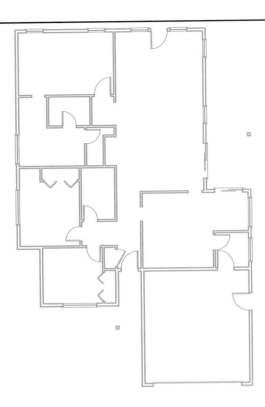

## Tips for Creating Door and Window Blocks

The previous discussion described offsetting walls to create the door and window openings, then adding the door and window blocks. This procedure can be eliminated by creating the door and window blocks with door jambs and window frames already added to the block. See **Figure 16-17.** By doing this, the doors and windows can be inserted directly into the wall with the jambs and frame already attached.

When creating the blocks, the blocks should be created on the 0 layer using the ByLayer setting for both the color and linetype. In this way, the block takes on the properties of the layer on which it is inserted.

As an option, try using a ByBlock color and linetype for the door jambs and window frame. The rest of the block should have the ByLayer color setting. Make sure the door and window layers have the same color as the wall layer. Then, when the door or window is inserted on the appropriate door or window layer, the block takes on the color of the wall layer, except the jamb and frame. These remain the ByBlock color. See **Figure 16-18.**

**Figure 16-17.**
Jambs and frames
can be included in
door and window
blocks.

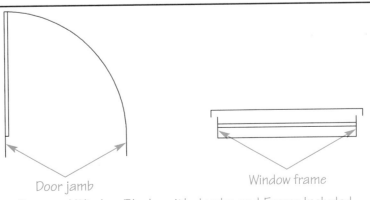

Door jamb

Window frame

Door and Window Blocks with Jambs and Frame Included

**Figure 16-18.**
One method for drawing door and window blocks is to use the **ByLayer** color for the door and window, and the **ByBlock** color for the jambs and frame.

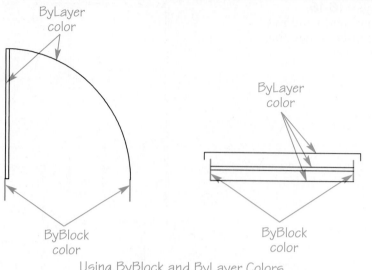

Using ByBlock and ByLayer Colors

After the door and window blocks are in place, the headers above the openings need to be trimmed. Use the **TRIM** command and select the jambs or frame edges as the cutting edges. Then, trim the walls. See **Figure 16-19.**

**Figure 16-19.**
A—Headers over the door and window. B—Select the jamb lines or frame lines within the block as the cutting edges. C—Trim away the wall lines.

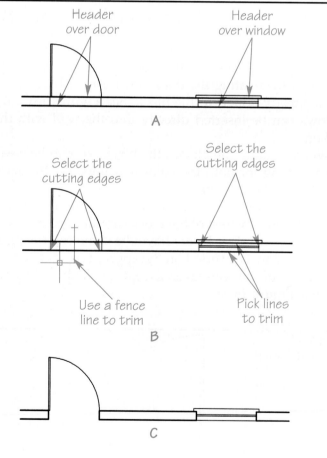

# Adding Stairs and Confirming the Layout

Depending on the design of the building, stairs may be required to provide access to a different level of the building. See **Figure 16-20.** Stairs are made up of risers and treads. The *riser* is the vertical component between the stairs. The *tread* is the actual horizontal step. Stairs need to conform to local building codes regarding staircase widths, maximum riser heights, and minimum tread depths. The layout of the stairs can be used to confirm the placement of adjoining walls.

Stairs are displayed in a floor plan in a manner similar to walls, doors, and windows. The stairs are shown with a break line and a note indicating the up or down direction. When stairs lead to a floor above the current floor, the bottom of the stairs is shown with an "up" note. For stairs that lead to a floor below the current floor, the top of the stairs is displayed with a "down" note. See **Figure 16-21.**

Before you begin drawing stairs on the floor plan, you need to consider how wide the stairway is, how many risers are required, and how deep the treads are. A recommended minimum stair width is 3'-0". To determine the total number of risers for the stair layout, first consult local building codes to determine the maximum allowed rise for each riser. This discussion assumes a maximum rise of 7-1/2".

The next step is to determine the total height for the stairs. This is called the *total rise.* The total rise is measured from the finished floor on the lower level to the finished floor on the upper floor. Refer to **Figure 16-20.** This discussion assumes a 9'-1 1/8" measurement between floors. Divide the maximum riser height into the total rise to give you the total number of risers required:

9'-1 1/8" = 109.125" ÷ 7-1/2" = 14.55

**Figure 16-20.**
The components making up stairs.

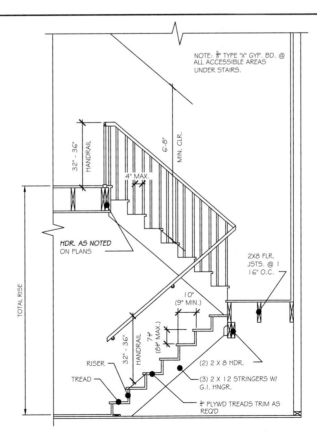

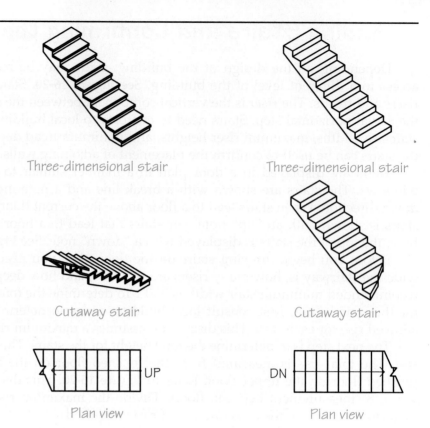

**Figure 16-21.**
Stairs in three-dimensional, cutaway, and floor plan views.

Three-dimensional stair

Three-dimensional stair

Cutaway stair

Cutaway stair

UP

DN

Plan view

Plan view

If there is any value after the decimal point, the number is rounded up. In this example, 14.55 becomes 15 risers. There is always one less tread than the total number of risers. Thus, there will be 14 treads.

Now, assume a minimum tread depth of 9″. To draw the stairs on the floor plan, use the **LINE** command to place the first riser. Then, use the **OFFSET** command to offset the depth of the tread. Generally, only enough treads are drawn as needed to clearly represent the stairs. Add an arrow for the direction of movement on the stairs and an up or down note, as shown in **Figure 16-21.**

**Professional Tip**

After drawing the stairs, it is a good idea to check hallway clearances, door and window placements, and any other feature that might interfere with the stairs.

# Exercise 16-5

◆ Open ex16-4.
◆ Create a layer named M-Stair and set it current.
◆ There will be a 20″ height difference from the ground to the finish floor of the house. Assume you will be using a rise of 7″.
◆ Add stairs to the front walk as shown.
◆ Add stairs at the patio area next to the dining room and the nook area. Refer to the drawing shown for placement.
◆ Save the drawing as ex16-5.

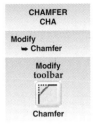

CHAMFER
CHA

Modify
➥ Chamfer

Modify
toolbar

Chamfer

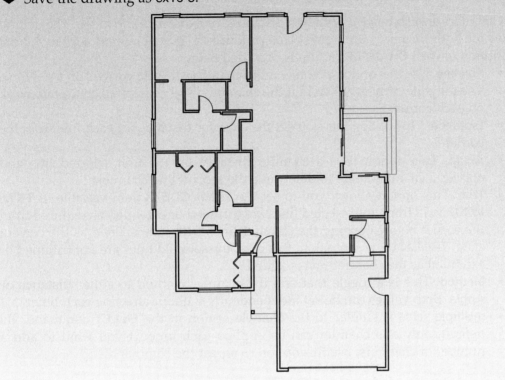

# Creating Angled Features

The **CHAMFER** command can be used to create an angled feature or wall. AutoCAD "thinks" of a chamfer as any angled corner on the drawing. The size of a chamfer is determined by its distance from the intersection of two lines. A 45° chamfer is the same distance from the corner in each direction, **Figure 16-22.**

**Figure 16-22.**
Examples of
different chamfers.

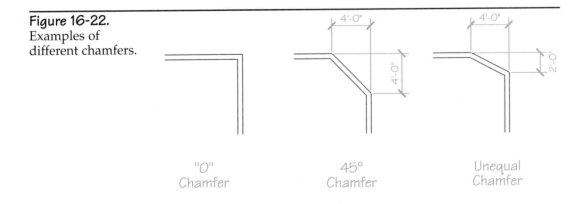

"0"
Chamfer

45°
Chamfer

Unequal
Chamfer

A chamfer is drawn between two lines that may or may not intersect. Chamfers can also connect polylines and rays. Access the **CHAMFER** command by picking the **Chamfer** button in the **Modify** toolbar, selecting **Chamfer** from the **Modify** pull-down menu, or entering cha or chamfer at the Command prompt. The following shows the default values and the options available when you enter the **CHAMFER** command. The current settings are displayed for reference.

Command: **cha** *or* **chamfer**↵
(TRIM mode) Current chamfer Dist1 = 0'-0 1/2", Dist2 = 0'-0 1/2"
Select first line or [Polyline/Distance/Angle/Trim/Method/mUltiple]:

Chamfers are established with two distances, or a distance and angle. The default values for both distances are equal. This produces a 45° chamfered corner. A brief description of each **CHAMFER** option is provided below.

- **Polyline.** Use this option if you want to chamfer all valid corners on a polyline. The polyline corners are valid if the chamfer distance is small enough to work on each corner.
- **Distance.** This option lets you set the chamfer distance for each line from the corner.
- **Angle.** This option uses a chamfer distance on the first selected line and applies a chamfer angle to determine the second line chamfer.
- **Trim.** This option allows you to set the **TRIMMODE** system variable. If **TRIMMODE** is 1 (**Trim**), the selected lines are trimmed or extended as required from the corner before creating the chamfer line. If **No trim** is listed as the current state, **TRIMMODE** is set to 0. In this case, the selected lines are not trimmed or extended as the chamfer line is added.
- **Method.** This is a toggle that sets the chamfer method to either **Distance** or **Angle**. Both values can be set independently without affecting each other.
- **mUltiple.** This is similar to the **Multiple** option in the **FILLET** command. By default, only one chamfer can be applied each time. If you want to add a number of chamfers, use this option to repeat the command.

## Setting the Chamfer Distance

The chamfer distance must be set before you can draw chamfers. The distances remain in effect until changed. Most drafters set the chamfer distances as exact values, but you can also pick two points to set a distance. The following procedure is used to set the chamfer distance.

Command: **cha** *or* **chamfer**↵
(TRIM mode) Current chamfer Dist1 = 0'-0 1/2", Dist2 = 0'-0 1/2"
Select first line or [Polyline/Distance/Angle/Trim/Method/mUltiple]: **d**↵
Specify first chamfer distance <*current*>: **2'0"**↵
Specify second chamfer distance <2'-0">: (*press* [Enter] *for the same as the first distance, or enter a new value*)

Specifying the same value for both distances creates 45° chamfers. Now, you are ready to draw chamfers. Select the first and second lines:

Select first line or [Polyline/Distance/Angle/Trim/Method/mUltiple]: (*pick the first line*)
Select second line: (*pick the second line*)

After the lines are picked, AutoCAD automatically chamfers the corner. Objects can be chamfered even when the corners do not meet. AutoCAD extends the lines as required to generate the specified chamfer and complete the corner if **TRIMMODE** is set to 1 (**Trim**). If **TRIMMODE** is set to 0 (**No trim**), AutoCAD does not extend the lines to complete the corner.

If the specified chamfer distance is so large that the chamfered objects will "disappear," AutoCAD does not perform the chamfer. If you want to chamfer additional corners, use the **mUltiple** option before adding the first chamfer. The results of several chamfering operations are shown in **Figure 16-23**.

---

**Figure 16-23.**
Using the **CHAMFER** command with the **mUltiple** option. First, the exterior lines are chamfered. Then, the interior lines are chamfered.

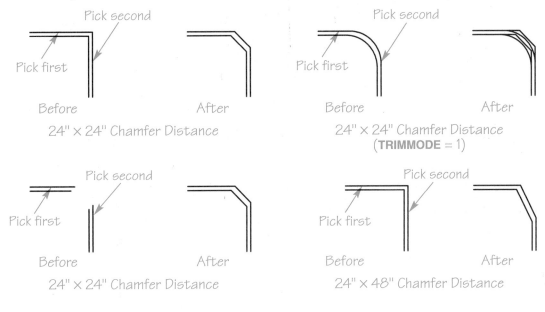

| | |
|---|---|
| Before — After | Before — After |
| 24" × 24" Chamfer Distance | 24" × 24" Chamfer Distance (**TRIMMODE** = 1) |
| Before — After | Before — After |
| 24" × 24" Chamfer Distance | 24" × 48" Chamfer Distance |

**Note**    The first chamfer distance is stored by the **CHAMFERA** system variable and the second chamfer distance is stored by the **CHAMFERB** system variable.

## Chamfering the Corners of a Polyline

All corners of a closed polyline can be chamfered in a single operation. Enter the **CHAMFER** command, set the chamfer distances if needed, enter the **Polyline** option, and then select the polyline. The command sequence is similar to that for drawing fillets for a polyline.

The corners of the polyline are chamfered to the distance values set. The current **TRIMMODE** setting also affects the chamfers drawn. If the polyline was drawn without using the **Close** option, the first corner is not chamfered. See **Figure 16-24**.

## Setting the Chamfer Angle

Instead of setting two chamfer distances, you can set the chamfer distance for one line and an angle to determine the chamfer to the second line. To do this, use the **Angle** option:

Command: **cha** *or* **chamfer**↵
(TRIM mode) Current chamfer Dist1 = 0'-0 1/2", Dist2 = 0'-0 1/2"
Select first line or [Polyline/Distance/Angle/Trim/Method/mUltiple]: **a**↵
Specify chamfer length on the first line <*current*>: *(enter a chamfer distance)*
Specify chamfer angle from the first line <*current*>: *(enter an angle)*

---

**Figure 16-24.**
Using the **Polyline** option of the **CHAMFER** command.

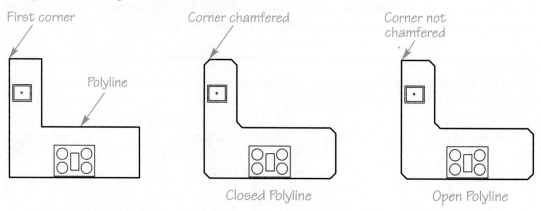

Next, you are prompted to pick the lines to be chamfered. See **Figure 16-25.** The example in the figure uses a distance of 4″ and an angle of 30°.

**Figure 16-25.**
Using the **Angle** option of the **CHAMFER** command.

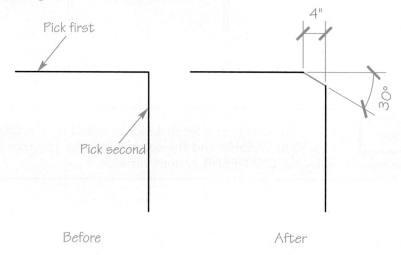

## Setting the Chamfer Method

AutoCAD maintains the chamfer distances and distance/angle settings independently. The settings remain in effect until you change them. Use the **Method** option to toggle between drawing chamfers by distance and by distance/angle. The set values are displayed after entering the command. From this, you can determine the current method:

Command: **cha** *or* **chamfer**⏎
(TRIM mode) Current chamfer Length = 0'-4", Angle = 30.0 *(the settings indicate the chamfer is drawn by distance/angle)*
Select first line or [Polyline/Distance/Angle/Trim/Method/mUltiple]: **m**⏎
Enter trim method [Distance/Angle]: <Angle>: **d**⏎
Select first line or [Polyline/Distance/Angle/Trim/Method/mUltiple]: *(pick the first line)*
Select second line: *(pick the second line)*
Command:

# Setting TRIMMODE Using the CHAMFER Command

You can set the **TRIMMODE** system variable within the **CHAMFER** command. This system variable determines how lines are trimmed when chamfered. See **Figure 16-26.** To set **TRIMMODE**, enter the **Trim** option in the **CHAMFER** command. Then, enter t for **Trim** (**TRIMMODE** = 1) or n for **No trim** (**TRIMMODE** = 0):

Command: **cha** *or* **chamfer**↵
Select first line or [Polyline/Distance/Angle/Trim/Method/mUltiple]: **t**↵
Enter Trim mode option [Trim/No trim] <Trim>: **n**↵ *(sets* **TRIMMODE** *to 0)*

You are then prompted to pick the lines to be chamfered.

---

**Figure 16-26.**
Using the **Trim** option of the **CHAMFER** command.

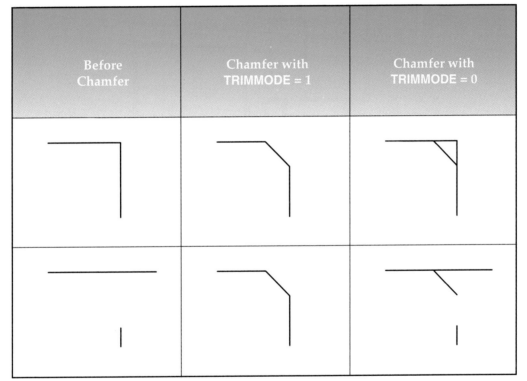

| Before Chamfer | Chamfer with TRIMMODE = 1 | Chamfer with TRIMMODE = 0 |
|---|---|---|

## Exercise 16-6

◆ Open ex16-5.
◆ Create a layer named M-Firebox and set it current.
◆ Refer to the drawing shown for the approximate size and location and add a 4′ × 6′ fireplace in the great room.
◆ Use the **CHAMFER** command to create the fireplace.
◆ Save the drawing as ex16-6.

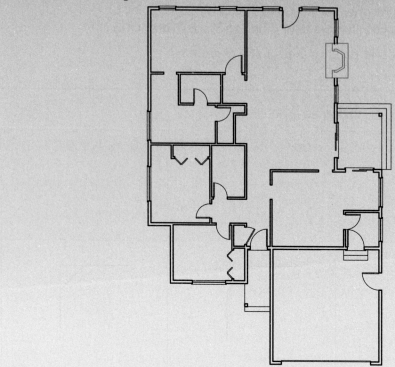

# Adding Casework and Fixtures

The wall, door, window, and stair locations are very important in the layout of a floor plan. These features show how the building is to be assembled. Once these components have been laid out on the drawing, other symbols are required to complete the floor plan. Casework (cabinets), plumbing fixtures, and appliances are added to finish the layout.

Like walls, casework, plumbing fixtures, and appliances are shown in relation to the cutting plane. In some cases, the symbols are shown complete, instead of cut. For example, toilets and bathtubs are not cut, but are viewed as if standing above them and looking down. See **Figure 16-27.**

## Drawing Casework

Casework is shown on a floor plan to represent the location of cabinets, counter-tops, built-in shelving, and kitchen cooking islands. Casework can vary in size from 12″ to 4′-0″ wide as a general rule. *Base cabinets* are the lower cabinets along a wall. They are usually no more than 2′-0″ wide. The reason for this is the average person can comfortably reach across a horizontal distance of 2′-0″.

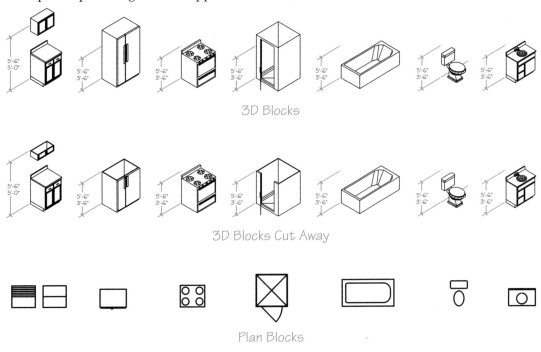

**Figure 16-27.**
Examples of plumbing fixtures, appliances, and casework.

3D Blocks

3D Blocks Cut Away

Plan Blocks

Cabinets deeper than 2'-0" are usually placed in the middle of the room. In this way, a person can reach horizontally 2'-0" from more than one direction. When placed in the middle of a room, cabinets are called *islands.*

The *upper cabinets* are placed above the base cabinets. These are also called *wall-hung cabinets* because they are "hung" on the wall when installed. Upper cabinets are typically half the width of the base cabinets.

There are a few ways to represent base cabinets and wall hung cabinets. One method uses a series of lines parallel to the length of the casework to represent the upper cabinet. Another method uses a hidden line around the perimeter of the upper cabinet to represent it. **Figure 16-28** shows different ways of representing casework in a building.

**Figure 16-28.**
Different methods of drawing casework on the floor plan.

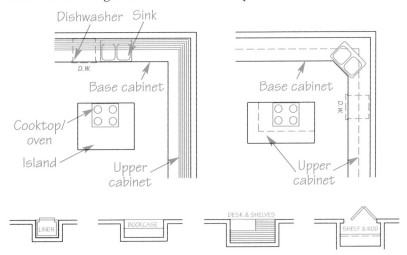

## Adding Plumbing Fixtures

Plumbing fixtures are items such as toilets, bathtubs, showers, sinks, and drinking fountains. They are drawn as symbols. The symbols represent where the bathrooms are located, indicate how many sinks are required, and let the plumber know where the plumbing lines are needed. **Figure 16-29** displays some typical plumbing symbols that are placed on a floor plan.

A *plumbing plan* indicates the locations of plumbing fixtures as well as piping runs and valves. Plumbing plans are discussed in Chapter 23 of this text. In residential design, a plumbing plan is not required. Normally, only the plumbing fixtures are placed on the floor plan. This may vary depending on the local building codes and ruling agency. However, in commercial and industrial design, a plumbing plan is often required in addition to the floor plans. In this case, the architect consults with the plumbing contractor. The plumbing contractor or a consulting engineer normally develops the plumbing plan.

## Adding Appliance Symbols

Some other symbols commonly found on floor plans represent appliances. Appliances include ranges, refrigerators, and dishwashers. Also included in this group are other manufactured products, such as elevators, which do not fall into any of the previously discussed categories. The symbols are drawn at full scale and placed on an appropriate layer.

**Figure 16-29.**
Typical plumbing fixture symbols.

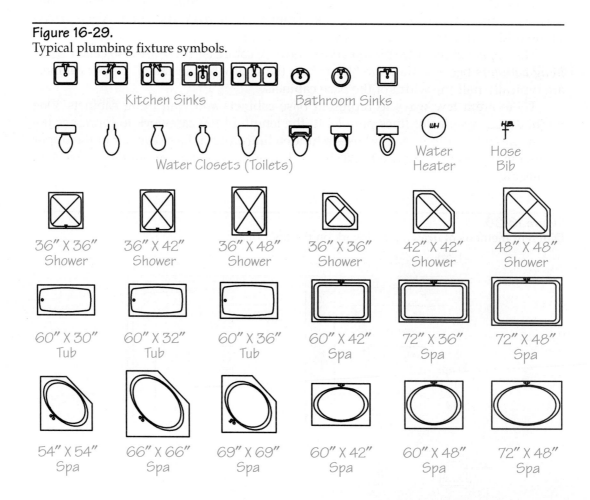

Architectural Drafting Using AutoCAD

Some appliance blocks are shown as hidden lines. These indicate items not included in the construction of the building. However, a space is reserved. Refrigerators, washers, and clothes dryers typically are shown as hidden lines. These items are not generally part of the building contract. If these items are to be installed during construction and are part of the contract, then they are drawn with solid lines. Dishwashers shown as hidden lines indicate an installation inside the cabinet. **Figure 16-30** displays some common appliance symbols.

**Figure 16-30.**
Common appliance symbols.

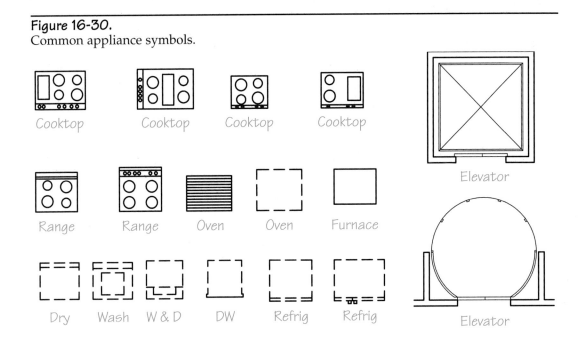

Cooktop    Cooktop    Cooktop    Cooktop    Elevator

Range    Range    Oven    Oven    Furnace

Dry    Wash    W & D    DW    Refrig    Refrig    Elevator

**Professional Tip**

As you continue making symbol blocks, use **DesignCenter** to drag and drop blocks into a separate drawing that can be used as a block library. The block library drawing can then be placed in a folder containing files observing company standards, and a tool palette can be created from the library. This way, you do not need to search several drawings for the blocks you need.

## Exercise 16-7

◆ Open ex16-6.
◆ Create the following layers:
  ◆ M-Casework
  ◆ M-Plumbing
  ◆ M-Appliances
◆ Add the cabinetry, plumbing fixtures, and appliances on the floor plan as shown. Be sure to place these items on the appropriate layers.
◆ Save the drawing as ex16-7.

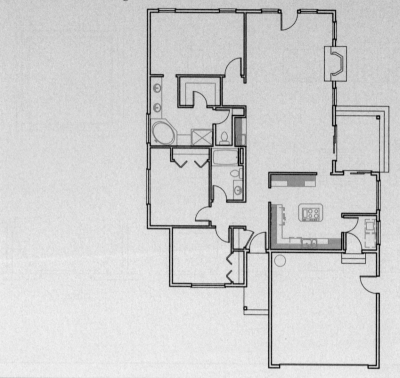

# Adding Dimensions and Text to the Floor Plan

Once the walls, doors, and windows and all symbols have been added to the drawing, you can begin dimensioning and adding notes. Dimension styles are discussed in Chapter 15. When placing dimensions, there should be adequate room around the building to keep the drawing "clean." The dimensions and notes need to provide enough information to make feature locations clearly understood. Dimensions in architectural drafting are often placed together in a straight line to make it easier for the builder to understand and to avoid calculating distances for feature locations. This method is called *continuous dimensioning,* as discussed in Chapter 15.

## Dimensions

There are normally four to five levels of dimensions around the floor plan. These dimensioning levels are often referred to as *dimension strings.* The first level, or string, away from the building provides dimensions for exterior wall openings and distances between interior wall centers. See **Figure 16-31.** The second level of dimensions is to the interior walls. See **Figure 16-32.** The third level of dimensions is to minor "jogs" or corners in a wall. Minor jogs include bays within a wall or pilaster locations along a wall. See **Figure 16-33.** The fourth level of dimensions is used for

**Figure 16-31.**
The first level of dimensions.

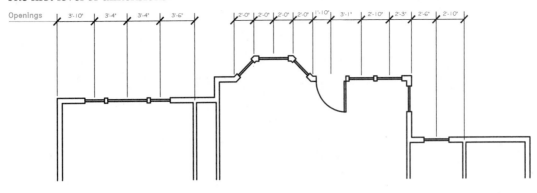

**Figure 16-32.**
The second level of dimensions.

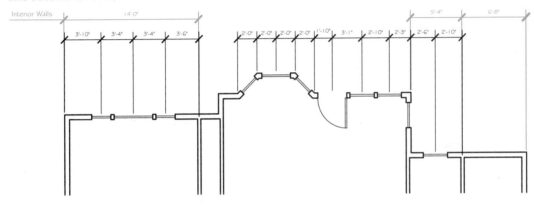

**Figure 16-33.**
The third level of dimensions.

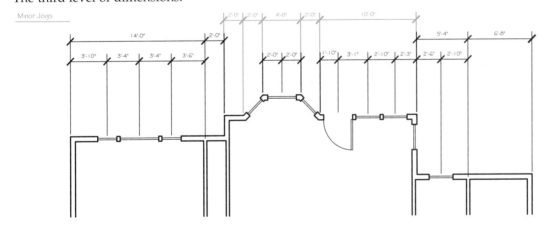

major jogs or corners in the building. See **Figure 16-34.** If there are no minor jogs in the building, major jogs are placed at the third level. The fifth level of dimensions is used for the overall dimensions of the building. See **Figure 16-35.** This is the fourth level if there are no minor jogs in the building.

Interior dimensions are also drawn as straight strings of dimensions. However, unlike exterior dimensions, interior dimensions do not have an established common format. Only interior wall or special feature dimensions are required for interior dimensioning. These dimensions need to be placed in a convenient location next to the feature being dimensioned. Careful placement is often required to provide the needed dimensions while keeping the drawing uncluttered and easy to read. "Clean" dimension placement is often difficult and requires planning. See **Figure 16-36.**

**Figure 16-34.**
The fourth level of dimensions.

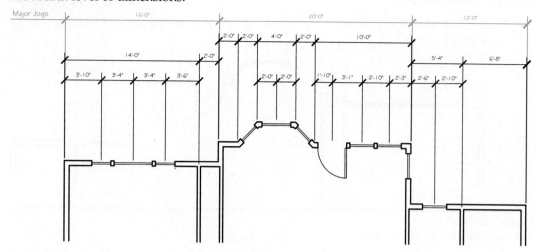

**Figure 16-35.**
The fifth level of dimensions.

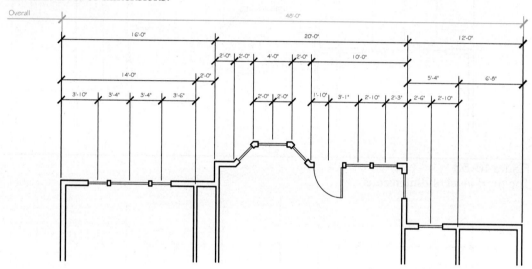

## Notes

After the dimensions have been placed, notes can be added into the drawing. Since they can be placed around blocks, walls, and dimensions, notes are one of the last elements to place in the drawing. *General notes* refer to common applications such as the framing lumber and nailing patterns. *Specific notes* or *local notes* point out a special feature or installation. **Figure 16-37** shows some general and specific notes.

The plotted text height for general and specific notes ranges from 3/32" to 5/32" high, with 1/8" high text most commonly used. The scale factor of the drawing must be taken into consideration when drawing text. For example, 3/32" text multiplied by a scale factor of 48 is equal to 4-1/2" high text for notes drawn in model space. Room tag notes and sheet names range in height from 3/16" to 1/4". If these notes are drawn on the floor plan in model space, multiply these heights by the scale factor to determine the correct model space text height.

Residential drawings may display a note for construction members on the floor plan or on a separate framing plan, or a combination of methods can be used. Construction members are items such as ceiling joists, headers, and beams. As you look at more floor plans and other architectural drawings, you notice these

## Figure 16-36.
Interior dimension strings. (Alan Mascord Design Associates, Inc.)

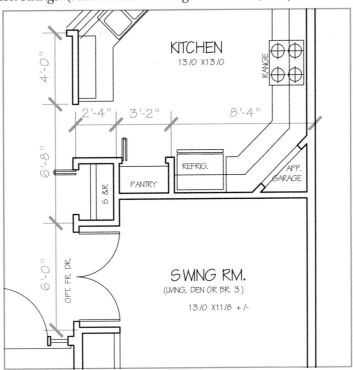

## Figure 16-37.
General notes are normally placed to the side of the floor plan. Specific notes are placed in the vicinity of the object to which they are referring. (Alan Mascord Design Associates, Inc.)

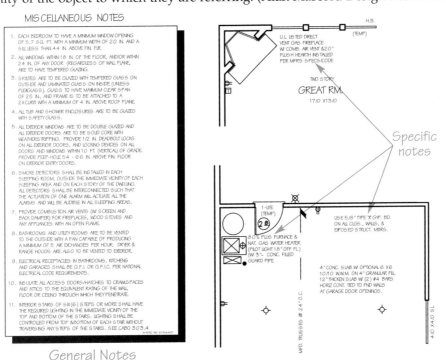

differences. This text discusses the placement of construction members on framing plans, covered in Chapter 22. However, the method you use depends on which practice your school or company follows. You need to become familiar with these standards and practices.

## Exercise 16-8

◆ Open ex16-7.
◆ Create the following layers:
  ◆ M-Dims
  ◆ M-Notes
◆ Create a dimension style using architectural units, an architectural text style, dimension values above the dimension line, and tick marks.
◆ Dimension the floor plan on the M-Dims layer.
◆ Add notes such as room names on the M-Notes layer. Label the appliances.
◆ Your floor plan should look like the plan below.
◆ Save the drawing as ex16-8.

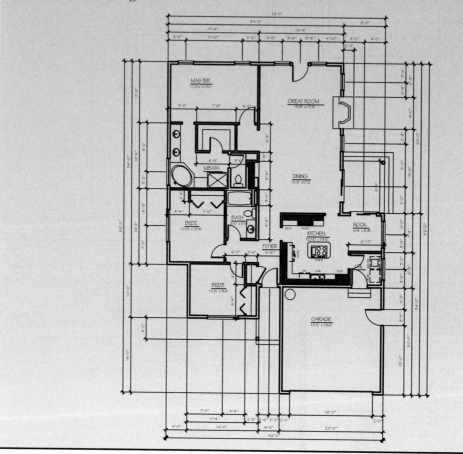

# Matching Properties

Throughout the drawing process, there will be many times when you need to change the properties of an object. This may be because you forgot to make a layer current before drawing new items or you placed text for notes in the wrong style. The **MATCHPROP** command allows you to copy the properties from one object to other objects. The command can be used within a single drawing or across multiple drawings.

To access the **MATCHPROP** command, select the **Match Properties** button in the **Standard** toolbar, select **Match Properties** from the **Modify** pull-down menu, or enter ma, matchprop, or painter at the Command prompt. When you first access the **MATCH-PROP** command, AutoCAD prompts you for the source object. The *source object* is the object that has the properties you want to copy to other objects.

MATCHPROP
MA
PAINTER

Modify
➥ Match
  Properties

Standard
toolbar

Match Properties

Command: **ma**, **matchprop**, *or* **painter**⏎
Select source object: *(pick the object that has the properties you want to copy to other objects)*
Current active settings: Color Layer Ltype Ltscale Lineweight Thickness PlotStyle Text Dim Hatch Polyline Viewport

Once the source object has been selected, AutoCAD displays which properties will be painted to the destination object, *not* the settings for the properties. As used here, the term "paint" means to apply the source properties to the destination object. The *destination object* is the object where the selected properties are to be applied. The next prompt is:

Select destination object(s) or [Settings]: *(pick all objects to which you want the properties copied)*
Select destination object(s) or [Settings]: *(press [Enter] to end the command)*
Command:

The cursor changes to a small paintbrush, indicating you are "painting" properties. To change which properties are to be painted, access the **Settings** option:

Select destination object(s) or [Settings]: **s**⏎

The **Property Settings** dialog box appears, showing the properties that can be painted. The setting of the source object for each property is also displayed. See **Figure 16-38**. The areas of the **Property Settings** dialog box are described below:

---

**Figure 16-38.**
The **Property Settings** dialog box for the **MATCHPROP** command. Select which properties to paint onto other objects.

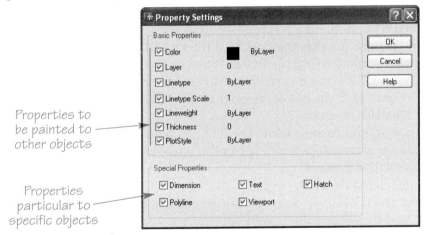

Properties to be painted to other objects

Properties particular to specific objects

- **Basic Properties.** This area lists the general properties of the selected source object. If you do not want the property to be copied, uncheck the appropriate check box. All active (checked) properties are painted to the destination objects.
- **Special Properties.** You can paint over dimension styles, text styles, some polyline and paper space viewport settings, and hatch patterns. These properties are replaced in the destination object if the appropriate check box in the **Special Properties** area is active. *Note:* Hatch patterns are "fill" patterns applied to a closed area. Hatch patterns are discussed later in the text.

Using the **Property Settings** dialog box, you can determine the exact properties painted onto the destination object. For example, if you want to paint only the color and text style of one text object to another text object, uncheck all check boxes *except* the **Color** and **Text** check boxes.

When using the **MATCHPROP** command on dimensions, the **Dimension** setting must be active for the command to work. You can check this after you have selected the source object. When the Current active settings: prompt line appears, Dim should appear with the other settings, as shown in the previous command sequence. If this setting does not appear, open the **Property Settings** dialog box. Then, check the **Dimension** check box in the **Special Properties** area and close the dialog box. You can now paint dimension properties to destination dimensions.

---

| Note | To use the **MATCHPROP** command between drawings, select the source object from one drawing and the destination object in the other drawing. |
| --- | --- |

---

## Chapter Test

*Answer the following questions on a separate sheet of paper.*

1. Briefly describe how a floor plan is created.
2. Calculate the exact wall thickness for a 2 × 6 stud wall with 1/2" gypsum on the inside, and 1/2" sheathing and 1/2" siding on the outside.
3. Name the pull-down menu where the **OFFSET** command is found. What is the keyboard alternative for this command?
4. Briefly describe how the **Through** option of the **OFFSET** command works.
5. What is the advantage of drawing the perimeter walls as a polyline as opposed to a line?
6. Suppose you want to draw a rounded corner with a 2' radius. Describe the procedure using the **FILLET** command.
7. What happens if you use the **Polyline** option of the **FILLET** command on a polyline that was drawn without using the **PLINE Close** option?
8. What does the **TRIMMODE** system variable control?
9. What happens to lines that do not connect at a corner when using the **FILLET** command with **TRIMMODE** set to 1?
10. How can you draw square corners using the **FILLET** command?
11. What is the advantage of creating a window block as a real block over a unit block?
12. Define "riser," as related to stairs.
13. Define "tread," as related to stairs.
14. Calculate the total rise if the main floor to ceiling height is 8'-1", the upstairs floor has 2 × 10 joists, and the second floor has 1" of subfloor and finish floor material. Show your calculations.
15. If a maximum 7" rise is suggested, calculate the number of risers in the stairs for the total rise calculated in the previous question. Show your calculations.
16. How many treads are there in the stairs calculated in the previous two questions? Show your calculations.
17. Give the function of the **CHAMFER** command.
18. What is *casework*?
19. Give another term used for "upper cabinets."
20. Briefly describe the five dimensioning levels.
21. Explain the difference between general and specific notes.
22. Briefly describe the function of the **MATCHPROP** command.

1. Open 12-ResA.
   A. Draw the floor plan shown, using the design sketch as a guide. Place objects on appropriate layers.
   B. Dimension the floor plan and add notes.
   C. Save the drawing as 16-ResA.

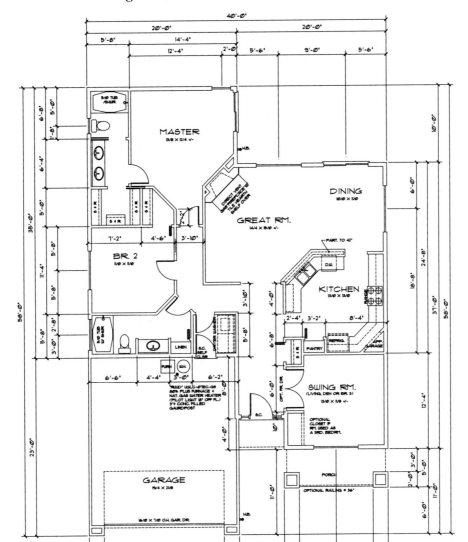

MAIN FLOOR PLAN
SCALE : 1/4" = 1'-0"

(Alan Mascord Design Associates, Inc.)

2. Open 12-ResB.
   A.  Draw the main floor plan shown below, using the M-Area layer objects as a guide. Place objects on appropriate layers.
   B.  Dimension the floor plan and add notes.
   C.  Freeze all the M- layers, and thaw all the U- layers.
   D.  Draw the upper floor plan shown on the following page, using the U-Area layer objects as a guide. Place objects on appropriate layers.
   E.  Dimension the floor plan and add notes.
   F.  Save the drawing as 16-ResB.

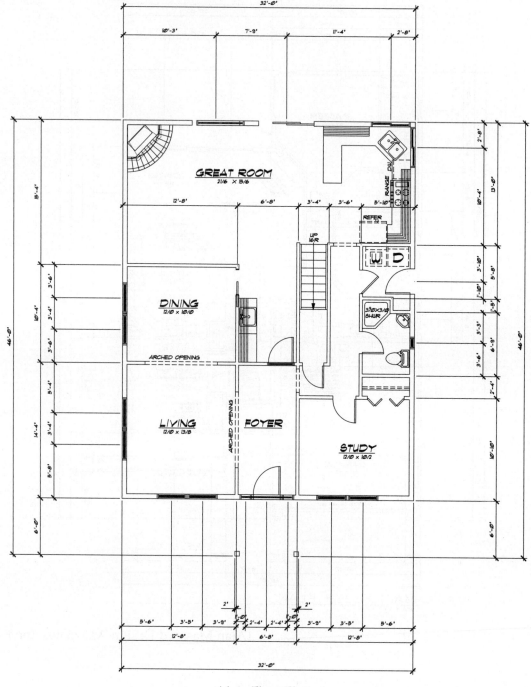

Main Floor Plan

(3D-DZYN)

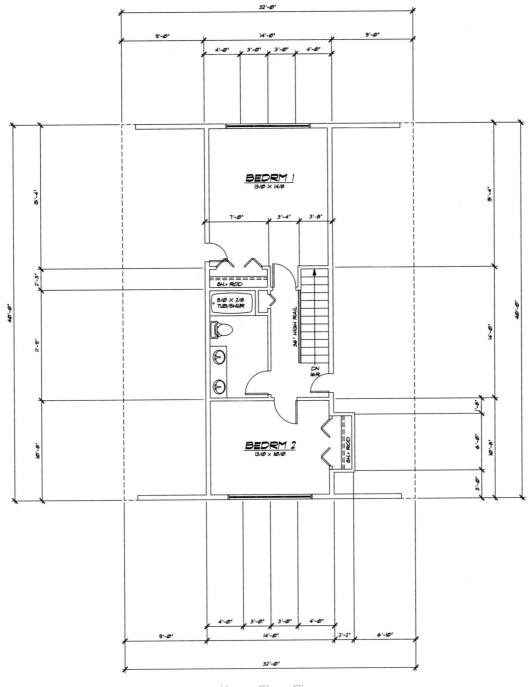

BEDRM 1
13/0 × 14/8

BEDRM 2
13/0 × 10/0

8H.+ ROD

3/0 × 2/0
TUB/SHWR

36" HIGH RAIL

DN
16R

8H.+ ROD

Upper Floor Plan

(3D-DZYN)

3. Open 12-Multifamily.
   A. Draw the main floor plan shown using the A-Area layer objects as a guide. Place objects on appropriate layers.
   B. Dimension the floor plan and add notes.
   C. Save the drawing as 16-Multifamily.

Multifamily

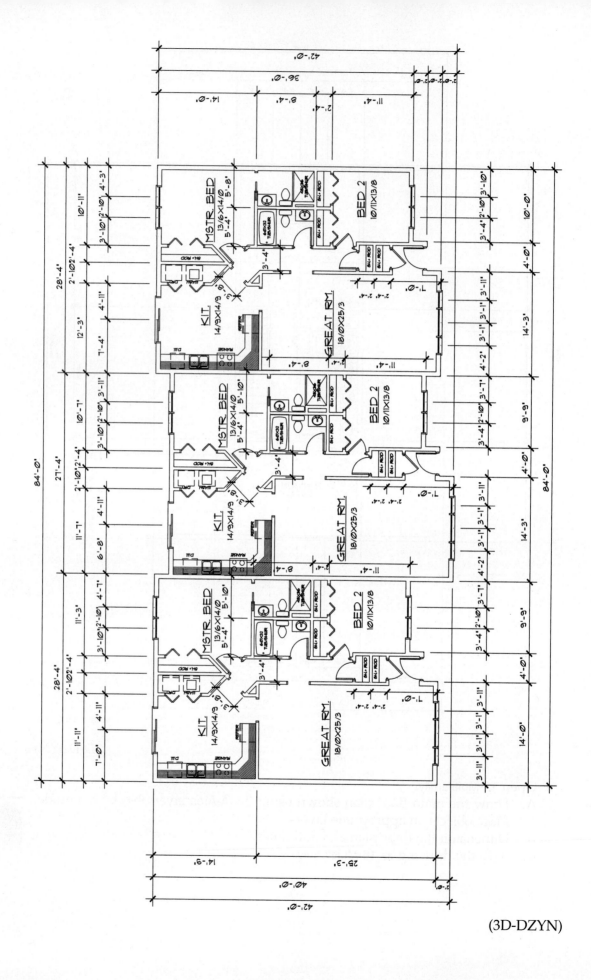

(3D-DZYN)

4. Open 12-Commercial-Main.
   A. Draw the main floor plan shown below, using the A-Area layer objects as a guide. Place objects on appropriate layers.
   B. Dimension the floor plan and add notes.
   C. Save the drawing as 16-Commercial-Main.
   D. Open 12-Commercial-Upper.
   E. Draw the upper floor plan shown on the following page, using the A-Area layer objects as a guide. Place objects on appropriate layers.
   F. Dimension the floor plan and add notes.
   G. Save the drawing as 16-Commercial-Upper.

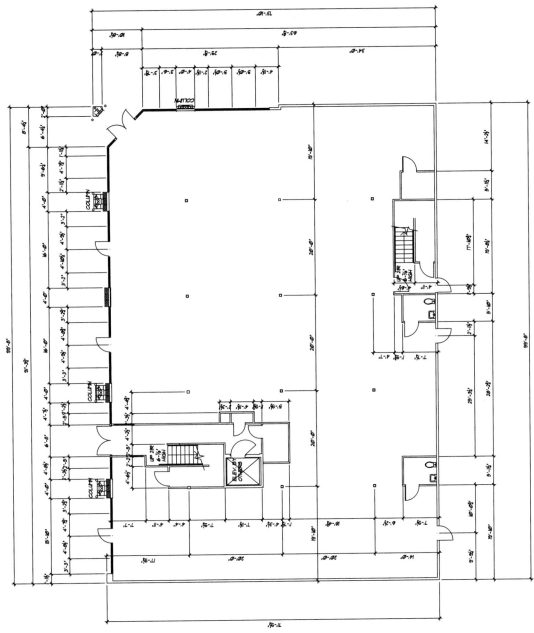

(Cynthia Bankey Architect, Inc.)

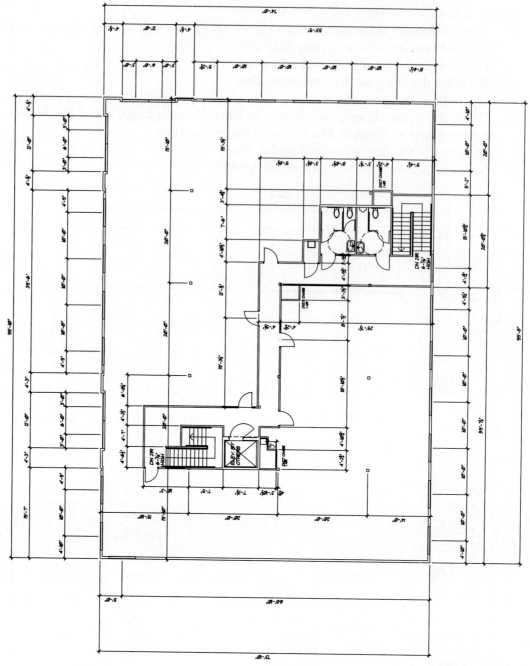

(Cynthia Bankey Architect, Inc.)

# CHAPTER 17

# Using External References

## Learning Objectives

After completing this chapter, you will be able to:

- Explain the function of external references.
- Attach an external reference to the current drawing using the **XREF** command.
- Use **DesignCenter** to attach external references.
- Overlay an external reference over the current drawing.
- Detach, reload, and unload external references.
- Update and work with xref paths.
- Bind an external reference and individual xref-dependent objects.
- Clip an external reference.
- Edit reference drawings.
- Configure AutoCAD to work with reference files.
- Explain the purpose of demand loading.
- Send drawings to other users with the **eTransmit** feature.

## Important Terms

binding
demand loading
dependent objects
external references
host drawing

nesting
projects
xrefs
working set

When creating a drawing, it is often necessary to reference another drawing that is similar, or one that is an additional part of the overall construction documents. For example, assume that a foundation plan is being drawn, and you need to base the layout of the foundation walls on the main floor walls. AutoCAD allows you to reference the main floor plan for this purpose. Referencing a drawing is similar to inserting an entire drawing file into the current drawing. However, reference drawings are treated differently, and they can be managed and displayed in different ways depending on the application.

In AutoCAD, reference drawings are called *external references*, or *xrefs.* A drawing that contains one or more reference drawings is called the *host drawing.* There are several advantages to using xrefs in drawing projects. If the original drawing file being referenced is modified by another drafter while you are working on the host drawing, any changes to the original file can be automatically applied the next time the host drawing is opened. Another advantage is that xrefs occupy very little file space in the host drawing as opposed to inserted drawings and blocks or copied objects.

External references are brought into a drawing and managed using the **XREF** command. This chapter discusses how xrefs are used in AutoCAD and how they can be applied in architectural drafting projects.

# Using Reference Drawings

In large architectural offices, work is often assigned to different groups within the company. For example, one group may be assigned to draw the plans of a building, another group may be assigned to draw the elevations and sections, and a third group may be assigned to draw the site plans. In this case, each group is working on a different part of the same set of construction documents. When this happens, one group may need to reference the drawings belonging to another group. Assume the group working on the elevations and sections needs to reference the plan group's floor plans to accurately draw the elevations. As you learned in Chapter 9, the **INSERT** command could be used to insert a floor plan drawing into the elevation drawings. However, inserting a drawing as a block reference also adds existing layers, blocks, dimension styles, text styles, and linetypes into the destination drawing. This dramatically increases the size of the drawing file. Also, if the plan drawings change and extensive revisions are made, any inserted plan drawings may need to be erased so that the drawings can be reinserted. Revising drawings in this manner can become a difficult and complex process.

When using xrefs, a host drawing can be automatically updated to display the latest changes to the externally referenced files by other users. In addition, when an existing drawing file is brought into the current drawing as an xref, the referenced drawing's geometry is not added to the current drawing. Instead, any objects belonging to the reference drawing are only displayed on screen. This keeps the host drawing's file size small. It also allows several drafters in a class or office to reference the same drawing file with the assurance that any changes to the reference drawing are applied to any drawing where it is used.

As previously discussed, the **XREF** command is used to reference existing drawing files into the current drawing. To access this command, pick the **External Reference** button from the **Reference** or **Insert** toolbar, pick **Xref Manager...** from the **Insert** pull-down menu, or enter xr or xref at the Command prompt. This displays the **Xref Manager** dialog box, **Figure 17-1.** This dialog box is a complete management tool for reference drawings and is discussed in detail in this chapter.

XREF
XR

Insert
➡ Xref Manager...

Reference
toolbar

Insert
toolbar

External Reference

Figure 17-1.

**Figure 17-1.**
The **Xref Manager**
dialog box lists any
externally refer-
enced drawings in
the current drawing
and provides tools
for managing xrefs.

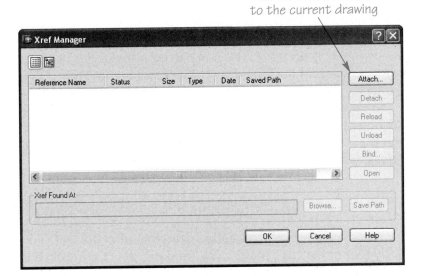

Pick to attach an xref
to the current drawing

## Advantages of Using External References

One of the greatest benefits of using xrefs is that whenever the host drawing is opened, the latest version of the xref is displayed. If the original referenced drawing is modified while the host drawing is closed, any revisions to the reference file will automatically be reflected once the host drawing is opened. This is because AutoCAD reloads each xref upon the opening of the host drawing.

Another benefit to using xrefs is that they can be referenced into a drawing that is then referenced into another drawing. This is called *nesting*. For example, individual details can be drawn in individual drawing files. Each detail is then referenced into a host drawing. The host drawing can then be referenced into yet another drawing that can be set up for plotting. If the original details are referenced into the host drawing and the host drawing is referenced into the plotting drawing, the details are displayed in the plotting drawing because they are nested inside the host drawing. See **Figure 17-2.** If any changes are made to the individual detail drawings and then the plotting drawing is opened, the latest versions of the externally referenced details are displayed.

**Figure 17-2.**
Examples of nesting
reference files. The
original detail
drawings are refer-
enced into the host
drawing and
displayed as nested
xrefs in the plotting
drawing.

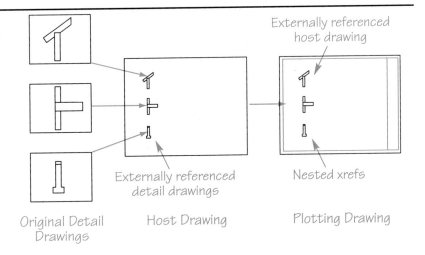

Externally referenced
host drawing

Externally referenced
detail drawings

Nested xrefs

Original Detail
Drawings

Host Drawing

Plotting Drawing

Xrefs are similar to inserted drawings in that when an xref is selected in the host drawing, all objects in the reference drawing are highlighted. However, the advantage of using an xref over an inserted drawing is that the drawing geometry of an xref is only displayed, and not added, to the host drawing. This significantly reduces the size of the host drawing file. You can also make the objects belonging to an xref a permanent part of the host drawing by binding the xref. This is discussed later in this chapter.

Xrefs are also useful when you wish to display only a portion of the reference drawing in the host drawing. This can be accomplished by defining clipping boundaries that eliminate the display of certain portions of the reference drawing. Clipping xrefs is discussed later in this chapter.

## Attaching an Xref to the Current Drawing

When you bring a reference drawing into the current drawing file, you are *attaching* it to the current drawing (making the current drawing a host). Referencing a drawing file in this manner is similar to inserting a block. To attach an xref to the current drawing, enter the **XREF** command and pick the **Attach...** button in the **Xref Manager** dialog box. This displays the **Select Reference File** dialog box. Use this dialog box to browse to the folder that contains the desired drawing that will be referenced. Select the file to attach and pick **Open** when you are finished.

Once a file to attach has been selected, the **External Reference** dialog box is displayed, **Figure 17-3.** This dialog box is used to indicate how and where the reference is to be placed in the current drawing. It is similar to the **Insert** dialog box used for blocks. The name of the reference file is shown in the upper-left corner of the dialog box. If you wish to change the drawing being attached, pick the **Browse...** button and select a different file in the **Select Reference File** dialog box. When attaching an xref, pick the **Attachment** option in the **Reference Type** area. This option

**Figure 17-3.**
The **External Reference** dialog box is used to specify how an xref is attached to the current drawing.

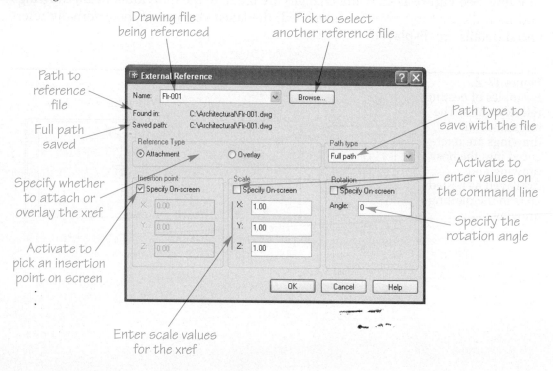

is active by default. If you are using the reference as an overlay, then select the **Overlay** option. The **Overlay** option is discussed later in this chapter.

The **Name:** window contains the name of the drawing file being referenced. Picking the drop-down arrow allows you to access a list of existing references in the current drawing. The **Insertion point**, **Scale**, and **Rotation** areas can be used to enter the xref insertion point, scaling, and rotation angle values. If the **Specify On-screen** check box is unchecked in the **Insertion point** area, you can enter absolute coordinates for the insertion point of the xref. Activate the check box if you want to pick the insertion location on screen. Scale values for the xref can be set in the **Scale** area. By default, the X, Y, and Z scale values are set to 1. In most situations, the values are left at 1. You can enter new scale values, or you can have AutoCAD prompt you for the values on the command line by checking the **Specify On-screen** check box. The rotation angle for the inserted xref is set at 0 by default. You can specify a different rotation angle in the **Angle:** text box. If you check the **Specify On-screen** check box, AutoCAD prompts you for the rotation angle on the command line as the reference is being added.

The **Path type** area includes a drop-down list with three options. These options control how the reference file is found each time the host drawing is opened. If the path is set to **Full path**, AutoCAD will look for the reference file in the specific path where it was originally referenced and attempt to reload it the next time the host drawing is opened. If the **Relative path** option is selected, AutoCAD searches for the reference in paths that are relative to the host drawing's path. If the **No path** option is selected, a path is not saved, and AutoCAD will first look in the host drawing's folder for the reference file. Then, it will look in the Support File Search Path locations to locate the reference file. The Support File Search Path locations are specified in the **Files** tab of the **Options** dialog box. If the xrefs used in your drawings are primarily stored as files on your local hard drive or a network drive, saving the xref path locations can be helpful. However, not saving xref paths may be more suitable when drawings are sent to other locations that do not have the same directory or folder structure that you have. Sending drawing files that contain xrefs to other students or offices is covered later in this chapter.

In the example given in **Figure 17-3,** the reference file Flr-001.dwg has been selected for attachment to the current drawing. Press the **OK** button to attach the reference. Because the **Specify On-screen** check box in the **Insertion point** area has been checked, the xref is attached to your cursor and you are prompted for the insertion point on the command line. Pick a point in the drawing, use object snaps, or enter absolute coordinates to place the reference into the drawing. The Flr-001 drawing has now been referenced into the current drawing. See **Figure 17-4.** In this example, the Flr-001 floor plan drawing has been referenced into a site plan drawing named Lot-16.

As you can see, the procedure for attaching an xref is similar to that used for inserting a block. Although the **XREF** and **INSERT** commands function in a similar manner, remember that externally referenced files are not added to the current drawing file's database, while inserted drawings are. This is why using external references helps keep your drawing file size to a minimum.

**Professional Tip**

As is the case with inserted blocks and drawings, an xref is placed on the current layer when attached to a drawing. When attaching reference files, it is advisable to create an xref layer for each reference that you plan on using. This makes it easier to manage xrefs in your drawing as the individual layers can be frozen or thawed to change the display of different files and create a combination of drawings.

**Figure 17-4.**
Attaching an xref to a drawing. The floor plan drawing named Flr-001 has been referenced into a site plan drawing named Lot-16 (shown in color).

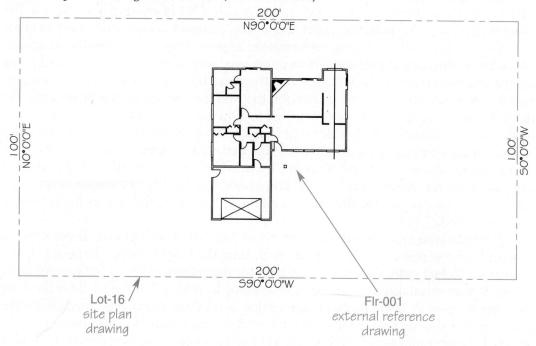

Lot-16
site plan
drawing

Flr-001
external reference
drawing

## Working with Dependent Objects in Xref Files

When an xref has been attached to a drawing, any named objects belonging to the reference drawing, such as blocks and layers, are referred to as *dependent objects.* This is because the objects are only displayed in the current drawing and the actual object definitions are stored in the reference drawing. Dependent objects are named differently by AutoCAD when an xref is attached to a drawing. Dependent objects are renamed so that the xref file name precedes the actual object name. The names are separated by a vertical bar symbol (|). For example, a layer named A-wall within an externally referenced drawing file named A-fp01 comes into the host drawing as A-fp01|A-wall. This is done to distinguish the xref-dependent layer name from the same layer name that may exist in the host drawing. This also makes it easier to manage layers when several xrefs are attached to the host drawing, because the layers from each reference file are prefixed with unique file names. Xref-dependent layers cannot be renamed.

It is important to remember that when an xref is attached, dependent objects such as layers are only added to the host drawing in order to support the display of the objects in the reference file. Any xref-dependent layers that are added are grayed out in the **Layer Control** box, **Figure 17-5.** This indicates that the layers cannot be set current or used to draw objects. However, xref layers can be turned off, frozen, or locked. In addition to controlling their display behavior, you can also change the colors or linetypes of xref layers. Changing a display property of an xref layer only affects the layer in the host drawing and does not modify the actual reference file(s). To assign a different color or linetype to an xref-dependent layer, access the **Layer Properties Manager** dialog box, select the layer, and change its color or linetype.

**Figure 17-5.**
Xref-dependent layers are renamed when an xref is attached to a drawing. The xref layers are grayed out in the **Layer Control** drop-down list and are unavailable for use.

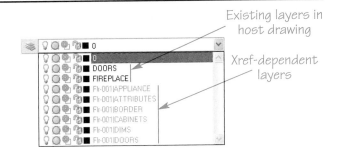

Existing layers in host drawing

Xref-dependent layers

**Professional Tip**

When attaching a drawing as an xref, the reference file comes into the host drawing with the same layer colors and linetypes used in the original file. If you are referencing a drawing to check the relationship of objects between two drawings, it is a good idea to change the xref layer colors to make it easier to differentiate between the content of the host drawing and the xref drawing. Changing xref layer colors only affects the display in the current drawing and not the original reference file. As discussed earlier, when attaching xrefs, it is also recommended to place them on specifically named layers so that they can be managed separately from other items in the host drawing.

## Attaching Xrefs with DesignCenter

**DesignCenter** provides a quick method for attaching xrefs to the current drawing. To attach an xref in this manner, first display **DesignCenter** and use the **Tree View** area to locate the folder containing the file to be referenced. When the drawing is displayed in the **Content** area, you can attach it as an xref using either of two methods. Right-click on the file icon and select **Attach as Xref...** from the shortcut menu, or drag and drop the drawing into the current drawing area *using the right mouse button* and select **Attach as Xref...** from the shortcut menu displayed. When the **External Reference** dialog box is displayed, enter the appropriate insertion values and pick **OK**.

## Overlaying an Xref

You may encounter many situations where you want to double-check the development of your drawing against another drawing in a project. In such cases, you can *overlay* a reference file over your drawing to compare the two. Overlaying an xref file on top of the current drawing allows you to view the xref without completely attaching it. This is accomplished by activating the **Overlay** option button in the **External Reference** dialog box after selecting the xref.

The difference between an overlaid xref and an attached xref relates to how nested xrefs are handled. As discussed earlier in this chapter, attached xrefs can be nested into other reference files. When an xref is overlaid, it cannot become a nested xref. In other words, assume an xref drawing of a stove top is overlaid when it is referenced into a drawing named Kitchen. The Kitchen drawing is then referenced into a host drawing named Floor. When the Kitchen drawing is referenced, and it is

**Figure 17-6.**
Differentiating
between overlaid
and attached xrefs.
When the host
drawing is refer-
enced into the plot-
ting drawing, only
the nested xrefs that
were attached are
displayed.

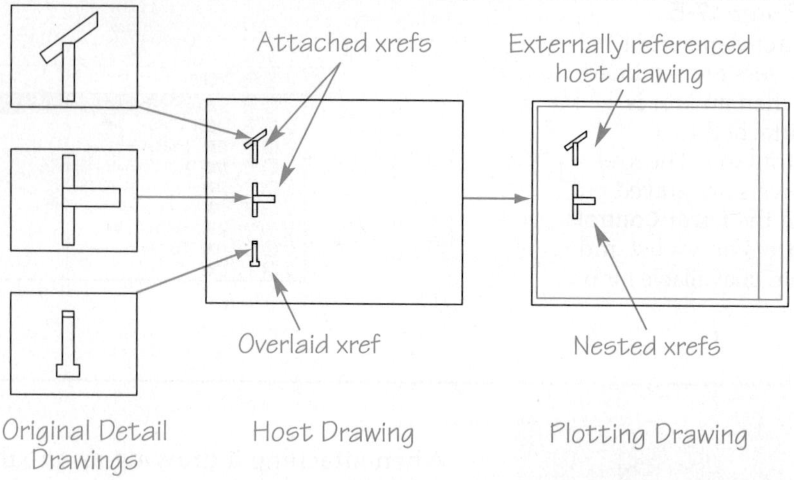

Attached xrefs

Externally referenced
host drawing

Overlaid xref

Nested xrefs

Original Detail
Drawings

Host Drawing

Plotting Drawing

attached *or* overlaid, the stove top xref that was previously overlaid in the Kitchen drawing will not be brought into the Floor host drawing. The manner in which nested overlays are handled is shown in **Figure 17-6.** The detail drawing that is overlaid in the host drawing is not displayed when the host drawing is attached to the plotting drawing. Only nested xrefs that have been attached (the attached detail drawings) are carried into the plotting drawing.

## The **Manage Xrefs** Icon

Once an xref has been attached to the current drawing, the **Manage Xrefs** icon is added to the status bar. This icon appears next to the **Communication Center** icon in the AutoCAD status bar tray and displays current information about xref files. See **Figure 17-7.** Picking the icon displays the **Xref Manager** dialog box, where you can reload, unload, detach, or bind an xref drawing. Managing xrefs with this dialog box is discussed in the following sections. If changes are made to an xref in the current file while the file is open, a notification appears along with the **Manage Xrefs** icon in the form of a balloon message. The message in **Figure 17-7A** indicates that the xref file needs to be reloaded to display the most current version. You can then pick on the file name or pick the **Manage Xrefs** icon to reload the file in the **Xref Manager** dialog box. In the example shown, dimensions have been added to the original Flr-001 xref file. Updating xref files in the host drawing is discussed in the next section.

## Figure 17-7.

The **Manage Xrefs** icon appears in the AutoCAD status bar tray when a reference file is attached to the current drawing. A—A balloon message is displayed with the icon when the original xref file has been modified. B—Reloading the Flr-001 xref file updates the current drawing.

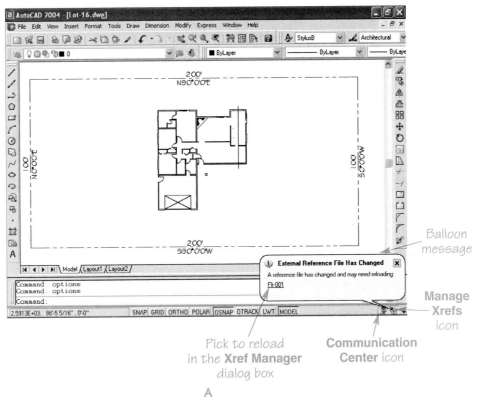

A

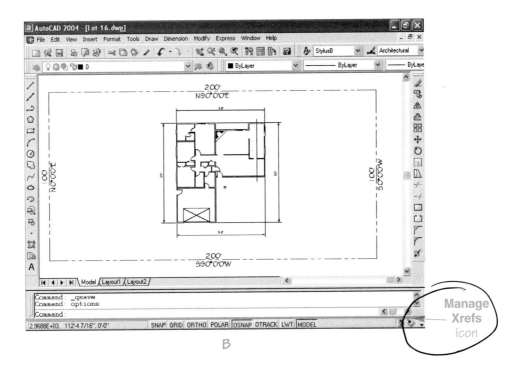

B

## Exercise 17-1

◆ Open the ex14-7 drawing you created in Chapter 14.
◆ Create a layer named Xref-Floor Plan. Set the layer current.
◆ Use the **XREF** command to reference the ex12-6 drawing created in Chapter 12.
◆ Insert at 0,0 with a uniform scale of 1 and a rotation angle of 0. The floor plan is now referenced into the site plan drawing.
◆ Use the **MOVE** and **ROTATE** commands to align the xref with the structure outline on the site plan.
◆ Save the drawing as ex17-1.

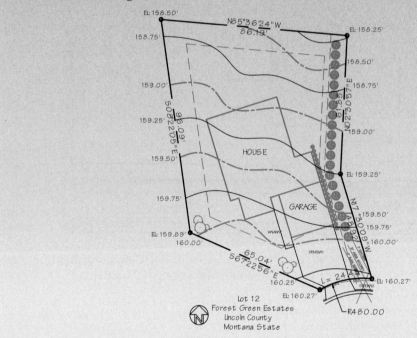

## Detaching, Reloading, Unloading, and Opening Xrefs

As discussed earlier in this chapter, every time you open a drawing file containing an xref, the xref is also loaded and appears on screen. Xref files loaded in the current drawing are listed in the **Xref Manager** dialog box, **Figure 17-8.** Attached and overlaid xrefs remain in a drawing until you *detach* them. This can be accomplished by highlighting the reference name in the **Xref Manager** dialog box and picking the **Detach** button. When you detach an xref file, any copies of the xref are erased, and all referenced data is removed from the current drawing. Any xrefs that are nested inside the detached file are also removed. The actual detachment does not occur until you press **OK** and close the dialog box.

If you are referencing a drawing that is being created by another drafter or group, you may need to update the reference or *reload* it to ensure you have the latest version. As previously discussed, the latest saved version of the xref is loaded upon opening the host drawing. However, there may be cases where another drafter is editing the file you are currently referencing. If the other drafter has made changes and saved the drawing, the displayed referenced version you have is not current. In this case, AutoCAD will display a notification next to the **Manage Xrefs** icon. To reload the xref file, access the **Xref Manager** dialog box, highlight the xref file name, and select the **Reload** button. This instructs AutoCAD to redisplay the most current version of the file being referenced.

**Figure 17-8.**
The **Xref Manager** dialog box lists currently loaded xref files and can be used to attach, detach, unload, and reload xrefs.

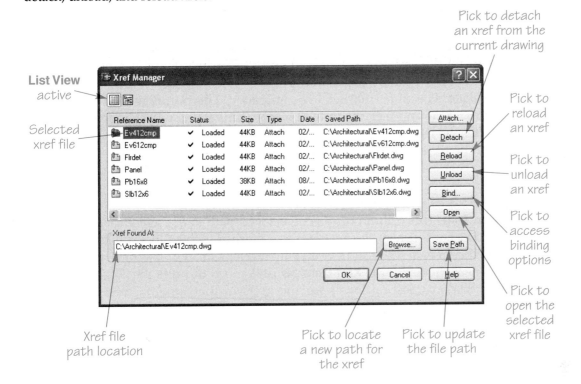

When a file is being referenced but is not being currently used, it may be desirable to temporarily remove the file or *unload* it to conserve system resources. When you unload an xref, the file is not detached, but it is no longer displayed on screen and is not regenerated. To unload an xref, highlight the xref file name in the **Xref Manager** dialog box and select the **Unload** button. To redisplay the xref again, use the **Reload** button to reload the xref.

The **Open** button allows you to select a reference file in the list and then open the drawing so that it may be edited. Editing xref files is discussed later in this chapter. Using the **Open** button saves time because AutoCAD knows the location of the reference file and you do not have to browse through several folders and directories manually to open the drawing.

## Using the **Xref Manager** Dialog Box

In addition to the attaching, detaching, reloading, and unloading functions previously discussed, the **Xref Manager** dialog box is used to access current information about any xref files in the current drawing. Refer to **Figure 17-8.** The list of file names in the **Reference Name** column can be displayed either in list view or tree view. The list view display mode is displayed by default. It can be activated by picking the **List View** button located at the upper-left corner of the dialog box, or by pressing the [F3] key. The labeled columns displayed in list view are described as follows:

- **Reference Name.** This column lists the names of xrefs in the current drawing.
- **Status.** This column describes the current status of each xref. The xref status can be classified as one of the following:
  - **Loaded.** The xref is attached to the drawing or overlaid and is currently being displayed.
  - **Unloaded.** The xref is attached or overlaid but is not currently being displayed or regenerated.

- **Not Found.** The xref file was not found in a valid search path.
- **Unresolved.** The xref file is attached but cannot be read by AutoCAD. This status may be due to a corruption to the reference drawing.
- **Orphaned.** The xref is attached, but it is a nested xref dependent upon the parent xref, which is unresolved or not found.
- **Reload.** The xref is marked to be reloaded. This occurs when you highlight an xref file and pick the **Reload** button. This status will change to **Loaded** after the **OK** button is picked.
- **Unload.** The xref is marked to be unloaded. This occurs when you highlight an xref file and pick the **Unload** button. This status will change to **Unloaded** after the **OK** button is picked.
- **Size.** The file size for each xref is listed in this column.
- **Type.** This column indicates whether the xref is attached or overlaid in the host drawing.
- **Date.** This column lists the last date the reference file was saved.
- **Saved Path.** This column displays the saved path to the reference file. If only a file name appears here, the reference was attached without the path location saved.

To view the xrefs in the tree view display mode instead of list view, pick the **Tree View** button near the top of the **Xref Manager** dialog box or press the [F4] key. The tree view listing displays nesting levels for the xrefs in the drawing. See **Figure 17-9.** When using the tree view display mode, the current drawing is indicated with the standard AutoCAD drawing file icon. Each xref file is listed below the current drawing icon as a sheet of paper with a paper clip. Nesting levels are shown in a format that is similar to the arrangement of file folders. The nesting levels indicate which xrefs belong to other drawing files. When using tree view mode, the xrefs can be selected and detached, reloaded, or unloaded using the same methods applied in list view mode.

The xref icons take on different appearances in tree view depending on the current status of each xref. An xref whose status is unloaded will have an icon that is grayed out. A question mark indicates that the file was not found. An upward arrow shown with the icon means the xref has just been reloaded, and a downward arrow means the xref has just been unloaded.

**Figure 17-9.**
The tree view display mode shows nesting levels for xref files and indicates the status of each xref.

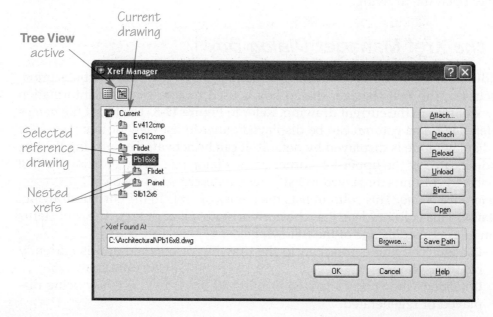

## Updating Xref Paths

As previously discussed, when attaching xrefs, you have the option of specifying the path location type. If an xref is attached with the **Full path** or **Relative path** option, the path appears in the **Saved Path** column in the **Xref Manager** dialog box. If an xref file cannot be found in the saved location when the host drawing is opened, AutoCAD searches a *library* path, which includes the current drawing folder and the Support File Search Path locations set in the **Files** tab of the **Options** dialog box. If a file with a matching drawing name is found, it is resolved. In such a case, the **Saved Path** location differs from where the file was actually found. You can check this in the **Xref Manager** dialog box by highlighting an xref name and then comparing the path listed in the **Saved Path** column with the listing in the **Xref Found At** area. To update the **Saved Path** location, pick the **Save Path** button at the bottom of the **Xref Manager** dialog box.

When a reference drawing has been moved and the new location is not in a relative path or the library path, the xref file status is indicated as **Not Found**. You can update the path to refer to the new location by selecting the **Browse...** button in the **Xref Found At** area. Using the **Select new path** dialog box, go to the new folder and select the desired file. Then, pick **Open** to update the path. When you pick **OK**, the xref is automatically reloaded into the drawing.

## Binding an External Reference

An xref file can be made a permanent part of the host drawing as if it had been a block inserted with the **INSERT** command. This is called *binding* an xref. Binding is useful when you need to send the full drawing file to a client, another student, or to a plotting service.

When a drawing is inserted into another drawing with the **INSERT** command, any blocks, layers, linetypes, dimension styles, and text styles that belong to the inserted file are carried into the destination drawing. Binding an xref to a host drawing has a similar effect. When an xref is bound, the reference file is converted into a block in the host drawing, and any blocks, layers, linetypes, dimension styles, and text styles belonging to the xref file are made a permanent part of the host drawing. Any bound objects from the xref file, such as layers, can then be used as desired in the host drawing. As previously discussed, when an xref is attached to a drawing, all dependent objects in the reference file are given unique names by AutoCAD. When an xref is bound to the host drawing, the dependent objects are renamed again to reflect that they have become a permanent part of the drawing.

To bind an xref, access the **Xref Manager** dialog box, highlight the xref to bind, and select the **Bind...** button. This displays the **Bind Xrefs** dialog box, which includes the **Bind** and **Insert** option buttons. See **Figure 17-10**.

When the **Bind** option is selected, the xref and any copies of the xref are converted to blocks in the drawing. All instances of the block are named using the same name as the reference drawing file's name. In addition, all dependent objects, such as blocks, layers, linetypes, dimension styles, and text styles, are added to the host drawing and renamed. The xref name is kept with the names of all dependent objects, but the vertical line in each name is replaced with two dollar signs ($$) with a number in between. For example, a layer named A-fp01|A-wall is renamed A-fp01$0$A-wall when the xref is bound using the **Bind** option. The number between the dollar signs is automatically incremented if there is already an object definition with the same name. For example, if A-fp01$0$A-wall already exists in the drawing, the layer is renamed to A-fp01$1$A-wall. In this way, unique names are created for all xref-dependent object definitions that are bound to the host drawing.

Figure 17-10.
The **Bind Xrefs**
dialog box allows
you to specify how
the xref will be
bound to the host
drawing.

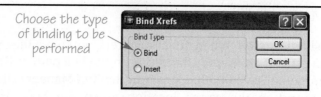

Choose the type
of binding to be
performed

Using the **Insert** option binds the xref as if you had inserted a drawing with the **INSERT** command. All copies of the xref are converted into blocks and named using the same name as the reference file's name. Also, all named objects, such as blocks, layers, linetypes, and styles, are added into the host drawing as named in the original xref file. For example, if an xref named S-fp03 is bound, and it contains a layer named S-beam, the xref-dependent layer S-fp03|S-beam is renamed to S-beam. The xref name prefix is removed from all xref-dependent objects, leaving only their original names from the reference drawing. If there is already a named object with the same name as the xref-dependent object, then the xref object takes on the properties of the host drawing's named object. For example, assume an xref containing a block named A-fp01|Toilet is bound into the drawing with the **Insert** binding option. If there is already a block named Toilet, any Toilet blocks from the reference file take on the same properties as the Toilet block in the host drawing. If the Toilet block definition from the xref is different from the Toilet block definition in the host drawing, the xref block is updated to match the host drawing's definition.

Binding a drawing is usually not an ideal option when using xrefs. Remember that the purpose of attaching an xref is to *reference* the drawing. When you bind an xref to the host drawing, the link to the reference file is broken, and any changes to the reference file are no longer automatically applied when the host drawing is opened. Also, when an xref is bound, the size of the host drawing is increased because the binding operation inserts the entire contents of the xref file.

In some cases, you may only need to bind one or more specific named objects from an xref into the host drawing, rather than the entire xref. If you only need to bind a selected item, such as a block or a layer, you can use the **XBIND** command. This command is discussed in the next section.

## Binding Individual Xref Objects

As previously discussed, it may be counterproductive to bind an entire xref to the host drawing when you only need selected objects from the original xref file. For example, you may want to use a block from a reference file after the xref is attached without binding the entire xref to the host drawing. This helps keep the size of the host drawing file small. Individual xref-dependent objects such as blocks, layers, linetypes, text styles, and dimension styles can be bound to the host drawing using the **XBIND** command.

Binding an individual object only inserts the definition of the item into the host drawing. For example, assume you want to bind a block from the xref file to the host drawing. When using the **XBIND** command, only the block definition is inserted into the host drawing. Any block instances in the xref file using the same definition remain in the reference file. The block can then be inserted into the host drawing, and since the entire xref was not bound, the host drawing can still be updated to display the latest version of the xref.

To access the **XBIND** command, pick the **External Reference Bind** button from the **Reference** toolbar, pick **Object** from the **Modify** pull-down menu and then pick **Bind...** from the **External Reference** cascading menu, or enter xb or xbind at the Command prompt. This displays the **Xbind** dialog box, **Figure 17-11.** This dialog box allows you to select individual xref-dependent objects for binding.

As shown in **Figure 17-11**, there are currently six reference files in the host drawing. Each xref file is indicated by a drawing icon. You can click the plus sign (+) next to an icon to display a list of items that are dependent upon an xref. The xref-dependent objects belonging to the Flr-001 xref file are shown in **Figure 17-12.** There are five types of dependent objects in an xref. These include blocks, dimension styles, layers, linetypes, and text styles. Each type has a group listing under the selected xref file in the **Xbind** dialog box.

To select an individual xref-dependent object, you must first expand the corresponding group listing by clicking on the plus sign next to the group icon. In **Figure 17-13**, the block group has been expanded to list the xref-dependent blocks in the xref drawing. To select an object for binding, highlight it and pick the **Add->** button. The names of all objects selected and added are displayed in the **Definitions to Bind** list on the right. Each xref-dependent object appears with the xref name prefix, the vertical bar symbol, and the object name. When all desired objects have been selected, pick the **OK** button. A message displayed on the command line indicates how many objects of each type were bound.

When an individual object is bound to the host drawing, it is automatically renamed. When using the **XBIND** command, objects are renamed in the same manner as objects bound with the **Bind...** option in the **Xref Manager** dialog box. The renaming method replaces the vertical bar symbol in the object name with two dollar signs and

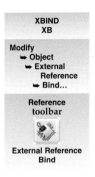

XBIND
XB

Modify
➥ Object
  ➥ External
     Reference
  ➥ Bind...

Reference
toolbar

External Reference
Bind

---

**Figure 17-11.**
The **Xbind** dialog box is used to individually bind xref-dependent objects to the host drawing.

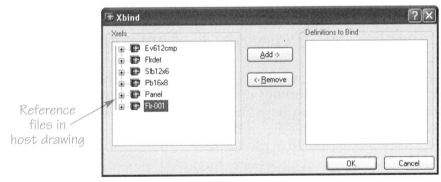

Reference files in host drawing

---

**Figure 17-12.**
Clicking the plus sign next to an xref icon will display the five xref-dependent group types.

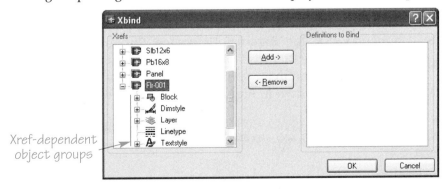

Xref-dependent object groups

---

**Figure 17-13.**
You can select an individual object to bind by expanding the corresponding group listing, selecting the desired item, and picking the **Add** button.

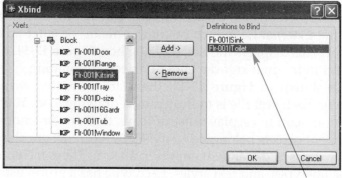

Block definitions added for binding

a number, typically 0. For example, after binding, a block named Sink belonging to the xref file named Flr-001 (Flr-001|Sink) would be named Flr-001$0$Sink.

If you bind an xref-dependent layer but not the linetype assigned to it, the line-type will be automatically bound to the host drawing by AutoCAD. A new linetype name, such as Flr-001|Hidden, will be assigned to the linetype.

## Exercise 17-2

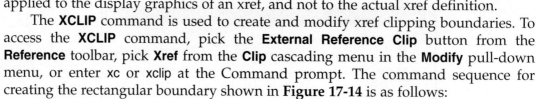

◆ Open ex17-1.
◆ Use the **XBIND** command to bind several layers, dimension styles, and text styles.
◆ Detach the ex12-6 xref.
◆ Check for the new bound definitions in the appropriate dialog boxes.
◆ Save the drawing as ex17-2.

# Clipping an External Reference

When creating architectural construction documents, it is often necessary to include many different views and portions of a building. Typically, the documents will contain detail drawings showing how building components are assembled or details of a particular design, such as the craftsmanship of a column. When using xrefs, a very useful feature is the ability to display specific parts of a drawing by clipping away the portions that are unnecessary. AutoCAD allows you to create a boundary that displays only a selected part of an external reference. All objects in the xref outside the border are removed, or clipped. Objects that fall partially within the boundary appear to be trimmed at the boundary line. Although these objects appear to be trimmed, the original reference file is not changed in any way. Clipping is applied to the display graphics of an xref, and not to the actual xref definition.

The **XCLIP** command is used to create and modify xref clipping boundaries. To access the **XCLIP** command, pick the **External Reference Clip** button from the **Reference** toolbar, pick **Xref** from the **Clip** cascading menu in the **Modify** pull-down menu, or enter xc or xclip at the Command prompt. The command sequence for creating the rectangular boundary shown in **Figure 17-14** is as follows:

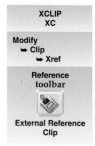

XCLIP
XC

Modify
➥ Clip
   ➥ Xref

Reference
toolbar

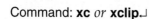

External Reference
Clip

Command: **xc** *or* **xclip**↵
Select objects: *(select any number of xref objects)*
Select objects: ↵
Enter clipping option
[ON/OFF/Clipdepth/Delete/generate Polyline/New boundary] <New>: ↵

**Figure 17-14.**
Creating an xref clipping boundary with the **XCLIP** command. A—The existing reference drawing of the main floor. B—The **Rectangular** boundary selection option is used to create a boundary around the kitchen area of the drawing. C—The kitchen area is displayed with the rest of the building clipped away.

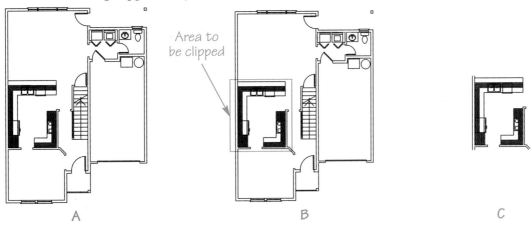

A           B           C

Specify clipping boundary:
[Select polyline/Polygonal/Rectangular] <Rectangular>: *(press* [Enter] *to create a rectangular boundary)*
Specify first corner: *(pick the first corner outside the area you wish to clip)*
Specify opposite corner: *(pick the opposite corner of the rectangular clip)*

The Select objects: prompt allows you to select any number of xrefs or copied xrefs to be clipped. Press [Enter] to accept the default **New boundary** option. This option allows you to select the clipping boundary. The other options of the **XCLIP** command include the following:

- **ON and OFF.** The clipping feature can be turned on or off as needed by using these options. Using the **OFF** option will turn off the clipped boundary edge, restoring the entire xref. The display of the clip can be restored by entering the **ON** option.
- **Clipdepth.** This option allows a front and back clipping plane to be defined. The front and back clipping planes define what portion of a 3D drawing is displayed. An introduction to 3D drawing is provided in Chapter 25.
- **Delete.** To remove a clipping boundary completely, use this option. The clipping boundary selected can be currently on or off. When deleted, it will no longer be part of the xref.
- **Generate Polyline.** This option allows you to draw a polyline object to represent the clipping border of the selected xref.

Note that the objects outside of the clipping boundary in **Figure 17-14** are no longer displayed once the command is completed. A clipped xref can be edited in the same way as an unclipped xref. Also, the clipping boundary moves with the xref. If the clipped xref contains nested xrefs, the nested xrefs outside the parent xref's clipping boundary are also clipped away.

In addition to the **Rectangular** clipping boundary option, two other options for defining a boundary are available. These options are described below:

- **Select polyline.** This option allows you to select an existing polyline object as a boundary definition. The border can only be composed of straight line segments, so any arc segments in the selected polyline are treated as straight line segments. However, a polyline that has been edited and turned into a splined or fit curve polyline can be used to create a curved border. If the polyline is not closed, the start and end points of the boundary are connected.

- **Polygonal.** This option allows you to pick points to create an irregular polygon to be drawn as a boundary. When finished selecting points for the polygonal shape, press [Enter] to close the start and end points of the clip.

When using the **XCLIP** command with the **Polygonal** or **Rectangular** clip options, the clipping boundary is invisible by default. The clipping boundary can be displayed by setting the **XCLIPFRAME** system variable to 1. The clipping frame is turned on and is placed on the layer clip the xref was inserted on. The clipping frame will plot if displayed. By default, the **XCLIPFRAME** system variable is set to 0 (off). The different types of clips with the clipping boundary turned on are shown in **Figure 17-15.**

Notice in **Figure 17-15** that a circular clipping boundary is used with the **Select polyline** clip option. A circular boundary can be created in the following manner. First, draw a polygon with multiple sides around the area you plan on clipping. Then, use the **PEDIT** command's **Spline** option to smooth the corners of the polygon. The resulting polygon should appear round. You can then use the **XCLIP** command with the **Select polyline** option to select the splined polygon as the clipping boundary.

**Figure 17-15.**
The three types of clipping boundaries. A—Using the **Rectangular** option. B—Using the **Polygonal** option. C—Using the **Select polyline** option with a splined polygon. (3D-DZYN)

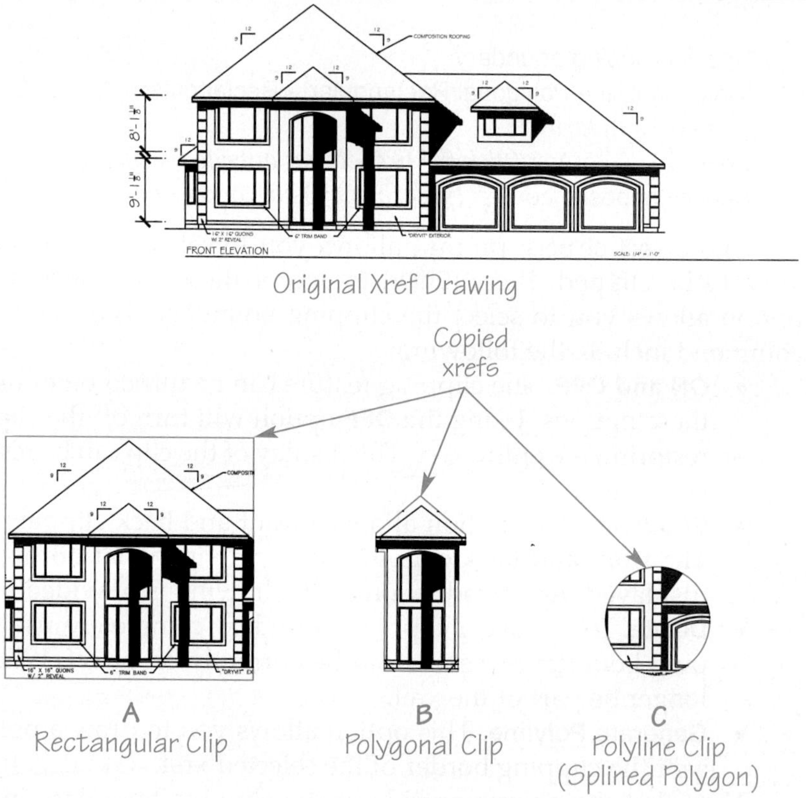

Original Xref Drawing

Copied xrefs

A
Rectangular Clip

B
Polygonal Clip

C
Polyline Clip
(Splined Polygon)

## Exercise 17-3

- Start a drawing using one of your templates.
- Create a layer named Xref-Floor plan. Set the layer current.
- Use the **XREF** command to reference the ex16-7 drawing you created in Chapter 16.
- Select **Attachment** in the **Reference Type** area.
- Insert at 0,0 with a uniform scale of 1 and a rotation angle of 0.
- Copy the xref three times in your drawing.
- Use the **XCLIP** command to create a rectangular and polygonal clip on the first two copies.
- Draw a polygon on the third copied xref. Use the **PEDIT** command to spline the polygon. Use the **Select polyline** option of the **XCLIP** command to create a clip from the splined polygon.
- Use the **XCLIPFRAME** system variable to turn on the clipping frames.
- Save the drawing as ex17-3.

# Editing Reference Drawings

There may be instances where you find that an xref attached to a host drawing requires editing. Xrefs may be edited using *in-place reference editing* with the **REFEDIT** command. Editing xrefs in place is similar to editing blocks in place. Blocks are discussed in Chapter 9. The **REFEDIT** command allows you to edit a reference drawing in the host drawing without having to open the original reference file. Any changes to the reference drawing can then be saved back to the original xref file without exiting the host drawing. You can also edit nested xrefs in this manner. This method of editing saves time when you notice something on the xref that is drawn incorrectly and you want to quickly revise it without having to find the reference file and open it for editing.

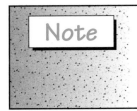 **Note**      Reference editing is best suited for minor revisions. Larger revisions should be done inside the original drawing. Making major changes with reference editing can decrease the performance of AutoCAD because additional disk space is used.

REFEDIT

➥ Modify
  ➥ Xref and Block
     Editing
    ➥ Edit
       Reference
       In-Place

Refedit
toolbar

Edit block or Xref

To use the **REFEDIT** command with an external reference, pick the **Edit block or Xref** button from the **Refedit** toolbar, pick **Edit Reference In-Place** from the **Xref and Block Editing** cascading menu in the **Modify** pull-down menu, or enter refedit at the Command prompt:

Command: **refedit**↵
Select reference: *(select the xref to edit)*

After you select an xref, the **Reference Edit** dialog box is displayed, **Figure 17-16.** This dialog box includes the **Identify Reference** tab and the **Settings** tab. In the **Identify Reference** tab, a preview image of the selected xref is shown in the **Preview** panel, and the name of the file is highlighted in the **Reference name:** list. Additionally, any blocks within the reference drawing are listed below the reference drawing name so that you can edit a specific xref-dependent block definition. Select the drawing name so you can edit parts of the drawing, or select a block reference so that you can edit the block definition.

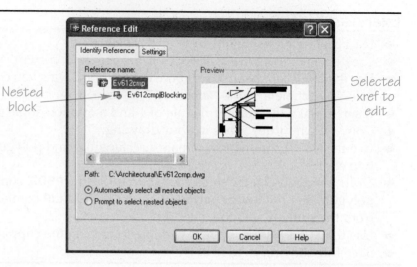

**Figure 17-16.**
The **Reference Edit** dialog box lists the name of the selected reference drawing and displays an image preview.

Nested block

Selected xref to edit

Below the **Reference name:** list box is a path to where the reference file was found and two radio buttons. The **Automatically select all nested objects** option is the default. When selected, any objects and blocks in the reference file are selected and placed in a work set where they can be edited. The **Prompt to select nested objects** option allows you to select only the items within the reference file that you want to edit.

The **Settings** tab includes three options for editing reference files. The check box labeled **Create unique layer, style, and block names** is active by default. This option renames xref-dependent objects that are *extracted,* or temporarily removed from the reference drawing, during editing. If this check box is selected, layer names and other dependent object names are given the prefix $n$, with *n* representing an incremented number. This is similar to the renaming method used when an xref is bound. If the check box is not checked, dependent objects are named as they appear in the original reference drawing. Once the editing sequence is finished, the objects are renamed again, using the original xref-dependent names created with the File name|Object name naming convention.

The **Display attribute definitions for editing** check box controls whether attributes in a selected block will be displayed so that you can edit them. This option is only available when a block object is selected in the **Identify Reference** tab of the **Reference Edit** dialog box. Attributes are discussed in Chapter 21. The **Lock objects not in working set** check box makes objects outside of the working set in the host drawing unavailable for selection while you are editing the objects that are in the work set.

Pick **OK** after selecting the reference to edit in the **Reference Edit** dialog box. If the **Automatically select all nested objects** option was selected, all objects within the reference file are available for editing. Any other geometry in the host drawing is grayed out and unavailable for editing. If the **Prompt to select nested objects** option was selected, the following prompt is displayed:

Select nested objects:

This prompt asks you to pick objects that belong to the previously selected xref or block. Pick any objects in the xref that are to be edited, and then press [Enter]. The nested objects that you select make up the *working set.* If multiple copies of the same xref are displayed, be sure to pick objects from the xref you originally selected when you entered the **REFEDIT** command.

After you are done selecting nested objects to be edited, the **Refedit** toolbar appears if it is not already displayed. The toolbar displays the name of the selected reference drawing that is being edited and is left on screen for the remainder of the reference editing session. You can use the toolbar to add objects in the host drawing to the working set, remove objects from the working set, and save or discard changes

Architectural Drafting Using AutoCAD

to the original xref file. The **REFSET** command can also be used to add objects to the working set or remove objects from the working set during reference editing.

If an object is added to the working set, it is extracted, or removed, from the xref or host drawing. Also, any object that is drawn during the reference edit is automatically added to the working set. After you have created the working set, any non-selected objects in the reference drawing are faded, or grayed out. The objects in the working set retain their normal property settings with no shading applied. You can then use any drawing or editing commands to alter the reference drawing objects. In the example shown in **Figure 17-17A,** the text objects have been selected from the Ev612cmp xref drawing so that they can be changed to a different color.

Once the necessary changes have been made, pick the **Save back changes to reference** button from the **Refedit** toolbar. If you wish to exit reference editing without saving changes, pick the **Discard changes to reference** button. You can also save or discard changes and end the editing session by using the **REFCLOSE** command. If you save changes, pick **OK** when AutoCAD informs you that all reference edits will be saved. All instances of the xref are then immediately updated. See **Figure 17-17B.**

---

**Figure 17-17.**
Editing an xref with the **REFEDIT** command. A—Objects that are not selected for the working set are grayed out. B—Once the reference edit is complete, the xref is updated and displayed with the changes. The text objects shown in color have been assigned a different display color.

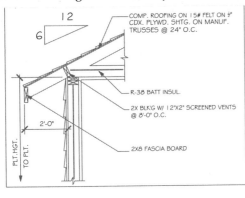
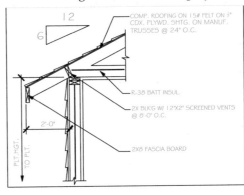

A                                        B

---

**Note**

All reference edits made using the **REFEDIT** command are saved back to the original reference drawing file and affect any other drawing that references the edited file. For this reason, it is critically important that external references be edited only with the permission of your instructor or supervisor.

# Configuring AutoCAD to Work with Xref Files

When working with external references, it is important to understand how AutoCAD finds and uses reference files. The following sections discuss the configuration options that should be considered when using xrefs.

---

As discussed earlier in this chapter, when you open a drawing that contains an xref, AutoCAD searches for the file path in order to load the xref file. If the file path was saved when the xref was attached to the drawing, AutoCAD looks to the saved path for the reference file. If the path is not found, AutoCAD looks in the Support File Search Path locations for the reference. The Support File Search Path locations are specified in the **Files** tab of the **Options** dialog box.

When you open a host drawing, you may find that an external reference file cannot be loaded because AutoCAD cannot locate the xref file. This can happen when the xref file has been moved to a different location and the saved path is no longer valid, or if the file was attached without a saved path location. To prevent this from occurring, you can store xref files in custom folders and add the folder locations to the Support File Search Path so that AutoCAD can find any files that need to be loaded. To add a path in this manner, access the **Options** dialog box and select the **Files** tab. Then pick the plus sign (+) next to the Support File Search Path listing to expand the list of search paths. These paths are created by AutoCAD and are required in order for AutoCAD to function.

Next, select the **Add...** button. This creates another level in the list. Type in the path name, or pick the **Browse...** button to locate the folder you are adding. When you are finished, press [Enter] or pick **OK**. AutoCAD's search for reference files will include the new path when a host drawing is opened.

**Professional Tip**

Avoid adding too many paths to the Support File Search Path listing. The more paths you add, the longer it will take for AutoCAD to access support files it needs in order to function. If you are using many different search paths for xrefs, you can add them to the Project Files Search Path folder. This is discussed next.

## Adding Search Paths to Project Folders

An efficient way to manage search paths for xref files is to assign the paths to *projects* associated with drawings. Drafters often work on projects that include a large number of drawings constructed from various sources. In AutoCAD, if you have several host drawings that are accessing xref files from different directories, you may find it useful to name a *project* that describes the drawings and stores the xref search paths. Each drawing can then be assigned to a project name so that when the drawing is opened, AutoCAD finds the search paths needed to load the xref files. Creating projects in this manner is useful when drawings are sent to other drafters or to locations that do not have access to the local directories you are using. Projects are defined as folders in the Project Files Search Path folder located in the **Files** tab of the **Options** dialog box.

If you are sharing drawing files with offices, contractors, or clients outside of the local computer directories in your office or classroom, do not save default search paths when attaching xrefs. If you select the **Full path** option in the **External Reference** dialog box when attaching an xref, and then send a drawing to an outside location, AutoCAD may not be able to find the reference file because the path locations are pointing to your local directories (not the directories of the recipient). Set up project folders and search paths so that AutoCAD will always look in the Project Files Search Path for the reference files.

When you create project names in the Project Files Search Path folder and assign search paths to them, AutoCAD will search these paths before searching in the Support File Search Path folder. This helps improve system performance, because AutoCAD does not have to sift through the files in the support directories.

You can create as many project folders as you need, but only one can be made active for AutoCAD to search at any given time. To create a project folder, first expand the Project Files Search Path folder in the **Options** dialog box and press the **Add...** button. By default, there are no project folders saved. Type in the name of the new project folder. Then, to add the search paths for the folder, press the **Add...** button and type in the first search path or use the **Browse...** button to select a directory. Each time you need to add another path, press the **Add...** button. When finished specifying the paths, select the project folder and press the **Set Current** button to set the project current. Now, if AutoCAD cannot find a reference file when a drawing is opened, it will look through the Project Files Search Path folder for the missing xref. In **Figure 17-18,** a project folder named Reference is shown with search paths added.

In many cases, drafters work on several different drawing projects at once throughout the lifetime of a project. For such applications, you may want to set up a project folder for each drawing project. Each folder can have its own set of search paths pointing to the xref files used in the project, and you can make each project name unique.

Only one project folder can be current at any time, so if you are working on a drawing in one project, set the appropriate folder current so that AutoCAD can search through it when locating xref files. Set a different folder current if you are working on a drawing in a different project. AutoCAD will only search through the current project folder for xref files. The files will not be found if the search paths are not listed in the currently active project folder.

If you have multiple project folders stored in the Project Files Search Path folder, you can ensure that xref files will be found regardless of the currently active project folder. This can be accomplished by using the **PROJECTNAME** system variable. This variable allows you to store the name of the project folder in each drawing belonging to the project. When a drawing containing xrefs is opened, AutoCAD will use the project name to search for xref files in all paths of the corresponding project folder regardless of the current folder. For example, if you set a project folder named Residence current but also want to work on commercial drawings, you can store a value for the **PROJECTNAME** system variable in each of the commercial drawings that points to a project folder named Commercial. When prompted for the value in each drawing, simply enter the name of the project folder (Commercial). This is a good way to complete the project search path definition for all drawings in a project.

**Figure 17-18.**
Creating a project folder and assigning search paths in the Project Files Search Path folder.

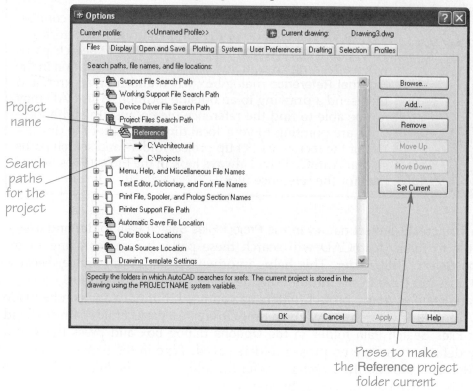

Project name

Search paths for the project

Press to make the **Reference** project folder current

## Understanding Demand Loading

When a drawing containing xrefs is opened, AutoCAD does not always load the entire contents of the xref files in order to display them on screen. This is because AutoCAD uses *demand loading* when loading an xref file into the host drawing. **Demand loading** controls how much of an xref is loaded when it is attached to the host drawing. When demand loading is enabled, the only portion of the xref file loaded is the part necessary to regenerate the host drawing. This improves performance and saves disk space, because the entire xref file is not loaded. For example, any objects in the reference file on frozen layers, as well as any data outside of clipping boundaries, is not loaded.

Demand loading is enabled by default. To check or change the setting, access the **Open and Save** tab of the **Options** dialog box. The three demand loading options are found in the **Demand load Xrefs:** drop-down list in the **External References (Xrefs)** area. The options are described as follows:

- **Enabled.** When this option is active, demand loading is turned on in the current drawing. If a drawing is being referenced into a host drawing, it becomes a read-only file and no other users can edit the reference file as long as the host drawing is open. Other users, however, can reference the file into another drawing.

- **Disabled.** When this option is active, demand loading is turned off in the current drawing. If a drawing is being referenced into the host drawing, it remains available so that another user can open and edit the reference file.

- **Enabled with copy.** When this option is active, demand loading is turned on in the host drawing, but the xref file can still be opened and edited by another user. This option is similar to the **Disabled** option. However, AutoCAD copies the xref file to a temporary directory and demand loads it, treating it as a completely separate file from the original xref file.

Two additional xref options are included in the **External References (Xrefs)** area of the **Open and Save** tab of the **Options** dialog box. These options are controlled by check boxes and have an AutoCAD drawing icon beside them. The icon represents that the option setting is saved in the active drawing. The two options are enabled by default and are described below:

- **Retain changes to Xref layers.** This option allows you to save changes to xref layer states in the active drawing. Any changes to layers in the host drawing take precedence over the layer settings from the xref file the next time the host drawing is opened. For example, if you decide to freeze several xref layers or assign different colors to them, the new layer states will be retained the next time the xref is loaded into the host drawing. This will not cause the layer changes to take effect in the original reference drawing.
- **Allow other users to Refedit current drawing.** This option controls whether other users can edit the currently open file with the **REFEDIT** command. If this option is enabled, the current drawing can be edited in place by others while it is open and when it is referenced by another file.

# Exchanging Drawings with Other Users

Many times in architectural projects, the construction documents are developed from several different sources. For example, the design, floor plans, and elevations are produced by the architect, the beams, columns, and structural elements are developed by a structural engineer, the site plan may be provided by a civil engineer, and the electrical plan is supplied by an electrical engineer. Each source requires some of the same drawings that the others are using or creating. When drawings have to be shared, they are commonly sent electronically using e-mail. The necessary files are attached to an e-mail message and transmitted on the Internet. Any files that are referenced by other drawings are included in the transmission.

As previously discussed, it is recommended that you do not save the path locations for xref files when they are attached to drawings and you are sending the drawings to an outside user. This is because each office will have a different computer directory structure. Search paths should be entered in the Project Files Search Path folder so they can be used by AutoCAD to find the files when loaded. This way, other users who receive all of the files in the project will be able to access any xref files provided they have the same listings in the Project Files Search Path folder.

When you e-mail drawings to an outside source, there may be instances where the recipient does not have all of the font files, plot style table files, and xref files after the transmission. When this occurs, the drawing features may be displayed differently on the recipient's computer, or critical components may be absent. To help prevent such problems, AutoCAD provides a tool that can be used to locate all files associated with a drawing file and copy them to a directory so that they can be quickly compiled and transmitted. This feature is called **eTransmit** and is discussed in the following section.

## Using the eTransmit Feature

The **eTransmit** feature simplifies the process of sending a drawing file by e-mail by creating a transmittal file. The transmittal file contains the DWG file and all font files, plot style table files, and xrefs associated with the drawing.

To use the **eTransmit** feature, select **eTransmit...** from the **File** pull-down menu, or type etransmit at the Command prompt. This accesses the **Create Transmittal** dialog box, **Figure 17-19.**

ETRANSMIT

File
➥ eTransmit...

**Figure 17-19.**
The **General** tab of the **Create Transmittal** dialog box provides options for transmittal features and format.

Add notes to be included in the transmittal report

Select type of transmittal

Path location of transmittal

**Create Transmittal**

Current Drawing: C:\Architectural\Sample\Foundation.dwg

General | Files | Report

Notes:

These notes will be included in the transmittal report.

Type:

Self-extracting executable (*.exe)

Password...

Location:

C:\Architectural\Sample\Foundation.exe

Browse...

☐ Convert drawings to:

AutoCAD 2000/LT 2000 Drawing Format

Transmittal options

☐ Preserve directory structure

☑ Remove paths from xrefs and images

☐ Send e-mail with transmittal

☐ Make web page files

OK | Cancel | Help

Use the **General** tab of the **Create Transmittal** dialog box to specify the settings for the transmittal file. The features and options in this tab are described as follows:

- **Notes: text box.** Text entered in this text box is included in the transmittal report, which is a text file included in the transmittal.
- **Type: drop-down list.** The transmittal can be created in one of three formats selected from this drop-down list. By default, the files can be compressed into a self-extracting executable (EXE) file. The recipient can then simply double-click on the file and the individual files are automatically extracted. Another option is to compress the files into a single zip (ZIP) file. With this option, the user must have a utility program designed to work with ZIP files. The third option is to create a folder containing all files to be transmitted.

**Professional Tip**

When transmitting files through e-mail, the smaller the size of the files being transferred, the quicker they are sent and received. Therefore, it is generally best to minimize the size of the files being transferred. If the recipient has a ZIP utility, sending a ZIP file is the best option because a ZIP file is smaller than a corresponding self-extracting zip file. The folder option results in the slowest transmittal.

- **Password... button.** Picking this button allows you to create a password for the transmittal when using a ZIP file or a self-extracting executable file. The recipient must then have the password in order to open the .zip or .exe file.

Architectural Drafting Using AutoCAD

- **Location: drop-down list.** The path listed in this drop-down list specifies the location where the transmittal is to be placed. You can pick the **Browse...** button to select a different path.
- **Convert drawings to: check box.** Check this check box if you want to convert the drawing files to an older version of AutoCAD. This option is useful when the recipient is using an older release of the software. Select the desired version from the drop-down list.
- **Preserve directory structure.** Using this option allows you to maintain the folder locations of the transmitted files. That is, every folder containing a file in the transmittal, plus every folder storing subfolders with transmitted files, is included in the transmittal.
- **Remove paths from xrefs and images.** Check this check box to remove the paths of the associated xref and image files. This allows the recipient to relocate the xrefs and image files. This option is active by default.
- **Send e-mail with transmittal.** Checking this check box automatically starts the default e-mail program when a transmittal is created and attaches the transmittal file to the e-mail.
- **Make web page files.** Select this option to produce a Web page with a link to the transmittal that can be posted on your Web site.

The **Files** tab of the **Create Transmittal** dialog box displays the files to be included in the transmittal. See **Figure 17-20.** These include font maps, shape files, plot style table files, and xrefs (additional DWG files referenced by the host drawing being transmitted).

The **Include fonts** check box determines whether font map files and shape files are included in the transmittal. If the drawings being transmitted use standard AutoCAD fonts, it is likely that the recipient already has these files, so there is no need to send them.

**Figure 17-20.**
The **Files** tab of the **Create Transmittal** dialog box shows the files to be transmitted.

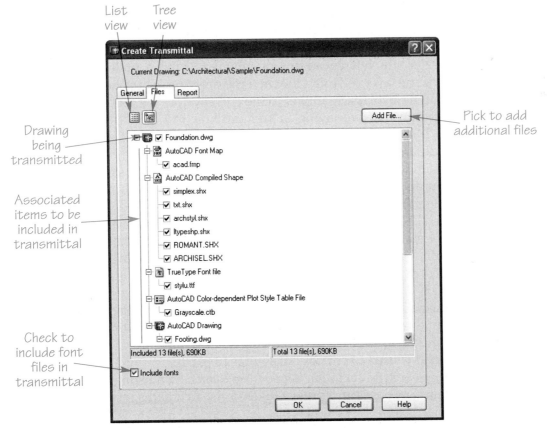

If you want to include any other files in the transmittal, you can pick the **Add File...** button to access the **Add file to transmittal** dialog box. Any files you select are added to the transmittal, and they are listed in the **Files** tab.

The **Report** tab of the **Create Transmittal** dialog box displays the text to be included in the transmittal report (the text file included in the transmittal). The report records the time and date when the transmittal is created, lists the files included in the transmittal, and provides some general notes regarding the file types included. The report is saved as a TXT file with the same name as that of the transmittal.

### Exercise 17-4

- Open ex17-3.
- Use the **eTransmit** feature to create a ZIP file containing the drawing and all related files.
- Create a second transmittal file using the self-extracting executable file format.
- Create a third transmittal using the **Folder (set of files)** option.
- Using Windows Explorer, compare the file size of the ZIP file, the self-extracting executable file, and the transmittal folder.

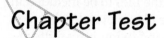

# Chapter Test

*Answer the following questions on a separate sheet of paper.*

1. What command is used to bring an external reference into a drawing?
2. A drawing that contains one or more xrefs is called the _____ drawing.
3. Name two advantages of using xrefs as opposed to inserting entire drawing files when referencing drawings.
4. Name two methods used to open the **Xref Manager** dialog box.
5. Briefly explain how to attach an external reference to the current drawing.
6. What is the function of the **Full path** option in the **External Reference** dialog box?
7. What is the function of the **Relative path** option in the **External Reference** dialog box?
8. Assume an externally referenced drawing named Flr-001 contains a layer named A-wall. What is the layer renamed to when the drawing is attached?
9. Briefly explain how to attach an xref to the current drawing using **DesignCenter**.
10. What is the purpose of overlaying an xref and how is it different from attaching an xref?
11. Explain the difference between detaching and unloading an xref.
12. How can you quickly reload an xref file in the current drawing?
13. How can you display nesting levels for xrefs in the current drawing in the **Xref Manager** dialog box?
14. If a referenced drawing has been moved and the new path location is not stored on the library path, how can you update the path to refer to the new location?
15. Briefly explain what occurs when you bind an xref to a drawing.
16. Give two reasons why binding a drawing is usually not an ideal option when using xrefs.
17. Which command is used to bind individual xref-dependent objects to a drawing?
18. Briefly explain how to bind an xref-dependent layer to a drawing.
19. What is the purpose of the **XCLIP** command?
20. What command is used to edit xref drawings in place?
21. Where are the search paths in the Support File Search Path listing accessed?
22. Briefly explain how to set up a project folder for search paths related to the drawings in a project.

23. Name the system variable that is used to store the name of a project folder in a drawing related to the project.
24. Define *demand loading*.
25. What is the function of the **Retain changes to Xref layers** option in the **Open and Save** tab of the **Options** dialog box?

# Chapter Problems

Project

Residential A

1. Open 14-ResA.
    A. Create a layer named Xref-Floor and set it current.
    B. Xref in 16-ResA.
    C. Change all the layers in the xref to one color.
    D. Freeze the xref dimension layer.
    E. Use the **ROTATE** and **MOVE** commands to place the xref directly over the building outline in the site plan.
    F. Verify that the building outline on the site plan matches the xref's exterior walls. If the outline does not match, adjust the building outline accordingly.
    G. Save the drawing as 17-ResA.

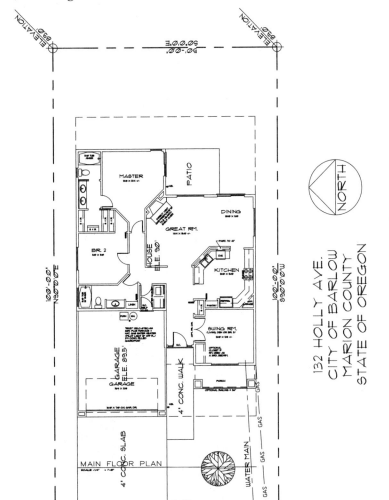

(Alan Mascord Design Associates, Inc.)

2. Open 14-ResB.
   A. Create a layer named Xref-Floor and set it current.
   B. Xref in 16-ResB.
   C. Change all the layers in the xref to one color.
   D. Freeze the xref upper floor layers and the main floor dimension layer.
   E. Use the **ROTATE** and **MOVE** commands to place the xref directly over the building outline in the site plan.
   F. Verify that the building outline on the site plan matches the xref's exterior walls. If the outline does not match, adjust the building outline accordingly.
   G. Save the drawing as 17-ResB.

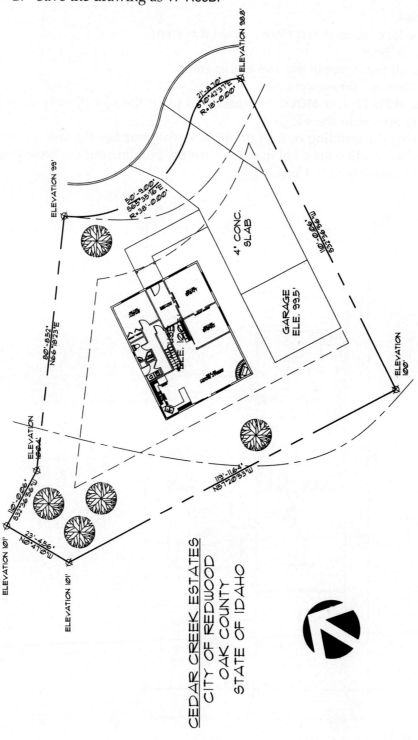

(3D-DZYN)

3. Open 14-Multifamily.
   A. Create a layer named Xref-Floor and set it current.
   B. Xref in 16-Multifamily.
   C. Change all the layers in the xref to one color.
   D. Freeze the main floor xref dimension layer.
   E. Use the **ROTATE** and **MOVE** commands to place the xref directly over the building outline in the site plan.
   F. Verify that the building outline on the site plan matches the xref's exterior walls. If the outline does not match, adjust the building outline accordingly.
   G. Save the drawing as 17-Multifamily.

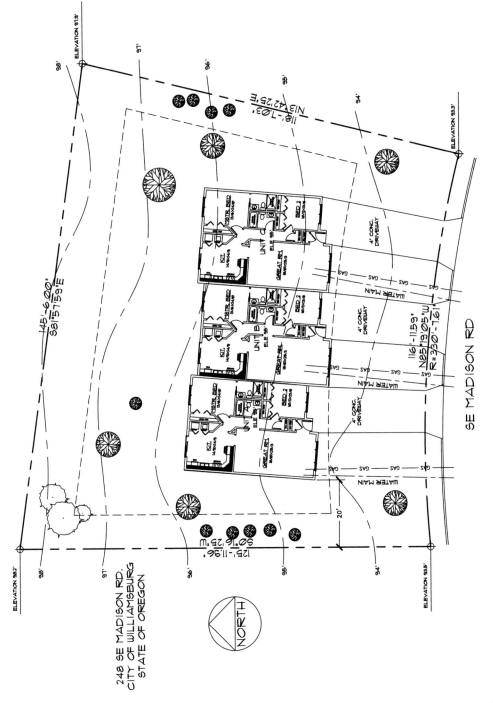

(3D-DZYN)

4. Open 14-Commercial.
   A. Create a layer named Xref-Main and set it current.
   B. Xref in 16-Commercial-Main.
   C. Change all the layers in the xref to one color.
   D. Freeze the main floor xref dimension layer.
   E. Use the **ROTATE** and **MOVE** commands to place the xref directly over the building outline in the site plan.
   F. Save the drawing as 17-Commercial.

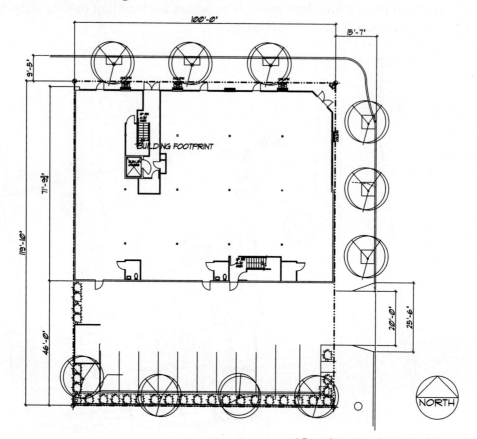

(Cynthia Bankey Architect, Inc.)

# CHAPTER 18

# Drawing Foundation Plans

## Learning Objectives

After completing this chapter, you will be able to:

- ◆ Describe a foundation plan.
- ◆ Identify and draw a floor joist foundation system.
- ◆ Describe and draw a post and beam foundation system.
- ◆ Explain and draw a concrete slab foundation system.
- ◆ Show exterior concrete construction on a foundation plan.
- ◆ Discuss brick veneer construction.
- ◆ Describe and show masonry block construction.

## Important Terms

beams
blocking
brick veneer construction
columns
concrete masonry unit (CMU)
concrete slab foundation system
decking
dry rot
floor joist foundation system
foundation plan
foundation vents
foundation wall

load bearing walls
mud sill
one-pour method
post and beam foundation system
rim joist
rows
span
span table
stem wall
subfloor
two-pour method
unit cell

Just as the floor plan is a two-dimensional representation of the floor layout, the *foundation plan* is a two-dimensional representation of the foundation system of a building. Foundation plans are viewed from above without the interference of the floor plan. The floor plan has essentially been lifted off the building and what remains is the foundation plan. This allows you to see where footings, structural components, and vents are located, as shown in **Figure 18-1**.

**Figure 18-1.**
A foundation plan is a two-dimensional representation of a three-dimensional building. (3D-DZYN)

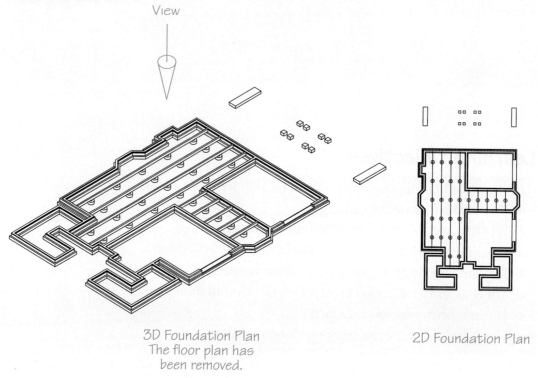

3D Foundation Plan
The floor plan has been removed.

2D Foundation Plan

# Foundation Systems

There are essentially three types of foundation systems. These are floor joist, post and beam, and concrete slab systems. Which type of system is used depends on the use of the building, code requirements, economical and structural considerations, and the geographic location. **Figure 18-2** shows the three types of systems.

## Floor Joist Foundation System

The *floor joist foundation system* is constructed of a concrete *stem wall* that sits on concrete footings. The stem wall is also commonly called a *foundation wall*. See **Figure 18-3**. The footing and stem wall vary in width depending on the number of floors in the building. Typically, for a single story building, the footing size is 12″ wide by 6″ high. The stem wall for a single story building is typically 6″ wide and can vary in height. **Figure 18-4** gives common footing and stem wall sizes.

The height of the stem wall varies depending on the floor system used, local codes, and the natural or excavated grade of the land. When drawing a foundation plan, the stem wall is drawn with a continuous linetype. The exterior stem wall should line up with the exterior wall of the floor plan. The inner stem wall line is offset the width of the stem wall.

**Figure 18-2.**

The three basic types of foundation systems.

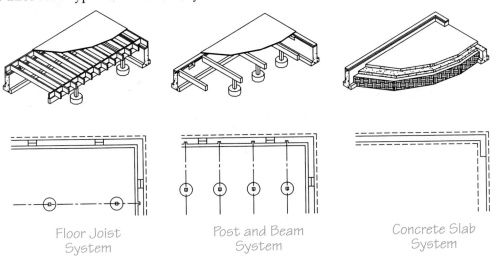

Floor Joist
System

Post and Beam
System

Concrete Slab
System

**Figure 18-3.**

The floor joist foundation system.

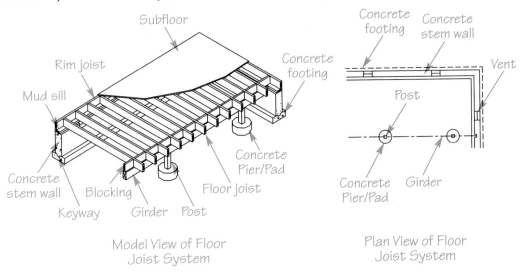

Model View of Floor
Joist System

Plan View of Floor
Joist System

**Figure 18-4.**

Common footing sizes.

| Footing and Stem Wall Size | | | |
|---|---|---|---|
| **Building Height** | **Footing Width** | **Footing Height** | **Stem Wall Width** |
| One Story | 12" | 6" | 6" |
| Two Story | 16" | 8" | 8" |
| Three Story | 18" | 10" | 10" |

The footing is normally drawn centered on the stem wall. The outer line of the footing is drawn with a hidden or dashed linetype indicating the footing is below the finish grade of the site. The inner footing line is drawn with a continuous linetype, because the inside of the footing is normally seen above grade when looking at the foundation plan. Some drafters prefer to show the inside footing line as a hidden or dashed linetype. If the footing is under a concrete slab, such as in a garage, the inside footing line is dashed. See **Figure 18-5.**

**Figure 18-5.**
The house drawing with the stem wall and footing laid out.

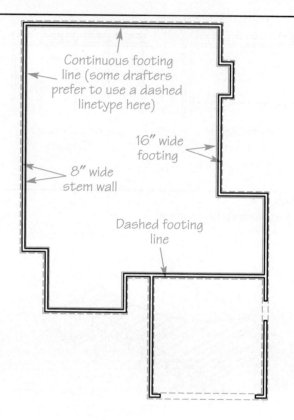

Continuous footing line (some drafters prefer to use a dashed linetype here)

16" wide footing

8" wide stem wall

Dashed footing line

## Drawing the Foundation Walls and Footings

To draw the foundation, start a new drawing. Create layers for the stem wall, the footings, and the xref layer for the main floor. Reference the main floor into the new drawing, inserting it to the 0,0 absolute coordinate. This ensures that if the plans are referenced together the floor plan and the foundation plan will line up. Trace over the exterior wall for the exterior stem wall location using the foundation wall layer. Freeze the xref layer or unload the xref when finished referencing the exterior walls.

If the foundation plan is to be incorporated into the same drawing file as the floor plan, freeze the floor plan layers except the main floor walls. Use the main floor walls as a reference and trace the exterior wall line onto the stem wall layer. This line becomes the exterior of the foundation. Freeze the main floor walls layer.

Next, use the **OFFSET** command to offset the exterior stem wall line to the inside of the building the width of the stem wall. Then, use the **OFFSET** command to offset the stem walls the width to the edge of the footing. Use the **Properties** window to change the footing lines to the footing layer.

On top of and bolted to the stem wall is a mud sill. The *mud sill* is usually a pressure treated piece of wood 2" thick on top of which the floor joists sit. The bolts used to anchor the mud sill are usually 1/2" diameter bolts. These anchor bolts tie the wood flooring system to the foundation.

In a floor joist system, a *rim joist* is placed along the exterior of the building. The floor joists are placed along the inside of the foundation. These construction members rest on the mud sill. The floor joist size is determined by the total span required between the ends of the joist. The sizes can range from a 2 × 6 joist to a 2 × 14 joist. Plywood sheeting, called a *subfloor,* is nailed on top of the floor and rim joists.

When drawing the foundation plan, the mud sill, rim joist, floor joists, and subfloor are not drawn. However, the joist size and a direction arrow indicating how they are placed is noted on the plan. Some local codes require the location of the anchor bolts to be shown on the foundation plan. The spacing between the anchor bolts is determined by code and engineering requirements. They are usually placed 12" from a corner and spaced no more than 8'-0" apart.

## Exercise 18-1

◆ Start a new drawing using one of your templates.
◆ Create three layers:
  ◆ F-Walls
  ◆ F-Footing          (Hidden linetype)
  ◆ F-Floor Plan
◆ Xref ex16-8 created in Chapter 16 using the overlay option.
◆ Freeze all the layers except the F-* layers and the M-Walls layer.
◆ Trace the exterior of the main floor using lines or polylines.
◆ Freeze the M-Walls layer.
◆ Offset the stem wall lines 6" to the inside of the building. The garage lines should also be offset to the inside of the house and not the inside of the garage.
◆ Offset the exterior stem wall 3" to the outside of the building and the interior stem wall 3" to the inside. These lines will represent the footing lines.
◆ Change the properties of the footing lines to place them on the F-Footing layer. Change the properties of the interior footing lines to a continuous linetype.
◆ Your drawing should look like **Figure 18-5.**
◆ Save the drawing as ex18-1.

## Drawing Anchor Bolts with Donuts and Solid Circles

Anchor bolts can be drawn as donuts in AutoCAD. Donuts are actually polyline arcs with width. The **DONUT** command allows you to draw a thick circle. It can have any inside and outside diameter, or it can be completely filled. See **Figure 18-6.** The **DONUT** command can be accessed by selecting **Donut** from the **Draw** pull-down menu or by entering do, donut, or doughnut at the Command prompt as follows:

DONUT
DO
DOUGHNUT

Draw
→ Donut

Command: **do, donut,** *or* **doughnut.**⏎
Specify inside diameter of donut <*current*>: *(enter an inside diameter; a 0 inside diameter produces a solid circle)*
Specify outside diameter of donut <*current*>: *(enter an outside diameter)*
Specify center of donut or <exit>: *(select the donut center point location)*
Specify center of donut or <exit>: *(select the center point for another donut, or press* [Enter] *to discontinue the command)*

After selecting the center point, the donut appears on the screen. Pick another center point to draw the same size donut in a new location. The **DONUT** command remains active until you press [Enter] or [Esc].

When **FILL** mode is turned off, donuts appear as segmented circles or concentric circles. **FILL** can be used transparently by entering 'fill while inside the **DONUT** command. Then, enter on or off as needed. The fill in existing donuts remains until the drawing is regenerated.

Figure 18-6.
Examples of donuts.

**Fill** on     **Fill** on
Interior
Radius = 0

**Fill** off     **Fill** off
Interior
Radius = 0

The anchor bolts are typically 1/2″ diameter. In a full-scale drawing, a 1/2″ diameter circle is very small. Therefore, anchor bolts are drawn at a larger size. Try using an anchor bolt with an outside diameter of 1″ to 2″. This will make the anchor bolts easier to spot on the foundation plan. Increase or decrease the diameter as needed.

## Drawing the Interior Support Girders

If the span for floor joists is so great that very large joists are required, girders are placed in the foundation to help support the joists, as shown in **Figure 18-7A.** When this happens, the joists can be downsized because the span of the joists has been shortened. The floor joists sit on top of the girder and can extend past the girder to create a cantilever. See **Figure 18-7B.** In a situation where there is not a cantilever, the end of a floor joist can stop on top of a girder. A new joist can start beside the first joist and extend to the next girder or mud sill. See **Figure 18-8.**

The girder is usually a 4 × 8, but it can be smaller or larger. The girder size can vary due to structural requirements. The girder sits on top of a post. The post is usually a 4 × 4. When girders must be spliced, a 4 × 6 post is used to support the ends of the girders. Posts rest on top of a concrete pier or concrete pad. The concrete pier or pad varies in size due to structural requirements. The pier is commonly round, generally 18″ diameter by 8″ high. The pad can be designed to hold more weight and varies in size and shape, depending on the structural requirements.

Girders are not always placed to support floor joists. Girders are also placed under walls that bear weight from above. These walls are known as *load bearing walls*, or bearing walls. Bearing walls are often placed roughly near the center of a building or along a staircase. However, they can be placed anywhere weight from above needs to be supported, such as under an upstairs bathroom. If a girder is placed in the foundation to support a bearing wall, a piece of wood is placed between the joists and sits on top of the girder, **Figure 18-9.** This piece of wood is known as *blocking.* Blocking is 2″ wide and the same height as the floor joist.

Figure 18-7.
A—A girder
supporting the
midspan of floor
joists.
B—Cantilevered
floor joists resting
on a girder for
support.

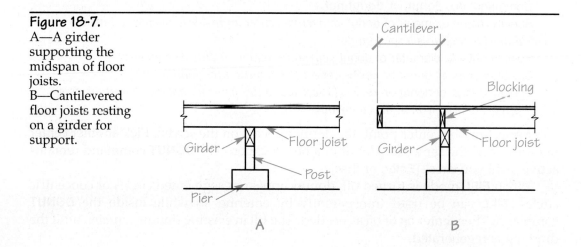

A       B

**Figure 18-8.**
Floor joists can end
on a girder.

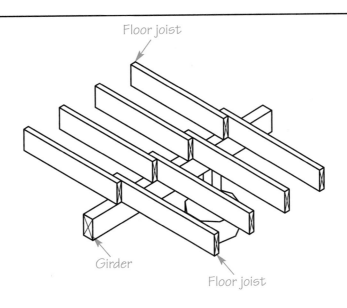

Floor joist

Girder

Floor joist

**Figure 18-9.**
A girder supporting
a bearing wall
above. Notice the
blocking added.

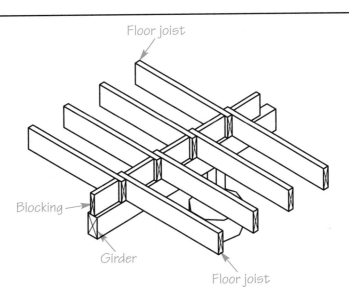

Floor joist

Blocking

Girder

Floor joist

   Although the foundation plan does not usually show each joist, the girders, posts, piers, and pads are shown on the plan. Girders are generally drawn with a heavy centerline representing the center of the girder. Piers and pads are drawn full scale along the girder, usually spaced no more than 8'-0" apart. The spacing depends on the structural engineering. Posts are drawn full scale (4" × 4"), centered on the piers or pads.

   Posts can be drawn with the **POLYGON** command. Center a four-sided polygon on the 18" diameter pier. Using the **Circumscribe** option of the **POLYGON** command, the post is measured from the center of the pier to a flat side of the post. To create a 4" × 4" post, the radius for the polygon is 2".

   An engineer will determine the exact location for girders. To figure out where girders are placed, the main floor walls are usually referenced. This provides a good idea where the bearing walls need to be placed. When drawing the girders, center the girder line on the bearing wall or walls. Start the piers and pads 8'-0" from the end of the girder. If the girder extends to the foundation wall, it is seated in a 3" deep "pocket" in the wall. The pocket in a stem wall is drawn on the stem wall layer, 2" to each side of the girder line, and 3" into the foundation. **Figure 18-10** shows a foundation with girders, posts, and piers added. The specifications provided here are for general applications and can vary depending on the structural engineering for the building.

**Figure 18-10.**
The house founda-
tion with the inte-
rior structural
components added.

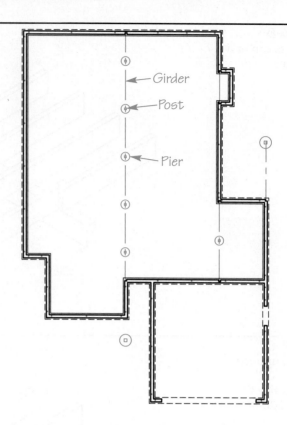

## Exercise 18-2

## Adding Vents to the Foundation

When building a foundation, adequate ventilation is required in order to keep moisture from collecting. If moisture collects, a condition called *dry rot* can destroy any wood structural components. *Foundation vents* are openings cut into the foundation stem wall with wire mesh placed over the opening. The number of vents required and their locations need to appear on the foundation plan.

Vents are typically 1'-6" wide × 8" high. This creates a 1 ft² opening. Vents are normally closeable so they can be blocked during the winter. See **Figure 18-11.** Vents are normally placed near corners to provide cross ventilation. The number of vents and sizes can vary depending on local building codes. In many areas, 1 ft² of ventilation area is required for every 150 square feet of foundation. In order to determine the minimum number of required vents in a foundation, the total square footage of the foundation is needed.

The square footage of the foundation is the total area beneath the floor joists. This area does not include areas with concrete slabs, such as a garage. Once the foundation is drawn, the square footage can be determined using the **AREA** command, discussed in Chapter 12. Measure the total area under the floor joists. Include the stem wall in the calculation because the joists sit on top of the stem wall. When using the **AREA** command, either pick the points around the floor joist locations for the area, or draw a polyline around the area and use the **Object** option of the **AREA** command to determine the area of the polyline.

In **Figure 18-12,** the total area for the house is 1620 ft². To determine the minimum number of vents required for the house, divide the square footage by 150 ft² (one vent for every 150 ft²):

1620 sq. ft. ÷ 150 sq. ft. = 10.8 vents

**Figure 18-11.**
Foundation vents in a foundation wall. Typically, a 1 ft² vent is placed for every 150 ft² of building, unless otherwise specified by the architect or local codes.

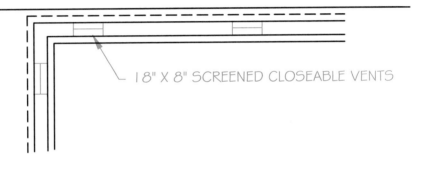

**Figure 18-12.**
The foundation vents added to the foundation.

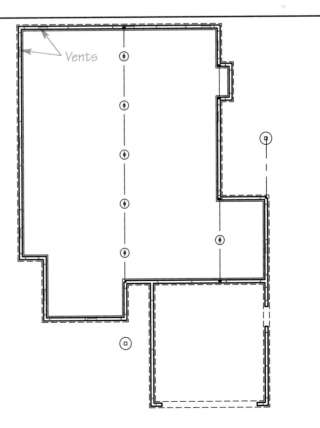

Round up to the nearest whole number to get the minimum number of foundation vents for each unit. In this case, 11 foundation vents are needed.

Draw the 11 vents in the foundation stem wall. Keep the vents in the exterior portion of the stem wall and not in the garage or shared wall. Place the vents 2'-8" from any corners and away from door openings. If there are any vents left over, space them evenly throughout the foundation, keeping in mind the criteria above. See **Figure 18-12.**

## Dimensioning Floor Joist Sizes and Span Directions

The size of the floor joists is determined by referring to a span table. *Span* is the distance apart of any two supports, or the end-to-end length of the joist. A *span table* is a table of information providing the minimum size floor joist that can be used to span a given distance. **Figure 18-13** shows a simple chart for floor joists spaced 16" on centers (OC). Consult local building codes for actual span charts.

The joist size can be determined by looking at the maximum span distance in the foundation. This is measured from the stem wall to the girder, or to the other side of the building if no girders are used. Looking at the foundation plan in **Figure 18-12,** the maximum span is measured from the left edge of the wall to the girder near the center of the foundation. Using the **DIST** command, this span is 17'-8". Consulting the chart in **Figure 18-13,** the floor can be 2 × 10 or 2 × 12 joists. Generally, select the smallest joist that can be used to span the distance for cost purposes. Therefore, select 2 × 10 joists.

## Adding Structural Notes, General Notes, and Dimensions

Now that the joists have been selected for 16" on centers, a note needs to be added to the drawing indicating the size and the direction that the joists are placed. Place the joist notes between each set of spans to indicate the placement of the floor joists.

Typically, a framing note is a line with two arrowheads at each end indicating the direction of the joist. To do this, a standard dimension can be used, with the text changed to reflect the note and extension lines removed. See **Figure 18-14.** Use the **Properties** window to remove the extension lines, change the dimension text and position, and change the type and size of arrowheads.

When the joist notes have been placed, the finishing structural notes can be added with the **MTEXT**, **TEXT**, and **LEADER** commands. Notes are added for the size of the girders, posts, and piers. General foundation notes are also added to the drawing. **Figure 18-15** shows an example of general foundation notes. Make sure the text is the correct plotted height using the scale factor of the drawing. Consult Appendix K for text height sizes used with different scales.

**Figure 18-13.**
A simple span table for floor joists spaced 16" on center. Consult local building codes for actual sizes.

| Allowed Spans for Floor Joists Spaced 16" on Centers | | |
|---|---|---|
| **Floor Joist Size** | **Minimum Span Distance** | **Maximum Span Distance** |
| 2 × 6 | 7'-9" | 10'-10" |
| 2 × 8 | 10'-2" | 14'-3" |
| 2 × 10 | 13'-0" | 18'-3" |
| 2 × 12 | 15'-10" | 22'-2" |

Architectural Drafting Using AutoCAD

**Figure 18-14.**
Changing a dimension line into a structural note.

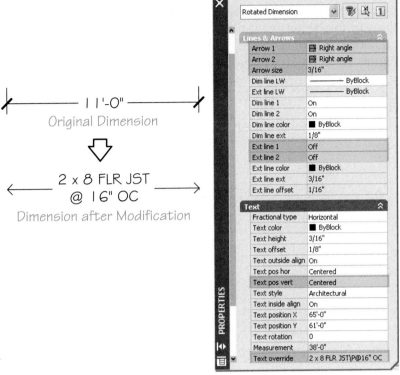

11'-0"
Original Dimension

2 x 8 FLR JST
@ 16" OC
Dimension after Modification

Modified Properties
Highlighted

---

**Figure 18-15.**
General foundation notes. (Alan Mascord Design Associates, Inc.)

## FOUNDATION NOTES

1. FOOTINGS TO BEAR ON UNDISTURBED LEVEL SOIL DEVOID OF ANY ORGANIC MATERIAL AND STEPPED AS REQUIRED TO MAINTAIN THE REQUIRED DEPTH BELOW FINAL GRADE.

2. SOIL BEARING PRESSURE ASSUMED TO BE 1500 PSI.

3. ANY FILL UNDER GRADE SUPPORTED SLABS TO BE A MINIMUM OF 4 INCHES GRANULAR MATERIAL COMPACTED TO 95%.

4. CONCRETE: BASEMENT WALLS & FOUNDATION WALLS NOT EXPOSED TO WEATHER: 2500 PSI
BASEMENT & INTERIOR SLABS ON GRADE: 2500 PSI
BASEMENT WALLS & FOUNDATIONS EXPOSED TO THE WEATHER: 3000 PSI
PORCHES, STEPS, & CARPORT SLABS EXPOSED TO THE WEATHER: 3500 PSI
(UBC APPENDIX CHAP 19 TABLE A-19-A)

5. CONCRETE SLABS TO HAVE CONTROL JOINTS AT 25 FT. (MAXIMUM) INTERVALS EACH WAY.

6. CONCRETE SIDEWALKS TO HAVE 1" TOOLED JOINTS@5'-0" (MINIMUM) O.C.

7. REINFORCED STEEL TO BE A-615 GRADE 60. OPTIONAL WELDED WIRE MESH TO BE A-185.

8. EXCAVATE SITE TO PROVIDE MINIMUM OF 18 INCHES CLEARANCE UNDER ALL WOOD GIRDERS AT FOUNDATION.

9. COVER ENTIRE CRAWLSPACE WITH 6 MIL BLACK "VISQUEEN" AND EXTEND UP FOUNDATION WALLS TO P.T. MUDSILL.

10. PROVIDE A MINIMUM OF 1 SQ. FT. OF VENTILATION AREA FOR EACH 150 SQ. FT. OF CRAWLSPACE AREA. VENTS TO BE CLOSABLE WITH ⅛ INCH CORROSION RESISTANT MESH SCREEN. POST NOTICE RE: OPENING VENTS @ELECTRIC PANEL.

11. ALL WOOD IN DIRECT CONTACT WITH CONCRETE OR GROUND TO BE P.T. (PRESSURE TREATED) OR PROTECTED WITH 55# ROLLED ROOFING MATERIAL.

12. BEAM POCKETS IN CONCRETE TO HAVE ½" MINIMUM AIRSPACE AT SIDES AND ENDS WITH A MINIMUM BEARING OF 3 INCHES.

13. WATERPROOF BASEMENT WALLS BEFORE BACKFILLING, PROVIDE A 4 IN. DIA. PERFORATED DRAIN TILE BELOW THE TOP OF THE FOOTINGS AS REQ.

Dimensions are the final information required on a foundation plan. Dimensions are measured to the outside of stem walls and the centers of girders. Also, add dimensions to the centers of the piers and pads. Footings are dimensioned with notes that call out the size. Drawing details are added to the construction documents later. **Figure 18-16** illustrates the finished foundation plan.

**Figure 18-16.**
The finished foundation plan.

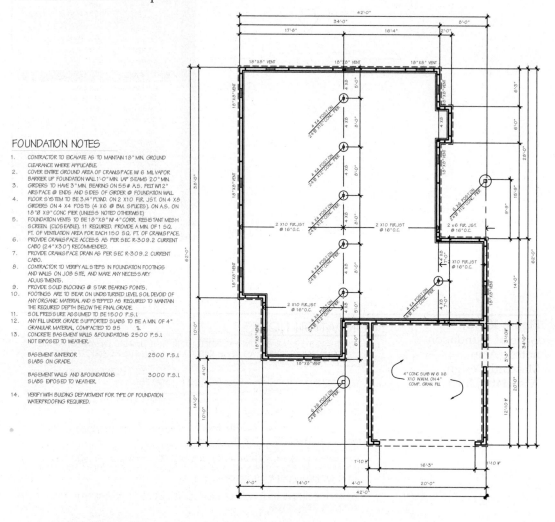

FOUNDATION NOTES

1. CONTRACTOR TO EXCAVATE AS TO MAINTAIN 18" MIN. GROUND CLEARANCE WHERE APPLICABLE.
2. COVER ENTIRE GROUND AREA OF CRAWLSPACE W/ 6 MIL VAPOR BARRIER UP FOUNDATION WALL 1'-0" MIN. LAP SEAMS 20" MIN.
3. GIRDERS TO HAVE 3" MIN. BEARING ON 55# A.S. FELT W/ 2" AIRSPACE @ ENDS AND SIDES OF GIRDER @ FOUNDATION WALL.
4. FLOOR SYSTEM TO BE 3/4" PLYWD. ON 2 X10 FLR. JST. ON 4 X8 GIRDERS ON 4 X4 POSTS (4 X6 @ BM. SPLICES). ON A.S. ON 18"Ø X9" CONC. PIER (UNLESS NOTED OTHERWISE).
5. FOUNDATION VENTS TO BE 18"X8" W/ 4" CORR. RESISTANT MESH SCREEN. (CLOSEABLE). 11 REQUIRED. PROVIDE A MIN. OF 1 SQ. FT. OF VENTILATION AREA FOR EACH 150 SQ. FT. OF CRAWLSPACE.
6. PROVIDE CRAWLSPACE ACCESS AS PER SEC R-309.2 CURRENT CABO. (24"X30") RECOMMENDED.
7. PROVIDE CRAWLSPACE DRAIN AS PER SEC R-309.2 CURRENT CABO.
8. CONTRACTOR TO VERIFY ALL STEPS IN FOUNDATION FOOTINGS AND WALLS ON JOB SITE, AND MAKE ANY NECESSARY ADJUSTMENTS.
9. PROVIDE SOLID BLOCKING @ STAIR BEARING POINTS.
10. FOOTINGS ARE TO BEAR ON UNDISTURBED LEVEL SOIL DEVOID OF ANY ORGANIC MATERIAL AND STEPPED AS REQUIRED TO MAINTAIN THE REQUIRED DEPTH BELOW THE FINAL GRADE.
11. SOIL PRESSURE ASSUMED TO BE 1500 P.S.I.
12. ANY FILL UNDER GRADE SUPPORTED SLABS TO BE A MIN. OF 4" GRANULAR MATERIAL, COMPACTED TO 95%.
13. CONCRETE BASEMENT WALLS & FOUNDATIONS 2500 P.S.I. NOT EXPOSED TO WEATHER.

    BASEMENT & INTERIOR        2500 P.S.I.
    SLABS ON GRADE.

    BASEMENT WALLS AND & FOUNDATIONS   3000 P.S.I.
    SLABS EXPOSED TO WEATHER.

14. VERIFY WITH BUILDING DEPARTMENT FOR TYPE OF FOUNDATION WATERPROOFING REQUIRED.

**Professional Tip**

General notes can be created in a separate drawing file, and then referenced into the drawing sheets as required. This can help ensure the note is the most recent version.

◆ Open ex18-2.
◆ Create the following layers:
  ◆ F-Vents
  ◆ F-Notes-FJ
  ◆ F-Dims
  ◆ F-Dims-FJ
◆ Add foundation vents as in **Figure 18-12.** Create the vents on the F-Vents layer.
◆ Create a dimension and modify with the **Properties** window to create a floor joist note.
◆ Add structural notes to the posts, piers, and girders.
◆ Add dimensions to the foundation plan, placing them on the F-Dims layer.
◆ Add dimensions for the girder and post locations, placing them on the F-Dims-FJ layer.
◆ Your drawing should look like **Figure 18-16.**
◆ Save the drawing as ex18-3.

## Post and Beam Foundation System

The *post and beam foundation system* is a flooring system using girders, posts, and piers, similar to the floor joist system. These girders are referred to as *beams.* Instead of having floor joists on top of the beams, a 2″ thick tongue and groove (T&G) subfloor is nailed directly over the top of the girders and mud sill. The T&G subfloor is made up of 2 × 6 or 2 × 8 boards with a "tongue" on one edge and a "groove" on the other. The boards are interlocked on top of the beams to form the subfloor. The T&G subfloor is also commonly called *decking.* See **Figure 18-17.**

The post and beam foundation system is built by using more girders (beams), posts, and piers on the interior of the foundation to create a solid flooring system. The beams for a post and beam foundation are generally spaced 4′-0″ apart and the posts and piers are commonly placed 8′-0″ on center along the beam. With the exception of the interior support beams and structural framing, both floor joist and post and beam foundation plans are drawn the same way.

### Drawing Post and Beam Girders

The girders in a post and beam system are drawn the same as girders for a floor joist system. As in the floor joist foundation, the girders extend into the stem wall 3″ and fit into beam pockets. A heavy centerline is typically used to represent the girder locations. If the girders are placed 4′-0″ apart, the **OFFSET** command can be used to offset the girders this distance. Start with one side of the foundation and offset the exterior stem wall 4′-0″ into the foundation. Then, use the **Properties** window to change the offset line to the girder layer with its linetype as a thick centerline. **Figure 18-18** displays the girders of a post and beam foundation for the house drawing.

**Figure 18-17.**
The post and beam foundation system.

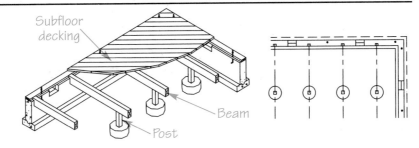

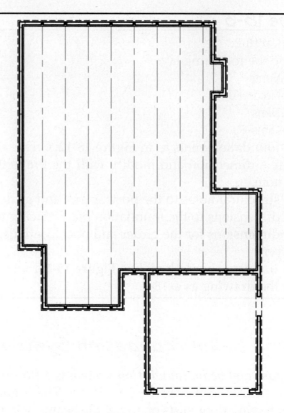

**Figure 18-18.**
The girders are laid out as centerlines for a post and beam foundation.

## Adding Posts and Piers to a Post and Beam Foundation

The posts and piers support the girders. They are spaced 8'-0" along each girder, unless otherwise specified by the architect or structural engineer. The **COPY** command can be used to individually copy each post and pier along each girder. However, the **ARRAY** command can be used to create all posts and piers in a single operation after the first set is drawn.

Before using the **ARRAY** command, the first set of objects you want copied needs to be drawn. The piers in a post and beam foundation are generally 18" diameter by 8" thick with a 4 × 4 post centered on the pier. The first pier and post set is drawn in the correct location on the first girder 8'-0" into the foundation, as measured from the outside of the stem wall. See **Figure 18-19.**

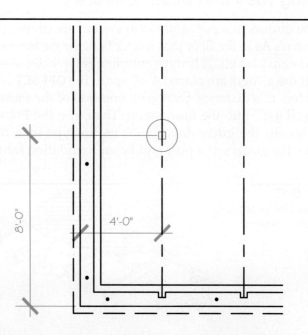

**Figure 18-19.**
Before using the **ARRAY** command, the objects to be arrayed need to be drawn on the plan. The centers of the first pier and post are placed 8'-0" from the outside of the stem wall.

8'-0"

4'-0"

ARRAY
AR

Modify
➞ Array

Modify
toolbar

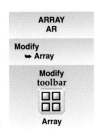

Array

Once the first post and pier set is drawn, the **ARRAY** command can be used to make multiple copies. The **ARRAY** command can be accessed by entering ar or array at the Command prompt, picking the **Array** button on the **Modify** toolbar, or selecting **Array** in the **Modify** pull-down menu. The **Array** dialog box appears, **Figure 18-20.**

The two radio buttons at the top of the **Array** dialog box specify whether the array is a rectangular array or a polar array. A rectangular array is discussed here.

If objects are selected before the command is entered, a message appears below the **Select objects** button indicating how many objects are selected. To select different or additional objects, pick the **Select objects** button to temporarily return to the drawing screen. Then, select *all* objects to array and press [Enter] to return to the **Array** dialog box. The "selected" message is updated to reflect the new selection set.

For rectangular arrays, you must specify the number of rows and columns. *Rows* are horizontal lines of arrayed objects. *Columns* are vertical lines of arrayed objects. In the **Rows:** and **Columns:** text boxes, enter the number of rows and columns for the array.

Finally, you must specify the offsets for the array. The offset is *not* the distance *between* objects. Rather, the offset is the distance (vertically *or* horizontally) from a given point on the original object to the same point on the first copy. In other words, the offset is the distance between objects *plus* the width (or height) of the object. Together, the vertical and horizontal offsets define the *unit cell.* Enter offset values in the **Row offset:** and **Column offset:** text boxes. You can also use the buttons to the right of the text boxes to pick the row offset, column offset, or unit cell in the drawing area.

If positive values are entered for both the row and column distances, the object is arrayed to the right and up. If negative values are entered for both the row and column distances, the object is arrayed to the left and down. By mixing a positive row distance and a negative column distance, the object is arrayed to the left and up. **Figure 18-21** shows how you can place arrays in four directions by entering either positive or negative row and column distance values.

**Figure 18-20.**
The **Array** dialog box is used to create copies of an original object in an array.

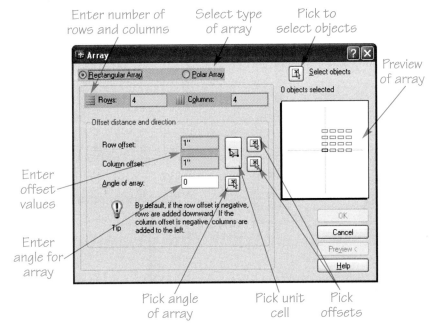

Figure 18-21.

By using positive and/or negative values for the row and column distances, the object can be arrayed in one of four directions.

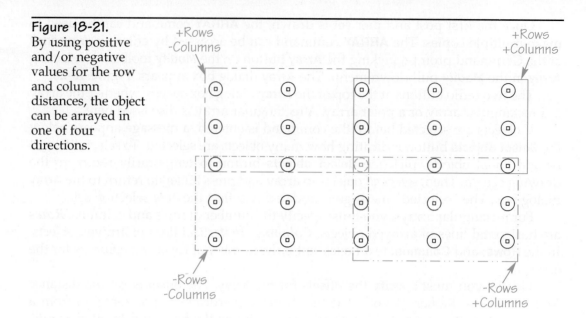

The image tile at the right of the **Array** dialog box provides a rough preview of the array. As settings are changed in the dialog box, the image tile updates. This preview is not necessarily accurate. To preview the array in the drawing area, pick the **Preview** button. When done previewing the array, you can accept or cancel the array. If you pick **Modify** in the small dialog box displayed during the preview, you are returned to the **Array** dialog box. Picking the **OK** button in the **Array** dialog box applies the array. **Figure 18-22** displays the posts and piers added to a post and beam foundation.

Figure 18-22.
The post and beam foundation with the posts and piers added.

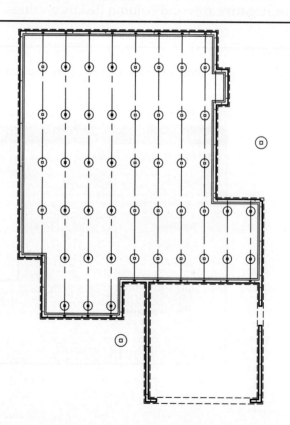

## Exercise 18-4

◆ Open ex18-3.
◆ Create the following layers:
  ◆ F-Girders-PB (Center linetype)
  ◆ F-Pads-PB
  ◆ F-Posts-PB
  ◆ F-Dims-PB
  ◆ F-Slab-PB
  ◆ F-Notes-PB
◆ Freeze the *-FJ layers.
◆ Set the F-Girders-PB layer current. Add the post and beam girders, spacing them 4'-0" apart as in **Figure 18-18.**
◆ Set the F-Pads-PB layer current. Draw the first pier in the lower left corner of the house, 8'-0" up from the outside stem wall as shown in **Figure 18-19.** Add a 4" × 4" post on the F-Posts-PB layer centered on the pier. Use the **ARRAY** command to array the post and pier, with a spacing of 8'-0" between the rows and 4'-0" between the columns.
◆ Finish the placement of the other piers as needed.
◆ Dimension the girder and post locations on the F-Dims-PB layer.
◆ Add notes to the drawing.
◆ Your drawing should look like **Figure 18-22.**
◆ You now have a foundation plan that can be used for either a floor joist or post and beam foundation.
◆ Save the drawing as ex18-4.

## Creating Polar Arrays

When a polar array is created, objects are arranged in a circular fashion around a center point. Examples of polar arrays include the decorative columns around the Jefferson memorial in Washington, D.C., structural columns in the Colosseum in Rome, and posts in a garden gazebo. See **Figure 18-23.**

**Figure 18-23.**
This is an AutoCAD 3D solid model of a proposed memorial building. The columns were placed using a polar array. Lights and materials were added and the scene rendered using 3ds max. (Blake J. Fisher)

For the following discussion on polar arrays, refer to the circular array of posts for the gazebo shown in **Figure 18-24.** First, enter the **ARRAY** command. Next, pick the **Select objects** button in the **Array** dialog box. Pick the original post and press [Enter] to return to the **Array** dialog box. Pick the **Polar Array** radio button at the top of the dialog box to specify a polar array.

Now, you must specify the center point for the array. You can manually enter the XY coordinates of the center using the **X:** and **Y:** text boxes. You can also select the **Pick Center Point** button to choose a location in the drawing area. For the gazebo, this button was used to pick the intersection of the plus symbol (+).

In the **Method and values** area of the **Array** dialog box, you must specify how the array is created. For the gazebo, there are eight posts. Therefore, 8 is entered in the **Total number of items:** text box. The **Angle to fill:** text box is used to specify the portion of the circle over which the arrayed objects are evenly spaced. For the gazebo, the posts should be spaced evenly around the entire circumference. Therefore, 360 is entered in this text box.

Finally, you must set whether or not the objects are rotated as they are placed around the array. When the **Rotate items as copied** check box is unchecked, the arrayed objects have the same orientation as the original. When checked, the objects are rotated as they are arrayed so the same "side" always faces the center point. See **Figure 18-25.** This is the option used for the posts in the gazebo.

When all settings have been made, pick the **Preview** button to preview the array in the drawing. When satisfied with the array, apply it to the drawing.

**Figure 18-24.**
Using the **ARRAY** command to create a polar array of posts around a gazebo.

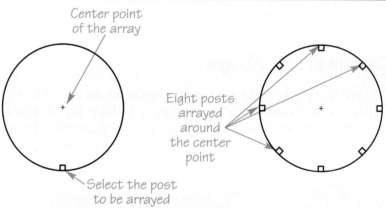

**Figure 18-25.**
You can specify whether or not arrayed objects are rotated as they are placed. A—Rotating the objects as they are copied. B—Objects are not rotated as they are copied.

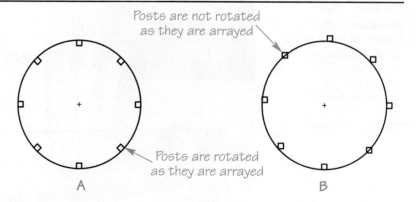

Architectural Drafting Using AutoCAD

## Exercise 18-5

- ◆ Start a new drawing or use one of your templates.
- ◆ Create a 36'-0" diameter circle.
- ◆ Create a layer named A-Cols and make it current.
- ◆ Draw a 22" diameter circular "column" centered on the bottom quadrant of the larger circle. Draw a 24" × 24" rectangle for the column base centered on the 22" diameter circle.

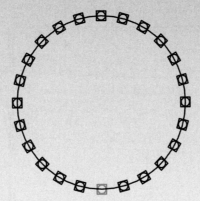

- ◆ Create a polar array of the column and base as shown. There should be 24 total items completely around the large circle.
- ◆ Save the drawing as ex18-5.

## Concrete Slab Foundation System

The previous foundation systems used wood as the main structural component on the interior of the foundation. The *concrete slab foundation system* also uses concrete footings and stem walls. However, a slab system does not use girders, beams, posts, or joists. Instead, the concrete slab foundation is filled with concrete. The concrete, or "slab," is normally 4" to 6" thick. To support interior bearing walls, additional footings are poured under the concrete slab to reinforce the load-bearing areas. **Figure 18-26** shows a typical concrete slab foundation system.

### Drawing the Footings and Stem Wall

The concrete footings and stem wall are drawn similar to the footings and stem walls for floor joist and post and beam systems. The difference is that both footing lines should appear as hidden or dashed lines. This indicates the exterior of the footing is under ground and the interior of the footing is under a concrete slab. To provide support for bearing walls, a concrete footing is placed under the concrete slab. In this case, the footings are centered under any bearing wall. **Figure 18-27** shows the placement of the footings and stem walls for a slab foundation used in the house plan.

**Figure 18-26.**
The concrete slab foundation system.

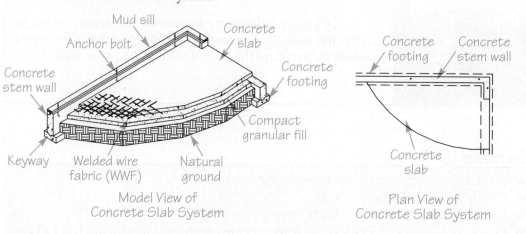

Model View of
Concrete Slab System

Plan View of
Concrete Slab System

**Figure 18-27.**
Placing the stem wall and footings for a slab foundation.

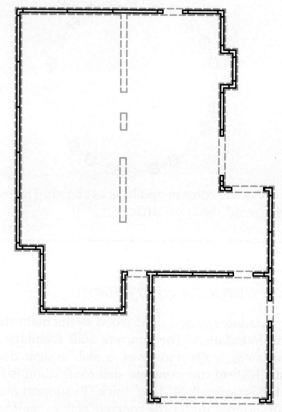

Notice in **Figure 18-27** the footings along the bearing wall are not one continuous footing but consist of three separate footings. The footings are placed directly under the wall locations. The gaps between the footings are where doors or openings in the bearing wall occur. There is not a wall above in the opening, so a footing is not placed there. This helps reduce cost by not having to pour extra concrete.

There is weight from the roof coming down on top of the bearing wall, so a beam is placed over the openings in the wall. To support the beams, a post is placed at either end of the door or opening. These posts in the main floor walls come down on top of the footing. In order to support the weight being transferred through the posts, additional thicker concrete pads need to be placed under the post locations.

Architectural Drafting Using AutoCAD

## Adding the Concrete Pads to the Foundation

When drawing the floor plans for the house, the engineer determined that some support columns should be placed in the walls in various locations on the floor plan. In order to support these columns, concrete pads are added to the foundation. Usually, a concrete pad is thicker than the footing to accommodate the extra weight it is supporting. The size and thickness of the pads is called out in the foundation notes.

The concrete pads are placed directly under any bearing points in the foundation. If a bearing point or column is lined up with the footing, the concrete pad is drawn on top of the footing, and the footing is then trimmed away from the pad. The concrete pads are drawn with a dashed linetype because the pad is under the concrete slab. See **Figure 18-28.**

In order to place the concrete pads correctly, use the main floor plan as a reference. During the initial design of the house and the development of the floor plans, columns were only specified for the porch locations. After more consideration, it was determined that structural columns should be placed on either side of any opening in the bearing wall down the center of the floor plan. **Figure 18-29** shows the placement of the concrete pads anywhere an opening is located along a bearing wall or footing.

The concrete slab system does not contain interior wood girders for support as does the other foundation systems. To reinforce the structure of the concrete slab, a wire mesh or sections of steel reinforcing bar are placed inside of the concrete slab. A common wire mesh is made up of number 10 wire spaced 6″ apart in two directions creating the mesh. In some cases, steel reinforcing bar is used. The bars are placed in two directions similar to the mesh. In either case, a note is added to the foundation plan indicating what type of reinforcing is planned for the slab.

The final item needed for the concrete slab system is the dimensions to the stem walls and the center of the concrete pads. Dimensioning is similar to the dimensioning for floor plans. Overall dimensions and "jog" dimensions are required. Instead of dimensioning to the center of openings in a foundation wall, the dimensions should indicate the size of the "cut" in the stem wall. The cuts for door openings are typically 3″ wider than the door opening (1-1/2″ on each side to provide for the door jamb).

**Figure 18-28.**
Adding concrete pads to a concrete slab foundation.

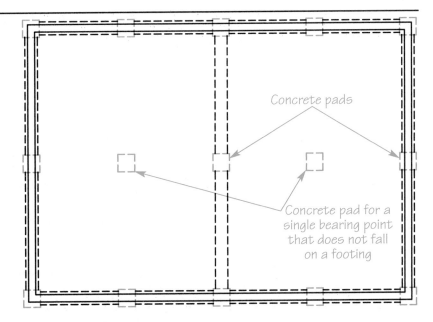

Concrete pads

Concrete pad for a single bearing point that does not fall on a footing

**Figure 18-29.**
The slab foundation with the concrete pads in place. Notice the concrete pads are placed where structural columns will be placed to support the header/beams at wall openings.

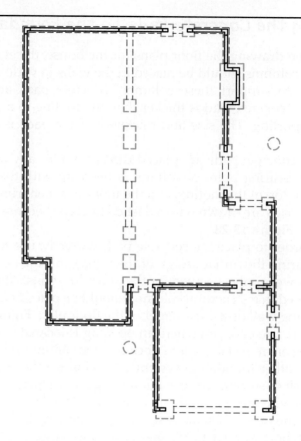

Figure 18-30 shows the completed concrete slab foundation for the house. Concrete slab foundations are also commonly used in commercial construction.

## Exercise 18-6

◆ Open ex18-4.
◆ Create the following layers.
  ◆ F-Dims-SL
  ◆ F-Footings-SL (dashed or hidden linetype)
  ◆ F-Notes-SL
  ◆ F-Pads-SL (dashed or hidden linetype)
  ◆ F-Slab-SL
  ◆ F-Walls-SL
◆ Freeze the *-PB layers.
◆ Freeze the F-Footing, F-Vents, and F-Walls layers.
◆ Thaw the M-Walls layer and trace the exterior wall line using the F-Walls-SL layer.
◆ Offset the wall line 6″ to the inside of the building.
◆ Add the stem wall "cuts" at the door locations. Add an additional 1-1/2″ to each side. Use the **TRIM** command to trim out the stem wall in the openings.
◆ Offset the stem walls 3″ to each side to establish the footing lines. Use the **Properties** window to place the new offset lines onto the F-Footings-SL layer.
◆ Add the footings under the bearing wall down the center of the building.
◆ Add pads on each side of any openings as indicated in **Figure 18-29.** Use the F-Pads-SL layer.
◆ Add notes and dimensions to the pad locations as indicated in **Figure 18-30** using the F-Dims-SL and F-Notes-SL layers.
◆ Freeze the M-Walls layer.
◆ Your drawing should look like **Figure 18-30.** You now have a foundation plan that can be used for the three different types of foundation systems.
◆ Save the drawing as ex18-6.

**Figure 18-30.**
The slab foundation with the dimensions and notes applied.

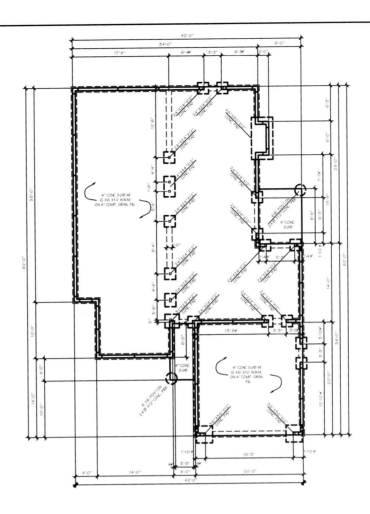

## Adding Exterior Concrete, Notes, and Dimensions

Exterior concrete slabs, porches, stairs, and ramps are commonly shown on the foundation plan, detail plans, or site plan. Where they are shown depends on the type of project being drawn. When working on the concrete slab foundation, a slab was drawn for the entry and rear porches with lines indicating the concrete slab areas and a note specifying the thickness of the slab. Refer to **Figure 18-30.** In a commercial project, exterior concrete slabs are usually an important part of the drawings.

When drawing the exterior concrete work, use lines or polylines to indicate the boundaries of the concrete slabs, risers for concrete stairs, and lower and upper edges of concrete ramps. **Figure 18-31** displays the placement of the exterior concrete work for a commercial building.

Notes also need to be added to indicate the size of concrete pads being used and any special construction features required. Other notes to consider include slab elevations in relation to the site and notes indicating any exterior concrete work, such as walks, stairs, and ramps. **Figure 18-32** displays a commercial building with notes and concrete stairs and ramps applied.

Figure 18-31.
The exterior concrete work applied to a commercial building.

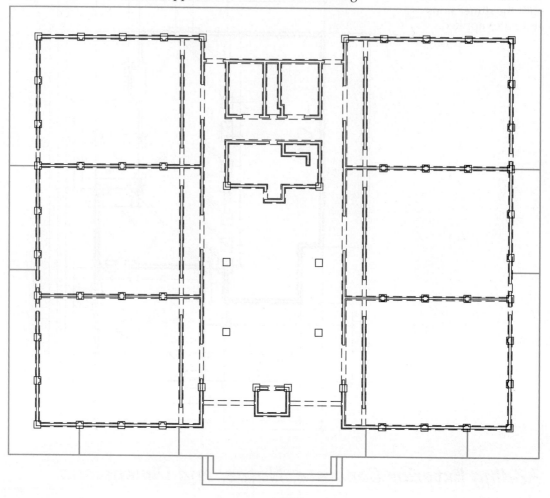

## Special Concrete Systems

Variations to the stem walls and footings may be required, depending on the design of the building. One common type of foundation is a footing that supports an exterior wall having a brick face. This is called *brick veneer construction.* The stem wall and footing width is the same as described earlier, except the footing is made wider to support the brick veneer. See **Figure 18-33.**

In some geographic locations, stem walls are made from poured concrete. The examples of stem walls presented to this point are poured walls. However, in some locations, concrete block is used for the stem wall, rather than pouring concrete. Concrete block is also called *concrete masonry unit (CMU).* This is a widely accepted variation to the concrete stem wall. See **Figure 18-34.** If CMU is used, it does not affect how the floor plan is drawn. The stem wall is shown with two lines representing each side of the wall. However, a note should be placed calling out the stem wall as constructed with CMU.

**Figure 18-32.**
Notes have been added to the commercial building.

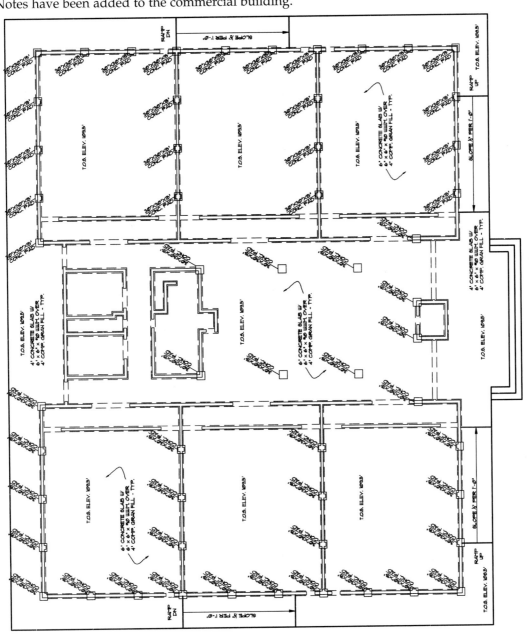

**Figure 18-33.**
A foundation wall with brick veneer on the outside of the wall.

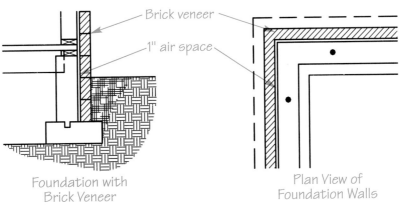

Brick veneer

1" air space

Foundation with
Brick Veneer

Plan View of
Foundation Walls

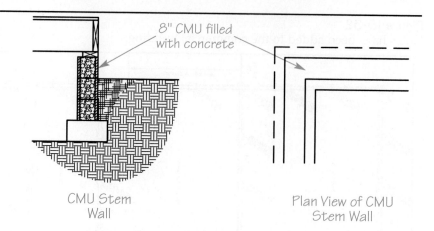

**Figure 18-34.**
A foundation wall made of 8" CMU blocks.

8" CMU filled with concrete

CMU Stem Wall

Plan View of CMU Stem Wall

Concrete slab systems can be built one of two ways: one-pour or two-pour. The *two-pour method*, shown in **Figure 18-26**, is used to create the slab foundation presented in this chapter. The footing is poured into forms built on site. When the footing has cured, the stem wall is poured. This is from where the "two-pour" name comes. The *one-pour method* involves digging trenches in the ground for the footing and pouring the footing at the same time as the slab. The one-pour method uses a modified footing/stem wall combination with the slab. See **Figure 18-35**. This is common for many small commercial projects.

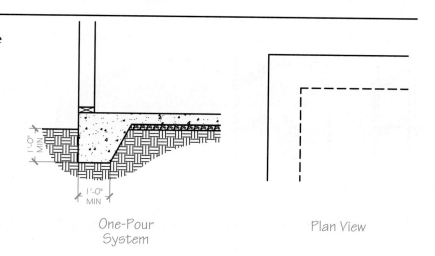

**Figure 18-35.**
A one-pour concrete slab. Notice the modified footing and how it is represented in a plan view.

1'-0" MIN

1'-0" MIN

One-Pour System

Plan View

*Answer the following questions on a separate sheet of paper.*

1. Define *foundation plan*.
2. Give another name for a stem wall. What does the stem wall sit on?
3. Identify three factors that influence the height of footings.
4. Why is the outside line of the footing normally drawn as a hidden or dashed line?
5. What is the purpose of the anchor bolts?
6. How are girders commonly represented on a foundation plan?
7. Name a command that can be used to easily draw posts.
8. Name the command you can use to calculate the square footage of the foundation. Why would you need to know foundation square footage?
9. Using the formula of 1 ft$^2$ of ventilation for every 150 ft$^2$ of foundation area, how many 1'-6" × 8" screened vents do you need for a 25' × 32' foundation? Show your calculations.
10. Define *span*.
11. What does OC stand for in the note "16" OC?"
12. Explain the basic difference between the floor joist foundation system and a post and beam foundation system.
13. How is the concrete slab foundation system different from the floor joist and post and beam systems?
14. Briefly explain how dimensions are shown to openings in the stem walls of a concrete slab system.
15. Give the name of the construction style that uses brick on the face of the building.
16. What happens to the footing when using the type of construction that places brick on the face of the building?
17. Give another name for concrete block.
18. Compare the one-pour method to the two-pour method for creating a concrete slab system.

# Chapter Problems

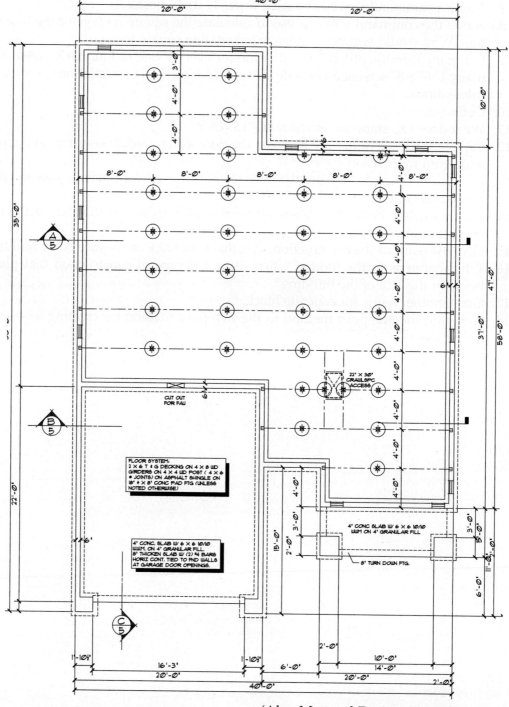

Project

Residential A

1. Open 16-ResA.
   A. Freeze all the layers but the main floor walls. Lock the main floor wall layer.
   B. Create the appropriate foundation layers. Manage your layers as you draw, ensuring that everything is placed on the proper layer.
   C. Draw the foundation plan shown, using the main floor as a reference.
   D. Dimension and note the foundation plan.
   E. Freeze the main floor layer.
   F. Save the drawing as 18-ResA.

(Alan Mascord Design Associates, Inc.)

2. Open 16-ResB.
   A. Freeze all the layers but the main floor walls. Lock the main floor wall layer.
   B. Create the appropriate foundation layers. Manage your layers as you draw, ensuring that everything is placed on the proper layer.
   C. Draw the foundation plan shown, using the main floor as a reference.
   D. Dimension and note the foundation plan.
   E. Freeze the main floor layer.
   F. Save the drawing as 18-ResB.

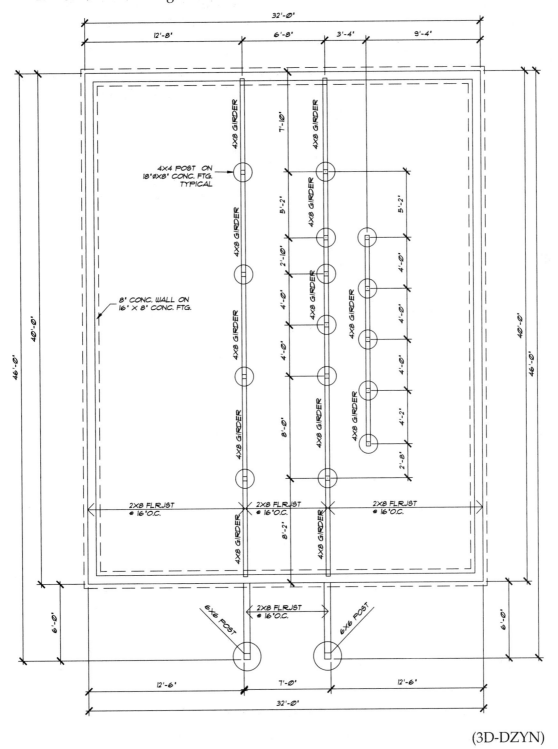

(3D-DZYN)

**Multifamily**

3. Start a new drawing from one of your templates.
   A. Create a layer named Xref-Main Floor.
   B. Xref the 16-Multifamily drawing from Chapter 16 into your drawing. Use the **Overlay** option.
   C. Freeze all the layers but the main floor walls.
   D. Create the appropriate foundation layers. Manage your layers as you draw, ensuring that everything is placed on the proper layer.
   E. Draw the foundation plan shown, using the main floor as a reference.
   F. Dimension and note the floor plan.
   G. Freeze the main floor layer.
   H. Save the drawing as 18-Multifamily.

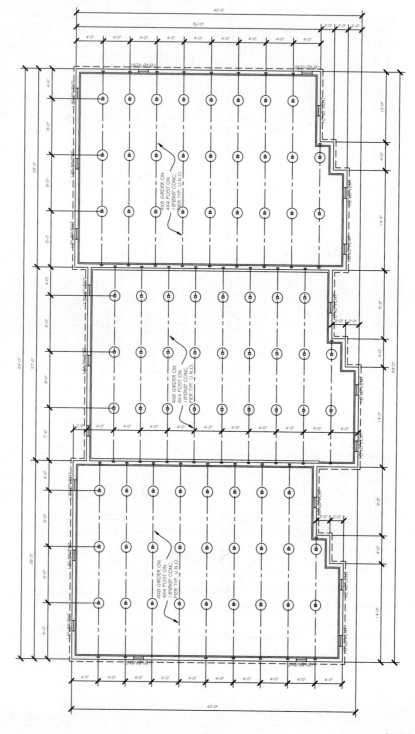

(3D-DZYN)

4. Start a new drawing from one of your templates.

   A. Create a layer named Xref-Main Floor.
   B. Xref the 16-Commercial-Main drawing from Chapter 16 into your drawing. Use the **Overlay** option.
   C. Freeze all the layers but the main floor walls.
   D. Create the appropriate foundation layers. Manage your layers as you draw, ensuring that everything is placed on the proper layer.
   E. Draw the foundation plan shown, using the main floor as a reference.
   F. Dimension and note the foundation plan.
   G. Freeze the main floor layer.
   H. Save the drawing as 18-Commercial.

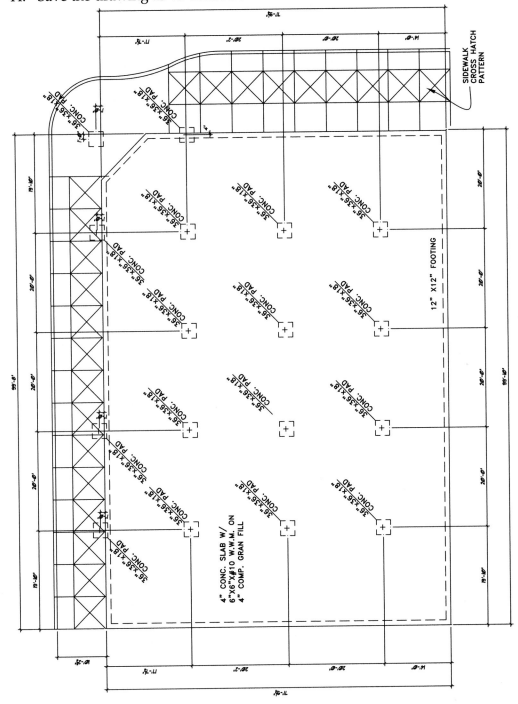

(Cynthia Bankey Architect, Inc.)

Elevation drawings provide details about exterior construction and other information. There are typically at least four drawings corresponding to each viewer direction in a set of elevations.

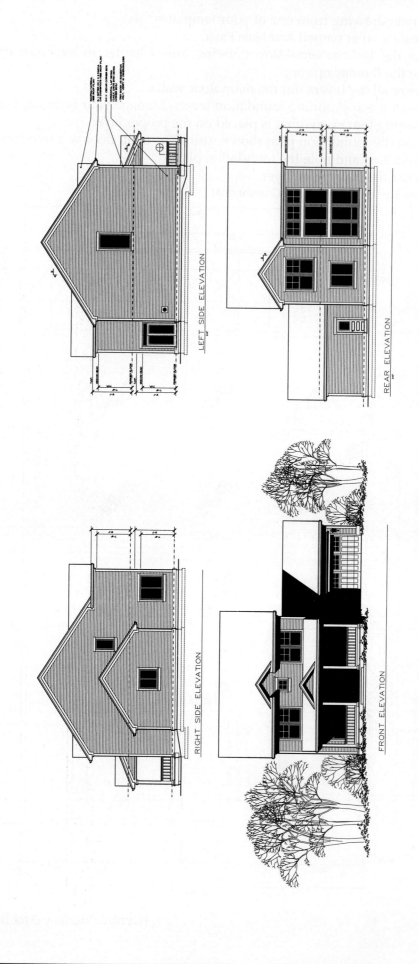

Architectural Drafting Using AutoCAD

# Drawing Elevations

## Learning Objectives

After completing this chapter, you will be able to:

- Draw exterior and interior elevations.
- Use xrefs to get information needed from floor plans for creating elevations.
- Define terminology related to construction and elevation design.
- Use the **BHATCH** command to add detail and patterns to your elevations.
- Edit hatch patterns.
- Improve boundary hatching speed.
- Place notes and dimensions on elevations and use keynotes.

## Important Terms

associative hatch patterns
birdsmouth
dimensional layout
direct projection
elevations
framed roofs
hatches
header
header line

islands
keynote system
nonassociative pattern
rafters
region
roof pitch
sill line
span
trusses

## Introduction to Drawing Elevations

*Elevations* graphically provide information about the face of a building or interior features such as cabinets. Exterior and interior elevations are an important part of the construction documents. They provide information that cannot be found on other sheets in the set of documents. Elevations contain information such as the exterior building materials used in the construction of the building; horizontal and vertical dimensions not found on other drawings; and specific detailing elements, such as the formation of brickwork in a design or cabinetry details along a kitchen wall.

Similar to a floor or foundation plan, an elevation is a two-dimensional projection of a three-dimensional building, as shown in **Figure 19-1.** This chapter discusses the process of creating both exterior and interior elevations.

# Exterior Elevations

Elevations are typically created from the four cardinal directions: north, south, east, and west. These views can also be referred to as front, rear, right, and left. See **Figure 19-2.** The north, south, east, and west elevations refer to the direction the building is facing.

The building need not be facing true north in order to draw the north elevation. If this is the case, the north elevation is the rear of the structure. The rear of the building is called the north or rear elevation because it is facing the "north" direction, or the top of the AutoCAD drawing screen. The side of the building that is facing the "south" direction, or the bottom of the AutoCAD drawing screen, is called the south or front elevation. The side of the structure facing the eastern direction, or the right side of the drawing screen, is called the east or right side elevation, and the side facing the west, or left side of the drawing screen, is called the west or left side elevation. The names of the elevations refer to the direction the building is facing, *not* the direction in which you are looking.

In some cases where the building is not a rectangular shape, such as a building with an angled wall, an elevation of the "skewed" side is drawn. The "skewed" side is also projected onto one of the cardinal elevations.

## Creating Elevations

Elevations can be created in one of two ways: direct projection and dimensional layout. Elevations created with the *direct projection* method use floor plans as a reference to project exterior building lines and jogs onto lines representing the floor and ceiling heights. This aids in accurately establishing the jogs in the building and begins laying out the elevations. **Figure 19-3** shows how elevations are created using the direct projection method.

---

**Figure 19-1.**
Elevations are two-dimensional projections of a three-dimensional surface.

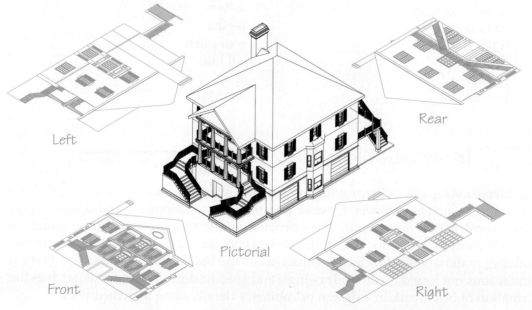

**Figure 19-2.**
Exterior elevation names and the directions they face.

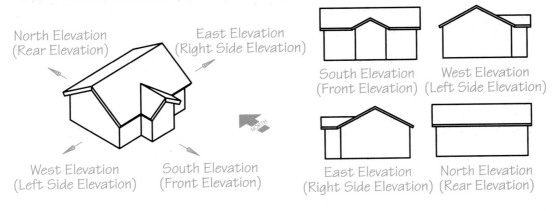

**Figure 19-3.**
Projecting the building lines from the floor plan to create elevations.

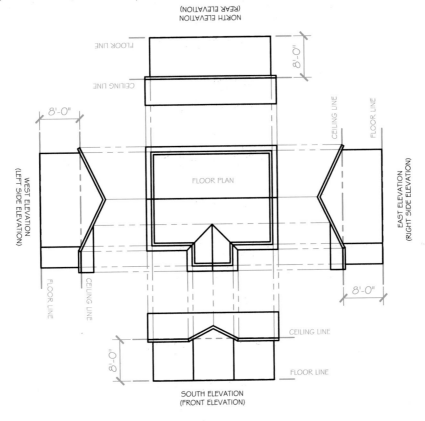

The *dimensional layout* method is similar to direct projection in that the floor and ceiling lines are laid out first. Then, referencing the dimensions from the floor plans, vertical lines are drawn over the top of the floor and ceiling lines representing the jogs in the building. This creates the basic shape of the building as shown in **Figure 19-4.**

Either method is commonly used in architectural offices. Both methods are used in the construction of exterior elevations as well as interior elevations.

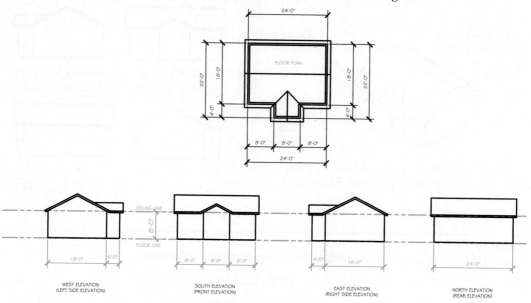

## Choosing a Scale

When choosing a scale for elevations, the largest practical scale that fits on the sheet should be selected. Listed below are the most common scales used in the construction of exterior and interior elevations.

- **Exterior Elevations.** 1/4″ = 1'-0″ for most plans, or 1/8″ or 1/16″ = 1'-0″ for larger structures.
- **Interior Elevations.** 1/2″ = 1'-0″, 1/4″ = 1'-0″, and 1/8″ = 1'-0″ are all commonly used.

No matter which scale is selected, the determining factors for a scale should be how accurately and clearly the elevations can be presented on the size of paper selected.

In residential design, a scale of 1/4″ = 1'-0″ is typical for small to average size homes. In commercial and industrial design, a scale of 1/8″ = 1'-0″ is normal because the buildings tend to be large.

## Drawing Elevations for Odd-Shaped Buildings

As mentioned earlier, not all buildings are rectangular in shape. In these cases, the four cardinal elevations (north, south, east, and west) are drawn. Any odd-shaped sides are projected onto these elevations. In addition to the cardinal elevations, an elevation is drawn so it appears to be perpendicular to the odd-shaped edge. **Figure 19-5** displays the elevations for an odd-shaped building.

## Creating Elevations for the House

The direct projection method will be used to draw the elevations of the house project discussed in previous chapters of this text. A new drawing is started, and the main floor plan is externally referenced into the drawing to be used as a reference for the projection. Once the drawing file has been referenced, lines representing the subfloor (floor line) and the plate lines (top of the wall) need to be drawn around the referenced floor plan.

**Figure 19-5.**
Each side of an odd-shaped building has its own elevation. The angled sides of the building are also projected onto the cardinal elevations where they are seen.

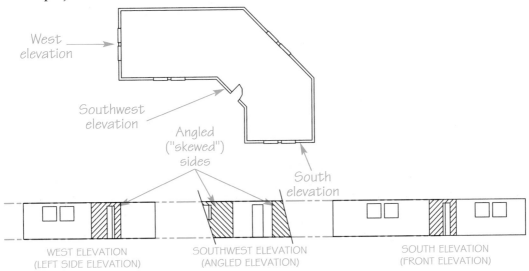

With direct projection, a line representing the subfloor is first drawn on each side of the building. Place the subfloor line far enough away from the floor plans to leave enough room for the elevations. A line representing the plate is also drawn above the subfloor line. The distance between the two lines is the total height of the wall. A typical main floor to upper floor height is 10'-1 1/8". This takes into consideration a 9'-1 1/8" main floor height, and 12" thick floor joists between the top plate of the main floor and the subfloor of the upper floor. The distance between the floors can be measured to 1/8" precision, but is often rounded to the nearest 1".

Once the main subfloor line is drawn, use the **OFFSET** command to offset the line toward the center of the drawing a distance of 9'-1", as shown in **Figure 19-6.** This establishes the top plate of the main floor. Do this for each side of the building. This gives you the floor and ceiling locations as well as the wall heights for the elevations.

Once the subfloor and plate lines have been established, refer to the main floor wall, window, and door layers. Then, begin projecting the main floor building jogs to the main subfloor line. Use the **LINE** command to draw a line from the endpoint of a corner of the building. Draw the line perpendicular to the main subfloor line. Once all of the jogs have been projected to the main subfloor line, use the **TRIM** command to trim the projected lines from the main plate line. This establishes the main floor building jogs. See **Figure 19-7.**

If you have a multistory building, after the main floor jogs and corners have been projected and trimmed, you need to reference the upper floor for any jogs or corners that can be projected to the upper subfloor and plate lines. Project the upper floor jogs to the upper subfloor line. If the upper floor aligns with the main floor, you do not need to project the line down. The main floor wall line can be used in this case. When finished projecting the upper floor lines, trim the projection lines from the upper plate line.

**Professional Tip**

In a multistory building, if the upper floor of the building aligns with the main floor, the projected lines from the main floor can also be used in the layout of the upper floor. This eliminates the need to trim the projected lines from the main plate. Instead, trim the projection lines from the upper plate.

**Figure 19-6.**
Layout of the subfloor and plate lines for the main and upper floors. Establish subfloor and plate lines for each side of the building, as well as for each floor in the building.

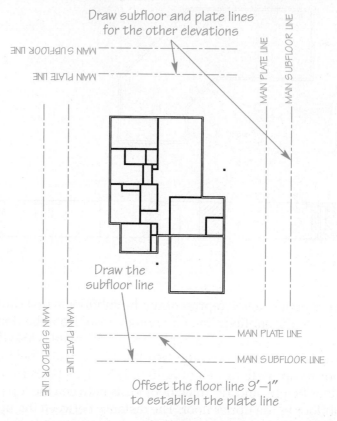

**Figure 19-7.**
Project building jogs and corners onto the main subfloor line. Then, trim the projection lines away from the main floor plate line.

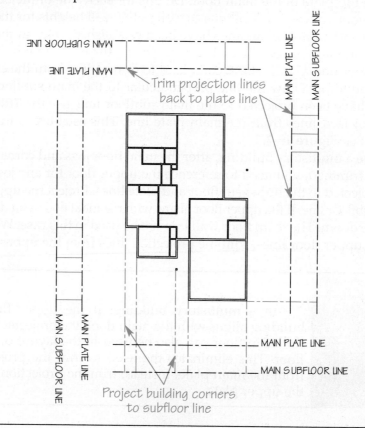

## Adding a Roof to the Elevations

The roof of a structure is generally constructed in one of two ways—framed or trussed. *Framed roofs* are built with structural members known as *rafters.* When creating a framed roof, the rafters sit on top of the plate line. The rafter is notched so the bottom of the rafter is placed on the inside of the wall. The notch in the rafter is called a *birdsmouth,* which sits on the top plate. See **Figure 19-8.** Rafter construction is similar to floor joist construction, except the "joists" are elevated. The angle at which the rafter is placed is based on the roof pitch. The *roof pitch* is the rise in roof elevation for a given unit of horizontal distance. Pitch is usually based on a run of 12″ of horizontal distance. For example, a 6:12 roof pitch means that for every 12″ of horizontal distance, the vertical elevation of the rafter is 6″ higher.

*Trusses* are preconstructed rafters that include a ceiling joist and diagonal web member supports between the rafters and the joist. Trusses do not use a birdsmouth. Instead, they sit directly on the top plate. See **Figure 19-9.** Truss roof pitches are measured in the same way as pitches for rafters.

The roof for this project is constructed with rafters. It has been determined that 2 × 8 rafters are to be used. The roof pitch is 6:12. With these specifications, the first thing to do is determine where the starting point of the rafter is located. The rafter sits on the top, inside corner of the top plate. A line representing the bottom of the rafter is drawn on the *inside* of the building corner. The exterior walls of the house are 6″ thick, so the start point of the rafter is 6″ from the outside corner of the building. See **Figure 19-10.** To draw the roofline with the correct pitch, draw the second endpoint of the rafter line using the relative coordinates @12″,6″.

After the bottom of the rafter has been determined, offset the rafter line the thickness of the rafter, 8″ in this case. You now have the angle and thickness of the rafter in the elevation. Offset the outside building line the distance the roof overhangs past the outer edge of the wall. A fascia board is often added at the end of the rafters. Extend the rafter lines to the fascia line. Trim the rafter lines to clean up the end of the rafter, as shown in **Figure 19-11.**

When the roof pitch, rafter, and fascia have been drawn, the rafter layout can be copied or mirrored to other parts of the building. When mirroring the rafter layout, it is often necessary to establish a mirror line half the distance of the roof span. *Span* is

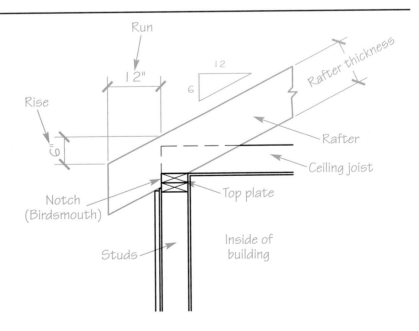

**Figure 19-8.**
A partial section view of a framed roof using rafters. Notice where the birdsmouth (notch) is located in relation to the wall.

**Figure 19-9.**
A partial section view of a trussed roof. Notice there is no birdsmouth in a truss.

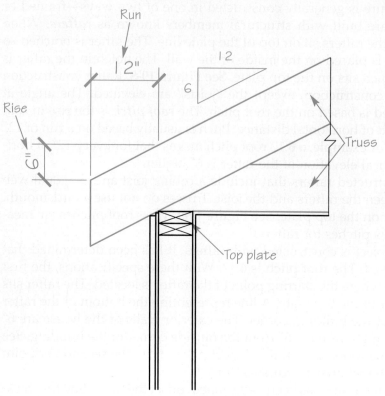

**Figure 19-10.**
Layout of the rafter and roofline.

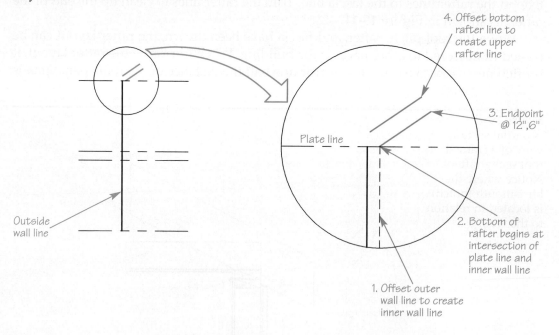

4. Offset bottom rafter line to create upper rafter line

3. Endpoint @ 12",6"

Plate line

2. Bottom of rafter begins at intersection of plate line and inner wall line

Outside wall line

1. Offset outer wall line to create inner wall line

the distance between any two supports. In the case of the elevation layout, the span is the distance from the outside of one exterior wall to the outside of the opposite exterior wall at the top plate. The geometry calculator can be used to establish the mirroring line in the process of using the **MIRROR** command. Two different expressions can be written at the command prompt. These are described as follows.

**Figure 19-11.**
Finishing the end of the roof and establishing the fascia board.

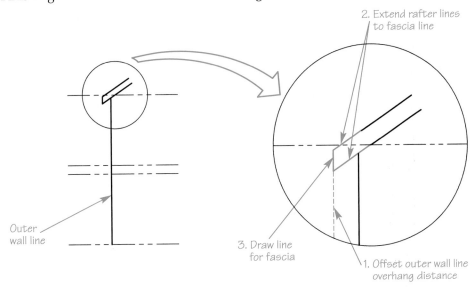

- **MEE.** After entering the **'CAL** command, mee can be entered at the Expression: prompt. **MEE** stands for "the middle of two endpoints." Once **MEE** has been entered, you are prompted to select two endpoints so the middle point between these two endpoints can be determined. This is the command sequence for establishing the mirror line in **Figure 19-12.**

Command: **mirror**↵
Select objects: *(select the rafter and fascia lines)*
Select objects: ↵
Specify first point of mirror line: **'cal**↵
Initializing...>> Expression: **mee**↵

**Figure 19-12.**
Finding the middle between two endpoints with the **MEE** calculator expression.

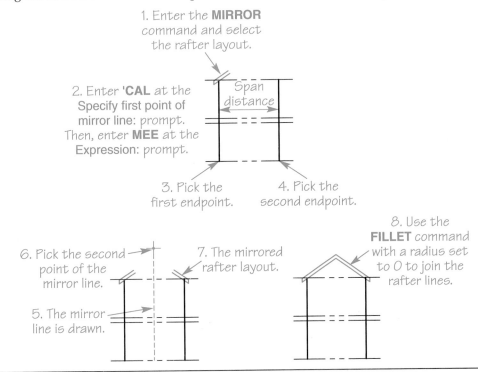

>> Select one endpoint for MEE: *(select the first endpoint)*
>> Select another endpoint for MEE: *(select the first endpoint)*
(xxx, xxx, xxx) *(coordinates of midpoint)*
Specify second point of mirror line: *(pick a point for the second mirror line point; use Ortho mode to your advantage)*
Delete source objects? [Yes/No] <N>: **n**↵

- **(CUR+CUR)/2.** Similar to **MEE**, the **(CUR+CUR)/2** expression finds the middle point between any two points you pick with the cursor. Object snaps can be used to select two points. AutoCAD calculates the distance between the points and divides this distance by two. The following command sequence is used.

  Command: **mirror**↵
  Select objects: *(select the rafter and fascia lines)*
  Select objects: ↵
  Specify first point of mirror line: **'cal**↵
  Initializing...>> Expression: **(cur+cur)/2**↵
  >> Enter a point: *(use an object snap to select the first endpoint)*
  >> Enter a point: *(use an object snap to select the second endpoint)*
  (xxx, xxx, xxx) *(coordinates of midpoint)*
  Specify second point of mirror line: *(pick a point for the second mirror line point; use Ortho mode to your advantage)*
  Delete source objects? [Yes/No] <N>: **n**↵

Once the rafter layout has been mirrored or copied, the rafter lines can be joined together. The **FILLET** command with a radius of 0 can be used to join the rafter lines to form the ridge lines and gable roof ends. **Figure 19-13** shows the layout of the front elevation for the house drawing.

**Figure 19-13.**
The layout of the front elevation. Note: The height of the roof over the garage was determined by creating the rafter layout in a side elevation.

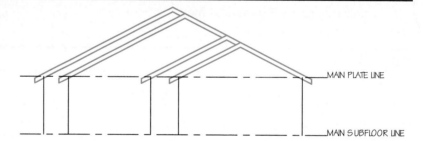

# Exercise 19-1

- Start a new drawing using one of your templates.
- Create the following layers:
  - X-Floor Plan
  - E-Floor & Plate (Center linetype)
  - E-Roof
  - E-Walls
- Xref in ex16-8 using the **Overlay** option.
- With the E-Floor & Plate layer current, draw four lines around the floor plan to represent the main subfloor (similar to **Figure 19-6**).
- Use the **OFFSET** command to create the main plate lines. The wall height for each floor is 9'-1".
- Use the E-Walls layer to project the corners/jogs of the floor plan to the subfloor and plate layout lines (similar to **Figure 19-7**).
- Create the roof on the E-Roof layer. The rafter thickness is 8". Use a roof pitch of 6:12. Determine an overhang for your elevations; try 12" to 18" past the edge of outside walls. Use the geometry calculator to establish mirror lines to aid in the construction of the roof.
- Use the **TRIM** and **FILLET** commands to clean up the elevation.
- Create the four cardinal elevations. Use **COPY**, **MIRROR**, **OFFSET**, **TRIM**, and **EXTEND** to create your elevations. Your drawing should look like the figure below.
- Save the drawing as ex19-1.

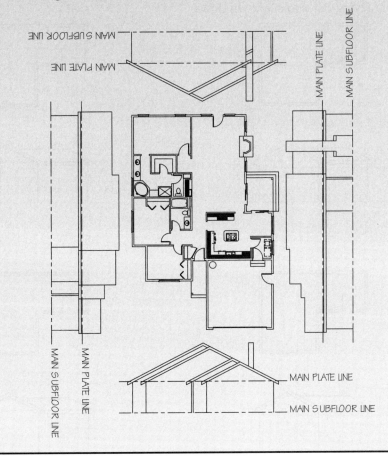

## Layout of the Doors and Windows

The next step in the elevation layout is to place doors and windows in their proper locations and with the proper sizes. The line at the top of the doors and windows is called the *header line.* A construction member, known as a *header,* is placed over the opening to support the wall and roof above. Typically, in a building with 8′ high walls, the tops of doors and windows are placed 6′-8″ from the subfloor. High walls that are 9′ generally start the header line 7′-0″ from the subfloor, and other options are possible depending on your design. Before laying out the locations of the doors and windows, first determine the header height. For the house drawing, a header height of 7′-0″ is used.

To create the header line, offset each subfloor line up 7′-0″. This is the top of the doors and windows. To determine the locations of the openings, project the windows and doors from the floor plans as you did when projecting the exterior wall lines. Once the header lines and locations have been drawn, determine the heights of the windows. Use the **OFFSET** command to offset the header lines down to create the bottom window line. This bottom window line is called the *sill line.*

Use the **Properties** window to place the header and sill lines on the door and window layer. Next, use the **TRIM** command to trim the header and sill lines. **Figure 19-14** displays the process for laying out doors and windows.

**Figure 19-14.**
The process of laying out doors and windows.

1. Offset the subfloor line to determine the header location.

2. Project the door and window locations.

3. Offset the header line to create the sill line for windows. Place the header and sill lines on the door and window layer.

4. Trim the door and window openings.

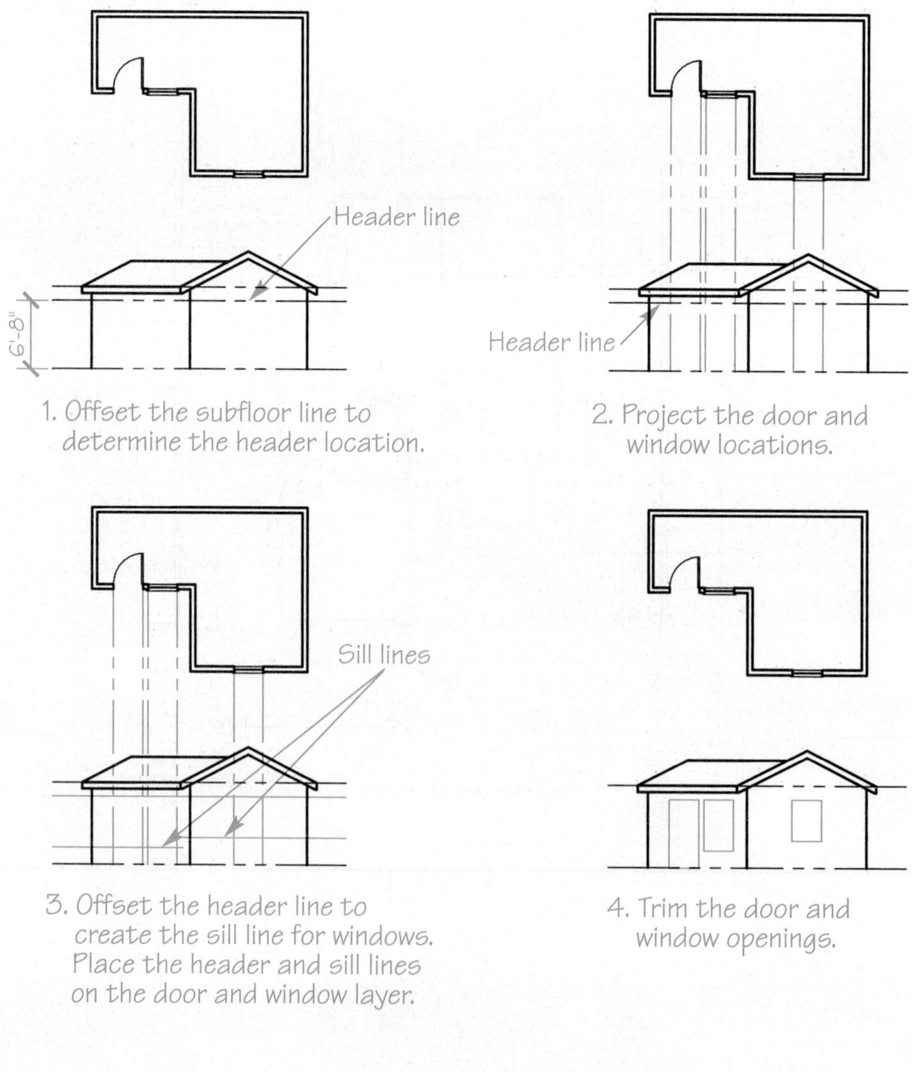

◆ Open ex19-1.
◆ Create the header lines for the elevations. The header lines should be 7'-0" from the subfloors.
◆ Create a layer named E-Door & Win. Set the layer current.
◆ Project the door and window locations for the main floor to the main subfloor line.
◆ Use **TRIM** to trim the projection lines from the main floor header lines.
◆ Use **TRIM** to trim the projection lines from the upper floor header lines.
◆ Use the **OFFSET** command to offset the header lines down to create the sill lines for the windows. Note: There may be several sill lines as all the windows may not be the same heights; however, all the windows will have the same header height.
◆ Use the **Properties** window to place the header and sill lines on the E-Door & Win layer.
◆ Use **TRIM** to clean up doors and windows.
◆ Your drawing should look similar to the diagram below.
◆ Save the drawing as ex19-2.

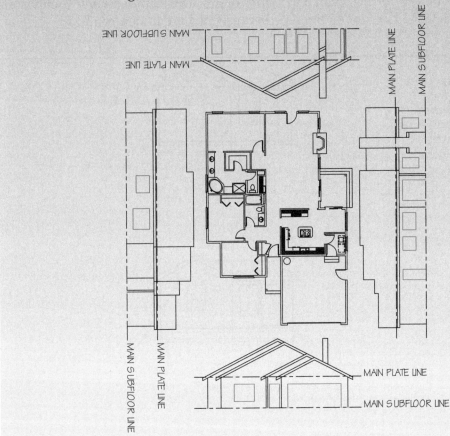

## Establishing the Foundation and Grading Lines

The final step in the layout of an exterior elevation is drawing the foundation locations and finished grading lines. In Chapter 18, three types of foundation systems were created for the house drawing. All three systems, to some degree, determine the final appearance of an elevation. In addition, the finished grade line is 8" below the top of the stem wall for each system.

In a floor joist system, the floor joists sit on top of the foundation stem wall. This height must be reflected in the total height of the elevation. So far, the wall lines have been projected to the subfloor line. With the floor joist system, the top of the stem wall is an additional 13″ below the subfloor. This value (13″) is calculated by adding a 1″ thick subfloor, plus 10″ tall floor joists, plus a 2″ thick mudsill. The calculated value may vary, depending on construction specifications.

With a post and beam foundation, the top of the stem wall is 4″ below the subfloor. This value (4″) is calculated by adding a 2″ thick tongue and groove floor plus a 2″ thick mudsill. An elevation for a post and beam foundation is shorter than an equivalent elevation for a floor joist foundation. This is because the tongue and groove subfloor sits directly on the mudsill. **Figure 19-15** illustrates these differences.

The exterior wall lines can now be extended to the top of the stem wall line using the **EXTEND** command. The stem wall line also becomes the bottom of the exterior siding. Therefore, draw it on the exterior wall layer.

The top of the footing is generally at least 12″ below the finished grade, or the distance below grade to the bottom of a basement floor. The bottom of the footing is offset the thickness of the footing.

To determine the corners of the foundation, project lines down from the foundation plan as you did for the main and upper floors. The stem wall and footings are drawn with a dashed or hidden linetype because they are underground.

**Figure 19-15.**
The heights of elevations for a floor joist system versus a post and beam system will cause the elevation height to vary.

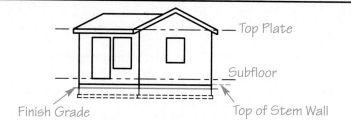

Floor Joist System

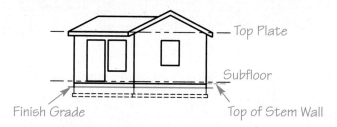

Post and Beam System

Architectural Drafting Using AutoCAD

# Exercise 19-3

- Open ex19-2.
- Determine which foundation system you would like to draw: floor joist or post and beam.
- Create a layer named E-Fnd Wall. Assign a hidden linetype to the layer and set current.
- **Floor Joist System:**
  - Offset the subfloor line down 13". Place this line on the E-Walls layer. Extend the exterior wall lines to this line.
  - Offset the bottom wall line down 8" to represent the finish grade line. Place this line on a layer named E-Grade.
  - Offset the grade line down 12" to represent the top of the footing. Then offset the top of the footing down 6" to represent the bottom footing line. Place these lines on the E-Fnd Wall layer.
  - Project the exterior stem wall and footing lines down to the footing lines. Trim the projection lines from the grading line.
  - Draw lines between the bottom of the siding and the grade line representing the stem wall that is above ground. These lines should be continuous.
- **Post and Beam System:**
  - Offset the subfloor line down 4". Place this line on the E-Walls layer. Extend the exterior wall lines to this line.
  - Offset the bottom wall line down 8" to represent the finish grade line. Place this line on a layer named E-Grade.
  - Offset the grade line down 12" to represent the top of the footing. Then offset the top of the footing down 6" to represent the bottom footing line. Place these lines on the E-Fnd Wall layer.
  - Project the exterior stem wall and footing lines down to the footing lines. Trim the projection lines from the grading line.
  - Draw lines between the bottom of the siding and the grade line representing the stem wall that is above ground. These lines should be continuous.
- Draw a line at the bottom of all the doors except the garage doors, representing the door threshold.
- For the doors at the garage level, set the header line to be 8' above the grade line, with the door jambs projected down to the grade.
- Use the **TRIM** command to clean up the foundation lines.
- Your drawing should look similar to the diagram on the next page. This was drawn using the floor joist foundation system.
- Save the drawing as ex19-3.

---

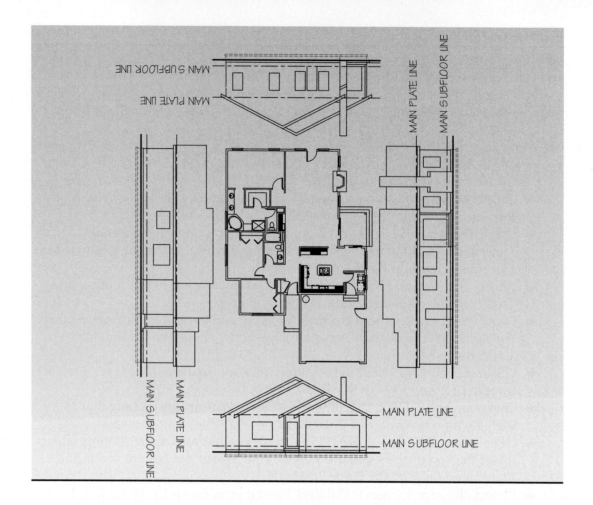

## Detailing the Elevations

Now that the elevations have been laid out, you can begin detailing the drawings to make them appear more realistic. For example, windows can be detailed to represent the exact type of window called for in the design. Or, a special type of door may be called for and can be added at this time. In addition, frames can be drawn around the doors and windows. **Figure 19-16** shows some examples of different types of door and window blocks used in architectural drawings. The frames around the openings are typically 2" thick. Create window and door blocks to reduce the amount of drawing time.

Other details can be added at this time as well, such as corner boards at the corners of the building or window/flower boxes under windows. Also, place trim boards on large walls to break up the "mass." Draw any decorative elements on the walls. By using different combinations of trim, windows, and doors, several different elevations can be created from the same floor plans. **Figure 19-17** shows different elevations created from the same house drawing. Adding the siding and roofing patterns is discussed in the next section.

**Figure 19-16.**
Examples of door
and window blocks.

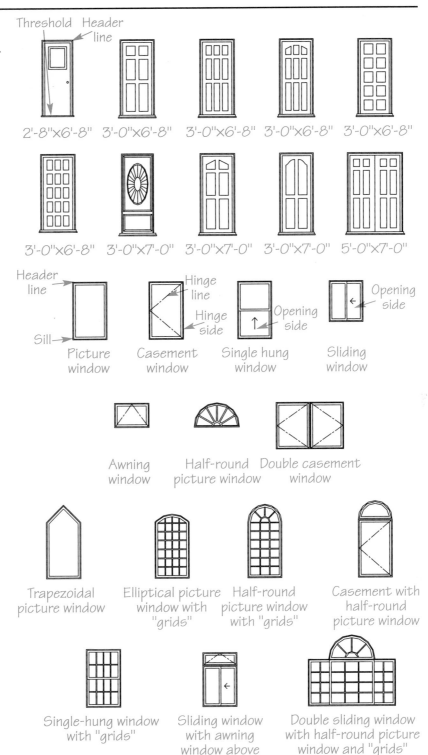

2'-8"x6'-8"   3'-0"x6'-8"   3'-0"x6'-8"   3'-0"x6'-8"   3'-0"x6'-8"

3'-0"x6'-8"   3'-0"x7'-0"   3'-0"x7'-0"   3'-0"x7'-0"   5'-0"x7'-0"

Picture
window

Casement
window

Single hung
window

Sliding
window

Awning
window

Half-round
picture window

Double casement
window

Trapezoidal
picture window

Elliptical picture
window with
"grids"

Half-round
picture window
with "grids"

Casement with
half-round
picture window

Single-hung window
with "grids"

Sliding window
with awning
window above

Double sliding window
with half-round picture
window and "grids"

## Exercise 19-4

◆ Open ex19-3.
◆ Begin detailing the windows and doors. Try using different frame widths such as 1" to 3". Refer to **Figure 19-17** for samples.
◆ If adding grid patterns to the doors and windows, use the **DIVIDE** command to create evenly spaced points that can be snapped to for the grid layout.
◆ Add trim components to the building. Do not add siding or roofing patterns.
◆ Save the drawing as ex19-4.

**Figure 19-17.**
Using different
combinations of
elements to create
different elevations.

# Adding Patterns to the Elevations

Using AutoCAD, you can add patterns representing building materials or shading to your drawing. These patterns are called *hatches.* Hatches can be used to symbolize siding, roofing, or shading on the elevations. They can also be added as a hatch pattern in sections or in walls. **Figure 19-18** shows the different hatch patterns available in AutoCAD.

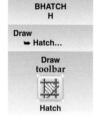

BHATCH
H

Draw
↪ Hatch...

Draw
toolbar

Hatch

The **BHATCH** command is used to draw a hatch by automatically filling an enclosed area with the selected pattern. Hatch patterns are selected and applied using the **Boundary Hatch and Fill** dialog box. You can access this dialog box by picking the **Hatch** button on the **Draw** toolbar, by picking **Hatch...** in the **Draw** pull-down menu, or by entering h or bhatch at the Command prompt.

The **Boundary Hatch and Fill** dialog box is divided into three tabs. See **Figure 19-19.** A series of buttons that determine the method of applying the hatch and a **Preview** button are also included.

**Professional Tip**

Hatch patterns can be edited using the **HATCHEDIT** command or the **Properties** window. The **HATCHEDIT** command is discussed later in this chapter.

**Figure 19-18.**
Predefined hatch patterns supplied with AutoCAD.

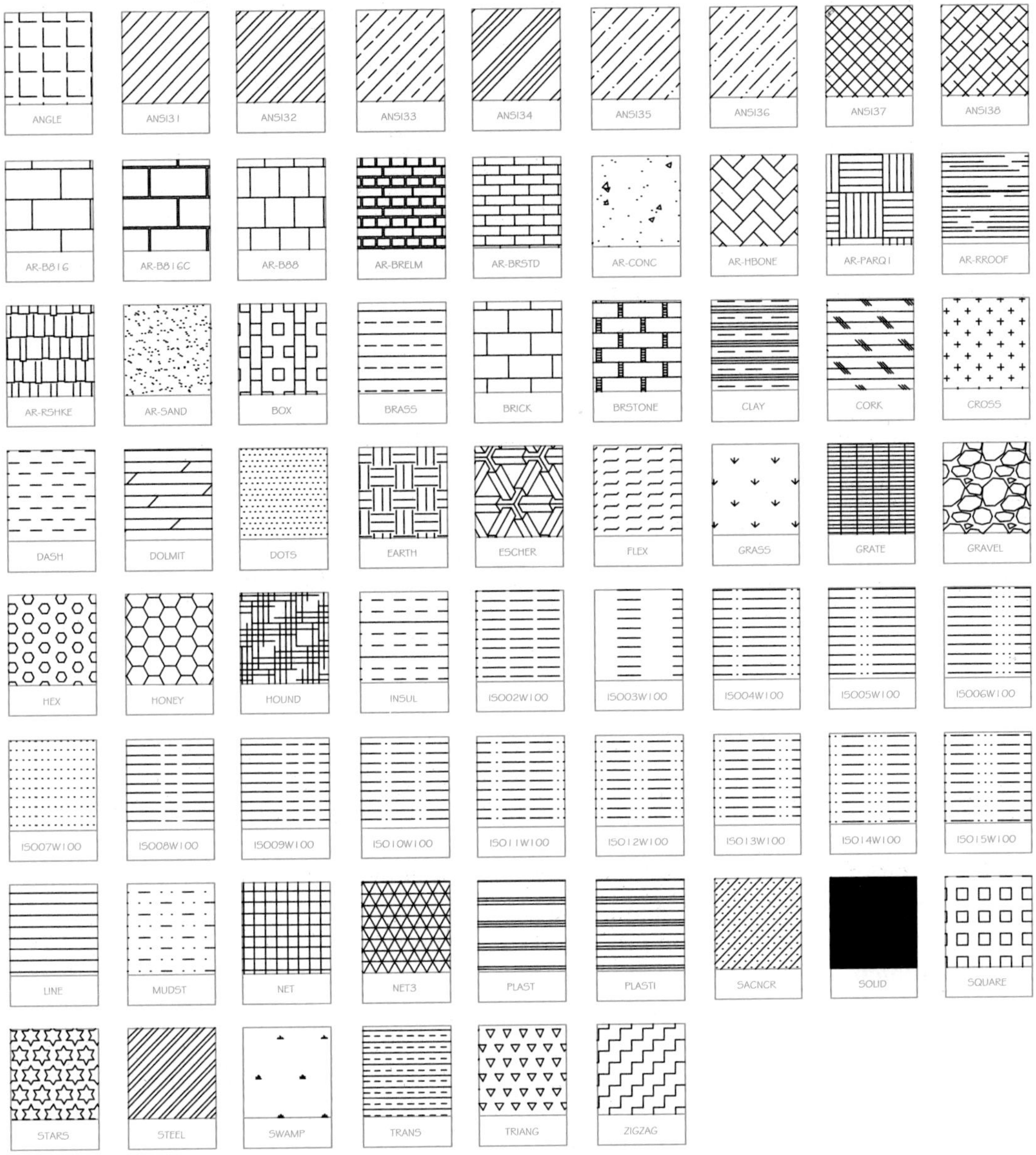

## Selecting a Hatch Pattern

The specific hatch pattern is selected in the **Hatch** tab of the **Boundary Hatch and Fill** dialog box. The following three categories of hatch patterns are available in the **Type:** drop-down list.

- **Predefined.** The predefined AutoCAD patterns are stored in the acad.pat and acadiso.pat files. The acad.pat file is used when you start a drawing using English units. The acadiso.pat file contains hatch patterns scaled for metric drawings. It is used when you start a drawing using metric units.
- **User defined.** Selecting this option creates a pattern of lines based on the current linetype in your drawing. You can control the angle and spacing of the lines. The **LTSCALE** system variable affects how this user defined hatch appears in the drawing.

Figure 19-19.
The **Hatch** tab of the
**Boundary Hatch and
Fill** dialog box.

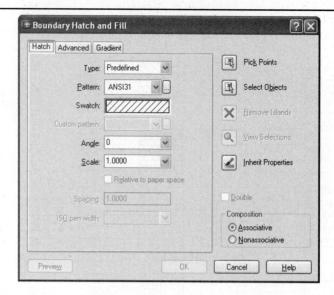

- **Custom.** This option allows you to specify a pattern defined in any custom PAT file that is added to the AutoCAD Support File Search Path locations. Custom hatch patterns can be created or found on the Internet. If you download patterns from the Internet, make sure you have the appropriate permissions to use the patterns.

## Predefined Hatch Patterns

AutoCAD has many predefined hatch patterns. After selecting **Predefined** in the **Type:** drop-down list, you need to select the specific predefined pattern. You can select the pattern name from the **Pattern:** drop-down list. You can also pick the ellipsis (...) button next to the **Pattern:** drop-down arrow or pick on the sample swatch to display the **Hatch Pattern Palette** dialog box, **Figure 19-20.**

The **Hatch Pattern Palette** provides sample images of the predefined hatch patterns. The hatch patterns are divided among the **ANSI**, **ISO**, **Other Predefined**, and **Custom** tabs. Highlight a pattern and pick the **OK** button or double-click on a pattern to select it and return to the **Boundary Hatch and Fill** dialog box. The selected pattern is displayed in the swatch and its name appears in the **Pattern:** drop-down list.

Figure 19-20.
The **Hatch Pattern
Palette** dialog box
contains image tiles
of the predefined
hatch patterns
supplied with
AutoCAD.

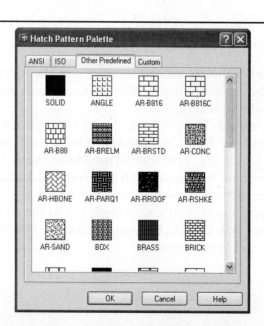

You can control the angle and scale of any predefined pattern using the **Angle:** and **Scale:** drop-down lists. These drop-down lists also function as text boxes so you can type values. For predefined ISO patterns, you can also control the ISO pen width using the **ISO pen width:** drop-down list.

Professional Tip

An object can be hatched solid by selecting the SOLID predefined pattern.

## User-Defined Hatch Patterns

A user-defined hatch pattern is a series of straight lines drawn using the current linetype. The angle for the pattern relative to the X axis is set in the **Angle:** text box. The spacing between the lines is set in the **Spacing:** text box.

Selecting the **Double** check box on the right side of the **Boundary Hatch and Fill** dialog box creates a pattern of lines intersecting at 90°. This check box is only available when **User defined** is selected in the **Type:** drop-down list. **Figure 19-21** shows examples of user-defined hatch patterns.

Figure 19-21.
Examples of different hatch angles and spacing for a user-defined hatch.

| Current Linetype | Fenceline 1 LTSCALE = .5 | Fenceline 1 LTSCALE = .5 | Fenceline 1 LTSCALE = .5 | Fenceline 1 LTSCALE = .5 |
|---|---|---|---|---|
| Angle | 0° | 45° | 0° | 45° |
| Spacing | 1/8" | 1/8" | 1/4" | 1/4" |
| Single Hatch | | | | |
| Double Hatch | | | | |

## Custom hatch patterns

You can create custom hatch patterns and save them in PAT files or download them from many websites on the Internet. When you select **Custom** in the **Type:** drop-down list, the **Custom pattern:** drop-down list is enabled. You can select a custom pattern from this drop-down list, or pick the ellipsis (...) button to select the pattern from the **Custom** tab of the **Hatch Pattern Palette** dialog box. In order to use the custom hatch patterns, the PAT file must be in one of the Support File Search Path locations. You can set the angle and scale of custom hatch patterns, just as you can with predefined hatch patterns. To create your own hatch patterns, refer to the AutoCAD Customization Guide accessed with the **HELP** command.

## Selecting an Existing Pattern

When specifying a hatch pattern, you can choose a pattern already drawn. All hatch settings of the existing hatch pattern are applied to the new hatch pattern. Pick the **Inherit Properties** button in the **Boundary Hatch and Fill** dialog box. The dialog box is temporarily closed and the "paint" cursor appears. In addition, you are prompted with the following on the command line:

Select associative hatch object: *(pick the desired hatch pattern)*
Inherited Properties: Name *<hatch name>*, Scale *<hatch scale>*, Angle *<hatch angle>*
Select internal point: ⏎

After the hatch is picked, the **Boundary Hatch and Fill** dialog box is again displayed. The settings of the selected pattern appear in the dialog box. You can now apply the hatch to the new object.

## Hatch Pattern Scale

Predefined and custom hatch patterns can be scaled by entering a value in the **Scale:** text box. The drop-down list contains common scales broken down in .25 increments. The scales in this list start with .25 and go up to a scale of 2. However, you can type any scale in the drop-down list text box. **Figure 19-22** shows examples of different scales.

The **Relative to paper space** check box is used to scale the hatch pattern relative to paper space units. Use this option to easily display hatch patterns at a scale appropriate for your layout in layout space. This option is only available when you are in a layout space viewport. Layout space is discussed in Chapter 24.

**Figure 19-22.**
The effect of different hatch pattern scale factors.

Hatch pattern: BRICK
Scale: 12

Hatch pattern: BRICK
Scale: 24

Hatch pattern: BRICK
Scale: 36

## Selecting Areas to Hatch

You can select the areas to hatch in one of two ways—picking points or selecting objects. Using the **Pick Points** button in the **Boundary Hatch and Fill** dialog box, you can select points inside a closed area to hatch. When you pick the button, the dialog box is temporarily closed. Pick a point within an enclosed area to hatch. AutoCAD automatically defines the boundary around the selected point and indicates the boundary with a dashed line. The following prompts are displayed.

> Select internal point: (pick a point inside the area to be hatched)
> Selecting everything visible...
> Analyzing the selected data...
> Analyzing internal islands...
> Select internal point: (pick an internal point inside an additional area or press [Enter] if you are done selecting objects)

When you are finished selecting points, press [Enter] and the **Boundary Hatch and Fill** dialog box is redisplayed. Pick the **OK** button in the dialog box and the feature is automatically hatched. See **Figure 19-23.**

The **Select Objects** button is used to select closed objects to define the hatch boundary, rather than an internal point. See **Figure 19-24.** Closed objects include circles, polygons, closed polylines, rectangles, and ellipses. The **Select Objects** button can also be used to exclude an object lying inside the area to hatch from the pattern. An example of this is the text shown inside the hatch area of **Figure 19-24.**

**Figure 19-23.**
Defining the hatch boundary by picking an internal point.

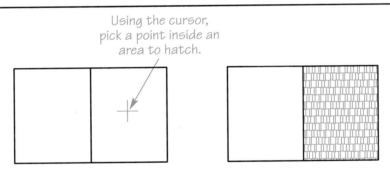

Using the cursor, pick a point inside an area to hatch.

The hatch pattern is applied inside the enclosed area.

**Figure 19-24.**
Using the **Select Objects** button to exclude an object from the hatch pattern.

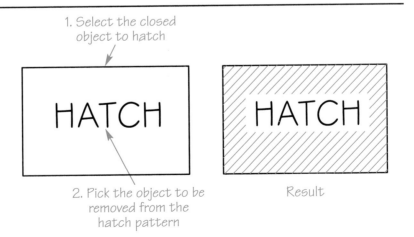

1. Select the closed object to hatch

2. Pick the object to be removed from the hatch pattern

Result

---

*Chapter 19   Drawing Elevations*

## Working with Islands

Enclosed areas within a boundary are known as *islands.* AutoCAD can either hatch through islands or around them. When you use the **Pick Points** button to hatch an internal area, islands are not hatched by default, as shown in **Figure 19-25B.** However, if you want islands to be hatched, pick the **Remove Islands** button in the **Boundary Hatch** dialog box after selecting the internal point. The dialog box is temporarily closed and the following prompts appear on the command line.

Select island to remove: (*pick the islands to remove*)
⟨Select island to remove⟩/Undo: ↵

Select the islands to remove and press [Enter] to return to the dialog box. The hatch is now applied through the islands. See **Figure 19-25C.**

The **Advanced** tab of the **Boundary Hatch and Fill** dialog box allows you to set the island detection style and the island detection method. See **Figure 19-26.** There are three options in the **Island detection style** area that allow you to set how features are hatched. These options have no effect if the boundary does not contain islands. The image tiles reflect the options.

**Figure 19-25.**
A—Original objects. B—Using the **Pick Points** button to hatch an internal area leaves the islands unhatched. C—After picking an internal point, use the **Remove Islands** button and pick the islands. The hatch is applied to islands.

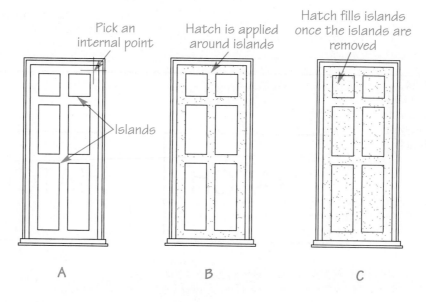

Figure 19-26.
The **Advanced** tab of
the **Boundary Hatch
and Fill** dialog box
contains options for
island detection and
boundary object
creation.

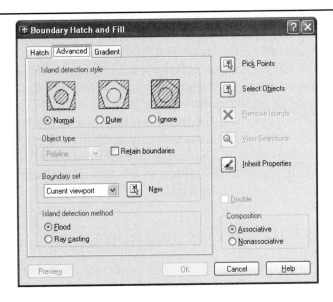

- **Normal.** This option hatches inward from the outer boundary. If AutoCAD encounters an island, hatching is turned off until another island is encountered. Then, hatching is turned back on. Another way to look at this is every other closed boundary has hatching applied. For example, a window in an elevation may have many islands. This option hatches every other island on the window.

- **Outer.** This option also hatches inward from the outer boundary. As with "normal" hatching, AutoCAD turns hatching off when it encounters an island. However, hatching is not turned back on even if other islands are detected. AutoCAD hatches only the outermost level of the structure and leaves the internal structure blank. This is a good option when hatching siding on a building and AutoCAD detects several islands on a window or door. The outer frame of the window is detected and AutoCAD does not place a hatch on the window.

- **Ignore.** This option ignores all islands and hatches everything within the selected boundary. Any islands within the boundary are filled with the hatch pattern.

The **Island detection method** area has two options—**Flood** and **Ray casting**. The **Flood** radio button is selected by default. This includes internal objects (islands) in the boundary calculation. The **Ray casting** option draws a line around the outermost enclosed area when calculating the boundary. This is similar to using the **Ignore** option in the **Island detection style**.

## Previewing the Hatch

Before applying a hatch pattern to the selected area, you can preview it to be sure the pattern and boundary are correct. The following buttons are located in the **Boundary Hatch and Fill** dialog box. They are used to preview the boundary and hatch pattern.

- **View Selections button.** The **View Selections** button is available after picking objects to be hatched. Pick this button and the drawing is displayed with the hatch boundaries shown as a dashed line. When you are finished, press [Enter] or right-click to return to the **Boundary Hatch and Fill** dialog box.

- **Preview button.** Pick the **Preview** button to see the hatch pattern as it will be applied to the boundary. This allows you to see if any changes need to be made before the hatch is drawn. When using this option, the **Boundary Hatch and Fill** dialog box is temporarily closed and the hatch is shown as it will be drawn with the current settings. When finished previewing the hatch, press [Esc] to return to the dialog box, or right-click or press [Enter] to accept the hatch pattern. If the [Esc] key is pressed, the **Boundary Hatch and Fill** dialog box is displayed again. You may change the hatch pattern, scale, or rotation angle as needed and preview the hatch again. When you are satisfied with the hatch, pick the **OK** button in the **Boundary Hatch and Fill** dialog box to apply the hatch to the drawing.

## Hatch Pattern Association

The **BHATCH** command creates associative hatch patterns by default. However, you can choose to create nonassociative patterns. The **Composition** area of the **Boundary Hatch and Fill** dialog box has two radio buttons. The **Associative** option is on by default.

*Associative hatch patterns* update automatically when the boundary is edited. If the boundary is stretched, scaled, or otherwise edited, the hatch pattern automatically fills the new area with the original hatch pattern as long as there is a closed area to fill. This is because the hatch is "associated" with the boundary.

A *nonassociative pattern* is not "associated" with the boundary and, therefore, is not updated when the boundary is edited. For example, if you scale the hatch boundary, the hatch pattern is not scaled. To scale both the boundary and the hatch, select both items before editing. If the boundary is stretched, the hatch will not update, even if it is part of the stretch selection.

**Professional Tip**

When creating an associative hatch, it is best to specify only one internal point per hatch placement. If you specify more than one internal point in the same operation, AutoCAD creates one hatch object from all points picked. This can cause unexpected results when trying to edit what appears to be a separate hatch object.

## Exercise 19-5

- ◆ Open ex19-4.
- ◆ Create a layer named E-Hatch and set it current.
- ◆ Freeze the E-Floor & Plate layer if it is thawed.
- ◆ Experiment with hatches for the elevations. Add patterns for the roofing and for the siding. Refer to **Figure 19-17** for samples.
- ◆ If the hatch is hatching parts of islands, try removing the island from the selection or use the **Advanced** tab to set the **Outer** island detection style current.
- ◆ Save the drawing as ex19-5.

## Correcting Errors in the Boundary

If there is an error in the hatch boundary, the **BHATCH** command will not work. The most common error is a gap in the boundary. This can be very small and difficult to detect, and results when you do not "close" geometry or do not use object snaps for accuracy. However, AutoCAD is quick to let you know by displaying the **Boundary Definition Error** alert box. See **Figure 19-27**. Pick the **OK** button. Then, find and correct the problem. This error message also appears if you pick a point outside of any areas that can be used as boundaries.

**Figure 19-28** shows an object where the corner does not close. The error is too small to see at the current zoom level. However, using the **ZOOM** command reveals the problem. Fix the error and use the **BHATCH** command again.

**Figure 19-27.**
A **Boundary Definition Error** alert box is displayed if problems occur during the boundary creation process.

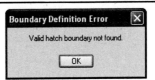

**Figure 19-28.**
An open boundary may not be visible at the current zoom level. However, when you zoom in on the area, the error is obvious.

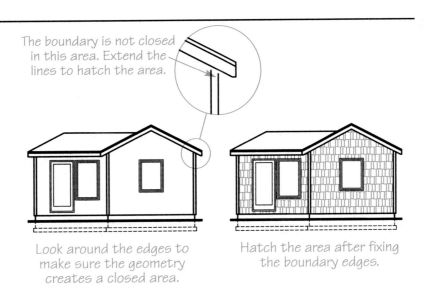

The boundary is not closed in this area. Extend the lines to hatch the area.

Look around the edges to make sure the geometry creates a closed area.

Hatch the area after fixing the boundary edges.

## Improving Boundary Hatching Speed

Normally, the **BHATCH** command evaluates all geometry visible on screen to establish the boundary. In most situations, boundary hatching works with satisfactory speed. However, this process can take some time on a large drawing or if many blocks are visible. You can improve the hatching speed and resolve other potential problems using options found in the **Advanced** tab in the **Boundary Hatch and Fill** dialog box. See **Figure 19-29**.

The drop-down list in the **Boundary set** area specifies what is evaluated when hatching. The default setting is Current viewport. If you want to limit what AutoCAD evaluates when hatching, you can define the boundary area so the **BHATCH** command only considers a specified portion of the drawing. To do this, pick the **New** button *before* selecting objects or internal points to hatch. Then, at the Select objects: prompt, draw a window enclosing the features to be hatched. You do not have to be very

Figure 19-29.
The **Advanced** tab of the **Boundary Hatch and Fill** dialog box provides options for improving hatching efficiency, including the ability to define a boundary set.

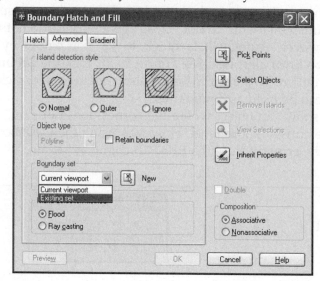

precise as long as all features to be hatched are enclosed in the window. This is demonstrated in **Figure 19-30.** After selecting the object(s), the **Boundary Hatch and Fill** dialog box returns. The drop-down list in the **Boundary set** area now displays Existing set, as shown in **Figure 19-29.** Only the objects inside the "existing set" are evaluated when the hatch is drawn. The "existing" boundary set remains defined until another is created.

When you use the **BHATCH** command and pick an internal area to be hatched, AutoCAD automatically creates a temporary boundary around the area. If the **Retain boundaries** check box is unchecked, the temporary boundaries are automatically removed when the hatch is applied. However, if you check the **Retain boundaries** check box, the hatch boundaries are kept when the hatch is applied.

Figure 19-30.
A boundary set limits the area evaluated by AutoCAD during a boundary hatching operation. (3D-DZYN)

When the **Retain boundaries** check box is checked, the **Object type** drop-down list is enabled. See **Figure 19-31.** The drop-down list has two options—**Polyline** (the default) and **Region**. If **Polyline** is selected, the boundary is retained as a polyline object around the hatched area. If **Region** is selected, the boundary is retained as a region. A *region* is a closed, two-dimensional area with mass, similar to a piece of paper.

**Figure 19-31.**
There are two options for the boundary object type. These options are only available if the **Retain boundaries** check box is checked.

Select an object type

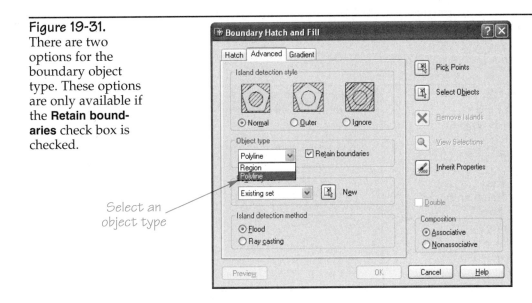

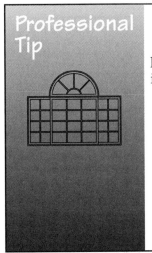

**Professional Tip**

There are several techniques to help save time when hatching, especially large and complex drawings. These include:

- Zoom in on the area to be hatched to make defining the boundary easier.
- Preview the hatch before you apply it. This allows you to make adjustments without undoing or editing the hatch.
- Turn off layers containing objects that might interfere with defining hatch boundaries.
- Create boundary sets of small areas within a complex drawing.

## Editing Hatch Patterns

You can edit hatch boundaries and hatch patterns with grips and editing commands such as **ERASE, COPY, MOVE, ROTATE,** and **SCALE**. If a hatch pattern is associative, editing the hatch boundary is automatically reflected in the hatch.

A convenient way to edit a hatch pattern is by using the **HATCHEDIT** command. You can access this command by picking **Hatch...** in the **Object** cascading menu in the **Modify** pull-down menu, picking the **Edit Hatch** button on the **Modify II** toolbar, or entering he or hatchedit at the Command prompt. You can also select a hatch pattern, right-click, and select **Hatch Edit...** from the shortcut menu, or simply double-click on the hatch pattern.

HATCHEDIT
HE

Modify
➥ Object
➥ Hatch...

Modify II
toolbar

Edit Hatch

When you select a hatch pattern, the **Hatch Edit** dialog box is displayed. See **Figure 19-32.** The **Hatch Edit** dialog box has the same features as the **Boundary Hatch and Fill** dialog box, except only the items controlling hatch pattern characteristics are available. You cannot create new boundaries or hatch new areas.

The available features work just like they do in the **Boundary Hatch and Fill** dialog box. You can change the pattern type, scale, or angle, remove the associative qualities, set the inherit properties of an existing hatch pattern, or use the **Advanced** tab options to edit the hatch pattern. You can also preview the edited hatch before updating it in the drawing.

**Figure 19-32.**
The **Hatch Edit** dialog box is used to edit hatch patterns and appears very similar to the **Boundary Hatch and Fill** dialog box. Notice that only the options related to hatch characteristics are available.

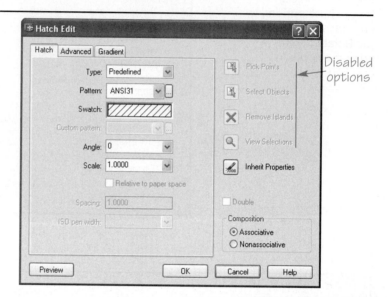

## Exercise 19-6

◆ Open ex19-5.
◆ Use the **HATCHEDIT** command to change the hatch patterns you used on the elevations.
◆ Try changing the scale of the hatch patterns.
◆ Save the drawing as ex19-6.

# Finishing the Elevations

Direct projection was used to create the house elevations, so the views need to be rotated for all of the elevations to be "right side up". Use the **MOVE** command and move the elevations to the side of the drawing. Then, rotate each elevation the appropriate rotation angle. For example, the right-side elevation is rotated 270° (–90°), the rear elevation is rotated 180°, and the left-side elevation is rotated 90° (–270°). Make sure all objects on all elevation layers are being moved and rotated. **Figure 19-33** displays the house elevations moved and rotated for readability.

After the elevations have been repositioned, notes reflecting the type of building materials are added. Any building-specific notes are also added to the elevations, such as the subfloor and plate line locations. Dimensions can be added to the elevations. The wall heights can be dimensioned from the subfloor to the plate lines. The roof overhangs are dimensioned on the elevations, and the chimney height is dimensioned for any fireplaces.

**Figure 19-33.**
The house elevations organized for readability.

Front Elevation

Left Side Elevation

Right Side Elevation

Rear Elevation

## Exercise 19-7

◆ Open ex19-6.
◆ Move the elevations to the side of the drawing.
◆ Rotate the right side elevation 270°, the rear elevation 180°, and the left side elevation 90°.
◆ Create the following layers:
  ◆ E-Notes
  ◆ E-Dims
◆ Use the **QLEADER** command to create notes that point to the building materials on your elevations.
◆ Dimension the wall heights and overhangs on the elevations.
◆ Your elevations should look similar to **Figure 19-33**.
◆ Save the drawing as ex19-7.

# Using Gradient Fills

As previously discussed, hatch patterns can be used to create shaded features. In **Figure 19-33**, a hatch pattern is used for the shading in the front elevation. Another way to apply shading is to use gradient fills. A *gradient fill* is a smooth transition between a darker shade of color and a lighter shade of color. See **Figure 19-34**. Gradient fills can be added by accessing the **Gradient** tab in the **Boundary Hatch and Fill** dialog box. See **Figure 19-35**.

When adding gradient fills to your drawings, you have the choice of using a one-color or two-color gradient fill. The **One color** option provides a smooth transition of your color choice, lightening it to a white color or darkening it to a black color. See **Figure 19-36A**. The **Two color** option uses a smooth transition of one color to another color. See **Figure 19-36B**.

**Figure 19-34.**
The use of gradient fills in this elevation provides the illusion of light hitting the building.

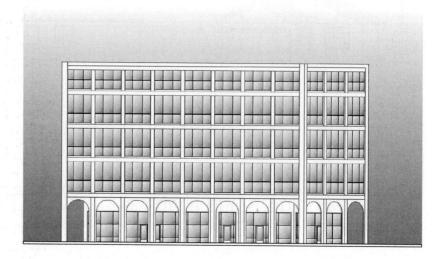

**Figure 19-35.**
The **Gradient** tab in the **Boundary Hatch and Fill** dialog box allows you to add gradient fills into an enclosed area similar to a hatch pattern.

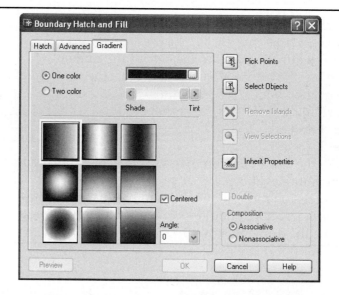

**Figure 19-36.**
A—A one-color gradient fill. B—A two-color gradient fill.

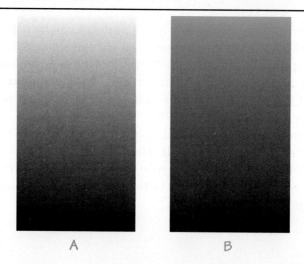

A                    B

When using a one-color fill, a color swatch is available to the right of the **One color** radio button. The swatch indicates the current color being used. Select the ellipsis button [...] to access the **Select Color** dialog box, where a different color can be chosen. Below the color swatch is the **Shade and Tint** slider. Sliding the bar changes the tint (the chosen color mixed with white) or shade (the chosen color mixed with black).

When using a two-color fill, the **Shade and Tint** slider is changed to another color swatch. This is used for the selection of the second gradient color.

Below the color radio buttons are nine different types of fills that can be used. When the color is changed, the gradient pattern buttons change to reflect your chosen settings. These patterns include linear sweep, spherical, and parabolic fills. Select the type of fill you wish to use.

To the right of the gradient patterns is the **Centered** check box. When a check is placed in the box, the gradient configuration remains symmetrical throughout the filled area. If this is not selected, the fill is shifted up and to the left, creating the illusion of a light source to the left of the fill area.

Below the **Centered** check box is an **Angle** drop-down list. This list specifies the angle of the gradient fill. You can select one of the predefined angles from the list or enter a different angle in the text box.

**Professional Tip**

Another way to insert hatch patterns is to use the **SUPERHATCH** command available with the AutoCAD Express Tools. If the Express Tools are installed, this command can be accessed from the **Draw** cascading menu in the **Express** pull-down menu. You can also enter superhatch at the Command prompt. Using the **SUPERHATCH** command is similar to normal hatching. However, instead of using predefined patterns, it allows you to use an image, block, external reference, or wipeout as a hatch pattern. Sample image files for hatching buildings can be found in the Textures folder in the AutoCAD 2004 Documents and Settings folder path. Access the **AutoCAD Express Tools Help** window for more information about the **SUPERHATCH** command.

# Creating Interior Elevations

At the beginning of this chapter, two different techniques for creating elevations were discussed. The direct projection method was used to create elevations for the house drawing. The following discussion explains how to lay out interior elevations for the house using the dimensional layout technique. Either technique can be used to lay out interior or exterior elevations.

Interior elevations are used to show how the interior of a structure is to appear. For example, an interior elevation may show details such as where a bathroom mirror is located or how the casework in the kitchen is to appear. In some offices, interior elevations are drawn for every room of a building. In this situation, simple walls with no details can contain extra information found on more detailed interior elevation walls. To eliminate unnecessary information, interior elevations may take a simple, common wall and note it as a typical interior wall.

In residential work, it is common to draw interior elevations of the kitchen, bathrooms, and any walls that have a special feature. Special features may include a bookcase, fireplace mantle, paneling, or archway entrance. In commercial work, interior elevations may include bathrooms, a typical office or room, or a wall with special features. Special features found in commercial construction include a library wall, food bar, or a decorative wall with pilasters, paneling, and arches.

## Interior Elevation Names

The names of exterior elevations are derived from the direction the side of the building faces. With interior elevations, the names of wall elevations are based on the direction from which the viewer is looking at the wall. See **Figure 19-37.** The cardinal direction plus the room name is the title of the elevation. If the location of an interior elevation is obvious by identification of the room from where it is created, the elevation may simply be labeled as KITCHEN, or BATH 1. Another basic practice is to place an interior elevation key symbol on the floor plan, correlating to the same symbol identifying the related interior elevation.

**Figure 19-37.**
Naming interior elevations. The arrows indicate the direction from which the elevation is viewed.

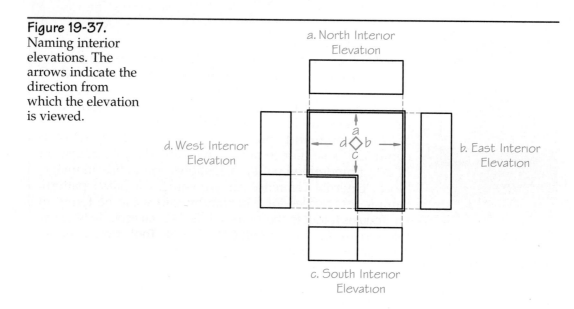

a. North Interior Elevation

d. West Interior Elevation

b. East Interior Elevation

c. South Interior Elevation

## Interior Elevation Layout

The dimensional layout technique uses a series of layout lines similar to the direct projection system. However, elevations are not created around the floor plans, as in the direct projection system. Instead, the dimensions of the floor plans are referenced to locate the walls, doors, and windows in the elevations.

The first step in the dimensional layout method is to reference the drawing. This can be done by either printing a copy of the dimensioned floor plans to use as a reference or by using xrefs. This discussion uses xrefs to reference the house floor plan.

The layout of the interior elevations includes only the interior wall lines, the finished floor and ceiling lines, and any detail on the wall itself. Knowledge of where the floor lines and ceiling lines are located is important and helps you "paint the picture" of how the interior of the building looks. Before creating the interior elevations, the types of cabinetry, sizes and heights of counters, and finishing materials should be known. Typical kitchen counters are 36" high. Typical bathroom cabinets are 30" to 33" high. **Figure 19-38** shows typical kitchen and bathroom cabinetry with dimensions for reference.

Architectural Drafting Using AutoCAD

**Figure 19-38.**
Kitchen and bathroom cabinets.

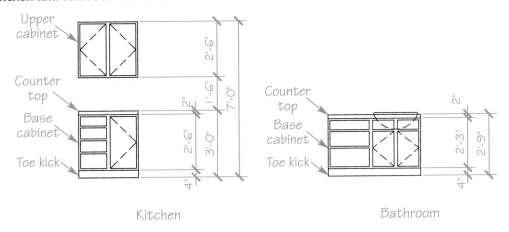

When creating the interior elevations, the elevation boundary represents the outermost edge of the interior of the room. When components such as cabinetry, beams, and soffits project toward the viewer, a line is drawn around the outermost edge of the component. Anything within the wall boundary line represents items along the wall being viewed, as shown in **Figure 19-39.**

Once you have a reference for the elevations, lay out the finished floor and ceiling lines as you did for the exterior elevations. This establishes the wall height for the interior elevations and is the beginning of the layout lines. You are not creating the elevations around the floor plans, so all floor and plate lines can be initially drawn parallel, as shown in **Figure 19-40.**

After the floor and plate lines are drawn, sketch the wall placements. Draw a vertical line through each of the floor and plate lines for each elevation. This line represents one edge of one of your elevations. Using the floor plan dimensions or the **DIST** command as a reference, offset the vertical line the distance to the other interior corners of the room. Next, draw lines for the floor and ceiling, connecting the wall lines for each elevation. **Figure 19-41** displays the interior elevation wall, floor, and ceiling lines laid out for the kitchen and two bathrooms.

**Figure 19-39.**
The outline of an interior elevation.

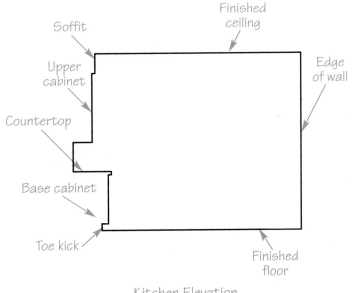

Kitchen Elevation

**Figure 19-40.**
As the different rooms are referenced, lay out floor and plate lines for each room.

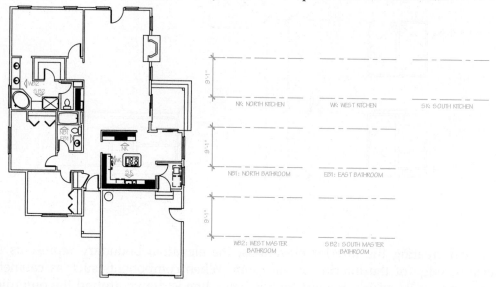

**Figure 19-41.**
Reference the floor plan for the placement of walls. Use the **DIST** command with the **OFFSET** command to lay out the walls in the elevations.

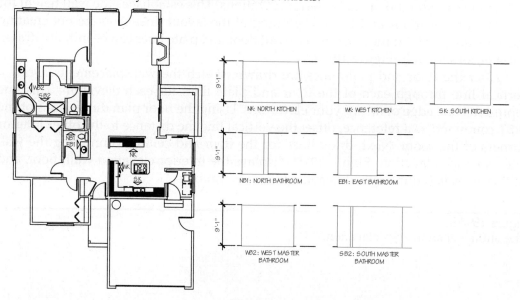

## Adding the Doors and Windows

After the walls have been laid out, the doors and windows are added to the elevations. Refer to the floor plan dimensions for locations. Place the doors and windows on the elevations at their correct sizes. Use the **DIST** command if needed to measure the width of doors on the floor plans.

Previously, in the exterior elevations, it was determined that the door and window headers would be 7'-0" from the floor. Offset the floor lines up 7'-0" to be used as a reference for the door and window heights. Refer to the exterior elevations for the height of the windows where required.

If doors are included in the elevations, detail them the way you would like interior doors to appear. In the case where an opening is present along a wall without a door, draw the opening as it should appear, such as arched or rectangular. You can also include trim boards and other detail, if you desire. **Figure 19-42** displays the interior elevations with door or window openings added.

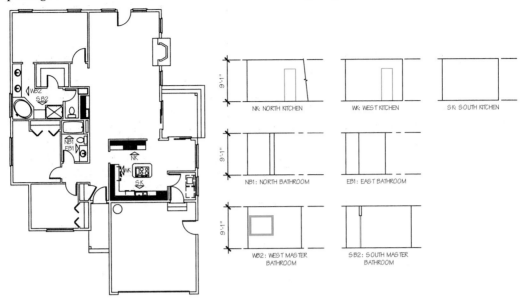

## Adding Detail

Now that the wall, door, and window locations have been added to the interior elevations, additional details such as casework, plumbing fixtures, and appliances can be added. This will help "tell the story" of how the interior of the building will look. Begin offsetting the wall, floor, and ceiling lines as required to establish casework, soffit, and appliance locations. **Figure 19-43** provides an example of different heights and widths for casework and appliances.

After the casework locations have been placed, use the **TRIM** and **EXTEND** commands as needed to clean up the detail. Notice in **Figure 19-43** the exterior boundary of each elevation follows the outlines of items that are being projected or coming toward the viewer (such as casework). This provides an odd-shaped elevation but displays to the viewer items that are viewed against the wall being viewed.

The next step, after the layout of the casework and appliances, is the detailing to be done on the casework and appliances. Add door and drawer locations to the casework. Add special casework detailing such as door configurations, trim, and glass. Tile can be added with hatching along the backsplash and counter edges. This provides the viewer with the sense of how the finished interior elevations will appear when the building is constructed.

## Adding Notes and Dimensions

After the interior elevations are completed, notes and dimensions are added to complete the drawings. Many architectural offices use a keynote noting system. A *keynote system* uses a number with a leader line pointing to an area or object that has an associated note. The number relates to a keynote legend. This legend explains the type of note the number is referencing. Appendix E provides examples of keynotes, legends, and a list of commonly used keynotes. **Figure 19-44** displays the final interior elevations for the house noted with keynotes and a keynote legend.

Dimensions are also placed on elevations. These dimensions show the different floor and plate heights. In addition, any features that cannot be dimensioned on the floor plans are dimensioned in an elevation.

## Figure 19-43.

Kitchen and bathroom plans with interior elevations. (Alan Mascord Design Associates, Inc.)

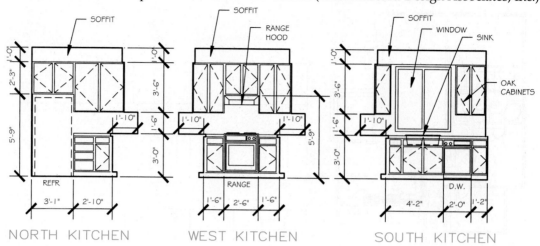

NORTH KITCHEN          WEST KITCHEN          SOUTH KITCHEN

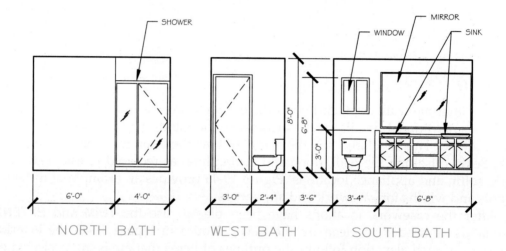

NORTH BATH          WEST BATH          SOUTH BATH

## Exercise 19-8

◆ Start a new drawing using one of your templates.
◆ Create the following layers:
  ◆ X-Floor Plan
  ◆ I-Walls
  ◆ I-Door & Win
  ◆ I-Casework
  ◆ I-Appliances
  ◆ I-Plumbing
  ◆ I-Dims
  ◆ I-Note
◆ Xref in ex16-8 using the **Overlay** option.
◆ Create interior elevations for the kitchen and the two bathrooms.
◆ Place any notes desired.
◆ Add dimensions to the elevations.
◆ Save the drawing as ex19-8. Your drawing should look similar to **Figure 19-44**.

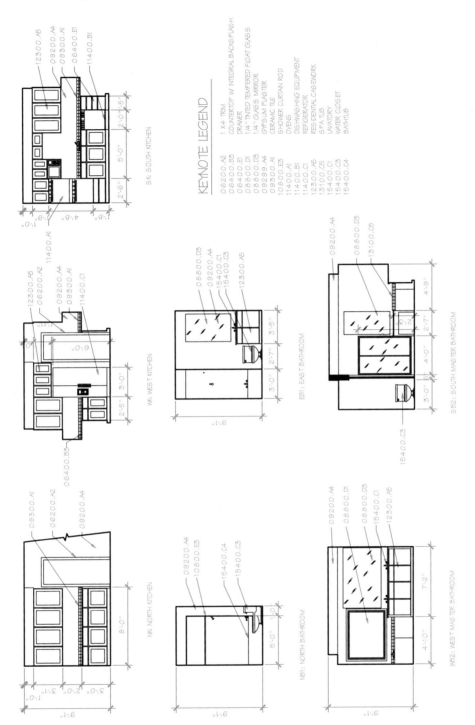

# Chapter Test

*Answer the following questions on a separate sheet of paper.*

1. Briefly describe elevations and the type of information they provide.
2. Describe the direct projection method of creating an elevation.
3. Explain the dimensional layout method of creating an elevation.
4. What is the determining factor when selecting a scale for elevations?
5. Name the two common roof framing methods.
6. In one of the common roof framing methods, a notch is cut in the rafter. What is this notch called?
7. Define *span*.
8. Name the construction member placed over door and window openings to support the wall and roof above.
9. Which AutoCAD command is used to automatically fill an enclosed area with a hatch pattern?
10. What are *islands*, as related to hatching?
11. Define *associative hatch patterns*.
12. What happens if you edit the boundary of a nonassociative hatch pattern?
13. What happens if you attempt to hatch an area inside of a boundary that is not completely closed?
14. Define *region*.
15. Name the command used to edit hatch patterns.
16. What is the definition of a *gradient fill*?
17. What is the purpose of interior elevations?
18. What is a *keynote system*?

# Chapter Problems

*For Problems 1–4, create elevations for the projects as shown on the following pages. Use the following general procedure:*

A. Start a new drawing and create appropriate layers.
B. Use the floor plan and elevation drawings for reference.
C. Draw and dimension the elevations for the assigned project.
D. Save the completed drawing as 19-ResA, 19-ResB, 19-Multifamily, or 19-Commercial, whichever is appropriate for the project.

1.

Residential A

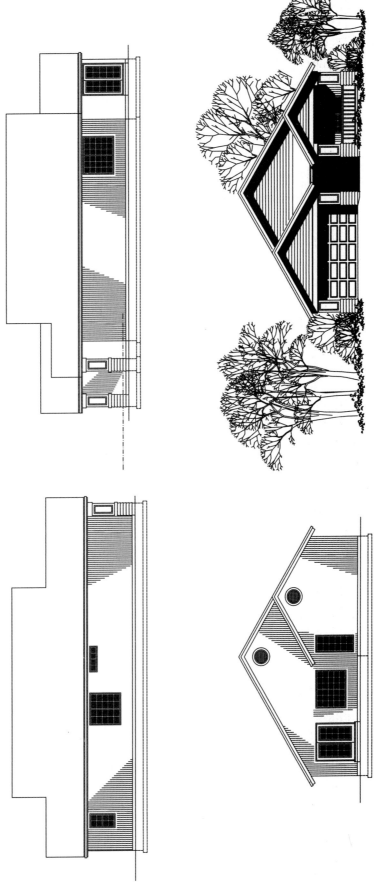

(Alan Mascord Design Associates, Inc.)

Residential B

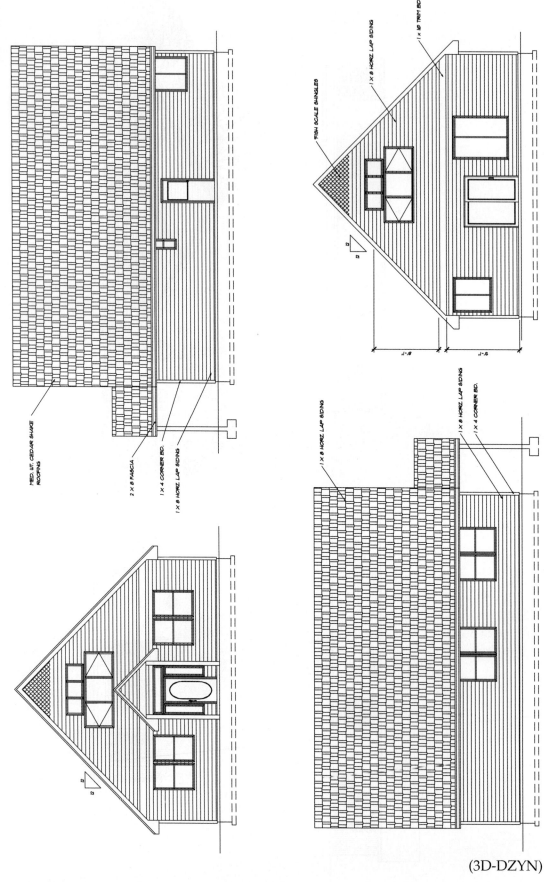

MED. WT. CEDAR SHAKE ROOFING

2 X 8 FASCIA

1 X 4 CORNER BD.

1 X 8 HORZ LAP SIDING

FISH SCALE SHINGLES

1 X 8 HORZ LAP SIDING

1 X 10 TRIM BD.

1 X 8 HORZ LAP SIDING

1 X 8 HORZ LAP SIDING

1 X 4 CORNER BD.

(3D-DZYN)

3.

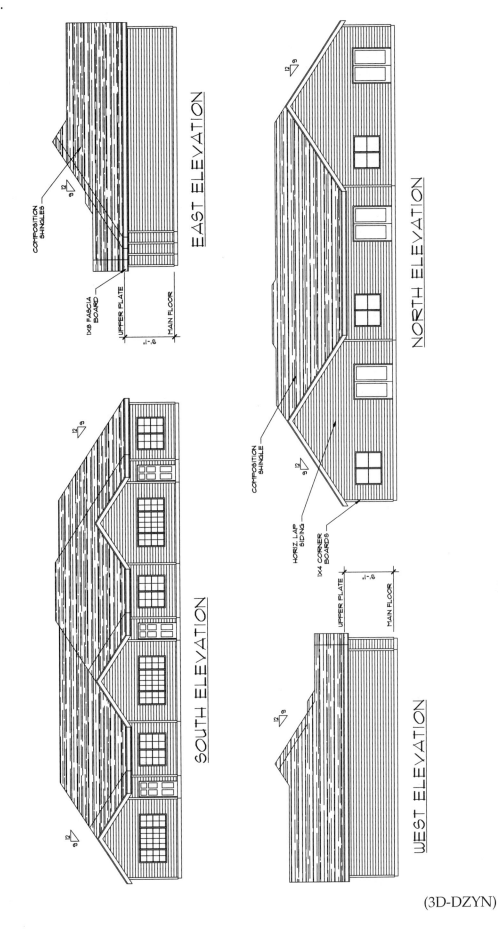

EAST ELEVATION

COMPOSITION
SHINGLES

IX8 FASCIA
BOARD

UPPER PLATE

MAIN FLOOR

9'-1"

NORTH ELEVATION

COMPOSITION
SHINGLE

HORIZ. LAP
SIDING

IX4 CORNER
BOARDS

UPPER PLATE

MAIN FLOOR

9'-1"

SOUTH ELEVATION

WEST ELEVATION

(3D-DZYN)

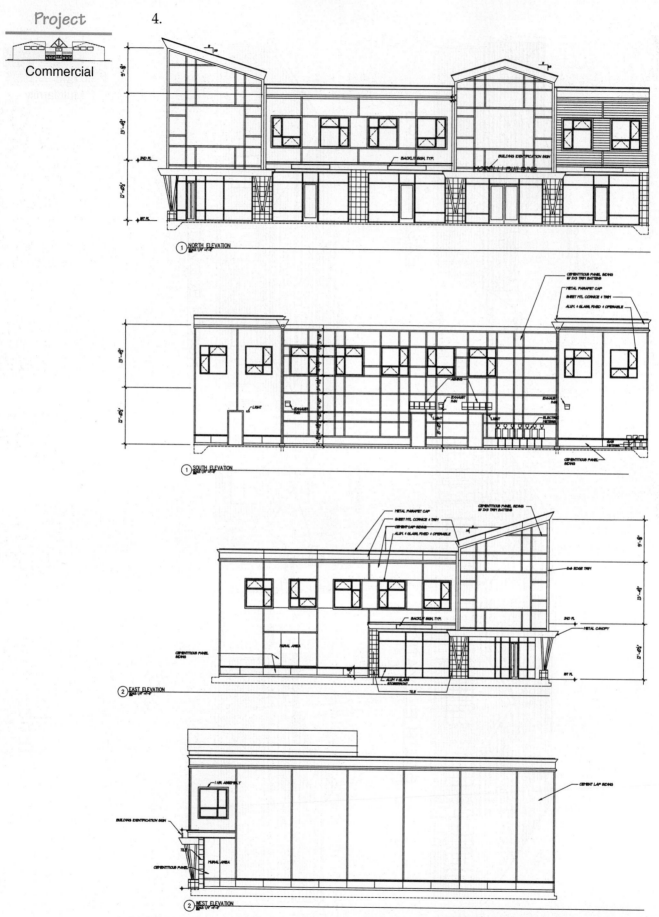

1 NORTH ELEVATION

1 SOUTH ELEVATION

2 EAST ELEVATION

2 WEST ELEVATION

(Cynthia Bankey Architect, Inc.)

C H A P T E R 20

# Drawing Sections and Details

## Learning Objectives

After completing this chapter, you will be able to:

- Identify different construction methods.
- Draw cutting-plane lines on plan drawings.
- Place detail bubbles on plans.
- Draw sections for different construction methods.
- Draw details.
- Create working views.
- Create and use tiled viewports.
- Use keynotes where appropriate.

## Important Terms

balloon framing
birdsmouth
blocking
bottom chord
bridging
cavity
cutting-plane line
detail sheet
details
double top plate
finish grade line
floating viewport
foundation details
full section

grout
partial section
platform framing
rake
rebar
roof details
room tag
section
stair framing details
tiled viewport
top chord
truss connector
view
wall details

Sections are very important in the design, drafting, and building processes. A *section* shows internal components of a structure or portion of a structure as they would appear if cut by an imaginary plane. After slicing the structure, you are able to view the internal construction of the building. See **Figure 20-1.** Sections are used to describe the construction methods used to create the structure, from the roof down to the foundation.

In the early stages of design, sections are used to study the vertical relationships of spaces in the building. Once the construction document phase is started, sections are used to verify vertical space, as well as explain construction methods and placements of walls, joists, and beams. During the construction process, sections are used to explain how the structure is put together.

**Figure 20-1.**
A section is created by slicing through the building.

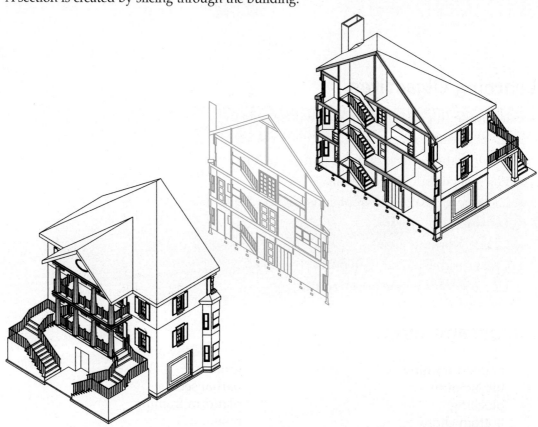

## Sectioning Basics

Before creating a section, you need to know where to "slice" the structure. Section "cuts" or "slices" are indicated on the floor plan. **Figure 20-2** shows how the cut lines are displayed on a drawing. The cut line is called a *cutting-plane line.* The cutting-plane line consists of a "bubble" with an arrow indicating the direction from which you are viewing the sectioned portion of the building. A letter at the top of the bubble indicates the section label. The number at the bottom of the bubble indicates the page where the section can be found. There are three types of sections that can be created for construction documents—a full section, partial section, and detail.

A *full section* creates a cross section through the entire building. See **Figure 20-3.** A full section shows the general construction practices of the building.

Architectural Drafting Using AutoCAD

## Figure 20-2.
The section cutting-plane lines on the floor plan (shown in color) indicate where each section will be sliced. The arrows indicate the direction from which the sectioned portion of the building is viewed.

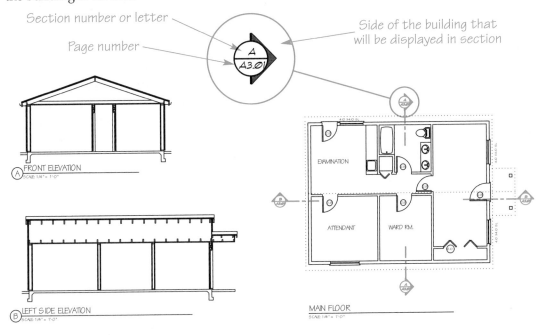

## Figure 20-3.
A full section drawing. (Alan Mascord Design Associates, Inc.)

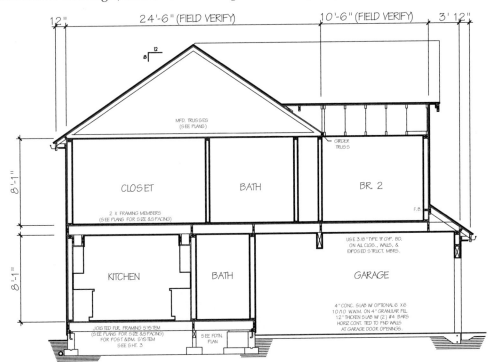

A *partial section* displays only a portion of the building. A partial section is used when more detail is required in a specific area. Usually, a partial section is used to indicate special framing or construction techniques used in a particular feature of the design. See **Figure 20-4.** There are two methods to indicate a partial section. The first method uses a bubble similar to the section cutting-plane line for a full section, except the cutting-plane line is not drawn through the entire floor plan. The second method uses a thick, dashed polyline drawn around an area on the full section, along with a bubble indicating the partial section number and page. See **Figure 20-5.**

*Details* provide more information than found in full sections. Similar to full and partial sections, a detail has a location bubble on the floor plan indicating where the detail can be found. See **Figure 20-6.** Details generally show one small area of the building, such as a foundation footing, floor framing, or roof framing section. These are drawn at a larger scale than the full or partial sections, because more information is presented. See **Figure 20-7.**

**Figure 20-4.**
A partial section drawing. (Cynthia Bankey Architect, Inc.)

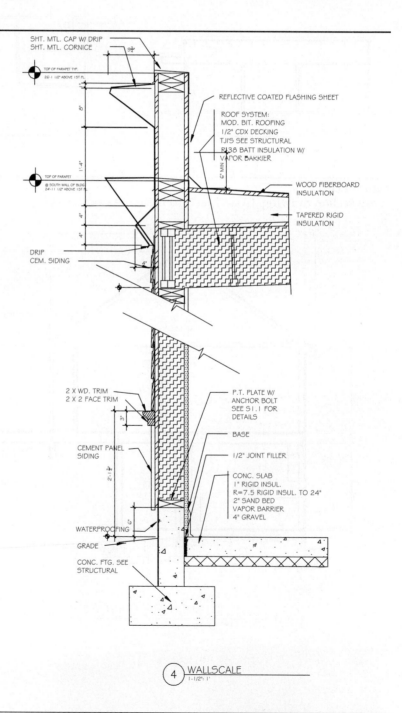

Architectural Drafting Using AutoCAD

**Figure 20-5.**
The two methods of indicating a partial section. (Cynthia Bankey Architect, Inc.)

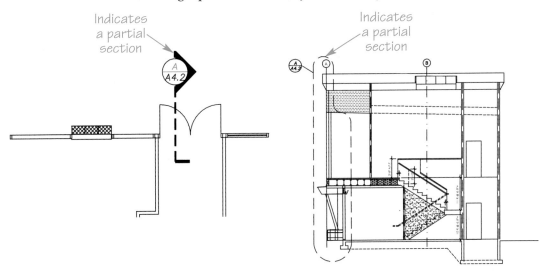

**Figure 20-6.**
Use a detail bubble on the floor plan to indicate the detail drawing for the specified location.

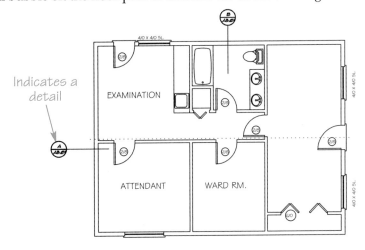

**Figure 20-7.**
A typical detail drawing. (Cynthia Bankey Architect, Inc.)

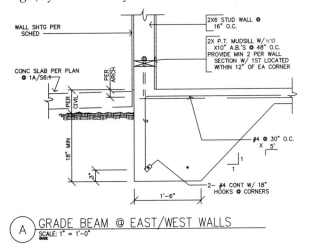

After indicating the cutting-plane line location, you should have an idea of how the building is constructed and what materials are used. Some things to consider before creating sections are:
- Type of foundation.
- Wall construction methods.
- Size of beams, joists, and columns.
- Plate heights.
- Roof pitch.
- Type of exterior building materials.

# Construction Techniques

In order to draw a section, it is very important to understand foundations, framing, and other typical construction techniques. The three main types of foundation systems are floor joist, post and beam, and concrete slab. Foundation systems are discussed in Chapter 18. The two main types of framing systems are balloon framing and platform framing. Framing systems can vary depending on the project, location, and building authority.

## Balloon Framing

*Balloon framing* uses exterior wall studs that are continuous from the first floor to the roof assembly. See **Figure 20-8.** Wood has a tendency to shrink as the moisture content decreases. Wood tends to shrink more in width than in length. With a single stud, vertical shrinkage is minimized, thus maintaining the height of the structure.

**Figure 20-8.**
Balloon framing construction.

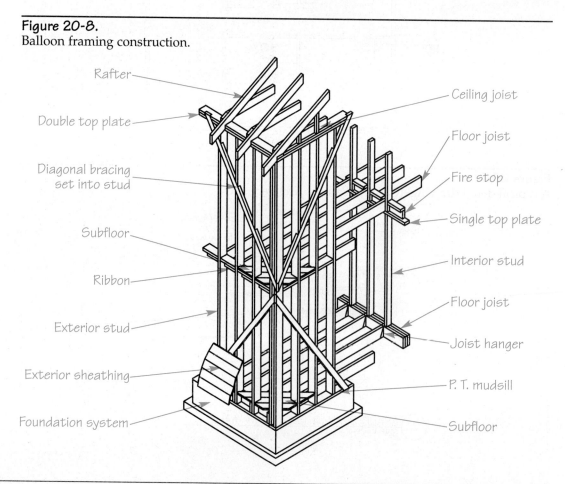

Labels: Rafter, Double top plate, Diagonal bracing set into stud, Subfloor, Ribbon, Exterior stud, Exterior sheathing, Foundation system, Ceiling joist, Floor joist, Fire stop, Single top plate, Interior stud, Floor joist, Joist hanger, P. T. mudsill, Subfloor

Architectural Drafting Using AutoCAD

Since balloon framing uses continuous studs, there is a problem with fire control. If a fire occurs on the lower floor, it can quickly spread to the upper levels because the wood studs extend the total height of the structure. To help prevent this, *blocking* is added at each level between the studs.

Another disadvantage of balloon framing is the required length of wood studs. For example, a two-story balloon framed house requires studs that are 18' or 20' in length.

Balloon framing was popular in the 19th century but is not commonly used anymore. However, a knowledge of balloon framing construction can be helpful. Balloon framing is quickly being replaced by platform framing techniques.

## Platform Framing

Platform framing is the most commonly used method of framing. With *platform framing,* each floor of a structure is built on a framed platform. Buildings with this type of framing can be built higher than with balloon framing because the stud length is not an issue. See **Figure 20-9.**

Each floor platform is used as the fire blocking between floors in platform framing. This eliminates the need to place individual blocking between the studs. Diagonal bracing may be added to brace the floors, as in balloon framing. However, this is less common in platform framing. Plywood sheathing is generally used to brace the structure. Check with the local building authority on the use of bracing for your area.

**Figure 20-9.**
Platform framing construction.

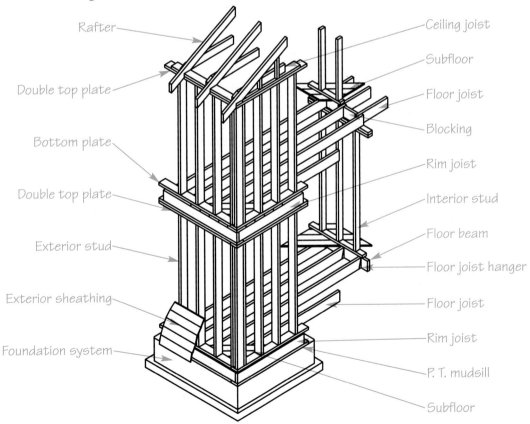

Chapter 16 introduced some wall framing conventions. Masonry, wood, and steel construction are all popular methods of wall framing. Masonry construction is often used where wood availability is limited and can be more common in warmer climates. Wood is a very common framing material, especially with residential and light commercial buildings. Steel framing competes with wood framing as it is not a fire danger and does not shrink. Any of these methods can be used when building a structure. Cost, availability, jurisdiction requirements, and building usage should be considered when choosing a type of framing material.

## Masonry Construction

Masonry construction can be found in commercial, industrial, and residential projects. The main elements used are brick and concrete blocks. Typically, the masonry walls are built on top of a concrete slab foundation with an expanded footing. See **Figure 20-10.** This is due to the weight of the masonry walls.

When using brick as a construction material, two rows of brick are laid, separated by a 2″ airspace. This airspace is called a *cavity* and is typically filled with insulation material. In areas of high winds, the cavity is filled with a bonding material known as *grout.* In these situations, iron bars, called *rebar,* are placed in the cavity. The grout and rebar provide reinforcement to the wall.

Concrete block can also be used for construction. The advantage of concrete block over brick is the lesser amount of materials and labor required. The block is generally wider than brick. Instead of two rows of brick, only one row of block is required. Just like the brick walls, the interior of the concrete wall can be filled with insulation or grout and rebar as the situation requires.

## Wood Construction

Wood construction is very popular across the country. Wood is easy to use, fairly economical, and readily available in most areas. Wood construction can be built on top of a floor joist, post and beam, or concrete slab foundation system. Wood construction consists of a bottom plate along the floor, studs sitting on top of the bottom plate, and a double top plate above the studs. See **Figure 20-11.**

**Figure 20-10.**
Masonry wall construction.

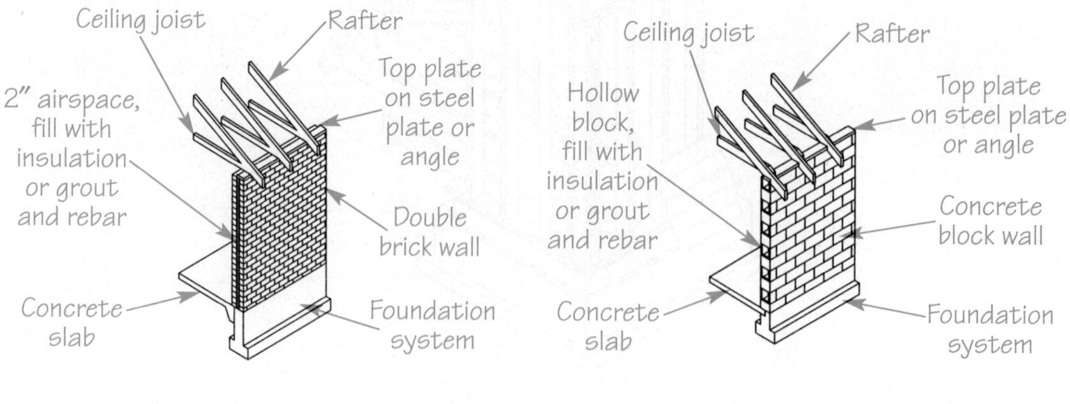

Architectural Drafting Using AutoCAD

**Figure 20-11.**
Wood framing
construction.

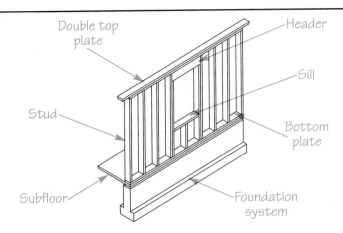

A *double top plate* is used to tie two or more walls together. The first top plate is placed above the studs along the total length of the wall. The second top plate is the piece tying the walls together. Blocking is sometimes used between the studs to help reinforce the wall section.

A masonry veneer is often applied to the exterior of wood construction. In this case, the wood walls are framed normally. Then, a masonry veneer is applied to the outside of the wall. When using a masonry veneer, the foundation wall is built with a ledge on which the masonry sits. See **Figure 20-12.**

**Figure 20-12.**
Wood construction
with a masonry
veneer applied to
the exterior.

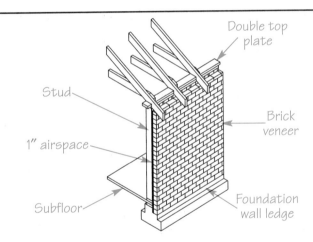

## Steel Construction

Steel construction has become a popular alternative to wood construction due to a number of advantages. Steel is lightweight, strong, preformed, and fireproof. A steel wall consists of a bottom channel, steel stud, and a top channel. See **Figure 20-13.** Sheathing can be applied to the exterior of the studs with self-tapping screws.

Steel studs can be used in construction similar to studs in balloon framing because there is no limit to the stud length. The studs can run through a few floors. The floor framing is attached to *bridging*. This is a steel channel running through the studs on which the joist can sit.

Steel framing also lends itself well to platform framing. In this case, a steel I-beam joist is placed on top of the top channel. The next floor is then framed in on top of the I-beam.

Figure 20-13.
Steel construction.

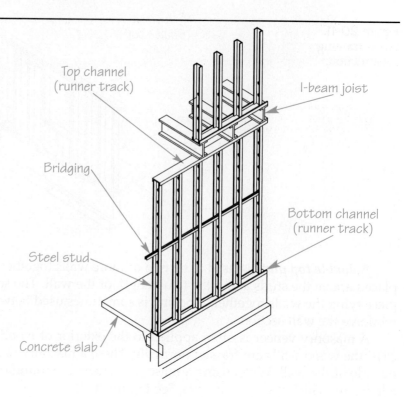

## Roofing Systems

There are two main conventions for drawing and building roofs—rafter construction and truss construction. Rafters are used in conventionally framed roofs. The rafter sits on top of the top plate of the wall and is seated in a notch cut into the rafter. This notch is called a **birdsmouth.** The birdsmouth is cut to fit on the top plate. To give the rafter support and create a ceiling, ceiling joists are also added beside each rafter. The ceiling joists also sit on the top plate and are nailed to the side of the rafter. See **Figure 20-14.**

Truss-framed roofs are prefabricated roofing systems. The truss consists of rafters, a ceiling joist, and diagonal webs. The ceiling joist, however, is not placed beside the rafter as in conventional framing. The rafter, which is also called the **top chord,** is placed on top of the ceiling joist, which is called the **bottom chord.** The top chord and bottom chord are nailed together with a **truss connector.** See **Figure 20-15.** The ends of the bottom chord are placed on the top plate. A birdsmouth is not used for trusses. Since trusses are prefabricated, they can be delivered to the job site and quickly placed into position.

Figure 20-14.
Rafter roof
construction.

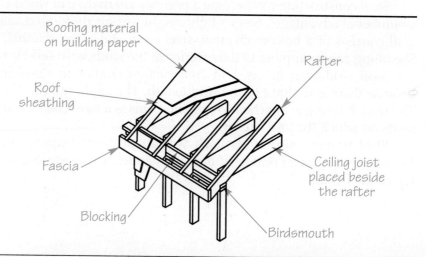

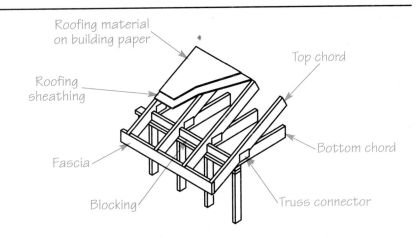

**Figure 20-15.**
Truss roof construction.

Labels: Roofing material on building paper, Roofing sheathing, Top chord, Fascia, Bottom chord, Blocking, Truss connector

# Locating the Section

Now that you have a basic understanding of how a building is constructed, the sections can be drawn. You must first determine where to place cutting-plane lines for the section on your floor plan. Things to consider when placing the cutting-plane lines are:

- What is to be shown?
- Are you going to show how the typical structural components are assembled?
- Is there a special building condition that needs to be shown?
- Are you trying to show a special feature, such as vaulted ceilings?

Once you have determined the placement for the cutting-plane lines, draw the lines on the floor plan. Cutting-plane lines for the house project from Chapter 16 are shown in **Figure 20-16.** The cutting-plane line bubble is typically a 1/2″ diameter circle with 3/32″ to 1/8″ lettering. Create an annotation block and insert it into the drawing using the scale factor of the drawing for the insertion scale. The arrow on the cutting-plane line bubble can be a separate block inserted and rotated as needed for the desired viewing direction.

Section cutting-plane lines should be added to each drawing through which the section cuts. For example, add the section cutting-plane lines to the foundation plan and all floor plans that can be seen in the section. However, this practice varies between offices. Some companies prefer to keep the section cutting-plane lines on only the foundation or floor plan, while other companies prefer to have the section cutting-plane lines on each plan.

Drawing sections is similar to drawing elevations. Subfloor and plate lines are used to obtain the spatial relationships of floors and establish where the vertical portions of the section are located on the drawing. Use the direct projection or dimensional layout procedures discussed in Chapter 19 to lay out the structural components of the section.

When using the direct projection method, you are often referring to a portion of the floor plan or the elevations to determine sizes of rooms or the location of doors and windows. If you find yourself referring to an area of the building often, use the **VIEW** command to create an enlarged view of the area. This saves you the time of zooming and panning around the drawing looking for a particular area to reference. Creating views is discussed in the next section.

**Figure 20-16.**
The section cutting-
plane lines for the
house drawing
project are deter-
mined and anno-
tated on the floor
plan.

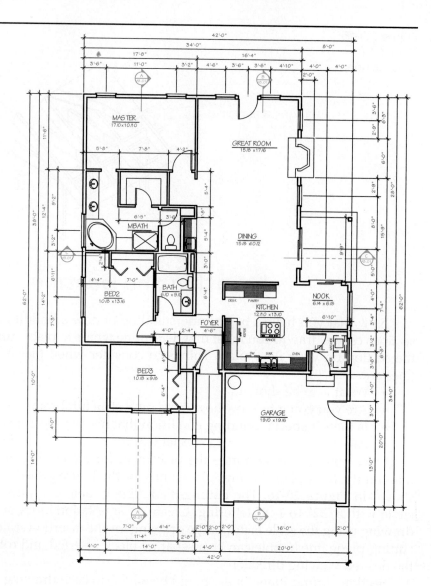

**Professional Tip**

If you create a cutting-plane line bubble block with text, the block must be exploded in order to change the text. Another way to add text to a bubble block is to define attributes with the block. Attributes can display text inside of the block. The advantage of attributes is the block does not have to be exploded in order to change the text. Attributes are discussed in Chapter 21 of this text.

## Creating a Working View

On a large drawing with a number of separate areas, using the **ZOOM** and **PAN** commands can be time-consuming. The **VIEW** command allows you to specify a certain part of the drawing and quickly restore that area. A *view* can be a small portion of the drawing, such as a zoomed-in area on a floor plan, or it can represent a large portion of the drawing, such as all the elevations. After the view is created, you can instruct AutoCAD to redisplay it at any time.

The **VIEW** command can be accessed by picking the **Named Views** button in the **View** toolbar, selecting **Named Views...** from the **View** pull-down menu, or entering v, view, or ddview at the Command prompt. This activates the **View** dialog box. See **Figure 20-17.** The **View** dialog box contains the **Named Views** and the **Orthographic & Isometric Views** tabs. The **Named Views** tab is where new views are defined. The **Orthographic & Isometric Views** tab provides preset views based on orthographic and isometric principles.

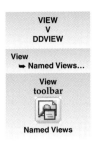

VIEW
V
DDVIEW

View
➥ Named Views...

View
toolbar

Named Views

## Named Views *Tab*

A list of currently defined views is shown in the **Named Views** tab. If you want to create a new view of what is currently displayed in the drawing window, pick the **New...** button to access the **New View** dialog box, **Figure 20-18.** Type a name for the view in the **View name:** text box. The **Current Display** radio button is active by default. This option creates a view based on the view currently displayed in the drawing area. Pick **OK** and the new view name is added to the list.

If you want to define a new view by windowing the view, pick the **Define window** radio button in the **New View** dialog box. Then, pick the **Define View Window** button. The **New View** and **View** dialog boxes are temporarily closed and the prompt Specify first corner: appears on the command line. Pick a first point and then a second point defining the corners of an area to use as a view. After the second corner is selected, the **New View** and **View** dialog boxes reappear. You can now add the new view based on the defined window.

**Figure 20-17.**
The **View** dialog box is used to save and restore views.

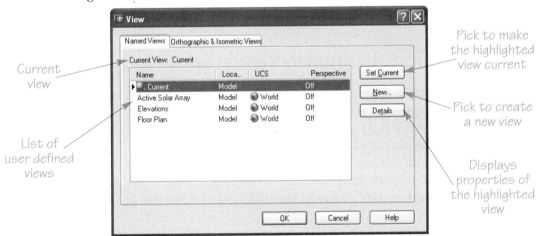

**Figure 20-18.**
The **New View** dialog box is used to define a new view.

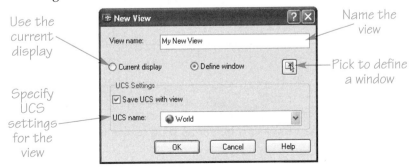

When creating a view, it is possible to save a named user coordinate system (UCS) with the view. The coordinate system determines where the origin (0,0,0) is for the X, Y, and Z axes. The world coordinate system (WCS) is the default coordinate system in AutoCAD. The **UCS** command is introduced in Chapter 25 of this text.

To make one of the listed views current, highlight its name in the list in the **Named Views** tab and pick the **Set Current** button. The name of the current view appears in the **Current View:** label. Pick the **OK** button to close the **View** dialog box and redisplay the drawing with the selected view.

To delete a saved view, open the **View** dialog box. Then, right-click on the view name in the list in the **Named Views** tab. A shortcut menu appears. Select **Delete** in the shortcut menu. The view name is removed from the list.

There are three other options in the shortcut menu displayed by right-clicking on a view name, **Figure 20-19.** You can set a view current with the **Set Current** option, use the **Rename** option to rename a view, or get a detailed description of the selected view by picking the **Details...** option. Selecting **Details...** from the shortcut menu opens the **View Details** dialog box, which provides a variety of information about the view. This dialog box can also be opened by selecting the **Details** button in the **View** dialog box.

**Figure 20-19.**
The shortcut menu displayed by right-clicking on a view name.

Set Current
Rename
Delete
Details...

## Orthographic & Isometric Views *Tab*

The **Orthographic & Isometric Views** tab in the **View** dialog box allows you to quickly choose a preset view based on orthographic or isometric principles. See **Figure 20-20.** The icons next to each view name represent the side of the drawing that will be viewed. The six orthogonal views are available. These are **Top, Bottom, Front, Back, Left,** and **Right**. There are also four standard isometric views available. These are **Southwest, Southeast, Northeast,** and **Northwest**. Highlight a view name and press the **Set Current** button to change the drawing view so you are looking at objects from the selected direction.

The isometric and orthographic views can also be selected from the **3D Views** cascading menu in the **View** pull-down menu or from the **View** toolbar. See **Figure 20-21.** The isometric and orthographic views are particularly helpful when drawing geometry in 3D. By using these different views, the front, back, and sides of a 3D building can be viewed. An introduction to 3D modeling is discussed in Chapter 25 of this text.

Professional Tip

Part of planning a project should include planning view names. A consistent naming system helps ensure all users know the view names without having to list them. The views can be set as part of the template drawings.

Figure 20-20.
The **Orthographic & Isometric Views** tab of the **View** dialog box contains six preset orthographic and four preset isometric views.

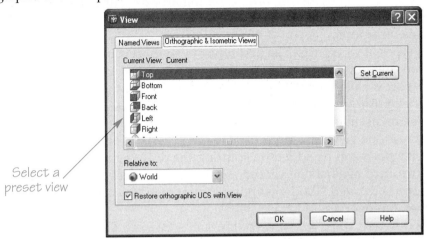

Select a preset view

Figure 20-21.
Preset orthographic and isometric views can be set current using the **View** toolbar or the **3D Views** cascading menu in the **View** pull-down menu.

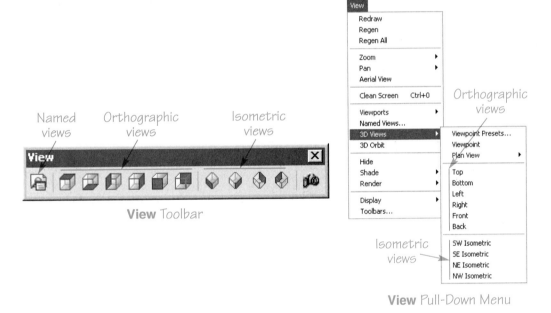

Named views | Orthographic views | Isometric views

**View** Toolbar

Orthographic views

Isometric views

**View** Pull-Down Menu

## Exercise 20-1

◆ Open ex16-8.
◆ Create a view of the floor plan named Flrplan.
◆ Create a view of the kitchen area named Kitchen.
◆ Create a view of the bathroom areas named Bathrooms.
◆ Restore the Flrplan view.
◆ Create a layer named M-Section Cut and set current.
◆ Draw section cutting-plane lines similar to those shown in **Figure 20-16**.
◆ Save the drawing as ex20-1.

---

# Using Tiled Viewports

Views can be very helpful by saving time zooming around a drawing. However, to further increase productivity, you can split the AutoCAD display into smaller windows, known as viewports.

There are two types of viewports. The first type of viewport is called a *tiled viewport.* The **Model** tab drawing area can be divided into various tiled viewports. The other type of viewport is called a *floating viewport.* The **Layout** tab, or paper space, is where floating viewports are created. Tiled viewports are discussed in this chapter. Floating viewports are discussed in Chapter 24.

By default, there is one viewport in the drawing area, which is the entire drawing area. Additional viewports can be added by splitting the drawing area. The edges of these viewports are butted against one another, similar to floor tiles. This is where the name tiled viewports is derived. Tiled viewports cannot overlap each other. Floating viewports, however, can overlap.

Viewports are different "tiles" or views of the same drawing. Only one viewport can be active at any given time. The active viewport has a bold outline around its edges. See **Figure 20-22.**

Viewports are created using the **Viewports** dialog box, **Figure 20-23.** This dialog box can be accessed by picking the **Display Viewports Dialog** button from the **Layouts** or **Viewports** toolbar. You can also enter vports or viewports at the Command prompt or select **New Viewports...** from the **Viewports** cascading menu in the **View** pull-down menu.

VIEWPORTS
VPORTS

View
→ Viewports
 → New
  Viewports...

Layouts
toolbar

Viewports
toolbar

Display Viewports
Dialog

**Figure 20-22.**
An example of three tiled viewports in model space. All viewports show the same drawing, just different portions of the drawing.

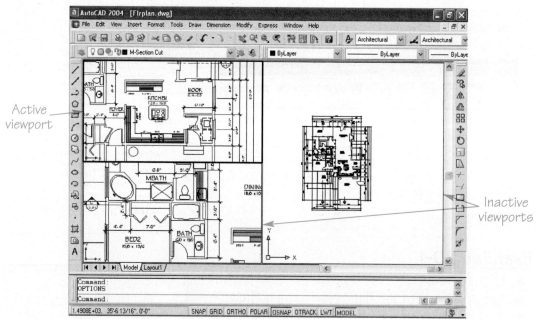

## Creating New Tiled Viewports

The **New Viewports** tab is shown in **Figure 20-23.** The **Standard viewports:** list contains AutoCAD's preset viewport configurations. The configuration name identifies the number of viewports and the arrangement or location of the largest viewport. In the case of a Right or Left four-viewport configuration, the "location" is where the small viewports will be placed. The preset configurations are shown in **Figure 20-24.** When you highlight a configuration name in the list, a preview of the configuration appears in the **Preview** area. Selecting the entry ***Active Model Configuration*** will preview the current configuration.

**Figure 20-23.**
The **Viewports** dialog box allows you to specify the number and arrangement of tiled viewports. Note the view names created in Exercise 20-1 are used in the different viewports.

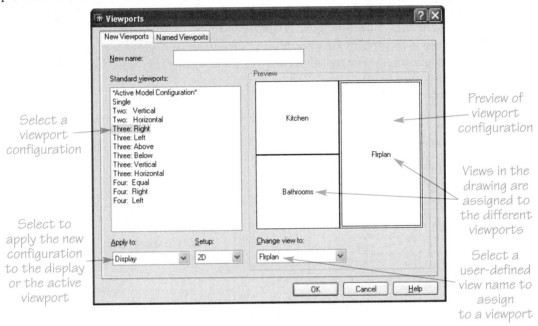

Viewports
New Viewports
Named Viewports
New name:
Standard viewports:
*Active Model Configuration*
Single
Two: Vertical
Two: Horizontal
Three: Right
Three: Left
Three: Above
Three: Below
Three: Vertical
Three: Horizontal
Four: Equal
Four: Right
Four: Left
Preview
Kitchen
Flrplan
Bathrooms
Apply to:
Display
Setup:
2D
Change view to:
Flrplan
OK
Cancel
Help
Select a viewport configuration
Select to apply the new configuration to the display or the active viewport
Preview of viewport configuration
Views in the drawing are assigned to the different viewports
Select a user-defined view name to assign to a viewport

**Figure 20-24.**
The preset tiled viewport configurations available in the **New Viewports** tab of the **Viewports** dialog box.

Single
Three Vertical
Three Horizontal
Four Equal
Two Vertical
Three Right
Three Left
Four Left
Two Horizontal
Three Above
Three Below
Four Right

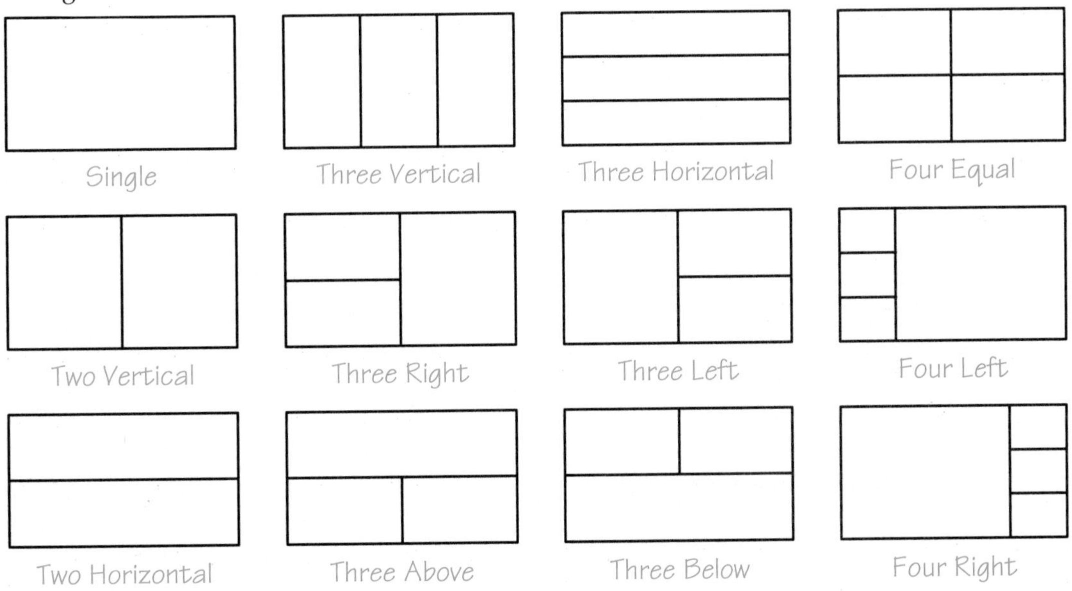

You can name and save a viewport configuration. Enter a name in the **New name:** text box at the top of the **New Viewports** tab. Use a descriptive and meaningful name. For example, if you are creating a four-viewport configuration for four elevations or sections, you might name the configuration Elevation Viewports or Section Viewports. When you pick the **OK** button, the configuration is applied. The next time you open the **Viewports** dialog box, the new named viewport configuration appears in the **Named Viewports** tab.

The **Apply to:** drop-down list allows you to specify how the viewport configuration is applied. Select **Display** to have the configuration applied to the entire drawing area. Select **Current Viewport** to have the new configuration added to the active viewport only. This, in effect, creates subdivisions within the viewport. See **Figure 20-25.**

The default setting in the **Setup:** drop-down list is **2D**. When this is selected, all viewports show the top view of the drawing. If the **3D** option is selected, the different viewports can display orthographic or isometric views of the drawing. Typically, at least one viewport is set up with an isometric view. The other viewports have orthographic views. The viewpoint or view is displayed within the viewport in the **Preview** image. To change a viewpoint or view that is assigned to a viewport, pick the viewport in the **Preview** image. Then, select the new viewpoint or view from the **Change view to:** drop-down list.

**Figure 20-25.**
Viewport configurations can be applied to the drawing area or the active configuration. The original tiled viewport configuration is shown on the left. On the right, a new viewport configuration is applied to a single viewport.

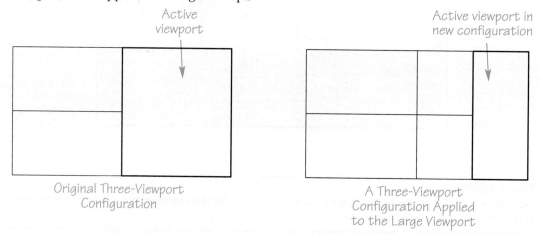

Original Three-Viewport Configuration

A Three-Viewport Configuration Applied to the Large Viewport

## Setting and Restoring Viewport Configurations

The **Named Viewports** tab displays the names of saved viewport configurations and gives you a preview of each. See **Figure 20-26.** Select the named viewport configuration and pick **OK** to apply it to the drawing area. Named viewport configurations cannot be applied to a single active viewport.

Certain preset viewport configurations can also be selected from the **Viewports** cascading menu in the **View** pull-down menu, shown in **Figure 20-27.** The following configuration options are available.

- **1 Viewport.** This option replaces the current viewport configuration with a single viewport.
- **2 Viewports.** When you select this option, you are prompted to select a vertical or horizontal arrangement. The arrangement you choose is only applied to the active viewport. This configuration does not replace the current viewport configuration.

Architectural Drafting Using AutoCAD

**Figure 20-26.**
The **Named Viewports** tab of the **Viewports** dialog box.

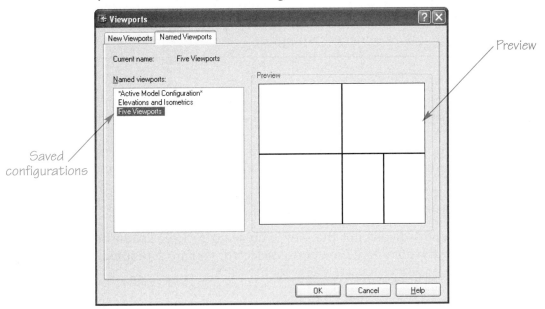

**Figure 20-27.**
The **Viewports** cascading menu in the **View** pull-down menu.

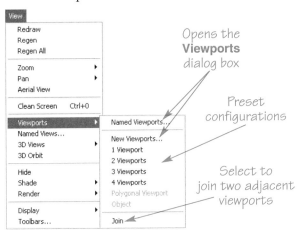

- **3 Viewports.** The following prompt appears when you select this option:

  Enter a configuration option [Horizontal/Vertical/Above/Below/Left/Right] <Right>:

  The arrangement you choose is only applied to the active viewport. This configuration does not replace the current viewport configuration.
- **4 Viewports.** This option creates four equal viewports within the active viewport. The current viewport configuration is not replaced.

**Note**

A maximum of 64 tiled viewports are available at one time. You can check this number using the **MAXACTVP** (maximum active viewports) system variable at the Command prompt.

## Joining Viewports

View
→ Viewports
→ Join

You can join two adjacent viewports into a single viewport. Pick **Join** from the **Viewports** cascading menu in the **View** pull-down menu. Once **Join** is selected, you are prompted:

Select dominant viewport <current viewport>:

Select the viewport displaying the view you want to keep in the resulting joined viewport. Once the dominant viewport is selected, you are prompted:

Select viewport to join:

Select the viewport to join with the active viewport. Once you select a viewport to join, AutoCAD "glues" the two viewports together and retains the dominant view.

The two viewports you are joining must be adjacent. In addition, they cannot create an L-shaped viewport. In other words, the two "shared" edges of the viewports must be the same size in order to join them.

## Working with Tiled Viewports

Once you have selected the viewport configuration and returned to the drawing area, move the pointing device around. Notice that only the active viewport displays the pointer as crosshairs. The pointer is displayed as the standard Windows pointer in the other viewports. To make a different viewport active, move the pointer into the viewport and press the left mouse button once.

As you draw in one viewport, the image is displayed in all viewports. Experiment by drawing lines and other shapes. Notice how the viewports are affected. Then, use a display command, such as **ZOOM**, in the active viewport and notice the results. Only the active viewport reflects the use of the **ZOOM** command.

## Exercise 20-2

◆ Start a new drawing using one of your templates.
◆ Create the following layers:
  ◆ X-Floor Plan
  ◆ S-Floor & Plate (Center linetype)
◆ Xref in ex20-1 using the **Overlay** option and the absolute coordinates 0,0,0 for the insertion point. Freeze any xref dimension and note layers as needed.
◆ Split the screen into three horizontal viewports with the largest viewport above.
◆ In the upper viewport, pan the floor plan to the side.
◆ In the lower-left viewport, perform a **Zoom Extents**.
◆ In the lower-right viewport, zoom into the horizontal section cutting-plane line.
◆ In the largest viewport, draw the subfloor and plate lines for the three sections. Refer to the elevations in Chapter 19 for the height of the main floor. Your drawing should look similar to the one shown.
◆ Save the drawing as ex20-2.

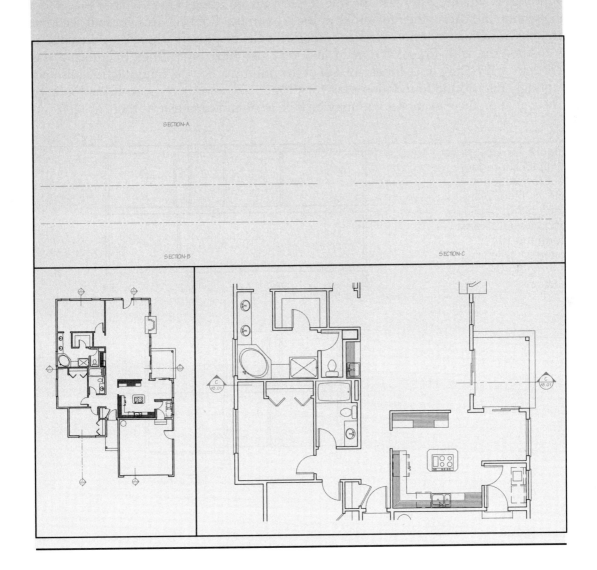

# Drawing the Section

In a section view, vertical lines are added between the subfloor and plate layout lines to distinguish where the walls are located. This is somewhat similar to the layout of elevations. Refer to the floor plan and section cutting-plane lines often to determine the placement of wall lines. All objects through which the cutting-plane line passes are displayed in the section. These include walls, doors, windows, and cabinets.

Once the vertical layout lines are drawn, refer to the floor plans for the wall widths. Use the **OFFSET** command to offset the vertical lines the correct widths. This establishes the internal workings of the structure. **Figure 20-28** shows the layout of the floor plan and foundation walls in a section view. As you are drawing these lines in the section, try to visualize what the cutting-plane line is passing through and where the "cut" pieces are placed in the section.

If there is a partial section indicated on the floor plan, as in **Figure 20-5,** the section only needs to be drawn as far as the cutting-plane line extends into the building. Where the cutting-plane line stops in the building, a break line is placed on the section indicating the remainder of the section has not been drawn. Full sections are drawn with all exterior walls and interior walls displayed where they are cut.

After the wall lines have been laid out, use horizontal lines to indicate the subfloor and ceiling lines for each level of the building. For the foundation walls and footings, refer to the foundation plan for proper size and placement. If the footings are drawn on the elevations, you may be able to obtain dimensions there as well.

**Figure 20-28.**
Wall locations laid out for section views. Floor plans, foundation plans, and elevations are continuously referred to when laying out the sections.

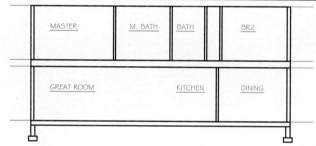

Full Section with a Floor Joist System

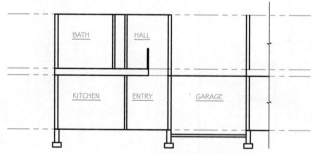

Partial Section with a Post and Beam System

## Exercise 20-3

- Open ex20-2.
- Use the largest viewport to draw the sections.
- In the smaller viewports, zoom into areas on the floor plan that you need to reference. Use the **DIST** command and osnaps to measure the different parts of the drawing.
- Create the following layers:
  - S-Framing (for wall, floor, and ceiling layout lines)
  - S-Notes (for section notes, labels, and break lines)
- Set the S-Framing layer current.
- Lay out the vertical walls for each section of the house. Exterior walls are 6″ thick. Interior walls are 4″ thick.
- Draw the subfloor and ceiling lines for each level.
- Determine which foundation system you want to draw (floor joist, post and beam, or concrete slab).
- Depending on the foundation system used, offset the floor line down the thickness of the subfloor. Add the joists or beams below the subfloor.
- Label the rooms to make it easier to identify the space.
- Your drawing should look similar to the one shown.
- Save the drawing as ex20-3.

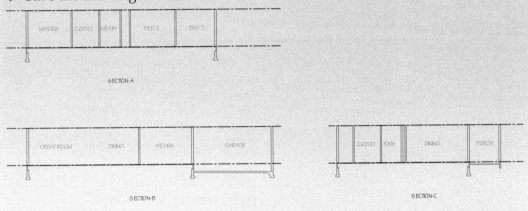

## Adding the Roof

After the walls are laid out, the roof needs to be added. A rafter or truss system can be drawn. For the house drawing, a rafter system is used. The rafter system uses ceiling joists, so both the rafters and ceiling joist need to be added at the top plate of any wall with a roof above it. Another consideration before drawing the roof is the pitch. Refer to the elevations for the roof pitch. In the case of the house drawing, $2 \times 8$ rafters with $2 \times 8$ ceiling joists are used and the roof pitch is 6:12.

Remember, a birdsmouth is used with a rafter system. Therefore, the bottom of the rafter starts on the inside part of an exterior wall. Use relative coordinates to determine the other end of the rafter. Offset the bottom of the rafter up 8″ to create a 8″ thick rafter. You can also draw the rafter as 7-1/2″, which is the actual size of 8″ dimensional lumber. **Figure 20-29** shows the steps involved in creating a roof section.

After the roof is laid out, use the **EXTEND** command or the **FILLET** command with a radius of 0 to join the opposite sides of the roof. Make a 16″ overhang on the outside of the building. Add a 8″ thick ceiling joist above the top plate to complete the roof. If the section is cut through a portion of the roof where there is not a slope, extend the exterior wall line up to the top of the roof. This type of section is used for a *rake*, which is discussed in the next section.

**Figure 20-29.**
The steps to creating a roof section.

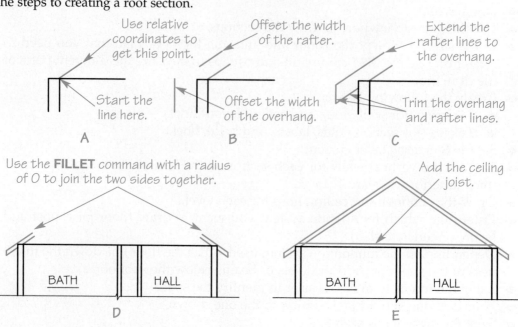

Use relative coordinates to get this point.

Offset the width of the rafter.

Extend the rafter lines to the overhang.

Start the line here.

Offset the width of the overhang.

Trim the overhang and rafter lines.

A          B          C

Use the **FILLET** command with a radius of 0 to join the two sides together.

Add the ceiling joist.

BATH    HALL          BATH    HALL

D                      E

## Exercise 20-4

◆ Open ex20-3.
◆ Ensure the S-Framing layer is current.
◆ Lay out the rafters for the sections.
◆ Use 8" thick rafters, an 8" thick ceiling joist, a 6:12 roof pitch, and a 16" overhang.
◆ For sections where the cut plane is not cutting a slope, but traversing it, draw the exterior walls up to the ends of the roof.
◆ Your drawing should look similar to the one shown.
◆ Save the drawing as ex20-4.

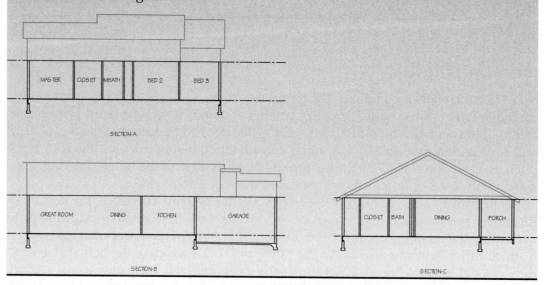

# Detailing the Section

The walls, roof system, and foundation system are the most important parts of a section. A section identifies where these components need to be placed in relation to each other, as well as how the structure is to be constructed. It is very important to understand how these components are laid out by referring to the existing floor plans. It is also important to understand how the cutting-plane lines "slice" through the structure and how "sliced" objects fit into the section.

After the components are drawn for the section, you can begin detailing the section. Typically, framing members sliced with the cutting-plane line are included in the section. These include floor joists, rafters, and beams. Keep the spacing between the framing members in mind as you draw the section. Typically, floor joists are spaced 16" on center (OC) and rafters are spaced 24" OC. This varies based on the structural engineering, construction material, construction members, construction methods, and building codes. Refer to engineering notes for the proper spacing between the joists.

Any construction member that is "cut" in a section view, such as a joist, plate, header, beam, or rafter, is drawn with a rectangle enclosing an X. This indicates the member is cut by a cutting-plane line. See **Figure 20-30.** Some office practices place the X only in the larger construction members, such as beams and headers. If the sections are to be plotted at a small scale, such as 1/8" = 1'-0", the X is often omitted so it will not interfere with the plot quality.

The top and bottom plates also need to be added, as shown in **Figure 20-8** and **Figure 20-9.** There are two top plates, each two inches thick, and one bottom plate two inches thick. If a window or door is sliced, the header above the door is also drawn. **Figure 20-31** displays some typical wall section conditions.

**Figure 20-30.**
Joists in a section view.

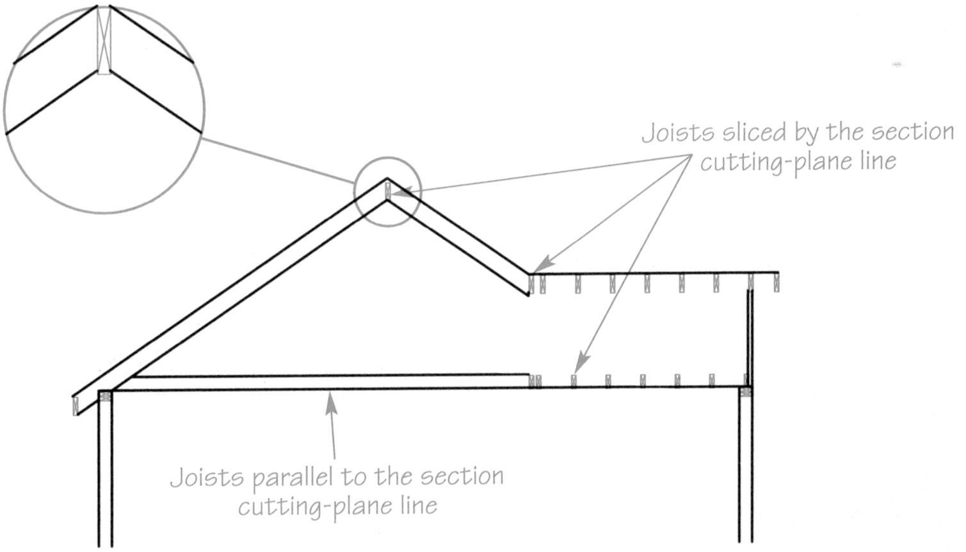

Joists sliced by the section cutting-plane line

Joists parallel to the section cutting-plane line

**Figure 20-31.**
Typical wall conditions in a section view.

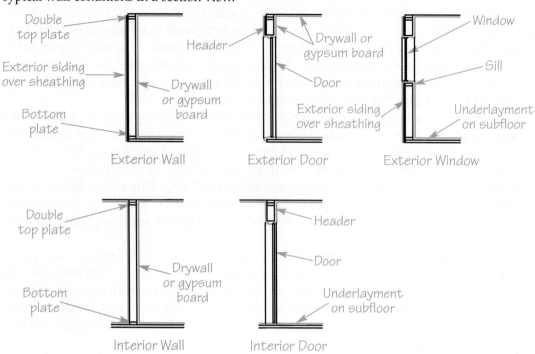

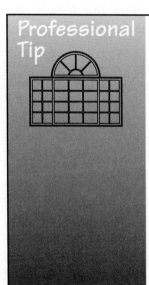

When drawing members constructed of dimensional lumber, you can draw them at nominal or actual size. The following list gives the nominal and actual sizes for common dimensional lumber.

| Nominal size | Actual dimensions |
|---|---|
| 2 × 4 | 1-1/2 × 3-1/2 |
| 2 × 6 | 1-1/2 × 5-1/2 |
| 2 × 8 | 1-1/2 × 7-1/2 |
| 2 × 10 | 1-1/2 × 9-1/2 |
| 2 × 12 | 1-1/2 × 11-1/2 |
| 4 × 12 | 3-1/2 × 11-1/2 |
| 6 × 12 | 5-1/2 × 11-1/2 |

Check with your CAD manager or instructor to see which method to use.

The interior drywall or gypsum board is typically shown on a section as 1" thick. Although this is dimensionally inaccurate, it plots nicely and ensures there is a visible division between the construction member and the finish wall. Two lines are drawn on the exterior of the wall. One line is for the exterior sheathing and the other is for the exterior siding. As with interior drywall, these lines are drawn 1" apart. Again, the 1" space ensures the lines plot clearly. The roof also has sheathing placed above the rafter. The roofing material is placed above the sheathing. In a section, these materials are typically drawn as 1″ thick. Your school or company may prefer the spacing between lines to be the actual thickness of the material, such as 1/2″ for drywall. Confirm the desired practice with your CAD manager or instructor.

If a rafter roofing system is used, ceiling joists are drawn "behind" the rafter. To represent this on the drawing, the top of the ceiling joist is displayed as a hidden line where the joist is behind the rafter. **Figure 20-32** shows typical roofing sections.

With a trussed roof, the ceiling joist stops at the bottom of the top chord. Blocking is added above the top plates on the rafter or truss. This is typically a 2″ thick piece designed to keep the weather and birds out of the attic. Blocking with a screened vent is placed at specified intervals to help provide attic ventilation. Confirm the proper spacing with building codes and design requirements.

If a fascia is used, it is added at the end of the rafter. The fascia is generally 1″ to 2″ thick and varies in height, depending on the exterior design. Some offices also prefer to display the gutter attached to the fascia.

The part of the roof displaying a gable end, such as the front of the house drawing, is called a *rake.* If the section cutting-plane line slices through the rake, draw the section as if it were a wall, but place a rafter at the top of the sliced roof line. Draw a vertical line extending from the rake down to the top plate.

Other components that may be sliced include cabinets, stairs, and special framing. Features that require special framing may include stepped or coved ceilings. A basic understanding of how these components are constructed will aid in drawing sections. See **Figure 20-33.**

Depending on the foundation system in use, you may need to add joists or girders, along with the posts and beams. Refer to the foundation plans for placement and size requirements for these construction members. A ground line is also added in the crawlspace area of the foundation to indicate that the foundation has been dug out (excavated). This should extend from the inside of one footing to the opposite footing in the section. An exterior grade line is also typically added. This indicates the finished grade of the site. This is discussed in the next section.

**Figure 20-32.**
Typical roof conditions in a section view.

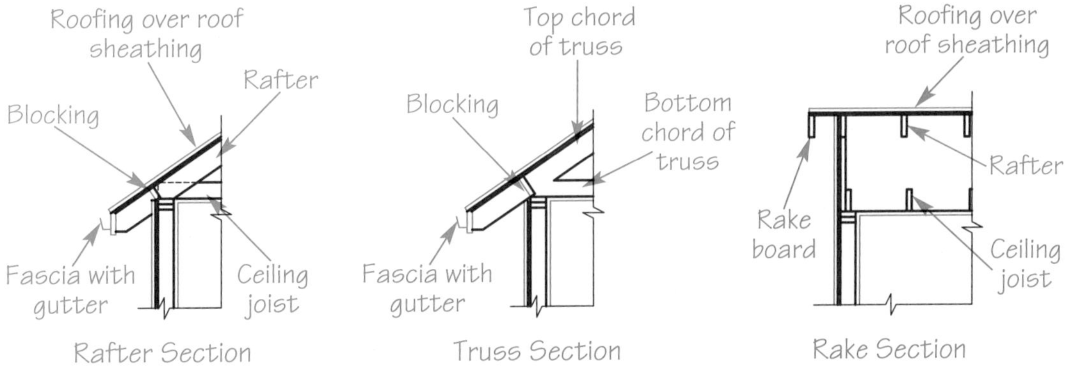

**Figure 20-33.**
Special sectioning conditions.

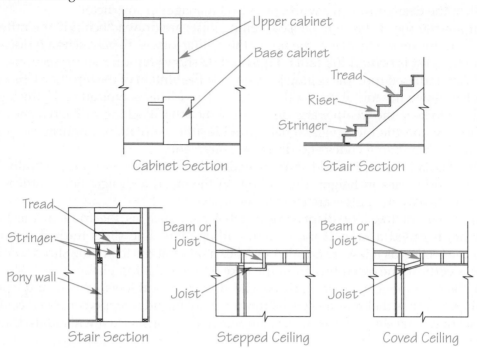

Cabinet Section

Stair Section

Stair Section

Stepped Ceiling

Coved Ceiling

# Exercise 20-5

◆ Open ex20-4.
◆ Create the following layers:
   ◆ S-Beams (for all joists and beams)
   ◆ S-Sheathing
◆ Begin adding the joists, ceiling joists, sheathing, and other detail components to the sections.
◆ Use 2 × 8 rafters and 2 × 8 ceiling joists. If you are drawing the floor joist foundation system, use the 2 × 10 floor joists specified in the foundation plan.
◆ Make the sheathing widths 1″.
◆ Your drawing should look similar to the one shown.
◆ Save the drawing as ex20-5.

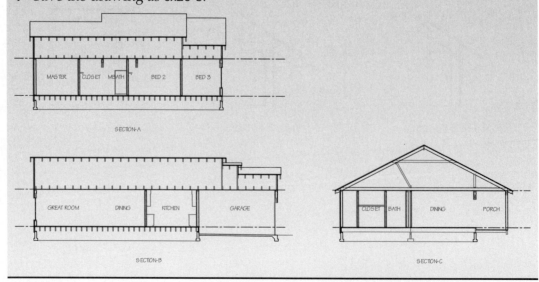

# Placing Notes and Dimensions on the Sections

The final step in drawing the sections is the placement of notes and dimensions, as well as adding a finish grade line and ground hatch pattern. When adding notes to the sections, call out any special conditions, such as special sizes for beams and joists. Also, any notes referring to the general construction of the structure are important to include in sections. If the section drawings are too crowded with geometry and notes, keynotes can be used.

Roof pitch symbols should also be drawn on the sections. Place the symbols in a location where the roof pitch is clearly seen. One of the reasons this is done is to ensure consistency between drawings. Roof pitch symbols are introduced in Chapter 19.

Foundation footing sizes are also noted in a section. Another note common in sections is room tags. A *room tag* indicates the intended function of a room, such as "kitchen" or "garage." Placing room tags in section drawings helps identify the area in relation to the floor plan. Dimensions are another important notation found on sections. Often, the locations of major beams, overhangs, and roof ridge lines are placed on the sections. Plate lines and any special dimensions that are not located on other plans should be placed on the section views.

The last component to place on a section is a *finish grade line.* In Chapter 19, a grade line was added to the elevations to show the exterior elevations in relation to the grading of the site. When placed on a section drawing, the grade line aids in the proper size and location of the foundation walls and footings. The grade line is generally drawn 8" below the mudsill or a minimum of 6" below exterior siding. A hatch pattern is often added under the footings and at the exterior of the building to represent ground. **Figure 20-34** shows an example of a finished section.

**Figure 20-34.**
An example of a finished section.

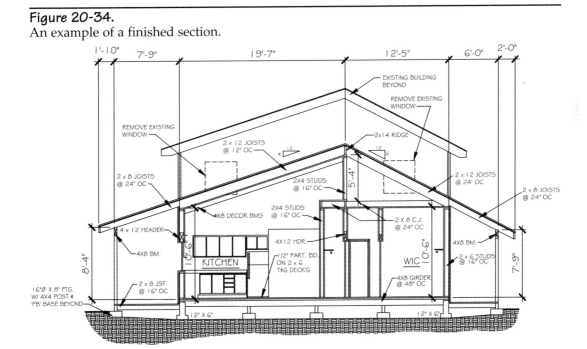

# Interior Details for Sections

As discussed in this chapter, a section represents the part of the building that can be seen after the building is "sliced." In some offices, it is standard practice to show the interior of the building that can be seen behind the cutting-plane line. Features are shown such as doors, windows, and columns that can be seen in the room that has been cut. These are plotted with a thin pen to give the impression that the rest of the building remains beyond the cutting-plane line.

This drawing is commonly plotted at a scale of 1/4" = 1'-0". However, smaller or larger scales such as 1/8" = 1'-0" or 1/2" = 1'-0" are used depending upon the size of the project. The 1/8" = 1'-0" and 1/4" = 1'-0" scales can result in crowding of notes. If that happens, use keynotes to place notes on the drawing and create a keynote schedule. Examples of keynotes are provided in Appendix E of this text.

## Exercise 20-6

◆ Open ex20-5.
◆ Create the following layers:
   ◆ S-Dims
   ◆ S-Grade (for ground line and hatch)
◆ Using the drawing provided, add notes to the sections.
◆ Add dimensions.
◆ Add a ground line and hatch the area.
◆ Your drawing should look similar to the one shown.
◆ Save the drawing as ex20-6.

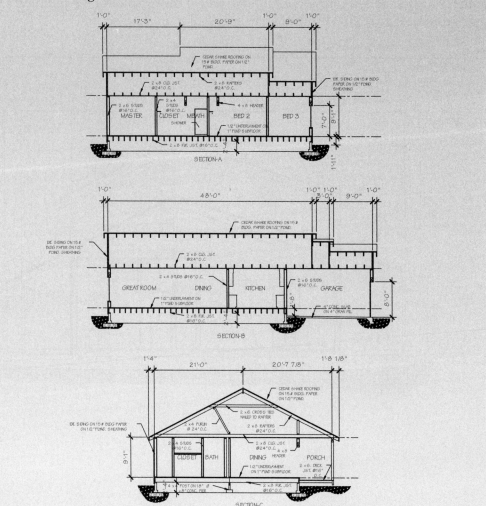

# Creating Details

*Details* are enlarged sections of a specific area. Details provide more information than found in a section. In addition, details can provide information specific to the construction of building components. The architectural office typically provides assembly and material details. A structural engineering office usually provides structural details.

Details are referenced from the floor plans using a detail bubble similar to the section cutting-plane line bubble. See **Figure 20-35.** The difference is the detail cutting-plane line only crosses the area to be shown in the detail and does not have a viewing direction arrow.

Details are drawn for many different construction assemblies. The number of details will vary, depending on the project and the complexity of the structure. For example, a residence may only have a few details, such as a foundation detail, a wall detail, and a roof eave detail. A commercial project, on the other hand, will have numerous details for all the different building conditions that may occur.

**Figure 20-35.**
The detail bubble points the viewer to the detail number and the page where it can be found.

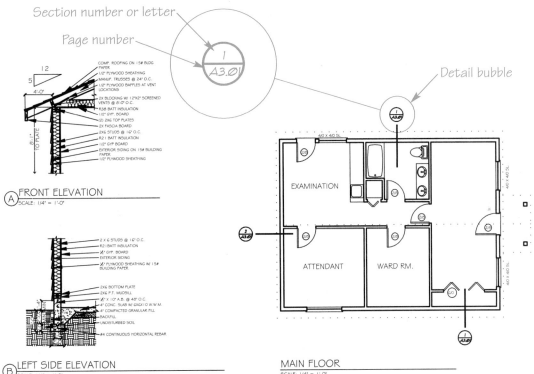

Details, just like all drawings in AutoCAD, are drawn to scale. The scale factor depends on the intended plotting scale. Details are typically printed at a scale of 1/2″ = 1′-0″ to 1″ =1′-0″. This can vary with offices or detail requirements. Details are normally assembled into a *detail sheet* that shows several details on a single page. It is common to have 12 to 16 details on a single sheet. Often, there are multiple detail sheets.

When placing details on a detail sheet, you need to consider how large the details are to be drawn. **Figure 20-36** displays a layout of nine details on a single detail sheet. Each detail can have its own border, or the details can be placed without individual borders. Either way, the details need to be placed in neat, uniform rows. Also, number the details consecutively from left to right and top to bottom.

**Figure 20-36.**
A typical detail sheet.

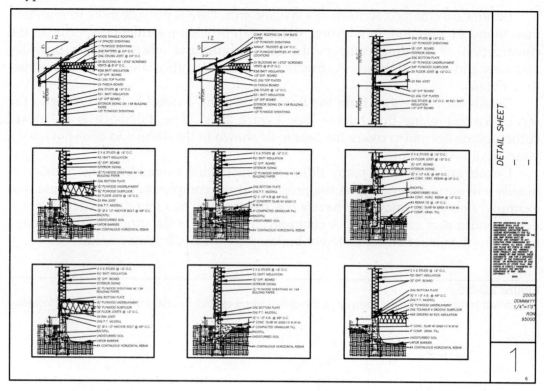

## Foundation Details

*Foundation details* are drawn for each condition that may occur in the construction of the building. Post and beam, floor joist, and slab construction techniques are all detailed. **Figure 20-37** displays some typical foundation details.

**Figure 20-37.**
Typical foundation details.

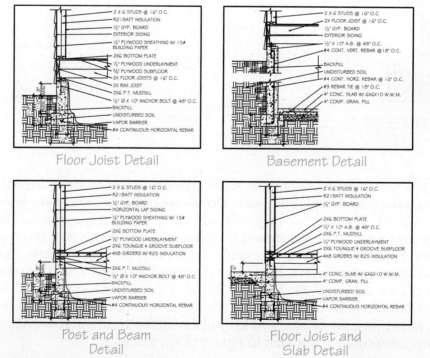

## Wall Details

**Wall details** are also drawn when necessary. Typical wall details include wall framing details, window framing details, and connection details. **Figure 20-38** shows some typical wall details.

## Roof Details

**Roof details** may include roof or truss framing. The framing details required for tile, shake, or composite roofing are often shown. Rake and eave details are often shown. **Figure 20-39** shows typical roof details.

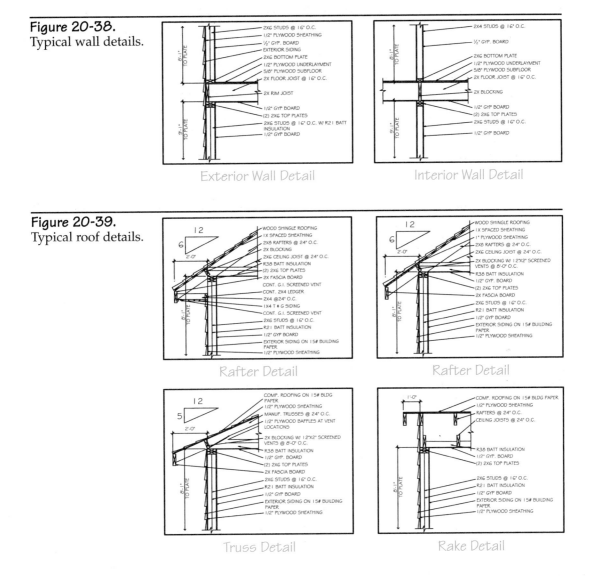

**Figure 20-38.**
Typical wall details.

**Figure 20-39.**
Typical roof details.

## Stair Details

Drawing **stair framing details** is also a part of the detailing process. Typically, a stair detail may be larger than other details. This is because the full wall height is often drawn. Stair construction details can also be drawn in a stair section. There may be no difference between a "stair detail" and a "stair section," except for the name. The actual practice varies between offices. All of the stair construction components and methods along with the dimensions and notes are shown in the stair detail. **Figure 20-40** shows a typical stair detail.

---

**Figure 20-40.**
A typical stair
detail.

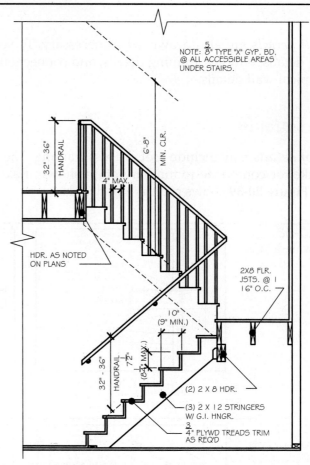

NOTE: $\frac{5}{8}$" TYPE "X" GYP. BD.
@ ALL ACCESSIBLE AREAS
UNDER STAIRS.

6'-8"

MIN. CLR.

32" - 36"

HANDRAIL

4" MAX.

HDR. AS NOTED
ON PLANS

2X8 FLR.
JSTS. @ 1
16" O.C.

10"
(9" MIN.)

32" - 36"

HANDRAIL

72"

(8¼" MAX.)

(2) 2 X 8 HDR.

(3) 2 X 12 STRINGERS
W/ G.I. HNGR.

$\frac{3}{4}$" PLYWD TREADS TRIM
AS REQ'D

Stair Detail

## Exercise 20-7

◆ Start a new drawing using one of your templates.
◆ Draw a foundation, wall, and roof detail. Use examples from **Figure 20-37,**
**Figure 20-38,** and **Figure 20-39** as reference.
◆ Use a scale factor of 24 for the dimensions and text heights.
◆ Save your drawing as ex20-7.

*Answer the following questions on a separate piece of paper.*

1. Define *section*.
2. What are sections used to describe?
3. Describe the purpose of a cutting-plane line.
4. Briefly describe a full section.
5. Briefly describe a partial section.
6. Explain the main difference between details and sections.
7. Describe balloon framing.
8. Explain platform framing.
9. Identify the two main elements used in masonry construction.
10. How is the foundation wall constructed when using masonry veneer?
11. List at least three advantages of steel construction.
12. Name the two main conventions used for roof construction.
13. Give the typical diameter of the bubble used with a cutting-plane line.
14. Identify the main function of the **VIEW** command.
15. Explain how you can create a new view based on the current drawing display.
16. How do you set a named view current?
17. The **Model** tab can be divided into various viewports. What are these viewports called?
18. How many viewports can be active at one time?
19. What should you consider when naming a viewport?
20. When **Current Viewport** is selected in the **Apply to:** drop-down list in the **Viewports** dialog box, how is the viewport configuration applied?
21. What condition(s) must exist before two viewports can be joined?
22. What types of dimensions are found on section drawings?
23. How is the grade shown on a section drawing?
24. When the interior of the building behind the cutting-plane line is drawn, how is that portion of the section plotted?

# Chapter Problems

For Problems 1–4, create sections and details for the projects as shown on the following pages. Use the following general procedure:

A. Start a new drawing and create appropriate layers.
B. Use the floor plan and elevation drawings for reference.
C. Refer to the sections shown and draw section lines on the floor plans associated with the sections.
D. Draw and dimension the sections and details for the assigned project.
E. Save the completed drawing as 20-ResA, 20-ResB, 20-Multifamily, or 20-Commercial, whichever is appropriate for the project.
1. Draw the following sections and details for the ResA project. Save the drawing as 20-ResA.

Project

Residential A

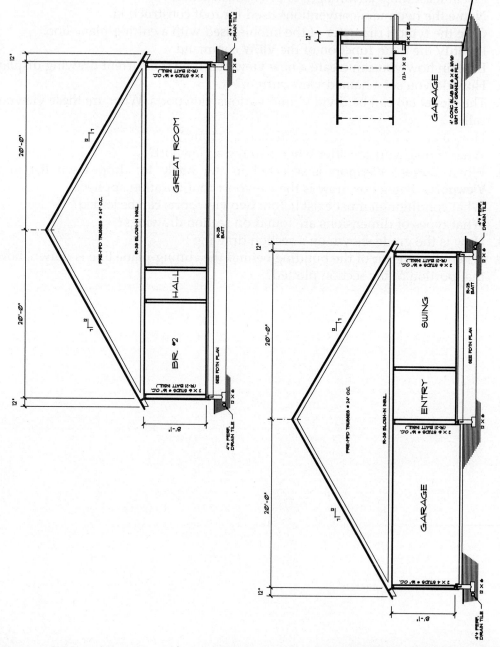

(Alan Mascord Design Associates, Inc.)

1. *(Continued)*

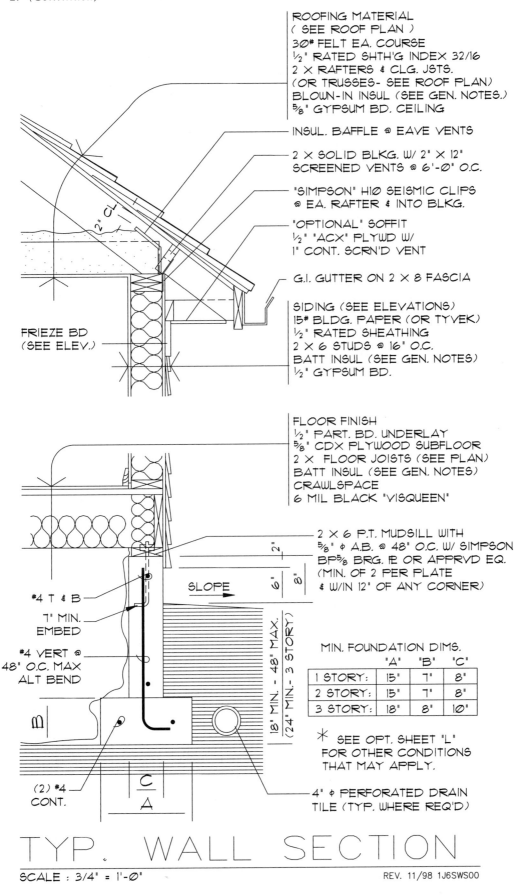

ROOFING MATERIAL
( SEE ROOF PLAN )
30# FELT EA. COURSE
½" RATED SHTH'G INDEX 32/16
2 X RAFTERS & CLG. JSTS.
(OR TRUSSES- SEE ROOF PLAN)
BLOWN-IN INSUL (SEE GEN. NOTES.)
⅝" GYPSUM BD. CEILING

INSUL. BAFFLE @ EAVE VENTS

2 X SOLID BLKG. W/ 2" X 12"
SCREENED VENTS @ 6'-Ø" O.C.

"SIMPSON" HIØ SEISMIC CLIPS
@ EA. RAFTER & INTO BLKG.

"OPTIONAL" SOFFIT
½" "ACX" PLYWD W/
1" CONT. SCRN'D VENT

G.I. GUTTER ON 2 X 8 FASCIA

SIDING (SEE ELEVATIONS)
15# BLDG. PAPER (OR TYVEK)
½" RATED SHEATHING
2 X 6 STUDS @ 16" O.C.
BATT INSUL (SEE GEN. NOTES)
½" GYPSUM BD.

FLOOR FINISH
½" PART. BD. UNDERLAY
⅝" CDX PLYWOOD SUBFLOOR
2 X FLOOR JOISTS (SEE PLAN)
BATT INSUL (SEE GEN. NOTES)
CRAWLSPACE
6 MIL BLACK "VISQUEEN"

2 X 6 P.T. MUDSILL WITH
⅝" ∅ A.B. @ 48" O.C. W/ SIMPSON
BP⅝ BRG. ℗ OR APPRVD EQ.
(MIN. OF 2 PER PLATE
& W/IN 12" OF ANY CORNER)

FRIEZE BD
(SEE ELEV.)

#4 T & B

7" MIN.
EMBED

#4 VERT @
48" O.C. MAX
ALT BEND

SLOPE

(2) #4
CONT.

4" ∅ PERFORATED DRAIN
TILE (TYP. WHERE REQ'D)

MIN. FOUNDATION DIMS.

|  | "A" | "B" | "C" |
|---|---|---|---|
| 1 STORY: | 15" | 7" | 8" |
| 2 STORY: | 15" | 7" | 8" |
| 3 STORY: | 18" | 8" | 10" |

✳ SEE OPT. SHEET "L"
FOR OTHER CONDITIONS
THAT MAY APPLY.

TYP. WALL SECTION

SCALE : 3/4" = 1'-Ø"

REV. 11/98 1J6SWS00

2. Draw the following sections and details for the ResB project. Save the drawing as 20-ResB.

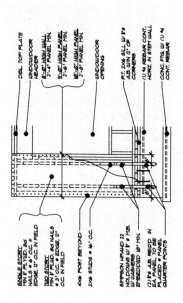

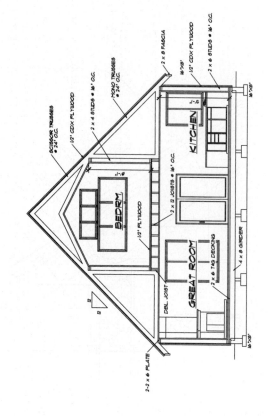

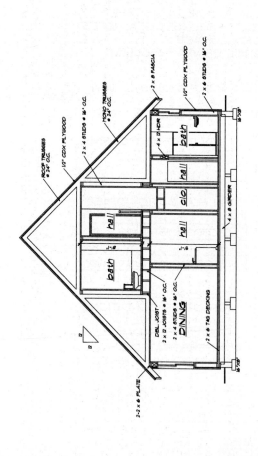

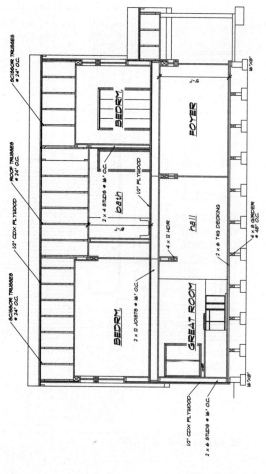

(3D-DZYN)

3. Draw the following sections and details for the Multifamily project. Save the drawing as 20-Multifamily.

Multifamily

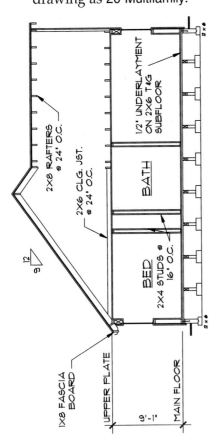

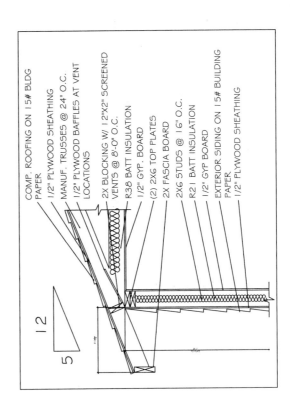

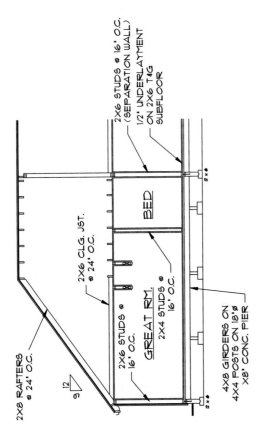

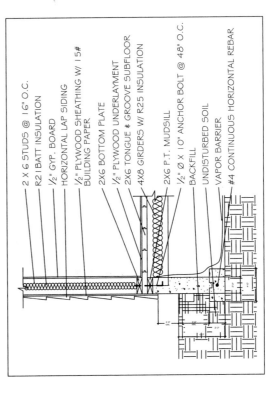

(3D-DZYN)

4. Draw the following sections and details for the Commercial project. Save the drawing as 20-Commercial.

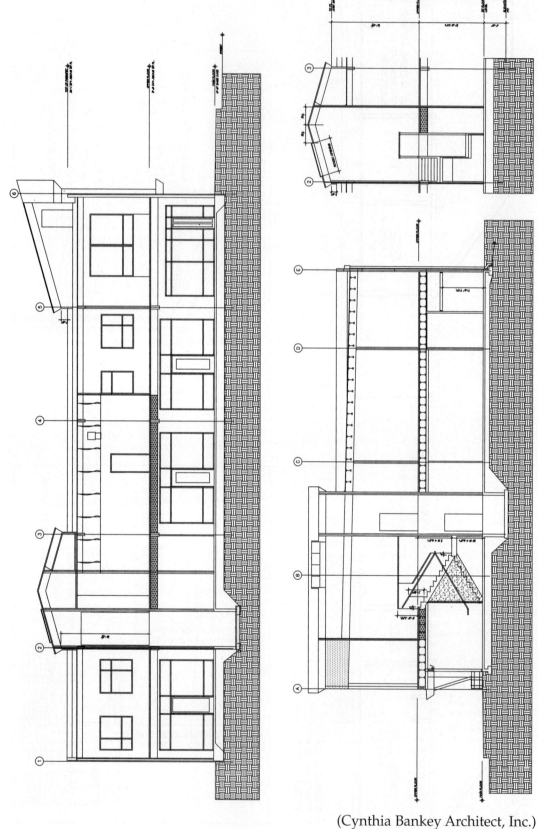

(Cynthia Bankey Architect, Inc.)

# Creating Schedules

## Learning Objectives

After completing this chapter, you will be able to:

- Create different types of schedules for your drawings.
- Use schedule symbols.
- Establish schedule information.
- Create smart tags by using attributes in your blocks.
- Edit attribute definitions.
- Insert blocks with attributes and control the display of attributes.
- Change attribute values.
- Redefine block attributes.
- Get attribute information.
- Use Windows Notepad to view an extracted file.
- Use object linking and embedding (OLE).
- Edit OLE objects.

## Important Terms

attribute extraction
attributes
block alias
embedded
finish schedules
furniture and equipment schedules

invisible attributes
linked
object linking and embedding (OLE)
schedule
tabulated schedules

A *schedule* is a chart of information that provides the details of building components. Schedules are generally created for doors, windows, and room finishes. However, schedules can be used to provide detailed information for anything. The purpose of creating a schedule is to provide clarity in the construction documents, as well as locations, sizes, and materials required. If care is not taken when placing information on the floor plan, the drawing can quickly become cluttered.

When creating a schedule, the items being added to the schedule list are tagged with a symbol. A symbol consists of a letter, number, or a combination of both inside a geometric shape, such as a circle, square, or polygon. **Figure 21-1A** shows examples of symbols that are commonly used by many architectural offices. Once the items have been identified, the details of the tagged item are added to a schedule. See **Figure 21-1B.**

## Using Schedule Symbols

Schedule symbols are commonly called tags, keys, marks, or symbols. An important aspect to adding tags is using a different symbol for each type of information. For example, doors should be represented by one symbol and windows by another. This helps clarify the specific type of information shown on the schedule. Whichever symbol is used, make sure the symbols are uniform in size. Also make sure that there is enough room inside the symbol to accommodate the number and/or letter.

There are four common methods of using schedule symbols. The first method identifies doors and windows with consecutive numbers until all doors and windows are tagged. The second method uses the floor number followed by the consecutive number. For example, the third door on the second floor would be identified with 203, where the 2 indicates the floor number and the 03 indicates the specific door.

The third method numbers the doors and windows with a room number plus a letter. In the case of doors, a door that starts in room 203 and swings into another adjacent room is assigned the number of 203A. Consecutively letter multiple doors that start in a room. Windows are then identified with the number of the room where they are located plus a letter. The distinguishing difference between the doors and windows, in this case, is the symbol.

The fourth method identifies the type of item being tagged with a letter in front of or above the tag number or letter. For example, D105 is used for door number 105 or W123 for window number 123. The letter *P* can be used for plumbing fixtures, *E* for electrical fixtures, and *A* for appliances.

**Figure 21-1.**
A—Common schedule tag symbols. B—A simple door schedule.

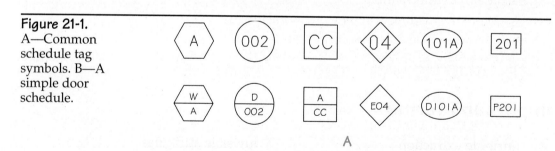

A

| KEY | SIZE | | | MATL | HC / SC | GLAZING AREA | NOTES |
|---|---|---|---|---|---|---|---|
| | WD | HGT | THK | | | | |
| 101 | 3'-0" | 6'-8" | 1 3/4" | STEEL | HC | - | 1-Hr self closing |
| 102 | 2'-8" | 6'-8" | 1 3/4" | WOOD | SC | 10 ⏚ | 1/4" Temp glass |
| 103 | 5'-0" | 6'-8" | 1 3/4" | WOOD | SC | 20 ⏚ | Dbl. Door |
| 104 | 3'-0" | 6'-8" | 2" | WOOD | HC | - | Pocket door |
| 105 | 6'-0" | 6'-8" | 1 3/4" | WOOD | SC | - | Bi-fold door |

DOOR AND FRAME SCHEDULE

B

Any of these methods is valid. Remember, it is important to be consistent throughout the entire set of drawings. Once you start with a method, use it for all drawings in the set. Most offices have standards established for identifying schedule items. Adhering to standards helps establish consistency on the drawings and ensures that multiple drafters have no question about conveying or understanding schedule items.

# Establishing Schedule Information

The information contained in the schedule varies depending on the item being identified. The identifying mark or number that refers to the tag is required, and is usually under a heading of Symbol, Key, or Mark. Other column headings that are common in a schedule include Width, Height, Thickness, Material, Manufacturer, and Notes (or Remarks). Specialized information columns can be added as necessary. This may include Fire Rating for a door, Glazing Area for a window, Quantity, or Type of Item.

The information added to a schedule depends on what is required to convey the message to the reader. It also depends on what is required by the manufacturer, supplier, or local building authority.

The schedule title, schedule border, header, and column lines are typically a heavier weight line than the row lines and can be created with a different color. This marks the difference between headings and item information.

# Using Smart Tags

The creation of symbols as blocks is discussed in Chapter 9 of this text. When creating symbol tags for schedules or annotations on a drawing, consider creating them as *annotation blocks*. Remember that annotation blocks are created at a 1:1 paper scale and inserted in model space by the scale factor. For example, if a door symbol is to appear as a 3/8" diameter circle on the finished plotted plan, create the door symbol with a 3/8" diameter circle and insert it in the drawing at the plot scale you plan to use.

Before you begin creating annotation symbols, however, you can make them "smart" by using attributes in the block. An **attribute** is a string of text that can be displayed within a block, but has the capability to be edited and changed while in the block format. If a window tag block is created using text instead of attributes, the value displayed in the tag is constant and cannot be changed unless the block is exploded. When a block is inserted with attributes, you specify the insertion point, scale, and rotation angle for the block. You are then prompted to enter the value for the attribute. This is particularly useful when creating tags for doors and windows because they are typically consecutively numbered or lettered.

## Creating Attributes in Blocks

Attributes can be created within block geometry or as stand-alone textual blocks. In most cases, attributes are created in the block symbol. The first step when creating the symbol is to draw the block geometry. Once the geometry has been drawn, the attributes can be placed within or around the symbol. See **Figure 21-2.**

When creating attributes for blocks, the type of information needed in the schedule is first determined. Each of these individual pieces of information can then be created as an attribute within the block. In many cases, the information required for the block does not need to be seen. For example, the only attribute that needs to be seen in a window tag is the tag number. However, other details, such as size,

**Figure 21-2.**
A—Block geometry with attributes before the block definition is created. B—The block symbols after the block definitions have been created.

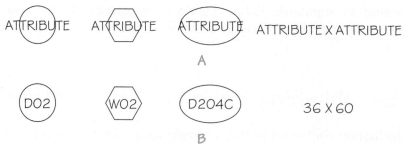

construction material, and glazing area, need to be placed in the schedule. In these situations, the attributes can be created as *invisible attributes* that do not display on the screen, but do contain specified information.

To create an attribute, the **ATTDEF** command is used. To access this command, pick **Define Attributes...** from the **Block** cascading menu in the **Draw** pull-down menu or enter att or attdef at the Command prompt. The **Attribute Definition** dialog box is displayed. See **Figure 21-3.** This dialog box is divided into four major areas. The four areas and their options are as follows:

ATTDEF
ATT

Draw
➥ Block
  ➥ Define
     Attributes...

- **Mode area.** Use this area to specify any of the attribute modes that affect how the attributes act and display. The mode options are as follows:
  - **Invisible.** If the attribute value is to be shown with the inserted block, leave this check box unchecked. If the box is checked, the attribute value is not displayed when the block is inserted. This is good for creating the schedule information that is not seen on the floor plan.
  - **Constant.** If the value of the attribute is always the same, place a check in this check box. This means that any insertion of the block displays the same attribute value; you are not prompted for a new value. If you wish to use different attribute values for inserted blocks, leave this check box unchecked. A check in this box will gray out the **Verify** and the **Preset** check boxes. If this tag is used for a specific manufacturer name, the manufacturer attribute may be made constant. Most offices tend to leave this unchecked because it allows the drafter the opportunity to change the attribute value as needed.
  - **Verify.** This check box prompts for two attribute values when the block is

**Figure 21-3.**
The **Attribute Definition** dialog box creates attributes that are added into a block definition.

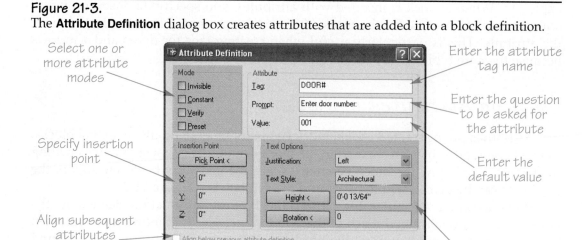

inserted. The first prompt asks for the value of the attribute and the second prompt asks you to verify the entry. If you do not wish to be prompted a second time for verification, leave this check box inactive.

- **Preset.** When creating attributes, a value can be specified. If a certain value is the desired value most of the time, place a check in this check box. The default value is displayed once the block is inserted. This option does allow you to go back and edit the default value to a unique value if so desired. When checked, the prompt for this individual attribute is disabled during a block insertion. Leave this check box inactive if you wish to display the normal prompts.

- **Attribute area.** This area lets you assign a tag name, prompt for the value, and default value to the attribute. The entries in the text boxes in this area can contain up to 256 characters. If leading blanks in the prompt or the default value are desired, start the string with a backslash (\). If the first character in the string needs to be a backslash, start the string with two backslashes. Each option is described as follows:

  - **Tag.** The name of the attribute tag is entered in this text box. You must enter a name or number. Any characters can be used, except spaces and exclamation marks. If you enter lowercase characters, AutoCAD converts them to uppercase when the attribute is added to the drawing. The tag name is displayed prior to defining the block and when using reference editing on a block with an attribute.

  - **Prompt.** This text box is used to enter a prompt statement that you want AutoCAD to display when the block is inserted. For example, if DOORTAG is the specified attribute tag name, you might enter What is the door number? or Enter door number: as the prompt. If the **Constant** attribute mode is set, this option is inactive. Any character can be used, including uppercase or lowercase characters.

  - **Value.** The value in this text box is used as a *default* attribute value when the block is inserted, unless the value is changed when you are prompted for the value at insertion time. A default value is not required for an attribute. The default value is displayed in chevrons (< >) when you are prompted for the attribute value. A possible application of a default value is to enter a message regarding the type of information needed, such as 4 spaces max or numbers only.

- **Text Options area.** This area allows you to specify the makeup of the attribute text. The justification, style, height, and rotation angle for attribute text can be set. The options in this area are described below:

  - **Justification.** This drop-down list is used to select a justification option for the attribute text. The default option is **Left**. If you are creating attributes that need to be centered on a tag shape, use the **Middle center** option.

  - **Text Style.** If the attribute is to use a specific text style, select the style from this list. Any styles currently in the drawing are included in this drop-down list. The default style is Standard.

  - **Height.** Enter the height of the attribute text in the text box to the right of the **Height** button. Selecting the **Height** button will temporarily return you to the drawing area where you can specify the text height by picking two points defining the height. Once the two points are picked, the dialog box returns and the corresponding height is shown in the text box. If the symbol you are creating will be used as an annotation block, make sure the height of the attribute is equal to the proper plotted height.

  - **Rotation.** The rotation angle for the attribute text is entered as an angular value in the text box next to the **Rotation** button. Selecting the **Rotation** button will temporarily return you to the drawing area where you can pick two points determining the rotation angle.

- **Insertion Point area.** This area is used to select the location, or insertion point, for the attribute based on its justification. Selecting the **Pick Point** button temporarily returns you to the drawing area and allows you to pick a point on screen. Once the insertion point is picked, the dialog box returns and the point is indicated by the coordinates in the **X:**, **Y:**, and **Z:** text boxes. You can also enter absolute coordinates in these text boxes to specify an insertion point. If placing the attribute in relation to block geometry, use osnaps and tracking to define the location relative to the geometry for the block.

- **Align below previous attribute definition check box.** When you first access the **Attribute Definition** dialog box, this check box is grayed out. After the first attribute is created and added to the drawing, additional attributes can be created. When the **Attribute Definition** dialog box is accessed for the next attribute, this check box can be activated. If you want the next attribute to be placed below the previous attribute created with the same justification, text height, rotation angle, and text style, pick this check box. When you do this, the **Text Options** and **Insertion Point** areas become inactive.

When finished defining the attribute, pick the **OK** button. The attribute tag is then placed on screen. If the attribute mode was set to **Invisible**, the tag name is still displayed on screen but becomes invisible once the attributes and symbol geometry have been created as a block definition. See **Figure 21-4.**

After the attributes have been created, use the **BLOCK** or **WBLOCK** command to create a block definition of the symbol geometry and the attributes. Block creation is discussed in Chapter 9. When creating the block, be sure to select all of the objects and attributes that go with the block. If you use the **Block Definition** or **Write Block** dialog box, it is recommended that you activate the **Delete** radio button. When the block is created, the selected objects should disappear, including the attributes. If any attributes remain on screen, undo the command and try again, making sure that all of the attributes are selected.

**Figure 21-4.**
The symbol geometry and any attributes created before the block definition is created.

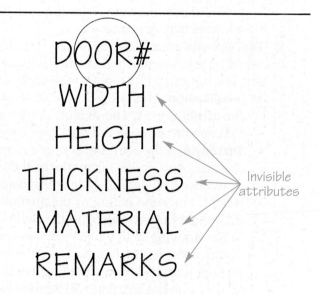

When selecting the items for the block definition, select the attributes in the order in which you wish to be prompted when inserting the block. Then, select the symbol geometry. In this way, you can control the specific order in which the prompts are displayed when the block is inserted.

When the block is inserted into the drawing, you are prompted on the command line with the questions you created for your attributes. Answer the questions to include the information in the tag. Invisible attributes do not display, but the information is included in the tag. See **Figure 21-5.** You will learn how to extract this information later in this chapter. The prompt sequence below answers questions for the symbol block in **Figure 21-4:**

Command: **i** *or* **insert**↵
*(select the block in the* **Insert** *dialog box and pick the* **OK** *button)*
Specify insertion point or [Scale/X/Y/Z/Rotate/PScale/PX/PY/PZ/PRotate]: *(Specify the insertion point of the block)*
Enter attribute values
Enter door number: <001>: **002**↵
Width of door? <36>: **2'-0"**↵
Enter door height: <7'-0">: ↵
Enter door thickness: <3/4">: ↵
What is the door made of? <WOOD>: **metal**↵
Enter any remarks: <->: **1-hour self closing**↵

Attributes can be added to any block symbol. Appliances, plumbing furnishings, and furniture can all have attributes describing features such as manufacturer, cost, and size to increase the amount of information included in the drawing. This information can then be extracted into schedules and spreadsheets, saving you time in preparing details for building materials required.

**Figure 21-5.**
The symbol geometry from **Figure 21-4** has been turned into a block. Notice that the invisible attributes do not display.

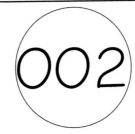

## Exercise 21-1

- Open the drawing ex20-1 you created in Chapter 20.
- Zoom in on a corner of a room.
- Create a circle that is 3/8″ in diameter.
- Add the following attributes similar to **Figure 21-4**. Develop your own prompts.

| Attribute | Text Parameters/Mode | Value |
|---|---|---|
| Door# | 1/8″ text height. Middle center justified | 01 |
| DWidth | Place below previous attribute. Invisible | #′-#″ |
| DHeight | Place below previous attribute. Invisible | #′-#″ |
| DThickness | Place below previous attribute. Invisible | #″ |
| DType | Place below previous attribute. Invisible | SNG. SWING |
| DMaterial | Place below previous attribute. Invisible | WOOD |
| DRemarks | Place below previous attribute. Invisible | — |

- Use the **Properties** window to change the block geometry to Layer 0, using ByBlock color, linetype, and lineweight.
- Use the **BLOCK** command to create a block definition called DoorTag. Make the insertion point the center of the circle. When selecting the items for the block, pick the attributes in the order you wish to have the prompts presented.
- Create a layer named M-Tags and set it current.
- Insert the DoorTag block next to all of the doors on the floor plan. Use the scale factor of 48 for the DoorTag block scale. Consecutively number the doors.
- Save the drawing as ex21-1. Your drawing should look like the one shown.

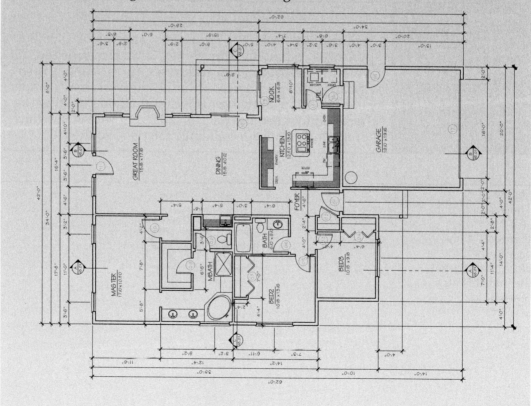

Architectural Drafting Using AutoCAD

# Editing Attribute Definitions

DDEDIT
ED

Modify
↳ Object
↳ Text
↳ Edit...

Text
toolbar

Edit Text

Once in a while it may be desirable to change certain aspects of text attributes *before* they are included in the block definition. If only the tag name, insertion prompt, or default value needs to be changed, the **DDEDIT** command can be used. To access the **DDEDIT** command, pick the **Edit Text** button on the **Text** toolbar, select **Text** and then **Edit...** from the **Object** cascading menu in the **Modify** pull-down menu, or enter ed or ddedit at the Command prompt. The **DDEDIT** command allows you to edit only one attribute definition at a time. The command sequence is as follows:

Command: **ed** *or* **ddedit**↵
Select an annotation object or [Undo]: *(select one attribute definition to change)*

This displays the **Edit Attribute Definition** dialog box. See **Figure 21-6**. The **Edit Attribute Definition** dialog box allows you to revise the **Tag**, **Prompt**, or **Default** values in the corresponding text boxes. When the changes are entered, pick **OK** to close the dialog box. The **DDEDIT** command prompt remains active should you want to select another attribute or text object to modify. When you are finished using the command, press [Enter] to end the command.

Figure 21-6.
The **DDEDIT** command allows you to modify an attribute before it has been added to a block.

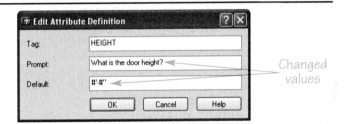

You can also double-click on an attribute before it is added to a block to open the **Edit Attribute Definition** dialog box. However, the **DDEDIT** command does not remain active after the **Edit Attribute Definition** dialog box is closed.

Professional Tip

# Using the Properties Window

The **Properties** window can be used to modify the attribute mode, text properties, or insertion point of the attribute before it is included in the block definition. When a text attribute is selected, **Attribute** appears in the drop-down list at the top of the window. The properties and defined values of an attribute are separated into four groups: **General**, **Text**, **Geometry**, and **Misc**. See **Figure 21-7**. These groups list all of the properties of the selected attribute and enable you to change their values.

The attribute tag, prompt, and default value entries are listed in the **Text** section. Change the **Tag**, **Prompt**, or **Value** values in the corresponding text boxes. Other properties that can be modified in the **Text** section include the text style, justification, height, rotation angle, width factor, and obliquing angle. Additional text options, such as the attribute mode options, are available in the **Misc** section.

**Figure 21-7.**
The **Properties** window can be used to adjust all of the properties of an attribute before the attribute is added to the block definition.

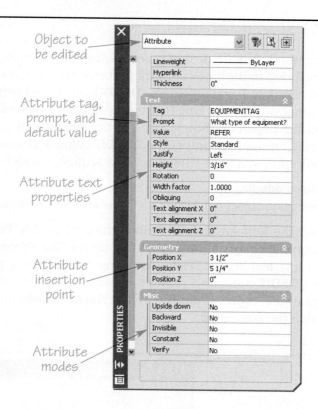

Object to be edited

Attribute tag, prompt, and default value

Attribute text properties

Attribute insertion point

Attribute modes

# Inserting Blocks with Attributes

When the **INSERT** command is used to place a saved block containing attributes into the drawing, you are prompted for the attribute information after picking the block's insertion point, specifying scale factors, and entering the rotation angle. The prompt statement that you created with the **ATTDEF** command appears on the command line and the default attribute value appears in brackets. Accept the default by pressing [Enter] or provide a new value at the prompt line. The attribute is then displayed with the block, if it is a visible attribute.

Attribute prompts can also be answered in a dialog box if the **ATTDIA** system variable is set to 1 (on). Answering attribute prompts in a dialog box allows you to quickly see all of the attribute prompts and change only the values desired. After inserting a block, the **Enter Attributes** dialog box appears. See **Figure 21-8**. To change a value, highlight the incorrect value and enter a new one. You can move forward through the attributes and buttons in the **Enter Attributes** dialog box by using the [Tab] key. Using the [Shift]+[Tab] key combination cycles through the attributes and buttons in reverse order. When you are finished, pick **OK** to close the dialog box. The inserted block with attributes then appears on screen.

The **Enter Attributes** dialog box can list up to eight attributes. If the block has more than eight attributes, the **Next** button at the bottom of the dialog box is highlighted. This allows you to navigate to different "pages" to answer all of the attribute prompts.

## Professional Tip

Set the **ATTDIA** system variable to 1 in your template drawings to automatically activate the **Enter Attributes** dialog box whenever you insert a block with attributes.

**Figure 21-8.**
The **Enter Attributes** dialog box appears after the insertion of the block and allows you to enter the attribute values in text boxes rather than at the Command prompt.

Enter Attributes

Block name:    DoorTag

What is the door number?        102
Width of door?                  2'-8"
Enter door height:              6'-8"
Enter door thickness:           1-3/4"
Enter the material:             WOOD
REMARKS

*Accept values or make changes as desired*

OK    Cancel    Previous    Next    Help

## Exercise 21-2

◆ Open ex21-1.
◆ Set the **ATTDIA** system variable to 1.
◆ Create a room tag that looks like the following room name attribute:

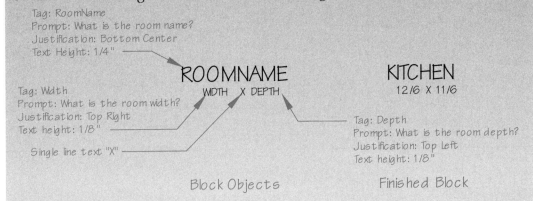

Tag: RoomName
Prompt: What is the room name?
Justification: Bottom Center
Text Height: 1/4"

Tag: Width
Prompt: What is the room width?
Justification: Top Right
Text height: 1/8"

Single line text "X"

ROOMNAME
WIDTH X DEPTH

KITCHEN
12/6 X 11/6

Tag: Depth
Prompt: What is the room depth?
Justification: Top Left
Text height: 1/8"

Block Objects                 Finished Block

◆ Use the **Properties** window to ensure all of the geometry is on Layer 0, using a ByBlock color, linetype, and lineweight.
◆ Create a block named RoomTag using the geometry created.
◆ Erase all of the room name text in the drawing and insert the RoomTag block for each room at a scale of 48. Insert it on the M-Tags layer.
◆ Save the drawing as ex21-2. The floor plan should look similar to the one shown on the following page.

*(Continued)*

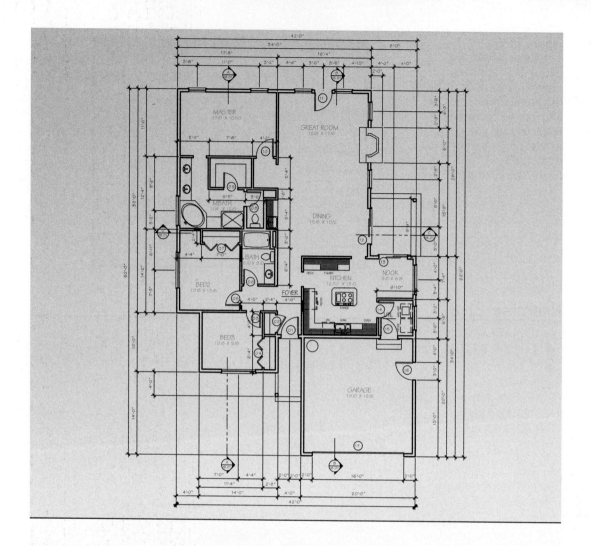

## Suppressing Attribute Prompts

If you are creating drawings that require the attribute values to always use the defaults, you can choose to suppress the attribute prompts. The **ATTREQ** system variable set to 0 is used to suppress the attribute prompts. The **ATTREQ** system variable setting is saved within the drawing.

After making this setting, try inserting the **DoorTag** block from Exercise 21-1. Notice that none of the attribute prompts appear. To display attribute prompts again, change the setting back to 1 and insert a block with attributes.

## Controlling the Display of Attributes

Attributes are intended to contain valuable information about the objects in your drawings. The main function of attributes is to generate schedules and materials lists, and to speed accounting. This information is often not displayed on screen or during plotting. In most cases, you can use the **TEXT** and **MTEXT** commands to create specific labels or other types of text.

To control how attributes are displayed in the drawing, use the **ATTDISP** (attribute display) command. This command can be accessed by picking **Attribute Display** from the **Display** cascading menu in the **View** pull-down menu or by entering attdisp at the Command prompt:

**ATTDISP**

**View**
↳ **Display**
↳ **Attribute Display**

Command: **attdisp**↵

Enter attribute visibility setting [Normal/ON/OFF] <Normal>:

- **Normal.** This option displays attributes exactly as they were created. This is the default setting.
- **ON.** This option will display *all* attributes in the drawing, including attributes that were set as *invisible* attributes.
- **OFF.** This option turns off the display of all attributes.

**Professional Tip**

After attributes have been created and defined within blocks, hide them by entering the **Off** option of the **ATTDISP** command. If attributes are left on, they clutter the screen and lengthen regeneration time. In a drawing where attributes should be visible, but are not, check the current setting of **ATTDISP** and adjust it if necessary.

# Changing Attribute Values

As discussed earlier, you can edit attributes before they are included in a block using the **DDEDIT** command or the **Properties** window. However, once a block containing attributes is inserted into a drawing, the **EATTEDIT** command is used to edit the inserted attributes. This command opens the **Enhanced Attribute Editor**, where inserted attribute values within a single block can be modified.

To open the **Enhanced Attribute Editor** dialog box, pick the **Edit Attribute** button on the **Modify II** toolbar, select **Attribute** and then **Single...** from the **Object** cascading menu in the **Modify** pull-down menu, or enter eattedit at the Command prompt. You are then prompted to select a block. Pick the block containing the attributes you wish to modify, and the **Enhanced Attribute Editor** is displayed. See **Figure 21-9A.** Double-clicking on a block containing attributes also opens the **Enhanced Attribute Editor** dialog box.

The **Enhanced Attribute Editor** contains three tabs. The **Attribute** tab is displayed when the dialog box is initially accessed, with the attributes within the selected block listed in the window. Pick the attribute to be modified. Enter a new value for the attribute in the **Value** text box.

Other properties of the selected attribute can be modified using the two other tabs. The **Text Options** tab allows you to modify the text properties of the attribute. See **Figure 21-9B.** The **Properties** tab, **Figure 21-9C,** contains settings for the object properties of the attribute.

After editing the attribute values and properties, pick the **Apply** button to have the changes reflected on screen. Pick the **OK** button to close the dialog box. If you want to modify a different block without closing the dialog box, pick the **Select block** button and select the block in the drawing area.

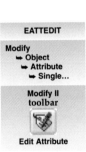

EATTEDIT

Modify
➥ Object
  ➥ Attribute
    ➥ Single...

Modify II
toolbar

Edit Attribute

## Exercise 21-3

- ◆ Open ex21-2.
- ◆ Issue the **ATTDISP** command and enter the **On** option to display all attributes.
- ◆ Use the **Enhanced Attribute Editor** to change the material attribute values of all the exterior doors to METAL.
- ◆ Change the material attribute value for the interior doors to WOOD.
- ◆ Set the **ATTDISP** command back to normal.
- ◆ Save the drawing as ex21-3.

**Figure 21-9.**
Select the attribute to be modified and change its value in the **Attribute** tab of the **Enhanced Attribute Editor**. A—The **Attribute** tab. B—The **Text Options** tab. C—The **Properties** tab.

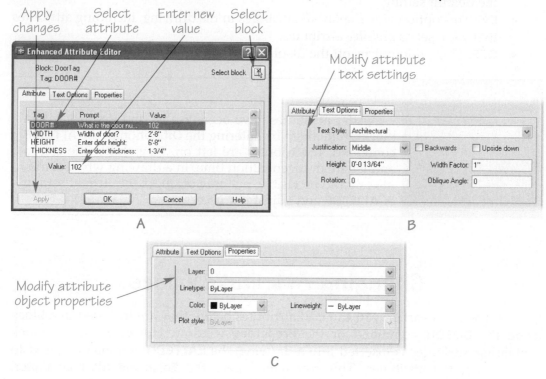

A

B

C

# Changing Attribute Definitions

Before saving an attribute within a block, you can modify the tag, prompt, and default value using the **DDEDIT** command. Once an attribute is saved in a block definition, you must use the **Block Attribute Manager** to change the attribute definition.

The **Block Attribute Manager** is accessed by picking the **Block Attribute Manager** button from the **Modify II** toolbar, selecting **Attribute** and then **Block Attribute Manager...** from the **Object** cascading menu in the **Modify** pull-down menu, or by entering battman at the Command prompt. The **Block Attribute Manager** is shown in **Figure 21-10**.

The **Block Attribute Manager** lists the attributes for the selected block. Select a block from the **Block:** drop-down list or pick the **Select block** button to return to the drawing area and pick the block. By default, the tag, prompt, default value, and modes for each attribute are listed.

The attribute list reflects the order in which prompts appear when a block is inserted. The attribute at the top of the list appears first. To change the order, select an attribute in the list and use the **Move Up** and **Move Down** buttons. To delete an attribute, select it in the list and pick the **Remove** button.

You can select which attribute properties are listed in the **Block Attribute Manager** by picking the **Settings...** button or right-clicking on the list and picking **Settings...** from the shortcut menu. This accesses the **Settings** dialog box, **Figure 21-11**. Select which properties to list in the **Display in list** area. When the **Emphasize duplicate tags** check box is active, attributes with identical tags are highlighted in red. Check the **Apply changes to existing references** option if you want the changes applied to existing blocks.

To modify an attribute definition, select the attribute in the **Block Attribute Manager** and then pick the **Edit...** button. This displays the **Edit Attribute** dialog box, **Figure 21-12**. The **Attribute** tab allows you to modify the mode, tag, prompt, and default value. Use the check boxes in the **Mode** area to select the desired mode(s). Enter new text strings in the **Tag:**, **Prompt:**, and **Default:** text boxes. The **Text Options**

**Figure 21-10.**
Use the **Block Attribute Manager** to change attribute definitions, delete attributes, and change the order of attribute prompts.

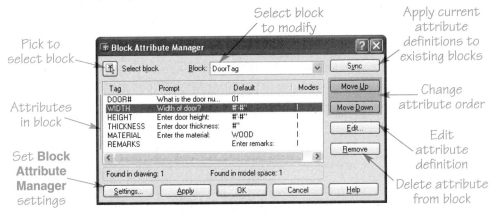

Select block to modify
Apply current attribute definitions to existing blocks
Pick to select block
Attributes in block
Set **Block Attribute Manager** settings
Change attribute order
Edit attribute definition
Delete attribute from block

**Figure 21-11.**
The **Settings** dialog box controls the display of the attribute list in the **Block Attribute Manager**.

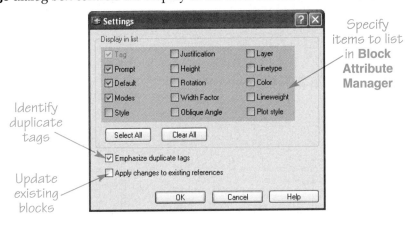

Specify items to list in **Block Attribute Manager**
Identify duplicate tags
Update existing blocks

**Figure 21-12.**
Use the **Edit Attribute** dialog box to modify attribute definitions and properties.

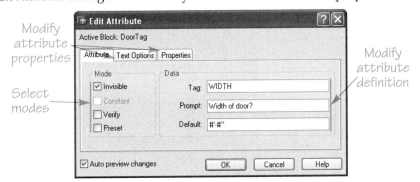

Modify attribute properties
Select modes
Modify attribute definition

and **Properties** tabs are identical to the tabs found in the **Enhanced Attribute Editor**, which is shown in **Figure 21-9**. These tabs allow you to modify the object properties of the attribute. After modifying the attribute definition in the **Edit Attribute** dialog box, pick the **OK** button to return to the **Block Attribute Manager**.

After modifying attributes within a block, all future insertions of the block will reflect the changes. Existing blocks are updated if the **Apply changes to existing references** option is checked in the **Settings** dialog box. If this option is not checked, the existing blocks retain the original attribute definition settings.

## Exercise 21-4

◆ Open drawing ex21-3.
◆ Insert the **DoorTag** block at a scale of 1. Explode the block.
◆ Replace the circle with a circumscribed hexagon with the same radius as the circle.
◆ Create a new block named WinTag from the exploded DoorTag block.
◆ Use the **Block Attribute Manager** to edit the WinTag attributes as shown and then pick the **Apply changes to existing references** check box in the **Settings** dialog box.

| Attribute | Text Parameters/Mode | Value |
|---|---|---|
| Win# | 1/8″ text height. Middle center justified | 01 |
| WWidth | Place below previous attribute. Invisible | #'-#" |
| WHeight | Place below previous attribute. Invisible | #'-#" |
| WGlazArea | Place below previous attribute. Invisible | # |
| WType | Place below previous attribute. Invisible | CSMT |
| WMaterial | Place below previous attribute. Invisible | WOOD |
| WRemarks | Place below previous attribute. Invisible | – |

◆ Insert the **WinTag** block for all of the windows in the floor plan at a scale of 48.
◆ Save the drawing as ex21-4. Your drawing should look similar to the one shown.

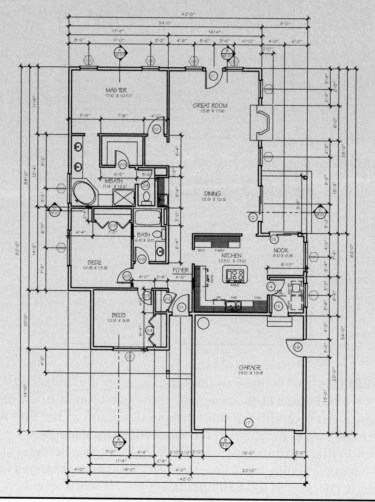

# Obtaining Attribute Information

The previous sections explained how to create and insert blocks containing user-specified information about a feature in a design. Once these blocks are created, the information can be extracted from every instance and placed into an extraction file. This extraction file can be opened to display the attributes on screen or imported into a spreadsheet, word processor, or database so they can be printed.

Attribute values and definitions can be extracted from a drawing and organized in a text file. This process, called *attribute extraction,* is useful for creating schedules. AutoCAD creates a text file containing the attribute information in a tabular format. You can select the specific blocks, attributes, and values to be extracted.

## Extracting Attributes

EATTEXT

Tools
➡ Attribute
  Extraction...

Modify II
toolbar

Attribute Extract

Attributes are extracted using the **Attribute Extraction** wizard. To access this wizard, pick the **Attribute Extract** button on the **Modify II** toolbar, select **Attribute Extraction...** from the **Tools** pull-down menu, or enter eattext at the Command prompt.

The first step in extracting attributes is to select the objects or drawings from which the information is to be gathered. The **Select Drawing** page of the **Attribute Extraction** wizard, shown in **Figure 21-13,** provides three options:

- **Select Objects.** Use this option if you want to include only some of the blocks in the current drawing. After picking the radio button, the **Select Objects** button is available. Pick this button to return to the drawing area and select the blocks to be included. You can select blocks from the current drawing only.
- **Current Drawing.** Pick this option to include all blocks in the current drawing.
- **Select Drawings.** Use this option to gather information from all blocks in multiple drawings. After picking the radio button, the ellipsis (...) button is available. Pick the ellipsis (...) button to open the **Select File** dialog box and select drawings. The selected drawings are then listed in the **Drawing Files** list.

After selecting the blocks to be included, pick the **Next>** button to advance to the **Settings** page. The options on this page allow you to include blocks from external reference files and blocks nested within other blocks. These boxes are checked by default. Uncheck the **Include xrefs** or **Included nested blocks** check box if you wish to exclude either type of object. Then, continue to the next page of the wizard by picking the **Next>** button.

**Figure 21-13.**
Select the blocks from which to extract information in the **Select Drawing** page.

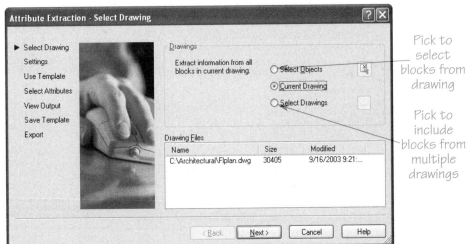

**Figure 21-14.**
Select a template of preset block and attribute values to be extracted in the **Use Template** page, or select no template.

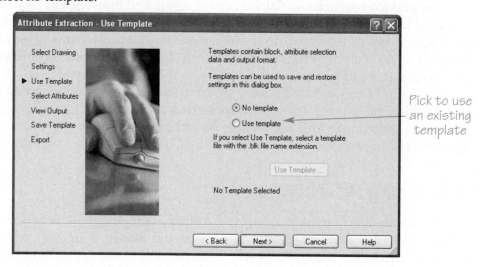

Pick to use an existing template

The **Use Template** page allows you to select a template file to automatically select the attributes to be extracted. See **Figure 21-14.** If this is the first use of the **Attribute Extraction** wizard, there will not be a template file saved and available for use. However, if attribute and block information have been extracted, a saved template file could be used. To select a template, pick the **Use template** radio button, which enables the **Use Template...** button. Pick this button to access the **Open** dialog box and select a block template file (BLK) file. Then, continue to the next wizard page by picking the **Next>** button.

The **Select Attributes** page, **Figure 21-15,** lists the selected blocks and the attributes contained in those blocks. This page is divided into two tables. On the left is a list of all selected blocks. This list shows the block name and the number of times the block appears in the drawing. You can enter a *block alias* in the **Block Alias Name** column. The alias is how the name of the block will appear in the extracted file. On the right is a list of the attributes for the selected block. By default, all attributes are selected. Uncheck all attributes by selecting the **Uncheck All** button and then check only those attributes to be extracted to the output file. If a template file was selected in the previous step, the blocks and attributes are automatically selected to match the template.

**Figure 21-15.**
Check the items to be extracted in the **Select Attributes** page.

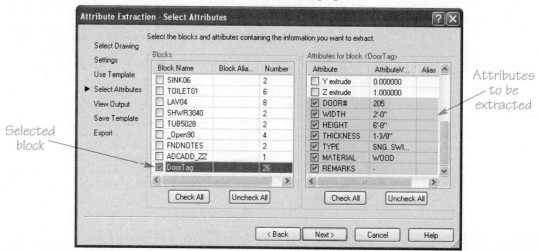

Selected block

Attributes to be extracted

Architectural Drafting Using AutoCAD

You often need to be selective when listing blocks and attributes. In most cases, only certain types of attribute data need to be extracted from a drawing. This requires guidelines for AutoCAD to use when sorting through a drawing for attribute information. The guidelines for picking out specific attributes from blocks are specified in the **Select Attributes** page. This information is then used by AutoCAD to list the attributes when you create an extract file.

In addition to extracting user-defined attributes, AutoCAD can extract information about certain block characteristics. These characteristics include:

- **Name.** The block name.
- **Number.** The number of block insertions made.
- **X insertion point.** The X coordinate of the block insertion point.
- **Y insertion point.** The Y coordinate of the block insertion point.
- **Z insertion point.** The Z coordinate of the block insertion point.
- **Layer.** The name of the layer the block is inserted on.
- **Orient.** The rotation angle of the block.
- **X scale.** The insertion scale factor for the X axis.
- **Y scale.** The insertion scale factor for the Y axis.
- **Z scale.** The insertion scale factor for the Z axis.
- **X extrude.** The X value of the block extrusion direction.
- **Y extrude.** The Y value of the block extrusion direction.
- **Z extrude.** The Z value of the block extrusion direction.

After selecting the attributes to be extracted, pick the **Next>** button to display the **View Output** page, **Figure 21-16.** A table displaying the results of the query is presented on this page. Two views of the information are available. Switch between the two views by selecting the **Alternate View** button. The view you select determines the format of the information when it is extracted. The information can also be copied to the Windows Clipboard. To do this, select the **Copy to Clipboard** button. The information is copied to the Clipboard in the same format as displayed in the table.

**Figure 21-16.**
Use the **View Output** page to select the format of the information being extracted.

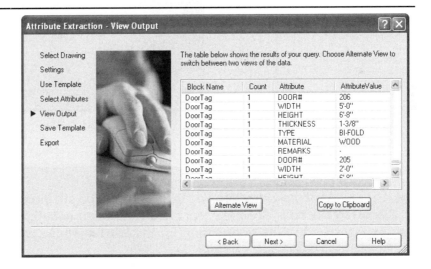

Alternate View

After viewing the output, pick the **Next>** button to display the **Save Template** page. This page provides an opportunity to save a template file. The template file stores the block and attribute selections made in the **Select Attributes** page as a BLK file. This template can then be used to automatically make the attribute selection for similar extractions in the future.

The last step in the wizard is the **Export** page, **Figure 21-17.** A file name and a file type are required on this page. The file name is entered in the **File Name** text box. Enter the entire path or pick the ellipsis (**...**) button to select a folder location.

The type of file to be saved is selected in the **File Type** drop-down list. If Microsoft Excel and Microsoft Access are installed, the XLS and MDB formats are available. The default formats that are always available are comma-separated (CSV) and tab-separated (TXT). Finally, pick the **Finish** button to export the file and return to the current drawing.

If the extracted file is a .csv or .txt file, it can be opened in Windows Notepad. You can print the file from Windows Notepad by selecting Print from the File pull-down menu. Examples of an extract file in comma-separated and tab-separated formats are shown in **Figure 21-18.** Decide which format is most suitable for your application.

**Figure 21-17.**
Type the file name and select the file type in the **Export** page.

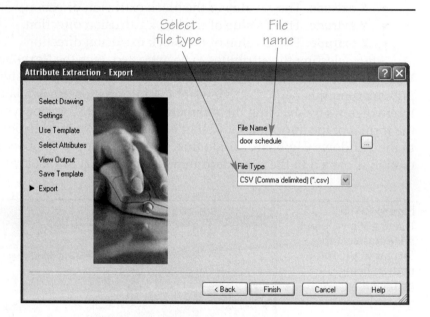

**Exercise 21-5**

◆ Open ex21-4.
◆ Use the **Attribute Extraction** wizard to extract the attribute information for the **DoorTag** blocks as a comma-separated file named ex21-5.csv.
◆ Extract the attribute information for the **WinTag** blocks as a tab-separated file named ex21-5.txt.
◆ Close the drawing.

**Figure 21-18.**
Extract files opened in Windows Notepad.

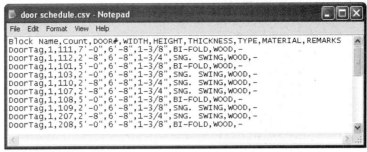

Comma-Separated Format

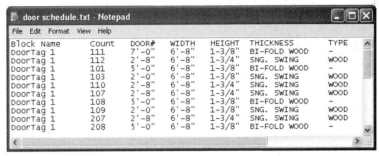

Tab-Separated Format

## Using Extracted Attributes in AutoCAD

Once the extraction file has been created, it can be used to create a schedule. The **MTEXT** command and the multiline text editor are used for this. When importing a document into the multiline text editor, the document must be either a text (TXT) or a rich text format (RTF) file. Attributes can be extracted to a tab-separated TXT file. However, to import attributes extracted to a comma-separated (CSV) file, you must first convert the file to TXT or RTF format. This can be done using a word processing program, such as Microsoft Word or Windows Notepad.

Now, enter the **MTEXT** command and pick the corners of the mtext object to display the multiline text editor. Adjust any settings, such as the text style, text height, or rotation angle. Remember that the text being imported into the drawing may need to have its height adjusted based on the scale factor of the drawing. Then, right-click in the multiline text editor and select **Import Text...** from the shortcut menu. Browse for the extract file and select it.

After the TXT or RTF file is selected, it appears in the multiline text editor. See **Figure 21-19.** You may need to adjust the tab settings. Use the [Tab] key to adjust the columns of the text so they appear presentable. Two pieces of information extracted in the previous example included the block name and the count. If you do not want these included, edit the text to remove them. Once you have formatted the text, press **OK** to create the multiline text object.

The width of the multiline text object may need to be adjusted to see the text properly. To do so, adjust the width with the grips. Then, draw lines around the text to create rows and columns for the schedule. **Figure 21-20** shows an example of a window schedule created this way.

**Professional Tip**

If you are importing a TXT file into the multiline text editor, the columns of information may not be lined up along one edge. Use the paragraph ruler or the **Indents and Tabs** dialog box to create proper columns of information.

Figure 21-19.
A tab-separated file is imported into the multiline text editor by right-clicking and selecting the **Import Text...** option.

| Block Name | Count | DOOR# | WIDTH | HEIGHT | THICKNESS | TYPE | MATERIAL |
|---|---|---|---|---|---|---|---|
| DoorTag | I | III | 7'-0" | 6'-8" | I -3/8" | BI-FOLD | WOOD |
| DoorTag | I | II2 | 2'-8" | 6'-8" | I -3/4" | SNG. SWING | WOOD |
| DoorTag | I | I0I | 5'-0" | 6'-8" | I -3/8" | BI-FOLD | WOOD |
| DoorTag | I | I03 | 2'-0" | 6'-8" | I -3/8" | SNG. SWING | WOOD |
| DoorTag | I | II0 | 2'-8" | 6'-8" | I -3/4" | SNG. SWING | WOOD |
| DoorTag | I | I07 | 2'-8" | 6'-8" | I -3/4" | SNG. SWING | WOOD |

**Figure 21-20.**
The finished window schedule.

| WINDOW SCHEDULE | | | | | | |
|---|---|---|---|---|---|---|
| NUMBER | WIDTH | HEIGHT | GLAZ AREA | TYPE | MATERIAL | REMARKS |
| 01 | 6'-0" | 5'-0" | 30 SQ FT | GLIDER | WOOD | — |
| 02 | 6'-0" | 5'-0" | 30 SQ FT | GLIDER | WOOD | — |
| 03 | 5'-0" | 4'-0" | 20 SQ FT | PICTURE | WOOD | TEMPERED |
| 04 | 3'-0" | 5'-0" | 15 SQ FT | CSMT | WOOD | — |
| 05 | 3'-0" | 5'-0" | 15 SQ FT | CSMT | WOOD | — |
| 06 | 3'-0" | 5'-6" | 16 1/2 SQ FT | AWNING | WOOD | — |
| 07 | 3'-0" | 5'-6" | 16 1/2 SQ FT | AWNING | WOOD | — |
| 08 | 3'-0" | 5'-6" | 16 1/2 SQ FT | AWNING | WOOD | — |
| 09 | 3'-0" | 5'-6" | 16 1/2 SQ FT | AWNING | WOOD | — |
| 10 | 5'-0" | 4'-0" | 20 SQ FT | GLIDER | WOOD | — |
| 11 | 4'-0" | 4'-0" | 16 SQ FT | GLIDER | WOOD | — |

## Exercise 21-6

◆ Open ex21-4.
◆ Set the layer M-Notes current.
◆ Enter the **MTEXT** command and import ex21-5.txt.
◆ Arrange the tab settings for the text as necessary. Press **OK** when done.
◆ Add lines around the multiline text object to make the schedule look similar to **Figure 21-20**.
◆ Save the drawing as ex21-6.

# Using Object Linking and Embedding

*Object linking and embedding (OLE)* is a Microsoft Windows feature that allows information to be shared between programs. With OLE, a certain relationship is maintained between the programs that share data. There are two aspects of OLE—linking and embedding. The following describes the key difference between linking and embedding:

• If the file containing the data is *linked,* the data can be edited in the original program and saved, which automatically updates the data in AutoCAD. If the file is edited in AutoCAD and saved, the original file is automatically updated.
• If the file containing the data is *embedded,* the data in AutoCAD is not automatically updated if the data in the original file is edited. The object becomes a static object in AutoCAD. However, you can launch the original program from which the data originated from within AutoCAD to edit the data.

You can only use the *"linking"* feature of OLE if the file you want to link to the drawing was generated by software that supports OLE. Linked OLE objects are similar to xrefs in that the drawing is referencing the original file.

The *"embedding"* feature refers to permanently storing a copy of the original file in the AutoCAD drawing. This is similar to binding an xref. If a file is embedded, it no longer has a link back to the original file; updating the original file does not update the data in AutoCAD. Any type of data that AutoCAD recognizes, such as a CSV or PCX file, can be embedded in a drawing.

## Linking and Embedding Data

The **INSERTOBJ** command is used for OLE in AutoCAD. This command can be accessed by picking the **OLE Object** button on the **Insert** toolbar, selecting **OLE Object...** from the **Insert** pull-down menu, or entering insertobj or io at the Command prompt. This displays the **Insert Object** dialog box.

When the **Insert Object** dialog box appears, the **Create New** radio button option is the default. See **Figure 21-21A.** This allows you to select a program listed in the **Object Type:** list in which to create a new file that is then linked to the AutoCAD drawing. The programs in the **Object Type:** list are the programs installed on your machine that support OLE. When you select one of the programs from the list and pick the **OK** button, that program opens and you can create the new file. Simply create the file and save it to the hard drive. The OLE object is then inserted into the drawing at the upper-left corner.

**Figure 21-21.**
The **Insert Object** dialog box is used to link or embed a file into your drawing. A—The **Create New** radio button allows you to open a program and create a file to link into AutoCAD. B—The **Create from File** radio button allows you to browse for an existing file to link into AutoCAD.

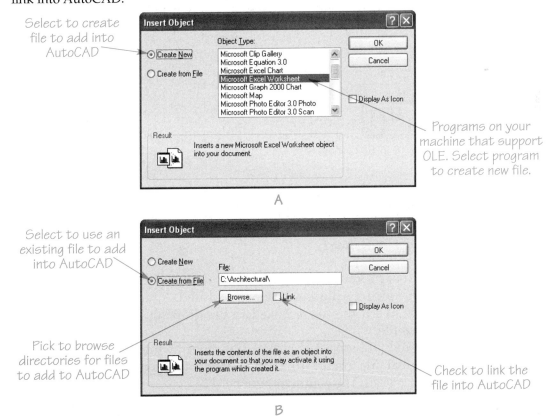

If the file has already been created, as with the .csv file created in Exercise 21-5, then select the **Create from File** radio button in the **Insert Object** dialog box. See **Figure 21-21B.** This displays the **File** text box, allowing you to enter a path location to the existing file to insert. The **Browse…** button can also be picked to browse for the file to insert into the drawing. After the file has been selected, the **Link** check box next to the **Browse…** button can be selected to *link* the file to the drawing. If the **Link** check box is not selected, the file is *embedded* into the drawing. **Figure 21-22** displays a window schedule inserted into a drawing as an OLE object.

The OLE object can be moved by picking on top of it to display the grips at each corner and edge. Move the cursor so that it displays a move cursor, press and hold the pick button, and drag to a new location. See **Figure 21-23.** The grip points can also be used to stretch the size of the OLE object. Simply move the cursor over the top of one of the grip points and wait for a double arrow symbol to display, indicating the direction of the stretch. Press and hold the pick button and resize the OLE object. To keep the object proportional, resize it using a corner grip.

**Figure 21-22.**
The AutoCAD drawing with an OLE object (shown in color) linked.

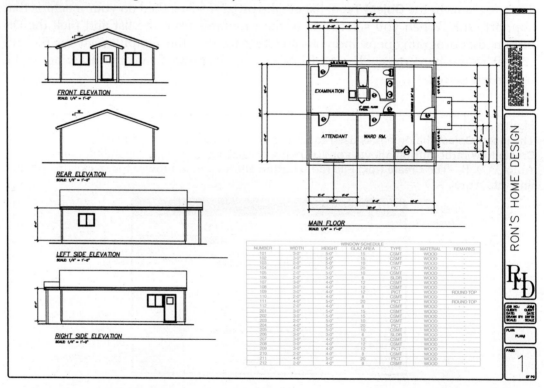

## Editing the OLE Object

To edit the OLE object from within AutoCAD, double-click on the object. This opens the program in which the file was originally created. After saving, any changes are updated in AutoCAD. If the file is linked to the drawing, the changes are also applied to the original file.

By default, a linked OLE object is updated in the drawing automatically when changes to the original file occur. To change the way linked files behave, the **OLELINKS** command is used. The command can be accessed by selecting **OLE Links…** from the **Edit** pull-down menu or by entering olelinks at the Command prompt. If there are no linked OLE objects in the drawing, this command is grayed out in the

OLELINKS

Edit
↳ OLE Links…

Architectural Drafting Using AutoCAD

**Figure 21-23.**
The resize grip points and the move cursor. Press and hold the pick button to relocate the OLE object in the drawing.

Resize using grip points

Move cursor

| Block Nam | Count | DOOR# | WIDTH | HEIGHT | THICKNESS | TYPE | MATERIAL | REMARK |
|---|---|---|---|---|---|---|---|---|
| DoorTag | 1 | 111 | 7'-0" | 6'-8" | 1-3/8" | BI-FOLD | WOOD | - |
| DoorTag | 1 | 112 | 2'-8" | 6'-8" | 1-3/4" | SNG. SW | WOOD | - |
| DoorTag | 1 | 101 | 5'-0" | 6'-8" | 1-3/8" | BI-FOLD | WOOD | - |
| DoorTag | 1 | 103 | 2'-0" | 6'-8" | 1-3/8" | SNG. SW | WOOD | - |
| DoorTag | 1 | 110 | 2'-8" | 6'-8" | 1-3/4" | SNG. SW | WOOD | - |
| DoorTag | 1 | 107 | 2'-8" | 6'-8" | 1-3/4" | SNG. SW | WOOD | - |
| DoorTag | 1 | 108 | 5'-0" | 6'-8" | 1-3/8" | BI-FOLD | WOOD | - |
| DoorTag | 1 | 109 | 2'-0" | 6'-8" | 1-3/8" | SNG. SW | WOOD | - |
| DoorTag | 1 | 207 | 2'-8" | 6'-8" | 1-3/4" | SNG. SW | WOOD | - |
| DoorTag | 1 | 208 | 5'-0" | 6'-8" | 1-3/8" | BI-FOLD | WOOD | - |
| DoorTag | 1 | 209 | 2'-0" | 6'-8" | 1-3/8" | SNG. SW | WOOD | - |
| DoorTag | 1 | 210 | 7'-0" | 6'-8" | 1-3/8" | BI-FOLD | WOOD | - |
| DoorTag | 1 | 211 | 2'-8" | 6'-8" | 1-3/4" | SNG. SW | WOOD | - |
| DoorTag | 1 | 212 | 2'-8" | 6'-8" | 1-3/4" | SNG. SW | WOOD | - |
| DoorTag | 1 | 201 | 5'-0" | 6'-8" | 1-3/8" | BI-FOLD | WOOD | - |
| DoorTag | 1 | 203 | 2'-0" | 6'-8" | 1-3/8" | SNG. SW | WOOD | - |
| DoorTag | 1 | 104 | 2'-8" | 6'-8" | 1-3/4" | SNG. SW | WOOD | - |
| DoorTag | 1 | 113 | 7'-0" | 6'-8" | 1-3/8" | BI-FOLD | WOOD | - |
| DoorTag | 1 | 102 | 2'-8" | 6'-8" | 1-3/4" | SNG. SW | WOOD | - |
| DoorTag | 1 | 106 | 5'-0" | 6'-8" | 1-3/8" | BI-FOLD | WOOD | - |
| DoorTag | 1 | 105 | 2'-0" | 6'-8" | 1-3/8" | SNG. SW | WOOD | - |
| DoorTag | 1 | 213 | 7'-0" | 6'-8" | 1-3/8" | BI-FOLD | WOOD | - |
| DoorTag | 1 | 202 | 2'-8" | 6'-8" | 1-3/4" | SNG. SW | WOOD | - |
| DoorTag | 1 | 204 | 2'-8" | 6'-8" | 1-3/8" | SNG. SW | WOOD | - |
| DoorTag | 1 | 206 | 5'-0" | 6'-8" | 1-3/8" | BI-FOLD | WOOD | - |
| DoorTag | 1 | 205 | 2'-0" | 6'-8" | 1-3/8" | SNG. SW | WOOD | - |

**Edit** pull-down menu or the entered command is ignored. If there is a linked file in the drawing, the **Links** dialog box appears, allowing you to make changes. See **Figure 21-24.**

The **Links** dialog box lists all linked files in the current drawing. When a file is selected from the list, the buttons along the right side and bottom of the dialog box are enabled. The **Automatic** radio button in the **Update:** area at the bottom of the dialog box is on by default. Select **Manual** if you want to manually update the object when the file changes. If you have selected a manual update, you must pick the **Update Now** button to update the data whenever there is a change to the original file.

The **Open Source** button allows you to open the source (original) program used to create the file so that changes can be made to the inserted file. This is the same as double-clicking on the OLE object to make changes. The **Change Source...** button allows you to change the current OLE object to link to a different file. If the **Break Link** button is selected, the *linked* file is *embedded* in the drawing.

**Figure 21-24.**
The **Links** dialog box displays all active links and allows you to specify how they are updated.

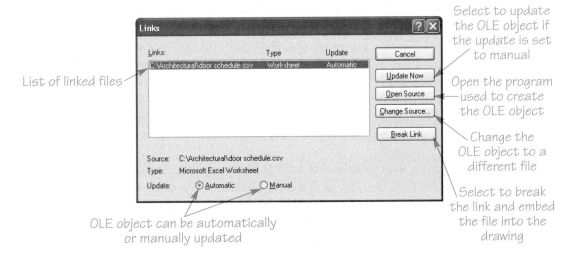

List of linked files

Select to update the OLE object if the update is set to manual

Open the program used to create the OLE object

Change the OLE object to a different file

Select to break the link and embed the file into the drawing

OLE object can be automatically or manually updated

When an OLE object has been inserted (linked or embedded) into the drawing, it is considered a raster image. In other words, it does not contain any coordinate values as far as location or size is concerned. You cannot use the **LIST** command on it. It is not a vector object, like AutoCAD text or a polyline. However, the OLE object does have a shortcut menu that can be accessed by right-clicking on the object. See **Figure 21-25.** The shortcut menu contains the following options:

- **Cut.** Removes the OLE object from the drawing and places it on the Windows Clipboard.
- **Copy.** Copies the OLE object to the Windows Clipboard.
- **Clear.** Removes the OLE object from the drawing without sending it to the Windows Clipboard. This is the same as erasing the object.
- **Undo.** Undoes the last operation performed on the OLE object. Does *not* undo changes made to the file in the original program.
- **Selectable.** When checked, this option allows you to select the OLE object so that it can be moved or stretched. If this option is unchecked, the object is "locked" into position and cannot be moved, stretched, or double-clicked. However, you can still right-click on the object to access the shortcut menu.
- **Bring to Front.** Brings the OLE object to the front of the screen. Similar to the **DRAWORDER** command.
- **Send to Back.** Sends the OLE object behind other objects. Similar to the **DRAWORDER** command.
- **Properties.** Displays the **OLE Properties** dialog box.
- **Object Type cascading menu.** Displays options for editing, opening, and converting the OLE object to other object types. This option will vary depending on the type of file linked to the drawing.

**Figure 21-25.**
Right-clicking on an OLE object displays this shortcut menu.

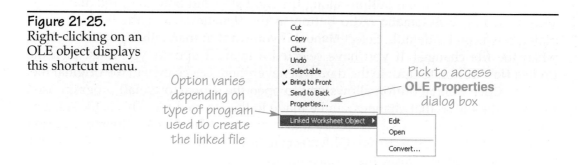

*Option varies depending on type of program used to create the linked file*

*Pick to access* **OLE Properties** *dialog box*

## OLE Object Properties

To adjust the properties of the OLE object, right-click on the object and select **Properties** from the shortcut menu. This displays the **OLE Properties** dialog box. See **Figure 21-26.** This dialog box contains options to set the size of the OLE object, scale the object, and control the plot quality of the object.

The size of the object can be set in drawing units or as a scale percentage. The text boxes in the **Size** area are used to set the size in drawing units. The text boxes in the **Scale** area are used to set the size as a percentage. If the **Lock Aspect Ratio** check box in the **Scale** area is checked, the current relationship between height and width is maintained.

The **Text size** area is available if the OLE object is text. This area contains two drop-down lists. The first is a list of fonts used within the OLE object. The second displays a list of point sizes used for the selected font in the OLE object. The text box to the right of the point size drop-down list allows you to specify the AutoCAD unit height for the selected point size to display in the drawing. For example, if you find

**Figure 21-26.**
The **OLE Properties** dialog box is used to make changes to an OLE object.

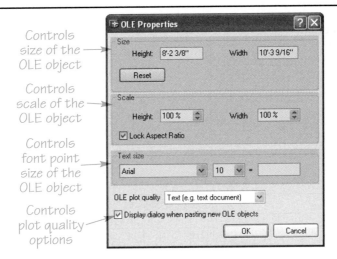

Controls size of the OLE object

Controls scale of the OLE object

Controls font point size of the OLE object

Controls plot quality options

that the Arial 10 point font is being used in the file and it needs to be 1/8″ in the AutoCAD drawing, specify that the Arial 10 = 1/8″. This scales the OLE object to meet the text size criteria. You can only scale one font.

The plot quality of the object is set in the **OLE plot quality** drop-down list. There are several options available. The lowest quality plot appears at the top of the list. The highest quality plot appears at the bottom of the list.

Professional Tip

When inserting an OLE object that contains text, use the **OLE Properties** dialog box to adjust the scale of the text. Keep the scale factor in mind. If the text is supposed to appear 1/8″ on the finished plot, set the 10 point font to be 1/8″ multiplied by the scale factor.

# Types of Schedules

A *schedule* is a list of information that defines the different characteristics or aspects of building objects such as doors, windows, equipment, finishes, fixtures, and walls. The information presented in the schedule explains to the plan reviewer what is required in the set of drawings. There are two main types of schedules in construction documents: tabulated and finish. *Tabulated schedules* are primarily used to list the tagged number of the object, what type of object it is, sizes, and remarks about the object. See **Figure 21-27.**

*Finish schedules* display information such as the room name, number of the tagged room, and the finishes used in each room, including wall, floor, and ceiling coverings. The information in the schedule lists all the different types of finishes used in the drawing. A dot, check mark, or "X" is added under the finish material columns, indicating which finish is to be applied in each room. **Figure 21-28** displays a typical room finish schedule. Dots are used in this example. Use the **LINE**, **PLINE**, and **DONUT** commands to construct the finish schedule.

A *furniture and equipment schedule* is often found on facility drawings and lists every chair, desk, computer, or other pertinent equipment found in a particular room. Information such as the tag number, manufacturer, and cost is often found in this type of schedule. **Figure 21-29** displays a typical furniture and equipment schedule.

**Figure 21-27.**
Examples of tabulated schedules.

| NO | NAME | LENGTH | WIDTH | HEIGHT | AREA |
|----|------|--------|-------|--------|------|
| 01 | BED 1 | 11'-0" | 10'-0" | 9'-0" | 110 sq.ft. |
| 02 | | 10'-0" | 11'-0" | 9'-0" | 110 sq.ft. |
| 03 | BED 2 M. BED | 12'-0" | 14'-0" | 9'-0" | 168 sq.ft. |
| 04 | LIVING | 12'-0" | 16'-0" | 9'-0" | 192 sq.ft. |
| 05 | DINING | 11'-0" | 12'-0" | 9'-0" | 132 sq.ft. |
| 06 | KITCHEN | 11'-0" | 10'-0" | 9'-0" | 110 sq.ft. |
| | | | | | 822 sq.ft. |

ROOM SCHEDULE

WINDOW SCHEDULE

| MARK | SIZE | | TYPE | MATERIAL | NOTES |
|------|------|------|------|----------|-------|
| | WIDTH | HEIGHT | | | |
| 01 | 3'-0" | 5'-0" | S.H. | WOOD | |
| 02 | 2'-6" | 1'-6" | SLDR. | VINYL | |
| 03 | 2'-6" | 3'-6" | SLDR. | METAL | |
| 04 | 3'-0" | 5'-0" | CSMT. | METAL | |
| 05 | 4'-0" | 6'-0" | PICT. | WOOD | ARCH TOP |
| 06 | 2'-6" | 5'-6" | S.H. | VINYL | |

DOOR AND FRAME SCHEDULE

| MARK | DOOR | | | | | LOUVER | | FRAME | | | | | FIRE RATING LABEL | HARDWARE | | NOTES |
|------|------|------|------|------|--------|--------|------|-------|------|--------|------|------|------|----------|------|-------|
| | SIZE | | | MATL | GLAZING | WD | HGT | MATL | EL | DETAIL | | | | SET NO | KEYSIDE RM NO | |
| | WD | HGT | THK | | | | | | | HEAD | JAMB | SILL | | | | |
| 01 | 36" | 84" | 1-3/4" | WOOD | 180 sq.ft. | | | WOOD | | | | | | | | |
| 02 | 30" | 84" | 1-3/8" | METAL | | | | METAL | | | | | | | | |
| 03 | 28" | 84" | 1-3/8" | WOOD | | | | WOOD | | | | | | | | |
| 04 | 30" | 84" | 1-3/8" | WOOD | | | | WOOD | | | | | | | | |
| 05 | 30" | 84" | 1-3/4" | METAL | | | | METAL | | | | | | | | |
| 06 | 28" | 84" | 1-3/8" | WOOD | | | | WOOD | | | | | | | | |

**Figure 21-28.**
An example of a room finish schedule.

### Schedule Table

| ROOM_NO. | ROOM | FLOOR | | | | WALLS | | | | CEILING | | REMARKS |
|----------|------|-------|-------|-------|-------|-------|-------|-------|-------|---------|---------|---------|
| | | CARPET | CONCRETE | LINOLEUM | TILE | AC. PLASTER | DRYWALL | PAINT | TILE | DRYWALL | EXP. BEAMS | |
| 101 | THEATER | | ● | | | ● | | | | | ● | All finishes are applied over cmu walls |
| 102 | THEATER | | ● | | | ● | | | | | ● | All finishes are applied over cmu walls |
| 103 | THEATER | | ● | | | ● | | | | | ● | All finishes are applied over cmu walls |
| 104 | THEATER | | ● | | | ● | | | | | ● | All finishes are applied over cmu walls |
| 105 | THEATER | | ● | | | ● | | | | | ● | All finishes are applied over cmu walls |
| 106 | THEATER | | ● | | | ● | | | | | ● | All finishes are applied over cmu walls |
| 107 | LOBBY | ● | | | | | ● | ● | | ● | | All finishes are applied over cmu walls |
| 108 | STORAGE | | | ● | | | ● | | | ● | | All finishes are applied over cmu walls |
| 109 | MEN'S REST. | | | | ● | | ● | ● | ● | | | All finishes are applied over cmu walls |
| 110 | WOMEN'S REST. | | | | ● | | ● | ● | ● | | | All finishes are applied over cmu walls |

## Exercise 21-7

◆ Open ex21-6.
◆ If you have Microsoft Excel installed, insert ex21-5.csv into the drawing as an OLE object.
◆ Double-click on the OLE object to open Excel. Remove the Block Name and Count columns.
◆ Use the **OLE Properties** dialog box to change the Arial 10 point text to be 6" in AutoCAD.
◆ Save the drawing as ex21-7.

Figure 21-29.
An example of a furniture and equipment schedule.

## FURNITURE SCHEDULE

| NO | DESCRIPTION | MANUFACTURER | MODEL | $ COST |
|----|-------------|--------------|-------|--------|
| 101 | DESK | PSM DESIGNS | 65421 | $249.00 |
| 102 | CHAIR | COMFY CHAIR CO. | 36685 | $119.00 |
| 103 | LAMP | M & L LIGHTING | L55321 | $48.00 |
| 104 | TABLE | PSM DESIGNS | 45931 | $332.00 |
| 105 | BOOKCASE | PSM DESIGNS | 58614 | $189.00 |
|  |  |  |  | $937.00 |

## EQUIPMENT SCHEDULE

| NO | DESCRIPTION | MANUFACTURER | MODEL | $ COST |
|----|-------------|--------------|-------|--------|
| 201 | COOKTOP | KITCHENS ETC. | C4521G | $249.00 |
| 202 | MICROWAVE | HOME FURNISHINGS | TR6984 | $119.00 |
| 203 | REFER. | KITCHENS ETC. | LKD658 | $357.00 |
| 204 | DISHWASHER | APPLIANCES INC. | 95483 | $149.00 |
| 205 | OVEN | KITCHENS ETC. | Y23559 | $189.00 |
|  |  |  |  | $1063.00 |

# Recording Information to the Drawing

Often, it is important to have information about the drawing accessible. AutoCAD can save the time the drawing was created and edited, and provide general information. The **DWGPROPS** command is used to view and edit this information. The command can be accessed by selecting **Drawing Properties...** from the **File** pull-down menu or entering dwgprops at the Command prompt. This opens the *drawing name* **Properties** dialog box. See **Figure 21-30**. The dialog box contains **General**, **Summary**, **Statistics**, and **Custom** tabs. Each tab contains different information, some that is read-only and other areas that can be modified.

The **General** tab contains read-only information regarding the drawing, such as the name of the file, when it was created, file size, and saved location. The **Attributes** area contains Windows system check boxes to show their state, but they cannot be modified.

The **Summary** tab contains text boxes for user-definable information, such as the title of the drawing, drafter, keywords, and comments. See **Figure 21-31**. The **Keywords** and **Comments** text boxes are utilized when using the **Search** option in **DesignCenter**. When searching for a drawing through **DesignCenter**, simply do a search on some keywords and **DesignCenter** locates the drawing file.

The **Statistics** tab includes read-only information, such as the drawing creation date and time, the last modified date and time, the name of the user who saved the file last, the revision number, and the total editing time. See **Figure 21-32**. The **Last saved by** area is utilized if your computer requires you to log onto the machine. The log on user name is displayed here.

DWGPROPS

File
➥ Drawing
Properties...

**Figure 21-30.**
The **Properties** dialog box is used to view information about the drawing.

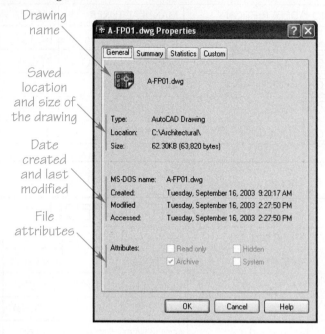

Drawing name

Saved location and size of the drawing

Date created and last modified

File attributes

**Figure 21-31.**
The **Summary** tab contains user-definable properties.

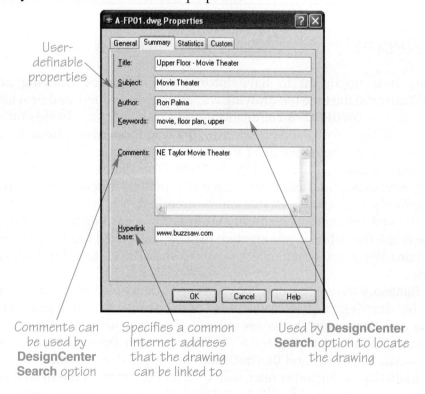

User-definable properties

Comments can be used by **DesignCenter Search** option

Specifies a common Internet address that the drawing can be linked to

Used by **DesignCenter Search** option to locate the drawing

The **Custom** tab includes several empty text boxes that can be used to keep track of drawing revisions. See **Figure 21-33.** There is a maximum of 10 rows that can be used. Enter the revision information or review notes when the drawing changes.

**Figure 21-32.**
The **Statistics** tab contains read-only information about the drawing file.

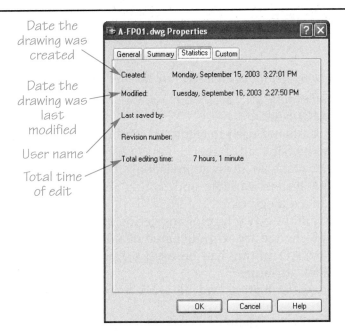

*Date the drawing was created*

*Date the drawing was last modified*

*User name*

*Total time of edit*

**Figure 21-33.**
The **Custom** tab includes 10 text boxes that can be used for revisions.

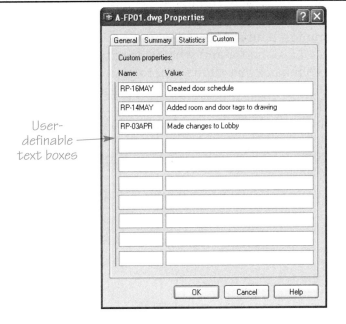

*User-definable text boxes*

**Professional Tip**

Establish office standards for filling out the **Properties** dialog box when first beginning a drawing. By filling out the information, the drawing can be searched for through **DesignCenter**. The **Total editing time** area in the **Statistics** tab can also be used for billing purposes.

# Chapter Test

*Answer the following questions on a separate sheet of paper.*

1. What is a *schedule?*
2. What is an *attribute?*
3. Name the command used to create an attribute.
4. Describe an invisible attribute.
5. How do you make an attribute invisible?
6. What is the system variable and setting that allows attribute prompts to be answered in a dialog box?
7. Briefly explain the advantage of answering attribute prompts in a dialog box.
8. How do you change an attribute value in a dialog box?
9. Which AutoCAD feature can be used to modify the values and properties of inserted block attributes?
10. Which AutoCAD feature can be used to modify attributes in existing block definitions?
11. Can changes to the existing attribute definitions be applied to inserted blocks?
12. Which AutoCAD wizard can be used to extract attribute data?
13. How do you specify only certain blocks and attributes to be used for the extraction file?
14. How do you insert an extracted file into AutoCAD with the **MTEXT** command?
15. What does *OLE* stand for and what is its basic function?
16. Name the command that allows you to place an OLE object into AutoCAD.
17. When an object is linked to AutoCAD, what happens when the original file is edited and saved?
18. When an object is embedded in AutoCAD, what is the relationship back to the original file?
19. Describe how to move and stretch an OLE file that has been inserted into AutoCAD.
20. Explain the use of tabulated schedules and finish schedules.

Residential A

1. Open drawing 20-ResA.
   A. Create a **Window tag** block with attributes as shown at the left below. Justification is middle center and text height is 3/32". All attributes are invisible except the **WIN#** attribute.
   B. Insert the **Window tag** at a scale of 48 for all of the windows. Fill out the attribute information completely. See the drawing on page 778 for reference.
   C. Create a **Door tag** block with attributes as shown at the right below. Justification is middle center and text height is 3/32". All attributes are invisible except the **DR#** attribute.

   D. Insert the **Door tag** block at a scale of 48 for all of the doors. Fill out the attribute information completely.
   E. Save the drawing as 21-ResA.

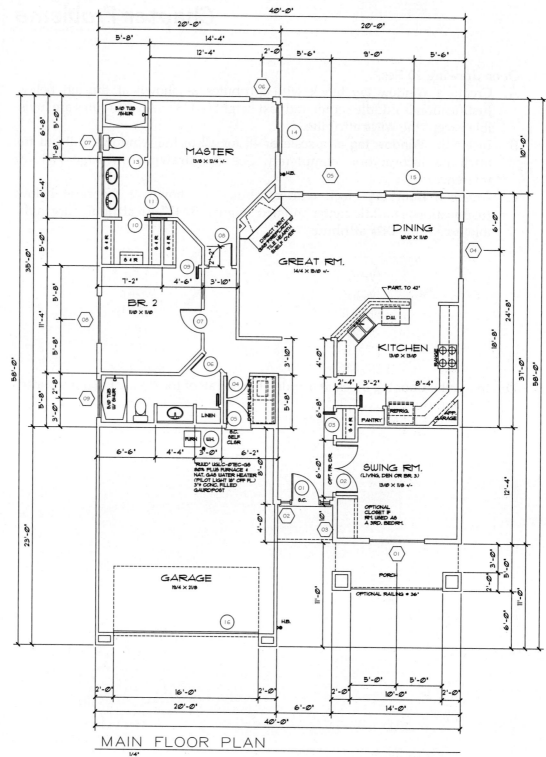

MAIN FLOOR PLAN
1/4"

(Alan Mascord Design Associates, Inc.)

2. Open drawing **20-ResB**.

Project

   A. Create a **Window tag** block with attributes as shown at the left below. Justification is middle center and text height is 3/32″. All attributes are invisible except the **WIN#** attribute.

   B. Insert the **Window tag** at a scale of 48 for all of the windows. Fill out the attribute information completely. See the drawing on page 780 for reference.

   Residential B

   C. Create a **Door tag** block with attributes as shown at the right below. Justification is middle center and text height is 3/32″. All attributes are invisible except the **DR#** attribute.

   D. Insert the **Door tag** block at a scale of 48 for all of the doors. Fill out the attribute information completely.

   E. Extract the window attribute values and create a window schedule.

   F. Extract the door attribute values and create a door schedule.

   G. Save the drawing as 21-ResB.

   (3D-DZYN)

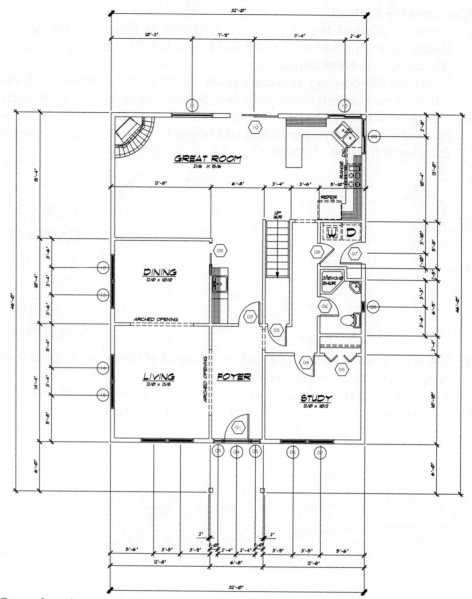

3. Open drawing 16-Multifamily.
   A. Create a door tag and a window tag and insert them into the drawing.
   B. Create the equipment tag as shown below. Insert the tag at a scale of 48 for all of the appliances. Justification is middle center and text height is 3/32". All attributes are invisible except the **ENO** attribute.
   C. If you have Microsoft Excel, extract the attribute values as a comma-separated file. Import the file into Microsoft Excel and format the schedule. If you do not have Microsoft Excel, extract the attribute values as a tab-separated file. Open the extracted data file in Microsoft WordPad and format it.
   D. Use the **INSERTOBJ** command to insert either the Excel or WordPad file.

Project

Multifamily

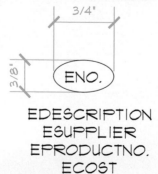

E. Save the drawing as 21-Multifamily.

(3D-DZYN)

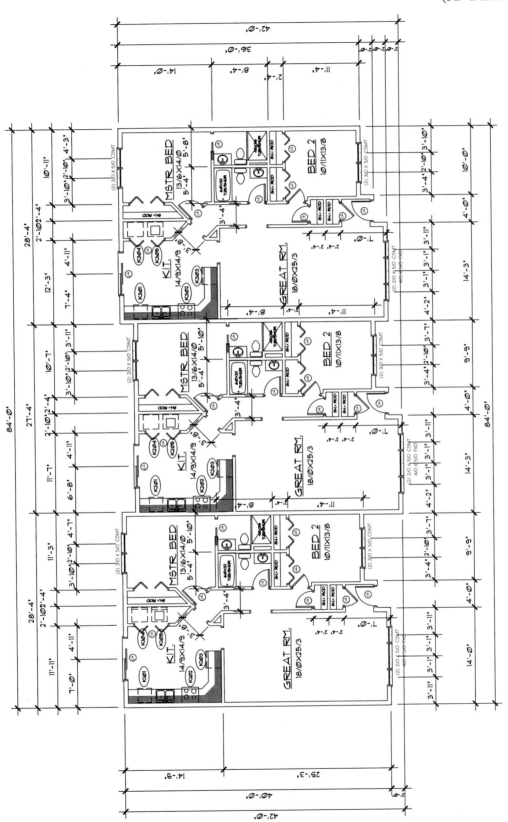

4. A. Open drawing 16-Commercial-Main.

B. Create a door tag as shown in Problem 1. Insert the tag at a scale of 96.
C. If you have Microsoft Excel, extract the attribute values as a comma-separated file. Import the file into Microsoft Excel and format the schedule. If you do not have Microsoft Excel, extract the attribute values as a tab-separated file. Open the extracted data file in Microsoft WordPad and format it.
D. Use the **INSERTOBJ** command to insert either the Excel or WordPad file.
E. Save the drawing as 21-Commercial.

(Cynthia Bankey Architect, Inc.)

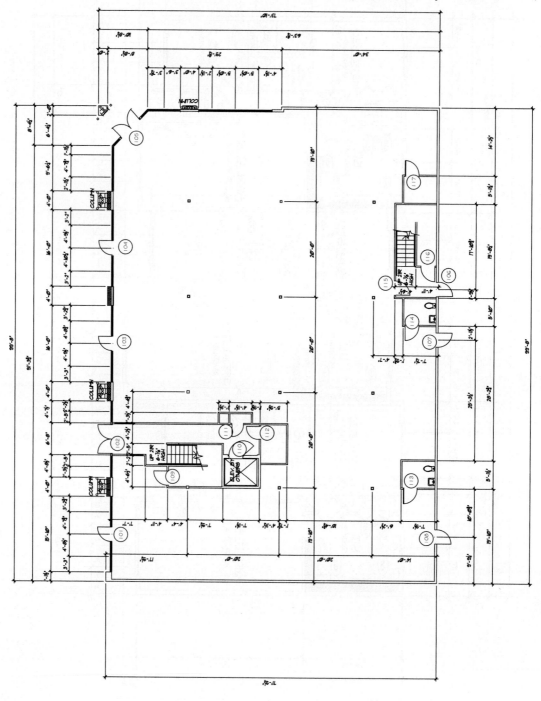

# CHAPTER 22

# Drawing Framing Plans and Roof Plans

## Learning Objectives

After completing this chapter, you will be able to:

◆ Use different techniques to draw framing plans for residential and commercial construction.

◆ Draw roof plans and roof framing plans for residential and commercial construction.

◆ Identify and define framing construction members.

◆ Use the AutoCAD geometry calculator for drawing applications.

## Important Terms

broken-out section
framing plan
header
hip
included angle
panelized roof system
purlins

ridge
roof framing plan
system variables
valley
variable
vertex

Chapter 18 introduced the framing found on a foundation plan. Foundation framing uses either a floor joist foundation system or a post and beam foundation system. In Chapter 20, balloon and platform framing techniques and typical framing details were discussed. Framing plans in a set of construction documents provide the locations and sizes of beams, headers, and framing members. This chapter explains how to create framing and roof plans.

# Creating Framing Plans

A *framing plan* is used to indicate the size and location of the framing members required to support the floor or roof. The framing plan is also used to indicate the direction in which the framing members run in the building and any supports for the framing such as beams, girders, and headers.

There are two main ways to represent framing in a set of construction documents. The first method is to indicate the size and direction of the framing with arrows and notes directly on the floor plan, similar to the way you add framing notes to a floor joist foundation. See **Figure 22-1.** The other method is to create a separate framing plan complete with each piece of framing, similar to adding each girder for a post and beam foundation. See **Figure 22-2.** In both cases, the framing plan is superimposed over the floor plan. This makes it easier to determine the framing locations within the building.

**Figure 22-1.**
A floor plan with framing notes applied.

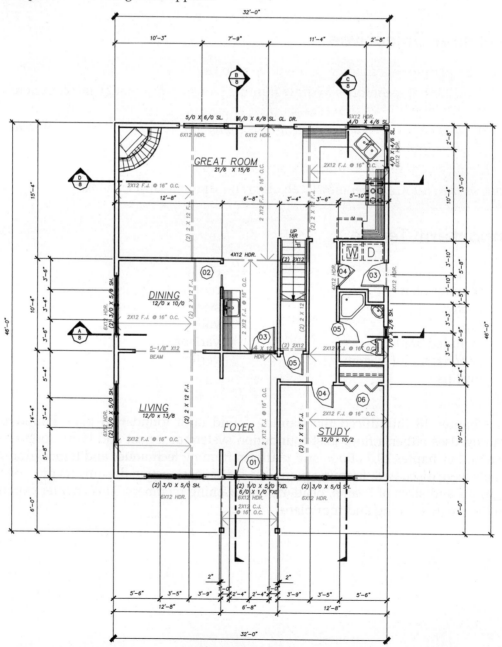

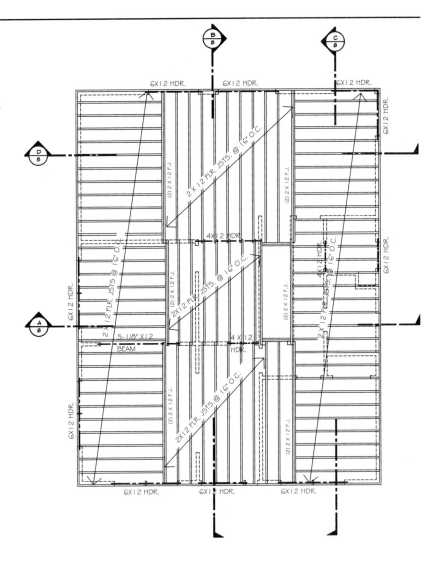

**Figure 22-2.**
Some practices require a separate framing plan indicating framing members and beam locations.

## Drawing Framing on the Floor Plan

In **Figure 22-1,** the framing is applied directly on the floor plan. A double arrow indicates the direction of framing runs. The size and type of framing member is indicated above the double arrow. Beams are shown as thick centerlines. The size of the beam is placed above the line. The method described in this section is commonly used, but can vary slightly between companies.

The advantage of placing the framing on the floor plan is eliminating the need for a separate framing plan. However, when using this method, the floor plan can quickly become cluttered with the addition of notes and symbols. Therefore, you may only want to use this method when the floor plan is large, has few notes, is not complex, or when the drawing will be plotted at a larger scale. Many offices prefer this method for residential construction because the framing is usually more simple than that found in a commercial building. Also, local building requirements may not require a separate framing plan for residences.

Before drawing the framing notes on the floor plan, you need to consider where the beams should be located. Most openings in a wall, such as doors, windows, or an open doorway, have a header placed over the opening. A *header* is a construction member placed over the opening for support of the joists above. The framing members on the next floor or the ceiling joist members can then be placed on top of the bearing walls and headers. Headers are normally placed directly over a door or window opening.

Large open areas in a room often have a beam at, or near, the center to support the framing above, allowing the spans of joists to be shorter. When determining beam locations, look for areas in the building that have long floor or ceiling joist spans. Place the beams where the joists above are best supported. In some instances where a beam is placed in the middle of a room, the bottom of the beam is placed flush with the ceiling with joists, which hang off the beam for support, instead of on top of the beam. In these cases, the note FLUSH is placed next to the beam size. Consult span tables or charts to determine the proper spans for the type of joists you are using.

Span tables can be obtained from the joist manufacturer. The tables are used to establish the joist size and maximum span. In wood construction, a good general rule is to place beams where the span is greater than 12'-0". With steel construction, the spans can be greater, depending on the material used and the loads applied.

When representing beams, use a line or polyline with a centerline linetype. Extend the ends of the beam into the component that supports the beams. The support for the beams can be a wall or a post. Beams are represented as a heavy line. This can be accomplished by adjusting the lineweight for the layer the beam is on or by using a wide polyline. **Figure 22-3** displays beams and headers for the house drawing. It is easier to determine where the runs for the framing should be after the beams are in place, as the beams indicate the support locations for joist spans.

**Figure 22-3.**
Beams on the main floor support the upper floor or the roof.

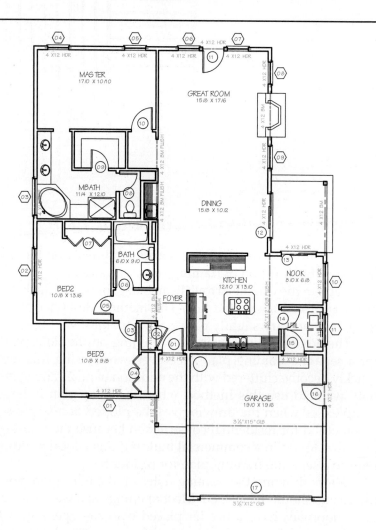

Architectural Drafting Using AutoCAD

## Exercise 22-1

◆ Open ex21-7.
◆ Create a layer named M-Beams. Assign a centerline linetype and set current.
◆ Add beams and headers in the locations indicated in **Figure 22-3**.
◆ Note that not all of the openings have beams over them. Typically, openings that run parallel to the framing members directly above do not require a beam.
◆ Add sizes for the beams on the M-Notes layer. Refer to **Figure 22-3** for the beam sizes.
◆ Save the drawing as ex22-1.

## Creating a Framing Notes Dimensioning Style

Dimensions can be drawn to construct the joist arrows. Then, edit the dimension text to reflect the note. First, create a dimension style for the joists. See **Figure 22-4.** Give the style a name that indicates it is to be used for framing notes, such as Framing. Suppress the extension lines and change the arrowheads to the **Right angle** type. Set the size for the arrowheads to be larger than the regular dimension arrowheads. See **Figure 22-5.** Next, set the text style to the style you want to use for notes. Set the dimension text height. Align the dimension text with the dimension and place the text above the dimension line. See **Figure 22-6.**

**Figure 22-4.**
Creating a dimension style to use for framing notes.

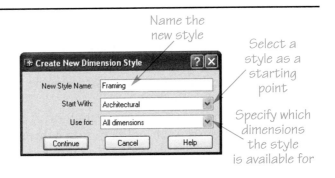

Name the new style

Select a style as a starting point

Specify which dimensions the style is available for

**Figure 22-5.**
Turning off the extension lines and adjusting the arrowheads.

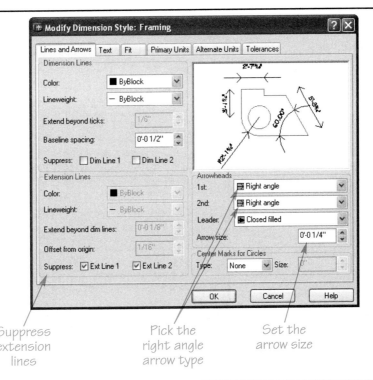

Suppress extension lines

Pick the right angle arrow type

Set the arrow size

**Figure 22-6.**
Adjusting the text parameters for the framing dimension style.

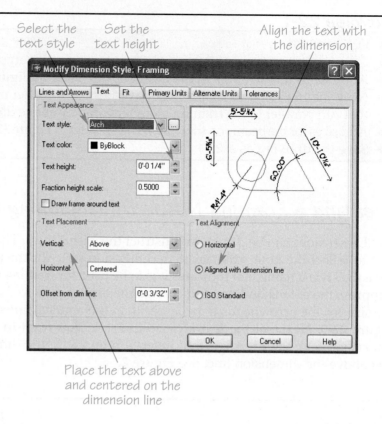

Select the text style

Set the text height

Align the text with the dimension

Place the text above and centered on the dimension line

The last things to check are the fit of the text and the scaling of the dimension. The fit can be your choice or the style used by your office. The framing note text should be the same as the text on the drawing dimensions. Therefore, use the same overall scale. See **Figure 22-7.**

Once the dimension style is created, set it current and add dimensions between the walls and beams in the direction in which the joists run. After the dimension strings are in place, use the **DDEDIT** command or the **Properties** window to edit the dimension text. The text should indicate the size and spacing of the framing members, as shown in **Figure 22-8.**

**Figure 22-7.**
Setting the fit variables of the text for the framing dimension style.

Select a fit option

Set the scale

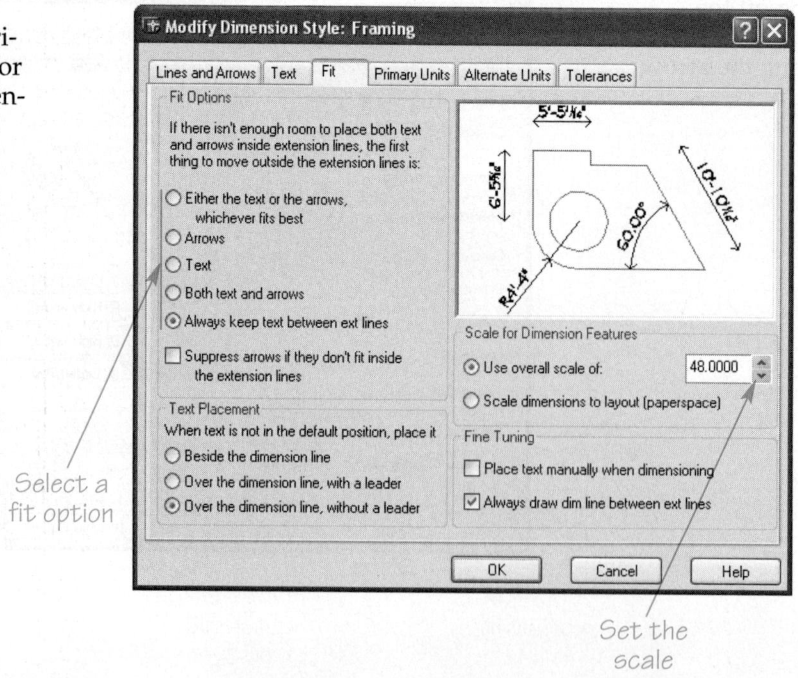

## Figure 22-8.

Process of creating framing joist notes. A—Add a dimension in the direction of the framing runs (shown in color). B—Use the **Properties** window (shown here) or the **DDEDIT** command to edit the dimension text for the size and spacing of the framing members. C—The finished notes.

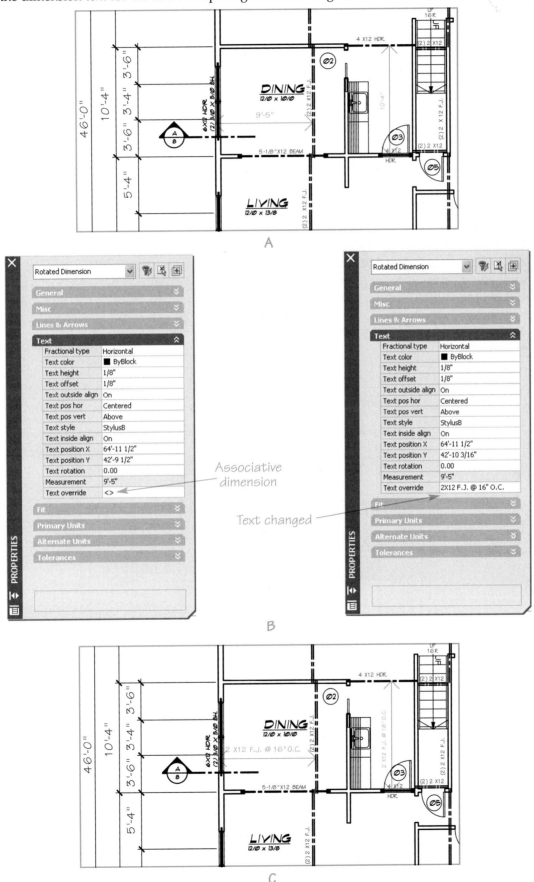

The final step in creating the notes on the floor plan is to indicate any supporting posts and their sizes. Use a diagonal line starting from a corner of the post. Add the size of the post above the line, **Figure 22-9.**

**Figure 22-9.**
A typical post note.

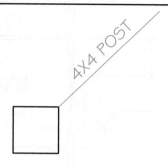

## Exercise 22-2

◆ Open ex22-1.
◆ Create a dimension style similar to the one described in the text. Set it current.
◆ Create a layer named M-Framing and set it current.
◆ Place dimensions to represent the framing runs. Use the diagram below as a guide.
◆ Use the **DDEDIT** command to edit the dimension text to display the size and spacing of the joists.
◆ Place notes on the posts to indicate the post size.
◆ Save the drawing as ex22-2.

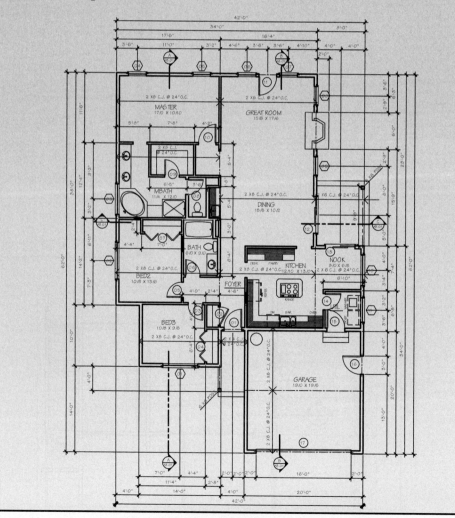

# Drawing a Separate Framing Plan

A *framing plan* is a separate drawing showing framing information such as framing members, beams, and posts. The framing plan includes only the framing construction components and the supporting floor plan walls. This can eliminate the clutter created by adding the framing runs, sizes, and notes directly on the floor plan.

There are two basic types of framing plans. One type of framing plan contains the beam locations and framing notes with double arrows, as described in the previous section. This eliminates extra information, such as door and window tags, specific floor plan notes, or symbols. See **Figure 22-10.** Notice how much cleaner the drawing looks without all of the floor plan information when compared to **Figure 22-1.**

**Figure 22-10.**
A simple framing plan.

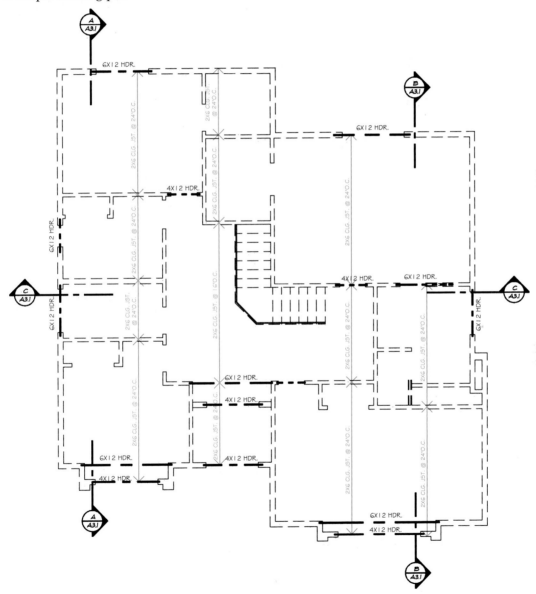

The second type of framing plan includes the individual framing pieces drawn over the walls of the supporting floor. There are two ways of representing the framing members in this type of framing plan. One way is to draw each piece of framing with double lines representing the width of the framing member. See **Figure 22-11A.** The other way is to draw a centerline for each framing member. See **Figure 22-11B.** This method is similar to using centerlines to represent the beam center locations in a post and beam foundation.

The process of drawing either type of framing plan is similar to placing the framing notes directly on the floor plan. First, draw or xref the supporting floor plan below the framing joists. Draw the rim joist around the perimeter of the building, if required. Next, add all of the beams that support the joists. Add the framing with centerlines, double lines, or as notes with a double arrow. Finally, place the framing notes on the drawing for the sizes of beams, joists, and posts. In some cases, the beam locations may need to be dimensioned.

**Figure 22-11.**
There are two basic types of framing plans. A—Double lines are used to represent the width of each framing joist. B—Centerlines are used to represent the center of each framing joist.

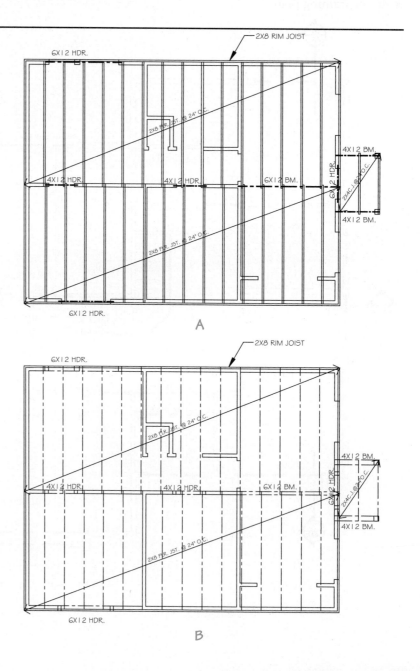

If required, a top section of the building materials at the floor level is drawn on the framing plan. This section is usually drawn where it will not obstruct the representation of the joists, such as in a corner. An arc indicates the "broken-out" part of the section and graphically displays the subfloor and finished floor over the joists. See **Figure 22-12**. This method is called a *broken-out section*.

The framing plan includes the floor plan of the supporting floor below to indicate the placement of the framing within the building. The walls are plotted with a thin lineweight or lighter color and with a dashed linetype because the walls are not the focus of the framing plan.

**Figure 22-12.**
A broken-out section is shown over the framing joists to indicate the flooring construction.

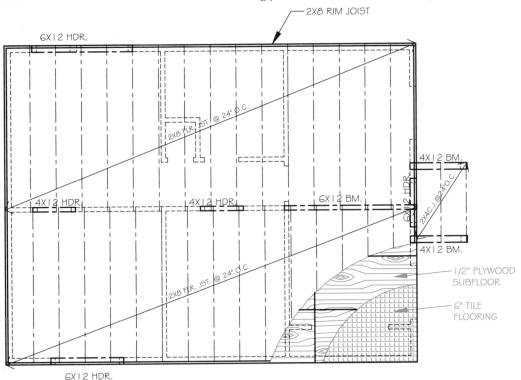

## Creating Roof Framing Plans

The *roof framing plan* is similar to the framing plan. The roof framing plan, however, shows rafter or truss locations and any beams supporting these framing members. Along with the framing members and beams, the roof framing plan needs to include construction information.

### Residential Roofing Plan

In residential design, roofs are often sloped and intersect with other portions of the roof. Hip, valley, and ridge are common roof framing terms. The *hip* is the part of a roof where two sides of a roof meet. The *valley* is the internal angle where two roof sides intersect. The *ridge* is the point at which two roofs come together at their highest point. See **Figure 22-13**. A roof may contain all, some, or none of these elements, depending on how the roof is designed. In commercial building, it is common to have a roof with a slight slope from one side of the structure to the other. In this case, the roof may not have a hip, ridge, or valley.

Figure 22-13.
Typical roof parts.

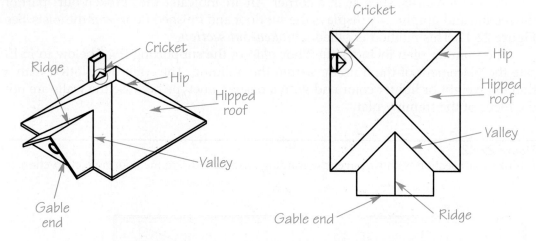

When drawing the roof framing plan for a roof with equal pitches, the ridge is formed halfway between the two intersecting sides of the roof. The elevations should show how the two sides of the roof come together. See **Figure 22-14.** If the roof has the same pitch on all sides, the hips and valleys are drawn with 45° angles from the corner of the building or from the ridge. When laying out the roof structure, refer to elevations often. Direct projection from the elevations to the floor plan can aid in the development of the ridge, hip, and valley lines. See **Figure 22-15.** Direct projection can be particularly helpful when laying out a roof having more than one pitch, such as a front porch with a different pitch from the rest of the house.

**Figure 22-14.**
Determining the ridge line for a roof.

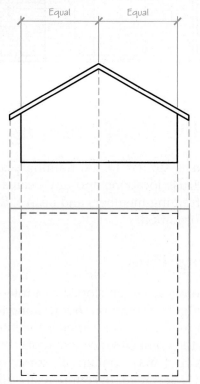

**Figure 22-15.**
Using direct projection to determine the roofline.

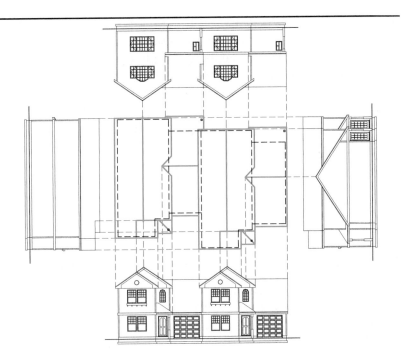

The roof framing plan also includes the overhang and an outline of the floor plan below. Other elements to include on the plan are roof vent locations and notes referring to the construction of the roof. **Figure 22-16** shows a typical roof framing plan.

Roof ventilation is typically 1/150 of the total roof area. To determine the required number of roof vents, first use the **AREA** command to calculate the roof area. Then, divide the roof area by 150 to determine the total ventilation area required. Use the formula:

Roof Square Footage ÷150 = Total Square Footage of Ventilation Required

**Figure 22-16.**
A roof framing plan for residential construction.

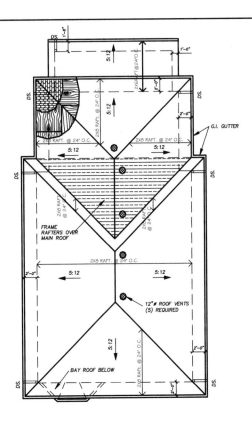

Roof vents are drawn as a 12″ × 12″ square or a ⌀12″ (diameter) circle. This creates a vent with approximately 1 ft² of ventilation. Therefore, the result from the given formula is the number of vents required on the roof. Place the roof vents toward the higher parts of the roof, near the ridge lines. This helps the warm air in the attic escape.

Roof drainage is also a part of the roof framing plan. In **Figure 22-16,** a 4″ gutter is shown on all sides of the roof that slope down. Downspout locations are indicated by a small circle within the gutter and two parallel lines leading to another circle along the building. The downspout is for rainwater to flow from the gutter to the ground or storm sewer. The downspouts are labeled **DS** on the plan. Place downspouts at the corners of the building where the roof slopes down.

Professional Tip

Similar to a framing plan, the roof plan includes notes for the framing members used to create the roof. You can create roof plans using dimension notes similar to those in **Figure 22-10,** double lines for each rafter similar to those in **Figure 22-11A,** or centerlines to represent rafters similar to those in **Figure 22-11B.**

## Exercise 22-3

◆ Start a new drawing using one of your templates.
◆ Create the following layers:
  ◆ X-Floor Plan
  ◆ R-Roofline
  ◆ R-Bldg_Outline (Dashed linetype)
  ◆ R-Framing
  ◆ R-Drainage (Hidden linetype)
  ◆ R-Vent
  ◆ R-Hatch
  ◆ R-Notes
  ◆ R-Dims
◆ Xref ex22-2 as an overlay at a location of 0,0.
◆ Use the R-Bldg_Outline layer to trace the outline of the house.
◆ Draw the roofline for the house. Use direct projection if needed.
◆ Add the notes, vents, and drainage systems.
◆ Your drawing should look similar to the diagram shown on the following page.
◆ Save the drawing as ex22-3.

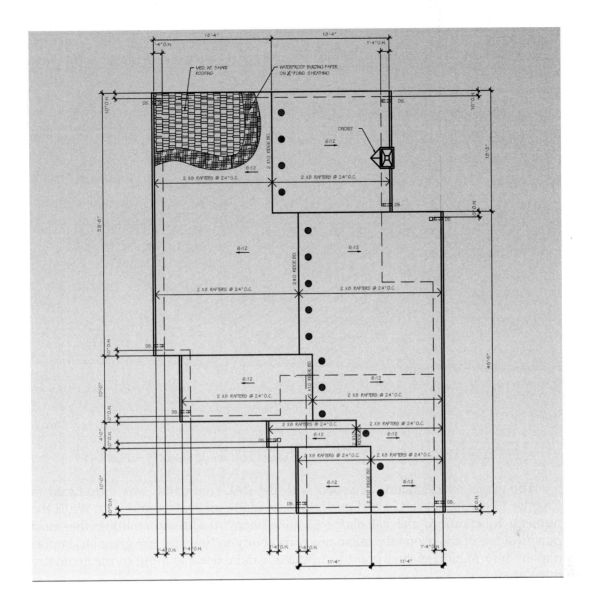

## Commercial Roof Framing Plan

Many commercial projects are built with a method called a ***panelized roof system.*** This system uses main support beams spread across the building at 20′ to 30′ intervals. Smaller beams, called ***purlins***, are added between or above the main support beams. The purlins are generally spaced 8′-0″ apart. Joists are then added between the purlins, commonly spaced 24″ on center. See **Figure 22-17.** The panelized roof is used mainly for flat or lower pitched roofs.

Commercial roof framing plans are similar to residential roofs with respect to the information required. Joists can be shown on top of support beams, as in the previous framing discussion. Another piece of information included on a commercial roof framing plan is the location of any mechanical equipment, such as air-conditioning units, and any special venting. A roof access door may need to be added to a plan for a flat roof. This door provides worker access to the mechanical equipment.

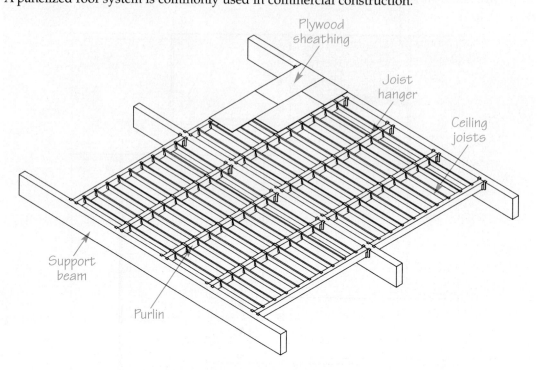

# Drawing Using the Geometry Calculator

The geometry calculator, accessed with the **CAL** command, was introduced in Chapter 13 to calculate areas and perform basic mathematical calculations. While the numeric functions of the calculator provide many useful capabilities, the most powerful use of the geometry calculator is its ability to find and use geometric information. Information such as point coordinates can be used as input to the geometry calculator.

A point coordinate is entered at the >> Expression: prompt as two or three numbers enclosed in square brackets and separated by commas. The numbers represent the X, Y, and Z coordinates. For example, [4,7,2], [2.1,3.79], or [2,7.4,0] are all valid entries. Any zero value coordinate can be omitted. For example:

| | | |
|---|---|---|
| [2,2] | is the same as | [2,2,0] |
| [,,6] | is the same as | [0,0,6] |
| [5] | is the same as | [5,0,0] |
| [ ] | is the same as | [0,0,0] |

Direction can be entered using any accepted AutoCAD format, including polar and relative coordinates:

| Coordinate system | Entry format |
|---|---|
| Polar | [dist<angle] |
| Relative | [@ x, y, z] |

These options provide the ability to determine locations, distances, and directions within a drawing.

For example, to determine the absolute coordinate value for a point six units from the absolute coordinate 2,2,0 at an angle of 45° within the XY plane, use the sequence:

Command: **cal**↵
\>> Expression: **[2,2,0]+[6<45]**↵
(6.24264 6.24264 0.0)

In an application of this type, the point answer is returned in parentheses with spaces separating the numbers instead of commas. Calculations can also be performed within the point coordinate specification:

\>> Expression: **[2+3,2+3,0]+[1,2,0]**↵
(6.0 7.0 0.0)

The current value of the **LASTPOINT** system variable can be determined using the geometry calculator. Enter the "@" symbol as follows:

Command: **cal**↵
\>> Expression: **@**↵

In addition to entering coordinates at the prompt, you can also specify point coordinates with the cursor. The **CUR** (cursor) expression is used to enter a point picked with the cursor:

Command: **cal**↵
\>> Expression: **cur**↵
\>> Enter a point: *(pick a point with the cursor)*
(4.12132 4.12132 0.0) *(the point coordinates will vary based on the selected point)*

A cursor pick can also be used as part of a calculation expression:

\>> Expression: **cur+[1,2]**↵
\>> Enter a point: *(pick a point with the cursor)*
(5.12132 6.12132 0.0) *(the point coordinates will vary based on the selected point)*

## Exercise 22-4

◆ Start a new drawing.
◆ Use the **CAL** command to find the following point coordinates. Enter values eliminating unneeded coordinates.

| Input | Returned Value |
|-------|----------------|
| [2,2,0]+[6<30] | (7.19615 5.0 0.0) |
| [4,3,0]+[2,2,0] | (6.0 5.0 0.0) |

◆ Use the **CAL** command to find the coordinates of a point selected with your cursor.
◆ Use your cursor to pick a point and add 3,2,0.
◆ Close the drawing without saving.

## Using the CAL Command Transparently

The **CAL** command can be used transparently within another command. To use the geometry calculator transparently, type 'cal (an apostrophe followed by cal) within a command. When the **CAL** command is used transparently, the result is supplied as the input to the current prompt.

---

The following example uses direct distance entry and the geometry calculator to provide the correct length of a line. The line being drawn is 1.006 times 8.0 inches. Note: When AutoCAD receives a single numeric value at a "point" prompt, the value is understood as a direct distance entry value.

> Command: l *or* **line**↵
> Specify first point: *(pick first point)*
> Specify next point or [Undo]: **'cal**↵ *(move cursor in correct direction, and the line will be drawn at this angle)*
> \>> Expression: **8\*1.006**↵
> 8.048
> Specify next point or [Undo]: ↵

The calculator evaluates the expression and supplies the result of 8.048 at the Specify next point or [Undo]: prompt. The line is drawn in the direction of the cursor location.

## Exercise 22-5

◆ Start a new drawing using one of your templates.
◆ Use the **CAL** command transparently within the **LINE** command to draw a line a length of 6 × 1.0625 from a point located at 2,4 using direct distance entry. The line should be drawn upward, from left to right, at an angle of approximately 45°.
◆ Save the drawing as ex22-5.

## *Using Object Snaps*

Object snaps can be used to select points as input for the geometry calculator. Object snaps provide the accuracy needed to precisely locate points on an object. The following example uses the **Endpoint** object snap to precisely locate a point on an object as the input for the calculator.

> Command: **cal**↵
> \>> Expression: **end**↵ *(the space bar cannot be used for [Enter])*
> \>> Select entity for END snap: *(pick the endpoint on an object)*
> (6.24264 6.24264 0.0) *(the point coordinates will vary based on the selected point)*

The next example uses the **Endpoint** object snap to find the end of a line and add the point coordinate of 2 at 45°:

> Command: **cal**↵
> \>> Expression: **end+[2<45]**↵
> \>> Select entity for END snap: *(pick the endpoint on an object)*
> (7.65685 7.65685 0.0) *(the point coordinates will vary based on the selected point)*

You can use the geometry calculator to provide information based on selected points. For example, the following sequence can be used to find the point midway between two points selected with the cursor.

> Command: **cal**↵
> \>> Expression: **(cur+cur)/2**↵
> \>> Enter a point: *(pick a point; use object snaps as needed)*
> \>> Enter a point: *(pick a point; use object snaps as needed)*
> (4.12132 4.12132 0.0) *(the point coordinates will vary based on the selected point)*

This same technique can be used with any desired object snap mode as part of the expression. The following example is used to find the midpoint of the distance between the center of a circle and the endpoint of a line.

Command: **cal**↵
>> Expression: **(cen+end)/2**↵
>> Select entity for CEN snap: *(pick the circle)*
>> Select entity for END snap: *(pick the endpoint of the line)*
(7.70597 2.29297 0.0) *(the point coordinates will vary based on the selected points)*

Suppose you want to draw a line starting from the point just calculated. Use the following sequence. Refer to **Figure 22-18.**

Command: **l** *or* **line.**↵
Specify first point: **'cal.**↵
>> Expression: **(cen+end)/2.**↵
>> Select entity for CEN snap: *(pick the circle)*
>> Select entity for END snap: *(pick the endpoint of the line)*
(7.70597 2.29297 0.0) *(the point coordinates will vary based on the selected points)*
Specify next point or [Undo]: *(pick the location of the second endpoint on the line)*
Specify next point or [Undo]: ↵

**Figure 22-18.**
Drawing a line halfway between the center of a circle and the endpoint of a line.

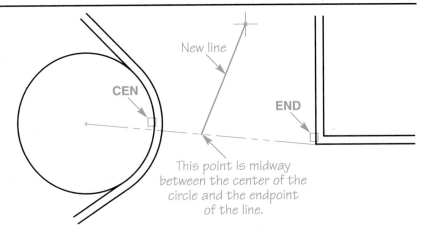

The following sequence is used to create a circle three units in diameter with its center located 12 units along the X axis from the midpoint of an existing line. Refer to **Figure 22-19.**

Command: **c** *or* **circle.**↵
Specify center point for circle or [3P/2P/Ttr (tan tan radius)]: **'cal.**↵
>> Expression: **mid+[12,0].**↵
>> Select entity for MID snap: *(pick the line)*
(7.75 2.25 0.0) *(the point coordinates will vary based on the selected point)*
Specify radius of circle or [Diameter] <*current*>: **d.**↵
Specify diameter of circle <*current*>: **3.**↵

The next sequence locates the center of mass, or centroid, of a pentagon. The centroid is located by picking the five endpoints of the pentagon and calculating the average. Refer to **Figure 22-20.**

Command: **cal.**↵
>> Expression: **(end+end+end+end+end)/5.**↵
>> Select entity for END snap: *(pick the first corner of the pentagon)*
>> Select entity for END snap: *(pick the second corner of the pentagon)*
>> Select entity for END snap: *(pick the third corner of the pentagon)*
>> Select entity for END snap: *(pick the fourth corner of the pentagon)*
>> Select entity for END snap: *(pick the fifth corner of the pentagon)*
(5.87785 8.09017 0.0) *(the point coordinates will vary based on the selected points)*

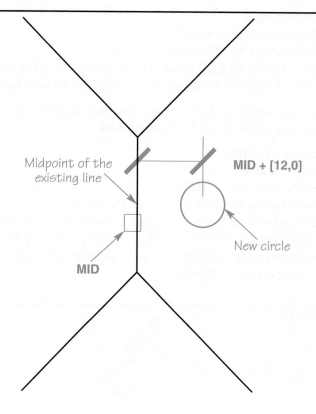

**Figure 22-19.**
Locating the center of a circle 12 units to the right (+X) of the midpoint of a line.

Midpoint of the existing line

MID

MID + [12,0]

New circle

## Exercise 22-6

◆ Start a drawing using one of your templates.
◆ Use the **CAL** command and object snaps as needed to create the drawings described below.
   ◆ Draw the square corner and double-line arc shown in **Figure 22-18**. Use **(CEN+END)/2** to draw a line starting halfway between the center of the arc and the endpoint of the outside line.
   ◆ Draw the roof peak shown in **Figure 22-19**. Use **MID+[2,0]** to draw a circle centered two units on the positive X axis from the midpoint of the vertical line.
   ◆ Draw two concentric pentagons, similar to those shown in **Figure 22-20**. Find the center of mass.
◆ Save the drawing as ex22-6.

## Calculating Distances

There are three basic geometry calculator functions used to calculate distances. These are the **DIST**, **DPL**, and **DPP** functions. The **DIST** (distance) function is entered as DIST($p1,p2$), where $p1$ = Point 1 and $p2$ = Point 2. The **DIST** function performs a simple distance calculation between the two specified points. Similar to all calculator functions, the points can be entered manually or picked. To find the distance between the endpoint and midpoint of a line, use the **DIST** function:

Command: **cal**↵
>> Expression: **dist(end,mid)**↵
>> Select entity for END snap: *(pick one endpoint of the line)*
>> Select entity for MID snap: *(pick the line)*
(5.87785) *(the distance value will vary based on the selected points)*

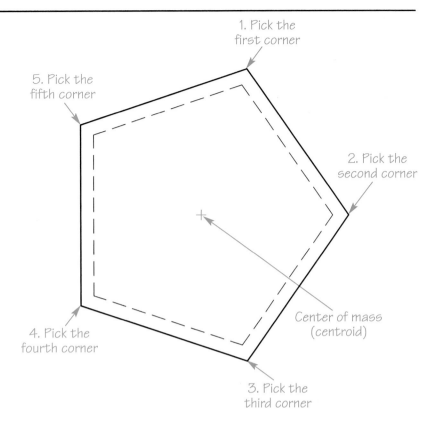

**Figure 22-20.**
Locating the center of mass of a polygon.

1. Pick the first corner

2. Pick the second corner

3. Pick the third corner

4. Pick the fourth corner

5. Pick the fifth corner

Center of mass (centroid)

The **DPL** (distance/point/line) function calculates the perpendicular distance between a point and a line passing through two other selected points. This function is written as DPL(*p,p1,p2*), where *p* is the point, *p1* is the first endpoint of the line, and *p2* is the second endpoint of the line. The points are selected in this order. See **Figure 22-21.** The following example uses **DPL** and the **Endpoint** object snap.

> Command: **cal**↵
> \>> Expression: **DPL(end,end,end)**↵
> \>> Select entity for END snap: *(pick an object)*
> \>> Select entity for END snap: *(pick an object)*
> \>> Select entity for END snap: *(pick an object)*
> (5.87785) *(the distance value will vary based on the selected points)*

The **DPP** (distance/point/plane) function works much like the **DPL** function, except it finds the shortest distance from a selected point to a plane defined by three other selected points. The **DPP** function is written as DPP(*p,p1,p2,p3*), where *p* is the selected point and *p1, p2,* and *p3* define the plane. See **Figure 22-22.** The points for **DPP** can be entered manually or picked. The following example calculates the distance between a point at absolute coordinate 2,2,6 and three points on the XY plane.

> Command: **cal**↵
> \>> Expression: **dpp([2,2,6],cur,cur,cur)**↵
> \>> Enter a point: *(pick a point)*
> \>> Enter a point: *(pick a point)*
> \>> Enter a point: *(pick a point)*
> 6.0 *(the point manually entered is six units above the XY plane)*

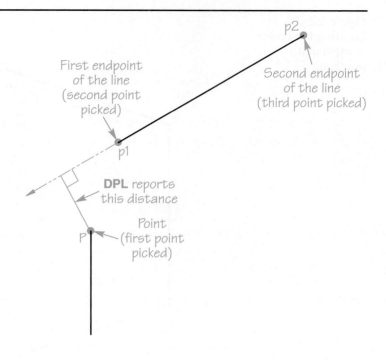

**Figure 22-21.**
Finding the shortest distance (perpendicular distance) between a point and a line.

First endpoint of the line (second point picked)

Second endpoint of the line (third point picked)

p2

p1

**DPL** reports this distance

Point (first point picked)

P

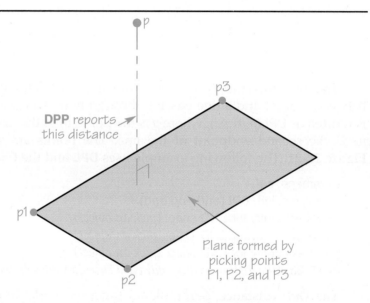

**Figure 22-22.**
Finding the perpendicular distance between a point and a plane.

p

p3

**DPP** reports this distance

p1

p2

Plane formed by picking points P1, P2, and P3

## Exercise 22-7

◆ Start a drawing using one of your templates.
◆ Draw a line. Draw another line that is not parallel to the first line.
◆ Use the **CAL** command to complete this exercise.
◆ Find the distance between the ends of the first line.
◆ Find one-half the length of the first line.
◆ Find the perpendicular distance between one endpoint of the second line and the first line.
◆ Save the drawing as ex22-7.

## Finding Intersection Points

The **ILL** (intersection/line/line) function locates an intersection point between two nonparallel lines. This function is written as ILL(*p1,p2,p3,p4*), where *p1* and *p2* define the first line and *p3* and *p4* define the second line. The selected points can be on a line or in space. This function finds a hypothetical intersection as if the lines are infinite in length. The following sequence uses **ILL** to find the intersection between an existing line and an imaginary line between the endpoint and midpoint of two other lines, as shown in **Figure 22-23**.

> Command: **cal**↵
> \>> Expression: **ill([2,5,0],cur,end,mid)**↵
> \>> Enter a point: *(pick the endpoint of the first line)*
> \>> Select entity for END snap: *(pick the endpoint of the second line)*
> \>> Select entity for MID snap: *(pick the midpoint of the third line)*
> (6.37637 6.01716 0.0) *(the point coordinates will vary based on the selected points)*

**Figure 22-23.**
Finding the intersection point between nonparallel lines defined by picking four points. In this example, one line exists (*p1/p2*) and the other line is imaginary (*p3/p4*).

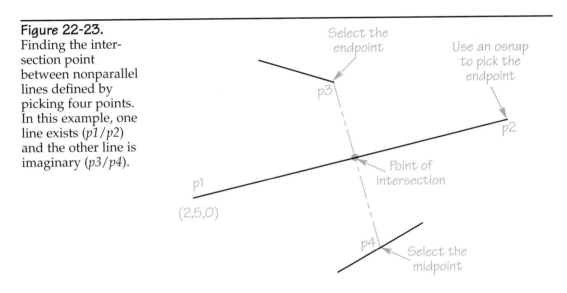

## Finding a Point on a Line

The **PLD** (point/line/distance) function finds a point on a line a specified distance from the start point. The line is defined by two picked points. A line does not need to exist between the two selected points. The function is written as PLD(*p1,p2,dist*). The following sequence finds a point along a line passing through 0,0 and 3,1 that is 10 units from the start point. Refer to **Figure 22-24**.

**Figure 22-24.**
Finding a point along a line a specified distance from the start point.

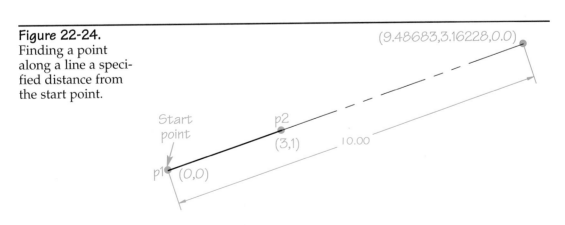

Command: **cal**↵
\>> Expression: **pld([ ],[3,1],10)**↵
(9.48683 3.16228 0.0)

The **PLT** (point/line/parameter t) function provides another means of finding a point along a line. Written as PLT(*p1,p2,t*), this function finds a point along a line passing through *p1* and *p2*. The point is located from the start point based on parameter *t*. The parameter *t* is simply a scale factor relative to the distance between *p1* and *p2*. If *t* = 0, the point is on *p1*. If *t* = 1, the point is on *p2*. If *t* = .5, the point is the midpoint between *p1* and *p2*. If *t* = 2.0, the point is located away from *p1* twice the distance from *p1* to *p2*. **Figure 22-25** shows several examples. The following sequence locates a point that is three quarters of the way along the length of a line between (0,0,0) and (2,2,0).

Command: **cal**↵
\>> Expression: **plt([ ],[2,2],.75)**↵
(1.5 1.5 0.0)

**Figure 22-25.**
Finding points along a line based on the scale of the line's length (parameter *t*).

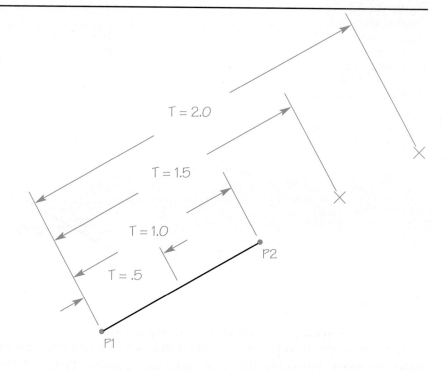

## Exercise 22-8

◆ Start a drawing using one of your templates.
◆ Draw a single line. Use the **CAL** command and **@** as needed to find the distance between the last point and the point 4,4,0.
◆ Draw two nonparallel lines that do not intersect. Use the **ILL** function to determine the point of intersection.
◆ Draw a line segment with two endpoints no more than 1" apart. Use the **PLD** function to find the coordinates of a point 3.375" from the start point.
◆ Draw a line and use the **PLT** function to find a point that is twice the distance from the start point.
◆ Save the drawing as ex22-8.

Architectural Drafting Using AutoCAD

# Finding an Angle

The **ANG** (angle) function finds the angle between two lines. As with other calculator functions, point specifications can be made and the lines do not need to exist in the drawing. This function can be entered in several different ways, depending on the nature of the angle you are trying to calculate.

To find the angle of a vector from the X axis in the XY plane, enter ang (*coordinates*). The coordinate values are entered within parentheses. The coordinates can be manually entered or a point can be picked with the cursor. The following sequence is shown in **Figure 22-26A.**

> Command: **cal**↵
> >> Expression: **ang([1,1,0])**↵ *(notice the use of square brackets)*
> 45.0

If the vector (line) is not known, two points along a line can be used to determine the angle of the line in the XY plane from the X axis. The formula is ang(*p1, p2*), as represented in **Figure 22-26B** and the following sequence:

> Command: **cal**↵
> >> Expression: **ang([2,2],[4,4])**↵
> 45.0

You can also calculate an included angle by specifying a vertex and a point on each side (leg) of the angle. A *vertex* is the intersection of two lines. An *included angle* is the angle formed between the vertex and the sides of the angle. The formula is entered as ang(*vertex,p1,p2*), **Figure 22-26C.** The following example determines the angle between two lines. The **Endpoint** object snap mode is used to select points.

> Command: **cal**↵
> >> Expression: **ang(end,end,end)**↵
> >> Select entity for END snap: *(pick vertex)*
> >> Select entity for END snap: *(pick end of first line)*
> >> Select entity for END snap: *(pick end of second line)*
> *(angle)*

---

**Figure 22-26.**
Finding an angle with the **ANG** function. A—Entering a single coordinate returns the angle from the X axis to the point with 0,0 as the vertex. B—Entering two coordinates returns the angle from horizontal to the line formed by the two points. C—Entering three coordinates finds the angle between the two lines formed from the three points.

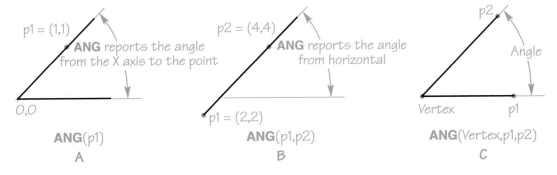

## Exercise 22-9

- Start a drawing using one of your templates.
- Draw a line using 0,0 as the start point. Do not draw a horizontal line. Use the **ANG** function to determine the angle of the line relative to horizontal.
- Draw a line at any angle that does not start or end at 0,0. Use the **ANG** function to determine the angle from horizontal.
- Draw an angle with a vertex and two sides, similar to **Figure 22-26C**. Use the **ANG** function to find the included angle.
- Save the drawing as ex22-9.

## Finding a Radius

You can use the **RAD** (radius) function to find the radius of an arc, circle, or 2D polyline arc. The command sequence is as follows:

Command: **cal**↵
\>> Expression: **rad**↵
\>> Select circle, arc or polyline segment for RAD function: *(select an appropriate object, such as a circle)*
5.25 *(the radius value will vary based on the selected object)*

You can easily draw objects to match the radius of an existing object using the **RAD** function. The following example uses **RAD** to supply the radius value of an existing circle for the radius of a new circle. Refer to **Figure 22-27**.

Command: **c** *or* **circle**↵
Specify center point for circle or [3P/2P/Ttr (tan tan radius)]: *(pick the center point)*
Specify radius of circle or [Diameter] <*current*>: **'cal**↵
\>> Expression: **rad**↵
\>> Select circle, arc or polyline segment for RAD function: *(select the existing circle)*
30.0 *(the radius value will vary based on the selected object)*
Command:

**Figure 22-27.**
Using the **RAD** function to create a circle with the same radius as an existing circle.

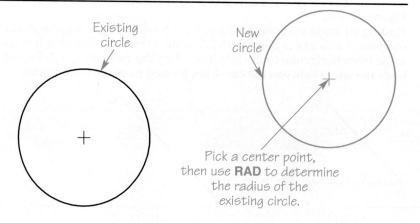

Existing circle

New circle

Pick a center point, then use **RAD** to determine the radius of the existing circle.

Calculator functions can be combined. For example, suppose you want to draw a circle 25% of the size of an existing circle with its center point halfway between the midpoints of two existing lines. Refer to **Figure 22-28** as you follow the procedure. First determine the center point of the new circle:

Command: **c** *or* **circle**↵
Specify center point for circle or [3P/2P/Ttr (tan tan radius)]: **'cal**↵
>> Expression: **(mid+mid)/2**↵
>> Select entity for MID snap: *(pick the first line)*
>> Select entity for MID snap: *(pick the second line)*
(150.125 85.5 0.0) *(the point coordinate value will vary based on the selected lines)*

Now, instruct AutoCAD to calculate a new radius 25% of the original radius:

Specify radius of circle or [Diameter] <*current*>: **'cal**↵
>> Expression: **.25*rad**↵
>> Select circle, arc, or polyline segment for RAD function: *(pick the original circle)*
7.5 *(the radius value will vary based on the selected object)*
Command:

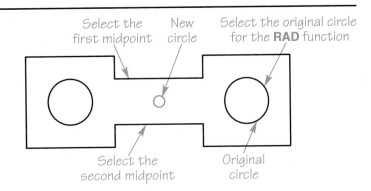

**Figure 22-28.**
Combining calculator functions to draw a new circle and place it in position.

Select the first midpoint
New circle
Select the original circle for the **RAD** function
Select the second midpoint
Original circle

The new circle is automatically drawn at the calculated location and is 25% the size of the original circle.

Another application of the **CAL** command is shown in **Figure 22-29**. A new circle is placed 3″ along a centerline from an existing circle and is 1.5 times larger than the original. The following command sequence can be used.

Command: **c** *or* **circle**↵
Specify center point for circle or [3P/2P/Ttr (tan tan radius)]: **'cal**↵
>> Expression: **pld(cen,qua,3.00)**↵
>> Select entity for CEN snap: *(pick the original circle)*
>> Select entity for QUA snap: *(pick the quadrant in the direction the new circle is to be drawn)*
(7.0 4.0 0.0) *(the point coordinates will vary based on the selected object)*
Specify radius of circle or [Diameter] <*current*>: **'cal**↵
>> Expression: **1.5*rad**↵
>> Select circle, arc, or polyline segment for RAD function: *(pick the original circle)*
1.5 *(the radius value will vary based on the selected object)*
Command:

**Figure 22-29.**
Creating a new
circle along a
centerline and
sizing it 50% larger
than the original
circle.

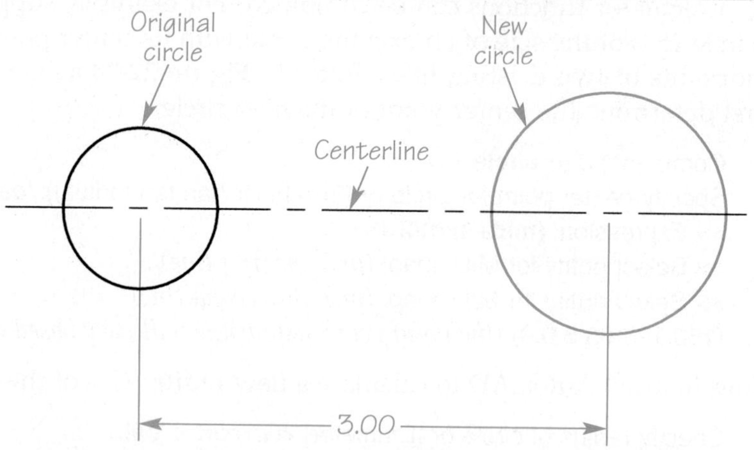

Original circle

New circle

Centerline

3.00

## Exercise 22-10

◆ Start a drawing using one of your templates.
◆ Draw a circle. Use the **RAD** function to draw another circle of equal diameter.
◆ Erase the two circles.
◆ Create a drawing similar to **Figure 22-28**. Use the **CAL** command as needed to locate lines and circles.
◆ Save the drawing as ex22-10.

## Geometry Calculator Shortcut Functions

To make using the geometry calculator as efficient as possible, some of the most commonly used calculator tasks have shortcuts. This makes typing the expression easier by reducing the number of keystrokes. The basic abbreviations are shown in the following table.

| Function | Replaces | Description |
|----------|----------|-------------|
| **DEE** | DIST(END,END) | Distance between two selected endpoints |
| **ILLE** | ILL(END,END, END,END) | Intersection of two lines defined by four selected endpoints |
| **MEE** | (END+END)/2 | Point midway between two selected endpoints |

These functions work exactly the same way as those using the longer format explained earlier. Refer to the earlier discussions for each of the functions associated with these shortcuts. The following are two examples using the function shortcuts. Refer to **Figure 22-30** as you go through the examples. To determine the length of a line:

**Figure 22-30.**
Centering a circle within a rectangle using the **CAL** command.

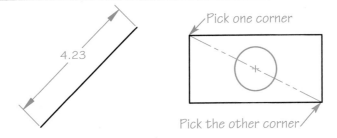

4.23

Pick one corner

Pick the other corner

Command: **cal**↵
>> Expression: **dee**↵
>> Select one endpoint for DEE: *(pick one end of the line)*
>> Select another endpoint for DEE: *(pick the other end of the line)*
4.23 *(the distance will vary based on the selected points)*

To draw a circle at the center of a rectangle using the **MEE** function:

Command: **c** *or* **circle**↵
Specify center point for circle or [3P/2P/Ttr (tan tan radius)]: **'cal**↵
>> Expression: **mee**↵
>> Select one endpoint for MEE: *(pick one corner of the rectangle)*
>> Select another endpoint for MEE: *(pick the opposite corner of the rectangle)*
3.25 4.0 *(the coordinates will vary based on the selected object)*
Specify radius of circle or [Diameter] <current>: *(type a radius and press [Enter])*

**Note**

When using the calculator to determine points, turn off your running object snaps as they can interfere with the calculator's accuracy. Once the points have been determined, turn the object snap modes back on.

## Exercise 22-11

◆ Start a drawing using one of your templates.
◆ Draw a line by randomly picking two points. Use **DEE** to determine the length.
◆ Draw two intersecting lines. Use the **ILL** function to find the coordinates of the intersection.
◆ Using the **MEE** function as needed, create a drawing similar to **Figure 22-30.**
◆ Save the drawing as ex22-11.

## Using Advanced Math Functions

Several advanced mathematical functions are also supported by the geometry calculator. These include logarithmic and exponential functions, as well as some data modification and conversion functions. The following table shows each of the advanced math operators supported by the geometry calculator.

| Function | Description |
|---|---|
| **ln**(*x*) | Returns the natural log of a number. |
| **exp**(*x*) | Returns the natural exponent (or natural antilog) of a number. Same as $e^x$. |
| **log**(*x*) | Returns the base-10 log of a number. |
| **exp10**(*x*) | Returns the base-10 exponent (or base-10 antilog) of a number. Same as $10^x$. |
| **sqr**(*x*) | Returns a number squared. |
| **sqrt**(*x*) | Returns the square root of a number. |
| **abs**(*x*) | Returns the absolute value (magnitude) of a number. |
| **round**(*x*) | Rounds a number up or down to the nearest integer value. |
| **trunc**(*x*) | Removes the decimal value of a number, returning the integer value. In other words, rounds all decimal values down to the nearest integer value. |

Note: *x* is a user specified number

For example, to calculate the square root of 25:

```
Command: cal⏎
>> Expression: sqrt(25).⏎
5.0
Command:
```

## Using Trigonometric Functions

To draw precisely, you often need to work with distances and angles. The geometry calculator supports several trigonometric functions for calculating distances and angles in a drawing. **Figure 22-31** shows the basic trigonometric operators and formulas. The available trigonometric operators are shown in the following table.

| Function | Description |
|---|---|
| **sin**(*angle*) | Returns the sine of the angle. |
| **cos**(*angle*) | Returns the cosine of the angle. |
| **tang**(*angle*) | Returns the tangent of the angle. |
| **asin**(*angle*) | Returns the arcsine of the angle. |
| **acos**(*angle*) | Returns the arccosine of the angle. |
| **atan**(*angle*) | Returns the arctangent of the angle. |
| **d2r**(*angle*) | Converts from degrees to radians. |
| **r2d**(*angle*) | Converts from radians to degrees. (Note: Do not use *r* suffix for this function.) |
| **pi** | The constant pi ($\pi$, 3.14159...) |

The constant pi ($\pi$) is used in circular formulas, such as $\pi R^2$ (circular area) or $2\pi R$ (circumference).

Architectural Drafting Using AutoCAD

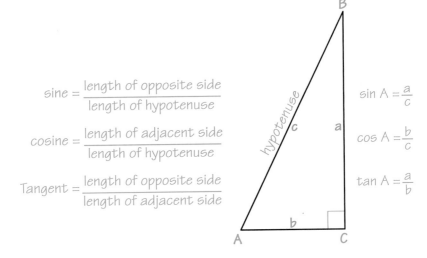

**Figure 22-31.**
The elements of a right triangle and related trigonometric functions.

$$\text{sine} = \frac{\text{length of opposite side}}{\text{length of hypotenuse}}$$

$$\text{cosine} = \frac{\text{length of adjacent side}}{\text{length of hypotenuse}}$$

$$\text{Tangent} = \frac{\text{length of opposite side}}{\text{length of adjacent side}}$$

$$\sin A = \frac{a}{c}$$

$$\cos A = \frac{b}{c}$$

$$\tan A = \frac{a}{b}$$

The geometry calculator assumes the numeric input for an angle is in degrees, unless otherwise specified, regardless of the current angular units setting in AutoCAD. AutoCAD can measure angles in degrees, radians, or grads.

To enter angular data as degrees (d), minutes (') and seconds ("), use the format 30d45'15". If the minute or second value is zero, it can be omitted from the entry. However, the degree value must be given, even if it is zero. For example, 0d0'30" can be written as 0d30" but *not* 30". To enter a value in radians, use an "r" as a suffix for the number, such as 1.2r. A suffix of "g" indicates the value is in grads, such as 50.00g. The geometry calculator output is always decimal degrees, regardless of the angular units style used for the input.

To provide an example of using trigonometric functions in the geometry calculator, the following sequence solves for angle *A* shown in **Figure 22-31**. The length of side *a* is 4.182 and side *c* is 5.136. Since the sine of angle *A* is side *a* divided by side *c*, the arcsine of *a*/*c* is equal to angle *A*:

Command: **cal**↵
>> Expression: **asin(4.182/5.136)**↵
54.5135

The returned value of 54.5135 means angle *A* is 54.5135°. Knowing the length of two sides and using the information in **Figure 22-31** and the geometry calculator, you can quickly solve for missing information needed to complete a drawing.

## Exercise 22-12

◆ Start a drawing using one of your templates.
◆ Solve the following math problems with the geometry calculator.
   ◆ Square root of 79.
   ◆ 23 squared.
   ◆ Sine of 30 degrees.
   ◆ Cosine of 30 degrees.
   ◆ Angle *A* of a right triangle (refer to **Figure 22-31**) with side *a* = 6 and side *b* = 2.5.
◆ Close the drawing without saving.

## Setting and Using Variables with the Geometry Calculator

In AutoCAD, many data values are given special names and stored for access whenever needed. These are called *system variables* and their values depend on the current drawing or environment. The geometry calculator can assign data values to a variable.

A *variable* is a text item representing a data value stored for later use. Calculator variables can only store numeric, point, or vector data. The following example sets a variable named *X* to a value of 1.25:

```
Command: cal↵
>> Expression: x=1.25↵
1.25
```

The variable can be recalled at a prompt by using the **CAL** command transparently:

```
Command: c or circle↵
Specify center point for circle or [3P/2P/Ttr (tan tan radius)]: (pick a center point)
Specify radius of circle or [Diameter] <current>: 'cal↵
>> Expression: x
1.25
Command:
```

The value of the variable *X* (1.25) is used as the radius of the circle. The following example sets a variable named *P1* to a point selected using the endpoint snap, then uses *P1* to assist in drawing a line.

```
Command: cal↵
>> Expression: p1=end↵
>> Select entity for END snap: (pick an object)
4.25 3.5 0.0 (point coordinate value will vary based on selected endpoint)
Command: l or line↵
Specify first point: 'cal↵
>> Expression: p1↵
4.25 3.5 0.0
Specify next point or [Undo]: (pick a second endpoint)
Specify next point or [Undo]: ↵
Command:
```

## Using AutoCAD System Variables with the Geometry Calculator

A specialized function named **GETVAR** can be used with the geometry calculator. This function allows you to use values stored in AutoCAD system variables. To retrieve a system variable, type getvar(*variable name*) at the >> Expression: prompt. In the following example, the drawing area is increased by multiplying the upper-right limit by 4. This limit is stored in the system variable **LIMMAX**.

```
Command: limits↵
Reset Model space limits:
Specify lower left corner or [ON/OFF] <0.0000,0.0000>: ↵
Specify upper right corner <12.0000,9.0000>: 'cal↵
>> Expression: 4*getvar(limmax)↵
(48.0 36.0 0.0)
```

If you use the **LIMITS** command again, you can see the upper-right value has increased to 48.00,36.00.

A complete listing of system variables and their current settings can be viewed in the AutoCAD text window. Use the **SETVAR** command as follows:

```
Command: setvar↵
Enter variable name or [?]: <(last variable set)> ?↵
Variable(s) to list <*>: ↵
```

The first "page" of system variables is displayed in the text window. Continue pressing [Enter] to see the complete list. Press the [F2] key to return to the drawing area.

# Chapter Test

*Answer the following questions on a separate sheet of paper.*

1. Describe the purpose of a framing plan.
2. Briefly describe the two main ways of representing framing in a set of construction documents.
3. Define *header.*
4. Explain how to set up a dimension style for use when placing arrows representing framing runs.
5. Give the name(s) of the command(s) used to change dimension text to indicate the size and spacing of the framing members.
6. Describe two ways of representing framing members in a detailed framing plan.
7. Briefly describe a broken-out section as it appears on a framing plan.
8. What is the *hip* on a roof?
9. Where is the *valley* located on a roof?
10. Define *ridge* in relation to a roof.
11. If a roof has the same pitch on all sides, what angle is formed at the hips and valleys?
12. Give the formula commonly used to calculate the total square footage of required roof ventilation.
13. Describe two typical ways to draw a roof vent.
14. If a roof vent has an area of 1 ft², how many of these vents are required for a roof that has an area of 2400 ft²?
15. In general, where should roof vents be placed?
16. Identify the two basic elements of the roof drainage system.
17. Briefly describe the panelized roof system that is commonly used in commercial construction.
18. What is the purpose of a roof access door and when would one be required?
19. How are point coordinates entered at the >> Expression: prompt?
20. Give the short way of representing the coordinates 2,2,0 at the >> Expression: prompt.
21. Give the expression used to determine a point coordinate value for a location six units from absolute coordinate 2,2,0 at an angle of 45° within the XY plane.
22. Identify the function of @ when used within the **CAL** command.
23. Name the **CAL** command function used to specify input as a point picked with the cursor.
24. How is the **CAL** command entered transparently within another command?
25. Give the calculator expression that can be used to find the point coordinates of a location midway between two points selected with the cursor.

26. Give the calculator expression that can be used to find the point coordinates of a location midway between the center of a circle and the endpoint of a line.
27. How is the **DIST** function entered at the >> Expression: prompt?
28. Identify the function used to calculate the perpendicular distance between a point and a line.
29. Identify the function used to calculate the shortest distance between a point and a plane.
30. Identify the function used to locate an intersection point between two nonparallel lines.
31. Identify the function used to find a point along a line passing through two other points, and is a specified distance from the start point.
32. Define *vertex*.
33. Define *included angle*.
34. Give the calculator expression that can be used to determine the angle between two lines.
35. Identify the calculator function used to find the radius of a circle.
36. Give the calculator expression that can be entered at the Specify radius of circle or [Diameter]: prompt to instruct AutoCAD to create a new circle 25% of the size of an existing circle you select. Assume you have already entered the calculator transparently.

*For the following questions, give the geometry calculator shortcut for the function being described.*

37. Distance between two selected endpoints.
38. The intersection of two lines defined by four selected endpoints.
39. Point midway between two selected endpoints.

*For the following questions, give the geometry calculator trigonometric function or value being described.*

40. Returns the sine of an angle.
41. Returns the square of a number.
42. Returns the square root of a number.
43. Converts from radians to degrees.
44. The constant $\pi$.

1. Open 21-ResA.
   A. Create the appropriate roof plan layers.
   B. Copy the main floor walls and place them on a hidden linetype layer for the roof plan.
   C. Draw the roof plan shown.
   D. Add the notes shown.
   E. Save the drawing as 22-ResA.

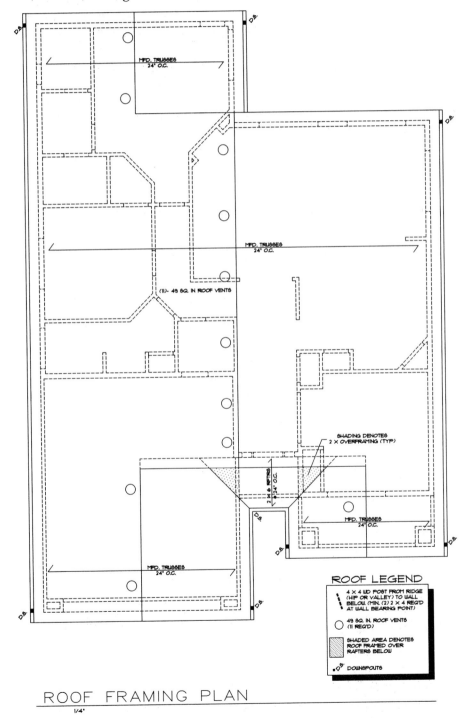

(Alan Mascord Design Associates, Inc.)

2. Open 21-ResB.
   A. Create the appropriate framing layers.
   B. Copy the main floor walls and place them on a hidden linetype layer for the framing plan.
   C. Draw the framing plan shown.
   D. Add the notes shown.
   E. Save the drawing as 22-ResB.

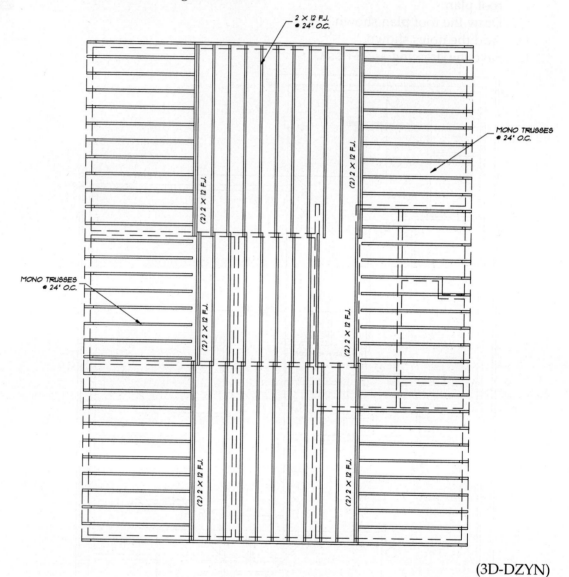

(3D-DZYN)

3. Start a new drawing from one of your templates.
   A. Xref 21-Multifamily into the drawing.
   B. Freeze all of the layers but the wall layer.
   C. Draw the framing plan shown.
   D. Save the drawing as 22-Multifamily.

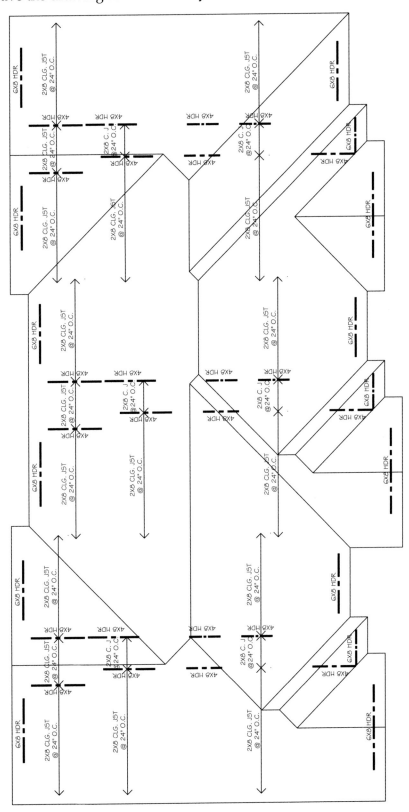

(3D-DZYN)

4. Start a new drawing from one of your templates.
   A. Xref 16-Commercial-Upper into the drawing. Use the floor plan as a reference as you draw the roof plan.
   B. Create the appropriate roof plan layers.
   C. Draw the roof plan shown.
   D. Note the roof plan as shown.
   E. Save the drawing as 22-Commercial.

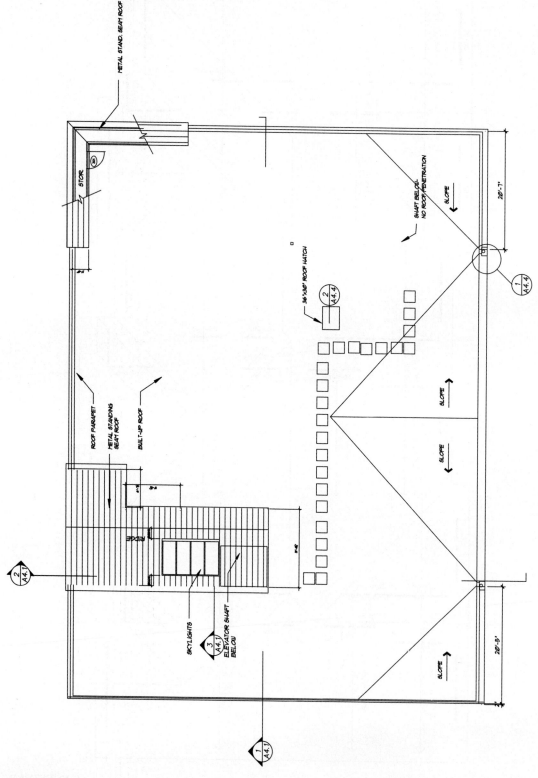

(Cynthia Bankey Architect, Inc.)

# CHAPTER 23

# Drawing Electrical, Plumbing, and HVAC Plans

## Learning Objectives

After completing this chapter, you will be able to:

- ◆ Create electrical symbols and draw electrical plans.
- ◆ Create plumbing symbols and draw plumbing plans.
- ◆ Construct isometric plumbing drawings.
- ◆ Create HVAC symbols and draw HVAC plans.
- ◆ Explain the function of revision clouds.
- ◆ Draw revision clouds and related notes.

## Important Terms

air return register
diffusers
duct
ductwork
duplex plugs
forced-air system
ground fault interrupter plugs
heating, ventilation, and air conditioning (HVAC)

industrial piping
isometric drawing
isoplane
reflected ceiling plan (RCP)
registers
residential plumbing
revision cloud
three-way switch

So far in this text, you have been introduced to the drawings that are included in a typical architectural set of construction documents. These drawings are developed in an architectural office by an architect or designer and created by drafters. Structural members in a design can be determined by the architect, but may also be determined by a structural engineer.

In addition to the drawings introduced to this point, there are three categories of construction documents typically created by firms outside of an architectural office. These documents are for electrical; plumbing; and heating, ventilating, and air conditioning (HVAC) systems. These plans are often created by specialists in the particular area. For residential construction, the designer or architect may develop these systems. However, in commercial and industrial projects, an office that specializes in a particular area develops the system and creates the drawings.

Typically, when electrical, plumbing, or HVAC drawings are needed to complete the set of construction documents, the architectural office contacts an appropriate firm and sends them a copy of the floor plans, sections, and elevations. On receiving plans from the architect, the specializing firm xrefs the drawings and adds its own symbols and diagrams to the plans. In this way, the original drawings are not modified by the specializing firm, but used to determine the types of systems needed in the design. Once these drawings are finished, they are returned to the architectural office where they are xrefed again into the construction documents.

# Electrical Plans

The electrical plans are commonly designed by electrical contractors, but can be added to the construction documents by the architect or designer. If the architect places electrical diagrams, the diagrams are often a suggested or recommended installation, rather than a specification to which the electrician must adhere. In this case, the electrician has the final say in the placement of the electrical fixtures to ensure appropriate electrical codes are met.

In residential design, the designer often meets with the client to determine the location and type of lighting used in the building. In commercial and industrial designs, the electrical firms are heavily relied on to determine the best locations for the electrical fixtures. Interior designers also work closely with the electrical firm to determine any special lighting effects desired in the design.

Once the lighting and any other special electrical needs have been addressed, the symbols are applied to the floor plans. See **Figure 23-1.** The architectural floor plans are xrefed into a new drawing and the electrical symbols applied over the xref.

**Figure 23-1.**
Electrical symbols (shown in color) are applied directly to the floor plans by the architectural office.

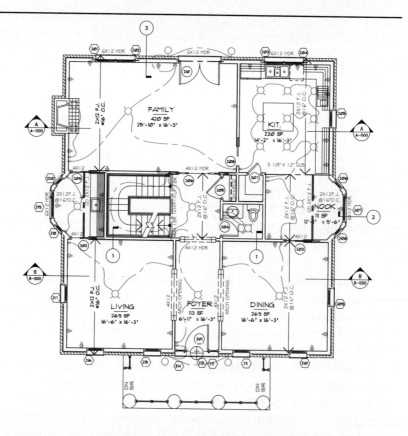

Architectural Drafting Using AutoCAD

There are two types of commercial electrical plans shown in **Figure 23-2**. The first plan is called a reflected ceiling plan, **Figure 23-2A.** The *reflected ceiling plan (RCP)* indicates the location of fluorescent light fixtures in a commercial building above the typical horizontal cutting plane for a floor plan. It is called a reflected ceiling plan because it displays items on the ceiling that would normally not be seen on a floor plan. These items are, in essence, a reflection of what is above the cutting plane. The acoustical panel locations, also known as "ceiling grids," are shown on the drawing as well. The second plan indicates the locations of the lighting and outlet plugs, **Figure 23-2B.** Typically, these plans are shown as separate drawings in commercial or industrial designs.

**Figure 23-2.**
Electrical symbols can be applied to a new drawing by referencing the floor plan. A—A reflected ceiling plan. B—The electrical plan.

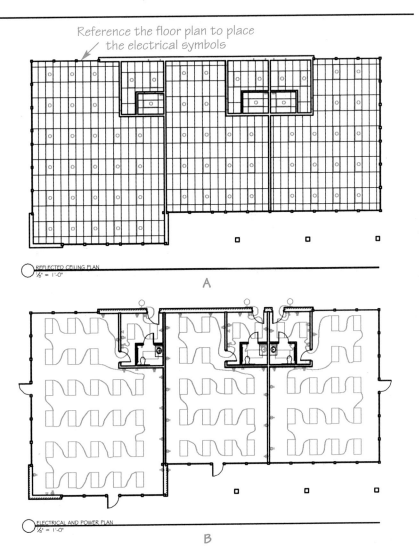

Reference the floor plan to place the electrical symbols

REFLECTED CEILING PLAN
⅛" = 1'-0"

A

ELECTRICAL AND POWER PLAN
⅛" = 1'-0"

B

## Considerations for the Electrical Plan

When adding electrical symbols to the drawing, considerations need to be made so local building codes are followed. Other considerations include matching client needs, functionality, ambience or atmosphere, and usage. Some basic rules to keep in mind are listed below.

- **Electrical Outlets, 110 volts.**
  - Wall outlets, known as *duplex plugs,* should be placed in any wall over 3'-0" in length and should never be placed more than 6'-0" away from a corner.
  - Duplex plugs should be placed no more than 12'-0" apart. A 6'-0" spacing is convenient, but cost can be a limiting factor.

- When designing a room, consider possible furniture layouts. Duplex plugs should be placed in relationship to furniture. For example, plugs should be placed near a possible desk or table location.
- Place duplex plugs in hallways as a convenience for vacuum cleaners.
- Place a waterproof duplex plug outside on patio areas for convenience.
- In kitchens, place plugs closer together than in other rooms. Duplex plugs should be located conveniently for kitchen appliances, such as blenders, electric can openers, and refrigerators.
- **Electrical Outlets, 220 volts.**
  - A 220 volt plug is needed for appliances such as ranges, ovens, and electric clothes dryers.
  - A garage or workshop area may need 220 volt plugs for large equipment, such as table saws, drill presses, and welders.
- **Specialty Duplex Plugs.**
  - Ground fault interrupter (GFI) plugs, also called ground fault current interrupter (GFCI) plugs, should be placed near any water or "wet" locations, and near metal fixtures where electrocution is a potential hazard. *Ground fault interrupter plugs* are designed to shut off the circuit in the event an unbalanced electric current is detected.
  - Each sink in a bathroom, kitchen, or laundry room should have a GFI plug nearby for household appliances, such as hair dryers or electric razors.
- **Ventilation.**
  - Bathrooms without a window that can be opened should have an exhaust fan. A bathroom with a window may also have a fan to vent steam from a bathtub or shower.
  - Laundry rooms and specialty rooms, such as a photo darkroom, may include an electrical fan.
- **Lighting.**
  - Include fixed lighting in rooms and around exterior doors. Large rooms may have more than one light. Consider placing lights in dark places, such as a walk-in closet or pantry.
  - Ceiling lights are common in bedrooms, bathrooms, and dining rooms.
  - Bathrooms commonly have lights over the mirror and may have additional ceiling lights if the bathroom is large.
  - Kitchens may have ceiling lights, commonly fluorescent lighting or recessed "can" lights. Placing a ceiling light over the kitchen sink increases lighting in the kitchen and can be used as an extra light or night-light.
  - A duplex plug wired to a switch may be included in rooms where a lamp is desired instead of a ceiling light.
  - Light switches should be placed in locations that are convenient when entering or leaving a room.
  - A *three-way switch* consists of two light switches that control one or more lights. Place three-way switches in hallways or rooms with two entrances, such as a kitchen or dining room.
- **Power Switches.**
  - Do not place switches in walls that contain a pocket door.
  - Place switches near room doors or entrances.
  - Do not place switches behind doors.
  - Do not place switches in a corner where they would interfere with framing.
  - If multiple lights are connected to a switch, run the wire from the switch to the first light, then from that light to the next. Do not run multiple electrical wires from one switch to each light.
  - Switches are drawn perpendicular to walls.
- **Electrical Panels.**
  - Place the electrical distribution panels in an easily accessible room, such as the garage, laundry room, or commercial building electrical room.

Architectural Drafting Using AutoCAD

- Electrical panels may be placed near appliances that require a heavy electrical load, such as clothes dryers.
- The electric meter is usually placed along the side of the building for easy access by the electric company.

All of these factors should be considered before placing electrical symbols on the drawing.

## Creating Electrical Symbols

Electrical symbols are used to show the placement of lighting, light switches, and electrical outlets. Electrical symbols are drawn at a scale so the plotted size of the symbol is approximately 1/8" in diameter. Notes indicating special conditions or types of fixtures are drawn with a plotted text height of 1/16" to 1/8". For example, symbols for ground fault interrupter plugs have the note GFI placed next to the symbol. **Figure 23-3** shows several types of electrical symbols commonly found on electrical plans.

**Figure 23-3.**
Common electrical symbols.

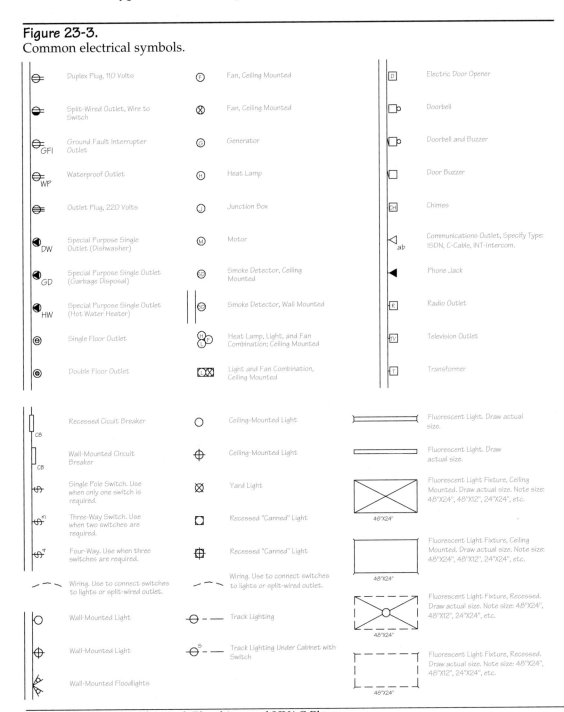

When placing lights, a corresponding switch or set of switches is required. To show which switches turn on which lights, use a curved line, such as an arc, spline, or splined polyline. This represents the electrical circuit path, not the actual conductor (wires). Draw the electrical circuit path line from the switch to the light(s) using a dashed linetype. Some companies use a centerline linetype. **Figure 23-4** shows typical placements for switches and lights.

**Figure 23-4.**
Typical switch locations and uses.

A single-pole switch is used to control one or more lights.

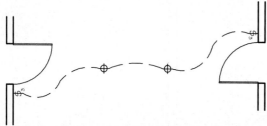

A three-way switch consists of two switches controlling the same set of lights.

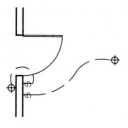

A single-pole switch can be connected to a wall-mounted light or a ceiling-mounted light.

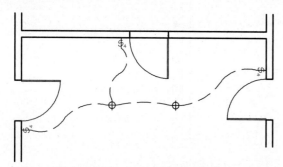

A four-way switch consists of three switches controlling the same set of lights.

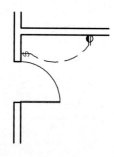

A single-pole switch can be connected to a split-wired outlet.

# Exercise 23-1

◆ Open ex22-2.
◆ Freeze the following layers:
  ◆ M-Beams
  ◆ M-Dims
  ◆ M-Framing
  ◆ M-Notes
  ◆ M-Tags
◆ Create a layer named M-Elec and set it current.
◆ Create some electrical symbol blocks and add them to the plan. Refer to **Figure 23-3** for types of electrical symbols.
◆ Use the guidelines for placements of the blocks as described earlier in this chapter.
◆ Add electrical circuit paths from the switches to the lights they are controlling.
◆ Your drawing should appear similar to the diagram below.
◆ Save the drawing as ex23-1.

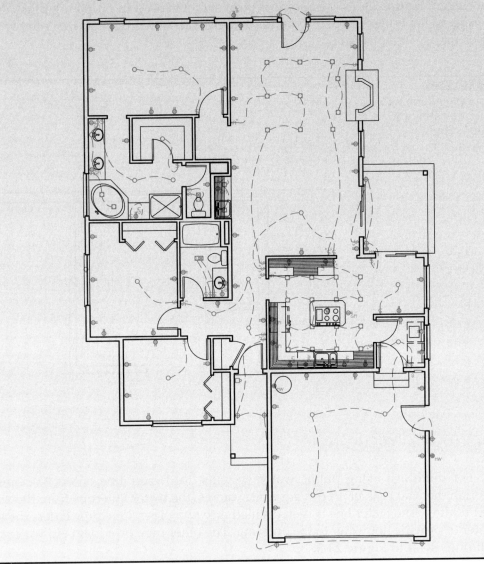

# Plumbing Plans

Plumbing plans can be broken down into two classifications—industrial piping and residential plumbing. *Residential plumbing* focuses on the transfer of water, gas, and waste water. The building plans usually only show the locations of plumbing fixtures, such as toilets, bathtubs, and sinks. In most residential applications, this is all that is required for the set of construction documents. **Figure 23-5** shows part of a simple plumbing plan that includes the cold and hot water supply line routing.

*Industrial piping* is used to transfer liquids and gases used in manufacturing processes. The construction documents require plumbing plans for the transfer of these materials. The plumbing plan is usually provided by the piping contractor. These piping plans are separate sheets with only the outline of walls, doors, openings, plumbing fixtures, and casework displayed. The piping runs are then added to the plans with the use of each pipe indicated.

Symbols are used to indicate the type of lines, valves, and connections used in the design. **Figure 23-6** shows some typical symbols used in plumbing plans. Notice the special linetypes. Chapter 27 of this text explains how to customize your own linetypes for use in AutoCAD.

**Figure 23-5.**
A simple plumbing plan indicating the water supply system.

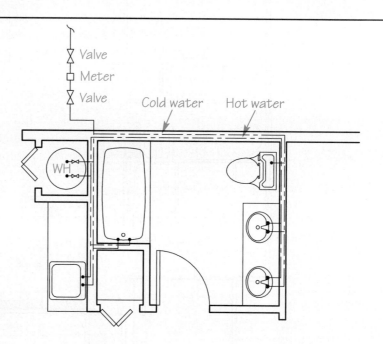

## The Water System

For buildings using public water systems, the water line enters the building through the water meter. In private well systems, the water line runs from the well to the building. The water line is then divided into two pipes. One pipe enters the water heater to provide hot water to the building. The other pipe provides cold water to the building. Refer to **Figure 23-5.**

Hot water and cold water lines run to plumbing fixtures throughout the building. When creating the plumbing plans, a hot water line and a cold water line are drawn on the plan indicating where the plumbing runs are located. When the pipes end at a fixture, a cap symbol or gate valve is shown to indicate the actual connection to the fixture. These symbols are shown in **Figure 23-6.**

## Figure 23-6.
Typical plumbing symbols and linetypes used in plumbing plans.

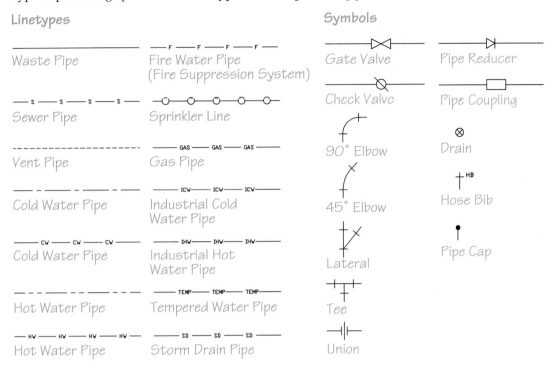

| Linetypes | | Symbols | |
|---|---|---|---|
| Waste Pipe | Fire Water Pipe (Fire Suppression System) | Gate Valve | Pipe Reducer |
| Sewer Pipe | Sprinkler Line | Check Valve | Pipe Coupling |
| Vent Pipe | Gas Pipe | 90° Elbow | Drain |
| Cold Water Pipe | Industrial Cold Water Pipe | 45° Elbow | Hose Bib |
| Cold Water Pipe | Industrial Hot Water Pipe | Lateral | Pipe Cap |
| Hot Water Pipe | Tempered Water Pipe | Tee | |
| Hot Water Pipe | Storm Drain Pipe | Union | |

When designing the building, it is often advantageous and cost effective to locate plumbing fixtures near each other. Back-to-back plumbing helps reduce the number of pipes required in the building, **Figure 23-7.** The stacking of plumbing fixtures in multiple floors also helps reduce the number of pipes and vents.

After the plumbing lines have been added, the method for removal of the waste water needs to be indicated. Drain symbols are shown for the plumbing fixtures and in any rooms that require extra drainage, such as a basement, utility room, or garage. The waste lines flow to the public sewer line for public plumbing or to a catch basin for private sewage systems.

## Figure 23-7.
Back-to-back plumbing reduces the number of pipes and vents used in the building.

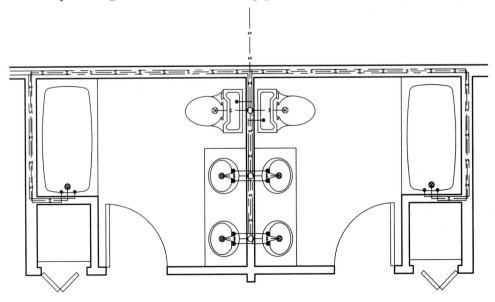

Waste lines require a ventilation system that allows air to flow from the pipes. This allows sewer gases and odors to vent outside the building, rather than come up through drains within the building. The vents run up through the roof, thus allowing the gases to escape. **Figure 23-8** displays a waste line and ventilation system.

In industrial design, additional piping lines may be added to indicate the flow of liquids and gases through the building. Sprinkler systems are also often required in the design of a commercial or industrial building. Generally, these fire suppression systems are shown on a separate plan with only the walls referenced. Fire suppression systems are indicated with the lines and symbols shown in **Figure 23-6**.

In both residential and industrial designs, a storm drainage line runs along the exterior of the building. Storm drainage provides a means of removing rainwater runoff from the building. Rainwater from the roof runs from downspouts to the drainage lines. From the drainage lines, the water flows to the municipal storm sewer lines. See **Figure 23-9**.

**Figure 23-8.**
A waste and ventilation system.

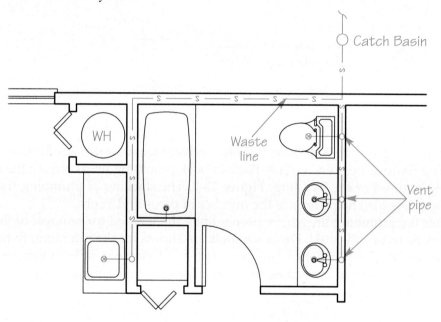

**Figure 23-9.**
A storm drainage system.

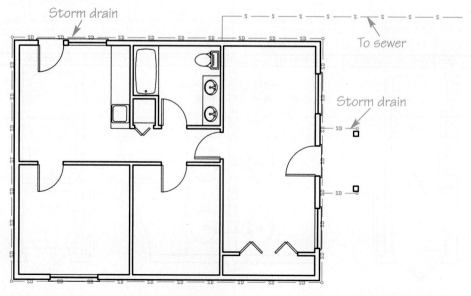

# Exercise 23-2

◆ Open ex23-1.
◆ Freeze the M-Elec layer.
◆ Create the following layers:
  ◆ M-Hot Water (Hot_Water-Supply linetype, use for hot water)
  ◆ M-Cold Water (Center2 linetype, use for cold water)
  ◆ M-Sanitary (Dashed2 linetype, use for sewer lines)
  ◆ M-Storm Drain (Phantom linetype, use for storm drains)
  ◆ M-Plumb Notes (Continuous linetype, use for plumbing notes)
◆ Add hot and cold water lines to the bathroom plumbing fixtures.
◆ Add waste lines from the bathroom fixtures to the exterior of the building.
◆ Add storm drainage lines to the exterior of the building.
◆ Your drawing should look similar to the diagram below.
◆ Save the drawing as ex23-2.

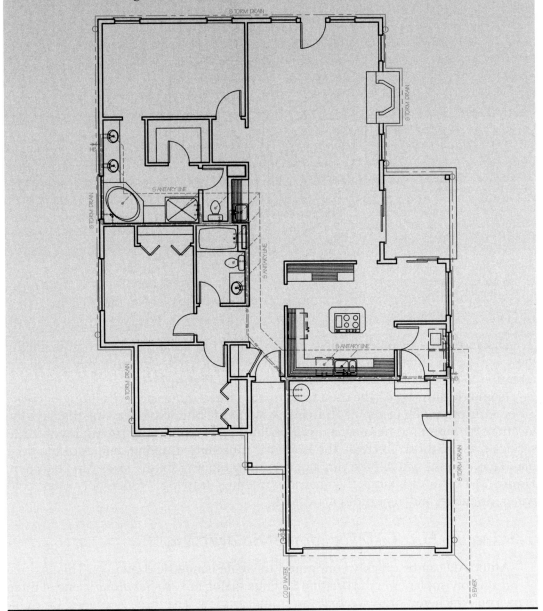

## Isometric Piping Diagrams

Isometric piping drawings provide an easy to understand diagram of the plumbing lines and fixtures used in a building. Isometric piping drawings are generally not created for residential construction, but they are commonly used for commercial projects. An *isometric drawing* is a form of pictorial drawing that appears as a three-dimensional (3D) drawing, but is not true 3D. The isometric drawing provides a single view of three sides of the object. Lines are drawn perpendicular and at 30° from horizontal. See **Figure 23-10.**

---

**Figure 23-10.**
An example of isometric drawing. The sides are drawn to form a 30° angle with horizontal. All measurements are full scale. Isometric circles (ellipses) are oriented so the major and minor axes are aligned with the corners of a cube.

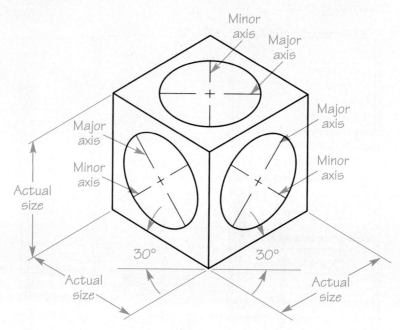

Distances in an isometric view are drawn at full scale. Circles in an isometric view appear as ellipses. When creating an isometric circle (ellipse), pay particular attention to the major and minor axes, as shown in **Figure 23-10.**

Isometric drawing can be used to simulate a three-dimensional building or create a isometric plumbing or piping drawing. A isometric plumbing drawing displays the locations of plumbing fixtures, as well as lines representing the piping involved to service these fixtures. To create the isometric plumbing drawing, reference the floor plan layout so the actual pipe run lengths and plumbing fixture sizes can be drawn. **Figure 23-11** shows a simple isometric plumbing drawing. Notice hot water, cold water, drainage, and vent pipes are drawn.

## Setting up AutoCAD for isometric drafting

AutoCAD can be quickly configured to create isometric drawings. This is done by turning on isoplanes in the **Drafting Settings** dialog box. An *isoplane* is one of three planes on which you draw to create an isometric view. The three isoplanes are right, left, and top.

**Figure 23-11.**
A simple plumbing isometric drawing for a building.

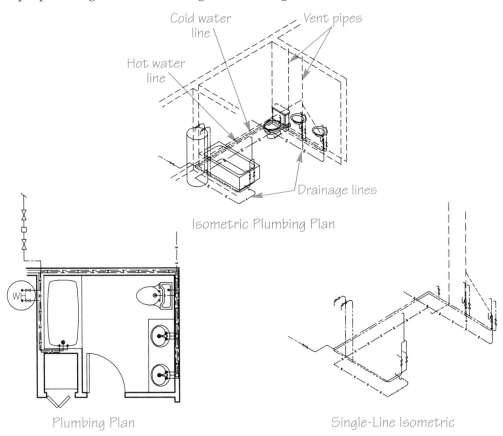

Isometric Plumbing Plan

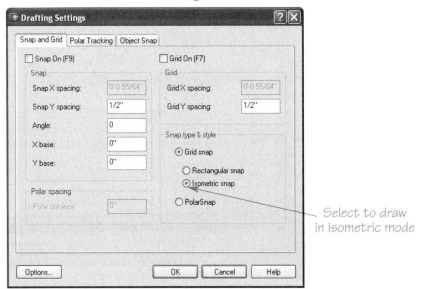

Plumbing Plan

Single-Line Isometric

To access the **Drafting Settings** dialog box, select **Drafting Settings...** from the **Tools** pull-down menu; type ds, se, dsettings, or ddrmodes at the Command prompt; or right-click on the **Snap**, **Grid**, or **Polar** buttons in the status bar and select **Settings...** from the shortcut menu. The **Drafting Settings** dialog box is opened. Pick the **Snap and Grid** tab so it is on top, **Figure 23-12.**

**Figure 23-12.**
Turn on isometric mode in the **Drafting Settings** dialog box.

To activate isometric mode, select the **Isometric snap** radio button in the **Snap type & style** area of the **Snap and Grid** tab. Once this radio button is selected, the **Grid X spacing:** and **Snap X spacing:** text boxes are grayed out. This is because isometric views are not drawn with horizontal measurements. However, the snap and grid spacing can be adjusted on the Y axis. To turn on the snap and grid, check the **Snap On** and **Grid On** check boxes. Finally, select the **OK** button to close the dialog box. If the grid is turned on, notice the dot pattern is changed from an orthographic display to an isometric display. See **Figure 23-13.**

The crosshairs also appear at an isometric angle. The isometric crosshairs help ensure lines are drawn at the proper angle. If the **ORTHO** button is selected, lines drawn with the cursor are limited to the angles represented by the crosshairs. In **Figure 23-14,** the side of a box is drawn on the left isoplane with ortho turned on.

**Figure 23-13.**
The AutoCAD grid changes when in isometric mode.

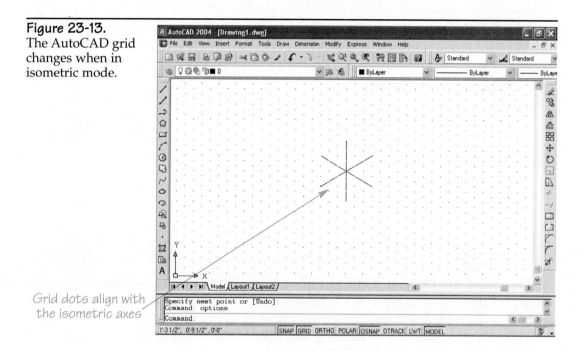

Grid dots align with the isometric axes

**Figure 23-14.**
The side of a box drawn on the left isoplane.

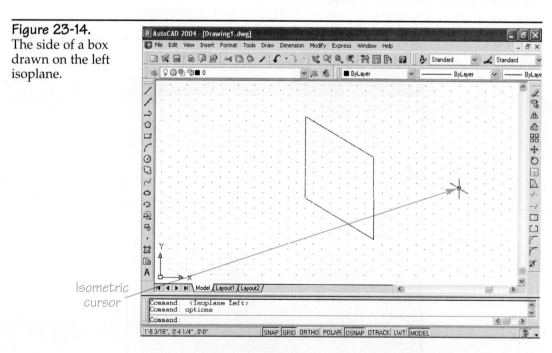

Isometric cursor

Architectural Drafting Using AutoCAD

## Changing the orientation of the crosshairs

In isometric mode, objects are drawn on the isoplane that matches the orientation of the crosshairs. Once isometric mode is on, the isoplanes can be cycled through by pressing the [F5] key or the [Ctrl]+[E] key combination. This rotates the crosshairs to the next isoplane. There are three crosshair orientations, one each for the left, right, and top isoplanes. See **Figure 23-15.**

The **ISOPLANE** command can also be used to change isoplanes. The command sequence to set the right isoplane current is:

Command: **isoplane.**↵
Current isoplane: Left *(assuming the left isoplane is current)*
Enter isometric plane setting [Left/Top/Right] <Top>: **r.**↵ *(the default is the "next" iso-plane in the order left-top-right)*
Current isoplane: Right
Command:

---

**Figure 23-15.**
The three isometric orientations for the crosshairs correspond to the three isoplanes. You can cycle through isoplanes by pressing the [F5] key or the [Ctrl]+[E] key combination.

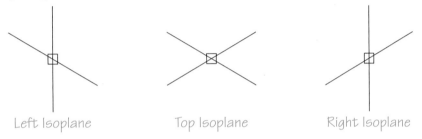

Left Isoplane          Top Isoplane          Right Isoplane

## Creating isometric circles

In an isometric drawing, circles appear as ellipses. To create an isometric circle, first select the appropriate isoplane. Then, use the **ELLIPSE** command to draw the isometric circle. Select the **Isocircle** option, then specify the center of the circle. Finally, set the radius of the circle. An ellipse is created in the correct orientation for the current isoplane. The following sequence is used to create the isometric circle shown in **Figure 23-16.**

---

**Figure 23-16.**
Circles appear as ellipses in isometric drawings.

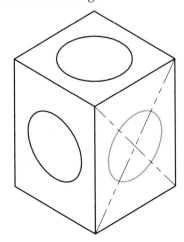

---

Command: **isoplane.**↵
Current isoplane: Left *(assuming the left isoplane is current)*
Enter isometric plane setting [Left/Top/Right] <Top>: **r.**↵
Current isoplane: Right
Command: **ellipse.**↵
Specify axis endpoint of ellipse or [Arc/Center/Isocircle]: **i.**↵
Specify center of isocircle: *(pick the center point using the construction lines shown in* **Figure 23-16***)*
Specify radius of isocircle or [Diameter]: **1.**↵
Command:

## Exercise 23-3

◆ Open ex23-2.
◆ Create a simple piping isometric plan based on the master bathroom of the house drawing.
◆ The isometric drawing should look similar to the diagram below.
◆ Save the drawing as ex23-3.

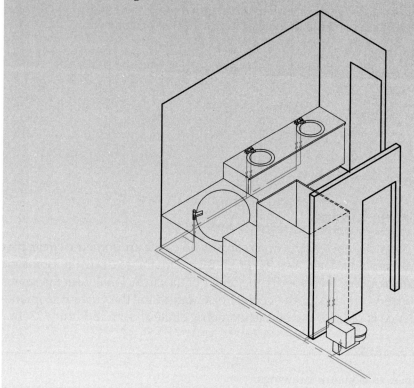

# Heating, Ventilation, and Air Conditioning

*Heating, ventilation, and air conditioning (HVAC)* is a building trade associated with maintaining proper climate control within a building. The HVAC system heats, cools, vents, and circulates air throughout the rooms of a building. The most common type of HVAC system is a forced-air system.

The *forced-air system* circulates air from room to room through special piping called *ductwork*. A *duct* is a metal or nonmetal tube that is normally round, oval, square, or rectangular. The duct transports air through the HVAC system and may be insulated or uninsulated. Ducts can be placed below the floor. In some cases, the ducts are placed above the ceiling. However, this practice should be avoided. Since hot air rises, venting warm air from a duct above the ceiling is not efficient. However, placing ducts in an attic space is often needed due to space limitations and access to rooms.

Ducts also move air through or around heating and cooling devices to warm or cool the air. The air is then forced from the heating or cooling device back through the air ducts with the aid of a fan. The ducts are connected to openings in the rooms called *diffusers* or *registers.* The air passes through the diffusers and enters the room. The air circulates through the room and flows back into the air ducts through an *air return register,* which starts the process again by reheating the air in the furnace.

Notice in **Figure 23-17** that some of the registers are placed near openings in the exterior wall, such as doors and windows. This is done so warmest air directly from the register is circulated near the coldest part of the room. As the warm air rises, circulation is created in a room. As the air cools, the circulation pushes the air toward the return air registers and back to the furnace.

The local building authority may require HVAC plans. However, for residential design, HVAC plans may not be required or, if required, only a minimum amount of information is shown. Often, only the furnace, supply registers, and air return registers need to be shown. **Figure 23-17** shows the minimum HVAC requirements for a residence.

**Figure 23-17.**
A simple HVAC plan for residential construction indicates the furnace and register locations.

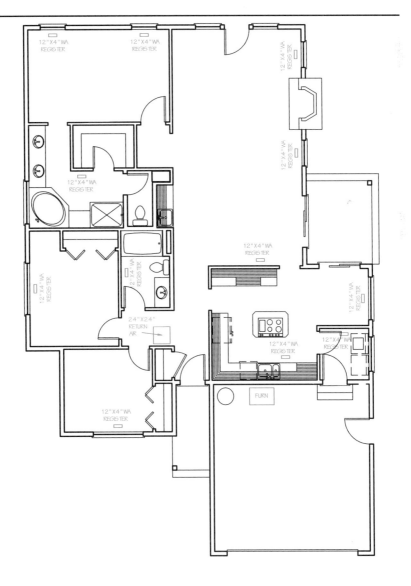

Registers vary in size depending on the cubic feet per minute (cfm) of air supplied to the room or returned to the central unit. A typical register is labeled as 12" × 4". Air return registers and furnaces vary in size depending on the area they are supporting. Typically, a 24" × 24" air return register is shown on the plans. The furnace may be drawn as a 30" × 24" or larger rectangle.

If a complete HVAC plan is required, the furnace, registers, air ducts, and air returns are shown over the floor plan. The furnace and air return sizes are also indicated on the plan, as well as the register and duct sizes. **Figure 23-18** illustrates a complete HVAC plan.

**Figure 23-18.**
A complete HVAC plan indicating the addition of ductwork.

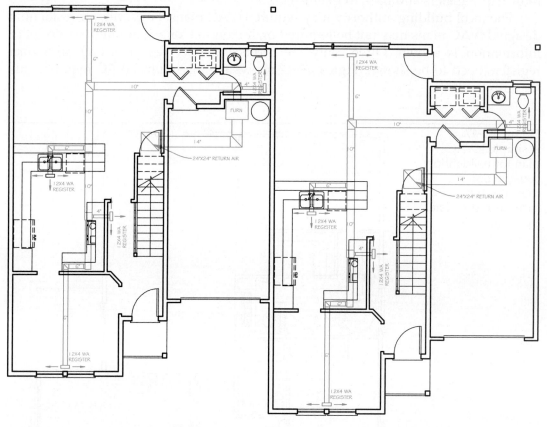

Architectural Drafting Using AutoCAD

# Exercise 23-4

- Open ex23-3.
- Freeze the following layers:
  - M-Cold Water
  - M-Hot Water
  - M-Plumb Notes
  - M-Sanitary
  - M-Storm Drain
- Create the following layers:
  - M-HVAC-Register (use for the heat registers)
  - M-HVAC-Duct (use for the ductwork)
  - M-HVAC-Furn (use for the furnace)
  - M-HVAC-Return (use for the air return)
  - M-HVAC Notes (use for the HVAC notes)
- Create an HVAC plan for the house.
- Add a 36″ × 24″ furnace in the garage.
- Place a 24″ × 24″ air return in the hall.
- Create 12″ × 4″ registers as indicated in the diagram below.
- Your drawing should look similar to the diagram below.
- Save the drawing as ex23-4.

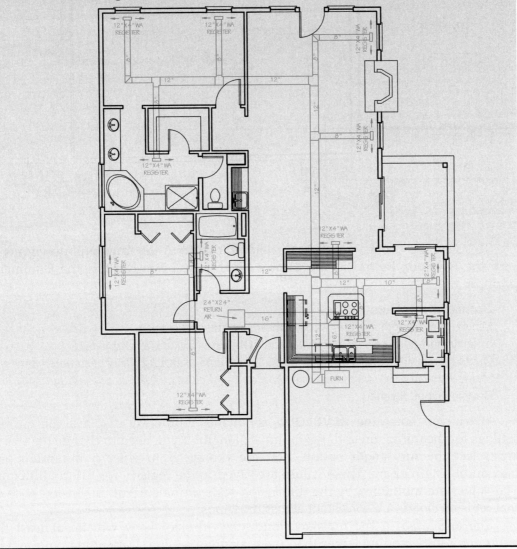

# Adding Revision Notes

After any plan is drawn, whether it is a floor plan, elevations, electrical plan, or HVAC plan, the drawings need to be reviewed for content and accuracy. A *revision cloud* is placed around any areas of the drawing that need modification or any special notes. See **Figure 23-19.** A revision cloud is used because it clearly indicates an area of the drawing that has been changed. The **REVCLOUD** command can be used to draw a revision cloud.

**Figure 23-19.**
A revision cloud indicates revisions that need to be made to a drawing.

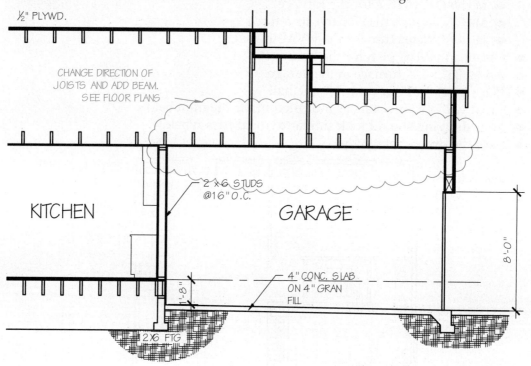

**REVCLOUD**

**Draw**
↳ Revision Cloud

**Draw
toolbar**

**Revcloud**

To access the command, select **Revision Cloud** from the **Draw** pull-down menu, pick the **Revcloud** button in the **Draw** toolbar, or type revcloud at the Command prompt:

Command: **revcloud.⏎**
Minimum arc length: *current* Maximum arc length: *current*
Specify start point or [Arc length/Object] <Object>: *(pick a starting point)*
Guide crosshairs along cloud path... *(move the cursor around the area to note; move the cursor toward the start point and the cloud will close and the command will end)*
Revision cloud finished.

When you enter the **REVCLOUD** command, AutoCAD displays the current settings for the minimum and maximum arc length. If you need to change the size of arc, select the **Arc length** option. You are prompted to enter a minimum and maximum length of arc. These values are saved in the registry for future drawings. The values are multiplied by the dimension scale of the current dimension style so that revision clouds are consistent across drawings.

The arcs used in the revision cloud vary in size. They will be at least the minimum setting and no larger than the maximum setting. Depending on how fast you move the cursor, the arcs will vary between these two settings. The completed revision cloud is a polyline object.

The **REVCLOUD** command also allows you to convert a closed object such as a circle, polyline, rectangle, polygon, or ellipse into a revision cloud. At the Specify start point or [Arc length/Object] <Object> prompt, press the [Enter] key to select a closed object to be converted.

## Chapter Test

*Answer the following questions on a separate sheet of paper.*

1. Describe the function of a reflected ceiling plan.
2. Give the approximate plotted size that electrical symbols should be.
3. Which type of line is used for electrical paths between switches and outlets?
4. What do residential plumbing drawings generally show?
5. How do industrial plumbing plans generally differ from residential plumbing plans?
6. How are hot water pipes distinguished from cold water pipes in a plumbing plan?
7. What is the purpose of the storm drainage system?
8. Describe an isometric drawing.
9. Name the dialog box where you can configure AutoCAD for making isometric drawings.
10. How are the crosshairs aligned when in isometric mode?
11. Identify the two keys or key combinations that can be used to change isoplanes.
12. How do circles appear in isometric view?
13. Name the command and option used to draw isometric circles.
14. Briefly describe a forced air system.
15. Define *duct*.
16. Why are heat registers often placed by an exterior opening in a wall?
17. What is the purpose of the air return register?
18. What is the purpose of a revision cloud?

## Chapter Problems

Project

Residential A

1. Open 22-ResA.
   A. Create the electrical plan shown below using appropriate layers and blocks.
   B. Save the drawing as 23-ResA.

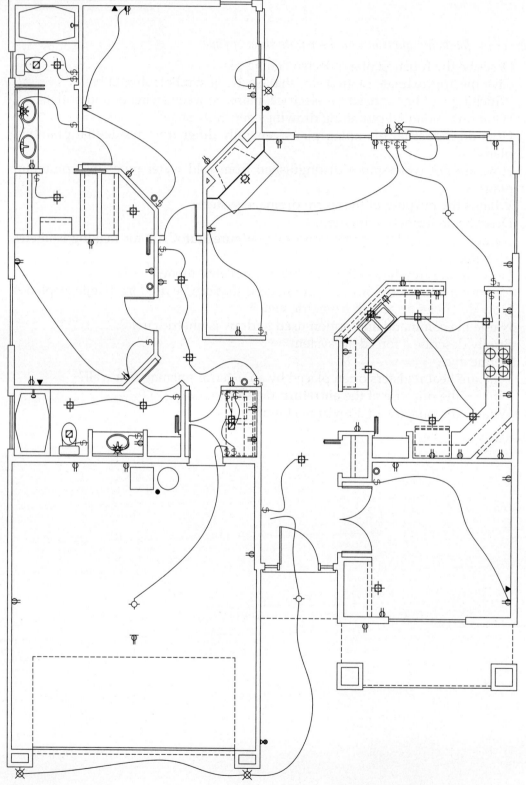

(Alan Mascord Design Associates, Inc.)

2. Open 22-ResB.
   A. Draw a piping isometric plan similar to the one shown below using appropriate layers.
   B. Save the drawing as 23-ResB.

Residential B

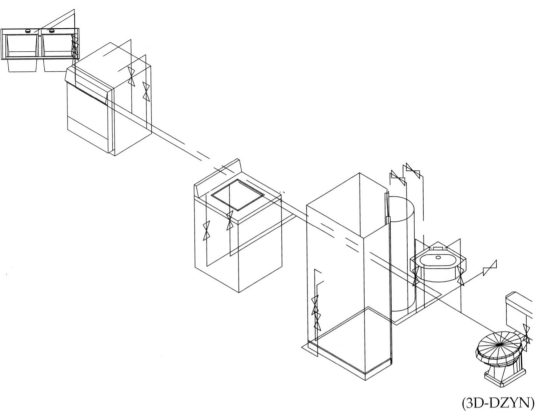

(3D-DZYN)

3. Start a new drawing from one of your templates.
   A. Xref 16-Multifamily into the drawing.
   B. Create a plumbing plan similar to one shown below using appropriate layers.
   C. Save the drawing as 23-Multifamily.

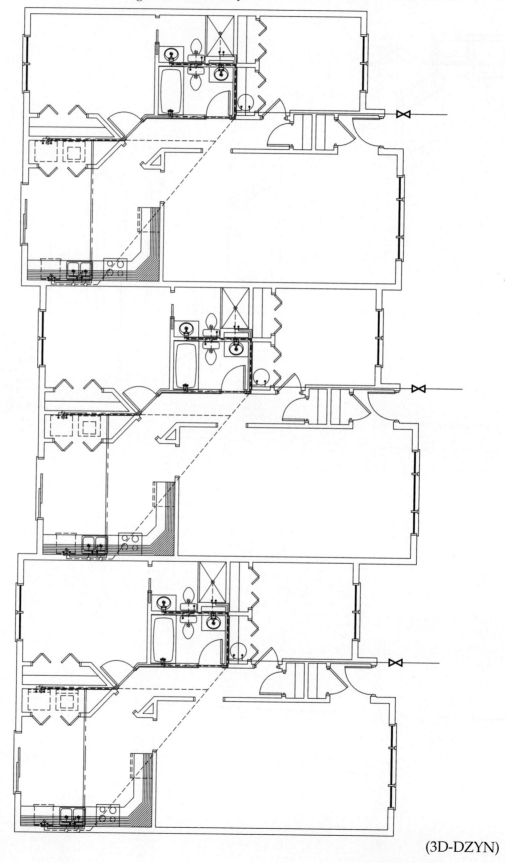

(3D-DZYN)

4. Start a new drawing from one of your templates.
   A. Xref 16-Commercial-Main into the drawing.
   B. Create a HVAC layout similar to the one below using appropriate layers.
   C. Save the drawing as 23-Commercial.

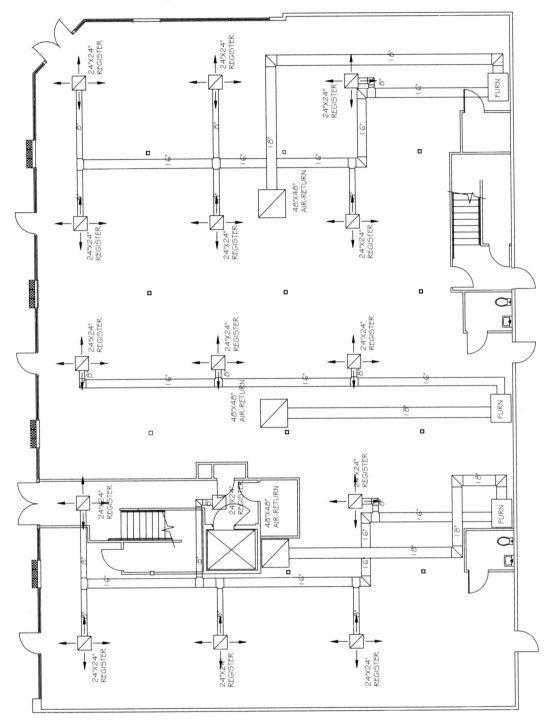

(Cynthia Bankey Architect, Inc.)

Viewports permit the display of several different views within the same drawing. In this isometric piping drawing, an isometric view is shown along with three orthographic views in model space. The process for creating viewports in paper space (layout space) is similar and is discussed in Chapter 24.

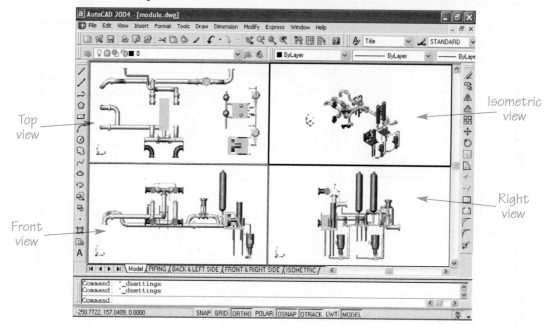

# Creating Layouts and Plotting

## Learning Objectives

After completing this chapter, you will be able to:

- Use model space and layout space.
- Set up a layout.
- Create and work with viewports.
- Create floating viewports.
- Control viewport, layer, and linetype display.
- Add annotations and dimensions to the layout.
- Use page setup.
- Specify a plotter.
- Specify pen settings.
- Specify layout settings.
- Configure plot styles.
- Use and edit color-dependent plot style tables and named plot style tables.
- Assign named plot styles to layers and objects.
- Use a plot stamp.
- Plot your drawing.
- Create plot files and drawing web format files.

## Important Terms

color tables
dithering
effective area
floating viewports
layout space

model space
named style tables
paper space
plot spooler
plot style table

So far you have learned how to produce drawings in model space. *Model space* can be thought of as the space where drawings and models are created. The term *model* refers to drawing in three dimensions, but can refer to a drawing created in two dimensions. Any drawings you create should be drawn full scale in *model space*.

*Layout space* is an area that is used to lay out the sheet of paper that is to be plotted. Also known as *paper space*, layout space allows you to set up a full size sheet of paper, add a title block, scale your drawing to fit on the paper, and arrange any views of the drawing around the paper. Geometry that is drawn on the paper is also drawn full scale as in model space.

When the drawing has been finished, and the sheet layout arranged and scaled, the layout sheet can then be plotted.

## Model Space and Layout Space

The best way to tell if you are in model space is to look at the UCS (User Coordinate System) icon. The UCS icon, usually in the lower-left corner of the drawing screen, represents the current positive X and Y coordinate directions. Once layout space has been entered, the UCS icon changes from two arrows to a triangle that indicates the X and Y coordinate directions. See **Figure 24-1.** The user coordinate system and UCS icon are covered in greater detail in Chapter 25.

In order to enter layout space, select one of the layout tabs at the bottom of the screen. See **Figure 24-2.** Model space can be reentered by selecting the **Model** tab next to one of the layout tabs.

**Figure 24-1.**
The UCS icons for model space and layout space.

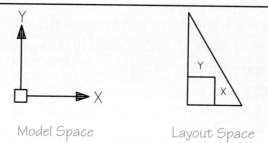

Model Space       Layout Space

Note

The first time you select a layout tab, the **Page Setup** dialog box appears. This dialog box is described in depth later in this chapter. For now, simply pick the **OK** button to access the sheet layout.

## Understanding Layout Space

As discussed throughout this text, model space is the area where the drawing or model is drawn. Every floor plan, elevation, or detail that you draw is drawn full scale in model space. The only geometry that is scaled in model space is text, dimensions, and annotation blocks. All of these items are scaled by the scale factor of the drawing. When you enter layout space, a real size sheet of paper is placed over the top of the model space drawing. Title blocks and notes are then added to the real size paper. A hole, or viewport, cut into the real size paper displays the entire drawing

**Figure 24-2.**
The layout tabs are located at the bottom of the drawing screen window. The **PAPER** button indicates that the layout space area is active. The button displays **MODEL** when working in model space.

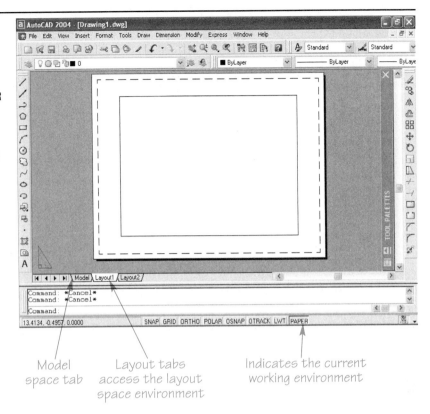

Model space tab

Layout tabs access the layout space environment

Indicates the current working environment

created in model space. See **Figure 24-3.** The viewport is then used to place the drawing so that it fits on the paper at a desired scale. This method does not physically scale the model space drawing but only the zoom scale at which it is displayed in the viewport. Once the geometry on the paper has been arranged, the paper layout can then be plotted.

Plotting can be accomplished from model space. However, only one viewport can be plotted at a time. Viewports are discussed in Chapter 20 of this text. The advantage of setting up a piece of paper in layout space is that multiple viewports can be arranged on the paper, given different scales, and plotted. For example, a foundation sheet may have the foundation plan in a viewport at a scale of 3/32″ = 1′-0″ with two details in separate viewports at a scale of 1/4″ = 1′-0″ on a 17″ × 11″ sheet of paper. See **Figure 24-4.** Remember that text drawn in model space is the plotted text height multiplied by the scale factor. The scale factor is determined from the scale that the drawing is to be given in a viewport. Text that is added to layout space is drawn at full scale.

As in model space, geometry that is drawn in layout space is drawn full scale. This includes title blocks and text. The only geometry that is scaled is the drawing geometry within a viewport.

## Setting Up the Layout

The layout can be set up prior to drawing any object in model space or after the drawing is completed. A time-saver is to build the layouts into your drawing templates. When a drawing is started using the acad.dwt or acadiso.dwt drawing template, two layout tabs are located next to the model tab at the bottom of the drawing screen. When using a predefined template that comes with AutoCAD, there may be one or more layout tabs.

---

*Chapter 24*   Creating Layouts and Plotting

849

**Figure 24-3.**
The layout space concept.

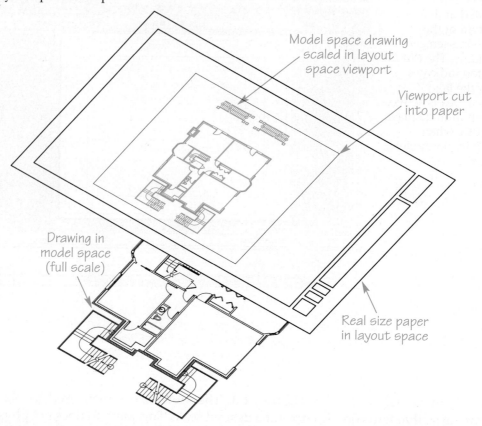

Model space drawing scaled in layout space viewport

Viewport cut into paper

Drawing in model space (full scale)

Real size paper in layout space

**Figure 24-4.**
A layout sheet ready to be plotted.

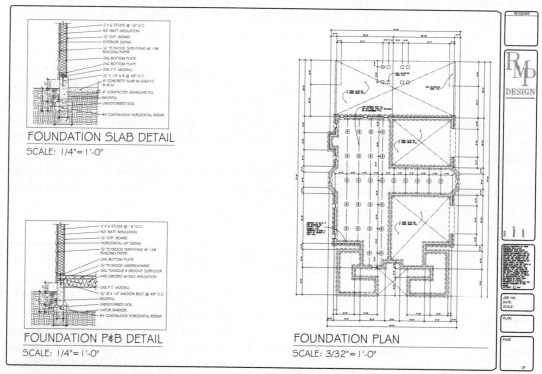

FOUNDATION SLAB DETAIL
SCALE: 1/4"=1'-0"

FOUNDATION P&B DETAIL
SCALE: 1/4"=1'-0"

FOUNDATION PLAN
SCALE: 3/32"=1'-0"

When working in model space, the model tab is active, indicating the space where you are currently working. There are three methods for switching between model space and layout space:

- **Selecting tabs.** Select the appropriate tab at the bottom of the drawing screen to switch between a layout and model space. See **Figure 24-5.**
- **Commands.**
  - **MODEL command.** Enter model at the Command prompt to switch to model space from a layout sheet.
  - **LAYOUT command.** Enter layout at the Command prompt to switch to a layout from model space. The following prompts are displayed for switching from model space to a layout:

    Command: **layout**↵
    Enter layout option [Copy/Delete/New/Template/Rename/SAveas/Set/?] <set>: ↵
    Enter layout to make current <Layout1>: *(enter a layout name to set current)*
    Regenerating layout.
    Regenerating model.
    Command:

  - **TILEMODE command.** Enter tilemode at the Command prompt. This issues a variable switch, where a 1 is equal to model space and a 0 is equal to layout space.
- **MODEL/PAPER button.** When model space is active, the **MODEL** button is displayed in the status bar. Picking the button switches to layout space. The button then reads **PAPER**. If the button is selected again, the viewport becomes active. This allows you to adjust how the model is displayed in the viewport. Selecting the button again closes the viewport and makes the layout space active. See **Figure 24-6.**

Once you have switched to layout space, the **Page Setup** dialog box appears, **Figure 24-7.** This dialog box appears by default the first time a layout is selected, allowing you to assign a printer or plotter and a piece of paper to the layout. This dialog box can be turned off in the **Options** dialog box so that the first time a layout is entered, the **Page Setup** dialog box does not appear. See **Figure 24-8.**

---

**Figure 24-5.**
The default layout tabs in a new drawing.

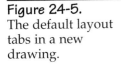

Model space active    Select to make a layout active

**Figure 24-6.**
The **MODEL/PAPER** button switches from model space to the first layout sheet.

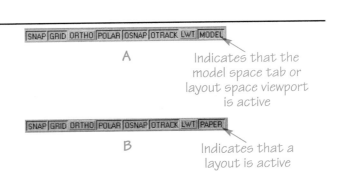

A    Indicates that the model space tab or layout space viewport is active

B    Indicates that a layout is active

---

## Figure 24-7.
The **Page Setup** dialog box sets up and assigns a plotter and paper size to your layout.

Page setup tabs

Plotter list

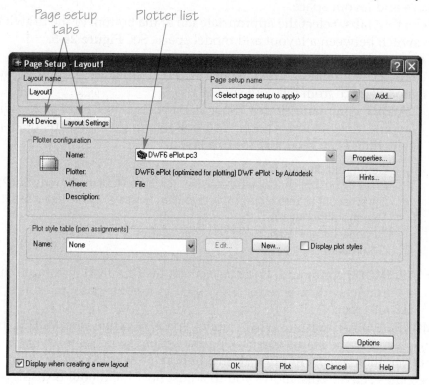

## Figure 24-8.
Page setup can be turned off in the **Options** dialog box so that when entering a new layout, the **Page Setup** dialog box does not appear.

Display tab

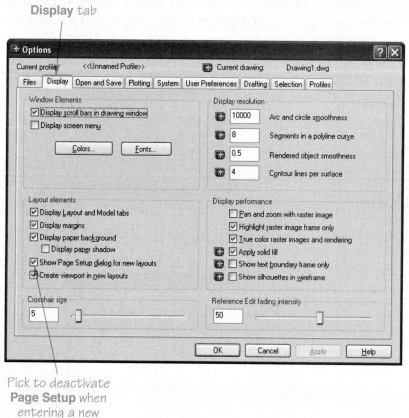

Pick to deactivate **Page Setup** when entering a new layout

**Figure 24-9.**
Selecting a printer
or plotter.

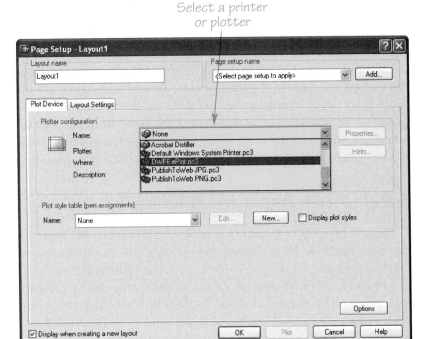

The **Page Setup** dialog box contains two tabs used for the paper sheet setup. To first set up the layout, pick the **Plot Device** tab, and select a plotter from the **Name:** drop-down list in the **Plotter configuration** area. The plotters listed are plotters that are configured in the Windows operating system and within AutoCAD. See **Figure 24-9.** After the plotter has been selected, access the **Layout Settings** tab. See **Figure 24-10.** Select the size of paper desired from the **Paper size:** drop-down list in the **Paper Size and paper units** area. The list of paper sizes available is dependent on the type of printer or plotter that you chose in the **Plot Device** tab.

**Figure 24-10.**
Selecting the paper
size.

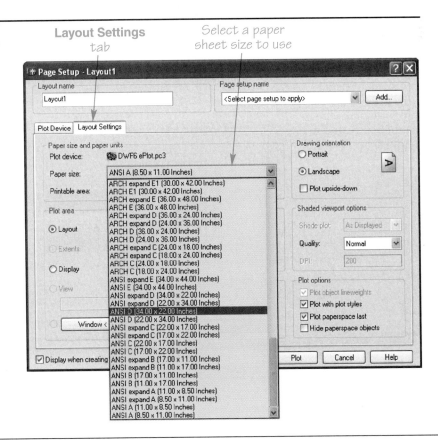

After specifying the plotter and the paper size, press the **OK** button. This displays the real size sheet of paper in layout space. A viewport is also automatically cut into the sheet of paper displaying the model space drawing. See **Figure 24-11.** The viewport is created on the current layer and plots unless the current layer is a nonplotting layer.

At this point, a title block can be drawn or inserted from a drawing file onto the sheet of paper. Create the appropriate layers and insert a title block you may have created for your company or school, or design one directly on the layout. See **Figure 24-12.** The dashed lines around the sheet indicate the paper margins. Anything outside of the margins does not plot. The margins of the paper can be adjusted by making changes to the plotter configuration. This is explained later in this chapter.

## Setting the Scale for a Viewport

The final step is to assign a scale to the viewport. Before a scale can be set, the viewport needs to be activated. To activate the viewport, move the crosshairs inside the viewport area and double-click, pick the **PAPER** button in the status bar to change it to **MODEL**, or enter mspace or ms at the Command prompt. This makes the viewport active. The viewport appears highlighted, indicating it is currently active. A model space UCS also displays in the corner of the viewport because you are now working directly in model space, through the layout space viewport. The layout space UCS is also removed. See **Figure 24-13.**

There are two methods of setting the scale for a viewport when it is active. The first requires that you know the scale factor for the viewport. Appendix K lists common scale factors. Remember that the scale factor is determined by the scale at which the drawing will be plotted. For example, if a drawing is to be plotted at a scale of 1/4″ = 1′-0″, the scale factor is equal to 48.

With the viewport active, enter zoom at the Command prompt. This displays the following prompt:

Command: **zoom**↵
Specify corner of window, enter a scale factor (nX or nXP), or
[All/Center/Dynamic/Extents/Previous/Scale/Window] <real time>:

**Figure 24-11.**
The sheet of paper with a viewport cut into it displays the geometry created in model space.

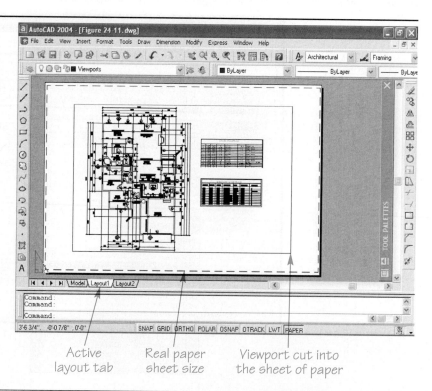

Active layout tab

Real paper sheet size

Viewport cut into the sheet of paper

Architectural Drafting Using AutoCAD

**Figure 24-12.**
Adding a title block
to the paper.

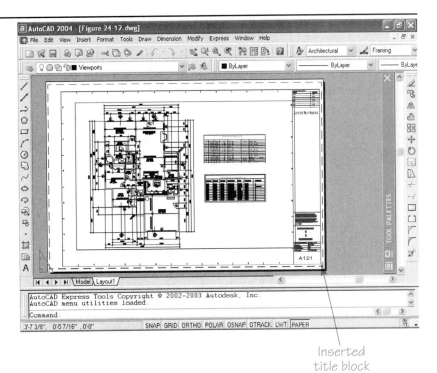

Inserted
title block

**Figure 24-13.**
Activating the view-
port.

Double-click inside
viewport to activate

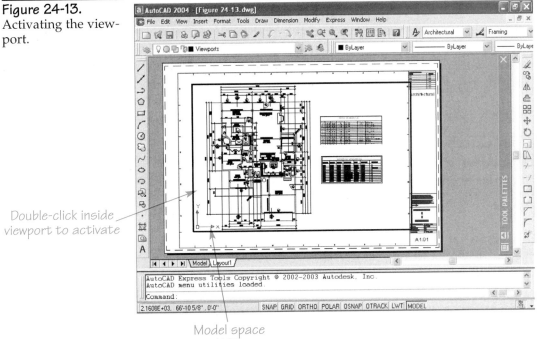

Model space
UCS

For a scale factor of 48, enter 1/48xp at the zoom prompt. This scales the drawing in the viewport so that it is 1/4" = 1'-0". The formula is 1/Scale Factor XP. This scales the zoom scale factor of the full scale drawing down to 1/48th its actual size. The *XP* stands for "times paper space." Thus, you are scaling the drawing to 1/48th its size relative to paper space (layout space). When the scale factor is applied, the drawing is resized in the viewport, reflecting the scale you have specified. The image is adjusted or zoomed from the center of the viewport.

The other method is to scale the active viewport from the **Viewports** toolbar. While the viewport is active, right-click on top of any toolbar and select **Viewports** to display the **Viewports** toolbar. The **Viewports** toolbar includes a drop-down list of scales that can be selected. See **Figure 24-14.** Choose the appropriate scale from the list and the model scales itself inside of the viewport.

**Figure 24-14.**
Scaling the model inside of the active viewport.

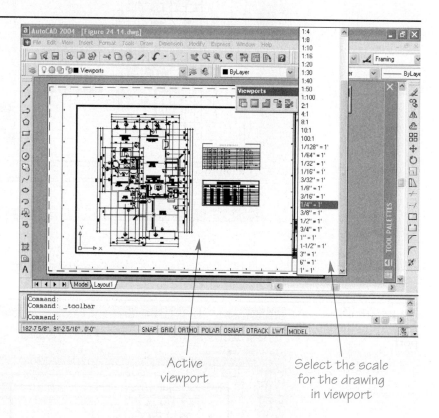

Active viewport

Select the scale for the drawing in viewport

Do not worry if the viewport edges appear to cut off the drawing. This can be adjusted. Once the scale has been set and layout space has been reentered, the viewport border can be adjusted. If the viewport is so large that there is no room to adjust the viewport edges, a different scale should be selected.

After the viewport is scaled, the layout space needs to be activated. Move the crosshairs outside of the viewport and double-click, pick the **MODEL** button to switch it to **PAPER**, or enter pspace or ps at the Command prompt. Now the viewport border can be adjusted. Simply select the viewport to obtain the grip boxes and stretch the borders until the whole drawing appears.

An alternative way of specifying a scale for a viewport is to select the viewport while you are in the layout mode, right-click, and select **Properties** from the shortcut menu. In the **Properties** window, select the **Standard** scale from the list, pick the drop-down arrow, and choose a scale. See **Figure 24-15.** The drawing is now ready to be plotted.

**Figure 24-15.**
Selecting a scale for
the viewport.

| Viewport | |
|---|---|
| **General** | |
| Color | |
| Layer | |
| Linetype | |
| Linetype scale | |
| Plot style | |
| Lineweight | |
| Hyperlink | |
| **Geometry** | |
| Center X | |
| Center Y | |
| Center Z | |
| Height | |
| Width | |
| **Misc** | |
| On | |
| Clipped | |
| Display locked | |
| Standard scale | |
| Custom scale | 1/16" |
| UCS per viewport | Yes |
| Shade plot | As Displayed |

Scale list: 1:4, 1:8, 1:10, 1:16, 1:20, 1:30, 1:40, 1:50, 1:100, 2:1, 4:1, 8:1, 10:1, 100:1, 1/128"=1', 1/64"=1', 1/32"=1', 1/16"=1', 3/32"=1', 1/8"=1', 3/16"=1', **1/4"=1'**, 3/8"=1', 1/2"=1', 3/4"=1', 1"=1', 1-1/2"=1', 3"=1', 6"=1', 1'=1'

Choose
**Standard Scale**

Pick drop-down
list button and
choose a scale

## Exercise 24-1

◆ Start a new drawing using one of your templates.
◆ Create a layer named X-Floor Plan and set it current.
◆ Xref ex22-2 from Chapter 22 to the absolute coordinate 0,0 using the **Overlay** option.
◆ Select one of the layout tabs.
◆ In the **Plot Device** tab in the **Page Setup** dialog box, select the **DWF6 ePlot.pc3** plotter.
◆ Pick the **Layout Settings** tab and select the **ARCH expand D (36.00 x 24.00 Inches)** paper size.
◆ Press the **OK** button.
◆ Create a layer named Viewports and make it a nonplotting layer.
◆ Change the viewport border to the Viewports layer using the **Properties** window.
◆ Create a layer named Title Block, and draw a new title block or insert an existing title block onto the sheet.
◆ Activate the viewport and give the viewport a scale of 1/4" = 1'-0".
◆ Activate the paper layout area.
◆ If the viewport cuts a portion of the drawing off, readjust the viewport border by using the viewport grips.
◆ Save the drawing as ex24-1.

**Professional Tip**

Additional layouts can be created for multiple sheets of paper by selecting **New Layout** from the **Layout** cascading menu in the **Insert** pull-down menu. Use multiple sheets with different sizes of paper, and different views to the drawing for the construction documents. This is discussed in greater depth later in this chapter.

# Working with Viewports

Viewports created in *layout space* are called floating viewports. *Floating viewports* are actually holes cut into the paper in the layout tab so that the *model space* drawing can be seen behind the paper. These viewports are separate objects and can be moved around, arranged, and overlapped—thus the term "floating viewports."

After floating viewports are created, display commands such as **VIEW**, **PAN**, and **ZOOM** can be used to modify the *model space* drawing "showing through" the viewport. This allows you to adjust how the drawing appears within the viewport. Editing commands such as **MOVE**, **ERASE**, **STRETCH**, and **COPY** can be used in *layout space* to modify the viewports and their borders.

As you work through the following sections describing floating viewports, be sure a layout tab is selected on your AutoCAD screen.

## Creating Floating Viewports

The process of creating floating viewports in layout space is nearly identical to the process of creating tiled viewports in model space. By default, AutoCAD creates a single viewport on the sheet of paper. Single viewports can be created with the **MVIEW** command, or multiple viewports can be created with the **Viewports** dialog box. Tiled viewports and the **Viewports** dialog box are discussed in Chapter 20 of this text.

As discussed earlier, when model space is active, the **Viewports** dialog box creates tiled viewports. When layout space is active, the **Viewports** dialog box creates floating viewports. This dialog box differs slightly depending on the current environment—model space or layout space. The **Apply to:** drop-down list found in model space becomes the **Viewport spacing:** text box in layout space. Use this setting to specify the distance or space around the edges of the floating viewports. See **Figure 24-16.**

**Figure 24-16.**
When layout space is active, the **New Viewports** tab in the **Viewports** dialog box contains the **Viewport spacing:** setting.

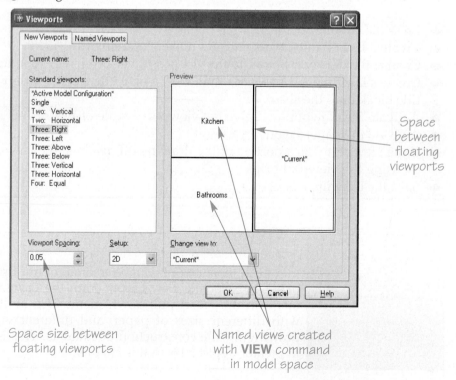

Architectural Drafting Using AutoCAD

**Figure 24-17.**
Picking two corners for a box designates the area in which your viewports will be created.

Three new
viewports created
in Figure 24-16

Pick the second
corner for viewport
configuration

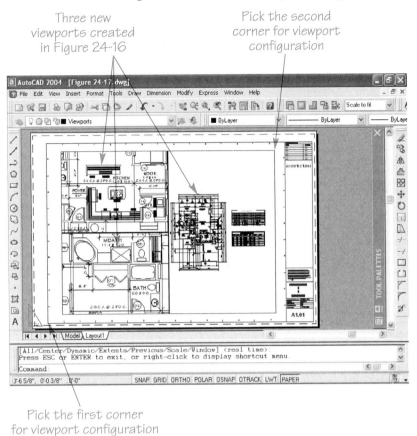

Pick the first corner
for viewport configuration

After selecting the configuration and picking the **OK** button, the drawing screen is returned, allowing you to pick two corners of a box on the layout sheet. The two corners that you select designate a boxed area in which to place the viewport configuration selected in the **Viewports** dialog box. See **Figure 24-17.**

Single floating viewports can also be created using the **MVIEW** command. The following prompt is displayed when entering mview at the Command prompt:

Command: **mv** *or* **mview**↵
Specify corner of viewport or
   [ON/OFF/Fit/Hideplot/Lock/Object/Polygonal/Restore/2/3/4] <Fit>:

At this point, you can define a rectangular floating viewport by selecting opposite corners. See **Figure 24-18.**

The **2**, **3**, and **4** options provide preset viewport configurations similar to those in the **Viewports** dialog box. These options can also be selected from the **Viewports** cascading menu in the **View** pull-down menu. The remaining options are described as follows:

- **ON and OFF.** These options activate and deactivate the display of the drawing within a viewport. When you enter the **OFF** option, you are prompted to select the viewports to be affected. Use the **ON** option to reactivate the viewport. Turning a viewport off is similar to turning off layers except the objects are only turned off in the floating viewport you select.
- **Fit.** This default option creates a single rectangular floating viewport that fills the entire printable area (area inside of the margins) on the sheet.
- **Hideplot.** This option prevents hidden lines in a 3D model from being plotted. This option is discussed in Chapters 25 and 26 of this text.

**Figure 24-18.**
Creating a rectan-
gular floating view-
port using the
**MVIEW** command.

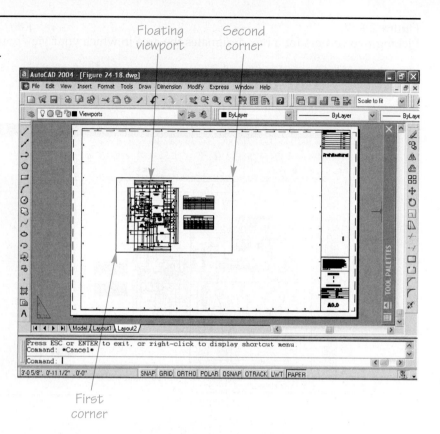

- **Lock.** This option allows you to lock the view in one or more viewports. When a viewport is locked, objects within the viewport can still be edited and new objects can be added, but you are unable to use display commands such as **ZOOM** and **PAN**. This option is also used to unlock a locked viewport. This is particularly useful after the viewport is scaled, because zooming in the viewport will change the scale of the viewport.
- **Restore.** This option converts a saved viewport configuration into individual floating viewports.
- **Object.** Use this option to change a closed object drawn in layout space into a floating viewport. Circles, ellipses, polygons, and other closed shapes can be used as floating viewport outlines. See **Figure 24-19.** This option can also be accessed by picking the **Convert Object to Viewport** button in the **Viewports** toolbar or by selecting **Object** from the **Viewports** cascading menu in the **View** pull-down menu.
- **Polygonal.** Use this option to draw a floating viewport outline using a poly-line. The viewport shape can be any closed shape composed of lines and arcs. See **Figure 24-20.** This option can also be accessed by picking the **Polygonal Viewport** button in the **Viewports** toolbar or by selecting **Polygonal Viewport** from the **Viewports** cascading menu in the **View** pull-down menu.

**Figure 24-19.**
Viewports can be created from closed objects. A—Draw the objects in layout space. B—Objects converted to viewports.

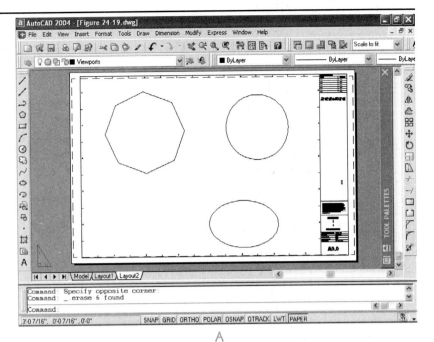

A

B

**Figure 24-20.**
Floating viewports
can be created from
a closed polyline
with arcs or line
segments.

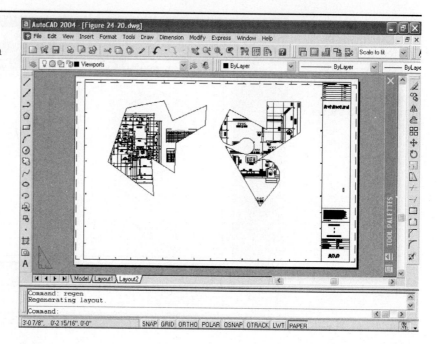

The **Viewports** toolbar can be used to create several of the same types of viewports described in this section, **Figure 24-21.** In addition to some of the options previously discussed, the **Viewports** toolbar includes a **Clip Existing Viewport** command that allows you to clip away parts of a viewport, similar to the **XCLIP** command described in Chapter 17.

**Figure 24-21.**
The **Viewports**
toolbar can be used
to create floating
viewports in layout
space.

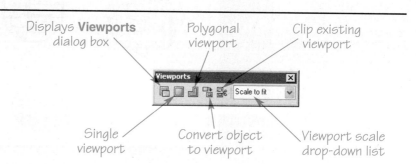

Architectural Drafting Using AutoCAD

◆ Open ex24-1 and switch to model space.

◆ Use the **VIEW** command to create a view of the kitchen area and a view of the bathroom area.

◆ Select Layout 1.

◆ Erase the viewport created in the previous exercise.

◆ Set the Viewports layer current.

◆ Enter the **Viewports** dialog box, and select the **Three: Right** configuration. Set the **Viewport Spacing:** to 1/2". Set the Kitchen and Bathroom views current in two of the viewports.

◆ Press **OK** and select two points of a box within the layout.

◆ Set the largest viewport to a scale of 1/4" = 1'-0". Use the **PAN** command to adjust the floor plan so that it is centered on the viewport. DO NOT use the **ZOOM** command after setting a scale.

◆ Set the Kitchen viewport to a scale of 1/2" = 1'-0" and the Bathroom view to a scale of 3/4" = 1'-0".

◆ Use the **Clip Existing Viewport** command to clip the smaller viewports. The final drawing should resemble the one shown below.

◆ Adjust the viewport borders as required using grips.

◆ Save the drawing as ex24-2.

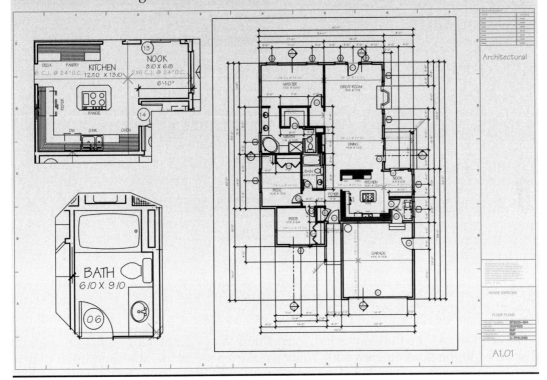

# Controlling Viewport Display

When a viewport is first created, AutoCAD performs a **ZOOM Extents** of the drawing in model space. This allows the drafter to view the entire contents in model space through the viewport. When the scale is then applied to the viewport, AutoCAD is readjusting the view from the center of the viewport. This is why the viewport edges appear to cut off some of the drawing geometry occasionally.

After the scale has been set in a viewport, the **ZOOM** command should never be used in the viewport again, because the drawing will be changed to the wrong scale. If you need to readjust the view, use the **PAN** command while in the viewport. Once the drawing has been adjusted in the viewport to reflect the scale and the area desired, the viewport can be locked so that the scale does not accidentally get changed. Locking the viewport was discussed previously through use of the **MVIEW** command.

There are two additional ways of locking a viewport. Both methods involve working in layout space. To get back to layout space, double-click outside of the viewport, pick the **MODEL** button in the status bar, or enter ps or pspace at the Command prompt. Pick the viewport that is to be locked to obtain the grip boxes. Right-click and select **Display Locked** from the shortcut menu. Selecting **Yes** in the cascading menu locks the viewport, and selecting **No** unlocks the viewport. This method only allows you to lock one viewport at a time. See **Figure 24-22.**

The other method is to select the viewport(s) that need to be locked, right-click, and select **Properties** from the shortcut menu. In the **Properties** window, select the **Display locked** option, pick the drop-down list button, and pick **Yes** from the list. See **Figure 24-23.**

**Figure 24-22.**
Locking a single viewport with the shortcut menu.

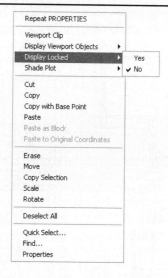

## Controlling Layer Display

Each time a viewport is created, everything that is displaying in model space is displayed in the floating viewport. This can take up a considerable amount of time if there are many items that AutoCAD is regenerating.

For example, in Figure 24-4, the model space area included the foundation plan and two details. When all three viewports were created, AutoCAD displayed the foundation plan and both details in each viewport. The desired effect was to have two details at a different scale from the larger foundation plan. One viewport in the layout is not enough, because the scale of the details could not be shown in a single viewport. So three viewports were created and scaled. Although each viewport is displaying a different portion of the drawing from model space, the whole drawing is present in each viewport. The foundation plan is not seen in either of the detail viewports, so a special tool is used to freeze the foundation plan layers in the detail viewports. Likewise, the detail drawings are not used in the foundation plan viewport so they also are frozen in the foundation viewport.

**Figure 24-23.**
Locking the view-
port scale from the
**Properties** window.

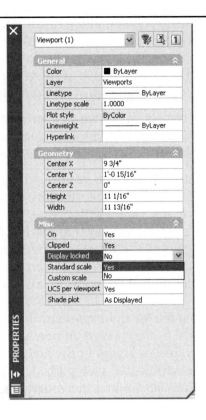

The tool used to control the display of layers in a floating viewport is the **VPLAYER** command. **VPLAYER** stands for *viewport layer*. This command is different from the regular freeze icon in the **Layer Properties Manager** dialog box because it only freezes layers in a floating viewport, whereas the freeze icon freezes layers globally in all floating viewports. An icon for thaw/freeze within a viewport is included in the **Layer Control** drop-down list in the **Object Properties** toolbar.

Before using the **VPLAYER** command, make the viewport that is to have frozen layers active. When vplayer is entered at the Command prompt, you are prompted with several options:

Command: **vplayer**⏎
Enter an option [?/Freeze/Thaw/Reset/Newfrz/Vpvisdflt]:

The **VPLAYER** command includes the following options:
- **?.** This option lists currently frozen layers in the currently active viewport.
- **Freeze.** Enter the name of the layer(s) to be frozen. The following prompts are displayed when using the **Freeze** option:

  Enter layer name(s) to freeze: *(enter the name of a layer or multiple layers by sepa-rating the names with commas)*
  Enter an option [All/Select/Current] <Current>:

    You can freeze the layer(s) in all of the floating viewports, select the viewport(s) to freeze the layer in, or have the layer frozen in the current viewport.
- **Thaw.** Enter the name of the layer(s) to be thawed in a floating viewport. The prompts and options are similar to the options for the **Freeze** option.
- **Reset.** This option resets layers to the default visibility status as they appear currently in the **Layers** dialog box (frozen or thawed). The prompts are the same as previously discussed. Specify a layer name to reset, and specify the floating viewports to which the layers will be restored.

- **Newfrz.** Specify layers that are to automatically freeze when creating any new floating viewports. This is a good option if new viewports are created and you do not want specific layers to display in any new floating viewports created.
- **Vpvisdflt.** This option thaws or freezes specified layers in newly created viewports. The following prompts are displayed with this option:

> Enter layer name(s) to change viewport visibility: *(enter the name of a layer or multiple layer by separating the names with commas)*
> Enter a viewport visibility option [Frozen/Thawed] *<current>*: *(enter an option)*

Layer visibility can also be controlled through the **Layer Properties Manager** dialog box. In order to control the visibility of the layers in a viewport, the viewport must first be active. If a viewport is active, the **Layer Properties Manager** dialog box can be opened by selecting the **Layer Properties Manager** button on the **Layers** toolbar. If the floating viewport is active and the **Layer Properties Manager** dialog box is accessed, a slider bar is located at the bottom of the layer list. Slide the bar to the right to display two columns that control layer visibility in floating viewports. See **Figure 24-24.**

The columns at the far right freeze or thaw layers in the currently active floating viewport and freeze or thaw layers in newly created floating viewports. The **Current VP Freeze** column freezes layers in the active viewport. The **New VP Freeze** column freezes layers in newly created viewports. Using the **Layer Properties Manager** dialog box to freeze or thaw layers in a viewport is often faster than entering layer names with the **VPLAYER** command.

**Figure 24-24.**
Additional layer columns used for controlling layer visibility in floating viewports.

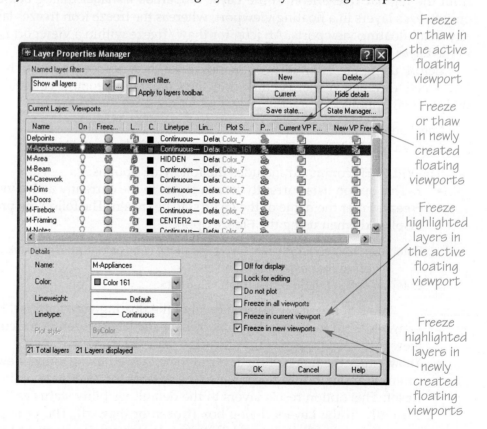

Freeze or thaw in the active floating viewport

Freeze or thaw in newly created floating viewports

Freeze highlighted layers in the active floating viewport

Freeze highlighted layers in newly created floating viewports

Throughout this text, you have been creating different types of plans. The house project includes several different drawings, and so far you have been using the freeze and thaw functions in model space to control what is being displayed as you draw. Layouts can be created within each of the drawing files to create each sheet for the construction documents. Another option is to create a plot drawing, then xref each of the drawing files into it.

When it is time for you to plot, you may consider creating a layout for each sheet or plan that you have drawn and referenced into the plot drawing. Thaw all of the layers in the drawing, and in each floating viewport, freeze the layers that do not need to be displayed in the active viewport.

For example, if a floor plan and a foundation plan are to be plotted, create a layout for the floor plan that only displays the main floor layers in one viewport. On the foundation sheet, display only the foundation layers and nothing else. This allows you to use one plotting drawing file, yet produce multiple sheets displaying different portions of the construction documents. See **Figure 24-25.**

---

**Figure 24-25.**
The house plan with all of the sheets created. Note all of the layers have been thawed in model space, but layers not needed in individual viewports have been frozen through the **VPLAYER** command or the **Active VP Freeze** column.

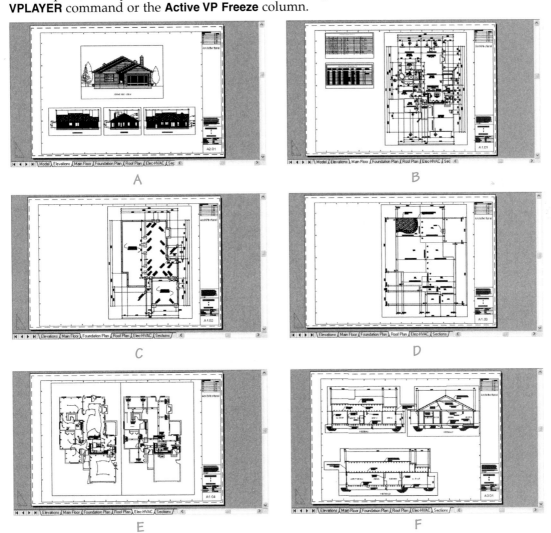

## Layer States

Layer settings, such as on/off, frozen/thawed, and locked/unlocked, determine whether or not a layer is displayed, plotted, and editable. The status of layer settings for all layers in the drawing can be saved as a named layer state. Once a layer state is saved, the settings can be reset by selecting the layer state. The **Save state...** and **State Manager...** buttons are available in the **Layer Properties Manager** dialog box. Refer to **Figure 24-24.** Layer states are covered in detail in Chapter 5 of this text.

### Exercise 24-3

◆ Open ex24-2.
◆ Create the following layers:
  ◆ X-Foundation    (use for the foundation xref, ex18-6.dwg)
  ◆ X-Elevations    (use for the elevations xref, ex19-7.dwg)
  ◆ X-Sections    (use for the sections xref, ex20-6.dwg)
  ◆ X-Roof Plan    (use for the roof plan xref, ex22-3.dwg)
  ◆ X-Elec-HVAC    (use for the electrical and HVAC plan xrefs, ex23-1.dwg and ex23-4.dwg)
◆ Access the **Model** tab and xref in ex18-6, ex19-7, ex20-6, ex22-3, ex23-1, and ex23-4 you created earlier. Place on the appropriate xref layers noted above, insert to 0,0 and use the **Overlay** option.
◆ Access the **Layer Properties Manager** dialog box and thaw all of the layers in the drawing.
◆ Access Layout 1. Erase all of the viewports. Create a single viewport on the Viewports layer. Set the scale to 1/4″ = 1′-0″. Make any adjustments to the viewport as required so that the floor plan is centered on the viewport.
◆ Use **VPLAYER** to freeze all of the xref layers, and then thaw only the main floor layers. Hint: the * wild card symbol can be used to freeze all of the xref layer names.
◆ Use **VPLAYER** to freeze all of the layers in the drawing in newly created viewports.
◆ Create two viewports for the schedules and place them to the left of the floor plan viewport. Scale these to 1/4″ = 1′-0″ and freeze the appropriate layers.
◆ Your drawing should look similar to the diagram below.
◆ Save the drawing as ex24-3.

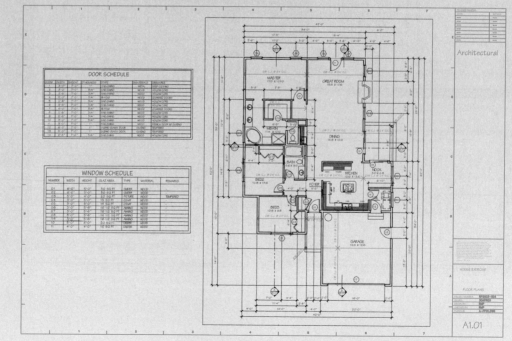

Architectural Drafting Using AutoCAD

## Controlling Linetype Display

When creating a set of construction documents, the drawings need to look consistent regardless of how many people have worked on them. One of the elements on a drawing that needs to appear consistent is the linetypes. The **LTSCALE** system variable controls the appearance and scale of linetypes in your drawing. A problem occurs when two viewports display the same linetype but have different scales side by side, and the linetypes can appear in two different sizes.

To remedy this, AutoCAD provides the **PSLTSCALE** system variable. When **PSLTSCALE** is set to 1 and the **LTSCALE** system variable is set to 1, then linetypes appear with the same lengths of dashes and dots regardless of scale. See **Figure 24-26**. **PSLTSCALE** set to 0 turns off the linetype scaling in floating viewports.

**Figure 24-26.**
Linetype scaling in floating viewports can be made to appear consistent by setting the **PSLTSCALE** variable to 1.

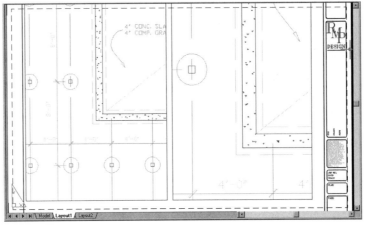

Viewports with Different Linetype Scales

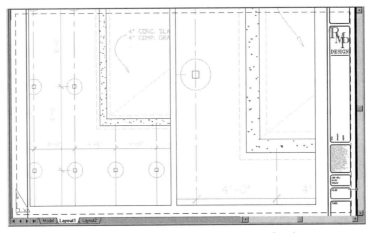

Viewports with Matching Linetype Scales

## Adding Annotations and Dimensions

The addition of text and dimensions to drawings was discussed earlier in this text. When you add notes or dimensions in model space, the scale factor is applied to adjust the text and dimensions so that they appear correctly when plotted. For example, if notes are to appear in the plotted drawing at 1/8″ in height and the plotted scale of the drawing is 1/4″ = 1′-0″, the 1/8″ high text is multiplied by the scale factor of 48, making the text height 6″. This way, when the drawing is scaled 1/48th its size in a floating viewport, the text appears as 1/8″ high.

If the model space drawing needs to appear at a 1/8″ = 1′-0″ scale in another viewport, freeze the dimension or text layer in that viewport, create a new layer to be used in the 1/8″ = 1′-0″ scale viewport, and create your notes 12″ high. This allows your notes to appear 1/8″ high in all of the viewports. The disadvantage is that this duplicates the text notes in model space, since you now have notes that appear 6″ high and the same notes again at 12″ high. But the advantage is that the layout space text is consistent.

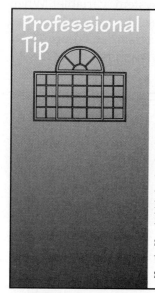

**Professional Tip**

If you are working with drawings that have many scales, you may decide to create several text styles, one for each scale. You might specify a naming convention such as Notes48, Notes96, and NotesDim for the style names that correspond to 1/4″ and 1/8″ = 1′-0″ scales and a text style that is used for the dimension style. Each of the styles then is given the same font. Then, in the **Height:** text box, enter the desired scaled text height for text. This requires additional management when it comes to adding notes, because you need to make sure the correct style is being used. It is important to remember to have a text style that uses a zero text height for your dimension style, because the dimension style looks to the text style for text heights and then scales them by the dimension style scale factor. Do not use a text style that has a nonzero text height in your dimension style.

Text and notes that are added directly to layout space and not in a floating viewport are drawn full scale. Remember that the layout sheet is full size so notes, tags, and drawing titles need to be created in the actual size you would like them to appear on the plotted sheet.

Dimensions are treated similarly to text for scaling purposes. Create a dimension style for each of the scales that will be represented in the floating viewports. Names such as DIM48 and DIM96 can be used for 1/4″ and 1/8″ = 1′-0″ scales, respectively. Dimension styles are discussed in Chapter 15. Dimensions can also be created in a floating viewport. They can be created so that the scale matches the viewport scale.

In order to create dimensions through a floating viewport, some setup needs to be accomplished. First, access the **Dimension Styles Manager** dialog box. Create a style named DimsPS. When the **New Dimension Style** dialog box appears, select the **Fit** tab. See **Figure 24-27**. In the **Scale for Dimension Features** area, select the **Scale dimensions to layout (paperspace)** radio button. This setting then looks to the current viewport for the scale to apply to the dimensions, similar to the way you set a scale for your dimensions with the **Use overall scale of:** radio button.

After the dimension style has been created and set current, access a layout sheet and add the floating viewports. Select a scale for the viewports and lock the viewport scale. Viewport locking was discussed earlier in this chapter. After the viewports have been locked, make a viewport active. If you zoom in a viewport that has been locked, AutoCAD remembers the scale and allows you to zoom into the drawing without changing the scale of the viewport. This aids in the placement of dimensions. Add dimensions while you are currently in the viewport. The dimensions are scaled by the viewport scale and appear correct in the layout. See **Figure 24-28**.

Architectural Drafting Using AutoCAD

**Figure 24-27.**
Setting the dimension scale for dimensioning in a floating viewport.

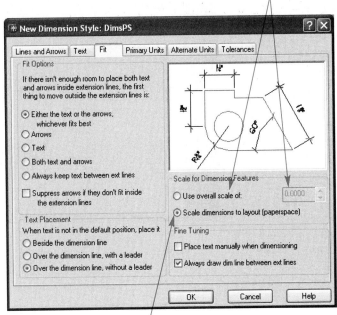

Use to scale the dimension by a scale factor

Select to dimension in a floating viewport

If you are dimensioning in the viewports, consider creating a layer for each set of dimensions that appear in different viewports. For example, in **Figure 24-28** a DIM32 layer was created for dimensions that were dimensioned in a 3/8″ = 1′-0″ scaled viewport, and a DIM24 layer was created for dimensions that were dimensioned in a 1/2″ = 1′-0″ viewport. This allows you to freeze the appropriate layers in each viewport, yet maintain the constant look of the dimension text and arrowhead sizes.

## Layout Setup Steps

The following are general steps to consider when creating your layout sheets:
1. Create the model space geometry.
2. Save any views in model space if desired to be used in the floating viewports.
3. Pick a layout tab to switch to layout space.
4. Select a plotter and paper size in the **Page Setup** dialog box.
5. Insert a title block.
6. Adjust the default viewport or create new viewports to arrange on the sheet. Arrange the viewports as needed.
7. Ensure the floating viewports are on a nonplotting layer.
8. Restore views from model space in the floating viewports as needed.
9. Apply a scale to the floating viewports and lock the viewports.
10. Apply any layer controls in each viewport as needed.
11. Add dimensions if you did not create them in model space.

**Figure 24-28.**
Creating dimensions through a viewport. A—Note the dimensions appear the correct size in the layout. B—The same dimensions displayed in model space. Note the differently scaled dimensions.

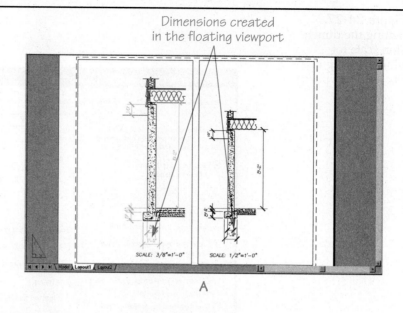

Dimensions created in the floating viewport

SCALE: 3/8"=1'-0"    SCALE: 1/2"=1'-0"

A

Both sets of dimensions at different scales in model space

B

12. Add annotations to the layout sheet, such as drawing titles and title block information.

# Plotting the Drawing

The end result of a project drawn in AutoCAD is to obtain a hard copy of the drawings so contractors, builders, engineers, and building officials can refer to the drawings as the structure is being built or reviewed. The previous discussion described how to set up a layout sheet and get it ready for plotting. Before you plot, consider where the drawing is going to be plotted, such as to a printer, plotter, or Internet file, and how the drawing will appear as it comes off the plotter. This section describes the settings involved with preparing the layout sheet and getting it plotted.

# Setting Up Layouts

Before setting up a layout sheet, you need to specify in the **Page Setup** dialog box where the drawing will be sent for plotting and the size of the layout sheet. This was discussed earlier in this chapter. After selecting a layout tab, the **Page Setup** dialog box displays by default. This dialog box allows you to adjust the layout settings.

Drawings that are created with the acad.dwt or the acadiso.dwt template automatically get created with two layout tabs named **Layout1** and **Layout2**. If other AutoCAD templates are used when starting a drawing, there may be one or more layout tabs with other names that you can choose from. See **Figure 24-29.** Most of the templates include a differently named layout tab and often include a title block drawn on the layout sheet.

**Figure 24-29.**
A drawing started from the Architectural, English units-color dependent plot styles.dwt template.

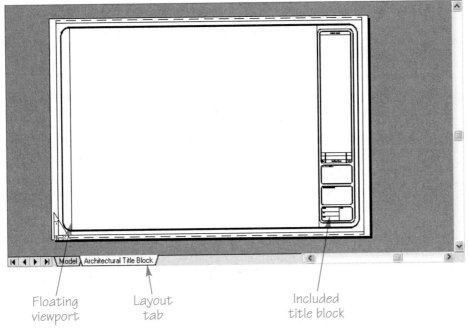

Floating viewport

Layout tab

Included title block

## Managing Layouts

A drawing file can contain as many layout tabs as desired. In addition to the model tab, there must always be at least one layout tab in the drawing. Layouts can be managed through the **LAYOUT** command. To access this command, enter lo or layout at the Command prompt. This displays the following prompt:

Command: **lo** *or* **layout**↵
Enter layout option [Copy/Delete/New/Template/Rename/SAveas/Set/?] <set>:

The following is a description of the options:
- **Copy.** This option copies an existing layout and places it after the current layout. If a name is not entered for the new layout, AutoCAD gives it the same name as the copied layout with an incremental number in parentheses. The following is the prompt sequence:

    Enter layout option [Copy/Delete/New/Template/Rename/SAveas/Set/?] <set>: **c**↵
    Enter layout to copy <current>: *(enter the name of the layout to be copied)*
    Enter layout name for copy <default>: *(enter the name of the new layout)*

- **Delete.** This option deletes a layout tab from the drawing. The current tab is the default.

  Enter layout option [Copy/Delete/New/Template/Rename/SAveas/Set/?] <set>: **d**↵
  Enter name of layout to delete <*current*>: (*enter the name of the layout to be deleted*)

  The **Model** tab cannot be deleted and there must be at least one layout tab.
- **New.** This option creates a new layout tab.

  Enter layout option [Copy/Delete/New/Template/Rename/SAveas/Set/?] <set>: **n**↵
  Enter new Layout name <Layout#>: (*enter the name for the new layout*)

- **Template.** This option creates a new layout based on an existing layout in a drawing template (DWT) or drawing (DWG) file. The layout and any geometry on the layout sheet from the template file is inserted into the current drawing. When entering the **Template** option, the **Select Template From File** dialog box appears. See **Figure 24-30.**

  Enter layout option [Copy/Delete/New/Template/Rename/SAveas/Set/?] <set>: **t**↵
  Enter layout name(s) or [?]: (*enter the name of a layout in the template*)

- **Rename.** This option renames layouts. The last current layout is used as the default layout to be renamed.

  Enter layout option [Copy/Delete/New/Template/Rename/SAveas/Set/?] <set>: **r**↵
  Enter layout to rename <*current*>: (*enter the name of a layout to rename*)
  Enter new layout name <*current*>: (*enter the new name for the layout*)

  Layout names cannot be duplicated in the same drawing file. The layout name can contain up to 255 characters and is not case sensitive. The first 32 characters are the only characters that will display on the tab.
- **SAveas.** This option saves the layout into a template file. Upon entering the **Saveas** option, the **Create Drawing File** dialog box is displayed, allowing you to create a new template utilizing the layout that you specify.

  Enter layout option [Copy/Delete/New/Template/Rename/SAveas/Set/?] <set>: **sa**↵
  Enter layout to save to template <*current*>: (*enter the name of the layout to be included in a new template*)

**Figure 24-30.**
Select a template or drawing file from which to copy a template.

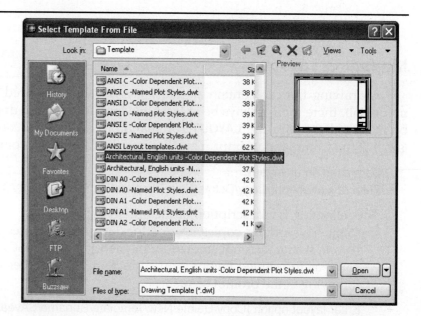

- **Set.** This option sets a layout current.

  Enter layout option [Copy/Delete/New/Template/Rename/SAveas/Set/?] <set>: **s**↵
  Enter layout to make current <*last*>: *(enter the name of a layout to set current)*

- **?.** This option lists all of the layouts currently defined in the drawing.

  Enter layout option [Copy/Delete/New/Template/Rename/SAveas/Set/?] <set>: **?** ↵
  Active Layouts:
  Layout: Elevations Block name: *Paper_Space.
  Layout: Foundation Block name: *Paper_Space409.
  Layout: Main Floor Block name: *Paper_Space408.
  Layout: Roof Block name: *Paper_Space412.
  Layout: Sections Block name: *Paper_Space411.
  Layout: Upper Floor Block name: *Paper_Space410.

New layouts can also be created from the **Layout** cascading menu in the **Insert** pull-down menu or from the **Layouts** toolbar. See **Figure 24-31.** The **Layout** cascading menu includes an option named **Layout Wizard**.

**Figure 24-31.**
Options for creating new layouts. A— The **Layout** cascading menu. B—The **Layouts** toolbar.

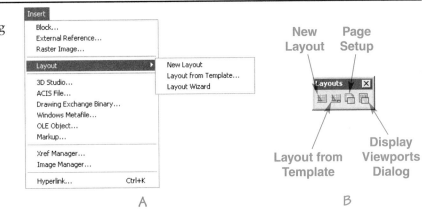

The **Layout Wizard** contains several steps that walk you through the process of creating a new layout. Settings such as the layout name, paper size, and the number of viewports are made. **Figure 24-32** displays the steps in order to create a new layout from this wizard.

Other layout options can also be accessed by moving the cursor over the top of any layout tab and right-clicking. This displays the layouts shortcut menu shown in **Figure 24-33.** The first four options act the same as the corresponding options in the **LAYOUT** command.

Selecting the **Move or Copy...** option displays the **Move or Copy** dialog box. See **Figure 24-34.** Pick the **Create a copy** check box to copy the tab you right-clicked on, and select a tab from the list to follow the new copy. The new copy is given the same name as the original layout tab with an incremental number in parentheses. Right-click the new tab, and select **Rename** from the shortcut menu to rename the new layout tab.

## Figure 24-32.
The **Layout Wizard** can be used to create a new layout.

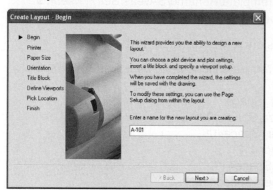

Step 1– Enter layout name

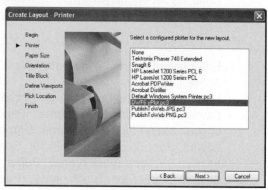

Step 2– Pick plotting device

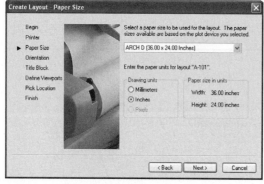

Step 3– Pick paper size

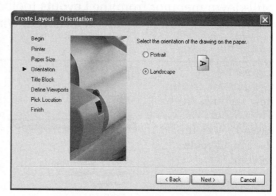

Step 4– Pick paper orientation

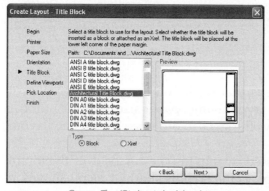

Step 5– Pick title block

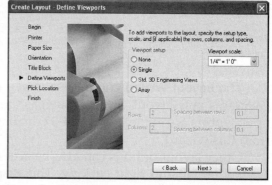

Step 6– Pick viewport options and locations

## Figure 24-33.
The layout shortcut menu can be accessed by right-clicking on a layout tab.

Architectural Drafting Using AutoCAD

**Figure 24-34.**
The **Move or Copy** dialog box is used to reorganize or copy layouts in the drawing. Right-click on a layout tab and select **Move or Copy...** to access this dialog box.

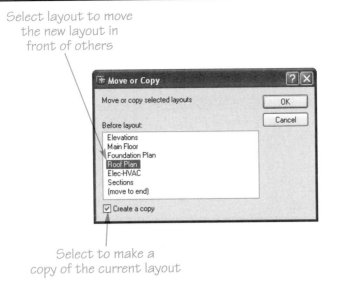

*Select layout to move the new layout in front of others*

*Select to make a copy of the current layout*

Layouts can also be added to your drawing by dragging and dropping them from **DesignCenter**. To copy a layout from **DesignCenter**, first locate the drawing that contains the layouts you wish to use from the **DesignCenter** tree view. Select **Layouts** in the tree view to list the layouts within the selected drawing. Pick the layout from the list and drag and drop the layout into the current drawing. See **Figure 24-35.**

When a layout is copied from **DesignCenter** into the current drawing, everything that is drawn on the original layout is also copied to the current drawing. If the original layout included a title block, three floating viewports, and drawing titles, all of the geometry is also copied over.

As you create multiple layouts in a drawing, layout tabs appear at the bottom of the drawing screen. See **Figure 24-36.** The arrows to the left of the model tab can be used to display the other tabs in the drawing so that you can access them.

**Figure 24-35.**
Layouts can be copied from existing drawings through the use of **DesignCenter**.

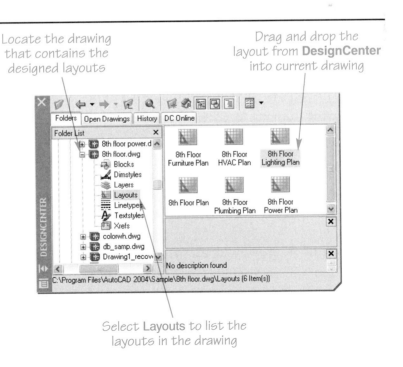

*Locate the drawing that contains the designed layouts*

*Drag and drop the layout from **DesignCenter** into current drawing*

*Select **Layouts** to list the layouts in the drawing*

**Figure 24-36.**
Use the arrows to view other tabs in the drawing.

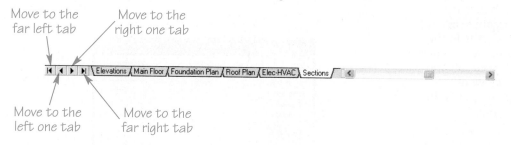

Move to the far left tab

Move to the right one tab

Move to the left one tab

Move to the far right tab

## Exercise 24-4

◆ Open ex24-3.
◆ Rename the **Layout 1** tab to Main Floor.
◆ Copy the **Main Floor** tab five times.
◆ Rename the copied layouts to the following names:

| Layout Name | Drawing(s) Displayed | Scale |
|---|---|---|
| Main Floor | ex22-2 | 1/4″ = 1′-0″ |
| Foundation Plan | ex18-6 | 1/4″ = 1′-0″ |
| Roof Plan | ex22-3 | 1/4″ = 1′-0″ |
| Elec-HVAC | ex23-1 (electrical) and ex23-4 (HVAC) | 1/4″ = 1′-0″ |
| Elevations | ex19-7 | 1/4″ = 1′-0″ (Front elevation) and 1/8″ = 1′-0″ (side and rear elevations) |
| Sections | ex20-6 | 1/4″ = 1′-0″ |

◆ Arrange and scale the viewports appropriately.
◆ Freeze and thaw layers in the floating viewports as required. Hint: In a floating viewport, freeze the layer that a particular xref has been inserted on. This will cause all the layers within that xref not to be displayed.
◆ Refer to **Figure 24-25** for arrangement of the drawings.
◆ Save the drawing as ex24-4.

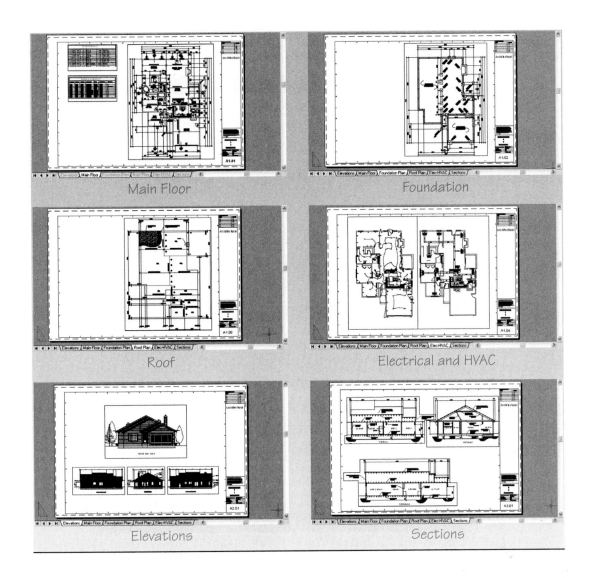

Main Floor

Foundation

Roof

Electrical and HVAC

Elevations

Sections

# Using Page Setup

When you first access a layout tab, the **Page Setup** dialog box displays, allowing you to select settings such as the plotter, pen settings, and the size of paper to use on the layout. Each layout can have a unique page setup. For example, you may create two layouts for a floor plan. One layout can be assigned a 36" × 24" sheet of paper and plotted with a plotter, and the second layout can be assigned to a printer and an 8-1/2" × 11" sheet of paper. This allows you to maximize the plotting possibilities with the same drawing.

After the **Page Setup** dialog box has automatically been accessed, it does not appear again if the layout is later selected. To access the **Page Setup** dialog box after it has already initially been set up, select **Page Setup...** from the **File** pull-down menu, pick the **Page Setup** button from the **Layouts** toolbar, right-click over the current layout tab and select **Page Setup...** from the shortcut menu, or enter pagesetup at the Command prompt. This displays the **Page Setup** dialog box, **Figure 24-37**.

The **Page Setup** dialog box contains two tabs, **Plot Device** and **Layout Settings**. The **Plot Device** tab is used to specify the printer or plotter assigned to the layout and the type of pen settings that are used when plotting the geometry. See **Figure 24-37**. The **Layout Settings** tab is used to set the size of paper, what is to be plotted, the scale, and the orientation of the layout sheet. See **Figure 24-38**. At the top of the **Page Setup** dialog box is a text box that contains the name of the current layout and a text box for the page setup name.

**Figure 24-37.**
The **Page Setup** dialog box.

Layout name

The **Plot Device** and **Layout Settings** tabs

Assign plotter to the current layout

Assign a pen style to the current layout

Page setup name

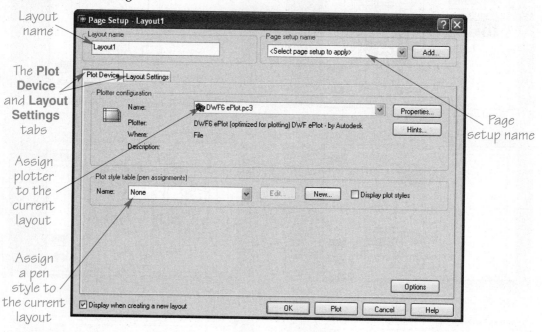

**Figure 24-38.**
The **Layout Settings** tab.

Select the size of paper

Paper orientation

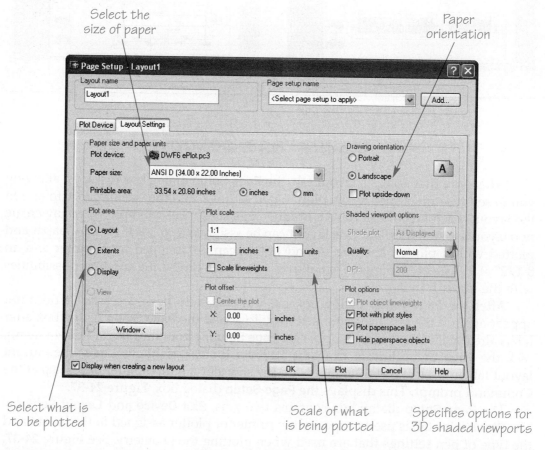

Select what is to be plotted

Scale of what is being plotted

Specifies options for 3D shaded viewports

The **Page setup name** drop-down list is used to assign page setup information to a layout. After the settings for a layout have been established, select the **Add...** button in the upper-right corner of the **Page Setup** dialog box to create a new page setup name. This displays the **User Defined Page Setups** dialog box. See **Figure 24-39.** Enter a name for your page setup in the **New page setup name:** text box. When page setup names are created, they remember all of the settings that were assigned in the **Plot Device** and **Layout Settings** tabs. If you have a drawing that contains page setup names, they can be imported and assigned to the current layout. The page setup name then adjusts all of the settings in the current **Page Setup** dialog box to match the settings from the drawing they were imported from.

**Figure 24-39.**
The **User Defined Page Setups** dialog box.

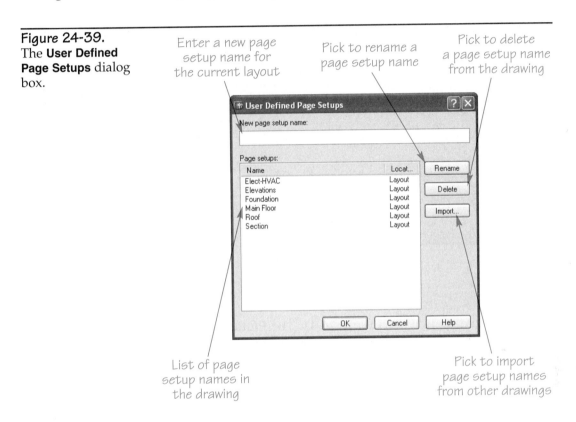

Enter a new page setup name for the current layout

Pick to rename a page setup name

Pick to delete a page setup name from the drawing

List of page setup names in the drawing

Pick to import page setup names from other drawings

## Specifying the Plotter

Earlier when setting up the layouts, the DWF6 ePlot.pc3 plotter was selected to be used on the layout. This is a plotter configuration that is included with AutoCAD, and it plots your drawings to a type of electronic file called a DWF (drawing web format) file. DWF files can be published to the Internet and viewed with a web browser. Drawing web format files are discussed in greater depth later in this chapter. The **Name:** drop-down list in the **Plotter configuration** area of the **Plot Device** tab contains a list of printers or plotters configured on your computer. AutoCAD includes a DWF plotter and two types of raster plotter configurations. If you have a printer or plotter configured in the Windows operating system, it also shows up in this list.

To assign a printer or plotter in the **Page Setup** dialog box, choose the appropriate configuration from the list. The printer or plotter you select directly affects the paper sizes available in the **Layout Settings** tab. See **Figure 24-40.**

If a plotter configuration needs to be adjusted, select the **Properties...** button next to the **Name:** drop-down list. This displays the **Plotter Configuration Editor** dialog box

Figure 24-40.
Selecting a plotter.

Select a plotter
from the
drop-down list

Adjust the plot
configuration settings

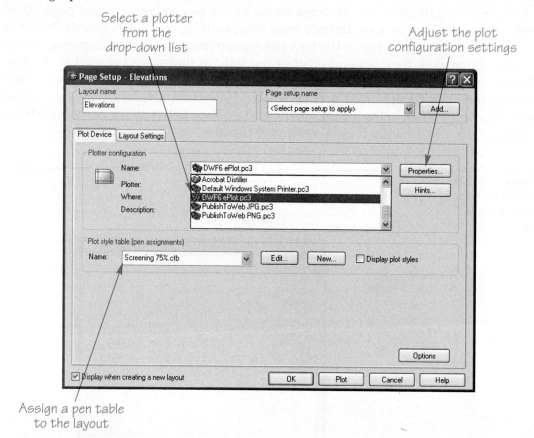

Assign a pen table
to the layout

for the selected plotter. See **Figure 24-41.** The **Plotter Configuration Editor** dialog box contains the following three tabs:

- **General tab.** This tab contains general information about the plotter configuration.
- **Ports tab.** This tab allows you to specify the port to send the plot information to.
- **Device and Document Settings tab.** This tab contains a list of settings for the current plotter that can be modified. This tab will vary depending upon the plotter selected, but it contains settings that can be modified. If an item is selected from the list, the options that can be set are displayed below the list. Items such as paper and margin sizes can be set here as well as color configurations for color plotters or printers.

When you are finished adjusting the settings for the plotter, select the **Save As...** button to save your changes as a new PC3 (plotter configuration) file. The new plotter configuration then appears as a choice when you select a plotter from the **Name:** drop-down list.

You can add printers and plotters to the **Name:** drop-down list by selecting **Plotter Manager...** from the **File** pull-down menu or by entering plottermanager at the Command prompt. This displays the **Plotters** window, where the **Add-a-Plotter Wizard** icon can be selected to add a plotter configuration.

**Figure 24-41.**
The **Plotter Configuration Editor** dialog box is used to adjust plotter settings such as paper size, colors used, and the margin sizes on a layout.

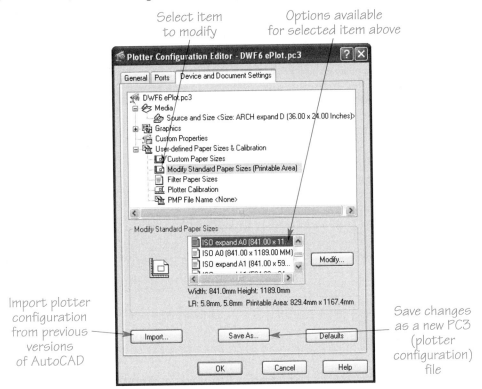

Select item to modify

Options available for selected item above

Import plotter configuration from previous versions of AutoCAD

Save changes as a new PC3 (plotter configuration) file

## Specifying Pen Settings

After the plotter has been selected, a plot style table can be attached to the layout. The **Plot Style Table (pen assignments)** area is located below the **Plotter configuration** area in the **Plot Device** tab. Refer to **Figure 24-40**. This area lists available plot style tables that can be assigned to a layout. A *plot style table* is a pen configuration that allows you to have complete control over how your drawing appears when plotted. There are two types of plot style tables: color tables and style tables. Only one of these types of tables can be active in a drawing. By default, color tables are used in any new drawings you create. Style tables can be selected for use with new drawings through the **Options** dialog box. See **Figure 24-42**. The **Options** dialog box can be activated by selecting **Options** in the **Page Setup** dialog box. After a drawing is started, the current Plot Style Table mode is current in the drawing.

Note

After a drawing is started, the current plot style table mode is used. By default, the color tables are the current mode. Style tables cannot be selected for the current drawing if it was started with color tables. The **CONVERTPSTYLES** command can be used to switch between color and style tables while in the same drawing.

Color tables assign different pen values to the colors in AutoCAD. For example, if the color Red is assigned a heavy pen that plots with a black color, then any objects AutoCAD finds with a red color will plot with heavy black lines. Style tables are names with pen settings that can be assigned to layers or objects. For example, a style table may include a named style called Walls, which has been assigned a heavy black

**Figure 24-42.**
The use of style tables in new drawings can be selected in the **Options** dialog box. Note after a drawing is started, the current plot style mode is active in that drawing.

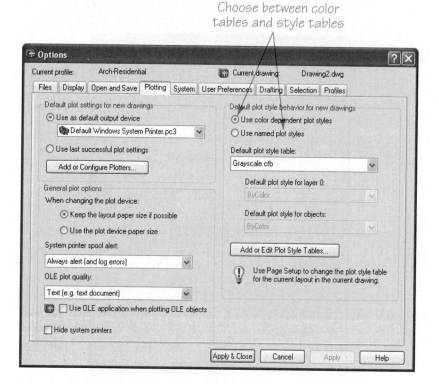

*Choose between color tables and style tables*

line. The Walls pen style can then be assigned to the Wall layers in the drawing. Anything that is drawn on the Wall layers then plots with a heavy black line.

To select a plot style for use, select one of the tables from the **Name:** drop-down list in the **Plot Style Table (pen assignments)** area. See **Figure 24-43.** By default, the list contains a number of color tables that can be assigned to the layout. These tables have a .ctb extension. The table you select plots the AutoCAD geometry with specific settings. For example, the monochrome.ctb color table plots the drawing in monochrome (black and white) colors. The grayscale.ctb color table plots the drawing using shades of gray, and the screening pen tables plot the drawing with faded colors.

The plot style tables can be edited by first selecting the appropriate table from the list, and then picking the **Edit...** button. Selecting this button displays the **Plot Style Table Editor** for the selected plot style table. See **Figure 24-44.** The **Plot Style Table Editor** is where settings can be assigned to AutoCAD colors if a color table is used or to a style if a style table is used. This dialog box is covered in greater depth later in this chapter. The **New...** button in the **Page Setup** dialog box walks you through a wizard in order to create your own plot style table.

Checking the **Display plot styles** check box displays a "What you see is what you get" view in layout space for how the layout will be plotted when assigned a plot style table. See **Figure 24-45.**

Architectural Drafting Using AutoCAD

## Figure 24-43.
Selecting a plot style table for use.

Edit selected pen table

Display how the plot style will appear in layout space

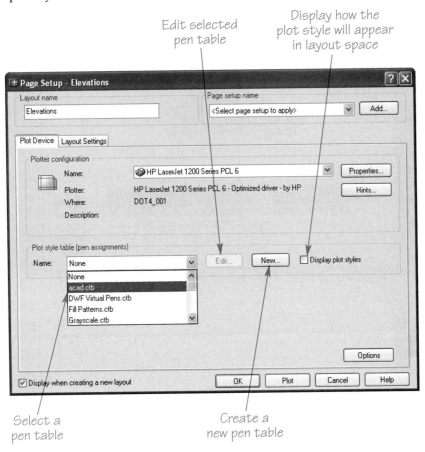

Select a pen table

Create a new pen table

## Figure 24-44.
The **Plot Style Table Editor** window is used to configure the way colors in AutoCAD will be plotted.

AutoCAD colors used for drawing geometry

Pen setting for selected color

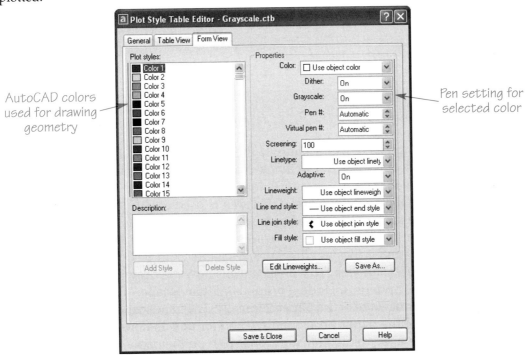

**Figure 24-45.**
A—The elevation layout with the monochrome.ctb table applied. B—The elevation layout with the Grayscale.ctb table applied.

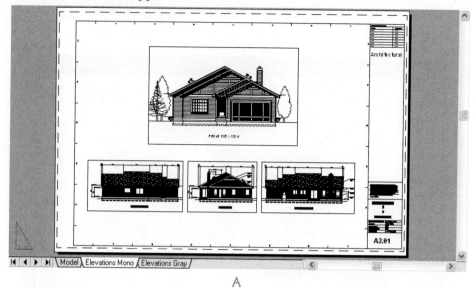

A

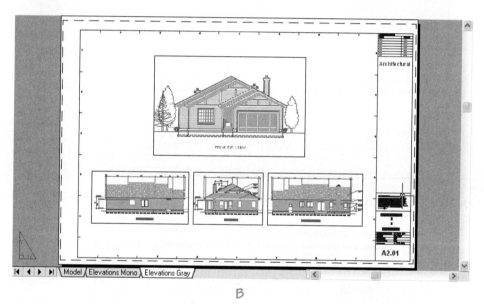

B

## Specifying the Layout Settings

After the settings have been made in the **Plot Device** tab, the settings for the layout need to be set. The **Layout Settings** tab is broken down into seven separate areas. See **Figure 24-46.** These areas are as follows:

- **Paper size and paper units area.** This area is used to specify a paper size and whether the paper is measured in inches or in metric units. The paper size list is dependent upon the printer or plotter selected in the **Plot Device** tab. For example, a printer does not display sizes larger than 17″ × 11″.
- **Drawing orientation area.** This area controls how the drawing is rotated in the layout. The options include **Portrait** and **Landscape**. The **Portrait** option orients the long edge of the paper vertically. The **Landscape** option orients the long edge of the paper horizontally. The **Plot upside-down** check box allows the drawing to be rotated an additional 180° on the paper.

**Figure 24-46.**
The **Layout Settings** tab is used to specify the settings used for the layout sheet.

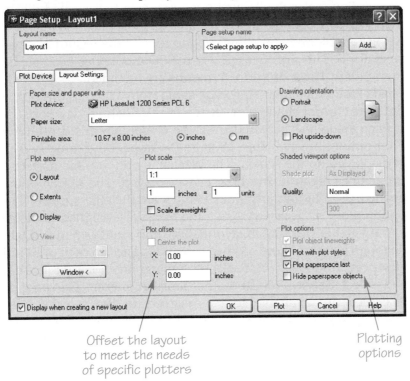

Offset the layout
to meet the needs
of specific plotters

Plotting
options

- **Plot area.** This area is used to plot a specified area of the drawing. The five options are described below:
  - **Layout/Limits.** The **Layout** option is selected by default when **Page Setup** is entered from a layout tab. This option plots the entire contents that appear on the layout sheet. This option is the best option if you have taken the time to set up the layout sheet. The **Limits** option replaces the **Layout** option if **Page Setup** was entered from the **Model** tab. This option plots everything within the limits of the drawing.
  - **Extents.** This option plots only the area of the drawing that contains geometry. AutoCAD plots anything within the edges of the geometry farthest out on the drawing.
  - **Display.** This option plots only what is currently being viewed on the drawing screen.
  - **View.** This option plots user-defined views. Views are discussed in Chapter 20 of this text. If **Page Setup** was accessed from a layout tab, views saved in layout space appear in this list. If **Page Setup** was accessed from the **Model** tab, views saved in model space appear in this list.
  - **Window.** This option is grayed out until the **Window** button is selected. AutoCAD returns you to the drawing screen in order to define two points of a rectangle in which to plot.
- **Plot scale area.** This area allows you to specify the scale for the area that you chose in the **Plot area**. If you chose to plot the layout, then set the scale to 1:1. This plots the layout area 1:1 on the plotter and the viewports reflect the scales you assigned them. If **Scaled to Fit** is selected, AutoCAD scales the layout to fit onto the plotter paper, changing the viewport scales you assigned. This area also contains an area for you to enter a custom plotting scale. This is primarily used when plotting portions of the drawing from model space.

A check box to scale the lineweights is included in this area. Lineweights normally plot with the weight of line they were assigned. However, checking this option scales the lineweights relative to the selected plotting scale.

- **Shaded viewport options area.** This area specifies how shaded and rendered viewports are plotted and allows you to specify the resolution levels and dots per inch (dpi). This area is used when a 3D model has been created and you want to plot it. Three drop-down menus are included:

  - **Shade Plot**. When accessing **Page setup** from a layout, this option is grayed out. The current shade plot setting to the floating viewports is displayed. If **Page setup** was accessed from the **Model** tab, this drop-down is active. Four options are available. With As Displayed, the geometry is plotted as it is displayed on the screen. The Wireframe option plots objects using wireframe lines regardless of how it is displayed. The Hidden option plots 3D geometry by hiding any lines behind another 3D surface. The Rendered option plots 3D geometry using the materials assigned to the geometry.

    If you are working in layout space and want to plot a 3D drawing in a floating viewport, these settings can be assigned to each individual floating viewport. To do this, first select the viewport in layout space, right-click, and select **Shade Plot** from the shortcut menu. The previous options discussed are available to be assigned to the selected viewport. 3D modeling and rendering is discussed in Chapters 25 and 26 of this text.

  - **Quality.** This drop-down allows you to select the resolution for shaded and rendered viewports. There are six options available. The Draft option sets shaded and rendered views to plot as wireframe. The Preview option allows shaded and rendered views to plot at a maximum of 150 dpi. The Normal option plots the shaded and rendered views to a maximum of 300 dpi. The Presentation option sets the shaded and rendered views to plot to the current plotting device resolution up to 600 dpi. The Maximum option plots the shaded and rendered views using the current plotting device's maximum resolution. The Custom option allows you to enter a custom dpi setting in the **DPI** text box up to the current plotting device's maximum print resolution.

  - **DPI**. This text box reflects the dpi chosen when selecting the Custom quality option.

- **Plot offset area.** This area determines how far the drawing is offset from the lower-left corner of the paper. The origin point for a plotter is the lower-left corner of the piece of paper. To begin plotting away from the origin point, adjust the values in relation to the lower-left corner of the paper.

- **Plot options area.** This area contains options that can affect how the drawing is plotted. The options are as follows:

  - **Plot object lineweights.** Objects and layers that have been assigned a lineweight plot using the assigned lineweight. This option is checked by default.

  - **Plot with plot styles.** This option is used if style tables are used in the drawing. This option allows any layers or objects that are assigned a style table to be plotted with the style table settings. This setting is ignored if color tables are being used.

  - **Plot paperspace last.** This option plots objects in layout space after the model space geometry has been plotted.

Architectural Drafting Using AutoCAD

- **Hide paperspace objects.** This option hides lines that appear behind another surface, such as lines on a 3D object. This option hides lines only on objects that appear in paper space. For example, 3D objects that appear in a floating viewport do not have hidden lines removed. However, a 3D object that appears on top of layout space does have its lines hidden. Three-dimensional objects that appear in a floating viewport can have hidden lines removed if the viewport has been set to hide objects in the **Shade Plot** cascading menu in the viewport shortcut menu. To access the shortcut menu, select the viewport and then right-click. Another method of hiding lines in a viewport is to use the **Properties** window. See **Figure 24-47.** First select the viewport that is to hide the lines of 3D objects, right-click, and select **Properties** from the shortcut menu. In the **Properties** window, select the **Shade Plot** property, then pick the **Hidden** option.

After the **Page Setup** values have been specified, the layout remembers the settings for all future plots. It is often an advantage to build all of the appropriate layouts and **Page Setups** within a template file. This helps eliminate the need to set up a drawing for plotting each time you start a new project. The layout is now ready for plotting.

**Figure 24-47.**
Hiding the lines of 3D objects in a floating viewport. In the **Properties** window for the viewport, select the **Hidden** property.

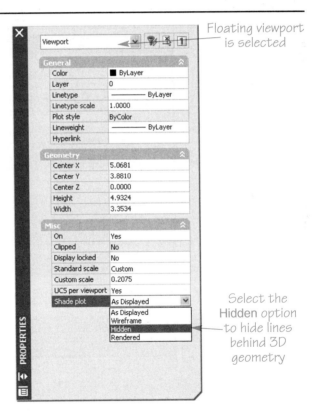

Floating viewport is selected

Select the Hidden option to hide lines behind 3D geometry

## Exercise 24-5

- ◆ Open ex24-4.
- ◆ Use the **Page Setup** dialog box to assign different color tables to the layouts.
- ◆ Place a check in the **Display plot styles** check box.
- ◆ Save the drawing as ex24-5.

# Configuring Plot Styles

The previous discussion introduced the use of plot style tables. *Color tables* are used by default in AutoCAD to control the way geometry colors are interpreted and plotted. If style tables are desired, access the **Options** dialog box *before* you start the project and change the **Default plot style behavior for new drawings** setting to **Use named plot styles**. Refer to **Figure 24-42**. This must be checked before you start the new project that uses style tables. This section covers the configuration and modification of both color tables and style tables.

## Color Tables

Color table (CTB) files interpret the colors used in your drawing and plot the colors with predefined settings. The settings for an existing CTB table can be modified by selecting the **Edit...** button in the **Page Setup** dialog box. New color tables can also be created by selecting the **New...** button in the **Page Setup** dialog box or by selecting the **Add or Edit Plot Style Tables...** button in the **Plotting** tab in the **Options** dialog box. See **Figure 24-48**.

**Figure 24-48.**
The **Options** dialog box allows you to create a new **Plot Style Table**.

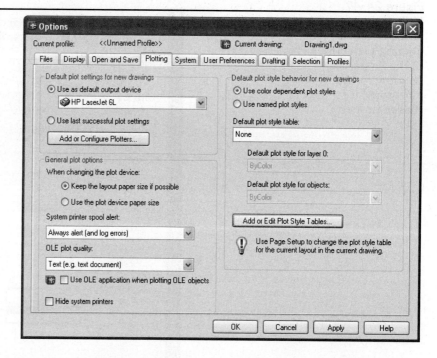

When the **Add or Edit Plot Style Tables...** button is selected from the **Options** dialog box, the **Plot Styles** window is displayed. See **Figure 24-49**. Double-click the **Add-A-Plot Style Table Wizard** icon. This displays the **Add Plot Style Table** wizard. AutoCAD displays an explanation of what the wizard does. Press the **Next** button. This displays the **Add Plot Style Table - Begin** window shown in **Figure 24-50**. Four options are included in this window:

- **Start from scratch.** This creates a new plot style table from scratch.
- **Use an existing plot style table.** This option allows you to base your new style on an existing plot style table to be used as a template.
- **Use My R14 Plotter Configuration (CFG).** This option copies the pen assignments from the acad14.cfg file and uses the settings as a template for the new plot style table.

**Figure 24-49.**
The **Plot Styles** window.

Double-click to create a new plot style table

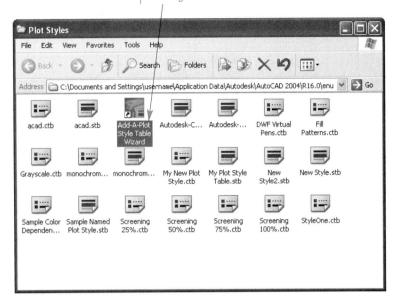

**Figure 24-50.**
The **Add Plot Style Table - Begin** window. Select an option.

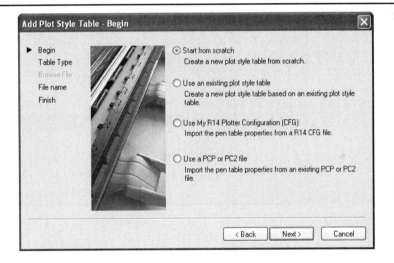

- **Use a PCP or PC2.** This option uses pen assignments stored in PCP or PC2 files from versions of AutoCAD prior to AutoCAD 2000 as a template for the new plot style table.

Choose an option and press the **Next** button. If the **Start from scratch** option is selected, the **Add Plot Style Table - Pick Plot Style Table** window is displayed. See **Figure 24-51A.** Select either color dependent or named plot styles to advance to the **Add Plot Style Table - File Name** window. See **Figure 24-51B.** Enter a name for the plot style table you are creating. Press the **Next** button to advance to the next page. The **Add Plot Style Table - Finish** window appears so you can edit the plot style table. See **Figure 24-51C.**

## Editing the Plot Style Table

The process of creating a new plot style table from the **Page Setup** dialog box is similar to the process above. Some of the dialog boxes may vary. After the wizard has stepped you through the process of creating the new plot style table, select the **Plot Style Table Editor...** button to modify the pen assignments.

**Figure 24-51.**
A—Select whether to create a color table or a style table. B—Enter a name for the new plot style. C—Select the **Plot Style Table Editor...** button to modify the plot style.

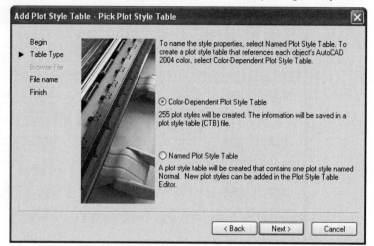

A

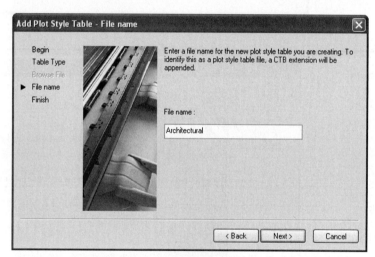

B

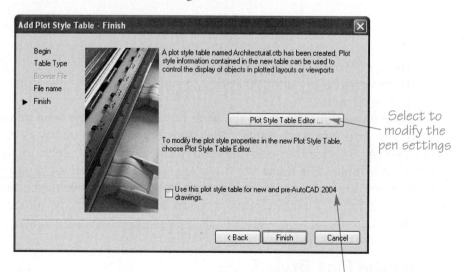

Select to modify the pen settings

Select to apply the new style to new and existing layouts in the drawing

C

The **Plot Style Table Editor** dialog box appears. It includes the **General, Table View,** and **Form View** tabs. See **Figure 24-52.** The **General** tab contains general information regarding the plot style table. A description can be entered in the **Description** area. The **Table View** and **Form View** tabs are used to modify the pen settings used in the drawing. Both tabs contain the same settings, except that the settings are organized a little differently between the two. See **Figure 24-53.**

The following properties can be set for AutoCAD object colors in a color table or for style names in a named style table. These settings can be adjusted through the **Table View** or **Form View** tabs of the **Plot Style Table Editor** in **Figure 24-53:**

- **Color.** This setting overrides any AutoCAD object's color. For example, assume that the Door layer is assigned Color 1 (Red). The red color in the **Plot Style Table Editor** can then be overridden with any color desired for plotting, such as black. When the drawing is plotted, AutoCAD interprets any red colors and plots them with a black color. The **Use object color** option is set as the default, which plots AutoCAD colors with the same color as they appear in the drawing.

- **Dither or Enable dithering.** *Dithering* is a form of simulating the depths of color by intermingling dots of varying colors to create what appears to be a new color. Dithering can be enabled or disabled. If the plotter or printer does not support dithering, this setting is ignored. When using the dithering option, the lines on your drawing appear as dotted linetypes, where the dots are spaced closer or farther away from each other in order to create the illusion of shaded color. Create test plots with the dither option on and off to determine the best method to be used for plotting.

Figure 24-52.
The **Plot Style Table Editor** contains three separate tabs.

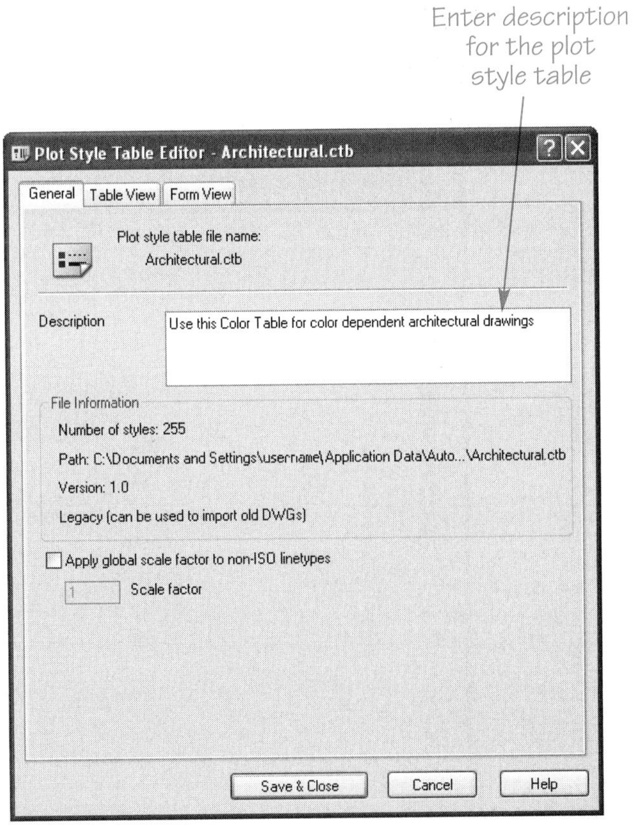

Enter description for the plot style table

## Figure 24-53.

A—The **Table View** tab organizes pen settings in a table format. B—The **Form View** tab organizes pen settings in a form format.

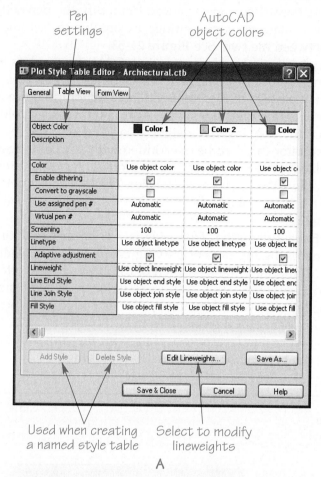

Pen
settings

AutoCAD
object colors

Used when creating
a named style table

Select to modify
lineweights

A

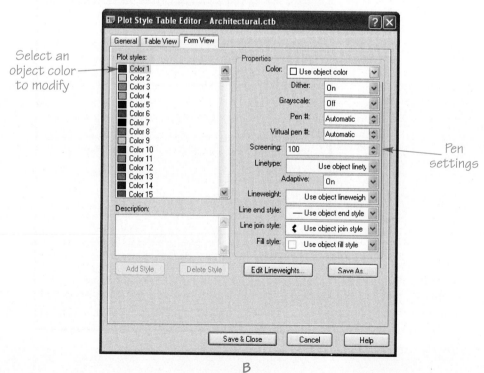

Select an
object color
to modify

Pen
settings

B

- **Grayscale or Convert to grayscale.** This setting is either turned on or off. If grayscale has been turned on, AutoCAD object colors are converted to shades of gray. As with *dithering,* some printers or plotters may not support grayscaling. Try plotting a sheet with the grayscale on and off to determine the best type of plotting method.
- **Pen number or Use assigned pen #.** This setting is used only for plotters that use actual pens for plotting. A total of 32 pens can be assigned to the AutoCAD object colors. The pen numbers range from pen #1 to pen #32. The pen number corresponds to the pen number in the plotter. For example, pen #1 may plot with a blue color that is 0.3 mm thick. If the dimension layer's color is to be plotted with a 0.3 mm thick line, then assign pen #1 to the color that is being used for the dimensions. If the setting is set to **Automatic** for each of the AutoCAD object colors, AutoCAD selects a pen based upon the plotter configuration.
- **Virtual pen or Virtual pen #.** This setting is used to simulate pen numbers for nonpen plotters such as inkjet plotters. Virtual pens use pen numbers ranging from 1 to 255. Refer to the *AutoCAD Installation Guide* for information on configuring plotters to use virtual pens. If the setting is **Automatic** for each of the AutoCAD object colors, AutoCAD selects a virtual pen from the AutoCAD Color Index (ACI).
- **Screening.** This setting controls the amount of ink that is applied to the plotted paper for each of the AutoCAD object colors. This setting is used to fade or "wash out" colors that are plotted. A value of 100 plots the object with the full intensity of color. A value of 50 plots the object color half the intensity, and a value of 0 plots the object color as white.
- **Linetype.** This setting overrides the linetype of objects in the drawing with a linetype in the drop-down list. The default value, **Use object linetype,** plots the colored objects in the drawing with the linetypes specified in the drawing.
- **Adaptive or Adaptive adjustment.** This setting adjusts the scale of the linetype to complete the linetype pattern. If this setting is not selected, the line might end in the middle of a pattern. Turn on this setting if complete linetype patterns are important to the plot.
- **Lineweight.** This setting assigns a lineweight to an AutoCAD object color. Specifying a lineweight for a color overrides the lineweight setting specified in the drawing. The default setting is **Use object lineweight.**
- **Line end style.** This setting applies a line end style to the ends of all lines, polylines, and arcs in the drawing that are using the associated color. See **Figure 24-54.** Note that the lines need to be thick in order for the line end style to be noticeable. The default setting is **Use object end style.**
- **Line join style.** This setting is used to add a line join style to the joint between two lines that join together. The default setting is **Use object join style.** The options include **Miter, Bevel, Round,** and **Diamond.**
- **Fill style.** This setting is used to adjust how a filled object appears. A filled object can be an object created with the **SOLID** command, a solid hatch pattern, a donut, or a wide polyline. The default setting is **Use object fill style,** which plots filled objects with a solid pattern. The options include **Solid, Checkerboard, Crosshatch, Diamonds, Horizontal Bars, Slant Left, Slant Right, Square Dots,** and **Vertical Bars.** To test this setting, create nine objects with a solid hatch pattern. Assign a different color to each object. Assign each of the used colors a different fill style and plot the drawing to view how the fill style is being applied.

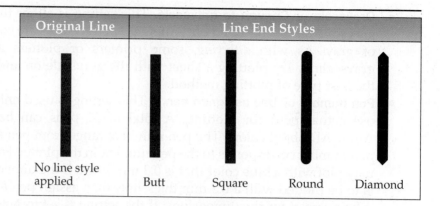

**Figure 24-54.**
Line end styles are
applied to the ends
of lines when
plotted.

| Original Line | Line End Styles | | | |
|---|---|---|---|---|
| No line style applied | Butt | Square | Round | Diamond |

After you have adjusted all of the AutoCAD object colors or named styles to meet the desired settings, pick the **Save & Close** button to apply the settings to the plot style table. If you entered the **Plot Style Table Editor** from the **Add Plot Style Table - Finish** page, pick the **Finish** button. Your plot style table is now ready to be assigned to your layouts through the **Page Setup** dialog box.

## Named Style Tables

*Named style tables* are configured using the same process for color tables. However, in order to configure a named style table, a style table (STB file) needs to be current in the active drawing. As discussed earlier in this chapter, new drawings use color tables (CTB files) by default. After a drawing is started using color tables, the only way to switch to named style tables is to use the **CONVERTPSTYLES** command. This command allows you to switch between style tables and color tables or vice versa.

You can switch to using **Named Style** tables for *new* drawings by selecting the **Use named plot styles** radio button in the **Plotting** tab of the **Options** dialog box. See **Figure 24-55.** After this radio button has been selected, new drawings you create use named style tables instead of color tables.

After the **Use named plot styles** option has been selected, named plot style tables can be used on *new* drawings. A new plot style table can be added the same way a color table is added. When the **Plot Style Table Editor** for a named plot style table has been accessed, you notice that the AutoCAD object colors are missing. If you are editing an existing named plot style, there may be one or more named styles in the style table. See **Figure 24-56A.** By default, any new style tables that are created will always have one style name called Normal.

When color tables are used, AutoCAD looks to the colors used in the drawing, and plots the colors according to the settings specified in the color table. Named style tables, however, can be assigned to layers or individual objects in the drawing. When AutoCAD finds a layer or an object that is assigned a named style, the objects are plotted using the settings specified for that named style.

To create a new style, select the **Add Style** button in either the **Table View** or the **Form View** tab. See **Figure 24-56B.** This opens the **Add Plot Style** window, where you can add a style name. Continue to add styles for any layers or objects as needed. Typically, you may create a named style for each layer used in the drawing or the type of lineweight to be used. For example, named styles can be called: Walls, Doors, Dimensions, Heavy lines, Medium lines, or Thin lines. If the drawing has several layers that are similar, such as M-Walls, U-Walls, and F-Walls, you may decide to create one named style called Walls that is assigned to all of the wall layers.

**Figure 24-55.**
The **Plotting** tab in the **Options** dialog box allows you to choose what type of plot style table will be used for new drawings.

Select a plot style table mode to use for new drawings

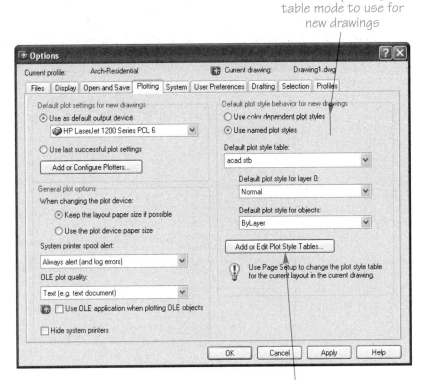

Edit or create plot style tables

**Professional Tip**

Named plot styles are often created with names that refer to the type of object they are assigned to. For example, named styles called Walls, Doors, Windows, Dimensions, and Notes may refer to the corresponding layers Wall, Door, Window, Dimension, and Notes, or to objects that are representing these types of items. A plot style name describing the lineweight is also common. For example, the style name Heavy lines can be used for walls or property lines.

As the style names are added, they begin showing up in the **Name** row of the **Table View** tab or in the **Plot styles:** list in the **Form View** tab. After the named styles are created, assign settings such as **Grayscale**, **Lineweight**, and **Line end style** to each. The process and the settings available are the same as those used with color tables. After you have created the styles and adjusted all of the settings, pick the **Save & Close** button to save the settings to the named plot style table.

## Exercise 24-6

◆ Open ex24-5.
◆ Create a new color table plot style named Arch.
◆ Modify the settings for the colors you have chosen throughout the project.
◆ Save the style and attach it to all of the layout tabs.
◆ Save the drawing.

**Figure 24-56.**
The **Plot Style Table Editor** for a named plot style.

Named styles

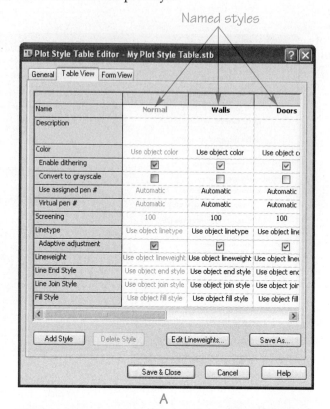

A

Named styles

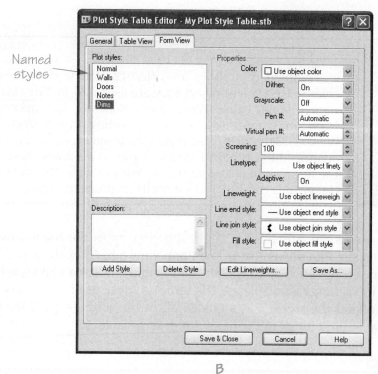

B

Architectural Drafting Using AutoCAD

## Assigning Named Styles to Layers and Objects

Named plot styles can be assigned to layers in the **Layer Properties Manager** dialog box. See **Figure 24-57.** Select the layer that you would like to assign a named plot style to and select **Normal** from the Plot Style column. This displays the **Select Plot Style** dialog box, listing the available plot styles. Select the named style that you would like to assign to the highlighted layer. See **Figure 24-58.**

Named plot styles can also be assigned by selecting a layer in the **Properties** window and selecting a plot style from the **Plot style** drop-down list. See **Figure 24-59A.** Any object drawn on a layer that has been assigned a plot style plots using the settings in the named plot style.

Named plot styles can also be assigned to individual objects. If a plot style is attached to an object that in turn has been drawn on a layer that is assigned a plot style, the plot style attached to the object overrides the plot style settings assigned to the layer. Plot styles can be assigned to objects with the **Properties** window or the **Plot Style Control** drop-down list on the **Properties** toolbar. See **Figure 24-59B.**

To attach the plot style to an object, first select the object(s) to highlight them. Right-click and select **Properties** from the shortcut menu. The selected objects are listed at the top of the **Properties** window. Pick the plot style setting and choose a plot style from the list. The alternate method is to select the object(s) to highlight them and select the desired plot style from the **Plot Style Control** drop-down list in the **Properties** toolbar.

**Figure 24-57.**
A named plot style can be assigned to a layer in the **Layer Properties Manager** dialog box.

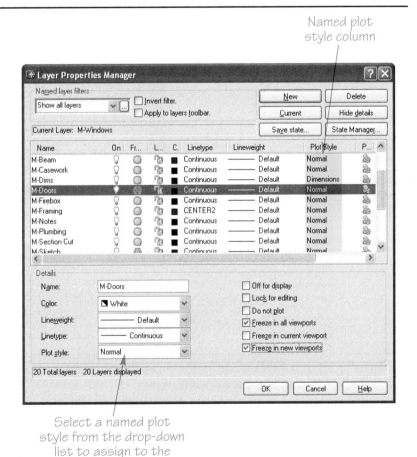

Named plot style column

Select a named plot style from the drop-down list to assign to the highlighted layer

**Figure 24-58.**
Select a named plot style from the list to assign to the highlighted layer in the **Layer Properties Manager** dialog box.

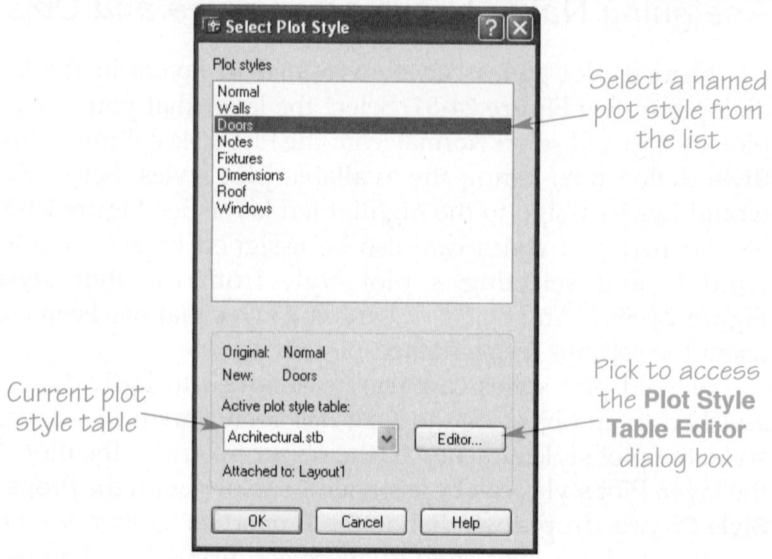

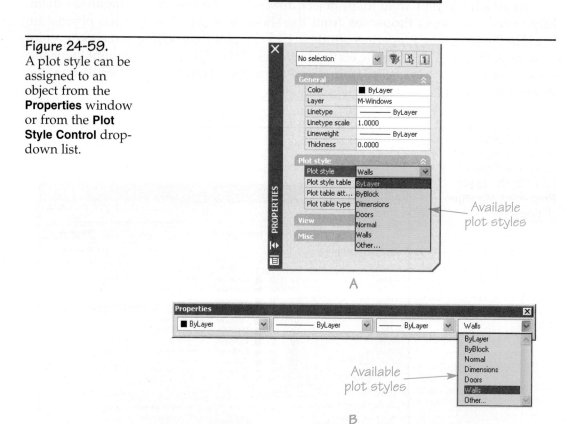

**Figure 24-59.**
A plot style can be assigned to an object from the **Properties** window or from the **Plot Style Control** drop-down list.

## Exercise 24-7

◆ Start a new drawing using the acad-Named Plot Styles.dwt template or the acadISO –Named Plot Styles.dwt template.
◆ This new drawing uses named plot style (STB) tables.
◆ Insert and explode ex22-2 in model space.
◆ Create a new named style table. Create style names (such as Walls, Doors, Windows, Notes, and Dimensions) and adjust their settings.
◆ Assign the plot styles to the layers in the drawing.
◆ Save the drawing as ex24-7.

# Plotting the Drawing

The previous discussions in this chapter have set up the layout sheets, assigned plotters and pen settings to the page setups, and discussed how to modify the plot style tables. If everything has been followed, you are ready to plot the drawing.

Before you plot the drawing, the layout or model tab that you want to plot needs to be active. Once the desired tab is active, the **PLOT** command can be accessed. To plot the drawing, select **Plot...** from the **File** pull-down menu, enter plot or print at the Command prompt, or right-click on the layout tab and select **Plot...** from the shortcut menu. This displays the **Plot** dialog box shown in **Figure 24-60**. This dialog box is similar to the **Page Setup** dialog box discussed earlier. The only additions to the **Plot** dialog box are on the **Plot Device** tab.

The **What to plot** area allows you to specify what layout tabs you would like to plot. By default, the **Current tab** radio button is selected. This plots only the current layout tab. The **Selected tabs** radio button is grayed out unless multiple layouts have been selected to plot. To select more than one layout tab, hold the [Ctrl] key while selecting the layout tabs. Then right-click on a layout tab and select **Plot...** from the shortcut menu. The **All layout tabs** radio button plots all the layouts if their page setup settings have been adjusted. When the **All layout tabs** radio button has been selected, the **Number of copies:** text box becomes highlighted, allowing you to specify the total number of copies to be made.

The **Plot to file** area is grayed out if you are plotting to a printer or plotter. To plot your drawing to an electronic file, select the **Plot to file** check box. This activates the **File name and path:** text box. The **File name and path:** text box contains the name and path of the layout tab with an extension of PLT (or DWF if you are plotting to a DWF file). A PLT file is a plot file that remembers all of the drawing geometry, plot styles,

**Figure 24-60.**
The **Plot** dialog box is similar to the **Page Setup** dialog box, but contains extra settings used for plotting.

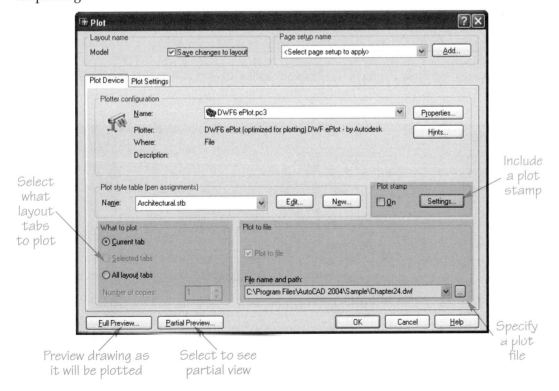

Select what layout tabs to plot

Include a plot stamp

Specify a plot file

Preview drawing as it will be plotted

Select to see partial view

and layout settings assigned to the drawing. A PLT file can be plotted using a plot spooler. A *plot spooler* is basically a smart disk drive with memory that allows you to plot files. In offices or schools with only one printer or plotter, a plot spooler may be attached to the printer or plotter. This device usually allows you to take a PLT file from a floppy disk and copy it to the plot spooler, which in turn plots the drawing.

As previously discussed, a DWF file is a drawing web format file. This type of file produces an electronic file that can be viewed through the Autodesk Express Viewer program. DWF files are discussed later in this chapter.

If you are plotting to a file, the location you would like to save the file can be entered before the file name. The ellipsis (**...**) button beside the **File name and path:** text box allows you to browse your hard drive or network drives to specify a folder for the PLT or DWF files to be saved.

The only other additions to the **Plot** dialog box include two preview buttons in the lower-left corner and the **Plot stamp** area. The **Full Preview...** button provides you with a preview of the entire drawing based on the settings in the **Plot** and **Page Setup** dialog boxes. See **Figure 24-61.** The preview window displays the drawing as it will look when it is plotted to reflect the colors, grayscales, and nonplotting layers (for the viewports) that have been assigned. By right-clicking in the preview window, you can zoom and pan around the drawing, checking for any errors before you plot the drawing.

The **Partial Preview...** button displays the **Partial Plot Preview** dialog box. See **Figure 24-62.** This preview displays a representation of the paper size selected, and the dashed line represents the actual printable area on the paper. The shaded blue area represents where on the paper your drawn geometry in layout space is located in relationship to the actual paper. This is known as the *effective area.* Below the preview is information for the **Paper size, Printable Area,** and the **Effective Area.** Any warnings to the plot are displayed at the bottom.

After previewing the drawing, specifying a location (if you are plotting PLT or DWF files) and verifying the paper size and scale, you can plot the drawing. Press the **OK** button in the **Plot** dialog box and the drawing is sent to the plotter. You can also send the plot directly to the plotter or printer from the plot preview by right-clicking in the plot preview window and picking the **Plot** option.

Figure 24-61.
The plot preview window displays the drawing as it will appear when it is plotted.

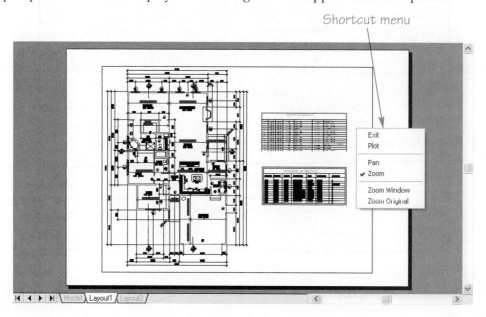

**Figure 24-62.**
The **Partial Plot Preview** dialog box provides information on where the geometry in layout space is in relationship to the paper.

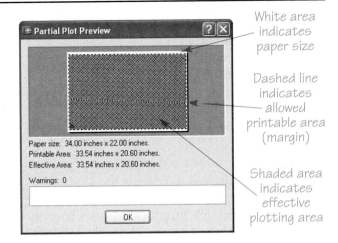

White area indicates paper size

Dashed line indicates allowed printable area (margin)

Shaded area indicates effective plotting area

## Adding a Plot Stamp

You can add a plot stamp to your drawings. A plot stamp is specific text information included on a printed or plotted drawing. A plot stamp may include information such as the drawing name or the date and time the drawing was printed.

In the **Plot** dialog box, the **Plot Stamp** area in the **Plot Device** tab allows you to activate and modify the plot stamp. If the **On** check box is activated, a plot stamp is printed on the drawing. You can also specify the items to be included in the plot stamp by picking the **Settings...** button. This accesses the **Plot Stamp** dialog box. See **Figure 24-63.**

**Figure 24-63.**
Use the **Plot Stamp** dialog box to specify the information included in the plot stamp. You can save plot stamp settings as PSS files.

Select items to be included in plot stamp

Pick to add new fields

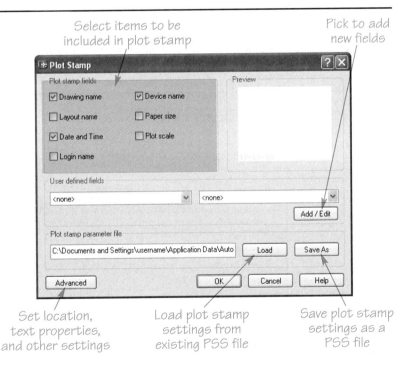

Set location, text properties, and other settings

Load plot stamp settings from existing PSS file

Save plot stamp settings as a PSS file

Specify the information to be included in the plot stamp in the **Plot stamp fields** area of the **Plot Stamp** dialog box. The following items can be included:

- Drawing name
- Layout name
- Date and time
- Login name
- Device name
- Paper size
- Plot scale

You can create additional plot stamp items in the **User defined fields** area. For example, you can add a field for the client name, the project name, or the contractor who will be using the drawing.

The **Preview** area provides a preview of the location and orientation of the plot stamp. The preview does not show the actual plot stamp text.

Plot stamp settings can be saved in a PSS (plot stamp settings) file. If you load an existing PSS file, the settings saved in the file are automatically set in the **Plot Stamp** dialog box.

Additional plot stamp options are set in the **Advanced Options** dialog box. To access this dialog box, pick the **Advanced...** button in the **Plot Stamp** dialog box. The **Advanced Options** dialog box is shown in **Figure 24-64.** The following options are available:

- **Location.** Pick the corner where the plot stamp begins from the drop-down list. If you want the plot stamp to print upside-down, pick the **Stamp upside-down** check box.
- **Orientation.** Pick **Horizontal** or **Vertical** from the drop-down list.
- **Offset.** Set the offset distance and pick where the offset distances are measured from (printable area or paper border).
- **Text properties.** Specify the text font and height. Pick the **Single line plot stamp** check box if you want the plot stamp contained to a single line. If this check box is not checked, the plot stamp will be printed in two lines.

**Figure 24-64.**
Specify the plot stamp location, orientation, text font and size, and units in the **Advanced Options** dialog box.

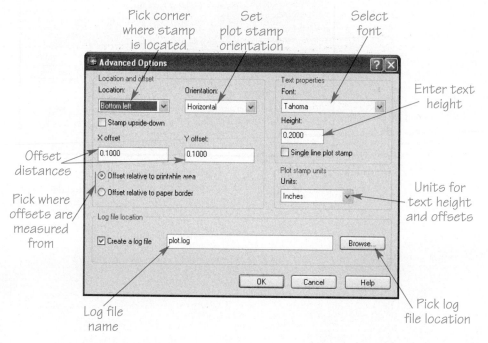

- **Units.** Select the plot stamp units. The plot stamp units can be different from the drawing units.
- **Log file.** Pick the check box to create a log file of plotted items. Specify the name of the log file in the text box. Pick **Browse...** to specify the location of the log file.

| Note | The log file settings are independent of the plot stamp settings. Thus, you can produce a log file without creating a plot stamp or have a plot stamp without producing a log file. |

## DWF Plots

As introduced earlier, a DWF (drawing web format) file is an electronic file similar to a drawing file, which can be viewed from the Autodesk Express Viewer. AutoCAD includes a DWF plotter configuration. The DWF6 ePlot.pc3 configuration creates an electronic drawing file with a DWF extension.

The advantage of plotting files to a DWF format is that the drawings can be shared by another person without them physically having AutoCAD to view your drawing file. Another advantage is that the drawings cannot be edited. This provides a great means for archiving projects, because the actual drawing files do not have to be opened and viewed from AutoCAD. The DWF files are also considerably smaller in file size and lend themselves to be easily sent to someone else through e-mail or posted to a website.

When viewing the DWF file, the viewer also has the capability of zooming and panning in the drawing, as well as the ability to turn layers on or off or displaying views of the drawing that you may have created. The person viewing the DWF file in the Autodesk Express Viewer can simply right-click in the program to display a menu of options for controlling what they are seeing in the DWF file. See **Figure 24-65.**

The Autodesk Express Viewer is included with your installation of AutoCAD. You can also download a free copy of the viewer by visiting the Autodesk Web site at www.autodesk.com. DWF files can also be viewed through another Autodesk program known as Volo View. Volo View allows you to add redlines to a DWF, DWG, or DXF file. For more information regarding the Volo View product, visit the Autodesk Web site.

**Figure 24-65.**
DWF files can be viewed with the Autodesk Express Viewer. The viewer also has the capability of zooming and panning in the drawing, as well as the ability to turn layers on or off and display views of the drawing.

Shortcut menu to control display options in the DWF file

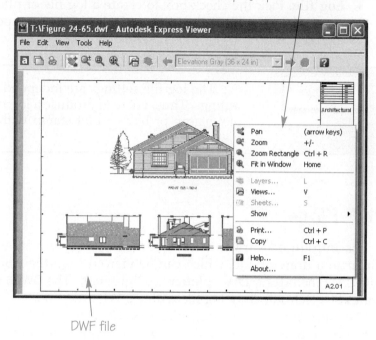

DWF file

## Chapter Test

*Answer the following questions on a separate sheet of paper.*

1. Define *model space*.
2. What scale do you use when drawing in model space?
3. Define *layout space*.
4. Describe the difference between the UCS icon when in model space and layout space.
5. Describe the two methods of setting the scale for a viewport when it is active. Use a 1/4″ = 1′-0″ scale as an example.
6. What are floating viewports?
7. After floating viewports are created, how can you change the display of the model space drawing inside the viewport?
8. What are the viewports called that are created in model space?
9. What are the viewports called that are created in layout space?
10. Explain what the **4** option of the **MVIEW** command provides.
11. After the scale has been set in a viewport, why should the **ZOOM** command never be used in the viewport again?
12. What should you do if you need to readjust the view in a viewport?
13. Why do you lock a viewport?
14. How do you freeze layers in a viewport?
15. Identify the two system variables and their settings that allow linetypes to appear with the same length of dashes and dots regardless of scale.
16. When drawing in model space and you know that the final plotted drawing will be at a scale of 1/4″ = 1′-0″, what text height value would you use if you want the final text to be 1/8″ high?

17. Text and notes that are added directly to layout space and not in a floating viewport are drawn at what scale?
18. Name the command that is used to manage layouts.
19. How do you add a layout to your drawing from **DesignCenter**?
20. Give the function of the **Plotter Configuration Editor**.
21. Define *plot style table* and name the two types.
22. Briefly explain the difference between the two types of plot style tables.
23. How many plot style tables can be active in a drawing?
24. Identify the **Plot area** option of the **Layout Settings** tab that is the best option if you have taken the time to set up the layout sheet.
25. Name the **Plot area** option of the **Layout Settings** tab that is used if page setup was entered from the model tab.
26. The **Plot scale** area of the **Layout Settings** tab allows you to specify the scale for the area that you chose in the **Plot area**. If you chose to plot the layout, what scale should you set?
27. What is the function of the **Color:** option in the **Plot Style Table** editor?
28. Define *dithering*.
29. After a drawing is started using color tables, the only way to switch to style tables is to use which command?
30. Describe how to assign named plot styles to layers.
31. Explain two ways to assign named plot styles to individual objects.
32. Which tab needs to be active before you can plot a drawing?
33. Explain how you can plot to a file.
34. What is a PLT file and a DWF file?
35. What is a plot stamp?

# Chapter Problems

1. Open 23-ResA.
   A. Thaw all of the layers in the model tab.
   B. Create a layer named Viewports and make it a nonplotting layer. Place viewports on this layer.
   C. Create the following layout tabs and necessary viewports:

Project

Residential A

| Sheet Name | Paper Size | Scale | Contents |
|------------|-----------|-------|----------|
| Elevations | 17″ × 11″ | Front: 1/8″ = 1′-0″ Rear and Sides: 1/16″ = 1′-0″ | Front Elevation Right Elevation Left Elevation Rear Elevation |
| Floor Plan | 17″ × 11″ | 3/32″ = 1′-0″ | Floor Plan |
| Foundation | 17″ × 11″ | 3/32″ = 1′-0″ | Foundation Plan |
| Framing | 17″ × 11″ | 3/32″ = 1′-0″ | Roof Framing Plan |
| Sections | 17″ × 11″ | 3/32″ = 1′-0″ | Building Sections Wall Details |

   D. Draw a title block on the layout sheets. Fill out any information on the title block.
   E. Use layer controls to display the appropriate layers in the layout sheet viewports.
   F. Add drawing titles below each plan.
   G. Set up any plot styles as desired.

H. Plot the set of drawings.

I. Save the drawing as 24-ResA.

Project

Residential B

2. Open 23-ResB.

A. Thaw all of the layers in the model tab.

B. Create a layer named Viewports and make it a nonplotting layer. Place viewports on this layer.

C. Create the following layout tabs and viewports:

| Sheet Name | Paper Size | Scale | Contents |
|---|---|---|---|
| Elevations | 34′ × 22″ | 1/4″ = 1′-0″ | Front Elevation Right Elevation Left Elevation Rear Elevation |
| Foundation and Plumbing | 34″ × 22″ | 1/4″ = 1′-0″ | Foundation Plan Plumbing Isometric |
| Main Floor | 34″ × 22″ | 1/4″ = 1′-0″ | Main Floor Plan |
| Upper Floor | 34″ × 22″ | 1/4″ = 1′-0″ | Upper Floor Plan |
| Framing | 34″ × 22″ | 1/4″ = 1′-0″ | Framing Plan |
| Section | 34″ × 22″ | 1/4″ = 1′-0″ | Building Sections Wall Detail |

D. Draw a title block on the layout sheets. Fill out any information on the title block.

E. Use layer controls to display the appropriate layers in the layout sheet viewports.

F. Add drawing titles below each plan.

G. Set up any plot styles as desired.

H. Plot the set of drawings.

I. Save the drawing as 24-ResB.

Project

Multifamily

3. Start a new drawing from one of your templates.

A. Xref the following files:

| File Name | Layer to Insert On |
|---|---|
| 16-Multifamily | Xref-Floor |
| 18-Multifamily | Xref-Found |
| 19-Multifamily | Xref-Elev |
| 20-Multifamily | Xref-Sect |
| 22-Multifamily | Xref-Roof |
| 23-Multifamily | Xref-Plumb |

B. Thaw all of the layers in the **Model** tab.

C. Create the following layout tabs:

| Sheet Name | Paper Size | Scale |
|------------|------------|-------|
| Elevations | 34″ × 22″ | 3/16″ = 1′-0″ |
| Floor Plan | 34″ × 22″ | 3/16″ = 1′-0″ |
| Foundation | 34″ × 22″ | 3/16″ = 1′-0″ |
| Roof | 34″ × 22″ | 3/16″ = 1′-0″ |
| Plumbing | 34″ × 22″ | 3/16″ = 1′-0″ |
| Section | 34″ × 22″ | 3/16″ = 1′-0″ |

D. Create a layer named Viewports and make it a nonplotting layer. Add the viewports on this layer.

E. Draw a title block on the layout sheets. Fill out any information on the title block.

F. Use layer controls to display the appropriate layers in the layout sheet viewports.

G. Add drawing titles below each plan.

H. Set up any plot styles as desired.

I. Plot the set of drawings as DWF files.

J. Save the drawing as 24-Multifamily.

4. Start a new drawing from one of your templates.

A. Xref the following files:

Project

Commercial

| File Name | Layer to Insert On |
|-----------|--------------------|
| 16-Commercial | Xref-Floor |
| 18-Commercial | Xref-Found |
| 19-Commercial | Xref-Elev |
| 20-Commercial | Xref-Sect |
| 22-Commercial | Xref-Roof |
| 23-Commercial | Xref-HVAC |

B. Thaw all of the layers in the **Model** tab.

C. Create the following layout tabs:

| Sheet Name | Paper Size | Scale |
|------------|------------|-------|
| Elevations | 34″ × 22″ | 3/16″ = 1′-0″ |
| Floor Plan | 34″ × 22″ | 3/16″ = 1′-0″ |
| Foundation | 34″ × 22″ | 3/16″ = 1′-0″ |
| Roof | 34″ × 22″ | 3/16″ = 1′-0″ |
| HVAC | 34″ × 22″ | 3/16″ = 1′-0″ |
| Section | 34″ × 22″ | 3/16″ = 1′-0″ |

D. Create a layer named Viewports and make it a nonplotting layer. Add the viewports on this layer.
E. Draw a title block on the layout sheets. Fill out any information on the title block.
F. Use layer controls to display the appropriate layers in the layout sheet viewports.
G. Add drawing titles below each plan.
H. Set up any plot styles as desired.
I. Plot the set of drawings.
J. Save the drawing as 24-Commercial.

# CHAPTER 25

# 3D Modeling

## Learning Objectives

After completing this chapter, you will be able to:

- Identify the three different ways to draw and represent three-dimensional models.
- Explain the function of the world coordinate system and user coordinate systems.
- Describe the rectangular, spherical, and cylindrical 3D coordinate systems.
- Display 3D views in a drawing.
- Hide lines in 3D views.
- Apply shading to 3D models.
- Create and manage user coordinate systems.
- Construct surface-modeled and solid-modeled objects.
- Extrude 2D objects into solid models.
- Create composite solids using Boolean operations.

## Important Terms

3D face
3D orbit view
3D UCS icon
arcball
Boolean operations
composite solid
cylindrical coordinate system
extruded
filter
intersection
isolines
isometric drawing
rectangular 3D coordinate system
region

solid model
solid primitives
spherical coordinate system
subtraction
surface model
tetrahedrons
UCS icon
union
user coordinate system (UCS)
virtual world
wireframe
world coordinate system (WCS)
world origin

Three-dimensional (3D) drawing is quickly becoming a standard design tool in architecture. The use of 3D modeling and design techniques helps architects visualize and evaluate an entire project without ever physically constructing a building. Building designs can be dropped into *virtual worlds* used with virtual reality systems so that they can be studied and revised before actual drawings are created. A *virtual world* is a visual representation created in a computer to appear real.

To be effective when constructing drawings in 3D, you must have good 3D visualization skills. It is important to be able to see the model in 3D in your mind and visualize it rotating in space. This chapter introduces you to 3D modeling and the various 3D drawing tools available in AutoCAD.

# 3D Basics

AutoCAD provides three means of drawing and representing objects in 3D. Objects drawn in 3D can be constructed as *wireframes, surface models,* or *solid models.* A *wireframe* can be thought of as a "skeleton" of a model with the "skin" removed. This type of model is simply a representation of basic objects such as lines, polylines, and circles. As shown in **Figure 25-1A,** the objects are combined into a three-dimensional model that appears to be made from wire. When working with a more complex model, a wireframe can be difficult to visualize because of the nature of the surfaces of the object. A *surface model,* on the other hand, is easier to visualize and appears as a more accurate version of the real object. A surface model can be thought of as a representation that applies the "skin" of a model over the wireframe. See **Figure 25-1B.**

Surface models are similar in appearance to solid models. However, a *solid model,* also known as a *solid,* can be thought of as a design of an object that uses solid material to create the model (rather than just the outer "skin"). Surface models that are shaded or rendered can be used to imitate solid models. However, where surface models are better suited for presentation purposes, solid models can be analyzed to determine such characteristics as mass and volume. Surface models can be distinguished from solids when displayed in wireframe and hidden-line form. See **Figure 25-2.** Displaying 3D models in wireframe and hidden-line views is discussed later in this chapter.

**Figure 25-1.**
Constructing objects as three-dimensional models.
A—A wireframe model has visible edges and appears to be constructed from wire.
B—A surface model of the same object appears to have "skin" applied over the object.

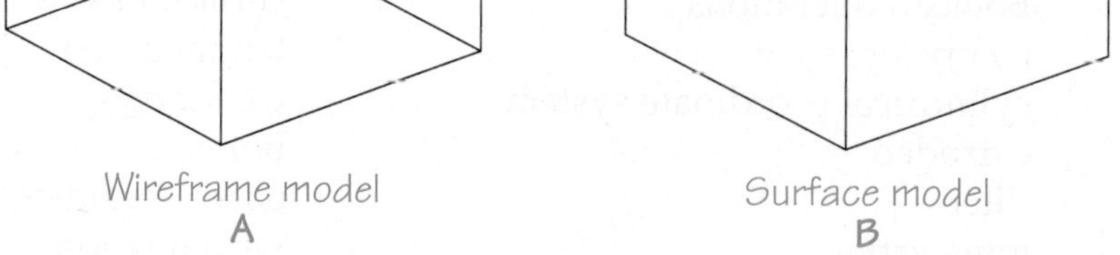

Wireframe model
A

Surface model
B

**Figure 25-2.**
Comparing three-dimensional models of a sphere. Surface models and solid models are similar in appearance, but they display differently when viewed in wireframe form or with hidden lines removed.

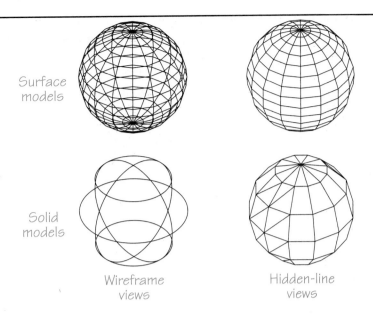

Surface models

Solid models

Wireframe views

Hidden-line views

Before constructing a 3D model, you should determine the purpose of your design. What will the model be used for—presentation, analysis, or manufacturing? Planning the type of model you create helps you determine which tools you should use to construct the model. This chapter discusses how 3D constructions can be created as wireframes, surface models, and solid models.

## Using Coordinate Systems in AutoCAD

Throughout this text, you have been drawing in two-dimensional space. In AutoCAD, this is represented as a drawing plane defined by the X and Y axes. This 2D drawing plane is part of the *world coordinate system (WCS),* the default coordinate system in AutoCAD. This is the coordinate system you have been using throughout this text.

When you first start a drawing, objects that you draw originate from the WCS origin (0,0). This is known as the *world origin.* Coordinate values you enter are measured from this origin and located along the X and Y axes. The WCS is a universal system. It is fixed and cannot be adjusted. The *user coordinate system (UCS),* on the other hand, can be moved to any orientation, allowing you to set your own coordinate origin. The ability to create different user coordinate systems is one of the most useful features of AutoCAD when constructing 3D drawings. Creating a UCS is discussed later in this chapter.

Coordinate systems are used in AutoCAD to establish a drawing plane. Any objects that are drawn are always parallel to the current plane, or coordinate system, you are working in. When using the WCS, for example, you are looking "down" at the XY drawing plane. Your view is considered to be "plan" to that plane. By changing the coordinate system, you can set a different drawing plane so that objects you draw are parallel to the new plane. For example, you may want to orient the UCS to the side of a wall or building after changing to a 3D view. This is discussed later in this chapter.

The orientation of the coordinate system you are currently working in is indicated by the *UCS icon.* By default, when you are in the WCS, this icon is located at the lower-left corner of the AutoCAD drawing area. If you create a new UCS, the appearance of the icon changes to reflect the orientation of the drawing plane. If the icon is not currently displayed in your drawing, you can turn it on by using the **UCSICON** command:

Command: **ucsicon.**⌐

Enter an option [ON/OFF/All/Noorigin/ORigin/Properties] <OFF>: **on.**⌐

The *3D UCS icon* is displayed by default. It appears as shown in **Figure 25-3A** when you are working in the default WCS. When you define a new UCS and place the icon at the origin of the new system, the icon appears as shown in **Figure 25-3B.** You can change the appearance of the UCS icon by using the **UCSICON** command. The options of this command are discussed in greater detail later in this chapter.

In **Figure 25-3,** the UCS icon axes indicate that you are in the XY drawing plane. When the coordinate system is changed, the icon changes to reflect the different orientation of the X and Y axes. For example, in **Figure 25-3B,** notice that the square is removed from the UCS icon. This indicates that the coordinate system is a user coordinate system and not the world coordinate system. Also, a cross appears in the UCS icon, indicating that the icon is displayed at the origin of the current UCS.

When you are using a 2D coordinate system and your drawing does not require a different UCS, you may want to turn off the display of the UCS icon. However, when constructing a 3D drawing, displaying the UCS icon may help you visualize the orientation of the current drawing plane. This is because 3D drawings are created using 3D coordinate systems. Using 3D coordinates in AutoCAD is discussed next.

**Figure 25-3.**
The **3D UCS** icon is displayed by default. A—The icon as it appears at the lower-left corner of the drawing area when working in the default world coordinate system. B—The icon as it appears when a new UCS is created.

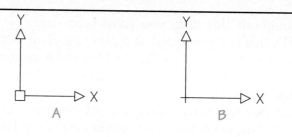

## Introduction to the 3D Coordinate System

As previously discussed, you have been drawing in two-dimensional space throughout this text. In a 2D coordinate system, objects are drawn using the X and Y axes and coordinates are entered as (X,Y). When you draw in three-dimensional space, a third axis, the Z axis, is used. See **Figure 25-4.** The positive values of this axis come up from the XY plane of a 2D drawing. If you consider the surface of your screen as the XY plane, anything behind the screen has a negative Z coordinate value, and anything in front of the screen has a positive Z coordinate value. Coordinates in a 3D coordinate system are entered as (X,Y,Z). In the WCS, objects you draw originate from the 0,0,0 origin.

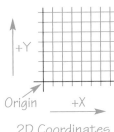
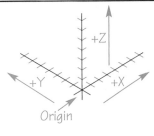

**Figure 25-4.**
Comparing the 2D and 3D coordinate systems. When drawing in three-dimensional space, a third coordinate value is specified for the Z axis.

2D Coordinates

3D Coordinates

The object shown in **Figure 25-5A** has been drawn in the 2D coordinate system with coordinate locations specified on the X and Y axes. The same object being constructed in three-dimensional form is shown in **Figure 25-5B.** Using the 3D coordinate system, this object has been drawn by specifying Z coordinate values for each vertex, or corner. This basic system of entering X, Y, and Z coordinates is known as the *rectangular 3D coordinate system.* As shown in the illustration, the vertices used for the top and bottom profiles have the same X and Y coordinate values, but different Z coordinate values. In this example, the three-dimensional model is being constructed with positive Z coordinates. The same model could have been drawn with negative Z coordinates. In this case, the object would extend behind the screen. Although the sign of the Z value makes no difference to AutoCAD, it is easier to work with positive values.

Study the nature of the rectangular 3D coordinate system. Be sure you understand Z coordinate values before you begin constructing 3D objects. As you gain more practice using this coordinate system, you will find it easier to visualize and plan your designs in three-dimensional space.

## Displaying 3D Views

When constructing 3D drawings, you will often find it necessary to adjust the display in AutoCAD so that you are looking at a 3D view of a model. Throughout this text, you have constructed drawings in plan view, with the angle of sight looking "down" on the top view of the drawing. Displaying this type of view is sufficient for 2D drawings. However, when working in 3D, you will frequently want to display 3D views so that you can better visualize the object and its sides. AutoCAD has several ways to display a 3D view of your drawing. The object in **Figure 25-5B**, for example, is shown in isometric view. As you learned in Chapter 23, an *isometric drawing* is a

**Figure 25-5.**
Constructing an object in two-dimensional and three-dimensional form. A—The object is drawn as a 2D representation by specifying X and Y coordinate values. B—A top profile is drawn to create a 3D construction using X, Y, and Z coordinate values.

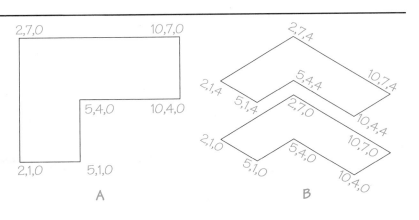

3D representation showing three sides of an object with axis lines drawn at 30° to horizontal. The entire object appears as if it is tilted toward the viewer. See **Figure 25-6.** Although an isometric drawing is not a true 3D drawing, an isometric view can be used to display a realistic 3D version of a model.

AutoCAD provides four preset isometric views that can be used to change the display to a 3D view. In addition, you can also change the display of your drawing to one of the six standard orthographic views. These include the top, bottom, left, right, front, and back views. Isometric and orthographic views can be accessed from the **3D Views** cascading menu in the **View** pull-down menu, the **View** toolbar, and the **Orthographic & Isometric Views** tab in the **View** dialog box. See **Figure 25-7.** The **View** dialog box is accessed by picking the **Named Views** button in the **View** toolbar, selecting **Named Views...** from the **View** pull-down menu, or by entering the **VIEW** command.

Study the button icons in the **View** toolbar and the icons in the **View** dialog box. Each icon identifies the side of a cube that will be displayed when the corresponding view is picked. The object in **Figure 25-6B,** for example, is displayed in southwest isometric view. This is accomplished by selecting the **SW Isometric View** button from the **View** toolbar, **SW Isometric** from the **3D Views** cascading menu, or **Southwest Isometric** from the **View** dialog box.

If you want to return to the previous 2D display after selecting an isometric view, you can select **Plan View** from the **3D Views** cascading menu and then **Current UCS**. This displays the current drawing in a plan view of the current user coordinate system. This option is not available in the **View** toolbar.

Creating an isometric view simplifies working in 3D. In many cases, it is helpful to create multiple model space viewports in a 3D drawing so that each viewport contains a different view. For example, you may want to display the drawing so that the top, front, and side views are shown, in addition to an isometric view. See **Figure 25-8.**

Referring to **Figure 25-5B,** the original object was created in the top view. When the top profile was added, the drawing was then displayed in southeast isometric view to show the entire object. Displaying the model in this manner helps you visualize it in three-dimensional space. In addition, the model can be quickly completed by drawing lines to connect the vertices with object snaps. See **Figure 25-9.** In this

**Figure 25-6.**
Displaying a drawing in isometric view provides a 3D representation of the model. A—A top view of a 3D model. B—The same model displayed in southwest isometric view.

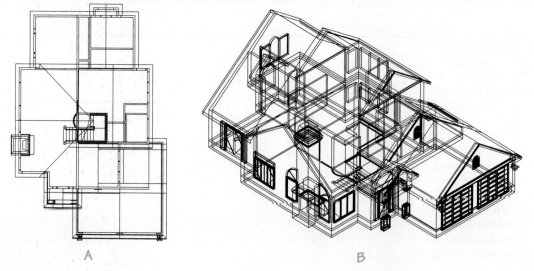

A

B

**Figure 25-7.**
Accessing AutoCAD's preset views. A—The isometric and orthographic viewing options can be selected from the **3D Views** cascading menu. B—Display options are also provided by the **View** toolbar. C—The **Orthographic & Isometric Views** tab in the **View** dialog box contains the same isometric and orthographic viewing options found in the **View** toolbar.

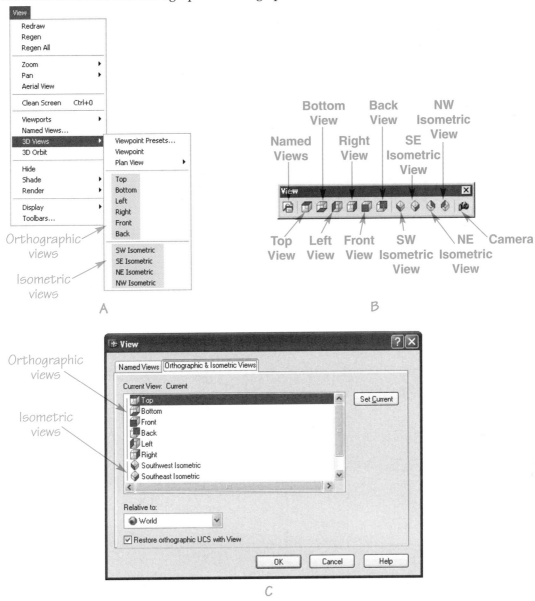

A

B

C

case, a wireframe model is created, because the model simply consists of lines combined into a three-dimensional representation. The model appears to be made from wire, and you can see through it.

When you change views in AutoCAD, the UCS icon changes to indicate the orientation of the drawing plane in relation to the view. For example, when you change the display to an orthographic view, the UCS icon is moved so that it is parallel, or plan, to the view. This indicates that the user coordinate system, or the drawing plane, is also plan to the view. See **Figure 25-10.** However, the origin point of the UCS is not moved. The origin remains the same as that of the world origin (0,0,0). If you wish to move the UCS origin to a point on a model, such as the corner of a wall, you must use the **UCS** command. This is discussed later in this chapter.

**Figure 25-8.**
Creating multiple viewports with different views aids in the development of a 3D model.

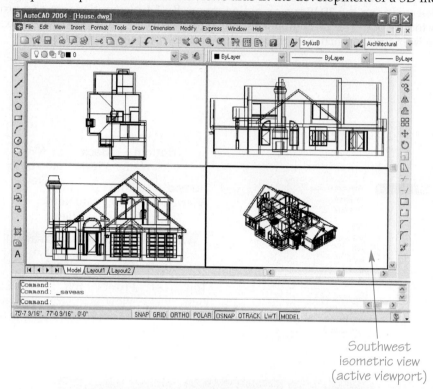

Southwest
isometric view
(active viewport)

**Figure 25-9.**
The 3D model is completed as a wireframe by drawing lines in southeast isometric view.

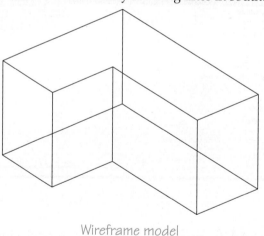

Wireframe model

When you change the display to an isometric view, the appearance of the UCS icon changes, but the drawing plane does not change. The axes of the icon change to reflect the type of isometric view selected. See **Figure 25-11.** However, the orientation of the axes does not change, and the drawing plane remains the same as the one previously used. You must manually move the UCS if you wish to establish a new drawing plane. As previously discussed, this is accomplished with the **UCS** command. Notice that in **Figure 25-11,** the 3D UCS icon displays the direction of the Z axis. This helps you visualize the orientation of the drawing plane in relation to the current 3D view.

**Figure 25-10.**
When an orthographic view is selected, the UCS is oriented so that the drawing plane is plan to the view. Note: The UCS icon has been moved to the UCS origin in each example for illustration purposes.

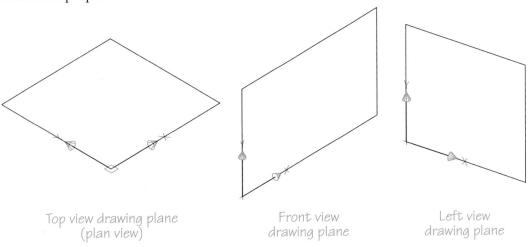

Top view drawing plane (plan view)

Front view drawing plane

Left view drawing plane

**Figure 25-11.**
When an isometric view is selected, the UCS drawing plane does not change from the one previously used. In this example, the current UCS is plan to the top view of the drawing. Note the direction of the Z axis in the UCS icon.

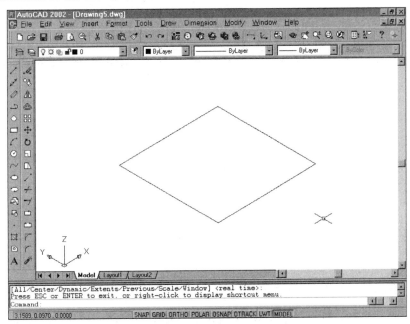

It is important to remember that the UCS icon indicates the current drawing plane and the direction of the X, Y, and Z axes. As you become more experienced in 3D drawing, you will find that establishing views and creating user coordinate systems is essential to constructing 3D models in AutoCAD.

## Exercise 25-1

◆ Start a new drawing using one of your templates.

◆ Using the **Viewports** dialog box, create a configuration of four equal model space viewports. Select the **3D** option in the **Setup:** drop-down list. This automatically sets a different view in each viewport.

◆ In the Top viewport, draw the 2D profiles for the top and bottom surfaces of the model shown using the coordinates provided.

◆ Activate the viewport displaying the isometric view of the object. Using the **Endpoint** object snap, draw vertical lines connecting the vertices of the bottom and top profiles to create a wireframe model.

◆ Save the drawing as ex25-1.

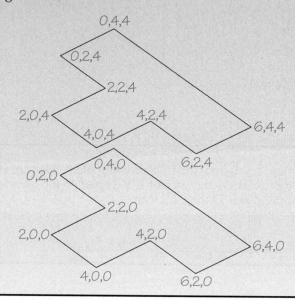

## Using Spherical and Cylindrical 3D Coordinates

In the previous exercise, you used rectangular 3D coordinates to construct a wireframe model. Coordinates entered in this manner are X, Y, and Z values measured from the UCS origin. Rectangular 3D coordinates can be entered simply as absolute coordinates, or as relative coordinates when you are specifying a point from a previous location.

You can also enter 3D coordinates in two other formats. These formats involve the use of spherical coordinates and cylindrical coordinates. Both systems are based on polar coordinate entry using angular values.

The method of point entry in the *spherical coordinate system* is similar to locating a point on the earth using longitudinal and latitudinal values, with the center of the earth representing the origin. The origin can be that of the default WCS or the current UCS. In this system, lines of longitude connect the north and south poles. These lines provide an east-west measurement on the earth's surface. Lines of latitude extend horizontally around the earth and provide a north-south measurement. See **Figure 25-12A.**

When entering spherical coordinates, the longitude measurement is expressed as the angle *in* the XY plane, and the latitude measurement is expressed as the angle *from* the XY plane. See **Figure 25-12B.** A distance from the origin is also provided. The coordinates represent a measurement from the equator toward either the north pole or the south pole on the earth's surface. Spherical coordinate entry is similar to polar

Architectural Drafting Using AutoCAD

coordinate entry. However, an additional angular value is provided. In **Figure 25-12B,** the absolute spherical coordinate 4<65<45 is used. This coordinate is located 4 units from the origin, at an angle of 65° in the XY plane and at an angle of 45° from the XY plane. As shown in the example, spherical coordinates are useful for locating features on a spherical surface or model.

Spherical coordinates can also be used as relative coordinates. For example, a point drawn with the relative spherical coordinate @2<35<45 means that the point is located 2 units from the last point, at an angle of 35° in the XY plane and at an angle of 45° from the XY plane.

Cylindrical coordinates are similar to spherical coordinates and are based on polar coordinate entry. However, the *cylindrical coordinate system* provides a method of point entry that specifies coordinate locations based on a cylindrical shape. As with spherical coordinates, cylindrical coordinates are entered using three values. The first value represents the horizontal distance from the origin. The second value represents the angle in the XY plane. The third value represents a vertical dimension, or Z dimension, measured up from the polar coordinate in the XY plane. In **Figure 25-13,** the absolute cylindrical coordinate shown is entered as 6<30,4. Like spherical coordinates, cylindrical coordinates can be entered as absolute or relative coordinates.

**Figure 25-12.**
Locating points using the spherical coordinate system. A—Lines of longitude, representing latitudinal segments, run from north to south. Lines of latitude, representing longitudinal segments, run from east to west. B—Spherical coordinates require a distance, an angle in the XY plane, and an angle from the XY plane.

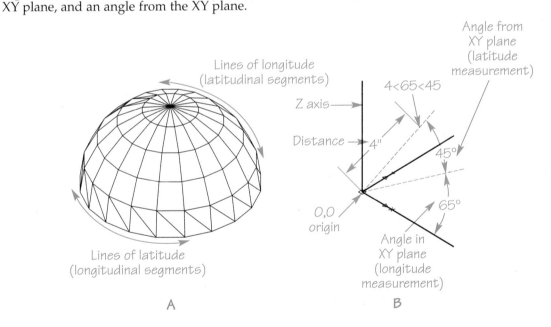

## Creating Basic Extruded 3D Shapes

So far in this chapter, you have seen how three-dimensional wireframe models can be created from objects drawn in 2D. In AutoCAD, there are many instances where 3D shapes are *extruded*. *Extruded* means that a 2D shape is given a base elevation and thickness. The object then rises up, or "extrudes" to its given thickness. The **EXTRUDE** command is most commonly used to extrude an object. This command is used to create solid models and is discussed later in this chapter.

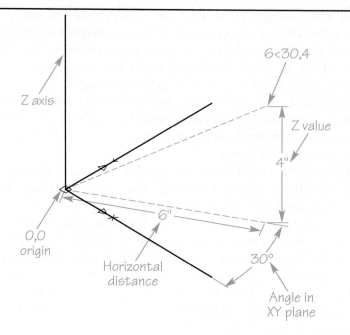

**Figure 25-13.**
Cylindrical coordinates are entered using a horizontal distance from the origin, an angle in the XY plane, and a Z dimension.

Z axis

6<30,4

Z value

4"

0,0 origin

6"

Horizontal distance

30°

Angle in XY plane

Another way to create 3D objects is to use the **THICKNESS** system variable to assign a thickness to the objects. The setting for this variable determines the height of the next object you draw. The thickness value can be applied to lines, polylines, polygons, arcs, and circles. When applying a thickness value, the two-dimensional object is "extended" in the Z direction, creating a 3D object from a simple 2D object. The resulting object is not a true solid, but it appears to have thickness. You can set the system variable to the desired thickness before drawing new objects, or you can assign a thickness value to an existing object by using the **Properties** window.

Objects that are not affected by the **THICKNESS** system variable include solids, ellipses, and splines. Rectangles drawn with the **RECTANG** command have a separate thickness setting that is applied during the command sequence.

To apply a thickness value to an existing object, access the **Properties** window and highlight **Thickness** in the **General** category. This method must be used when assigning a thickness value to a text object.

**Professional Tip**

Wide polylines can be drawn with a thickness value to represent walls in a building. To draw walls in this manner, set the **PLINE** width option to the width of the walls, and set the **THICKNESS** system variable to the desired height of the walls.

## Removing Hidden Lines and Shading the Model

HIDE
HI

View
↳ Hide

Render toolbar

Hide

When displaying 3D models as wireframes, every edge can be seen. This makes it difficult to visualize the model and distinguish its features. The simplest way to mask all features that would normally be hidden is to remove hidden lines using the **HIDE** command. This command regenerates the drawing and removes all lines that are behind objects. Invisible edges of 3D faces are also removed. To display a hidden-line view, enter hi or hide at the Command prompt, pick the **Hide** button from the **Render** toolbar, or select **Hide** from the **View** pull-down menu. The effects of using the

**Figure 25-14.**
A—A wireframe model of a cube. B—The same model after using the **HIDE** command to remove hidden lines.

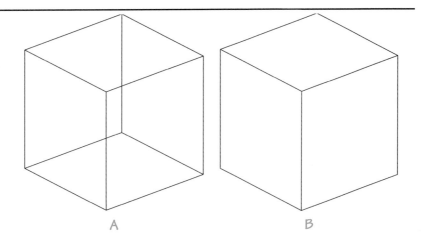

A          B

**HIDE** command are shown in **Figure 25-14.** The **HIDE** command should only be used after displaying a 3D view of a model. After removing hidden lines, you can restore the previous view by performing a **REGEN**.

You can apply shading to a model by using the **SHADEMODE** command. This command allows you to create a simple rendering of a 3D model. The color of the shaded image is controlled by the color of the model. There are several different shading options that can be applied, and you can also use the command to create a hidden-line or basic wireframe display. The command options can be accessed from the **Shade** cascading menu in the **View** pull-down menu, or from the **Shade** toolbar. See **Figure 25-15.** You can also enter shademode at the Command prompt.

When using one of the shading options, the UCS icon changes to a shaded version of the 3D UCS icon. This icon identifies the positive direction of the X, Y, and Z axes and is also used with the **3DORBIT** command, which is discussed later in this chapter. The following options are available with the **SHADEMODE** command:

- **2D Wireframe.** This is the default option. It displays the 3D model in normal wireframe view. The UCS is displayed as the normal 2D or 3D UCS icon.
- **3D Wireframe.** This option also displays the 3D model in wireframe view. However, the UCS icon is displayed as a shaded 3D UCS icon.
- **Hidden.** The effects of this option are similar to those obtained with the **HIDE** command. The lines representing back faces are hidden. The UCS icon is displayed as a shaded 3D UCS icon. Using **REGEN** does not affect a hidden view created with this option. To return to a wireframe view, use the **2D Wireframe** or **3D Wireframe** option.

**Figure 25-15.**
Shading options can be accessed from the **Shade** cascading menu or the **Shade** toolbar.

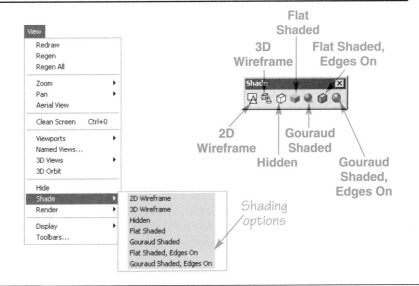

- **Flat Shaded.** This option shades the faces of 3D objects with the existing object colors. The edges of the faces are not shown, and smoothing is not applied.
- **Gouraud Shaded.** This option shades the faces of 3D objects with the existing object colors and applies smoothing to the edges between faces. This produces a smoother, more realistic type of shading than flat shading.
- **Flat Shaded, Edges On.** This option combines flat shading and 3D wireframe shading. Objects are shaded using the existing object colors, but wireframe edges are displayed.
- **Gouraud Shaded, Edges On.** This option combines Gouraud shading and 3D wireframe shading. Objects are shaded using the existing object colors, but wireframe edges are displayed.

Examples of displaying wireframe and hidden views with the **SHADEMODE** command are shown in **Figure 25-16.** Examples of flat shading and Gouraud shading are shown in **Figure 25-17.** After using the **SHADEMODE** command to shade your model, performing a **REGEN** will not restore a wireframe view. You must use the **2D** or **3D Wireframe** option of the **SHADEMODE** command.

Figure 25-16.
The **SHADEMODE** command options allow you to display wireframe and hidden-line views.

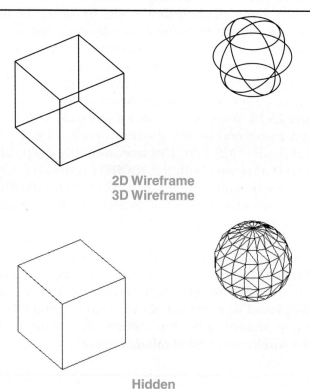

2D Wireframe
3D Wireframe

Hidden

Note

As discussed in Chapter 24, hidden or shaded models can be plotted. To do so when plotting from the **Model** tab, select the appropriate setting in the **Shaded viewport options** area of the **Layout Settings** tab in the **Plot** dialog box. To do so when plotting model space objects in a floating viewport, you must select the floating viewport, right-click to display the shortcut menu, and then select the appropriate option in the **Shade Plot** cascading menu. The **Properties** window can also be used to access the **Shade plot** options for a floating viewport.

**Figure 25-17.**
Displaying flat shaded and Gouraud shaded views with the **SHADEMODE** command. Not shown are views resulting from the **Edges On** options. Note the appearance of the **3D UCS** icon.

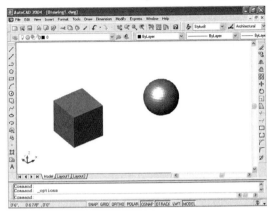

*Flat Shading*

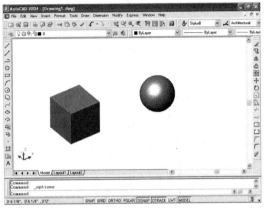

*Gouraud Shading*

**Professional Tip**

Enabling grid mode when working in 3D can help you visualize the current UCS drawing plane. If the default grid display of dots becomes confusing when zooming in on features, you can change the grid to a display of lines oriented in the current X and Y axis directions by entering the **3D Wireframe** option of the **SHADEMODE** command.

## Viewing the Model Dynamically

Earlier in this chapter, you learned how to display 3D models in standard orthographic and isometric views. AutoCAD also offers a powerful tool for viewing models in 3D dynamically. The *3D orbit view* enables you to rotate, pan, and zoom a 3D model in real time so that any part of the model can be viewed. The model can be viewed in wireframe, hidden, or shaded form. The 3D orbit view is easy to use and can be applied throughout the 3D modeling process.

The 3D orbit view is accessed with the **3DORBIT** command. To initiate the view, pick the **3D Orbit** button from the **3D Orbit** toolbar, select **3D Orbit** from the **View** pull-down menu, or enter 3do or 3dorbit at the Command prompt. The 3D orbit view first appears as shown in **Figure 25-18.** The large circle displayed with four smaller circles at the quadrant points is called the *arcball.* If the UCS icon is turned on, it is displayed as a shaded 3D UCS icon. You can right-click to display a shortcut menu listing a variety of viewing options, or you can select display options from the **3D Orbit** toolbar. See **Figure 25-19.**

You can use the shortcut menu to toggle between orbiting, panning, and zooming modes. A check mark appears next to the current setting, with **Orbit** being the default. When you are in orbiting mode, moving the cursor around the arcball results in the display of four different cursor icons, depending on where you place the cursor. You can then press and hold the pick button and move the pointing device to adjust the view. When you move the cursor inside the arcball, you can pick and drag to move the object horizontally, vertically, or diagonally. Moving the cursor outside the arcball allows you to "roll" the object around an axis that projects perpendicular

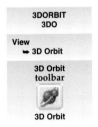

**3DORBIT**
**3DO**

**View**
➥ **3D Orbit**

**3D Orbit**
**toolbar**

**3D Orbit**

**Figure 25-18.**
The 3D orbit view allows you to rotate, pan, or zoom the display. The arcball is displayed by default in orbiting mode.

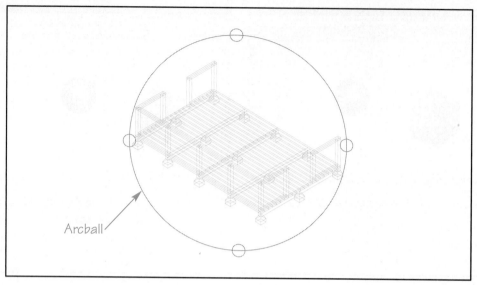

**Figure 25-19.**
A—Viewing options can be selected from the **3D orbit view** shortcut menu. B—Display options are also provided in the **3D Orbit** toolbar.

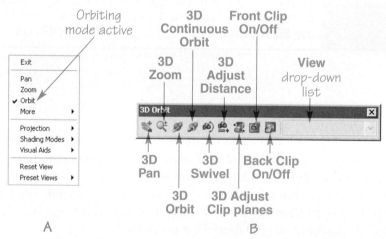

to the screen. When the cursor is placed in one of the smaller circles to the left or right of the arcball, the object can be rotated about the Y axis. When the cursor is placed in one of the smaller circles on the top or bottom of the arcball, the object can be rotated about the X axis.

When using the shortcut menu, zooming options can be selected by first picking **More**, and then the option. The **More** options also allow you to change the display based on the functions of a camera, and apply front and rear clipping planes to the model. Clipping planes are used to "slice" through the model so that certain portions can be displayed. Selecting **More** and then **Continuous Orbit** sets the model into motion so that you can view it rotating in space continuously. These options are also available in the **3D Orbit** toolbar.

The shortcut menu also contains options for establishing a parallel or perspective projection, applying shading to the model, and displaying visual aids such as a spherical 3D compass, grid lines, and the UCS icon. You can also display the previous view, a saved view, or one of AutoCAD's preset orthographic or isometric views.

# Creating User Coordinate Systems

As discussed earlier in this chapter, the UCS is used to establish a drawing plane where objects can be drawn "plan" to the plane. When working in 3D, you will frequently find it necessary to change viewing angles and drawing planes. A UCS can be defined at any orientation desired. It can then be saved and reused as necessary. When a UCS is created and moved from the default WCS, a new 0,0,0 origin is generated, allowing you to locate X, Y, and Z coordinates in relation to the origin. You may want to create several user coordinate systems based on different features in your drawing.

User coordinate systems are created and managed with the **UCS** command. This command is used to change the origin, position, and rotation of the coordinate system. For example, you can move or rotate an existing UCS on an axis, align it to an object or solid face, or orient it to an orthographic view. Options for creating and managing the UCS are also available in the **Tools** pull-down menu, and the **UCS** toolbar. See **Figure 25-20.** The options in the **Tools** pull-down menu are described below:

**Figure 25-20.**
Accessing UCS options. A—The UCS selections in the **Tools** pull-down menu. B—The UCS toolbar. This toolbar is identical to the UCS flyout in the **Standard** toolbar.

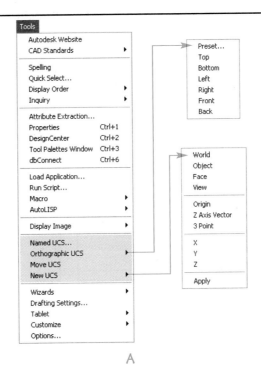

A

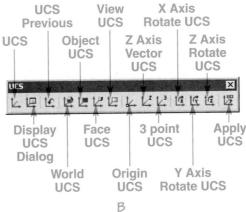

B

- **Named UCS.** This option displays the **UCS** dialog box. This dialog box contains three tabs that you can use to control the orientation of the UCS. These tabs are shown in **Figure 25-21** and described below:
  - **Named UCSs.** This tab is used to create, rename, set current, and delete named coordinate systems. You can also pick the WCS and the previous UCS. See **Figure 25-21A.**
  - **Orthographic UCSs.** This tab is used to select one of six preset UCS orientations in relation to the standard orthographic views. When a preset UCS is selected, the UCS is oriented so that it is plan to the corresponding view. See **Figure 25-21B.**
  - **Settings.** This tab contains options for displaying the UCS icon and controlling how the UCS operates in a viewport. See **Figure 25-21C.**
- **Orthographic UCS.** This option displays a cascading menu listing the six preset UCS orientations. Picking the **Preset...** option displays the **Orthographic UCSs** tab of the **UCS** dialog box.

---

Figure 25-21.
The **UCS** dialog box tabs. A—The **Named UCSs** tab lists named coordinate systems and allows you to set them current. B—The **Orthographic UCSs** tab allows you to select a preset UCS based on a viewing direction. C—The **Settings** tab controls the display of the **UCS** icon and lists additional options for managing the UCS in viewports.

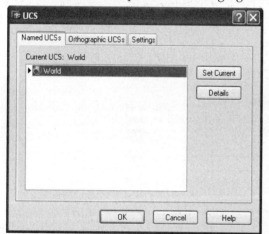

A

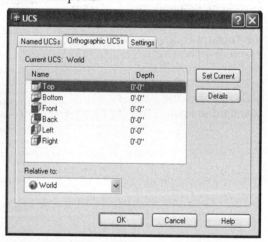

B

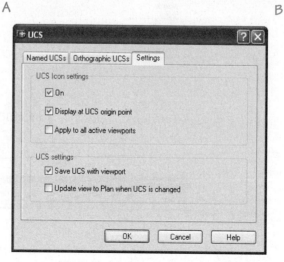

C

- **Move UCS.** This option allows you to specify a new UCS origin point or change the Z depth of the UCS. Adjusting the Z depth moves the UCS drawing plane along the Z axis.
- **New UCS.** This option displays a cascading menu listing options for changing and creating a new UCS. The same UCS options listed are available in the **UCS** toolbar and are described as follows:
  - **World.** This option restores the default WCS.
  - **Object.** This option allows you to select an object and create a new UCS based upon the object's positive X and Y directions.
  - **Face.** This option orients the UCS to the face of a solid object. The face selected establishes the positive X and Y coordinates for the drawing plane.
  - **View.** This option rotates the UCS so that the drawing plane is perpendicular to the viewing direction. This option is useful for adding text that appears horizontal in a 3D view.
  - **Origin.** This option enables you to select a new origin point for the UCS drawing plane. The orientation of the XY plane remains parallel to that of the current UCS, but a new origin point is defined.
  - **Z Axis Vector.** This option allows you to create a new UCS by selecting a point on the positive Z axis. You are prompted to specify an origin location, and then the positive direction of the Z axis. You can use 3D coordinates or object snaps with existing objects to designate the positive Z direction.
  - **3 Point.** This option creates a new UCS based on positive X and Y axis points that you specify. You are prompted to specify a new origin point, a point designating the positive X direction, and then a point designating the positive Y direction. The UCS drawing plane is then moved based on the three points selected. See **Figure 25-22.** This option can also be accessed by picking the **3 Point UCS** button on the **UCS** toolbar.
  - **X, Y, and Z.** Each of these options is used to rotate the UCS around the corresponding axis by a specified angle. Rotating the UCS can be accomplished by looking "down" on the XY drawing plane and visualizing the UCS icon rotating in space. In **Figure 25-23,** the UCS is shown rotated 90° about the X, Y, and Z axes. In each example, the direction of rotation is positive (counterclockwise). You can also use negative rotation values. Each of the UCS rotation options can be accessed from the **UCS** toolbar by picking the **X, Y,** or **Z Axis Rotate UCS** button.

Figure 25-22.
Creating a new UCS by using the **3 Point UCS** option. A—After selecting an origin point, points are specified on the positive X and Y axes. B—The new UCS.

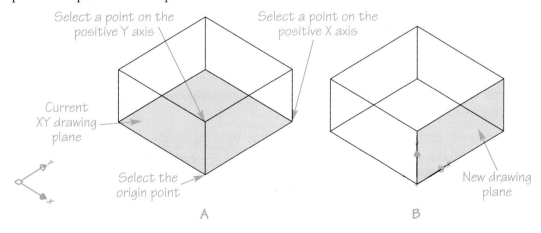

Select a point on the positive Y axis

Select a point on the positive X axis

Current XY drawing plane

Select the origin point

New drawing plane

A

B

**Figure 25-23.**
The UCS can be rotated about the X, Y, or Z axis by selecting an axis and entering a rotation angle. Positive or negative values can be used.

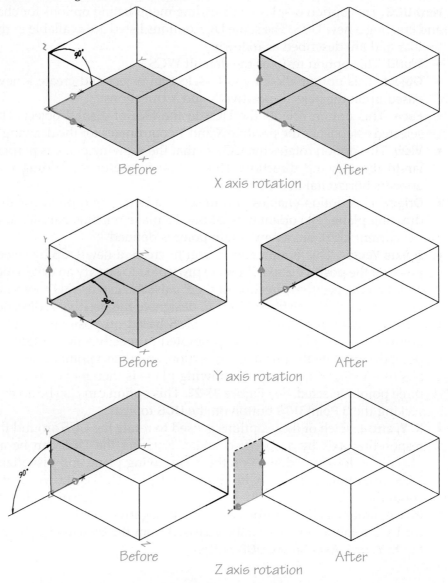

- **Apply.** This option allows you to apply the active UCS setting to a specified viewport or to all viewports.

As previously discussed, UCS options can also be accessed by entering the **UCS** command. The command sequence is as follows:

Command: **ucs.**↵
Current ucs name: *current*
Enter an option [New/Move/orthoGraphic/Prev/Restore/Save/Del/Apply/?/World]
<World>: *(enter an option)*

Once you understand a few of the basic options of creating user coordinate systems, drawing 3D models becomes an easy and quick process. The following sections show how to display the UCS icon, change the UCS in order to work on different drawing planes, and name and save a UCS.

## Displaying the UCS Icon

As discussed earlier in this chapter, the display of the UCS icon is controlled by the **UCSICON** command. This command can also be used to move the icon to the UCS origin after a new UCS has been created. The command sequence is as follows:

Command: **ucsicon**⏎
Enter an option [ON/OFF/All/Noorigin/ORigin/Properties] <*current*>:

The **UCSICON** command options are described below:
- **ON.** This option displays the UCS icon in the current viewport.
- **OFF.** This option turns off the display of the UCS icon in the current viewport.
- **All.** When this option is entered, changes made to the UCS icon are applied to all viewports.
- **Noorigin.** Entering this option places the UCS icon in the lower-left corner of the current viewport.
- **ORigin.** This option places the UCS icon at the 0,0,0 origin of the current UCS. This is a useful option after a new UCS is created. If you zoom in on the origin point and AutoCAD cannot redraw the UCS icon at the origin, then the icon reverts to the lower-left corner of the drawing area.
- **Properties.** Entering this option displays the **UCS Icon** dialog box, which can be used to change the style, size, and color of the icon.

## Applying UCS Basics in 3D Modeling

As you have learned in this chapter, defining user coordinate systems and manipulating views is essential to visualizing and constructing 3D objects in AutoCAD. Previous discussions introduced you to the various methods used to change the UCS and construct objects in 3D space. Now these principles can be applied to create a 3D model. In the following example, you will construct a wireframe model of a cabin using different named coordinate systems and 3D point entry methods. You will construct the walls, roof, windows, and front door to create the model shown in **Figure 25-24.**

**Figure 25-24.**
The completed wireframe model of the cabin.

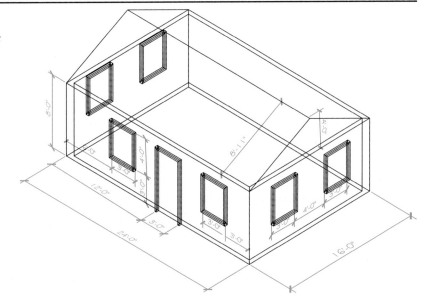

First, begin a new drawing and turn on the UCS icon if necessary. Make sure that you are using architectural units. When starting a new drawing, the default UCS is the WCS, with the origin at 0,0,0. The UCS is oriented so that you are looking "down" on AutoCAD's default XY drawing plane. Think of this drawing plane as the cabin floor. By naming and saving this UCS, you know that this drawing plane can be used to construct anything on the "floor" plane. Name the UCS using the **UCS** dialog box, or enter the **UCS** command:

Command: **ucs.**↵
Current ucs name: *WORLD*
Enter an option [New/Move/orthoGraphic/Prev/Restore/Save/Del/Apply/?/World] <World>: **s.**↵
Enter name to save current UCS or [?]: **Floor.**↵

After naming the UCS, you can draw walls by using the **PLINE** command and the **THICKNESS** system variable. The walls are 8'-0" high, so set the **THICKNESS** variable to 8'-0". Then use the **PLINE** command to draw a closed polyline representing the outside walls, which are 24' × 16'. Using the **OFFSET** command, offset the polyline 6" inside the building to make the walls 6" thick. See **Figure 25-25A**. Now, display a southeast isometric view of the building. The model should appear as shown in **Figure 25-25B**.

**Figure 25-25.**
A—The top view of the walls for the cabin. B—The walls in southeast isometric view.

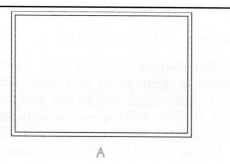
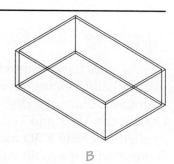

A                                                                              B

The next step is to add the door and windows to the front of the building. To do so, create a new UCS that is "plan" to the front. First, move the UCS to the lower-left front corner of the building:

Command: **ucs.**↵
Current ucs name: Floor
Enter an option [New/Move/orthoGraphic/Prev/Restore/Save/Del/Apply/?/World] <World>: **n.**↵
Specify origin of new UCS or [ZAxis/3point/OBject/Face/View/X/Y/Z] <0,0,0>: *(pick the lower-left corner of the front wall)*

The UCS icon is moved to the corner, indicating the new 0,0,0 origin. See **Figure 25-26A**. Now that the origin has been specified, the UCS needs to be rotated so that the X and Y axes are parallel to the front of the building. Using the following procedure, rotate the UCS about the X axis, and then save it with the name Front:

Command: **ucs.**↵
Current ucs name: *NO NAME*
Enter an option [New/Move/orthoGraphic/Prev/Restore/Save/Del/Apply/?/World] <World>: **n.**↵
Specify origin of new UCS or [ZAxis/3point/OBject/Face/View/X/Y/Z] <0,0,0>: **x.**↵
Specify rotation angle about X axis <90>: **90.**↵

Architectural Drafting Using AutoCAD

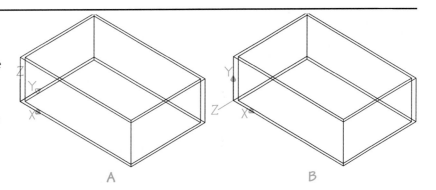

Figure 25-26.
A—A new origin
point is specified
for the UCS. B—The
UCS is rotated 90°
about the X axis to
orient the drawing
plane to the front of
the building.

A          B

Command: ↵
Current ucs name: *NO NAME*
Enter an option [New/Move/orthoGraphic/Prev/Restore/Save/Del/Apply/?/World]
<World>: **s**↵
Enter name to save current UCS or [?]: **Front**↵

The new UCS should appear as shown in **Figure 25-26B**. The door and the windows can now be drawn. The door and window frames are 2″ wide and 4″ thick. First, change the setting for the **THICKNESS** system variable to 4″. Then, enter the **PLINE** command and draw the door using the dimensions from **Figure 25-24**. Use the **Width** option to set the polyline width to 2″. The door is 3′ × 7′, and it originates 12′ from the new UCS origin. You can simply enter XY coordinates when specifying point locations, since all coordinates will have a Z value of 0.

Professional Tip

When working in 3D, it is often easier to work with at least two tiled viewports in the drawing. One viewport can display an isometric view of the model, and the other the "plan" view of the current UCS. To display a "plan" view of the current UCS, activate a viewport, then enter plan at the Command prompt. Next, enter the **Current** option. Use the **Ucs** option to set your view plan to a named UCS.

Add the window to the left of the door in the same manner. The window is 3′ × 4′, and it originates at the coordinate location 6′,3′. You can then copy the window to the other side of the door by specifying the base point as the UCS origin and the second point of displacement as 12′,0′. When you are finished, the model should appear as shown in **Figure 25-27**.

Next, add the windows to the right side of the building. A new UCS needs to be created so that the drawing plane is oriented to the right side. You can use the **3 Point** UCS option to move the UCS origin to the lower-left corner of the right side of the building. After selecting the new origin point, pick the lower-right corner of the right side wall to specify the positive X axis. Pick the upper-left corner of the right wall to specify the positive Y axis. Finally, name the new UCS Right_Side. It should appear as shown in **Figure 25-28**.

Command: **ucs**↵
Current ucs name: Front
Enter an option [New/Move/orthoGraphic/Prev/Restore/Save/Del/Apply/?/World]
<World>: **n**↵
Specify origin of new UCS or [ZAxis/3point/OBject/Face/View/X/Y/Z] <0,0,0>: **3**↵

**Figure 25-27.**
The door and two
windows are added.

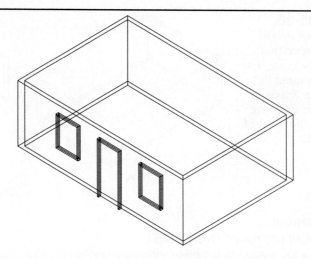

**Figure 25-28.**
The UCS is moved
to the right side
wall using the
**3 Point** option.

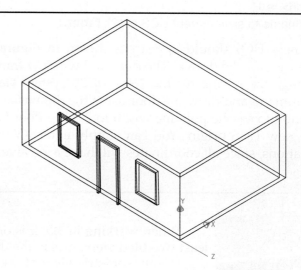

Specify new origin point <0,0,0>: *(pick the lower-left corner of the right side wall)*
Specify point on positive portion of X-axis <24'-1",0'-0",0'-0">: *(pick the lower-right corner of the wall)*
Specify point on positive-Y portion of the UCS XY plane <24'-0",0'-1",0'-0">: *(pick the upper-left corner of the wall)*
Command: ↵
Current ucs name: *NO NAME*
Enter an option [New/Move/orthoGraphic/Prev/Restore/Save/Del/Apply/?/World]
<World>: **s**↵
Enter name to save current UCS or [?]: **Right_Side**↵

Add the first window using the **PLINE** command, with the start point at the coordinate location 3',3'. You can then create a copy for the second window. Specify the base point as the UCS origin and specify the second point of displacement as 7',0'.

The windows on the left side of the building also need to be added. One way to do this is to move the UCS to the left side wall and display a different isometric view. However, you can mirror the two windows from the right side to the left side by restoring the Floor UCS. Use the middle of the front wall as the mirror line:

Command: **ucs**↵
Current ucs name: Right_Side
Enter an option [New/Move/orthoGraphic/Prev/Restore/Save/Del/Apply/?/World]
<World>: **r**↵
Enter name of UCS to restore or [?]: **Floor**↵

```
Command: mirror↵
Select objects: (pick one window)
Select objects: (pick the second window)
Select objects: ↵
Specify first point of mirror line: mid↵
of (pick the midpoint of the front wall line)
Specify second point of mirror line: @1<90↵
Delete source objects? [Yes/No] <N>: ↵
```

Now you will add the roof. The roof can initially be constructed as a wireframe object by drawing lines without thickness. Later in this chapter, you will use surface modeling to apply a "skin" to the roof surface. To draw the roof, create a new UCS at the top of the walls and name it Top_Plate:

```
Command: ucs↵
Current ucs name: Floor
Enter an option [New/Move/orthoGraphic/Prev/Restore/Save/Del/Apply/?/World]
<World>: n↵
Specify origin of new UCS or [ZAxis/3point/OBject/Face/View/X/Y/Z] <0,0,0>: (pick the
    upper-left corner of the front wall)
Command: ↵
Current ucs name: *NO NAME*
Enter an option [New/Move/orthoGraphic/Prev/Restore/Save/Del/Apply/?/World]
<World>: s↵
Enter name to save current UCS or [?]: Top_Plate↵
```

The new UCS should appear as shown in **Figure 25-29.** Next, change the value of the **THICKNESS** system variable to 0. Add the first roof line using 3D cylindrical coordinates as follows:

```
Command: line↵
Specify first point: 0,0↵
Specify next point or [Undo]: @8'<90,4'↵
Specify next point or [Undo]: ↵
```

Copy this line to the other end of the building to create the second roof line. Specify the base point as the UCS origin and specify the second point of displacement as 24',0'. Next, draw a ridge line connecting the two roof lines using the **Endpoint** object snap. Finally, mirror the two roof lines to the other side of the ridge line. Select the midpoint of each side wall when defining the mirror line. When finished, save the drawing with the name wfcabin. The wireframe cabin with the roof completed is shown in **Figure 25-30.**

**Figure 25-29.**
The UCS is moved to the top of the walls to add the roof.

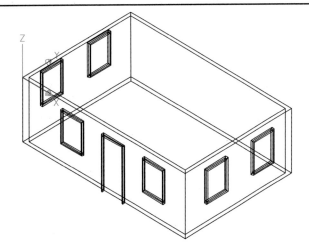

**Figure 25-30.**
The completed
model after adding
the roof.

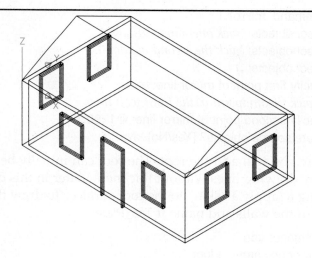

**Professional Tip**

Using layers with different color and linetype settings is very important in 3D modeling. In many cases, objects can be visualized more clearly in a 3D drawing when layers are used to distinguish features. In addition, rendering materials can be assigned to individual layers or colors for rendering purposes. Creating renderings from drawings is discussed in Chapter 26.

## Exercise 25-2

◆ Start a new drawing using one of your templates.
◆ Follow the steps in the *Applying UCS Basics in 3D Modeling* section to create the cabin.
◆ Save the drawing as ex25-2.

# Surface Modeling

Wireframe modeling is a basic form of 3D drawing that is suitable for some drafting applications. Surface modeling, on the other hand, provides much more realistic representations of 3D objects. A surface model is a wireframe model with "skin" added. A surface model looks more like a real object and can be used in presentations requiring rendered images. There are several different surface modeling techniques available in AutoCAD. This chapter discusses the construction of three-dimensional faces and the use of AutoCAD's predrawn surface-modeled objects to create basic 3D shapes.

A surface that appears solid in a 3D model is called a *3D face.* It can be thought of as a surface with "skin" that is drawn directly over the "skeleton" of a wireframe model. Three-dimensional faces are drawn with the **3DFACE** command. This command can be used to create a three- or four-sided face. Points are picked in a clockwise or counterclockwise manner to designate the corners of the face. See **Figure 25-31.**

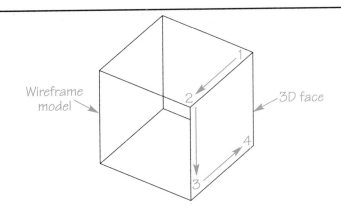

**Figure 25-31.**
Adding a 3D face to a wireframe model with the **3DFACE** command.

Wireframe model

3D face

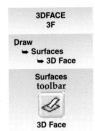

3DFACE
3F

Draw
➥ Surfaces
  ➥ 3D Face

Surfaces toolbar

3D Face

To access the **3DFACE** command, select **3D Face** from the **Surfaces** cascading menu in the **Draw** pull-down menu, pick the **3D Face** button from the **Surfaces** toolbar, or enter 3f or 3dface at the Command prompt. A 3D face drawn with this command must have at least three corners, but it cannot have any more than four corners. During the command sequence, upon selecting the fourth point of a face, you are prompted to select the third point again. This is because AutoCAD assumes that the previous third and fourth points are the first and second points of the next face. This allows you to continue selecting points for additional faces.

The object in **Figure 25-32A,** for example, could be constructed as a surface model by first drawing the bottom and top profiles with the **3DFACE** command. Two 3D faces are required for the bottom profile, as shown in **Figure 25-32B.** First, draw the first face of the bottom profile by using the coordinates provided and the following sequence:

Command: **3f** *or* **3dface**↵
Specify first point or [Invisible]: *(pick the first point for the first face)*
Specify second point or [Invisible]: *(pick the second point for the face)*
Specify third point or [Invisible] <exit>: *(pick the third point for the face)*
Specify fourth point or [Invisible] <create three-sided face>: *(pick the fourth point for the face)*
Specify third point or [Invisible] <exit>: ↵

**Figure 25-32.**
A—A surface model created from 3D faces. B—Using the **3DFACE** command to construct the two faces for the bottom profile.

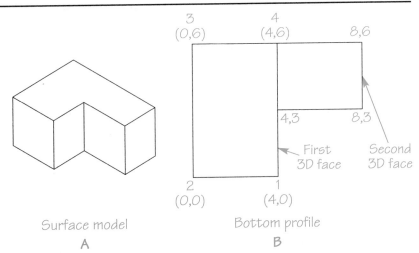

Surface model

A

Bottom profile

B

3 (0,6)    4 (4,6)    8,6

4,3    8,3

First 3D face    Second 3D face

2 (0,0)    1 (4,0)

Next, draw the second face for the bottom profile using the same procedure. You can then create the top profile by copying the bottom profile "up" 4 units along the Z axis. This can be accomplished by picking a base point on the object, such as 0,0, and specifying the second point of displacement with a Z value of 4 (0,0,4). Faces can then be added to the sides by reentering the **3DFACE** command and using the sequence shown in **Figure 25-33A**. After removing hidden lines, the model appears as shown in **Figure 25-33B**.

Notice in **Figure 25-33** that an intersection line between the faces on the top surface is visible in the display. This surface can be drawn so that the intersecting edge will be invisible. The **Invisible** option of the **3DFACE** command allows you to hide edges that should not appear as lines on a surface. The option is entered before picking the first point of the invisible edge. In the previous example, when drawing the bottom profile for the model, the **Invisible** option would be entered after picking the first two points of the first face (refer to **Figure 25-34**):

Command: **3f** *or* **3dface**⏎
Specify first point or [Invisible]: *(pick the first point for the first face)*
Specify second point or [Invisible]: *(pick the second point for the first face)*
Specify third point or [Invisible] <exit>: **i**⏎
Specify third point or [Invisible] <exit>: *(pick the third point for the first face)*
Specify fourth point or [Invisible] <create three-sided face>: *(pick the fourth point for the first face)*
Specify third point or [Invisible] <exit>: *(pick the third point for the second face)*
Specify fourth point or [Invisible] <create three-sided face>: *(pick the fourth point for the second face)*
Specify third point or [Invisible] <exit>: ⏎

---

**Figure 25-33.**
A—Adding 3D faces to the sides of the model. B—The model after using the **HIDE** command.

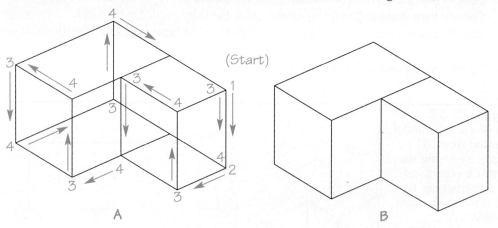

Edges of 3D faces can also be made visible or hidden using the **Properties** window. After selecting a 3D face object, the visibility of any edge can be changed by selecting the desired edge listed under the **Geometry** category and changing the setting.

Another method of turning the edge of a 3D face from a visible edge to invisible is to use the **EDGE** command. This command can be accessed by picking the **Edge** button from the **Surfaces** toolbar, selecting **Edge** from the **Surfaces** cascading menu under the **Draw** pull-down menu, or by entering edge at the Command prompt. Upon entering the command, you are prompted for the following:

Specify edge of 3dface to toggle visibility or [Display]:

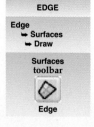

EDGE

Edge
↪ Surfaces
 ↪ Draw

Surfaces
toolbar

Edge

Architectural Drafting Using AutoCAD

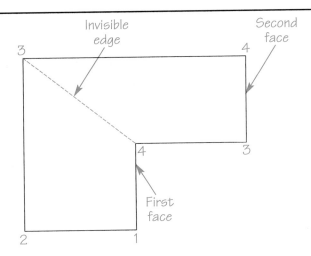

**Figure 25-34.**
Using the **Invisible** option of the **3DFACE** command to remove the intersecting edge between faces in the original profile.

Select any edges that need to be turned invisible. The **Display** option is used to make invisible edges visible. When you enter this option, the following prompt appears:

Enter selection method for display of hidden edges [Select/All] <All>:

The **Select** option allows you to select any 3D face that has invisible edges. The **All** option makes all hidden edges visible in the drawing. After the selection method has been chosen, any invisible edges are displayed as hidden lines. Selecting the hidden edges will toggle them back to visible edges.

## Exercise 25-3

- ◆ Open ex25-2.
- ◆ Using the **3DFACE** command, add two rectangular 3D faces to the top of the wireframe roof.
- ◆ Add triangular 3D faces at the gable ends of the roof.
- ◆ Save the drawing as ex25-3.

## Creating Surface-Modeled Objects

As previously discussed, AutoCAD provides several predrawn surface-modeled objects that can be used when constructing surface models. These objects can be quickly placed in a drawing by specifying an insertion location and basic dimensions. They can be accessed by using the **3D Objects** dialog box, the **Surfaces** toolbar, or the **3D** command. See **Figure 25-35.** To access the **3D Objects** dialog box, select **3D Surfaces...** from the **Surfaces** cascading menu in the **Draw** pull-down menu.

To select an object from the **3D Objects** dialog box, select the image icon or the name of the object in the list box and press the **OK** button. Depending on the type of object you select, you are then prompted for the dimensions, such as the length, width, height, diameter, or radius. The resulting object is created as a 3D mesh made up of 3D faces. Rounded objects, such as spheres, cones, and tori, can appear to be segmented, depending on the number of segments specified when creating the object. This is because the 3D faces are polygonal in shape. Entering the **HIDE** command makes the object appear solid.

A surface-modeled object is treated as one object. Minor editing can be accomplished by picking the object to display grips and selecting a grip to modify. Exploding the object turns it into a display of individual 3D faces that can be modified. The following sections discuss how each type of object is created.

**Figure 25-35.**
A—A predefined surface-modeled object can be drawn by selecting the appropriate object from the **3D Objects** dialog box. B—The same objects can be selected from the **Surfaces** toolbar.

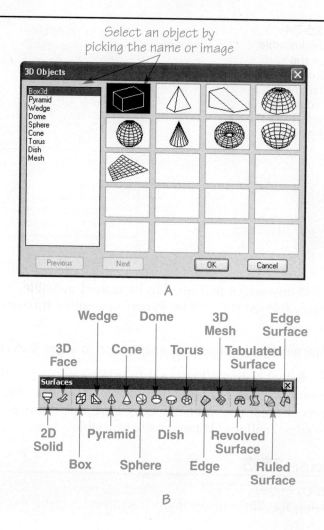

## Drawing a Box

Surfaces toolbar

Box

A surface-modeled box can be constructed by selecting the **Box** image in the **3D Objects** dialog box, picking the **Box** button on the **Surfaces** toolbar, or by entering the **Box** option of the **3D** command. You must specify a location for one of the corners, the box dimensions, and the rotation angle. The following command sequence is used to create the box in **Figure 25-36**:

> Command: **3d**↵
> Enter an option
> [Box/Cone/DIsh/DOme/Mesh/Pyramid/Sphere/Torus/Wedge]: **b**↵
> Specify corner point of box: *(pick a location or enter coordinates)*
> Specify length of box: **2**↵
> Specify width of box or [Cube]: **2**↵
> Specify height of box: **4**↵
> Specify rotation angle of box about the Z axis or [Reference]: **30**↵

After the length is specified, you are prompted to enter the width. If you enter the **Cube** option, the length value is used for the width and height.

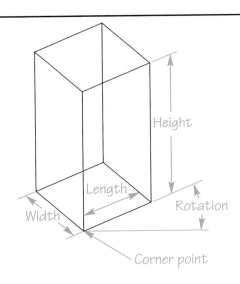

**Figure 25-36.**
When drawing a surface-modeled box, you must specify a corner point, the box dimensions, and a rotation angle.

## Drawing a Wedge

A right-angle, surface-modeled wedge can be created by selecting the **Wedge** image in the **3D Objects** dialog box, picking the **Wedge** button on the **Surfaces** toolbar, or by entering the **Wedge** option of the **3D** command. You must specify a location for one of the corners, the wedge dimensions, and a rotation angle. The following command sequence is used to create the wedge in **Figure 25-37**:

```
Command: 3d↵
Enter an option
[Box/Cone/DIsh/DOme/Mesh/Pyramid/Sphere/Torus/Wedge]: w↵
Specify corner point of wedge: (pick a location or enter coordinates)
Specify length of wedge: 4↵
Specify width of wedge: 2↵
Specify height of wedge: 3↵
Specify rotation angle of wedge about the Z axis: 30↵
```

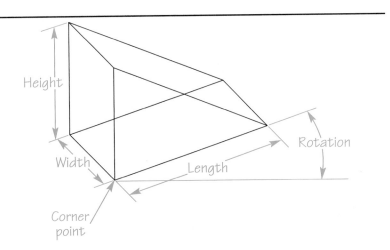

**Figure 25-37.**
A corner point, the object dimensions, and a rotation angle are specified when drawing a surface-modeled wedge.

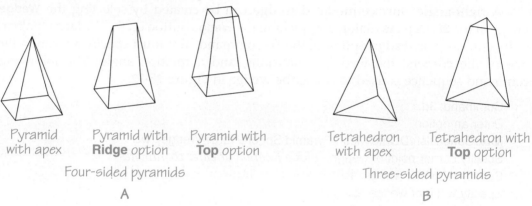

# Drawing a Pyramid

**Surfaces toolbar**

**Pyramid**

Five types of surface-modeled pyramids can be created with the **Pyramid** option. There are three types of four-sided pyramids available. See **Figure 25-38A.** You can also draw two types of three-sided pyramids known as *tetrahedrons.* See **Figure 25-38B.** To create a pyramid, select the **Pyramid** image in the **3D Objects** dialog box, pick the **Pyramid** button on the **Surfaces** toolbar, or enter the **Pyramid** option of the **3D** command.

When constructing a pyramid, you must first draw the base of the object. After entering the third corner point for the base, you can specify a fourth point, or you can enter the **Tetrahedron** option to draw a three-sided pyramid. Once the base is drawn, you are prompted for the apex point. When drawing a four-sided pyramid, you can make the top pointed, ridged, or truncated. When drawing a three-sided pyramid, you can enter coordinates for the apex, or you can make the top truncated. Refer to **Figure 25-38.**

**Figure 25-38.**
A—Examples of four-sided pyramids drawn with the **Pyramid** option. B—Examples of tetrahedrons drawn with the **Pyramid** option.

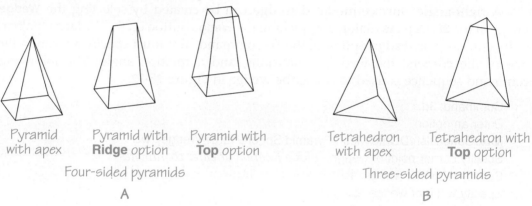

Pyramid with apex · Pyramid with **Ridge** option · Pyramid with **Top** option

Four-sided pyramids

A

Tetrahedron with apex · Tetrahedron with **Top** option

Three-sided pyramids

B

Points specified for the pyramid apex point, ridge line, and truncated top require Z coordinates. You can enter XYZ coordinates for these points, or you can use *filters* so that the Z coordinate can be entered based on an existing point. A *filter* is an existing point in a drawing used to locate a new coordinate relative to that point. The new coordinate is specified by entering the missing X, Y, or Z value, or a combination of values. For example, an XY filter can be used to establish a known point in the XY drawing plane. You are then prompted for the Z coordinate to be used with the XY coordinate. This method is useful when drawing a pyramid, because an XY filter can be used to apply an XY coordinate on the base of the object for the apex point. The Z coordinate you specify is then measured "up" from the XY coordinate. The following sequence uses filters to create the four-sided pyramid in **Figure 25-39:**

Command: **3d**↵
Enter an option
[Box/Cone/DIsh/DOme/Mesh/Pyramid/Sphere/Torus/Wedge]: **p**↵
Specify first corner point for base of pyramid: **4,2**↵
Specify second corner point for base of pyramid: **@2,0**↵
Specify third corner point for base of pyramid: **@0,2**↵
Specify fourth corner point for base of pyramid or [Tetrahedron]: **@–2,0**↵
Specify apex point of pyramid or [Ridge/Top]: **.xy**↵ *(enter this filter to filter out a known xy coordinate value)*
of **5,3**↵ *(enter the known xy coordinate)*
(need Z): **3**↵ *(enter the new z value measured up from the known xy coordinate)*

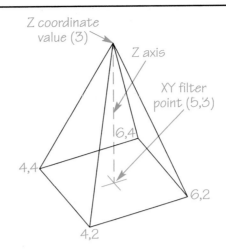

**Figure 25-39.**
Using XY filters allows you to apply XY coordinates from the pyramid base when specifying the Z coordinate for the apex.

After the fourth point of the base is picked, the **Ridge** option can be used to create a ridge at the top of the pyramid instead of an apex. This requires two Z coordinates for the ridge line. Use XY filters or XYZ coordinates to specify these points. The prompt sequence is as follows:

Specify apex point of pyramid or [Ridge/Top]: **r**↵
Specify first ridge end point of pyramid: **.xy**↵
of (*pick a point to specify an XY filter*)
(need Z): **3**↵
Specify second ridge end point of pyramid: **.xy**↵
of (*pick a second XY filter point*)
(need Z): **3**↵

The **Top** option is similar to the **Ridge** option. However, four coordinates with Z values are required to create the truncated top. Use XY filters or XYZ coordinates to locate these points. When the fourth top point is entered, the pyramid is complete.

**Professional Tip**

When creating pyramids, use construction objects and object snaps in plan view to specify corner points and XY filter points. This will help you locate apex points and ridge lines relative to the XY drawing plane.

The process for creating tetrahedrons is similar to that used for four-sided pyramids. As previously discussed, the resulting shape can have an apex or truncated top. To draw a tetrahedron, enter the **Tetrahedron** option after picking the third point for the pyramid base. You can use XY filters or XYZ coordinates to locate the apex or top points. If you enter the **Top** option, you will be prompted for three points designating the top of the tetrahedron.

## Drawing a Cone

The **Cone** option can be used to create a pointed cone, a truncated cone, or a cylinder. When creating a surface-modeled cone, you are prompted for the center base point, the radius for the base, the radius for the top of the cone, and the height of the cone. A pointed cone has a top radius value of zero. A truncated cone has a top radius value other than zero. See **Figure 25-40.** You can draw a cylinder by entering the same radius value for the base and the top.

**Surfaces toolbar**

**Cone**

To create a cone, select the **Cone** image in the **3D Objects** dialog box, pick the **Cone** button on the **Surfaces** toolbar, or enter the **Cone** option of the **3D** command. The command sequence for creating a pointed cone is as follows:

Command: **3d**↵
Enter an option
[Box/Cone/DIsh/DOme/Mesh/Pyramid/Sphere/Torus/Wedge]: **c**↵
Specify center point for base of cone: *(pick a center point)*
Specify radius for base of cone or [Diameter]: **1**↵
Specify radius for top of cone or [Diameter] <0>: ↵
Specify height of cone: **3**↵
Enter number of segments for surface of cone <16>: ↵

After specifying the height, you are prompted for the number of segments. This refers to the number of faces used to create the cone. Using more segments creates a smoother cone. However, this also increases the drawing regeneration time. Use the default number of segments whenever possible.

**Figure 25-40.**
Examples of surface-modeled cones with hidden lines removed.

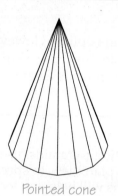
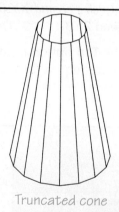
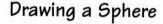

*Pointed cone*          *Truncated cone*

## Drawing a Sphere

**Surfaces toolbar**

**Sphere**

A surface-modeled sphere can be created by selecting the **Sphere** image in the **3D Objects** dialog box, picking the **Sphere** button on the **Surfaces** toolbar, or entering the **Sphere** option of the **3D** command. You must specify a center point and a radius.

Drawing a sphere also requires values for the number of longitudinal and latitudinal segments. As discussed earlier in this chapter, a spherical object has longitudinal segments that run east to west and latitudinal segments that run north to south. The default number of longitudinal and latitudinal segments is 16. See **Figure 25-41.** As with a cone, the more segments added, the smoother the sphere appears. The command sequence for creating a sphere is as follows:

Command: **3d**↵
Enter an option
[Box/Cone/DIsh/DOme/Mesh/Pyramid/Sphere/Torus/Wedge]: **s**↵
Specify center point of sphere: **3,5,2**↵

**Figure 25-41.**
A surface-modeled sphere created with the default number of segments and displayed with hidden lines removed.

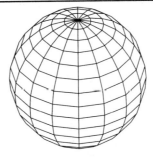

16 × 16 Segments

Specify radius of sphere or [Diameter]: **2**⏎
Enter number of longitudinal segments for surface of sphere <16>: ⏎
Enter number of latitudinal segments for surface of sphere <16>: ⏎

## Drawing a Dome and Dish

A dome can be thought of as the top half of a sphere, or the upper hemisphere of the earth. A dish can be thought of as the bottom half of a sphere, or the lower hemisphere of the earth. See **Figure 25-42.** When drawing a dome or dish, you must specify a center point and radius. As with a sphere, values are required for the number of longitudinal and latitudinal segments.

To draw a surface-modeled dome or dish, select the **Dome** or **Dish** image in the **3D Objects** dialog box, pick the **Dome** or **Dish** button on the **Surfaces** toolbar, or enter the **DOme** or **DIsh** option of the **3D** command. The command sequence is the same for each object. The following sequence is used to draw a dome:

Surfaces toolbar

Dome

Surfaces toolbar

Dish

Command: **3d**⏎
Enter an option
[Box/Cone/DIsh/DOme/Mesh/Pyramid/Sphere/Torus/Wedge]: **do**⏎ *(or **di** for a dish)*
Specify center point of dome: *(pick a point)*
Specify radius of dome or [Diameter]: **2**⏎
Enter number of longitudinal segments for surface of dome <16>: ⏎
Enter number of latitudinal segments for surface of dome <8>: ⏎

**Figure 25-42.**
Surface-modeled dome and dish objects with hidden lines removed.

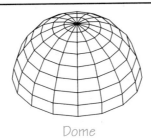

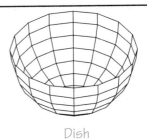

Dome          Dish

## Drawing a Torus

A torus resembles a three-dimensional donut or inner tube. Two radius values are required to draw a surface-modeled torus, one for the overall size of the torus and one for the tube. See **Figure 25-43.** You must also specify the number of segments around the tube and around the torus itself.

**Figure 25-43.**
A surface-modeled
torus is drawn with
radius (or diameter)
values for the torus
and the tube.

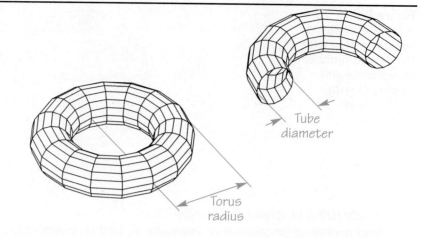

**Surfaces
toolbar**

**Torus**

To create a torus, select the **Torus** image in the **3D Objects** dialog box, pick the **Torus** button on the **Surfaces** toolbar, or enter the **Torus** option of the **3D** command. The command sequence is as follows:

Command: **3d**↵
Enter an option
[Box/Cone/DIsh/DOme/Mesh/Pyramid/Sphere/Torus/Wedge]: **t**↵
Specify center point of torus: (*pick a point*)
Specify radius of torus or [Diameter]: **3**↵
Specify radius of tube or [Diameter]: **1**↵
Enter number of segments around tube circumference <16>: ↵
Enter number of segments around torus circumference <16>: ↵

## Exercise 25-4

◆ Start a new drawing using one of your templates.
◆ Construct the building shown using surface-modeled objects and 3D drawing techniques. Create viewports containing orthographic and isometric views. Define user coordinate systems and display 3D views as needed. Remove hidden lines as necessary. Use the objects and dimensions listed for each portion of the building in the following table:

| Feature | Object | Length | Width | Height | Radius |
|---------|--------|--------|-------|--------|--------|
| West wing | Box | 24'-0" | 48'-0" | 36'-0" | |
| West hall | Box | 24'-0" | 16'-0" | 36'-0" | |
| Main building | Box | 36'-0" | 36'-0" | 48'-0" | |
| East wing | Box | 24'-0" | 48'-0" | 36'-0" | |
| East hall | Box | 24'-0" | 16'-0" | 36'-0" | |
| Columns (16) | Cylindrical cone | | | 36'-0" | 1'-0" |
| Wing roof sections (4) | Wedge | 12'-0" | 48'-0" | 12'-0" | |
| Hall roof sections (4) | Wedge | 12'-0" | 24'-0" | 12'-0" | |
| Dome | Dome | | | | 18'-0" |
| Spindle | Pointed cone | | | 10'-0" | 6" |

◆ You may want to create the individual objects first and then move them to the correct locations using object snaps.

*(Continued)*

- Align the columns underneath the hall roof sections as shown in the top view. The spacing between columns is 4'-0".
- After the roof sections are in place, the roof sections for the halls need to be modified to "lay" on top of the wing roofs. You can use grips to accomplish this. For the west side hall roof sections, pick the westernmost ridge line grip box and stretch it 12'-0" to the west. For the east side hall roof sections, pick the easternmost ridge line grip box and stretch it 12'-0" to the east. Use the illustration provided as a guide.
- Add a 3D face for the ground plane.
- Save the drawing as ex25-4.

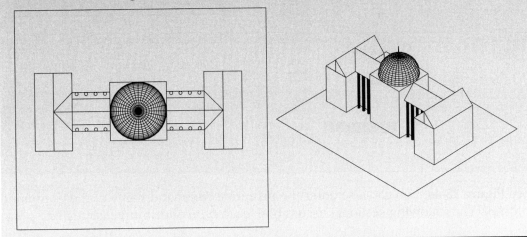

# Solid Modeling

Solid modeling is similar to surface modeling. However, solid modeling provides a more realistic way to represent objects. Unlike surface models, solid models have the mass properties of a solid rather than only the skin of a surface. In addition, solids can be used as "building blocks" to construct complex models and are more suited for editing than surface models. As with surface models, solid models can be shaded and rendered for presentation purposes.

Solid modeling involves the use of solid primitives, solid extrusions, and editing techniques that enable you to manipulate solids when creating other objects. For example, solids can be joined together or subtracted from other solids to create different shapes. This section introduces how to draw solid primitives, create extrusions from basic 2D objects, and apply solid editing tools.

The material in this section is intended as an overview of solid modeling. Additional information about AutoCAD's advanced solid modeling and surface modeling commands is provided in Appendix H of this text. For greater coverage on three-dimensional modeling, refer to the text *AutoCAD and its Applications—Advanced*, available from Goodheart-Willcox Publisher.

## Constructing Solid Primitives

*Solid primitives* are basic 3D objects such as boxes, cones, and spheres. The basic solid primitives available in AutoCAD are similar to the surface-modeled objects previously discussed. However, solid primitives contain mass and can be used as construction objects when creating more complex models. AutoCAD's predefined solid primitives can be accessed from the **Solids** cascading menu in the **Draw** pull-down menu or by picking the appropriate button in the **Solids** toolbar.

**Figure 25-44.**
A—Solid primitives can be selected from the **Solids** cascading menu in the **Draw** pull-down menu. B—The same objects can be accessed from the **Solids** toolbar.

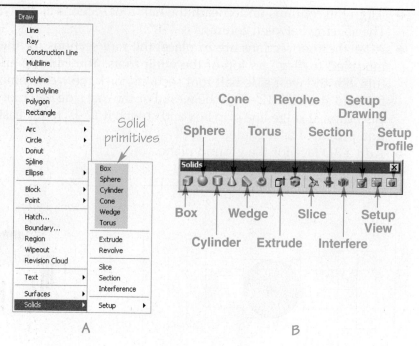

A

B

See **Figure 25-44.** You can also enter the primitive command name at the Command prompt. The following sections discuss how each type of primitive is created.

## Creating a Box

BOX

Draw
➥ Solids
➥ Box

Solids toolbar

Box

A solid box is created by picking two opposite corners at the base of the box, or by specifying a center point from which the box is constructed. To draw a box, select **Box** from the **Solids** cascading menu in the **Draw** pull-down menu, pick the **Box** button on the **Solids** toolbar, or enter box at the Command prompt. The following command sequence is used to create the box in **Figure 25-45:**

Command: **box**↵
Specify corner of box or [CEnter] <0,0,0>: *(pick a starting point for the box)*
Specify corner or [Cube/Length]: **@28',20'**↵
Specify height: **9'**↵

The **Cube** option allows you to create a solid cube. The length specified is applied to all dimensions. If the **Length** option is entered, you are prompted for the length and width dimensions in addition to the height.

**Figure 25-45.**
A solid box created by specifying corner points. The object is shown in wireframe view.

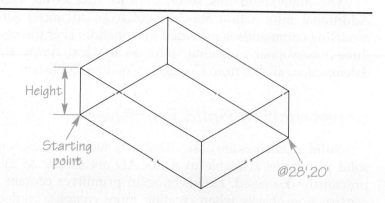

Architectural Drafting Using AutoCAD

## Creating a Sphere

**SPHERE**

Draw
➥ Solids
➥ Sphere

**Solids toolbar**

Sphere

A solid sphere is created by specifying a center point and a radius. To draw a sphere, select **Sphere** from the **Solids** cascading menu in the **Draw** pull-down menu, pick the **Sphere** button on the **Solids** toolbar, or enter sphere at the Command prompt. The following command sequence is used:

Command: **sphere**↵
Current wire frame density: ISOLINES=4
Specify center of sphere <0,0,0>: *(pick a center point)*
Specify radius of sphere or [Diameter]: **12'**↵

The sphere shown in **Figure 25-46A** is displayed in wireframe mode as a series of lines defining the shape. The lines that form the wireframe of a solid are called *isolines.* By default, four isolines are displayed. This value is controlled by the **ISOLINES** system variable. After using the **HIDE** command, the sphere is displayed as shown in **Figure 25-46B**.

**Figure 25-46.**
Creating a solid sphere. A—In wireframe mode, the shape of the object is represented by isolines. B—The object after using the **HIDE** command.

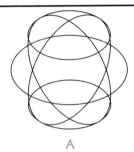 

A            B

## Creating a Cylinder

**CYLINDER**

Draw
➥ Solids
➥ Cylinder

**Solids toolbar**

Cylinder

A solid cylinder can be created as a circular or elliptical cylinder. To draw a cylinder, select **Cylinder** from the **Solids** cascading menu in the **Draw** pull-down menu, pick the **Cylinder** button on the **Solids** toolbar, or enter cylinder at the Command prompt. When drawing a circular cylinder, you must specify a center point, a radius, and a height. The following command sequence is used to create the cylinder in **Figure 25-47A**:

Command: **cylinder**↵
Current wire frame density: ISOLINES=4
Specify center point for base of cylinder or [Elliptical] <0,0,0>: *(pick a center point)*
Specify radius for base of cylinder or [Diameter]: **4'**↵
Specify height of cylinder or [Center of other end]: **8'**↵

**Figure 25-47.**
Examples of solid cylinders displayed in wireframe view. A—A circular cylinder. B—An elliptical cylinder.

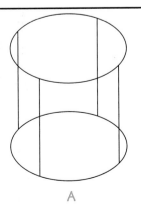 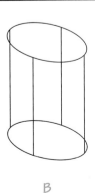

A            B

The **Center of other end** option can be used to pick a point that represents the center point of the opposite end of the cylinder. This is useful when you are locating the cylinder inside another solid object for modeling purposes. For example, you may want to subtract a cylinder from another solid to create a hole. Subtracting solids is discussed later in this chapter.

An elliptical cylinder can be created by specifying the first and second axis endpoints for the cylinder base. The second axis distance is then specified. The following command sequence is used to create the cylinder in **Figure 25-47B**:

Command: **cylinder**⏎
Current wire frame density: ISOLINES=4
Specify center point for base of cylinder or [Elliptical] <0,0,0>: **e**⏎
Specify axis endpoint of ellipse for base of cylinder or [Center]: *(pick a point)*
Specify second axis endpoint of ellipse for base of cylinder: **@0',6'**⏎
Specify length of other axis for base of cylinder: **2'**⏎
Specify height of cylinder or [Center of other end]: **8'**⏎

You can also draw an elliptical cylinder by first specifying the center point of the base by entering the **Center** option. You are then prompted for the endpoint of the first axis and the second axis distance.

## Creating a Cone

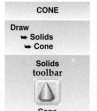

CONE

Draw
➡ Solids
➡ Cone

Solids
toolbar

Cone

As is the case with a cylinder, a solid cone can be created with a round or elliptical base. To draw a cone, select **Cone** from the **Solids** cascading menu in the **Draw** pull-down menu, pick the **Cone** button on the **Solids** toolbar, or enter cone at the Command prompt. The following sequence is used to create the cone in **Figure 25-48A**:

Command: **cone**⏎
Current wire frame density: ISOLINES=4
Specify center point for base of cone or [Elliptical] <0,0,0>: *(pick a center point)*
Specify radius for base of cone or [Diameter]: **3'**⏎
Specify height of cone or [Apex]: **10'**⏎

The **Apex** option allows you to locate a point for the opposite end of the cone and orient the object at any angle. This option is similar to the **Center of other end** option for a cylinder. If you place the cone inside another solid, you can create a tapered cutout by subtracting the cone.

**Figure 25-48.**
Examples of solid cones displayed in wireframe view. A—A cone with a circular base. B—A cone with an elliptical base.

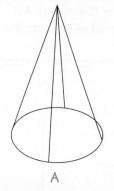

A

B

Architectural Drafting Using AutoCAD

The process for creating a cone with an elliptical base is similar to that used for an elliptical cylinder. You can specify the endpoints of the first axis and then enter the second axis distance, or you can enter the **Center** option to specify the center of the base. The following sequence is used to create the cone in **Figure 25-48B**:

Command: **cone**↵
Current wire frame density: ISOLINES=4
Specify center point for base of cone or [Elliptical] <0,0,0>: **e**↵
Specify axis endpoint of ellipse for base of cone or [Center]: *(pick the first axis endpoint)*
Specify second axis endpoint of ellipse for base of cone: **@0',4'**↵
Specify length of other axis for base of cone: **3'**↵
Specify height of cone or [Apex]: **10'**↵

## Creating a Wedge

A solid wedge can be created by specifying opposite corners of the base and a height, or by locating a center point from which the object is constructed. You can also specify the length, width, and height dimensions individually. The procedure is similar to that used for a solid box. To draw a wedge, select **Wedge** from the **Solids** cascading menu in the **Draw** pull-down menu, pick the **Wedge** button on the **Solids** toolbar, or enter we or wedge at the Command prompt. The following sequence is used to create the wedge in **Figure 25-49A**:

Command: **we** *or* **wedge**↵
Specify first corner of wedge or [CEnter] <0,0,0>: *(pick the first point for the base)*
Specify corner or [Cube/Length]: **@8',9'**↵
Specify height: **4'**↵

Entering the **CEnter** option allows you to specify the center of the wedge, which is located in the middle of the angled surface. See **Figure 25-49B**. You are then prompted for a corner point and the height. You can also use the **Length** option to specify the length, width, and height dimensions separately. The **Cube** option applies the length value for all three dimensions. The following sequence uses the **CEnter** and **Length** options to create the wedge in **Figure 25-49B**:

Command: **we** *or* **wedge**↵
Specify first corner of wedge or [CEnter] <0,0,0>: **ce**↵
Specify center of wedge <0,0,0>: *(pick the center point)*
Specify opposite corner or [Cube/Length]: **l**↵
Specify length: **5'**↵
Specify width: **4'**↵
Specify height: **6'**↵

**Figure 25-49.**
A solid wedge can be created by picking corner points or by specifying dimensions after selecting a center point. A—Selecting opposite corners to designate the base. B—Constructing a wedge from the center point of the object.

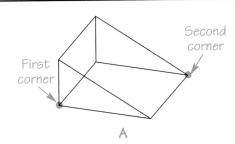
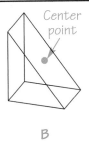

TORUS
TOR

Draw
➡ Solids
  ➡ Torus

Solids
toolbar

Torus

## Creating a Torus

A solid torus can be created by specifying a center point, a torus radius, and a tube radius. Three types of tori can be created. See **Figure 25-50.** To draw a torus, select **Torus** from the **Solids** cascading menu in the **Draw** pull-down menu, pick the **Torus** button on the **Solids** toolbar, or enter tor or torus at the Command prompt. The following sequence is used to create the torus in **Figure 25-50A:**

Command: **tor** *or* **torus**↵
Current wire frame density: ISOLINES=4
Specify center of torus <0,0,0>: *(pick the center point)*
Specify radius of torus or [Diameter]: **3'**↵
Specify radius of tube or [Diameter]: **6"**↵

A torus that does not have a center hole through itself is called a *self-intersecting* torus. Refer to **Figure 25-50B.** This type of torus is created by making the tube radius larger than the torus radius:

Command: **tor** *or* **torus**↵
Current wire frame density: ISOLINES=4
Specify center of torus <0,0,0>: *(pick the center point)*
Specify radius of torus or [Diameter]: **2'**↵
Specify radius of tube or [Diameter]: **30"**↵

The third type of torus resembles a football. It is created by entering a negative value for the torus radius and a positive value for the tube radius. The following sequence is used to create the torus in **Figure 25-50C:**

Command: **tor** *or* **torus**↵
Current wire frame density: ISOLINES=4
Specify center of torus <0,0,0>: *(pick the center point)*
Specify radius of torus or [Diameter]: **–4'**↵
Specify radius of tube or [Diameter]: **6'**↵

---

**Figure 25-50.**
A solid torus can be created in three different ways. The objects shown are displayed in wire-frame view and with hidden lines removed.

A                                      B                                      C

## Exercise 25-5

◆ Start a new drawing using one of your templates.
◆ Referring to the surface model you created in Exercise 25-4, construct the same model using solid primitives.
◆ The roof sections above the halls should be an additional 12'-0" in width. Place these objects so that the hall roofs intersect the wing roofs.
◆ Use a sphere primitive in place of the surface-modeled dome. Place the sphere so that the lower half intersects the main building.
◆ Save the drawing as ex25-5.

## Creating Solid Extrusions

The basic solid primitives available in AutoCAD provide a useful starting point for solid modeling. However, constructing models in 3D requires many different types of objects and shapes. You can create unique solid shapes from existing 2D objects by *extruding* them. Extruding an object into a 3D solid gives it thickness and converts it into the same type of object as a basic primitive. Closed objects such as polylines, circles, rectangles, ellipses, and polygons can be extruded in this manner. Extrusions are created with the **EXTRUDE** command.

Solid extruded objects can also be created from *regions*. A *region* is a closed two-dimensional solid treated as a single object. This type of object has all the properties of a 3D solid model, except thickness. Regions are created with the **REGION** command. Because objects that are extruded must be closed, creating regions from existing 2D objects is often required before using the **EXTRUDE** command.

To access the **REGION** command, select **Region** from the **Draw** pull-down menu, pick the **Region** button on the **Draw** toolbar, or enter reg or region at the Command prompt. The following command sequence is used to create a region from the object shown in **Figure 25-51A**:

REGION
REG

Draw
➥ Region

Draw
toolbar

Region

Command: **reg** *or* **region**↵
Select objects: (*pick the lines making up the object*)
Select objects: ↵
1 loop extracted.
1 Region created.

**Figure 25-51.**
Extruding a region created from an existing 2D object. A—The lines making up the closed object are selected to define the region. B—The region is extruded in the positive Z direction, creating a 3D solid.

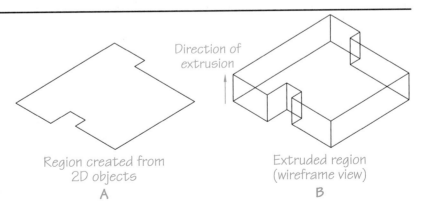

Direction of extrusion

Region created from 2D objects
A

Extruded region (wireframe view)
B

EXTRUDE
EXT

Draw
➥ Solids
➥ Extrude

Solids
toolbar

Extrude

After creating the region, the object is ready to be extruded. To access the **EXTRUDE** command, select **Extrude** from the **Solids** cascading menu in the **Draw** pull-down menu, pick the **Extrude** button on the **Solids** toolbar, or enter ext or extrude at the Command prompt. Closed objects and regions can be extruded in a positive or negative direction along the Z axis. The following command sequence is used to create the extruded solid in **Figure 25-51B**:

Command: **ext** *or* **extrude**↵
Current wire frame density: ISOLINES=4
Select objects: *(select the region)*
Select objects: ↵
Specify height of extrusion or [Path]: **9'**↵
Specify angle of taper for extrusion <0>: ↵

After specifying the extrusion height, you are prompted for a taper angle. This angle applies a taper to the inside or outside of the extruded object along the Z axis. See **Figure 25-52**. A positive taper angle results in the object tapering inward. A negative taper angle results in the object tapering outward.

---

**Figure 25-52.**

A taper angle can be applied when extruding an object into a solid. The object shown is tapered 15° in both the positive and negative directions.

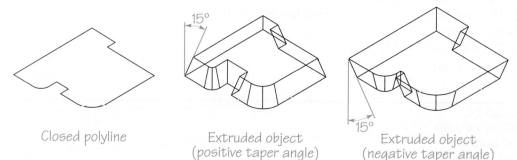

Closed polyline      Extruded object (positive taper angle)      Extruded object (negative taper angle)

## Extruding Objects along a Path

Extrusions can be created along a straight line or along a path curve. The **Path** option of the **EXTRUDE** command is used to extrude an object along a path. The path can be a line, circle, arc, ellipse, polyline, or spline. See **Figure 25-53.** The following command sequence is used:

Command: **ext** *or* **extrude**⌐
Current wire frame density: ISOLINES=4
Select objects: *(select the object to extrude)*
Select objects: ⌐
Specify height of extrusion or [Path]: **p**⌐
Select extrusion path: *(pick the path)*

**Figure 25-53.**
Extruding objects along paths. A—A path object is selected to define the extrusion direction. B—The objects after extruding with hidden lines removed.

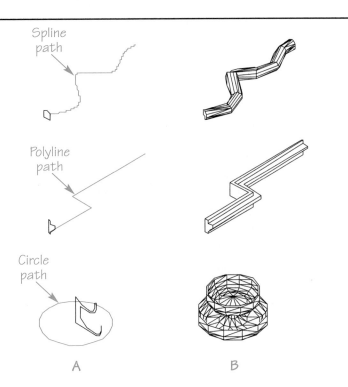

Spline path

Polyline path

Circle path

A

B

## Using Solid Editing Operations

One of the most powerful 3D modeling tools in AutoCAD is the ability to construct solid models from a variety of objects. A solid model that is constructed from two or more solid primitives is called a *composite solid.* Solid primitives can be joined together, subtracted from one another, and overlapped to create new models. These solid editing methods are known as *Boolean operations.* When two or more solids are joined together, the resulting shape is called a *union.* When the volume of one solid is removed from another solid, a *subtraction* occurs. An *intersection* is created when a common area shared by two solids is used to make a new solid. The commands for these operations can be accessed from the **Solids Editing** cascading menu in the **Modify** pull-down menu or the **Solids Editing** toolbar. See **Figure 25-54.** Composite solids are discussed in the following sections.

**Figure 25-54.**
Boolean operation commands are accessed from the **Solids Editing** cascading menu in the **Modify** pull-down menu. The same commands are available in the **Solids Editing** toolbar.

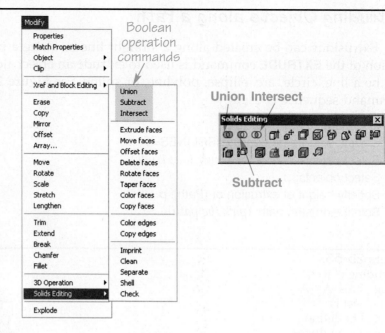

## Joining Solids

A union of two or more solid primitives can be created with the **UNION** command. The objects that are unioned are joined into a composite solid. The original solids do not need to touch or intersect in order to be unioned. To create a union, select **Union** from the **Solids Editing** cascading menu in the **Modify** pull-down menu, pick the **Union** button on the **Solids Editing** toolbar, or enter uni or union at the Command prompt. The command sequence is as follows:

Command: **uni** or **union**↵
Select objects: (select the solids to be joined)
Select objects: ↵

Examples of joining solids together with the **UNION** command are shown in **Figure 25-55.**

**Figure 25-55.**
A union is created from two or more solid primitives. A—The original solid objects. B—The objects after using the **UNION** command with hidden lines removed.

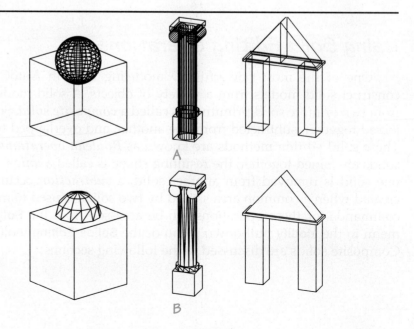

## Subtracting Solids

The **SUBTRACT** command is used to subtract the volume of one or more solids from another solid. This allows you to "cut out" portions of a solid model, such as openings for doors and windows. After entering the **SUBTRACT** command, the first object you select is the object that will have volume removed (the solid you are subtracting *from*). The next object selected is the solid that will be subtracted. To subtract solids, select **Subtract** from the **Solids Editing** cascading menu in the **Modify** pull-down menu, pick the **Subtract** button from the **Solids Editing** toolbar, or enter su or subtract at the Command prompt. The command sequence is as follows:

SUBTRACT
SU

Modify
➥ Solids Editing
➥ Subtract

Solids Editing
toolbar

Subtract

Command: **su** *or* **subtract**↵
Select solids and regions to subtract from…
Select objects: *(select the object that will have volume removed)*
Select objects: ↵
Select solids and regions to subtract…
Select objects: *(select the object(s) that will be removed)*
Select objects: ↵

Examples of solid models with other solids subtracted out are shown in **Figure 25-56.**

Figure 25-56.
Subtracting solid primitives to create composite solids.
A—The original solid objects.
B—The objects after using the **SUBTRACT** command with hidden lines removed.

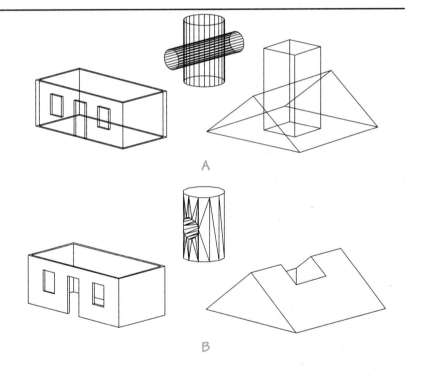

A

B

**Professional Tip**

If you have extruded polylines to create walls, place solid primitive boxes where the windows and doors are located. Subtract the primitives from the extruded walls to create the openings. You can later insert 3D door and window blocks created with solids to fill in the openings.

## Exercise 25-6

◆ Open ex25-5.
◆ Union the wings and halls to the main building.
◆ Add windows to the building using your own dimensions. Use solid primitive boxes or extruded objects and place them in an arrangement of your own design. Use the figure shown for reference. Locate the windows so that they intersect "into" the walls of the building. Use the UCS accordingly.
◆ Subtract the solid windows from the building.
◆ Union the roof sections together.
◆ Union the sphere representing the dome to the main building.
◆ Save the drawing as ex25-6.

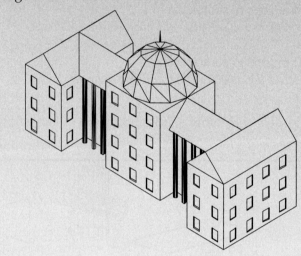

## Creating Solids from Intersections

INTERSECT
IN

Modify
↪ Solids Editing
  ↪ Intersect

Solids Editing
toolbar

Intersect

When two or more solid primitives occupy a common space, they share volume. The shared space can be used to create a new solid by using the **INTERSECT** command. This command creates a composite solid from the shared space, or intersection, of the objects. To create a solid in this manner, select **Intersect** from the **Solids Editing** cascading menu in the **Modify** pull-down menu, pick the **Intersect** button on the **Solids Editing** toolbar, or enter in or intersect at the Command prompt. The command sequence is as follows:

Command: **in** *or* **intersect**.↵
Select objects: *(select the objects that intersect)*
Select objects: ↵

Examples of solids created from intersections are shown in **Figure 25-57**.

**Figure 25-57.**
Creating composite solids from intersections. A—The original solid objects. B—The objects after using the **INTERSECT** command with hidden lines removed.

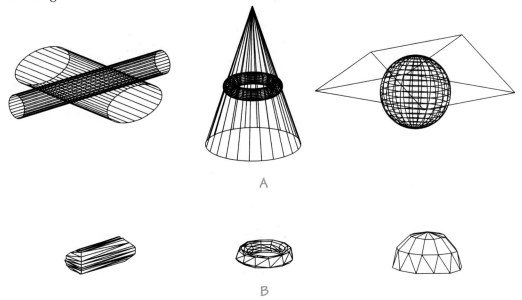

A

B

## Exercise 25-7

◆ Start a new drawing using one of your templates.
◆ Change the view to southwest isometric.
◆ Create a new UCS by rotating it 90° about the X axis so that the Y axis is pointing "up."
◆ Referring to the wireframe drawing shown, create a rectangle 3'-0" wide by 4'-0" high.
◆ Use the **EXTRUDE** command to extrude the rectangle 8".
◆ Move the UCS to the "front" of the extruded rectangle.
◆ Create a layer named Glass and assign it color number 151. Set it current.
◆ Draw a rectangle 15" wide by 21" high located 2" to the right and 2" up from the lower-left corner of the extruded rectangle.
◆ Use the **ARRAY** command to array the small rectangle into 2 rows and 2 columns, with a spacing of 23" for the rows and 17" for the columns.
◆ Extrude the four small rectangles –8" with a taper angle of 10°.
◆ Subtract the small rectangles from the large rectangle.
◆ Save the drawing as ex25-7.

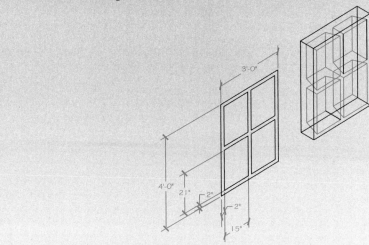

## Creating a Solid Model

In Exercise 25-3, you created the cabin as a surface model. You can use the solid modeling methods discussed in this chapter to construct the same model. For the walls, draw closed polylines and extrude them to the desired height. The roof can be extruded or unioned from solid primitives. The windows and the door can be created by subtracting openings from the walls and then adding extruded or composite solids at the necessary locations. In each operation, consider where to locate the UCS and display orthographic or 3D views as needed.

A solid model of the house project discussed in this text is shown in **Figure 25-58**. The representation is a basic rendering. Rendering is discussed in greater detail in Chapter 26.

**Figure 25-58.**
A basic solid model rendering of the finished house project.

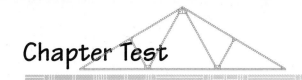

*Answer the following questions on a separate sheet of paper.*

1. Identify and briefly describe the three basic ways to represent three-dimensional objects.
2. What is the default coordinate system used in AutoCAD?
3. What is the purpose of a user coordinate system?
4. What command is used to control the appearance of the UCS icon?
5. What are the three coordinate axes used in the rectangular 3D coordinate system?
6. If you visualize the current XY drawing plane as the surface of your monitor screen, anything behind the screen has a _____ Z coordinate value and anything in front of the screen has a _____ Z coordinate value.
7. What are the four basic isometric views available for displaying 3D objects in AutoCAD?
8. Name three ways to access one of AutoCAD's preset orthographic and isometric views.
9. Explain the difference between spherical and cylindrical coordinates.
10. Identify the coordinate entry used to specify cylindrical coordinates for the end of a line 6″ from the last point, at an angle of 30° in the XY plane and 4″ along the Z axis.
11. What is the purpose of the **THICKNESS** system variable?
12. Name the command that can be used to remove hidden lines or shade a 3D model.
13. What is the function of the 3D orbit view?
14. List two ways to enter the **3DORBIT** command.
15. What is the large circle that appears with four smaller circles at the quadrant points after entering the **3DORBIT** command?
16. List three ways to access the options for creating and managing user coordinate systems.
17. What is the purpose of the **Named UCSs** tab in the **UCS** dialog box?
18. What is the function of the **3 Point UCS** option?
19. Briefly explain how to use the **UCS** command to create and save a UCS.
20. If the UCS icon is not displayed at the origin of the current UCS, how can you move it to the origin?
21. Which command is used to draw three-dimensional faces?
22. Name three ways to access the predrawn surface-modeled objects available in AutoCAD.
23. What dimensions and other specifications are required to draw a surface-modeled box?
24. What is a *tetrahedron*?
25. Define *filter*.
26. How can you draw a surface-modeled cone with a truncated top?
27. Briefly describe the differences between solid models and surface models.
28. List three ways to access AutoCAD's predrawn solid primitives.
29. What are *isolines*?
30. What specifications are required to draw a solid primitive cylinder with a circular base?
31. What is a self-intersecting solid torus and how can it be created?
32. What is the function of the **EXTRUDE** command? What types of objects can be used with this command?
33. What is a *region* and how is it created?

---

34. What is the effect of entering a positive taper angle when using the **EXTRUDE** command?
35. What is the purpose of the **Path** option of the **EXTRUDE** command?
36. What is a *composite solid?*
37. What are *Boolean operations?*
38. What is the function of the **UNION** command?
39. When using the **SUBTRACT** command, which object selected will have volume removed?
40. What command is used to create a new solid from the intersection of two solid objects?

# Chapter Problems

1. Draw the door shown using surface-modeled objects. Change the UCS and use 3D views as needed. Draw the frame using the dimensions provided. Draw and locate the door and the panels using your own dimensions. Construct the doorknob from a sphere and a cylindrical cone. Remove hidden lines as needed. When finished, save the door as a block named Door. Save the drawing as p25-1.

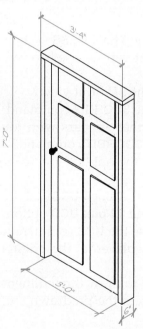

2. Draw the window shown using surface-modeled objects. Change the UCS and use 3D views as needed. Draw the frame using the dimensions provided. Make the cross members 2″ wide and 1″ thick and center them in the frame. Draw four 3D faces at the "front" of the cross members to represent panes of glass. Remove hidden lines as needed. When finished, save the window as a block named Window. Save the drawing as p25-2.

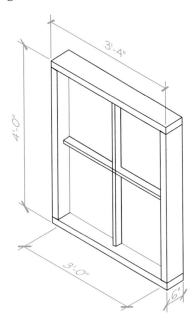

3. Draw the house shown as a surface model. Begin by drawing the walls as a single 2D polyline using the dimensions provided. Set the polyline width to 6″ and the **THICKNESS** system variable to 8′-0″ so that the walls are 6″ thick and 8′-0″ high. Draw the four roof sections using surface-modeled wedges and your own dimensions. Change the UCS and use 3D views as needed. Use grips to edit the two smaller roof sections so that they extend "into" the larger roof sections. Insert the Door block from drawing p25-1 and locate it as shown. Insert the Window block from drawing p25-2 and use it to locate the three windows as shown. Save the drawing as p25-3.

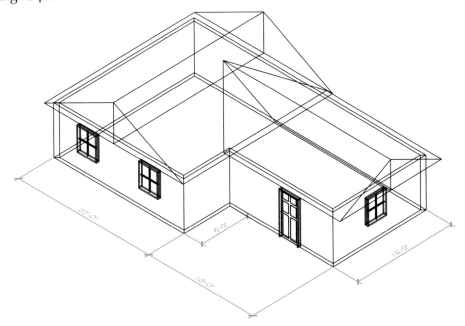

4.  Draw the deck shown using surface-modeled objects or solid primitives. Use the dimensions provided as a guide. Change the UCS and use 3D views as needed. If you draw the deck as a surface model, construct the piers from boxes and four-sided pyramids with truncated tops. If you draw the deck as a solid model, construct each pier from a solid box and an extruded solid with a taper angle. The remaining objects can be drawn using surface-modeled boxes or solid boxes. Make the pier footings 1'-0" wide and 8" high. Make the posts 6" square and 18" high. The floor slats for the deck are 6" wide and 2" thick. The floor joists are 10" wide and 2" thick. The horizontal cross beam is 1'-0" wide and 6" thick. Draw the rails and rail posts using your own dimensions. When finished, remove hidden lines as needed. Save the drawing as p25-4.

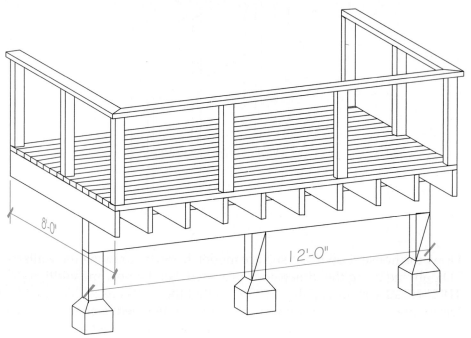

5.  Draw the appliances and sink fixture shown as surface models or solid models. Use surface-modeled objects, lines with thickness, and 3D faces if you construct the objects as surface models. Use solid primitives, extruded solids, and Boolean operations if you construct the objects as solid models. Use the dimensions provided as a guide. When finished, save each object as a block with the names Range, Sink, and Refrig. Save the drawing as p25-5.

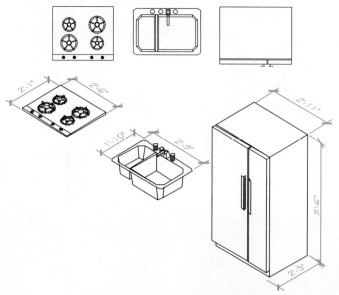

Architectural Drafting Using AutoCAD

6. Draw the kitchen shown as a surface model or solid model. Use surface-modeled objects, lines with thickness, and 3D faces if you construct a surface model. Use solid primitives, extruded solids, and Boolean operations if you construct a solid model. Use your own dimensions. Insert the Range, Sink, and Refrig blocks from drawing p25-5 and locate them as shown. Save the drawing as p25-6.

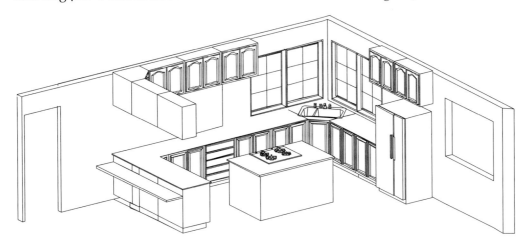

7. Draw the house shown as a solid model. Create the outer edge of the floor plan as a closed polyline. Draw each of the interior rooms as a closed polyline. Make the spacing between the rooms and the walls 6″ and the spacing between the rooms 4″. Extrude the inside and outside polylines 8′-0″. Then, subtract the room solids from the main building solid. Design solid windows and doors using your own dimensions. Draw solid boxes with the same dimensions and use them to subtract openings from the walls to create "holes" for the windows and doors. Then, locate the windows and doors in the openings. Save the drawing as p25-7.

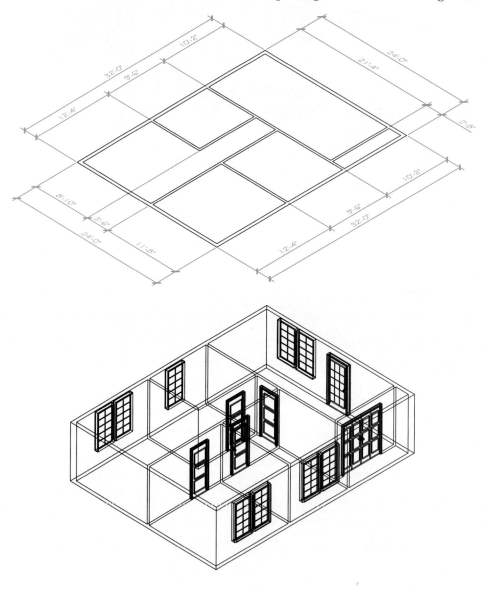

Architectural Drafting Using AutoCAD

# CHAPTER 26

# Presentation Drawings

## Learning Objectives

After completing this chapter, you will be able to:

- Create a hand-sketched perspective.
- Use the **3DORBIT** command to create desired views.
- Render a drawing.
- Add materials to your model.
- Add lighting to your model.
- Create scenes.
- Add a background to your model.
- Create and modify landscape objects.

## Important Terms

altitude
ambient light
antialiasing
attenuates
attributes
azimuth
back face normal
background
cache file
distant light
falloff
fog
front face normal
gradient

hotspot
landscape objects
mapping coordinates
material
material library
material mapping
normal
point light
presentation drawings
rendering
scene
shading sample
spotlight
target

# Presentation Drawings

*Presentation drawings* are used to convey basic design concepts from the architectural team to the client. These drawings can take many forms, from hand-sketched perspectives to color renderings of the design. AutoCAD provides tools to help create presentation drawings, including hidden-line drawings and color renderings. With either of these two presentation techniques, a solid grasp of three-dimensional (3D) space is required to model your design. See **Figure 26-1.**

**Figure 26-1.**
This presentation sheet contains a plan view, hidden-line perspective, and rendered perspective. (3D-DZYN)

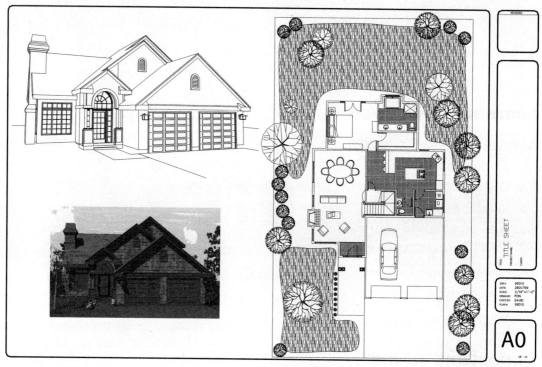

## Creating a Hidden-Line Drawing

A simple hidden-line or shaded drawing of a 3D model can be displayed in AutoCAD. First, use the **3DORBIT** or **VPOINT** command to obtain a pictorial view. If using the **3DORBIT** command, you can further refine the view with the **3D Swivel** and **3D Adjust Distance** buttons on the **3D Orbit** toolbar. See **Figure 26-2.** After an appropriate view is displayed, use the **VIEW** command to save the view with a name. Then, use the **SHADEMODE** command to display a hidden-line or shaded view.

You can also create a viewport in layout space that displays the hidden-line or shaded drawing. Use the **VIEW** command to restore the named hidden-line or shaded view in the viewport. Also, use the **MVIEW** command with the **Shadeplot** option to assign the viewport to plot the model with hidden lines removed or shaded. The drawing can then be plotted.

## Creating a Hand-Sketched Perspective

You can create a hand-sketched perspective by plotting a hidden-line drawing and tracing the plot by hand. You can also create a traditional hand sketch using a hidden-line display on screen as a reference.

Another way to create a "hand-sketched" perspective is to take a screen capture of the hidden-line display. Then, adjust the screen capture in photo-editing software. To do this, configure the view and viewports. Then, display a hidden-line view in the viewport. Press the [Print Screen] key on the keyboard. This creates a "snapshot" of what is displayed on the monitor and places that image on the Windows Clipboard. The image can then be pasted into photo-editing software and adjusted to make it look hand drawn or sketched. See **Figure 26-3.** If you do not have advanced photo-editing software, the screen capture can be pasted into the Windows Paint program and adjusted by tracing over the lines with the various paint tools.

Once the image has been adjusted and saved in the photo-editing software, the image can be brought into AutoCAD with the **IMAGE** command and plotted. Within AutoCAD, you can incorporate the image into other line drawings or color renderings to create a presentation drawing.

**Figure 26-2.**
The **3D Orbit** toolbar contains commands that can be used to obtain a pictorial view.

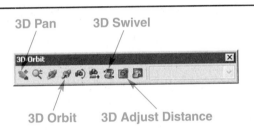

**Professional Tip**

Before doing a screen capture to use for a "hand sketch," make the background color of the drawing area white. A dark blue background with white lines can also be used to create the look of a traditional blueprint.

## Figure 26-3.
A—A hidden-line drawing of a 3D model. B—A screen capture of the hidden-line drawing pasted into photo-editing software and adjusted. C—Further adjustments in the photo-editing software.

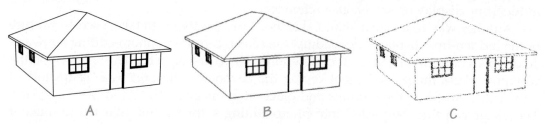

A        B        C

## Exercise 26-1

- Open ex25-6 you created in Chapter 25.
- Using the **3DORBIT** or **VPOINT** command, obtain a 3D view similar to the view shown in the layout sheet below. Save the view using a name of your choice.
- Obtain a hidden-line display. Then, using the [Print Screen] key, copy the image to the Windows Clipboard.
- Paste the image into Windows Paint or, if available, an advanced photo-editing software.
- Adjust the image to create a hand-sketched look. Then, save the image.
- In AutoCAD, set up three viewports. Select the Three:Right configuration.
- In the large viewport, display the top view of the building. In the top-left viewport, display the 3D view you saved earlier. In the bottom-left viewport, use the **IMAGE** command to insert the "hand-sketched" perspective view.
- Set up a layout for plotting with three viewports. Plot the drawing.
- Save the drawing as ex26-1.

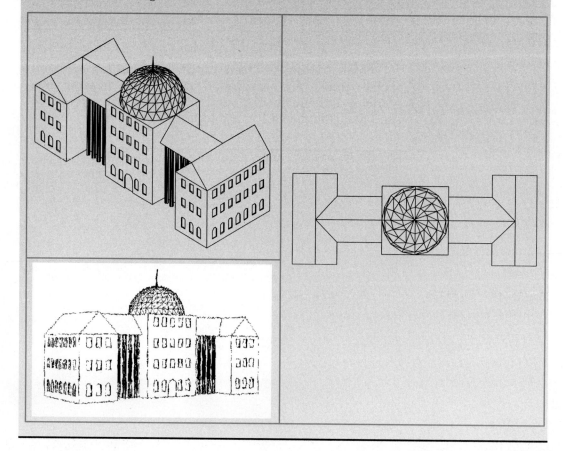

## Rendering a Drawing

A *rendering* is an image that has been shaded with color to create a pictorial view. In AutoCAD, a rendering is usually made from a three-dimensional model that has materials, lights, and other details added to create a realistic pictorial view.

A drawing can be rendered at any time during the creation process. By default, models do not have materials or lights placed in the drawing. There is, however, default lighting. Without adding lights to the scene, AutoCAD uses a default light source. Without materials assigned to the geometry, AutoCAD renders the model with the object color. This is similar to using **SHADEMODE**.

The options found in the **Render** cascading menu in the **View** pull-down menu and on the **Render** toolbar are used to create renderings of your drawings. See **Figure 26-4.** These options and the process of rendering a drawing are covered in the next sections.

Figure 26-4.
A—The **Render** cascading menu in the **View** pull-down menu. B—The **Render** toolbar.

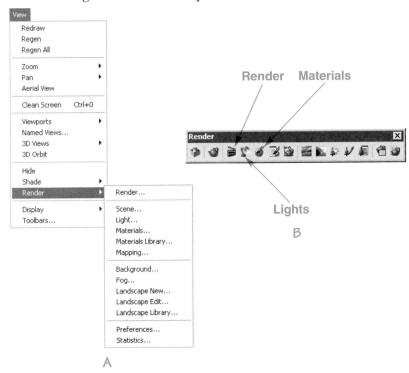

## The **Render** Dialog Box

To render the drawing, first open the **Render** dialog box with the **RENDER** command. See **Figure 26-5.** This dialog box is opened by selecting **Render...** from the **Render** cascading menu in the **View** pull-down menu, picking the **Render** button on the **Render** toolbar, or entering rr or render at the Command prompt. The **Render** dialog box is the "control center" for the type of rendering created, rendering procedures, and rendering options. It is also where the rendering is initiated.

The **Rendering Options** area in the lower-right corner of the **Render** dialog box contains four options to refine the rendering. Which check boxes are available depends on the selected rendering type, which is discussed later in this section. The rendering options are:

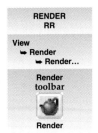

RENDER
RR

View
➥ Render
　➥ Render...

Render
toolbar

Render

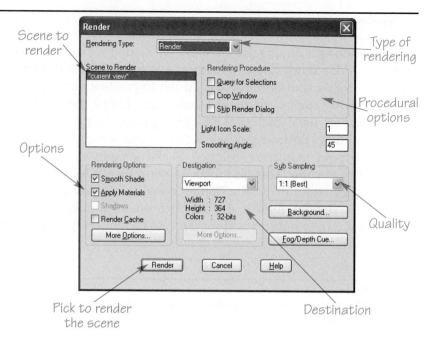

**Figure 26-5.**
The **Render** dialog box contains settings for creating renderings.

Scene to render

Options

Pick to render the scene

Type of rendering

Procedural options

Quality

Destination

- **Smooth Shade.** When this check box is checked, faceted surfaces, such as curved objects, are smoothed during the rendering process.
- **Apply Materials.** When materials are assigned in the scene, checking this check box renders the materials. If unchecked, the materials are not rendered. This option is ignored when the rendering type is **Render**.
- **Shadows.** This option applies shadows in the scene when the rendering type is **Photo Real** or **Photo Raytrace**. Shadows only appear if lights are added to the drawing and those lights are configured to cast shadows.
- **Render Cache.** Checking this check box sends rendering information to a *cache file,* or temporary storage, on the hard drive. The first time a rendering is created, the renderable objects are "cached" so AutoCAD can render them faster the next time. Only the geometry that has been modified is re-rendered the next time the scene is rendered.

Picking the **More Options...** button accesses different options for each of the rendering types. The options available for each rendering type are described in the sections that follow.

Before you render a scene, you need to set the type of rendering that will be created. You can select from the **Render, Photo Real,** and **Photo Raytrace** rendering types. At the top of the **Render** dialog box is the **Rendering Type:** drop-down list. This list contains the three rendering types. The default rendering type is **Photo Real**.

Each rendering type has options to improve the rendering quality. These options are found by picking the **More Options...** button in the **Rendering Options** area of the dialog box. The options available vary based on which rendering type is selected.

## Render *Rendering Type*

The **Render** rendering type produces the lowest-quality rendering. The scene is rendered using the object colors. Any materials assigned in the scene are ignored and not rendered. This rendering type also does not add shadows. The **Shadows** check box in the **Rendering Options** area of the **Render** dialog box is grayed out. Selecting the **More Options...** button displays the **Render Options** dialog box for the **Render** rendering type. See **Figure 26-6.** You can set the type of shading and control how faces are calculated. These options are:

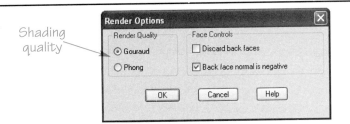

Figure 26-6.
The **Render Options** dialog box for the **Render** rendering type.

Shading quality

Render Options

Render Quality
- ● Gouraud
- ○ Phong

Face Controls
- ☐ Discard back faces
- ☑ Back face normal is negative

OK    Cancel    Help

- **Phong.** This type of shading calculates the light intensity at each pixel in the rendering. This creates a rendering with realistic lighting.
- **Gouraud.** This type of shading calculates light intensity at each vertex in the model. The light intensity between the vertices is then estimated. This option produces a less realistic rendering than the **Phong** option.
- **Discard back faces.** When this option is checked, AutoCAD does not calculate or render faces hidden from view. Using this option can speed up rendering time for large scenes.
- **Back face normal is negative.** A *normal* is a vector perpendicular to a given face. When creating 3D geometry in AutoCAD, the face that points toward the viewer is considered the *front face normal* and is positive. The *back face normal* is the face of the object pointing away from the viewer and is negative. When this check box is checked, AutoCAD reverses the normal. When this option is on, back faces are the faces closest to the view.

The **Render** rendering type provides a quick rendering. This is helpful after lighting is added and you are trying to adjust the light sources. **Figure 26-7** shows an example of a rendering created with the **Render** rendering type.

Figure 26-7.
The house project rendered with the **Render** rendering type. Notice shadows and materials are not displayed, but the colors of the objects are rendered.

## Photo Real *Rendering Type*

The **Photo Real** rendering type is the default type. It can render materials and provides a more realistic rendering than the **Render** rendering type. If lights are added to the scene, this rendering type can produce shadows in the rendering. AutoCAD must calculate the materials and lights to create a realistic rendering. As a result, the **Photo Real** rendering type can take much longer to render than the **Render** rendering type.

Selecting the **More Options...** button displays the **Render Options** dialog box for the **Photo Real** rendering type. See **Figure 26-8.** The rendering options for the **Photo Real** rendering type are:

**Figure 26-8.**
The **Photo Real Render Options** dialog box for the **Photo Real** rendering type.

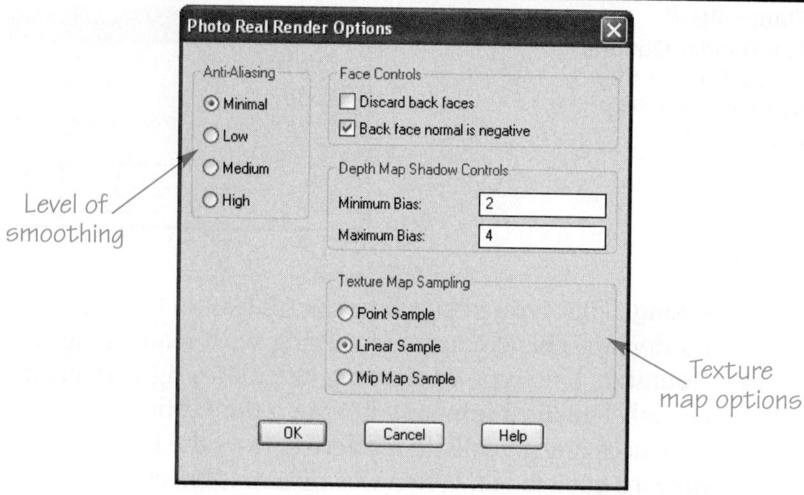

Level of smoothing

Texture map options

- **Anti-Aliasing.** *Antialiasing* is the process of smoothing the jagged edges that can appear on text and images, especially at lower resolutions. AutoCAD provides four levels of antialiasing, from minimal to high. Each successive level requires more time to render. The four levels are:
  - **Minimal.** This level of antialiasing requires the least amount of time to calculate and render. This option instructs AutoCAD to use only horizontal antialiasing.
  - **Low.** This level of antialiasing uses horizontal antialiasing with four shading samples per pixel. A *shading sample* is a variety of colors and shades used to create a smoother edge. This option requires more time to calculate and render than the **Minimal** option.
  - **Medium.** This level of antialiasing uses horizontal antialiasing and up to nine shading samples per pixel. This option requires more time to calculate and render than the **Minimal** and **Low** options.
  - **High.** This level of antialiasing uses horizontal antialiasing and up to 16 shading samples per pixel. This option requires the longest amount of time to calculate and render.
- **Face Controls.** The options in this area are the same as those found with the **Render** rendering type discussed in the previous section.
- **Depth Map Shadow Controls.** The settings in this area control the location of shadows in relation to the shadow-casting objects. These controls prevent "detached" shadows in the rendering. The higher the value for each option, the greater the distance between the shadow and the object.
  - **Minimum Bias.** The default value for this text box is 2. Generally, a value no greater than 20 should be used.
  - **Maximum Bias.** This text box default setting is 4. Generally, this value should be no more than 10 greater than the minimum bias value.
- **Texture Map Sampling.** The settings in this area determine how a mapped material is sampled when projected onto an object smaller than the texture material. A "sampling" of the mapped material is taken in order to map the material to the object correctly. The options in this area are:
  - **Point Sample.** This sampling method selects a pixel within the bitmap that is nearest to a given pixel as the sample material. This option requires the shortest amount of time to calculate.
  - **Linear Sample.** This option selects four pixels nearest to a given pixel within the bitmap. An average of the four pixels is used as the sample material.

Figure 26-9.
The house project
from **Figure 26-7**
rendered with the
**Photo Real**
rendering type.
Notice materials are
applied and
shadows are
created.

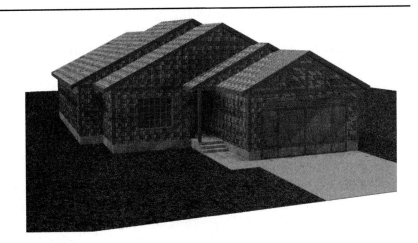

- **Mip Map Sample.** This sampling option calculates a pyramidal average based on square sample areas. This calculation is called mip. The average is used as the sample material. This option takes the most time to calculate.

**Figure 26-9** shows the scene from **Figure 26-7** rendered with the **Photo Real** rendering type.

## Photo Raytrace *Rendering Type*

The third rendering type is **Photo Raytrace**. This rendering type produces the most realistic rendering. It provides more options to control antialiasing and allows for raytraced lights. Raytracing calculates how light rays from a source bounce off reflective surfaces onto other objects. Raytrace calculations require tremendous computer resources and take much longer to process than other rendering types.

Picking the **More Options...** button in the **Rendering Options** area of the **Render** dialog box displays the **Render Options** dialog box for the **Photo Raytrace** rendering type. See **Figure 26-10**. In addition to the same options for the **Photo Real** rendering type, the **Photo Raytrace** rendering type includes two additional options. These are:

Figure 26-10.
The **Photo Raytrace**
**Render Options**
dialog box includes
the same options as
those for the **Photo**
**Real** rendering type,
plus two additional
areas to control
raytracing.

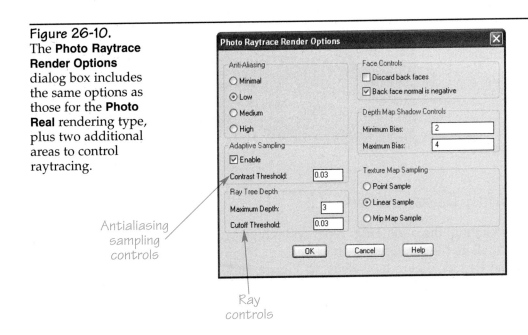

Antialiasing
sampling
controls

Ray
controls

- **Adaptive Sampling.** The settings in this area allow AutoCAD to process fewer samples than specified in the **Anti-Aliasing** area to achieve an acceptable rendering. This area is grayed out if antialiasing is set to **Minimal**.
  - **Enable.** Checking this check box turns on adaptive sampling.
  - **Contrast Threshold.** This text box sets the number of samples needed to arrive at the specified antialiasing level. A low threshold value uses small differences between the initial sample. This forces more samples to be taken. With a higher threshold value, differences in the initial sample must be greater to force more sampling. The valid values are 0.0 up to 1.0.
- **Ray Tree Depth.** As a ray bounces from one object to the next, it "branches" from the light source. Thus, the settings in this area control the "ray tree." This area includes two options that control how far a light ray can reflect off of an object.
  - **Maximum Depth.** This setting determines the maximum distance a light ray can bounce from a surface. If the light ray reflects off of an object and does not encounter another reflective surface before the **Maximum Depth:** value is reached, the light ray is terminated. The higher the value, the more accurate the rendering. The largest value is 9999, but never use this value. This will take a considerable amount of time to render. Generally, values between 3 and 10 produce quality renderings without taxing the system too much.
  - **Cutoff Threshold.** This setting determines the percentage that a branch must add to the last pixel in the branch in order for the ray to continue. A value of .10 indicates that 10% of the branch must be added to the end of the branch in order for the ray to continue. If after adding 10% the ray does not encounter another object, the ray is terminated at the total branch length plus the 10% length.

**Figure 26-11** shows the scene from **Figure 26-7** rendered with the **Photo Raytrace** rendering type.

**Figure 26-11.**
The house project from **Figure 26-7** rendered with the **Photo Raytrace** rendering type. Notice the difference in shadows and "resolution" of materials.

## Rendering Destination

After setting the rendering type and adjusting the options, you must tell AutoCAD where the rendering is to be shown. The location is set in the **Destination** area of the **Render** dialog box. Refer to **Figure 26-5.** You can specify to show the rendered scene in the current viewport or in the **Render Window**, or you can save the rendering to a file. The **Destination** area contains a drop-down list with these three options.

## Viewport *option*

The default destination is the current viewport. When the **Viewport** option is selected, AutoCAD displays the rendered scene in the current viewport, whether the viewport is in model or layout space. A rendering displayed in a viewport can be printed by using the **As Displayed** option in the **Plot** dialog box.

Rendering to a viewport is intended to help quickly visualize the scene so adjustments can be made as needed. If a viewport displays the rendered scene, use the **REGEN** command to clear the rendering from the viewport.

## Render Window *option*

If the **Render Window** option is selected, AutoCAD loads the ObjectARX application **Render**. This application is the "engine" that renders the scene. Once the rendering is initiated, AutoCAD displays the **Render Window** and renders the scene in the window. See **Figure 26-12.**

A rendering created in the **Render Window** can be saved as an image file and printed. To save the rendering, pick the **Save** button on the toolbar or **Save...** in the **File** pull-down menu of the **Render Window**. The only file type available is bitmap (BMP). Pick the **Copy** button on the toolbar or **Copy** in the **Edit** pull-down menu to copy the image to the Windows Clipboard for pasting into another program. Picking the **Options** button on the toolbar or **Options...** in the **File** pull-down menu allows you to specify the size and color depth of renderings created in the window.

**Figure 26-12.**
A rendering can be created in the **Render Window**, then saved, printed, or copied to the Windows Clipboard.

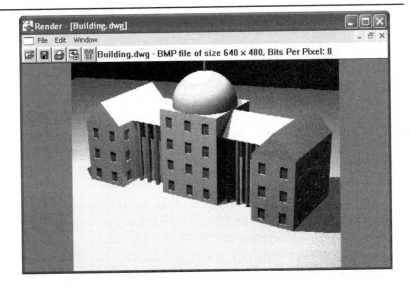

## File *option*

When **File** is selected as the destination for the rendering, AutoCAD saves the rendered scene to an image file. The rendering cannot be viewed in AutoCAD unless the saved image is brought back into AutoCAD using the **IMAGE** command. When **File** is selected, the **More Options...** button is enabled. Selecting the **More Options...** button displays the **File Output Configuration** dialog box. This dialog box allows you to specify what type of image file is saved and contains options for controlling the image file. See **Figure 26-13.**

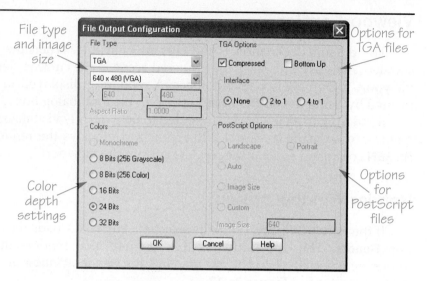

**Figure 26-13.**
The **File Output Configuration** dialog box allows you to specify the type of image file, the dimensions in pixels, and the color depth used to render the drawing.

*File type and image size*

*Options for TGA files*

*Color depth settings*

*Options for PostScript files*

The **File Output Configuration** dialog box contains four areas with options to control the image file. The options that are available depend on the selected file type. These areas and their options are:

- **File Type area.** This area is used to specify the type of file and the size of the image. The available file types are BMP, PCX, PostScript, TGA, and TIFF. Select the type of file to create from the upper drop-down list in this area. The **BMP** and **PCX** options result in lower-quality renderings. The lower drop-down list in this area allows you to specify the image size. The size is measured as "pixels wide" by "pixels tall." The drop-down list contains many common image sizes. A user-defined "size" is also available. When this is selected, the **X:** and **Y:** text boxes are enabled so a custom image size can be specified.

- **Colors area.** This area allows you to specify the color depth, or number of colors, AutoCAD can use to create a rendering. Depending on the selected file type, some options are unavailable.

- **TGA Options area.** The options contained in this area are only available when **TGA** is selected as the file type. Check the **Compressed** check box to apply file compression to the saved image. Checking the **Bottom Up** check box instructs AutoCAD to scan the scene from the bottom left instead of the top left. Options are also available for creating an interlaced image file.

- **PostScript Options area.** The options in this area are available when **PostScript** is selected as the file type. The file can be created with the image in landscape or portrait orientation. Also, image sizing options are available. The **Auto** option automatically scales the image. The **Image Size** option uses the exact image size. The **Custom** option allows you to enter the image size in pixels.

## Rendering the Model

After you have selected the rendering type, adjusted options, and specified where the rendering will be created, the scene can be rendered. Pick the **Render** button at the bottom of the **Render** dialog box. If the destination is **File**, AutoCAD displays the **Rendering File** dialog box. This is where you specify a file name and location for the saved image. AutoCAD then processes and renders the scene. If the destination is **Viewport** or **Render Window**, the rendering is displayed. If the destination is **File**, the rendered image is saved without being displayed.

## Printing a Viewport Rendering

A model space viewport in layout space can be set up to print a rendered view. Select the floating viewport and right-click to display the shortcut menu. Then, select the **Rendered** option from the **Shade Plot** cascading menu.

If plotting the rendering from model space, open the **Plot** dialog box. Then, select the **Rendered** option in the **Shade plot:** drop-down list in the **Shaded viewport options** area. If the viewport currently displays a rendered view, you can also use the **As Displayed** option.

# Adding Materials

A *material* in AutoCAD is a definition of the color, surface characteristics, and type of finish or design applied to 3D geometry. AutoCAD includes some basic materials in a material library. A *material library* is a collection of material definitions saved to a file. Materials can be recalled from a material library so they do not have to be recreated. Materials can also be created from scratch and saved to a material library. As part of a material definition, an image or design can be placed, or "mapped," onto the material.

The material library supplied with AutoCAD contains a wide variety of materials. These materials are suitable for architectural, civil, and mechanical applications. By applying even the most basic materials in the AutoCAD material library, the realism of your drawing is increased.

## Managing Material Definitions

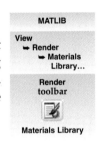

MATLIB

View
➥ Render
  ➥ Materials
    Library...

Render
toolbar

Materials Library

The **Materials Library** dialog box is used to manage materials in the current drawing and material library. See **Figure 26-14.** This dialog box is opened by selecting **Materials Library...** from the **Render** cascading menu in the **View** pull-down menu, picking the **Materials Library** button on the **Render** toolbar, or entering matlib at the Command prompt.

**Figure 26-14.**
The **Materials Library** dialog box lists the materials available in the current drawing and those in the current library. You can view a preview of the selected material and import a material into the drawing.

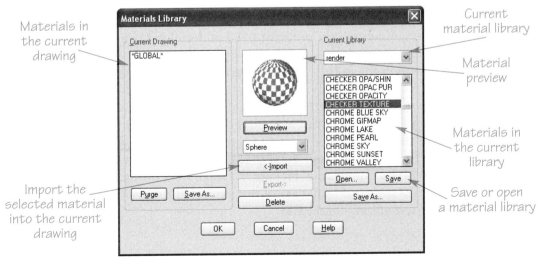

The **Current Drawing** area of the **Material Library** dialog box lists all materials loaded into the current drawing. The *GLOBAL* "material" in this list is rendered as if no material is assigned to an object. This "material" cannot be assigned to objects. When a material is imported into the drawing, the list is updated to display the material. If materials in the list are not assigned in the drawing, they can be removed from the drawing by picking the **Purge** button.

The drop-down list in the **Current Library** area contains any loaded material libraries. The current material library is selected in the drop-down list. The default material library file is Render. The materials in the current library are listed below the drop-down list. Material library files have the MLI file extension. Picking the **Open...** button in the **Current Library** area allows you to load a saved material library file.

The middle area of the **Materials Library** dialog box is used to preview materials, import materials into the drawing, and export materials from the drawing into the current library. Picking the **Preview** button renders a small preview image of the material selected in either the **Current Library** area or in the **Current Drawing** area. The rendered preview appears in the square above the **Preview** button. Below the button is a drop-down list from which you can select **Sphere** or **Cube**. This specifies the shape of the object in the preview.

To make a material available in the current drawing, select the material name in the list in the **Current Library** area. Then, pick the **<-Import** button. The material is loaded into the current drawing and its name appears in the list in the **Current Drawing** area. A material cannot be assigned to an object until it is imported into the current drawing.

## Creating a Material Library

As you make changes to the current material library, you will want to save it or create a new library. A new library can also be created from only the materials in the current drawing. The **Materials Library** dialog box is used to save or create a material library.

To save all material definitions in the current drawing as a new library, pick the **Save As...** button in the **Current Drawing** area. The **Library File** dialog box appears. This is a standard Windows "save as" dialog box. The only file type available is the MLI file type. Name the library file and specify a location. Then, pick the **Save** button to save the file.

If a material definition is created or modified, you can add it to the current material library. Highlight the material name in the list in the **Current Drawing** area. Then, pick the **Export->** button. The material definition is added to the current material library. If a material with the same name already exists in the current material library, a dialog box appears allowing you to rename the material being added or overwrite the existing definition.

The **Delete** button in the middle of the **Materials Library** dialog box permanently removes the selected material. If the material is selected in the **Current Library** area, the material is removed from the current material library. If the material is selected in the **Current Drawing** area, the material is removed from the current drawing.

When changes are made to the current material library, they are not automatically saved to file. The **Save** button in the **Current Library** area saves the current material library to file with its same name. Picking the **Save As...** button opens the **Library File** dialog box. This is the same "save as" dialog box used to save the materials in the current drawing to a material library file.

# Exercise 26-2

- Start a drawing using one of your templates.
- Create a layer named Floor and draw a 10′ × 10′ floor with the **3DFACE** command.
- Create a door and window by referring to projects P25-1 and P25-2 from Chapter 25. Draw the door, door frame, and window frame on a layer named Frame. Create a layer named Glass for the faces used for the window glass.
- Create a layer named Walls, and use the **3DFACE** command to draw walls around the door and window. Refer to the drawings shown.
- Create a layer named Table, and use solids to construct the table shown below. Make the table 3′ × 3′ and 32″ high with 2″ × 2″ legs. Union the legs and the tabletop together.
- Create a layer named Chair and use solids to construct the chair shown below. Union the legs, seat, and back together. Add a cushion to the chair on a Cushion layer but do not union it to the chair.
- Add a drinking glass to the top of the table on a layer named Cup.
- Add a bowl on the table on a layer named Bowl.
- Access the **Materials Library** dialog box and import the following materials:
  - Copper
  - Glass
  - Mottled Marble
  - Red Gouraud
  - Semicircle Patrn
  - Stitched Pattern
  - White Plastic
  - Wood - White Ash
  - Wood Inlay - B
- Save the drawing as ex26-2.

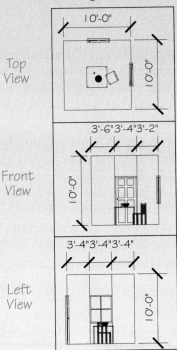

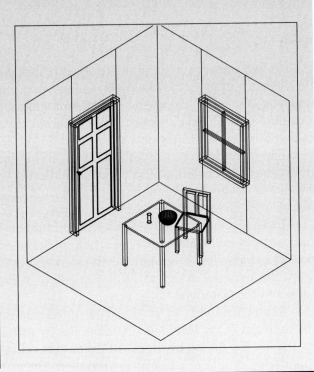

## Applying Materials

RMAT

View
➥ Render
➥ Materials...

Render
toolbar

Materials

Once materials are loaded into the current drawing, they are assigned to objects. The **Materials** dialog box is used to assign materials to geometry, **Figure 26-15.** To access this dialog box, select **Materials...** from the **Render** cascading menu in the **View** pull-down menu, pick the **Materials** button on the **Render** toolbar, or enter rmat at the Command prompt.

The **Materials** dialog box includes a list of materials in the current drawing. This list is the same list that appears in the **Current Drawing** area of the **Materials Library** dialog box. Only materials that appear in this list can be assigned to geometry in the drawing. To open the **Materials Library** dialog box, you can pick the **Materials Library...** button in the **Materials** dialog box.

Figure 26-15.
The **Materials** dialog box is used to assign materials to objects. It is also the "starting point" for creating new materials or modifying existing materials.

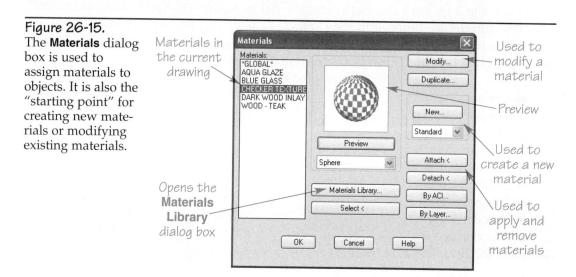

Materials in the current drawing

Opens the **Materials Library** dialog box

Used to modify a material

Preview

Used to create a new material

Used to apply and remove materials

To find out which material is currently assigned to an object in the drawing, pick the **Select** button in the **Materials** dialog box. The dialog box is temporarily hidden and you can select an object. The **Materials** dialog box is then redisplayed with the material assigned to the object highlighted in the list. A message at the bottom of the dialog box also indicates how the material is attached to the object.

There are three basic methods that can be used to apply a material to objects in the scene. You can choose to pick individual objects using the cursor. You can also choose to assign a material to all objects on a given layer. Finally, you can assign all objects of a given color the same material.

To assign a material by picking individual objects, you must first select the material to apply in the **Materials:** list. Then, pick the **Attach** button in the **Materials** dialog box. The dialog box is temporarily hidden and you can select the objects to which you want the material assigned. When finished picking objects, press the [Enter] key to return to the **Materials** dialog box.

To attach a material to all objects of the same color, you do *not* need to first select the material in the **Materials:** list. Pick the **By ACI...** button in the **Materials** dialog box to display the **Attach by AutoCAD Color Index** dialog box, **Figure 26-16.** On the left of this dialog box is a list of all materials in the current drawing. On the right of the dialog box is a list of all AutoCAD Color Index (ACI) numbers, from 1 to 255. Select a material on the left and a color on the right. Then, pick the **Attach->** button in the middle of the dialog box to assign the material to the color. The material name now appears next to the ACI number. Continue assigning materials as needed. Then, pick the **OK** button to return to the **Materials** dialog box.

Figure 26-16.
The **Attach by AutoCAD Color Index** dialog box is used to assign a material to all objects of the same color.

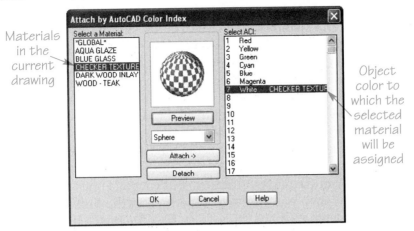

To assign a material to all objects on a given layer, pick the **By Layer...** button in the **Materials** dialog box. You do *not* need to first select a material. The **Attach by Layer** dialog box is displayed, **Figure 26-17.** The options in this dialog box are similar to those in the **Attach by AutoCAD Color Index** dialog box. On the left of the dialog box is a list of all materials in the current drawing. On the right is a list of all layers in the drawing. Select a material on the left and a layer on the right. Then, pick the **Attach->** button. The material name now appears next to the layer name. Continue assigning materials as needed. Then, pick the **OK** button to return to the **Materials** dialog box.

If an object has a material assigned to it, you can remove the material by picking the **Detach** button in the **Materials** dialog box. The dialog box is closed and you can select objects from which to detach any assigned materials. If materials are assigned by color or layer, the material must be detached by color or layer. The **Attach by AutoCAD Color Index** and **Attach by Layer** dialog boxes each have a **Detach** button. These buttons are used to detach by color or detach by layer.

Figure 26-17.
The **Attach by Layer** dialog box is used to assign a material to all objects on the same layer.

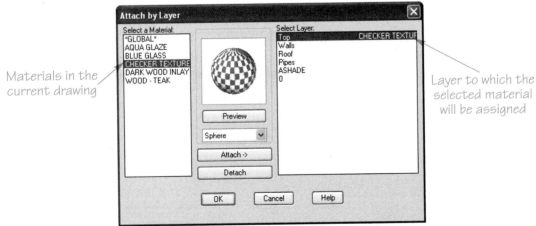

# Modifying and Creating Materials

There may be times when the materials supplied in the default material library do not meet your needs. Existing materials can be customized. In addition, new materials can be created. The **Materials** dialog box is the starting point for modifying an existing material or defining a new material.

To change the definition of an existing material, first import the material into the drawing. Then, in the **Materials** dialog box, select the material name and pick the **Modify...** button. The **Modify Material** dialog box is displayed, **Figure 26-18**. Adjust the material definition as needed. When finished modifying the material, pick the **OK** button to return to the **Materials** dialog box.

You can create a new material from scratch based on one of four basic material types. The basic material types are standard, granite, marble, and wood. These material types share many of the same attributes, but each also has its own unique attributes. To create a new material, first select the type in the drop-down list below the **New...** button in the **Materials** dialog box. Then, pick the **New...** button. A **New Material** dialog box is displayed. See **Figure 26-19**.

**Figure 26-18.**
The **Modify Material** dialog box is used to modify an existing material.

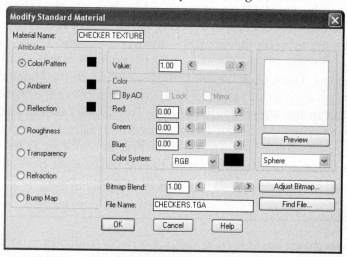

**Figure 26-19.**
The **New Standard Material** dialog box is used to create a new standard material.

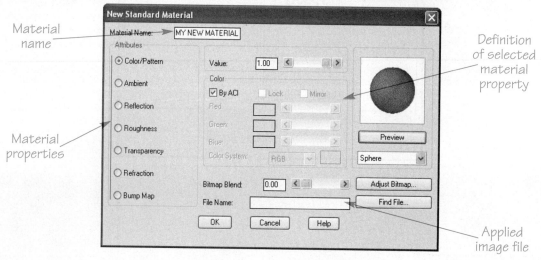

Material name

Material properties

Definition of selected material property

Applied image file

First, name the new material in the **Material Name:** text box. Use a logical name that indicates what the material represents, such as GREEN BOTTLE or RUSTED METAL. After the material is named, you must adjust the material properties. The material properties define how the material appears when rendered. AutoCAD calls material properties *attributes.* As you adjust material attributes, use the **Preview** button to view a sample of the material.

Some material attributes can have an image file applied to create special effects. This is called *material mapping.* When an image is applied to an attribute and the material is applied to an object, mapping coordinates are used to orient the image on the object. *Mapping coordinates* are instructions on how an image or material is to be placed. If an image is specified at the bottom of the **New Material** dialog box, mapping coordinates can be adjusted by picking the **Adjust Bitmap...** button to display the **Adjust Material Bitmap Placement** dialog box.

## Exercise 26-3

- ◆ Open ex26-2.
- ◆ Open the **Materials** dialog box.
- ◆ Assign the following materials to the objects indicated below. Attach some materials directly to objects, assign some materials to layers, and assign other materials by the AutoCAD color index.
  - ◆ Copper (Assign to the doorknob)
  - ◆ Glass (Assign to the glass and window glazing)
  - ◆ Mottled Marble (Assign to the table)
  - ◆ Red Gouraud (Assign to the bowl)
  - ◆ Semicircle Patrn (Assign to the walls)
  - ◆ Stitched Pattern (Assign to the chair cushion)
  - ◆ White Plastic (Assign to the chair)
  - ◆ Wood - White Ash (Assign to the door and frames)
  - ◆ Wood Inlay - B (Assign to the floor)
- ◆ Render the drawing with the **Render** rendering type. Set the destination as the viewport.
- ◆ Render the drawing with the **Photo Raytrace** rendering type. Set the destination as the **Render Window**. Make sure the **Apply Materials** check box is checked.
- ◆ Do a raytrace rendering again, this time with the destination set as a file named ex26-3.bmp.
- ◆ Save the drawing as ex26-3.

# Lighting the Model

Lighting is a very important part of a quality rendering. Lights can cast shadows and provide a realistic atmosphere in the rendering process. Without lighting, there are no shadows in the scene. Shadows are needed to "ground" objects, thus preventing "floating" objects. There are four types of lights in AutoCAD. Lighting can be set with ambient light, distant lights, point lights, and spotlights. Lights, other than ambient, are represented in a viewport by icons. See **Figure 26-20.**

*Ambient light* is similar to natural outdoor light just before sunrise. It has the same intensity everywhere in the drawing. All geometry in the scene receives the same amount of ambient light. Ambient light cannot create highlights or shadows. The intensity of the ambient light can be adjusted. However, do *not* use ambient light to provide the primary illumination for a scene. Ambient light can be turned off by setting the intensity to 0. The renderings you have created so far are lighted with only ambient light and the default AutoCAD light source. Ambient light does *not* have an icon representation in the viewports.

A *point light* is a light source that projects light rays in every direction, similar to a household lightbulb. The light rays are not parallel. The intensity of a point light *attenuates,* or "falls off," over distance. This means that the effect the light has on an object is less the farther the object is from the light. The intensity of a point light can be adjusted. In addition, a point light can be placed at any location in the drawing.

A *distant light* is a light source that projects parallel light rays in one direction. This is very similar to sunlight. The sun is so far from Earth that when sunlight rays arrive, they are essentially parallel. The intensity of a distant light can be adjusted. In addition, a distant light can be placed at any location in the drawing.

A *spotlight* is a light source that projects light rays in one direction. Unlike a distant light, the light rays from a spotlight are not parallel. They are projected in a cone shape. Spotlights have a hotspot and a falloff. The *hotspot* is in the center of the light's cone and represents the brightest part of the light. Light rays outside the hotspot attenuate to the edge of the light's cone. This area is called the *falloff.* A spotlight provides no illumination outside the falloff cone. The intensity of a spotlight can be adjusted. In addition, a spotlight can be placed at any location in the drawing.

**Figure 26-20.**
When placing lights in a drawing, an icon representing the light is displayed. Each light, with the exception of ambient light, has a unique symbol representing the type of light.

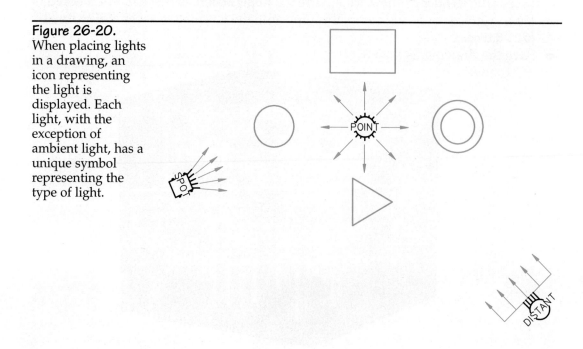

Before adding lights, think about your model and how lights can be used to enhance specific design features. Some things to consider may be the brightness of lights, the number of lights used, whether the lights cast shadows or not, and the color of the lights. You can add as many lights to a drawing as you need. All lights can be turned on or off as needed.

Lights are added to the drawing using the **Lights** dialog box, **Figure 26-21.** Open this dialog box by selecting **Light...** from the **Render** cascading menu in the **View** pull-down menu, picking the **Lights** button on the **Render** toolbar, or entering light at the Command prompt.

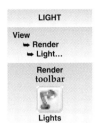

LIGHT

View
➡ Render
  ➡ Light...

Render
toolbar

Lights

### Figure 26-21.
The **Lights** dialog box contains settings for adjusting the ambient light source and for creating and modifying point lights, distant lights, and spotlights.

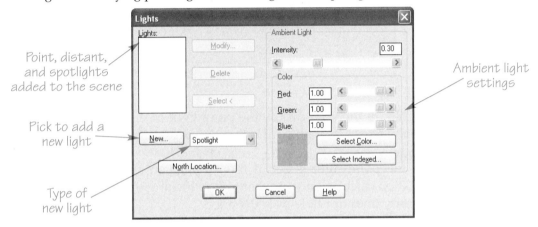

Point, distant, and spotlights added to the scene

Pick to add a new light

Type of new light

Ambient light settings

## Setting Ambient Light

The **Ambient Light** area of the **Lights** dialog box contains settings to control ambient light. The slider bar and text box at the top of this area set the intensity of ambient light. The higher the value, the brighter the light. Turn off ambient light by setting the intensity to 0.

By adjusting the **Red, Green**, and **Blue** slider bars, the color of ambient light can be changed. The **Select Color...** and the **Select Indexed...** buttons also can be used to select a predefined color for ambient light. There can only be one ambient light source in a drawing.

## Adding a Point Light

To create a point light, open the **Lights** dialog box. Select **Point Light** from the drop-down list next to the **New...** button. Then, pick the **New...** button. The **New Point Light** dialog box is displayed, **Figure 26-22.**

Name the point light in the **Light Name:** text box. The name can be a total of eight characters. Spaces are not allowed in the light name.

The intensity of the point light is controlled with the slider bar and text box. These settings are similar to those for ambient light. The higher the value, the brighter the light.

By default, AutoCAD creates the light in the center of the current viewport. To change the location, pick the **Modify** button in the **Position** area. The dialog box is temporarily hidden and you can pick a new location. When the location is picked, the dialog box is redisplayed.

**Figure 26-22.**
The **New Point Light** dialog box is used to create a new point light.

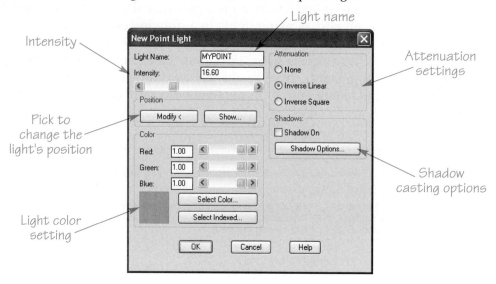

Intensity

Pick to change the light's position

Light color setting

Light name

Attenuation settings

Shadow casting options

You can set the color of the light cast by the point light in the **Color** area. Use the slider bars, the **Select Color...** button, or the **Select Indexed...** button to adjust the color for the point light.

Attenuation for the point light is set in the **Attenuation** area. Select the radio button for the attenuation calculation you want to use. Picking the **None** radio button means the light intensity does not fade over distance.

For the point light to cast shadows in the drawing, the **Shadow On** check box must be checked. Picking the **Shadow Options...** button displays a dialog box where you can make adjustments to the shadows.

When all settings are made in the **New Point Light** dialog box, press the **OK** button. The light is created and you are returned to the **Lights** dialog box. The new light name is listed in the **Lights:** list. To modify the light, select it from the list and pick the **Modify** button. The "modify" dialog box that is displayed is the same as the "new" dialog box.

**Professional Tip**

If you want shadows rendered in the scene, the shadows must be turned on for each light that will cast a shadow and the **Shadows** check box must be selected in the **Render** dialog box.

## Adding a Distant Light

To create a distant light, open the **Lights** dialog box. Select **Distant Light** from the drop-down list next to the **New...** button. Then, pick the **New...** button. The **New Distant Light** dialog box is displayed, **Figure 26-23.**

Name the distant light in the **Light Name:** text box. The name can be a maximum of eight characters with no spaces. The intensity, color, and shadow settings are the same as those for a point light.

Figure 26-23.
The **New Distant Light** dialog box is used to create a new distant light. It is also used to access the **Sun Angle Calculator** dialog box.

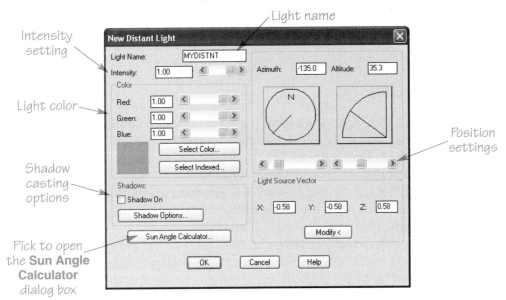

The right-hand side of the **New Distant Light** dialog box is used to define the orientation of the light in the viewport. The **Azimuth** and **Altitude** settings determine the location of the distant light relative to the current UCS. The *azimuth* is the location in degrees from the north position. The *altitude* is the angular location up from the XY plane of the current UCS. Enter values in the text boxes or pick on the image tiles. The light source vector, or direction of travel from the light, is indicated in the **Light Source Vector** area. The vector settings and azimuth/altitude settings are interrelated.

If using the distant light to simulate the sun, you may want to replicate the sun's position at an exact date and time for an actual geographic location. Select the **Sun Angle Calculator...** button to display the **Sun Angle Calculator** dialog box. See **Figure 26-24.** Enter the date, time, and geographic location. When all settings are entered, pick the **OK** button to close the **Sun Angle Calculator** dialog box and load the settings in the **New Distant Light** dialog box. You can also load settings for a predefined location by picking the **Geographic Location...** button in the **Sun Angle Calculator** dialog box.

Figure 26-24.
The **Sun Angle Calculator** dialog box can be used to set a distant light to simulate light from the sun at a specific time, date, and place.

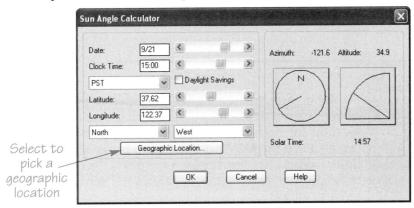

When all settings are made in the **New Distant Light** dialog box, press the **OK** button. The light is created and you are returned to the **Lights** dialog box. As with the point light, the distant light is added to the center of the current viewport. The new light name is listed in the **Lights:** list. To modify the light or the location, select it from the list and pick the **Modify...** button. The "modify" dialog box is the same as the "new" dialog box.

## Adding a Spotlight

To create a spotlight, open the **Lights** dialog box. Select **Spotlight** from the drop-down list next to the **New...** button. Then, pick the **New...** button. The **New Spotlight** dialog box is displayed, **Figure 26-25.** This dialog box is similar to the **New Point Light** dialog box, except there are two additional settings.

At the top right of the dialog box are the **Hotspot:** and **Falloff:** sliders and text boxes. These settings determine the angle of the cone for the hotspot and falloff. The falloff angle cannot be less than the hotspot angle.

The default location for the spotlight is the center of the viewport pointed away from your eye. When modifying the location of the spotlight, you are first prompted for the target point. The *target* is the point at which the light is aimed. Then, you are prompted for the light location. Try using the **.xy** filter when working in a top view and adjusting the Z height for the target and light location.

When all settings are made in the **New Spotlight** dialog box, pick the **OK** button. The light is created and you are returned to the **Lights** dialog box. The new light name is listed in the **Lights:** list. To modify the light or location, select it from the list and pick the **Modify** button. The "modify" dialog box is the same as the "new" dialog box.

**Figure 26-25.**
The **New Spotlight** dialog box is used to create a new spotlight and includes settings for hotspot and falloff.

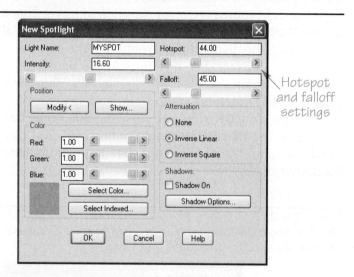

Hotspot and falloff settings

**Professional Tip**

By default, all new lights are added to the center of the current viewport. As mentioned earlier, you can modify the location for each light through the **Lights** dialog box. You can also use the **MOVE** command to move the location of a light. Work in multiple viewports set to different orthographic and isometric views to see the results of moving a light.

Architectural Drafting Using AutoCAD

## Exercise 26-4

◆ Open ex26-3.

◆ Using the **Lights** dialog box, turn off the ambient light by adjusting the slider to a value of 0.

◆ Add a point light centered above the table approximately 8′ from the floor. Turn on shadow casting for the light. In the **Render** dialog box, turn on the **Shadows** check box. Create a raytrace rendering with shadows in the **Render Window**.

◆ Add a distant light to the scene. Use your hometown, today's date, and the current time for the position and direction of the distant light. Turn on shadow casting for the light. Create a raytrace rendering with shadows in the **Render Window**.

◆ Add a spotlight pointed between the glass and bowl on the table. Turn on shadow casting for the light. Also, set the light color to a deep green. Create a raytrace rendering with shadows in the **Render Window**.

◆ Make any adjustments to the lights as needed. Then, save a raytrace rendering with shadows to a file named ex26-4.bmp.

◆ Save the drawing as ex26-4.

## Adjusting the Light Icon Scale

In some cases, the icon representing a light may be too small to be useful. You can change the size of the light icon when needed. This is done in the **Rendering Preferences** dialog box. You can also change the light icon scale in the **Render** dialog box. However, you must actually render the drawing to set the change. Open the **Rendering Preferences** dialog box by selecting **Preferences...** from the **Render** cascading menu in the **View** pull-down menu, picking the **Render Preferences** button on the **Render** toolbar, or by entering rpref or rpr at the Command prompt.

The **Rendering Preferences** dialog box is exactly the same as the **Render** dialog box, except you cannot render from it. See **Figure 26-26.** In the **Light Icon Scale:** text box, enter a scale for the light icon. Generally, the scale factor for the drawing is a good scale factor to use for the light icon. After the light icon scale is changed, pick **OK** to close the **Render Preferences** dialog box. *All* light icons in the drawing are updated to reflect the new size.

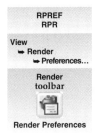

RPREF
RPR

View
➥ Render
   ➥ Preferences...

Render
toolbar

Render Preferences

**Figure 26-26.**
Changing the light
icon scale.

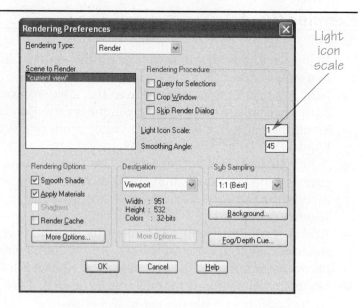

Light
icon
scale

# Creating Scenes

A scene in AutoCAD is similar to a photo studio. A *scene* consists of a named view and at least one light other than ambient. After a scene is defined and saved, it can be selected as the "object" to render. When a scene is rendered, the defined view is rendered regardless of what is currently shown in the current viewport.

Before a scene can be created, at least one named view and one light should be created. Use the **3DORBIT** or **VPOINT** command to obtain an appropriate view of your model. Then, save the view with a logical name. Create as many views as desired. Next, add lights to the drawing as needed.

After views are created and lights added, a scene can be defined. To define a scene, select **Scene...** from the **Render** cascading menu in the **View** pull-down menu, pick the **Scenes** button on the **Render** toolbar, or enter scene at the Command prompt. This displays the **Scenes** dialog box. See **Figure 26-27.**

Select the **New...** button to create a new scene. This displays the **New Scene** dialog box. See **Figure 26-28.** Enter a name in the **Scene Name:** text box at the top of the dialog box. Then, select one of the named views from the **Views** list at the left of the dialog box. You can also choose to use the current view. In this case, the view displayed in the viewport when the scene is rendered is used as the "named" view in the scene. Next, select the lights to include in the scene. Hold down the [Ctrl] key to pick multiple lights. You can also choose to use "all" lights. Many scenes with different light combinations can be created. Pick the **OK** button to add the new scene to the drawing.

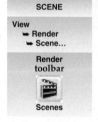

SCENE

View
➥ Render
  ➥ Scene...

Render
toolbar

Scenes

**Figure 26-27.**
The **Scenes** dialog
box is used to
manage defined
scenes.

Defined scenes

Pick to create
a new scene

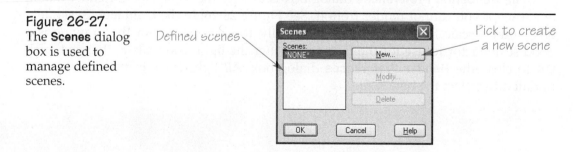

**Figure 26-28.**
The **New Scene** dialog box is used to define a scene.

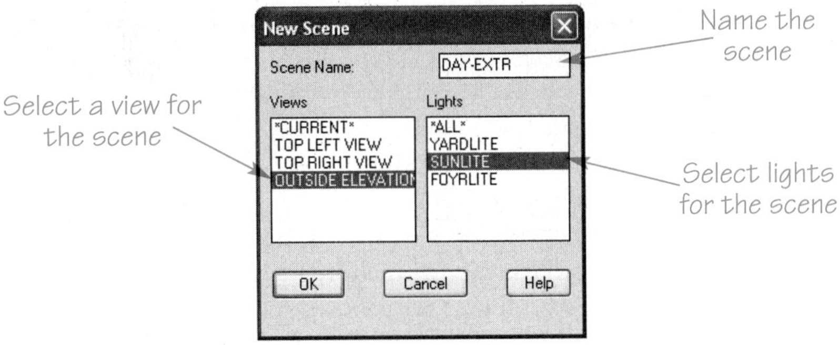

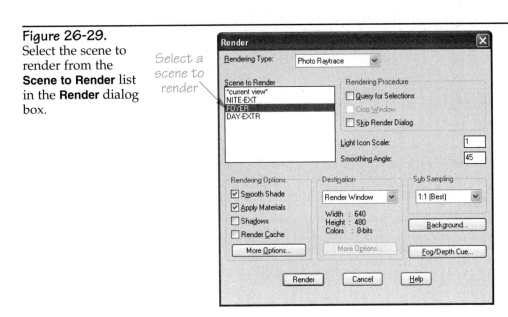

Name the scene

Select a view for the scene

Select lights for the scene

To render a scene, open the **Render** dialog box. Select the scene you would like to render from the **Scene to Render** list. See **Figure 26-29.** Make any adjustments needed in the **Render** dialog box and pick the **Render** button. AutoCAD renders the scene to the current destination. If the destination is set to **Viewport**, the view defined in the scene is rendered in the viewport, regardless of the current view in the viewport.

**Figure 26-29.**
Select the scene to render from the **Scene to Render** list in the **Render** dialog box.

Select a scene to render

## Exercise 26-5

◆ Open ex26-4.

◆ Create two named views similar to those shown below. Name one view Table View and the other Left View.

◆ Create a scene named Table displaying the table top, glass, and bowl. Use the spotlight and the point light.

◆ Create a scene named Left displaying the table, chair, and window from the left side of the room. Use the point light.

◆ Create raytrace renderings of both scenes. First render each to the **Render Window**, then to files named ex26-5a.bmp and ex26-5b.bmp.

◆ Save the drawing as ex26-5.

# Rendering Background

A *background* in AutoCAD is similar to a backdrop on a movie set. It provides an image or color behind the rendered objects. By default, the background is the color of AutoCAD's drawing area. A background can be a solid color, a gradient of colors, an image, or the color of the drawing area.

To change from the default background, select **Background...** from the **Render** cascading menu in the **View** pull-down menu, pick the **Background** button on the **Render** toolbar, or enter background at the Command prompt. The **Background** dialog box is displayed. See **Figure 26-30**.

At the top of the **Background** dialog box are the **Solid**, **Gradient**, **Image**, and **Merge** radio buttons. Pick the radio button corresponding to the type of background you want to use. The **Merge** option uses the background color of the AutoCAD drawing area as the background for the rendering. The other three options are described in the next sections. Use the **Preview** button to see a preview of the defined background.

The **Environment** area of the **Background** dialog box is used to specify what is reflected from the background by reflective surfaces. By default, the **Use Background** check box is checked. This specifies that reflective surfaces reflect the current background. However, if this check box is unchecked, you can select an image file that is reflected in place of the current background. The image is mapped to an invisible sphere surrounding the model. This is called the environment. Environmental reflections can only be seen in raytraced renderings.

**BACKGROUND**

View
➡ Render
➡ Background...

Render
toolbar

Background

---

**Figure 26-30.**
The **Background** dialog box is used to add a background to your model.

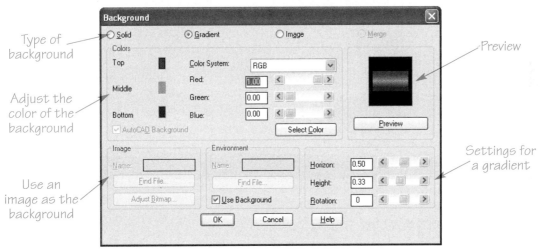

## Solid Background

When the **Background** dialog box is first opened, the default setting is **Solid** with the **AutoCAD Background** check box in the **Colors** area checked. With this check box checked, the background in the rendering is the same as the color of the drawing area. In effect, this is the same as selecting the **Merge** radio button. Uncheck the **AutoCAD Background** check box to choose a different solid color. Use the slider bars in the **Colors** area to adjust the background color.

## Gradient Background

A *gradient* background consists of two or three colors with a gradual transition between the colors. **Figure 26-31** displays a rendering using a three-color gradient. Pick the **Gradient** radio button to define a gradient background. The **Top**, **Middle**, and **Bottom** color swatches in the **Colors** area can be selected separately and adjusted using the slider bars. Additionally, the lower-right corner of the dialog box contains options for setting the gradient colors:

- **Horizon.** The value in this text box is a percentage that determines where the center of the gradient is to be placed. The slider bars or text box can be used to adjust this value.
- **Height.** The value in this text box is the percentage of the gradient dedicated to the middle color. If this value is 0, a two-color gradient of the bottom and top colors is created.
- **Rotation.** The value in the text box is measured in degrees and controls the angle at which the gradient is created.

**Figure 26-31.**
A three-color gradient background.

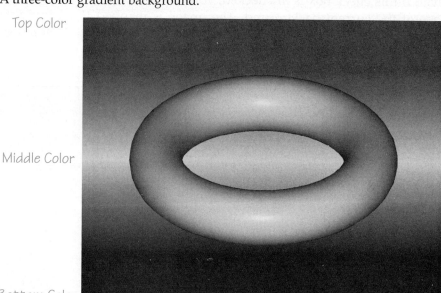

Top Color

Middle Color

Bottom Color

## Image Background

Picking the **Image** radio button allows you to use a bitmap image as a background. For example, you may want to use an image of an empty lot on which a building will be constructed. In this way, a 3D model of the proposed building can be created. The rendering then shows a realistic view of the proposed design on the existing property. **Figure 26-32** illustrates the use of a background image.

When the **Image** radio button is selected, the **Image** area in the lower-left corner of the dialog box is enabled. Pick the **Find File...** button to open the **Background Image** dialog box. This dialog box is a standard Windows file selection dialog box. Locate the image file and pick the **Open** button. The name and path of the image file now appear in the **Name:** text box in the **Image** area. Use the **Adjust Bitmap...** button to adjust the orientation of the background image.

**Figure 26-32.**
An image can be used as a background, such as the clouds shown in this rendering.

## Exercise 26-6

◆ Open ex26-5.
◆ Add a background using an image. Use one of the TGA images in the AutoCAD 2004 Textures folder as a background.
◆ Render the scene Left first to the **Render Window**, then to a file named ex26-6.bmp.
◆ Save the drawing as ex26-6.

## Fog

FOG

View
➡ Render
  ➡ Fog...

Render
toolbar

Fog

As you look far off into the distance, objects become obscured from the haze in the sky. This is considered to be *fog* in AutoCAD. Colors are used to represent the distance between your eye and the model. To use fog, select **Fog...** from the **Render** cascading menu in the **View** pull-down menu, pick the **Fog** button on the **Render** toolbar, or enter fog at the Command prompt. The **Fog/Depth Cue** dialog box is displayed. See **Figure 26-33.**

Figure 26-33.
The **Fog/Depth Cue** dialog box is used to enable and adjust fog.

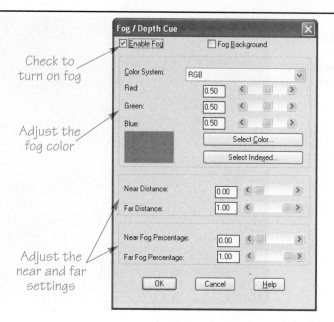

Check to turn on fog

Adjust the fog color

Adjust the near and far settings

By default, fog is not turned on in a new drawing. Check the **Enable Fog** check box to turn fog on and enable the options in the dialog box. Checking the **Fog Background** check box applies fog to the background as well as the objects. After fog is enabled, use the settings in the top area of the dialog box to adjust the color of the fog.

The **Near Distance:** and **Far Distance:** slider bars control where the fog starts and stops. The settings are percentages in relation to the viewer and the back clipping plane. A value of 0 is the point at which the viewer is "standing" in the model. A value of 1.0 is the back of the model. Use the slider bars to adjust the fog toward or away from the viewer. The **Near Fog Percentage:** and **Far Fog Percentage:** slider bars control the percentage, or "thickness," of fog at the near and far distances. A value of 0 creates no fog and a value of 1.0 creates 100% fog.

# Landscaping

The purpose of presentation drawings is to visually communicate the final product, whether it is a building, road, park, bridge, or other constructed feature. In order to more fully represent the final product, accessory items that are not part of the actual model can be added. These "accessories" can include trees, bushes, people, and road signs. Architects call these accessories *entourage.* In AutoCAD, objects making up entourage are called *landscape objects.* Landscape objects are simply bitmap images attached to vector objects.

## Adding Landscape Objects

LSNEW

View
↳ Render
 ↳ Landscape New...

Render toolbar

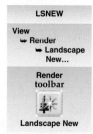

Landscape New

To add landscape objects to your drawing, select **Landscape New...** from the **Render** cascading menu in the **View** pull-down menu, pick the **Landscape New** button on the **Render** toolbar, or enter lsnew at the Command prompt. This displays the **Landscape New** dialog box. See **Figure 26-34.**

The list on the left contains the available landscape objects. Select an object from the list and pick the **Preview** button to view it. The height of the object can be specified below the preview window. Use the slider bar or enter the value directly in the text box to adjust the height. The height of the object is measured in current drawing units.

Figure 26-34.
The **Landscape New** dialog box allows you to add landscape objects to the drawing.

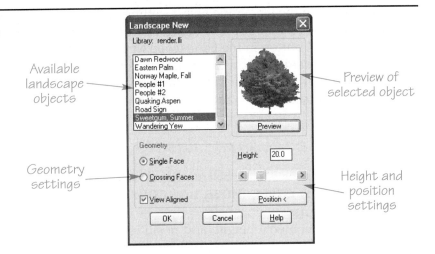

The **Geometry** area is used to specify whether the landscape object is made from a single face or two crossing faces. See **Figure 26-35.** To help understand this, you can think of a landscape object as a single 3D face or two intersecting 3D faces. The landscape images are attached to a single face when the **Single Face** radio button is selected. If the **Crossing Faces** radio button is selected, the image is attached to two faces intersecting at 90°. This type of object creates a more realistic image in the rendering, but takes longer to render than the single face object. Checking the **View Aligned** check box keeps a single face object perpendicular to the view in the rendering. This allows the full detail to be seen in the rendering. If a crossing face object is used with the **View Aligned** check box selected, the crossing faces are oriented at 45° to the view.

**Figure 26-35.**
A landscape object set to "single face" is represented in the drawing with one triangular face. A landscape object set to "crossing faces" is represented in the drawing by two intersecting triangular faces. Notice how the two objects render slightly different. A—The wireframe representations.
B—Rendered versions.

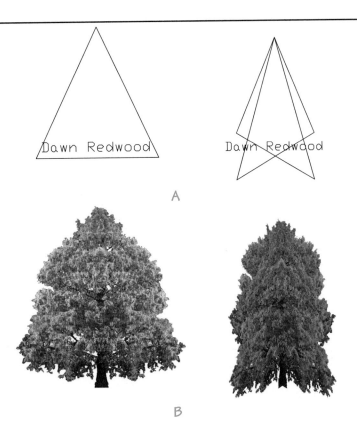

After selecting the landscape object, setting the height, and specifying the type of geometry, use the **Position** button to select a position for the object in the drawing. Then, pick the **OK** button in the **Landscape New** dialog box to place the object.

When the **View Aligned** check box is used on the objects, AutoCAD always rotates the objects so they are perpendicular to the view. If the **View Aligned** check box is unchecked, the objects can be rotated with the **ROTATE** command.

## Modifying Landscape Objects

Landscape objects can be modified with standard AutoCAD modifying commands such as **ERASE**, **MOVE**, and **COPY**. The objects can also be selected and modified using grips.

**LSEDIT**

View
  → Render
    → Landscape
    Edit...

**Render toolbar**

Landscape Edit

The type of geometry, height, and position can be modified using the **Landscape Edit** dialog box. Open this dialog box by selecting **Landscape Edit...** in the **Render** cascading menu in the **View** pull-down menu, picking the **Landscape Edit** button on the **Render** toolbar, or entering lsedit at the Command prompt. You are prompted to select a landscape object. After the object is picked, the **Landscape Edit** dialog box appears. This dialog box has the same features as the **Landscape New** dialog box, except that the landscape object list is unavailable. Adjust any of the other values to modify the landscape objects and pick **OK** to update the object.

**Professional Tip**

This chapter has introduced you to the basic concepts of rendering an AutoCAD model. Additional information about rendering and advanced rendering techniques can be found in the AutoCAD help file or in the text *AutoCAD and its Applications—Advanced*, published by Goodheart-Willcox Publisher.

# Exercise 26-7

◆ Open ex26-6.
◆ Add a single-face landscape object to the model. Select **People #1** or **People #2** and place the object near the corner of the room.
◆ Render the scene Left to the **Render Window**.
◆ Edit the landscape object so it is a crossing-face object. Render the scene Left to the **Render Window**.
◆ Make any adjustments needed. Then, render the scene Left to a file named ex26-7.bmp.
◆ Save the drawing as ex26-7.

# Chapter Test

*Answer the following questions on a separate sheet of paper.*

1. Which command is used to create a hidden-line display?
2. Describe how you can simulate a hand-drawn perspective view starting with an AutoCAD drawing.
3. Define *rendering*.
4. How are objects rendered if a material has not yet been assigned?
5. Identify the function of the **Render** dialog box.
6. List the three rendering types.
7. When creating 3D geometry in AutoCAD, is the face that points toward the viewer considered the "front face" or "back face?" Is this positive or negative?
8. Define *raytrace*.
9. Define *antialiasing*.
10. What is the function of the **Destination** area of the **Render** dialog box?
11. What are the three options located in the drop-down list in the **Destination** area of the **Render** dialog box?
12. List three things that can be done with a rendering created in the **Render Window**.
13. When rendering to a file, which types of image files can be created?
14. Define a *material* in AutoCAD.
15. How can the materials in the current drawing be saved as a new material library?
16. What is the default material library in AutoCAD?
17. Explain the importance of lights in a rendering.
18. Describe a *point light*.
19. Explain the function and purpose of a *distant light*.
20. Describe the function and effect of a *spotlight*.
21. What is the purpose of the **Sun Angle Calculator** dialog box?
22. What items are defined to create a scene in AutoCAD?
23. Define a *background* in AutoCAD.
24. List the four types of backgrounds available in AutoCAD.
25. Define *fog* in AutoCAD.
26. What is a *landscape object?*
27. Which command(s) can be used to modify a landscape object once it is created?

1. Construct a 3D model of the house project created in the earlier chapters of this text. Import or create your own materials and apply the materials to the appropriate objects. Add a distant light set for your location, today's date, and the current time. Add a background and landscape objects. Save the drawing as P26-1.

2. Open ex14-3 you created in Chapter 14. Create a region of the site, extrude the building outline up 9'-0", and add the roof. Add a driveway and create some trees with solid cylinders and spheres. Assign materials and a distant light to create a shadow study of the site plan. Save the drawing as P26-2.

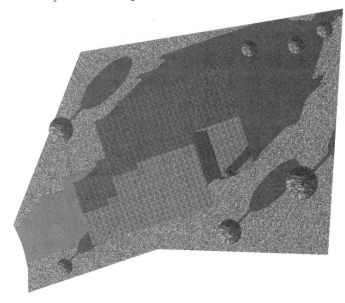

3. Open p25-3. Using the **3DORBIT** command, obtain a perspective view of the building similar to the one shown below. Obtain a screen shot of the building and paste it into photo-editing software, such as Windows Paint or Microsoft Photo Editor. Adjust the drawing to make it appear hand sketched. Save the drawing as P26-3.

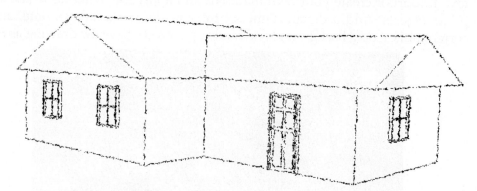

4. Open P25-4. Add materials and lights as needed. Assign a gradient background. Add a 3D face under the deck for a ground plane. Render the scene. Try creating scenes for daytime and nighttime. Save the drawing as P26-4.

5. Open ex26-1. Draw a 3D face under the building to represent a ground plane. Add materials and lights as desired. For the window openings, try using the **Color Faces** command in the **Solids Editing** toolbar to change the window faces to an ACI color to which a glass material can be assigned. Render the scene in the top left viewport above the hand sketch in the layout. Print the drawing. Save the drawing as P26-5.

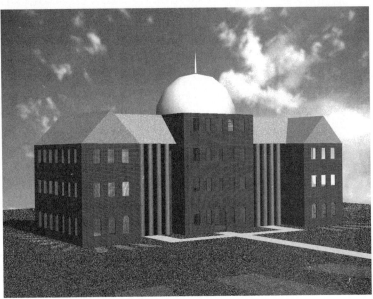

6. Open P25-6. Add materials, lights, and a background to the kitchen. Render to the **Render Window**. Save the drawing as P26-6.

7. Open P25-7. Use the **BOUNDARY** command to create a region of the inside of each room to be used as a floor. Assign a point light to each room. Add materials to the walls, doors, windows, and floors. Use the **3DORBIT** command to create a perspective top view of the floor plan. Render to the **Render Window**. Save the drawing as P26-7.

# CHAPTER 27

# Customizing AutoCAD

## Learning Objectives

After completing this chapter, you will be able to:
- Insert hyperlinks into a drawing.
- Create a script file to automate drafting applications.
- Customize toolbars.
- Create custom linetypes.

## Important Terms

complex linetypes
hard code
hyperlink
linetype definition files

macro
script file
simple linetypes

AutoCAD provides many options to customize the way you interact with and use the AutoCAD environment. By adjusting these options, you can configure AutoCAD to suit your own preferences as well as office standards. Custom toolbars and linetypes can be created to streamline workflow. This chapter introduces some of the customization features found in AutoCAD.

## Using Hyperlinks in a Drawing

A *hyperlink* is a feature common to many Web sites. By picking on a hyperlink, you are "transported" to a different location on the Web. You can incorporate hyperlinks in your AutoCAD drawings to open another drawing file, a text document, or a Web page. The use of hyperlinks in a drawing allows a set of drawings to be tied together. In this way, the person reviewing the drawing does not have to search for all related drawings. Hyperlinks can also link to text documents or Web pages containing additional information about a particular feature, such as a piece of furniture.

## Inserting a Hyperlink

**HYPERLINK**
[Ctrl]+[K]

**Insert**
↳ **Hyperlink...**

To add a hyperlink to the drawing, first draw an object to which the hyperlink will be attached. Then, to attach the hyperlink, pick **Hyperlink...** from the **Insert** pull-down menu, press [Ctrl]+[K], or enter hyperlink at the Command prompt. If the drawing has not been saved, an alert box appears suggesting you save the drawing before attaching the hyperlink. Select the object to which the hyperlink should be attached and press the [Enter] key. This displays the **Insert Hyperlink** dialog box. See **Figure 27-1**.

The **Type the file or Web page name:** text box near the top of the **Insert Hyperlink** dialog box is where you can type the complete path to the file or Web site being hyperlinked. If you are unsure of the location, use the **Browse for:** buttons. Pick the **File...** button to locate a file in a standard Windows file selection dialog box. Pick the **Web Page...** button to launch AutoCAD's **Browse the Web** dialog box.

The **Text to display:** text box at the top of the **Insert Hyperlink** dialog box is used to enter a label for the object. The label is the help text displayed when the cursor is over an AutoCAD object with a hyperlink attached to it. Since this is a label, use a descriptive name. For example, you can have the label be the same as the hyperlink path. However, this may not be descriptive. Instead, use a short description of where the hyperlink leads.

Once the hyperlink path and label are entered, pick the **OK** button to close the dialog box. The hyperlink is attached to the object selected during the command sequence.

---

**Figure 27-1.**
The **Insert Hyperlink** dialog box allows you to attach a hyperlink to an object in the drawing.

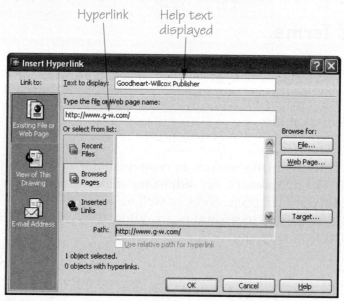

## Using a Hyperlink

When the crosshairs are moved over an object that includes a hyperlink, a world icon appears next to the crosshairs. See **Figure 27-2**. To view the hyperlink, select the object to obtain the grip boxes. Then, right-click to display a shortcut menu, **Figure 27-3**. Select **Hyperlink** from the menu to access the hyperlink options. Pick the **Open** option to open the hyperlinked file in its native application.

---

**Figure 27-2.**
When the cursor is moved over an object with a hyperlink, an icon is displayed next to the crosshairs indicating a hyperlink is attached.

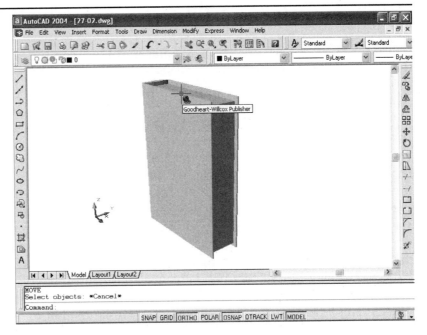

**Figure 27-3.**
After displaying grips on an object with a hyperlink, right-click to display this shortcut menu. Then, select **Hyperlink** to display the cascading menu and open the hyperlink.

## Exercise 27-1

- ◆ In Windows Notepad, type a short description of a desk. Save the document as Desk Desc.txt.
- ◆ Start a new drawing using one of your templates.
- ◆ Draw a 48″ × 30″ desk.
- ◆ Draw a personal computer.
- ◆ Use the **HYPERLINK** command to attach the Desk Desc.txt file you created in Notepad.
- ◆ Select the desk, right-click, and open the hyperlinked file.
- ◆ Save the drawing as ex27-1.

# Creating Script Files to Automate Drafting

A *script file* is a list of commands that AutoCAD can run without input from the drafter. Scripts can be created to run a series of commands to perform repeated tasks, thus saving drafting time. Before creating a script, a good working knowledge of AutoCAD commands is needed.

A script file can be written in any ASCII text editor, such as Windows Notepad. Essentially, the text you type in the script file is exactly what you would type on the AutoCAD command line. When creating a script file, one command or option is typed per line, just as when you type on the command line. A return at the Command prompt is represented in the script by pressing the [Enter] key. While you can use the space bar in place of [Enter] when working on the command line, *do not use a space as a return in your script routines.* The script will not function correctly.

You cannot use a command that opens a dialog box in a script file. You may think this presents difficulty, since many commands normally display a dialog box. However, some of these commands have a command-line-only equivalent. Many of these equivalent commands are simply the command preceded by a dash, such as **-UNITS**. The following is a list of common commands that display a dialog box and their command-line-only equivalents.

| Command | Dialog Box Displayed | Command-Line-Only Equivalent |
| --- | --- | --- |
| ATTDEF | Attribute Definition | -ATTDEF |
| ATTEDIT | Edit Attributes | -ATTEDIT |
| BHATCH | Boundary Hatch and Fill | -BHATCH |
| BLOCK | Block Definition | -BLOCK |
| BOUNDARY | Boundary Creation | -BOUNDARY |
| GROUP | Object Grouping | -GROUP |
| INSERT | Insert | -INSERT |
| IMAGE | Image Manager | -IMAGE |
| LAYER | Layer Properties Manager | -LAYER |
| LINETYPE | Linetype Manager | -LINETYPE |
| OSNAP | Drafting Settings | -OSNAP |
| PLOT | Plot | -PLOT |
| RENAME | Rename | -RENAME |
| TOOLBAR | Customize | -TOOLBAR |
| UNITS | Drawing Units | -UNITS |
| VIEW | View | -VIEW |
| VPORTS | Viewports | -VPORTS |
| XBIND | Xbind | -XBIND |
| XREF | Xref Manager | -XREF |

In addition to using commands that are command-line only, you can use the **FILEDIA** command to turn off any "select file" dialog boxes that appear in certain commands. These dialog boxes are used when AutoCAD prompts you to select a file or to save a file to a location. The default value of 1 allows the dialog boxes to be displayed. A value of 0 disables the dialog boxes so a path name can be entered at the Command prompt.

# Writing a Script File

The following is a command-line-only example of changing units, increasing limits, creating a layer and setting it current, and creating a rectangle on the current layer around the limits for a new drawing. The script file for this series of commands is shown in **Figure 27-4.**

Command: **-units**↵
Report formats:            (Examples)
1.  Scientific              1.55E+01
2.  Decimal              15.50
3.  Engineering          1'-3.50"
4.  Architectural         1'-3 1/2"
5.  Fractional            15 1/2
With the exception of Engineering and Architectural formats,
these formats can be used with any basic unit of measurement.
For example, Decimal mode is perfect for metric units as well
as decimal English units.
Enter choice, 1 to 5 *<default>*: **4**↵
Enter denominator of smallest fraction to display
(1, 2, 4, 8, 16, 32, 64, 128, or 256) *< default >*: **16**↵
Systems of angle measure:     (Examples)
1.  Decimal degrees        45.0000
2.  Degrees/minutes/seconds  45d0'0"
3.  Grads                50.0000g
4.  Radians             0.7854r
5.  Surveyor's units       N 45d0'0" E
Enter choice, 1 to 5 *< default >*: **1**↵
Enter number of fractional places for display of angles (0 to 8) *< default >*: **0**↵
Direction for angle 0:
East                 3 o'clock     = 0
North               12 o'clock   = 90
West                9 o'clock     = 180
South              6 o'clock     = 270
Enter direction for angle 0 *< default >*: **0**↵
Measure angles clockwise? [Yes/No] *< default >* **n**↵
Command: **limits**↵
Reset Model space limits:
Specify lower left corner or [ON/OFF] *< default, default >*: **0,0**↵
Specify upper right corner *< default, default >*: **144',96'**↵
Command: **zoom**↵
Specify corner of window, enter a scale factor (nX or nXP), or
[All/Center/Dynamic/Extents/Previous/Scale/Window] <real time>: **all**↵
Command: **-layer**↵
Enter an option
[?/Make/Set/New/ON/OFF/Color/Ltype/LWeight/Plot/PStyle/Freeze/Thaw/LOck/Unlock/
    stAte]: **make**↵
Enter name for new layer (becomes the current layer) *<current>*: **border**↵
Enter an option
[?/Make/Set/New/ON/OFF/Color/Ltype/LWeight/Plot/PStyle/Freeze/Thaw/LOck/Unlock/
    stAte]: **color**↵
New color [Truecolor/COlorbook] <7 (white)>: **1**↵
Enter name list of layer(s) for color 1 (red) <BORDER>: **border**↵
Enter an option

**Figure 27-4.**
This script file, displayed in Windows Notepad, changes units and limits, creates a new layer, and draws a rectangle. Notice only one command or option appears on each line.

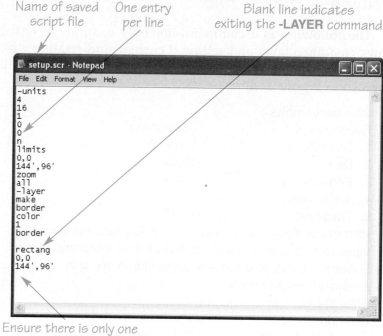

Name of saved script file

One entry per line

Blank line indicates exiting the **-LAYER** command

Ensure there is only one blank line at the end

```
[?/Make/Set/New/ON/OFF/Color/Ltype/LWeight/Plot/PStyle/Freeze/Thaw/LOck/Unlock/stAte]: ↵
Command: rectang↵
Specify first corner point or [Chamfer/Elevation/Fillet/Thickness/Width]: 0,0↵
Specify other corner point or [Dimensions]: 144',96'↵
Command:
```

When creating the script file, press the [Enter] key after the last command line so AutoCAD knows there is a return after the last entry. Make sure there is only one blank line at the end of the script file. The final step is to save the text file with an SCR extension.

## Running a Script File

To run the script file, select **Run Script...** from the **Tools** pull-down menu or enter scr or script at the Command prompt. The **Select Script File** dialog box is opened. See **Figure 27-5.** Locate and select the script file you want to run, then pick the **Open** button. The script file is initiated.

Once the script file is initiated, AutoCAD reads the file one line at a time. Each function is performed in order. You may see the AutoCAD text window open and close several times during the script, depending on which commands are used in the script. If you watch the command line as the script runs, you can see all the commands and options appear in the same order they were typed in the script file.

SCRIPT
SCR

Tools
➡ Run Script...

## Troubleshooting a Script File

If AutoCAD stops the script before completion, a problem in the script has occurred. Use the [F2] key to display the AutoCAD text window. Determine where the script failed, open the script file in an ASCII text editor, fix the problem, and save the script file. The most probable causes of a script not running are a space in a line or too many or too few returns at the end of the script. You should only have one blank line at the end of the script. Also, double-check the spelling of commands and options. Make sure all entries are valid.

**Figure 27-5.**
Use the **Select Script File** dialog box to locate and open a script file to run.

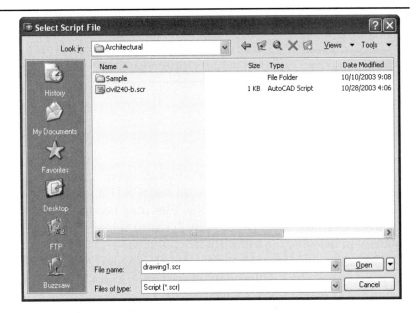

## Exercise 27-2

- Start a new drawing using one of your templates.
- Type the command sequence given in the section *Writing a Script File* to change the units and limits, create a layer, and draw a rectangle. If correctly completed, a red rectangle should be created on the Border layer.
- Close the drawing without saving.
- Using Windows Notepad, create the script file shown in **Figure 27-4.**
- Save the file as setup.scr.
- Open a new drawing and run the script file. The result should be exactly the same as it was when the commands were entered on the command line.
- If the script file does not run properly, look over the file in Notepad. Fix any errors and save the file. Then, rerun the script.
- Save the drawing as ex27-2.

# Customizing Toolbars

Many AutoCAD commands have button equivalents that can be found on a toolbar. Toolbars generally contain a group of buttons for commands that logically go together. For example, many dimensioning commands have button equivalents in the **Dimension** toolbar.

The default toolbar button configurations work well for most drafters in most situations. However, you may find that you always use certain commands in "groups" but the buttons are located on different toolbars. By creating your own toolbar with the "group" of commands you frequently use, your drafting can be streamlined.

**Professional Tip**

A toolbar can contain many buttons. Create buttons that will insert blocks, create layers, or set up drawing sheets. Any repetitive task can be automated and assigned to a toolbar button to help save time.

## Philosophies on Customization

There are two philosophies among users concerning the customization of AutoCAD. The first is to customize AutoCAD and replace the default settings. In some cases, AutoCAD or its support files may become corrupted. This situation may be difficult to correct and you may have to reload AutoCAD. Reloading AutoCAD means you lose any customization.

The second philosophy is to customize AutoCAD and save the customization as a separate "version." This keeps the original AutoCAD default settings intact. Then, if AutoCAD needs to be reinstalled or a new version of AutoCAD is installed, the customized settings are not lost. In addition, if the customized settings corrupt AutoCAD, you can simply reload the default settings and start over without reinstalling AutoCAD.

This text promotes the second philosophy where the default AutoCAD settings are retained. Your school or office may choose to use the "overwriting" philosophy. Check with your instructor or CAD manager before customizing AutoCAD in any way.

**Professional Tip**

See Appendix I, *File Management*, for ideas on how to manage drawing and customization files.

## Understanding the Menu System

Before you begin customizing toolbars, a few concepts regarding AutoCAD's menus and toolbars must be understood. Toolbar information in AutoCAD is written to a file called acad.mnu, or the AutoCAD menu file. The MNU file extension indicates the file is a menu file. The acad.mnu file contains all of the information needed to run all AutoCAD commands. This file is the default menu system loaded when AutoCAD is installed (before any customization). It may be helpful to think of the menu file as a command "template" to configure AutoCAD.

After AutoCAD reads the acad.mnu file, another file is generated. This file is called acad.mns and is referred to as a menu source file. This file is the acad.mnu file reduced to the core AutoCAD commands. All user or programmer "comments" are removed. When a toolbar is customized or created, the information for the toolbar is saved to the acad.mns file by default, not the acad.mnu file. Once the acad.mns file is created, AutoCAD no longer reads the acad.mnu file unless the **MENU** command is used.

At the same time AutoCAD generates the acad.mns file, a file named acad.mnr is created. This is a menu resource file. It is a binary file containing all the images used for toolbar buttons.

Once the MNS file and the MNR file are created, AutoCAD generates a final file that is actually loaded each time AutoCAD is opened. This file is the acad.mnc file. The MNC file is a binary file that combines the commands from the MNS file and the images from the MNR file into a single file.

The **MENU** command is used to load a menu, either the default menu or a customized menu. When the **MENU** command is entered, the **Select Menu File** dialog box is displayed, **Figure 27-6.** This dialog box allows you to search for an MNU, MNC, and MNS file to load. If you load an MNU file, AutoCAD redefines and overwrites the existing MNS, MNR, and MNC files. When the selected MNC, MNS, or MNU file is loaded into AutoCAD, all other menus are removed.

The **MENULOAD** command can be used to load additional menus or parts of additional menus. This command opens the **Menu Customization** dialog box. See **Figure 27-7.** In the **Menu Groups** tab, pick the **Browse...** button to select a menu file to load. Then, in the **Menu Bar** tab, pick the custom menu in the **Menu Group:** drop-down list. Highlight the pull-down menu to add in the **Menus:** area. Then, pick the **Insert** button. The new pull-down menu is inserted before the pull-down menu that was highlighted in the **Menu Bar:** area.

**Figure 27-6.**
The **Select Menu File** dialog box allows you to load the MNC, MNS, or MNU files.

## Creating a Custom Menu File

With an understanding of how menus work within AutoCAD, you can create a menu file (MNU file) to load into AutoCAD before customizing any toolbars. An MNU file can be written in an ASCII text editor, such as Windows Notepad. For this discussion, Notepad is used. When Notepad is started, a blank document appears on the screen. Press the [Enter] key to create a blank line.

A menu must have a unique name when loaded into AutoCAD. The menu name is listed in the **Menu Customization** dialog box when the menu is loaded. The name can be anything as long as it is not named the same as one of the AutoCAD menus. On the second line of the Notepad file, type ***MENUGROUP=*menu file name*. See

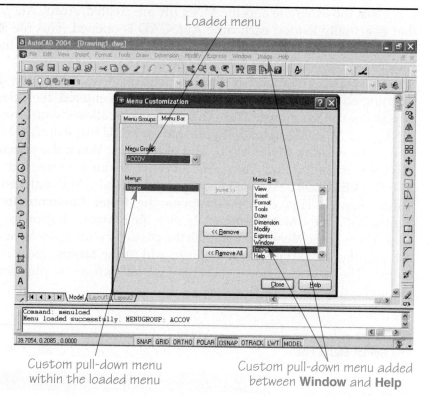

Loaded menu

Custom pull-down menu within the loaded menu

Custom pull-down menu added between **Window** and **Help**

**Figure 27-8.** The three asterisks (\*\*\*) in the menu represent a major section in the menu. The word MENUGROUP indicates the following menu strings belong to the name specified in the line.

Now, save the Notepad file with the MNU extension. Name the file using the same name as the menu. In this example, the file name is Custom_Menu.mnu. If you save the menu file in the AutoCAD \Support folder, AutoCAD will find the menu file when it is loaded. However, to keep AutoCAD "stock," it is better to save the menu file in a folder you create that will be used strictly for menu-related items. Refer to Appendix I for ideas on how to create a file structure for saving customized files.

**Figure 27-8.**
The \*\*\*MENUGROUP= string indicates any menu strings in the menu file belong to the name of the menu identified after the = sign, CUSTOM_MENU in this case.

Second line of the menu file

Menu name

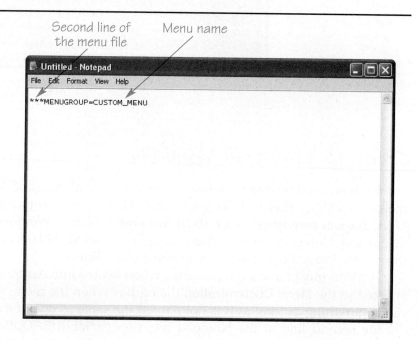

## Exercise 27-3

◆ Open Windows Notepad.
◆ On the second line, type ***MENUGROUP= My_Menu.
◆ Save the file to the folder that will contain your custom menu items. Name the file My_Menu.mnu.
◆ This file is used in later exercises.

## Loading the Menu File into AutoCAD

Once you have created the menu file, the menu needs to be loaded into AutoCAD. The AutoCAD profile keeps track of which menus are loaded so future sessions of AutoCAD using the profile have all of the menus loaded. To load the custom menu, enter menuload at the Command prompt. The **Menu Customization** dialog box is displayed. Use the **Browse...** button in the **Menu Groups** tab to locate your menu file.

Picking the **Browse...** button displays the **Select Menu File** dialog box. By default, this dialog box is looking for MNC and MNS files. Use the **Files of type:** drop-down list to change to the **Menu Template (*.mnu)** option. This allows you to search folders for custom menu files. Once you have located your menu file, pick the **Open** button. This opens the menu and returns you to the **Menu Customization** dialog box.

The path and the menu file name are now displayed in the **File Name:** text box. However, the file is not yet loaded. Pick the **Load** button to load the menu file, **Figure 27-9.** Once you pick the **Load** button, a warning appears indicating that loading a menu file overwrites the menu source file and deletes any toolbar customizations. See **Figure 27-10.** If you have not created any customizations, pick the **Yes** button.

**Figure 27-9.**
The **Menu Customization** dialog box is used to load additional menus.

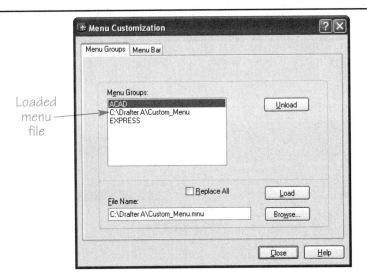

**Note**

Add the folder where menu files are saved to the AutoCAD support file search path in the **Options** dialog box. Otherwise, AutoCAD will not find the menus the next time it is launched.

**Figure 27-10.**
When loading a
menu file,
AutoCAD displays
a warning message.
If previous
customizations have
been made, do not
select **Yes**.

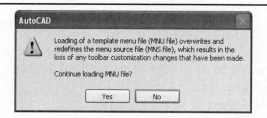

## Exercise 27-4

◆ Launch AutoCAD.
◆ In the **Files** tab of the **Options** dialog box, add the folder where you saved the
   menu file from Exercise 27-3 to the search path. Close the **Options** dialog box.
◆ Enter menuload at the Command prompt.
◆ Use the **Browse...** button in the **Menu Customization** dialog box to locate and
   open your custom menu file.
◆ Use the **Load** button to load the menu file.
◆ Close the **Menu Customization** dialog box.

## Creating a Custom Toolbar for Your Menu

After you have loaded your custom menu file, you can begin creating toolbars.
Right-click on any toolbar to get the toolbar list. At the bottom of the list, select the
**Customize...** option. See **Figure 27-11A.** This displays the **Customize** dialog box with
the **Toolbars** tab active. See **Figure 27-11B.** You can also open the dialog box by
selecting **Toolbars...** from the **View** pull-down menu or by entering toolbar at the
Command prompt.

TOOLBAR

View
➥ Toolbars...

**Figure 27-11.**
A—Right-clicking
on a toolbar
displays this
shortcut menu. B—
Select **Customize...**
to open the
**Customize** dialog
box with the
**Toolbars** tab
displayed.

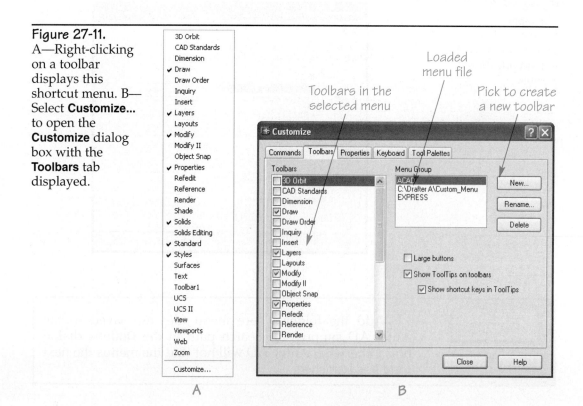

Figure 27-12.
The **New Toolbar**
dialog box. Enter a
name for your
toolbar and assign a
menu group so that
your custom toolbar
is assigned.

*Name the toolbar*

*Select which menu the toolbar is associated with*

Select the **New...** button in the dialog box to create a new toolbar. This displays the **New Toolbar** dialog box. See **Figure 27-12.** Enter a name for your toolbar in the **Toolbar Name:** text box. In the **Save toolbar in menu group:** drop-down list, select the name of the custom menu. By assigning the toolbar to the custom menu group, it is added to the custom menu source file and not AutoCAD's. When you press the **OK** button, a new "blank" toolbar is created at the top of the AutoCAD screen. The **Customize** dialog box remains open. See **Figure 27-13.** Drag the toolbar to a blank area on the drawing screen to make it more accessible.

Figure 27-13.
Drag the new
"blank" toolbar to
an open area so it is
easier to see.

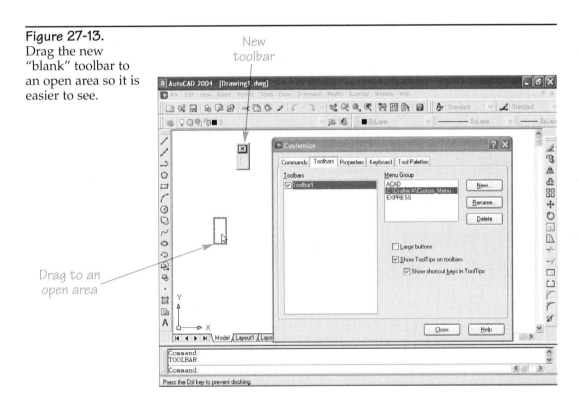

*New toolbar*

*Drag to an open area*

## Exercise 27-5

- ◆ Open the **Customize** dialog box.
- ◆ In the **Toolbars** tab, pick the **New...** button.
- ◆ Create a new toolbar named **My Toolbar**. Save the toolbar with the My_Menu file created earlier.
- ◆ Move the new toolbar to an open area beside the **Customize** dialog box. Leave the dialog box open.

# Adding Commands to the Custom Toolbar

With the "blank" toolbar created, you can begin adding buttons. Open the **Customize** dialog box if it is not already open. Then, pick the **Commands** tab. See **Figure 27-14.**

The AutoCAD commands are grouped in different categories. The categories are shown in the **Categories** list in the **Commands** tab. The commands available in the category selected in the list are shown in the **Commands** list on the right side of the tab. When a command is picked in the **Commands** list, a description for the command appears in the **Description:** area at the bottom of the tab.

To add a command to the new toolbar as a button, first locate the command. For example, if you want to add the **3DORBIT** command to the new toolbar, select **View** in the **Categories** list. Next, locate the command in the **Commands** list. Select the command with the mouse and hold down the mouse pick button. Drag the command to the new toolbar and drop it where you want it. See **Figure 27-15.** Continue adding commands to the toolbar as needed.

---

**Figure 27-14.**
The **Commands** tab of the **Customize** dialog box contains commands that can be added as buttons to your custom toolbar.

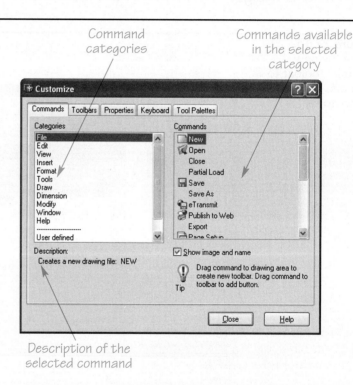

Command categories

Commands available in the selected category

Description of the selected command

---

Commands from different categories can be placed on one toolbar. As you drag and drop the desired buttons to the toolbar, AutoCAD assembles the menu information for the toolbar's menu source file (MNS file).

There is a category at the bottom of the **Categories** list called **User defined**. This category does not include any commands, but has two blank buttons that can be added to a toolbar. These buttons can be customized to perform AutoCAD functions.

When you are finished adding buttons to the toolbar, press the **Close** button in the **Customize** dialog box. AutoCAD writes the toolbar information to the menu source file. Since the toolbar was set to be saved to the Custom_Menu file, the button information is written to the Custom_Menu.mns file.

**Figure 27-15.**
Drag and drop the desired command onto a toolbar to create a button.

Button added

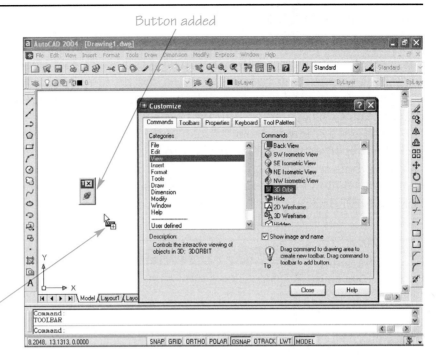

Dragging a button to the toolbar

**Professional Tip**

If you drag a command from the **Customize** dialog box and drop it on an open area of the drawing screen, a new toolbar is created.

## Removing Buttons from a Toolbar

If you add a toolbar button to a toolbar, you are not stuck with it. You can remove any button from any toolbar. Open the **Customize** dialog box. Then, select the button on the toolbar and drag and drop it to a blank part of the AutoCAD screen. This removes the button from the toolbar. It is also discarded from the menu.

## Exercise 27-6

◆ Open the **Customize** dialog box.
◆ Select the **Commands** tab.
◆ Browse through the list of categories and commands. Drag and drop three commands of your choice onto your custom toolbar.
◆ Select the **User defined** category. Drag and drop the **User Defined Button** onto your toolbar.
◆ Close the **Customize** dialog box.

# Customizing Toolbar Buttons

After commands are assembled as buttons on the toolbar, the buttons can be customized to perform any function desired. If you add a **User Defined Button** to a toolbar, you must then define the action the button should perform. You can also change the function of a command button added to a toolbar. However, do not alter default AutoCAD command buttons.

To assign a command to a "blank" button, open the **Customize** dialog box. Then, pick the **Properties** tab. See **Figure 27-16A**. The tab is blank except for a tip indicating to pick a button to customize. Pick the blank button on the toolbar. The tab label changes to **Button Properties** and the tab displays information related to the button. See **Figure 27-16B**.

**Figure 27-16.**
A—The **Properties** tab of the **Customize** dialog box is used to modify a button's properties. Select the tab and then pick a button on the toolbar to modify. B—Once a button is selected, the tab is labeled **Button Properties** and displays the properties of the selected button.

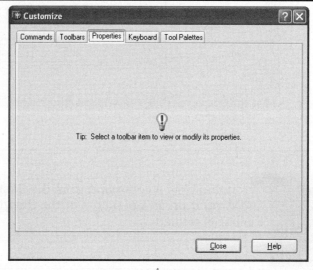

A

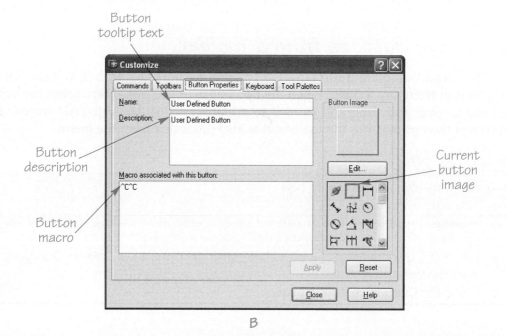

B

In the **Name:** text box, enter a name for the button. This name is used for the button tooltip. Below the **Name:** text box is the **Description:** text box. Type a short description of the button and its function in this text box. This description is displayed on the AutoCAD status bar when the cursor is over the button.

At the bottom of the **Button Properties** tab is the **Macro associated with this button:** area. This area is the "computer code" for the function performed by the button. This area is described in the next section.

On the right side of the **Button Properties** tab are options for changing the image on the button. A preview of the current image is shown large size in the upper-right corner. Changing the button image is discussed later in this chapter.

## Button macro

A *macro* is a set of multiple commands and options that run automatically once started. A script file is a type of macro. The **Macro associated with this button:** area at the bottom of the **Button Properties** tab is where a macro is entered for a button. For a "blank" button, the entry ^C^C is placed in this area. This entry stands for "cancel" "cancel," which means the default action of the button is the same as pressing the [Esc] key twice. In many cases you want to start your macros with two cancels. This ensures any active command is completely exited before performing any functions. However, if the macro performs a transparent function, you would *not* start the macro with ^C^C.

A macro is written much like a script file. However, the commands in a macro are written in one long line as opposed to one command on each line, as in a script file. The information you add to the macro must consist of commands that can be typed at the Command prompt. If a command displays a dialog box, AutoCAD reads the macro up to that command, displays the dialog box, and stops. Refer to the list of commands given earlier in this chapter that do not bring up dialog boxes. The following syntax characters can be used in a macro.

| Syntax Character | Meaning |
| --- | --- |
| ^C (carat C) | [Esc] This function performs a single cancel of the current prompt on the command line. Two cancels are used to exit from some commands. |
| ; (semicolon) | [Enter] The semicolon acts as a return or enter on the keyboard. |
| \ (backslash) | User input. The backslash pauses the current command so the drafter can enter information at the Command prompt. For example, if the button will prompt for a location, the backslash can be used to pause the macro so a coordinate can be entered. Once the coordinate is entered, the rest of the macro can be carried out. |

**Figure 27-17A** displays a macro that performs the same functions as the script you created in Exercise 27-2. Notice each command or entry is separated by a semi-colon. The semicolon is where you would normally press the [Enter] key if typing the commands at the Command prompt. Also notice how the commands are automatically "wrapped" to the next line in the text box. This does *not* mean there is a return at the end of the line.

**Figure 27-17.**
A—The script file commands from Exercise 27-2 written in macro form and entered for the button. B—The macro that loads and runs the script file created in Exercise 27-2 is entered for the button.

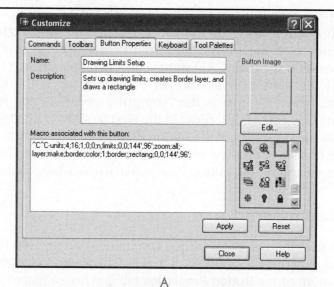

A

B

Figure 27-17B displays a macro that loads and runs the script file you created in Exercise 27-2. In the macro, the **FILEDIA** system variable is set to 0. This is used to turn off the **Select File** dialog box, which would normally be displayed when using the **SCRIPT** command. The path to the script file location is added so the **SCRIPT** command can locate the file. The path directories are separated with forward slashes instead of backslashes. This is because the backslash is used in a macro for user input information. Also, the entire path is enclosed in quotation marks so AutoCAD understands the complete path. At the end, the **FILEDIA** system variable is set to 1 so dialog boxes are enabled again.

## Modifying a button image

After the macro has been entered, a button image can be created and assigned to the button. At the bottom of the **Button Image** area of the **Button Properties** tab is a graphic listing of button images currently used by AutoCAD. You can scroll through the listing and select one of the images for the button. An image can also be selected from the listing and modified.

Architectural Drafting Using AutoCAD

To modify an existing image, pick the image in the list. The image is displayed large size in the preview. Then, pick the **Edit...** button above the list. To start a new image from scratch, simply pick the **Edit...** button with a blank image shown in the preview. The **Button Editor** dialog box is displayed, **Figure 27-18.**

The **Button Editor** contains drawing tools and a color palette. By default, the button includes $16 \times 16$ pixels. If AutoCAD is set to use large buttons, the button displays $32 \times 32$ pixels. Create an image using the tools available. To use a saved image file as the button image, pick the **Open** button and open the image. Once open, the image can be modified.

To save the button image to a file for future use, pick the **Save As...** button. Then, specify a name and location. If you pick the **Save** button, AutoCAD saves the bitmap under a generic name. Generic names can make it hard to find and modify a bitmap at a later date.

**Figure 27-18.**
The **Button Editor** dialog box allows you to customize a button image.

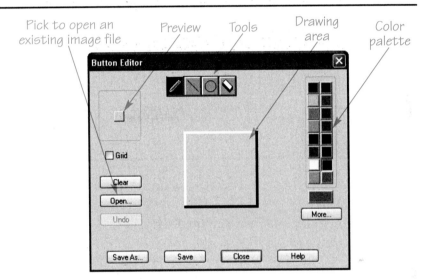

When you are finished creating or customizing the button, press the **Close** button. If you have not saved the changes, you are prompted to do so. Then, the **Button Properties** tab of the **Customize** dialog box is returned. Press the **Apply** button to apply this information to your button. See **Figure 27-19.** When the **Customize** dialog box is closed, the changes are written to the menu source file.

When saving button images, place them in the same folder as your custom menu files. Since AutoCAD must be set up to look in that folder for the menu, it will find the image files for the buttons as well.

**Figure 27-19.**
When the **Apply** button in the **Button Properties** tab is picked, the button is updated with all changes.

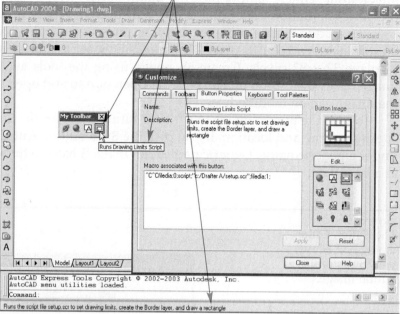

Button image, tooltip, and description reflect changes

## Exercise 27-7

◆ Open the **Customize** dialog box.

◆ Pick the **Properties** tab. Then, pick the "blank" button on your custom toolbar (**My Toolbar**).

◆ Name the button **Drawing Limits Setup**.

◆ Type a short description of the button indicating it sets up a new drawing.

◆ Write the following macro in the **Macro associated with this button:** area.

    ^C^C-units;4;16;1;0;0;n;limits;0,0;144',96';zoom;all;
    -layer;make;border;color;1;border;;rectang;0,0;144',96';

◆ Starting with the "blank" button, edit the button image to create an image of your own design. It should be representative of what function the button performs.

◆ Save the button image as setup.bmp in the same folder where the custom menu file is saved. Close the **Button Editor** dialog box.

◆ Add another blank button to your custom toolbar.

◆ Pick the **Button Properties** tab in the **Customize** dialog box. Pick the blank button you just added to display its properties.

◆ Name the button **Detail Bubble**.

◆ Add a description indicating this button draws detail bubbles.

◆ Write the following macro. Notice the user input steps, which allow the drafter to select the circle center and specify the starting point for the text.

    ^C^Ccircle;\.5;text;justify;mc;cen;\.25;0;

◆ Edit the blank button image. Save the button image as detail_bubble.bmp in the same folder where your custom menu file is saved. Close the **Button Editor** dialog box.

◆ Test the two custom buttons. If the buttons do not function correctly, double-check the macros to ensure the correct commands and options are being used, and semicolons are correctly placed.

When a toolbar is customized, the information is saved to the MNS file of the menu group to which the toolbar is associated. In the above examples, **My Toolbar** is created in the MNS file for the Custom_Menu menu group. However, if the Custom_Menu.mnu (not MNS) file is reloaded, toolbar customization is lost. To prevent this problem, the information from the menu source file needs to be placed in the menu file (MNU). Then, if the menu file (MNU file) is reloaded, the custom toolbar information is also reloaded. In addition, the custom menu file is available for use with future versions of AutoCAD.

The menu file (MNU file) and the menu source file (MNS file) are both ASCII text files. This means you can use Windows Notepad to open and modify these files. When the menu source file (MNS file) is opened in Notepad, notice that AutoCAD has written the toolbar information into the file. See **Figure 27-20.** Under the **\*\*\*MENUGROUP=** section you added earlier, a new section named **\*\*\*TOOLBARS** has been added. This section contains the information for your toolbar. Multiple toolbars are listed below the **\*\*\*TOOLBARS** section in separate minor sections preceded by two asterisks (\*\*). In **Figure 27-20,** the toolbar named "**MY TOOLBAR**" is preceded by two asterisks (\*\*) indicating this toolbar section.

Below the **\*\*\*TOOLBARS** section, a **\*\*\*HELPSTRINGS** section has also been added. This section contains the help strings you entered for the buttons as well as the help strings for the AutoCAD buttons.

**Figure 27-20.**
The new toolbar information is saved to the Custom_Menu.mns file, shown here opened in Windows Notepad.

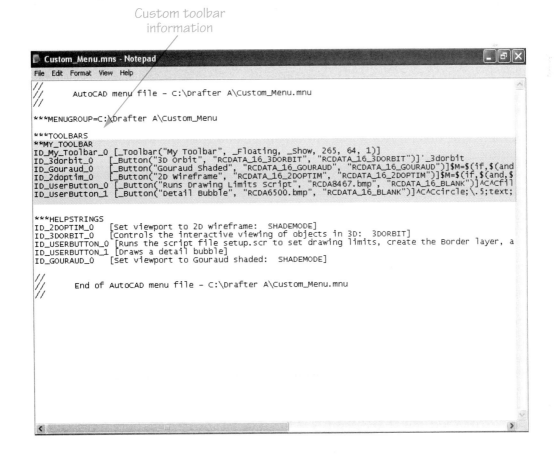

To save the information to the MNU file, simply save the MNS file from Notepad with an MNU file extension. Save in the same menu folder and overwrite the initial MNU file you created. This ensures the toolbar information is reloaded if the menu is ever reloaded.

The last thing to do is "hard code" your saved button image file names into the menu. *Hard code* means to fix the image file name to the desired button. The toolbar button string includes two areas for button names to be hard coded. See **Figure 27-21**. The first area after the button name is for the name of the 16 × 16 button image. Replace the *named*.bmp file in quotes with the name of the image file you created when customizing the button. The second area after the button name is for the name of the 32 × 32 button image.

**Figure 27-21.**
The "code" for a toolbar indicates the name and current on-screen location. The "code" for a button indicates the name for the button. You can also embed the name of a button image in the "code" by replacing the default 16 × 16 or 32 × 32 image name.

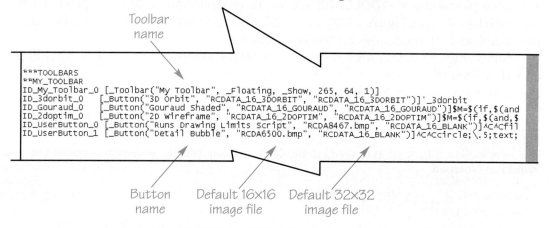

**Exercise 27-8**

◆ Open your Custom_Menu.mns file in Windows Notepad.
◆ Change the default AutoCAD button image name for the **Drawing Limits Setup** button to setup.bmp.
◆ Change the default AutoCAD bitmap name for the **Detail Bubble** button to detail_bubble.bmp.
◆ Save the file as Custom_Menu.mnu, overwriting the existing file.

# Customizing Linetypes

AutoCAD *linetype definition files* contain the information needed by AutoCAD to create and display a given linetype. These files have a LIN file extension. Linetype definition files are ASCII text files that can be opened and edited in Windows Notepad.

AutoCAD linetypes are made up of dots, dashes, and spaces, and can contain embedded shape or text objects. There are two general categories of linetypes. Linetypes that contain only dots, dashes, and spaces are considered *simple linetypes.* Linetypes that contain shapes and text in addition to dots, dashes, and spaces are considered *complex linetypes.*

The **Linetype Manager** dialog box is introduced in Chapter 5 of this text. When loading linetypes, the **Load or Reload Linetypes** dialog box is displayed and lists the linetypes available to load into AutoCAD. See **Figure 27-22**. The default linetype definition file is the acad.lin file. At the top of the **Load or Reload Linetypes** dialog box is the **File...** button. Picking this button allows you to open different linetype definition files.

To begin creating a custom linetype, first open the acad.lin file in Windows Notepad. The file is located in the AutoCAD \Support folder. Once the file is open in Notepad, you can see the existing linetype definitions. See **Figure 27-23**. Before modifying the default acad.lin file, do a "save as" in Notepad and save the file under a different name. In this way, the original linetype definition file remains unaltered.

**Figure 27-22.**
A—Pick the **Load...** button in the **Linetype Manager** dialog box to open the **Load or Reload Linetypes** dialog box. B—In the **Load or Reload Linetypes** dialog box, pick the **File...** button to open a custom linetype definition file. The acad.lin file is shown open here. Then, select the linetypes to load in the **Load or Reload Linetypes** dialog box and pick the **OK** button.

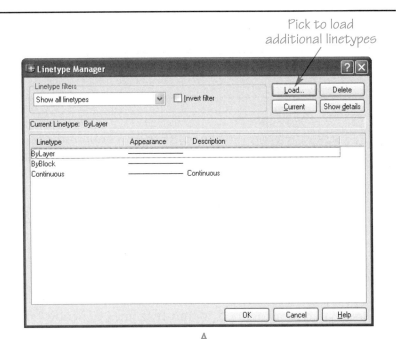

**Figure 27-23.**
The acad.lin file opened in Windows Notepad.

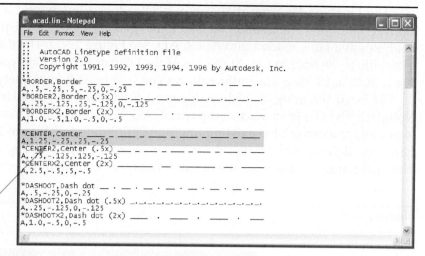

A single linetype definition

**Professional Tip**

The **-LINETYPE** command can be used to create new linetypes using command line prompts. Once you are experienced in creating linetypes by editing the linetype definition file, this command may be a way to save time.

## Defining Linetypes

Each linetype is defined within two lines of "code." The first line includes the linetype name and optionally provides a description. The second line of code is the actual definition for the linetype.

The first line begins with an asterisk and is immediately followed with the linetype name.

*linetype name, linetype description*

The linetype name can be up to 256 characters, including spaces. The description is not used by AutoCAD. It is only used as a representation of the linetype appearance. If the description is included, it must be separated from the linetype name by a comma and cannot be any longer than 47 characters.

The second line begins with an alignment field (A). This entry balances the linetype on each end of the line, ensuring each end of a line, arc, or circle is equal. This character is required at the beginning of the definition.

A,*pattern descriptor,pattern descriptor,pattern descriptor*

The alignment field is followed by a comma and the pattern descriptors. The pattern descriptors form a series of numbers to indicate dots, dashes, and spaces in the linetype. Each dot, dash, and space in the linetype is indicated by a number and separated by a comma. A positive number in the descriptor indicates the length of a dash. A negative number in the descriptor indicates the length of a space. A value of 0 in the descriptor indicates a dot.

**Professional Tip**

The length values for dashes and spaces should be assigned using the size of the dash or space as it appears on a plotted sheet of paper. Remember, the **LTSCALE** system variable controls the scaling of linetypes.

## Creating a Simple Linetype

Once you have saved the acad.lin file under a different name, you are ready to create a custom linetype definition. If you choose, you can also start with a "blank" LIN file in Notepad. Follow the guidelines given in the previous section. Remember, the first line of the definition must have an asterisk followed by the name of the linetype. The description is separated from the name with a comma. The second line begins with the letter A followed by a comma and the size of the dashes, spaces, and dots.

The linetype you will be creating in this example is a dash followed by three dots, all separated by spaces. On the first line of the definition, type:

*DASH_DOT_DOT_DOT

See **Figure 27-24.** Now, you can choose to enter a description of the linetype. Use any characters, such as hyphens, periods, and underscores, to create a visual description of what the linetype should look like. Remember, the description is optional. Be sure a comma separates the name. For example, type:

*DASH_DOT_DOT_DOT,—— . . .

See **Figure 27-25.** Now, you must provide the "code" definition of the linetype. Press the [Enter] key to start a new line. Type the letter A at the beginning of the line to specify alignment. Then, type a comma. Use a positive value for the length of the dash, a negative value for the length of the space, and a 0 for the dots. Each value must be separated by a comma. However, a comma does not need to be placed at the end of the string (line). To define the line, type:

*DASH_DOT_DOT_DOT,—— . . .
A,.5,−.25,0,−.125,0,−.125,0,−.25

**Figure 27-24.**
The name of the custom linetype is typed on the first line of the definition using Windows Notepad. The file is saved with a LIN file extension.

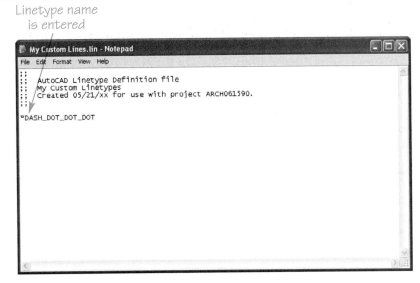

**Figure 27-25.**
An optional descriptor is typed after the linetype name. This is a visual reference only and not used by AutoCAD.

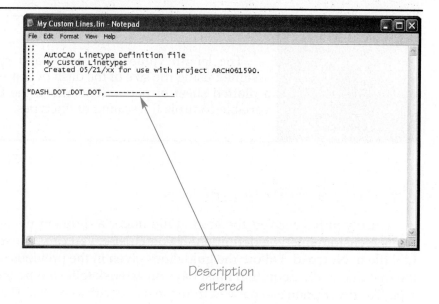

Description entered

See **Figure 27-26A.** Finally, you must save the LIN file. When you load the custom linetype file, the custom linetype is available. See **Figure 27-26B.**

**Professional Tip**

You may want to separate linetype definitions in a LIN file with a blank line between definitions. This does not affect the "usability" of the file and makes it easier to read.

## Exercise 27-9

◆ Open Windows Notepad. Save the "blank" file as My Linetypes.lin in the same folder as your custom menus.
◆ Type the following custom linetype definition in the file.

   *Dot Dash Dash Dot *(enter a description if you like)*
   A,0,–0.125,0.5,–0.25,0.5,–0.125,0,–0.125

◆ Save the file and close Notepad.
◆ Open AutoCAD. Open the **Linetype Manager** and open the custom linetype definition file. Then, load the custom linetype.
◆ Draw a line and a circle. Change the linetype to your custom linetype.
◆ Change the **LTSCALE** system variable several times. Notice the effect on the linetype.
◆ Open the custom linetype definition file in Notepad.
◆ Add the following linetype definition.

   *Longdash Shortdash Dot *(enter a description if you like)*
   A,.5,–.125,.125,–.125,0,–.125

◆ Save the file and close Notepad.
◆ In AutoCAD, change the line to the new custom linetype.
◆ Change the **LTSCALE** system variable several times. Notice the effect on the linetype.
◆ Save the drawing as ex27-9.

**Figure 27-26.**
A—The second line of a custom linetype definition is the actual definition of the line. B—The custom linetype definition file is opened in the **Load or Reload Linetypes** dialog box. Notice the custom linetype is available for loading into AutoCAD.

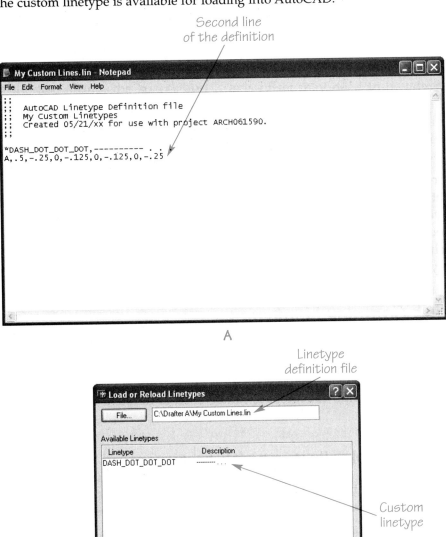

## Creating a linetype with the Express Tools

Throughout this text, the AutoCAD Express Tools in AutoCAD 2004 are discussed where applicable. The **MKLTYPE** command available with the Express Tools provides a quick way to create a linetype from a series of objects. If the Express Tools are installed, they can be accessed from the **Express** pull-down menu. To create a linetype with the **MKLTYPE** command, first draw a series of lines, spaces, and dots. Use lines, polylines, and points to draw the linetype desired. See **Figure 27-27.** Once the linetype is drawn, select **Make Linetype** from the **Tools** cascading menu in the **Express** pull-down menu, or enter mkltype at the Command prompt.

This displays the **Select Linetype File** dialog box. Select an existing .lin file or create a new file. If you select an existing file, you are asked whether you want to overwrite it. If you select **Yes**, AutoCAD will take the existing file and append it with the new linetype definition.

## Exercise 27-10

◆ In Notepad, open the My Linetypes.lin file you created in Exercise 27-9.
◆ Add the following linetype definition. Be sure to pay attention to the correct syntax of the text string.

    *COLD_WATER_SUPPLY,Cold water supply —— CW —— CW —— CW ——
    A,0.5,–0.2,["CW",STANDARD,S=0.1,R=0.0,X=–0.1,Y=–.05],–0.2

◆ Save the file from Notepad.
◆ Create a linetype with the word "SEWER" between lines. Use the **MKLTYPE** command to create the new linetype.
◆ Load the new custom linetypes. Draw a few lines with the new linetypes.
◆ Adjust the **LTSCALE** system variable as needed.
◆ Save the drawing as ex27-10.

## Creating complex linetypes with shapes

A complex linetype can have a shape embedded into the definition instead of a text string. Before a shape can be assigned to a linetype definition, the shape must exist within AutoCAD. By default, AutoCAD loads a shape file named ltypeshp.shx whenever a complex linetype containing shapes is loaded into the drawing. The ltypeshp.shx file contains five shapes. These five shapes are used in the complex shape linetypes found in the acad.lin file. See **Figure 27-29**.

When a linetype containing a shape is loaded, AutoCAD loads the appropriate SHX file. If a shape file is not loaded, the **LOAD** command can be used to load a shape file (SHX file). The ltypeshp.shx file is found in the AutoCAD \Support folder. When the **LOAD** command is used, the **Select Shape File** dialog box is displayed, allowing you to load a shape file.

**Figure 27-29.**
The five shapes shown here are included in the default ltypeshp.shx file.

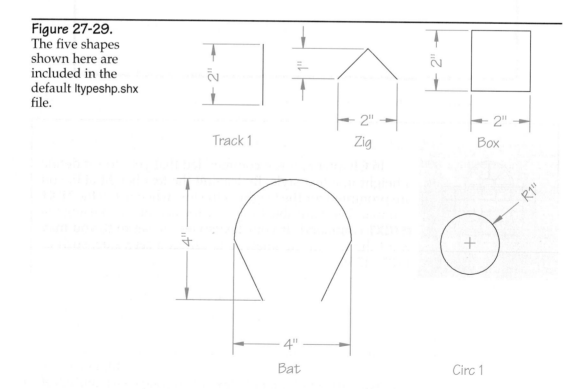

Track 1        Zig        Box

Bat        Circ 1

After a shape file is loaded, the shapes contained within can be listed. To list the shapes in the ltypeshp.shx file, type shape at the Command prompt. You are prompted for a name or you can use the **?** option to list the available shapes. The following sequence is used to list the shapes.

Command: **shape.⏎**
Enter shape name or [?]: **?** ⏎
Enter shape name(s) to list <*>: ⏎
Available shapes:
File: *path*\SUPPORT\ltypeshp.shx
TRACK1    ZIG
BOX        CIRC1
BAT

The **SHAPE** command can also be used to insert a shape into the drawing:

Command: **shape.⏎**
Enter shape name or [?]: **circ1.⏎**
Specify insertion point: *(pick insertion point)*
Specify height <1.0000>: ⏎
Specify rotation angle <0>: ⏎
Command:

The shape is added to the drawing. A shape cannot be exploded, but most editing commands can be used on a shape. Only the Insert object snap mode can be used on shapes. Shapes can be plotted.

The AutoCAD Express Tools include a command to create shapes and write their definitions to a .shx file. This is the **MKSHAPE** command. Before creating a shape definition, you need to draw the symbol. You can use lines, polylines, arcs, and circles. When creating the shape, keep in mind what the shape will be used for. If a shape will be placed in a linetype definition, then you probably want the shape to be drawn at the scale you intend on seeing in the finished plot. If you are creating a fancy linetype or inserting a shape that does not have to conform to a specific scale, then the shape can be drawn at any size. **Figure 27-30** displays some examples of shapes that can be incorporated into a linetype.

Once the symbol has been drawn, the shape can be created. To create the shape, select **Make Shape** from the **Tools** cascading menu in the **Express** pull-down menu or enter mkshape at the Command prompt. This displays the **Select Shape File** dialog box. Assign a name for your shape file and pick **Save**. You will next be prompted for the name of the shape. Enter a name and press the [Enter] key. The next prompt requires a resolution for the shape. The value can be a number between 8 and 32,767. The higher the value, the more accurate the appearance of the shape in the drawing.

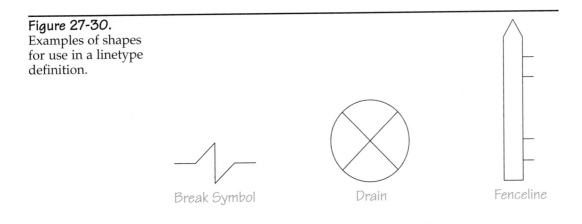

**Figure 27-30.**
Examples of shapes for use in a linetype definition.

Break Symbol          Drain          Fenceline

After setting the resolution, you must specify an insertion point for the shape and select the objects for the shape. The following prompt sequence is used to create a shape named Break:

Command: **MKSHAPE**⏎
Enter the name of the shape: **Break.**⏎
Enter resolution <128>: **10000.**⏎
Specify insertion base point: *(specify the insertion point)*
Select objects: *(Pick an object(s))*
Select objects: ⏎

After selecting objects and pressing [Enter], the shape file is compiled. This example creates a shape for the break line from **Figure 27-30.** When a shape is created with the **MKSHAPE** command, AutoCAD creates a .shp and a .shx file. The .shp file is used to create the shape and the .shx file is used to compile a number of different shapes together for use with the **SHAPE** command.

As is the case with the **MKLTYPE** command, selecting an existing .shp file when creating a shape with the **MKSHAPE** command causes the resulting .shx file to be appended with the new shape definition.

After your shapes have been created, they can be inserted into the drawing and placed between lines that will make up the linetype. Then use the **MKLTYPE** command to create the linetype. The linetype can also be created manually by editing the appropriate linetype file. The syntax for a complex linetype with a shape is very similar to the syntax for a linetype with text. The following syntax is used for linetype definitions with shapes:

[*shape name,shape file name,*S=*scale,*R=*rotation,*X=*X axis offset,*Y=*Y axis offset*]

The first two entries are the only entries that are different from those used for custom linetypes with text. These are described below.
- **Shape name.** This is the name of the shape that will be drawn. This field is required in order to draw the shape within the linetype.
- **Shape file name.** This is the name of the compiled .shx shape definition file. This field is also required to generate the shape. If the .shx file path is not in the Support File Search Path, the shape will not be drawn. The path to the shape file name can be added here.

For additional information on customization in AutoCAD, refer to the AutoCAD help file or the text *AutoCAD and its Applications—Advanced,* available from Goodheart-Willcox Publisher.

## Exercise 27-11

◆ Start a new drawing using one of your templates.
◆ Draw the symbols shown in **Figure 27-30.**
◆ Use the **MKSHAPE** command to create a shape from each symbol.
◆ Enter CustShp.shp for the shape file name. Use the CustShp.shp file for each shape and overwrite it when prompted by AutoCAD. This will ensure that the shapes are compiled together into the CustShp.shx file.
◆ To check the creation of the shapes, start a new drawing and use the **LOAD** command to load the CustShp.shx file. Then use the **SHAPE** command to list and insert each shape.

# Chapter Test

*Answer the following questions on a separate sheet of paper.*

1. Define *hyperlink.*
2. Identify at least two uses for hyperlinks.
3. How do you open a hyperlink in its native application?
4. What is a script file?
5. In a script file, how many AutoCAD commands or options can be entered on each line?
6. Which commands *cannot* be used in a script file?
7. How is a return at the Command prompt represented in the script?
8. What happens if a space is placed as a return in a script file?
9. How do you run a script file?
10. Name the file where the AutoCAD toolbar information is written.
11. Give the file extension of the file AutoCAD creates after "reading" a menu file.
12. Where is the information saved by default when a toolbar is customized or created?
13. What happens if you reload a MNU file instead of the MNC or MNS file?
14. Name the command used to load additional menus.
15. To create a menu named Custom Menu, what is entered on the second line in Notepad?
16. Which dialog box do you open to start creating a custom toolbar?
17. How do you add a command to a customized toolbar?
18. How do you modify a toolbar button?
19. Define *macro.*
20. What does ^C^C placed in the **Macro:** area of the **Button Properties** tab mean?
21. When typing the path to a script file, why are forward slashes used in place of the normal backslashes?
22. How do you create a button image from scratch?
23. Why is it a good idea to do a "save as" when saving a button image?
24. How can you make sure menu customizations are reloaded and not lost?
25. What is the name of the default linetype definition file for AutoCAD? In which folder is it located by default?
26. Compare simple linetypes to complex linetypes.
27. Describe the contents of the first line of code for a linetype definition.
28. Describe the contents of the second line of code for a linetype definition.
29. What does a positive number, a negative number, and zero indicate in a pattern descriptor?
30. How is a custom linetype made available in AutoCAD?
31. What are the two types of complex linetypes that can be created?
32. Which command is used to list the shapes in the drawing?
33. When a shape is embedded into a complex linetype, how can you ensure AutoCAD will find the shape when the linetype is loaded?

*For the following problems, check with your instructor or employer before creating folders or altering the default AutoCAD files.*

1. Create a folder on your computer named Custom. In the Custom folder, add a folder named Menu. In the **Options** dialog box, add the Custom and Menu folders to the Support File Search Path.

2. Write a script file to set units to architectural, set up model space limits to 36' × 88', and create a layer named Walls assigned the color blue and set current.

3. Write a script file that creates the following layers. At the end, Layer 0 should be set current.

| Layer Name | Color | Linetype |
|------------|-------|----------|
| M-WALL | Red | Continuous |
| M-DOOR | Blue | Continuous |
| M-WIND | Green | Continuous |
| M-DIMS | Cyan | Continuous |
| M-NOTE | Magenta | Continuous |
| U-WALL | Red | Continuous |
| U-DOOR | Blue | Continuous |
| U-WIND | Green | Continuous |
| U-DIMS | Cyan | Continuous |
| U-NOTE | Magenta | Continuous |

4. Create a menu file with a menu group named Custom. Use the **MENULOAD** command to load the menu file. Then, create a toolbar named **Layers** assigned to the Custom menu group.

   - Create a button that runs the script file. Hint: If the button does not work, you may need to set **FILEDIA** to 0 and add the path and file name to the script. Remember to set **FILEDIA** back to 1 at the end of the button macro.
   - Create a button that sets Layer 0 current, freezes all the layers, and then thaws any layers that begin with the letter M. The macro could be written as follows.

     ^C^C-LAYER;SET;0;FREEZE;*;THAW;M*;;

   - Create a button that sets Layer 0 current, freezes all the layers, and then thaws any layers that begin with the letter U.
   - After the menu is created, save the MNS file as an MNU file.

5. Load the custom menu created in Problem 4. Create a toolbar named **Tools** on the Custom menu group.
   - Create a button that finds the midpoint between two cursor picks. The macro could be written as follows.

        'CAL;(CUR+CUR)/2;

   - Notice there is no "cancel" in the macro. This is also a transparent command.
   - Create a button that will make a Dimension layer, initiate the **DIMLINEAR** command to draw linear dimensions, and immediately open the **Drafting Settings** dialog box with the **Object Snap** tab displayed to select and turn on object snaps.
   - Create a button to offset objects 6".
   - After creating the buttons, save the MNS file as an MNU file.
6. Create definitions for the following linetypes. Start with a "blank" text file in Windows Notepad. When done, save the file as p27-6.lin. Finally, test the linetypes in a new AutoCAD drawing.

Waste Water ———— W W ———— W W ———— W W ————

Cold Water ————C W————C W————C W————

TV Wire ————T V————T V————T V————

Coaxial Cable ————CABLE————CABLE————

Stone Path

# AIA Layering Standards

The American Institute of Architects (AIA) is a professional organization devoted to architects and the architectural field. The organization specializes in continuing education, seminars, and information that architects need to be proficient in their careers. More recently, the AIA has become a focal point for the standardization of CAD drawings. One of the most important contributions to CAD from the AIA is the development of a layering standard.

Layering standards help multiple disciplines (such as the architectural, mechanical, plumbing, and electrical disciplines) work together by eliminating confusion as to what the layers in a project are representing. The following describes the AIA layering system as developed by the AIA in the second edition of the *CAD Layer Guidelines*. This document is available through The American Institute of Architects, 1735 New York Avenue NW, Washington, DC 20006.

## Naming Layers

The AIA layering standard consists of a layer name that can be broken down into four distinct categories. The four categories contain specific information regarding the type of architectural feature the layer is representing. The four categories are listed below.

- Discipline code
- Major group
- Minor group (or user defined)
- Status

The format of the four categories is displayed in **Figure A-1**.

At a minimum, the layer name must include the first two groups: the discipline code and the major group.

The *discipline code* consists of a letter and a hyphen. The letter used in the code corresponds to the discipline related to the objects on the layer. The following tables list some common discipline codes. Refer to the *CAD Layer Guidelines* for a complete listing of discipline codes.

**Figure A-1.**
Layer names may include a discipline code, major group, minor group, and status field.

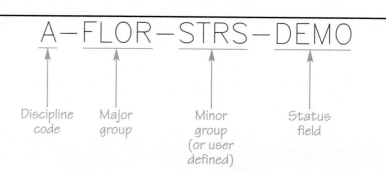

| Discipline Code | Description |
| --- | --- |
| A- | Architectural |
| C- | Civil |
| E- | Electrical |
| M- | Mechanical |
| P- | Plumbing |
| S- | Structural |

The *major group* identifies the type of objects in the layer. For example, walls, doors, and windows are building components that fit into the major group category. The major group consists of four letters, abbreviating the component. Some common major groups are included in the layer names listed in the following table. Refer to the *CAD Layer Guidelines* for a complete list of major group classifications.

| Layer Name | Description |
| --- | --- |
| A-DOOR | Doors |
| A-CLNG | Ceilings |
| C-TOPO | Contour lines |
| C-STRM | Storm drainage |
| E-LITE | Lighting |
| E-DATA | Data outlets |
| M-HVAC | HVAC system |
| M-REFG | Refrigeration system |
| P-DOMW | Domestic water system |
| P-FIXT | Fixtures |
| S-FNDN | Foundations |
| S-COLS | Columns |

The major groups in the layer names listed in the table above identify the type of objects drawn on the layer. Major groups can also be used to identify the drawing type or text items. The following table lists these additional major codes.

| Major Code | Description |
| --- | --- |
| *-ANNO | Text, dimensions, symbols, and borders |
| *-ELEV | Elevations |
| *-SECT | Sections |
| *-DETL | Details |

The optional *minor group* is a four-character designation that further identifies the objects on the layer. For example, the layer name A-GLAZ-SILL indicates the layer is used for window sills. Although there is a list of common designations, you can create your own minor codes. The following table lists some common layer names that include minor groups. Refer to the *CAD Layer Guidelines* for a complete list.

| Discipline Code, Major Group, and Minor Group | Description |
|---|---|
| A-WALL-PRHT | Partial-height walls |
| C-ROAD-CURB | Curbs |
| E-POWR-PANL | Power panels |
| M-EXHS-EQPM | Exhaust equipment |
| P-STRM-PIPE | Storm drainage piping |
| S-SLAB-RBAR | Slab reinforcing |

Remember that the minor group is also considered a user-definable group. If there is a need to further describe a major group, create a minor group.

The *status field* is also an optional, four-character designation. This provides additional information about the objects on the layer. The status field can be used to identify existing objects, specify objects to be demolished, or indicate when an object will be installed. The status field is always placed at the end of the layer name. This way a full description of the item is made with its current status. The following table contains some common layer names including status fields. Refer to the *CAD Layer Guidelines* for a complete list of status fields.

| Layer Name | Description |
|---|---|
| A-FURN-FILE-MOVE | File cabinets to be moved |
| C-PKNG-ISLD-DEMO | Existing parking lot islands to be demolished |
| E-SITE-OVHD-RELO | Relocated electrical overhead lines |
| M-STEM-MPIP-FUTR | Medium pressure steam piping to be installed in the future |
| P-SANR-FLDR-EXST | Existing floor drains to remain |
| S-GRID-INTR-NEWW | New interior column grid |

## Typical Layer Example

A drawing may contain a few layers or many layers. Architectural layers can be mixed with structural layers or mechanical layers. However, standard practice places layers for different disciplines in separate drawing files. These separate files are then referenced together.

A typical floor plan might contain the following layers:

|  |  |
|---|---|
| A-ANNO-DIMS | Annotation dimensions |
| A-ANNO-LEGN | Schedules and legends |
| A-ANNO-NOTE | Annotation notes |
| A-AREA | Area boundary lines |
| A-COLS | Architectural columns |
| A-COMM | Communication lines |
| A-CLNG-GRID | Ceiling grid |
| A-DOOR | Doors |
| A-DOOR-DEMO | Doors to be removed |
| A-DOOR-IDEN | Door numbering symbols |
| A-FLOR | Floor plan information |
| A-FLOR-CASE | Floor plan casework (cabinets) |
| A-FLOR-FIXT | Floor plan fixtures |
| A-FLOR-HRAL | Stair and balcony handrails |
| A-FLOR-IDEN | Room numbering symbols |
| A-FLOR-OVHD | Overhead features on floor plan |
| A-FLOR-PATT | Floor plan hatch patterns |
| A-FLOR-PFIX | Plumbing fixtures |
| A-FLOR-RISR | Stair risers |
| A-FLOR-STRS | Floor plan stairs |
| A-FURN | Furniture plans |
| A-GLAZ | Windows |
| A-GLAZ-IDEN | Window numbering symbols |
| A-GLAZ-SILL | Window sills |
| A-LITE | Light fixtures |
| A-LITE-SWCH | Light switches |
| A-POWR | Power lines |
| A-ROOF-OTLN | Roof outline |
| A-WALL | Walls |
| A-WALL-IDEN | Wall numbering symbols |
| A-WALL-FIRE | Fire wall patterning |
| A-WALL-FULL | Full height walls |
| A-WALL-PATT | Wall hatch patterns |
| A-WALL-POWR | Wall power outlets |
| A-WALL-PRHT | Partial height walls |
| S-BEAM | Structural beams |
| S-COLS | Structural columns |
| S-FNDN | Structural foundation |
| S-JOIS | Structural joists |
| S-WALL | Structural bearing walls |

There are many more layers that can be used when creating construction documents. Refer to the *CAD Layer Guidelines* for a complete guide to layering standards.

# Drawing Name Conventions

Drawing name conventions can vary between offices. One office may choose to save drawing names by assigning a job code along with a designator indicating the sheet where the file belongs. Another office may combine all of the drawings into one file and save the name with only a job number. Other offices may name drawing files according to the discipline and type of drawing and store the individual drawings in a file folder with the job number. No matter how the drawing names are determined, it is important to establish and maintain a standard for consistency in the office. The following provides a few ideas on how to determine the name for a drawing file.

When working in a small architectural office that specializes in residences or small commercial structures, all drawing sheets can be combined into the same drawing file for each project. To separate the drawing sheets, paper space layouts are used, each showing a different sheet in the set of drawings. In this case, it is often an advantage to name the drawing using a job number. **Figure B-1** provides suggestions in creating a file name based on a job number.

**Figure B-1.**
Some drawing name systems are based on the project number of the job.

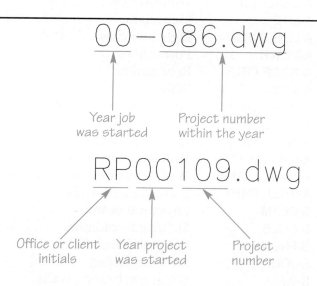

In larger architectural firms, drawing sheets may be separated into individual drawing files so many people can work on them. In this case, a drawing file may be saved with the job number and a designator indicating the sheet in which the drawing belongs. **Figure B-2** gives examples of file names using this method.

The disadvantage to the above system is that if a drawing file is referenced into another drawing, the file name becomes a part of the layer name. This creates long layer names. If drawings are continuously referenced into one another, nested xrefs are created and the layer names may exceed their 255-character limit.

The AIA *CAD Layer Guidelines* standard includes standards for naming files. In this system, the file name includes a discipline code, drawing type code, and user-defined descriptor. **Figure B-3** illustrates samples of this system.

**Figure B-2.**
These drawing name systems include the project number and the sheet designator.

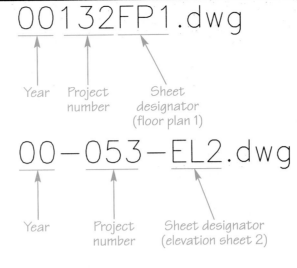

**Figure B-3.**
Sample drawing file names using standard naming conventions from the AIA *CAD Layer Guidelines*.

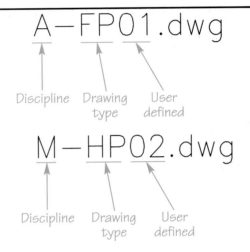

The discipline codes are identical to the discipline codes used when naming layers, as outlined in Appendix A. Some drawing type codes are used for all disciplines, while others are specific to a single discipline. The following table lists some common drawing types. Refer to the *CAD Layer Guidelines* for a complete listing.

| Discipline and Drawing Type | Description |
|---|---|
| *-FP | Floor Plan |
| *-SP | Site Plan |
| *-EL | Elevation |
| A-CP | Ceiling Plans |
| C-GP | Grading Plans |
| E-LP | Lighting Plans |
| M-HP | HVAC Ductwork Plans |
| P-PP | Plumbing Plans |
| S-FP | Framing Plans |

* identifies drawing type codes that apply to all disciplines.

# Typical Sheet Numbering Conventions

A typical set of architectural construction documents includes building drawings, structural drawings, mechanical drawings, plumbing drawings, electrical drawings, and schematic drawings. Depending on the office and the specialties in the firm, an architectural office may draw only the architectural drawings, and contract out the electrical, plumbing, structural, and mechanical drawings to organizations that specialize in those areas. A larger firm may draw most of the set in house, contracting only when necessary.

Sheet numbers are broken down into a discipline code and a sheet type designator. The sheet type designator always remains the same, no matter how large or small the project. Not all of the designators may be required for a set of construction documents.

**Figure C-1** shows a few sheets from a construction document set. Notice the discipline code is followed by the sheet type designator. Typical codes are identified in the following tables.

| Discipline Code | Description | Discipline Code | Description |
|---|---|---|---|
| A | Architectural | P | Plumbing |
| C | Civil | Q | Equipment |
| E | Electrical | R | Resource |
| F | Fire Protection | S | Structural |
| G | General | T | Telecommunications |
| H | Hazardous Materials | X | Other Disciplines |
| I | Interiors | Z | Contractor/Shop Drawings |
| L | Landscape | | |
| M | Mechanical | | |

**Figure C-1.**
Numbered drawings in a construction document set.

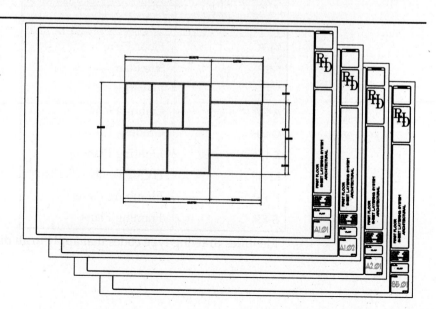

| Sheet Type Designators | Description |
|---|---|
| 0.01–0.99 | General (index, symbols, legend, notes, abbreviations, location map) |
| 1.01–1.99 | Plans (floor, foundation, ceiling, framing, roof, plumbing, lighting, mechanical) |
| 2.01–2.99 | Elevations (exterior, small scale) |
| 3.01–3.99 | Sections |
| 4.01–4.99 | Large Scale (plans, interior elevations, sections that are not details) |
| 5.01–5.99 | Details |
| 6.01–6.99 | Schedules and Diagrams |
| 7.01–7.99 | User Defined |
| 8.01–8.99 | User Defined |
| 9.01–9.99 | 3D Views (isometrics, perspectives, photographs) |

The following table lists typical sheet numbering conventions for an architectural set of construction documents.

| Sheet Number | Description |
|---|---|
| A1.01 | Architectural floor plan, first floor, sheet number 1 |
| A1.02 | Architectural floor plan, second floor, sheet number 2 |
| A2.01 | Architectural elevation sheet, sheet number 1 |
| A2.02 | Architectural elevation sheet, sheet number 2 |
| A5.01 | Architectural detail sheet, sheet number 1 |
| S3.01 | Structural section sheet, sheet number 1 |
| S5.10 | Structural detail sheet number 10 |
| E6.03 | Electrical schedule sheet number 3 |

Residential design drawings often do not conform to a typical standard. Sheet numbers are determined by the need for the number of drawings. Often, any required information is added onto the floor plans, foundation plans, sections, and detail sheets, eliminating the need for a large number of drawings.

**Figure C-2** shows a few sheets from a residential drawing set. A typical set of residential plans might contain the following sheets in the listed order:
- Cover Sheets (when required, often containing a presentation drawing)
- Site Plans
- Exterior Elevations
- Floor Plans, often containing the following:
  - Electrical
  - Structural
  - Plumbing Fixtures
- Foundation Plans, often containing the following:
  - Structural
  - Plumbing Fixture Locations
- Roof Plans, often containing the following:
  - Vent Locations
  - Downspout Locations
- Sections
- Details

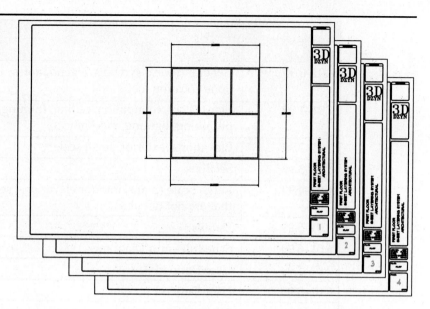

**Figure C-2.**
Numbered sheets in a residential drawing set.

APPENDIX D

# Introduction to the Construction Specifications Institute (CSI)

The Construction Specifications Institute (CSI) is a group of professionals devoted to the standardization of the Architectural, Engineering, and Construction (AEC) fields. This group has created a system of organization for the architect, engineer, and contractor called the MasterFormat. The system is broken down into 16 major groups called *divisions*. Within each division is a series of subdivisions called *sections*. Items that can be organized under this system could include block names, keynotes, and products such as furniture, bathroom hardware, and fixtures.

When organizing CAD information under this system, file names and product names are often prefixed with the appropriate division number. A listing of businesses or professional people are listed under the appropriate division number. For example, the beginning name of the product may have the division number and possibly the section number within the name. Appendix E introduces keynotes organized under the CSI system with a general listing of the sections organized under each division.

## CSI MasterFormat Divisions

**Division 1—General Requirements**
General notes, miscellaneous blocks not covered in other divisions, and general contractors

**Division 2—Sitework**
Site notes, water lines, elevation blocks, and civil engineers

**Division 3—Concrete**
Foundation notes, footing blocks, and concrete companies

**Division 4—Masonry**
Fireplace notes, chimney details, and masons

**Division 5—Metals**
Steel notes, metal bracket blocks, and structural engineers

**Division 6—Wood and Plastic**
Joist notes, glulam beam details, and carpenters

**Division 7—Thermal and Moisture Protection**
Moisture protection notes, flashing details, and insulation manufacturers

**Division 8—Doors and Windows**
Installation notes, door blocks, and window manufacturers

**Division 9—Finishes**
Painting notes, finish symbol blocks, and flooring companies

**Division 10—Specialties**
Specialty notes, signage blocks, and handrail manufacturers

**Division 11—Equipment**
Installation notes, medical equipment blocks, and commercial kitchen manufacturers

**Division 12—Furnishings**
Manufacturing notes, furniture blocks, and furniture manufacturers

*Appendix D*                                                                 **1051**

**Division 13—Special Construction**

Engineering notes, ADA blocks, precast concrete manufacturers

**Division 14—Conveying Systems**

Escalator notes, conveyor belt blocks, and elevator manufacturers

**Division 15—Mechanical**

HVAC notes, plumbing blocks, and plumbers

**Division 16—Electrical**

Ceiling grid notes, lighting blocks, and electricians

# Keynote Glossary

A keynote system is a system of tags designed to annotate a drawing through the use of symbols. Too many notes clutter and confuse the drawing. The tags refer back to a keynote legend where the full note can be found. Each tag is typically a number pointing to the area to be noted. Some offices place an elongated hexagon or oval around the number to make the tag more distinguishable. **Figure E-1** displays typical keynotes.

When developing keynotes, write down the list of common notes you use when annotating your drawing, and then assign a number tag to each of them. The following table lists some examples of typical keynotes based upon the Construction Specifications Institute (CSI) numbering system.

**Figure E-1.**
Different types of keynotes and their corresponding legends.

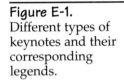

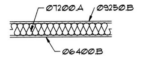

KEYNOTE LEGEND
06400.B  FLUSH PANELING
07200.A  BATT INSULATION
09250.B  GYPSUM BOARD± ⅝" TYPE'X'

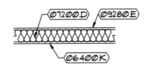

KEYNOTE LEGEND
06400.K  PARTICLE BOARD
07200.D  LOOSE-FILL INSULATION
09280.E  ACOUSTICAL SEALANT

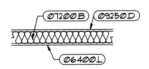

KEYNOTE LEGEND
06400.L  PLYWOOD
07200.B  RIGID BOARD INSULATION
09250.D  GYPSUM BOARD± 2LAYERS ½"

## Keynote System Examples

| Keynote Tag | Note | Keynote Tag | Note |
|---|---|---|---|
| 01010.B | EXISTING CONSTRUCTION | 03300.C7 | 4" THICK CONCRETE SLAB |
| 01010.A1 | WORK BY OTHERS | 04200.B3 | 8" CONCRETE BLOCK |
| 01500.B1 | TEMPORARY ACCESS ROAD | 04400.A5 | MARBLE |
| | | 05200.A2 | STEEL JOISTS |
| 01500.B8 | TEMPORARY PARK ING AREA | 05300.E1 | CORRUGATED METAL DECK |
| 02060.D2 | REMOVE BUILDINGS | 06100.D4 | 2 × 4 T&G DECKING |
| 02200.B1 | REMOVE DIRT | 06100.H17 | DBL 2 × 10 HEADER |
| 02500.B10 | 4" CONCRETE WALK W/ BROOM FINISH | 06100.J14 | 2 × 12 JOISTS @ 16" O.C. |
| 03300.A11 | 1'-6" THICK CONT FOOTING | 06110.A1 | ROOF TRUSSES |

*(Continued)*

| Keynote Tag | Note | Keynote Tag | Note |
|---|---|---|---|
| 06400.B3 | COUNTERTOP W/ INTEGRAL BACKSPLASH | 11100.A1 | CENTRAL VACUUM SYSTEM |
| | | 11100.C3 | SAFE |
| 07100.A5 | NEOPRENE SHEET WATERPROOFING | 11300.A1 | BEVERAGE VENDING MACHINE |
| 07200.A3 | 1″ BOARD INSULATION | 11400.A1 | FOOD COOKING EQUIPMENT |
| 07300.A1 | ASPHALT SHINGLES | | |
| 07400.B3 | VINYL CLADDING/ SIDING | 11400.B2 | GARBAGE DISPOSAL |
| | | 11400.C1 | REFRIGERATOR |
| 07800.A1 | METAL FRAMED SKYLIGHT | 11400.C2 | REFRIGERATED CASE |
| | | 11400.C3 | FREEZER |
| 08100.A1 | HOLLOW METAL DOOR | 11500.A2 | DARKROOM PROCESSING EQUIPMENT |
| 08200.A1 | 1-3/4″ SOLID CORE WOOD DOOR | | |
| | | 12300.C3 | LIBRARY CASEWORK |
| 08500.C2 | VINYL CASEMENT WINDOW | 12500.A1 | HORIZONTAL LOUVER BLINDS |
| 08600.B3 | WOOD BAY WINDOW | 12500.A2 | VERTICAL LOUVER BLINDS |
| 08800.B4 | 1/4″ CLEAR TEMPERED FLOAT GLASS | | |
| | | 12500.A3 | CURTAIN |
| 08900.A3 | STAINLESS STEEL CURTAIN WALL SYSTEM | 12700.A1 | AUDITORIUM SEAT-ING |
| | | 13030.D1 | CLEAN ROOM |
| 09200.A4 | GYPSUM PLASTER | 13030.D2 | DARKROOM |
| 09250.A3 | 5/8″ GYP. BD. CEILING | 14200.A1 | PASSENGER ELEVATOR, HYDRAULIC |
| 09250.B6 | 3-5/8″ METAL STUDS @ 16″ O.C. | | |
| 09300.A1 | CERAMIC TILE | 14300.A1 | ESCALATOR |
| 09300.A6 | QUARRY TILE | 14400.A2 | WHEELCHAIR LIFT |
| 09500.A4 | ACOUSTICAL WALL-TREATMENT | 15050.A3 | MOTOR |
| | | 15050.A4 | PUMP |
| 09550.B4 | WOOD STRIP FLOORING | 15300.A3 | SPRINKLER HEAD |
| 09600.A4 | MARBLE FLOORING | 15400.A4 | ROOF DRAIN |
| 09600.C1 | CARPETING | 15400.D1 | WATER FOUNTAIN |
| 09800.A2 | ANTI-GRAFFITI COATING | 15500.A2 | ROOFTOP HVAC EQUIPMENT |
| 09800.B5 | WALLPAPER | 15500.A5 | DUCT |
| 10100.A3 | ERASABLE MARKER BOARD | 16050.A3 | ELECTRICAL CONDUIT |
| 10200.A5 | METAL GRILLE | 16500.C1 | RECESSED CAN FIXTURE |
| 10350.A1 | AUTOMATIC FLAG POLE | | |
| 10500.A1 | METAL LOCKERS | | |

# Construction Specifications Institute (CSI) Block Naming Conventions

Block names can contain up to 255 characters. If an AutoCAD drawing is saved as a Release 14 or earlier drawing, AutoCAD truncates the block name to 31 characters. When blocks with long file names are used in xrefs, the drawing name of the xref is added to the beginning of the block name. This can also be a problem when saving the drawing as a Release 14 or earlier drawing. Due to these limitations, it is generally a good idea to try to limit the characters in a block name.

This appendix provides suggestions for assigning block names using the CSI MasterFormat system in an attempt to standardize the way you work with AutoCAD. The suggested format is a 10-digit block name with four parts. The parts are shown in **Figure F-1** and described below:

- **CSI division number.** The first two digits correspond to the CSI MasterFormat division number.
- **Block type.** The third entry identifies the type of block, such as P (plan block), E (elevation block), or Z (3D block).
- **Symbol type.** The fourth through seventh entries identify the type of symbol, such as TOIL (toilet), BTUB (bathtub), or DTAG (door tag).
- **Block number.** The last three values assign a block number to differentiate between items within a class of symbols. For example, if there are several types of sinks used in a project, each would have a unique block number.

**Figure F-1.**
In this block naming system, the block name has four components.

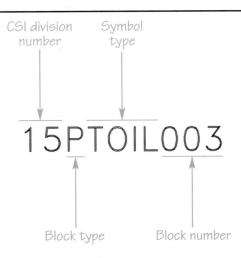

The following page lists a few examples of block names for each division. Remember, this is only a suggested format for organization and is designed to help limit the number of characters used in a block name. You can add more characters as needed, such as in the symbol type area. Remember, when creating a block, you can also add a description to the block for use with **DesignCenter**.

# Block Name Examples

| Block Name | Type of Block | Block Name | Type of Block |
|---|---|---|---|
| 01PREVT001 | Plan view—Revision note tag #1 | 10PSTPT002 | Plan view—Straight movable block #2 |
| 01PDWGT001 | Plan view—Drawing tag #1 | 10PCVPT001 | Plan view—Curved movable block #1 |
| 02ETREE002 | Elevation view—Tree block #2 | 10PFLPT001 | Plan view—Folding partition block #1 |
| 03EFNDT006 | Elevation view—Foundation detail #6 | 10PHDRL001 | Plan view—Hand rail block #1 |
| 03ZFTNG003 | 3D view—Footing block #3 | 11PDWSR001 | Plan view—Dishwasher block #1 |
| 04PFPLC004 | Plan view—Fireplace block #4 | 11PREFR003 | Plan view—Refrigerator block #3 |
| 04ECHIM002 | Elevation view—Chimney block #2 | 11PRANG002 | Plan view—Range block #2 |
| 04PCOLM002 | Plan view—Column block #2 | 11EOVEN001 | Elevation view—Oven block #1 |
| 04ZCOLM002 | 3D view—Column block #2 | 12PQBED001 | Plan view—Queen size bed block #1 |
| 05PPIPE011 | Plan view—Pipe block #11 | 12PCHAR005 | Plan view—Chair block #5 |
| 05PANGL014 | Plan view—Angle iron block #14 | 12EBKCS002 | Elevation view—Bookcase block #2 |
| 05PCHNL009 | Plan view—Steel channel block #9 | 12ZDESK001 | 3D view—Desk block #1 |
| 05PBOLT007 | Plan view—Bolt block #7 | 13PPOOL001 | Plan view—Swimming pool block #1 |
| 06PMLDG12 | Plan view—Wood molding block #12 | 13ZCVLT003 | 3D view—Concrete vault block #3 |
| 06EWLDT003 | Elevation view—Wall detail #3 | 13EGRNH002 | Elevation view—Greenhouse block #2 |
| 06PSTRS001 | Plan view—Stair block #1 | 13PADAB001 | Plan view—ADA bathroom block #1 |
| 06ZFRMG002 | 3D view—Wood framing block #2 | 14PELEV001 | Plan view—Elevator block #1 |
| 07EGTDT2 | Elevation view—Gutter detail #2 | 14EELEV001 | Elevation view—Elevator block #1 |
| 07PRFPT001 | Plan view—Roof pitch tag #1 | 14ZCNVR003 | 3D view—Conveyor belt block #3 |
| 07EVBAR001 | Elevation view—Vapor barrier block #1 | 14PESCL002 | Plan view—Escalator block #2 |
| 07PINSL002 | Plan view—Insulation symbol #2 | 15PBTUB004 | Plan view—Bathtub block #4 |
| 08PSIDR003 | Plan view—Single door block #3 | 15PSHWR002 | Plan view—Shower block #2 |
| 08PDBDR001 | Plan view—Double door block #1 | 15ZTOIL003 | 3D view—Toilet block #3 |
| 08ESHWN001 | Elevation view—Single hung window #1 | 15PSINK002 | Plan view—Sink block #2 |
| 08ZCSWN004 | 3D view—Casement window #4 | 16PCFAN002 | Plan view—Ceiling fan block #2 |
| 09PFINT002 | Plan view—Room finish tag #2 | 16PFLLT001 | Plan view—Fluorescent light block #1 |
| 09PCLGT001 | Plan view—Ceiling tag #1 | 16PINLT003 | Plan view—Incandescent light block #3 |
| 09PFNOT001 | Plan view—Finish note #1 | | |
| 09EMLDT003 | Elevation view—Molding detail #3 | 16PPWER002 | Plan view—Power outlet block #2 |

# Typical Architectural Blocks

The following pages display some common blocks used in the development of architectural drawings. Note that the dimensions provided are only the most common sizes and provide only a generic size. Sizes of blocks may differ depending on manufacturer and specific office practices. Also, the insertion points displayed are the suggested insertion points. Modify them as you see fit.

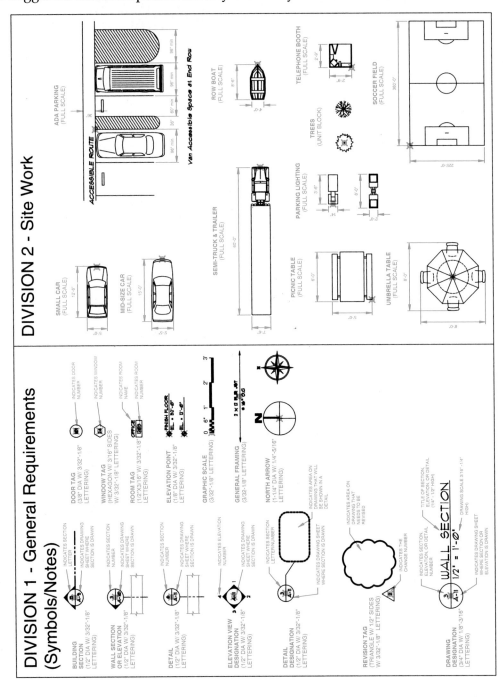

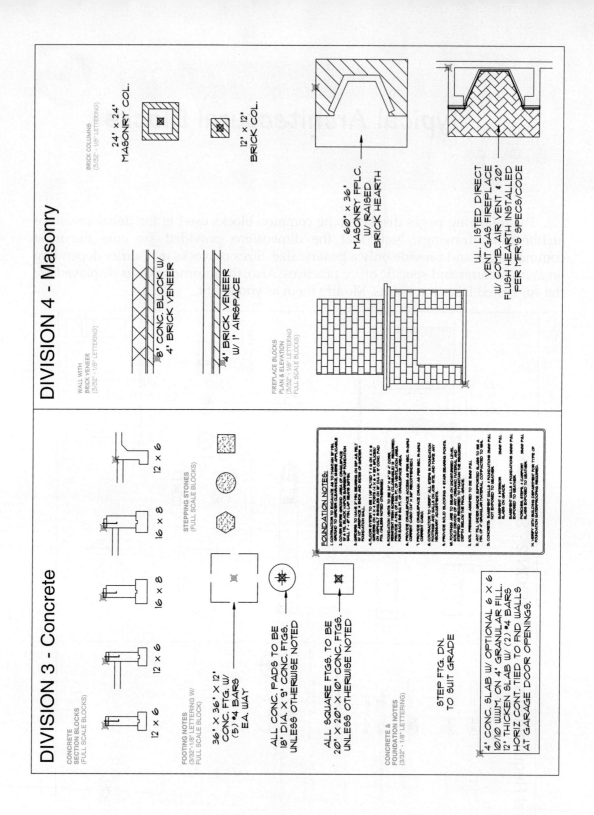

# DIVISION 4 - Masonry

BRICK COLUMNS
(3/32" - 1/8" LETTERING)

24" x 24"
MASONRY COL.

12" x 12"
BRICK COL.

WALL WITH
BRICK VENEER
(3/32" - 1/8" LETTERING)

8" CONC. BLOCK W/
4" BRICK VENEER

4" BRICK VENEER
W/ 1" AIRSPACE

60" x 36"
MASONRY FPLC.
W/ RAISED
BRICK HEARTH

FIREPLACE BLOCKS
PLAN & ELEVATION
(3/32" - 1/8" LETTERING
FULL SCALE BLOCKS)

U.L. LISTED DIRECT
VENT GAS FIREPLACE
W/ COMB. AIR VENT & 20"
FLUSH HEARTH INSTALLED
PER MFR'S SPECS/CODE

# DIVISION 3 - Concrete

CONCRETE
SECTION BLOCKS
(FULL SCALE BLOCKS)

12 x 6    12 x 6    16 x 8    16 x 8    12 x 6

STEPPING STONES
(FULL SCALE BLOCKS)

FOOTING NOTES
(3/32"-1/8" LETTERING W/
FULL SCALE BLOCK)

36' x 36' X 12'
CONC. FTG. W/
(5) #4 BARS
EA. WAY

ALL CONC. PADS TO BE
18" DIA. X 9" CONC. FTGS,
UNLESS OTHERWISE NOTED

ALL SQUARE FTGS. TO BE
20" X 20" X 10" CONC. FTGS.
UNLESS OTHERWISE NOTED

CONCRETE &
FOUNDATION NOTES
(3/32" - 1/8" LETTERING)

STEP FTG. DN.
TO SUIT GRADE

FOUNDATION NOTES:

1. CONTRACTOR TO EXCAVATE AS TO MAINTAIN 18" MIN.
   GROUND TO GIRDER CLEARANCE WHERE APPLICABLE.
2. COVER ENTIRE GROUND AREA OF CRAWLSPACE
   WITH 6 MIL POLY VAPOR BARRIER UP FOUNDATION
   WALL 7 - 8" MIN. LAP SEAMS 12"MIN.
3. GIRDERS TO HAVE 3" MIN. BEARING ON 8" MIN A.B. FELT
   ON FOUNDATION WALL.
4. FLOOR SYSTEM TO BE 1-3/4" PLYWD T & G ON 2 X 8
   SPF#2 @ 16" O.C. U.N.O. W/ 2 X 8 W/ R-30 BATTS INSUL.
   ON APPROVED SHINGLES ON 18" DIA. X 9" CONC. PAD
   FTG. U.N.O.W. NOTED OTHERWISE.
5. PROVIDE 12" MIN SCREEN, CLOSABLE AS REQUIRED,
   PROVIDE 1 SQ. FT. OF VENTILATION AREA
   FOR EACH 150 SQ. FT. OF CRAWLSPACE AREA.
6. CONTRACTOR TO VERIFY ALL STEPS IN FOUNDATION
   FOOTING AND WALLS ON JOB SITE, AND TAKE ANY
   CURRENT CARD (24" X 36" RECOMMENDED)
7. PROVIDE CRAWLSPACE DRAIN AS PER SEC. R-3612.
8. PROVIDE CRAWLSPACE ACCESS AS PER SEC. R-3612
   24" X 36" RECOMMENDED.
9. PROVIDE SOLID BLOCKING @ STAIR BEARING POINTS.
10. FOOTINGS ARE TO BEAR ON UNDISTURBED LEVEL
    SOIL DEVOID OF ANY ORGANIC MATERIAL AND
    POURED OVER 4" OF COMPACTED FILL BELOW THE REQUIRED
    DEPTH BELOW THE FINAL GRADE.
11. SOIL PRESSURE ASSUMED TO BE 2000 PSF.
12. ANY FILL UNDER GRADE SUPPORTED SLABS TO BE A
    MIN. OF 4" GRANULAR MATERIAL COMPACTED TO 2000.
13. CONCRETE: BASEMENT WALLS & FOUNDATION 2500 PSF.
    EXTERIOR PORCHES & GARAGE SLABS 3000 PSF.
    BASEMENT & INTERIOR
    SLABS ON GRADE.                3000 PSF.
    BASEMENT WALLS & FOUNDATION 3500 PSF.
    EXPOSED TO WEATHER.
    PORCHES & GARAGE SLABS        3500 PSF.
    SLABS EXPOSED TO WEATHER.
14. VERIFY WITH BUILDING DEPARTMENT FOR TYPE OF
    FOUNDATION WATERPROOFING REQUIRED.

4" CONC. SLAB W/ OPTIONAL 6 X 6
10/10 W.W.M. ON 4" GRANULAR FILL.
12" THICKEN SLAB W/ (2) #4 BARS
HORIZ CONT. TIED TO FND WALLS
AT GARAGE DOOR OPENINGS.

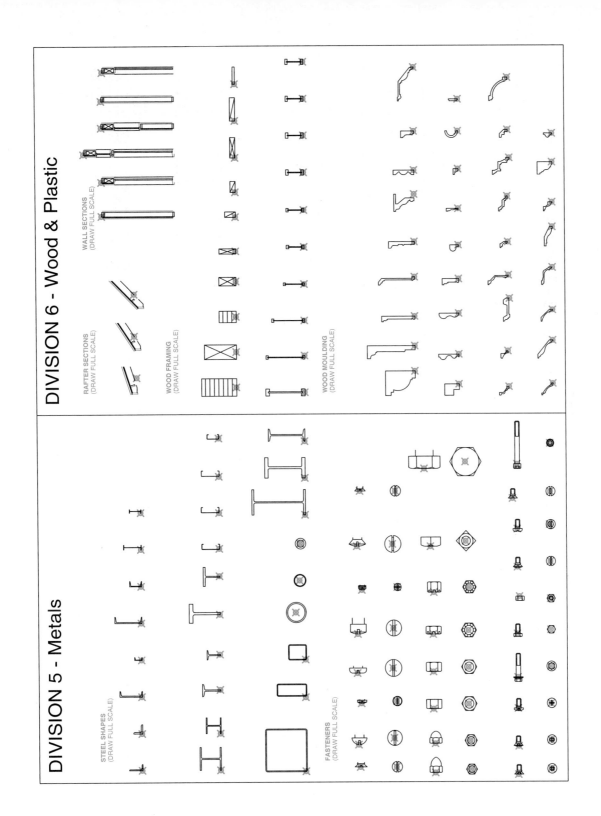

# DIVISION 6 - Wood & Plastic

**WALL SECTIONS**
(DRAW FULL SCALE)

**RAFTER SECTIONS**
(DRAW FULL SCALE)

**WOOD FRAMING**
(DRAW FULL SCALE)

**WOOD MOULDING**
(DRAW FULL SCALE)

# DIVISION 5 - Metals

**STEEL SHAPES**
(DRAW FULL SCALE)

**FASTENERS**
(DRAW FULL SCALE)

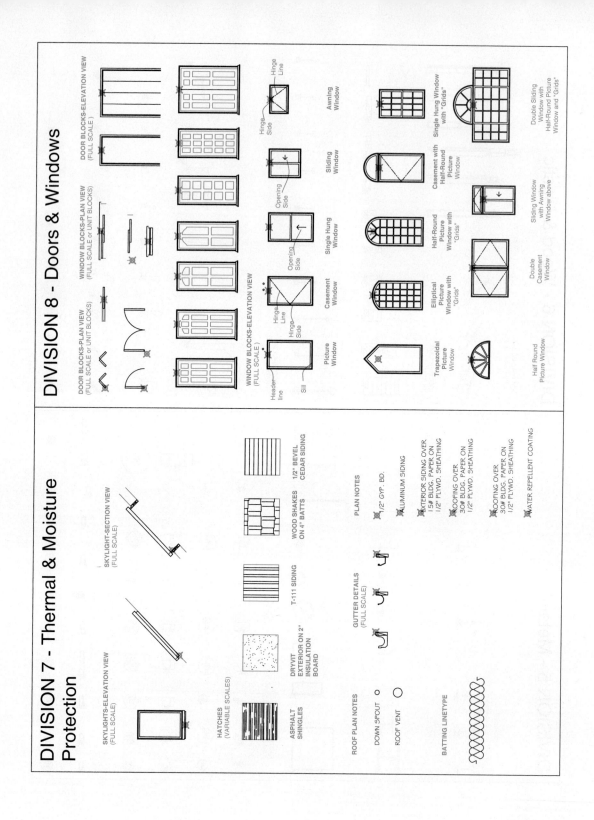

# DIVISION 7 - Thermal & Moisture Protection

**SKYLIGHTS-ELEVATION VIEW**
(FULL SCALE)

**SKYLIGHT-SECTION VIEW**
(FULL SCALE)

**HATCHES**
(VARIABLE SCALES)

1/2" BEVEL
CEDAR SIDING

WOOD SHAKES
ON 4" BATTS

T-111 SIDING

DRYVIT
EXTERIOR ON 2"
INSULATION
BOARD

**ASPHALT
SHINGLES**

**ROOF PLAN NOTES**

DOWN SPOUT

ROOF VENT

**GUTTER DETAILS**
(FULL SCALE)

**PLAN NOTES**

1/2" GYP. BD.

ALUMINUM SIDING

EXTERIOR SIDING OVER
15# BLDG. PAPER ON
1/2" PLYWD. SHEATHING

ROOFING OVER
30# BLDG. PAPER ON
1/2" PLYWD. SHEATHING

ROOFING OVER
30# BLDG. PAPER ON
1/2" PLYWD. SHEATHING

WATER REPELLENT COATING

**BATTING LINETYPE**

# DIVISION 8 - Doors & Windows

**DOOR BLOCKS-PLAN VIEW**
(FULL SCALE or UNIT BLOCKS)

**WINDOW BLOCKS-PLAN VIEW**
(FULL SCALE or UNIT BLOCKS)

**DOOR BLOCKS-ELEVATION VIEW**
(FULL SCALE)

**WINDOW BLOCKS-ELEVATION VIEW**
(FULL SCALE )

Header
line

Sill

Hinge
Line

Hinge
Side

Opening
Side

Opening
Side

Hinge
Line

Hinge
Side

Hinge
Side

**Picture
Window**

**Single Hung
Window**

**Casement
Window**

**Sliding
Window**

**Awning
Window**

**Trapezoidal
Picture
Window**

**Picture
Window**

**Elliptical
Picture
Window with
"Grids"**

**Casement
Window**

**Half-Round
Picture
Window with
"Grids"**

**Casement with
Half-Round
Picture
Window**

**Single Hung Window
with "Grids"**

Half Round
Picture Window

Double
Casement
Window

Sliding Window
with Awning
Window above

Double Sliding
Window with
Half-Round Picture
Window and "Grids"

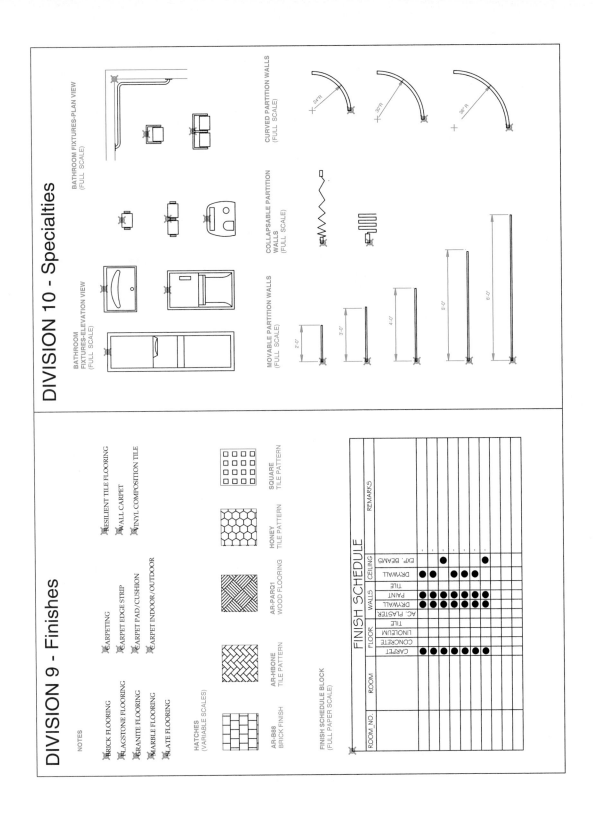

## DIVISION 9 - Finishes

NOTES

- BRICK FLOORING
- FLAGSTONE FLOORING
- GRANITE FLOORING
- MARBLE FLOORING
- SLATE FLOORING

- CARPETING
- CARPET EDGE STRIP
- CARPET PAD/CUSHION
- CARPET INDOOR/OUTDOOR

- RESILIENT TILE FLOORING
- WALL CARPET
- VINYL COMPOSITION TILE

HATCHES
(VARIABLE SCALES)

AR-B88
BRICK FINISH

AR-HBONE
TILE PATTERN

AR-PARQ1
WOOD FLOORING

HONEY
TILE PATTERN

SQUARE
TILE PATTERN

FINISH SCHEDULE BLOCK
(FULL PAPER SCALE)

### FINISH SCHEDULE

| ROOM_NO. | ROOM | FLOOR | | | | | WALLS | | | | CEILING | | REMARKS |
|---|---|---|---|---|---|---|---|---|---|---|---|---|---|
| | | CARPET | CONCRETE | LINOLEUM | TILE | AC. PLASTER | DRYWALL | PAINT | TILE | DRYWALL | EXP. BEAMS | |
| | | ● | | | | | ● | ● | | ● | | |
| | | ● | | | | | ● | ● | | ● | ● | |
| | | ● | | | | | ● | ● | | | | |
| | | ● | | | | | ● | ● | | ● | | |
| | | ● | | | | | ● | ● | | ● | | |
| | | ● | | | | | ● | ● | | | ● | |

## DIVISION 10 - Specialties

BATHROOM
FIXTURES-PLAN VIEW
(FULL SCALE)

BATHROOM
FIXTURES-ELEVATION VIEW
(FULL  SCALE)

MOVABLE PARTITION WALLS
(FULL  SCALE)

2'-0"
3'-0"
4'-0"
5'-0"
6'-0"

COLLAPSABLE PARTITION
WALLS
(FULL SCALE)

CURVED PARTITION WALLS
(FULL SCALE)

24"R
30"R
36" R

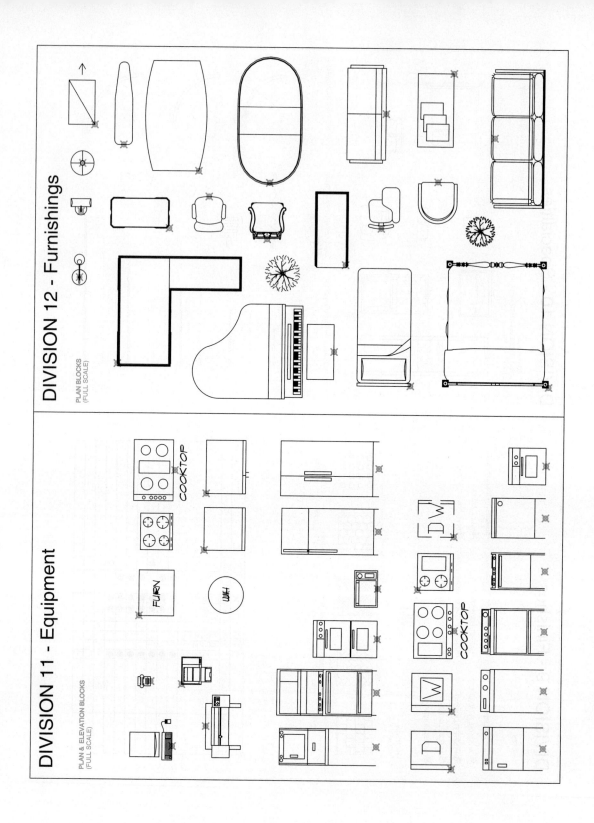

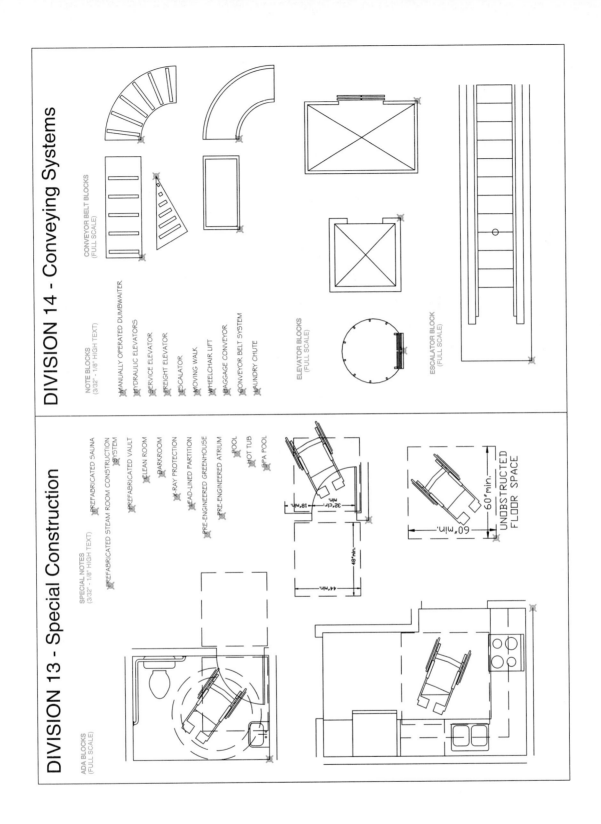

# DIVISION 14 - Conveying Systems

CONVEYOR BELT BLOCKS
(FULL SCALE)

NOTE BLOCKS
(3/32" - 1/8" HIGH TEXT)

MANUALLY OPERATED DUMBWAITER
HYDRAULIC ELEVATORS
SERVICE ELEVATOR
FREIGHT ELEVATOR
ESCALATOR
MOVING WALK
WHEELCHAIR LIFT
BAGGAGE CONVEYOR
CONVEYOR BELT SYSTEM
LAUNDRY CHUTE

ELEVATOR BLOCKS
(FULL SCALE)

ESCALATOR BLOCK
(FULL SCALE)

# DIVISION 13 - Special Construction

SPECIAL NOTES
(3/32" - 1/8" HIGH TEXT)

PREFABRICATED SAUNA
PREFABRICATED STEAM ROOM CONSTRUCTION
SYSTEM
PREFABRICATED VAULT
CLEAN ROOM
DARKROOM
X-RAY PROTECTION
LEAD-LINED PARTITION
PRE-ENGINEERED GREENHOUSE
PRE-ENGINEERED ATRIUM
POOL
HOT TUB
SPA POOL

ADA BLOCKS
(FULL SCALE)

18" min.
32" clr.
min.
48" min.
44" min.

60" min.
60" min.
UNOBSTRUCTED
FLOOR SPACE

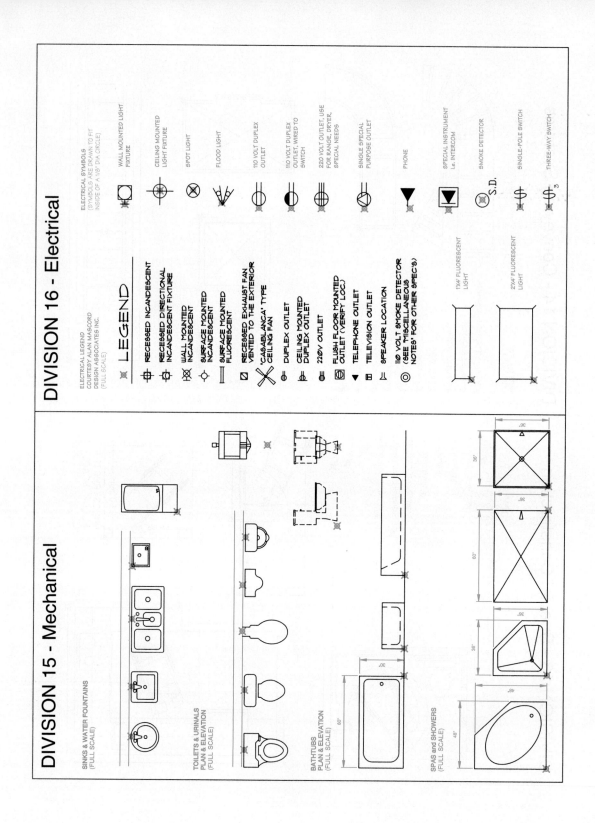

# DIVISION 15 - Mechanical

**SINKS & WATER FOUNTAINS**
(FULL SCALE)

**TOILETS & URINALS**
**PLAN & ELEVATION**
(FULL SCALE)

**BATHTUBS**
**PLAN & ELEVATION**
(FULL SCALE)

30"

60"

**SPAS and SHOWERS**
(FULL SCALE)

48"

48"

36"

36"

36"

36"

60"

# DIVISION 16 - Electrical

**ELECTRICAL LEGEND**
COURTESY ALAN MASCORD
DESIGN ASSOCIATES INC.
(FULL SCALE)

**LEGEND**

⊕ RECESSED INCANDESCENT

⊕ RECESSED DIRECTIONAL INCANDESCENT FIXTURE

⊗ WALL MOUNTED INCANDESCENT

⊕ SURFACE MOUNTED INCANDESCENT

‖ SURFACE MOUNTED FLUORESCENT

▨ RECESSED EXHAUST FAN VENTED TO THE EXTERIOR

✕ 'CASABLANCA' TYPE CEILING FAN

⊕ DUPLEX OUTLET

⊕ CEILING MOUNTED DUPLEX OUTLET

⊟ 220V OUTLET

⊟ FLUSH FLOOR MOUNTED OUTLET (VERIFY LOC.)

▼ TELEPHONE OUTLET

⊡ TELEVISION OUTLET

⊬ SPEAKER LOCATION

◎ 110 VOLT SMOKE DETECTOR (SEE 'MISCELLANEOUS NOTES' FOR OTHER SPEC'S)

☐ 1'X4' FLUORESCENT LIGHT

☐ 2'X4' FLUORESCENT LIGHT

**ELECTRICAL SYMBOLS**
(SYMBOLS ARE DRAWN TO FIT INSIDE OF A 1/8" DIA. CIRCLE)

◻ WALL MOUNTED LIGHT FIXTURE

⊕ CEILING MOUNTED LIGHT FIXTURE

⊗ SPOT LIGHT

⊻ FLOOD LIGHT

⊖ 110 VOLT DUPLEX OUTLET

◑ 110 VOLT DUPLEX OUTLET, WIRED TO SWITCH

⊕ 220 VOLT OUTLET, USE FOR RANGE, DRYER, SPECIAL NEEDS

⊖ SINGLE SPECIAL PURPOSE OUTLET

▼ PHONE

▼ SPECIAL INSTRUMENT i.e. INTERCOM

S.D. SMOKE DETECTOR

S SINGLE-POLE SWITCH

S₃ THREE-WAY SWITCH

# Advanced 3D Modeling Commands

Three-dimensional modeling is introduced in Chapter 25 of this text. In addition to the commands and methods discussed in Chapter 25, there are a number of other commands for advanced surface and solid modeling in AutoCAD. The following sections provide a brief introduction to these commands.

## 3D Object Editing Commands

It is often useful to reorient the position of objects in space when constructing a three-dimensional model. The following table lists 3D-based commands used for editing. These commands can be accessed in the **3D Operation** cascading menu under the **Modify** pull-down menu. See **Figure H-1**.

**Figure H-1.**
Editing commands for 3D objects can be accessed from the **3D Operation** cascading menu in the **Modify** pull-down menu.

| Command | Description |
|---------|-------------|
| **3DARRAY** | Arrays objects about the X, Y, and Z axes of the current UCS. |
| **MIRROR3D** | Mirrors objects about a 3D drawing plane. |
| **ROTATE3D** | Rotates objects around a three-dimensional axis. |
| **ALIGN** | Aligns 3D objects in space. |

# Advanced Surface Modeling Commands

The following table lists commands that can be used in surface modeling. These commands can be accessed in the **Surfaces** cascading menu under the **Draw** pull-down menu or from the **Surfaces** toolbar. See **Figure H-2**.

---

**Figure H-2.**
Surface modeling commands are available in the **Surfaces** cascading menu under the **Draw** pull-down menu and in the **Surfaces** toolbar.

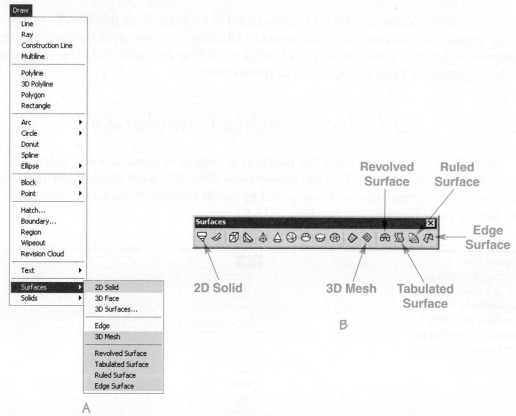

| Command | Description |
|---|---|
| **SOLID** | Creates solid-filled 2D objects similar to a 3D face or region. Access by selecting **2D Solid** from the **Surfaces** cascading menu under the **Draw** pull-down menu or from the **Surfaces** toolbar. |
| **3DMESH** | Creates a freeform polygon mesh. A *mesh* is a series of individual four-sided polygon faces joined together to form a single "meshed" object. |
| **REVSURF** | Creates a revolved surface object by revolving a 2D section profile around an axis. |
| **TABSURF** | Extrudes a section profile along a path, turning the resulting object into a tabulated surface. |
| **RULESURF** | Creates a surface between two pieces of 2D geometry, such as points, lines, polylines, splines, arcs, or circles. |
| **EDGESURF** | Creates a surface between four adjoining pieces of geometry, such as lines, polylines, splines, or arcs. The object endpoints must touch in order to create the mesh object. |
| **SURFTAB1 and SURFTAB2** | System variables controlling the number of tabulations or faces created in a revolved surface, tabulated surface, ruled surface, or edge surface. |

# Advanced Solid Modeling Commands

The following table lists commands that can be used in solid modeling. These commands can be accessed in the **Solids** cascading menu under the **Draw** pull-down menu or from the **Solids** toolbar. See **Figure H-3**.

**Figure H-3.**
Solid modeling commands are available in the **Solids** cascading menu under the **Draw** pull-down menu and in the **Solids** toolbar.

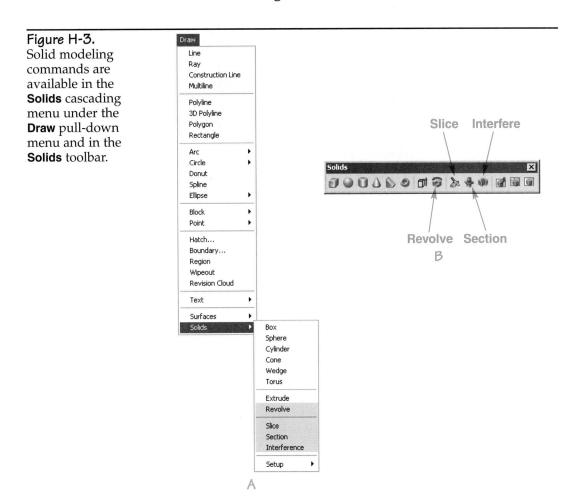

| Command | Description |
|---------|-------------|
| **REVOLVE** | Creates a solid object by revolving a 2D section profile around an axis. |
| **SLICE** | Cuts a solid into two parts using a three-dimensional plane. |
| **SECTION** | Creates a 2D section of a solid object through the intersection of a plane and the solid. |
| **INTERFERE** | Creates a solid from the common area of two or more solid objects and retains the original interfering objects. |

# Advanced Solid Editing Commands

There are a number of ways to alter the object faces or edges making up a solid. The following table lists commands used for editing solids in this manner. These commands can be found in the **Solids Editing** cascading menu under the **Modify** pull-down menu or in the **Solids Editing** toolbar. See **Figure H-4**. They can also be accessed within the **SOLIDEDIT** command.

## Figure H-4.
Solid editing commands are available in the **Solids Editing** cascading menu under the **Modify** pull-down menu and in the **Solids Editing** toolbar.

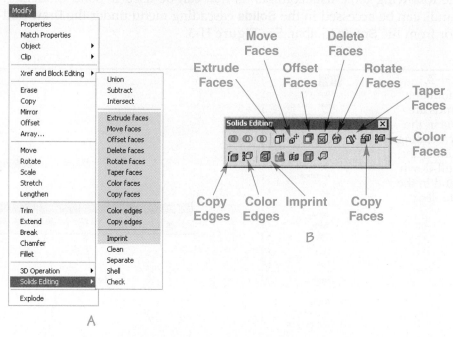

| Command | Description |
|---|---|
| **Extrude Faces** | Extrudes an existing face of a solid object to a specified height. |
| **Move Faces** | Moves an existing face of a solid a specified height or distance. |
| **Offset Faces** | Offsets an existing face of a solid a specified distance. |
| **Delete Faces** | Deletes or removes existing faces from a solid. |
| **Rotate Faces** | Rotates an existing face of a solid around an axis. |
| **Taper Faces** | Tapers the face of an existing solid. |
| **Copy Faces** | Copies an existing solid face as a region. |
| **Color Faces** | Changes the color of an existing solid face regardless of the layer the solid is on. |
| **Copy Edges** | Copies existing edges on a solid and turns the copies into lines, arcs, circles, ellipses, or splines. |
| **Color Edges** | Changes the color of an edge on an existing solid object. |
| **Imprint** | Imprints objects onto the face of an existing solid. Objects such as arcs, circles, lines, polylines, ellipses, splines, and regions can be used. The imprint then becomes a separate face on top of the solid face and can be extruded with the **Extrude Faces** command. |

# File Management

When applying CAD office standards, a very important part of the process should include addressing how drawings are organized and filed, as well as any customization done to AutoCAD. An effective office or school implements and practices file management techniques in order to be productive.

## Understanding File Structure

The computer is used as an electronic desk. It is the electronic drafting table, typewriter, and file cabinet. At the base of the computer is a hard disk drive. This hard disk drive can be thought of as the file cabinet. The hard drive stores files that allow the operating system (the electronic desk), as well as any programs and files it creates, to function.

The hard drive contains a folder called the *root directory*. The root directory (usually named the C: drive) is the door to other folders or files stored on the hard drive. The Windows operating system files are stored in the Windows folder (if you are using Windows XP, Windows 2000, or Windows 98). See **Figure I-1**. With the Windows operating systems, a folder named Program Files is also present in the root folder. This folder is where most Windows-compliant programs are installed and stored.

When AutoCAD is installed, it is placed in the Program Files folder by default. Any other folders and files that AutoCAD uses are placed in the AutoCAD folder. See **Figure I-2**.

---

**Figure I-1.**
The root folder with the operating system folder.

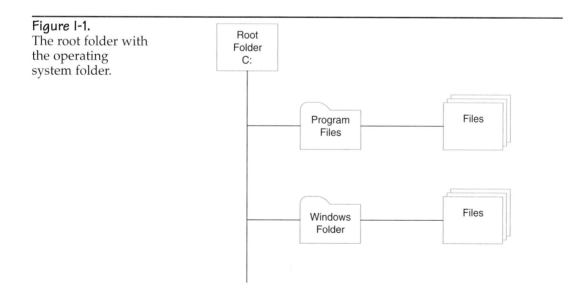

**Figure I-4.**
Organizing drawing files.

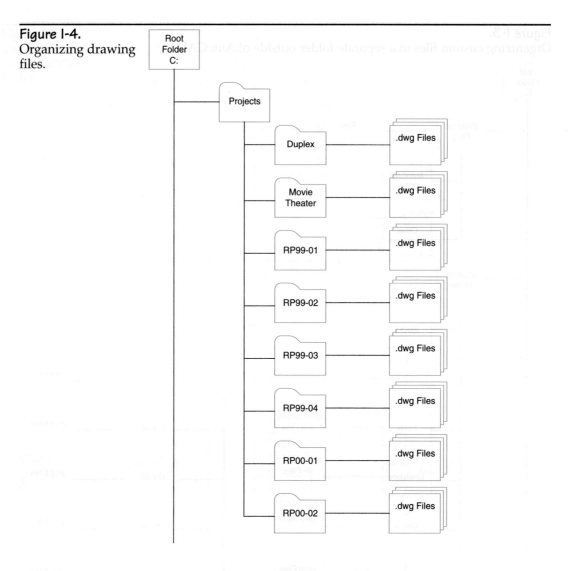

The files in each project subfolder may include drawing files, xref drawings, word processing documents, and spreadsheets. This helps keep the entire project together, making it easier to manage.

## Creating Folders

Windows Explorer is used to manage folders, subfolders, and files. This program can be accessed by selecting Windows Explorer in the Programs menu in the Windows Start menu. Windows Explorer can also be accessed from within AutoCAD by entering explorer at the Command prompt. This opens the Windows Explorer window. See **Figure I-5**.

To create a new folder, select the hard drive in the Folders pane. This displays the folders and files for the hard drive in the Contents pane. Right-click in the Contents pane to display a shortcut menu. See **Figure I-6**. Select New and then Folder from the shortcut menu. This creates a new folder. Type the name of the new folder.

To create subfolders under the new folder, select the new folder in the Folders pane. Right-click in the Contents pane and select New and then Folder from the shortcut menu. By following this process, you can quickly create the folders and subfolders to organize files on your computer. See **Figure I-7**.

**Figure I-5.**
The Windows
Explorer window.

Folders pane

Contents pane

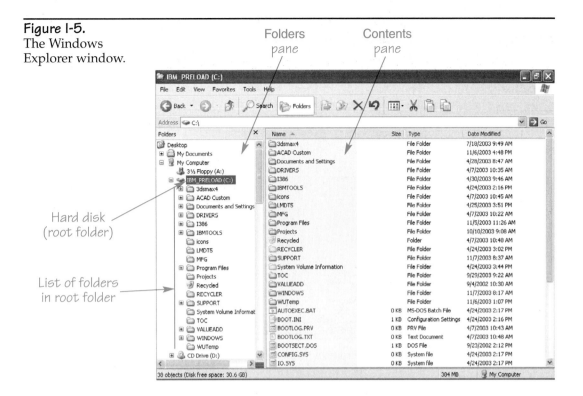

Hard disk
(root folder)

List of folders
in root folder

**Figure I-6.**
Select Folder from
the shortcut menu
to create a new
folder.

Right-click
to access
shortcut menu

Pick **Folder** in the
cascading menu

Once you have created an organized system of folders, be sure to keep files in the appropriate folders. In addition, add new folders to your system when appropriate. Maintaining an organized desktop system is a continuous process.

**Figure I-7.**
The Custom and
Project folders with
the subfolders
beneath.

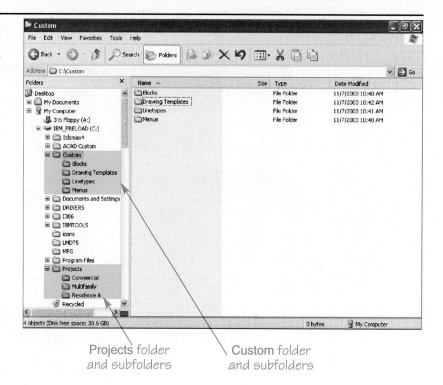

Projects folder
and subfolders

Custom folder
and subfolders

Architectural Drafting Using AutoCAD

# Command Aliases

AutoCAD has a number of keyboard shortcuts known as *command aliases*. The list of aliases can be found in the acad.pgp file in the AutoCAD \Support folder. To edit the aliases, open the file in Microsoft Notepad. Scroll down through the file until you see the following:

> ; — Sample aliases for AutoCAD commands —
> ; These examples include most frequently used commands.

> 3A, *3DARRAY

This is the area for the AutoCAD shortcuts. The first line, 3A, *3DARRAY, tells AutoCAD that entering 3A at the Command prompt instructs AutoCAD to perform the **3DARRAY** command. The list of shortcuts begins with the **3DARRAY** command and ends with the **ZOOM** command. There are also additional shortcuts for other functions within AutoCAD.

To create a shortcut, determine what you would like to enter at the Command prompt and what function you would like AutoCAD to perform. In the shortcut list, type your keyboard shortcut followed by a comma, then type in the * (asterisk) followed by the full command name. For example, typing a Q at the keyboard could access the **LINE** command. The format to use looks like this:

> Q, *LINE

Command aliases can access only one command. Command options cannot be accessed with aliases. To access a command and then select an option, use a custom button, create a LISP routine, or modify the Accelerators section of the AutoCAD menu. Refer to the AutoCAD Customization Guide for more information on these topics.

The following is a list of the default aliases in the acad.pgp file.

| Alias | Command | Alias | Command |
|-------|---------|-------|---------|
| 3A | 3DARRAY | ATTE | -ATTEDIT |
| 3DO | 3DORBIT | B | BLOCK |
| 3F | 3DFACE | -B | -BLOCK |
| 3P | 3DPOLY | BH | BHATCH |
| A | ARC | BO | BOUNDARY |
| ADC | ADCENTER | -BO | -BOUNDARY |
| AA | AREA | BR | BREAK |
| AL | ALIGN | C | CIRCLE |
| AP | APPLOAD | CH | PROPERTIES |
| AR | ARRAY | -CH | CHANGE |
| -AR | -ARRAY | CHA | CHAMFER |
| ATT | ATTDEF | CHK | CHECKSTANDARDS |
| -ATT | -ATTDEF | COL | COLOR |
| ATE | ATTEDIT | COLOUR | COLOR |
| -ATE | -ATTEDIT | CO | COPY |

| Alias | Command | Alias | Command |
|-------|---------|-------|---------|
| D | DIMSTYLE | IAT | IMAGEATTACH |
| DAL | DIMALIGNED | ICL | IMAGECLIP |
| DAN | DIMANGULAR | IM | IMAGE |
| DBA | DIMBASELINE | -IM | -IMAGE |
| DBC | DBCONNECT | IMP | IMPORT |
| DC | ADCENTER | IN | INTERSECT |
| DCE | DIMCENTER | INF | INTERFERE |
| DCO | DIMCONTINUE | IO | INSERTOBJ |
| DDA | DIMDISASSOCIATE | L | LINE |
| DDI | DIMDIAMETER | LA | LAYER |
| DED | DIMEDIT | -LA | -LAYER |
| DI | DIST | LE | QLEADER |
| DIV | DIVIDE | LEN | LENGTHEN |
| DLI | DIMLINEAR | LI | LIST |
| DO | DONUT | LINEWEIGHT | LWEIGHT |
| DOR | DIMORDINATE | LO | -LAYOUT |
| DOV | DIMOVERRIDE | LS | LIST |
| DR | DRAWORDER | LT | LINETYPE |
| DRA | DIMRADIUS | -LT | -LINETYPE |
| DRE | DIMREASSOCIATE | LTYPE | LINETYPE |
| DS | DSETTINGS | -LTYPE | -LINETYPE |
| DST | DIMSTYLE | LTS | LTSCALE |
| DT | TEXT | LW | LWEIGHT |
| DV | DVIEW | M | MOVE |
| E | ERASE | MA | MATCHPROP |
| ED | DDEDIT | ME | MEASURE |
| EL | ELLIPSE | MI | MIRROR |
| EX | EXTEND | ML | MLINE |
| EXIT | QUIT | MO | PROPERTIES |
| EXP | EXPORT | MS | MSPACE |
| EXT | EXTRUDE | MT | MTEXT |
| F | FILLET | MV | MVIEW |
| FI | FILTER | O | OFFSET |
| G | GROUP | OP | OPTIONS |
| -G | -GROUP | ORBIT | 3DORBIT |
| GR | DDGRIPS | OS | OSNAP |
| H | BHATCH | -OS | -OSNAP |
| -H | HATCH | P | PAN |
| HE | HATCHEDIT | -P | -PAN |
| HI | HIDE | PA | PASTESPEC |
| I | INSERT | PARTIALOPEN | -PARTIALOPEN |
| -I | -INSERT | PE | PEDIT |
| IAD | IMAGEADJUST | PL | PLINE |

| Alias | Command | Alias | Command |
|---|---|---|---|
| PO | POINT | SPL | SPLINE |
| POL | POLYGON | SPE | SPLINEDIT |
| PR | PROPERTIES | ST | STYLE |
| PRCLOSE | PROPERTIESCLOSE | SU | SUBTRACT |
| PROPS | PROPERTIES | T | MTEXT |
| PRE | PREVIEW | -T | -MTEXT |
| PRINT | PLOT | TA | TABLET |
| PS | PSPACE | TH | THICKNESS |
| PTW | PUBLISHTOWEB | TI | TILEMODE |
| PU | PURGE | TO | TOOLBAR |
| -PU | -PURGE | TOL | TOLERANCE |
| R | REDRAW | TOR | TORUS |
| RA | REDRAWALL | TP | TOOLPALETTES |
| RE | REGEN | TR | TRIM |
| REA | REGENALL | UC | UCSMAN |
| REC | RECTANG | UN | UNITS |
| REG | REGION | -UN | -UNITS |
| REN | RENAME | UNI | UNION |
| -REN | -RENAME | V | VIEW |
| REV | REVOLVE | -V | -VIEW |
| RO | ROTATE | VP | DDVPOINT |
| RPR | RPREF | -VP | VPOINT |
| RR | RENDER | W | WBLOCK |
| S | STRETCH | -W | -WBLOCK |
| SC | SCALE | WE | WEDGE |
| SCR | SCRIPT | X | EXPLODE |
| SE | DSETTINGS | XA | XATTACH |
| SEC | SECTION | XB | XBIND |
| SET | SETVAR | -XB | -XBIND |
| SHA | SHADEMODE | XC | XCLIP |
| SL | SLICE | XL | XLINE |
| SN | SNAP | XR | XREF |
| SO | SOLID | -XR | -XREF |
| SP | SPELL | Z | ZOOM |

# Standard Tables

## Architectural–Traditional Paper Sizes

| Paper Size | Scales | Scale Factor | Model Space Limits | Text Height 3/32″ | 1/8″ | 3/16″ | 1/4″ | 1/2″ | Line Type Scale | Dimension Scale Factor |
|---|---|---|---|---|---|---|---|---|---|---|
| A<br>11″ × 8-1/2″ | 3/32″=1′-0″<br>1/8″=1′-0″ | 128<br>96 | 117′-4″ × 90′-8″<br>88′ × 68′ | 12″<br>9″ | 16″<br>12″ | 24″<br>18″ | 32″<br>24″ | 64″<br>48″ | 64<br>48 | 128<br>96 |
| | 3/16″=1′-0″<br>1/4″=1′-0″ | 64<br>48 | 58′-8″ × 45′-4″<br>44′-0″ × 34′ | 6″<br>4 1/2″ | 8″<br>6″ | 12″<br>9″ | 16″<br>12″ | 32″<br>24″ | 32<br>24 | 64<br>48 |
| | 3/8″=1′-0″<br>1/2″=1′-0″ | 32<br>24 | 29′-4″ × 22′-8″<br>22′ × 17′ | 3″<br>2 1/4″ | 4″<br>3″ | 6″<br>4 1/2″ | 8″<br>6″ | 16″<br>12″ | 16<br>12 | 32<br>24 |
| | 3/4″=1′-0″<br>1″=1′-0″ | 16<br>12 | 14′-8″ × 11′-4″<br>11′ × 8′-6″ | 1 1/2″<br>1 1/8″ | 2″<br>1 1/2″ | 3″<br>2 1/4″ | 4″<br>3″ | 8″<br>6″ | 8<br>6 | 16<br>12 |
| B<br>17″ × 11″ | 3/32″=1′-0″<br>1/8″=1′-0″ | 128<br>96 | 181′-4″ × 117′-4″<br>136′ × 88′ | 12″<br>9″ | 16″<br>12″ | 24″<br>18″ | 32″<br>24″ | 64″<br>48″ | 64<br>48 | 128<br>96 |
| | 3/16″=1′-0″<br>1/4″=1′-0″ | 64<br>48 | 90′-8″ × 58′-8″<br>68′ × 44′ | 6″<br>4 1/2″ | 8″<br>6″ | 12″<br>9″ | 16″<br>12″ | 32″<br>24″ | 32<br>24 | 64<br>48 |
| | 3/8″=1′-0″<br>1/2″=1′-0″ | 32<br>24 | 45′-4″ × 29′-4″<br>34′ × 22′ | 3″<br>2 1/4″ | 4″<br>3″ | 6″<br>4 1/2″ | 8″<br>6″ | 16″<br>12″ | 16<br>12 | 32<br>24 |
| | 3/4″=1′-0″<br>1″=1′-0″ | 16<br>12 | 22′-8″ × 14′-8″<br>17′ × 11′ | 1 1/2″<br>1 1/8″ | 2″<br>1 1/2″ | 3″<br>2 1/4″ | 4″<br>3″ | 8″<br>6″ | 8<br>6 | 16<br>12 |
| C<br>22″ × 17″ | 3/32″=1′-0″<br>1/8″=1′-0″ | 128<br>96 | 234′-8″ × 181′-4″<br>176′ × 136′ | 12″<br>9″ | 16″<br>12″ | 24″<br>18″ | 32″<br>24″ | 64″<br>48″ | 64<br>48 | 128<br>96 |
| | 3/16″=1′-0″<br>1/4″=1′-0″ | 64<br>48 | 117′-4″ × 90′-8″<br>88′ × 68′ | 6″<br>4 1/2″ | 8″<br>6″ | 12″<br>9″ | 16″<br>12″ | 32″<br>24″ | 32<br>24 | 64<br>48 |
| | 3/8″=1′-0″<br>1/2″=1′-0″ | 32<br>24 | 58′-8″ × 45′-4″<br>44′ × 34′ | 3″<br>2 1/4″ | 4″<br>3″ | 6″<br>4 1/2″ | 8″<br>6″ | 16″<br>12″ | 16<br>12 | 32<br>24 |
| | 3/4″=1′-0″<br>1″=1′-0″ | 16<br>12 | 29′-4″ × 22′-8″<br>22′ × 17′ | 1 1/2″<br>1 1/8″ | 2″<br>1 1/2″ | 3″<br>2 1/4″ | 4″<br>3″ | 8″<br>6″ | 8<br>6 | 16<br>12 |
| D<br>34″ × 22″ | 3/32″=1′-0″<br>1/8″=1′-0″ | 128<br>96 | 362′-8″ × 234′-8″<br>272′ × 176′ | 12″<br>9″ | 16″<br>12″ | 24″<br>18″ | 32″<br>24″ | 64″<br>48″ | 64<br>48 | 128<br>96 |
| | 3/16″=1′-0″<br>1/4″=1′-0″ | 64<br>48 | 181′-4″ × 117′-4″<br>136′ × 88′ | 6″<br>4 1/2″ | 8″<br>6″ | 12″<br>9″ | 16″<br>12″ | 32″<br>24″ | 32<br>24 | 64<br>48 |
| | 3/8″=1′-0″<br>1/2″=1′-0″ | 32<br>24 | 90′-8″ × 58′-8″<br>68′ × 44′ | 3″<br>2 1/4″ | 4″<br>3″ | 6″<br>4 1/2″ | 8″<br>6″ | 16″<br>12″ | 16<br>12 | 32<br>24 |
| | 3/4″=1′-0″<br>1″=1′-0″ | 16<br>12 | 45′-4″ × 29′-4″<br>34′ × 22′ | 1 1/2″<br>1 1/8″ | 2″<br>1 1/2″ | 3″<br>2 1/4″ | 4″<br>3″ | 8″<br>6″ | 8<br>6 | 16<br>12 |
| E<br>44″ × 34″ | 3/32″=1′-0″<br>1/8″=1′-0″ | 128<br>96 | 469′-4″ × 362′-8″<br>352′ × 272′ | 12″<br>9″ | 16″<br>12″ | 24″<br>18″ | 32″<br>24″ | 64″<br>48″ | 64<br>48 | 128<br>96 |
| | 3/16″=1′-0″<br>1/4″=1′-0″ | 64<br>48 | 234′-8″ × 181′-4″<br>176′ × 136′ | 6″<br>4 1/2″ | 8″<br>6″ | 12″<br>9″ | 16″<br>12″ | 32″<br>24″ | 32<br>24 | 64<br>48 |
| | 3/8″=1′-0″<br>1/2″=1′-0″ | 32<br>24 | 117′-4″ × 90′-8″<br>88′ × 68′ | 3″<br>2 1/4″ | 4″<br>3″ | 6″<br>4 1/2″ | 8″<br>6″ | 16″<br>12″ | 16<br>12 | 32<br>24 |
| | 3/4″=1′-0″<br>1″=1′-0″ | 16<br>12 | 58′-8″ × 45′-4″<br>44′ × 34′ | 1 1/2″<br>1 1/8″ | 2″<br>1 1/2″ | 3″<br>2 1/4″ | 4″<br>3″ | 8″<br>6″ | 8<br>6 | 16<br>12 |

Architectural Drafting Using AutoCAD

# Architectural–Standard Plotter Paper Sizes

| Paper Size | Scales | Scale Factor | Model Space Limits | Text Height 3/32" | 1/8" | 3/16" | 1/4" | 1/2" | Line Type Scale | Dimension Scale Factor |
|---|---|---|---|---|---|---|---|---|---|---|
| A 12"×9" | 3/32"=1'-0" | 128 | 128'×96' | 12" | 16" | 24" | 32" | 64" | 64 | 128 |
| | 1/8"=1'-0" | 96 | 96'×72' | 9" | 12" | 18" | 24" | 48" | 48 | 96 |
| | 3/16"=1'-0" | 64 | 64'×48' | 6" | 8" | 12" | 16" | 32" | 32 | 64 |
| | 1/4"=1'-0" | 48 | 48'×36' | 4 1/2" | 6" | 9" | 12" | 24" | 24 | 48 |
| | 3/8"=1'-0" | 32 | 32'×24' | 3" | 4" | 6" | 8" | 16" | 16 | 32 |
| | 1/2"=1'-0" | 24 | 24'×18' | 2 1/4" | 3" | 4 1/2" | 6" | 12" | 12 | 24 |
| | 3/4"=1'-0" | 16 | 16'×12' | 1 1/2" | 2" | 3" | 4" | 8" | 8 | 16 |
| | 1"=1'-0" | 12 | 12'×9' | 1 1/8" | 1 1/2" | 2 1/4" | 3" | 6" | 6 | 12 |
| B 18"×12" | 3/32"=1'-0" | 128 | 192'×128' | 12" | 16" | 24" | 32" | 64" | 64 | 128 |
| | 1/8"=1'-0" | 96 | 144'×96' | 9" | 12" | 18" | 24" | 48" | 48 | 96 |
| | 3/16"=1'-0" | 64 | 96'×64' | 6" | 8" | 12" | 16" | 32" | 32 | 64 |
| | 1/4"=1'-0" | 48 | 72'×48' | 4 1/2" | 6" | 9" | 12" | 24" | 24 | 48 |
| | 3/8"=1'-0" | 32 | 48'×32' | 3" | 4" | 6" | 8" | 16" | 16 | 32 |
| | 1/2"=1'-0" | 24 | 36'×24' | 2 1/4" | 3" | 4 1/2" | 6" | 12" | 12 | 24 |
| | 3/4"=1'-0" | 16 | 24'×16' | 1 1/2" | 2" | 3" | 4" | 8" | 8 | 16 |
| | 1"=1'-0" | 12 | 18'×12' | 1 1/8" | 1 1/2" | 2 1/4" | 3" | 6" | 6 | 12 |
| C 24"×18" | 3/32"=1'-0" | 128 | 256'×192' | 12" | 16" | 24" | 32" | 64" | 64 | 128 |
| | 1/8"=1'-0" | 96 | 192'×144' | 9" | 12" | 18" | 24" | 48" | 48 | 96 |
| | 3/16"=1'-0" | 64 | 128'×96' | 6" | 8" | 12" | 16" | 32" | 32 | 64 |
| | 1/4"=1'-0" | 48 | 96'×72' | 4 1/2" | 6" | 9" | 12" | 24" | 24 | 48 |
| | 3/8"=1'-0" | 32 | 64'×48' | 3" | 4" | 6" | 8" | 16" | 16 | 32 |
| | 1/2"=1'-0" | 24 | 48'×36' | 2 1/4" | 3" | 4 1/2" | 6" | 12" | 12 | 24 |
| | 3/4"=1'-0" | 16 | 32'''×24' | 1 1/2" | 2" | 3" | 4" | 8" | 8 | 16 |
| | 1"=1'-0" | 12 | 24'×18' | 1 1/8" | 1 1/2" | 2 1/4" | 3" | 6" | 6 | 12 |
| D 36"×24" | 3/32"=1'-0" | 128 | 384'×256' | 12" | 16" | 24" | 32" | 64" | 64 | 128 |
| | 1/8"=1'-0" | 96 | 288'×192' | 9" | 12" | 18" | 24" | 48" | 48 | 96 |
| | 3/16"=1'-0" | 64 | 192'×128' | 6" | 8" | 12" | 16" | 32" | 32 | 64 |
| | 1/4"=1'-0" | 48 | 144'×96' | 4 1/2" | 6" | 9" | 12" | 24" | 24 | 48 |
| | 3/8"=1'-0" | 32 | 96'×64' | 3" | 4" | 6" | 8" | 16" | 16 | 32 |
| | 1/2"=1'-0" | 24 | 72'×48' | 2 1/4" | 3" | 4 1/2" | 6" | 12" | 12 | 24 |
| | 3/4"=1'-0" | 16 | 48'×32' | 1 1/2" | 2" | 3" | 4" | 8" | 8 | 16 |
| | 1"=1'-0" | 12 | 36'×24' | 1 1/8" | 1 1/2" | 2 1/4" | 3" | 6" | 6 | 12 |
| E 48"×36" | 3/32"=1'-0" | 128 | 512'×384' | 12" | 16" | 24" | 32" | 64" | 64 | 128 |
| | 1/8"=1'-0" | 96 | 384'×288' | 9" | 12" | 18" | 24" | 48" | 48 | 96 |
| | 3/16"=1'-0" | 64 | 256'×192' | 6" | 8" | 12" | 16" | 32" | 32 | 64 |
| | 1/4"=1'-0" | 48 | 192'×144' | 4 1/2" | 6" | 9" | 12" | 24" | 24 | 48 |
| | 3/8"=1'-0" | 32 | 128'×96' | 3" | 4" | 6" | 8" | 16" | 16 | 32 |
| | 1/2"=1'-0" | 24 | 96'×72' | 2 1/4" | 3" | 4 1/2" | 6" | 12" | 12 | 24 |
| | 3/4"=1'-0" | 16 | 64'×48' | 1 1/2" | 2" | 3" | 4" | 8" | 8 | 16 |
| | 1"=1'-0" | 12 | 48'×36' | 1 1/8" | 1 1/2" | 2 1/4" | 3" | 6" | 6 | 12 |

# Civil–Traditional Paper Sizes

| Paper Size | Scales | Scale Factor | Model Space Limits | Text Height 3/32" | 1/8" | 3/16" | 1/4" | 1/2" | Line Type Scale | Dimension Scale Factor |
|---|---|---|---|---|---|---|---|---|---|---|
| A 11" × 8-1/2" | 1"=10'<br>1"=20' | 120<br>240 | 110' × 85'<br>220' × 170' | 11 1/4"<br>22 1/2" | 15"<br>30" | 22 1/2"<br>45" | 30"<br>60" | 60"<br>120" | 60<br>120 | 120<br>240 |
| | 1"=30'<br>1"=40' | 360<br>480 | 330' × 255'<br>440' × 340' | 33 3/4"<br>45" | 45"<br>60" | 67 1/2"<br>90" | 90"<br>120" | 180"<br>240" | 180<br>240 | 360<br>480 |
| | 1"=50'<br>1"=60' | 600<br>720 | 550' × 425'<br>660' × 510' | 56 1/4"<br>67 1/2" | 75"<br>90" | 112 1/2"<br>135" | 150"<br>180" | 300"<br>360" | 300<br>360 | 600<br>720 |
| | 1"=100'<br>1"=120' | 1200<br>1440 | 1100' × 850'<br>1320' × 1020' | 112 1/2"<br>135" | 150"<br>180" | 225"<br>270" | 300"<br>360" | 600"<br>720" | 600<br>720 | 1200<br>1440 |
| B 17" × 11" | 1"=10'<br>1"=20' | 120<br>240 | 170' × 110'<br>340' × 220' | 11 1/4"<br>22 1/2" | 15"<br>30" | 22 1/2"<br>45" | 30"<br>60" | 60"<br>120" | 60<br>120 | 120<br>240 |
| | 1"=30'<br>1"=40' | 360<br>480 | 510' × 330'<br>680' × 440' | 33 3/4"<br>45" | 45"<br>60" | 67 1/2"<br>90" | 90"<br>120" | 180"<br>240" | 180<br>240 | 360<br>480 |
| | 1"=50'<br>1"=60' | 600<br>720 | 850' × 550'<br>1020' × 660' | 56 1/4"<br>67 1/2" | 75"<br>90" | 112 1/2"<br>135" | 150"<br>180" | 300"<br>360" | 300<br>360 | 600<br>720 |
| | 1"=100'<br>1"=120' | 1200<br>1440 | 1700' × 1100'<br>2040' × 1320' | 112 1/2"<br>135" | 150"<br>180" | 225"<br>270" | 300"<br>360" | 600"<br>720" | 600<br>720 | 1200<br>1440 |
| C 22" × 17" | 1"=10'<br>1"=20' | 120<br>240 | 220' × 170'<br>440' × 340' | 11 1/4"<br>22 1/2" | 15"<br>30" | 22 1/2"<br>45" | 30"<br>60" | 60"<br>120" | 60<br>120 | 120<br>240 |
| | 1"=30'<br>1"=40' | 360<br>480 | 660' × 510'<br>880' × 680' | 33 3/4"<br>45" | 45"<br>60" | 67 1/2"<br>90" | 90"<br>120" | 180"<br>240" | 180<br>240 | 360<br>480 |
| | 1"=50'<br>1"=60' | 600<br>720 | 1100' × 850'<br>1320' × 1020' | 56 1/4"<br>67 1/2" | 75"<br>90" | 112 1/2"<br>135" | 150"<br>180" | 300"<br>360" | 300<br>360 | 600<br>720 |
| | 1"=100'<br>1"=120' | 1200<br>1440 | 2200' × 1700'<br>2640' × 2040' | 112 1/2"<br>135" | 150"<br>180" | 225"<br>270" | 300"<br>360" | 600"<br>720" | 600<br>720 | 1200<br>1440 |
| D 34" × 22" | 1"=10'<br>1"=20' | 120<br>240 | 340' × 220'<br>680' × 440' | 11 1/4"<br>22 1/2" | 15"<br>30" | 22 1/2"<br>45" | 30"<br>60" | 60"<br>120" | 60<br>120 | 120<br>240 |
| | 1"=30'<br>1"=40' | 360<br>480 | 1020' × 660'<br>1360' × 880' | 33 3/4"<br>45" | 45"<br>60" | 67 1/2"<br>90" | 90"<br>120" | 180"<br>240" | 180<br>240 | 360<br>480 |
| | 1"=50'<br>1"=60' | 600<br>720 | 1700 × 1100'<br>2040' × 1320' | 56 1/4"<br>67 1/2" | 75"<br>90" | 112 1/2"<br>135" | 150"<br>180" | 300"<br>360" | 300<br>360 | 600<br>720 |
| | 1"=100'<br>1"=120' | 1200<br>1440 | 3400' × 2200'<br>4080' × 2640' | 112 1/2"<br>135" | 150"<br>180" | 225"<br>270" | 300"<br>360" | 600"<br>720" | 600<br>720 | 1200<br>1440 |
| E 44" × 34" | 1"=10'<br>1"=20' | 120<br>240 | 440' × 340'<br>880' × 680' | 11 1/4"<br>22 1/2" | 15"<br>30" | 22 1/2"<br>45" | 30"<br>60" | 60"<br>120" | 60<br>120 | 120<br>240 |
| | 1"=30'<br>1"=40' | 360<br>480 | 1320' × 1020'<br>1760' × 1360' | 33 3/4"<br>45" | 45"<br>60" | 67 1/2"<br>90" | 90"<br>120" | 180"<br>240" | 180<br>240 | 360<br>480 |
| | 1"=50'<br>1"=60' | 600<br>720 | 2200' × 1700'<br>2640' × 2040' | 56 1/4"<br>67 1/2" | 75"<br>90" | 112 1/2"<br>135" | 150"<br>180" | 300"<br>360" | 300<br>360 | 600<br>720 |
| | 1"=100'<br>1"=120' | 1200<br>1440 | 4400' × 3400'<br>5280' × 4080' | 112 1/2"<br>135" | 150"<br>180" | 225"<br>270" | 300"<br>360" | 600"<br>720" | 600<br>720 | 1200<br>1440 |

# Civil–Standard Plotter Paper Sizes

| Paper Size | Scales | Scale Factor | Model Space Limits | Text Height 3/32" | 1/8" | 3/16" | 1/4" | 1/2" | Line Type Scale | Dimension Scale Factor |
|---|---|---|---|---|---|---|---|---|---|---|
| A 12" × 9" | 1"=10'<br>1"=20' | 120<br>240 | 120' × 90'<br>240' × 180' | 11 1/4"<br>22 1/2" | 15"<br>30" | 22 1/2"<br>45" | 30"<br>60" | 60"<br>120" | 60<br>120 | 120<br>240 |
| | 1"=30'<br>1"=40' | 360<br>480 | 360' × 270'<br>480' × 360' | 33 3/4"<br>45" | 45"<br>60" | 67 1/2"<br>90" | 90"<br>120" | 180"<br>240" | 180<br>240 | 360<br>480 |
| | 1"=50'<br>1"=60' | 600<br>720 | 600' × 450'<br>720' × 540' | 56 1/4"<br>67 1/2" | 75"<br>90" | 112 1/2"<br>135" | 150"<br>180" | 300"<br>360" | 300<br>360 | 600<br>720 |
| | 1"=100'<br>1"=120' | 1200<br>1440 | 1200' × 900'<br>1440' × 1080' | 112 1/2"<br>135" | 150"<br>180" | 225"<br>270" | 300"<br>360" | 600"<br>720" | 600<br>720 | 1200<br>1440 |
| B 18" × 12" | 1"=10'<br>1"=20' | 120<br>240 | 180' × 120'<br>360' × 240' | 11 1/4"<br>22 1/2" | 15"<br>30" | 22 1/2"<br>45" | 30"<br>60" | 60"<br>120" | 60<br>120 | 120<br>240 |
| | 1"=30'<br>1"=40' | 360<br>480 | 540' × 360'<br>720' × 480' | 33 3/4"<br>45" | 45"<br>60" | 67 1/2"<br>90" | 90"<br>120" | 180"<br>240" | 180<br>240 | 360<br>480 |
| | 1"=50'<br>1"=60' | 600<br>720 | 900' × 600'<br>1080' × 720' | 56 1/4"<br>67 1/2" | 75"<br>90" | 112 1/2"<br>135" | 150"<br>180" | 300"<br>360" | 300<br>360 | 600<br>720 |
| | 1"=100'<br>1"=120' | 1200<br>1440 | 1800' × 1200'<br>2160' × 1440' | 112 1/2"<br>135" | 150"<br>180" | 225"<br>270" | 300"<br>360" | 600"<br>720" | 600<br>720 | 1200<br>1440 |
| C 24" × 18" | 1"=10'<br>1"=20' | 120<br>240 | 240' × 180'<br>480' × 360' | 11 1/4"<br>22 1/2" | 15"<br>30" | 22 1/2"<br>45" | 30"<br>60" | 60"<br>120" | 60<br>120 | 120<br>240 |
| | 1"=30'<br>1"=40' | 360<br>480 | 720' × 540'<br>960' × 720' | 33 3/4"<br>45" | 45"<br>60" | 67 1/2"<br>90" | 90"<br>120" | 180"<br>240" | 180<br>240 | 360<br>480 |
| | 1"=50'<br>1"=60' | 600<br>720 | 1200' × 900'<br>1440' × 1080' | 56 1/4"<br>67 1/2" | 75"<br>90" | 112 1/2"<br>135" | 150"<br>180" | 300"<br>360" | 300<br>360 | 600<br>720 |
| | 1"=100'<br>1"=120' | 1200<br>1440 | 2400' × 1800'<br>2880' × 2160' | 112 1/2"<br>135" | 150"<br>180" | 225"<br>270" | 300"<br>360" | 600"<br>720" | 600<br>720 | 1200<br>1440 |
| D 36" × 24" | 1"=10'<br>1"=20' | 120<br>240 | 360' × 240'<br>720' × 480' | 11 1/4"<br>22 1/2" | 15"<br>30" | 22 1/2"<br>45" | 30"<br>60" | 60"<br>120" | 60<br>120 | 120<br>240 |
| | 1"=30'<br>1"=40' | 360<br>480 | 1080' × 720'<br>1440' × 960' | 33 3/4"<br>45" | 45"<br>60" | 67 1/2"<br>90" | 90"<br>120" | 180"<br>240" | 180<br>240 | 360<br>480 |
| | 1"=50'<br>1"=60' | 600<br>720 | 1800' × 1200'<br>2160' × 1440' | 56 1/4"<br>67 1/2" | 75"<br>90" | 112 1/2"<br>135" | 150"<br>180" | 300"<br>360" | 300<br>360 | 600<br>720 |
| | 1"=100'<br>1"=120' | 1200<br>1440 | 3600' × 2400'<br>4320' × 2880' | 112 1/2"<br>135" | 150"<br>180" | 225"<br>270" | 300"<br>360" | 600"<br>720" | 600<br>720 | 1200<br>1440 |
| E 48" × 36" | 1"=10'<br>1"=20' | 120<br>240 | 480' × 360'<br>960' × 720' | 11 1/4"<br>22 1/2" | 15"<br>30" | 22 1/2"<br>45" | 30"<br>60" | 60"<br>120" | 60<br>120 | 120<br>240 |
| | 1"=30'<br>1"=40' | 360<br>480 | 1440' × 1080'<br>1920' × 1440' | 33 3/4"<br>45" | 45"<br>60" | 67 1/2"<br>90" | 90"<br>120" | 180"<br>240" | 180<br>240 | 360<br>480 |
| | 1"=50'<br>1"=60' | 600<br>720 | 2400' × 1800'<br>2880' × 2160' | 56 1/4"<br>67 1/2" | 75"<br>90" | 112 1/2"<br>135" | 150"<br>180" | 300"<br>360" | 300<br>360 | 600<br>720 |
| | 1"=100'<br>1"=120' | 1200<br>1440 | 4800' × 3600'<br>5760' × 4320' | 112 1/2"<br>135" | 150"<br>180" | 225"<br>270" | 300"<br>360" | 600"<br>720" | 600<br>720 | 1200<br>1440 |

# Metric—Standard Plotter Paper Sizes

| Paper Size (mm) | Scales | Scale Factor (mm) (sf × 25.4) | Model Space Limits (mm) (paper size × sf) | Text Height | | | | | Linetype Scale (.5 × sf) |
|---|---|---|---|---|---|---|---|---|---|
| | | | | 3/32" (n × sf) | 1/8" (n × sf) | 3/16" (n × sf) | 1/4" (n × sf) | 1/2" (n × sf) | |
| A4 297 × 210 | 1 = 2 | 50.8 | 594 × 420 | .188 | .250 | .375 | .5 | 1 | 1 |
| | 1 = 5 | 127 | 1485 × 1050 | .469 | .625 | .938 | 1.25 | 2.50 | 2 |
| | 1 = 10 | 254 | 2970 × 2100 | .938 | 1.25 | 1.875 | 2.50 | 5.00 | 5 |
| | 1 = 20 | 508 | 5940 × 4200 | 1.875 | 2.50 | 3.75 | 5.00 | 10.00 | 10 |
| | 1 = 50 | 1270 | 14850 × 10500 | 4.688 | 6.25 | 9.375 | 12.50 | 25.00 | 25 |
| | 1 = 100 | 2540 | 29700 × 2100 | 9.375 | 12.50 | 18.75 | 25.00 | 50.00 | 50 |
| A3 420 × 297 | 1 = 2 | 50.8 | 820 × 594 | .188 | .250 | .375 | .5 | 1 | 1 |
| | 1 = 5 | 127 | 2100 × 1485 | .469 | .625 | .938 | 1.25 | 2.50 | 2 |
| | 1 = 10 | 254 | 4200 × 2970 | .938 | 1.25 | 1.875 | 2.50 | 5.00 | 5 |
| | 1 = 20 | 508 | 8400 × 5940 | 1.875 | 2.50 | 3.75 | 5.00 | 10.00 | 10 |
| | 1 = 50 | 1270 | 21000 × 14850 | 4.688 | 6.25 | 9.375 | 12.50 | 25.00 | 25 |
| | 1 = 100 | 2540 | 42000 × 29700 | 9.375 | 12.50 | 18.75 | 25.00 | 50.00 | 50 |
| A2 594 × 420 | 1 = 2 | 50.8 | 1188 × 840 | .188 | .250 | .375 | .5 | 1 | 1 |
| | 1 = 5 | 127 | 2970 × 2100 | .469 | .625 | .938 | 1.25 | 2.50 | 2 |
| | 1 = 10 | 254 | 5940 × 4200 | .938 | 1.25 | 1.875 | 2.50 | 5.00 | 5 |
| | 1 = 20 | 508 | 11880 × 8400 | 1.875 | 2.50 | 3.75 | 5.00 | 10.00 | 10 |
| | 1 = 50 | 1270 | 29700 × 21000 | 4.688 | 6.25 | 9.375 | 12.50 | 25.00 | 25 |
| | 1 = 100 | 2540 | 59400 × 42000 | 9.375 | 12.50 | 18.75 | 25.00 | 50.00 | 50 |
| A1 841 × 594 | 1 = 2 | 50.8 | 1682 × 1188 | .188 | .250 | .375 | .5 | 1 | 1 |
| | 1 = 5 | 127 | 4205 × 2970 | .469 | .625 | .938 | 1.25 | 2.50 | 2 |
| | 1 = 10 | 254 | 8410 × 5940 | .938 | 1.25 | 1.875 | 2.50 | 5.00 | 5 |
| | 1 = 20 | 508 | 16820 × 11880 | 1.875 | 2.50 | 3.75 | 5.00 | 10.00 | 10 |
| | 1 = 50 | 1270 | 42050 × 29700 | 4.688 | 6.25 | 9.375 | 12.50 | 25.00 | 25 |
| | 1 = 100 | 2540 | 84100 × 59400 | 9.375 | 12.50 | 18.75 | 25.00 | 50.00 | 50 |
| A0 1189 × 841 | 1 = 2 | 50.8 | 2378 × 1682 | .188 | .250 | .375 | .5 | 1 | 1 |
| | 1 = 5 | 127 | 5945 × 4205 | .469 | .625 | .938 | 1.25 | 2.50 | 2 |
| | 1 = 10 | 254 | 11890 × 8410 | .938 | 1.25 | 1.875 | 2.50 | 5.00 | 5 |
| | 1 = 20 | 508 | 23780 × 16820 | 1.875 | 2.50 | 3.75 | 5.00 | 10.00 | 10 |
| | 1 = 50 | 1270 | 59450 × 42050 | 4.688 | 6.25 | 9.375 | 12.50 | 25.00 | 25 |
| | 1 = 100 | 2540 | 118900 × 84100 | 9.375 | 12.50 | 18.75 | 25.00 | 50.00 | 50 |

sf = scale factor before multiplying by the inch:mm conversion of 25.4
n = text height value

Architectural Drafting Using AutoCAD

# Lengths and Areas of Arc Segments

The following table lists data for the length of an arc (*l* = radians), height of the segment (*h*), chord length (*c*), and the area of the segment (*A*). The values are for angles between 1° and 180° and are based upon an arc with a radius of 1″. For radii greater than 1″, multiply the distance values by the radius (r × l = l, r × h = h, r × c = c). For the area of radii greater than 1″, multiply the square of the radius by the area value (r² × A = A).

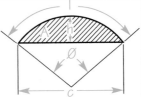

| Angle ø | l | h | c | Area (A) | Angle ø | l | h | c | Area (A) | Angle ø | l | h | c | Area (A) |
|---|---|---|---|---|---|---|---|---|---|---|---|---|---|---|
| 1 | 0.0175 | 0.0000 | 0.0175 | 0.0000 | 61 | 1.0650 | 0.1384 | 1.0150 | 0.0950 | 121 | 2.1220 | 0.5076 | 1.7410 | 0.6273 |
| 2 | 0.0349 | 0.0002 | 0.0349 | 0.0000 | 62 | 1.0820 | 0.1428 | 1.0300 | 0.0996 | 122 | 21290 | 0.5152 | 1.7490 | 0.6406 |
| 3 | 0.0524 | 0.0003 | 0.0524 | 0.0000 | 63 | 1.1000 | 0.1474 | 0.0450 | 0.1043 | 123 | 2.1470 | 0.5228 | 1.7580 | 0.6540 |
| 4 | 0.0698 | 0.0006 | 0.0698 | 0.0000 | 64 | 1.1170 | 0.1520 | 1.0600 | 0.1091 | 124 | 2.1640 | 0.5305 | 1.7660 | 0.6676 |
| 5 | 0.0873 | 0.0009 | 0.0872 | 0.0000 | 65 | 1.1340 | 0.1566 | 1.0750 | 0.1141 | 125 | 2.1820 | 0.5383 | 1.7740 | 0.6813 |
| 6 | 0.1047 | 0.0014 | 0.1047 | 0.0001 | 66 | 1.1520 | 0.1613 | 1.0890 | 0.1191 | 126 | 2.1990 | 0.5460 | 1.7820 | 0.6950 |
| 7 | 0.1222 | 0.0019 | 0.1221 | 0.0002 | 67 | 1.1690 | 0.1661 | 1.1040 | 0.1244 | 127 | 2.2170 | 0.5538 | 1.790 | 0.7090 |
| 8 | 0.1396 | 0.0024 | 0.1395 | 0.0002 | 68 | 1.1870 | 0.1710 | 1.1180 | 01298 | 128 | 2.2340 | 0.5616 | 1.7980 | 0.7230 |
| 9 | 0.1571 | 0.0031 | 0.1569 | 0.0003 | 69 | 1.2040 | 0.1759 | 1.1330 | 0.1354 | 129 | 2.2510 | 0.5695 | 1.8050 | 0.7372 |
| 10 | 0.1745 | 0.0038 | 0.1743 | 0.0004 | 70 | 1.2220 | 0.1808 | 1.1470 | 0.1410 | 130 | 2.2690 | 0.5774 | 1.8130 | 0.7514 |
| 11 | 0.1919 | 0.0046 | 0.1917 | 0.0006 | 71 | 1.2390 | 0.1859 | 1.1610 | 0.1468 | 131 | 2.2860 | 0.5853 | 1.8200 | 0.7658 |
| 12 | 0.2094 | 0.0055 | 0.2091 | 0.0008 | 72 | 1.2570 | 0.1910 | 1.1760 | 0.1528 | 132 | 2.3040 | 0.5933 | 1.8270 | 0.7803 |
| 13 | 0.2269 | 0.0064 | 0.2264 | 0.0009 | 73 | 1.2740 | 0.1961 | 1.1900 | 0.1589 | 133 | 2.3210 | 0.6013 | 1.8340 | 0.7950 |
| 14 | 0.2444 | 0.0075 | 0.2437 | 0.0012 | 74 | 1.2920 | 0.2014 | 1.2040 | 0.1651 | 134 | 2.3390 | 0.6093 | 1.8410 | 0.8097 |
| 15 | 0.2618 | 0.0086 | 0.2611 | 0.0015 | 75 | 1.3090 | 0.2066 | 1.2180 | 0.1715 | 135 | 2.3560 | 0.6173 | 1.8480 | 0.8245 |
| 16 | 0.2793 | 0.0097 | 0.2784 | 0.0018 | 76 | 1.3260 | 0.2120 | 1.2310 | 0.1781 | 136 | 2.3740 | 0.6254 | 1.8540 | 0.8395 |
| 17 | 0.2967 | 0.0109 | 0.2956 | 0.0022 | 77 | 1.3440 | 0.2174 | 1.2450 | 0.1848 | 137 | 2.3910 | 0.6335 | 1.8610 | 0.8546 |
| 18 | 0.3142 | 0.0123 | 0.3129 | 0.0026 | 78 | 1.3610 | 0.2229 | 1.2590 | 0.1916 | 138 | 2.4090 | 0.6416 | 1.8670 | 0.8697 |
| 19 | 0.3316 | 0.0137 | 0.3301 | 0.0030 | 79 | 1.3790 | 0.2284 | 1.2720 | 0.1986 | 139 | 2.4260 | 0.6498 | 1.8730 | 0.8850 |
| 20 | 0.3490 | 0.0152 | 0.3473 | 0.0035 | 80 | 1.3960 | 0.2340 | 1.2860 | 0.2057 | 140 | 2.4430 | 0.6580 | 1.8790 | 0.9003 |
| 21 | 0.3665 | 0.0167 | 0.3645 | 0.0040 | 81 | 1.4140 | 0.2396 | 1.2990 | 0.2130 | 141 | 2.4610 | 0.6662 | 1.8850 | 0.9158 |
| 22 | 0.3839 | 0.0184 | 0.3816 | 0.0047 | 82 | 1.4310 | 0.2453 | 1.3120 | 0.2205 | 142 | 2.4780 | 0.6744 | 1.8910 | 0.9314 |
| 23 | 0.4014 | 0.0200 | 0.3987 | 0.0054 | 83 | 1.4490 | 0.2510 | 1.3250 | 0.2280 | 143 | 2.4960 | 0.6827 | 1.8970 | 0.9470 |
| 24 | 0.4189 | 0.0219 | 0.158 | 0.0061 | 84 | 1.4660 | 0.2569 | 1.3380 | 0.2358 | 144 | 2.5130 | 0.6910 | 1.9020 | 0.9627 |
| 25 | 0.4363 | 0.0237 | 0.4329 | 0.0069 | 85 | 1.4840 | 0.2627 | 1.3510 | 0.2437 | 145 | 2.5310 | 0.6993 | 1.9070 | 0.9786 |
| 26 | 0.4538 | 0.0256 | 0.4499 | 0.0077 | 86 | 1.5010 | 0.2686 | 1.3640 | 0.2517 | 146 | 2.5480 | 0.7076 | 1.9130 | 0.9945 |
| 27 | 0.4712 | 0.0276 | 0.4669 | 0.0086 | 87 | 1.5180 | 0.2746 | 1.3770 | 0.2599 | 147 | 2.5660 | 0.7160 | 1.9180 | 1.0105 |
| 28 | 0.4887 | 0.0297 | 0.4838 | 0.0096 | 88 | 1.5360 | 0.2807 | 1.3890 | 0.2683 | 148 | 2.5830 | 0.7244 | 1.9230 | 1.0266 |
| 29 | 0.5061 | 0.0319 | 0.5008 | 0.0107 | 89 | 1.5530 | 0.2867 | 1.4020 | 0.2768 | 149 | 2.6010 | 0.7328 | 1.9270 | 1.0428 |
| 30 | 0.5236 | 0.0340 | 0.5176 | 0.0118 | 90 | 1.5710 | 0.2929 | 1.4140 | 0.2854 | 150 | 2.6180 | 0.7412 | 1.9320 | 1.0590 |
| 31 | 0.5411 | 0.0364 | 0.5345 | 0.0130 | 91 | 1.5880 | 0.2991 | 1.4270 | 0.2942 | 151 | 2.6350 | 0.7496 | 1.9360 | 1.0753 |
| 32 | 0.5585 | 0.0387 | 0.5513 | 0.0143 | 92 | 1.6060 | 0.3053 | 1.4390 | 0.3032 | 152 | 2.6530 | 0.7581 | 1.9410 | 1.0917 |
| 33 | 0.5759 | 0.0412 | 0.5680 | 0.0157 | 93 | 1.6230 | 0.3116 | 1.4510 | 0.3123 | 153 | 2.6700 | 0.7666 | 1.9450 | 1.1082 |
| 34 | 0.5934 | 0.0437 | 0.5847 | 0.0171 | 94 | 1.6410 | 0.3180 | 1.4630 | 0.3215 | 154 | 2.6880 | 0.7750 | 1.9490 | 1.1247 |
| 35 | 0.6109 | 0.0463 | 0.6014 | 0.0186 | 95 | 1.6580 | 0.3244 | 1.4750 | 0.3309 | 155 | 2.7050 | 0.7936 | 1.9530 | 1.1413 |
| 36 | 0.6283 | 0.0489 | 0.6180 | 0.0203 | 96 | 1.6760 | 0.3309 | 1.4860 | 0.3405 | 156 | 2.7230 | 0.7921 | 1.9560 | 1.1580 |
| 37 | 0.6458 | 0.0517 | 0.6346 | 0.0219 | 97 | 1.6930 | 0.3374 | 1.4980 | 0.3502 | 157 | 2.7400 | 0.8006 | 1.9600 | 1.1747 |
| 38 | 0.6632 | 0.0545 | 0.6511 | 0.0238 | 98 | 1.7100 | 0.3439 | 1.5090 | 0.3601 | 158 | 2.7580 | 0.8092 | 1.9630 | 1.1915 |
| 39 | 0.6807 | 0.0574 | 0.6676 | 0.0257 | 99 | 1.7280 | 0.3506 | 1.5210 | 0.3701 | 159 | 2.7750 | 0.8178 | 1.9670 | 1.2084 |
| 40 | 0.6981 | 0.0603 | 0.6840 | 0.0277 | 100 | 1.7450 | 0.3572 | 1.5320 | 0.3803 | 160 | 2.7930 | 0.8264 | 1.9700 | 1.2253 |
| 41 | 0.7156 | 0.0633 | 0.7004 | 0.0298 | 101 | 1.7630 | 0.3639 | 1.5430 | 0.3906 | 161 | 2.8100 | 0.8350 | 1.9730 | 1.2422 |
| 42 | 0.7330 | 0.0664 | 0.7167 | 0.0319 | 102 | 1.7800 | 0.3707 | 1.5540 | 0.4010 | 162 | 2.8270 | 2.8436 | 1.9750 | 1.2592 |
| 43 | 0..7505 | 0.0696 | 0.7330 | 0.0343 | 103 | 1.7980 | 0.3775 | 1.5650 | 0.4117 | 163 | 2.8450 | 0.8522 | 1.9780 | 1.2763 |
| 44 | 0.7679 | 0.0728 | 0.7492 | 0.0366 | 104 | 1.8150 | 0.3843 | 1.5760 | 0.4224 | 164 | 2.8620 | 0.8608 | 1.9810 | 1.2934 |
| 45 | 0.7854 | 0.0761 | 0.7653 | 0.0391 | 105 | 1.8330 | 0.3912 | 1.5870 | 0.4333 | 165 | 2.8800 | 0.8695 | 1.9830 | 1.3105 |
| 46 | 0.8030 | 0.0795 | 0.7810 | 0.0418 | 106 | 1.850 | 0.3982 | 1.5970 | 0.4444 | 166 | 2.8970 | 0.8781 | 1.9850 | 1.3277 |
| 47 | 0.8200 | 0.0829 | 0.7970 | 0.0445 | 107 | 1.8680 | 0.4052 | 1.6080 | 0.4556 | 167 | 2.9150 | 0.8868 | 1.9870 | 1.3449 |
| 48 | 0.8380 | 0.0865 | 0.8130 | 0.0473 | 108 | 1.8850 | 0.4122 | 1.6180 | 0.4669 | 168 | 2.9320 | 0.8955 | 1.9890 | 1.3621 |
| 49 | 0.8550 | 0.0900 | 0.8290 | 0.0502 | 109 | 1.9020 | 0.4193 | 1.6280 | 0.4784 | 169 | 2.9500 | 0.9042 | 1.9910 | 1.3794 |
| 50 | 0.8730 | 0.0937 | 0.8450 | 0.0533 | 110 | 1.9200 | 0.4264 | 1.6380 | 0.4901 | 170 | 2.9670 | 0.9128 | 1.9920 | 1.3967 |
| 51 | 0.8900 | 0.0974 | 0.8610 | 0.0565 | 111 | 1.9370 | 0.4336 | 1.6480 | 0.5019 | 171 | 2.9850 | 0.9215 | 1.9940 | 1.4140 |
| 52 | 0.9080 | 0.1012 | 0.8770 | 0.0598 | 112 | 1.9550 | 0.4408 | 1.6580 | 0.5138 | 172 | 3.0020 | 0.9302 | 1.9950 | 1.4314 |
| 53 | 0.9250 | 0.1051 | 0.8920 | 0.0632 | 113 | 1.9720 | 0.4481 | 1.6680 | 0.5259 | 173 | 3.0190 | 0.9390 | 1.9960 | 1.4488 |
| 54 | 0.9420 | 0.1090 | 0.9080 | 0.0667 | 114 | 1.9900 | 0.4554 | 1.6770 | 0.5381 | 174 | 3.0370 | 0.9477 | 1.9970 | 1.4662 |
| 55 | 0.9600 | 0.1130 | 0.9230 | 0.0703 | 115 | 2.0070 | 0.4627 | 1.6870 | 0.5504 | 175 | 3.0540 | 0.9564 | 1.9980 | 1.4836 |
| 56 | 0.9770 | 0.1171 | 0.9390 | 0.0741 | 116 | 2.0250 | 0.4701 | 1.6960 | 0.5629 | 176 | 3.0720 | 0.9651 | 1.9990 | 1.5010 |
| 57 | 0.9950 | 0.1212 | 0.9540 | 0.0780 | 117 | 2.0420 | 0.4775 | 1.7050 | 0.5755 | 177 | 3.0890 | 0.9738 | 1.9990 | 1.5184 |
| 58 | 1.0120 | 0.1254 | 0.9700 | 0.0821 | 118 | 2.0590 | 0.4850 | 1.7140 | 0.5883 | 178 | 3.1070 | 0.9825 | 2.0000 | 1.5359 |
| 59 | 1.0300 | 0.1296 | 0.9850 | 0.0863 | 119 | 2.0770 | 0.4925 | 1.7230 | 0.6012 | 179 | 3.1240 | 0.9913 | 2.0000 | 1.5533 |
| 60 | 1.0470 | 0.1340 | 1.0000 | 0.0956 | 120 | 2.0940 | 0.5000 | 1.7320 | 0.6142 | 180 | 3.142 | 1.0000 | 2.0000 | 1.5708 |

# Solutions to Triangles

$A + B + C = 180°$

$S = \dfrac{a + b + c}{2}$

Right

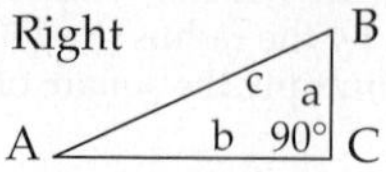

Oblique

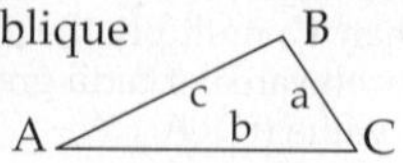

| Have | Want | Formulas for Right | Formulas for Oblique |
|------|------|--------------------|-----------------------|
| abc | A | $\tan A = a/b$ | $1/2A = \sqrt{(s-b)(s-c)/bc}$ |
| | B | $90° - A$ or $\cos B = a/c$ | $\sin 1/2B = \sqrt{(s-a)(s-c)/a \times c}$ |
| | C | $90°$ | $\sin 1/2C = \sqrt{(s-a)(s-b)/a \times b}$ |
| | Area | $a \times b/2$ | $\sqrt{s \times (s-a)(s-b)(s-c)}$ |
| aAC | B | $90° - A$ | $180° - (A + C)$ |
| | b | $a \cot A$ | $a \sin B/\sin A$ |
| | c | $a/\sin A$ | $a \sin C/\sin A$ |
| | Area | $(a^2 \cot A)/2$ | $a^2 \sin B \sin C/2 \sin A$ |
| acC | A | $\sin A = a - c$ | $\sin A = a \sin C/c$ |
| | B | $90° - A$ or $\cos B = a/c$ | $180° - (A + C)$ |
| | b | $\sqrt{c^2 - a^2}$ | $c \sin B/\sin C$ |
| | Area | $1/2a \sqrt{c^2 - a^2}$ | $1/2 ac \sin B$ |
| abC | A | $\tan A = a/b$ | $\tan A = a \sin C/b - a \cos C$ |
| | B | $90° - A$ or $\tan B = b/a$ | $180° - (A + C)$ |
| | c | $\sqrt{a^2 + b^2}$ | $\sqrt{a^2 + b^2 - 2ab \cos C}$ |
| | Area | $a \times b/2$ | $1/2ab \sin C$ |

# Fraction, Decimal, and Metric Equivalents

| Imperial | Metric | |
|---|---|---|
| Inch | Decimal | Millimeter |
| 1/32″ | .03125 | .7938 mm |
| 1/16″ | .0625 | 1.5875 mm |
| 3/32″ | .09375 | 2.3813 mm |
| 1/8″ | .125 | 3.175 mm |
| 5/32″ | 1.5625 | 3.9688 mm |
| 3/16″ | .1875 | 4.7625 mm |
| 7/32″ | .21875 | 5.5563 mm |
| 1/4″ | .250 | 6.35 mm |
| 9/32″ | .28125 | 7.1438 mm |
| 5/16″ | .3125 | 7.9375 mm |
| 11/32″ | .34375 | 8.7313 mm |
| 3/8″ | .375 | 9.525 mm |
| 13/32″ | .40625 | 10.3188 mm |
| 7/16″ | .4375 | 11.1125 mm |
| 15/32″ | .46875 | 11.9063 mm |
| 1/2″ | .500 | 12.70 mm |
| 17/32″ | .53125 | 13.4938 mm |
| 9/16″ | .5625 | 14.2875 mm |
| 19/32″ | .59375 | 15.0813 mm |
| 5/8″ | .625 | 15.875 mm |
| 21/32″ | .65625 | 16.6688 mm |
| 11/16″ | .6875 | 17.4625 mm |
| 23/32″ | .71875 | 18.2563 mm |
| 3/4″ | .750 | 19.05 mm |
| 25/32″ | .78125 | 19.8438 mm |
| 13/16″ | .8125 | 20.6375 mm |
| 27/32″ | .84375 | 21.4313 mm |
| 7/8″ | .875 | 22.225 mm |
| 29/32″ | .90625 | 23.0188 mm |
| 15/16″ | .9375 | 23.8125 mm |
| 31/32″ | .96875 | 24.6063 mm |
| 1″ | 1.000 | 25.4000 mm |

## Area Formulas

| | | |
|---|---|---|
| | Square | Area = $a^2$ |
| | Rectangle | Area = $l \times w$ |
| | Triangle | Area = $\frac{1}{2}(a \times b)$ |
| | Circle | Area = $\pi r^2$<br>Circumference = $2\pi r$ |
| | Ellipse | Area = $\pi ab$ |

# Roof Pitch Angles

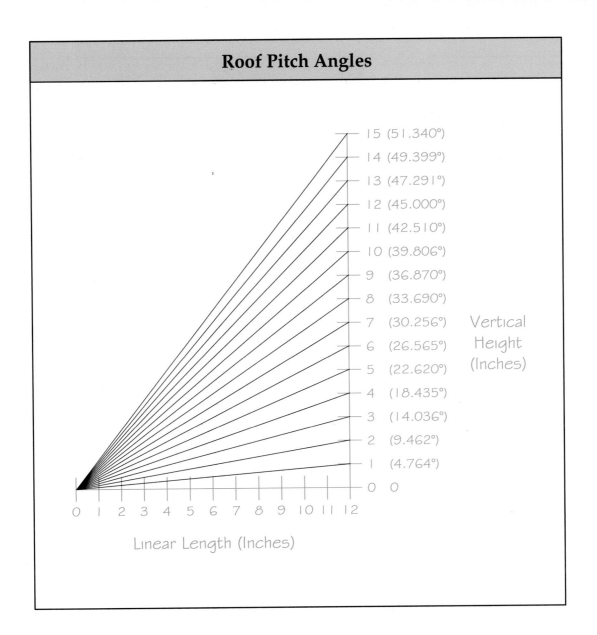

15 (51.340°)
14 (49.399°)
13 (47.291°)
12 (45.000°)
11 (42.510°)
10 (39.806°)
9 (36.870°)
8 (33.690°)
7 (30.256°)
6 (26.565°)
5 (22.620°)
4 (18.435°)
3 (14.036°)
2 (9.462°)
1 (4.764°)
0  0

Vertical Height (Inches)

0  1  2  3  4  5  6  7  8  9  10  11  12

Linear Length (Inches)

# Index

# C

Cache file, 972
CAD manager, 25–26
**CAL** command, 443–446, 798–815
Careers, 23–32
Cartesian coordinate system, 75
Cascading menu, 54
Casework and fixtures, 580–584
Cavity, 712
Center dashes, 539
Centerlines, 539
Chain dimensioning, 533
**CHAMFER** command, 575–580
Chamfers, 108, 575–580
    angles, 577–578
    distance, 576–577
    method, 578
**Character Map** dialog box, 299–300
Check boxes, 57
**Check Spelling** dialog box, 315
Child dimension style, 520
Chord, 97
Chord length, 470
**CIRCLE** command, 90–94
**CIRCLERAD** system variable, 91
Circles, 90–94
    dimensioning, 531, 539–540
Circular reference error, 351–352
Circumscribed, 105
Civil drafter, 26
Clipping boundary, 423
**Close** option, 84–85, 470
Color tables, 890–896
Command aliases, 74
Command buttons, 56
Command line editing, 291
Commands,
    **3DFACE**, 936–939
    **3DORBIT**, 925–926
    **ARC**, 95–100, 470–471
    **ARCTEXT**, 321–322
    **AREA**, 426–433, 637, 795
    **ARRAY**, 642–645
    **ATTDEF**, 748, 754
    **ATTDISP**, 756
    **BACKGROUND**, 995
    **BASE**, 346–347
    **BATTMAN**, 758–760
    **BHATCH**, 678–690
    **BLIPMODE**, 426
    **BLOCK**, 330, 333–335, 750
    **BOUNDARY**, 429–430
    **BOX**, 948
    **BREAK**, 234–236
    **CAL**, 443–446, 798–815
    **CHAMFER**, 575–580
    **CIRCLE**, 90–94
    **CONE**, 950–951
    **CONVERTPSTYLES**, 883, 896
    **COPY**, 211–213, 265–266
    **CYLINDER**, 949–950
    **DDEDIT**, 312, 753, 788–789
    **DIMALIGNED**, 528–529
    **DIMANGULAR**, 529
    **DIMBASELINE**, 504, 535–537
    **DIMCENTER**, 507
    **DIMCONTINUE**, 537–538
    **DIMDIAMETER**, 539–540
    **DIMEDIT**, 550
    **DIMLINEAR**, 523–527
    **DIMORDINATE**, 533
    **DIMOVERRIDE**, 546–548
    **DIMRADIUS**, 541
    **DIMREASSOCIATE**, 549
    **DIMSTYLE**, 500
    **DIMTEDIT**, 549
    **DIST**, 425–426, 559, 695
    **DIVIDE**, 485
    **DONUT**, 247, 633–634
    **DRAWORDER**, 418–419, 770
    **DSETTINGS**, 832
    **DWGPROPS**, 773
    **EATTEDIT**, 757–758
    **EATTEXT**, 761
    **EDGE**, 938
    **ELLIPSE**, 110–113, 835
    **ERASE**, 88–89, 347, 548
    **EXPLODE**, 233–234, 350–351, 550
    **EXTEND**, 238–240, 473, 674, 697, 727
    **EXTRUDE**, 953–955
    **FILLET**, 564–567, 727
    **FILTER**, 453–460
    **FIND**, 316–317
    **FOG**, 997–998
    **GRID**, 136–137, 402
    **GROUP**, 450
    **HATCHEDIT**, 678, 689–690
    **HELP**, 65–69
    **HIDE**, 922–925
    **HYPERLINK**, 1008
    **IMAGE**, 412–414, 969, 977
    **INSERT**, 330, 336–347, 569, 754
    **INSERTOBJ**, 767
    **INTERSECT**, 958–959
    **ISOPLANE**, 835
    **JUSTIFYTEXT**, 315, 322
    **LAYER**, 177